REGGAE & CARIBBEAN MUSIC

Dave Thompson

Backbeat Books

San Francisco

Published by Backbeat Books
600 Harrison Street, San Francisco, CA 94105
www.backbeatbooks.com
email: books@musicplayer.com
An imprint of the Music Player Network
United Entertainment Media

Distributed to the book trade in the US and Canada by
Publishers Group West 1700 Fourth Street, Berkeley, CA 94710

Distributed to the music trade in the US and Canada by
Hal Leonard Publishing P.O. Box 13819, Milwaukee, WI 53213

Cover Design by Richard Leeds
Text Composition by Impressions Book and Journal Services, Inc.
Front Cover Photo of Bob Marley: MICHAEL OCHS ARCHIVES.com
Back Cover Photo by Ebet Roberts

Library of Congress Cataloging-in-Publication Data

Thompson, Dave.
    Reggae and Caribbean music / by Dave Thompson.
      p. cm. — (Third ear)
    Includes discographies, bibliographical references, and index.
    Contents: Carnival history & winners—Artist/genre profiles—The producers—Directory of singles.
    ISBN 0-87930-655-6
      1. Popular music—West Indies, British—Encyclopedias. 2. Reggae
    music—Encyclopedias. I. Series.

ML102.P66 T46 2001
781.64'09729—dc21   2001043710

Printed in the United States of America
02 03 04 05 06 5 4 3 2 1

TABLE OF CONTENTS

ACKNOWLEDGMENTS

Any book this size necessarily demands the help and dedication of an army of people — I'd like to thank everybody who threw something into the pot, but most especially Jo-Ann Greene, tireless sounding board and co-review writer; Amy Hanson for fearlessly proof-reading beyond the call of duty; Dreadnought Skanga and Matt Green for pointing me in the direction of sundry obscure and unknown records; and Miles and Arthur at Holy Cow Records of Seattle, for having so many of them.

Further thanks are due to the staff and publicists at the following record companies: Heartbeat, Blood & Fire, Greensleeves, Music Club, Cleopatra, Universal, Koch International, Trojan, Pressure Sounds, Mango, Caroline, Motion/ Guava Jelly, New Millennium/Orange Street.

Thanks also to everybody else who helped bring the beast to life — my agent, Sherrill Chidiac; Dorothy Cox, Richard Johnston, and all at Backbeat Books; Anchorite Man; Back Ears (whose ears are apparently still on backwards); Bateerz, family and the Reverend Crab; Blind Pew; Veronique Cordier/V Entertainment; Barb East; Ella and Sprocket; Gaye and Tim; Gef the Talking Mongoose; the Gremlins who live in the furnace; K-Mart (not the store); Geoff Monmouth; Nutkin; Rita, Eric, and Samantha; Snarleyyowl The Cat Fiend; Sonny; Mrs Nips and Grabby; a lot of Thompsons, and Neville Viking.

INTRODUCTION

There is no such thing as Caribbean music.

Across a chain of 30 major islands or island groups, which stretches more than 2,500 miles in length, encompasses over 30 million people and occupies 90,000 square miles of land, four different European nations have held sway and left their imprint — the Dutch, the English, the French and the Spanish.

The Danes and the Germans made further marks on the landscape; East India, West Africa and North America have also thrown their own contributions into the cultural melting pot. And just as nobody could possibly mistake the music and culture of any one of those nations for that of one of the others, neither can that of the Caribbean islands be neatly swept into one convenient catch-all.

However, as innumerable works on that most all-encompassing of musical genres, "World Music," have shown, there are similarities and relationships between the music of individual islands.

Those which fell beneath, and have retained the culture of, the Spanish conquerors form one group, evidenced in the Latin sounds of Cuba, Puerto Rico, the Dominican Republic, and so forth. Those formerly ruled by the French — Haiti, Guadeloupe, Martinique, etc. — form a second; and those which came into the English sphere of influence comprise a third.

It is this latter category with which this book is concerned, the sounds of reggae, calypso, pan, soca, and chutney which are familiar to everybody, whether they are experienced in their natural form, or absorbed via their (now so common-place) incorporation into other Anglo-American musical forms.

Even in their pre-eminence, however, much remains unknown about these musical styles — how and why they developed, the men and women who forged that development, the ideas and ideals which dictated the direction which that development would take. Those are the unknowns which inspired the creation of this encyclopedia.

Of course, it is intended first and foremost as a reference tool and, as such, offers up a number of tables, indexes, and listings which have never previously been compiled in one single volume. But it is also hoped that, via both inference and statement, the reader will gain an understanding of how the music came to be, what gives it its unique flavor and character, and how it has managed to retain that spirit, even after it arrived at the forefront of the global market.

Similarly, the essays and artist biographies within aim not only to provide a straightforward chronological survey of their subjects, but also a discussion of the vast, but so seldom acknowledged, common ground which exists between the different musical styles.

HOW TO USE THIS BOOK

This encyclopedia is divided into four main sections.

PART ONE   is devoted to the carnival traditions which now characterize each of the featured islands. Reference is made to leading artists not featured elsewhere in the book, while select listings of carnival victors (Calypso Monarch, Road March, Panorama) are also included wherever possible. In addition, brief historical surveys have been incorporated, to place into context many of the traditions and events discussed elsewhere in the book.

PART TWO   offers career biographies and discographies for close to 100 key artists and performers, selected as representing the best in their personal musical field. Essays interspersed alphabetically within this section discuss the primary musical genres included within this book. Also included are listings of releases from several key record labels.

Weight of numbers alone demands that calypso and reggae (and the manifold sub-genres of each) consume the bulk not only of this section, but of the book itself. But there is room, too, for lesser-known musical forms, and for discussion of artists who fit no acknowledged Caribbean precedent, but whose music is of profound importance all the same.

PART THREE   offers brief biographies of many of the record producers whose work over the past four decades has played a crucial role in the development and popularization of Caribbean music.

PART FOUR   looks at the development of what was, until the emergence of the US and Japan during the 1990s, the largest single overseas market for Caribbean music, the United Kingdom.

This takes the unique form of a near-comprehensive directory of singles (45rpm records) released in Britain during the period 1957–72, arranged chronologically by year (and alphabetically by artist/record label therein) to indicate the growth of the market and the changing fashions within the music itself. Pocket biographies of key performers and reviews of selected songs are also included.

SPELLING/TERMINOLOGY: In general, the British Caribbean adheres to British spelling ("labour" for "labor," "-ise" for "-ize" etc.). This is reflected in song and album titles, etc, and has been retained here. Similarly, patois song titles are given as they appear in original sources.

The following spellings have been adopted throughout this book: the spelling "nyahbingi" has been preferred over the popular alternatives nyabingi and nyabinghi. The local "Pukumina" is preferred over the Anglicized Pocomania. The Rastafarian religion as a whole is described as thus; its adherents as Rastas, its theology as Rastafarianism. The term Ras Tafari, except where incorporated into speech or song titles, refers to the historical figure Prince (Ras) Tafari.

Ethnic terms follow established island assignations: in general, the term "Creole" indicates those people, whether of African or European origin, born and raised in the region. More specific terms (Black, white, East Indian, Chinese, British, etc.) are applied when necessary.

LPs, TV programs, movies, newspapers and magazines, stage plays are noted in *italics*. Song titles appear in double quotes. Rock'n'roll is spelled thus; rhythm and blues is abbreviated to R&B. The terms 45 (for 45 rpm), single and 7-inch are applied interchangeably.

ABBREVIATIONS: Abbreviations are used as follows: ANG — Anguilla; ANT — Antigua & Barbuda; BARB — Barbados; BVI — British Virgin Islands; CAY — Cayman Islands; DOM — Dominica; GREN — Grenada; GUY — Guyana; JA — Jamaica; STK — St Kitts & Nevis; STL — St Lucia; STV — St Vincent & Grenadines; T&T — Trinidad & Tobago; T&C — Turks & Caicos Islands. Other country and state names appear as their most familiar abbreviation: UK — United Kingdom; US — United States; CA — California; NY — New York, etc.

ENTRY FORMAT: Artist entries adhere to the same format.

PERFORMING NAME: Artists are listed alphabetically by their surname except in those instances where a title (King, Lord, Mighty, Prince, Ras etc) has been adopted as an integral part of their name — King Tubby, Lord Kitchener etc. In these instances, the listings are alphabetical by title.

STYLE refers to the type of music best (although not exclusively) associated with the artist: calypso, chutney, dance hall, lovers rock, mento, ringbang, roots, ska/rock steady, soca, toasting/DJ. Each of these styles refers back to an essay within Part Two, to provide an overview of the genre.

Birthdates, names and places (for solo artists), and the original, or earliest-documented line-up (for bands) follow, together with instruments played. Thereafter, full career synopses include subsequent line-up changes and major career events.

DISCOGRAPHIES: No attempt has been made to note every single and LP release in the text. However, major releases are noted, together with the producers responsible for each. Thumbnail biographies of around 100 leading producers will be found in Part Three. In addition, releases by artists active between 1957–62 are documented in Part Four. LP/CD discographies are included for every featured artist, noting the year of release and original record label where possible.

Except where noted, LP/CD listings are complete. All are US releases unless otherwise stated, however the availability of releases is not addressed. As labels dig deeper into the vault in search of fresh material for reissue, "new" material is appearing on the racks on a weekly basis (and often disappearing again soon after).

Neither are formats (vinyl, tape, CD, etc.) considered. In general, pre-1986 releases were originally available on vinyl and cassette only; post 1986, CDs came to dominate, although many releases continued to appear on vinyl (some exclusively). The discographies strive to differentiate between albums intended to showcase fresh material — a group's "new album"; and those (***SELECTED COMPILATIONS & ARCHIVE RELEASES***) which collect previously unreleased material from earlier in a band's career, rare and unavailable cuts, or greatest hits/best of selections.

In many instances, this may lead to some controversy. Particularly during the early (pre-1975) period, many artists' recent singles were compiled onto albums for both domestic and international release, and a number of other references describe these as regular LP releases. Here they are considered compilations and are cataloged accordingly. These listings are not complete. Among the titles omitted are those whose contents have not been verified, and those which either duplicate or have been superseded by other collections. Where relevant, solo, side project, and other related releases follow the main artist discography.

REVIEWS AND RATINGS: Reviews of selected albums are included as a general guide to the band's music and impact. All reviews were written by Jo-Ann Greene and Dave Thompson. Albums are rated on a scale of **1** – **10**, with (**1**) representing a very poor release, and (**9**) the best in the band's catalog. It should be noted that these ratings apply only within an individual band's discography — a rating of (**7**) in one band's catalog does not necessarily imply it is superior to a (**5**) in another's.

REGGAE & CARIBBEAN MUSIC

A rating of (**1**) is not, therefore, intended to suggest that an album is one of the worst ever made (although it probably is), simply that it is the worst the band in question has ever made. The majority of releases are rated between (**5**) and (**7**), indicating that while the band may not have attained its (potential) peak, the album is definitely worthy.

In addition, a rating of **10** has been reserved for those albums which can be considered essential listening, not only for their content, but also for their historical and/or cultural impact. A full listing of these follows. NOTE: 45s and LPs included as *RECOMMENDED LISTENING* following the essays are not rated.

ACCURACY: Caribbean music in general, and reggae in particular, has been the victim of more informed misinformation than virtually any other mainstream musical genre, a consequence of the absolute disdain for record-keeping which was, until recently, an immutable fact of life in the local music industry.

Secondary sources — contemporary press reports, record release data, and so forth — are also frequently distorted, while first hand accounts from the people who were actually there are constantly at odds with both the known facts and with one another.

It is astonishing, too, how many times an utterly unfamiliar name will be encountered within otherwise familiar circumstances, only to be revealed — usually after several hours of frenzied research — as nothing more than a phonetic transliteration of a misheard and uncorrected name. Owners of records by the late 60s Jamaican band The Richus Flames, are thus directed to the Righteous Flames.

Recent research by a number of authors has gone some way toward clearing up this confusion, or at least confirming an accepted wisdom for certain areas — the bibliography acknowledges these sources. However, in many instances the non-existence of original source documentation leaves one with no alternative but to choose between informed estimates and educated guesses. It is inevitable, therefore, that this book will be populated with errors, omissions, and misconceptions which subsequent (or existing, but obscure) research will correct. For these, I apologize in advance.

PART ONE: CARNIVAL HISTORY & WINNERS

INTRODUCTION: BACKGROUND TO CARNIVAL

The vivid spectacle of the Caribbean Carnival dates back to the era of the Spanish conquest and the introduction of the traditional Shrovetide festivities, the prelude to the 40 days of fasting which begin on Ash Wednesday. (This tradition is responsible for the fluctuating date of each annual event: Shrove Tuesday is determined by counting back 40 days from Easter, which shifts according to the lunar cycle.) The word "carnival" itself reflects these religious origins — "carne" is the Latin word for meat, "vale" means goodbye.

If the tradition of making merry in the last days before Lent was an invention of the early Catholic church, however, it merely supplanted the even earlier Roman tradition of Saturnalia, during which slaves were given seven days of freedom in which to party as they saw fit. Very early on in its history, the church realized that it was easier to adopt and adapt existing rituals, than to try and suppress them altogether. Hence the proximity of such religious holidays as Easter, Christmas and Halloween to earlier pagan events.

The pre-Lent Carnival was originally celebrated throughout the Catholic world and, while it gradually fell away in Europe, Catholic strongholds in the new world maintained the tradition — Mardi Gras in New Orleans and carnival in Brazil are both descendants of what was once a semi-global phenomenon.

It is in the Caribbean, however, that the tradition survived the longest and strongest, imported by French and Spanish settlers and shared (willingly or otherwise) with the slaves who, so the plantation owners believed, were themselves in need of some form of religious discipline. That the slaves simply adapted this indulgence to beliefs and traditions they themselves had brought with them is, according to modern anthropologists, beyond doubt, and there is a wry irony indeed in knowing that a non-Christian ceremony which was hijacked by the church had, in many respects, turned full circle and been returned to other gods entirely.

In the British-controlled islands, carnival was at its peak around the middle of the 19th century, following the passage of the Abolition Act of 1833. Under that act, all slaves were to be freed by August 1, 1834, with the exception of domestics, who could be kept on until August, 1838, and agricultural workers, who were reclassified as apprentices and held until 1840 (this was eventually changed, and apprenticeship, too, ended in 1838).

Having previously celebrated their version of carnival on the plantations, where they were subject to the whims of both the law and their former masters, the newly freed slaves quickly took the event to the streets. Only as the harshest realities of freedom forced other issues to the fore did the exuberance slow. Abolition brought an end to slavery, but replaced it with the struggle to find employment, food and medicine within a social system which now felt its duties had all been discharged.

By the end of the 19th century, only Trinidad and Barbados still enjoyed a carnival worthy of its modern reputation; by the 1940s, Trinidad alone maintained the tradition. Not until the 1960s and 1970s, and the drive towards a tourist industry, did the other islands look again at their carnival traditions and begin to slowly revive them.

Not all of the modern events retain their original religiously inspired dates. The sheer enormity and popularity of the Trinidad carnival prompted many of the island's neighbors to seek out alternative dates worthy of celebration — hardly surprisingly, many chose either August, to mark the anniversary of Emancipation, or their own Independence Day.

The nature of the festivities, however, remain unchanged. It is a period of vibrant color and rampant excitement, of music and dance, costume and competition. It is, in one fabulously expressive word, carnival.

NOTE: The following documents carnival or its equivalent in each of the English-speaking islands of the Caribbean. Included where available are indices of winners in the Calypso and Soca Monarch and Road March (Lavway) competitions. The Jamaican Independence Festival is also detailed. In addition, brief histories of each island are included, to facilitate contextualization of events referenced elsewhere.

With the exception of the opening Trinidad & Tobago (T&T), all islands and festivals appear alphabetically.

TRINIDAD/TOBAGO

HISTORY

Europeans first visited Trinidad in 1498, when Christopher Columbus made landfall during his third voyage. The Spanish made several attempts to establish a permanent settlement on the island but, because of fierce resistance from the native Arawak and Carib people, it was 1592 before the first city, San Jose de Oruna, was founded. Unfortunately, the Spanish crown had not sanctioned the settlement and, when the city's founder, Antonio de Berrio, refused to renounce his claim, Trinidad was effectively shut out of the empire.

The island's distance from the established shipping routes compounded its isolation — between 1592 and 1613, and again between 1702–16, not one Spanish ship visited Trinidad. This isolation has since been credited with the development of the island's "parang" musical tradition, an Hispanic folkloric style rediscovered and popularized over the past decade.

If the Spanish paid Trinidad little heed, British, Dutch and French vessels did, and the island was subject to regular raids throughout the 17th and 18th centuries. More peacefully, 1783 saw a number of French Creole settlers take refuge on Trinidad, escaping the revolution which their homeland had exported to its own West Indies possessions. However, February, 1797, saw the British seize Trinidad for themselves, and, in 1802, the island was formally ceded to Great Britain.

Emancipation in 1834 dealt a staggering blow to the island's economy, thus, between 1845 and 1917, more than 150,000 Muslim and Hindu East Indians were brought to the island as indentured servants.

In 1889, Trinidad was twinned with the nearby island of Tobago, a British possession since 1814 and previously part of the shortlived Windward Islands union with Grenada, St Lucia and St Vincent. A constituent part of the Federation of the West Indies from April 22, 1958 until May 31, 1962, Trinidad & Tobago were granted independence on August 31, 1962.

Immediately things began to look up. Not for T&T the financial and social problems which were to bedevil neighboring Jamaica throughout the 1960s and 1970s, nor the political uncertainties which left that island forever teetering on the brink of revolution or worse. Although there were hard times on T&T, they came from within — climaxing with the failed Black Power/military coup in 1970.

The Peoples National Movement (PNM), in power from independence until 1986, oversaw a period of incredible economic growth as Trinidad took advantage of the oil crisis to become the third leading exporter of oil in the western hemisphere.

Externally, Prime Minister Eric Williams' government's decision to attract foreign investment in the island's principle resources (oil, sugar and banking), and then all but nationalize them in 1973, was the cue for a period of unimaginable wealth. The Arab oil embargo that November quadrupled the price of oil; by 1975, Williams was able to inform the electorate, "Money is no problem."

Oil revenues funded a mass of public, education and welfare programs, and allowed the government to maintain consumer goods at almost farcically low prices. Inflation was tamed, while crippling unemployment numbers were slashed. So what if outsiders glanced in and mumbled darkly about socialism (of the islands' neighbors, only Castro's Cuba exerted more control over the national economy)? Trinidad simply thumb its nose at them. "Money is no problem."

By the early 1980s, however, oil revenues were beginning to fall drastically. Suddenly a society which had grown luxuriously accustomed to the good life found itself tightening its belt. And a government used to swimming in funds, saw its budget dry up, a critical problem, since the public sector employed a whopping two-thirds of T&T's work-force.

Civil unrest shook the country during 1980–81, a period which culminated with Williams' death in 1981. He was succeeded by Agriculture Minister George Chambers, but the 1986 elections saw the National Alliance for Reconstruction (NAR) win 33 of the 36 seats in the House of Representatives, electing Arthur Robinson Prime Minister.

The country continued to suffer internal dissent. In July, 1990, Muslim militants bombed the police headquarters, seized the parliament building and held Robinson and other government officials hostage for several days in an abortive coup attempt.

After a PNM victory in the December 1991 elections, Patrick Manning became Prime Minister; his government was succeeded in 1995 by a coalition of the NAR and the United National Congress (UNC), headed by East Indian UNC leader Basdeo Panday.

THE BEGINNINGS OF CARNIVAL

Although carnival appears to have been celebrated on T&T since the founding of the first Spanish settlement in 1592, almost 200 years elapsed before the first written evidence of an actual carnival event appears, following the arrival in Trinidad of French Creole planters in 1783, escaping the after-effects of the recent French Revolution. The predominantly Catholic Spanish island offered a safe haven, both politically and religiously.

When the British took control of Trinidad in 1797, they found carnival already firmly entrenched in the local calendar — so much so that for many years, the celebration was actively resisted by the new overlords, all the more so for its Catholic origins. The British, of course, were Protestant and suspicious of anything remotely resembling Catholic ritual. The bacchanalian excesses of carnival reeked of unimaginable Papist shenanigans, and the authorities spent much of the next century seeking a successful cure for the cancer.

In 1801, a new law was passed concerning the "Prohibition of Negro Dances in Town"; six years later, "balls and assemblies" were permissible only if the organizers made a $16 donation to "paupers." Slaves were banned from dancing after ten P.M., assuming they were granted any kind of liberty whatsoever.

But carnival lived on, growing stronger by the year. For those whites who wished to participate (and there were some, albeit mostly of French or Spanish descent) and for the freedmen who already constituted a sizeable portion of the population, it was a time of balls and dances, street fairs and fireworks, masquerades (mas) and music.

Then came the 1834 Emancipation and, suddenly, it was a free-for-all. Emancipation Day itself, August 1, saw a massive, spontaneous celebration throughout the entire Caribbean region, an event which is still recalled by annual carnivals elsewhere.

Even in the aftermath of this momentous date, however, Trinidad reserved its greatest celebration for Shrovetide. And what a celebration it was. Former slaves who had hitherto been subject to all manner of governmental prohibitions (but who celebrated their own variation on carnival regardless, for whom among their overlords would have been sober enough to stop them?), descended upon what, by comparison, now seemed such mild-mannered events and literally took control.

Where once genteel men and women had sedately danced the quadrille, now were wild, uncontrolled, lascivious and violent displays of movement and passion. Where once, the dancers had sipped decorously from tumblers of rum, there were communal pots of steaming hard liquor into which cups, pots, hands, heads and entire bodies plunged.

No taboo was sacred, no hedonism too profane. The British, it was said, ruled Trinidad for 360 days every year. But for anything up to a week in February, they could not even step out on the street, for fear of being washed away by a tidal wave of dancing, screaming, copulating, murdering humanity.

No wonder they regarded the tradition with uneasiness, and who could blame them for continuing to seek new ways of quelling the revel? Regular disturbances at the annual event saw a plethora of new laws enacted, all aimed at suppressing carnival. Trouble in 1838 saw the following year's carnival restricted to just two days. In 1846, the high incidence of crime among masquerade revellers led to masks being outlawed in public. Additional restrictions on dancing and playing music were instituted two years later. Still, carnival remained barely contained, and in 1858, the army was brought in to control and disperse the crowds.

Few of these laws remained in force for long, largely because they were so difficult to enforce. However, the authorities remained opposed to carnival throughout much of the remainder of the century, with periodic outbreaks of rioting bringing further, inevitable, clampdowns.

These outbreaks worsened during the 1870s, with the greatest unrest occurring during the opening ceremony of Canboulay (modern J'Ouvert), the symbolic extinguishing of a sugar cane fire which was first adopted following emancipation.

Even vivid descriptions of the components of elaborate masques, stick-fighting, singing and dancing cannot begin to illustrate the immensity of the celebration, nor the potential for problems unleashed once the revellers began their parade through the streets. Drunken singing and chanting, impromptu halts for wild dancing and — naturally, given that so many revellers were "armed" with sticks — fighting and vandalism consumed the city.

1878 and 1879 saw mounted police quell the worst of the trouble. The following year, the police acted to prevent, rather than simply halt, the violence, descending before the festival-goers were even aware of their presence, scrutinizing the revellers and arresting anybody who even looked like stepping out of line. Stick-fights were broken up before the first blow was struck; lewd dancers were carted off before their first gyration; obscene singers were gagged as they took their first breath.

Polite Trinidad society celebrated a major victory and looked forward to another night of righteous crackdown the following year. Instead they got a full fledged riot as the police, intent on improving on the previous year's triumph, attempted to halt Canboulay altogether. Utterly unexpectedly, they encountered massive, well-organized resistance. On Market Street, police and stick-men battled ferociously for three hours beginning at midnight, ending only when the stick-men, apparently responding to a pre-arranged signal, broke away and simply melted into the night.

The riot was confined to just one part of Port of Spain — other areas seem to have been totally unaffected by either the fighting or the police. The result of even this localized conflict, however, was inevitable. Calls for carnival to be outlawed altogether grew louder than ever before.

Acting with a degree of forethought which is frequently unimaginable in government circles, the authorities opted not to heed those calls, and were rewarded when the 1882 event passed off both peaceably and unmolested. But trouble the following year returned carnival to the very epicenter of the political agenda.

Again, the decision was taken not to outlaw the festivities. Rather, a series of new legislative measures were put in place, including the banning of musical instruments. Most significantly percussion was forbidden, the pounding cause, it was believed, of the violent frenzies into which crowds were so easily whipped, and the inspiration behind the vile obscenities which still passed for dancing and songs.

Certain costumes were outlawed. Transvestites, another apparent hotbed of lewdness, were banned from appearing.

The stick-dance was prohibited; so were lighted torches and anything else which could be even remotely described as inciting riotous assembly. Carnival itself was not banned. But so many traditional aspects of it were now illegal, that it might as well have been.

At least, that's how the authorities looked at it. The revellers themselves, however, were not going to let a few prohibitions stand in their way. A full month before Canboulay, a crowd of drum dancers forced their way through a police barricade with stone-throwing and sticks. In one daring raid, police were forced to surrender an arrested man to a crowd which leaped to his aid. And while the carnival itself passed off without any serious disturbances in Port of Spain, San Fernando, Couva and Prince Town all saw rioting deep into the night.

The turning point in carnival's relations with the authorities, ironically enough, came later in 1884, following the government's attempts to similarly suppress the East Indian festival of Muharram, or Hosien — not because it had ever been problematic, but because not doing so would further enflame the Creole carnival-goers. On October 30, police opened fire on a Muharram parade, killing a number of people and injuring many more.

The so-called Hosien Massacre shocked even carnival's most vociferous opponents and, when the 1885 event passed off without incident, the pressure began to lift. Although there were sporadic outbreaks of serious trouble in the future, by the turn of the century carnival was entrenched not only within the Creole community, but elsewhere as well.

As early as 1887, a second carnival was organized by the authorities themselves, to commemorate Queen Victoria's Golden Jubilee. A decade later, the centenary of British rule over Trinidad was celebrated with similar enthusiasm and pageantry. Newspapers, once numbered among carnival's most implacable foes, now embraced it — in 1902, the *Port of Spain Gazette* was even calling for the event to be enlarged to celebrate the coronation of King Edward VII.

CARNIVAL COMPETITIONS

One of the principle factors in both the calming, and the acceptance, of carnival from the days of apparently Bacchanalian wildness, was the sense that the event itself was becoming organized, in the form of competitions between dancers, bands, drummers and, most popular of all, singers.

The first of these was staged in 1900, when a former City Councillor, Ignatio "Papa" Bodu, offered a cup for the best-dressed, or "fanciest" band at carnival. Titled, of course, the Fancy Band Cup, it was won by the White Rose Social Union, whose rousing repertoire included a song celebrating Britain's military prowess (this was the height of the Boer War, after all), which they published in the *Port of Spain Gazette* a few days earlier.

Further competitions were added. In 1911, an organization called the Jubilee Establishment offered a trophy for "the most original song on a local topic," won that first year by a band called Peep Of Day; runners up were the Fighting Cocks.

By 1919, when carnival returned after a two year wartime hiatus, "valuable cash prizes" were offered in seven different categories, including Best Patriotic Song, Best Creole Song, Best Band, Best Dressed Band, Best Fancy Dress Band and Best Individual Masqueraders, plus a special Good Conduct prize.

The competitive spirit continued to flourish throughout the 1920s and 1930s — by which time Trinidad was the only island in the entire region to still celebrate carnival. Finally, in 1939, the greatest competition of them all, the Calypso King, was inaugurated.

Carnival was suspended in 1942, following the already three year old World War Two's arrival in the Americas. Small scale events were staged unofficially throughout the war years, and impromptu carnival-like celebrations inevitably erupted in 1945, following the surrender of Germany in May and Japan in August.

The traditional Shrovetide carnival then returned in 1946, in much the same form as the modern event. Carnival itself is celebrated over just two days, the Monday and Tuesday, with the early hours of the former given over to the impromptu, and utterly unlicensed J'Ouvert celebrations — the unofficial opening of carnival.

The preceding weekend, however, is itself awash in the panoply of the main event. It is the Saturday and Sunday which see the fevered preparations for the various competitions reach their climax. The finals are staged in the Queen's Park Savannah, and the winners selected so that they might take their own places of honor in the festivities to come. Many people, approaching carnival from a musical or artistic point of entry, regard the crowning of the Calypso Monarch as the climax of the affair. In fact, it is only the beginning.

Since its reintroduction, carnival has operated without interruption. Following independence in 1962, one of the incoming government's first actions was to assume responsibility for the future well-being of carnival. They have remained true to their word — indeed, only once has the event ever deviated from its traditional berth, in 1972 when the official celebration was shifted to May, because of a polio outbreak on the island. A number of private carnivals took place at the traditional time regardless.

THE INDEPENDENCE CALYPSO COMPETITION

On August 15, 1962, to mark T&T's newly attained independence, an Independence Calypso Competition was staged at the New Town Hall, Port of Spain. Organized by a special celebrations sub-committee chaired by Senator Marguerite Wyke, and offering prizes of between $400 for second runner-up and $1,000 for the winner, 36 contestants were drawn from auditions staged by Radio Trinidad. This field was then whittled down to a final of 12 performers, including: Lord Pretender, Nap Hepburn, The Hawk, Mighty Power, Brynner, Mighty Bomber, Lord Dougla, Lord Cristo, Mighty Sparrow, Chang Kai Shek, Striker and Lazy Harrow.

Bert Innis and his Combo provided the music, with backing vocals supplied by the March of Dimes Quartet. The event was won by Lord Brynner, performing "Trinidad & Tobago Independence." Mighty Sparrow finished second, Nap Hepburn came third.

Two subsequent Independence Calypso competitions have been staged. In 1972, Chalkdust won the Tenth Anniversary Independence competition with "We Are Ten Years Old" and "Who Next"; in 1987, Cro-Cro triumphed at the silver jubilee celebrations with "Happy Anniversary."

TRINIDAD CALYPSO CROWN COMPETITION WINNERS

Official records were not kept until the 1953 carnival. Prior to that, unofficial monarchs were crowned, generally according to either consensus or the perceived importance of individual competitions.

CALYPSO KING

1939 Growling Tiger: "Trade Union"

1940 Roaring Lion: "Rise and Fall of the British Empire"

1941 Mighty Destroyer: "Adolf Hitler"

1942–1945 no competition

1946 Atilla The Hun: "Daily Mail Report"

1947 Atilla The Hun: "Million Dollar Jail" (some sources state Mighty Killer)

1948 Mighty Spoiler: "Royal Wedding"

1949 Lord Melody: "Glory Mama Glory"

1950 no competition

1951 Lord Melody: "Jonah and the Bake"

1952 no competition

1953 Mighty Spoiler: "Bed Bug"

1954 Lord Melody: "Second Spring"

1955 Mighty Spoiler: "Pick Sense Out of Nonsense"

1956 Mighty Sparrow: "Yankees Gone" (aka "Jean and Dinah")

1957 Lord Pretender: "Que Sera Sera"

1958 Striker: "Don't Blame The PNM," "Can't Find a Job to Suit Me"

1959 Striker: "Ban the Hoola Hoop," "Comparison"

1960 Mighty Sparrow: "May May," "Ten to One Is Murder"

1961 Lord Dougla: "Lazy Man," "Split Me in two"

1962 Mighty Sparrow: "Model Nation," "Sparrow Come Back Home"

1963 Mighty Sparrow: "Dan is the Man in the Van"

1964 Mighty Bomber: "Joan and James," "Bomber's Dream"

1965 Sniper: "Portrait of Trinidad," "More Production"

1966 Mighty Terror: "Pan Jamboree," "Last Year's Happiness"

1967 Mighty Cypher: "Last Elections," "If the Priest Could Play"

1968 Mighty Duke: "What is Calypso," "Social Bacchanal"

1969 Mighty Duke: "One Foot Visina," "Black is Beautiful"

1970 Mighty Duke: "Brotherhood of Man," "See Through"

1971 Mighty Duke: "Mathematical Formula," "Melvin & Yvonne"

1972 Mighty Sparrow: "Drunk and Disorderly" + 1

1973 Mighty Sparrow: "School Days," "Same Time, Same Place"

1974 Mighty Sparrow: "We Pass that Stage," "Miss Mary"

1975 Lord Kitchener: "Tribute to Spree Simon," "Fever"

1976 Chalkdust: "Three Blind Mice," "Ah Put on meh Guns Again"

1977 Chalkdust: "Juba Dubai," "Shango Vision"

CALYPSO MONARCH

In 1978, the competition was won for the first time by a woman, Calypso Rose. The title was promptly, and properly, changed to Calypso Monarch, which it has retained ever since.

1978 Calypso Rose: "I Thank Thee," "Her Majesty"

1979 Black Stalin: "Caribbean Man (Caribbean Unity)," "Play One"

1980 Lord Relator: "Food Prices," "Take ah Rest Mr Prime Minister"

1981 Chalkdust: "Things that Worry Me," "I Can't Make"

1982 Scrunter: "The Will," "Lee Kee Ting"

1983 Tobago Crusoe: "Don't Cry Now," "South Africa"

1984 Penguin: "We Living in Jail," "Sorf Man"

1985 Black Stalin: "Ism Schism," "Wait Dorothy Wait"

1986 David Rudder: "The Hammer," "Bahia Girl"

1987 Black Stalin: "Mr Pan Maker," "Burn Them"

1988 Cro-Cro: "Three Bo-rats," "Corruption in Common Entrance"

1989 Chalkdust: "Chauffeur Wanted," "Carnival Is the Answer"

1990 Cro-Cro: "Political Dictionary," "Party"

1991 Black Stalin: "Black Man Feeling to Party," "Look on the Bright Side"

1992 Mighty Sparrow: "Both of Them," "Survival"

1993 Chalkdust: "Misconception," "Kaiso in the Hospital"

1994 (tie) De Lamo: "31 Years Old," "Trinity Is my Name"

1994 (tie) Luta: "Good Driving," "Licensed Firearm"

1995 Black Stalin: "In Time," "Tribute to Sundar Popo"

1996 Cro-Cro: "All Yuh Look for Dat," "Dey Cyah Stop Social Commentary"

1997 Gypsy: "Rhythm of a People," "Little Black Boy"

1998 Mystic Prowler: "Vision of T&T in the Year 2010," "Look Beneath the Surface"

1999 Singing Sandra: "Voices from the Ghetto," "Song for Healing"

2000 Shadow: "What's Wrong with Me," "Scratch meh Back"

2001 Denyse Plummer: "Heroes," "Nah Leaving"

ROAD MARCH (LAVWAY) WINNERS

The Road March, or Lavway, has been an integral part of carnival since the beginning, when the first bands gathered to play favorite songs as they made their way through the streets. Absolutely informal for many years (and the cause, therefore, of much of the violence for which early carnival was renowned), Road March began to organize during the 1940s, before being formalized with the introduction of the

Road March award. This is presented to the composer of the most popular song played by the massed bands, as noted by judges stationed at various points along the route.

1932 "Tiger Tom Playing Tiger Cat" — composed by King Radio

1933 "Wash Pan Wash" — King Radio

1934 "After Johnny Drink" — Railway Douglas

1935 "Dingolay Oy" — Roaring Lion

1936 "Advantage Could Never Done" — Roaring Lion

1937 "Netty Netty" — Roaring Lion

1938 "No Norah Darling" — Roaring Lion

1939 "Matilda" — King Radio

1940 "Run Yuh Run" — Lord Beginner

1941 "Whoopsin Whoopsin" — Roaring Lion 1942–1946 no competition

1947 ? — King Pharaoh

1948 "Canaan Barrow" — Lord Melody

1949 "Ramgoat Baptism" — Lord Wonder

1950 "In a Calabash" — Mighty Killer

1951 "Tiny Davis" — Mighty Terror

1952 "Post, Post Another Letter for Thelma" — Spitfire

1953 "Bow Wow Wow" — Spitfire

1954 "Steelband Clash" — Blakie

1955 NO LOCAL WINNER — award presented for "The Happy Wanderer," a popular US song composed by Anne & Milton DeFugg

1956 "Yankees Gone" aka "Jean And Dinah" — Mighty Sparrow

1957 "PNM" — Spitfire

1958 "P.A.Y.E." — Mighty Sparrow

1959 "Run the Gunslingers" — Lord Caruso

1960 "May May" — Mighty Sparrow

1961 "Royal Jail" — Mighty Sparrow

1962 "Maria" — Blakie

1963 "The Road" — Lord Kitchener

1964 "Mama dis Is Mas" — Lord Kitchener

1965 "My Pussin'" — Lord Kitchener

1966 "Melda (Obeah Wedding)" — Mighty Sparrow

1967 "'67" — Lord Kitchener

1968 "Miss Tourist" — Lord Kitchener

1969 "Sa Sa Yae" — Mighty Sparrow

1970 "Margie" — Lord Kitchener

1971 "Mas in Madison Square Garden" — Lord Kitchener

1972 "Drunk and Disorderly" — Mighty Sparrow

1973 "Rain-O-Rama" — Lord Kitchener

1974 "Bassman" — Shadow

1975 "Tribute to Spree Simon" — Lord Kitchener

1976 "Flag Woman" — Lord Kitchener

1977 "Tempo" — Calypso Rose

1978 "Soca Jam" — Calypso Rose

1979 "Ah Tell She" — Poser

1980 "Soca Baptist" — Blue Boy

1981 "Ethel" — Blue Boy

1982 "Deputy" — Penguin

1983 "Rebecca" — Blue Boy

1984 "Doh Back Back" — Mighty Sparrow

1985 "Soucouyant" — Crazy

1986 "Bahia Girl" — David Rudder

1987 "Thunder" — Mighty Duke

1988 "This Party Is It" — Tambu

1989 "Free Up, Free Up" — Tambu

1990 "No, No, We Eh Going Home" — Tambu

1991 "Get Something an' Wave" — Superblue

1992 "Wine on Something" — Superblue

1993 "Bacchanal Time" — Superblue

1994 "Jump an' Wave" — Preacher

1995 "Signal for Lara" — Superblue

1996 "Movin'" — Nigel Lewis

1997 "Big Truck" — Machel Mantano

1998 "Footsteps" — Xtatik

1999 "River" — Sanell Dempster

2000 "Pump Up" — Superblue

2001 "Stranger" — Shadow

ANGUILLA
HISTORY

Anguilla lies within the Leeward Island group, which also comprises Antigua, St Kitts-Nevis, Montserrat and the British Virgin Islands of Anegada, Tortola and Virgin Gorda. Visited by the Dutch in 1631, it was settled by the British in 1650. A founding member of the short-lived West Indies federation in 1958, the island was incorporated alongside St Kitts-Nevis as an associated state with internal self-government in 1967. It was not a popular arrangement, however; the Anguillans promptly evicted the St Kitts authorities (including the police force) and commenced a period of self rule, until the British agreed to return the island to colonial status in 1969.

In 1982, a new constitution was drawn up, granting the island its own status of associated state under British jurisdiction.

CARNIVAL

A carnival was launched in Anguilla in 1974, taking place in late July-early August, to mark Emancipation Day, August 1, 1834. Events are spread over some two weeks of music, boat races, fireworks, street dancing and parades, launched by the extravagant opening celebration of J'Ouvert. The main parade features appearances from the newly-crowned Calypso Monarch, the Carnival Queen and the winners of lesser events — Miss Talented Teen and the primary school-age Prince and Princess.

The most successful Calypso Monarch in recent years is Mighty Splinter (aka Dr Splinter); his 1997 winning song, "Anguilla Must Rise Again," has since become a permanent island favorite. 1997 also saw the Anguilla Carnival host the first ever Leeward Islands Calypso Monarch competition, featuring national champions from across the island chain, including the Dutch island of St Maarten, St Thomas (in the US Virgin Islands), St Kitts, Nevis and Tortola.

The inaugural winner of this competition was the Antigua-born Zacare; while 1998 brought a major upset when Burning Flames frontman King Onyan, representing Antigua, finished third behind Anguilla's Mighty Springer and the defending champion, Zacare. Springer also took the Anguilla Calypso crown; among the performers he defeated were his own brother, Gossip (who finished second), Ziggy, Controller, Upsetter, Thunder and Monarch.

Anguilla also hosts the Moonsplash Music Festival in March, an annual event since 1990. Organized by local reggae performer Bankie Banks, recent stars have included fellow Anguillans Kingniah I, the Reggae Groovers, High Tension, St Croix's Midnight Band and New York's Sheriff Uncle Bob.

ANTIGUA
HISTORY

Antigua is situated in the Leeward Island group, which also comprises Anguilla, St Kitts & Nevis, Montserrat and the British Virgin Islands of Anegada, Tortola and Virgin Gorda. The island was settled in 1632 by the British, who arrived from nearby St Kitts. Antigua was one of the islands plundered by French forces in 1665–66, an event which led to the creation of the Leewards as a political entity in their own right (hitherto they were governed from Barbados).

The island was the scene of a bloody revolt in 1710, during which the hated British governor, Colonel Daniel

Parkes, was assassinated and his 70 man bodyguard either slain or wounded. There were also major slave uprisings in 1701 and 1831. A founding member of the short-lived West Indies Federation in 1958, Antigua was granted full independence in 1982.

CARNIVAL

Antigua's Carnival has been staged annually in the capital, St John's, since 1957, and has built a reputation for grandeur second only to T&T. The carnival was originally conceived to boost tourism during the traditionally light May to July period, but was eventually shifted to coincide with the Emancipation celebration.

It now runs from the last week in July to the first Monday and Tuesday in August, although preparations begin several months earlier, with calypso tents opened on the weekends. The actual festivities take place at "Carnival City," the Antigua Recreation Grounds in the capital, St John's. The festivities include the Party Monarch and Calypso Monarch competitions, the Panorama steel band competition, the Parade of Bands, the Miss Antigua Pageant and the Caribbean Queen's Competition. Other events contested include Most Improved Performer, Best Arranged and Most Humorous Calypso, First Band On The Road and Sweetest Band on the Road.

The island's best known acts include calypsonian King Short Shirt and the soca band Burning Flames, whose original vocalist, King Onyan, has now established himself among the most successful Monarchs of all time.

CALYPSO MONARCHS

1957 Styler: "Water Wet Me Bed," "Don't Back Back on Me"
1958 Obstinate: "Dance Dance Dance," "Obsti Will Sing Again"
1959 Peculiar: "Chemist," "Shimmy"
1960 Canary: "Slapping Hands," "Gem of the Caribbean"
1961 Zemakai: "Tribute to Radio Antigua," "Fidel Castro"
1962 Canary: "Island Peoples' Names," "Immigration Bill"
1963 Tennyson: "Racial Tension," "Gagarin"
1964 Lord Short Shirt: "No Place Like Home," "Hermitage"
1965 Lord Short Shirt: "Blessed," "Beatles MBE"
1966 Lord Short Shirt: "Paradox of Life," "They Scorning Me"
1967 Creole: "Independence Carnival," "Neighbour Neighbour"
1968 Creole: "Martin Luther King," "Proud Antiguans"
1969 Lord Short Shirt: "Heart Transplant," "Carnival on the Moon"
1970 Lord Short Shirt: "Black Like Me," "Technical School"
1971 Calypso Joe: "Educate the Youths," "Recorded in History"
1972 Lord Short Shirt: "Star Black," "Pull Together"
1973 Swallow: "March for Freedom," "Push Ya Push Dey"
1974 Lord Short Shirt: "This Land," "Lucinda"
1975 Lord Short Shirt: "Awake," "Cry For A Change"
1976 Lord Short Shirt: "In Spite of All," "Tourist Leggo"
1977 Swallow: "Dawn of a New Day," "Jam Dem Back"

1978 Swallow: "One Love One Hope One Destiny," "Whining"
1979 Lord Short Shirt: "Not by Might," "Kangaroo Jam"
1980 Lord Short Shirt: "Help," "Summer Festival"
1981 Obstinate: "Independence," "Fat Man Dance"
1982 Obstinate: "Coming to Talk to You," "Elephant Walk"
1983 Obstinate: "Antigua's True Heroes," "Children Melee"
1984 Progress: "Madness," "You Getting It"
1985 Swallow: "All Is Not Lost," "Tong Mash Dong"
1986 Lord Short Shirt: "World in Distress," "Jennifer"
1987 Lord Short Shirt: "Hari Kari," "J'Ouvert Rhythm"
1988 Lord Short Shirt: "AIDS," "Fire"
1989 Fiah: "Faithful Nationals," "Family Affair"
1990 Zero: "Kneel in Prayer," "Speculation"
1991 Zacari: "Jail Dem," "Guilty of Being Black"
1992 Lord Short Shirt: "Share the Honey," "Last J'Ouvert"
1993 Smarty Jr: "Never Again," "Role of the Calypsonian"
1994 Smarty Jr: "What Black Power Means," "Cry for Change"
1995 Smarty Jr: "Draw the Line," "Follow the Leader"
1996 Bankers: "Mas de Ras," "Fire Go Bun Dem"
1997 King Onyan: "Crazy Man," "Wile Out"
1998 King Onyan: "Stand Up for Antigua," "Ghetto Life"
1999 King Onyan: "Family," "Swim"
2000 King Onyan: Criteria," "Money"

ROAD MARCH CHAMPIONS

1970 "Bum Bum" — Calypso Joe
1971 "Shake You" — Razor Blade
1972 "Pow Pow" — Swallow
1973 "Push Ya Push Dey" — Swallow
1974 "Lucinda" — Short Shirt
1975 "Shake and Break You Bam Bam" — Swallow
1976 "Tourist Leggo" — Short Shirt
1977 "Supa Jam" — La Tumba
1978 "Benna Music" — Short Shirt
1979 "Kangaroo Jam" — Short Shirt
1980 "Summer Festival" — Short Shirt
1981 "Up and Jumping" — Redding
1982 "Push" — Short Shirt
1983 "Party in Space" — Swallow
1984 "Satan" — Swallow
1985 "Stylie Tight" — Burning Flames
1986 "Rudeness Mek Me" — Burning Flames
1987 "J'Ouvert Rhythm" — Short Shirt
1988 "Bad Girl" — Lion
1989 "Workey Workey" — Burning Flames
1990 "Congo Man" — Burning Flames
1991 "Piece ah Iron" — Burning Flames
1992 "Donkey" — Burning Flames
1993 "Wet Down de Place" — Burning Flames
1994 "Dress Back" — Vision Band
1995 "Gym Jam and Stampede" — Burning Flames

1996 "Fire unda Me Foot" — Burning Flames
1997 "Crazy Man" — King Onyan
1998 "Sweet Song" — Burning Flames
1999 "Magician I Command You" — Burning Flames
2000 "Exercise" — Calypso Jim

THE BAHAMAS
HISTORY

The group of 700+ islands and cays which constitute the Bahamas represent the most populous of the British Caribbean territories after Jamaica and Trinidad. Christopher Columbus made his first landing in the New World in the Bahamas, on an island then inhabited by Arawak people. He named the island San Salvador (most likely modern Samana Cay) and, though no permanent settlement was established, by the 1520s, the Spaniards had effectively wiped out the islands' indigenous people.

The Bahamas remained largely uninhabited for more than a century. The first European settlers were British Puritans fleeing Bermuda, after that island was caught up in the English Civil War of the 1640s. They settled Eleuthera and New Providence in 1647, however, their settlement was repeatedly attacked by the Spanish during its early years. Later, the islands became a pirate stronghold, most notably harboring the infamous Blackbeard.

The Bahamas were ruled by the proprietary governors of the British colony of Carolina from 1670 to 1717, when the British crown assumed direct control of civilian and military affairs. The capital, Nassau, was held briefly by revolutionary colonials during the American war of 1776; the Bahamas were also occupied by the Spanish during 1782–83; they became a British colony in 1787.

The abolition of slavery in 1834 brought about a serious decline in both the economy and the population of the islands, as plantations closed and their owners left the region. An epidemic of cholera in the middle of the 19th century was similarly damaging. However, prosperity returned during the American Civil War when the Bahamas became an important base for blockade-runners; the islands were also popular with rum runners during Prohibition.

In 1964 Britain granted the Bahamas internal autonomy, with independence following on July 10, 1973.

CARNIVAL: CROP OVER

The Bahamas' carnival, Junkanoo, has its roots in the tradition of allowing slaves three days off to celebrate Christmas. This temporary freedom developed into a musical masquerade named, it is believed, in honor of John Canoe, an African tribal chief who demanded he be allowed to celebrate with his people, even after he was brought to the West Indies as a slave. The name has also been traced to the French "gens inconnus" ("the unknown people") — a reference to the elaborate masks and disguises which were so much a part of the festival.

Following the abolition of slavery in 1834, Junkanoo fell into both disrepute and obscurity. The Street Nuisance Act of 1899 did much to crush the event — a mere five hours, four A.M. — nine A.M., were set aside for celebration on Christmas Day and New Year's Day. Further restrictions were enacted during both World Wars, however, spontaneous celebrations of Junkanoo began to re-emerge on a major level during the 1950s. Today, the event is wholly official and a vital part of the islands' tourism industry, which prides itself on the unique nature of the festival.

With events occurring simultaneously across the island group (the largest, of course, takes place in the capital, Nassau), Junkanoo involves parades, arranged in groups of up to a thousand participants, organized around a particular theme and reflected in music, dance and costume. There are two parades, on December 26 and January 1; uniquely, they are nocturnal events, beginning at two A.M. and wrapping up around eight A.M. Prizes are awarded for Best Music, Best Costume and Best Overall Group Presentation. (There is no conventional Monarch competition.) A smaller Junkanoo celebration occurs to mark Independence day, July 10.

The musical style associated with the original celebration has also survived. The traditional music of the Bahamas is "goombay," taken from the Bantu word for rhythm, and performed, then and now, by so-called rake-and-scrape bands.

Although today's practitioners add electric guitars, saxophones and keyboards to the brew, the equipment required by a rake and scrape band has barely changed in three centuries. With a drum fashioned from a pork barrel and goatskin, a carpenter's saw that was scraped with a metal file, a washtub bass, maracas and rhythm sticks, goombay combined half-remembered African music with the European sounds of the island's colonial masters. Outside of Junkanoo, goombay is most frequently heard accompanying the Bahamian Quadrille and the Heel and Toe Polka dances.

Attempts to market goombay to a wider audience have been limited to specialist musicologist circles for the most part — Blind Blake, who regularly performed for the Duke of Windsor during his stint as Governor during the 1940s, has had a number of recordings made available.

Of a more contemporary nature, Kirkland Bodie is generally credited with fusing junkanoo with rock for a string of local hits during the 1980s. The Baha Men, the most successful band ever produced by the islands, also utilize certain goombay rhythms and traditions in their music, and are frequently accompanied by authentically costumed goombay dancers.

BARBADOS
HISTORY

Located in the Lesser Antilles island chain, Barbados was originally discovered by the Portuguese during the early 16th century. The first settlers, however, were two rival syndicates of English merchants who arrived in 1627, and Barbados swiftly grew into the most successful of all the early Caribbean colonies. Over 100 miles from its nearest neighbor, it was less susceptible to attack and thus developed quickly.

Between 1635 and 1655, the island's population grew from less than 1,500 to over 43,000, the most densely populated landmass in the region and soon to become one of the richest, as Barbados was established as the world's largest producer of sugar. Massive influxes of slaves saw the population hit around 70,000 by the mid-1680s. Barbados was declared a Crown possession in 1663.

The colony's prosperity was severely affected by the 18th century wars between the French and the British. A century later, in 1876, the islanders themselves rebelled after the British government proposed a confederation of Barbados and the Windward Islands.

Poor economic conditions caused further unrest and, in 1937, a British Royal Commission was sent to Barbados, resulting in a series of much needed social and political reforms, including universal suffrage (1951). In 1958, Barbados joined the short-lived Federation of the West Indies; and was granted full internal self-government in 1961.

Following the collapse of the Federation in 1962, Prime Minister Grantley Adams attempted to create a smaller federation of eastern Caribbean islands. His plans went nowhere, however, and Barbados was granted independence on November 30, 1966. In 1973, Barbados helped form the Caribbean Community.

CARNIVAL

Barbados' Crop Over carnival was launched in July, 1974, as part of the island's drive towards a tourism-based economy. It was rooted in a festival which dated back to the 1780s, when a massive celebration marked the end of the annual sugar harvest. The decline of the industry saw the festivities become increasingly muted and, by the mid-1940s, Crop Over was a thing of the past.

Its revival in July, 1974, received considerable attention overseas, and might even have been the inspiration behind what became the first ever calypso (or, at least, calypso-style) record ever to top the UK chart — summer, 1975's joyously celebratory "Barbados" by Typically Tropical. It was ironic, therefore, that the record was both written and performed, in cod-Caribbean accents, by two white English sessionmen, Jeff Calvert and Max West.

Echoing its 19th century counterpart, Crop Over begins with the Ceremonial Delivery of the Last Canes, followed by the crowning of the King and Queen of the Festival — titles once awarded to the most productive male and female cane cutters of the season. However, where once the event lasted for a single day, today it expands over a full month, July–August.

Other events include the popular Decorated Cart Parade and Cohobblopot, a huge carnival-like show in its own right, featuring the extravagantly costumed "Kadooment" bands which are themselves a survivor of Crop Over's oldest traditions.

Calypso moved into focus during the late 1970s. Although the music had existed on the island for decades, it needed the impetus of carnival and competition to truly bring it to prominence. Supplanting the Folk Singer of the Year competition as Barbados' principle contest, the Pic-o-de-Crop Calypso Competition involves up to a dozen calypso tents, from whom the eventual monarch is chosen. Road March was inaugurated in 1979, when it was won by Gabby.

Notable Crop Over Calypso Monarchs have included Krosfyah's Edwin Yearwood (whose 1995 victory was accompanied by Road March and Party Monarch titles, the first time one artist ever won all three events) and Square One's Alison Hinds, who became the first ever female victor in 1996, before emulating Yearwood's triple crown in 1997. Hinds' bandmates Andy "Young Blood" Armstrong and Cecil "O'Shaka" Riley are also Pic-o-de-Crop regulars — the band's 1999 album, 25, was so titled in honor of Crop Over's silver jubilee that same year.

DOMINICA
HISTORY

Located within the Lesser Antilles island chain between the French-owned islands of Guadeloupe and Martinique (and not, therefore, to be confused with the Dominican Republic), Dominica was first sighted and named by Christopher Columbus on November 3, 1493. The indigenous Carib people successfully resisted early European attempts at colonization, and Dominica remained one of their last strongholds. In 1632, the French gained a foothold on the island, but as late as 1660, the Caribs and the French were still in a state of open warfare, until a peace treaty was signed in that year.

Political control of the island passed to the British in 1763, under the Treaty of Paris. The French regained control in 1778, retaining the island until the Treaty of Versailles returned it to the British in 1783. However, it was 1814 before the government could truly say they had control of Dominica, as rebellious slaves and the surviving Carib led regular revolts. There were also a number of thriving Maroon communities in the mountainous interior, formed by runaway slaves; while these were common to most of the islands, Dominica's community seems to have been especially troublesome. Between 1785–90, the British were embroiled in what history records as the First Maroon War. A second such conflict burned between 1809–14.

Under British rule, Dominica became part of the Leeward Islands dependency in 1833, and was attached to the Windward Islands group in 1940. Dominica became a member of the West Indian Federation in 1958, and was granted internal self-government in 1967. Dominica finally attained full independence on November 2, 1978.

CARNIVAL: MAS DOMINIK

Dominica's annual carnival, Mas Dominik, is staged annually during two weeks in February, a colorful celebration centered around the traditional "lapo kabwit" drumming which forms the pounding backdrop to every event. Alongside the Miss Dominica Queen pageant, the Calypso Monarch competition is, of course, a centerpiece of Mas Dominik.

The first Calypso competition was staged in Windsor Park by St Havis Shillingford in 1959. It was won by The Idol, whose record of three consecutive victories (1959–61) was finally equalled in 1975–77 by Lord Solo, whose overall tally of four wins has yet to be beaten. Other notable past winners have included Lord Breaker (1967, 1968), Zeye (1979) and the controversial De Rabbit (1984), while Dominica is also home to soca pioneer Lord Tokyo. Among Dominica's other leading artists are De Hunter, Lazo (winner of the Juno Award in 2000 for Best Reggae Recording) and the heavyweight Young Bull, who dominated local airwaves in 1992 with his *Too Fat to Soca* album.

CALYPSO MONARCHS

1989 Wizzard
1990 Wizzard
1991 De Scrunter
1992 De Scrunter
1993 De Hurricane
1994 De Hurricane
1995 De Scrunter
1996 De Hurricane
1997 De Brakes
1998 De Hunter
1999 De Brakes
2000 De Hunter

GRENADA
HISTORY

Grenada was discovered in 1498 by Christopher Columbus, but the hostility of the indigenous Carib people ensured that the island remained uncolonized until 1650, when the French founded the city of Saint George's.

The British captured the island in 1762. It was retaken by the French in 1779, but was ceded to Britain under the Treaty of Paris in 1783. However, a slave rebellion in 1795 saw the authorities lose all control of Grenada for over a year. Nevertheless, sugar plantations on the island proved a major success, while Grenada also became one of the world's largest producers of nutmeg.

Grenada was the administrative headquarters of the British Windward Islands from 1885 to 1958, uniting St Vincent, St Lucia and Tobago under one governor, but with its own treasury, police force and legislative council — in fact, the only common link between the four islands was a shared lunatic asylum on Grenada.

From 1958 to 1962 the island was part of the Federation of the West Indies. Grenada became independent on February 7, 1974, under the initially popular, but increasingly corrupt, cruel and eccentric government of Prime Minister Eric Gairy. His reign was finally overthrown by the Marxist People's Revolutionary Government (PRG) in 1979 — Gairy himself was in New York at the time, trying to convince the UN to recognize the existence of UFOs.

The PRG was an extraordinarily popular movement within Grenada, forging alliances which alienated the "democratic" world superpowers, but saw foreign aid pour into the island's infrastructure from Cuba, the USSR, Algeria, Iraq, Syria and Libya. However, flamboyant overspending led Grenada into serious economic problems in 1983, and divisions within the government saw the dismissal, arrest and execution of PRG Prime Minister, Maurice Bishop, that fall.

A new Revolutionary Military Council was installed to govern the island; their actions, however, were widely condemned throughout the remainder of the Caribbean, prompting the US invasion of Grenada just six days later. Following equally controversial elections overseen by the invaders, a new government favoring free market forces was elected in December, 1984. Regardless of these political upheavals, Grenada has managed to create a thriving tourism industry.

CARNIVAL

Grenada's carnival was originally staged during the run-up to Lent, but was shifted to Emancipation Day in August to avoid competing with the T&T event. It now overlaps with the island's other principle summer events, the Carriacou Regatta and the Rainbow City Festival, with preparations beginning in May, a full three months before the actual event. In 2000, the city of Gouvaye also launched a "Carnival City" program, with free, officially sanctioned, street parties every Friday night beginning in mid-June, leading up to the main event.

Grenada's first truly successful calypsonian was Zebra. He moved to Trinidad as a child and appeared in the Young Brigade tent performing "No Pan, No Pan in the Band" in 1948. Zebra subsequently relocated to the Virgin Islands around 1952, although he made several reappearances at the T&T carnival, performing at the Original Young Brigade tent during the late 1950s/early 1960s. He recorded at least one album for RCA (T&T) in 1956, combining original material with Radio, Terror and Spoiler covers.

Grenada was also the birthplace of both Mighty Sparrow (see entry on page 184) and the great Lord Caruso, who debuted at the T&T carnival in 1954, and won the Road March in 1959. Caruso recorded a number of weighty songs during the late 1950s/early 1960s, including "Africa," "We Encouraging the Criminals," "Death Row Cell 2455" and "Burn Them." In 1967, he returned to Grenada, where he became a dominant force at his homeland's carnival, until his death from kidney failure in the late 1970s.

Leading present-day Grenada calypsonians include Ajamu, Black Wizard, Flyin' Turkey (Calypso King for 1976–78, 1984), Flying Cloud, Inspector, Darius Thomas (Calypso Monarch, 2000), Mighty Squeeze and Tallpree (Road March winner, 2000). Evlyn Alexander was Grenada Soca Monarch for 2000.

GUYANA
HISTORY

Although Guyana is located on the South American mainland, political considerations have long seen it included within the Caribbean — indeed, it is frequently referred to as the gateway to the Caribbean from South America.

Although Spanish explorers first charted the area in 1499, it was the Dutch who first established a permanent colony, on an island in the Essequibo River, in the 1620s. The English and French also founded settlements, with all three nations claiming rights in the region.

By the mid-18th century, the Dutch had established two further colonies, Berbice and Demerara, but lost their holdings after France occupied their homeland during the French Revolution in 1789. In 1795, the Dutch offered the colonies to the British to prevent the French from moving in, and, in 1814, the British officially took possession. In 1831, the British merged the three Dutch settlements into a single colony known as British Guiana. (Other Dutch settlements on the coast were retained and formed the foundation of modern Suriname.) Following the abolition of slavery in 1834, the British recruited indentured servants from East India to work the plantations, a system which survived until 1917. Modern Guyana's unique population mix of Africans and East Indians stems from this policy.

Guyana received its first constitution under the British administration in 1928. And although independence was originally scheduled to take place in 1962, it did not occur until 1966, at which time the country took the name Guyana.

CARNIVAL

Guyana enjoys a number of major festivals throughout the year, each significant to one of the three major religious groupings which call the country home — Hindus, Muslims and Christians. The most significant — and certainly the most colorful — however, is Mashramani or Mash, staged annually since 1970 in late February, to celebrate the foundation of the Guyanan Republic (February 23). Masquerades, floats and street dancing are all a major part of the event, which climaxes with the Calypso competitions.

The best-known modern Guyanan calypsonian is Lord Canary, who debuted at the T&T carnival in 1966, and appeared in the 1985 King of Kings competition singing "Wicket Cricket." The following year, he presented the paper "The Nature and Function of Calypso in Guyana" at the University of the West Indies conference on Calypso and Society. Also in the 1980s, Lord Canary was selected as the government's Cultural Affairs minister, and he was elected Calypso Monarch in 1988.

Recent Mash favorites have included Tempest (the first female victor, in 1994), the Kaiso Kid, the Mighty Intruder and Special Lady Nima. Among the artists competing for Calypso and Soca Monarch crowns at Mash 2000 were reigning (1999) rulers Winfield James and the Mighty Rebel, plus Angel Gabriel, Black Hat, Blazing Fire, Lady Explainer, Mighty Destroyer, Mighty Raja, Mighty Roots, Prince Solomon, Ras Marcus and Winston Gray.

Guyana is also the homeland of international stars Eddy Grant and Terry Gajraj, both of whom have composed songs in praise (and otherwise) of the country. Gajraj, in particular, represents the country's long-established East Indian community, which itself did much to bring about the chutney revolution elsewhere in the region.

JAMAICA
HISTORY

When the first Europeans reached the Caribbean, Jamaica was inhabited by the Arawak tribe (the island is named from the Arawakan word Xaymaca, meaning isle of springs). Christopher Columbus sighted the island during his second voyage and it became a Spanish colony in 1509, with the first colony established at Saint Jago de la Vega (now Spanish Town) around 1523.

Much as they did elsewhere in the Caribbean, the Spaniards lost interest in the island once it became clear that it contained no gold. A handful of settlers remained, with the island under the nominal control of Christopher Colum-

bus' descendants, until it was captured by an English naval force, commanded by Sir William Penn, in 1655. Jamaica was formally transferred to England in 1670 under the Treaty of Madrid.

Heavy immigration from England saw the sugar, cacao and other agricultural and forest industries expand rapidly during the second half of the century, with the consequent demand for plantation labor leading to the large-scale importation of African slaves.

By the 1700s, Jamaica was an immensely wealthy sugar producer, ruled by the most powerful plantation owners with minimal interference from London. Their success continued despite a series of cataclysms later in the century — an earthquake in 1692 damaged the entire country and destroyed the capital, Port Royal (the modern city of Kingston was founded as a consequence); yellow fever was endemic; and a French invasion in 1694 came close to capturing the island. Between 1730 and Emancipation in 1834, the island's population more than quadrupled, from 82,000 to 376,000.

Jamaica's economy suffered severe difficulties in the aftermath of Abolition. Although a number of workers were recruited from northern Europe and Portuguese Madeira, disease wiped most of them out. By 1860, replacements simply could not be lured to the island, even among the indentured East Indians who flocked to British Guiana (modern Guyana) and Trinidad. Jamaican exports fell by one-half, one-third of all plantations closed, and with local government devising ever more punitive taxes, the inevitable finally occurred. In October, 1865, a massive insurrection occurred at Port Morant. Imposing martial law, the government swiftly quelled the uprising and declared Jamaica a crown colony. Local government was not even partially restored until 1884.

Internal autonomy returned to Jamaica in 1953, under Alexander Bustamente's Jamaican Labour Party (JLP). In elections two years later, Norman Manley's People's National Party (PNP) came briefly to power, leading Jamaica into the Federation of the West Indies in 1958. However, Bustamente's opposition party forced a plebiscite in late 1961, which removed the island again. The JLP returned to government soon after, and oversaw independence on August 6, 1962. Bustamente retired in 1967, and was succeeded by Hugh Lawson Shearer; the JLP remained in government until their defeat at the hands PNP, under the leadership of Manley's son Michael, in 1972.

Violence scarred that election, but worse was to follow during the 1976 campaign, as the rival ideologies of socialism (PNP) and conservatism (JLP) fought for control of the country — and whether one viewed those ideologies as conservative versus socialist, or traditionalist versus radical, the outcome remained the same, bully versus bully.

1976 opened with some of the worst rioting in years, as uptown Kingston hosted the International Monetary Fund's annual conference, and downtown rose up in protest. Rumors that Prime Minister Manley's eternal foes in the JLP were responsible for much of the unrest were stoked by the proximity of the next general election, a contest during which Manley's increasingly militant program of socialism was to receive its toughest test yet.

Manley's admiration for Castro's Cuba was no secret; nor was his government's support of the Communist revolution in Angola. Jamaica's wealthy plantocracy had been seeing figurative reds under the bed ever since the PNP came to power in 1972. Now they were beginning to find real ones there as well. Other horrors, too, were abroad. Three years earlier, American fears that Chile was preparing to take a similar political path were ended when the CIA assisted the country's military in rising up and snatching power for itself.

There were no guarantees that the same fate did not await Jamaica, all the more so since the strict new currency laws imposed by the IMF had seen Manley outlaw the possession of American dollars. Already there seemed to be more guns and fire arms on the island, supplied by the Americans and smuggled in, it was whispered, by the JLP. On June 19, the government declared a state of emergency. It remained in force for the rest of the year, until elections in December finally confirmed the PNP's mandate.

The 1980 campaign, which saw Manley voted out, was even more violent, leaving over 800 Jamaicans dead, mainly as a result of clashes between political gangs.

Manley was succeeded by Edward Seaga of the JLP, former finance minister but, prior to that, a leading force in the birth of the modern Jamaican music industry. Seaga swiftly severed relations with Cuba, established close ties with the United States, and tried hard to attract foreign capital. However, a weak market for Jamaica's mineral exports hampered economic recovery, a plight worsened in September, 1988, when Hurricane Gilbert caused an estimated $8 billion in property damage and left some 500,000 Jamaicans homeless.

Manley returned to power in 1989, and immediately swept away the excesses of the JLP's "free market" policies. Although he was forced to resign in 1992 due to poor health, Percival J. Patterson, his successor as Prime Minister and PNP leader, easily won re-election a year later. In 1997, the PNP won an unprecedented third consecutive electoral victory, capturing 56 percent of the vote.

THE INDEPENDENCE FESTIVAL

Despite boasting the most successful musical tradition in modern Caribbean history, the modern carnival arrived late in Jamaica. It had, of course, existed during the slavery era, but the dire economic state in which Jamaica wallowed for much of the 19th and 20th centuries, neither encouraged its continuation, nor regretted its demise.

It was 1962 before carnival returned, in the form of the Independence Festival, a full fledged celebration of the arts nurtured by then Minister of Community Development, Edward Seaga, to showcase literary, fine and performing artists in a variety of contests.

Set to climax on the first Monday in August, the event coincides with the anniversary of both Independence and Emancipation (the two events share the same public holiday). The other highlighted features are queen shows and agricultural exhibitions, all culminating in an array of street parades with floats and effigies, which reach their apex at a grand gala show at Kingston's National Stadium. Supporting events take place in the 14 parish capitals and other main commercial centers.

While burru, johncanoe and a mento band competition certainly have their adherents, for music fans the absolute highlight of the Festival is the Independence Festival Song Competition (from 1990, Popular Song). Inaugurated in 1966, it can be compared, in both organization and significance, to the calypso Monarch competitions elsewhere in the Caribbean — indeed, that was the model upon which the competition was based, with Jamaica's own unique musical complexion then coloring the event itself.

FESTIVAL/POPULAR SONG COMPETITION WINNERS

1966 The Maytals: "Bam Bam"

1967 The Jamaicans: "Baba Boom"

1968 Desmond Dekker & the Aces: "Music Like Dirt"

1969 The Maytals: "Sweet and Dandy"

1970 Hopeton Lewis: "Boom Shacka Lacka"

1971 Eric Donaldson: "Cherry oh Baby"

1972 Toots & The Maytals: "Pomps and Pride"

1973 Morvin Brooks: "Jump in the Line"

1974 Tinga Stewart: "Play de Music"

1975 Roman Stewart: "Hooray Festival"

1976 Freddie McKay: "Dance this Ya Festival"

1977 Eric Donaldson: "Sweet Jamaica"

1978 Eric Donaldson: "Land of My Birth"

1979 The Astronauts: "Born Jamaican"

1980 Stanley & The Turbines: "Come Sing with Me"

1981 Tinga Stewart: "Nuh Wey Nuh Betta Dan Yard"

1982 The Astronauts: "Mek wi Jam"

1983 Ras Karbi: "Jamaica I'll Never Leave You"

1984 Eric Donaldson: "Proud to Be Jamaican"

1985 Roy Rayon: "Love Fever"

1986 Stanley & The Turbines: "Dem a fe Squirm"

1987 Roy Rayon: "Give Thanks and Praise"

1988 Singer Jay: "Jamaica Land We Love"

The Maytals, winners of the first Festival Song Competition.

1989 Michael Forbes: "Stop and Go"

1990 Robbie Forbes: "Island Festival"

1991 Roy Rayon: "Come Rock"

1992 Heather Grant: "Mek wi Put Things Right"

1993 Eric Donaldson: "Big it Up"

1994 Stanley & The Astronauts: "Dem a Pollute"

1995 Eric Donaldson: "Join de Line"

1996 Zac Henry & Donald White: "Meck We Go Spree"

1997 Eric Donaldson: "Peace and Love"

1998 Neville Martin: "Jamaica Whoa"

1999 Cheryl Clarke: "Born inna JA"

2000 Marvin Harriott: "Feel the Boom"

CARNIVAL

A rival to the Independence Festival arrived on the scene in the late 1980s, through the efforts of veteran musician/ entrepreneur Byron Lee. A long time devotee of calypso, and a regular attendant at T&T's annual event, Lee launched what he described as a true carnival, as opposed to an arts festival, during the week of April 14–22, 1990, with events in Kingston, Ocho Rios and Montego Bay. Cos-

tumes were designed by some of T&T's best known designers; music was provided by Lee and his Dragonaires.

The event was a success despite intense opposition from both religious groups and organizers of the Independence Festival and, since that time, carnival has established itself among the island's largest and most vibrant events (over 40,000 people took part in 1998).

The range and complexity of the festival, too, have mushroomed. Local designers and Mas Camps have emerged, and a Road March has come into being. In 1993, Eddie Chai (manager of the Humming Birds Steel Orchestra) introduced pan to the event, while that same year saw another T&T tradition, the Ole Mas, enacted for the first time. Two years later, the first J'Ouvert Parade took place.

1996 saw the creation of a National Committee to oversee the organization of the carnival, and, in 1998, Byron Lee formally handed over the reigns to promotor Russell Hadeed. However, Lee returned to the scene the following year to celebrate its 10th anniversary. As always, the song he cut for Carnival that year, "Soca Prang," proved one of the inescapable hits of the event.

MONTSERRAT
HISTORY

Located within the Lesser Antilles island group, Montserrat was settled by Irish Catholics departing the neighboring British colony of St Kitts in 1632 — their legacy is source of both the island's nickname of "the Emerald isle" and the distinct Gaelic flavor which permeates traditional Montserrat folk music.

The island's history echoes that of others in the Leewards chain. Its early sugar prosperity was eclipsed by neighboring Barbados to such an extent, that in the century preceding Emancipation in 1834, Montserrat's white population declined from over a thousand, to just 330. Merged into the Leeward Islands federation (alongside Anguilla and the British Virgin Islands) during the 19th century, Montserrat was a member of the West Indies Federation, but became a crown colony in 1962, following that group's collapse. It remains a British possession to this day.

The 1980s saw the island make an aggressive, and extraordinarily successful, attempt to build the country's infrastructure — between 1985 and 1994, Montserrat's economy grew by more than 10% a year, with per capita income higher than almost every island in the region. Offshore banking increased the island's prosperity (at least until 1992, when over 90% of the institutions were closed down during British investigations into corruption and criminal activities).

This period of growth ended in July, 1995, when the Chances Peak volcano erupted after more than a century of dormancy. With geologists insisting that the entire southern portion of the island was in immediate danger, over 5,000 residents were evacuated to the north, including the entire population of the capital city, Plymouth. That city itself was destroyed by a subsequent eruption. At the time of writing (early 2002), the volcano remains active.

CARNIVAL

Montserrat's Carnival is staged annually between Christmas and New Year. The best known Monarch is Arrow, who won the first of four titles while still a schoolboy in 1971, before going on to become the first soca superstar a decade later. (Two of his brothers, Justin "Hero" Cassell and Lorenzo "Young Challenger" Cassell, were also Calypso Monarchs during the 1960s.)

Around the same time as Arrow broke through, in 1982, another Montserrat act, the Goombay Dance Band, became the island's first act to crack the international market, when their calypso-style "Seven Tears" single topped the UK chart. A follow-up, "Sun of Jamaica," reached #50.

Montserrat also made musical headlines when George Martin, producer of the Beatles, built his AIR Studios on the site of the old Sturges Farm water works in 1978. A number of top British and American acts recorded there over the next decade — so, of course, did Arrow. However, the studio sustained serious damage from Hurricane Hugo in 1989 and was soon closed down.

Martin retained an affection for Montserrat, however. He was one of the driving forces behind the September, 1997, Music for Montserrat benefit concert in London, which raised over a million dollars for the volcano's victims, and featured performances by Arrow, Elton John, Paul McCartney, Eric Clapton and more. That same night, British rock act Climax Blues Band (famous as the first European act to record at the Montserrat AIR studios) and Anguillan Bankie Banks headlined the Many Happy Returns concert at Gerald's Bottom, Montserrat.

A similar show was planned for the following fall, with parallel events in Anguilla and, again, London. The arrival of Hurricane Georges, however, forced the postponement of the two Caribbean shows (the London event went ahead), and Many Happy Returns II was eventually staged in Montserrat alone on St Patrick's Day, 1999. Appearing were Arrow, the Irish band Kissing Stone, and Montserrat calypsonians Cupid, Hustler and Hero, plus Muscovada, a band formed in 1998 by Randall "Zunky" Greenaway, Cecil "Cepeke" Lake and Dave "Pregu" Williams. Greenaway was ex-the duo Zunky & Dem, Lake was best known for the solo hit "My Redemption."

ST KITTS-NEVIS
HISTORY

St Kitts was first colonized by the English in 1624 — it was their earliest Caribbean settlement and, for some years, their most important. The island's first successful tobacco harvest reached England in 1625, igniting a frenzy of subsequent settlements in the region; Nevis, Montserrat and Antigua were all settled by colonists heading out from St Kitts. Nevis and St Kitts were united as one administrative body in 1882. Following its involvement in the short-lived West Indies federation, St Kitts-Nevis was granted independence in 1983.

CARNIVAL

St Kitts-Nevis stages carnival annually during the period between Christmas and New Year's. Of the islands' leading performers, Mighty Pat placed fourth in the 1998 Leeward Islands Calypso Monarch competition.

CALYPSO MONARCHS

1971–72 Entertainer
1972–73 Entertainer
1973–74 Ellie Matt
1974–75 Ellie Matt
1975–76 Sweeney
1976–77 Mallet
1977–78 Starshield
1978–79 Ellie Matt

1979–80 Mallet
1980–81 Ellie Matt
1981–82 Ellie Matt
1982–83 Ellie Matt
1983–84 Mark the First
1984–85 Ellie Matt
1985–86 Phonsie
1986–87 Ellie Matt
1987–88 Starshield
1988–89 Socrates
1989–90 Socrates
1990–91 Ellie Matt
1991–92 Lord De Maths Too Hard
1992–93 (unknown)
1993–94 (no carnival)
1994–99 (unknown)
1999–2000 Ayatollah

ROAD MARCH CHAMPIONS

1971–72 Sundar Popo: "Play You Mas"
1972–73 Controller: "Right On"
1973–74 Ellie Matt: "All Day, All Night"
1974–75 Mark The First: "Come Forward"
1975–76 Arrow: "Rummy Song"
1976–77 Ellie Matt: "Jam Back"
1977–78 Ellie Matt: "Shang Shang"
1978–79 Ellie Matt: "Sugar City Jam"
1979–80 Ellie Matt: "Tune for de Children"
1980–81 Ranger: "Seven Day Mas"
1981–82 Starshield: "Hooray Mas"
1982–83 Ellie Matt: "Patsy"
1983–84 (no competition)
1984–85 Shango: "Chin Chin Bar"
1985–86 Mic Stokes: "One Shot Man"
1986–87 (tie) De Coach: "De Boops"/Contender: "Living in de Band"
1987–88 Grand Masters: "Master's Jam"
1988–89 Small Axe: "Big League"
1989–90 Small Axe: "Who Is de Dan"
1990–91 Small Axe: "Pan Man"
1991–92 Mic Stokes: "All Kinda Tings"
1992–93 (unknown)
1993–94 (no carnival)
1994–95 (unknown)
1995–96 Nu Vybes: "Hands Up"
1996–97 Nu Vybes: "Hand Signal"
1997–98 Nu Vybes: "Street Style"
1998–99 Grand Masters: "Masters Massive"
1999–2000 Grand Masters: "Millennium Jam"

ST LUCIA
HISTORY
St Lucia was probably first visited by Europeans about 1500. The first successful colony was established in 1635 by the French, a venture which ended in 1654, when the indigenous Carib people rose and massacred the entire settlement. A new colony was more successful, and St Lucia's sugar plantations prospered (today, the principle crop is bananas), despite periodic changes in the island's ownership.

Three times between 1762 and 1796, British invasions brought the island under that country's control, three times treaties handed it back to France. In 1803, a fourth invasion proved more permanent, and the island was finally ceded to Britain in 1814.

Representative government was first introduced to the island in 1924. From 1958 to 1962 Saint Lucia was a member of the Federation of the West Indies. In 1967 it became a member of the West Indies Associated States with full internal self-government. On February 22, 1979, Saint Lucia became an independent state within the British Commonwealth of Nations.

CARNIVAL
St Lucia's carnival takes place annually in June–July. A calypso competition has formed a part of the event since 1957, although the first local calypsonians of note began appearing during the 1940s, when the Mighty Bonnet, the Mighty Session, Battle Axe, Lord Scrubb, Ezekial and Piti Quart staged impromptu performances in the streets. Regular competitions followed during the early 1950s and, in 1955, Mighty Session won the newly instituted Road March with his calypso "The Flying Cask."

The first calypso monarch of St Lucia was Terra, a schoolteacher who held the crown for five years running, 1957–1961, and again in 1965.

The first calypso tents opened in St Lucia in 1976, under the aegis of Lord Jackson, the locally born son of a Trinidadian. Lord Jackson was also a founding member of the St Lucia Calypsonian Association, and was elected Calypso Monarch in 1980. St Lucia crowned its first female Monarch in 2000, Lady Spice (performing "This Woman Vex").

Other successful performers have included Madame Sequin, the New York based Mighty Jaunty and 2000 Soca Monarch and Road March winner Rootsy.

ST VINCENT/GRENADINES
HISTORY
St Vincent was first visited and named by Christopher Columbus in 1498. Although St Vincent subsequently fell within the French sphere of influence, the island itself was left unsettled, as a treaty reserved it as a homeland for the indigenous Carib people (Dominica was similarly left at peace). This agreement remained in force until 1763, when the Treaty of Paris passed the island to England. The Caribs

were subdued and many were deported, following an uprising in 1795.

In 1902, St Vincent received worldwide attention following the eruption of the volcano Mount Pele, which killed over 2,000 people and all but obliterated the northern half of the island (a similar disaster has threatened Montserrat since 1996).

St Vincent was a member of the Federation of the West Indies from 1958 to 1962 and, in 1969, it became an internally self-governing member of the West Indies Associated States. On October 27, 1979, it received full independence within the Commonwealth of Nations as Saint Vincent and the Grenadines, the administrative title for the chain of some 600 islands which stretch south to Grenada. A separatist movement in the Grenadines resulted in a brief uprising in 1979, on Union Island.

CARNIVAL

St Vincent's carnival, Vincy Mas, was originally staged in the days preceding Lent. It was moved to the last week of June/first week of July to avoid coinciding with the larger T&T event.

TURKS & CAICOS ISLANDS
HISTORY

The Turks & Caicos Islands take their name from the indigenous Turk's Head "fez" cactus, and the indigenous Lucayan term "caya hico," meaning string of islands. Columbus is widely believed to have sighted the islands in 1492, although the matter is disputed — Ponce de Leon is also credited as their European discoverer.

Both the Spanish and French occupied the islands during the 15th/16th centuries, before British colonists arrived from Bermuda during the 17th century, settling on the islands of Grand Turk, Salt Cay and South Caicos. (The other main islands in the group are Middle Caicos, North Caicos, Providenciales and the uninhabited East and West Caicos.)

Initially, the islands' principle industries were salt and cotton; however, the thin native soil saw the latter crop deteriorate during the 18th century, with the death blow to the industry being dealt by a hurricane in 1813.

Between 1776–1848, Turks and Caicos were under the administration of the Bahamas colony. The islands became a British Crown Colony in 1862 and were granted a resident governor in 1972. They remain a British Overseas Territory, one of five remaining dependencies in the Caribbean (alongside Anguilla, the Cayman Islands, Montserrat and the British Virgin Islands).

CARNIVAL

Until 2000, Turks & Caicos had no official carnival, the chief local celebration being a National Youth Day. That September, however, the Legislative Council announced plans for a Cultural Awareness Week, embracing sport, dancing and music. The motion itself stated, "WHEREAS it is said that the people of the Turks and Caicos Islands have no culture. AND WHEREAS the importance of knowing and defining who you are as a people is inextricably linked to instilling and encouraging national pride . . . the Honourable House deems the week immediately preceding National Youth Day each year to be Cultural Awareness Week during which all aspects of local culture will be displayed and celebrated" under the aegis of the newly formed Turks and Caicos Islands Cultural Commission (TCICC).

VIRGIN ISLANDS
HISTORY

The British Virgin Islands comprise 36 islands east of Puerto Rico, forming part of the Lesser Antilles chain. Just 16 of the islands are inhabited, the principle settlements being Tortola, Virgin Gorda, Anegada, Jost Van Dyke, Peter Islands, and Salt Island. The capital and only town in the group is Road Town, on the southeastern coast of Tortola.

First visited by Christopher Columbus in 1493, the islands were originally settled by the Dutch in 1648. They passed to Britain in 1666 during the Second Dutch War, but attempts to establish the islands as a sugar producer finally ended in the 1830s.

From 1871 to 1956 the islands were part of the Federation of the Leeward Islands. They opted not to join the West Indies federation in 1958, and remain affiliated to Great Britain.

CARNIVAL

The British Virgin Islands Emancipation Festival Celebrations take place annually in late July/early August. (Emancipation Day is celebrated on August 1.) The neighboring US Virgin Islands festivities take place earlier in the year; St Thomas celebrates around Easter, while St John's festivities fall on July 4th.

The Islands boast their own indigenous variation on goombay, named "fungi" after a traditional local food based on corn bread, combined with onions, peppers and okras — a fiery stew which sums up the music perfectly! The Lashing Dogs, whose fungi is further flavored with reggae and calypso, are the music's prime modern exponents.

The other best known BVI performer is Enriquito "Quito" Rymes, whose five album catalog includes two CDs (*Searchin'*, *Paradise*) and three cassettes (*Mis up World*, *Caribbean Run* and *Reggae Express*). Recent USVI stars have included St Claire Alphonso DeSilva, St Thomas' 2000 Calypso Monarch.

PART TWO: ARTIST/GENRE PROFILES

THE ABYSSINIANS

STYLE *reggae*
FORMED *1968 (Kingston, JA)*
ORIGINAL LINE-UP *Bernard Collins (vocals), Lynford Manning (vocals), Donald Manning (vocals)*

The crucial Rastafarian rebels of the late 1960s, the Abyssinians' smokey rootsiness pointed out a new direction to a multitude of inner city aspirants, physically delineating the path Jamaican music took during the 1970s. Their best known recording, the hymnal "Satta Amasa Gana" ("give thanks and praise" in Amharic), has been described as the national anthem of roots reggae. It is an accolade with which few would disagree.

The Abyssinians came together in early 1968 when Bernard Collins and Donald Manning, friends since their teens in the 1950s, composed "Satta Amasa Gana" during a late night songwriting session. Instantly aware of the song's potential, they sought out a third vocalist and launched themselves onto the Kingston scene.

This initial incarnation of the group did not survive; the newcomer was still at school, and was often unable to attend rehearsals and shows. He was dismissed and, in his stead, came one of Donald's brothers, Lynford — at that time a member of the vocal trio Carlton & The Shoes with another Manning sibling, Carlton. (A fourth brother, Estefanos, was an Ethiopian Orthodox priest, and officiated at the funerals of both Bob Marley and Peter Tosh.)

Ironically, one of the Shoes' own songs, "Happy Land" (the b-side of 1968's chart-topping "Love Me Forever"), has subsequently been singled out by onlookers as a primary influence on "Satta Amasa Gana." According to Donald Manning, however, "Carlton did sing a song like that, but we sing ours in a different perspective." Although he alone was a Rastafarian at that time, it was his faith which both colored the song and dictated its fate.

With "Happy Land" producer Coxsone Dodd, the Abyssinians recorded "Satta Amasa Gana," together with several other tracks, at Studio One in March, 1969 — and single-handedly illustrated the split now appearing in the Kingston scene between the older musicians whose intentions and ideals were formed in an earlier age, and the new generation of street-wise revolutionaries.

Unable to discern an iota of commercial potential in a performance which swam in what he perceived as cultural subversion, Dodd refused to release either "Satta Amasa Gana" — or anything else by the band. Their material remained on the shelf for the next two years.

In 1971, the Abyssinians purchased the session tapes back from producer Dodd for the sizeable sum of 90 pounds, and

released it on their own Clinch label. Immediately, Dodd's misgivings were crushed. Not only was "Satta Amasa Gana" an immediate hit, it was swiftly joined in the chart by Dodd's own rush-released instrumental and DJ versions of the song (including efforts by Tommy McCook — "Cool It"; and Jackie Mittoo — "Night in Ethiopia"). Clinch hit back with its own variations by Big Youth ("I Pray Thee" and "Dreader than Dread"), Tommy McCook again ("Mandela") and Dillinger ("I Saw E Saw").

The Abyssinians themselves followed through with another cut from the same Dodd sessions, the similarly evocative "Declaration of Rights." The next few years brought further hits with "Let My Days Be Long" (1971) and "Leggo Beast" (1972). Dodd also released competing versions of several Abyssinians tracks, albeit in limited editions.

1973 brought a new version of "Satta Amasa Gana," "Mabrak," featuring the group members reciting verses from the Old Testament. Collins alone released another 45 utilizing the same rhythm track, "Satta Me No Born Yah" (1976). Clinch remained the Abyssinians' primary outlet, but the trio also recorded with other producers, including Lloyd Daley ("Reason Time" and "Yim Mas Gan" — 1972/73), Tommy Cowan ("Love Comes and Goes" — 1975) and Geoffrey Chung (another Amharic anthem, "Tenayistillin Wandimae" — 1975).

The Abyssinians cut their first album, *Forward on to Zion*, with producer Clive Azul Hunt in 1976. Recent singles "Forward Jah" and "Prophecy" were included, together with both "Satta Amasa Gana" and "Mabrak," and a dramatic new recording of "Declaration of Rights." The record sold well, although its most successful pressings were bootlegs manufactured in the UK, which were rarely off that country's turntables all year.

In 1978, Clinch linked with Bob Marley's Tuff Gong label for a second Abyssinians album, the self-produced *Arise*, and the accompanying single, "Hey You." After a decade together, however, the trio was becoming increasingly fractious and Collins left soon after the album's completion. He was replaced by Carlton Manning, thus reuniting all three performing brothers, and in this form, the Abyssinians performed at the 1979 Reggae Sunsplash. However, the group split in 1980, but were remembered with the *Forward* compilation that same year.

Donald Manning launched a short-lived solo career as Donald Abyssinians in the early 1980s, releasing the "Peculiar Number" 45 on his own Dahna Dimps label. Interest from the UK and US, meanwhile, saw the old band name resurface in 1989, as Collins relaunched the long-dormant Clinch label, leading with the singles "African Princess" and "Swing Low," both credited to the Abyssinians, and appearing under that name at Reggae Sunsplash.

The Mannings (with Collins appearing as a singing, but not writing, partner) then launched their own Abyssinians, issuing a new album, *Reunion*, in 1998. Collins' own Abyssinians album followed in 1999.

DISCOGRAPHY

🔟 Forward onto Zion (Different—JA) 1976

One of the most awe inspiring album debuts of the era, *Zion* remains the yardstick against which all other roots records must be judged. The record's soundscapes are lovingly sculpted by the Abyssinians' flawless close harmonies, through which the heavy rhythms stride majestically. The trio's vision, too, is absolutely breathtaking. Across such crucial songs as the title track, recut versions of "Declaration of Rights" and "Yim Mas Gan," and the magnificent "Satta Amasa Gana," *Zion* presents a vivid, devotional manifesto of Rastafarianism.

7️⃣ Arise (Tuff Gong—JA) 1978

Less spirited than its predecessor, but worthwhile for Collins' moving "This Land Is for Everyone" and "Let My Days Be Long." "Wicked Men" reprises the earlier single "Leggo Beast."

5️⃣ Reunion (Artists Only) 1998

SELECTED COMPILATIONS & ARCHIVE RELEASES

8️⃣ Forward (Alligator) 1980

A collection of high quality rarities, notably "Jerusalem" (the original flip from the first pressing of "Satta Amasa

Gana"—it was subsequently replaced by the semi-dub "Thunder Storm"), the exquisite "Prophesy" and a solo Bernard Collins' "Forward Jah Jah."

9️⃣ Satta Massagana (Heartbeat) 1993

The best of the Abyssinians almost inevitably revolves around their debut album, appended by four bonus cuts including "Leggo Beast" and "Peculiar Time."

8️⃣ The Best of the Abyssinians (MusicDisc—FRA) 1994

Solid collection sweeping up much of the trio's non-Clinch output. Placed alongside the *Satta* compilation, and forgiving occasional duplication, the group's greatest strengths are revealed in all their glory.

8️⃣ Satta Dub (Tabou—France) 1998
7️⃣ Declaration of Dub (Heartbeat) 1998

Two enjoyable dub sets concentrating on *Forward to Zion*, but with ten tracks duplicated, there's little reason to pick up both. The 14 song Heartbeat set features a new version of "Declaration of Rights," mixed by Karl Pitterson and Pablo Black; "Dub Abendigo," "Mark of the Dub" and "Reasonable Dub" wrap up the exclusive cuts. The Tabou issue features 15 cuts, including the otherwise unavailable "Jah Loves Dub" and "Dem a Dub," and probably has the edge via the inclusion of Tommy McCook's two part "Mandela"/"Satta" instrumental, plus its dub.

BERNARD COLLINS & THE ABYSSINIANS
6️⃣ Last Days (Tabou) 1999

Opening with a dedication to Bob Marley ("Jah Marley") and reprising "African Princess" and "Swing Low," a warm but none too remarkable set.

DENNIS ALCAPONE

STYLE *reggae (toasting/DJ)*
BORN *Dennis Smith, 6 August, 1947 (Clarendon, JA)*

A lynch-pin of Jamaica's early 1970s DJ-ing scene, Alcapone was an obvious disciple of the pioneering U-Roy and King Stitt, but still an absolute break in what was already becoming a well-established pattern. In a genre which had seemingly confirmed itself as little more than a succession of shouted interjections and catch-phrases, Alcapone's easygoing singing style not only introduced a new sound, but also perfected a new technique.

Alcapone's forte was to answer back to the vocal lines in the records he toasted over, or to expand upon sentiments raised in that original performance. That he was able to do this without breaking the rhythm of the performance, or obscuring the existing vocals, were equally signs of his talent. Besides, who else could toast along with Slim Smith in one song, then hold his own against "Mule Train" in another?

Alcapone first came to local prominence after he launched the El Paso Hi Fi sound system in 1969, with fellow DJs Lizzy and Samuel the First. One of the most successful systems of the era, drawing crowds so massive they often blocked entire streets, El Paso Hi Fi operated into early 1970, when Alcapone shifted his attention towards recording.

He cut sides with producers Niney Holness ("You Must Believe," "False Prophet") and Rupie Edwards ("You Must Believe Me"), but it was his unions with producers Coxsone Dodd and Keith Hudson which allowed him to spend the rest of 1970 machine-gunning singles into the marketplace.

Overseen by Hudson, "Shades Of Hudson," "Spanish Amigo," "Revelation," "I Don't Want to See You Cry," and "The Sky's the Limit" soon saw Alcapone attain unimagined local heights. At the same time, his debut album, *Forever Version*, rounded up a number of Dodd's productions, including "Power" and the title track, performed over the backing track of Carlton & The Shoes' "Love Me Forever."

Alcapone's talent was equal to his reputation. Producers queued to offer him the hottest rhythms, and the DJ effortlessly made them his own. Often visiting two or three studios a day, he cut over 100 singles in Jamaica between 1970–73. This impressive tally included its fair share of makeweight efforts, but also incorporated many of the tracks now considered essential to any "best of" Alcapone.

In 1971, Alcapone moved on to Bunny Lee's stable for a handful of hits: "Horse and Buggy," "Ripe Cherry," "Alcapone's Guns Don't Argue," "Tell It Like It Is," "Togetherness," "Jumping Jack" "Shake It Up" and "Lorna Banana" (a duet with fellow DJ Prince Jazzbo).

From there, Alcapone relocated to Duke Reid's studio, from whence he continued to dominate the Jamaican hit parade. "The Great Woggie," "Wake Up Jamaica," "Number One Station" and "Mosquito One" in 1971, "Rock to the Beat," "Love is Not a Gamble," and "Teach the Children" (1972) were highlights, with the boisterous latter remaining a favorite on Jamaican broadcasting's juvenile literacy programs.

Other highlights from this period included efforts with producers Phil Pratt ("This Is a Butter"); Byron Lee ("Go Johnny Go"); Lee Perry ("Well Dread," "Alpha Omega," "Rasta Dub," "Wonderman," "Master Key," "Back Biter"); Prince Buster ("Let It Roll," "Giant"); Prince Tony ("Fine Style," "Dub Up a Daughter"); Winston Riley ("Look into Yourself"); Byron Smith ("Out the Light, Baby"); Alvin Ranglin ("Milk and Honey," "King of Kings," "Honey Comb," "Musical Alphabet"); Harry J ("Party Time" and "Sorry Harry"), Joe Gibbs and JJ Johnson, among others.

Pairing up with Alton Ellis, Alcapone cut the popular "Big Bad Boy Version." Another well-received collaboration linked him with Dennis Brown for "Get in the Groove." Alcapone also began producing in his own right, recording Augustus Pablo ("Ape Man") and Delroy Wilson ("Little Village").

In 1972, Alcapone toured the UK for the first time. He returned home to be named Best DJ by the Jamaican magazine *Swing*, and reunited with Bunny Lee to record the immortal "Cassius Clay" with Slim Smith. Then it was back to Britain for another tour, during which time he determined to make London his home. He later explained, "I was on tour there, I met a girl and just kind of never got round to going home." From a personal point of view, it was the right move to make. From a musical perspective, however, it spelled the end of his stardom.

In 1974, following the low-key *Belch It Off* album with producer Sydney Crooks, Alcapone was among the first artists to sign with the newly formed British label Magnet. Releases included the Bunny Lee-produced *King of the Track* and the singles "Freedom Skank" and "Muhammad Ali," but Alcapone's visibility declined as the company's once pronounced interest in reggae faded.

A handful of 45s cut with UK producer Larry Lawrence included "Brixton Hall," "London Town" and "The Bounce" for the short-lived Ethnic Fight label; 1975–76 also saw the release of "Epsom Derby" and "Fattie Pum Pum" for Jamatel, and "Here I Come" for Justice.

Alcapone then shifted to the ambitious north London-based Third World label, joining a stable already dignified by the likes of Errol Dunkley, Johnny Clarke and I-Roy. The *Dread Capone* album, produced by Count Shelly, appeared on Third World's Live & Love subsidiary, before he was switched to the parent label for 1976's Lorraine "Ronnie Bop" Williams produced "Answer to My Commandments."

However, two albums in 1977, *Six Million Dollar Man* and, back with Bunny Lee, *Investigator Rock*, did little, while the death of his mother in 1979 saw Alcapone withdraw from recording for much of the next decade. His final single was a collaboration with producer KC White, "Throw Me Corn."

Following a tentative return to live work in 1988, Alcapone was one of the star attractions at the 1989 WOMAD festival. An enquiring interest in the digital scene now dominating his homeland saw him back in Jamaica in 1990, working again with Bunny Lee. He was also a guest on English dub producer Adrian Sherwood's *Two Bad Card* DJ album.

Despite such activity, Alcapone remains a shadowy figure on the fringes of the modern scene, his most significant release of the last decade being his collaboration with Mad Professor, 1997's *21st Century Version*. However, a hearty package of reissues and an explosion of mid-90s interest in his catalog have seen him finally attain the international prominence which should have been his three decades before.

SELECTED DISCOGRAPHY

8 Forever Version (Studio One — JA) 1971
Dynamic selection of Coxsone Dodd-produced sides, highlighting the colossal impact Alcapone had on a scene still accustomed to traditional DJ dub. Included are combination style assaults on Larry Marshall's "Nanny Goat," Delroy Wilson's "Run Run," several Heptones classics and cuts by the Wailers, John Holt, Alton Ellis, the Cables and Carlton & The Shoes. Since reissued by Heartbeat.

6 King of the Track (Magnet — UK) 1974
Alcapone is in fine form and the material is generally strong. But this is one of those albums better experienced piecemeal on 45s (the irrepressible "Lorna Banana") and cuts on compilations (*Musical Liquidator* is recommended) than in its own right.

6 Belch It Off (Attack — UK) 1974
Worth hearing for Alcapone's stylized revisions of "Little Jack Horner" and "Old King Cole," and packing one classic in the uncouth title track.

7 Dread Capone (Live & Love — UK) 1976
7 Six Million Dollar Man (Third World — UK) 1977
Alcapone's most openly Rastafarian set, with highlights "Babylon Set Rasta Free" and "Prophets of Jah" equal to any similarly themed performances since "Rocking to Ethiopia."

6 Investigator Rock (Third World — UK) 1977
6 21st Century Version (Ariwa — UK) 1997

Either one loves Mad Professor's work or one doesn't. Approached from a partisan Alcapone point of view, this set disappoints.

SELECTED COMPILATIONS & ARCHIVE RELEASES

8 Guns Don't Argue (Attack — UK) 1971
Subsequently released on the Jamaican Gold label, nonstop Bunny Lee from the 1971 Dynamic Sounds sessions, featuring all the crucial cuts. The album takes its title, of course, from Alcapone's version of "Love of the Common People."

8 Soul to Soul: DJ's Choice (Treasure Isle — JA) 1973
Although fellow DJs Lizzy, U-Roy and Little Youth also feature, the heart of *Soul to Soul* represents producer Duke Reid's own, utterly unimpeachable, view of Alcapone's golden years.

9 My Voice Is Insured for Half a Million Dollars (Trojan — UK) 1989
Originally available only as a 15 track vinyl collection, this near-definitive sampling of crucial Alcapone was upgraded to a 25 track CD collection of 1970–73 era sides. The sound quality is occasionally rough ("This Is a Butter" is one of several songs taken from a flawed vinyl source), but there is no better Alcapone compilation available today.

7 Universal Rockers (RAS) 1992
A representative, if somewhat tight-fisted, collection of tracks drawn from Alcapone's late 1970s Third World label releases.

7 Musical Liquidator (Jamaican Gold) 1995
Another Jamaican Gold reissue, Lee, Ephraim Barrett, Ronnie Bop and Alcapone himself are credited producers on a set which picks up much of Alcapone's lesser-known, but no less deserving, mid-1970s material.

See also entries: TOASTING: THE ART OF THE DJ on page 280, and DIRECTORY OF SINGLES on pages 321–388.

ADISA ANDWELE
STYLE *rhythm poetry/soca*
BORN *Mike Richards (BARB)*

One of the most exciting of the rhythm poets to have emerged outside of the music's traditional strongholds in Jamaica and T&T, Andwele first came to the public's notice in 1978–79 when he published the collection, *Whispers in the Spirit*, issued under his given name, Mike Richards. He began experimenting with rhythmic accompaniment over the next three years, forming the Re-emergence Band to back him at live performances.

The popularity of a second collection of poems, *Rhythms and Roots*, published in 1989, encouraged Andwele and the

Re-emergence Band to greater heights and, in 1990, And-wele became the first poet ever to stage a solo performance in Barbados. Still operating under his birthname, he released the well-received *Mike Richards & the Re-Emergence Band Live* album the following year, shortly before being named Barbados Poet of the Year. A second honor, Author of the Year, awaited 1992's *Black Distant Voice* poetry collection, published just as he changed his name to Adisa Andwele.

Andwele's second album, *Conscious*, appeared in November, 1993, as he was nominated for Barbados Entertainer of the Year. It was a deserved honor—on June 12, Andwele became the first poet in Barbados (and only the third in the Caribbean) to perform at a carnival tent, during the island's Crop Over festivities. He also made his debut excursions to the US and Canada that year.

The mid-1990s saw Andwele join Eddy Grant's Ice label. He became a vociferous exponent of Grant's ringbang style, and immediately incorporated ferocious new beats into a musical approach which has, from the outset, been built upon a relentless comprehension of the power of rhythm.

Alongside Viking Tundah, Gabby, Square One, Grynner and Panta Brown, he contributed to the *Fire in de Wave* compilation, turning in the infectious "Jump in the Ringbang Tide." Three further performances appeared on a second Ice sampler, *Ringbang Rebel*—"Low Blow," "Play Jooky Jooky" and "Believe in de Party."

By 1998, however, Andwele was keen to return to mainstream poetry, this time fused with traditional jazz. Linking with the Barbados band Jamari (Andre Daniel—keyboards; Rick Aimey—bass; James Lovell—drums), he began work on what became *Doin' it Saf*, recorded at Eddy Grant's Blue Wave studios. Andwele also became a leading figure at Holders performing arts center near Sandy Lane, Barbados.

DISCOGRAPHY

8 **Mike Richards & the Re-Emergence Band Live (- BARB) 1991**
An extraordinarily powerful performance, the band's instinctive awareness of the poet's presence all but translating rhythm into words, giving the impression of a choir of voices in intuitive harmony.

6 **Conscious (- BARB) 1993**
The studio environment strips some of the immediacy from the performance, although words like "sterile" and "disappointing" can never be applied to Andwele's work.

7 **Doin' It Saf (Ice—UK) 2000**
Andwele's poetry/jazz hybrid (with the jazz little more than a half-heard whisper behind him) resurrects several poems from earlier works—"Black Distant Voice" dates back to 1992, "Antiquity" first appeared in the Caribbean poetry anthology *Voices* in 1998.

HORACE ANDY

STYLE *reggae (roots)*
BORN *Horace Hinds, 2/19/51 (Allman Town, Kingston, JA)*

One of the greatest vocalists Jamaica — or anywhere else, for that matter — has ever produced, possessed of an emotional strength which utterly belies his sometimes feather-light delivery, Horace Andy is one of those singers who can make his work seem utterly effortless—not for nothing was he long ago nicknamed "Sleepy."

Andy was 16 when, operating under his given name, he cut his first single, "This is a Black Man's Country," with producer George "Phil" Pratt at the West Indies Recording Studio in 1967. The record went nowhere and Andy remained unknown until January, 1970, when he and a friend, Frank Melody, auditioned for producer Coxsone Dodd at Studio One. The duo failed the test, but a few days later, Andy tried again on his own, and this impressed the producer.

It was Dodd who renamed the singer, partly as a tribute to former Paragon vocalist Bob Andy, then at the peak of his commercial success; but also to distance him from his chart-topping cousin Justin Hinds, with whom the youngster's singing style then had a great deal in common. With faultless, rootsy backing from the Horsemouth Wallace/Leroy Sibbles rhythm section, "Got to Be Sure," the self-composed ballad he performed at the solo audition, became his first single for Dodd. "See a Man's Face" and "Night Owl" followed during 1971, with "Fever" and "Mr Bassie" arriving in 1972, before Andy unveiled the classic "Skylarking."

The song was originally released on Dodd's *Jamaica Today* compilation album, but was culled as a single after it caused a sensation at a Tippertone sound system dance. It soared to the top of the Jamaican chart, and remains one of the best loved 45s of the entire era.

Over the next few years, Andy was seldom out of the Jamaican chart. "Something on My Mind," "Love of a Woman," "Just Say Who," "Every Tongue Shall Tell," "Christmas Time" and many more chased one another up the listings. Andy also covered "Oh Lord Why Lord," a song best associated with the early George Clinton/Parliament, and created a minor gem from Cat Stevens' mawkish "Where Do the Children Play."

At the height of this success, however, Andy quit Dodd's set-up to work again with Phil Pratt, cutting the classic "Get Wise," "Feel Good" and "Money Is the Root of All Evil," one of several songs he subsequently returned to.

Other early 1970s sessions saw Andy freelance for a number of different producers: Derrick Harriot ("Lonely Woman"); Ernest and JoJo Hookim ("Girl I Love You"); Gussie Clarke ("Love You to Want Me" and "Delilah");

Trio International ("Reggae Rhythm"); Count Shelly ("Jah Jah Children") Harry J ("God Is Displeased"). He was also responsible for a fine version of pop songwriter Tony Orlando's "Bless You", cut for Robbie Shakespeare's Bar-Bell label.

Leonard Chin produced Andy's second Jamaican chart-topper with "Children of Israel" in 1973. Niney Holness oversaw "Nice and Easy" and "I'm in Love" in 1975, while JoJo Hookim captured the stunning "Beware of a Smiling Face" that same year. A duet with Freddie McKay brought the hit "Talking Love." It was Andy's early-mid 1970s union with Bunny Lee, however, which paid the greatest dividends. Kicking off with new recordings of "Skylarking" and the King Tubby fired "Just Say Who," the pair followed through with a succession of classic 45s: "Don't Try to Use Me," "You Are My Angel," "Rasta Saw Them Coming," "Zion Gate," Tappa Zukie's "Better Collie," John Holt's brooding "Serious Thing" and "I've Got to Get Away" (aka "Man Next Door") and "Pure Ranking," alongside new versions of "Money Is the Root of All Evil" (retitled "Money Money"), "Love of a Woman" and "Something on My Mind."

The sheer majesty of Andy's vocals, meantime, ensured that he was in constant demand by other artists — Jah Stitch and Doctor Alimantado both joined the queue for Andy's services (Andy supplied characteristically distinctive backing vocals on Alimantado's 1975 hit "Poison Flour," written and recorded after several dozen people died from eating bread made with contaminated flour.) Andy also teamed up with DJ Clint Eastwood for 1978's "Problem Times."

Andy relocated to the US in 1977, moving to Connecticut with his first wife, Claudette, and teaming up with New York-based Everton DaSilva, head of the Hungry Town label. The classic *In the Light* and the Prince Jammy mixed *In the Light Dub* albums followed, together with the singles "Do You Love My Music," "Youths of Today," "Fever" and "Government Land."

Over the next two years Andy and DaSilva cultivated an astonishing partnership, including the formation of Andy's own label, Rhythm. Debuted with the single "Don't Let Problems Get You Down" (a song Andy originally recorded with Leonard Chin in 1972), Rhythm released a number of Andy 45s over the next two years, including "Control Yourself," "Good Vibes" and "Ital Vital." The duo's plans, however, were shattered when DaSilva was murdered in 1979. Two years later, Andy had his own brush with death, when he, too, was shot — caught in the crossfire of a gunfight, he was hit in the right arm as he tried to take cover.

1979 brought a collaboration with producer Morwells for the single "Black Cinderella" and, as the 1980s dawned, Andy was deeply embroiled in formulating what became dance hall. His 1978 *Pure Ranking* album is almost prescient in its anticipation; 1982's *Dance Hall Style* (recorded in New York with fellow Jamaican expatriate Lloyd "Bullwackie" Barnes) confirms its intent.

Other important releases from this period include a collaboration with Tappa Zukie for the album *Natty Dred a Weh She Want* and two singles, "Revolution" and a reworking of another of Andy's Studio One era hits, "Earth Must Be Hell." He then joined with producer Ossie Hibbert for "Sitting on a Hillside" (1980), "Have You Ever Been in Love" (1981), "Cool And Deadly" (1983), "Ain't No Love," "You Are My Angel" and "Eternal Love" (1984).

Linking with the Sonny Peddie and Jackal studio team, Andy's next sessions produced a string of excellent singles during 1983/84 including "Sweet Music," "Confusion" and "Walking on Ice." 1984 also saw Andy join Chaka Demus, Don Carlos, Super Liki and others on the raw *Prince Jammy & The Striker Lee Posse Presents Music Maker Live at the Halfway Tree Jamaica* album.

In 1985, Andy and his new wife, Caroline, relocated to London, settling in the Ladbroke Grove neighborhood and signing with the independent Rough Trade label. A single, "Elementary," and an album of the same title followed. The next year saw Andy try self-production for the first time, teaming with Rhythm Queen for the exquisite "User."

He continued visiting Jamaica, and 1986 also saw him reunite with Prince Jammy. Backed by Steely and Clevie and the Fire House Crew, Andy recorded "My Baby Knows How," "Do Your Thing," "Come in a This" and "Must Have to Get It" during 1986/87. Further confirmation of

Andy's continued significance was forthcoming when the fast-rising Garnett Silk recording a version of Andy's signature "Skylarking."

Back in London, in 1988, Andy paired with English DJ Tonto Irie for the "Bangarang" 45; two years later, the Bristol-based trip hop pioneers Massive Attack contacted him, mailing him the rhythm to their song "One Love" and requesting a vocal. Andy has since appeared on all three of Massive Attack's albums to date, his contributions include a new version of the *Dance Hall Style* album track "Spying Glass," "Exchange (Part Two)" and a claustrophobic revision of "Man Next Door."

1994 also saw Andy record "Seek and You Will Find" with London producer Dennis "Mixman" Bedeau; a full album of the same name followed in 1995. That year also brought the album (and single) *Life Is for Living*, cut with occasional Massive Attack collaborator, dub producer Mad Professor. A second single, "Zion," was well received in 1996, while another Mad Professor set, *Roots and Branches*, followed in 1997. (Andy also played Sunsplash 96.)

In 1998, Andy cut a new version of "I May Never See My Baby," a song he has regularly revisited since his teens, for release as a single on Sarse Perellar, while the Japanese label Tachyon released the self-explanatory *Horace Andy Sings Bob Marley* album, produced by Bullwackie.

Amid a sea of compilations unleashed by Andy's new-found pre-eminence within trip-hop circles, Massive Attack's own Melankolic label released the powerful *Skylarking* in 1997, following up with a new Andy album, *Living in the Flood*, in 1999. Included were the title track collaboration with punk-reggae maven Joe Strummer.

SELECTED DISCOGRAPHY

10 In the Light (Hungry Town) 1977
9 In the Light Dub (Hungry Town) 1977

In the Light is one of Andy's strongest sets, highlighted by such classic songs as "Problems," "Government Land" and the title track, but of course best distinguished by one of the most incredible voices on the planet. Prince Jammy's dub album version, therefore, could be said to miss the point of Andy's art somewhat. In fact, the spectral interjections which float in the ether are all the more powerful for their sparsity and the only complaint is, more attention isn't paid to the scintillating guitar lines that haunt "Hey There Woman" (played by Privy Dub and Andy himself). The Blood & Fire reissue pairs both sets on one CD.

8 Pure Ranking (Clocktower) 1978

An intriguing album that arguably lays the foundation for dance hall with its sparse production and cultural themes, highlighted by the title track's discussion of the eponymous West Kingston gang, which also foreshadowed the rise of the raggamuffin.

6 Bim Sherman Meets Horace Andy & U Black (Yard International) 1980
8 Natty Dread a Weh She Want (New Star—JA) 1980

Produced by Tappa Zukie and as much a product of his fervent imagination as Andy's. "Ragamuffin" and "Run Babylon" are classics, while Zukie insists that the lilting title track was so affecting that Andy himself grew dreadlocks in tribute to it. "I just wear beaver hat and not shave, but Horace, ha ha ha, him have dreads specially for *Top of the Pops*."

8 Dance Hall Style (Wackies—JA) 1982

Lloyd Barnes' production played to Andy's strengths creating a classic record that featured both new material and rerecordings of older songs, "Money Money" and "Lonely Woman" amongst them. A revised version of this album appeared in the UK as *Exclusively*, and is generally considered superior, adding extra tracks and new mixes to an already powerful, and powerfully cognitive, album.

8 Showcase (Vista Sounds—UK) 1984

Ted Dawkins produced set which offers a near-definitive version of "Cherry O Baby" and a moving "Ain't No Sunshine," together with the harder hitting "Chant Rastaman Chant" and "Babylon System."

5 Confusion (Music Hawk—UK) 1984

The full Sonny Peddie/Jackal sessions. In fairness, Andy doesn't seem to be paying attention throughout, giving the album a disjointed and somewhat over-produced feel.

8 Elementary (Rough Trade—UK) 1985

Co-credited to Rhythm Queen, an album firmly in the tradition of contemporary British lovers rock, fused with an exhilarating electro pulse. The title track, in particular, has a compulsive jerkiness, and some delightfully dated keyboard sounds, but there's not a dull moment (or sound) in sight.

6 Haul & Jack Up (Live & Love—UK) 1987

Prince Jammy produced set, with Andy a somewhat perfunctory sounding addition to the Steely & Clevie rhythm tracks.

7 Everyday People (Wackies) 1988
6 Shame And Scandal (—JA) 1988
4 Rude Boy (Shanachie) 1993

Guest appearances from Ricky General and Bunny Clarke (on the closing "That's How I Feel") distinguish an album otherwise most notable for a sweet cover of "Just My Imagination."

8 Seek and You Will Find (Blakamix Int'l—UK) 1995
6 Seek and You Will Find—The Dub Pieces (Blakamix Int'l—UK) 1995

One of the most convincing British-made reggae albums of the mid-1990s, Andy's vocals as hypnotic as the rhythms. The mantric "African Girl" is a triumph, both in its original form and stripped back for the dub companion set. The second half of the album is less spectacular, but still closes with the album's finest number, the rapid rhythmic title track.

7 Life Is for Living (Ariwa — UK) 1995
7 Roots and Branches (Ariwa — UK) 1997

The Mad Professor era, with Andy obviously enjoying himself, but never breaking a sweat on the songs.

7 See and Blind (Heartbeat) 1998

An extraordinarily schizophrenic set, mixing old and new material under the aegis of producer Bunny Gemini. The Fire House Crew cause a few flare-ups, but Andy is still conserving his strength.

9 Living in the Flood (Melankolic) 1999

Andy's most fulfilled vision since *Elementary*, and his best album since *In the Light*. Clive Hunt's production is disturbingly claustrophobic, all fluid bass and slow burning backing vocals, while Andy's voice glowers majestically. The title track, so redolent of co-writer Joe Strummer's own recent reggae excursions, is a masterpiece, while "Johnny Too Bad" includes one of the most disorienting effects of all, the sound of badly worn vinyl panning from channel to channel. The US edition includes a bonus Mad Professor remix of the opening "After All," plus the uncredited "Dance to the Reggae Beat."

HORACE ANDY & PATRICK ANDY
5 Clash of the Andys (Thunderbolt — JA) 1985

HORACE ANDY & DENNIS BROWN
7 Reggae Superstars Meet (Striker Lee — JA) 1986

HORACE ANDY & JOHN HOLT
7 From One Extreme to Another (Beta — JA) 1986

HORACE ANDY & WINSTON JARRETT
8 Earth Must Be Hell (Atra — JA) 1974
6 Earth Must Be Hell — Dub (Atra — JA) 1974

HORACE ANDY & ERROL SCORCHER
6 Unity Showcase (Pre — UK) 1981

HORACE ANDY & JAH SHAKA
5 Jah Shaka Meets Horace Andy (Jah Shaka Music — UK) 1994
4 Dub Salute 1 Featuring Horace Andy (Jah Shaka Music — UK) 1994

One of Andy's less impressive albums, with correspondingly non-essential dub counterpart.

SELECTED COMPILATIONS & ARCHIVE RELEASES
8 Skylarking (Studio One — JA) 1972

The cream of Andy's Studio One recordings, including original (although not necessarily) definitive versions of "Something's on My Mind," "Every Tongue Shall Tell" and "See a Man's Face."

6 Best of Horace Andy (Coxsone — JA) 1974

Further highlights from the Studio One vault, including his original take on "Ain't No Sunshine," together with stylized covers of the international hits "Everything I Own," "Rock Your Baby" and "I Can See Clearly Now." The preponderance of covers lessens the validity of the title, but completists won't be disappointed.

8 Sings for You and I (Clocktower) 1985

More Bunny Lee material, with a slapdash approach to chronology and a handful of mistitled tracks. But "I've Got to Get Away" serves up a quirkily breakneck prelude to Massive Attack's discomforted "Man Next Door" revision, and "Our Jamaican National Heroes" offers DJ-style cliff notes to local history. Leroy Sibbles' "My Guiding Star" and Tappa Zukie's "Better Collie" open and close the album with deathless elan.

9 Good Vibes (Blood & Fire — UK) 1997

Fascinating trawl through Andy's late 1970s output, including work with Lee, DaSilva and Trio International. The extended/dub (and, a sign of the times, disco) mixes include an ambitiously subtitled "Better Version" of "Skylarking" — which is!; and a "Serious Version" of "Serious Thing." Although Andy is rightfully best regarded as a singer/songwriter, his choice of producers is often as inspired as the material he hands them.

9 Skylarking (Melankolic) 1997

Solid assemblage of harder to find hits (plus the Studio One title track), proving that even during the fallow 80s, Andy was still on top of his game. That super-scarce collaboration with Tappa Zukie rubs shoulders with Channel One, Wackies and Rough Trade material, and while there is more here to interest the collector than the novice, even first-time listeners will come away impressed.

8 Mr Bassie (Heartbeat) 1998

Much needed digest of Andy's Studio One hits, featuring the key singles, plus a heavenly unreleased version of Jimmy Cliff's "Come into My Life" (one of two previously unavailable tracks) and a dynamic assault on Parliament's "Oh Lord, Oh Why." A remake of "Mother and Child Reunion" lets the side down a little, but it is the only weak link.

8 The Prime of Horace Andy (Music Club) 1998

16 track collection highlighting Andy's collaboration with Bunny Lee, much of which previously appeared as *You Are My Angel* (Trojan — UK, 1973). Rerecordings of several Studio One successes, dramatic versions of "Ain't No Sun-

shine" and "Skylarking" and Marley's "Natural Mystic" are unsurpassable.

8 The Wonderful World of Horace Andy (Cleopatra) 2000

Basically, an excellent round-up of otherwise lost Niney Holness and Bunny Lee productions from the mid-1970s, but straying into the early 1980s via Andy's cover of Michael Jackson's "The Girl Is Mine." Four modern remixes close the album.

ARROW

STYLE *calypso/soca*
BORN *Alphonsus Cassell 11/16/54 (Montserrat)*

The first superstar of soca, and still one of the greatest names in the entire genre, Arrow was named for his "piercing" lyrics, a talent which was evident even during his school years. He first performed aged 10 at a concert at the Montserrat Secondary School, and began singing calypso in 1967, immediately taking the junior monarch title.

He turned professional in 1969, taking second place to Lord Short Shirt at the Montserrat Calypso King competition. Arrow triumphed the next year, becoming the third member of his family to take the title, following his two older brothers Hero (Justin Cassell) and Young Challenger (Lorenzo Cassell). Overall, Arrow would take four Montserrat Calypso King titles.

Arrow's first single, "Dance with Me, Woman," was released in 1972, as he made his debut at carnival in Trinidad, performing in the Original Young Brigade tent. The following year "Let the Music Play"/"Invitation to the Caribbean" launched his own Arrow label. 1974 brought his debut album, *The Mighty Arrow on Target*, home to the smash hit "On Target." He followed up with *Arrow Strikes Again* in 1975, with the song "Rummy Song" becoming Road March champion at that year's St Kitts carnival. The album *Keep on Jamming* appeared in 1976, and "Bills" proved a politically sharp hit in 1978.

Arrow's 1980 album, *Instant Knockout*, only amplified the vast strides he was making in an apprenticeship which allowed him to hone a unique musical fusion of calypso, salsa and R&B. In the process, critics accused him of single-handedly destroying the islands' original calypso traditions; in fact, Arrow's greatest achievement lay in so effortlessly updating them, ushering the genre into a whole new age of both musical and commercial impact.

Backed by his Multi National Force band, Arrow scored further successes with the early 1980s hits "Double Trouble" and "Instant Knockout." Then, in 1982, having spent much of his career working with producer Ed Watson, Arrow switched to arranger Leston Paul and recorded the album *Hot, Hot, Hot*. Debuting rock lead guitarist Christopher 'Columbus' Newland, the result was his first

pan-Caribbean hit and the biggest selling soca record of all time.

"Hot Hot Hot" was subsequently adopted as the theme song of the 1986 soccer World Cup in Mexico, and has enjoyed cover versions by reformed New York punk rocker David Johansson (as Buster Poindexter), Latin teens Menudo and East Indian stars Babla & Kanchan (under the Hindi title "Kuchh Gadbad Hai").

Even this global success, however, was swiftly left behind as Arrow and the Multi National Force continued to expand their — and their audience's — musical horizons. Their next album, 1983's *Heat* (aka *Rush Hour*) launched the smash "Rub Up," 1984's *Soca Savage* was recorded at studios in Jamaica (Dynamic), New York and Montserrat, with a band line-up of Newland (guitar), Burning Flames founder members Toriana Edwards (guitar) and his brother Clarence Edwards (bass), Leston Paul (keyboards), Errol Wise (drums) and others. The set brought Arrow's next major hit, as "Long Time" reached #30 in the UK in July, 1985. A remixed "Hot Hot Hot" followed — the original version had faltered at #58; this time, it climbed to #38. Musical horizons, too, expanded — Arrow made heavy use of brass, with the hit "Party Mix" finding him toying expertly with a Latin feel. That song also featured the prescient promise "a musical revolution crossing over," one which was born out by his next release.

Wholly recorded in the US, 1986's *Heavy Energy* brought an intriguing taste of merengue to the brew; 1988's *Knock Dem Dead* album was an unabashed rock effort; 1990's "Zouk Me" introduced a now international audience to the local stylings of the French island of Guadeloupe.

Knock Dem Dead was Arrow's first for the Island Records subsidiary Mango, and pushed him to the brink of international superstardom. "Groovemaster" was featured in the soundtracks to *The Mighty Quinn* and *Cutting Edge*, while Arrow also shot his first music videos, for "Groovemaster" and "Crazy Mama."

He remained with Mango for three years, but further hits "Hey Pocky Way" and "Limbo Calypso," and the *O La Soca* and *Soca Dance Party* albums failed to recapture the earlier excitement. In 1991, Arrow returned to his own label. That year he released *Zombie Soca*, followed by *Model in de Bam-Bam*. 1993 brought *Outrageous*, while 1994 saw Arrow take stock of the last frenetic decade with the collection *Classics Plus* and a full CD of *Hot Hot Hot* remixes.

Aside from music, Arrow also established himself among his homeland's leading businessmen, albeit at a time when the very existence of Montserrat was under threat from the Soufriere Hills volcano. His original enterprise, the clothing, gifts and record store Arrow's Manshop, in the capital, Plymouth, was destroyed in 1995; he then relocated to the town of Salem.

Arrow: the first superstar of soca.

Arrow contributed heavily to Montserrat's disaster relief fund both financially and musically, and organized a fund-raising calypso festival on the island during 1996. He was also a special guest at the Caribbean Song festival in Barbados in October, 1997, raising money for disaster relief, and increasing awareness of the islanders' plight, at a time when the British government was dragging its feet over anything more than the most nominal assistance.

In addition, Arrow's brother (and long-time vocal arranger) Justin Cassell was appointed to the organizing committee of the massive Many Happy Returns benefit concert at London's Royal Albert Hall that September — the event itself was the brainchild of English producer George Martin, owner of Montserrat's famed AIR Studios. A similar event was staged simultaneously in Montserrat, featuring Anguilla's Bankie Banks and Britain's Climax Blues Band.

In the midst of the turmoil at home, Arrow co-headlined (alongside Third World) Bermuda's Soca '96 festival, his fourth appearance at the event in its seven year history. He released the acclaimed *Phat* that same year, and in 1997, *Ride De Riddim*. His next set, *Turbulence* (early reports ti-

tled it *Hold Your Breath*), was released in December, 1998, shortly after Arrow appeared at a second Many Happy Returns concerts in London that year. Plans to stage similar shows throughout the Caribbean were wrecked, ironically, by another natural disaster, Hurricane Georges.

1998 also saw Arrow presented with the Living Legends award by the organizers of the Caribbean Song festival and the Bahamas Tourist Board.

SELECTED DISCOGRAPHY

6 **The Mighty Arrow on Target (—MONT) 1974**
7 **Arrow Strikes Again (Arrow—MONT) 1975**
6 **Keep on Jamming (Arrow—MONT) 1976**
8 **Instant Knockout (Charlie's) 1980**

Tentative by later standards, but pure as well. The grooves are jumping throughout, and the soca doesn't stop!

9 **Hot Hot Hot (Arrow/Chrysalis) 1982**

Home of the hit and the first port of call for anybody investigating Arrow's tumultuous dance fusion.

7 Heat (Arrow) 1983

7 Soca Savage (Arrow) 1984

"Party Mix" is essentially a shopping list of the musical styles Arrow's aiming at, set to a rambunctious Latin beat. That sets the mood — *Soca Savage* is, contrarily, less soca than a lot of other things ("Beating Round de Bush" is brutal disco), but the blend is never less than exuberant, peaking with the honking "Prum Prum," host to some truly wicked bass tones.

7 Deadly (Arrow) 1986

5 Heavy Energy (Arrow) 1986

The aerobically saucy "Get Fit" opens Arrow's least captivating album, one which relies too heavily on quick phrases and easy rhythms ("Tit for Tat") for comfort. But even its darkest depths are dignified by Clarence Edwards' ever-slinky bass, while the exuberantly nonsensical "Aye Merengue" (key lyric, "aye aye I love merengue, mucho mucho mucho merengue") is irresistible.

6 Massive (Arrow) 1989

7 Knock Dem Dead (Mango) 1988

Long-time Arrow guitarist Chris Newland dominates what has ascended into legend as Arrow's rock album. That's rock, of course, with dance beat enough for the most tireless reveller.

7 O'La Soca (Mango) 1989

Remixed for the US market, and purists will probably flinch a little at the thought. But the album is as exuberant as any — indeed, if anything, the party's even wilder than before.

6 Soca Dance Party (Mango) 1990

8 Zombie Soca (Arrow) 1991

6 Zombie Remixes (Arrow) 1991

With Arrow now feted as one of the giants of "World Music," *Zombie Soca* acquired something of a reputation as his "political" album. There is some social commentary, but the hit "Wine Yuh Body" proves that the old infectiousness remains loud and proud. *Zombie Remixes* is precisely that, a redundant but nevertheless enjoyable listen.

6 Model in de Bam-Bam (Arrow) 1992

5 Outrageous (Arrow) 1993

7 Phat (Arrow) 1996

6 Ride de Riddem (Arrow) 1997

8 Turbulence (Arrow) 1998

"Come Girl," a duet with DJ Lady Saw, prompted the *Montserrat Reporter* to request, "prophylactic, please." It is a heavy, sultry piece, highlighting the best of Arrow's later albums.

SELECTED COMPILATIONS & ARCHIVE RELEASES

9 Best of Arrow (Red Bullet) 1988

8 Hot Soca Hot (Arrow) 1990

9 Best of Arrow (Arrow) 1992

There is little to separate these three albums in terms of Arrow's overall ouvre. Just look for the one containing your favorite songs!

8 Classics Plus (Arrow) 1994

Marvelous collection of 12-inch mixes, extended jams and general greatest hits, stretching into infinity. Soca at its sexiest.

THE BAHA MEN

STYLE *soca*

FORMED *1981 (BAH)*

ORIGINAL LINE-UP *Nehemiah Hield (vocals), Ron Butler (vocals), Herschel Small (guitar), Steve Kelly (guitar), Tony Curtis (guitar), Eddie Rolle (keyboards), Jeffrey Chea (keyboards), Mark Johnson (organ), Isiah Taylor (b 1940 — bass, percussion), Colyn Grant (drums)*

One of the most audacious of Caribbean area bands, the Baha Men specialize in an electrifying junkanoo blend of island motifs and western rock motivations. It is a hybrid which has proven especially popular in Japan — each of the Baha Men albums to date have gone platinum in that country. Elsewhere, however, the Baha Men waited two decades to make an impact.

Already in his late 30s when the Baha Men got off the ground, founder and band leader Isiah Taylor explained, "My ambition was to take the instruments from the Bahamas' street festival and put them together with stage instruments like bass, drums and guitar. I wanted to blend them all together in order to get the junkanoo music out into the world."

What became the Baha Men originally formed in the early 1980s as High Voltage, a disco-funk band who swiftly became regulars on the local nightclub and hotel circuit. High Voltage released a number of cassettes in the Bahamas, but remained utterly unknown elsewhere. That changed in 1991, when Atlantic Records A&R man Steve Greenberg was handed one of the group's tapes by a friend. He signed them to the American label's Big Beat subsidiary, changing their name to the Baha Men at the same time.

The ensuing album *Junkanoo* was buoyed by the local hit "Back to the Island," a song which has since become a staple of Bahamas' tourism commercials, while "Mama Lay Lay Lay," "Home Sweet Home" and "Gin and Coconut Water" also proved popular. *Kalik*, similarly themed, followed, raising some eyebrows with the inclusion of a Lenny Kravitz song ("Just a Sunny Day"), but retaining the band's roots sensibilities regardless. The single "Dancing in the Moonlight" proved an international hit, and the Baha Men set about broadening their outlook by linking with mainstream producers Tommy D, Trevor

Steele (the Escape Club) and others, as they prepared their next album.

When Steve Greenberg joined the Mercury label, the Baha Men followed, but the glossy production of 1997's *I Like What I Like* album utterly divided the Baha Men's audience. 1998's *Doong Spank* pursued this same direction to even more divisive results — according to the *New York Times*, it sold less than 700 copies in the US, and that despite the band touring the country with teen stars Hanson — another of Greenberg's discoveries. Hardly surprisingly, the Baha Men were dropped from the Mercury roster; Steve Greenberg departed the company at the same time, establishing his own S-Curve label and making the Baha Men his first signing.

Having survived several line-up changes over the years, the 1999 departure of vocalist Nehemiah Hield (to tour with Lenny Kravitz) did not disturb the Baha Men's equilibrium. He was replaced, appropriately, by his nephew, Omerit Hield (then working as a bank teller), together with Marvin Prospect and Rick Carey, considerably younger musicians whose input and enthusiasm had an immediate impact on the band.

Greenberg, too, was looking into ways of revitalizing the group's fortunes. Their 1999 album *2 Zero 0–0* was released only in the band's traditionally loyal stronghold of Japan. Finally Greenberg suggested they cut a cover of soca star Anslem Douglas' 1998 carnival hit, "Who Let the Dogs Out," for their next US release.

Taylor initially resisted the proposal, but Greenberg's advice won out — with astonishing results. Throughout the summer of 2000, "Who Let the Dogs Out" — with its quirky rhythms and even quirkier video — was in constant rotation on MTV and effortlessly stormed the charts around the world. (The band was renamed the Baha Boys in Europe.) An album of the same name naturally followed suit.

The first hit for the S-Curve label was also one of the most memorable smashes of the entire year. It certainly struck a chord with America's sporting fraternity — the Seattle Mariners made the song their team victory anthem as they bid for the 2000 World Series, while the new year saw the Baha Men play Super Bowl XXXV in Tampa, among numerous other events.

In addition, "Who Let the Dogs Out" won the 2001 Grammy for Best Dance Recording, even as the Baha Men's latest single, "You All Dat?" commenced its assault on the dance charts of the world.

DISCOGRAPHY

7 Junkanoo (Big Beat) 1992

The most traditional of the Baha Men's efforts, concentrating on updating Bahamian music for modern instruments.

The single "Back to the Island" was an especially strong reminder of the traditions behind the band's contemporary sheen.

6 Kalik (Big Beat) 1994
6 I Like What I Like (Polygram) 1997

While the band's roots in American funk-lite are given a convincing work out via a medley of old KC & the Sunshine Band hits ("That's the Way I Get Down"), the group's natural buoyancy struggles with the studio polish.

7 Doong Spank (Polygram) 1998

Conventional wisdom (and contemporary sales figures) insist this is the Baha men's worst album. In fact it is a marked improvement on its predecessor — still slick, still overproduced, it nevertheless shows the band adapting to their R&B ambitions, and threatening to break out sometime soon.

7 2 Zero 0–0 (—Japan) 1999

Finally released in the US in 2001 (Universal), a punchy re-awakening helmed by newcomers who give the band more than a fresh frontline; they also infuse the raw hip-hop street smarts highlighted by a skewered version of "Hooked on a Feeling."

8 Who Let the Dogs Out (S-Curve) 2000

And the kids are at it again, driving the title track to the top of the chart, sending the infectious "You All Dat" soaring in its wake (the "Lion Sleeps Tonight" sample is truly irresistible), and establishing *Dogs* among the most surprising reinventions of the year. Wow, a Grammy winner which actually deserved it.

SELECTED COMPILATIONS & ARCHIVE RELEASES

8 The Best of the Baha Men (Polygram) 2000

Two years earlier, the label could not wait to be rid of these under-performing islanders. Now they're the biggest band on the planet, so here's a sampling of the best bits of their last two albums. Now, why did we drop them in the first place?

BANKIE BANKS

STYLE *reggae*
BORN *1953 (ANG)*

Known to his admirers as the "Anguillan Bob Dylan" (an honor compounded when he jammed with the real thing), Banks dates his musical career from 1963 when he built his own first guitar. Inspired by the local radio station broadcasting from a British frigate moored off the coast, and feeding the island's youth with non-stop UK Top 40 music, Banks formed his first band around 1967, and spent the next decade working his way up the Anguilla nightclub circuit.

In 1978, Banks and his regular band, the Dune People, cut his first album, the reggae classic *Roots & Herbs*, a success both locally and in Jamaica. Following the release of 1982's *Where I and I Abide*, he became the first Anguillan performer ever to appear at Reggae Sunsplash, in 1983. Banks has since toured with a number of Jamaican acts, including Jimmy Cliff.

Having spent the late 1980s in New York where he recorded his third album, *Terrestrial Spirits*, Banks returned to Anguilla in 1990 to launch the Moonsplash Music Festival, staged in the grounds of his own bar, the Dune Preserve, on Anguilla's Rendezvous Bay. An annual event, Moonsplash is now established as one of the most important local events in the region. Recent headliners have included Ritchie Havens and American actor Kevin Bacon's Bacon Brothers Band. The destruction of the Dune Preserve during Hurricane Lenny in November, 1999, did not delay the following year's Moonsplash 2000 event. Banks simply rebuilt.

Banks has also distinguished his career with regular charity and benefit work. He appeared alongside Paul Simon and Gloria Estefan at a hurricane relief concert in Miami; and in 1996, Banks channelled proceeds from his *Mighty Wind* album into rebuilding traditional Anguillan sailing boats destroyed by Hurricane Luis the previous year. The following September, he took part in the Many Happy Returns concert at Gerald's Bottom, Montserrat, benefitting victims of that island's volcano disaster.

SELECTED DISCOGRAPHY

8 Roots and Herbs (Urban Country—ANG) 1978

Banks' rootsiest album does spend some time searching for its own identity, but that isn't necessarily a drawback. Reissued through Zemi Music, it's paired with the early 1980s set *Where I and I Abide*.

7 Where I And I Abide (Urban Country—ANG) 1982
7 Terrestrial Spirits (Zemi Music) 1989

Recorded in New York, a varied set adds R&B, jazz and folk guitar to a brew characterized by Banks' best known hit, "Night Bird."

8 Island Boy (Zemi Music) 1991

"Suburban Princess" and the title track offer further reflections on Banks' time in New York, although the entire set is flavored with a sense of homesickness.

9 Mighty Wind (Zemi Music) 1996

If nothing else, Banks' version of "Amazing Grace" captures the emotions which went into this album, cut in the aftermath of Anguilla's most destructive hurricane in decades.

7 Stuck In Paradise (Zemi Music) 1999

BUJU BANTON
STYLE *reggae (toasting/dance hall)*
BORN *Mark Myrie, 1973 (Kingston, JA)*

The young Buju Banton gained his nickname from his mother ("buju" is a Maroon word for breadfruit, corresponding to the youth's chubbiness); Banton was adopted in tribute to the boy's hero, DJ legend Buro Banton. Fittingly, "banton" is also slang for a great story-teller.

The youngest of 15 brothers and sisters, Banton was just 12 when he began DJ-ing around his childhood home Denham Town, working with the Sweet Love and Whitehall Avenue's Rambo Mango sound systems, where he came under the aegis of DJ Flourgon.

In 1986, another of Banton's fellow DJs, Clement Irie, introduced the boy to producer Robert Ffrench, who handled Banton's first single, "The Ruler." 1987 brought sessions with Patrick Roberts, Digital B, Bunny Lee, Winston Riley and Red Dragon and, the following year, he recorded what subsequently became his most notorious song, "Boom Bye Bye"—widely interpreted as a call for the random shooting of homosexuals.

However, it was in partnership with Dave Kelly, engineer at Donovan Germain's Penthouse Studios, which saw Banton widely feted as the brightest upcoming star of dance hall. Together they wrote and recorded a string of early singles, commencing in 1990 with "Man fi Dead" and "Jackie and Joyce," released on the studio's own Penthouse label.

Banton scored his first major hit with "Love Mi Browning," the next year, extolling the virtues of his light-skinned girlfriend. Swamped by complaints from darker maidens, he sensibly followed up with "Love Black Woman." The DJ also enjoyed a string of Jamaican hits alongside other members of the Penthouse stable—Beres Hammond, Wayne Wonder, Carol Gonzales, Capleton (the slacker anthem "Good Hole") and Marcia Griffiths among them.

Banton linked again with Winston Riley to cut the classics "Stamina Daddy" and "Gold Spoon"; and teamed with '80s dance hall legend Frankie Paul (blind from birth, he was briefly labeled "the Jamaican Stevie Wonder") for the duet "Bring You Body Come to Me." Other successes during the 1991–92 period included "Woman Nuh Fret," "Bogle," "Yardie" and "Good Looking Gal." A duet with Don T, 1992's "Big It Up," became the first release on Dave Kelly's Mad House label, and was followed by "Batty Rider" and the awesome "How Massa God World a Run."

January, 1992, also brought Banton's debut album, *Mr Mention*. The fastest selling album in Jamaican history, it set Banton up for appearances at Reggae Sunsplash (he returned in 1993 and 1994) and Sting '92. That summer, he was signed to Mercury Records after being seen at Sunsplash by label executive Lisa Cortes. However, Banton's next release, a rerecording of "Boom Bye Bye" (to the rhythm of Cobra's "Flex") came close to shattering his career.

Released on a Shang label compilation, "Boom Bye Bye" was singled out for outraged attention both in the US and Europe. Banton suddenly found his work mentioned in the same breath as some of the more extreme rap and hip hop artists, a controversy which eventually grew so vast that Banton was even withdrawn from the Penthouse Revue's appearance at the WOMAD Festival.

Shaken, Banton issued a public apology, acknowledging that sentiments which might have been appropriate from a 15 year old struggling to survive in west Kingston had no place in the wider world. Banton's major label debut arrived in spring, 1993, with proof that his apologies were sincere. While the single "Make My Day" climbed to #72 in Britain, the *Voice of Jamaica* album became one of the year's top sellers, a hard-edged slice of social comment interspersed with sexual braggadocio, but again tempered with concern.

Banton's "Willy (Don't Be Silly)" single championed safe sex (since immortalized as the first pro-condom song in dance hall history), with proceeds from the release being donated to a charity supporting children with AIDS. He was invited to meet Jamaican Prime Minister PJ Patterson, another dance hall first, while he garnered further international attention with victories at the Caribbean Music Awards, the Canadian Music Awards and the Tamika ceremony.

In an interview with *Vibe* magazine, Banton attempted to explain the attraction of the violent imagery which had hitherto characterized dance hall. "A different generation arise and that is what we saw through the media and what was shown to us as lessons to be learned." Those lessons came in for serious revision after two of Banton's friends, fellow DJ Pan Head and "Hot This Year" hitmaker Dirtsman were gunned down in separate, but inextricably linked, murders.

Banton responded with November, 1993's "Murderer," a dramatic condemnation of gun violence which has since been described as singlehandedly reversing the lyrical mood of dance hall, and relegating the still unrepentant rude boyisms of Cutty Ranks, Supercat, Ninjaman and the like to the dustbin of history.

Banton's transformation continued apace. He shed his b-boy hairstyle and began growing dreadlocks. He joined Tony Rebel, at that time the paragon of roots consciousness, Papa San and General Degree in the aptly named Yardcore Collective, recording the swaggering "Can't Stop the Dance." He also took a leading role in what the US media termed a Rastafarian revival, the first of a number of hitherto unrepentant bad boys to publicly embrace the religion.

New lyrics were composed for much of his earlier material and, by 1995, when Banton toured the US aboard Reggae Sunsplash, the *Chicago Tribune* was marveling, "His spirituality seemed to be one with his person; he performed in the rapt way of a Miles Davis."

1994, meanwhile, saw Banton perform sold out shows throughout Europe and Japan; he appeared before 20,000 people in T&T, while a concert at Trafalgar Park in Queens, NY, attracted the attention of riot police. Later in the year, Banton launched his own label, CB (Cell-Block/Riddim In Custody) 321 in partnership with Syl Gordon, debuting it with the "Rampage" single.

In 1995, having joined Lisa Cortes at her own new label, the Island Records subsidiary Loose Cannon, Banton released the singles "Champion" and "Untold Stories," the latter readily comparable to Bob Marley's "Redemption Song." His next album, *Til Shiloh* (a Biblical phrase meaning forever), was recorded with Donovan Germain and Bobby Digital, and featured songwriting contributions from Coxsone Dodd and Leroy Sibbles among others.

Banton closed CB321 in 1996 and opened a new label, Gargamel, releasing the "Love Song" single (his variation on the "Under Mi Sensi" rhythm). Singles by Don T, Tru Blacks, Alley Cat and Little Kirk followed that same year. 1997 brought Banton's own "Run de Place," "Legalise It," "Talking" and "Principle," cut with Beenie Man, heralds to Banton's own next album, 1998's *Inna Heights*. It proved a consolidatory disc, although it continued to spit out hits — Toots Hibberts was numbered among the guests, appearing on a sizzling version of his own "54 46 Was My Number."

Preluded by the 1999 singles "Fake Smile" (co-produced with Syl Gordon) and "Probation" (Steely and Clevie), 2000's *Unchained Spirit* was Banton's first for the California-based label Epitaph. It featured guest appearances from Luciano, Morgan Heritage, Stephen Marley and the punk band Rancid, the latter repaying Banton for guesting on their earlier *Life Can't Wait* album. The album's collaboration with Beres Hammond, "Pull It Up," received Record of the Year award at the 12th annual Tamika Reggae Awards in New York.

DISCOGRAPHY

🎱 Mr Mention (Penthouse — JA) 1992

Banton entered the big time in early 1992, and his debut was heavily reliant on recent hit singles, from the breakout hit "Love Mi Browning," to "Batty Rider"'s tribute to dance hall girls' short shorts. With songs this strong, a hits collection was not out of place.

7️⃣ Voice of Jamaica (Mercury) 1993

The DJ refused to compromise one iota of his island roots for his US major label debut, and with Donovan Germain producing, and Cutty Ranks, Tony Rebel and Terry Ganzie guesting, this was still very much a JA album, packed with cultural themes. Banton was clearly leaving his raggamuffin past behind, but the odd slacker song still made the set.

9 Til Shiloh (Loose Cannon) 1995

The unaccompanied opening hymn sets the spiritual stage, but "Til' I'm Laid to Rest" proves that Banton's religious conversion has not diminished his power in the slightest. "Murderer," spurred by the killings of two friends, remains shocking even after familiarity has dulled its original impact, while a duet with Garnett Silk, "Complaint," isn't simply heartfelt, it also rides an intriguing rhythm. Elsewhere, the hard edge that has always been Banton's forte remains through upbeat anthems and juttering hardcore hiphop.

8 Inna Heights (Jet Star) 1997
9 Unchained Spirit (Epitaph) 2000

Completing the 180 degree turn begun on 'Til Shiloh, Banton's spirit is freed to sail across the musical spectrum, at times moving far from his dance hall roots—a beautifully rearranged "23rd Psalm" and the gospelly "Voice of Jah." But there's also a rip-roaring ska recreation of Delroy Wilson's "Better Must Come," and the suitably Wailers-esque "Poor Old Man," featuring Stephen Marley. The Rancid-fired "No More Misty Days," meanwhile, boasts a guitar motif which sounds just like U2!

SELECTED COMPILATIONS & ARCHIVE RELEASES

7 Stamina Daddy (Techniques—JA) 1992
7 Quick (Exworks) 1998

Similar collections feature many of Banton's early singles, notably the Winston Riley productions.

8 Dubbing with the Banton (Penthouse—JA) 2000

Excellent dub restructuring drawn from the *Til Shiloh* and *Inna heights* albums, and related singles.

6 Rude Boys inna Ghetto (Jamaican Vibes) 2000

Credited to Buju Banton & Posse, another airing for the early '90s Winston Riley material, coupled with cuts by Comanche, Zarro, Simpleton and others.

7 The Ultimate Collection (Hip-O) 2001

BEENIE MAN

STYLE *reggae (toasting/dance hall)*
BORN *Anthony Moses Davis, 8/22/73*
  (Waterhouse, Kingston, JA)

The nephew of former Jimmy Cliff drummer Sydney Wolfe, Beenie Man was just 5 when he began showing an interest in DJ-ing. At age 8, he won a national Teeny Talent contest, following which he was introduced to producer Junjo Lawes by radio personality Barry G. Another early partnership linked him with Shocking Vibes producer Pat-

rick Roberts, who made tapes at King Tubby's for the DJ to play to his friends.

Lawes produced Beenie Man's first single, "Too Fancy" in 1981, and showcased him on the compilation *Junjo Presents Two Big Sounds*, alongside such elder statesmen as Dillinger, Michael Irie, Fathead and Ringo. The set was recorded at a continuous live session from 82 Chisholm Avenue, Kingston, Jamaica on 2/27/83. By then, Beenie was a regular on the sound system circuit, appearing at Prince Jammy's, Volcano and Bunny Lee's Unlimited set-ups, among others. That same year, he recorded his debut album with Bunny Lee, appropriately titled *The Invincible Beenie Man, The 10 Year Old DJ Wonder*, and scored his first hit single under the aegis of Niney Holness, "Over the Sea." Another 45 that year, "Code Black," was credited to DJ Beenie Man.

In 1984, the young DJ cut a handful of tracks with Barrington Levy, including "Under Mi Sensi" and "Two Sounds" (both were remixed and reissued a decade later). However, it was another six years before Beenie Man truly resurfaced. In the interim he completed school, then took time off traveling to the UK, US and Canada.

Together with his brother Little Kirk, he reunited with producer Patrick Roberts and released the singles "Wicked Man" and "Kip Whey" in 1990–91, on the Shocking Vibes label. "Mobster," "Never dis a Mobster," "Veteran," "Tiger Rides in Town" and "Cu-Cum Looks," plus a well-received Sunsplash 92 showing furthered Beenie Man's dance hall renown to the point where he was ready to challenge the scene's established figureheads.

Particularly noteworthy was his feud with Bounty Killer, ignited after the latter began borrowing Beenie Man's "people dead" catch-phrase. The pair went head to head following Sting '93 — the performance was recalled on the *Guns Out* album.

However, Beenie Man was also to be embroiled in controversy after he performed at a show welcoming Nelson Mandela on a visit to Jamaica. Included within his set was one song which was widely condemned as being utterly inappropriate — booed offstage, in the ensuing fall-out, Beenie Man left Jamaica for almost a year.

Beenie Man's embrace of Rastafarianism in 1994 was ignited when he went into the studio with Sly & Robbie to cut versions of Bob Marley's "Crazy Baldhead" (with Luciano) and "No Woman No Cry." Retitled "No Mama No Cry," the latter echoed Buju Banton's "Murderer" in condemning the wave of violence which had ended the lives of so many of the island's top performers in recent years. The record went to #1 in Jamaica.

"Press Button" (produced by Andrew Thomas), the Rasta-conscious "World Dance" (Patrick Roberts), "Name Brand"

and "Yu Better Listen" (Redrose & Malvo) and "Praise Him" (Jack Scorpio) kept the heat on during 1994, as Beenie Man celebrated the first of four consecutive DJ of the Year awards. He also proved a major success at Sunsplash 95.

Early Beenie Man albums concentrated on gathering together either singles or popular live routines. Now he signed with Island Jamaica for *Blessed*, his first full LP, and his debut international release. His much-photographed romance with singer Carlene Davis confirmed his stardom, while 1995 brought massive hits with "Healer" (produced via Buju Banton's CB 321 organization), "Defend Apache" and "Big Up And Thrust" (Patrick Roberts).

Inevitably, Beenie Man's fame spread. Touring the UK that same year, the DJ paired up with Barrington Levy and came close to charting with "Under Mi Sensi X Project Jungle Spliff," a jungle remix of "Under Mi Sensi." Back home, he furthered comparisons with Buju Banton when he linked with longtime Banton associate Dave Kelly to record "Wicked Ride" and "Slam," the earthy insistence that downtown girls made better lovers than their wealthier counterparts. Other notable releases that year included "Girls Way" and "Blackboard" (produced by Aidan Jones), "So Many Things to Say" (Garfield Phillips) and "Ban Mi fi di truth" (Jack Scorpio).

Collaborations with performers Lady Saw ("Healing"), Triston Palma (the *Three Against War* album), Sanchez ("Refugee"), Michael Prophet ("Gun'n'Bass") and Silver Cat ("Chronic") furthered Beenie Man's acclaim. He also joined roots veterans Third World for a version of "Papa Was A Rolling Stone," featured on their *Live It Up* album.

In September, 1997, his duet with Chevelle Franklin, "Dance Hall Queen," broke Beenie Man into the UK chart. Six months later, the Jeremy Harding produced "Who Am I" hit the Top 10, while the autobiographical *Many Moods of Moses* album also proved a sizeable success. A third UK hit single, "Foundation," followed in August, 1998. All three, incidentally, topped the Jamaican chart during 1997, while four other Beenie Man singles that same year proved similar successes: "Oysters & Conch," "Romie," "Missing You" and "Girls Dem Sugar."

Having headlined Sunsplash 98, Beenie Man now signed a five year contract with Virgin Records. That year's hits included "Nah Bow" (produced by Redrose & Malvo), "Year Four" (Steely & Clevie), "Gwaan So" (Shane Richardson), "Let Him Go" (D Brownie & D Juvenile), "Walla Wiss" (P Giscombe), "Always Be My Baby" (Desmond & Rupert Blake), "Sleep with Me" (Jeremy Harding).

The onslaught continued through 1999, with the release of "100 Dollar Bag" and "LOY" (produced by Goofy), "Battery Dolly" (Steely & Clevie), "In this Together" (Murray & Smith), "Mi Nuh Walla" and "Heights of Great Man"

(King Jammy), "Study Me" (Jack Scorpio) and "Forget You" (Harvel Hart). Beenie Man also collaborated with Buccaneer ("Hot Bwoy" — produced by Steely & Clevie), Silver Cat ("So Nice") and Angel Doolas ("Skettel Tune" — both King Jammy) and Redrose ("Ruff Like We" — Harvel Hart).

Beenie Man's *Art of Life* album won Best Reggae Grammy in February, 2001. Later in the year, he joined Fugee Wyclef Jean as co-producer of the debut album by actor Steven Seagal.

DISCOGRAPHY

6 The Ten Year Old DJ Wonder (Bunny Lee—JA) 1983
The diminutive DJ was already a studio veteran by the time he recorded this album for Bunny Lee. Obviously a child's view is somewhat limited, but the attitude and confidence were already in place, and it was evident that this boy wonder was going places.

8 Defend It (VP) 1994
1994 was the year of Beenie's breakthrough, and this strong collection shows why. Fueled by hardcore dance hall with strong beats, the DJ's incisive lyrics and verbal skills are showcased on a set that leads off with "Wicked Man" and includes the hardhitting hit title track.

7 Dis Unu fi Hear (High Tone—JA) 1994
8 Blessed (Island Jamaica—UK) 1995
The DJ's public retreat from raggamuffin culture and into rastafarianism is made plain on the album's title track, a theme he returned to on such singles as the "Freedom," "Heaven Vs Hell," and the anthemic "Acid Attack." It was the infectious "Slam" however, that brought him international attention, and prompted this singles' package, which doubled as Beenie's international full-length debut.

7 Maestro (Greensleeves—UK) 1996
Brother Little Kirk is among the guests duetting with Beenie Man; Sly & Robbie and the Shocking Vibes Crew are among the producers. After so many albums that were really no more than hits sets, *Maestro* was an unexpected pleasure, hanging wonderfully together even as the moods shift, another surprising side of the DJ that few people imagined, all set to some excitingly fresh rhythms.

8 Many Moods of Moses (Greensleeves—UK) 1997
"Oysters & Conch," "Foundation" and "Bad Man" were already proven JA hits by the time this album was released, while the presence of Sly & Robbie and Buju Banton, and a surprisingly effective reworking of Bobby Brown's "My Prerogative," "Bad Mind Is Active," rendered this among Beenie Man's most instantly impressive albums.

8 The Doctor (VP) 1999
It has been called one of the year's definitive dance hall albums, and 70s' MOR duo Captain & Tenille can take

some of the credit. A cover of their hitherto grisly "Do that to Me One More Time" is a stand-out.

⁊ Y2K (Artists Only) 1999

King Jammy production which seemingly deals with everything but the so-called Millennium Bug. "Illiterate Girl" and "AIDS Victim" are rightfully pinpointed as highlights, while "Feel Good" features a passing Leroy Sibbles and ranks with the best of Beenie Man.

9 Art & Life (Virgin) 2000

Arturo Sandoval and Wyclef Jean guest on a multi-faceted album, the Cuban and hip hop extremes bookending some of Beenie's best work ever. With 17 tracks, the album may be a little overlong, but at its best (which certainly includes the maddeningly infectious "Ola") *Art & Life* is a purposefully, pleasingly ramshackle exploration of the point where dance hall bursts into the modern American mainstream.

BEENIE MAN & BOUNTY KILLER
6 Guns Out (Greensleeves—UK) 1994

The guns may be out, but thankfully the DJs are not aiming them at each other. After their notorious feud, the public reconciliation between the pair resulted in this set to settle their grudges once and for all. They get six cuts apiece and, while the sound system clash was an essential purchase for fans at the time, both artists have moved on, and it's of little more than historical note today.

BEENIE MAN & DENNIS BROWN & TRISTON PALMA
4 Three Against War (VP) 1995

BEENIE MAN & MAD COBRA & LT STITCHIE
4 Mad Cobra Meets Lt Stitchie & Beenie Man (VP) 1995

SELECTED COMPILATIONS & ARCHIVE RELEASES
⁊ Gold (Charm—UK) 1994

Wicked selection of 1993–94 period 45s, drawn from his work outside of the Sly & Robbie/Taxi stable.

BIG YOUTH

STYLE *reggae (toasting/DJ)*
BORN *Manley Augustus Buchanan, 4/19/49 (Kingston JA)*

Possibly the greatest of the classic DJs, Big Youth learned his trade as far from the sound systems as it was possible to get, employed as a diesel mechanic at the Kingston Sheraton hotel, toasting to himself as he worked (it was there, too, that he gained his stage name, from older and smaller co-workers).

Only slowly did he graduate to the public arena, taking the mike at various dances and, as he grew in experience, so his popularity soared. By 1970, he was a regular at Lord Tippertone's, and within a year had established himself as resident DJ, attracting the attention of various producers.

None, however, seemed capable of drawing the talent out further. Big Youth's debut single, "Movie Man" (utilizing the rhythm from Errol Dunkley's "Movie Star") was released in January, 1972, on the African Museum label set up by Dunkley and Gregory Isaacs, but did little. The same fate awaited follow-ups, "The Best Big Youth" (aka "Black Cindy," with producer Jimmy Radway), "Moving" (Lee Perry), and "Phil Pratt Thing" and "Tell It Black" (versioning Dennis Brown's "Black Magic Woman," produced by Phil Pratt). Even Niney Holness only scratched the surface of Big Youth's abilities—the pair cut "Fire Bunn," around the producer's already legendary "Blood and Fire" rhythm.

However, Big Youth's minor league status was finally shattered in 1972, when producer and fellow youthful ingenue Augustus "Gussy" Clarke took the DJ under his wing, and began allying his toasting with some serious roots. "The Killer," in July, 1972, was a hit, and "Tippertone Rocking" followed.

Shortly after, Big Youth linked with Keith Hudson and enjoyed his greatest smash yet. "S.90 Skank," a tribute to the then in-vogue Honda motorbike, was a Jamaican chart-topper (and also appeared in a TV commercial for the same machine); the Hudson/Youth duet "Can You Keep a Secret" offered a solid followup. The same day he recorded "S90 Skank," incidentally, Big Youth cut two tracks with Glen Brown, "Opportunity Rock" and "Come into My Parlour." Less than a week later, he cut four more with Prince Buster—"Chi Chi Run," "Leave Your Skeng," "Leggo Beast" and "Cain and Abel."

Visually, Big Youth captured the country's imagination—who else could boast front teeth inlaid with red, gold and green jewels? Musically, too, he created headlines. His serene, almost laid-back delivery, in a half-chanted, half-sung style which oozed melody, was the virtual antithesis of the yelps and exhortations of his contemporaries. At the same time, his flawless precision timing allowed him to chatter away in perfect synchronization with the rhythms, and while his relaxed style made it all seem so easy, his competitors quickly realized it wasn't.

Released in 1973, Big Youth's first album, titled for the now-legendary "Screaming Target" hit, reunited him with Gussie Clarke across a string of well-chosen rhythms from Gregory Isaacs, Leroy Smart and Lloyd Parks among others. Further hits followed with Sonia Pottinger ("Facts of Life"), Joe Gibbs ("A So We Stay," "Foreman Versus Frazier," "Chucky No Lucky" and Derrick Harriott ("Cool Breeze"). At one point, Big Youth had seven singles on the Jamaican chart at the same time; during 1973, "Chi Chi Run," "Cool Breeze," "Screaming Target" and "A So We Stay" remained on the Top 20 for a full year.

However, by now frustrated by the labyrinthine and often dubious finances of the Jamaican music industry, Big Youth

Big Youth, the greatest of the classic DJs.

set up his own record labels, Negusa Nagast (Amharic for "King of Kings") and Augustus Buchanan, in 1974. The former debuted with the singles "Hot Cross Bun," "Children Children," "Mr Bunny" and "Streets in Africa," cut over funk band War's "The World Is a Ghetto" with Dennis Brown and the Heptones.

These were followed by the aptly titled *Reggae Phenomenon* album, its title track one of several variations on Dennis Brown's recent "Money in My Pocket" hit. Featuring hot hits "Natty Dread No Jester" and "Dread inna Babylon," alongside remakes of several earlier cuts, the album also boasted the first stirrings of what became one of Big Youth's strongest characteristics, a penchant for American pop and R&B hits. Over the years, his idiosyncratic versions of Otis Redding's "Dock of the Bay," Diana Ross' "Touch Me in the Morning," Gene Pitney's "Town Without Pity" and the Temptations' "Papa Was a Rolling Stone" have become cross-over milestones. His version of Al Green's "Love and Happiness" is an especial triumph.

And the hits continued piling up. With Glen Brown, Big Youth cut "Dubbie Attack"; Tony Robinson conjured "House of Dreadlocks" and "Mammy Hot and Daddy Cold"; Harry J paired him with Dennis Brown for "Wild Goose Chase"; Holness retained the same duo for "Ride on Ride On." (Big Youth and Brown also released a powerful version of Bob Marley's "Get Up Stand Up.") Buddy Davidson produced the infectious "Johnny Dead," while an even more promising union saw Big Youth working with Vivian "Yabby You" Jackson on a version of the producer's already trademark "Conquering Lion," "Yabby Youth." (Youth utilized the same rhythm for "Lightning Flash," while Jackson also produced the favorite "Big Youth Dread.")

Toasting over the Abyssinians' "Satta Amasa Gana," Big Youth scored another memorable smash with the mighty "I Pray Thee." At Tuff Gong, he took Bob Marley's "Craven Choke Puppy" and developed "Craven Version"; Bunny Wailer's "Bide Up" became "Black on Black"; Burning Spear's "Marcus Garvey" was developed into "Mosiah Garvey." The latter became one of several highlights on 1975's *Dreadlocks Dread* album, a massive underground hit in the UK that summer, following its release on the Klik label. Big Youth visited Britain the following year.

By the mid-1970s, the DJ was confidently producing himself, usually recording with Earl Smith's Soul Syndicate—renamed the Ark Angels for the occasion. 1976's *Natty Cultural Dread* and *Hit the Road Jack* albums not only spun off hit title tracks, but were positively loaded with major Jamaican smashes—"Wolf in Sheep's Clothing," "Jim Squashey," "Ten Against One."

A reunion with Holness saw Big Youth release "Four Sevens," a response to Culture's "Two Sevens Clash," scheduled to coincide with July 7, 1977—the seventh day of the seventh month. The same team's "Six Dead, 19 Gone to Jail" was as eloquent as it was heartfelt. Another Observer-led masterpiece reworked Niney's own "Blood and Fire" as "Whole Lot of Fire."

Another intriguing collaboration saw Big Youth co-write at least one song with bassist Boris Gardiner and American actor Calvin Lockhart. The result, "Every Nigger Is a Star" was recorded with the I-Threes (Rita Marley, Marcia Griffiths and Judy Mowatt), and was the first record ever to feature the trio.

In 1977, Big Youth signed with the UK label Virgin's Frontline subsidiary for the album *Isaiah First Prophet of Old*, and also appeared in the cult movie *Rockers*. The following year, the DJ helped feed the national outrage after troops massacred a group of Rastafarians at Green Bay, cutting the incendiary "Green Bay Killers." However, Virgin passed on three further albums, *Progress*, the Sylvan Morris dub *Reggae Gi Dem Dub*, and *Rock Holy*. As the new decade loomed, Big Youth's popularity as both a DJ and a recording artist seemed increasingly uncertain, with a corresponding dip in the quality of his work consigning him to the shadows for much of the next two decades.

He resurfaced only sporadically. A single with Lloyd Parks, "No War in the Dance," emerged in 1982, commenting upon the increasingly fractious dance hall scene. That same summer, Big Youth turned in a strong hits-heavy set at Reggae Sunsplash. (He made further appearances in 1983, 1987, 1992 and 1996.)

A pair of weak albums during the late 1980s was followed by another renaissance in 1990–91, the Niney Holness-produced "Chanting," and the powerful "Free South Africa" on the Mikey Bennett produced protest album *One Man One Vote*. He guested on albums by Mutabaruka (*Gathering of the Spirits*, Capleton (*I Testament*) and Creation Rebel (*Feat of a Green Planet*), but it was 1995 before Big Youth truly re-emerged, with the enjoyable (if not exactly classic) *Higher Grounds*. He also keeps a fatherly eye on Tug Hype, a rap act formed by his sons.

DISCOGRAPHY

9 Screaming Target (Trojan—UK) 1973

Sheer dynamite. The title track (appearing twice) is the unimpeachable highlight, but Youth never puts a foot wrong throughout, and even tired singles ("Solomon Grundy") re-emerge invigorated under his guiding raps and Gussie Clarke's production.

10 Reggae Phenomenon (Negusa Nagast—JA) 1974

Though hindsight makes it look like a hits collection, there was a time when everything on this album was fresh—and if you forget the repackages, it still is. Youth at his rollicking peak, knowing both his audience and their demands, and delivering on target every time.

9 Dreadlocks Dread (Klik—UK) 1975

Prince Tony produced set features Big Youth with the underrated Skin Flesh & Bones Band, for "House of Dread Locks," "Natty Dread She Want," "Marcus Garvey Dread," "Dread Organ," "Lightning Flash." Almost half the album comprises dubs, but is still an essential set. Subsequently reissued by Front Line.

8 Natty Cultural Dread (Trojan—UK) 1976

The DJ raps, produces and even sings on this self-confident rootsy set, which included such seminal cultural songs as the title track, "Every Nigger Is a Star" and the equally dread chant "Wolf in Sheep's Clothing." The stand-out, however, is the penultimate "Keep Your Dread," a churning riff keeping time behind Big Youth's mantric invocation—"dreadlock, dread, natty dread, natty congo. . . ."

7 Hit the Road Jack (Trojan—UK) 1976

Picking up where its predecessor left off, self-produced once more, and equally self-assured, Big Youth versions and reconstructs old chestnuts like the title track, which transmogrifies into a wonderful medley; "Jah Man of Syreen"—which threatens to turn into "If I Had a Hammer"!; and the equally spectacular "Ten Against One," a rootsified take on the Mad Lads' "Ten to One." A couple of tracks let the side down, but given Youth's workload at this time, that's hardly surprising.

8 Isaiah First Prophet of Old (Front Line—UK) 1978

"World in Confusion" sets the scene for a seething roots set characterized by D Russell's booming production and some seriously impassioned Youth vocals. "Reaping Time," "Writing on the Wall" and the title track are indispensable.

8 Live at Reggae Sunsplash (Sunsplash) 1983

"I Pray Thee"/"Satta Amasa Gana" opens, "Hit the Road Jack" closes and in between, Big Youth pre-empts a binful of compilation albums with a magnificent performance topped by the savage "Green Bay Killers."

7 A Luta Continua (Heartbeat) 1985

A surprising set finds Big Youth moving away from his traditional toasting style, preferring to sing his messages in the company of Jamaican jazz-man Herbie Miller. The title track is a remarkable study in Fela Kuti-esque Afrobeat.

5 Manifestation (Heartbeat) 1988

Not one of the Youth's finest hours, although the casual toast of "Superman Meets the Hulk" offers up a thoughtful highlight, and "No Way to Treat a Lady" levels its sights on raggamuffin traditions of downgrading women.

8 Jamming in the House of Dread (ROIR) 1991

Great hits-heavy live set recorded at the Japansplash festival in Osaka.

5 Higher Grounds (VP) 1995

Oddball fusion of reggae, R&B and beyond was produced by Junior Reid and includes the popular "Cuba Yi Gong."

SELECTED COMPILATIONS & ARCHIVE RELEASES

6 Chi Chi Run (Fab—UK) 1972

Just four Big Youth cuts are included, vying for attention with Prince Buster productions for Alton Ellis, Dennis Brown, John Holt and Little Youth, but the title track, based on "Rain from the Skies," remains a gem.

8 Everyday Skank: The Best of Big Youth (Trojan—UK) 1980

The title accurately sums up the contents, a slew of hits both self-produced and recorded for others that spans the DJ's career.

6 Some Great Big Youth (Heartbeat) 1981

Negusa Nagast 45s collection concentrating on the early 80s, and picking up the rap-inflected "Get on Up," the near-balladic "Living" and a bizarrely lounge-like version of "I'm In A Dancing Mood." However, we also get "Green Bay Killing" and a roots-meets-pop mangling of the Beatles' "We Can Work It Out."

8 The Chanting Dread inna Fine Style (Heartbeat) 1983

A companion volume to the above, tracking back to pick up 1973's somewhat more crucial "Street in Africa," "Sky-juice" and more.

9 Tell It Black (Snapper—UK) 2000

Fabulous two-CD, 31 track round-up of Big Youth's 1972–75 output, omitting the Buster material but otherwise touching upon all the crucial bases.

9 Natty Universal Dread (Blood & Fire—UK) 2000

51 tracks spread across three discs cover the period 1973–79, rounding up the majority of his self-productions. A handful of tracks are familiar from the earlier Heartbeat collections, but the majority have not been seen since their original Negusa Negast label releases. Too many gems to even begin to list, but if you've ever wondered what would have happened if Sly Stone was born in Kingston, catch "Love and Happiness" (Leroy Smart supplies vocals), while any discussion on who was the greatest DJ of them all is

answered by "Battle of the Giants," a titanic tussle between Youth and U-Roy.

BLACK STALIN

STYLE *calypso/soca*
BORN *Leroy Calliste, 9/24/41 (San Fernando, T&T)*

Possibly the greatest of all calypso lyricists and certainly the most militant, Black Stalin is a devout Rastafarian who sees carnival as simply another stage from which to broadcast his strident demands for Pan-African unity. To this end, he has been described as everything from an unrepentant Garveyite to the Martin Luther King of Trinidad calypso, titles which sit equally comfortably upon his head.

Growing up on San Fernando's Coffee Street, Stalin's earliest influences were the schoolteachers who wove their lessons like traditional African storytellers, and the steel bands which practiced in the pan yard next door to his childhood home. Both unlocked ambitions within the boy, although his first job in entertainment saw him working as a limbo dancer, while running through a stream of short-lived day jobs.

It was a Lord Pretender concert in Skinner Park, San Fernando, which turned Stalin's head towards performing and, in 1959, he made his debut as a vocalist at the Good Shepherd Hall in St Madeline. Three years later, he appeared at the Southern Brigade calypso tent; around 1964, calypsonian Blakie, who ran his own tent, gave him the name Black Stalin in tribute to the youth's fiery lyrical style and steely self-belief.

In 1967, under the tutelage of Lord Kitchener, Stalin made the Calypso King finals for the first time, performing "Beat My Tune" and "Culture First." He became a familiar fixture at the T&T carnival over the next decade, but it was 1979 before Stalin finally won the crown, taking honors with the prayer for unity, "Caribbean Man" and "Play One," a tribute to the father of pan, Winston "Spree" Simon.

That same year brought Black Stalin's debut album, also titled *Caribbean Man*, followed in 1981 by *In ah Earlier Time*. Fiercely outspoken throughout, a steady sequence of albums appeared during the 1980s, highlighted by *You Ask for It* (1984), *I Time* (1986) and *To de Master* (1989), Stalin's first and only album for the Warner Brothers major label.

Stalin continued to dominate carnival throughout this period, reaching the calypso monarch finals eight times. He won again in 1985 with "Ism Schism" and "Wait Dorothy," a calypso dedicated to those fans who insisted he write either party or sexually-themed music, rather than the socio-political commentary which was his forte. That same year, he finished second behind Mighty Sparrow at the BUCKS Calypso King of the World competition, featuring the cream of Caribbean, European and North American performers.

1987 brought Stalin's third Carnival victory, performing "Mr Pan Maker" and "Bun 'Em," an astonishingly popular plea to St Peter to cast Margaret Thatcher and Ronald Reagan into the deepest pits of hell. Further victories arrived in 1991 ("Look on the Bright Side," "Black Man Feelin' to Party") and 1995, when the social commentary "In Time" was joined by "Tribute to Sundar Popo," a whimsical song dedicated to the veteran chutney performer.

1994, meanwhile, saw Black Stalin join Eddy Grant's Ice label stable, cutting the aptly titled *Rebellion* album, with backing vocals throughout supplied by Legend, Ice's own in-house vocal trio (Nicole and Simone Niles, and the intriguingly named Indra Rubber). In addition, "Black Woman Lament," a tremendous duet with labelmate Viking Tundah, also appeared. "Tribute to Sundar," of course, emerged a central prop of 1995's *Message to Sundar* and a highlight of the *Soca Carnival 95* compilation.

SELECTED DISCOGRAPHY

8 Caribbean Man (—T&T) 1979
7 In ah Earlier Time (Makossa—T&T) 1981
7 You Ask for It (Charlies—T&T) 1984
7 Wait Dorothy Wait (Charlies—T&T) 1985
9 I Time (B's) 1986

Six tracks include both vocal and instrumental versions of the hits "Bun 'Em" and "Peace in de World," but neither Stalin's message nor his fascination with calypso's past ("Mister Pan Maker") are diluted by the brevity.

8 We Can Make It (—T&T) 1988

A club mix of "We Ready" is the weakest of the five cuts-stick with the original (also included), then marvel at "No Way" as well.

6 To de Master (Warner Bros) 1989
6 The Bright Side (Straker—T&T) 1991
7 Cry of the Caribbean (—T&T) 1992

With both "Come with It" and "Monday Night Mas" repeated as remixes, *Caribbean* could have emerged one of Stalin's weakest albums. The title track, however, is remarkable, a reminder of his strongest suits.

5 Rebellion (Ice—UK) 1994

The Dylan cover ("I Shall Be Released") may be taking things too far, even if the lyrics do blend perfectly in with Black Stalin's normal surroundings, while a super-sheen production also wrinkles Stalin's customary rough style. But the only real complaints are reserved for "Black Woman Ring Bang" and the multiple mixes of "Let the Soca Play," marginal pieces which neither exercise Black Stalin nor deserve his attention.

8 Message to Sundah (Ice—UK) 1995

9 Roots Rock Soca (Rounder) 1991

Gripping compilation heavy on hits, but still catching Black Stalin at his most purgative. Eleven tracks close with the foreboding "Kaiso Gone Dread." For more of an unabashed soca party flavor, the albums *Best of Straker's: Ah Feel to Party* and *The Best of Black Stalin Volume One* are worth checking out.

BLACK UHURU

STYLE *reggae (roots)*
FORMED 1972 *(Kingston, JA)*
ORIGINAL LINE-UP *Garth Dennis (vocals — b Rudolph Dennis, 12/2/49), Derrick "Ducky" Simpson (vocals — 6/24/50), Don Carlos aka Don McCarlos (vocals — b Ervin Spencer 6/29/52)*

Of all the artists primed to step into Bob Marley's shoes in the aftermath of his death at the dawn of the 1980s, none seemed more likely than Black Uhuru. Unquestionably the band was a phenomenon. When they visited the UK in early summer, 1982, opening for the Rolling Stones, many observers insisted they wiped the floor with the headliners, while the preceding twelve months had already seen three of the band's albums make the UK chart. *Red* even broke the Top 30, the most successful (non-Marley) Jamaican album in years.

That so much promise did eventually evaporate can, in part, be laid at the door of the group's never-disguised militancy. Their popularity never waned, at least in the years before the band's "classic" line-up disintegrated; but it never increased, either. Nevertheless, Black Uhuru remain one of the best known and, certainly, best loved reggae groups of all time, with a catalog constantly in the process of rediscovery by another generation.

The original band line-up was known simply as Uhuru (Swahili for "freedom"). Of the three founding members, only Garth Dennis had any kind of musical background, albeit of a vicarious nature — his sister, Joey, was one half of the Studio One duo Andy and Joey. The new group debuted on the Top Cat label with a version of Curtis Mayfield's "Romancing to the Folk Song," following up with "Time Is on Our Side" (Randy's).

Neither was a success, and the group disbanded soon after. Don Carlos launched a solo career, only to see his first single, "Please Stop Your Lying, Girl," a duet with Errol Dunkley, released with Dunkley's vocal alone. He later recorded for Gregory Isaacs' Zairena label, scoring a minor hit with the Drifters' "Magic Moment," while 1982 brought the minor classic album *Day To Day Living* (Greensleeves).

Dennis, too, went solo, releasing the single "Slow Coach,"

Black Uhuru in the late 1990s: Simpson, Connally, and Bees.

before joining the Wailing Souls, just as that band moved to Channel One and into their period of greatest local success. Coincidentally, Ducky Simpson also worked with the Wailing Souls, cutting the "Liberty" single with them shortly before Dennis joined the group. However, Simpson also persisted with the Uhuru vision, recruiting two new vocalists, Jayes frontman Errol Nelson and Michael Rose.

Rose had been operating as a solo artist since the early 1970s, when his debut single, "Woman a Gineal fe True," appeared under the name Tony, the b-side of Andel Forgie's performance of the same song on producer Newton Simmons' SRS label. From there, Rose moved onto the tourist circuit, playing the north coast hotels for a couple of years before returning to Kingston and hooking up with drummer Sly Dunbar.

Dunbar introduced Rose to producer Niney Holness, and 1972 saw the release of the original version of what became one of Black Uhuru's signature hits, "Guess Who's Coming to Dinner."

Other pre-Uhuru Rose singles included "Love Between Us," "Clap the Barber" and "Freedom Over Me," before

Dunbar engineered another crucial introduction, to producer Lloyd "Prince Jammy" James, who in turn suggested the singer meet with Simpson.

As Black Sounds Uhuru, this new line-up recorded one album, *Love Crisis*, released by Prince Jammy during 1977 (a dub version, *Jammy's in Lion Dub Style*, later appeared). A cover of Bob Marley's "Natural Mystic" appeared around the same time; a second 45, featuring the non-album "Bad Girl," was issued in 1979.

However, aside from spawning the future live favorite, Rose's rousing funk inflected "I Love King Selassie" (another Jamaica-only 45), the album did little. A second Marley cover, "The Sun Is Shining," was recorded with JoJo Hookim at Channel One shortly after but, by the end of the year, Nelson had returned to the Jayes.

He was replaced by American Sandra "Puma" Jones (b 10/5/53, Columbia SC; d 1/28/90), hitherto a dancer with nyahbingi band Ras Michael and the Sons of Negus. In this form, the newly renamed Black Uhuru linked with Sly & Robbie's Taxi label, recording a stream of instant classic singles.

Most were composed by Rose — "General Penitentiary" and a classy reworking of "Guess Who's Coming to Dinner" appeared during 1978. 1979 brought "Plastic Smile," "Abortion" and "Shine Eye Gal," a crucial performance rendered even edgier by guest guitarist Keith Richard (the previous year, the Stone had indicated his grasp of roots with a dubbed-out version of Jimmy Cliff's "The Harder They Come.") These tracks were swiftly compiled as Black Uhuru's second album, *Showcase*, and the band turned in a magnificent performance at the 1980 Reggae Sunsplash. (They returned there in 1981 and 1983.)

The trio next recorded two singles for Dennis Brown's DEB label, "Wood for My Fire" and "Rent Man," an album was scheduled, but never released. Back at Taxi, meanwhile, "Observe Life" kicked the new decade off in dynamic style and, soon after, Island Records moved in for the band. Months later, *Sinsemilla* formally introduced the Black Uhuru to the international audience they courted for the next five years.

Recorded with the beating heart of the Channel One studio house band, the Revolutionaries — Sly and Robbie, of course, plus Ansell Collins (keyboards), Radcliff Bryan and Ranchie McLean (guitar) and Sticky Thompson (percussion), the album spawned another major hit via its title track. The sessions also threw up what is now regarded as the definitive version of "Guess Who's Coming to Dinner," originally a UK b-side, but subsequently included in the *Liberation* anthology.

Their follow up album, the UK #28 hit *Red*, was accompanied by the "Sponji Reggae" single, while the *Showcase* album resurfaced in Europe (through Virgin Records) as *Black Uhuru* and climbed to #81 just weeks later. Completing the hit triumvirate, Black Uhuru's own next album, *Chill Out* made #38 in June, 1982, as the band — augmented now by Sly and Robbie, guitarists Darryl Thompson and Mikey Chung, keyboard player Keith Sterling and percussionist Sly Juice — toured with the Rolling Stones.

Tear It Up, an essential (if criminally short) live recording offered a memento of the excitement, but it was over a year before the band resurfaced, a hiatus broken only by the *Dub Factor* remix album and, of course, a burgeoning string of outside engagements for Sly & Robbie. Their work with Black Uhuru had already prompted Island label head Chris Blackwell to pair them with Grace Jones; now, the self-styled Riddim Twins developed into one of the most in-demand session teams of the decade.

1984's *Anthem* delineated the gulf forming between the Jamaican market's taste in music and that intended for an international market. A near faithful version of Sly Stone's "Somebody's Watching You" was only one of the shocks in store. Even more incredibly, the entire album was remixed and resequenced for Europe and the US; indeed, the Ja-maican version itself was soon replaced by this oddly fash-ioned new mix, with one of its finest tracks, "Party Next Door," physically removed from the album and buried instead on an import-only single.

The sacrifices were not in vain, as *Anthem* became the first ever winner of the Grammy Awards' newly instituted Reggae category (it beat out releases by Peter Tosh, Yellowman, Jimmy Cliff and Steel Pulse). Despite its success, however, Rose quit the band to resume his solo career. At the same time, the group parted company with Island Records.

Rose was replaced by Junior Reid (b Delroy Reid, 1963, Kingston, JA), whose own solo career had seen him regularly working alongside Black Uhuru founder member Don Carlos, most recently within the Worry Struggle & Problem conglomerate (completed by Sugar Minott).

In this form, the band signed to the American label RAS, and a new Black Uhuru single, Reid's "Fit You Haffe Fit," promised business as usual. "Conviction or a Fine" echoed its promise, but five years spent on the cusp of a major break-through had left the group almost desperate to push forward, and their next steps were to prove cruelly ill-advised. The single "The Great Train Robbery" paired them with New York dance producer Arthur Baker, while the *Brutal* album served only to alienate the band's original roots audience, even as it earned Black Uhuru their second Grammy nom-ination.

The trio was in disarray. Despite returning to producer Prince Jammy, sessions for their next album were never completed — the tracks were later salvaged for the *Love Dub* album, and a new single from the same sessions was nothing more than an instrumental retake of "I Love King Selassie." Ill health then forced Jones to quit the band — she returned to the US, where she died of cancer 1/28/90. She was re-placed by Olafunke (born Janet Reid, JA) and, with the group intent now on reclaiming their earlier credibility, Black Uhuru began a parallel career recording for Reid's own JR Productions label.

While RAS released "Conquer the Tanker" (1987), the JR singles "Pain on the Poor Man's Brain" and "Nah Get Rich and Switch" were the true highlights of this period and did go some way towards recapturing the majesty of the early 80s line-up. However, problems with his US visa, which in turn affected his ability to tour, forced Reid to quit Black Uhuru following the *Positive* album in 1988. Ola-funke left at the same time, and Simpson was on his own again.

Fortune stepped in when Black Uhuru were booked to perform at an awards ceremony in California, a function at which original vocalists Don Carlos and Garth Dennis were also scheduled to appear. Simpson promptly invited the pair to reform the original Black Uhuru line-up for the event, and they carried on from there.

The "new" line-up debuted in 1990 with the "Reggae Rock" single, backed by a version of "Hey Joe." 1991 brought the moody *Now*, an album which addressed both current world events (the Gulf War and the end of apartheid in South Africa) and more personal tragedies — the deaths of friend Peter Tosh and former bandmate Jones. It garnered another Grammy nominee, and saw the group finally settle into their true role as elder statesmen of Jamaican music, as opposed to burdening themselves with the frustrating, but so unnecessary, tag of post-Marley nearly men.

Mystical Truth emerged in 1992, while 1996 brought *Strongg*. However, the storm clouds were once again gathering over the band. By the end of the year, Simpson had quit to tour Europe with dub poet Yasus Afari, under the name Black Uhuru — even as his bandmates went on the road in the US, also as Black Uhuru.

Of course the matter moved into the courts, preventing either band from recording (the Carlos/Dennis line-up appeared on the *Reggae on the Rocks* live album); in 1997, however, Simpson's Black Uhuru issued a new version of "General Penitentiary" as a single, shortly before an LA court awarded him the legal rights to the band name.

While Carlos cut his first solo album in a decade, *7 Days a Week*, Simpson pieced together a new Black Uhuru line-up, featuring Andrew Bees and Jennifer Connally, for the King Jammy produced album *Unification*. Simpson and Bees alone cut 2001's *Dynasty*.

SELECTED DISCOGRAPHY

6 Love Crisis (Third World — JA) 1977

Prince Jammy produced set subsequently remixed and reissued as *Black Sounds of Freedom* (Greensleeves — UK) 1981, a title taken from the coda of the opening "I Love King Selassie." A revelation in hard roots, and from their awe inspiring cover of Marley's "Natural Mystic" to their own, equally superb, "African Love," *Crisis* was awash in cultural and Rastafari themes, stunning vocals, and deep rhythms.

10 Showcase (D-Roy — JA) 1979

It's only a string of singles, not always expertly segued into their dub counterparts, but if Black Uhuru should be remembered for any one album, this is it. The original interpretations of seven of their best-known numbers, "Guess Who's Coming to Dinner" included, still draw wallflowers out of their corners, while the vocals are so brilliant you barely notice the rhythm section. And vice versa.

8 Sinsemilla (Island) 1981

The group solidify their sound and vision, with the title track, "Endurance" and "World Is Africa" remaining roots classics.

8 Red (Island) 1981

It's not their best, just their best known. Still, "Carbine" and "Youth of Eglington" live up to the band's revolutionary reputation, while "Sponji Reggae" has an irredeemably hypnotic bounce to it.

9 Tear It Up [live] (Island) 1982

And tear it up they did. Onstage the group were one of the most powerful roots performers around, and their two nights at London's Rainbow Theatre in July, 1981, captured them at their height, with an unforgettable set of classic songs, delivered with passion and power.

7 Chill Out (Island) 1982

At the same time as laying the groundwork for the group's Grammy success with *Anthem*, this album rocketed Sly & Robbie to international fame. The duo's series of heavy, pulsing rhythms and palpitating electronics might have swamped a lesser group, but Uhuru merely used them as a launching pad for their own soaring work, in a sublime meeting between studio wizardry and the trio's own magical stylings.

5 The Dub Factor (Mango) 1983

This could have been sublime, and it's not quite ridiculous. Rather, 10 tracks are stripped down to more or less their component parts, but when that all sounds too ordinary, they're then echoed and reverbed just enough to make them "different." Dub for soothing the savage dinner guest, but not really much use any other time.

6 Anthem (Island) 1984

The Jamaican version disappeared quickly from the shops, but its US counterpart, which included more tracks but was resequenced and remixed, lives on. Songs such as "Black Uhuru Anthem," "Elements" and the hypnotically infectious "What Is Life" were the more powerful tracks, but too much of *Anthem* hovers around the "average" mark.

5 Brutal (RAS) 1986
7 Brutal Dub (RAS) 1986

Times were indeed brutal, what with the departure of Michael Rose (replaced by dancehall hitmeister Junior Reid) and the dangerously shifting musical sands of the mid-'80s; trapped between their rootsy sound and the electro-lightness of the day, *Brutal* contains some good songs, but overall sounds sadly lightweight. The dub, contrarily, is often superlative.

5 Positive (RAS) 1988
6 Positive Dub (RAS) 1988
7 Live in New York (Rokit — UK) 1988

Raw reminder that no matter what was going down in the studio, live Black Uhuru remained awe-inspiring.

6 Now (Mesa) 1991
6 Now Dub (Mesa) 1991

5 Iron Storm (Mesa) 1991
5 Iron Storm Dub (Mesa) 1991

A guest appearance from rapper Ice T (on "Tip of the Iceberg") prompted a flurry of interest; a Grammy nomination (the band's fourth) lent the album further respect.

6 Mystical Truth (Mesa/East West) 1992

Despite puzzling versions of War's "Slipping into Darkness" and Peter Gabriel's "Mercy Street," plus Jimi Hendrix's "Hey Joe," *Mystical Truth* actually emerges one of the strongest latter day Uhuru albums.

4 Strongg (Mesa) 1996
7 Strongg Dub (Mesa) 1996

It's too easy to overlook the parent album, but the dub set is remarkable, strong overtones of early 80s technique haunted by horns which baffle the first time, but quickly become essential.

7 Unification (5 Star General) 1998

"Wood for My Fire," a classic from the band's early days, is revisited as the Rastafarian warning "Babylon Fall With John Paul."

7 Dynasty (RAS) 2001

A worthy return to the old deep roots sound.

SELECTED COMPILATIONS & ARCHIVE RELEASES

9 Black Uhuru (Virgin—UK) 1980

Despite packing just seven tracks, all Jamaican hit 45s (and mostly available on *Showcase*), the dawn of the Sly & Robbie years could not be better served.

8 Uhuru In Dub (CSA—UK) 1982

Equally credited to Sly & Robbie and Black Uhuru, the dub companion to *Love Crisis* unveils "Eden Dub," "Mystic Mix," "Firehouse Special" and the rest, stripped to the bone, then bludgeoned back together. Dirty dub at its darkest.

8 Liberation—The Island Anthology (Island) 1994

A good portion of this two-CD set reprises the long lost original *Anthem*, the extended versions and heavier mix proving a stunning corollary to the familiar, so-breezy set. Rare single mixes and choice album cuts complete the story of the band's Island years, but infuriatingly omitting the classic Taxi period, replacing those tracks with rerecordings and live versions. It's a major shortcoming — we already know this band was great. But we don't get to hear just *how* great.

6 Love Dub (Rohit) 1994

The aborted Prince Jammy sessions — nothing special.

8 Ras Portraits (RAS) 1997

Despite having just the two Junior Reid era albums to choose from, highlights of the dub counterparts blend neatly to create a remarkably ambitious and forward-looking package.

MICHAEL ROSE SOLO

9 Michael Rose (Heartbeat) 1995

An awe inspiring blend of dance hall and roots. Niney's immaculate production is an epiphany, peppered with beats so fat that they're positively obese, while even the most synthetic tracks throb with a deep rootsy quality. Rose's vocals have retained their power, although his occasional dance hall stylings are just a touch tentative.

7 Be Yourself (Heartbeat) 1996
8 Big Sound Frontline (Heartbeat) 1996

Left to his own production devices, Rose turns in a comparatively lighter weight album than the last; conversely though, this works as a masterful vocal showcase which glows with a sense of joie de vivre across both old songs and new. The accompanying dub version adds a little more weight, plenty of bounce and two bonus tracks.

5 Dance Wicked (Heartbeat) 1997
6 Dub Wicked (Heartbeat) 1997
8 Party In Session—Live (Heartbeat) 1997

Aptly titled album recorded at a variety of US shows during 1996–7, featuring faves old and new and totally capturing the excitement of the singer and his S.A.N.E. band, and the absolute jubilation of the crowd and performance.

8 Bonanza (Heartbeat) 1999

Rose's most diverse album to date, and his hardest hitting. From the easy going "It's Alright" to the toughest dance hall, from revisions of Uhuru songs to nods towards the Beatles and Michael Jackson, lovers rock and social bite, this has it all.

7 Never Give It Up (Heartbeat) 2001

MICHAEL ROSE AND SLY & ROBBIE

8 X Uhuru (Tabou) 1999

Gripping recreations of former hits, updated and upgraded.

BLUE BOY see SUPER BLUE

BROTHER RESISTANCE

STYLE *rhythm poetry*
BORN *Roy Lewis aka Lutalo Masimba (East Dry River, T&T)*

Taking his lead from the pioneering work and research of early 1970s performer Lancelot Layne, Brother Resistance emerged on the T&T live circuit in 1979, fronting the Network Riddum Band and espousing a new poetic soca hybrid which he christened rapso. It was a movement destined to reshape the Caribbean scene.

Despite an immense, immediate live impact, the Network Riddum Band was never going to fit into the easy-going milieu of carnival. Constantly questioning and inciting, and breeding an audience which was as disruptive as the group themselves, the Network Riddum Band's very existence was considered so subversive that, on June 27, 1983, the band's offices, which included rehearsal rooms, a performance area and a drug rehab center, were stormed by the police, accompanied by a demolition squad. The building was razed and equipment was confiscated. Until they could locate new headquarters, the group rehearsed and performed on the streets.

It was 1984 before the group — with Resistance its undisputed focus — cut its first record, *Roots of de Rapso Riddum*. Two further sets appeared during 1985–86, but the band's most profound impact lay in their live work. Their first UK tour in 1986 was covered by the BBC, and included an appearance at the Commonwealth Festival, at London's Royal Albert Hall.

That honor caused an abrupt change in government response to both Resistance and rapso and, in 1989, the singer was selected as T&T's cultural delegate to the World Festival of Youth and Students in Korea, where he was certified for Excellence in the Arts.

The band's single releases have tended to be very well received — "Dancing Shoes," "Ring de Bell," "Drum and de Bass," "Drip Dry," "De Power Move," "RAPSO Energy," "From de Rapso Tradition Make," "De Right Move" and "Tonight Is de Night" (the first rapso song to top the carnival chart, in 1988) rank among their biggest sellers. However, the group's albums remained sporadic, with their fourth set, *Rapso Uprising*, not appearing until 1989.

The emergence of a new wave of T&T based rapso bands, headed by Kindred, 3 Canal and Ataklan, confirmed Resistance's status as an elder statesman of the local music scene — even as he became one of the star attractions at the somewhat oxymoronically named New Music Festival in New York in 1992. The year after, he appeared at the first International Dub Poetry Festival in Toronto, Canada. Other important international appearances include the U.N. Environment Conference, Barbados, in 1994; MIDEM in France in 1997 (Kindred had appeared there the previous year); and California's Reggae on the River in 1998.

Resistance's recording schedule, meanwhile, has remained erratic. Since the albums *Touch de Earth with Rapso* and *From de Heart of de Rapso Nation* in 1991/92, Resistance has released just one further CD, the anthology *De Power of Resistance* in 1996.

He continues touring regularly, however; 2000 saw Resistance appear at the Berlin WOMEX Festival and the United Nation's 55th anniversary celebration in Bonn, during a three month European jaunt (Resistance is especially popular in Germany). 2000 also brought a new single, "Rally," recorded with the French producer Sodi, best known for his work with Femi Kuti.

Resistance was also featured on the *Jouvay 2000* rapso compilation that year, while completing his own next album, *No Communion*, featuring contributions from Steely & Clevie, Kindred and London musician Nitin Sawhney.

SELECTED DISCOGRAPHY

8 **Roots of de Rapso Riddum (—T&T) 1984**
The fusion of steel drum and African rhythm which sets up Resistance's assault grabs you from the opening moment. Compared to later Resistance sets, *Roots* is well-named, and as the first blow in what became a virtual revolution, it is unstoppable.

6 **Rapso Explosion (—T&T) 1985**
8 **Rapso Takeover (—T&T) 1986**
"Big Dirty Lie," "Ring de Bell" and "Tonight Is de Night" head the strongest of Resistance's early albums, dark and rumbling, with the words a wall of rage.

6 **Rapso Uprising (—T&T) 1989**
7 **For RAPSO Lovers de World Over (—T&T) 1990**
7 **Touch de Earth with Rapso (—T&T) 1991**
7 **From de Heart of de Rapso Nation (—T&T) 1992**

SELECTED COMPILATIONS & ARCHIVE RELEASES

9 **De Power of Resistance (Rituals—T&T) 1996**
A dramatic collection which highlights exactly what it was that Resistance passed onto the younger generation. "Big Dirty Lie" is the most dramatic of his soca-dance hall anthems, but the presence of "Cyan Take Dat," "Mother Earth" and "Drum and de Bass," plus a handful of remixes, ensure that every track emerges a classic.

DENNIS BROWN

STYLE *reggae (lovers rock/roots)*
BORN *1957 (Kingston, JA), d 7/1/99*

His admirers called him "Emmanuel, the Crown Prince of Reggae" and, through a career which was cruelly cut short by his death in 1999, Dennis Brown (Emmanuel was actually his middle name) did everything required to justify and retain that title.

Some of the greatest reggae records of the past 30 years were Brown's. The *Super Reggae and Soul Hits* album cut in 1972 with producer Derrick Harriott, revealed a teenaged talent unparalleled in the annals of Jamaican music. The dance hall stylings of 1990's *Unchallenged* reinvented the now veteran Brown for a new generation of fans. In between, the singer established himself — alongside Bob Marley and Gregory Isaacs (with whom he also formed a remarkable singing duo) — among the greatest performers of his age, with a repertoire to match.

Brown grew up on Kingston's Orange Street, spending his childhood watching and listening as the stars of the day filed past on their way to the studios which pocked the

Dennis Brown, the Crown Prince of Reggae.

neighborhood. He had still to hit his teens when he scored his first hit in 1968, working with producer Coxsone Dodd on a cover of the Impressions' "No Man Is an Island" — at the session, he had to stand on a box to reach the microphone. Further Dodd productions "Love Grows," "Never Fall in Love," "Silky," "Little Green Apples" and "If I Follow My Heart," and the Prince Buster produced "If I Had the World" proved this early success was no fluke. Unlike so many of the other child stars then populating the Jamaican hit parade, Brown was obviously built for the long haul.

Dodd released two albums of the young singer's recordings during this period, before he broke away in 1972 and began freelancing around the studios. Sessions with Clive .Chin (among others) were followed by a liaison with Harriott, where Brown was soon wrapping his super-cool vocals around such pop standards as "Wichita Linesman" and "Silhouettes." Another unlikely success came courtesy of producer Phil Pratt, who oversaw Brown's reading of the Fleetwood Mac/Santana hit "Black Magic Woman."

In 1972, he hooked up with Joe Gibbs to record the song which became Brown's best known number, the infectious "Money in My Pocket." Rerecorded at the end of the decade, the single gave him one of the biggest international hits in Jamaica's history.

Although it was recorded at Gibbs' Duhaney Park studio and released on the producer's own Record Globe label, the original "Money in My Pocket" was in fact produced by Niney the Observer. He was just 20 and the similarities in their ages alone was enough to ensure a friendship. As they worked, however, both knew instinctively that they had a chemistry worth nurturing. The quality of Brown's releases from this era, including the classic "He Can't Spell," ensured that, by the summer of 1973, Holness was Brown's official producer.

It was a dramatic move for both men. While Holness was renowned for the experimental roots approach which characterized his 1970 smash "Blood and Fire," and was now refined to near perfection, Brown's success and reputation were based upon sweet lovers rock, delivered with an innocence which matched his gentle voice. But the singer was growing up fast, politicized in the cauldrons of both Jamaican everyday life and his Rastafarian faith. So, while local critics wondered what good could possibly come out of the union between Brown and Holness, in the studio the pair were blueprinting the future.

The first fruits of their union arrived in the form of a string of peerless singles released through Holness's own Observer label over the next two years — the electrifying "Westbound Train," "Have No Fear," "Cassandra," "Go Now," "No More Will I Roam," "I Am the Conqueror," "Ride on Ride On" (with Big Youth) and the classic "Africa" (reworking an old Gaylads rhythm) among them. By the time the pair unleashed "Tribulation" in 1975, Brown's days as an adolescent balladeer seemed far behind him.

Working from the rock solid foundations of the accompanying Soul Syndicate backing band, Brown evinced a passion, a commitment and, most of all, a militancy which utterly defied his still tender years. He was 16 when he and Holness launched their partnership, 18 when they cut "Tribulation." When Bob Marley described Brown as the best reggae singer in the world, it was in the awareness that the youth was only going to get better.

Brown and Holness parted company following "Tribulation," and the singer cut a handful of singles elsewhere around Kingston — "Change Your Style" with Sydney Crooks; "Let Love In" with Phil Pratt; "My Time" with Castro Brown; and the self-produced "Life Goes in Circles" and "Life's Worth Living."

None had the visceral impact of his work with the Observer, however and the pair soon reunited for a fresh batch of recordings. "Wolf and Leopard," cut at composer Lee Perry's recently opened Black Ark studios in Kingston, was a massive hit in Jamaica in 1977, and received a warm welcome in the UK too, where Brown's increasingly rebellious stance found a greedy echo in the burgeoning punk movement.

Alongside near simultaneous offerings from the similarly outspoken Tappa Zukie, Dillinger and Max Romeo, "Wolf and Leopard" (and such successors as "Take a Trip to Zion") consummated the already ripe union between Anglo punks and Rastas. When Holness himself visited London to work with the local reggae band the Cimarrons, his fame actually eclipsed his clients'. Although the Cimarrons themselves received an inestimable boost when they laid down the backing track for Brown's next crucial 45, "Here I Come."

Though Brown and Holness cut just two albums together (1975's *Just Dennis* and the deeply Rastafarian *Wolf and Leopard* two years later), it is a sign of their relentless prodigy that almost every song on both became a hit single. And while it is true that none was ever to prove as universally successful as "Money in My Pocket," still they laid the groundwork for all that Brown was to achieve later in the decade.

1978 saw the singer establish his own DEB label, where early successes included Brown-produced recordings by Junior Delgado, Desi Roots and 15–16–17, an English female lovers rock trio. Other intriguing releases included Gregory Isaacs' "Mr Know It All," and cuts by Field Marshall Buckors, the Tamlins, Alton Ellis, the Gaylads, Errol Dunkley and Black Uhuru. Brown was also responsible for a pair of albums by the so-called DEB Players, 1978's *Umoja Love and Unity* and *20th Century DEBwise*.

Of course DEB maintained a solid stream of releases by Brown himself, many of which were also scintillating self-productions: "Oh What a Day," John Holt's "Man Next Door," "I Don't Want to Be No General," "Cup of Tea," "Troubled World," "Death Before Dishonor" and "What About te Half" among them. Featuring many of the singles so far, Brown's own next albums, *So Long Jah Rastafari* and *Joseph's Coat of Many Colours*, were also DEB releases.

DEB closed down in 1979 and Brown returned to the studio rounds. Winston Riley produced the single "I've Got To Find You"; Bunny Lee hit with "Love Me Forever"; and Ossie Hibbert handled "Whip Them Jah" (a remake of one of Brown's 1976 Holness-era hits). A liaison with Tad Dawkins resulted in the "Unite Brotherman," "If This World Is Mine," "Easy Take It Easy," "You Are," "Armagideon," "How Sweet It Is," "Any Way You Want It" and "Here I Come" singles, released over a five year period.

His most important partnership, however, was with Joe Gibbs. They reunited in 1978, cutting the *Visions* album, and scoring with the "Equal Rights" and "How Can I Leave" 45s. That same year, Brown proved one of the runaway successes at both the epochal One Love Peace Concert at Kingston's National Stadium and the inaugural Reggae Sunsplash. (Brown returned to Sunsplash in 1980, 1981, 1983, 1984 and then annually from 1986.)

In 1979, the revival of "Money in My Pocket" spun off the *Words of Wisdom* album and gave Brown the monster hit his reputation had always sworn he was due. Further gems from this period included a cover of the Sharks' "How Can I Leave," and a duet with Trinity, "Funny Feeling." Brown's own pen supplied "Ghetto Girl" (aka "Stay at Home"), and "Three Meals A Day." The singer himself produced 1981's "The Little Village" and "Do I Worry?" before returning to Joe Gibbs for "Should I," "So Jah Say" and an excellent remake of Alton Ellis' "Ain't that Loving You."

With interest in his activity still peaking, Brown signed an international deal with A&M this same year. Having moved to London, he and Gibbs now cut the albums *Foul Play* and *Love Has Found a Way*. Despite the major label's intentions, this was not an especially successful period and in 1983, *The Prophet Rides Again* marked the end of Brown's relationship with both Gibbs and the label.

Intrigued by the now flourishing dance hall scene, Brown was a participant in DJ Brigadier Jerry's *Live at the Controls at Jack Ruby Sound Ocho Rios J.A.* album in 1983, alongside Sammy Dread and Michael Prophet. He also cut the singles "It's Magic" and "Slow Down Woman" with Prince Jammy, at the same time as allowing his spiritual side a voice with a lovely version of "The Lord Is My Shepherd."

In 1984, a union with Gregory Isaacs produced the album *Two Bad Superstars Meet* and the hit single "Let Off Supm," recorded with Sly and Robbie and Prince Jammy. A second album by this remarkable pairing, *Judge Not* arrived later in 1985. Brown also cut "To the Foundation" with Gussie Clarke, "Summer Holiday" and "I've Been Trying" with Starlight Productions, "Hold Tight" and "Mischief" with Delroy Wright and "Revolution" with Sly and Robbie.

With a ferocious appetite for work, Brown became a willing member of the mid-1980s conspiracy of vocalists which resolved to flood the dance hall market with new material, in a bid to overwhelm the then ubiquitous DJ explosion, the belief being DJs were only succeeding in such quantities because there weren't sufficient singers releasing records at the time. (The song "Stop Your Fighting So Early in the Morning" was dedicated to their struggle.) For the remainder of his life, Brown thought nothing of releasing up to six albums a year, either on his own new label, Yvonne's Special (named for his wife) or elsewhere.

In 1986, Prince Jammy produced Brown's acclaimed *The Exit* album and his successful revision of Slim Smith's "Never Let Go" rhythm, "I Can't Stand It" (one of several dozen versions of that track to appear during the mid-late 1980s). However, Brown's biggest hits of the decade came in 1989/90 — another duet with Gregory Isaacs, "Big All Round" (produced by Gussie Clarke), and the triumphant and so aptly titled *Unchallenged*.

In 1991, Brown was recruited to Mikey Bennett's *One Man One Vote* artists collective — paired with Third World's Bunny Clarke and Cocoa Tea, he delivered an impassioned "Warning," then served up the solo "No More Walls." Another collaboration pitched Brown alongside Twitch and Brian and Tony Gold for the dance hall smashes "Hypocrite Corner" and "Poison"; while 1992's *Blazing* album brought Brown voice-to-voice with Shabba Ranks and Maxi Priest for a raging "Fever." (Brown also worked with Tiger, Fabiana, Reggie Stepper, Platinum and Bounty Killer during this period.)

Indeed, Brown's continued importance was signalled when he collaborated with Beenie Man and Triston Palma for 1995's *Three Against War* album. His international profile, meantime, was maintained when the American RAS label picked up a series of albums Brown recorded during the early-mid 1990s with Leggo Beast (*Victory Is Mine*) and

Roots Radics bassist Flabba Holt (*Blood Brothers, Milk and Honey*).

A string of hits during 1995–97 saw producer Musclehead continue pairing Brown with some of the modern era's hottest names — Roger Robin ("Keep It Burning"), Saxon ("Whip Dem"), Peter Hunningale ("Cupid"), while the singer maintained his solo profile with "Keep It Up," "Rainbow Country," "Feeling The Spirit," "Rocky Love," and the album *You Got the Best of Me*.

Behind the scenes, however, Brown's health was failing. He had developed a serious cocaine habit and, on July 1, 1999, was taken to a Kingston hospital emergency room, unconscious and suffering from a collapsed lung — a direct result of his drug use. He died while doctors tried to reinflate it.

The first anniversary of his passing, in July, 2000, was marked with a massive memorial concert in Brooklyn, featuring Johnny Osbourne, Micky Jarrett, Delano Tucker, Half Pint and others.

SELECTED DISCOGRAPHY

Brown is estimated to have released over 100 albums during his lifetime, with probably twice as many compilations.

7 No Man Is an Island (Studio One — JA) 1970

7 If I Follow My Heart (Studio One — JA) 1971

8 Super Reggae & Soul Hits (Trojan — UK) 1972

An awesome mix of teenaged Brown classics ("He Can't Spell," "Changing Times") and American MOR covers ("Wichita Linesman," "Silhouettes"), with a sharp Derrick Harriott production to smooth the stylistic edges.

9 Best Of (Joe Gibbs — JA) 1975

A deceptive title if you're searching for the hits alone, but also one of Brown's most accomplished and cohesive sets. His first with producer Gibbs includes a remarkable reading of Al Wilson's "Poor Side of Town," alongside a clutch of great Brown originals.

8 Just Dennis (Observer — JA) 1975

Ostensibly a hits collection, padded with a few previously unreleased tracks, and featuring some of Brown's most evocative songs, all for producer Holness, including "Westbound Train," "Cassandra," and "Conqueror."

10 Westbound Train (Third World — UK) 1977

Visionary, violent and totally a child of its time, *Westbound Train* is best remembered for "Tribulation," although any of its inclusions are utterly representative — not only of Brown's talent, but also the turbulent era which it epitomized.

8 Sledgehammer Dub (Observer — JA) 1977

Credited to producer Holness, a dynamite recounting of great swathes of *Westbound Train* reduced to raw thunder.

7 Wolf & Leopard (Weed Beat — JA) 1978

Niney knows roots and Brown sings like a charm.

7 So Long Jah Rastafari (DEB — UK) 1979
8 Visions of Dennis Brown (Lightning — UK) 1979

Joe Gibbs and Errol Thompson keep Brown on the high where Holness left him, while smoothing some of the coarser edges. "Concrete Castle King" and the heartfelt "Malcolm X" manage to fray the seams some, though.

8 Joseph's Coat of Many Colours (DEB — UK) 1979

The second Gibbs/Thompson production, Brown's pairing with Ranking Joe for a remarkable rendering of Bob Marley's "Slave Driver" places much of the rest of the album in the shade. But only until you reach Brown's take on "Man Next Door," a song which seems to get better every time someone else covers it.

7 20th Century Dubwise (DEB) 1979
6 Words of Wisdom (Laser — UK) 1979
5 Live at Montreux (Laser — UK) 1979

Lackadaisical (by Brown's studio standards) live rendering of the hits.

8 Spellbound (Laser — UK) 1981

Brown and producer Gibbs are both in fine form, highlighting the strengths of their partnership just in time for the major labels to come calling.

6 Foul Play (A&M) 1981

The best of Brown's A&M albums features the remarkable "The Existence of Jah" and "The World Is Troubled," two of the greatest roots cuts in major label history.

4 Love Has Found a Way (A&M) 1982

Tri-produced by Brown, Willie Lindo and Joe Gibbs, a masterful blending of lovers rock with a more suave, urban pop styling. But is this a good thing? Given the anonymity of much of the album, probably not.

5 The Prophet Rides Again (A&M) 1983

An album of two halves — side two (on the original vinyl) is Brown composed and includes some of his moodiest work yet, including the deeply foreboding title track. Side one, however, is bright and largely disposable, with the opening "Out of the Funk" and Joe Gibbs' "Jamming My Way to Fame" surely a deaf record company executive's idea of a good time, MTV R&B style.

7 Satisfaction Feeling (Tads — JA) 1983
6 Love's Gotta Hold on Me (JGM — JA) 1984
7 Revolution (Yvonne's Special — JA) 1985
7 Slow Down (Greensleeves — UK) 1985

The title track and "They Fight I" are unimpeachable, as Brown (and producer Jammy) continue their investigation of dance hall roots.

8 Wake Up (Natty Congo — JA) 1985

His master's voice roars — co-producer Trevor Bow wrings a passionate, yearning and deeply spiritual performance from Brown, resulting in the rootsiest of his later albums. "Ray of Light" (aka "Deepest Love") was a stand-out 45.

7 The Exit (Jammy's — JA) 1986

The title track was one of Brown's sharper 80s singles; "Fire" and "Israel" likewise.

6 Smile Like an Angel (Blue Moon) 1986
8 Brown Sugar (Taxi — JA) 1986

Seven scintillating tracks, including three extended mixes, round up Brown's most successful singles for the Taxi, Powerhouse and Yvonne's Special labels, including "Revolution," the falsetto-flavored "Sitting and Watching" and "Hold onto What You've Got." A US release arrived through RAS (1988).

6 Slow Down (Shanachie) 1987

Medium weight album best distinguished by Prince Jammy's production, and the presence of "Can't Keep A Good Man Down." Reissued 2001 by Greensleeves' newly launched US operation.

6 More (Black Scorpio — JA) 1988
5 My Time (Rohit) 1989
8 Unchallenged (VP) 1990

Mutabaruka guests on the stand-out "Great Kings of Africa"; Beres Hammond appears on "Mama's Love," but even the greatest duetting partner is going to come in a distant second behind Brown. Strong material and a crisp Gussie Clarke production.

4 Overproof (VP) 1990

Nowhere near as strong as its predecessor — producer Mikey Bennett seems somewhat in awe of his charge, and guest vocalist (on "Freedom Fires") Erica Newell has done a lot better elsewhere. Brown, meanwhile, simply cruises.

6 Good Tonight (Greensleeves — UK) 1990
7 Go Now (Rohit) 1991
8 Victory Is Mine (RAS) 1991

Brown's first at Leggo Beast's studios is also one of his best sounding. "Should I" is clean and punchy, a choppy cover of the 50s pop classic "Sea of Love" maintains his unpredictable taste in remakes, while the title track makes such a fuss that it surely portends more than it lets on.

6 If I Didn't Love You (Jamaican Gold — UK) 1992

A sensitive cover of the Beatles' "Long and Winding Road" summarizes the mood of this gentle, but distinctly featherweight offering.

5 Friends for Life (Shanachie) 1992
6 Blazing (Greensleeves — UK) 1992

4 General (VP) 1993

The Dennis Brown jukebox! "Green Green Grass of Home," "Just My Imagination" and "The Last Thing on My Mind" highlight an at-times nightmarishly MOR covers collection, performed without a single surprise in store.

5 Hotter Flames (VP) 1993

Brown's take on Bob Marley's "Natural Mystic" has few peers. The rest of the album, sadly, has a lot.

3 Unforgettable (VP) 1993

Just what the world needed, Dennis' version of John Holt's "OK Fred." And that's one of the highlights. Unforgettably forgettable.

8 Cosmic Force (Heartbeat) 1993

Reunion with Niney Holness, remarkable for the title track, a passionate revival of Motown's "(My World Is Empty) Without You" and an almost tribal assault on "Groovin' on a Sunny Afternoon." The electronics which underpin the album are never less than electrifying, while almost every track cuts in, freakishly, with what could well be an excerpt from another piece of music entirely. Even if the songs don't sell you, the sound will.

7 Light My Fire (Heartbeat) 1994

A more conventional sounding album than its predecessor, but remarkable, still, for the revolutionary remake of Leiber/Stoller's "Fools Fall in Love," the turbulent "House on the Rocks" and "More Liberation." Gregory Isaacs' "To Be My Lover" is another stand-out, while the sessions themselves are noteworthy as one of the final performances of the classic Roots Radics line-up, before the death of guitarist Eric "Bingy Bunny" Lamont.

7 Nothing Like This (Greensleeves—UK) 1994

Brown and Gregory Isaacs guested on Reid's 1993 album *Visa*; Reid returns the favor by co-producing (with Brown) an album which certainly has its share of classic sounding moments.

4 Blood Brothers (RAS) 1994

The plaintive "Give Thanks to the Father" would have dignified many of Brown's early-70s albums—its use of the 23rd Psalm, in fact, echoes the classic "Here I Come" from precisely that period. The rest of the album, however, is so lackluster that even the label's "best of" Brown collection all but ignored it.

7 Milk and Honey (RAS) 1996

"Your Love" has an adorable rinky-dink keyboard line running through it, symptomatic of an album which doesn't touch a single peak, but nevertheless remains genuinely enjoyable.

7 Dennis (Burning Sounds—UK) 1996

All hail Sir Niney, who ensures that even when the material is weak, the album still sounds magical. Not essential Brown, even by 90s standards, but an informative listen.

8 You Got the Best of Me (Saxon—UK) 1996

The finest of the Musclehead-produced 45s are joined by skilful reworkings of "Equal Rights" and "Wolf and Leopard." The best of him indeed.

6 Tribulation (Heartbeat) 1997

Alvin Ranglin produced set looking back from a computer consul. "Tribulation" doesn't really enjoy its revision, but rock band Buffalo Springfield's "For What It's Worth" is at least freakishly weird.

7 Hold Tight (Heartbeat) 1997

7 Bless Me Jah (RAS) 1999

A radical cover of Kenny Rogers' "Decorate My Life" retains enough of its country origins to posit some interesting questions about reggae's links to early Americana, while "Black Magic Woman" receives a neat Flabba revision and "Everybody's Talking" rounds up the covers quotient in lackadaisically lovely style. Elsewhere, Brown's own compositions are, if nothing else, unmistakably Brown.

6 Stone Cold World (VP) 1999

A widescreen Gussie Clarke production unleashes some lovely ballads, a soupcon of soul and even some funk.

4 Let Me Be the One (VP) 2000

One of several albums claiming to be Brown's last recorded work, a love song heavy Don Hewitt production marked out by the exemplary "Catch Me if You Can," but scarcely notable for anything else.

DENNIS BROWN & HORACE ANDY

7 Reggae Superstars Meet (Striker Lee—JA) 1986

DENNIS BROWN & BEENIE MAN & TRISTON PALMA

4 Three Against War (VP) 1995

DENNIS BROWN & JOHN HOLT

5 Wild Fire (Natty Congo—JA) 1986

DENNIS BROWN & GREGORY ISAACS

7 Two Bad Superstars Meet (Burning Sounds) 1984

Three tracks apiece, Brown's contributions—"Funny Feeling," "Let Love In" and "To the Foundation" are part of the very bedrock upon which his reputation lies. The dub versions affixed to each track make for double pleasure.

6 Judge Not (Greensleeves—UK) 1985

Again, not a duet set; rather, the Linval Thompson produced tracks are divided equally between the pair. The CD bonus tracks do include one joint performance, the hit "Let Off Supm."

7 No Contest (Greensleeves—UK) 1989

A mix of duets, dubs and solo tracks highlighted by "Big All Round," but also featuring Brown's excellent "No Camouflage."

DENNIS BROWN & JANET KAY
6 So Amazing (Body Work) 1987

DENNIS BROWN & FREDDIE MCGREGOR/COCOA TEA
7 Legit (Greensleeves—UK) 1993

Three full on collaborations vie with generally excellent solo contributions.

DENNIS BROWN & ENOS MCLEOD
6 Baalgad (Goodies) 1986

SELECTED COMPILATIONS & ARCHIVE RELEASES
8 Money in My Pocket (Trojan—UK) 1983

Impossible to quibble with any album which includes "Cassandra," "Africa," "Yagga Yagga" and "Changing Times," a digest of early 70s material which serves up "Silhouettes" as well. The label also drew the collections *Super Hits* and *Musical Heatwave* from the same chronological source.

5 Halfway Up, Halfway Down (A&M) 1986

Uncomfortable collection culled from the three A&M albums, but primarily highlighting the lesser moments of each.

8 Some Like It Hot (Heartbeat) 1992
8 Open The Gate (Heartbeat) 1995

Excellent collections of Holness productions, rounding up the occasional rarity (the 12-inch mix of the classic "Africa," "Here I Come" featuring Dillinger), but concentrating more on simply documenting one of the most fertile partnerships of the age.

7 RAS Portrait (RAS) 1997

Reasonable selection of cuts from *Brown Sugar*, *Victory Is Mine*, *Blood Brothers* and *Milk and Honey*, four albums spanning eight years of distinct ups and downs.

8 The Prime of Dennis Brown (Music Club) 1998

The 1973–95 subtitle suggests a full career round-up; in fact, 1973 *and* 1995 would be more accurate, as *The Prime* alternates between the two dates to serve up an utterly schizophrenic, but strangely satisfying vision of Brown at these totally unrelated peaks. Of the early inclusions, the original "Money in My Pocket" is segued into its "Ah So We Say" flip (with Big Youth), while "Black Magic Woman" and "Yagga Yagga" receive welcome airings. Later offerings include "The Closer I Get to You" with Janet Kay and Marley's "I'm Still Waiting." A more satisfying effort would have spread both periods over entire single discs, but there's no complaints about the music.

7 The Golden Years 1974–76 (Cleopatra) 2000

Two-CD set investigates the Niney years—again! Highlights include the full length "Here I Come" with I-Roy, "Home Sweet Home" and a strong appreciation of the more incendiary elements of the partnership. Sensibly avoids too much duplication with the Heartbeat collections.

6 May Your Food Basket Never Empty (RAS) 2000

Scouring the Flabba Holt archives for recordings dating back to the dawn of his collaborations with Brown, a smattering of new songs dignifies an otherwise covers- and revivals-heavy collection. We really didn't need another version of "Money in My Pocket," but Brown does a nice job with the Beatles' "Lady Madonna" and Alton Ellis' "Just Another Girl," while "Emmanuel" is a fine slab of autobiography. Israel Vibration's "Same Song" also gets a neat work out.

7 The Ultimate Collection (Hip-O) 2000

Hardly "ultimate," but at least further reaching than most Brown collections, nibbling at most crucial eras, and putting the A&M highlight "Prophet Rides Again" on CD at last.

BUCCANEER

STYLE *reggae (toasting/dance hall)*
BORN *Andrew Bradford, 1974 (JA)*

Instantly recognizable in his eye patch and pirate garb, and armed with a repertoire which has swung from raucous ragga to dramatic operatic aria, Buccaneer exploded onto the DJ scene in 1994 courtesy of the Shocking Vibes label.

Building from Beenie Man's "Press Button" rhythm, "Hey Yah Hey Yah" became his signature hit that same year, to be succeeded by a slew of further singles—"Chatty Chatty Mouth," "Yu Nah Beg," "Yu Nuh Care," "Call Me." There was also success for the King Jammy produced "Police in a Pocket" and "Set the Pace," "Romeo," "Ganga Pipe," "Good Director," "Unity," "Disaster Pipe," "Sensi Ride" and "Trust" (the latter pair with Wayne Wonder).

Shocking Vibes' Patrick Roberts was also among the producers responsible for Buccaneer's debut album, *There Goes the Neighbourhood*, released in January, 1995—Bobby Digital, Dave Kelly and Danny Browne were also involved. But it was live that Buccaneer made the greatest impact, running away with the honors at that year's Reggae Sumfest.

Summer brought the release of "Oven" and "Hotter this Year," a remembrance of Dirtsman, the DJ brother of Papa San who was murdered shortly after signing a major label deal with BMG in 1993. However, it was another of Buccaneer's releases that year which truly demonstrated his powers, when he took the operatic "Marriage of Figaro" and converted it into the ragga anthem "Skettel Concerto."

Though Buccaneer remained the epitome of ragga slackness when he put his mind to it (1996's "Buccaneer Medley" fulfills a lot of promises, 1997's "Invasion" likewise), the overwhelming popularity of "Skettel Concerto" ensured that further classical assaults inevitably awaited.

Buccaneer's sophomore album, 1997's *Classic*, featured the hits "Bad Man Sonata" and the utterly outrageous "Man Tief Sonata," which looks to both the Moonlight Sonata and the Blue Danube Waltz for its inspiration. Even more audaciously, 1998's *Opera House* saw the DJ sample new age songstress Enya's "Orinoco Flow" for the hit "Fade Away"—an incongruous companion indeed for his other major hits that year, the hard rock inflected "Bruk Out," recorded with US punks Rancid, "Sha La La La," "Father Joe Joe" and "We Own Show."

"Hot Bwoy," a Steely & Clevie led union with Beenie Man, "Kill a Sound," the deliciously named "Little John Hits Medley," "Keep di Hype" and "Dash-Weh" were hits during 1999, while 2000 brought "Hot to Ratid" and "Freedom of Speech" (produced by Lexxus).

DISCOGRAPHY

LPs

5 **There Goes the Neighborhood (VP) 1995**
9 **Classic (Greensleeves—UK) 1997**

"Moonlight Sonata" drifts politely in, before Buccaneer steps to the fore with "Bad Man Sonata," a great joke told well. "Gal Skin fi Bore" (featuring Red Rat), "Hold on pon Him" and "Real Ganja Man" of course keep the old guard happy, but the presence of both "Skettel Concerto" and "Man Tief Sonata" reminds us of Buccaneer's true ambition. Maria Callas, look out.

6 **Opera House (VP) 1998**

The operatic rap (ope-rap-ic?) "Fade Away" is such a treasure that much of the rest initially pales by comparison. Give it time, though, and while *Opera House* isn't a patch on its audacious predecessor, Buccaneer's approach transcends both gimmick and novelty to reveal a fusion which has a lot of life left in it.

BURNING FLAMES

STYLE *soca*
FORMED *1984 (St John, Antigua)*
ORIGINAL LINE-UP *Toriana "King Onyan" Edwards (vocals, guitar), David "Bubb-l" Edwards (vocals, bass), Clarence "Oungku" Edwards (vocals, keyboards), Rone "Foxx" Watkins (drums)*

The three Edwards brothers—Toriana, David and Clarence—started their career busking on the streets of the Antiguan capital, St John, before briefly separating to pursue their own musical directions. David and Toriana worked as entertainers on Caribbean cruise ships for a time, while Clarence joined Montserrat soca star Arrow's band, the

Multi National Force, in 1983. He was on board for the massive hit "Hot Hot Hot," and soon recruited Toriana to the group.

Having completed Arrow's 1984 *Soca Savage* album, the pair broke away to form their own band with brother David and drummer Rone Watkins. (Clarence remained with Arrow for 1986's *Heavy Energy* album.) Burning Flames premiered at the Antiguan carnival Road March in August, 1985, debuting the infectiously high energy synthesized soca sound which became their trademark. "Stiley Tight" emerged the all-conquering hit at carnival that year (it became Burning Flames' debut 45 in early 1986), a triumph which the group confirmed with 1986's "Rudeness Mek Me" and 1989's "Workey Workey," a heavyweight zouk inflected number which became their first international smash. (Byron Lee & the Dragonaires subsequently turned in a similarly successful cover.)

1990's "Congo Man" single and the *Mek E Bark* album both reaped the rewards of this new recognition and, in 1991, the band was picked up by Mango for *Dig*, a compilation of older material remixed and reworked under the supervision of Gloria Estefan's production team (Joe Galdo, Lawrence Dermer, Rafael Virgil). Past local hits "Island Girl" and "Chook and Dig" were included, alongside the inevitable "Workey Workey."

However, the hoped for international breakthrough never materialized and Burning Flames' recording career remained tied to their homeland. Annual album releases and almost equally regular carnival triumphs have maintained the group's Antiguan stranglehold. They took Road March titles in 1991 ("Piece ah Iron"), 1992 ("Donkey"), 1993 ("Wet Down de Place"), 1995 ("Gym Jam and Stampede") and 1996 ("Fire Unda Me Foot"); while also making major inroads elsewhere in the Caribbean via 1997's "Showdown," a collaboration with T&T soca superstars Xtatik.

1997 also saw Toriana Edwards launch a successful solo career with the album *Crazy Man*—that same year, he won the first of four (to date) consecutive Antiguan Calypso Monarch titles, plus Soca Monarch and Road March. He eventually quit the band to concentrate on his career as King Onyan. 1998's Road March champion, "Sweet Song," was his last with Burning Flames.

Introducing new vocalists Bryan Fontanelle and Onika Bostic, Burning Flames bounced back with *Hokuspokus*, an album designed, Clarence Edwards insisted, to prove there was life after Onyan. This fact was amplified when the new-look Burning Flames first won Road March once again, with "Magician (I Command You)"; then when they emerged as one of the stars of the Labor Day, 1999, Brooklyn carnival. The search for their music in the US, however, is complicated by the existence of a hardcore punk band of the same name.

8 Mek E Bark (Dr G) 1990

A truly contagious rash of electrifying soca erupts with the opening "Squeeze Me," a showcase for the Congo Women backing troupe. The wild jumping "Nuff Problem" and the horn-laden seduction of "Chook and Dig" are highlights, but the masterpiece is "Karate," a hard Arrow influence colliding with a joyous pseudo-Asian motif.

4 Dig (Mango) 1991

Unfortunately, the easiest Burning Flames album to find in America is also the most unrepresentative, a high gloss monster which paints its crossover ambitions in mile high neon. "Forbidden Fruit," "Island Girl," "If You Get What You Want" and "Chook and Dig" are among the better revisions.

7 As You Were (Tropical Vibes) 1995

"Jungleypso" and "Jumbee Jamboree" stand out in the band's traditional party vibe; "What the Hell Can the Police Do" offers gleeful soca subversion.

6 Oh Behave: Nothing Personal Just Business (Tropical Vibes) 1998

The densely driving "Twone Drunk," "Groove" and the marginally hip-hopping "Spunks" (featuring Baja Jedd) push Burning Flames in a heavier direction than usual, occasionally at the cost of the band's original effervescence.

9 Hokuspokus/Magical Music (Tropical Vibes) 1999

Onyan's departure doesn't extinguish any of the Flames' natural fire. "Magician (I Command You)" emerges as one of their finest efforts ever, "Steel Band Power" is an astonishing invocation of pan and "Chook Chook" is almost ridiculously infectious. Add the bonus inclusion of the Xtatik-fired "Showdown" and the entire set is a triumph.

5 Jam Eulus (Tropical Vibes) 2000

Disappointing set revisits some of the last album's highlights, but with considerably less conviction — the infectious "De Romans" is simply "I Command You" part two, while "Super Festival" is a weak stab at pan.

BURNING SPEAR

STYLE reggae (roots)
BORN Winston Rodney, 1948 (St Ann's Bay, JA)

No artist presents a more cogent and coherent view of Rastafarian beliefs than Burning Spear. Alongside Black Uhuru and Bob Marley, Spear completes a roots triumvirate which incorporates the most crucial roles any artist (or group of artists) can aspire to, those of unifier, militant, educator and spokesmen, with Spear's work frequently touching upon all four. It is this which remains the key to his enduring popularity.

Given his future importance, it is, perhaps, only appropriate that Winston Rodney was introduced to his first producer, Coxsone Dodd, by Bob Marley — the pair first met in 1969, in the St Ann's hills where Marley owned a farm. In the course of conversation, Rodney mentioned he wanted to break into the music business, and Marley suggested he check out Studio One.

Rodney took his advice, auditioning for Dodd one Sunday in 1969. Accompanied by bass singer Rupert Willington, he performed three songs, including the spiritual chant "Door Peep," which Dodd promptly earmarked for the duo's debut single. It was released under the name Burning Spear — a title previously borne by Kenyan President and former Mau Mau tribal leader Jomo Kenyatta.

Burning Spear became a trio soon after, with the arrival of tenor Delroy Hinds (brother of rock steady veteran Justin). In this form the group cut several further Studio One releases, including "We Are Free," "Zion Higher," "This Population," "New Civilization," "Ethiopians Live It Out" and the 1972 Jamaican Top 5 hit "Joe Frazier (He Prayed)." The trio also recorded two albums together, 1973's *Studio One Presents* and *Rocking Time* the following year.

However, further commercial success remained elusive and, in 1975, Burning Spear teamed up with producer Jack Ruby (b Lawrence Lindo, d 1990), owner of the Ocho Rios sound system. Together they recorded "Marcus Garvey," a tribute to St Ann's most famous son, the pre-World War One founder of the pioneering Universal Negro Improvement Society. Ruby initially intended the song simply as a sound system exclusive, but demand was so great that he eventually had no choice but to release it. "Marcus Garvey" was an immediate hit, as was a second single from the same sessions, "Slavery Days."

While Studio One returned to the vault for further singles "Ethiopia Live It Out," "Swell Headed" and "Foggy Road," work began on Burning Spear's own next album. Produced by Ruby, and featuring accompaniment from the Black Disciples — Earl "Chinna" Smith and Valentine "Tony" Chin (guitars), Robbie Shakespeare (bass) and Leroy Wallace (drums), among others — the *Marcus Garvey* album was an immediate smash, prompting Island Records to sign the group.

Marcus Garvey was released internationally in 1976, although not without some controversy. Island not only remixed the album before release, they also sped up some of the tracks, prompting a firestorm of outrage from listeners familiar with the original recordings. The release of a dub companion to the album, *Garvey's Ghost*, went some way towards stilling the complaints, but Rodney himself was so incensed by the label's actions, that he promptly formed his own label, Spear, through which he could release music as he saw fit.

The new label debuted with "Travelling," a reworking of the Studio One era "Journey" and, during 1976, two further

The original three-man Spear: Rodney, Willington, and Hinds.

45s appeared, "Spear Burning" and "The Youth." (Spear also released singles by Phillip Fullwood and Burning Junior.) 1976 also brought Burning Spear's second Island album, *Man in the Hills*, a remarkable set which included a revision of Spear's first ever release, "Door Peep," and spawned the club hit single "The Lion."

Rodney broke with producer Ruby in late 1976, around the same time as he parted company with Willington and Hinds. (They resurfaced as members of the Arrows and the Original Survivors). Taking the name Burning Spear for his own, he self-produced his next album, *Dry and Heavy* at Harry J's studio; again returning to some of his earlier material, updating "Swell Headed" (as "Black Disciples") and "Creation Rebel" (as "It's a Long Way Around"). Again, too, the Spear label provided a subsidiary outlet, releasing the singles "Institution," "Free" and an alternate version of "Dry and Heavy."

Encouraged by the admiration of Britain's punk community, Burning Spear visited London in October, 1977, recruiting local reggae band Aswad as his backing musicians. A show at the London Rainbow Theatre was sold out well in advance, and was recorded for release as *Live*.

Aswad remained alongside him when he returned to the studio to record his next album, *Social Living* aka *Marcus Children*. Karl Pitterson co-produced, Sly Dunbar and Rico Rodriguez also appeared on the set. (Sylvan Morris' dub mix of *Social Living* subsequently appeared as *Living Dub*.) Burning Spear's visibility increased further when he appeared in the movie *Rockers*, alongside drummer Wallace. He also appeared at the inaugural Reggae Sunsplash in 1978, making return appearances in 1979, 1980, 1982, 1984, 1986, 1987, 1990, 1993 and 1996.

Social Living was Burning Spear's final album for Island, even as the "Nyah Keith" single rung down the curtain on Spear Records. In 1980, Rodney signed his newly renamed Burning Spear label to EMI and, retiring to Bob Marley's Tuff Gong studios, recorded *Hail H.I.M.* with co-producer Family Man Barrett. Again Sylvan Morris cut a dub mix, *Living Dub Volume Two*.

1982 saw Burning Spear (the artist and the label) link with Heartbeat, launching the union with the album *Farover* and singles "She's Mine" and "Jah Is My Driver." He was now backed by a new aggregation, the Burning Band, comprising Devon Bradshaw (guitar), Anthony Bradshaw (bass), Nelson Miller (drums), plus horn players Bobby Ellis and Herman Marquis, the latter pair veterans of the *Marcus Garvey* sessions.

This line-up cut the album *Fittest of the Fittest*; 1985's Grammy nominated *Resistance* followed; and, in 1986, with the California independent label Slash now releasing his albums in the US, Burning Spear unleashed the mighty *People of the World*, another Grammy contender. *Mistress Music* appeared in 1988, while an accompanying European tour was documented by a second live album, recorded at the Paris Zenith. (The latter album earned Burning Spear his third Grammy nomination in 1989).

The Burning Band broke up after this tour. Retaining only drummer Miller and latter day guitarist Lenford Richards, Burning Spear pieced together a new backing group and signed again with Island Records in 1990. He was promptly rewarded with yet another Grammy nomination, for that year's *Mek We Dweet*, while his appearances on the Sunsplash US Tour were widely acclaimed among the best of his career.

Further proof of Burning Spear's growing renown was delivered when he was invited to appear on the Grateful Dead tribute album *Deadicated* in 1991; he contributed a version of "Estimated Prophet," while his own new album, *Jah Kingdom*, again received a slew of critical raves.

Burning Spear departed Island in 1992 (his two terms with the label were later anthologized on the *Chant Down Babylon* collection), and the remainder of the 1990s saw him adopting a somewhat lower profile than ever before.

Now widely acclaimed the Elder Statesman of Roots — a title he did not necessarily cherish — Burning Spear continued touring vigorously, but released just three new albums over the next six years, *The World Should Know*, *Rasta Business* and the experimentally folk-inflected *Appointment with His Majesty*. Astonishingly, all three were Grammy nominees. He also collaborated with roots singer Fred Locks on the album *12 the Hard Way*.

1999's *Calling Rastafari* album marked the 30th anniversary of Burning Spear's entry into the music business — with his opinions on the subject perhaps best summed up by "As It Is," a savage reworking of his first album's "Slavery Days," retooled to ask "someone remember Burning Spear?" Triumph, however, was just around the corner: having already garnered him his eighth Grammy nomination, *Calling Rastafari* became his first winner.

A 70+ date American tour that summer/fall proved his best publicized outing since Sunsplash a decade previous.

DISCOGRAPHY

6 Studio One Presents Burning Spear (Fab—JA) 1973

7 Rocking Time (Fab—JA) 1974

The cover art doesn't give a hint as to what's within, a pensive Spear outlined against the blue sky, the water calm

behind him — all a far cry from the 12-inches of black wax raging inside.

10 Marcus Garvey (Island—UK) 1975

This groundbreaking set burst onto the scene like a nuclear explosion, one which still resonates today. Producer Jack Ruby's deep roots mix (which was softened for white consumption by Island) flawlessly captures the group's moody atmospheres, while Rodney's distinctive and passionate vocals are indistinguishable from the record's twin themes of oppression (past and present) and Rastafarian devotion.

4 Garvey's Ghost (Island—UK) 1976

. . . is rattling his chains at this dub version of the parent album. The mix dissipates all the power of the original; though the rhythm tracks are handled well, the moods are destroyed by focusing on the lightest weight and poppiest instrumentation, muzak dub for the non-discriminating masses. Both *Garvey* and *Ghost* were subsequently packaged together as *100th Anniversary* (Mango — 1987), a single disc marking the centenary of Garvey's birth. Island (UK) also released a commemorative EP

8 Man in the Hills (Island—UK) 1976

The title track sums up the album's overall rural theme, while a rerecording of "Door Peep" adds an even stronger religious element.

8 Dry and Heavy (Island—UK) 1977

Rodney exudes self-confidence on his production debut, while the musicians, together since *Marcus Garvey*, are equally self assured. *Dry* is awash in sound, jams and instrumental flourishes, while the singer polishes his intertwined historical, political and religious messages.

8 Live (Island—UK) 1977

Accompanied by UK reggae band Aswad, the Spear burned especially bright onstage, as *Live*, recorded at a 1977 London gig, demonstrates. The band flames while Rodney's exuberance immediately electrifies the crowd.

8 Social Living (Stop—UK) 1978

The single "Civilised Reggae" is a highwater mark. While Spear's sound expands into jazz, most notably on "Marcus Say Jah No Dead," the anthemic roots of crucial cuts like the title track and "Marcus Children Suffer" rule on this Rodney/Pitterson produced opus.

6 Living Dub (Burning Spear—JA) 1979

Sylvan Morris's original *Social Living* was dangerous, but a little dead in places. The Heartbeat CD reissue features a surprisingly sparkling new mix by Barry O'Hare.

8 Hail H.I.M. (Heartbeat) 1980

Completing the quintet of roots masterpieces kicked off by *Marcus Garvey*, Spear consolidates his sound and vision over a clutch of crucial cuts, including the classic "Cry Blood Africans."

6 **Living Dub Vol 2 (Burning Spear—JA) 1981**

Hail H.I.M. dub companion, again, revised on CD with a 1990s O'Hare remix.

6 **Farover (Heartbeat) 1982**

Dark roots and deeply meaningful as always, but the reprise of past themes and a growing interest in less "conscious" material ("She's Mine") conjures up Spear's first non-essential release.

6 **The Fittest of the Fittest (Heartbeat) 1983**

The sense that Burning Spear has settled in to a roots-heavy rut, haunting on *Farover*, grows louder—the album's not bad, but it simply doesn't do anything.

5 **Resistance (Heartbeat) 1985**
6 **People of the World (Slash) 1986**

A strong set opens with the title track, but peaks towards the end, with "Built this City" and "No Worry You'self." The Burning Band take a lot more of the limelight than Spear shakers might prefer, but the mood is the most important thing and this album oozes it.

5 **Mistress Music (Slash) 1988**

"Negril" and "Love Garvey" are highlights of an occasionally bland, and certainly over-produced collection.

7 **Live in Paris: Zenith (Slash) 1988**

14 tracks recorded 5/21/88, include "Spear Burning," "The Youth" and a triumphant "Door Peep." As gripping as any career-spanning Spear compilation.

7 **Mek We Dweet (Mango) 1990**

Rodney enters the new decade with the same lightened load as scarred *Mistress Music*. The message remains on track, but the dread sound has been diluted to a listener-friendly roots lite, the perfect commercial blend of jam guitar and jazzy horns ("Recall Some Great Men"), infectious reggae-pop (the title track) and easy-dance-able electro-pop (the infectious "African Woman").

7 **Jah Kingdom (Mango) 1991**

A tight set that shows little musical change from its predecessor. The atmosphere remains light, yet hypnotic, "Should I" is the definite standout, and remains a crowd pleasing part of the band's live set, while the inclusion of the previously released Grateful Dead's "Estimated Prophet" allowed more fans to experience this epic revision.

6 **The World Should Know (Heartbeat) 1993**
7 **Love and Peace: Live 1993 (Heartbeat) 1994**

A high energy performance is overwhelmed by the horns and, possibly, a sense that Spear is more enjoyable when the mood is a little more subdued. The 10 minute "Take A Look" gallivants around on searing rock guitar leads, while

almost every other track opens with a funky brass serenade, and just gets more frantic from there. The closing "Peace," however, is a revelation, riding a dreamy synth line while the rhythm builds in intensity behind it.

7 **Rasta Business (Heartbeat—UK) 1995**
6 **Living Dub Vol 3 (Declic) 1996**
6 **Appointment With His Majesty (Heartbeat) 1997**
7 **Live in Concert 1997 (Musidisc—UK) 1998**

Live recording from the 1997 WOMAD Festival and Maritime Hall, San Francisco.

4 **Living Dub Vol 4 (Declic) 1999**

Very disappointing (if not pointless) dub remix of *Appointment With His Majesty*.

7 **Calling Rastafari (Heartbeat) 1999**

All it took to finally grab a Grammy was to soft peddle the social commentary. So the Spear doesn't so much burn as simmer slightly across a set of moody introspection. But the band cooks, and the overall vision has a surprisingly sharp edge.

BURNING SPEAR/FRED LOCKS

6 **12 the Hard Way (Tribesman—UK) 1994**

SELECTED COMPILATIONS & ARCHIVE RELEASES

7 **Harder than the Rest (Island—UK) 1979**

Island era album tracks plus a few unreleased offerings—the trancy, dub inflected "Civilize Reggae" and "The Invasion (A.K.A. Black Wa-Da-Da)."

6 **The Fittest Selection (EMI—UK) 1987**

1980–83 compilation

9 **Chant Down Babylon—The Island Anthology (Island) 1996**

Well compiled two-CD set traces Spear's 1975–80 and 1990–91 Island epochs via key album cuts, rarities, live and 12-inch mixes. The decade which divides the two phases does spell disorientation—the gap between "Civilize Reggae" (1979) and "Mek We Dweet" (1990) is more than chronological, after all. But there is no better introduction.

7 **The Ultimate Collection (Hip-O) 2001**

Essentially, a condensed version of the above, lacking the rarities but adding cuts from *Hail HIM* and *The Fittest of the Fittest*.

9 **Behold the Spear Burning (Pressure Sounds) 2001**

Mighty collection of Spear label rarities includes cuts by Phillip Fullwood and Big Joe, alongside *shattering* discomix versions of "Institution," "Free the Whole Wide World," and "Jah No Dead."

JUNIOR BYLES

STYLE *reggae (roots)*
BORN *Kerrie Byles, 1948 (Kingston, JA)*

One of the most understated and (perhaps consequently) under-rated vocalists of the "classic" roots period, the richly baritoned Junior Byles formed his first band, the Versatiles, in early 1967.

Lining up as Byles, the East Indian-born Earl Dudley and Louis Davis (born Ben C Davis), the group were just one of the countless vocal trios working the local scene at that time, and may have remained unknown had Lee Perry not spotted them at auditions for Kingston's 1967 Festival Song Contest, where they were hoping to find a sponsor for Byles' composition, "The Time Has Come."

Perry was then employed as chief recording engineer at Joe Gibbs' studio, and was actively scouting talent for the producer's newly launched Amalgamated label. Instantly impressed by Byles' slight, but so emotional vocal flair, he signed the Versatiles, but departed Gibbs' organization soon after, having produced and engineered a mere handful of tracks with them — "The Time Has Come," "Trust the Book," "Lu Lu Bell," "Long Long Time," and "Worries a Yard" among them.

The Versatiles remained with Gibbs and his new chief engineer, Niney Holness and, over the next two years cut a handful of further 45s, the risque "Push It In," "Pick My Pocket" and "Give It to Me" among them.

They then returned to Lee Perry, and cut seven more songs with him, including the hits "Children Get Ready" and "Teardrops Falling" released on Deltone, a label run by Coxsone Dodd's former secretary, Dorothy Barnett. From there they moved to Treasure Isle, cutting "I Love You Baby" with Duke Reid, while also recording a handful of tracks with Laurel Aitken and Joe Gibbs.

The trio sundered in 1970 at the conclusion of further Perry sessions ("Cutting Razor," a version of Peter Tosh's "Stepping Razor," among them). Davis joined the Morwells, Byles began working for the Jonestown fire department, but continued to record with Perry. By the end of the year, the pair had released the single "What's the World Coming To?"

A minor hit, it opened the door to a partnership which, over the next five years, unleashed some of Perry's finest work of the period — militant Rastafarian anthems "Beat Down Babylon" (with its ear-catching whip effects) and "King of Babylon," the almost hymnal "Place Called Africa," "Got the Tip" and the suggestive "Rub Up Festival 71," Byles' entry for the 1971 Festival Song Festival. Amazingly, the song actually reached the final eight selections before radio objected to its lyric, at which point it was disqualified. Byles responded with the laid-back singsong "Festival Da Da," second runner-up at the 1972 event. That same year, Byles also began self-producing singles for release on his own Love Power label.

"Pharaoh Hiding," Byles' contribution to the overwhelming roots support for Michael Manley's PNP (Peoples' National Party) in the 1972 general election, offered another hit, together with a deliciously skewed dub b-side, "Hail to Power." Year's end then brought Byles' greatest success yet, an atmospheric version of the Peggy Lee standard "Fever" (Perry himself so liked the dubby rhythm concocted for the performance that he employed it again three years later with Susan Cadogan.)

Byles' debut album, *Beat Down Babylon* arrived in 1973, a manifesto of dread intent backed up by a barrage of further 45s — "Break Up To Make Up," cut with Duke Reid, and a string of further Perry productions. "Rasta No Pickpocket," "Gwane Joshua Gwane," "Fun and Games," the wonderfully understated cry of "When Will Better Come," "Now Generation," the whimsical "Auntie Lulu" and "Pretty fe True," issued during 1973–74, not only consolidated Byles' Jamaican renown, they also firmly established his UK profile. The plaintive "Curley Locks" picked up considerable radio and club play in the UK during 1974.

The yearning, jamming "The Long Way," one of his final sessions with Perry, maintained Byles' stranglehold on the Jamaican chart; thereafter, work with other producers seemingly established him among the most indefatigable performers on the scene.

Joining Dudley Swaby and Leroy Hollett's Ja-Man label, 1975 saw Byles score with three duets with singer Rupert Reid, "Chant Down Babylon," "Know Where You're Going" and "Remember Me." He also scored with "Bury-O-Boy" (produced by Lloyd Campbell), and covers of the Temptations' "Ain't too Proud to Beg" and the ska classic "Oh Carolina," (Pete Weston), taken from Byles' second album, *Jordan*.

His greatest moment, however, came with "Fade Away," produced by JoJo Hookim in 1975. A massive hit, it impacted so hard in the UK that, five years later, it was among the first tracks recorded by Adrian Sherwood's New Age Steppers dub conglomerate.

Behind the scenes, however, Byles was disintegrating. His moodiness had long been factored into his relations both with producers and musicians; bouts of depression now saw even the closest of those friendships fluctuate wildly. By 1975, Byles' health was an open cause for concern among his associates, but still nobody foresaw the tragedy to come.

The death of the Rastafarian figurehead Haile Selassie in August 1975 (one year after he was deposed as Emperor of Ethiopia), sent Byles over the edge. While Jamaica, where Haile Selassie's presumed divinity had always been open to debate, seethed with confusion, Byles attempted suicide. He was checked into Bellevue Hospital, precipitating a traumatic decline in both his personal and professional lives.

Dividing his time between hospital, the hills and the recording studio, 1975–76 saw Byles link with producer Niney Holness for an apocalyptic reworking of "King of Babylon" (elements of Holness' "Blood and Fire" rhythm had been borrowed by Lee Perry for Byles' "Dreader Locks" dub) and a cover of Delroy Wilson's "Run Run." Return engagements with Lloyd Campbell ("Weeping," "Can You Feel It") and Swaby/Hollett ("Pitchy Patchy") were successful, while Byles also linked with Big Youth on a version of the Archies' "Sugar Sugar." But no matter how healthy his career, Byles remained shattered and, by the end of 1976, he had all but vanished.

In 1978, an attempted comeback saw Byles cut two singles with Joe Gibbs, "Heart and Soul" and "Dreadlocks Time." They were released close to a year apart as it became apparent that Byles was not yet ready to resume operations. It was 1982 before he resurfaced again, working with the New York based label Bullwackies, and beginning a new album with producer Blacka Morwell.

Progress, however, was slow. Byles' beloved mother passed away; he lost his home in a fire and his own family shattered when his wife and children emigrated to the US. Morwell released two new singles, "Better Be Careful" and "Don't Be Surprised," but Byles' next release, the *Rasta No Pickpocket* album did not appear until 1986. It was prefaced by the Winston Riley produced "Dance Hall" 45, but Byles was again fading away. In November, 1987, *Weekly Gleaner* journalist Balford Henry found Byles living on the streets, eating from dumpsters, unknown and unrecognized even by his friends.

Since that time, his name has been kept alive more by a healthy reissue program than through his own efforts. Byles reunited with Niney Holness in 1989 for the excellent "Young Girl" (three years later, the pair recorded "Little Fleego"). He played a handful of live shows in Jamaica during 1997–98, with guitarist Earl "Chinna" Smith; the pair also appeared at the Sierra Nevada Music festival that same year.

That brief flicker notwithstanding, Byles' recording career has remained silent for close to two decades. Compilations documenting both the Lee Perry and later eras remain firm Heartbeat and Trojan catalog items, however, and the rediscovery of that legacy by successive new generations of fans has ensured that Byle's prodigious talent remains as vibrant today as it ever was in his prime.

DISCOGRAPHY

🔟 Beat Down Babylon (Trojan—UK) 1973

Byle's debut album was one of the most remarkable albums of the age, and features one of Lee Perry's most coherent productions. That said, there is no mistaking the renegade genius behind the controls—it's the one racing to keep up with the renegade genius at the microphone. Both "Beat Down Babylon" and "Coming Home" make creative use of limited sound effects, a whip in one, a machine gun in the other, while Byles' dread lyricism brings a foreboding spirituality to even the most playful song. *Beat Down Babylon* has since been repackaged as an anthology of the Byles/Perry sessions, packed with bonus tracks drawn from period singles and evincing a remarkable understanding not only of roots, but also rock dynamics.

9️⃣ Jordan (Micron—UK) 1976

Produced by Pete Weston, Byles' second album is almost as great as his first. Almost. Hits "Lorna Banana" and a sensational reading of the Temptations' "Ain't too Proud to Beg" are joined by the definitive retread of Prince Buster's "Oh Carolina."

6️⃣ Rasta No Pickpocket (Night Hawk) 1986

A patchy collection certainly evinces the occasional moment of brilliance, but the lost potential is louder than the lyrics. Best left for collectors alone.

SELECTED COMPILATIONS & ARCHIVE RELEASES

9️⃣ Curly Locks: The Best Of (Heartbeat) 1997

Close to half the album duplicates Trojan's bonus stacked CD reissue of *Beat Down Babylon* collection, but that still means half doesn't, and this alternative look at the Lee Perry archive draws out a number of b-sides and oddities which might otherwise have been forgotten. The Versatiles' "Cutting Razor" is among the album's primal rarities, while two unissued versions of "Curly Locks" highlight half a dozen unheard performances—a version of Clodagh Rodgers' UK hit "Jack in the Box" is another.

SUSAN CADOGAN

STYLE *reggae (lovers rock)*
BORN *Alison Anne Cadogan, 11/2/51 (Kingston, JA)*

The Queen of Lovers Rock in its earliest, purest, form, with a voice which could swing from total vulnerability to stunning sexuality in the space of a breath, Susan Cadogan was the daughter of singer Lola Cadogan, who cut a number of 78s of devotional music during the 1950s.

She spent some of her childhood in Belize, where her family moved during the mid-1950s. They returned to Jamaica at the end of the decade and, having completed her schooling, Cadogan took a job at the library at the University of the West Indies in Mona.

She was "discovered" by DJ Jerry Lewis, boyfriend of one of her schoolfriends; he produced her first single (one of his own compositions), "Love My Life" at JBC. Apparently Perry was at the studio at the same time and was immediately impressed by Cadogan's voice; it was he who renamed her Susan.

Having recorded an album's worth of material, Cadogan's first single for Perry was a rocking cover of American soul singer Millie Jackson's "Hurts So Good," featuring bassist Boris Gardiner and the Zap Pow horns. Released that spring, it did little in Jamaica, where it was an early release on Perry's new Perries label. Licensed to the DIP label in London, however, a remix of the track mashed up the annual Notting Hill Carnival in August, 1974, and was soon topping the UK specialist reggae charts.

In the new year, the mainstream label Magnet licensed "Hurts So Good" for national distribution and, in March, 1975, the single reached #4 on the UK chart. Cadogan was flown to London to promote the record — among her backing band for TV appearances was Gene Rondo, a Jamaican vocalist resident and recording in the UK since 1962.

With Cadogan signing directly to Magnet for future releases, Perry immediately arranged for the Birmingham, England, based Black Wax label to issue an unofficial follow-up 45, a reissue of "Love My Life." Other UK labels, Klik and Lucky, were equally swift to leap aboard with two further Perry cuts "In The Ghetto" and "Congratulations." None of these speculative releases charted, and the remainder of the Perry-produced material eventually appeared on the album *Hurts So Good*, a collection of covers ranging from a bubbling version of "Fever" (a song Perry also recorded with Junior Byles) to the action-packed "Shame."

Magnet, meanwhile, teamed Cadogan with English pop producer Pete Waterman and were rewarded when the "official" UK follow-up, "Love Me Baby" reached #22 in July, 1975. However, successive singles including "How Do You Feel the Morning After" (1975) and "Keep It Coming" (1977) failed and, with a second Cadogan album, *Does It Her Way*, also steadfastly refusing to sell, one of the most distinctive female vocalists of the age apparently vanished from sight.

Cadogan returned to Jamaica and the University library, before resurfacing in 1982 with Jamaican hit versions of "Tracks of My Tears" and "Piece of My Heart." 1983 saw her teamed with producer Hawkeye for "Love Me" and a chart-topping duet with Ruddy Thomas, "(You Know How to Make Me) Feel So Good." A second Thomas duet, "Only Heaven Can Wait," followed, while 1984 saw Cadogan score again with "Cause You Love Me Baby" and "Don't Know Why."

Despite such success, however, she again retreated for close to a decade, before linking with English producer Neil "Mad Professor" Fraser. A stunning version of "Together We Are Beautiful" opened Fraser's Ariwa label's *12th Anniversary* compilation in 1992; the song then reappeared on the album *Soulful Reggae*, a fine set which again found Cadogan tackling some impressive covers. Fraser also oversaw a rerecording of "Hurts So Good," itself utilized by U-Roy, again under Fraser's aegis, for "The Hurt Is Good," a cut from his *Smile a While* album. Cadogan herself contributed another non-album cut, "Take Time with Me," to Ariwa's *This Is Lovers' Reggae Volume Three* compilation, and appears on the Professor's own *Dub Maniacs on the Rampage* album (1993).

"Hurts So Good" returned to the UK chart in 1995, when singer Jimmy Somerville released a straightforward cover of Cadogan's own interpretation. That same year brought Cadogan's own fourth album, *Chemistry of Love.*

DISCOGRAPHY

7 Doing It Her Way (Magnet—UK) 1975

Easily dismissed as a lightweight collection with lukewarm island undertones — just another bad British bash at reggae, with a track listing which includes "Swinging on a Star," "Will You Still Love Me Tomorrow" and "Something." Cadogan's international debut nevertheless boasts pristine production, strong arrangements and what has been described as the sexiest voice in reggae.

8 Hurts So Good (Trojan—UK) 1976

A more representative glimpse of Cadogan's capabilities, with Lee Perry's production as restrained as he's ever been, allowing voice and song to melt together. "In the Ghetto" is heartbreakingly sincere, "Don't You Burn Your Bridges" painfully admonitory and, of course, no praise is too high for "Hurts So Good."

8 Soulful Reggae (Ariwa—UK) 1992

"Be My Baby" is the tour de force, but "I Say a Little Prayer" comes close and even a trite reworking of Eddy Grant's "Baby Come Back" sounds fresh in Cadogan's hands. Like Perry before him, Mad Professor reins in some of his more outlandish production tendencies for the occasion, and again the results are spellbinding.

6 Chemistry of Love (—UK) 1995

CALYPSO/SOCA
THE EARLY YEARS

Calypso is an evolving tradition. After close to a century of study, scholars and musicologists remain absolutely divided on where it comes from, or even what it means.

Any one of several roots has its fierce adherents — "calypso" is drawn from the French "carrousseaux," meaning a drinking party. Or it is based upon a Carib term, "carieto," a song sung to take one's mind off a drudging workload. Or perhaps it is Spanish, from "caliso," a song about current events. Or maybe it dates back to the Hausu people of west Africa, whose culture remains the strongest link with the original (Spanish and French-owned) slaves' homeland. In its earliest written form, the word calypso appears as "kaiso," a Hausu term roughly approximating to the Spanish "ole."

African traditions can be isolated in its musical form as well, the poly-rhythmic base which is believed to derive from original African Shango religious songs; the tradition of call and response; an eye for relating contemporary news and gossip in an amusing, insulting, innuendo-laden manner; the ability to quickly ad-lib a song in and out of troubled waters (or unexpectedly hostile listeners).

All of these were the talents of the wandering African poets, or griots, who communicated the latest news from village to village; all, too, were rapidly adapted to the New World, where a largely illiterate and ostensibly subservient slave population had no other access to "current affairs."

Glibly, Caribbean history records most early singers were female—"chanterelles," in French patois. How this arose, and why the situation changed remains as open to conjecture as everything else. But over time, the chanterelle became the chantwell, which in turn came to mean exactly what it says, somebody who could chant (or sing) well.

Perhaps it was the rise of stick-fighting which relegated women to the sidelines. Though singing and stick-fighting were by no means mutually exclusive pastimes, the "kalinda" songs which traditionally accompanied the bouts were themselves so much a part of the event that they could not help but become part of the action, too, until the fighters themselves used kalinda to warm up themselves and wind up their opponents.

It was the fighters, too, who first began to adopt the grandiose nicknames which have long since become a calypso tradition, with further titles—King this and the Mighty that—conferred by their peers as the victories mounted up. Of course, those victories, and the ensuing reputations, then passed into song; the songs passed into common usage and, long before anything approaching what we today understand to be a star-making system was in place, stars were being born.

The chantwells first appeared in the carnival record during the 1830s, just one more wave in the sea of innovations which the newly emancipated slave population brought to the fete they had so neatly hijacked—the drums, the sticks and the dances, of course, accompanied them. But whereas those other accouterments were forced to change, to adapt to the swirling eddies of sundry government prohibitions, the chantwells were left more or less unscathed.

Maybe the bawdier songs needed to be toned down and the harsher political observations sugared. But such necessities simply sharpened the singer's wit, forcing him to seek out ever more subtle innuendo and craftier satire, usually delivered in French. In the eyes of the governing British authorities, a good chantwell was one who sang in plain English. To his audience, a great chantwell was one who could then make that same plain English do his own vicious bidding.

The first calypsonians to make this transition were Henry Inventor and Richard Couer de Lion. Inventor began performing in English around 1898, although little of his work has survived to the modern day. Couer De Lion introduced the Jamaican mento "Not a Cent" and "Jerningham the Governor" to his repertoire around the same time.

The local press began to refer to these songs as calypsos around 1900, with more attentive onlookers then dividing that basic genre down into a number of sub-types. There was the kalinda, of course; there was the "belair," topical songs performed in French patois (and of particular annoyance to the English); there was the "bongo," funereal dirges which frequently accompanied wakes. And there was the "lavway," which essentially summed up any song whose popularity and appeal was so great that vast crowds of people marched through the streets, spontaneously singing it at the top of their lungs. Today, the lavway lives on as the road march.

One of the foundations of the modern calypso circuit, the carnival tent, was launched in the first years of the 20th century, originally to shelter performers from the elements and also to allow singers, musicians and dancers a little privacy away from the revelry surrounding them. Richard Couer de Lion is credited with opening the first tent, at carnival in 1899.

The earliest were makeshift affairs constructed of bamboo poles and cocyea branches, but they proved an immediate attraction. First performers, then enterprising entrepreneurs, learned that the public was more than willing to pay an extra few pennies for the opportunity to witness singers rehearsing their material.

By the 1910s, tents were opening around T&T's capital city, Port of Spain, days—sometimes weeks—before carnival actually got underway. Each one vying with the others to attract the biggest name calypsonians, who then provided patrons with a sneak preview of the songs they intended performing at the main event. Every year saw ever more, and ever larger, structures spring up in the weeks leading up to the carnival itself; and, in 1921, calypsonian Railway Douglas opened a 300 seater venue on Duncan Street, with performances scheduled three nights a week.

The massive success of the tents was also an indication of the success of calypso. At least into the 1920s, most calypso singers were, if not members of, then at least affiliated with individual bands. The large tents, however, allowed them to experiment beyond those confines—just one band would be hired for the season, to provide accompaniment for a host of different singers, all competing both with one another and with the other tents, for the various calypso prizes which were simultaneously coming into being, including several which were distinct precursors of the modern Calypso Monarch competition.

One of the earliest recorded victors here was the Duke of Albany, a schoolteacher calypsonian who served in the West Indian Regiment during World War One, and won an event staged by the Carnival Improvement Association in 1927.

By the 1930s, almost every component of the modern calypso circuit was in place, with the final piece of the jigsaw, the Calypso King competition, inaugurated in 1939. From a field which included Lord Caresser, King Radio, Lord Pretender, Atilla The Hun and Roaring Lion, Growling Tiger emerged with the winning song, "Trade Union" (Lord Pretender was runner up). A former boxer, flyweight champion of Trinidad in 1929, Growling Tiger had only been singing professionally for five years at that point, although his career had certainly moved fast.

Within a year of his launch, Decca Records' T&T agent Eduardo Sa Gomes had arranged for Tiger to accompany Atilla and Lord Beginner on a trip to New York to record, a trip which came close to ending on Ellis Island, when it was discovered that the necessary paperwork had not been completed. The trio were left on the island for three weeks before Decca's New York office finally agreed to bail them out, and over the next decade, Tiger recorded 46 songs for Decca.

With the struggle for calypso supremacy now formalized by competition, the pace began heating up even further. The tents began auditioning for the new season shortly before Christmas, then opened to the public in the new year. Anything up to 30 different singers were engaged, each performing two songs a night to a crowd which, even with carnival itself several weeks away, was itself already getting into the party spirit.

Successful calypsonians were called back for encore after encore; failures were dragged off the stage with a sheep-crook. Heckling was not merely allowed, it was positively encouraged. Come carnival itself, a tent's very honor depended upon its star performers being able to withstand, even deflect, the harshest criticism, not only from the audience, but also from supporters of the other competing tents.

It was a fiercely partisan atmosphere, and there was no room whatsoever for ambiguity — either a performer was great, in which case he lived to sing another day, or he was rubbish, in which case he was despatched with a few kind words from the older performers, and encouraged to try again when he'd written some new material.

For it was the material which mattered — that, and the ability to maintain a constant flow of it. The greatest calypso performers weren't simply those whose songs spoke directly to the listener, whether their subject matter was topical, sexual, personal or humorous; they were those who were able to continue speaking just as persuasively year in, year out.

Neither were the singers simply addressing the patrons of an individual tent. The 1930s also saw the institution of the "picong" duels (from the French "piquant," — "hot and spicy"), battles of wit in which two performers went head to head with one another, hurling lyrical insults until the crowd — the crowd was always the final arbitrator — declared a victor. Originally a live event, the success of picong was such that, by the late 1930s, duels were also taking place on record, rival calypsonians delighting their fans with discs devoted to belittling one another.

Lord Executor (c1880/d c1955), generally regarded as the first ever professional calypsonian, was party to the first picong battle ever fought on gramophone record, taking on Houdini during the 1930s. American musicologist Emory Cook captured the first stirrings of another titanic tussle on tape in 1957, when the Mighty Sparrow and Lord Melody inaugurated a rivalry which was to continue for years to come.

Sparrow opened. "Well, Melody, come close to me/I will tell you plain and candidly/Don't stop in the back and smile/Because you have a face like a crocodile."

Melody hit back instantly. "Sparrow, you shouldn't tell me that at all/I mind you when you was small/Many of the nights I used to mash your head/In crossing to go on your mother."

No exchange in the recorded canon of the music better sums up the spirit of calypso than that.

CALYPSO GOES INTERNATIONAL

If one had mentioned calypso to the average American or European of the 1950s, chances are they would have responded with just one name — Harry Belafonte. A native New Yorker of Trinidadian parentage (and Jamaican upbringing), Belafonte was never a calypsonian per se; rather, he performed Caribbean folk music of all persuasions.

But between 1945, when he replaced Roaring Lion as the resident performer at the Village Vanguard club in New York, and 1970, when he scored his final Top 200 album, the multi-talented Belafonte took what had hitherto been a cultish infatuation with West Indian music and transformed it into a multi-million dollar business. Indeed, his 1956 album *Calypso* topped the *Billboard* chart for an incredible 31 weeks, becoming in the process the first ever album by a solo artist to sell a million copies.

Neither did Belafonte's steadfast determination to tackle every musical style he could wrap his tonsils around dent either his popularity or his reputation. Quite deliberately, Belafonte released only four calypso-themed albums, and only three of them (*Calypso*, 1961's *Jump Up Calypso* and 1966's *Calypso In Brass*) made the US chart.

But his adaptation of the Jamaican mento "Banana Boat Song," a #5 smash in 1957, was more than simply his biggest hit. It became as instantly identifiable with Belafonte, as he himself was with the Caribbean and, even as he plied his audience with everything from Gershwin to Guthrie, cowboy blues to urban folk, still it was not at all difficult to imagine him smashing the mood with a single well-timed cry of "day-oh." Which, of course, was precisely what he did on 1960's *Belafonte at Carnegie Hall* live album, a set which spent a staggering three years on the American chart. No wonder the audience sounded ecstatic.

Strictly speaking, then, Belafonte was not at all representative of the music which the average listener could expect to find should they ever venture out on a Caribbean vacation. He was far more important than that. More adroitly than any artist before or (at least until the advent of Bob Marley) since, Belafonte took a music which he knew and understood on the most instinctual level, then *translated* it for an audience which did not have that same advantage. And in so doing, he laid the foundations upon which almost every subsequent strand of Caribbean music has been built.

It was Belafonte's success in the UK, for instance, which opened the doors for the first specialist West Indian-themed record labels to flourish. They, of course, traced not only calypso as it moved into the 1960s, but also the development of Jamaican mento and R&B into ska and, ultimately, reggae. Of course those labels existed before Belafonte came along, and they would have continued to exist even if he had proved to be a simple flash in the pan of one hit wonderdom. But both they and their audience were marginal concerns at least. Before Belafonte, they merely dreamed of survival. After Belafonte, they dreamed of having hits.

It was a similar story in the United States, or at least in those parts of the country where circumstance and opportunity had already opened up a niche in the market — southern California, isolated strongholds across the mid-west, and New York City, Belafonte's home town and, then as now, the beating heart of America's entire Caribbean culture. For while it was Belafonte who gifted calypso to America, it was New York which gifted it to Belafonte, through the blood, sweat and joyous tears of an entire generation of earlier pioneers.

Throughout the first half of the 20th century, calypso and its makers originated in the Caribbean, performing for a West Indian audience, then reached out to America and the UK from there. Beginning in the 1930s, however, a new wave of performers arose for whom the primary audience was American, and whose impact in their homeland was minimal.

It was an uneasy existence. On the one hand, the rewards of American success were far greater than anything T&T had to offer. But they were also far more tenuous. In T&T, it was not at all unusual for a great calypsonian to remain a carnival superstar for his entire career — a lifetime, in other words. In America, fame was driven by momentary fads and generally lasted for little longer.

Neither was there any hope of moving adroitly back into the carnival mainstream once Stateside glory had faded away. Of the greatest names in American calypso during the 1930s and 1940s, the peak of that country's initial flirtation with the music, few are even dimly recalled today, either in the US or the Caribbean. Names like the Duke of Iron, Lord Caresser and Houdini live on only in the writings of calypso's archaeologists, or within the heaps of scratched old 78s which even the modern CD age has not yet gotten around to exhuming.

Others are even more obscure, seemingly surviving only in the small print of advertisements published by the New York based record labels Black Swan (motto: "The Only Record Made By Colored People") and Gennett ("West Indians! Stop! Look! Listen!"). Yet, clumsy though these early era attempts at niche-marketing may seem today, they were astonishingly effective, creating an audience by appealing for one, and then cornering it with both imported and home-made talent.

Of the biggest names on the New York calypso scene in these early years, the Venezuelan born Lionel Belasco (1882–1967) and the Trinidadians Gerald Clark (1899–19??) and Houdini (1895–1973) arrived in New York with carnival blood already coursing in their veins, having regularly performed in T&T during their teens. By the late 1920s, however, American talent — or at least, West Indians who had never sung a note in anger prior to emigrating to the US — was coming to the fore.

Belasco goes down in history as the first calypsonian ever to record in America, cutting his first sides for Victor in 1915. Houdini was a seaman who had played with the African Millionaires mas (masquerade) band at carnival in 1919, and appeared in the calypso tents. Not until he migrated to New York in the late 1920s, however, did his singing career take off. He recorded a vast number of calypsos (and other Trinidadian songs) for the Victor company; somewhat dishonestly, he also claimed to have written many of them, a common tactic in those days, but one which has left modern-day historians still trying to establish the true magnitude of Houdini's talent.

British Guiana-born Sam Manning, on the other hand, was a former jockey and motor mechanic who did not take up professional performance (as a singer and a comedian) until he reached New York following World War One. The Duke of Iron was similarly otherwise employed before taking up singing in the city under the aegis of band leader Gerald Clark (born 1899, T&T).

A former guitarist with Lionel Belasco, Clark relocated to New York in 1927. Since that time, his Caribbean Serenaders had become the most popular West Indian band in North America, while Clark himself was hired as an agent for Decca Records, charged with feeding the country's growing appetite for calypso. It was he who discovered the greatest of all the so-called calypso hucksters, Sir Lancelot.

Born around 1910, Lancelot was the son of a wealthy T&T bureaucrat who spared no expense on his son's education. The boy attended the best parochial schools in T&T and was a regular at the most exclusive operas. The notion that he might make his career singing calypso never even crossed his parents' minds — nor the child's. If he had any musical inclinations whatsoever, they lay towards German lieder and Italian aria.

Having completed his secondary schooling, Lancelot was sent to New York City, where he intended studying medicine. Of course he gravitated towards the city's already burgeoning Trinidadian community, and it was there that he first began singing professionally, performing his beloved European classics at small halls and gatherings — and there that he, too, first encountered Gerald Clark, during the mid-1930s.

Lancelot met Clark at an especially fortuitous moment. The band leader had a recording date for the Varsity label looming, and was searching for a suitable singer when he heard one of Lancelot's classical performances. Immediately sensing the young man's abilities, Clark offered him the job, and Lancelot — to what was reportedly his own surprise — accepted.

Things moved quickly. His studies forgotten, Lancelot began recording regularly with Clark; he also became a regular at the Village Vanguard, the Greenwich Village nightspot renowned for its calypso evenings. He adopted the name Sir Lancelot and, by the early 1940s, was widely considered the hottest calypsonian in the city.

It was a different story at home. Early in the decade, he returned to T&T to visit his family. They all but disowned him — "gentlemen," as Lancelot later recalled, "did not sing calypsos at that time." Apparently his brothers were so convinced of this particular truism, that they begged their father to keep Lancelot as far out of sight as possible. They were convinced that his very presence on the island was likely to bring ruin down upon the entire Pinard dynasty. Though he changed the scenario, Lancelot composed the hit "Shame and Scandal on the Family" with this episode in mind.

In 1941, Lancelot joined Lionel Belasco on a tour of Oregon and California. One of the final shows of the outing was in Los Angeles, which is where Lancelot was offered a minor singing role in the latest Pat O'Brien/Janet Blair movie, *Two Yanks in Trinidad*. He accepted.

Opting to remain in California, Lancelot's next two movie engagements, in 1943, have both been adjudged classics — albeit for very different reasons. He appeared in Jacques Tournier's cult horror flick *I Walked with a Zombie*, performing "Shame and Scandal on the Family" (it accompanies one of the voodoo sequences); he was also a highlight of the Rudy Vallee/Betty Hutton vehicle *Happy Go Lucky*, performing Roaring Lion's "Ugly Woman."

Having already outraged his family by turning out to be an adept calypsonian, he now heaped disgrace upon their dismay by becoming a proficient actor as well. By the end of 1943, he had carried off his first non-singing role, in director Mark Robson's *The Ghost Ship*. The following year, he appeared as Horatio in the Humphrey Bogart/Lauren Bacall movie *To Have and Have Not*, and as Edward in Robert Wise's *Curse of the Cat People*. 1945 then brought a return to calypso as a singer in the admittedly low grade *Zombies on Broadway*.

(Other Lancelot movie roles included: *Linda Be Good* (1947), *Brute Force* (1947), *Romance on the High Seas* (1948), *The Unknown Terror* (1957) and Anthony Quinn's *The Buccaneer* (1958). He also appeared in an episode of *The Andy Griffith Show* in 1967.)

Lancelot's visibility was at an all time high. His cultured British colonial tones were instantly familiar to a generation of radio listeners, not only as a performer but also — will the shame never cease? — as the voice behind a number of calypso-flavored advertising jingles, most of which he wrote himself.

Throughout the World War Two years, in particular, Lancelot recorded regularly, delivering some of his best loved material at a time when his apparently left wing politics were least likely to offend mainstream America — "Century of the Common Man," "Defenders of Stalingrad" and "Walk in Peace" were all substantial hits.

He also enjoyed great success with *Calypso*, an album (three 78s in a colorful package) cut for the Keynote label around this same time. But perhaps the most indelible sign of Lancelot's influence upon the American scene became apparent when the country's own first calypsos began to emerge (usually from the pens of white professional songwriters). For it was not the complex Trinidadian models of Kitchener, Lion and Melody which they followed, it was Lancelot's easy rhyming couplets and simple lockstep rhythms.

If World War Two was to give West Indian music in America its greatest foothold yet — US troops based in T&T during the conflict seem to have been unanimously converted to the cause — it contrarily robbed the UK of her own most beloved Caribbean talent, the legendary, and still much lauded, band leader Snakehips.

Ken Johnson (b 1915, T&T d 3/8/41, London) was called Snakehips because that is what he appeared to have. At a time when most band leaders still performed all but stock still, Johnson slipped and slithered across the stage — a sexual exhibitionist by the standards of the time, but one at whom it was impossible to take offense.

Indeed, for five years during the late 1930s and early 1940s, Snakehips was universally regarded as the single most important West Indian musical personality in Britain — with the emphasis on the word personality. He was certainly among the most influential, both musically and socially. Famed society photographer Roye shot a number of striking images of Snakehips in 1937 at the Cafe Florida. (Many of these were included in a major retrospective of the photographer's work at London's Ebury Galleries in October, 1999.)

Johnson arrived in the UK during the mid-1930s, forming his own band, the grandly titled West Indian Orchestra, in 1937. The core of both group and repertoire hailed from the Caribbean; in fact, the bulk of the orchestra itself was drawn from the Trinidad Police Band: Carl Barriteau (clarinet), George Roberts (reeds), Dave Williams (sax — brother of famed orchestra leader John "Buddy" Williams) and trumpeter Dave Wilkins were all former members of that outfit.

By 1939, the West Indian Orchestra was both recording regularly and broadcasting live on the BBC, and the outbreak of World War Two in Europe, in September that same year, barely dented the workload. Indeed, it may well have increased it, as London filled with both British and Empire troops on leave, or awaiting orders. The West Indies supplied thousands of men to the war effort (the Royal Air Force recruited 8,000 as ground crew alone), and Snakehips' performances at the Jigs Club became a renowned home away from home for many of them — assuming they could get in through the crush of other nationalities battling for what were often the hottest tickets in town.

The onset of the Blitz in September, 1940, did briefly halt the Orchestra's operations, as German bombers attempted to pound London into submission from the air, and the city's once vibrant night-life began to constrict. Fear, however, swiftly transformed into fatalism, and less than three weeks after the daily raids began, London's west end was as bustling as ever. The Cafe De Paris, sheltered securely beneath the Rialto cinema, was the runaway success story of all London's clubs, for not only had owner Martin Poulsen cornered the local supply of champagne, he had also booked Snakehips as the nightly entertainment.

It was there that Snakehips died, onstage in a dance hall modelled on the main ballroom aboard the liner *Titanic*. On the evening of March 8, 1941, two 50 kilo bombs fell on the Rialto, crashing through both roof and floor to impact on the dance floor. The first bomb failed to explode; the second, a fraction of a second later, detonated instantly, killing 34 people and injuring over a hundred. Aside from Snakehips, saxophonist Williams and club owner Poulsen also perished in the blast.

Without their charismatic leader, the West Indian Orchestra shattered, although many of the musicians remained in the UK, to have their own impact upon the next, peacetime, generation of fans of West Indian music.

Barbados born trumpeter Wilkins, for example, joined Cyril Blake's Calypso Serenaders in 1950 — after more than two decades playing popular music and jazz in both England and France (one of his engagements in the latter country was backing Josephine Baker at the Folies Bergere). Blake had turned to calypso at the request of the BBC during the war, and his band was soon regarded as the most proficient of its kind in the country. When the EMI label recorded its first calypsonians in 1951, Roaring Lion and the Lords Kitchener and Beginner, the Serenaders were their inevitable accompanists.

Snakehips' death, then, did not mark the end of a musical era, so much as that of a musical phenomenon. He was the first and, for the generation which grew up listening to him, the last West Indian who was truly, again that word, a personality.

Trinidad-born pianist Winifred Atwell, a cousin of calypsonian The Mighty Atwell, enjoyed a string of British hits during the 1950s, and was certainly a major star. But her talents leaned towards orchestral and music hall. Lord Kitchener, during his twelve year sojourn in Britain, also rivaled Snakehips' popularity at times, but even at the height of his own newsworthiness, the great Lord remained in many ways a novelty — good for singing about cricket, sunshine and similar themes of levity, but never a part of the fabric of daily life.

Snakehips, on the other hand, was, accorded a respect which rose above any of the petty boundaries — social, racial, class and, of course, musical — of the day. Had he lived, he might have become one of the legends of British music. As it was, it would take decades of both strife and struggle before any other Caribbean musicians were granted the same effortless, border-less acceptance.

THE YOUNG BRIGADE TAKE OVER

Calypso is timeless. Descriptions laid down in its infancy, during the opening years of the 20th century, were still relevant as it approached middle-age, emerging out of World War Two into a world which had changed beyond all recognition, but into a society which did not seem to have altered one iota.

T&T society was still choking on the decay of its once glorious colonial legacy, even though that legacy had brought nothing but a lonely foreign death to so many of her citizens. The British Empire was in terminal decline — soon, even the British admitted that and restyled their international possessions a "commonwealth."

But there were forces abroad who desired more than that — politicians who rose from the shattered promises of colonial government to press for independence; writers and scholars who bled ink for the salvation of their homeland; and a new wave of calypsonians who put those convictions to the harshest test of all — the carnival audience.

World War Two brought about massive changes in the nature of calypso, not least of all in its content, and ability to confront the most contentious themes. Indeed, even before the conflict broke out, Gorilla had his "Jews in the West Indies" banned by authorities discomforted at his criticism of British policy towards refugees. In 1941, too, Gorilla raised local hackles with his playful "Hitler, the Scampish Devil," but he was not alone in treating the war with an unbecoming irony. Although calypsos themselves can in no way be blamed, few observers were surprised when the government banned carnival "for the duration" in 1942. It finally returned in 1946.

The spirit of rebellion was not quashed, however. In 1947, two of the pre-war era's brightest hopes, Lord Kitchener and the Mighty Killer, launched an audacious new venture, the Young Brigade tent. Age, however, was not the criteria by which they judged their fellow performers. It was attitude which counted, the belief that just as the world was embracing a new dawn, so should T&T. It was time to shake off the shackles of colonialism, it was time for the island to stop helping to fight other people's wars. The Young Brigade wanted change, and they wanted singers and songs which might help affect that.

Kitchener himself did not remain on the scene for long — little more than a year later, he decamped for Britain itself, to spread his message into the heart of the beast. Neither was the Young Brigade tent to remain a seething hotbed for agitation. But the seeds it planted blossomed regardless.

In 1956, when Dr Eric Williams' People's National Movement (PNM) swept to power on an independence-minded ticket, most observers agreed it wasn't the political rhetoric alone which pushed the people to the ballot boxes. It was the calypsonians, who had taken that rhetoric as the theme for their songs, and put it into language which everyone understood.

In 1955, Spoiler won the Calypso King title with the pointed "Pick Sense Out of Nonsense." In 1956, Sparrow won the Road March with "Yankees Gone" (aka "Jean & Dinah"), a song celebrating the long-overdue departure of American troops from Trinidadian soil. The following year, Spitfire took the same title with the quite unequivocally titled "PNM." The year after that, it was Sparrow again, with "Pay as You Earn," extolling the virtues of the Williams government's newly instituted tax laws. It was all a very far cry from "Ugly Woman."

The Young Brigade ushered in more than a simple new wave of political consciousness, however. The late 1940s were an era of musical change as well — partly in response to the newly emergent impetus of the steel bands, partly because music must adapt to survive.

To the older generation of calypsonians, the hard horns and flamboyant rhythms which now underpinned calypso were an aberration; as perilous to the established order as the unpatriotic rantings which now passed muster for lyrics. To the new performers, excited beyond words by the limitless horizons now opening before them, it was the established order which was the aberration, and blind acceptance which was perilous. And the audience apparently agreed with them.

The audience itself had undergone a seismic shift, of course, and that, too, was absorbed into the new sounds of calypso. In Jamaica, the late-1950s saw the dawn of the rude boys, unemployed/unemployable teenage hoodlums who strutted the streets as though they owned them (usually because they did, as Kingston was partitioned off between rival, ratchet-wielding gangs), and struck fear into every law-abiding citizen.

In T&T, it was the Saga Boys who took over, and they were just as rough and tough as their counterparts over the water, and just as demanding musically, as socially. The first scratchy wails of rock'n'roll were now filtering into T&T, just as they were in Jamaica. On that island, the local musicians competed by reinventing the wheel — they tried to play authentic rhythm'n'blues and ended up discovering ska. In T&T. . . well, they started playing calypso, and they continued playing calypso. But that was only because nobody came up with a better name for the new sounds which jangled the island's ears.

ESSENTIAL COMPILATIONS

Calypso at Midnight! The Live Midnight Special Concert — Town Hall, New York City 1946 (Rounder) 1999

An astonishing discovery, a miraculous survivor. Across two CDs, a full evening of calypso hosted by Alan Lomax (who recorded the event), featuring three of the greatest New York-based calypsonians, Lord Invader, the Duke of Iron and Macbeth the Great, accompanied by Gerald Clark & his Invaders.

Calypso Awakening (Smithsonian Folkways Collection) 2000

A 21 track sampling drawn from the full Emory Cook Caribbean catalog. The majority of cuts date from the mid-1950s period, many recorded live — Sparrow and Melody's "Picong Duel" is included, alongside a couple of subsequent assaults; there's also a superb recounting of "Yankees Gone," recorded at a steel band procession. An excellent taste of what the tents were all about.

Calypso Breakaway 1927–1941 (Rounder) 1990

Lord Beginner, Atilla the Hun, Roaring Lion, Growling Tiger, King Radio, Lord Caresser, Houdini and Belasco headline a collection centered around calypso's arrival in New York. Growler's "An Excursion into Grenada," and "Guests of Rudy Vallee" from Lion and Atilla are among the better known of 20 titles.

Calypso Calaloo (Rounder) 1993

The earliest years of calypso recording are the theme of this excellent collection — it opens in 1914, with a piano roll cut by Lionel Belasco, then passes through the next 25 years via Lion, Babb & Williams, Tiger, Houdini, Executor and the Duke of Lion. A steelband interlude from 1950 spoils the mood a little (although there's no denying the significance of "Last Train io San Fernando"), but overall there can be few better primers to a crucial era.

Calypso Carnival (Rounder) 1993

Twenty-five classic performances from the golden age round up classics performances not included on Rounder's 1912–41 collections. Lion's "Ba Boo La La," Gerald Clark's "Si O No," Belasco's "Depression," and a string of songs on the pros and cons of buying a bungalow (!) have a period charm which cannot be matched.

Calypso Kings (Cook) 1957

Live in the tents, the definitive Cook compilation features Melody's "Creature from the Black Lagoon" and "Jonah & The Bake," the immortal "Picong Duel" with Sparrow, plus contributions from the Mighty Cypher, King Solomon, the March of Dimes Quartet and King Fighter's "Silly Meal — Coocoo Soup." An essential look inside carnival.

Calypso Pioneers 1912–1937 (Rounder) 1989

Impeccable collection highlighting some of the rare survivors of calypso's first recordings, featuring Lovey's Band, Merrick's Orchestra, Houdini, White Rose, Atilla the Hun, Gerald Clark & His Night Owls and Executor.

Don't Stop the Carnival (Pavilion—UK) 2000

There's no such thing as the definitive calypso anthology, but this comes close. Drawn from the 1940s era Decca archive, a solid survey of the era opens with the Lion's "Ugly Woman," and only gets better from there. MacBeth, Houdini, King Radio, Lionel Belasco, Tiger, Invader, Executor, Lancelot and more come to life through surprisingly vibrant sound quality, reminding us that it's very easy indeed to become bound up in the socio- musico-cultural significance of calypso. But at the end of the day, a lot of it is also incredibly funny.

Fall of Man: Calypsos on the Human Condition 1935–1941 (Rounder) 1999

The title gives it away. Tiger, Lord Beginner, King Radio, Executor, Lord Caresser, Lion, Growler and the Mighty Destroyer are among the stars giving their advice on matters philosophical, financial, social and, most of all, sexual: Atilla's "Women Will Rule the World" and "Vagaries of Women," Beginner's "Women Are Good and Women Are Bad, Lion's "Malicious Neighbours" and King Radio's "Man Smart, Woman Smarter" are absolute stand-outs.

Roosevelt in Trinidad: Calypsos of Events, Places, and Personalities 1933–1939 (Rounder) 1999

An hysterical collection of calypsos about British royalty, American movie stars, local politicians and international disasters ensure this collection sounds like a singing newspaper. Hurricanes from Houdini, fires from Belasco, cricket from Beginner, abdications from Lord Caresser and Atilla's title track serve up some good laughs, but also some homespun philosophy. Truly one of the best collections of its type.

INDEX OF LEADING CALYPSONIANS

The following documents the stage- and real names of 250 leading calypso and soca performers from throughout the region, listed alphabetically by performing name. This avoids repetition of identical information elsewhere within this encyclopedia.

CHALKDUST: Hollis Liverpool

CHARLO: Charles Thorne

CHIEFTAIN DOUGLAS aka RAILWAY DOUGLAS: Walter Douglas

CHILLER: Cedric Pierre

CLIPPER: Joseph Aansalum

COBEAU: Nap Hepburn

COMMANDER: Alan Daniel

COMMENTOR: Brian Honore

COMPOSER: Fred Mitchell

CONQUEROR: Leroy Paul

CONTENDER: Mark John

COUNT ROBIN: Randolph Hilliaire

CRAVAT: David Noel

CRAZY: Edwin Ayong

CREOLE (ANT): Manroy Hunte

CREOLE (T&T): Winston Barker

CRO-CRO: Weston Rawlins

DE ALBERTO: Winston Albert

DE BRAKES: Brancker John

DE HUNTER: Derrick St Rose

DE LAMO: Franz Lambkin

DE ORIGINAL DE FOSTO: Winston Scarborough

DE SCRUNTER: Irwin Reyes Johnson

DEPLE: Tyrone Hernandez

DESIGNER: Keith Prescott

DEE DIAMOND: Denesian Moses

DOCTOR SOCA: Dr Kongshiek Achong Low

DUKE OF ALBANY: Charles Jones

DUKE OF IERE: G R Plummer

DUKE OF IRON: Cecil Anderson

DUKE OF MARLBOROUGH: George Jamesie Adilla

DUPPI: Patrick Sadlow

EAGLE: Ewart Isaac

EBONY: Fitzroy Joseph

EL DRAGO: Ainsley Mayers

EXPLAINER: Winston Henry

EXPOSER: Moses Monroe

FIAH: Julian Lawrence

FIGHTER: Shirland Wilson

FLAMINGO: Winston Pitts

FLUKE: Cecil Duke Taylor

FLYIN' CLOUD: Francis Daniel

FLYIN' TURKEY: Cecil Belfon

FROSTY: Andy Brooks

FUNNY: Donrick Williamson

GABBY: Tony Carter

GABILANG: David Bereaux

GIBRALTAR: Sydney Benjamin

GORILLA: Charlie Grant

GRABBER: Ellis Clarke

GROWLER: Errol Duke

GROWLING TIGER: Neville Marcano

GRYNNER: McDonald Blenman

GYPSY: Winston Peters

HAPPY: Gilbert O'Connor

HENRY INVENTOR aka MODERN INVENTOR: Henry Forbes

HERO: Justin Cassell

HINDU PRINCE: Kenneth Nathaniel

HOUDINI: Wilmoth Hendricks (aka Edgar Leon Sinclair)

IMPULSE: Wayne Modeste

INSPECTOR: Elymus Gilbert

IRON DUKE: Brylo Ford

IWER GEORGE: Neil George

JAGUAR: Alfred Carlton Marryshow

RIKKI JAI: Ricky Samraj Jaimungal

JAYSON: John Perez

JOHNNY MA BOY: John King

JOKER: Winsford Devine

JUST COME, JOHN: John Walcott

KASSMAN: Wayne McDonald

KING AUSTIN: Austin Lewis

KING ONYAN: Toriana Edwards

KING PHARAOH: Andrew Bernard

KING RADIO: Norman Span

KING SOLOMON: Samuel Ryan

KING SOUL: Rannie Peters

KING WELLINGTON: Hawthorne Stephen Wellington Quashie

DANNY KING: Clifford Caesar

KINTE: Carey Stephens

LADY B: Beulah Bobb

LADY CHACONIA: Christiana Balbosa

LADY GYPSY: Lynette Steele

LADY HOTSPOT: Easlyn Orr

LADY IERE: Maureen St John

LADY PAULA: Paula Salandy

LADY SMASHER: Genelle Wilson-Moore

LADY TANTALIZER: Joan St John

LADY VENUS: Marilyn Jimenez

LADY WONDER: Diane Hendrickson-Jones

LAZO: Lazarus Finn

LIONESS: Suzanne John

LORD BAKER: Alex King

LORD BEGINNER: Egbert Moore

LORD CANARY: Malcolm Corrica

LORD CARESSER: Rufus Callender

LORD CARUSO: Emmanuel Pierre

LORD CRISTO: Christopher Laidlow

LORD DOUGLA: Claytis Ali

LORD EXECUTOR: Philip Garcia

LORD INVADER: Rupert Grant

LORD INVEIGLER: MacDonald Borel

LORD INVENTOR: Lloyd Merchant

LORD IVANHOE: Clinton George

LORD JACKSON: Mark Jackson

LORD KITCHENER: Aldwyn Roberts

LORD MELODY: Fitzroy Alexander

LORD MENTOR: Mentor Trimm

LORD NELSON: Robert Nelson

LORD ORLANDO: Thomas Ollivierre

LORD PRETENDER: Aldric Farrell

LORD SHORT SHIRT aka BROTHER SHORT SHIRT: Emmanuel McClean

LORD SHORTY aka RAS SHORTY I: Garfield Blackman

LORD SURPRISER: Calvin Romero

LORD TOKYO: Hayden Desiree

LORD WONDER aka MIGHTY ATWELL: Victor Atwell

LUTA aka SUGAR STICK: Morel Peters

MAESTRO: Cecil Hume

MANCHILD: Carlton Collins

MARVELOUS MARVA: Marva Joseph

MASTERTONE: Anthony Salloum

MBA: Gary Thomasos

MERCHANT: Dennis Franklyn Williams

MESSENGER: Dennis Cudjoe

MIGHTY ATWELL aka LORD WONDER: Victor Atwell

MIGHTY BOMBER: Clifton Ryan

MIGHTY DESTROYER: Clifford Morris

MIGHTY DICTATOR: Kenny St Bernard

MIGHTY DUKE: Kelvin Pope

MIGHTY FEARLESS: Mikey Hamit

MIGHTY INDIAN: Hosein Mohammed

MIGHTY JAUNTY: Pierre Regis

MIGHTY KILLER: Cephas Alexander

MIGHTY PANTHER: Vernon Roberts

MIGHTY PANTI: Bernard Pantin

MIGHTY POWER: Sonny Francois

MIGHTY SPARROW: Slinger Francisco

MIGHTY SPOILER: Theophilus Phillip

MIGHTY TERROR: Fitzgerald Henry

MIGHTY TRINI: Robert Elias

MIGHTY VIKING: Victor Springer

MIGHTY ZEBRA: Charles Harris

MODERN INVENTOR aka HENRY INVENTOR: Henry Forbes

MYSTIC PROWLER: Roy Lewis

NIGHTINGALE: Bertie Hicks

NINJA: Kenson Neptune

OBSTINATE: Paul Richards

ORGANISER: Leydon Charles

PAMPERS: Jazzy Blackman

PECULIAR: Fitzroy Richards

PENGUIN: Seadley Joseph
PINK PANTHER: Eric Taylor
PLAIN CLOTHES: Clinton Moreau
POET: Joseph Cummings
POODY: Everol Cooper
POPO: Reginald Blondell Alphonse
POSER: Sylvester Lockhart
PREACHER: Barnett Henry
PRINCE: Clifton De Labastide
PRINCE GALLOWAY: E Galloway, Jr
PRINCE UNIQUE: Jeffrey Thomas
PRINCESS: Teresa De Labastide-Campbell
PRINCESS SURPRISER: Janice Romero
PROGRESS: Glenmore Sheppard
PRONTO: Elvis Escayg
PROSPECTOR: Carl Robinson
PROTECTOR: Michael Leggerton
RAILWAY DOUGLAS aka CHIEFTAIN DOUGLAS: Walter Douglas
RAJAH: Dhanni-O-Gopal
RANDY DARLING: Clarinda Wickham
RAS ILEY: Darcy Small
RAS KOMMANDA: Stephen Pascal
RAS SHORTY I aka LORD SHORTY: Garfield Blackman
RED PLASTIC BAG: Stedson Wiltshire
RELATOR: Willard Harris
RICHARD COUER DE LEON: Norman Le Blanc
RINGO: D Pernell
ROARING LION aka THE LION FLAPS: Hubert Raphael Charles aka Raphael de Lion
ROOTSMAN: Yafei Osei
SALTY: Winston Smith
SANTA: Dennis Williams

SECRET RIVAL: Wayne Brooks
SERENADER: E Brewster
SHADOW: Winston Bailey
SHAKABAKA: Andre McEachnie
SHORT PANTS: Llewellyn McIntosh
SINGING B: Bernadette McFarlane
SINGING FRANCINE: Francine Edwards
SINGING SANDRA: Sandra De Vignes
SINGING SONIA: Sonia Francis
SIPPY: Chotilal Seecharan
SIR LANCELOT: Lancelot Victor Edward Pinard
SKUNKY: Odian Cyrus
SMALL ISLAND PRIDE: Theo Woods
SMARTY JR: Ira Harvey
SMILEY: Gaston Nunes
SNIPER: Mervyn Hodge
SOCA VAN: Colin Jackman
SOCA GENERAL: Irwin Williams
SPITFIRE: Carlton Gumbs
SPRANGALANG: Dennis Hall
SQUIBBY: Stanley Cummings
STAMONE: Victor Cardenas
STINGER: Dexter Parson
STRIKER: Percy Oblington
STYLER: Samuel Ryan
SUGAR ALOES: Michael Anthony Osouna
SUGAR STICK aka LUTA: Morel Peters
SUPERBLUE aka BLUE BOY: Austin Lyons
SUPER KELLY: Kelly Des Vignes
SUPER ROD: Wilston Legendre
SUZANNE: Suzanne Wallace-Romero
SWALLOW: Rupert Philo
TALLISH: Francis Edwards
TAMBU: Christopher Herbert

TAN TAN: Alyson Brown
TEMPO: Joe Caesar
TENNYSON: Kenneth George
TERRA: Pancras Theodore
THE KING: David Baptiste
THE LION FLAPS aka ROARING LION: Hubert Raphael Charles aka Raphael de Lion
TOBAGO CRUSOE: Orthniel Bacchus
TRINIDAD BILL: Paul Trotman
TRINIDAD RIO: Daniel Brown
TWIGGY: Ann Marie Parks
UPRISING: Peter Edwards
VERSATILE: D Hector
VIPER: Roderick Lewis
WANDERER: Peter Herbert
WARRIOR: Glenroy Preddie
WATCHMAN: Wayne Hayde
REX WEST: Richard Chen
WHITE ROSE: Henry Julien
WINSTON SO SO: Winston Lockhart
WIZZARD: Merlin St Hilaire
WOUNDED SOLDIER: Leslie Palmer
WRANGLER: Kenneth Wynne
YOUNG BULL: Val Cuffy
YOUNG CARESSER: Rudolph Benoit
YOUNG CHALLENGER: Lorenzo Cassell
YOUNG KILLER: Emmanuel Jardine
ZACARE: Trevor King
ZANDOLIE: Sylvester Anthony
ZEBRA: Charles Harris
ZEMAKAI: George Edwards
ZERO: Lynwall Joseph
ZHIVAGO: Felix Scott
ZOOM: Michael Salloum

CALYPSO ROSE

STYLE *calypso*
BORN *McCartha Lewis (Bethel, Tobago)*

One of the first women to successfully challenge — and triumph — in the hitherto male dominated world of calypso, Calypso Rose was just 15 when she first came to attention, performing around her home village of Bethel. With a rich repertoire of songs designed to deflate the engorged sexuality of many male performers, she made her debut at carnival in Port of Spain in 1963.

She gave calypso one of its most enduring anthems when "Fire in Meh Wire" became the first calypso ever sung two years running at carnival, in 1966 and 1967. 1968's "Too Much Vitality" proved almost as popular.

Calypso Rose began working regularly with Lord Kitchener, but continued on her own course as well. For five years around the early-mid 1970s, Calypso Rose dominated the race for the Calypso Queen title, but it was clear that her abilities and impact stretched beyond that honor alone. "Constable Rose" and her first gold disc, "Do Dem Back," were major hits during 1974, and in 1975 she was awarded the Medal of Merit Class 2 by the government of T&T for her services to calypso.

1975 brought the massive hit "Labour Day Breakaway"; 1976 saw her score with "The Bomb" and "Pan Rhapsody"; finally, in 1977, Calypso Rose became the first ever female winner of the Road March competition, with "Gimme More Tempo."

In 1978, she took the title again with "Come Leh We Jam." But even that triumph was to be overshadowed as she swept the finals of that same year's Calypso King competition, to become the tournament's first ever female winner, with the calypsos "I Thank Thee" and "Her Majesty." In her honor, the competition's title was promptly changed to Calypso Monarch, while international acclaim for her victory arrived in the form of an "Award for Unprecedented Achievement by a Calypsonian" from the Trinidad and Tobago Alliance of the USA.

In 1983, Calypso Rose was named Top Female Calypsonian by the Smithsonian Institute, Washington D.C., while her 1984 album, *Trouble*, won the CEI's Best Female Recording Artist Award. 1989 then saw Calypso Rose scoop the Best Party Song and Best Female Vocalist titles at the annual Sunshine Music Awards. In 1991, the National Woman's Action Committee named her Outstanding Female in the Field of Music and Most Outstanding Woman in Trinidad and Tobago, and in 1993 Calypso Rose became a charter member of the Tobago Walk of Fame.

After more than a decade with the New York based Straker label, Calypso Rose joined Eddy Grant's Ice in 1993, for the album *Soca Diva*. Plans for a swift return, however, were delayed when she was diagnosed with breast cancer. She underwent surgery in 1996 and spent much of the next year convalescing, both from the surgery and from depression. Calypso Rose finally bounced back in early 1998 with the Eddy Grant produced *Tobago*, reflecting upon her past hits. She also performed at London's Royal Albert Hall in a massive calypso concert staged by Grant.

Since that time, Calypso Rose has moved away from calypso and soca to concentrate on gospel, a process highlighted by the *Jesus Is My Rock* album. However, May, 1999, saw her appear in concert in Tunapuna, T&T, with American soul legend Roberta Flack. Also in 1999, a new hospital in Tobago was named after her, the McCartha Lewis Memorial Hospital.

SELECTED DISCOGRAPHY

8 **Action Is Tight (Charlies — T&T) 1977**
The hit title track, "Give More Tempo" and "My Little Pussy" place the sexual ball firmly in the girls' court, as Calypso Rose storms out with a voice like warm kittens and a band that wraps like a blanket. An incredibly sensuous album.

7 **Mass Fever (Charlies — T&T) 1978**
"Soca In Guyana" gives credit where credit is due; "Gunplay on de Parkway" is an effective anti-violence song, but the highlights are the distinctly partisan party song "J'Ouvert Tobago" and the mighty "Mass Fever."

8 **We Rocking for Carnival (Charlies — T&T) 1979**
The "Hold I Say" single missed out on an album appearance, but the rest of this set is just as good. The title track is a joyous storm, while "Satan Music" has a wry charm of its own.

7 **Her Majesty (Charlies — T&T) 1980**
7 **Trouble (Strakers) 1984**
8 **Pan in Town (Strakers) 1985**

"Pussy Cat Bawl" is a throwback to Rose's early sexual put downs; "Put It on the Table" could be. Non-stop fun regardless.

6 **Steppin' Out (Strakers) 1986**
5 **Leh We Punta (Strakers) 1987**
Not one of Rose's strongest efforts, although "The Other Woman" is a classic.

8 **Soca Explosion (Strakers) 1988**
7 **Jump with Power (Strakers) 1991**
7 **Rosie Doh Hurt Them (Straker's — T&T) 1992**
Reprising oldies "Leh We Punta" and "Give Me More Tempo," a neatly updated introduction to Rose's 80s output.

8 **Soca Diva (Ice — UK) 1993**
Rose's most produced album, as Eddy Grant brings all his biggest technological guns to bear. Long time fans need not be alarmed, however; the trademark growl is still in place and her lyrics are as pertinent as ever. "Jamming in Jamaica" and "Pump Up de Base" are excellent.

8 **Tobago (— T&T) 1998**
Eddy Grant produced set includes a reworking of the seminal "Fire in Meh Wire" and the fiery "I Want It Hotter."

7 **Soul on Fire (— T&T) 1999**
The jumping "Pepper Soup," an earth-rich "Dark End of the Street" and the ubiquitous "Fire In Meh Wire" are highlights. Elsewhere, "Amazing Grace" and "Coombya" form a heartstopping medley.

6 **Jesus Is My Rock (— T&T) 2000**

CAPLETON

STYLE *reggae (toasting/dance hall)*
BORN *Clifton Bailey, 4/13/67 (Islington, St Mary, JA)*

Having grown up in a small farming village, Capleton moved to Kingston when he was 18. He worked a handful of smaller sound systems, including Muzoo and Maestro, before he was recruited to Toronto, Canada-based Stewart Brown's Africa Star set-up in early 1987. Performing alongside Brown, the DJ shared the stage with stars Ninjaman, Anthony Malvo and Flourgon, and returned to Kingston overflowing with confidence.

In 1989, Capleton was signed by producer Philip "Fatis" Burrell, releasing his first single, the risque (and banned) "Bumbo Red" in early 1990. By the end of the year, he scored the hit which established him as a major power on the slacker dance hall scene, the swaggering "Number One (On the Good Look Chart)."

Over the next year, Capleton maintained a solid output of further hits, alternating between slacker than slack anthems and some genuinely cultural material: "Bible fi Dem" (with Burrell), "Oow" (Patrick Brown), "The Red" and "Gun Talk" (King Jammy), "Somebody" and "Ghetto Youth" (Scorpio), "Dem No Like Me" (Roof International), "Rough Rider" (Uncle T), "Too Warsome" (Fresh Breed), "God Mi Love Me Nuh Love Satan" (Bravo the Best Baby Father).

Many of these hits were compiled together as his debut album in 1991 and predictably, *Capleton Gold* became an aptly titled monster. "We No Lotion Man" (produced by Peterkins) also gave its name to a best selling album, while Capleton attracted further attention by combining with Ninjaman and Tony Rebel for the *Real Rough* collection.

Capleton made his Sunsplash debut that same year (he returned annually 1992–94); 1991 also saw his "Special Guest" open the Outernational compilation *Joe Frazier: Knocked Out* — another hit, of course. He followed that with collaborations with Gussie P and General Levy (the *Double Trouble* album), Cutty Ranks and Reggie Stepper (*Three the Hard Way*), Bobby Zarro ("Young, Fresh and Green"), Junior Reid ("After Dark"), and Buju Banton ("Good Hole").

Capleton's first British dates (alongside Pan Head) in December, 1991, ended in controversy in the aftermath of a shooting incident at one of the London shows. He also recorded the popular "Dance Can't Done" during the visit, but indications that Capleton was moving away from the overt violence of his early work came with a pair of singles recorded back in Jamaica during 1992, "Almshouse" (with Burrell) and "Prophet" (Donovan Germain).

Both looked forward to a peaceful solution to the strife rending the dance hall scene and beyond. Capleton's public declaration of his Rastafarian faith followed, informing his subsequent releases with a deep spirituality.

Remaining with Burrell and the formidable rhythm section of Sly Dunbar and Donald Dennis, Capleton scored further hits with "FCT," "Matey a Dead," "Unno No Hear," "Husband Goody-Goody," "Hard to Believe" and "Make Hay," leading up to 1993's *Almshouse* album. "Living in a Dream" (produced by Redrose & Malvo), "Stampede" and "Good Love" (Mad House) and "Everybody Need Somebody" and "Mankind" (Colin Fat) maintained Capleton's hit making record into 1993.

He also charted alongside Nadine Sutherland with "More Than Loving" (Gussie Clarke), but it was with a return to Stewart Brown that Capleton made the greatest impact. "Buggering" and "Good So" (from the album of the same name) were both major releases. "Taxi" was triumphant at the 1994 Caribbean Music Awards, while a hip-hop mix of 1994's driving "Tour" single made #57 on the US chart in January, 1995, prompting the Def Jam label to sign him. "Chalice," a variation on the same rhythm, fronted by a powerful nyahbingi drum beat, was next, and late 1995 brought the militant Rastafarian *Prophecy* album. Further

hits "Wings of the Morning" (a collaboration with Wu-Tang Clan rapper Method Man) and "Heathen Rage" followed.

Three years later, *I Testament* was a less impressive set, seemingly aimed wholly at Capleton's newfound American audience (although a guest appearance from Big Youth restored some roots sensibility to the proceedings); the album's failure to pursue *Prophecy* into the charts, however, proved that whatever America wanted from Capleton, it wasn't his R&B approach.

Capleton broke with Def Jam and found immediate success with 1997's "Rising Up" (produced by the Firehouse Crew). The hits continued through 1999/2000 including "Never Get Down" (C Parchment & R Bailey), "Final Assassin" (Steely & Clevie), "High Grade" (Harvel Hart), "More Prophet" (Desmond & Rupert Blake), "Bun Dun Dreadie" (Jazzwad), "Who Dem?" (Ward 21) and "Caan Hold We Dung" (Madd Dawgz).

A new album, *One Mission*, also appeared in 1999, followed by the controversial *More Fire* in 2000. American audiences apparently misconstrued Capleton's calls for symbolic flames with a demand for real ones, a confusion which climaxed at an April, 2000, show at Miami's Mahai Temple, where the crowd began setting fires inside the building. In another much publicized incident, a mother discovered her house burning, and her daughter chanting "more fire." A bemused Capleton responded that the woman shouldn't have left matches lying around.

DISCOGRAPHY

7 **Capleton Gold (Charm) 1991**

7 **We No Lotion Man (Charm) 1991**

Essentially the story so far, hit after hit after hit, all performed in what was then an inimitable, but so cool slacker style.

8 **Almshouse (RAS) 1993**

A Fats Burrell set dominated by "Mate a Dead," "GCT," "Hole Good" and a duet with Singing Apache, "Falling in Love." The title track, another massive hit, debuted the DJ's shift to the "cultural" themes that form the lyrical focus of this album.

9 **Prophecy (African Star/Def Jam) 1995**

The DJ sharpens his social commentary on such crucial cuts as "Heathen Reign," "Obstacle," and "Tour," the latter a hit in the US in a remixed hiphop version. The addition of nyahbingi drumming to the hard dance hall sounds kicked off a revival of African beats that quickly slammed their way into the dance hall scene.

7 **I-Testament (Def Jam) 1998**

Disappointing major label sophomore set, marred by Capleton's apparent submersion beneath a surfeit of too many MTV rap shows.

7 One Mission (J&D — JA) 1999
8 More Fire (VP) 2000

One of the year's most outspoken albums, from one of the decade's most outspoken artists. Capleton's penchant for roaring throatily when he runs out of words never loses its impact, while "Critics," roasting the Pope and British royalty, is as tough as they come.

8 Still Blazin' (VP) 2002

Dramatic, rootsy set featuring contributions from Luciano and Morgan Heritage.

CAPLETON & GENERAL LEVY
6 Double Trouble (Gussie P — JA) 1991

CAPLETON & CUTTY RANKS & REGGIE STEPPER
5 Three the Hard Way (Techniques — JA) 1991

CAPLETON & TONY REBEL & NINJAMAN
6 Real Rough (— JA) 1990

SELECTED COMPILATIONS & ARCHIVE RELEASES
6 Good So (VP) 1994

A round up of the DJ's best "cultural" songs, most, appropriately enough, recorded for African Star. Included are three of his 1993 hits, while a track each from Black Scorpio and Colin Fat round out the set.

CHUTNEY
HISTORICAL BACKGROUND

In May, 1838, a very strange cargo was delivered to the shores of British Guiana (modern Guyana). For months, rumor had insisted that the tiny nation's British overlords had a ready solution to the acute labor shortage which had afflicted the land since the emancipation of the slaves. Now, pouring down the gangplanks of a newly arrived sailing ship, came confirmation of those stories — an army, or so it seemed, of exotic looking foreigners, chattering in a strange language, draped in unimaginable clothing, and gazing about at their new homeland with exactly the same expressions of wonder, as the gathering Guyanans felt as they watched them.

They came from India, it was said, lured halfway around the world by the promise of regular work and reasonable wages in the sugar plantations which were British Guiana's principle source of wealth. In the parlance of the time, they were "indentured servants," contracted to work out a set period of time, and then free to do as they would. Today, we say it was little better than slavery. But that, in a way, was the point. It was a little better.

The majority of the newcomers — close to 400,000 altogether — were drawn from India's western and southern states of Bihar, Uttar Pradesh, Bengal and the area around Madras, and were settled primarily in the British colonies of British Guiana, T&T and Jamaica. (Others, recruited by the Dutch, were employed in Dutch Guiana/Surinam.)

Once their contracted time was up, the workers were then given the option of returning to India, or remaining in their new homeland. Many chose the latter, and today their descendants constitute the largest ethnic group in T&T (around 43%), and a majority in Guyana (52%).

The nature of their employment, and the people's own strict social codes, ensured that the East Indians remained somewhat isolated from mainstream life in the region. So did the prejudices of both the British authorities and the Creoles, who nicknamed the East Indians "coolies" (a term borrowed from the British Indian lexicon), and despised the apparent grace with which the immigrants did what had once been a slave's work.

Even after indentureship was abandoned, the colonial government not only ignored the peoples' rights to education, employment and the vote, they even refused to legally recognize East Indian marriages. It was 1946 before a child born to such a union was acknowledged as anything other than illegitimate. So developed a state of affairs which ensured that whatever elements of their native culture accompanied them to the New World remained largely untouched by outside influences.

These elements, of course, permeated every aspect of East Indian life, but perhaps "home"'s most profound manifestation was musical, where traditional instruments such as the harmonium, sitar, tabla, dholak (barrel drum) and the metal dhantal readily survived the transition to the Americas, alongside the traditional bhajans (devotional songs) which were one of the centerpieces of Bhojpuri music. There, they were supplemented by the loud, excitable sound of tassa drums, a backdrop which grew more pronounced as players and singers picked up on other traditional Creole elements and incorporated them into their music. Hindu lyrics shot through with local slang and, even more pronounced, accents became as much a part of the music as the instrumentation. It was these elements which ultimately evolved into the folk song, or tan, tradition which lies at the soul of modern chutney.

HOSEIN

Across T&T, the high point of the East Indians' cultural year throughout the 19th century was the festival of Muharram, celebrated every October. Muharram's origins lay in the Muslim community, a small (around 20%), but culturally vibrant component of the early Indo-Caribbean population. The festival originally re-enacted events leading up to the deaths, eleven years apart, of the Prophet Mohammed's grandsons, Husayn and Hasan (the festival's alternate names, Hosay and Hosien, are derived from these).

Model mausoleums, or tajahs, were constructed, then carried by torchlight through the countryside and towns before being deposited in the sea. The entire parade route was lined by tassa drummers, who themselves first began playing several days before the procession itself. In a community undisturbed by religious rivalry, the Hindu population was naturally attracted to this colorful, often riotous, event, and so Muharram expanded until it became an expression of faith and national identity for all people of sub-continental extraction.

Like carnival, it was celebrated throughout the island, with the largest event taking place in San Fernando. Unlike carnival, however, it was largely overlooked by the authorities, a situation which offers an interesting corollary to the Creole festivities of the age. While carnival and, in particular, the opening Canboulay ceremony was under constant attack from the authorities, both physically (in terms of police presence) and legislatively, Hosien was left untouched. Indeed, the wording of laws passed against carnival was often deliberately drafted to exclude the East Indian festivities. Observers of the day frequently remarked upon this apparent discrimination; the authorities responded by explaining that the new laws were intended not to discriminate against the blacks, but to encourage them to behave in the same orderly fashion as the East Indians — they, too, enacted vast torchlight parades (the so-called Coolie Processions), but rarely was there any cause for public alarm.

Neither did the growing Creole participation in Hosien appear to affect the good natured mood of the revel (Hosien bands were also a familiar sight at carnival). However, the official mood changed considerably following the riots at Canboulay in 1883. Suddenly, all large public gatherings seemed a threat to law and order, all the more so since the authorities realized that suppressing one carnival while permitting another was a certain recipe for disaster. Public opinion, too, favored a crackdown. An editorial in the *Port of Spain Gazette* summed up the prevalent feeling among T&T's upper classes by thundering, "It is utterly absurd to pretend that the monster processions which . . . inundate our principal towns with thousands of fanatical drunken coolies can form any necessary part of [the Indians'] religious ceremonies."

In July, 1884, acting under powers granted by the newly introduced Ordinance for Regulating the Festivals of Immigrants, the government announced that henceforth, Hosien could be celebrated only on the plantations where its participants were employed (a similar restriction had existed in British Guiana for several decades). The East Indian population, of course, was incensed, and over the next few months, several petitions were made to the government, in the hope of having the restrictions lifted. Governor Sir Sanford Freeling held firm, however, and ordered Police Chief Arthur Baker — chief architect of the assaults on Canboulay — to arm his men in readiness for trouble at the next Muharram. On October 30, 1884, in clear defiance of the law, a procession gathered behind two tajahs and began making its way towards San Fernando. Encountering a police cordon, the protestors stood their ground — until they were mowed down in a hail of police bullets. No definitive tally of the resultant deaths appears to have been published, but the so-called Hosien Massacre passed effortlessly into the darkest annals of British colonial rule in the Caribbean.

THE MOHAMMED BROTHERS TAKE CONTROL

Although Muharram continued to be celebrated, subsequent events were understandably muted affairs. By the early 20th century, the practice appears to have been abandoned altogether, both in T&T and British Guiana (where the increasing influx of other local people had, in any case, dispirited all but the most hardcore East Indian revellers).

Minor musical competitions continued to be held within the community, however, the larger of which took on at least some of the symbolism of the older gatherings. But for many years, East Indian music was rarely heard outside of Hindu wedding ceremonies and similar affairs. This was not wholly the consequence of the massacre. The indentureship system was abandoned in 1917 and, though the Indian community remained close-knit, earlier communities themselves began to break up. Many families moved away from the plantation and into their own small holdings and businesses, others moved into the cities themselves, a dispersement which relegated the further transmission of folk music and culture to both a social and geographical backwater.

The launch of Radio Trinidad in early September, 1947, marked the beginning of the music's resurgence, both in folk and pop terms. On September 26 that year, East Indian presenter Kamalludin Mohammed became the first man to play an Indian record on the station, when he spun Imam Farook's "Kush Raho Tum Allah Wale," a popular song from the movie *Noor-E-Yeman*. Thereafter, Mohammed's *Indian Talent on Parade* became one of the most popular shows on the station. The Naya Zamana Orchestra enjoyed a six month residency on the show; when they moved on, the Young Indian National Orchestra took their place.

By the early 1950s, local talent was stepping forward in increasing numbers. Tarran Persad, Isaac Yankarran, the SM Aziz Orchestra, Naya Tarana, Basant Bahar, Jameer Hosain and Nau Jawan were all regulars on Mohammed's show and, in 1958, East Indian music finally made its recorded debut with the release of the debut album by the self-styled King of Surinam, Ramdeo Chaitoe. The album ostensibly comprised traditional devotional bhajans, but they were performed with a remarkable twist. Chaitoe sung in Creoleized Hindi, above a backdrop of wild tassa, dhantal and dholak beats which gave the music the sheen of unabashed dance music. Some of the performances were old, dating back to the centuries before the first Indians arrived in the

Caribbean; others were of more recent vintage. But all had been touched by their environment—the result, as Trinidadian sitar player Mungal Patasar once explained, of taking "a capsule from India, [leaving] it here for a hundred years . . . this is what you get."

In 1962, American musicologist Alan Lomax visited the region; his East Indian field recordings captured the local music in its purest form—at probably the last opportunity for that to happen. 1962 also saw Kamalludin Mohammed retire from broadcasting, to concentrate on the political career he had launched in 1953, and a successful sideline in songwriting (he composed Tarran Persad's winner at the 1962 Independence Singing Contest). He was succeeded at Radio Trinidad by his younger brothers Sham and Moean, ambitious young men who swiftly proved even brighter visionaries than their sibling.

By the end of 1962, the pair had supplemented their radio broadcasts with another first for the island's East Indians, a weekly televised talent show, *Indian Variety*. The following year, the brothers arranged for Ramdeo Chaitoe to tour T&T, in the company of a number of other Surinamese performers. As with Chaitoe's album, the outing was expected to appeal primarily to T&T's East Indian community, for whom the music and, just as importantly, the dancing, was otherwise in short supply.

Other locals, however, also attended the shows, to be stunned by a style of music which seemed as deeply rooted in Caribbean traditions as in those of the performers' own Asian homeland. Hearsay alone guaranteed the tour was a success. Emboldened, the Mohammeds arranged for further tours, launched their own record label, Windsor, and equally significantly began encouraging local performers to make themselves known.

By the mid 1960s, public fetes were taking place across T&T, each pushing forward their own local superstars (the legendary Sundar Popo emerged from this circuit). In 1968, another Surinamese artist, Dropati (a veteran, too, of the groundbreaking 1963 tour) released the album *Let's Sing and Dance*, a collection of traditional Hindu wedding songs, again put through the wringer of Caribbean culture. No less than Ramdeo Chaitoe a full decade before, her revolutionary arrangements of the traditional "Gowri Pooja" and "Lawa" established Dropati as a superstar not only within the East Indian community, but across T&T as a whole. Throughout the land, aspiring young performers set about creating their own, similar fusion.

MASTANA BAHAR

By the late 1960s, East Indian "pop" music was the most exciting new sound around, and the cue for the Mohammeds to inaugurate what has since become the most spectacular celebration of East India in the West Indies, the television show *Mastana Bahar*, named for the network of amateur talent contests which had long been a staple of community life. Filmed in front of an audience so large and enthusiastic that some observers have compared it to a carnival in its own right (and its champions to the Calypso Monarchs of Carnival), *Mastana Bahar* was launched in 1970. With the Mohammeds stressing their intentions to encourage a new wave in Indo-Trinidadian music, *Mastana Bahar* was initially oriented towards showcasing new Indian ("Bollywood") movies, via local interpretations of the songs and dances popularized by the biggest hits.

Original musical performances rapidly became an integral part of the event, however, together with ever more extravagant prizes, presented by a flood of willing sponsors. In 1972, a tan singer named Jameer Hosein won a car on *Mastana Bahar* and, by 2000, it was estimated that some 80,000 people had performed for the cameras. These hopefuls offered everything from distinctly amateurish renditions of the ubiquitous film themes and pop songs, to the startlingly original hybrids which saw East Indian music in general, and Indo-Trinidadian music in particular, assume such significance over the past decade. "Chutney," a term first voiced by broadcaster Hansrahjie Muragh, and named for the similarly spicy East Indian condiment, was born.

In addition, *Mastana Bahar* has become a recognized springboard to success across the musical spectrum. Gabrielle Hosein, Queen of the 2000 event with "Chutney Love," also performed that year at the Breaking New Ground event during National Rapso Month. Other successful *Mastana Bahar* performers include Sherlon, winner of the first ever Canadian Road March; Michael Salickram, of the globally renowned Shiv Shakti dance troupe, and the only male dancer ever to have taken the grand prize, in 1992; and jazz fusion legend Mungal Patasar. Ironically, the best known East Indian performer of them all, Sundar Popo, never won *Mastana Bahar*.

CHUTNEY TAKE-OVER

Throughout this period, specialist circles continued to view the now-independent Guyana and neighboring Surinam as the spearheads of the scene. However, the former's thenincumbent Peoples National Congress (PNC) government's open discrimination against the East Indian community did little to encourage the music's indigenous growth. Indeed, the PNC has subsequently been blamed for (among a multitude of other sins) the almost painfully slow gestation of Guyana's own East Indian music scene, which in turn forced the most gifted artists overseas.

It was close to two decades before artists of the caliber of Nisha Benjamin and Joyce Urmela Harris were heard by anything like a wide audience, but in the meantime, Guyana's loss could only be T&T's gain. By the late 1970s, Benjamin had followed Popo to the top of the T&T chart with her hits "Na Manu Na Manu" and "O'Maninga," describing the hardships of life for a woman employed on a sugar plantation. (She was also an outspoken opponent of the PNC.) By the early 1980s, chutney's popularity among East Indian youth was at an all-time high. For so many years, they had cast envious eyes towards the reggae of Jamaica, the calypso of the Creoles and the disco-fied pop being churned out on Bollywood movie soundtracks, and mourned their own culture's failure to create anything so exciting.

Now, through the magic of Popo, and those who were so swift to follow his lead, chutney was the equal to any of those other role models. No matter that its roots remained tangled in the tight traditions of folk-song and tan. With modern instrumentation and stinging rhythms, chutney could make the dead get up and dance. Or, at least, it could make them cease their interminable tan singing, and let the audience enjoy themselves for once — as chutney soared, so tan declined, until the streets of Barrackpore seemed strewn with old timers, lamenting the sweeping away of music that "meant something," to be replaced by the idiot gyrations of the latest chutney shouter.

Even more excitingly, chutney was still evolving, absorbing fresh influences from all over the world, but most immediately, from within the Creole community elsewhere in T&T. Soca-chutney was coming. East Indians had long figured in calypso imagery — Atilla The Hun's legendary "Dookanii" was written as early as 1939. 1947 brought Killer's popular "Grinding Masala," while the Mootoo Brothers formed one of the most important back-up bands for calypsonians in the 1950s.

Now in the early-mid 1980s, soca giants like Baron ("Raja Rani"), the Mighty Trini ("Curry Tabanca" — later covered by *Mastana Bahar* discovery Atiya), Sugar Aloes ("Roti and Dhalpourie"), Crazy ("Nani Wine"), Scrunter ("Nanny"), Becket ("Nanny Revival") and the Mighty Sparrow ("Marajin") were weighing in with their own contributions to that tradition. It was not an altogether happy relationship. "Marajin," discussing Sparrow's love for the wife of a Hindu Pandit, or priest, was banned in Guyana and frowned upon in T&T, where the very concept of mixed marriages remained alien to many older East Indians.

There was also a problem surrounding the preponderance of songs seemingly dedicated to that most venerable of souls, the maternal Indian grandmother, or Nani. By one of those peculiar quirks of linguistic fate, the word was very similar to local slang for "vagina," thus loading these songs with a wealth of double entendres — to be adored by one segment of the community, but abhorred by another.

East Indian artists were initially slow to respond to this latest musical innovation; indeed, among the first to venture into the soca-chutney field were the veteran husband and wife team Babla & Kanchan, natives of India itself. Reacting to their own long standing success in the Caribbean, they released a pair of mid-1980s albums largely covering Sundar Popo oldies in a soca style, following up with hit covers of Arrow's "Hot Hot Hot" and Baron's "Buss Up Shot."

By the end of the decade, however, T&T's own East Indian community was in action. Drupatee Ramgoonai was the movement's first superstar, breaking through in 1987 with "Pepper Pepper." She followed it up with the ribald "Lick Down Me Nani," a song which was ostensibly concerned with her grandmother being run over by a truck ("lick down" — "knock down"), but so certainly played on an equally familiar double-meaning that it generated massive controversy within the East Indian community.

The trouble did not, of course, hurt Ramgoonai. The following year, "Mr Bissessar (Roll Up de Tassa)" became one of the biggest soca hits of the year, topping the charts throughout the English-speaking Caribbean, then repeating that feat on soca listings in the US, UK and Canada. 1989's "Hotter Than a Chulha" spoke to all young East Indians whose family and friends maybe denigrated their interest in the new music — "they give me blows . . . for doing soca/ but it shows how much they know about the culture."

1989 also saw the emergence of Kancha, with the hit "Give Me Paisa." Then, in 1993, with a more tolerantly governed Guyana back in the picture, Terry Gajraj emerged from the Corentyne coastal village of Fyrish, to score one of the best selling Indo-Caribbean albums of all time, *Guyana Baboo*. Indian-inflected soca continued to explode during the 1990s. New record labels concentrating on the genre proliferated — Jamaican Me Crazy (JMC), Spice Island, Mohabir and JTS Productions were suddenly making the music available internationally, to be played in such nightclubs as New York's Calypso City and Toronto's Calypso Hut. And with the success of this new musical hybrid, so chutney's own roots began to stir once more.

With predominantly Hindi lyrics, and fresh emphasis on traditional instrumentation, T&T-born Anand Yankarran (the son of Isaac) broke through with the album *Zindabad*, a collection of tan-style folk songs; while 1996 saw Cecil Funrose score a massive hit with "Kirki Na Din."

Even more remarkable, however, were the events of 1995. Marking the 150th anniversary of the arrival of the first indentured East Indians to T&T, the year had already taken on massive significance for the community, after the government declared May 30 was a new national holiday marking "Indian Arrival Day."

The mood was obviously contagious. At carnival that February, Black Stalin won the Calypso Monarch prize with

"Sundar Popo," a tribute to the father of chutney. That fall, one of the biggest hits in the weeks leading up to the national General Election was Jairam Dindial's insistent "We're Voting UNC," referring to the predominantly East Indian led United National Congress party headed by Basdeo Panday. And in November, T&T's electorate agreed with him, electing a coalition formed between the UNC and the once distinctly anti-Hindu NAR (National Alliance For Reconstruction).

Not everybody was thrilled by that particular turn of events. 1996 Calypso Monarch Cro-Cro won his title with a song openly critical of the Creole community for allowing Panday's victory. But against his bad-tempered triumph could be balanced the remarkable success of Sonny Mann, a 61 year old East Indian chutney and tan singer, suddenly jolted out of semi-obscurity when a song he recorded four years earlier, "Lotay La," became one of the biggest hits of the season, despite being largely performed in the Bhojpuri dialect. An anthem at the road march, "Lotay La" had already earned Mann the inaugural Chutney Monarch title during the pre-carnival season; now, Mann announced he intended competing for the Soca Monarch crown as well.

Unfortunately, that appears to have been a step too far. Tradition dictated that entrants for that competition perform new material only, but when the organizing committee pointed this prohibition out to Mann, he countered by threatening legal action. Faced with such a threat, the committee relented, but the crowd was less understanding. As Mann took the stage, he was met with a hail of boos, bottles and the unmistakable message that the audience had come to hear new soca, not old chutney. Mann left the stage without singing a note, but in his ignomy, scored a victory regardless. The following year saw a Chutney-Soca Monarch competition added to the carnival bill itself.

Other performers, meanwhile, were swift to protest, in word or song, Cro-Cro's winning performance at the 1996 event, and the ugly scenes which marred the event for Mann himself. Brother Marvin came close to taking the Monarch title with "Jihaaji Bhai" ("shipmate"), a song in praise of the racial unity which Panday's government promised. General Grant scored with a dub-chutney hybrid which he described as "bhangra- muffin," while Luta (1994 Calypso Monarch), Crazy, Marcia Miranda and Tony Ricardo also rallied behind the chutney flag.

Each of these records was enormous in the Caribbean. Sales records were, and still are, established and then broken on an almost monthly basis — the days when Ramdeo Chaitoe and Dropati topped the table were long gone. Sponsorship blossomed. Contestants at the 2001 Chutney Soca Monarch competition were guaranteed a $1,000 prize from sponsors WITCO simply for appearing. The winner collected a purse of $125,000; the runner-up received $40,000; third place $20,000.

Sharlene Boodhram's "Calcutta Woman" not only took the Caribbean by storm, it also entered several US charts; while her "Joe Le Taxi" clashed so many cultures (including perky Europop) that it should be irresistible to everyone. Other major sellers have included Anand Yankarran's "Nand Baba," Double D's "Ragga Dulahin," Madain Ramdas' "Chutney Genie" and Nirmal "Massive." Gosine's "Bhabuni" (banned by several radio stations because of a perceived reference to fellatio) was also a major seller. Angela Ramoutar, 1998 Chutney Queen, also boasts vast international popularity.

Today, American chain stores carry chutney collections as carelessly as any other musical genre.

CHUTNEY SOCA MONARCHS

1997 Heeralal Rampartap
1998 Rikki Jai
1999 Rikki Jai
2000 Rooplal Girdharrie
2001 Rikki Jai

RECOMMENDED LISTENING

Caribbean Voyage: East Indian Music in the West Indies (Rounder) 1999

Recorded in 1962, wedding, funereal and devotional performances naturally pinpoint the ceremonial nature of the music, and of course there is little reference to the growing popularity of "pop." But still this far reaching sampling is essential listening for anybody anxious to trace the manifold strands woven into the modern sound.

East Indian Drums of Tunapuna, Trinidad (Cook Records) 1956

Possibly the earliest field recording was made by American Emory Cook and revolves, as the title suggests, around the manifold ceremonial purposes to which the drums (primarily tassa) were put.

East Indian Music in the West Indies (Peter Manuel) 2000

Only available with author Manuel's book of the same name (see bibliography), this 12 song disc attempts the impossible — and very nearly achieves it. Surveying its subject from tan to chutney (via examples of thumri, ghazal and holi), including several tracks from the Mohammed brothers' indispensable Windsor records catalog, the album features contributions from traditional performers Isaac Yankarran, Jeevan Dhanram and Dino Boodram vying with modern stars Manradjie Lachman, Anand Yankarran and Rasika Dindial (the compulsive "D'Lazy Man").

Tent Singing by Our Classical Masters (Windsor Records) 1974

Produced by Moean Mohammed, a raw recording of some

of T&T's most important tan performers, including Sook-deo Sookhraj, Abdul "Kush" Razack, Dev Bansraj Ramkis-soon and Sharm Yankarran.

Chutney Gold (JMC) 1998–date

On-going series collecting the greatest chutney/chutney-soca hits of the year gone by.

Hot & Spicy Chutney (Music Club) 1998

Enjoyable, if slightly one-dimensional 14 track collection highlighting some of the bigger names on the contemporary soca-scene — Home Front, Double D, Cecil Fonrose, An-and Yankarran. The inclusion of Sundar Popo adds some historical resonance to the collection, while Sally Edwards' irrepressible "Lotayla," a response to Sonny Mann's 1995 hit, highlights the modern era's reliance on his early model.

JOHNNY CLARKE

STYLE *reggae (roots)*
BORN *January, 1955 (Whitfield Town, JA)*

Clarke first came to attention in 1971, when he won one of impresario Tony Mack's talent contests in Bull Bay, and was rewarded with a meeting with producer Clancy Eccles. (Mack himself had recorded several sessions with Eccles, usually as a backing vocalist — he appears on several Slim Smith singles from the time).

Clark's debut single, "God Made the Sea and the Sun," did not sell and, disappointed by the lack of promotion which Eccles put into the record, Clarke moved on, linking with producer Rupie Edwards. Backed by a stellar band including Jackie Jackson (bass), Carlton Davis (drums), Hux Brown (guitar), Tommy McCook (sax), Edwards oversaw Clarke's first hits in 1973, "Everyday Wondering" and "Ju-lie," before transforming the former into his own worldwide hit "Ire Feelings (Skanga)." Even more than the original version (which didn't actually give Clarke's name on the label), "Ire Feelings" catapulted the singer into the head-lines, one of the new breed of roots conscious radicals burst-ing out of JA, and one of the most in-demand.

Breaking with Edwards, Clarke cut "Jump Back Baby" with producer Glen Brown (1974) and "Golden Snake" for the little-known Atom label (produced by Stamma), before linking with Bunny Lee and the Aggrovators in 1974. "None Shall Escape the Judgement" was originally cut with com-poser Earl Zero's own vocal trio backing Clarke, however, the song was rerecorded as a solo effort and became an im-mediate smash. (It also titled Clarke's debut album.)

Clarke now launched into an era of unparalleled bril-liance, swinging effortlessly between militant dread ("Cold I Up," "Enter into His Gates with Praise," "Joshua's Word") and superb lovers rock — "Rock with Me Baby." He also proved a remarkable interpreter of other people's material.

John Holt was an especial favorite, and Clarke scored with versions of his "Fancy Make-Up," "Stranger in Love," "So Much Pain" and "Left with a Broken Heart." Many of these were originally released on bassist Robbie Shakespeare's own Bar-Bell label.

In 1975, Clarke's "Move Out a Babylon Rastaman" (itself set to another Holt rhythm, "Sad News") produced another DJ sensation, as Dillinger took it for his "Commercial Locks." Clarke and Dillinger subsequently combined for the late 1970s hits "Babylon Yard," "Waiting in Vain" and "Empty Chair."

The singer won Jamaica's Artist of the Year award for 1974, and took it again in 1975, after scoring further Lee-led hits "Too Much War," "Rebel Soldiering," "Joyful Fes-tival," "Bring It on Home to Me" and "You Keep on Run-ning." Added to the list were versions of Derrick Morgan's "Don't Call Me Daddy" and a pair of Bob Marley covers, "Put It On" and a monster hit recounting of "No Woman No Cry," which went onto sell more than 40,000 copies in Jamaica alone.

After two further albums, *Movin' Out* and *I'm Gonna Put It On*, Clarke was among the Jamaican contingent signed to Virgin Records' Front Line subsidiary in 1976. Again pro-duced by Lee, the *Authorized Version* and *Rockers Time Now* albums followed, sensational sets which combined some of the finest yet Clarke originals with covers of Burn-ing Spear, the Mighty Diamonds, the Abyssinians and Hopeton Lewis. The singles "I Wish It Could Go on For-ever," "Roots Natty Roots Natty Congo" are crucial.

Into the late 1970s, Clarke and Lee continued to collab-orate for some excellent recordings — "My Woman's Love," "Age Is Growing," "Blood Dunza" (dunza is slang for money), "Peace and Love in the Ghetto," Delroy Wilson's "Riding for a Fall" and "Every Knee Shall Bow" (subject to a mighty U-Roy toast on the Jamaican 12-inch). 1978's *Sweet Conversation* album, with its excellent take on John Holt's classic "Wear You to the Ball Tonight," and Clarke's duets with Hortense Ellis on Lee's 1978 *Lovers' Rock* album were career stand-outs.

Other highlights from this period included the self-produced "Jah Love Is with I," cut with the Revolutionaries, and "Can I Change Your Mind" (both 1979), while Clarke also undertook some outside production, with Biddy Brown and Alphonso Love.

Frequently in tandem with producer S Douglas, Clarke continued scoring hits during the early 1980s — "Babylon" (1980), "Can't Get Enough," "Guide Us Jah," "You Better Try," "Give Me Love" (1982), "Do I Do I" and "Young Rebel" (1983). A reunion with Bunny Lee provoked the *I Man Come Again* album, and the singles "Rude Boy," "Get in the Groove" and "Stop Them Jah." He also enjoyed another major hit with the Joe Gibbs' produced "Like a Soldier" (1983).

Throughout this period, however, Clarke's profile was unquestionably and, apparently unaccountably, dipping — with dire consequences for his record sales. Year after year he was conspicuously absent from Reggae Sunsplash. Year after year, too, the man who was voted Jamaica's top vocalist five years running, was suddenly having trouble even getting radio play.

The singer himself put the blame on a dispute with Bob Marley's estate which dated back to his cover of "No Woman No Cry" — Marley himself had refused to release his own version of the song as a single in Jamaica, hoping to encourage album sales. Clarke's cover version neatly circumvented that strategy and, in an interview with journalist Chuck Foster, Clarke insisted he was never forgiven. Though Clarke continued releasing quality records (including one album with fellow Striker veteran Cornell Campbell), it took a complete change of scenery to prompt a major resurgence.

Relocating to London in 1983, Clarke linked with Englishman Neil "Mad Professor" Fraser for the *Yard Style* (1983) and *Give Thanks* (1985) albums, while recordings with King Tubby (whose dubs had frequently backed Clarke's Striker-era b-sides), Errol Thompson and Prince Jammy saw him move effortlessly into the dance hall era. Periodic comebacks have linked him with Prince Jazzbo (1992's *Rasta Nuh Fear*) and Niney Holness (1997's *Rock with Me*). He also — finally — appeared at Sunsplash 95. Clarke continues to tour regularly.

DISCOGRAPHY

8 **None Shall Escape the Judgement (Total Sounds — JA) 1974**
With Bunny Lee's "flying cymbals" sound still a novelty, Clarke's debut album sounded like nothing on earth — and that despite being comprised almost exclusively of recent hits. Of the more unusual inclusions, the Tams' US soul hit "Hey Girl Don't Bother Me" takes some beating.

7 **Moving Out (Total Sounds — JA) 1975**
Another Lee-led classic, fairly evenly split between original rootsy songs and Studio One covers, with John Holt and Delroy Wilson obviously Clarke's favorites.

7 **I'm Gonna Put It On (Vulcan — UK) 1975**
Like the same period *Wondering* (Third World — UK), drawn from the cream of Clarke's 1975 sessions with Lee . . . the hit title track, "No Woman No Cry," "Creation Rebel" and "Joyful Festival". . . oh, and a redundant "The Tide Is High."

8 **Authorised Version (Virgin) 1976**
10 **Rocker's Time Now (Virgin) 1976**

The title track grabs you by the throat and the album never lets go. One of the all-time greats, it features Clarke's luxurious vocals, dramatic roots with a dub edge (King Tubby mixes), and a dreamy cover of "Satta Amasa Gana." Other highlights include "African Roots," "Ites Green and Gold," "Declaration of Rights" and "Natty Dreadlocks Stand Up Right," but you cannot play favorites with an album like this.

9 **Don't Stay Out Late (Paradise — UK) 1976**
Any album featuring the mighty "Blood Dunza" has to be considered more or less essential; add "Judgement Day" and "They Can't Conquer I and I," and this Bunny Lee production ranks among Clarke's very finest.

7 **Up Park Camp (Justice — UK) 1977**
7 **Girl I Love You (Justice — UK) 1977**
8 **Sweet Conversation (Third World — UK) 1978**
The album that reaffirmed the majesty of "Wear You to the Ball Tonight" also includes "Sinners Repent," "A Real Rastaman" and, for a change of pace, "Put on Your Dancing Shoes."

6 **King of the Arena (Third World — UK) 1978**
7 **Satisfaction (Third World — UK) 1979**
6 **Down in a Babylon (1980) (Cha Cha — UK)**
8 **I Man Come Again (Black Music — UK) 1982**
No-one coaxes Clarke like Bunny Lee, with the "Don't Want to Be No Rude Boy" anthem a statement of defiant intent par excellence.

7 **Yard Style (Ariwa — UK) 1983**
The incendiary "Nuclear Weapon" (a 1984 single) is the most obvious highlight; other first rate inclusions are "Mount Zion," "Dread Like a Lion" and "Top Fight."

7 **Sly & Robbie Present the Best of Johnny Clarke (Vista Sounds — UK) 1985**
Not quite the best, but certainly a strong collection which includes an updated "Bring It on Home to Me," plus "I'll Never Fall in Love Again," "Love Me Forever" and "We a Africa." The sharp mid-1980s production does get a little wearing after a while, but Clarke's vocals remain angelic.

7 **Give Thanks (Ariwa — UK) 1985**
"When I Fall in Love" isn't the most promising opener, but once it hits its stride, *Give Thanks* is at least the equal of its predecessor as Clarke mixes up his winning formula with the addition of a searing soul song and a pair of tracks featuring African beats.

7 **Rasta No Fear (Sonic Sounds — UK) 1992**
Intriguing comeback collusion with Prince Jazzbo. The clash of Clarke's earthy tones and Jazzbo's techno sheen

occasionally jars, but more often it adds an almost surprisingly satisfying edge.

7 **Rock with Me (—JA) 1997**

JOHNNY CLARKE & CORNELL CAMPBELL

6 **Johnny Clarke Meets Cornell Campbell in New Style (Vista Sounds—UK) 1983**

One side apiece leaves Clarke just enough room to pack punchy takes on "None Shall Escape," "Jah Jah in Idea" and "The Ruler"; Campbell strikes back with a surprisingly effective "Duke of Earl."

JOHNNY CLARKE & PAT KELLY/HORTENSE ELLIS

7 **Lovers Rock (Third World—UK) 1978**

Kelly's cuts are solo only (but do include a wonderful "People Get Ready"), alternating with five great Clarke/Ellis duets — "Baby Come Back to Me," "In Paradise," "Dearest," "You're Mine" and "This Is My Story."

JOHNNY CLARKE & DELROY WILSON/DOREEN SCHAEFFER

5 **Lovers Rock Vol. 2 (Third World—UK) 1979**

Weak attempt to duplicate the first volume, but we really didn't need Clarke's versions of "Perfidia" and "She Wears My Ring."

SELECTED COMPILATIONS & ARCHIVE RELEASES

7 **Showcase (Paradise—UK) 1979**

Enjoyable, if scarcely essential gathering of recent Bunny Lee singles ("Again," "Loving Rock," "Wide Awake in a Dream," "Disgraceful" among them) in both vocal and version style.

8 **Don't Trouble Trouble (Attack—UK) 1989**

A stunning collection of early Bunny Lee productions omitted from Clarke's debut album, with even the weaker material (a cover of "Tears on My Pillow" could have stayed at home) working in the context of the entire set.

9 **Johnny in the Echo Chamber (Trojan—UK) 1989**

Credited to the Aggrovators, a dramatic restructuring of Clarke's greatest hits — "A Crabit Version," "A Colder Version," "Soldering Version," "Dub on My Pillow" and "Dub It on Home" included.

8 **Authorised Rockers (Front Line) 1991**

There should be no reason on earth not to own the two Front Line albums in their original form. But just in case you can think of one, this sampling divides the pair into one magnificent whole.

7 **Originally Mr Clarke (Clock Tower) 1995**

Clarke is at his most radical on this compilation of Bunny Lee produced rebel fired songs, including such cries against the West as "Blood Dunza" and "Every Knee Shall Bow."

8 **Dreader Dread 1976–78 (Blood & Fire—UK) 1998**

Full blooded Bunny Lee compilation includes a handful of lost 12-inch mixes (including a stunning "Every Knee"), the brittle "Fire & Brimstone a Go Burn the Wicked" and a loose take on Peter Tosh's "I'm the Toughest," retitled "Top Rank."

JIMMY CLIFF

STYLE *reggae*
BORN *James Chambers, 4/1/48 (St Catherine, JA)*

Before Bob Marley burst onto the international scene in the mid-1970s, the term "reggae" meant just one thing to many people — Jimmy Cliff. Composer and performer of some of the genre's biggest hits during the early 1970s and star of the midnight theater classic *The Harder They Come*, he was also, for anybody interested in delving deep into the music's history, one of the most consistent names on both the Jamaican and British scenes since the early 1960s.

An accomplished child performer (he once appeared before 7,000 people at a county fair, performing Fats Domino's "Be My Guest"), Cliff moved to Kingston from St Catherine at the age of 14, intent only on carving himself a career in music — he adopted the surname Cliff because it implied the heights he aspired to.

Pioneering producer Count Boysie was first to sense his potential, but "Daisy Got Me Crazy" went nowhere, a fate which also attended the Sir Cavalier produced "I'm Sorry." Derrick Morgan then entered the scene, introducing the boy to producer Leslie Kong and, in late 1962, Cliff's next single, "Hurricane Hattie," became a major hit almost precisely one year after the storm of the same name ravaged the Caribbean.

Island Records chief Chris Blackwell was another of Cliff's early admirers, releasing a constant stream of his singles in the UK throughout the 1960s, initially aimed towards the West Indian community alone but, increasingly, with an eye towards a wider market as well. Island label issues included songs which remain the crown jewels in any modern ska collection — "Miss Jamaica," "Since Lately" (1962), "My Lucky Day," "King of Kings," "Miss Universe," "The Prodigal," "The Man," "You Are Never too Old" (1963), "One Eyed Jacks," "Call on Me" and "Pride and Passion" in 1964. Finally, Blackwell persuaded Cliff to relocate to the UK on a permanent basis.

Cliff was no stranger to attempts to export Jamaica's music. In August, 1964, he joined Byron Lee and Prince Buster among Jamaica's cultural representatives at the New York World's Fair; in 1965, he enjoyed a residency at the Bus Palladium in Paris; all the while maintaining a stream of quality singles.

By 1967, Island Records' own emphasis had moved away from Caribbean music, and the label was now actively courting the rock underground. Cliff was one of the mere handful of Jamaican artists who remained on the roster,

The King of Kings—Jimmy Cliff.

clearly with an eye towards the then burgeoning singer-songwriter market.

With Cliff focussing his own writing accordingly, "Aim and Ambition," "Give and Take," "I Got a Feeling," "Hard Road to Travel," "That's the Way Life Goes" (1967), "Set Me Free," "Here I Come" and International Song Festival winner "Waterfall" (1968) all garnered increasing attention from this new target audience, both in their own right and via Cliff's appearances on Island samplers of the day, rubbing shoulders with such giants of underground rock as Mott The Hoople, Jethro Tull and King Crimson.

However, he was not to remain in the UK for long. In 1968, Cliff relocated to Brazil, where "Waterfall" proved a massive hit; he was there when he heard he had finally broken through internationally. In fall, 1969, the Leslie Kong produced "Wonderful World, Beautiful People" made #6 in the UK and #25 in America. Cliff promptly followed through with "Vietnam," a righteous protest song which confirmed his place in the same arena of thoughtful adult-oriented troubadours as Curtis Mayfield, Cat Stevens and the like.

A lesser hit than its predecessor, "Vietnam" nevertheless prompted a warm reception for his *Jimmy Cliff/Wonderful World* sophomore album. It also drew passionate responses from both Bob Dylan, who called "Vietnam" the best protest song he had ever heard, and Paul Simon, who was so enamored with Cliff's sound that he later traveled to Kingston to record his "Mother and Child Reunion" single at Dynamic Sounds Studio with the same producer (Kong) and musicians Cliff had employed — Neville Hinds (organ), Jackie Jackson (bass), Winston Grennan (drums).

July, 1970, brought Cliff another massive hit with a cover of Island labelmate Cat Stevens' own "Wild World" (Stevens also produced the recording). Weeks later, Desmond Dekker made #2 in the UK with a buoyant cover of Cliff's "You Can Get It if You Really Want."

However, critical disappointment greeted the soulful *Another Circle* album and the singles "Synthetic World" and the brooding "Sitting in Limbo" (written while mourning the death of Leslie Kong in August, 1971), and when Cliff returned to Jamaica, it was to discover that much of his home support, too, had faded. But while Cliff's roots credibility was undoubtedly in tatters (a consequence, of course, of his vast musical shift), still his next move resulted in one of the most significant events in the entire history of Jamaican music, the movie *The Harder They Come*.

The story was loosely based on the life of Ivanhoe "Rhygin" Martin, a late 1940s outlaw whose escapades thrilled the populace and who history has determined to be the archetypal rude boy. (Prince Buster's "Rhygin" instrumental also paid tribute to Martin.) Updating Martin's own downtown Kingston haunts to the early 1970s, the story emerged a hard-hitting epic set equally in the streets and recording studios of Kingston, with Cliff starring as a musical hopeful inextricably involved in the city's gangland.

The Harder They Come was written and produced by Perry Henzell, but the soundtrack — predominantly Cliff, but also featuring the Melodians, the Maytals, Desmond Dekker, the Slickers and the then hot DJ Scotty — was no less powerful. Cliff's title track, in particular, appeared to sum up the aspirations, and the eventual fate, of every soul in the film and, by extension, on the streets which the film graphically depicted. While the movie became the most successful Jamaican release of all time, the soundtrack likewise became one of the biggest selling albums.

Despite *The Harder They Come* not being granted a US release until 1975, Cliff was nevertheless poised on the brink of superstardom. But while neither his reputation nor the quality of his music have ever declined, he was never to take that one final step. Perhaps assuming the job was already done, Island Records turned its marketing muscle towards another superstar in waiting, Bob Marley, employing many of the same techniques in his favor as had been designed for Cliff — not least of all the targeting of his music towards a non-reggae audience.

Cliff himself was allowed to leave the label after a decade on the roster; he joined Reprise (EMI in the UK), but 1973's *Unlimited* album did not begin to capitalize on the success of its predecessor. It was with wry irony indeed that he titled his next album after one of his less successful pre-movie singles, 1972's *Struggling Man*.

1973 also saw Cliff embrace the Muslim faith, adopting the name Na'im Bashir, and in 1974, he journeyed to Africa to research his ancestry. Of course this new spirituality flavored his future work; it also led Cliff towards some of the best music of his career beginning with 1975's *Follow My Mind* album.

Buoyed by the long awaited American theatrical release of *The Harder They Come*, *Follow My Mind* became Cliff's first ever US chart entry (it peaked at #195). The next year saw Cliff paired with the legendary English producer Andrew Loog Oldham (Rolling Stones, Immediate Records) to record a live album, which the Reprise label had already decided was to be cunningly disguised as a greatest hits collection.

But if his label, Reprise, hoped it might promote Cliff on the nostalgia circuit, the singer had other ideas. Taped at shows in Massachusetts and New York, with a band led by Ernest Ranglin (guitar) and also featuring Joe Higgs (vocals, percussion) and the rhythm section of Carlton Davis and Earl Walker, Cliff's performance is as abrasive as it's electrifying.

Cliff's next studio albums, 1978's *Give Thanx*, 1979's *Oh Jamaica* and 1980's *I Am the Living*, echoed Cliff's determination to remain contemporary — an admirable resolution at a time when many of his Jamaican peers were enjoying a whole new lease of retro-flavored life courtesy of Britain's 2-Tone ska revival. While Desmond Dekker, Prince Buster, Rico Rodriguez, Laurel Aitken and more readily leaped aboard the reborn ska bandwagon, Cliff continued pursuing his own path.

He launched his own Sunpower label, and one of his acts, Full Experience, recorded an entire album with Lee Perry, then at the peak of his Black Ark experimentation (sadly, the album was never released).

After nine years with Reprise/Warners, *Give the People What They Want* proved Cliff's final album for the company. He had just performed major concerts in Nigeria and Soweto, South Africa, and this latest, deeply roots-conscious collection reflected his concerns over those countries' policies. (A concert film, *Bongo Man*, captured the strength of Cliff's current live show.)

He moved next to the Columbia label, forming a new backing band, Oneness, around Earl "Chinna" Smith and Radcliff Bryan (guitars), Bertram McLean (bass), Ansell Collins and Phil Ramocan (keyboards), Mikey Boo Richards (drums) and Sticky Thompson (drums). This line-up cut the *Special* album (highlighted by the singles "Roots Radical" and "Peace Officer"), before launching onto a six week US tour with Peter Tosh.

Cliff was still capable of delivering major surprises, too. He was well-received at Sunsplash 81, while 1983's *The Power and the Glory* album featured one track, "Reggae Nights," co-written with LaToya Jackson, and two recorded in New Jersey with disco funk kings Kool & The Gang. Though sales were unspectacular, the album was nominated for the inaugural Best Reggae Album Grammy.

Kool & The Gang were again present on Cliff's next album, 1985's *Cliff Hanger* and, this time around, the pairing won the Grammy. Equally exciting, that same year saw Cliff involved personally in the Artists United Against Apartheid movement, and indirectly with USA For Africa — Bruce Springsteen covered Cliff's 1972 single "Trapped" for the organization's album. A return to movies, meanwhile, saw

Cliff co-star with Peter O'Toole and Robin Williams in the comedy *Club Paradise*; the attendant soundtrack featured seven Cliff songs, including a duet with English songwriter Elvis Costello, "Seven Day Weekend."

Cliff and the Oneness Band (now featuring Glen Browne — bass; and Anthony Williams — drums) cut one final album for Columbia — his last, too, to feature any input from the now disbanded Kool & The Gang. That group's Khalis Bayyan produced the bulk of *Hanging Fire* at Tuff Gong; two further songs dated from sessions at Congo's Industrie Africane du Disque studios, and featured members of the Grand Zico Band of Zaire ("Love Me Love Me") and Afriza International Band of Zaire ("Girls and Cars").

Over the next two years, two further Cliff albums appeared in Jamaica and the UK, together with the excellent single "Pressure" (1989); then, in 1993, Cliff's version of Johnny Nash's "I Can See Clearly Now" leaped from the movie soundtrack *Cool Runnings*, to hit the US Top 20 — his first chart hit since "Come into My Life," 23 years before. Two years later, Cliff joined with Lebo M to record a version of "Hakuna Matata," from the *Lion King* movie. Cliff's most recent album, *Humanitarian*, appeared in 1999.

DISCOGRAPHY

7 **Hard Road to Travel (Island — UK) 1968**
8 **Wonderful World UK title *Jimmy Cliff* (A&M) 1969**

Cliff's early years and greatest hits have been recycled so many times that it's easy to overlook two albums which themselves are the equal of any of his most famous songs. "My Ancestors," "Time Will Tell," "Come into My Life"... the reggae may be restrained, but Cliff is like a pitbull.

8 **Another Cycle (Island — UK) 1971**

The magnificent "Sitting In Limbo," "Opportunity Only Knocks Once" and "Take a Look at Yourself" are the masterpieces this time, on an album which may not be quite as consistent as its predecessors, but certainly doesn't lack for impact.

10 **The Harder They Come — Original Soundtrack (Island — UK) 1972**

Not a Cliff album per se, but so integral to his career and catalog that few consider it anything else. The Maytals' "Pressure Drop" and the Slickers' "Johnny too Bad," of course, are the equal of anything else in sight, but still "You Can Get It if You Really Want," "Sitting in Limbo" and the title track are the musical personification of the life the movie depicts — all three, too, have spawned crucial covers, by Desmond Dekker, the Neville Brothers and Rolling Stone Keith Richard respectively. A fully remastered version was released on CD in 2001.

6 **Unlimited (Reprise) 1973**
7 **Struggling Man (EMI — UK) 1974**

There's an uneasy sense of discontent hanging over much of this album, but that is also one of its strengths. The ever-popular title track is joined by the admonitory "Sooner or Later" among Cliff's finest ever compositions.

6 **Music Maker [UK title *House of Exile*] (Reprise) 1974**
5 **Brave Warrior (EMI — UK) 1975**
8 **Follow My Mind (Reprise) 1975**

Arguably Cliff is never going to write a song that surprises you, but he can still crank out the classics. "Who Feels It (Knows It)," "Wahjahka Man" and bandmate Joe Higgs' "Dear Mother" are uniformly excellent, while Cliff also turns in such a stunning version of Marley's "No Woman No Cry" that it could have been written purposefully for him.

9 **Live — In Concert (Reprise) 1976**

If it walks like a hits collection and talks like a hits collection. . . chances are it's a complete reinvention of Cliff's ouvre. While roots meet rock with a seamless majesty which even Bob Marley had yet to visualize, Cliff positively refused to rest on past laurels — and that despite just two tracks ("Struggling Man" and "Fountain of Life") representing his last three years' work.

8 **Give Thanx (WB) 1978**

Cliff mixes up his winning formula with the addition of a searing soul song and a pair of tracks featuring African beats. For the rest, the vocalist does what he does best, belt out the best reggae pop-lite in the world.

7 **Oh Jamaica (EMI — UK) 1979**
6 **I Am the Living (WB) 1980**
6 **Give the People What They Want (WB) 1981**
8 **Special (CBS — UK) 1982**

With guests Sly Dunbar, Dean Fraser and Rolling Stone Ron Wood, a powerful musical vision bolstered by some of Cliff's heaviest rhythms and moodiest themes yet ("Peace Officer," "Roots Radical"). Some odd vocal trickery, however, leaves one of the best songs, "Love Is All," sounding as though it was recorded at slightly the wrong speed. Either that, or there was a helium leak in the studio that day.

7 **The Power And The Glory (Columbia) 1983**
6 **Cliff Hanger (Columbia) 1985**

With hindsight, teaming up with Kool & The Gang probably wasn't Cliff's best commercial decision — all the more so since they themselves were nosediving into the doldrums at the time. But while the album is largely (and sometimes laughably) superficial, "Hot Shot" leaps out like a rocket on album and, if you can track it down, burns even brighter across the six minute dub mix on the 12-inch single.

4 Hanging Fire (Columbia) 1988

Even if the title, a slang expression for "waiting around" (or maybe "sitting in limbo"!) was ironic, Cliff has been marking time too long. The African elements of the album suggest he's getting ready to start moving again, but too much (the futile "Reggae Down Babylon" most of all) is lazy Cliff-by-numbers.

5 Images (UK title *Save Our Planet Earth*) (Cliff) 1989
6 Breakout (JRS) 1992

The self-affirming "Stepping Out of Limbo" and a clutch of heartfelt political message songs see Cliff return to past concerns, at the same time as striving for modern studio credibility. The result is not always comforting, but after the tech-for-tech's sake late 80s albums, this is a veritable return to form.

6 The Cool Runner—Live in London (More Music) 1995
5 Samba Reggae (Lagoon) 1995

Blandly entertaining album built upon the hit credentials of the title track, but not offering much more than a fistful of new songs in a similar vein.

5 Humanitarian (Eureka) 1999

Disappointing comeback which blends strong Cliff compositions like "Giants" and the title track with bland reggae muzak covers of the Beatles' "Ob-La-Di Ob-La-Da" and Carole King's "You've Got a Friend."

SELECTED COMPILATIONS & ARCHIVE RELEASES

8 The Best of Jimmy Cliff (Island—UK) 1976

No surprises included, but a non-stop barrage of brilliance all the same.

7 Gold Collection (Tristar—FRA) 1994

The Columbia years condensed around a generally well-chosen 15 songs. A similar, but shorter, domestic collection, *Reggae Man*, appeared two years later.

9 Ultimate Collection (Hip-O) 1999

A solid 19 song collection tracking powerfully from 1969–74, then sporadically through to '99, clearly indicating the gaping need for an all encompassing Cliff box set. You can't argue with the inclusions (the Leslie Kong produced "Bongo Man," unreleased until 1984's *Reggae Greats* collection, is especially welcome), but the absentees are heartbreaking.

8 The Best of Jimmy Cliff (Music Club) 2000

13 track collection drawing from the *Wonderful World* album and associated 1969–70 45s. At its best, Cliff is revealed as one of the most thoughtful bards on a scene which was overflowing with earnest muse — his strength, however, is that he was never po-faced about it.

8 The Messenger (Metro) 2000

Excellent Island-era digest, reminding us once again of just how much the young Cliff had to offer the hearts and souls of mature rock listeners everywhere.

EMORY COOK/COOK RECORDS

musicologist/producer
BORN *San Francisco, USA*

"Sound is a way of daydreaming, an escape into the wild blue. A bad recording interferes with that escape, forcing the listener's imagination to strain against natural elements." With that quotation as his personal mantra, US-born recording engineer and audio pioneer Emory Cook set about amassing (and releasing) a vast body of recordings, all captured on equipment designed by Cook himself. Among his most notable inventions were a method of reducing the distortion then considered an unavoidable by-product of record manufacture, and the "binaural," or two channel recordings which we today know as stereo.

Between 1952–66, his own Cook Records label released over 140 albums, drawing from sources all over the world. It was his work in the Caribbean, however, which stands out the furthest — at a time when recorded calypso music was still the province of either tight American studio orchestras or poor local efforts, Cook swung into the region with an unquenchable enthusiasm for the excitement of the music, and a refusal to accept that that excitement could not be captured on wax.

Frequently recording live wherever singers and bands gathered (as opposed to the then accepted method of bringing the performers into a studio), he not only caught the music in its native environment, he did so at a time when calypso itself was at its most exciting high in years, the post-war period which was thrusting a whole new generation of performers and styles into the spotlight. He was especially fascinated by the still developing pan tradition, and many of Cook's most prized recordings feature steel bands.

Neither was Cook concerned with carnival alone. Traveling the Trinidadian countryside, he recorded music wherever he heard it — the funereal "bongo," the violent "kalinda," the percussive "tamboo bamboo." In later years, musicologists compiled the calypsonian family tree which incorporated each of these musical styles; for Cook, it was enough simply that they were preserved. Other crucial recordings took place in Antigua, British Guiana, Cuba, Grenada, Haiti, Jamaica, Martinique, Puerto Rico, St Lucia and the Virgin Islands.

Cook donated his entire collection to the Smithsonian in 1990; a full restoration and reissue program is currently underway.

COOK RECORDS SELECTED SINGLES

The following catalogs a sampling of Cook label 45s, listed chronologically by catalog number.

5838 Lord Melody: Peddlers/Michael (1958)

5873 Johnny Gomez: Scandal/Mr Allison (1959)

5875 Fitzvaughn Bryan: Calypso Vicki/Cook's Cooking (1959)

5901 Fitzvaughn Bryan: Mangoes/Mi Beso (1959)

5905 Merrymakers Steel Band: Explorer/Lillit (1959)

5925 Rafie Camacho: Lost Generation/Play Ball (1959)

5926 Georges Trio: I Want a Hula Hula Girl/Calypso Christmas (1959)

5930 King Striker: Two Smart Calypsonians/West Indians in England (1959)

5932 Teentones: Mangoes/Mathilda (1959)

5939 The Woodpeckers: Woodpeckers' Christmas Party/I Want a Hula Hula Girl (1959)

5962 Lord Melody: The Iceman/Polly Carr (1960)

5964 Mighty Spoiler: Twin Brother/Tarzan (1959)

5976 Olive Walke's La Petit Musical: Etat Bon/Beaubeen Chapeau (1959)

5994 Young Killer: Cutting Cane/Spreading Joy (1960)

6006 Mighty Sparrow: Short Little Shorts/No More Rocking & Rolling (1960)

6014 Nerlynn Taitt: Cupid/Mambo Rhythm (1961)

6019 Bing Serrao & The Ramblers: Three in One Saga/Nothing in Common (1960)

6025 Rod Borde & Orchestra: Yellow Bird/Sad Sack (1959)

6038 Johnny Gomez: Gloria/Cameraman (1960)

6047 St Joseph Convent Choir: Little Shepherd Boy/Rejoice It's Christmas (1960)

6077 Clarence Curvan: My Last Date with You/La Donna E Mobile (1961)

6079 Bentley Jack: Barbara/Saga Thing (1961)

6083 Ed Watson: Pachanquita/Stephanie (1961)

6099 Clarence Curvan: No Royal Jail/Honeymoon on Bombshell (1961)

6106 Nesbit Changur: Santa's Samba/Moon Ride (1961)

6108 Mighty Bomber: Lacatan/Do the Twist (1961)

6110 Cyril Diaz: Begin the Beguine/Te Oui Wa (1962)

6117 Rafie Camacho: Praise Sparrow/CYRIL DIAZ: Spider Limbo (1962)

6123 Lord Inventor & Joe Sampson: Be Careful with the Twist/Ah Going to Catch Up with You (1962)

6140 Tropical Harmony Steel Orchestra: Doorway to Paradise/Montevideo (1962)

6144 Guyana All Stars Steel Orchestra: Guyana Twist/El Reloj (1962)

6159 Tropical Harmony Steel Orchestra: Brazilian Love Song/Stranger on the Shore (1962)

CARIBBEAN LP DISCOGRAPHY

The following catalogs only releases relevant to this encyclopedia. LPs are listed chronologically, by catalog number.

00103 various: *Music of St Lucia* (1953)

01040 various: *Steel Band Clash* (1955)

01042 Brute Force Steel Band: *Of Antigua with Big Shell Band* (1955)

01043 various: *Three Rituals* (1955)

00105 spoken word: *Jose Ramon & Olga Comma Maynard Nancy Stories* (1956)

01045 various: *Drums of Trinidad* (1956)

01072 various: *Jump Up Carnival: Calypso Tent* (1956)

01180 various: *Dance Calypso* (1956)

05016 spoken word: *Calypso Lore And Legend* (1956)

05017 various: *Bamboo Tamboo Bongo & Belair* (1956)

05018 various: *East Indian Drums of Tunapuna, Trinidad* (1956)

05020 various: *Epilogue to the String Band Tradition* (1956)

10850 Rupert Clemendore: *Le Jazz Trinidad* (1956)

00101 spoken word: *Grenada Stories & Songs* (1957)

00106 various: *Afro-West Indian Cultural Practises* (1957)

00906 Lord Melody: *Lord Melody Sings Calypso* (1957)

00914 Lord Melody: *Again! Lord Melody Sings Calypso* (1957)

00916 various: *Calypso Cross Section* (1957)

01046 various: *Champion Steel Bands of Trinidad* (1957)

01047 The Katzenjammers: *The Enchanted Steelband* (1957)

01048 Brute Force Steel Band: *Music to Awaken the Ballroom Boast* (1957)

01049 Brute Force Steel Band: *Beauty & the Brute* (1957)

01185 various: *Calypso Kings & Pink Gin* (1957)

00104 various: *Rada* (1958)

01021 Groupe Mi-O: *Un Tim Bo* (1958)

01121 various: *Island in the Moonlight* (1958)

01140 various: *Steelband Promenade* (1958)

01186 Ensemble Aux Calebasses: *Meringue* (1958)

01188 various: *Dirty Jazz from Down South: Trinidadian Instrumentals* (1958)

00911 Tom Charles & His Syncopater Orchestra: *Fate for Sol* (1959)

00920 Mighty Sparrow: *King Sparrow's Calypso Carnival* (1959)

00927 Lord Melody: *Calypso Through the Looking Glass* (1959)

01123 various: *Calypso Atrocities* (1959)

00930 Fitzvaughan Bryan etc: *Belly to Belly* (1960)

01125 Lord Myrtle/Cecil Mitchel/James Convery: *Calypso Jamaica* (1960)

01023 various: *The Ramayana* (1961)

01082 Rupert Clemendore/John Buddy Williams: *Le Jazz Primitif from Trinidad* (1961)

01189 various: *Calypso Exposed* (1961)

00931 Lord Melody: *Lord Melody* (1962)

01122 various: *Hellish Calypso* (1962)

01126 Mighty Sparrow: *Sparrow in Hi Fi* (1963)

01101 The Invaders: *Steel Band in San Juan* (1964)

01102 10th Naval District Steel Band: *New Paths for Steel Band* (1965)

01280 various: *Caribbean Limbo Music* (1965)

CRAZY

STYLE *calypso/soca*

BORN *Edwin Ayoung, 1948 (Port of Spain, T&T)*

As a child, there was considerable debate as to where the young Ayoung's talents lay most prominently, as a cricketer or a musician, and the West Indies sporting world's loss was carnival's gain. Having spent some time working under the names Wong Ping (in tribute to his father's Chinese descent; Ayoung's mother is Venezuelan) and the Mighty Arawak, he was singing in a chorus when calypsonian Fred Farrell spotted him, and encouraged him to step out solo. It was Farrell, too, who dubbed the newcomer Crazy, in deference to his extravagant performing style.

Crazy made his solo debut in 1975 at the Mighty Sparrow's Original Young Brigade tent with the risque "The Electrician." A popular song, "The Electrician" became Crazy's debut single, and won him a guest spot as the token male at the Calypso Queen competition.

In 1976, Crazy joined the Charlies' label and released "Satan's Coming," with "A Great Achievement" following on Belini the next year. In early 1978, Crazy was recruited to Eddy Grant's Ice label and scored his first hit, the double A-sided "Dustbin Cover"/"Listen Joffre Serrette." Those two songs were Crazy's contribution to the 1978 National Calypso Monarch finals, where he finished second behind Calypso Rose. Another sure sign of his potential arrived in the run up to Christmas, when he hit with "Parang Soca," a devastating blend of soca and the hymnal Latin music which traditionally ruled T&T during the festive season.

The new year opened with Crazy's first full length record, *Super Album*, reviving the eponymous label he'd debuted back in 1976 with "The Electrician." It was an immediate hit, with sales topping 35,000 in T&T alone. Crazy's confidence was now so high, that even before the final selections for the Calypso Monarch finals were made, he offered to add $10,000 of his own money to the prize winner's purse, on the condition that the Mighty Sparrow and Lord Kitchener competed against him. Neither did, and Crazy's own challenge ("Guadeloupe Chick," "Back to Pan") finished a poor fourth in a competition dominated from the start by Black Stalin's formidable "Caribbean Man."

Nevertheless, Crazy scored another Christmas hit with "Muchacha," a cut from his forthcoming *Madness Is Gladness* album, with a second single, "Don't Try That," also performing well. However, delays in getting the album into the stores ensured that he was too late to even enroll in one of the calypso tents for the 1980 carnival, and he sat the event out.

Crazy was back in 1981, of course, and in 1982, he came joint second in the Road March with "Uncle Crazy." From carnival, Crazy then embarked on a European tour as a member of the Trinidad All Theatre Productions' travelling re-enactment of carnival's traditional J'Ouvert opening ceremony. (He had previously appeared in the same company's *Cinderama* in 1980 and *Snokone and the Seven Dwens* in 1981.)

With Crazy appearing as the masquerade character Chief Crazy-Without-A-Horse, J'Ouvert toured Britain, France, Switzerland, Berlin and Italy during May–June, 1982. He and co-star Lord Relator also made their London debut that August, performing at the Pickett's Lock Center in an event timed to coincide with the annual Notting Hill Carnival.

Back in T&T, Crazy joined Lord Kitchener's Calypso Revue tent for the 1983 carnival (he remains there to this day); an inauspicious performance, however, saw him finish last in the Calypso Monarch finals. He repeated this sad showing in 1984, and that despite performing one song especially written for him by Blue Boy, "Ain't Boung for You,"

and another, "Soca Tarzan," which had already finished third in the Road March. 1984 also saw Crazy play Reggae Sunsplash, one of the first soca musicians ever to do so.

1985's risque "Suck Meh Soucouyant" was the 1985 Road March winner, and "I Want It Back" brought Crazy third place in 1986. Soon after, another UK visit saw him appearing alongside Lord Relator and Brigo with the Caribbean Calypso Tent Road Show in London.

Crazy made little impact during the 1987/88 carnivals, while his 1989 campaign was marred by press controversy. His Road March entry, "Nani Wine," was co-written with Blue Boy, and it was widely rumored that Crazy had refused to pay his collaborator for his work. In fact, Blue Boy had been happy to gift his friend with the song, and said so himself.

That explanation barely satisfied the rapacious newsmen, of course, but more trouble was to arise, when Crazy was accused of trying to influence the outcome of the Road March itself, by soliciting bands and DJs to play the song as they approached the judging points during the event. Crazy did not deny the accusations. Rather, he retaliated by claiming the previous year's victor, Tambu, had already been set up as winner long before the competition began, and that he was simply trying to level the playing field. In the event, his efforts came to naught — Tambu won, "Nani Wine" finished second.

Crazy remained in comparative obscurity during the early 1990s, despite continuing to write and record popular songs for the Road March. These included 1990's "Gimme More"; "De Party Now Start" and "Advice to Married People" in 1992; "OPP in de Party" and "Dis Is How" in 1994; "Cough Remedy" and "Heat Up de Place" in 1995. It was 1997 before Crazy truly re-emerged, celebrating his 25th anniversary in calypso with the album *Still Crazy After 25 Years*, and finishing third in the Soca Chutney Monarch competition with "Jammania" and "Phulbasia." He also reached the International Soca Monarch finals with "Jump & Mash Up."

Crazy returned to the Calypso Monarch finals in 2000, one of eleven performers set to challenge Singing Sandra for the title she won the previous year. He finished seventh with "In Time to Come" and "They Don't Like de Government" — the latter song written in support of the judging committee's own disapproval of recent carnival funding cutbacks.

2001 brought the compulsively agonized "Streets of Fire," a rapso armageddon effectively punctuated with snatches of the militant folk melody "When Johnny Comes Marching Home."

SELECTED DISCOGRAPHY

7 Crazy's Super Album (Crazy) 1979

A raucous celebration, the artist's singing style sending lyrics and band skittering all over the place, but still nailing down some tremendous performances — "Guadeloupe Chick," "Is War" and the amusing "Cricket Commentary."

8 Madness Is Gladness (Crazy) 1980

"Muchacha" might not sound like a Christmas offering, but it mashed up the festive season just the same. The brutal "Our Values Are Wrong" and "One for the Road" are contrarily sober.

6 New Direction (Kalico) 1983

The title is no misnomer, as Crazy moves towards a highly stylized soca vibe. Although "Soca Tarzan" and "Can Yuh Feel It" are classics, he hasn't quite got there on this album.

7 Fire (Crazy) 1985

"Tina Turner" is as amazing as Crazy's reputation (and Miss Turner's image) suggests it should be.

7 Here I Am (Crazy) 1986

"Suck Meh Soucouyant" sounds ruder every time you hear it, but Crazy's appeal was never his subtlety!

6 Chief Crazy (Crazy) 1987

8 Crazy Crazy (Kai Soca) 1988

Swings, in effortless Crazy style, from the silliness of "Tac Tikki Tac" to the bitter "No Face No Vote."

8 Nani Wine (Trinity) 1989

Blue Boy's chutney inflected title track ode to East Indian matriarchs took the headlines, both during carnival and later, when the song's alternate meaning became apparent ("Nani" is also Creole slang for "vagina"). It also emerged the strongest song of the five tracks here (two of which are soca mix reprises), although Crazy's performance remains fluid throughout.

7 Soca Beti (Benab) 1990

10 Jump Leh We Jump (Dynamic) 1991

Brilliant Byron Lee production features the Road March warrior "Fools," and the somewhat self-celebratory "Mas in Jamaica" (that island's carnival, a Lee creation, was launched the previous year). Best of all, though, is "Scoogie Woogie," and with a title like that, it should be.

6 Crazymania (JWP) 1992

5 Let's Go Crazy (JWP) 1993

Disappointing set, with the predictably double-entendre ridden "Paul" the best thing in sight.

6 Craziah than Ever (JWP) 1994

6 Crazy for You (JWP) 1995

With eight tracks, Crazy's most ambitious album yet! Sadly, "Heat Up de Place," "Cough Remedy" and a bizarre "Route 66" don't really match the best of his past efforts.

7 Wildness (JWP) 1996

The sly admonishments of "Put Yuh House in Order" and a raw cover of Winston "Shadow" Bailey's "Wildness" highlight Crazy's finest album in half a decade.

8 Still Crazy After 25 Years (JWP) 1997

"We Want Uncle Crazy" is fabulous, a jump up and chant shout- a-long driven by infection, insurrection and maybe just a hint of nostalgia. 25 years have flashed by in mere moments.

7 Ah Crazy Again (Back To Basics) (JWP) 1999

Eleven tracks certainly give value for money in a field best known for six songs and out. "A for Apple, B for Bat" is a charming musical alphabet, "Limbo Like Me" is an absurd invitation and the recent single "D Ride"/"Mosquito" reappears in a different mix to the hit.

CULTURE

STYLE *reggae (roots)*
FORMED *1976 (Kingston, JA)*
ORIGINAL LINE-UP *Joseph Hill (vocals), Albert "Ralph" Walker (vocals), Kenneth Dayes (vocals)*

The first superstar roots vocal trio of the 1970s, Culture thrust to prominence in both Jamaica and the UK with 1976's "Two Sevens Clash," a fearsome rendering of Rastafarian portent on the eve of the year in which the two sevens would, indeed, clash — a date which tradition allegedly believed would ignite the end of the world.

The culmination, of course, of several years of increasing roots militancy (Burning Spear, the Abyssinians, much of Lee Perry's recent output), the song exploded over Jamaica like a thunder crash, and found a fascinated, sympathetic ear within England's burgeoning punk community, too. Neither did armageddon's failure to materialize throw Culture off their stride. More than two decades later, and despite a stream of albums which have never even threatened to match their debut, Culture remain a force to be reckoned with.

Of the three band members, frontman Joseph Hill had the longest track record. A former member of the Studio One houseband Soul Defenders, whose dub and version sides were already familiar to a generation of listeners, he also released one fine solo single, "Behold the Land," produced by Coxsone Dodd in 1972. (Another cut from this period, "Take Me Girl," appears on the Soul Defenders anthology *At Studio One* — Heartbeat, 1991.)

It was Hill's cousin, Albert Walker, who initially suggested they form a band together. Joined by Kenneth Dayes, the trio originally called themselves the African Disciples, but had already switched to Culture by the time they auditioned for producers Joe Gibbs and Errol Thompson in early 1976.

With Sly & Robbie and the Revolutionaries studio band laying down the rhythm, Gibbs cut Culture's debut single, "See Dem a Come," following through with "Two Sevens Clash," a record of such strength that its vision held Jamaica enthralled throughout the next year.

Throughout the first six months of 1977, as the two sevens clashed, the island was in a state of suspended animation. During the first week of July, as three sevens clashed, the Jamaica Defense Force was placed on alert, and private citizens armed themselves. On July 7, when four sevens clashed, businesses closed for the day, and there was scarcely a soul of the street.

It was brilliant political theater, then, when Prime Minister Manley chose to unveil a new Jamaican constitution at precisely 7 P.M. that evening — as the five sevens clashed. And it was several years before Hill admitted that the whole business was a hoax. Nowhere in Rastafarian lore were the two (or any other quantity of) sevens imbibed with such powerful significance.

Two Sevens Clash, Culture's debut album, ruled supreme throughout this entire period, with Joe Gibbs releasing a second Culture album, *Baldhead Bridge*, in early 1978. Culture, meanwhile, linked with Sonia Pottinger for the Jamaica-only *Cumbolo*.

Culture were one of the attractions at the inaugural Reggae Sunsplash event in summer, 1978. (They returned to the festival in 1980 and 1981.) In Britain, booming UK sales had finally pushed *Two Sevens Clash* into the national Top 60, spawning near-hit singles with "Jah Pretty Face" and, inevitably, the title track. Virgin Records promptly signed the band to the Front Line label and released Culture's third album in a year, the Pottinger produced *Harder than the Rest*. The "Stop the Fussing and Fighting" and "Trod On" 45s also appeared.

Pottinger's own High Note label released *Culture in Dub*, a dreadnought of Revolutionaries-heavy *Harder* remixes. Other Pottinger/Culture sessions from this same period appeared on the quasi-legal *Africa Stands Alone* album in 1978 and, 15 years later, as *Trod On*, the latter largely drawn from an abandoned LP project, *Black Rose*.

Buoyed by excellent sales for *Harder Than The Rest*, Front Line picked up *Cumbolo* for a full international release, also issuing the "Natty Never Get Weary" 45. But Culture released just one further album through Front Line, *International Herb*, together with a single of the title track, then effectively broke up. Hill alone helmed 1981's disappointing *Lion Rock*, the final Culture release for five years.

Hill re-emerged at Sunsplash in 1985; Walker and Dayes returned in 1986 and, produced now by Enos McLeod, Alvin Ranglin and Hill himself, Culture were reborn with *Culture in Culture* and the Sly & Robbie led *Culture at*

Work. Since that time, Culture have maintained a steady stream of reliable, if seldom sense-shattering new albums, most of which are de facto Hill solo shots. He alone appears on the majority of the 1990 album sleeves, and the departure of Dayes around the time of 1996's *One Stone* album barely caused a ripple.

DISCOGRAPHY

🔟 Two Sevens Clash (Joe Gibbs) 1977

It was the apocalyptic title track which etched Culture's legacy in stone, but this album is filled with equally memorable gems. Righteous reggae vies with resurrected sounds of the past (nods to the vocal trios of yore, hints of calypso, and some stunning rock steady) to create a rich tapestry within which Hill weaves his vivid lyrics with a true poet's passion.

8️⃣ Baldhead Bridge (Joe Gibbs) 1978

Though nothing has the visceral impact of its predecessor's title track, "Them a Payaka," "So Long Babylon" and more retain the same sense of impending doom, roots at its darkest.

7️⃣ Cumbolo (High Note — JA) 1978

Some of the trio's finest singing is matched by a seamless production, although the overall feel is considerably lighter on the dread. The swaggering "Poor Jah People" and the sing-song "Natty Never Get Weary" are undeniable delights, while the title track has genuine style.

6️⃣ Harder than the Rest (Front Line — UK) 1978
7️⃣ Culture in Dub (High Note — JA) 1978

Hill's earnest delivery isn't always matched by either the music or his fellow vocalists — "Stop the Fighting and Fussing," for example, marries an already weak lyric to a frail keyboards-led melody, while "Behold" simply sounds curmudgeonly. The entire album is served far better by its dub counterpart.

8 International Herb (Front Line — UK) 1979

Joseph Hill is no Peter Tosh and "International Herb" is no "Legalize It." If you enjoyed Pato Banton's "Do Not Sniff the Coke," on the other hand, the jolly title track, at least, takes on gleefully anthemic qualities. "Too Long in Slavery," too, has a boyish buoyancy, rendering this the best of Culture's Front Line albums, and one of their finest all round.

6 Lion Rock (Sonic Sounds) 1981

An extremely melodic album, with Hill's increasingly Marley-like vocals appealing even if the material sometimes seem slight. Includes the singles "Forward to Africa" and "Disobedient Children." Since reissued by Heartbeat.

8 Culture in Culture (Blue Track) 1986

Culture return as strong as ever for an album as notable for its intriguing musical blends as the strength of the songs. Highlights include a simmering "Peace & Love," a brilliant dub in a dancehall style. Memorable melodies and sublime singing just add to the pleasure.

4 Culture at Work (Shanachie) 1986
5 Nuff Crisis! (Blue Mountain) 1988
5 Good Thing (RAS) 1989
5 Wings of a Dove (Shanachie) 1993

The fallen mighty remain fallen. Culture can usually be relied upon to serve up one good song — here they muster two.

6 One Stone (RAS) 1996
6 Stoned (RAS) 1997
5 Trust Me (RAS) 1997
7 Cultural Livity — Live 1998 (RAS) 1998

Sad that Culture's finest release in 10 years should be an in concert set, but understandable, too. A career-spanning set highlights most of the band's strongest moments so far, while Hill's wife Pauline offers up some delicious harmonies. The only downside is the downsizing of the band, sparse and rhythmic, while replicating horns on keyboards is rarely a good idea.

5 Payday (RAS) 2000

Despite the inclusion of the sterling "War in Sierra Leone," this Clive Hunt produced set starts out weak and never really strengthens.

4 Humble African (VP) 2000

Drawn from the same Collin York/Lynford Marshall sessions which spawned 1999's "Poor People Hungry" and "Revolution" singles. Whatever its merits may be, most of them come from outside — Sly & Robbie's energetic rhythms, Marcia Griffiths' so-sweet duet and Ernie Smith's "Home Grown."

SELECTED COMPILATIONS & ARCHIVE RELEASES

6 Africa Stand Alone (April) 1978

Now painfully rare, reportedly an alternate (but barely superior) view of *Harder than the Rest*, released simultaneously to much fussing and fighting.

7 Vital Selection (Virgin — UK) 1981

Strong compilation of the Pottinger produced Front Line albums, highlighted for international collectors by the Jamaica-only "Natty Never Get Weary" dub, "Citizen as a Peaceful Dub." A CD upgrade appeared as 1989's *Too Long in Slavery*. Elsewhere, neither *International Herb* nor *Cumbolo* receive as much attention as they deserve, but their highlights are unquestionably THE highlights.

8 Trod On (Heartbeat) 1993

Salvaging an unreleased album from the band's Pottinger period, 1979's *Black Rose*, plus period singles. A great sounding set, reflective and bitter in equal portions ("Trod On" itself packs some charming echoes of Jacob Miller's "Tenement Yard"), the package climaxes with two tracks (but several songs, including a snatch of "Rivers of Babylon") recorded at Treasure Isle with Count Ossie & The Mystic Revelation of Rastafari, shortly before Ossie's death in 1976. As such, they are somewhat out of place here, but no Culture fan should miss the opportunity to hear them.

6 Culture in Dub — 15 Dub Shots (Heartbeat) 1994

A clutch of Pottinger dubs, sensibly avoiding too much duplication with other collections of the same era.

7 The Production Something: The 12-inch Mixes (Heartbeat) 1995

Even more Pottinger, although little that the CD age will recognize. The 12-inch mixes, all segued vocal/dub sides, are uniformly excellent, despite the sometimes weak nature of the material. But nine minutes of "Too Long in Slavery" could never be too many.

6 RAS Portraits (RAS) 1997

Deceptively strong selection from some generally disappointing albums. Arguably, this is all the later Culture you need.

5 Scientist Dubs Culture into Parallel Universe (RAS) 2000

DANCE HALL

The dance hall movement which commenced in the late 1970s was the sound of the Jamaican music industry taking control of its own destiny once again, after the increasingly internationally-oriented adventures (and internationally fu-elled political upheavals) of the decade. Dance hall re-turned the music, as its name implies, to the dance halls from whence it sprang in the first place.

Internally and externally, Jamaica was changing. After close to a decade of Michael Manley's experimental socialist government, the right wing JLP had finally swept back into power, ushering in a new era of globalism and promises of prosperity. For the first time in a long while, people were being offered the chance to determine their own future, a bright future, and one which had absolutely no use for the apocalyptic grumblings of the discredited Manley era.

That this also ignited a move away from the cultural and spiritual "roots" concerns which had fired reggae's explosion into the world marketplace was less a consequence of the shift, then, than a cause. Though religious leaders have claimed that six out of every ten Jamaicans are either Rastafarians or sympathizers, music serves many purposes other than religion. Christianity can claim even greater infiltration in the USA, but not every club-goer wants to dance nightly to "The Lord Is My Shepherd."

Observations on weightier themes were joyously swept away, to be replaced by ruminations on dancing, violence and (yet another throwback) explicit sexuality. Christened by General Echo's *Ranking Slackness* album in 1979, and firmly rooted in the latter themes, "slacker" or "yard style" music itself evolved a virtual sub-genre in itself, one which was to dance hall what "rude reggae" had been to its late 1960s counterpart.

Even more encouragingly (at least for its fans), it was greeted by exactly the same outpourings of horror and shock from more "responsible" listeners as its earlier counterpart had been. The fact that many of those "responsible" listeners were themselves now old enough to have been a part of the original movement only added to the delight.

It is also true that reggae's international breakthrough (as evidenced by Bob Marley, Inner Circle, Third World and others) and reputation never truly impacted in the Jamaican dance halls themselves. There, the key to success remained an individual record's ability to excite an audience in its own right, as opposed to consolidating or complimenting the rest of an artist's canon, and the first stars of dance hall were the solo vocalists and disc jockeys who managed to maintain a constant stream of such recordings.

The fact that many of them chose to impose new songs over old, 60s-era rhythms only added to the new music's popularity. Put bluntly, the kids were bored with artists growing ever more obscure as they struggled to remain "original"; all they really wanted to do was dance. And if their heroes couldn't help them, they'd just have to find new artists who could.

Sugar Minott is generally credited as the artist who first

hit upon the most obvious solution to this growing dissat-isfaction, working as a sessionman at Coxsone Dodd's Studio One set up, and knocking up new lyrics to old tunes during studio down-time. His first singles, all cut to these standards, were instant dance hall smashes; inevitably, others swiftly followed in his footsteps.

At the same time as Sugar Minott was experimenting with old rhythms over at Studio One, producer Don Mais was similarly turning out some quite radical reinterpretations of old rhythms over at Channel One, usually in the company of the Roots Radics band.

The near obsessive creativity of the Sly & Robbie rhythm section notwithstanding, the greatest records created during the entire early dance hall period featured Roots Radics' reinterpretations of classic oldies. The musicians themselves were already comparative veterans — bassist Errol Holt and guitarist Eric Lamont had been playing together since 1974 (drummer Lincoln Valentine Scott joined them in 1978). However, the Roots Radics could also call upon a virtual who's who of session men to join them in their recreations.

Guitarists Dwight Pickney and Roy Hamilton, drummers Carlton Davis and Eric Clarke, and keyboardist Wycliffe Johnson were all regular auxiliaries. By the time Roots Radics joined another up and coming producer, Junjo Lawes, in 1979, to record the similarly little known Barrington Levy, the group had already acquired a ubiquity to match the greatest session bands of the past. It only followed that at least a trace of that same magic rubbed off on the artists with whom they worked.

Some became international giants — Barrington Levy was the first unassailably dance hall oriented singer to attain large-scale renown, while the early 1980s launched new stars into orbit with almost casual aplomb: Frankie Paul, Half Pint and Junior Reid were all pioneering entrants.

Many more, however, sank just as swiftly as they arose and, again, the parallels to the 1960s ska and rock steady eras are inescapable. More one-off artists emerged from the Jamaican studios during 1980–85 than at any time in the previous 20 years, with the emergence of this new musical culture (some called it freedom) naturally encouraging the birth of a new generation of both producers and sound systems as well.

Suddenly high-profile, operations like Killimanjaro, Black Scorpio, Stereophonic, the Emperor Faith Hi Fi, the Gemini Disco, Virgo Hi Fi and Aces International were among the earliest entrants to the new scene, bringing with them an equally new wave of top DJs.

Almost without trying, rising stars like Captain Sinbad, Ranking Joe, Clint Eastwood, the Lone Ranger, Josey Wales, Charlie Chaplin, General Echo and Yellowman dis-placed the toasters of old, just as they had dismissed the generation before them. As early as 1981, an album titled A

Whole New Generation of DJs, produced by Junjo Lawes, could offer listeners precisely that.

Undoubtedly fired, at least in part, by the braggadocio and aggression of this first wave of disc jockeys, dance hall became renowned as both an aggressive and a violent music — in later years, it would even become allied with American gangsta rap, such was the level of violence, misogyny and homophobia it espoused.

Again there were precedents, in the bloodletting which surrounded the early wars for supremacy between Coxsone Dodd and Duke Reid, in Kingston in the late 1950s — gun and knifeplay were rife then as well. But the media today is not only quicker to condemn than it once was, it is also faster to sensationalize, and what were once local scuffles swiftly took on the tone of an all-out generational crisis — one which the DJs themselves were swift to exploit.

1982–83 saw the record racks explode with a plethora of "sound clash" recordings, albums (and, more commonly, home-made cassettes) capturing two putative rival DJs going head-to-head, turntable-to-turntable, in front a large and wildly partisan crowd. The winner, of course, was the DJ who drew the most consistent applause from an audience which had no doubt as to why it was present.

The majority of sound clashes actually released through official outlets tended towards simply showcasing the DJs and allowing the listener to decide who was the "victor." Cassettes, recorded live and then distributed via the underground, were less cautious, not only capturing some excellent performances, but also some horrifying violence. This, of course, was then passed into the folklore surrounding individual DJs and sound systems, and ensured that the next sound clash was even more on edge, as a new challenger sought to prove that he (and his supporters) was even tougher.

Of course there were DJs whose very style and persona stood far above the melee. The albino Yellowman (a graduate of the same Alpha Boys School that produced the Skatalites) and the superbly named Eek-A-Mouse both utilized a wildly humorous delivery which was hard to resist — and even harder to fight about. Hardly surprisingly, both enjoyed periods during which they were, undisputedly, the biggest names on the scene — indeed, a full decade after his peak, Yellowman remained one of the biggest selling artists on the UK Greensleeves label's roster, while he also became the first Jamaican DJ ever to be signed to an American major label (Columbia).

Female DJs, too, began emerging, a development which had hitherto scarcely even been contemplated. Lady Saw, Shelly Thunder and Sister Nancy led the pack and, if their very presence was surprising, their actual acts could be absolutely shocking. The super-slack Lady Saw and, in her wake, Lady Shabba, often made their male counterparts sound positively prudish.

Although the DJs remained the most visible (or, at least, audible) face of dance hall, a plethora of producers were soon stepping into an equally bright spotlight. In the first five years of the dance hall movement, somewhere between 3,000 and 5,000 new singles were released in Jamaica every year. The vast majority were the output of maybe 30–50 different producers.

Despite (or, more likely, because of) its rapid-fire growth from underground cult to overnight sensation, the initial response to dance hall from within traditional reggae circles was negative. Though the heart of much of dance hall's early popularity remained the familiarity of the backing tracks which pounded beneath both singers and DJs, to untutored ears the music fell into two camps. Either it was blatantly unoriginal, or it was blindingly offensive, the sound of misguided youth pushing the barriers of "free expression" as far as it could, without any regard for what it might do when it got there.

What none among these nay-sayers could have imagined was how readily their prejudice worked to the "new" music's advantage. By so ghetto-izing an entire generation of talent, it permitted the movement's most reactionary talents to ally themselves with their contemporaries elsewhere, eschewing not only the "traditions" in which their music was founded, but those upon which the Jamaican music industry itself was built.

Dance hall grew out of reggae. But it grew into so much more — by the late 1980s, a number of Jamaican performers, the hard- rapping DJs in particular, were regularly appearing on the US R&B chart, attracting the attention of the hip hop community, even catching the eye of major US labels who had never ventured south of the Florida Keys in the past. If the Jamaican music establishment didn't want to know what its own children were doing, they'd take their sound to one which did.

The jaundiced eye which the old guard turned towards dance hall did not, of course, translate to the dance halls themselves. There, the music remained as popular as ever, and soon the older bands were themselves beginning to drift away. How ironic it was then, that this compulsory relocation should become the key to the ultimate survival not only of the veteran bands who were squeezed out of focus in their homeland; but also of many of the artists who displaced them to begin with.

Heading in the main to the US and Canada, Culture, Israel Vibration, Third World and more formed a diaspora whose universal popularity mushroomed even as its domestic profile slipped off the radar. This, in turn, formed a fertile international bed for the so-called slackers when, during the early-mid 1990s, they began turning away from traditional dance hall themes, to embrace the roots they had once stood in such firm opposition to.

Before that latter convolution could occur, however, dance hall had a number of issues of its own to work out. Dance hall, in its original form, was at its peak during the first half of the 1980s. Singer Cocoa Tea, another Junjo Lawes discovery, was launched onto the same stage as Barrington Levy and proved just as popular.

Studio One, the most renowned of all classic ska era Kingston studios (and, in terms of rhythms, one of the most revisited) followed Sugar Minott with General Smiley. Channel One, headed by JoJo Hookim and now employing producers as disparate as Niney Holness, Scientist, Soljie and Chemist, unleashed Michael Palmer, Sammy Dread, Little John and Don Carlos.

Amid so much activity, producers often became at least as well known as their artists — the likes of Gussie Clarke, Jah Thomas and Linval Thompson probably even more so. Sly Dunbar and Robbie Shakespeare, already established as the most inventive rhythm section of the late 1970s, now grabbed a similar crown for their production work — and then added a third, with their ready embrace of that strand of recording technology which, harnessed to Jamaica's latest sounds, gave rise to an entire new genre, ragga.

Ragga was built almost wholly around computer generated rhythms, a field which Dunbar in particular had been investigating since the early 1980s, and the arrival in the marketplace of the first readily affordable electronic instruments. As early as 1978/79 his inventive employment of syndrums had utterly outstripped the efforts of musicians and producers in even the best-appointed American and British studios and, as the duo's Taxi studio's arsenal of equipment increased, the greatest challenge facing Sly & Robbie's listeners was often to determine exactly what they were listening to — "real" drums or digital ones?

Both King Tubby and Prince/King Jammy joined Dunbar in pioneering and popularizing the new methods, with Jammy's 1985 production of Wayne Smith's "Under Mi Sleng Teng" emerging a defining moment in musical history — computer generated reggae. Utilizing a rhythm originally discovered on a Casio Rhythm Box, "Sleng Teng" became one of the predominant features of the next decade of dance hall, and the instantly recognizable hook behind an estimated 200 subsequent recordings.

Within weeks of "Sleng Teng" hitting the floor, Half Pint, a DJ first recorded in 1982 by Myrie Lewis and John Marshall, slammed to stardom when his variation on the Casio theme, "Greetings" (a computerized approximation of Vin Gordon's 1967 hit "Heavenless") became a best seller in both the US and Europe, a success he swiftly followed with 1987's "Buss Out" (recorded with the Firehouse Crew) and 1988's Victory album.

Although ragga (and, indeed, "Sleng Teng") was a technological development more than a musical advance, again the shift in style provoked an explosion of new talents to compliment the already established pioneers. Performers arose of the caliber of Paul Blake & the Blood Fire Posse, Buccaneer, Capleton and Shabba Ranks — at one point, widely described as the biggest ragga star in the world.

They were swiftly joined by now legendary producers Philip Burrell's Xterminator empire, Dave "Rude Boy" Kelly, Courtney Cole's Roof International, George Phang (producer of Junior Delgado's defining "Raggamuffin Year"), Hugh "Redman" James, Donovan Germain and the so-aptly named Bobby Digital, a former engineer at Prince/King Jammy's, whose Digital B label and sound helped dominate the late 1980s.

The duo of Wycliffe "Steely" Johnson and Cleveland "Clevie" Browne, meanwhile, emerged from the Kingston sessions scene (Roots Radics included) to become, in the words of many contemporary observers, the "new Sly & Robbie," hitting with distinctive singles by Ninjaman, Cutty Ranks and Leroy Gibbons. The first single on their Steely & Clevie label, in fact, launched one new local fad, pairing a new talent (Gibbons) with a fading one (Dillinger) for a record guaranteed to appeal to young and old fans alike.

The duo were also integral to the short-lived (but so enjoyable) Poco Dance Hall boom of 1989–90, following the success of DJ Lloyd Lovindeer's One Day Christian album with a string of tracks based on rhythms borrowed from Pukumina religious songs. The new rhythms — the Poco style, perhaps surprisingly, included — provided a fertile backdrop for the slacker style which had been percolating since the early 1980s. Spouting lyrics which left ever less to the imagination, ragga made stars of Bounty Killer (whose "Benz & the Bimma" offers yet another "Sleng Teng" permutation), Cobra, Little Lenny, Major Bones and Grindsman, before another of their number, Buju Banton, reversed the trend in 1992, ironically with a record (the virulently anti-gay "Boom Bye Bye") which could have opened the floodgates to even harder lyrical excesses. Instead, it slammed the door shut forever.

Across the US, where Banton had just signed a major record deal, and Europe, where he was scheduled to perform at the WOMAD Festival, "Boom Bye Bye" was greeted with absolute horror, a backlash which not only consumed a year of Banton's own career, but threatened to engulf Jamaica as well.

The slackers became extinct practically overnight. Soon after, Banton converted to Rastafarianism and embraced a sincere and moving musical spirituality; a slew of others followed. And though the dance hall scene didn't suddenly turn into the warm ocean of peace and love which was now most observers' fondest memory of the earlier roots movement (how quickly people forget!), it did remember that there is a massive difference between singing about reality, and simply shocking people for the sake of it.

Of course, not every early 90s dance hall artist needed that reminder. Even as the headline writers dwelt on the savage excesses of the most notorious slackers, an entire so-called "conscious ragga" scene grew up, for whom Rastafarianism was already an integral part of their life and outlook, and whose music bore a direct line of descent from the roots of old.

Popularized by DJs Icho Candy, Tony Rebel, Brigadier Jerry and Charlie Chaplin; and furthered by such singers as Sanchez, Yami Bolo, Jack Radics, Luciano and Daweh Congo, it was ultimately slammed into the mainstream in 1992 by Garnett Silk.

It was Silk, too, who began to reverse the trend away from digital recordings in the early 1990s, and prepare reggae for the consciousness explosion which was to reshape the scene in the late 1990s. Indeed, shortly before his death in 1994, he responded to the (primarily US) media's obsession with comparing him to Bob Marley, with the insistence that the only real correlation was that he, too, recorded with his musicians playing alongside him, as opposed to being sampled and stored on a hard drive. At a time when the robots ruled, that touch of humanity really made all the difference.

RECOMMENDED LISTENING

DONOVAN Banzani! (Mango) 1989
It might have been 1989, and everything's electro, but *Banzani!* harks back to the rootsy Seventies with a passion which would not be revisited for another five or six years. The modern touches lurk in the harmonies, keyboards and production. But it's Donovan's exhilarating performance and storytelling lyrics which make this album a stand-out.

MAD COBRA *Milkman* (EMI America) 1996
The king of the double entendre (and straight-ahead come-on), Mad Cobra is dance hall at its most suggestive and seductive, with *Milkman* proof positive that this charmer can chat up women in any genre. Like a snake shedding his skin, each stylistic change on the album invents the Cobra anew, yet his vocals sinuously coil around the sound, bringing it under his entrancing spell.

SHABBA RANKS As Raw as Ever (Epic) 1991
"Where does slackness comes from?" Ranks ponders early into his major label debut. Three guesses — a trailer load of girls, a chamber full of bullets and an album full of wicked raw rhythms. Indisputably Ranks was the master of all he surveyed by the time this album hit; it earned him the first ever Grammy to go to a DJ (the follow-up *X-Tra Naked*, repeated the feat), but one wonders whether the jury ever realized what they were listening to?

SHAGGY Midnite Lover (Virgin) 1997
Finally, a Shaggy album that doesn't fade behind one hit track ("Oh Carolina," "Boombastic"). Love may be the dominant theme, but there's also biting social commentary, a religious number (a cover of Marley's "Thank You Lord," featuring Ky-Mani Marley), and a brilliant summary of the DJ's story so far ("Think Ah So It Go"). Robert Livingston's production shines across the album's many moods, notably on the darkly atmospheric "Sex Body Girls," while musical stylings range from r&b to light hearted pop and onto the breezy ska-esque "The Mission."

SPANNER BANNER Chill (Island) 1996
For his US debut, Spanner Banner brought in the big guns — older brother Pliers and his partner Chaka Demus, the duo's producers Sly and Robbie, and singers/rappers DJ Tony Rebel and Luciano. Yet *Chill* remains a magnificent showcase of Spanner's sweet, smooth vocals and formidable writing talents, slipping effortlessly from emotive R&B, punchy dance hall to bouncy reggae.

TERROR FABULOUS Yaga Yaga (East West) 1994
Raggamuffin with a conscience, Fabulous' debut album shoots down the rude boys with cautionary tales of gangsta life, while enticing the girls with a string of sexy songs that advance from flirtatious to pure sexual boasting.

YELLOWMAN Burn It Down (Shanachie) 1987
Prozac just not doing the job? Then try Yellowman, guaranteed to cheer up all but the terminally depressed. The toaster brings such a sense of playfulness and joy to everything he does that you can't help but smile. 1982's *Mr Yellowman* (reissued in 2001 by Greensleeves) is probably his most archetypal album, but *Burn It Down* just edges it, even when the rapping remonstrates against recalcitrant wife beaters, wards off illnesses by chanting down "Diseases," or agitates for the legalization of sinsemilla. What else?

VARIOUS ARTISTS

Hardcore Ragga: The Music Works Hits (Greensleeves — UK) 1990
One of several late 1980s/early 1990s compilations highlighting the prodigious output of producer Gussie Clarke, via Shabba Ranks, JC Lodge, Papa San, Deborahe Glasgow and more. A decade on a few tracks sound dated, but vital collisions between Ranks, Cocoa Tea, Rebel Princess and Home T stand as brittle reminders of ragga's once boundless possibilities. Reissued in 2001 by Greensleeves' newly opened US operation.

VARIOUS ARTISTS

Ragga Essentials in a Dance Hall Style (Hip-O) 2000

The "Under Mi Sleng Teng" story . . . or part of it, anyway. A collection of ragga classics following Jammy into the bowels of the Casio beat box, via classic cuts by Half Pint, JC Lodge, Ini Kamoze, Born Jamericans and others.

VARIOUS ARTISTS

Presenting A Live Session With Aces International vols 1 and 2 (Greensleeves, Intense — UK) 1983

A taste of dance hall at its most furious. Fiery clashes feature Eek-A-Mouse, Buru Banton, Little John, Ringo, Peter Metro, Little Harry, Yellowman, Billy Boyo, Fathead, Toyan, Sinbad and the minuscule Beenie Man (plus Aces International's Stereo and Shaggy), the majority recorded live October 1982 at 82 Chisholm Ave. Kingston. Volume one was reissued in the US in 2001 (Greensleeves).

DESMOND DEKKER

STYLE *reggae (ska/rock steady)*
BORN *Desmond Dacres, 7/16/41 (some sources state 1942/43), (Kingston, JA)*

For more than 30 years, the name Desmond Dekker has been synonymous with the sound of ska and rock steady, not only as a leading light in the music's original incarnation, but also via revivals at the end of the 1970s and again in the mid-1990s.

As the epitome of the Jamaican rude boy, Dekker became the first island artist to enjoy a #1 hit in the UK, with the immortal "The Israelites," and the first to score any kind of chart success in America. He was also the first to be signed to the legendary UK independent label Stiff Records during his late 1970s resurgence, while 1993 saw him link with British 2-Tone superstars the Specials, themselves recently reformed after a decade-plus furlough, to record the album *King of Kings*. Indeed, like his best-known contemporary, Jimmy Cliff, Dekker has remained a constant presence in the development of Jamaican music, the timelessness of his greatest hits ensuring his rediscovery by generation after generation of listeners.

As an orphaned teen, Dekker apprenticed as a welder, entertaining his workmates with his singing. It was they who persuaded him to try and break into the music business and, overcoming rejections from both Duke Reid and Coxsone Dodd, Dekker finally struck gold with Leslie Kong, owner of the now legendary Beverley's label.

Kong produced Dekker's self-penned debut single, "Honour Your Father and Mother" in 1963, with accompaniment by Australian guitarist Dennis Cindry, Lloyd Mason (bass), Theo Beckford (piano), Stanley Webbs and Deadly Headly (horns). A swift Jamaican chart topper, it became the first in a string of monstrous local hits for the young vocalist.

"Sinners Come Home," a gospel-based number which reflected Dekker's own influences (Sam Cooke and Nat King Cole among them), and "Labour for Learning" followed, before Dekker linked with the similarly fast-rising Maytals (here called the Cherrypies), to record the epochal "King of Ska."

In 1963, Dekker recruited his own backing band, the [Four] Aces, featuring the brothers Barry, Carl, Clive and Patrick Howard, and thenceforth maintained a solid stream of Jamaican hits, all with producer Kong — "Parents," "Dracula," "Get Up Edina" and "This Woman" rank among the most notable. In total, the Dekker/Kong partnership scored 20 Jamaican #1s during the mid-late 1960s, while he and half-brother George Dekker were also an audible feature on several of Derrick Morgan's rude boy hits during this same period.

If Dekker's Jamaican success was prodigious, abroad his impact was even more astonishing. In July, 1967, the rock steady classic "007 (Shanty-Town)" gave him a UK Top 20 hit and, while he would not return to the British chart for another two years, his singles continued to sell well. "Unity" (runner-up at the 1967 Festival Song Competition), "Bongo Gal," "Hey Grandma," "Rudie Got Soul," "Sabotage," "Rude Boy Train" and a cover of the movie hit "To Sir with Love" all scored on the British club scene.

"Hippopotamus," was enormous on the same circuit, while "The Israelites," originally released in 1968, spent some six months percolating into the national consciousness before finally breaking into the UK chart in March, 1969. Even more incredibly, the song also made the US Top 10, the first undiluted reggae record ever to do so. "It Mek," a rerecording of another 1968 release (when it was titled "A It Mek" — "that's why it happened") proved a successful follow up, although few listeners realized that, beneath its tone of knowing righteousness, the song was actually written about Dekker's sister, Elaine, after she fell off a wall.

The hits continued into the new decade. With Dekker now living in the UK and touring constantly, the effortlessly singalong "Pickney Girl" reached #42, while a cover of Jimmy Cliff's "You Can Get It if You Really Want" soared to #2. There was also a Top 30 berth for the album *This Is Desmond Dekker*, a round-up of past hits drawn from the earlier *007 (Shanty-Town)*, *Action* and *The Israelites* sets.

Like Jimmy Cliff, Dekker's career was completely thrown off of its stride by the death of producer Kong in August, 1971. Although he continued releasing some fine records including several recorded before Kong's passing ("Mother Nature," "Beware") and remained a force in Jamaica, the singer did not enjoy another British hit until 1975 brought a Top 10 reissue of "The Israelites."

The previous year, Dekker had launched a relationship with pop producers Tony Cousins and Bruce White (who worked under the single name Bruce Anthony), cutting the

Desmond Dekker: Both beautiful and dangerous.

(admittedly lightweight) "Everybody Join Hands" and "Busted Lad" for the UK Rhino label. Now "Sing a Little Song" from those same sessions proffered a successful successor to the reissue, while a new album, again titled *Israelites*, also sold well. No further hits appeared, however, and Dekker returned to the shadows until 1979/80 brought Britain's 2-Tone explosion.

Created under the aegis of confirmed UK ska revivalists the Specials and Madness, 2-Tone was a frantic, punk-inspired update of the classic 60s Jamaican sound. Both bands frequently covered the era's biggest hits, and Madness were themselves named after a Prince Buster song. As a host of classic oldies hit the reissues rack, Dekker was one of the first of the legendary performers to resurface, signing to Stiff and recording 1980's amusingly titled *Black and Dekker* album with the English rock band, the Rumour.

Produced by Lol Gellor and Syd Bucknor, a rerecorded "Israelites" made #12 in Belgium that year, while further 45s "Please Don't Bend" and Jimmy Cliff's "Many Rivers to Cross" (backed by an updated "Pickney Girl") also received their share of praise. So did "Book of Rules," a dy-

namic performance recorded with English powerpop producer Will Birch, and effortlessly lining up among Dekker's finest cuts in a decade. A second album, *Compass Point*, appeared in 1981, produced by Robert Palmer and attended by another entertaining 45, the non-album "Hot City." Neither record sold well, but Dekker's live shows (generally backed by the Rumour) remained popular.

As the 2-Tone scene faded away, however, Dekker, too, drifted out of sight once more. In 1984, the financial misdoings of past management forced him into bankruptcy, and he retired from music for much of the decade. In 1990, however, the appearance of a revised version of "The Israelites," retitled "My Ears Are Alight," in a Maxell tape commercial reawakened interest in him once again. He returned to the live circuit and, in 1993, Dekker linked with the reformed Specials to cut *King of Kings*, an enthusiastic selection of songs from the golden age of ska — updated to celebrate an equally glittering rebirth.

DISCOGRAPHY

8 007 (Shanty-Town) (Beverley's—JA) 1967

7 Action! (Beverley's—JA) 1968
8 The Israelites (Beverley's—JA) 1969

. . . backed by the superb Beverley's All Stars, three albums featuring a peerless round-up of Dekker's greatest Jamaican hits, including "007" and "The Israelites" of course, but also "Rudy Got Soul," "Beautiful & Dangerous," "Unity". . . the list is practically endless.

9 The Israelites (Uni) 1969

UK title *This Is Desmond Dekker*; Dekker's international debut album, culled from the first three Jamaican releases and cutting out everything but the finest hits.

7 You Can Get It if You Really Want (Trojan—UK) 1970
4 The Israelites (Cactus—UK) 1975

A very different record from either of its 1969 namesakes, the peerless title track devours the rest of the album, then spits it out. Dekker's voice remains sweet, but "Sugar Dumpling" is only the first of the saccharin nadirs to which it is bound. "Sing a Little Song" is especially gruesome.

6 Black and Dekker (Stiff—UK) 1980

Doubling as a greatest hits package, albeit a rerecorded one. "Israelites," "It Mek," "Lickin' Stick," "Pickney Girl," "007" and "Rude Boy Train" all get fresh airings, and come through in finer fettle than one might expect. It's not Dekker's most imaginative album, but it's certainly a likeable one.

5 Compass Point (Stiff—UK) 1981

New material dominates, with producer Robert Palmer doing his best to keep things interesting, even when the songs flag. "Allemanna" and the "I Do Believe"/"My Destiny" medley are highlights, but Dekker might have been advised to have saved some of the old hits for this set as well. (CD bonus tracks include "Book of Rules," Hot City" and "Movin' On.")

5 Officially Live & Rare (Trojan—UK) 1987

A listenable recording of Dekker at his 60s peak would be priceless. But we have to make do with a hits heavy recording from the post-traumatic mid 1980s, at a late night London watering hole. Dekker's in good voice, the band are competent and the audience knows all the words.

4 King of Ska (Trojan—UK) 1991

Trojan should be ashamed, not just for the laughable liner notes which refer to Dekker's rerecordings of "classic hits from the 1950s," but also for a host of misleading, truncated and mistitled songs. That said, this album is proof positive of Leslie Kong's genius, for though Dekker delivers the vocal goods, and the performances remain fairly true to their predecessors, they still don't hold a candle to the originals.

4 Moving On (Trojan—UK) 1996

Loaded down with redundant remixes (dub, rocksteady, a cappella) and not especially strong in the songs department either, only the constant perfection of Dekker's voice raises the temperature above lukewarm.

DESMOND DEKKER & THE SPECIALS
5 King of Kings (Trojan—UK) 1993

A classic covers' collection high on peppy trad sound, but let down by both the unimaginative arrangements and Dekker, who seems to lose interest halfway through.

SELECTED COMPILATIONS & ARCHIVE RELEASES
7 Double Dekker (Trojan—UK) 1974
7 Sweet 16 Hits (Trojan—UK) 1978
8 The Original Reggae Hitsound (Trojan—UK) 1985
8 Music Like Dirt (Trojan—UK) 1992

Dekker stirs, Trojan rush out a compilation. The 70s releases tend towards the more familiar material; the latter pair present a more rounded appreciation.

7 The Original Rude Boy (Music Club) 1997

A useful single disc Dekker collection, lining up 12 classic hits, then allowing listeners to make up their own minds about Dekker's 1990s activities.

JUNIOR DELGADO

STYLE *reggae (dance hall)*
BORN *Oscar Hibbert, 8/25/58 (Kingston, JA)*

One of the crucial roots performers of the mid-late 1970s and, equally importantly, one of the few who was able to sustain his impact during the dance hall era, the grittily voiced Junior Delgado made his debut as a member of Time Unlimited, a band formed with Junior Marshall, Orville Smith and Glasford Manning (later members of the Jewels — Manning was also the youngest brother of the Abyssinians/Carlton & The Shoes family members). Delgado at this time worked under the name Junior Hibbert.

In early 1973, Time Unlimited auditioned for Lee Perry at Black Ark, cutting three songs — one, Manning's "African Sound," was released on the Upsetter label. Other sessions followed, but the vast majority of the group's work with Perry went unreleased. However, he did spend a lot of time molding them into a top rate harmony group, and they eventually scored one hit under his aegis, "Reaction," released on Joe Gibbs' Reflections label.

A second 45, "23rd Psalm," followed later in 1973, while 1974 paired Delgado with Rupie Edwards to ride the "Ire Feelings" rhythm with "Rasta Dreadlocks," released under the name of the Heaven Singers. Edwards also produced another Delgado performance, "Run Baldhead," under the name Junior Hibbert. Sessions with producer Tommy Cowan (backed by members of Third World) went nowhere and, while a new single, "Really for a Reason," appeared in 1975, a series of aborted sessions for Bunny Lee's Total Sounds label was the last straw. Delgado quit the group and went solo under his now familiar pseudonym. ("Delgado" means "skinny" in Spanish.)

From sessions with producer Niney Holness, further singles "Everyday Natty" and a version of Ken Boothe's "Thinking" followed. A short-lived change of name to Jooks produced the enjoyable, but unsuccessful "Every Natty" 45. Delgado remained a comparative unknown until late 1975, when he went over to Dennis Brown's DEB label and recorded "Tition" (as in "poli-tician") with producer Earl "Chinna" Smith.

An immediate success, "Tition" set Delgado and DEB on course for a string of Jamaican hits, including "Devil's Throne," "She Gonna Marry Me," "Famine," "The Raiders," "Trickster," "Warrior No Tarya" and a cover of the Heptones' "Love Won't Come Easy," plus 1978's acclaimed *Taste of the Young Heart* debut album. In 1979, Delgado launched his own label, Incredible Jux, debuting it with a reworking of the "Tition" rhythm, "Jah Stay," and a dub companion to his sophomore DEB album, *Effort*.

During this same period, Delgado recorded additional sides with Prince Jammy — "Love Tickles Like Magic"; Joe Gibbs — "Armed Robbery," "United Dreadlocks"; Augustus Pablo — "Blackman's Heart Cries Out" (a variation on Pablo's own "Zion High" rhythm) and "Away With Your Fussing and Fighting" (featuring toaster Hugh "Jah Levi" Mundell). Turning to self-production, Delgado then recorded 1982's "Rich Man Poor Man" and "First on Sunday," among others; while a reunion with Lee Perry spawned the mighty "Sons of Slaves."

With his UK popularity set to rival his Jamaican standing, Delgado spent much of the early 1980s touring that country, promoting such singles as "Merry Go Round" and "Fort Augustus" (produced by Sly & Robbie), "Personality," "Loving You Girl," "Midnight Raver" and "Part Time Lover" (produced by S Douglas). In 1983, however, he was forced off the scene by an 18 month jail sentence.

He was released in 1985 and, back in London, recorded "Broadwater Farm," a ferocious condemnation of life on the north London housing estate of the same name. Incredibly, the estate was shortly to be the scene of some of the worst civil unrest the city had ever seen, during which a police officer was hacked to death. (According to some sources, Delgado's record was promptly banned in the aftermath of the clash, although by whom, nobody seems certain.)

Delgado followed up with "Nine Fence" (1985), "Rockers Non-Stop" (produced by Prince Jammy) and "Poverty" (Mikey Carrol — both 1986). But his greatest triumph reunited him with Augustus Pablo, now a master of the modern digital technology, for "Raggamuffin Year," a celebration of

the current state of Jamaican music and the new wave of musicians erupting around him — a wave which embraced Delgado as one of their own, and ensured he was not left behind. The *Raggamuffin Year* album followed to similar success.

Delgado repaid that loyalty by taking two of this new generation under his own wing. White Mice and Yami Bolo both enjoyed Delgado/Pablo-produced hits, including Bolo's "Ransom of a Man's Life" (1987), "Love Me with Feeling" (1989), "Struggle in Babylon" (1990) and the album *Ransom*.

Delgado's own profile, meanwhile, was maintained by the hits "Illegal Gun" (Prince Jammy, 1987), "Forward Revolution," "Hanging Tree"/"Hey Good Looking," "Riot inna Juvenile Prison," "Dub School" and the *One More Step* album (all with Pablo) and the self-produced "We a Blood." He made his Sunsplash debut in 1988, while the UK connection remained intact via a link-up with the Fashion label — the self-produced album *It Takes Two to Tango* and singles "Bus I Skull," "Daydreaming" and "We a Blood" were strong sellers during 1987–89.

Perhaps surprisingly in the light of such success, the 1990s saw Delgado adopt a somewhat lower profile, highlighted only by the release of an excellent dub reunion with Pablo, *Ragamuffin Dub*, and a 1990 revision of "Titian" (Fashion). 1998's *Fearless*, however, proved he was still firing on all cylinders, and featured collaborations with guests Naked Funk, Kid Loops, trip hop stars Smith & Mighty, the Specials' Jerry Dammers, Faithless rapper Maxi Jazz and superstar remixers the Jungle Brothers.

He was a success at 1999's Glastonbury and Roskilde festivals and, still based in London, Delgado's next release, *Reasons*, was recorded with UK producer Adrian Sherwood. 2001 brought *Junior Delgado Sings Dennis Brown*, a tribute to his late friend and mentor, cut at Delgado's own Incredible Music Studios.

DISCOGRAPHY

8 Taste of the Young Heart (DEB — UK) 1978
Co-produced with labelhead Brown, a crop of recent Delgado 45s is topped by "Black Man Heart," "Trickster" and the foreboding "Famine."

7 Effort (DEB) 1979
A lesser set than its predecessor, although Bob Marley's "Caution," the Shades' "She's Gonna Marry Me" and "Sisters and Brothers" hold up well.

7 Dance a Dub (Jux — JA) 1979
The *Effort* dub companion. Just 500 copies were pressed at the time; the album has since been reissued by Big Cat.

6 More She Love It (Yvonne's Special) 1981
7 Disco Style Showcase (Yvonne's Special) 1981

Don't be fooled by the title, as Delgado continues moving in on the dance hall floor with a strong set.

8 Bushmaster Revolution (Jux) 1982

Packed with enough heavy hitting guest musicians to field a baseball team, the deliciously dichotomous *Bushmaster* divides its time between hefty rootsy numbers and pop ballads, social commentary and love songs, all performed with Delgado's signature emotive style.

6 Sisters & Brothers (Blue Moon) 1985
9 Raggamuffin Year (Mango) 1986

Indisputably Delgado's latter-day classic, built around the title track but proving time and again that its precognitive brilliance was no accident.

7 Stranger (Skengdon) 1987
6 Moving Down the Road (Live & Love—UK) 1987
6 Roadblock (Blue Track—UK) 1987
7 It Takes Two to Tango (Fashion—UK) 1987
8 One More Step (Mango) 1988

Delgado aims for a balance of styles from lover's rock — the title track, "Magic of Love" and "It's True"; through cultural concerns — the powerful "Rebel Sold in Captive"; and onto the tremendous dance hall styled "Labba Labba."

6 Another Place in Time (Vision) 1994
7 Fearless (Big Cat—UK) 1998

Brave and generally successful lurch into the late 1990s arena, Delgado and a host of friends reinvent oldies "Fussin' and Fightin'," "She's Gonna Marry Me," "Armed Robbery," "23rd Psalm" and others, often dipping into a ragbag of both American and Caribbean sounds as they do so.

7 Reasons (Big Cat—UK) 1999
8 Junior Delgado Sings Dennis Brown (Incredible Music) 2001

JUNIOR DELGADO & AUGUSTUS PABLO
6 Ragamuffin Dub (Rockers International) 1990
7 Dub School (Buffalo) 1990
6 Showcase (Rockers International) 1993

SELECTED COMPILATIONS & ARCHIVE RELEASES
9 20 Classic Hits (Sonic Sounds) 1991

20 indeed, including the incredible "Mascerade," "Armed Robbery," "Trickster," "Bushmaster" and "Rub a Dub."

9 Treasure Found (Incredible) 2000
8 More Treasure Found (Incredible) 2000
9 Treasure Found 3: No Baby Lion (Incredible) 2000

From crucial partnerships with Lee Perry, Rupie Edwards and Augustus Pablo in the 1970s, to the cutting edge collaboration with Junjo Lawes, three separate volumes round-up the best of both Delgado's classic and overlooked recordings.

CHAKA DEMUS & PLIERS

STYLE *reggae (toasting/dance hall)*
ORIGINAL LINE-UP *Chaka Demus (b John Taylor, 1965, West Kingston, JA—vocals); Pliers (b Everton Banner, 1965, Kingston, JA—vocals)*

When Chaka Demus & Pliers landed a #1 British single in early 1994 with their dance hall revision of the Isley Brothers' "Twist and Shout," they not only became the first Jamaican act to top the UK chart in eight years (since Boris Gardiner's "I Want to Wake Up with You"), they also confirmed a status which critics had conferred upon them a full year earlier, as the most successful DJ-led pairing in reggae history.

It was not difficult to understand the enthusiasm. Though Chaka Demus and Pliers had only been working together since 1991, they had already racked up a string of hits both at home and abroad, while their earlier solo careers, too, had thrown up some captivating releases.

Pliers, the older brother of fellow DJ Spanner Banner, cut his first singles under his given name in the mid-1980s with producer Maurice Johnson (Black Scorpio). He also recorded sides for Harry J, Studio One, George Phang's Arrival (1985's "Youth Wise"), Jammys, Pickout and Pioneer Music.

It was with the latter that he recorded the original version of the future hit "Murder She Wrote," an adaptation of the Maytals' 1966 hit "Bam Bam." (Other releases included "Love Is Burning," "Let the Good Times Roll," "I Want to Be Your Man," "Request to Brenda," "Hot Pepper" and "Revolution Song.") Surprisingly, however, the DJ's pretty tenor, clear as a bell with an almost delicate, vulnerable quality, failed to capture Jamaica's heart.

In 1988, he linked with fellow DJ Pinchers for the set

which gifted him his future identity, the *Pinchers with Pliers* album. 1989 brought "I Found Love" with Beenie Don (produced by Dennis Star & June Hayes). Pliers was also a familiar figure around the Penthouse studios, where he first encountered his next partner.

Chaka Demus originally worked under the name Nicodemus Jr (in tribute to early 1980s DJ Nicodemus — born Cecil Wellington, 1957; died 8/26/99) at the Jammys and Supreme sound systems. He changed his name shortly before cutting his first single, 1985's "Increase Your Knowledge." With Jammys, he enjoyed a string of minor hits, including "2 Foot Walk" and a version of the R&B stomper "One Scotch, One Bourbon, One Beer" with Admiral Bailey. All were notable for the DJ's relaxed style, ready wit and his signature hearty chuckle.

He also recorded with Yellowman ("Everybody Loves Chaka"), Scotty ("Bring It to Me") and fellow Jammys DJ Shabba Ranks (the album *Rough and Rugged*). In 1987, he moved to Penthouse for "Chaka on the Move"; while the next three years brought another successful collaboration with Ranks, *Best Baby Father*, together with two solo albums and the single "Vanity Crazy" (produced by Ini Kamoze). Chaka Demus also appeared at Sunsplash 1990.

In 1991, in the wake of another mini hit, "Stallion," Chaka Demus traveled to Miami with Pliers for a series of shows, where the pair made the decision to team up on a full time basis. Returning to Jamaica, they recorded "Gal Wine" with producer Ossie Hibbert. It was an instant hit and the cue for a succession of successful follow-ups.

The duo's most notable releases include: "Brenda" (produced by Ranking Joe), "Dem a Watch Wi" and "Bad Mind" (Jah Screw), "Bogle Dance," "Sweet Jamaica" and "Love Up de Girl" (Lloyd "Pickout" Dennis), "Rough this Year" (Blackbeard), "Thief" (Adrian Genius), "A Nuh Me" and "You Send Come Call Me" (Prince Jammy), "World A Girlz" (Donville Davis), "Winning Machine" (Mafia & Fluxy), "Blood in a Eyes" (Peter Chemist) and "Pretty Face" (Bobby Digital). Many of these were included on the 1992 album *Gal Wine Wine Wine*.

The pair appeared at Sunsplash 1992 (and again in 1994), then rejoined Hibbert for an easy going, rock steady-esque union with Spanner Banner, "A Terror," while solo ambitions were kept alive by a warm reception for Pliers' "Clare" (Jah Screw).

"Tease Me," produced by Sly & Robbie, was a 1993 hit and it was this same pairing, resplendent across a reworked "Murder She Wrote," which gave Chaka Demus & Pliers their international breakthrough, and paved the way for their signing to Island Records in 1993.

That year their fourth album together, *Tease Me* (US title *All She Wrote*), made #26 in the UK, while the singles "Tease Me" and "She Don't Let Nobody" both made the UK Top 5. The chart-topping "Twist and Shout," featuring guest appearances from Jack Radics and Sly & Robbie's Taxi Gang, followed in the new year and, during 1994, Chaka Demus & Pliers were virtual fixtures on the British chart. "Murder She Wrote," "I Wanna Be Your Man" and a breezy rerecording of their first ever 45, "Gal Wine," all made the Top 30.

Close to two years elapsed before the duo returned with the *Every Kinda People* album. Inevitably less successful than its monster predecessor, it nevertheless spawned a hit title track, and a remarkable reworking of the calypso classic "Man Smart, Woman Smarter." The duo's final hit was a cover of the Police's "Every Little Thing She Does Is Magic," in summer, 1997.

That same year brought Chaka Demus' solo "Come Ya Mi Darlin' Come." The pair were well-received at Sunsplash in 1998, and their next album, *Help Them Lord*, finally appeared in early 2001.

DISCOGRAPHY

8 **Gal Wine (Greensleeves — UK) 1992**

Producer Ossie Hibbert's pairing of the DJ and singer was a brilliant move immediately rewarded by the public. The gruffly voiced, but jovial Demus was the perfect foil for the sweetly singing Pliers across this album filled with hits, and the duo's careers, individually stuck in a rut, collectively moved into the bigtime.

7 **Ruff This Year (RAS) 1992**
7 **Chaka Demus & Pliers (Charm — UK) 1992**
10 **All She Wrote (Mango — UK)**

Released in the UK as *Tease Me*. Sly and Robbie (who produced, co-wrote, and performed) strip down the sound and beats for the funk and dance hall, turn up the heat and lushness on the R&B, and pay their respects to JA's musical past with unerring precision to give dance hall a whole new sound. The hits "Twist and Shout" and "Murder She Wrote" are impeccable; elsewhere "I Wanna Be Your Man" simply drowns in syrupy vocals and sensuous bass, and the recut "Gal Wine" casts the duo's contrasting vocals in crystalline light. Even their attempts at redefining American funk ("One Nation Under a Groove") and R&B ("She Don't Let Nobody") have a sublime magnificence and the only regret is, the penultimate "Tracy" is their own composition, and not the early 1970s pop classic. That could have been phenomenal.

6 **For Every Kinda People (Island) 1996**
8 **Help Them Lord (RAS) 2001**

CHAKA DEMUS

6 **Everybody Loves the Chaka (Scorpio) 1988**
7 **The Original Chaka (Witty) 1989**

5 Rough & Rugged (Jammys) 1988

Both artists had a clutch of attention grabbing singles to their own names before they recorded their debut full length for Jammy. Considering future events, though, neither DJ was particularly well served here, as the record fails to capture either's true strengths and talents.

6 Best Baby Father (John John—JA) 1989

Now working with Bobby Digital, this set was a vast improvement on the last, and featured a slew of hits by both artists. Arguably, Demus won the last round in this battle of the dueling DJs, but this time, Ranks took the title, and entered the world of superstardom.

PLIERS & PINCHERS

4 Pinchers with Pliers (Black Scorpio) 1988

It sounds great in theory, but the reality was somewhat disappointing, perhaps because the pair's sweet tenor vocals are just a little too close in timbre, at times making it virtually impossible to distinguish them. It's all pleasant enough, but Pliers needed to search on for a more musically challenging partner.

SELECTED COMPILATIONS & ARCHIVE RELEASES

8 Gold (Charm—UK)

Anybody tracking back from the hits won't be too surprised by what they find—and this is the easiest way to find it. Twelve tracks from eight producers include the crucial original "Gal Wine," plus the best of those excellent Prince Jammy sessions.

THE (WITCO) DESPERADOES

STYLE *pan*

FORMED *1945 (Laventville, T&T) CURRENT ARRANGER Clive Bradley*

Ten times winner of Panorama since 1966, the Desperadoes' were among the rash of bands which emerged on the carnival scene in 1946. The group was originally known as the Dead End, partially from the popular *Dead End Kids* movies of the late 1930s. Led by pannists "Benyeh" and "Brains," the Dead End were notorious for their regular battles with police and other bands, and were among the principle offenders responsible for the formation of a government committee to look into the steel band phenomenon.

Around 1950, Wilfred "Speaker" Harrison and Donald Steadman became involved with the group, responsible forces whose chief aim was to encourage the band to focus their energies on their music. This was accomplished so swiftly that, in 1955, the group had concluded a sponsorship agreement with Coca Cola, changing their name to the Coca Cola Gay Desperadoes.

In 1961, Rudolph Charles became the band's leader (he joined in 1958), and led the Gay Desperadoes through their first period of prominence. A taste of the group's sound from this time can be found on the live RCA (T&T — 1962) compilation *Steelband Music Festival*, where a supremely delicate rendition of the "Emperor Waltz" lies alongside contributions from the Tropoli Steel Orchestra, the Shell Invaders, the Dixieharps and the Metronomes.

Having been a regular carnival masquerade success, the Gay Desperadoes were among the bands entering the first ever Panorama in 1963, where they placed third with Lord Kitchener's "The Road." 1964 saw "Mama Dis Is Mas" give them second place.

In 1965, the West Indian Tobacco Company (WITCO) took over the Gay Desperadoes' sponsorship, a relationship which flourishes to this day. The band began repaying the company's interest immediately; they conquered Panorama for the first time in 1966, performing Beverly Griffith's spirited arrangement of Mighty Sparrow's "Obeah Wedding."

Sparrow's "Governor Ball" gave the Gay Desperadoes' the runner-up place at Panorama in 1967; and in 1970, they took Panorama once more, with Clive Bradley's arrangement of Lord Kitchener's "Margie." A US tour that same year saw the band drop the "Gay" from their name.

The Desperadoes returned to the Kitchener songbook for victory in 1976 ("Pan in Harmony") and 1977 ("Crawford"). They also scored two consecutive runners-up places with 1978's "Pan in the 21st Century" and 1980's "No Pan"— there was no Panorama staged in 1979. 1977, meanwhile, also brought a hit single with "Hello Africa," on the local Hildrina label.

In 1982, the Desperadoes took third place at Panorama with arranger Clive Bradley's own "Party Tonight"; in 1983, Blue Boy's "Rebecca" gave them their fifth Panorama title; two years later, they tied for first place with the Renegades, both bands performing Kitchener's "Pan Night and Day."

Charles passed away in 1985 (David Rudder's 1986 hit "The Hammer" was composed in his memory), but the Desperadoes triumphed at the Trinidad Music festival in 1986 (further victories came in 1988 and 1992), and continued to perform well at Panorama. They placed third in 1987 with Kitchener's "Pan in a Minor," and again in 1988 with David Rudder's "Panama," both arranged by Griffith. In 1991, they won Panorama again with arranger Robert Greenidge's spectacular "Musical Volcano."

Indeed, the 1990s proved the Desperadoe's most successful decade yet. Under the captaincy of Elias Emmanuel Phillip, the band scored further Panorama triumphs in 1994 (with another Greenidge composition, "Fire Coming Down"), 1999 (with arranger Clive Bradley's version of Oba Synette's "In My House") and 2000 (a second Synette composition, "Picture on My Wall"). They also placed third in 1995 ("Pan Parang") and 1996 ("Blast Off").

In addition, the band's touring schedule regularly takes them across North America and Europe, where they are widely regarded among their homeland's premier ambassadors. 2000 saw them perform with the tenor superstar Pavarotti.

RECOMMENDED LISTENING

8 Steel in the Classics (—)

Trevor Valentine arranges nine classical pieces (plus Scott Joplin's "The Entertainer") for pan, including "Orpheus in the Underworld," "Finlandia," "Amazing Grace" and, spectacularly, Handel's "Hallelujah Chorus."

7 The Jammer (—) 1991

Featuring the Panorama winning "Musical Volcano," alongside the title track, "Moliendo Cafe," "Rebecca" and more, a magnificent recounting of the Desperadoes' full fiery performance — the best of their work is otherwise most easily found on steelband compilation albums.

7 Live at Holder's, Barbados (—) 1998

Fabulous concert performance runs the band through all their paces, including decisive versions of "It Ain't Necessarily So" (one of several *Porgy & Bess* selections), "The Can Can" and "The Greatest Love of All."

DILLINGER

STYLE *reggae (toasting/DJ)*
BORN *Lester Bullocks, 6/25/53 (Kingston, JA)*

For many listeners, Dillinger will forever be the man who gave the world "Cocaine in My Brain," the 1976 single which, while it never charted outside of Jamaica, was nonetheless positively endemic on the late-1970s UK and US club scenes, and remains a constant favorite today.

In fact, deeper investigation of Dillinger's early catalog reveals one of the most stylish and innovative of all the 1970s DJ crew. It's an achievement rendered even greater when one considers the man's own confession that when he started out, he simply copied what he'd heard U-Roy, Big Youth and Dennis Alcapone doing.

It took him some three years to find his own, lightheartedly rude style, and almost as long to find his moniker. Having launched his career under his given name on Prince Jackie's sound system, he then moved on to the El Paso set up, where he replaced the great Dennis Alcapone. The young DJ promptly began trading as Dennis Alcapone Jr, until Lee Perry told him, "you're different from Al Capone. You're Dillinger."

In 1973, Perry produced Dillinger's first session at his Black Ark studios, drawing the "Dub Organiser" debut single from the tapes. Other Perry produced 45s included

"Tighten Up Skank," "Cane River Rock" (both riding the same "Tighten Up" rhythm), "Uncle Charley Version," "Connection," "John Devour," "Headquarters," "Ensome City Skank" and "Me Nah Tell a Man."

Dillinger's career did not take off, however, until 1974, when Vivian "Yabby You" Jackson produced the hit "Freshly," built upon the same "Jah Vengeance" rhythm as fired Tappa Zukie's "Natty Dread on the Mountain Top."

That opened the floodgates. Over the next year Dillinger unleashed a slew of generally excellent material, including: "Bump Skank," "Brace a Boy" (produced by Augustus Pablo), "Flat Foot Hustling" (Niney Holness, reworking Dennis Brown's "Have No Fear"), "Take a Dip" (Count Ossie) and the mountainous pun "Killer Man Jaro" (Coxsone Dodd). The latter track also previewed Dillinger's debut album, *Ready Natty Dreadie*, the title track a stunning revision of Burning Spear's "Creation Rebel."

Another Dodd production, "Natty Kung Fu," tied Dillinger to the then epidemic craze for martial arts launched into the international music scene by Jamaican-born R&B veteran Carl Douglas. However, it was his sophomore album, *CB200*, produced by JoJo Hookim, which truly drove the DJ onto the world reggae stage. Any number of cuts from the album held the clubs in their thrall. But "Cocaine In My Brain" rose above all of them.

Brought to Britain by the sheer weight of local demand, Dillinger was a familiar figure on the London scene just as it moved into the punk era. "Cocaine" was everywhere, blasting out of nightclub PAs and trendy boutiques alike, and expectations were high for Dillinger's third album, a duel with Trinity produced in London by Clement Bushay.

Sadly, *Clash* sold poorly, a fate which also befell a second

Hookim-produced set, *Bionic Dread*, and while a pair of albums for the London-based Third World label certainly boasted their fair share of powerful material, the continued pre-eminence of "Cocaine" remained a self-made rod for Dillinger's own back.

"Dread Called Fred," "Cornbread" (from the album of the same name), "Loving Pauper," "Out the Light," "Woody Woodpecker," "Funky Punk" and a pair of humorous discussions of crab lice, "Mickey Mouse Crab Louse" (surely the only song ever to rhyme "fire" with "gonorrhoea") and "Crab in My Pants," were swallowed in its slipstream. A fine collaboration with Sugar Minott, "Lamb's Bread," was all but ignored. Other excellent, but overshadowed releases from 1977–79 include a clutch recorded with producer Bunny Lee: "Empty Chair" (a duet with Johnny Clarke), "Mark My Word" (with Hortense Ellis) and a pair of exhilarating vinyl battles with Ronnie Davis and Delroy Wilson.

In 1979, Dillinger sought to reverse his decline with a direct follow-up to "Cocaine in My Brain," "Marijuana in My Brain." The record promptly topped the chart in the Netherlands (the only country where the drug is legal), while an album of the same name did well enough to prompt the A&M major to sign Dillinger to an international deal. The relationship survived just one album, 1980's *Badder than Them*.

1981 saw the release of Dillinger's own *Live at the Music Machine*, and a second *Live in London* set recorded with Clint Eastwood. In 1982, his interest in production work was given a boost, when the UK Oak Sound label unleashed a host of 12-inch singles overseen by Dillinger: his own "Send Another Moses" and "Mr Mikey" were accompanied by singles by Johnny Osbourne, Anthony Johnson and the singularly named Diana. Dillinger's latest album, *Join the Queue*, offered further evidence of his production skills.

Back in Kingston, Dillinger was an elder statesmen of sorts at a February, 1983, live session staged by Junjo Lawes as a showcase for some of Jamaica's younger DJ-ing talent — Ringo, Little Harry and the 10 year old Beenie Man among them. The show was recorded and released as *Junjo Presents Two Big Sound*. New Dillinger material, however, was restricted to just a handful of barely noticed albums in the mid-1980s, as he all but retired from the music business.

He was finally lured back during the early 1990s, but though his subsequent output proved frequently ironic (the "Say No to Drugs" single) and generally enjoyable ("Bruk Camera," a duet with Leroy Gibbons which debuted producers Steely & Clevie's eponymous label), it was also patchy. Dillinger continues touring today; he also operates his own Scandal Bag label.

DISCOGRAPHY

9 Ready Natty Dreadie (Studio One) 1975

Oddly, only the first pressing contains the title track, a version of Burning Spear's "Creation Rebel," later purchasers had to settle for Dillinger's take on Roy Richards' "Freedom Blues," cleverly titled "Natty Kung Fu." The rest of the album remains the same, a brilliant updating of Channel One hits from the likes of Horace Andy and Alton Ellis, fleshed out by the DJ's always intriguing cultural raps.

10 CB 200 (Island) 1976

Utterly seminal album, home to the irrepressible "Cocaine In My Brain," but in no way subservient to it. Dillinger's toasting is exemplary throughout, with other highlights including "Plantation Heights," "Crank Face" — where he's joined by Trinity (Clint Eastwood's kid brother), and the title track ode to his motorbike, a version of Gregory Isaacs' "Sun Shines for Me."

7 Bionic Dread (Black Swan—UK) 1976

Disappointing? Hardly. Classic Hookim production and some brutal toasts.

6 Talkin' Blues (Magnum—UK) 1978
8 Top Ranking (Third World—UK) 1978

If "Cocaine" had not already ascended to legend, this is the album which should have assured Dillinger's legend. Not a dull note in sight, as "Rat a Cut Bottle," "Mr Wicked Man Know Yourself" and "King Pharaoh Is Baldhead" blister by.

8 Corn Bread (Vista Sounds—UK) 1978

"Dread Called Fred" was a phenomenal way to open an album, and the remainder of the set keeps up the pace, a war of wills between Dillinger and producers Shrowder and Sevitt. The CD reissue adds "Cocaine" and "Funky Punk."

7 Answer My Questions (Third World) 1979
8 Marijuana in My Brain (Burning Sounds—UK) 1979

Despite the commercial desperation inherent in the title track (whatever next, after all?), an overall excellent set features "Addis Ababbaithiopia," "Stop Stealing in the Name of Jah" and the dread "African Roots Rock Reggae."

7 Badder than Them (A&M) 1980

A remarkable set, as much for its production as for its contents. Watching as the UK new wave scene came to grips with synthesizers and electronics, Dillinger employed many of the same devices himself, creating an album which pre-empted developments which shook his homeland later in the decade, at the same time, ironically, as distancing many of his homeland acolytes.

8 Live at the Music Machine (Vista Sounds) 1981

It was a phenomenal show and the CD loses none of the excitement, as Dillinger launches with "Natty Don't Need Glasses" and "Roots Natty Congo," drops a dynamic "CB 200" in midset, then wraps up with "Cocaine" and "Judgement Time," a packed house knowing the words as well as he does. Appropriately if misleadingly, the album was subsequently reissued as *Best of Live*.

6 Join the Queue (Oak Sounds — UK) 1983

"Jennifer Naurd," "Mr Mickie" and "Duddle Oley" say little, but sound great.

4 Funky Punk (Jamaica Sounds — UK) 1983

Cocaine, marijuana . . . we asked, whatever next? LSD, of course, although the novelty is certainly thinning by now. The Sevitt/Shrowder electro disco-funk adds to the distaste, particularly when applied to reprises of "Cocaine" and "Funky Punk." Not an essential album by any means.

6 King Pharaoh (1984) (Blue Moon)

The title track is classic Dillinger, "Know Yourself Wicked Man" and "When the Sevens Meet" only marginally less so.

5 Blackboard Jungle (Vista Sounds — UK) 1984

Sevitt/Shrowder produced set which has the occasional peak ("Cup of Tea," "Chinese Soul Train") but, heinously, is just a little boring. Just a little.

5 Tribal War (New Cross — UK) 1986
6 Say No to Drugs (Lagoon) 1993

Co-produced with Bunny Lee and Superblack, an interesting comeback but, the title track aside, hardly an enduring one. Since reissued as *Freedom Fighter* (Orange Street).

DILLINGER & CLINT EASTWOOD
7 Live In London (Echo Jazz) 1981

The Freedom Fighters start the show with the first of several solo shots; thereafter, Dillinger and Clint battle one side apiece, and though the material isn't always familiar (no "Cocaine"), it soon will be.

DILLINGER & TRINITY
8 Clash (Burning Sounds — UK) 1976

Clem Bushay takes the production credits on an album which is DJ mayhem all the way. The slow burning hit "Rizla Skank," "Cricket Lovely Cricket" and an ode to TV's "Starsky & Hutch" indicate a light-hearted mood and the exuberance is contagious.

SELECTED COMPILATIONS & ARCHIVE RELEASES
3 3 Piece Suit (Lagoon) 1993

Generous collection of Bunny Lee productions, including "Three Piece Suit and Thing," "Babylon Leggo Jah Children," "Natty Dread a the Ruler" and a host of Tubby dubs.

8 Rebel with a Cause (Culture Press) 1999

The first half of this two-CD set includes both "Cocaine" and its "Rockers" counterpart, before moving into later electro-flavored territory, and winding up with the intriguing (if non-Dillinger) "Bunny Hop," rapped over the "Funky

Punk" rhythm. Over on disc two, 1976's "Killer Man Jaro," "Freedom" and "Natty Kung Fu" appear alongside a handful of excellent vocal and dub sides produced by Roderick "Blackbeard" Sinclair. The frankly daft "Rapping on the Bus" brings things nicely up to date.

9 Cocaine in My Brain (Trojan — UK) 2000

Much needed anthology of Dillinger's 70s peak, featuring all the expected hits ("Cocaine," "Loving Pauper," "Micky Mouse Crab Louse," "Crab in My Pants"), plus 11 Lee Perry productions.

MIKEY DREAD

STYLE *reggae (toasting/dub)*
BORN *Michael Campbell, 1948 (Port Antonio, JA)*

Arguably, Mikey Dread's UK and US fame rests largely on his work with British dub-punks the Clash, and a career which has seemingly seen him divide much of the last two decades between British and American television. However, the clutch of crucial albums he recorded for his own DATC (Dread At The Controls) label at the outset of that period also marked the culmination of several years of equally essential and influential work in Jamaica, beginning when he launched his weekly four hour *Dread at the Controls* radio program on the national JBC station.

At a time when mainstream Jamaican radio generally concentrated on imported sounds, eschewing homegrown talent (but, simultaneously, providing it with a world of covers to choose from), *Dread at the Controls* was priority listening. Dread's playlist ranged across the spectrum, frequently airing new material within hours (or less!) of it being pressed onto acetate — the very first step in manufacturing a record.

Even Dread's jingles were remarkable, recorded at King Tubby's studios with whatever rhythms, sound effects and vocalists were to hand. One team he especially favored, Althea Forrest and Donna Reid, worked up a jingle based around a DJ cut they had made with Joe Gibbs, answering Trinity's "Three Piece Suit" with a reworking of Alton Ellis' classic "I'm Still in Love." Overwhelmed by listener response, Gibbs released "Uptown Top Ranking" in late 1977 and was rewarded with a #1 hit both at home and in the UK.

Of course Dread's popularity (and his manic broadcasting style) soon led him to the recording studio in his own right. Lee Perry cut what became Dread's signature piece, "Dread at the Controls," as well as "Schoolgirls" and the powerful "Homeguard"; Sonia Pottinger released his "Rootsman Revival" 45. He also recorded with Joe Gibbs and, after resigning from JBC in 1979, having endured one row too many with the staid old broadcasters, he swiftly found work as an engineer at Treasure Isle.

From there, Dread linked with producer Carlton Patterson, both as an artist (the "Barber Saloon Haircut" single) and co-producer—he and Patterson handled Ray I's "Weatherman Skank" smash. By the end of the year, Dread had established DATC, again in conjunction with Patterson, and the pair began releasing a stream of singles by Edi Fitzroy, Sugar Minott, Earl Sixteen and more. Dread, too, continued recording, his singles invariably featuring revolutionary Patterson/King Tubby dubs on the flip—"African Anthem," "Parrot Jungle," "Robbers Roost" and more.

The label's first LP release was *Dread at the Controls Master Showcase*, a non-stop celebration of dub into which Dread interspersed toasts, jingles, spoken word, until the experience was nothing less than an evening in the company of the old show itself. The album was completed shortly before Dread traveled to England where he was booked as opening act on the Clash's January, 1980, tour. Within a month, he was supervising the recording of that band's next single, "Bankrobber," in the process completely restyling the song's original ska backing to a threatening dub. Dread himself toasted a version of the same track, eventually released as "Rocker's Galore—UK tour."

Weeks later, Dread joined the Clash in New York to cut versions of Eddy Grant's "Police on My Back" and the group's own "One More Time" (for their gestating *Sandinista!* album), plus what became his own next single, the brutal "Rockers' Delight." Casting a jaundiced eye over the then-prevalent British 2-Tone ska movement, he chastised all of its figureheads, before moving on to some of their punk brethren, too. Further Clash sessions took place at the Channel One studios in Kingston—abandoned when the punks found themselves the targets for every hoodlum in town.

Following the vital *African Anthem: The Mikey Dread Show Dubwise* set, *World War III*, Dread's second album, arrived in 1981. Although it lacked some of the anarchic approach of its predecessors (a "failing" exaggerated by the largely lovers rock-enhanced *SWALK*), it nevertheless found fertile soil in the UK. There, Dread was now being courted by the newly launched television station, Channel Four, who recruited him to narrate 1982's six part *Deep Roots* exploration of Jamaican music. In 1983, he hosted the channel's live music *Rockers Road Show*—the show's theme appeared on his 1984 album *Pave the Way* (Clash bassist Paul Simonon was included amongst that album's guest musicians).

Dread's recording career slowed to a comparative trickle as further outside opportunities presented themselves. In 1983, the UK label Earthquake released the Alton Ellis-produced "Paradise" single, but his next album, 1989's *Happy Family* received little attention. A spell with the US Rykodisc label in the early 1990s similarly produced a less-than-classic album.

Dread's most recent projects have included the reggae video history *Deep Roots Music* and British TV's ten part *Rockers' International*. He was also involved with former Guns n'Roses member Izzy Stradlin's 1992 debut album, *Izzy Stradlin & The Ju Ju Hounds*.

DISCOGRAPHY

9 **Dread at the Controls Master Showcase (DATC) 1979**
9 **African Anthem Dubwise (DATC) 1979**

Two blindingly spontaneous slabs of magic, dub after dub after radio jingle, a night in what must have been the staid JBC directors' vision of hell.

8 **World War III (DATC) 1981**
7 **Beyond World War III (DATC) 1981**
7 **Jungle Signal (DATC—UK) 1982**
7 **Dub Merchant (DATC) 1982**

Dubby diversions between the main attractions—*Dub Merchant* features eight crunching remixes of the hit single "Jumping Master."

5 **SWALK (DATC) 1982**

A weak point in one of the strongest chains in the DJ catalog, Dread goes in search of lovers rock, and finds it in the arms of the latest studio technology. Plus, the collision with his occasionally nasal singing voice is an acquired taste in its own right.

8 **Pave the Way (Heartbeat) 1984**
8 **Pave the Way Parts 1/2 (DEP) 1985**

Like a steppin' razor, Dread shreds rock's rich tapestry than reties the threads into previously unimaginable new patterns. Disco whistles collide with rocker guitars, lush keyboards clash with whiffs of punk, dubby electro bleeps bleed across brass solos, and Sixties vocal trios rub shoulders with soca. It sounds chaotic, and that's exactly how it should be.

5 **Happy Family (RAS) 1989**
5 **Portrait (RAS) 1991**
6 **African Anthem Revisited (RAS) 1991**

Portrait is essentially another of Dread's lovers rock excursions; its evocatively titled dub companion offers a return to the mechanics of its better known predecessor, but not necessarily to the sound.

5 **Obsession (Rykodisc) 1992**

A lovers rock inspired selection of songs that lack sizzle, and although Dread gives his best, it just ends up sounding limp.

7 **Come to Mikey Dread's Dub Party (ROIR) 1996**

Rekindling the mood of his earliest albums, albeit with the benefit of mid-1990s studio tech, an occasionally earth-shaking reminder that Dread was one of dub's most powerful pioneers.

8 Best Sellers (Rykodisc) 1991

Grabbing a handful of early 45s, then cherry-picking the albums for some of Dread's most memorable efforts, a mighty introduction to the world of Dread. "Jah Jah Love," "Warrior Stylee" and "Barber Saloon Haircut" receive welcome revivals, while the unreleased "Choose Me" is another of his "SWALK"-like soul-flavored gems.

8 Prime of Mikey Dread: Massive Dub Cuts 1978–92 (Music Club—UK) 1999

Despite a smattering of duplication with the Rykodisc set, a worthwhile companion which rounds out the best of Dread, even if the original album releases remain the true essentials.

DUB

Few musical forms have proven as influential, and internationally important, as dub. Though the term is now virtually interchangeable with remixing, particularly on rock and dance records, in its purest and most vibrant form dub is better described as an entire reconstruction, a process by which an existing piece of music is stripped down to its barest rhythmic bones, then rebuilt in its entirety.

A genuinely successful dub, therefore, is not simply a familiar tune with a handful of sonic alternations, but a piece of music which stands on its own terms, to be appreciated in its own right. That the vast majority of dubs, even among the classic Jamaican artists, can be viewed more as exercises in sound effects and technical wizardry cannot be held against the art form in itself. For every ten dubs which are simply annoying, random sound effects thrown together because they can be, there is always one which doesn't merely overwhelm the listener, it has the potential to possess him as well. Some can even change the way you listen to music.

The undisputed king of the dub is, as his name suggests, the late King Tubby. Indeed, to an audience raised on the reggae reissues and retrospection of the past decade, King Tubby *is* dub. It's an understandable assumption and, if one overlooks chronology and contemporary international recognition, an accurate one. More than any other musician or producer experimenting within the dub field of the 1970s and 1980s, King Tubby took the music to its limits, both sonically and technically. An entire generation of future producers and remixers learned their trade from King Tubby, either in person or by example.

Equally impressive is the roster of established artists whose career at some point or another, intersected with Tubby's, there to be dissected, devolved, stripped to the bone, and sent back out into the world with that most magical of credits engraved within its grooves — "remix by King Tubby."

It was, of course, King Tubby who first developed the dub process, while working as a disc cutter at Duke Reid's Treasure Isle studios around 1968. DJs had long since learned how to fade out the vocal track alone, creating the instrumental "version" b-sides which, by 1968, were de rigueur on Jamaican 45s. Treasure Isle itself had also taken the lead in terms of remixing, as engineer and sound system opener "Ruddy" Redwood reworked popular instrumental versions to emphasize the bass — a key element during the rude boy/rock steady era.

King Tubby, however, went so much further than that. Taking an existing tape, he stripped out the vocals and then replaced them with anything that came to hand, dropping instrumental tracks in and out of the mix, overdubbing new sounds and effects, and all the while increasing and echoing the bass lines, reinventing the performance to create what ultimately became dub.

Having pressed the results up as acetates, or dub plates (the term existed before the genre), King Tubby's favorite tracks were exclusive to his own sound system. Other DJs, however, were soon commissioning their own dubs from him. The likes of U-Roy (a Tubby's Hi Fi regular), I-Roy, Big Youth, Dean Beckford and Berry Simpson, all future giants of the toasting scene, learned to ply their trade with King Tubby dub-plates and, of course, it wasn't long before other producers and engineers began emulating his techniques.

As the medium developed during the early 1970s, the young Augustus Pablo was in constant demand to add his trademark melodica to dub sides, to the point where an instrument which hadn't even figured in the reggae arsenal two or three years earlier, was now considered a vital component to the newest musical form. When Rupie Edwards was hatching his "Ire Feelings (Skanga)" variation "Buckshot," Pablo was one of the first musicians he asked to contribute. And when Pablo declined to perform, Edwards simply played the melodica himself.

Such elements as this, however, were merely the icing on the dub cake. The true beating heart of dub is the bass guitar, cranked up to impossible earthquake proportions, to echo and reverberate first through the rhythm of the record, then through the soul of anybody caught within earshot. King Tubby understood this from the outset; other pioneers — Pablo, Edwards, Lee Perry, Niney Holness and Keith Hudson among them — simply took his extremes even further.

All made some frighteningly unlistenable records as they strove to discover their own signature dub sound, but again, all knew that when a dub worked, there was no end to the possibilities. Soon, dubs of dubs were appearing; and dubs of dubs of dubs, each one stripping its predecessor back, then rearranging it in a whole new direction.

Niney Holness' "Blood and Fire" variations offer a classic early example. The aforementioned "Ire Feelings (Skanga)" another, and if the first dub pioneers were at all restrained by the primitive equipment with which they were, for the most part, working, they rarely let it show.

Again, the best of King Tubby's work was created on an obsolete second-hand four track mixer he bought from Byron Lee's Dynamic Sounds studio in 1971 and, at a time when the greatest American producers felt themselves under-privileged with less than eight tracks to work on, King Tubby turned out masterpieces by using no more than two. Lee Perry's infamous Black Ark studio was similarly equipped.

Far from being hamstrung by these limitations, however, Perry and Tubby were encouraged by them. Indeed, one can argue very convincingly that as technology and equipment improved through the 1970s and (especially) 1980s, the actual quality and inventiveness of dubs declined. It would not, after all, be the first musical format to suffer for such reasons.

Dub reached its peak, in terms of both quality and quantity, during the mid-late 1970s, not at all coincidentally the last years during which Perry and King Tubby were actively blazing the trail. Thereafter, its commercial value declined — the days when an artist's latest album was inevitably accompanied by a dub counterpart were over, and even the once-near-obligatory practice of placing a dub mix on the back of new singles was supplanted by a return to the earlier "version" side, a more or less straightforward instrumental take.

There were exceptions, of course. Both Scientist and Prince/King Jammy remained deft dub practitioners, while Sly Dunbar and Robbie Shakespeare's very ouvre is based in dub technique. Their recreation of Black Uhuru's early 1980s output, the *Dub Factor* album, arrived in 1983, the equally inflammatory *Brutal Dub* in 1987, and the duo's own Taxi label was still pumping out dub sides (and corresponding compilation albums), even after dub itself was utterly reinvented by the onset of digital technology.

British producers Adrian Sherwood and Neil "Mad Professor" Fraser, too, perpetuated dub into the 1990s and beyond, arguably creating some of the finest aural sculptures of the age, but seldom working within the field's own natural parameters. Sherwood's On-U Sound empire in particular has proven almost absurdly eclectic, plowing a furrow which zigzags between reggae, punk, indie rock and hip hop (often simultaneously), while maintaining a ferocious working relationship with the likes of Lee Perry, Prince Far-I and Dennis Alcapone.

The Mad Professor, too, works within his own unrestricted field, although his most satisfying projects have undoubtedly been his own dub collaborations with Perry, Alcapone and a number of other Jamaican artists — he also successfully revitalized the careers of both Susan Cadogan and U-Roy during the mid 1990s.

Few, however, even dream of comparing these efforts with the primal creations of dub's now-distant past, the days when record buyers inspected the remix credits even before they played their new purchase, then checked out the dub before spinning the hit. Time and technology have marched too far for dub to ever return with the passion it once wore, and the music, too, has moved far away from the basics which underpinned the genre's finest moments. But, the reissue racks continue to bulge with rereleased and recently rediscovered dub classics, living proof that, if the creativity is locked into the past, the experience lives on.

RECOMMENDED LISTENING

Dub Chill Out (Music Club) 1996

With its 18 tracks dominated by Perry and Tubby, with token entries for Prince/King Jammy, Scientist and Sly & Robbie, this is very much a budget priced entry level collection, the chance for ingenues to find out what dub's all about before they start spending serious money. The liner notes provide minimal information, but there is little quibbling with a song list which includes "Zion Gate," "Rasta Dub It Everywhere" and "Hypocrite."

VARIOUS ARTISTS

Dub Reggae Essentials (Hip-O) 2000

An extraordinarily aptly titled collection hits more high spots than even the (generous) track listing lets on. The majority of inclusions are drawn from either long lost Jamaican b-sides or out of print UK/US albums and, while the chronology is again skewed, the liner notes document source, producer, remixer and even the original cuts that are being assaulted. Primal offerings from Dillinger, Mikey Dread, Black Uhuru and the Congos join surprisingly effective contributions from Steel Pulse, Linton Kwesi Johnson and even British 2-Tone heroes The Selecter.

VARIOUS ARTISTS

Dubwise & Otherwise (Blood & Fire—UK) 1997

Radical round-up of dubs drawn from throughout Blood & Fire's (excellent) catalog of compilations and reissues. Bunny Lee, Keith Hudson, Winston Rodney, Vivian Jackson, Lee Perry and Tappa Zukie are all present and correct, while the lesser known Bertram Brown, Pete Weston, Everton DaSilva and Don Mais prove that ferocious dub beauty is not the province only of the genre's biggest names. Chronologically the collection is a mess. But musically, it's unstoppable.

VARIOUS ARTISTS

Front Line in Dub (Caroline) 1997

Dramatic selection drawn from the Front Line label's surprisingly thorough dub archives. Culture, Prince Far I, the Mighty Diamonds, the Twinkle Brothers and I-Roy all recorded some startling dub sides during their late 70s sojourn at Front Line; Sly & Robbie, and the lesser feted Vivian Weathers and Poet & the Roots (featuring dub poet Linton Kwesi Johnson) likewise. This 15 track set highlights some of the best offerings, drawing both from albums and period 12-inch singles, the source for two positively brobdingagian offerings from the Twinkle Brothers.

VARIOUS ARTISTS

Timewarp Dub Clash (Island Jamaica) 1993

Past and present collide on a dramatic set which merges classic Black Uhuru, Burning Spear, Junior Delgado and even the Paragons (a spooky Steve Stanley mix of "Man Next Door"), with 1992–93 efforts from the Mad Professor/Jah Shaka/Adrian Sherwood/Alpha & Omega axis. Half of the album was originally released as *Raiders of the Lost Dub* during the mid-1980s, but the package as a whole hangs together as both a musical masterpiece and a solid history lesson.

VARIOUS ARTISTS

Trojan Dub Box Set (Trojan—UK) 1998

Far reaching three-CD box showcasing a variety of producers and artists, unhappily without too much explanation of who or what is behind the mix. Perry and Tubby dominate, of course, but Bunny Lee and Niney Holness are also well-represented in a collection which concentrates on the less anthologized b-side material.

RUPIE EDWARDS

STYLE *reggae*

BORN *Rupert Edwards, 7/4/45 (Goshen, nr Brownstown, St Anns, JA)*

Born in the rural St Ann's region, Edwards was 13 when his family moved to Kingston. There his earliest musical strivings included performing a Pat Boone song at a Joseph Verejohn talent show in 1958, and ultimately won him a spot on the broadcast talent show *Opportunity Hour* in 1962.

Spotted by producer SL Smith, whose Hi-Lite label operated out of the haberdashery of the same name, Edwards cut his first single, "Guilty Convict," later that year, although it did little. The Little Wonder label also released a couple of 45s by the 17 year old, including "Just Because."

Further 45s emerged on President Bell's label before Edwards linked with Paragons vocalist Junior Menz and guitarist Eric Frater in 1965, to form the Virtues. They cut several singles for Harry J, including "Mother's Choice," "Your Wife and Mother" and a fine cover of Curtis Mayfield & The Impressions' recent hit "Amen." "High Tide" and "Burning Love" (Edwards' first ever production, recorded at Studio One and released as Rupie Edwards and the Virtues) were among the band's follow-ups before they broke up in 1968. Frater went on to become a respected sessionman, Edwards turned to establishing himself among the era's most in-demand young producers.

Based out of his Success record store on Orange Street, the next few years saw Edwards work with Dennis Alcapone, Bob Andy, Errol Dunkley, the Ethiopians, the Heptones, Hugh Roy Junior and the Meditators. Backing was provided from his aptly named All Stars session band, whose line-up at this time included Hux Brown (guitar), Jackie Jackson (bass), Gladstone Anderson (piano), Winston Wright and Tyrone Downie (organ), Tommy McCook (tenor sax), Stanley Ribbs (baritone sax) and Carlton Davis (drums).

Edwards continued releasing singles under his own name, including "I Can't Forget" (1968), "Long Lost Love" (1969), "Sharp Pan Ya Machete," "Full Moon," "Census Taker," "Handicap" and "Love at First Sight" (1970), "I'm Gonna Live Some Life," "Black Man" and "Soulful Stew" (1971).

In addition, the All Stars commenced their own string of dynamic instrumentals and versions — "Kinky Funky," "Bee Sting," "The Return of Herbert Splifington" (continuing a saga which Edwards launched on an earlier single with Winston Blake), "Promotors Grouse," "Grandfather Clock," "Rock In," "Tender Waltz," "Solid as a Rock," "Riot" and "Christmas Parade," plus version sides of the Meditators' "Music Alone Shall Live" and "Stop the Party" and Laurel Aitkens' "Mary's Boy Child."

In 1971, Edwards began working with vocalist Gregory

Isaacs, producing the classic "Lonely Man" single. That same year, the UK reggae label Trojan handed him what amounted to his own imprint, Big Records, which became home to some sterling work with Dave McClaren, the Itals, the Gaylads, Keith Cole, Froggy Ray, Joe Higgs, BB Seaton and Max Romeo. He also released material on the Success label, distributed by Pama, before linking exclusively with another Trojan subsidiary, Cactus.

The singles "Press Along," "Jimmy Has a Job Card" (both 1972), "Boloman a Come" and "Mysterious Nature" (1974) did well in both Jamaica and the UK, while a strong collection of his 1973–74 material, *Rupie's Gems*, was released in 1974. Edwards also caused a stir that year with the release of the *Yamaha Skank* album, the entire set based upon multiple reworkings of just one rhythm, taken from Slim Smith and the Uniques' "My Conversation."

Yamaha Skank was unlike anything heard before. Although it was common for the same rhythm to reappear again and again over the course of various singles by different artists, the idea of actually building a full LP around the same notion was an absolute revelation — and one which would soon become a staple of the Jamaican scene.

Edwards' next move, however, was — if anything — even more remarkable. The previous year, 1973, he scored a major Jamaican hit as producer of Johnny Clarke's "Everyday Wondering." Now he revamped that song's rhythm for his own next 45, the proto-dub masterpiece "Ire Feelings (Skanga)."

The record caught everybody off-guard. "Ire Feelings" made #9 in the UK in late 1974 and, while many observers wrote it off as a simple novelty hit, other ears were attuned to some more lasting qualities. A full year later, the British *Street Life* magazine acknowledged, "'Irie Feelings'. . . helped create an unprecedented neo-commercial demand for [dub]," pointing out that hitherto, the genre had been all but unknown outside of specialist listening circles.

Now the floodgates opened, with Edwards himself leading the charge. He ultimately recorded some twenty different variations of "Ire Feelings" for release as singles, ranging from such relatively straightforward approximations as Jah Woosh's "The Wanderer" and Milton Henry's "What Can I Do," to deep dub experiments with titles to match — "Dub Master Special," "Spangy Dub," "Strictly Dub."

One of these, "Buckshot," was released as Edwards' next UK 45, and was characterized by the lead instrumentation being taken by a melodica. (Augustus Pablo was his first choice as soloist; he refused the offer, so Edwards played it himself). Despite, or perhaps because of, its marked similarities to the original hit, "Buckshot" failed to take off in Britain.

The less derivative, although markedly inferior, "Leggo Skanga," however, made #32 in February, 1975, and there was also high praise for the hastily compiled *Ire Feelings*

album, rounding up a number of Edwards' other recent singles and sessions.

Edwards relocated to the UK soon after, remaining there even after it became apparent that a third hit was not on the horizon — neither "Boogooyaga" (1975) nor "Three Pan One, a Murder" (1976) registered in the mainstream. However, his production work continued to be successful. Cactus provided an outlet for a stream of 45s by Jah Woosh, the Heaven Singers (featuring Junior Delgado), Errol Carter, Flabba, Gladstone Anderson and Shorty the President, while Edwards' own subsequent releases included two volumes of his distinctive dubs and versions, the *Dub Basket* compilations.

In the aftermath of Cactus' demise around 1977, Edwards' own visibility declined. A number of his earlier recordings were reissued — "My Little Red Top," from the *Ire Feelings* album, appeared on the Sensations Sounds label later that same year. Production work with the same label included new releases for Errol Dunkley and Dobby Dobson. In 1980, Edwards released his first new album in almost half a decade, *Conversation Stylee*; since that time, his attentions have been directed towards inspirational and sentimental music. He remains a UK resident, insisting he will never return to Jamaica until he receives full payment for recordings made back in the 1960s and early 1970s.

DISCOGRAPHY

9 Yamaha Skank (Success) 1974

Slim Smith's "My Conversation," warped and wrapped around so many new sounds and symbols that half the time it is all but unrecognizable. Only the odd floating passage serves to remind the listener just what is going on here, and the ensuing sense of disorientation is worth the price of admission alone. At the time, this album was considered a work of demented genius. Today it is simply genius.

7 Ire Feelings (Cactus — UK) 1975

Though the stellar title track and its even freakier version flip open the album, the remainder of the set proves surprisingly diverse. "Do the Skanga," of course, leaves little to the imagination, but "Love Is a Wonderful Wicked Thing," "Burning Love" and "My Little Red Top" must have come as a shock to anyone expecting simply a dozen retreads of the same rhythm. Of course, that came later.

6 Conversation Stylee (Tad's — UK) 1980

Worth investigating from the "whatever happened to" point of view, but generally an unfocused collection of seemingly unfinished ideas.

SELECTED COMPILATIONS & ARCHIVE RELEASES

8 Rupie's Gems (Cactus — UK) 1974
8 Rupie's Gems Volume Two (Cactus — UK) 1976

And indeed they are — hits from the Heptones, the fabulous Errol Dunkley, Johnnie Clarke, Dobbie Dobson and more make for a crucial collection of Edwards' greatest productions.

8 Rupie Edwards Dub Basket (Cactus — UK) 1976
8 Dub Basket Chapter 2 (Cactus — UK) 1976

Two companions to the *Rupie's Gems* production compilation, but emphasizing material hitherto released in Jamaica only.

9 Jamaica Serenade (Cactus — UK) 1976

British and Jamaican 45s are presented with versions intact — and one wonders why no-one thought to release "Free Up de Ganja," "Baby It's You" and "That Wonderful Sound" before this.

6 Dub Classic (Cactus — UK) 1977
7 Hit Picks Vol 1 (Cactus — UK) 1977
10 Ire Feelings: Chapter & Version (Trojan) 1990

16 years on (and with the possible exception of Pluto Shervington's "Dat"), "Ire Feelings" remains one of the most divisive reggae/dub recordings ever to take up residence in the UK chart. Utterly dislocated, fragments fly, bass lines burble, a cuckoo coos, a cowbell clangs and over it all, the endless refrain of "skanga skanga skanga." And that's only the first time you hear it. 20 versions (plus the original "Everyday Wondering") later . . . this might be the greatest album ever made. Equally gratifyingly, it might also be the most annoying.

9 Let There Be Version (Trojan) 1990

Three bonus tracks chase *Yamaha Skank* towards its own irresistible state of overkill.

EEK-A-MOUSE

STYLE *reggae (toasting/dance hall)*
BORN *Ripton Joseph Hilton, 1957 (Kingston JA)*

Ripton Hilton was still at college in the mid-1970s when he cut his first singles, "My Father's Land" and "Creation," produced by his mathematics tutor, Mr Dehaney and heavily influenced by roots singer Pablo Moses. They did little, and he spent much of the remainder of the decade moving between sound systems and studios, issuing a series of sporadic 45s — "Georgy Porgy" (produced by Banny Riley/Hyman Wright), "No Wicked" and "Trying to Be Free." All appeared under his given name.

Hilton was already known to his friends as Eek-A-Mouse, taken from a racehorse he regularly bet upon, and which lost every race, until the one time he decided to place his wager elsewhere. "Once a Virgin," his first single with Joe Gibbs, introduced this distinctive new name to the record buying public in 1979.

In tandem with an exhilarating song, it also made an im-

mediate star of the DJ who bore it, all the more so since both his extravagantly costumed appearance and quirky, "bingy-boingy" sound only exaggerated the sheer bizarreness of the Eek-A-Mouse experience. No matter that he dressed like a mouse and toyed with giant lumps of cheese while squeaking loudly, even his vocal style was unique — neither singing nor DJ-ing, it was eventually christened singjay.

"Wa-Do-Dem" (produced by Douglas Boothe) and "Modelling Queen" (Linval Thompson) followed during 1980, together with another Thompson production, the album *Bubble Up Yu Hip*. By the end of the year, Eek-A-Mouse had linked with Junjo Lawes, backing band Roots Radics and remixer Scientist. Minor hits "Virgin Girl" and "Noah's Ark" warmed the partnership up, but it was a remake of "Wa-Do-Dem" which truly broke things open.

Further attention came when Eek-A-Mouse proved an unexpected smash at Reggae Sunsplash in 1981. At a show utterly overshadowed by the death of Bob Marley, Eek-A-Mouse's exuberant personality and repertoire could have appeared horribly out of place. Instead, he brought the house down, cementing his "biddy biddy beng" refrain among the most pervasive catch-phrases of the decade. (Eek-A-Mouse returned to Sunsplash in 1982, his set captured on 1983's *Live At . . .* album.)

The festive hit "Christmas A-Come" wrapped up Eek-A-Mouse's breakthrough year. 1982 brought more hits including "Do You Remember," "Ganja Smuggling," "Wild Like a Tiger" and "For Hire and Removal," all leading up to the release of his second album, *Wa-Do-Dem*.

"Operation Eradication," meanwhile, proved that there was a deeply sensitive side to Eek-A-Mouse — the song was prompted by the vigilante shooting death of his close friend, DJ Errol Scorcher. Further albums *Skidip* (1982) and *The Mouse and the Man* (1983), and the singles "Terrorists in the City," "Anarexol" and "Teacher" ensured both Eek-A-Mouse's reputation and his stature remained high.

Aside from his own vinyl excursions, Eek-A-Mouse became a ubiquitous feature on dance hall live collections. Alongside Yellowman and Fathead, he was one of the stars of a Junjo Lawes-arranged live session from 82 Chisholm Avenue, on 10/13/82, preserved aboard the *Aces International* album; further suitably demented performances can be found on the seminal *Live at Skateland* set.

In 1984, following the Lawes-produced *Mouseketeer* album (and another memorable Sunsplash showing), Eek-A-Mouse joined producers Anthony and Ronald Welch. They cut 1985's *Assassinator* album, destined to become Eek-A-Mouse's US debut.

The King and I arrived later that same year. Recorded in England with producer Cliff Carnegie, the set was a clear nod towards the rock cross-over audience to which Eek-A-Mouse, quite uniquely among the Jamaican DJ crowd, was appealing to. Noel Alphonso, of the US label RAS, determined that his next album, *Eek-A-Nomics*, should confront this new opportunity head on.

The scheme was rewarded when "The Freak," a distinctive revision of the theme from television's *The Adams Family*, became a club hit in 1988, in turn prompting Island Records to sign Eek-A-Mouse in 1989. He also landed the role of Fat Smitty in the movie *New Jack City*.

Co-produced by Gussie Clarke, Eek-A-Mouse's Island debut, 1991's *U-Neek*, continued its predecessor's rock drive with an effective cover of Led Zeppelin's cod reggae number "D'Yer Maker" and the single "You're The One I Need." Two years later, Eek-A- Mouse stood in for Buju Banton at a charity show in Pasadena, CA, after the scheduled headliner was forced to pull out in the wake of the "Boom Bye Bye" scandal.

Departing Island, Eek-A-Mouse then lapsed into a period of uncharacteristic silence, finally broken by 1996's *Black Cowboy*.

DISCOGRAPHY

7 Bubble Up Yu Hip (Greensleeves — UK) 1980
9 Wa-Do-Dem (Shanachie) 1982

Or, the best of the early years. From the smash hit title track debut, fueled by a Roots Radics rhythm, to the conspiratorially gleeful "Ganja Smuggling," and on through "Noah's Ark," "Long Time Ago" and "Operation Eradication," Eek-A-Mouse proves that even weird voices can prove enduring if the material (and production) is strong enough. And here, they are. The album was reissued on CD in 2001 by Greensleeves' newly opened US operation.

7 Skidip (Shanachie) 1982

"Always On My Mind" is not necessarily the first song one equates with the Eek-A-Mouse treatment, but he pulls it off with breathless daring, before confirming his abilities with an album which doesn't rely on hit singles for its hardest hitters.

8 The Mouse and the Man (Shanachie) 1983

With Linval Thompson producing and the Roots Radics slinging the rhythms, this set returned to classic form and includes such crucial cuts as "Terrorists in the City," "Hitler" and the title track.

7 Mouseketeer (Greensleeves — UK) 1984

"Star, Daily News or Gleaner" is worthy of any Eek-A-Mouse best of; past hits "Anarexol" and "Wild Like a Tiger" are already there. And "How I Got My Name" tells the story of one man and a horse. . . .

6 Assassinator (Shanachie) 1985

An oddly downbeat album, or at least as downbeat as you can be with a voice like that. "Penni-Walli" discusses the consequences of being knocked off his bicycle; "Gun Shot a Cry" discusses the prevalence of gunfire in the city; "Assassinator" is self explanatory.

7 The King & I (RAS) 1987
8 Eek-A-Nomics (RAS) 1988

Hello . . . it's him . . . he's on the loose again. "The Freak" has to be one of the most compulsively annoying songs of the year, and a slice of clinical self-analysis which would be seriously disturbing if it wasn't so silly. Elsewhere, Mouse must be the only person who can make a police siren sound like . . . well, sound like Eek-A-Mouse.

6 U-Neek (Mango) 1991

Led Zeppelin's "D'Yer Maker" probably wasn't written with a tall, skinny Jamaican fruitcake in mind, but in Eek-A-Mouse's hands, it sounds like it was. American band Dread Zeppelin were making a similar virtue of reggae-ing up the heavy rock leviathans, but Mouse does more in one song than they achieved in their entire career. And the rest of the album's not bad, either.

7 Black Cowboy (Explicit) 1996

EEK-A-MOUSE & MICHIGAN & SMILEY
7 Live at Reggae Sunsplash (Sunsplash) 1983

Five Eek-A-Mouse cuts open the album, all past hits, all absurdly contagious.

SELECTED COMPILATIONS & ARCHIVE RELEASES
8 The Very Best Of (Shanachie) 1987

With five albums to choose from (*Wa-Do-Dem* through *Assassinator*), plus a string of crucial singles, how could this album be anything but aptly titled?

Surprisingly strong set drawn from a period which most commentators regard as a definite lull in the Mouse's progress. "The Freak" opens, while rarity hunters are treated to a very (very) distinctive rendering of "The Night Before Christmas," originally cut for a 1988 RAS label sampler.

FRONT LINE RECORDS

Throughout the first half of the 1970s, the UK-based Virgin label was widely regarded as the home for a string of increasingly avant-garde progressive rockers — the label's first release, in 1973, was Mike Oldfield's *Tubular Bells*, and little of its output since that time had deviated too far from its model. Beginning in 1975, however, label head Richard Branson attempted broadening the Virgin image by signing a number of leading roots artists, and swiftly establishing the company as the only mainstream rival to Island records.

U-Roy, the Mighty Diamonds, Keith Hudson, Johnny Clarke, Peter Tosh, the Gladiators, I-Roy and Delroy Washington all had success with albums released during 1976–77 — indeed, it was said that the Sex Pistols' Johnny Rotten wanted to sign with Virgin because of the company's progressive policy towards reggae. In 1978, therefore, Virgin announced the formation of a new subsidiary devoted entirely to reggae, Front Line.

According to legend, Branson and Rotten holed up in a Kingston hotel for a week, while the lobby filled with musicians anxious to check out reports of these crazy Englishmen who were giving away money. Aside from confirming Virgin's existing stable of reggae artists (released on the Virgin and Caroline labels), the two also cemented deals with Prince Far-I, Big Youth, Prince Hammer, Tappa Zukie, Sly Dunbar, the Twinkle Brothers and more, a roster which established Frontline among the most serious players on the entire reggae scene.

Frontline survived just two years before the operation was folded. In that span, however, the label was responsible for giving mainstream UK releases to a host of now-classic albums, many of which have since been reissued, or at least compiled onto, CD with 2001 bringing an excellent four-CD box set. In addition, original UK pressings are considered eminently collectible.

FRONT LINE AND ASSOCIATED LABEL LISTING

VIRGIN 7-inch SINGLES

VS 111 BB SEATON: Dancing Shoes/Moon River (1974)

VS 137 THE MIGHTY DIAMONDS: Have Mercy/Them Never Love Poor Marcus (1975)

VS 138 U-ROY: Runaway Girl/Chalice in the Palace (1975)

VS 140 PETER TOSH: Legalize It/(Version) (1976)

VS 151 KEITH HUDSON: Thank You Baby/Too Expensive (1976)

VS 152 JOHNNY CLARKE: I Wish It Would Go on Forever/—(1976)

VS 155 THE MIGHTY DIAMONDS: Shame & Pride/—(1976)

VS 165 GREY EZEKE & GREIG TONY: We're the Greatest (1977)

VS 168 THE MIGHTY DIAMONDS: Country Living/Coming Through (1977)

VS 173 JOHNNY CLARKE: Roots Natty Roots Natty (Congo/Version) (1977)

VS 174 THE GLADIATORS: Chatty Chatty Mouth/Hearsay (1977)

VS 179 PETER TOSH: African/Stepping Razor (1978)

VS 182 THE MIGHTY DIAMONDS: Sneakin Sally Through the Alley/—(1978)

VS 208 THE DIAMONDS: Sweet Lady/Jah Will Work It Out (1978)

VS 221 THE MIGHTY DIAMONDS: Planet Called Earth/Lovely Lady (1978)

FRONT LINE 7-inch SINGLES

FLS 101 I-ROY: Fire Stick/Casmas Town (1978)

FLS 102 THE GLADIATORS: Stick a Bush/Music Makers from Jamaica (1978)

FLS 103 JAH LLOYD THE BLACK LION: This Ya Sound/Upfull Rastaman (1978)

FLS 104 THE TWINKLE BROTHERS: Free Africa/—(1978)

FLS 106 PRINCE HAMMER: Bible/Morwell Esquire (1978)

FLS 107 ALTHEA & DONNA: Puppy Dog Song/—(1978)

FLS 108 JOYELLA BLADE: Cairo/Cairo Dub (1978)

FLS 109 TAPPA ZUKIE: She Want a Phensic/Rastaman Skank (1978)

FLS 110 ALTHEA & DONNA: Going to Negril/—(1978)

FLS 111 THE GLADIATORS: Dreadlocks the Time Is Now/Pocket Money (1978)

FLS 112 PRINCE FAR I: No More War/Version (1978)

FLS 113 THE ABYSSINIANS: Hey You/This Land Is for Everyone (1978)

FLS 114 VIVIAN WEATHERS: Hip Hug/—(1978)

FLS 115 TAPPA ZUKIE: Oh Lord/First Street Rock (1978)

FLS 116 CULTURE: Natty Get Weary/Dub (1978)

FLS 117 TWINKLE BROTHERS: Distant Drums/Dub (1978)

FLS 118 THE GLADIATORS: Struggle/Praises to the Most High (1979)

FLS 125 CULTURE: International Herb/Down in Jamaica (1979)

FLS 126 THE GLADIATORS: Holiday Ride/No Disturbance (1979)

VIRGIN 12-inch SINGLES

VDJ 13 U-ROY: Runaway Girl/Chalice in the Palace (1975)

VDJ 22 DELROY WASHINGTON: Give All the Praise to Jah/Stand Up and Be Happy (1977)

VOLE 1 DR. ALIMANTADO: Slavery Let I Go/Find the One (1978)

VOLE 4 U-BROWN: Black Star Liner/River John Mountain (1978)

VOLE 5 U-ROY: *Live at the Lyceum* EP (1978)

VOLE 6 SLY DUNBAR: A Who Say/Cocaine Cocaine (1978)

VOLE 7 ALTHEA & DONNA: Going to Negril/The West (1978)

VOLE 8 POET & THE ROOTS: It Dread inna Ingland/—(1978)

VS 18712 U-ROY: Small Axe/(Version) (1977)

VS 19012 POET & THE ROOTS: All Wi Doin Is Defendin/Five Nights of Bleedin/(Version) (1977)

VS 19312 THE GLADIATORS: Pocket Money/(Version)/Evil Doers/(Disco Mix) (1977)

FRONT LINE 12-inch SINGLES

FLS 11912 THE TWINKLE BROTHERS: Keep on Trying/King Pharaoh (1979)

FLS 12012 SLY DUNBAR: Rasta Fiesta/Dirty Harry (1979)

FLS 12112 GREGORY ISAACS: Soon Forward/Uncle Joe (1979)

FLS 12212 THE MIGHTY DIAMONDS: Bodyguard/One Brother Short (1979)

FLS 12312 THE TWINKLE BROTHERS: Jahoviah/Free Africa (1979)

FLS 12412 I-ROY: Fire in a Wire/Hill and Gully (1979)

CAROLINE LPS

C 1521 VARIOUS: *The Front Line* (1976)

CA 2002 BB SEATON: *Dancing Shoes* (1976)

CA 2011 I-ROY: *Crisis Time* (1976)

VIRGIN LPS

ONLY 1 I-ROY: *Ten Commandments* (1980)

ONLY 2 BLACK UHURU: *Black Uhuru* (1980)

PZ34454 THE MIGHTY DIAMONDS: *Ice on Fire* (1977)

V2048 U-ROY: *Dread in a Babylon* (1975)

V2052 THE MIGHTY DIAMONDS: *Right Time* (1976)

V2055 THE REVOLUTIONARIES: *Vital Dub* (1976)

V2056 KEITH HUDSON: *Too Expensive* (1976)

V2058 JOHNNY CLARKE: *Rockers Time Now* (1976)

V2059 U-ROY: *Natty Rebel* (1976)

V2060 DELROY WASHINGTON: *I Sus* (1976)

V2061 PETER TOSH: *Legalize It* (1976)

V2062 THE GLADIATORS: *Trenchtown Mix Up* (1976)

V2075 I-ROY: *Musical Shark Attack* (1976)

V2076 JOHNNY CLARKE: *Authorized Version* (1976)

V2081 PETER TOSH: *Equal Rights* (1977)

V2088 DELROY WASHINGTON: *Rasta* (1977)

V2092 U-ROY: *Rasta Ambassador* (1977)

V2102 THE MIGHTY DIAMONDS: *Planet Earth* (1978)

V2161 THE GLADIATORS: *The Gladiators* (1980)

V2164 ROY REID: *Whap'n Bap'n* (1980)

V2169 THE TWINKLE BROTHERS: *Countrymen* (1980)

VC503 VARIOUS: *The Front Line* (1976)

FRONTLINE LPS

FCL 5001 THE TWINKLE BROTHERS: *Love* (1979)

FL 1001 I-ROY: *Heart of a Lion* (1978)

FL 1002 THE GLADIATORS: *Proverbial Reggae* (1978)

FL 1003 U-BROWN: *Mr. Brown Something* (1978)

FL 1004 PRINCE HAMMER: *Bible* (1978)

FL 1005 JAH LLOYD THE BLACK LION: *The Humble One* (1978)

FL 1006 TAPPA ZUKIE: *MPLA* (1978)

FL 1008 SLY DUNBAR: *Simple Sly Man* (1978)

FL 1009 TAPPA ZUKIE: *Peace in the Ghetto* (1978)

FL 1010 THE ICEBREAKERS WITH THE DIAMONDS: *Planet Mars Dub* (1978)

FL 1011 BIG YOUTH: *Isaiah, First Prophet of Old* (1978)

FL 1012 ALTHEA & DONNA: *Uptown Top Ranking* (1978)

FL 1013 PRINCE FAR I: *Message from the King* (1978)

FL 1014 BIG YOUTH: *Dreadlocks Dread* (1978)

FL 1015 RANKING TREVOR: *In Fine Style* (1978)

FL 1016 CULTURE: *Harder than the Rest* (1978)

FL 1017 POET & THE ROOTS: *Dread Beat an' Blood* (1978)

FL 1018 U-ROY: *Version Galore* (1978)

FL 1019 ABYSSINIANS: *Arise* (1978)

FL 1020 GREGORY ISAACS: *Cool Ruler* (1978)

FL 1021 PRINCE FAR I: *Long Life* (1978)

FL 1023 U-ROY: *Jah Son of Africa* (1978)

FL 1025 VIVIAN WEATHERS: *Bad Weather* (1978)

FL 1028 I-ROY: *Ten Commandments* (1978)

FL 1029 TAPPA ZUKIE: *In Dub* (1979)

FL 1030 U-BROWN: *Can't Keep a Good Man Down* (1979)

FL 1031 JAH LLOYD: *Black Moses* (1979)

FL 1032 TAPPA ZUKIE: *Tappa Roots* (1979)

FL 1033 I-ROY: *World on Fire* (1979)

FL 1034 VARIOUS ARTISTS: *Hottest Hits* (From the Vaults of Treasure Island) (1979)

FL 1035 THE GLADIATORS: *Naturality* (1979)

FL 1040 CULTURE: *Cumbolo* (1979)

FL 1041 THE TWINKLE BROTHERS: *Praise Jah* (1979)

FL 1042 SLY DUNBAR: *Sly Wicked and Slick* (1979)

FL 1044 GREGORY ISAACS: *Soon Forward* (1979)

FL 1045 MIGHTY DIAMONDS: *Deeper Roots* (Back to the Channel) (1979)

FL 1047 CULTURE: *International Herb* (1979)

FL 1048 THE GLADIATORS: *Sweet So Till* (1979)

FL 1052 VIVIAN WEATHERS: *Bad Weather* (1979)

FLB 3001 VARIOUS: *The Front Line II* (1978)

FLB 3002 VARIOUS: *Front Line III* (1979)

FLD 6001 MIGHTY DIAMONDS: *Deeper Roots* (Back To The Channel) (1979)

FLD 6002 I-ROY: *The General* (1979)

FLX 4001 I-ROY: *Cancer* (1979)

FLX 4002 PRINCE FAR I: *Cry Tuff Dub Encounter Part 2* (1979)

FLX 4003 THE TWINKLE BROTHERS: *Love* (1979)

FLX 4004 U-ROY: *With Words of Wisdom* (1979)

GABBY

STYLE *calypso*

BORN *Anthony Carter, 1949 (Emmerton, BARB)*

The youngest artist ever to claim the throne of Barbados' Calypso King, Gabby was 19 when his "Heart Transplant" — a timely offering dealing with the then pioneering research of South African physician Christian Barnard — swept all before it in 1968.

Gabby did not pursue his victory further. Rather, he turned his attention to acting and, in 1971, he joined Paul Webster's New York-bound Barbados Theater Workshop (later, the Caribbean Theater Workshop). As well as taking the lead role, Pa John, he also composed much of the music for the play *Under the Duppy Parasol*, which enjoyed a successful run at the Harlem Cultural Center and The Billie Holiday Theater in Brooklyn.

It was 1976 before Gabby returned to the carnival scene, scoring with the viral political commentary, "Licks Like Fire," the first in a chain of successes which saw him dominate Barbados' Crop Over carnival for the remainder of the decade. In 1977, "Riots in the Land" earned him the title of Folk Singer of the Year, an honor he retained in 1978 ("Bridgetown"). 1979 saw Gabby make it three in a row with "Bajan Fisherman."

That same year, "Burn Mr Harding" won Barbados' first

ever Crop Over Road March. (Since that time, Gabby's own Battleground Calypso Tent has won every Road March in which it has competed.) 1979 also brought a successful tour of Cuba, a trip which became the inspiration behind Gabby's 1981 hit "Gisella."

Gabby's eye for violent political confrontation rarely wavered. In 1984, he scored with "Boots," written in the shocked aftermath of the unpopular US invasion of neighboring Grenada. Hardly surprisingly, then, Gabby is also notoriously Barbados' most banned calypsonian, and became the first musician ever to be sued by the island's government, when Prime Minister Tom Adams launched legal proceedings against him in 1985.

At the heart of the controversy lay Gabby's newly composed calypso "Cadavers." It concerned the Adams' government's agreement to accept and store dead bodies from the U.S., regardless of cause of death — in fact, the terms of the agreement did not even raise that particular subject. With AIDS already casting an ever deepening shadow over the Caribbean, local opinion was outraged, with the island's medical establishment especially incensed. Gabby's words were no stronger than those of many other commentators; they were, however, more specific in who they blamed for the situation — and why.

Perhaps fittingly, Adams himself died before the case against Gabby came to court, while the storage plan was eventually shelved. Still the singer's concerns were given fresh emphasis by the full-fledged onset in the Caribbean of AIDS, and in 1988 Gabby became one of the first calypsonians to discuss the disease in song, "The List." 1988 also delivered "Jack," a savage assault on the local tourist industry, and the legal loopholes which seemed to exist for its benefit alone.

Such controversial material brought Gabby to the attention of Eddy Grant, owner of the local Blue Wave studio. Their first collaboration was a career-encompassing anthology, *Til Now*, released in 1994 and closing with the two songs Gabby performed at Carnival in T&T in 1995, "Dr Cassandra" and "Debra." The album finally broke Gabby out into the wider Caribbean scene,

It was followed by *Soca Trinity*, a collaboration with Bert "Panta" Brown and Grynna; in 1999, Gabby celebrated another carnival win with the two-CD *Well Done*.

RECOMMENDED LISTENING

9 Til Now (Ice) 1994

Touted as a celebration of Gabby's 30 years in calypso, a 14 track collection of his best known, and most controversial material, together with a taste of the broad range at his disposal — the folky "Bridgetown" and "Emmerton," the soca of "Hit It," the Latin rhythms of "Gisella" and so on. Also included are "Cadavers," "Boots," "Jack" and "West Indian Politician."

TERRY GAJRAJ

STYLE *chutney*
BORN *Fyrish, Guyana*

The most prolific artist in Guyana's musical history, releasing an impressive 14 albums between 1990–2000, Terry Gajraj is best known to his international audience as a chutney performer. In fact, his repertoire is as vast as his output, embracing bhagans, pop, reggae and ballads; he has performed with Arrow, the Mighty Sparrow and India's Babla and Kanchan, and represented Guyana at every major carnival in the world, including Toronto's Caribana, London's Notting Hill and, of course, T&T.

The son of a school teacher, Gajraj launched his professional singing career at age 5, appearing onstage with his chacha (uncle), Butch Ramdeo, and the Dil Bahar orchestra, conducted by Lakhan Sookray. Under Ramdeo's instruction, the youth learned to play the harmonium and drums, and was soon performing at local weddings, fairs and dances.

During his teens and early 20s, Gajraj worked with both the Star Rhythm Combo in West Coast, Berbice, and the Original Pioneers and the Melody Makers in the Guyanan capital, Georgetown. However, music was little more than a part time interest, as he followed his father into teaching, working at a high school in Georgetown.

Although Gajraj himself never learned to speak Hindi, he was able to incorporate the language into the songs he was writing. By the late 1980s, with chutney breaking out all over the region, he took the momentous decision to dedicate himself to the music full time, moving to New York in 1989. There he linked with a handful of short-lived bands before going solo the next year. Working with New York based producer Herman Singh, he released his debut album, the landmark *Soca Lambada*, that October, recorded with the acclaimed New York/East Indian Tropical Vibes session band: Larry Marsden (guitar), Patrick LaTouche (bass), Don Lynch (keyboards), Gerald Rampersaud (sax), Paul Litrenta (trumpet), Eric Goletz (trombone), Feroz Mohammed (congas), Jay Kewla (percussion).

The album's cunning soca-soaked chutney proved an immediate success and, within a year, Gajraj was recording *Caribana '92*, an ambitious self-produced and written set featuring contributions from DJ Daddy Scano and, again, the Tropical Vibes Band. 1992 brought his first major regional hit, "Tun Tun Dance," inspired by the Indian movie comedy duo of Tun Tun and Keshto Mukerjhee. Firmly establishing his musical credentials, Gajraj played all the instruments on the record, but despite the success of the project, he turned to outside production thereafter, teaming with Derek DeSouza and arranger Brian Chaitoo.

The *Guyana Baboo & Pack Up: New York* album, split between Gajraj and singer David Ramoutar was a hit in early 1993, leading off with Gajraj's latest single, also titled "Guyana Baboo." "Guyanese Ting" followed, while 1994 brought another collaboration, this time with Apache Waria, *Tun Tun Dance/Guyana Baboo 2*.

That same year, Gajraj was invited to appear at Trinidad Spektakula, a festival featuring the cream of Caribbean musical talent. He also made his debut on T&T television, which led in turn to his becoming the first Guyanese artiste to represent his nation at the islands' carnival, in 1995.

1994's *Phagwah Songs* and 1995's *Roti & Dall* accompanied this spate of activity. They were succeeded by 1996's *Baboo Bruk Dem Up*, Gajraj's last with long time collaborator Brian Chaitoo — he died at age 40 on December 16, 1995, *Baboo Bruk Dem Up* was dedicated to his memory.

Fall, 1996's *Funky Chatni* saw Gajraj back in the producer's seat. In 1997, he contributed to a pair of Mohabir label compilations, *Happy Birthday to You* (five tracks including "Chutney Birthday" and "Reggae Birthday") and *Mother's Day*. Featured alongside him was the cream of modern chutney talent — Ramdew Chaitoe, Sangeetha, Bisoondat Ram, Manisha, Harry Panday and more.

Gajraj's first live album also appeared that year. Recorded at Soca Paradise in Trinidad, 1997's *Summer Jam* was swiftly joined by a second volume featuring additional performances from Gajraj, Sheila Basdeo, Devindra Pooran and Tony Gill.

Gajraj's own next album was an absolute change of pace as he linked with the Supertone Orchestra for 1998's *Sweet Love Songs*, a collection of, indeed, love songs ranging from Elvis Presley to the Bee Gees, Chris DeBurgh to George Michael.

Boom, later in 1998, returned Gajraj to basics, a collection which peaked with the massive hit "Saki Boom," but also included an excellent interpretation of the traditional "Banaras." *Boom*, however, was Gajraj's last chutney project for two years. He wrapped up 1998 with *Christmas Dancemix*, an only marginally successful attempt to present various festive songs in a variety of Caribbean settings, recorded in New York and India. Two further volumes of *Sweet Love Songs* were followed by the self-explanatory *Ragga Ding-A-Ling*, a Gajraj produced compilation featuring Apache Waria, Ragga Don, Princess Anisa and more.

Gajraj returned to chutney in 2000 with "Baka Bana," a song which marked the final recorded appearance of Sundar Popo, Gajraj's co-vocalist in the song's chorus. "Baka Bana" was included on X, Gajraj's celebration of ten years of recording, a compilation of past hits and the first double CD ever issued by an individual chutney artist.

SELECTED DISCOGRAPHY

6 Soca Lambada (Mohabir) 1990

The revolution which Gajraj presaged is scarcely apparent in this lightweight debut, featuring two versions of the reggae-ish "Happy Birthday," and three of the title track. The decidedly anti-social calypso "Guyana Nice," however, more than makes up for other disappointments — "Guyana nice but it's ugly, the people are friendly but they're hungry."

6 Caribana 92 (Mohabir) 1992

The opening "Sweet 16 Soca" apparently revolves around the joys of sticking various things in the air and shaking them, but the album swiftly settles down, peaking with the compulsive "Mashramani" (dedicated to his homeland's annual carnival) and a very successful, and unabashedly reggae version of "Happy Birthday."

7 Phagwah Songs (Mohabir) 1994
8 Roti & Dall (Mohabir) 1995

If *Phagwah Songs* and *Guyana Baboo* were the sound of Gajraj finally coming of musical age, *Roti & Dali* sees him hit full maturity, secure in both his heritage and its importance to his music. Titles are split almost equally between English language and Hindi, and the music is similarly, joyfully accommodating. The hits "Oh My God" and "Raat Ke Sapna" are the most immediate stand-outs; "Bhool Biesar Mati" comes close behind.

7 Baboo Bruk Dem Up (Mohabir) 1996
10 Funky Chatni (Mohabir) 1996

An adventurous "Macarena" was the highlight last time out; now it's "Cheese," a surreal six minute exercise in sound effects, disembodied voices and, indeed, cheese. The house-influenced "I Love Roti" is equally infectious, while "Gimme Chatni" offers precisely that, a frenetic tassa-led chant. Also included are a crucial reprise of "Mashramani," the drifting "Richmond Hill" and the self-affirming "Indo-Caribbean Man," but even with 17 tracks, it's hard to play favorites.

8 Summer Jam (Mohabir) 1997

An excellent taste of the Gajraj live experience, its 24 songs including Gajraj's own biggest hits, plus such classic titles as "Big Truck," "Nani Wine" and "Hot Hot Hot."

4 Sweet Love Songs (Mohabir) 1998

It's cover version time, lost in love and layering some sickly-sweet sentimentality with a Carib-lite backing. It isn't hard to see why the album (and several similarly themed/titled successors) was so successful, but "Lady in Red," "Help Me Make It Through the Night" and "Always on My Mind" really did not need such reinventions. "Wild World," contrarily, is excellent.

7 Boom (Mohabir) 1998

3 Christmas Dancemix (RP) 1998

"Little Drummer Boy" chutney-fied; "Feliz Navidad" reggae soul fashion; "Christmas He Wrote" dance hall style . . . it was probably a lot of fun to make.

5 Sweet Love Songs Volume 2 (Mohabir) 1999

A tougher selection of songs includes "Stand by Me," "Tell Laura I Love Her" and "Red Red Wine." Tougher, of course, is a relative term.

5 Sweet Love Songs Volume 3 (Mohabir) 2000

Gregory Isaacs' "Night Nurse" and Bob Marley's "One Love" prove that Gajraj can handle reggae as effectively as you like, but the excitement remains in recognizing the songs, rather than the actual performances. Background music for chic whole food restaurants sounds a lot like this.

TERRY GAJRAJ & DAVID RAMOUTAR

7 Guyana Baboo & Pack Out: New York (Mohabir) 1993

Though only half the album features Gajraj, this was the set which launched his stardom, thanks largely to the inescapable "Guyana Baboo." The remainder of the set pales in its shadow, and several of Ramoutar's contributions are actually stronger than Gajraj's, but the album is worth persevering with.

TERRY GAJRAJ & APACHE WARIA

6 Tun Tun Dance/Guyana Baboo 2 (Mohabir) 1994

SELECTED COMPILATIONS & ARCHIVE RELEASES

9 X (Mohabir) 2000

Excellent comp hits all the right places, 30 tracks highlighting hits, oddities ("Dear Mummy," from the *Mother's Day* comp), his bizarre version of Chuck Berry's masturbatory "My Ding-A-Ling," and the excellent "My Land"—basically a recitation of all the countries which are not his land.

EDDY GRANT

STYLE *reggae/rock, soca*

BORN *Edmond Montague Grant, 3/5/48 (Plaisance, GUY)*

Eddy Grant is, depending on the age of the listener, best remembered for his UK chart topping stint with the Equals in the late 1960s, the chain of righteously politicized reggae-funk hits which slammed into the MTV consciousness of the early 1980s, or the emergence of his own soca variant, "ringbang," in the early 1990s.

He is also, however, one of the most tireless musical historians in the West Indies, owner of a record label, Ice Records, dedicated to preserving and reissuing the calypso catalogs of the genre's greatest practitioners. Roaring Lion, the Mighty Sparrow, the Lords Melody and Kitchener, early steel bands and orchestral giants Ron Berridge, Clarence Curvan, Joey Lewis and Johnny Gomez all feature in the Ice label catalog.

Grant's childhood was spent listening to the unique Indo-Caribbean tan singing which was the sound of his native Guyana. This education was curtailed in 1960, when Grant's family migrated to England, to a home in the north London area of Stoke Newington. There the young Grant added rock'n'roll and the blues to his musical experiences and, in 1965 he formed his first band, the Equals.

Emphasizing the pop side of Grant's musical background, but never losing sight of his early influences either, the Equals are most frequently eulogized today as the first multi-racial British band to attain international prominence. The Equals comprised three West Indians—Grant was joined by Jamaican born twins Derv (guitar) and Lincoln Gordon (vocals—both b 6/29/48)—and two white Englishmen, drummer John Hall (b 10/25/47) and bassist Patrick Lloyd (b 3/17/48).

The Equals gigged heavily around London for over a year before being picked up by President Records and, in early 1967, their first single "I Won't Be There" became a strong radio hit. Buoyed by tremendous live support, their debut album, *Unequalled Equals*, made #10; its successor, *Equals Explosion*, reached #32 in early 1968, trailing the mini hit "I Get So Excited."

President, meanwhile, picked up on Grant's insatiable energy, and put him in the studio with the Pyramids, the UK based reggae band who backed Prince Buster on his 1967 UK tour. Grant wrote and produced several tracks for them, including their debut single, 1967's "Train Tour to Rainbow City." He also wrote Prince Buster's "Rough Rider," one of the songs which kicked off a boom of rude reggae songs during the late 1960s. Later in that particular cycle, it was Grant who advised the visiting Max Romeo to play down the sexual connotations of his hit "Wet Dream," by telling interviewers it was a song about a leaking roof.

Meanwhile, the Equals' career was set to go into hyperdrive. In March, 1968, a track first issued as the b-side to the unsuccessful "Hold Me Closer" single, "Baby Come Back," was released as an A-side in Germany, to capitalize on a successful recent tour. It promptly topped the chart there and elsewhere across the continent and, in late spring, President reissued the song in the UK.

"Baby Come Back" soared to #1 that summer, establishing the Equals as virtual superstars. Inexplicably, however, another year elapsed before they even glimpsed such heights again, as three further 45s, "Laurel And Hardy," "Softly Softly" and "Michael and the Slipper Tree," foundered in the lower reaches of the UK Top 50. The *Sensational Equals* album failed to chart, and while "Viva Bobby Joe" returned the group to the Top 10 during summer, 1969, "Rub a Dub Dub" crashed at a lowly #34.

In 1970, Grant launched his own record label, Torpedo. Specializing in British-made reggae, Grant produced singles by Errol English, Les Foster, Silkie Davis and others. There, too, he launched a short solo career under the pseudonym Little Grant, cutting the single "Let's Do It Together." His attention was soon drawn back to the Equals, however.

Late 1970 saw the group back on top with the #9 hit "Black Skinned Blue Eyed Boys," a tough number which proved that songwriter Grant was already moving away from the lovable pop which had made his name (and, equally importantly, his bleached afro hair style) a household fixture. But it was the band's final hit. On New Year's Day, 1971, the 23 year old teetotal vegetarian Grant suffered a heart attack and a collapsed lung and was rushed to hospital.

He withdrew from the Equals altogether. While his bandmates sank into the obscurity of the nightclub circuit, churning out their hits for an audience which wanted to hear nothing more, Grant turned his attention to the other side of the studio.

Selling the Torpedo label, Grant opened his own recording studio, the Coach House, in 1972, and continued his production work. He handled resurgent reggae legends The Pioneers' 1976 album *Feel the Rhythm*, while his brother, DJ Mexicano, released three albums on Grant's own newly-formed Ice label during the 1970s. Grant's own recording career, however, seemed stalemated by his own refusal to compromise, or even share, his musical vision.

His first solo album, 1977's *Message Man*, took some three years to record, with Grant handling every instrument himself. A dark, highly politicized album which was barely noticed at the time, *Message Man* has since ascended to legend on the strength of one track, the unquenchable celebration of "Hello Africa" — the first European manifestation of what was, even in the Caribbean a brand new musical force.

Grant himself christened it "kaisoul," blending the traditional alternate term for calypso, kaiso, with American soul music. Others — including Lord Shorty, the acknowledged father of this hybrid — preferred Solka, in tribute to the other Caribbean musical forms which he inserted into this bold, rhythmic sound. But the T&T music press had a better name for it. Soca started here.

Two years later, with the *Walking on Sunshine* set proving a uncharacteristically swift follow-up, Grant scored a major hit with "Living on the Front Line," a growling funk reggae anthem which slipped readily into the climate of riot and urban discontent which then characterized English inner city life.

Love in Exile, and 1981's *Can't Get Enough* albums spawned further hits "Do You Feel My Love," "Can't Get Enough of You" and "I Love You, Yes I Love You," while

Grant also triumphed with the double *Live at Notting Hill* album, ten tracks spread across four sides of vinyl.

Grant relocated to Barbados in 1982, combining his own still massive career with a renewed interest in fostering the burgeoning talent now pouring out behind the soca banner. Future stars David Rudder, Tamu Herbert, Gabby and Grynner were all Grant proteges, his support and encouragement playing a major part in soca's rapid ascent onto the world stage during the 1980s.

Grant's own fame, too, ballooned anew, as "I Don't Wanna Dance" (from the Top 10 hit *Killer on the Rampage* album) topped the British chart in late 1982, with the pounding "Electric Avenue" reaching #2 on both sides of the Atlantic in the new year.

A reissue of "I Don't Wanna Dance" reached the US Top 60, and while further British singles "War Party," "Till I Can't Love No More" and "Romancing The Stone" (written for, but not used in the movie of the same name) barely brushed the Top 50, the latter gave him another American Top 30 hit in spring, 1984. Four years later, having spent the intervening time working at his newly opened Blue Wave studio, Grant scored his last major hit, the anti-apartheid "Gimme Hope Jo'Anna," a #7 UK smash.

As his 40th birthday approached in 1988, Grant's interests swung away once more from pursuing commercial success. He opened a Barbados nightclub, the Pepperpot, and moved into music publishing, concentrating his efforts on the aforementioned calypso greats. He has also remained busy administering his own back catalog — unlike so many other artists, Caribbean or otherwise, Grant has maintained control over his entire solo output, allowing him a freedom and control which few others have ever managed to attain.

The Blue Wave studio, too, was flourishing (clients have included Mick Jagger, Sting and Elvis Costello, while the Rolling Stones used the studio to prepare for their decade's-end *Steel Wheels* tour). Throughout the early 1990s, Grant produced albums by Black Stalin, Duke, Calypso Rose and others, as well as releasing his own latest album, the calypso covers collection *Soca Baptism*.

Simultaneously, Grant was formulating what he considered the next major wave in Caribbean music, ringbang, a term of his own invention which made its public debut at Barbados' Crop Over festival in 1994. That same year, calypso veteran Black Stalin became the first artist to refer to ringbang on record, in two cuts from his Ice Records album *Rebellion*, "All Saints Road" and "Black Woman Ring Bang." Both Square One ("Ringbang Pickiney") and Viking Tundah ("Ringbang Souljah"), plus Grant himself of course, also recorded songs within the genre for the same label.

Ringbang's roots lie in a number of different directions. Geography demands that *tuk*, a traditional Barbados drumming style incorporating both British military and African tribal rhythms, be considered an influence, an assumption which Grant readily agrees to; soca, rapso and dance hall are also primal ingredients. He explained, "What Ringbang seeks to do is envelop all the rhythms that have originated from Africa so that they become one, defying all geographical boundaries."

Yet since the music's emergence onto a major scene in 1994, when it seemed set to dominate the Barbados Crop Over carnival, and spawned two local hit singles, Viking Tundah's "Ringa Ringa Ringbang" and Gabby's "Doctor Cassandra," little development has occurred. This is an acknowledgement, perhaps, that the genre itself is still very much in its formative phase; but also a consequence of Grant's decision to trademark the term, thus ensuring that only artists operating under his aegis can actually use the word "ringbang" in lyric or title.

Therefore, although ringbang has certainly been investigated by the likes of Calypso Rose, Superblue, Ajala, Chinese Laundry, Chris Garcia and Marvin & Nigel Lewis, the trademark issue has prevented them from actually acknowledging it in song—which, in turn, holds the music itself back from finding a wider audience. (To put this in context, imagine, for example, if somebody had trademarked the word "reggae," back in 1968.)

Ringbang moved into focus in T&T in 1996, albeit in a generally negative sense. In that year, Grant agitated loudly (and not, one assumes, unreasonably) for his artists to receive fair copyright fees from the organizers, establishing himself—as T&T journalist Terry Joseph put it, "public enemy number one in this country. He has continued to anger locals with his contentious claim that he is the father of soca music."

It was, therefore, extraordinarily courageous of Grant to even dream of organizing a ringbang festival, Ringbang Celebration 2000, at Shaw Park, Tobago, as a centerpiece of the island's millennium celebrations on January 31, 1999. The festival featured performances from Superblue, Ray Cape & the Kaiso All-Stars, Machel Montano & Xtatik, Black Stalin, Signal Hill Choir, Viking Tundah, Lord Kitchener, Calypso Rose, Len "Boogsie" Sharpe, Duke, the Yoruba Singers, Adisa Andwele, Dread & the Bald Head, Shadow, Mighty Terror, Gabby, BWIA Invaders, Calypso Prince, Tobago Crusoe and Grant himself.

The event was plagued by controversy from the outset, but all the more so as costs—largely born by the Tobago House of Assembly—increased. Ringbang Celebration was finally estimated to have cost some T&T $41 million (US $6.5 million), with Grant adding further fuel to the outrage when he very correctly pointed out that that amount was "a pittance to showcase our culture."

Grant himself performed two songs at the event, "Gimme Hope Jo'Anna" and "East Dry River," and in the new year he cut a ska version of the latter during a trip to Jamaica.

DISCOGRAPHY

8 Message Man (Ice) 1977

Grant's most politicized album was a somewhat tentative opening shot—at least in terms of garnering radio play. But it is impressive in execution, aggressive in both outlook and delivery, and absolutely indispensable for its highlights—"Hello Africa," of course, but also "Curfew," "Cockney Black" and "Race Hate."

9 Walking on Sunshine (Epic) 1979

A seamless tapestry of Caribbean sounds, merging with funk, pop, rock and even New Wave. "Walking on Sunshine" was effortless pop, while "Living on the Front Line" and the freakish chorale dub "The Front Line Symphony" swaggered beneath a tough message and an aggressive electro sheen which appealed across the board. Side two of the original vinyl is, perhaps, weaker, but "Dancing in Guyana" is a fitting tribute to his homeland.

7 Love in Exile (Epic) 1980
7 Can't Get Enough (Epic) 1981
10 Live at Notting Hill (Ice—UK) 1981

Recorded at the 1981 Notting Hill Carnival, and originally released as both a double LP and a video, Grant and his Front Line Orchestra in full flight, impressively jamming across a side-long "Hello Africa" and delivering a truly sublime "Living on the Frontline." The music, however, is only part of the appeal—the entire performance packs a hard-nosed punch which not only captures the exuberance of the carnival, but also the underlying tensions which were such a part of the event through the late 1970s and early 1980s.

7 Killer on the Rampage (Portrait) 1982

"Electric Avenue" is the potent point of entry, "I Don't Wanna Dance" keeps the beat going in the clubs, while "War Party" pounds funk into roots; the rest of the record leans more heavily towards pop, but sparkles with snippets of rock, New Wave, and funk strewn throughout.

8 Going for Broke (Portrait) 1984

The superb "Political Bassa Bassa," "Boys In The Street" and "Telepathy" are joined by a sensational remake of the Equals' "Baby Come Back."

6 Born Tuff (Portrait) 1987
5 File Under Rock (Enigma) 1988
7 Barefoot Soldier (Enigma) 1990

After a brace of less than compulsive albums, Grant returns to form with a passionate, somewhat reflective set which touches on reggae, pop and country flavors, but is best remembered for the anti-apartheid "Gimme Hope Jo'Anna."

6 Paintings of the Soul (Ice) 1992
8 Soca Baptism (Ice) 1993

Grant digs into the calypso past to deliver some of the warmest performances of his recent career, a 15 strong collection of covers which ranges from a handful of classics ("Ugly Woman," "Miss Tourist," "Bajan Girl"), through to a handful of songs he must really have dug around to find. The performances are thoroughly modern, without losing sight of the songs' original purity, and though Grant's choices tend to shy away from calypso's more political/controversial highlights, the ingenue will find precious few more enjoyable introductions.

7 Hearts and Diamonds (Ice) 1999

SELECTED COMPILATIONS & ARCHIVE RELEASES

9 Hit Collection (Ice) 1999

Although other Grant hits collections exist, all feature basically the same material. Disc one of this set doesn't break that mold, but it is at least up to date (the final cut, "Don't Back Down," introduces the just-released *Hearts and Diamonds* album), while disc two serves up nine original 12-inch mixes, including the brutal "Living on the Frontline," the essential "Hello Africa" and the seldom heard (but so deserving) "African Kings."

THE HEPTONES

STYLE *reggae (rock steady/roots)*
FORMED *1965 (Kingston, JA)*
ORIGINAL LINE-UP *Leroy Sibbles (b 1949, JA — vocals), Barry Llewellyn (b 12/25/47, JA — vocals), Earl Morgan (b 11/25/45, JA — vocals)*

Of all the vocal groups to come to the forefront in the years before the Wailers' international breakthrough, the Heptones had the fewest peers, even after the rock steady boom which brought them to prominence had faltered. Indeed, many observers tipped them as the act most likely to accompany the Wailers to prominence and their failure to do so remains baffling.

Llewellyn and Morgan paired up first in a Kingston Senior School band called Earl Morgan & The Swinging Squirrels. It did little and soon they were one half of the Sylastians, with Clive Campbell (of the Aces) and Keble Drummond (the Cables). Again the group made little progress, and broke up after Llewellyn and Morgan met Sibbles at a talent contest in 1965.

Under the aegis of Sidney Crooks, a member of the vocal group The Pioneers, the trio became the Heptones in 1965 (taking the name from an old bottle of Heptones Tonic which Morgan saw lying in a pile of refuse one day.) The band first recorded with producer Ken Lack at the Caltone label.

Of the clutch of singles he made with them, "Gun Men Coming to Town" was the most instantly memorable, taking

Rossini's "William Tell Orchestra" into the very heart of rudie territory — others, "I Am Lonely," "We've Got Love," "Ain't that Bad" and "Schoolgirl," released during 1966–67, were less remarkable.

In 1967, the Heptones shifted to Coxsone Dodd and Studio One, moving into the organization just as the Wailers moved out. Dodd saw immediately that they had the potential to replace the errant stars. Having enjoyed some minor success with "Why Did You Leave," "Only Sixteen" and "Party Time," the Heptones scored their first major hit with "Fattie Fattie" (aka "Fat Girl") — a song which arguably launched the late 1960s boom in "adults only" music with its plaintive demand, "I need a very fat girl because I'm in the mood . . . I'm feeling rude."

Slapped with an immediate radio ban, the single sold by word of mouth alone, while the Heptones followed up with a succession of similar gems, each one riding the trio's gorgeous harmonies (plus "Deadly" Headley Bennett's killer horn parts), and Sibbles' ability to turn his hand to anything, from sentimental love songs through social realism and politics and on again to ribald innuendo. They could even make misogyny sound heavenly, although the frequently cited (and so downbeat) "Tripe Girl" and "I Hold the Handle" are comparatively minor league songs when compared with the best of the Heptones' Studio One output.

Hits through the end of the 1960s included "Schoolgirls," "Cry Baby Cry," "We've Got Love," "A Change Is Gonna Come," "If I Knew" and "Why Must I?" (1967); "Christmas Time," "I Got a Feeling," "Love Won't Come Easy," "Gee Wee," the spiritual "Oil in Your Lamp," "If You Knew" "Giddy Up" and a lovely cover of the late Otis Redding's "Dock of the Bay" (1968); "Sweet Talking," the Beatles "Ob-La Di Ob-La-Da," Bob Dylan's "I Shall Be Released," "Love Me Always" and the militant classic "Soul Power" (1969); the Whatnauts' American hit "Message from a Blackman," "Jamaica Underground," "Young Generation," "Be a Man" and the Bob Andy/Marcia Griffiths smash "Young Gifted & Black" (1970).

Neither was the Heptones' influence limited to their own records. Sibbles was regularly called upon as a talent scout, and arranger and bassist on other artists' sessions, while the band's harmonies can be heard on records by Bob Andy, Freddie McKay, Alton Ellis, the Freedom Singers, the Brentford Road All Stars and the Underground Vegetables. The group also appear prominently on the Abyssinians' "Declaration of Rights."

Despite so much activity, a severe lack of financial enumeration saw the band's relations with Dodd slowly sour and, in 1971 (shortly after they cut one of the first great Jamaican albums of the 1970s, *Freedom Line*), the Heptones quit Studio One for a stint with Joe Gibbs. There they recut the Dodd-era classic "Hypocrites," while "Save the Last

Dance for Me," "Freedom to the People," "Every Day and Every Night," "Be the One" and "Love Has Many Faces" all kept the quality high. The band's Gibbs era material was spread over two albums by the UK label Trojan, *The Heptones & Friends Meet the Now Generation.*

Breaking with Gibbs in 1972, the Heptones launched their own label, Hep-Ic Scorch Unlimited, cutting a warmly compulsive version of the Supremes' "My World Is Empty Without You, Babe." It was a short-lived enterprise—in common with so many other hopeful would-be entrepreneurs, the Heptones found it impossible to sort out reliable distribution and radio play, and the label folded.

The band now launched into the kind of nomadic existence around Kingston which sustained so many other acts. Over the next two years, they worked with Winston Blake ("Mood for Love"), Prince Buster ("God Bless the Children," a gracious cover of "Our Day Will Come"), Alvin Ranglin ("Old Time," "Meaning of Life"), Niney Holness ("Keep on Pushing"), Harry J ("Book of Rules," "Mama Say," "Country Boy"), Phil Pratt ("Swept for You, Baby"), Lee Perry ("I Do Love You"), Sonia Pottinger ("I've Been Trying," "Help," "I'll Take You Home"), Geoffrey Chung ("Let Me Hold Your Hand") and Rupie Edwards ("You've Lost that Loving Feeling." They also provided backing vocals on Edwards' work with Gregory Isaacs).

Exhilarating, too, were their collisions with Alton Ellis ("Big Bad Boy") and Big Youth ("I Am Crying"), while the Heptones also spun out a string of enjoyable 45s recutting their Studio One classics: "Love Won't Come Easy" (with Blacka Morwell), "Tripe Girl" (Pete Weston & Alton Ellis), "I'm Crying" (Raphael Allen) and "Party Time" (Phil Pratt).

With the band now signed to Island Records, 1975 brought the Harry J produced *Night Food*, reiterating several of the singles they'd cut with him earlier in the decade. It did not sell well; a second set, the Lee Perry masterminded *Party Time*, suffered likewise, and that despite since proving the Heptones' best loved and most popular album.

Among the wealth of material cut with Perry during this period were masterful adaptations of "Na Na Hey Hey Kiss Him Goodbye" (retitled "Babylon's Falling"), Ken Boothe's "Crying Over You," and the driving "Mystery Babylon." Again their harmonies washed over much of Perry's other output—Max Romeo's "War in a Babylon," Junior Murvin's "Police and Thieves," and Perry's own *Super Ape* album.

A reunion with producer Niney Holness for the hopefully titled *Better Days* could not break the Heptones' international misfortunes, despite a string of Jamaican hit singles including "Book of Rules," "Losing You," "Mr Do Over Man" and a cover of the American pop classic "Crystal Blue Persuasion." Finally, in spring 1976, Sibbles quit

the band midway through a three month US tour with the Wailers and the Maytals, and relocated to Canada as a solo artist.

For a time it looked like Morgan and Llewellyn, too, would abandon the cause, but finally, Sibbles was replaced by Naggo Morris and the new look Heptones debuted on Dennis Brown's DEB label in 1978, with the "Love Has Many Faces" single. They also appeared at the inaugural Reggae Sunsplash festival. (The solo Sibbles appeared at the festival two years later, returning in 1981, 1983, 1986 and 1990. The Heptones played the 1988 event.)

In 1979, they signed with Greensleeves for international releases, and cut the *Good Life* album with producer JoJo Hookim. (Both the title track and the stirring "Can't Hide from Jah" proved hit singles in Jamaica.)

Augustus Pablo paired the Heptones with his All Stars for the dub anthem "Love Won't Come Easy"; with Morgan producing, the group scored another hit with "The World Has Begun," a 1979 collaboration with Earl Sixteen. 1980 brought a return engagement with Alton Ellis. That year also saw the band work with producer Flabba Holt for the gentle "Lovers Feeling."

The self-produced "What It Is" and "You Decorated My Heart" singles appeared in 1982—both were gathered onto 1985's acclaimed *Swing Low* album. Subsequent albums, however, were muted affairs, meaning Sibbles' eventual return to the band in 1991 went largely unheralded. However, the group acquitted themselves well at Reggae Sunsplash in 1992, while 1995's *Pressure* album, featuring the classic Sibbles/Llewellyn/Morgan line-up, emerged the group's most powerful set in a decade, thanks in part to a stunning Tappa Zukie production.

DISCOGRAPHY

9 The Heptones (Studio One—JA) 1967
Subsequently reissued as *Fattie Fattie*, the Heptones' debut is a stunning document of the band's capabilities. All three members wrote and sang and, though much of the set has since surfaced on sundry "best of"'s, the overall vision remains unimpeachable. "Land of Love" alone is worth the price of vinyl admission.

8 On Top (Studio One) 1968
Still expanding their sound, and now moving into reggae, the Heptones' early promise is fulfilled by "Heptones Gonna Fight" and "Pretty Looks Isn't All."

8 Freedom Line (Studio One) 1971
Though purists decry the increasing influence of US radio on Jamaican music at this time, the Heptones' take on Elvis Presley's "Suspicious Minds" and the Beatles' Let It Be" can only be commended, with the latter's original hymnal qualities now imbibed with additional soulfulness.

6 Night Food (Island) 1975

Under the ambitious eye of arranger Danny Holloway, a string section rearranges some familiar old tracks ("Fattie Fattie," "Book of Rules"), and a handful of new ones. The end result sounds lovely, but it's also very slick.

7 Party Time (Island) 1976

A rerecorded "Crying Over You" packs more power than any other version of the song, the Heptones' own original included. Elsewhere, "Mr President" and the driving "Sufferer's Time" allow producer Lee Perry as much room to move as he needs, while never letting the Heptones' own powers out of sight.

8 Better Days (Third World—UK) 1978

Niney drives the band through a handful of revivals, an excellent "Suspicious Minds," and a sweet "Crystal Blue Persuasion" among them. Too late to do the band any good (Sibbles had long since quit by the time this appeared), better days indeed arrive with a sublime set of rootsy tracks varying from stirring soulful numbers to sundry spirituals, with the emotive vocals and gorgeous harmonies a total treat.

7 Good Life (Greensleeves—UK) 1979

A stunningly realized cover of Marley's "Natural Mystic" proves that Sibbles' presence will not be missed—at least for the time being.

6 On the Run (Shanachie) 1982
6 Back on Top (Vista Sounds—UK) 1983

The title, of course, plays on their Studio One classic, although the material doesn't come too close to a similar recreation. The Beatles' "Yesterday" makes a mawkish inclusion.

5 In a Dance Hall Style (Vista Sounds—UK) 1983
6 Swing Low (Burning Sounds—UK) 1985

Earl Morgan's production is clean and crisp, as his bandmates float through the title track, "You Decorated My Life," "Heaven" and more. The overall album is a little light (and occasionally slight), but moments of sublime glory shine through.

4 Place Called Love (Thunderbolt—UK) 1986
5 Changing Time (Thunderbolt—UK) 1987

Two generally mediocre albums are nevertheless distinguished by a handful of interesting cuts—"Get Up Chant," "African Child" and, hard to believe, a rock steady recreation of Culture Club's "Do You Really Want to Hurt Me." The two have since been paired on one-CD (MIL Multimedia).

5 Sing Good Vibes (Clarendon—JA) 1988
7 Pressure (RAS) 1995

Recutting "Country Boy," adding Marley and Burning Spear covers, and closing with a stunning Llewellyn/Zukie

composition, "Old Time Gang Leader"—the band barely put a foot wrong on an inspired Sibbles-led comeback.

5 Rainbow Valley (House of Reggae) 1996

Scarcely crucial Heptones as the band serve up a platter packed with lightly reggae-fied AOR balladry—and that despite a deceptively authentic return to roots via "Susa Pan Rasta." A rerecorded "Beggie Beggie" is catchy enough, but doesn't really get past a dynamite chorus; the falsetto led "Tenderness" has its moments; and "Between the Sheets" has a soulful softness.

5 On the Road Again (Warriors) 1999

THE HEPTONES & ALTON ELLIS
5 Mr Ska-Beana (Cha Cha—UK) 1980

A marriage made in heaven, and the most soulful voices this side of it united across . . . unfortunately, some considerably weaker material than either deserves. Marvel, mortals, but mourn as well.

THE HEPTONES & THE NOW GENERATION
8 Heptones & Friends Meet the Now Generation (Joe Gibbs—JA) 1972
8 Heptones & Friends Meet the Now Generation Volume Two (Joe Gibbs—JA) 1972

In truth, the two albums contain no more than one album's worth of Heptones, an admission made by the subsequent CD release. Still, no worries—with Gibbs' Now Generation studio band firing behind them, Peter Tosh, the Ethiopians, Jackie Brown, Alton Ellis, Delroy Wilson, Nicky Thomas and Julie Ann (actually Judy Mowatt) are among the "friends" serving up some powerful material, but "Hypocrite" (opening volume one) and "The Magnificent Heptones" (Volume Two) beat them all hands down.

SELECTED COMPILATIONS & ARCHIVE RELEASES
7 In Love with You (United Artists)

Short but effective overview of the Studio One days.

8 Sea of Love (Heartbeat) 1995

Studio One again, although 16 tracks allow plenty of room to reach into lesser known corners of the band's repertoire.

9 The Meaning of Life (Trojan—UK) 1999

Opening with four super-rare Caltone sides, an excellent 25 track selection skips over the bulk of the Studio One era (well covered elsewhere), to concentrate on early 1970s studio hop. The Heptones' obsession with 60s US R&B is evident not only in their choice of material, but also their vocal arrangements, although the disc ends with some Lee Perry cuts which are strictly roots.

ALISON HINDS see SQUARE ONE

JOHN HOLT

STYLE *reggae*

BORN 7/11/47 *(Greenwich Farm, Kingston, JA)*

He is one of the sweetest vocalists, the most prolific writers and the most accomplished interpreters in Jamaican musical history, author of the definitive anthem of sufferer paranoia, "A Quiet Place" (aka "Man Next Door"), but also the epitome of reggae easy listening, who took the soul standard "Help Me Make It Through the Night" to #1 across Europe in 1974. And if the latter success has diminished his importance to "serious" reggae fans, the former ensures they can never ignore him.

A familiar sight around the King Edwards sound system, Holt was just 12 when he began appearing at (and invariably winning), promotor Joseph Verejohn's talent contests during 1958–62. The youth eventually took a record 28 titles, including several which were broadcast live on Radio Jamaica.

Holt turned professional following his final victory, where he performed Solomon Burke's "Just Out of Reach," and cut his debut single, "Forever I'll Stay"/"I Cried a Tear" for producer Leslie Kong soon after. From there, he moved to Clive Chin's Randy's label, where he was teamed with singer Alton Ellis for the infectious "Rum Bumper." However, his career did not truly get underway until 1965, when he joined the Paragons, one of the fastest rising vocal groups on the scene.

The Paragons were originally formed (as the Binders) by vocalists Keith "Bob Andy" Anderson (b 1944), Garth "Tyrone" Evans (d 10/2000), Junior Menz and Leroy Stamp. Holt replaced Stamp in 1964, and, with Howard Barrett coming in for Menz around the same time, the band re-corded their first singles for producer Coxsone Dodd — the somewhat prophetic "Good Luck and Goodbye" among them. Shortly after its release, Bob Andy departed to launch a solo career. (After a string of classy Studio One singles, Andy made an international impression as one half of Bob & Marcia (Griffiths), UK hitmakers in the early 1970s with "Pied Piper" and the anthemic "Young Gifted And Black.")

With Holt confirmed as the band's writer and arranger (Evans had full time work as a technician with a bauxite company, Barrett worked for the telephone company), the Paragons opted not to replace the errant Andy, preferring to remain a trio. In this form, they linked with producer Duke Reid, just as the musical landscape was moving towards the rock steady beat.

It was the ideal marriage. For all his expertise as a producer, Reid had never viewed ska as anything more than a convenient musical form to make money from; his personal jazz and R&B roots were far more at ease with rock steady and, through 1966–67, his work with the Paragons was a virtual permanent fixture in the Jamaican chart.

The group cut a definitive reworking of the old calypso classic "Island in the Sun"; elsewhere, with Holt's pen and voice firmly to the fore, "Talking Love," "If I Were You," "Only a Smile," "Mercy Mercy Mercy," "Riding on a High & Windy Day," "The Same Song," "So Depressed," "We Were Meant to Be," "You Mean the World to Me," "Happy Go Lucky Girl" and "Love Brings Pain" were all monster hits.

Given the strength of the Paragons' vocal line-up, it is ironic that the group were present at the birth of what soon became a Jamaican institution, the instrumental (or version) b-side. It occurred when a vocal-less version of their "On the Beach" hit was unintentionally included in a batch of dub-plates prepared for sound system kingpin Ruddy Redwood — aka — Mr Midnight, the Supreme Ruler of Sound.

"On the Beach" was already a favorite at his dances. On this particular evening, he cued up both the vocal and the instrumental versions of the song on his turntables, and began switching between the two, much to the delight of the audience. Immediately, Redwood requested similar versions of other big Treasure Isle hits; Duke Reid began preparing and issuing them himself soon after.

One of the first, naturally, graced the next big Paragons hit, "My Best Girl," with former Skatalite Tommy McCook's exquisite sax taking the lead on what Reid retitled "My Best Dress." Soon, there was scarcely a producer on the island not making similar recordings.

The Paragons marched on with "Wear You to the Ball Tonight" and "The Tide Is High," Holt compositions which have since become undisputed staples not only in Jamaica, but in the rock world as well — New York band Blondie scored an international chart topper with the latter in 1981, while UB40 covered the former.

This impressive barrage was maintained through the end of the decade, with the Paragons absorbing the gradual change to reggae without any apparent ill-effects. Both "A Quiet Place" (aka "Got to Get Away" and "Man Next Door" — subsequently covered by British acts The Slits and Massive Attack) and "Left with a Broken Heart" date from this period. Holt was also responsible for bringing DJ U-Roy to Duke Reid's attention, after catching the toaster at a King Tubby dance on Gold Coast Beach and hearing his revolutionary assault on Holt's own "Wear You to the Ball."

In 1968, Holt launched a solo career alongside the Paragons, cutting tracks with producers Bunny Lee (including "Tonight") and Harry J. The group, meanwhile, moved to Coxsone Dodd's Studio One during 1969, both collectively and for a handful of solo recordings. Evans reunited with Bob Andy for the hit "I Don't Care"; he also scored with "You Done Me Wrong" and "If This World Were Mine." Despite the promise of these latter-day recordings, however, the Paragons split in 1970, after both Evans and Barrett were awarded scholarships in the US.

Holt immediately began recording with a variety of producers: Prince Buster ("For Your Love," "Get Ready," "Rain from the Skies" and "Oh Girl"); Duke Reid ("Stealing Stealing," "Write Her a Letter" and "Ali Baba"); Coxsone Dodd ("Let's Build Our Dreams," "My Heart Is Gone," "OK Fred," "A Love I Can Feel," "A Stranger In Love," "Tonight" and "Fancy Make-Up"); Alvin Ranglin ("Strange Thing," "Son of the Wise" and "Keep It Up") and Phil Pratt (a swift rerecording of "My Heart is Gone").

It was Holt's union with Bunny Lee which really paid dividends, however, producing a handful of collaborations with Dennis Alcapone ("Jumping Jack" and "Togetherness") and the massive solo hits "A Little Tear," "Sometimes" and "Stick by Me." The latter, a cover of the American hit by Shep & The Limelites, became the biggest selling Jamaican single of the year, remaining top of the chart for 23 weeks.

"I Am the One to Blame" and "Time and the River" highlighted a powerful reunion with Duke Reid (1973), while 1974's Harry Mudie produced Time Is the Master album unleashed Holt's voice on a clutch of exquisitely chosen cover versions, to the accompaniment of orchestral arrangements cut in London by Tony Ashfield. Effortlessly, too, the album spun off the hits "Again," "Love Is Gone" and "Everybody Knows," while Holt's version of Ivory Joe White's "It May Sound Silly' was held back only by its proximity to Gladstone Anderson's best-selling version of the same song — which was also produced by Mudie.

Aware that a crossover breakthrough was distinctly possible, Mudie's UK distributors, Trojan Records, brought Holt to London in 1974, again pairing him with pop producer Ashfield and a suitcase full of MOR gems. By the end of the year, all concerned were enjoying a Top 10 UK hit with "Help Me Make It Through the Night" (a song previously reggaefied by Joyce Bond).

Despite the attendant 1000 Volts of Holt album positively overflowing with further such material, Holt was never able to match that solitary hit. Back in Jamaica, however, he continued to march from strength to strength. His compositions were regularly visited by other artists (Marcia Griffiths cut a great version of "Reggae From The Ghetto"), while his "There's a Jam in the Streets," loosely applicable to the chaotic aftermath of the recent Hurricane Gilbert, became an anthem of sorts. Holt's 1976 reworking of the Heptones' "Get in the Groove," "Up Park Camp" (produced at Channel One) proved he was as adept at roots as with ballads. Riding the Heptones' "Got in the Groove" rhythm, the song documented life in a government youth detention camp.

Further sessions with Bunny Lee that same year produced the 45s "Winter World of Love," "The Next Tear Drop," "Wasted Days and Nights" and "You're All I Got," and even a blatant attempt to regain Anglo-American favor with 1977's John Holt Goes Disco album had its high points. The hits did begin to slow as the musical climate shifted again at the end of the decade, but Holt continued releasing classy material. Numbered among his more significant releases were "Lovely Woman," and versions of "If I Were a Carpenter," the Isley Brothers' "This Old Heart of Mine" and Lou Rawls' "You'll Never Find a Love Like Mine."

Holt's appearance at the 1982 Reggae Sunsplash was one of the highlights of the entire event, while a union with Junjo Lawes brought the dance hall hit "Fat She Fat" that same year. A modern revival of the Studio One-era "A Love I Can Feel" followed, while "Private Doctor," "Peeping Tom" and "Youths' Pon the Corner" restated the continued relevance of Holt's natural strengths.

But it was another Lawes production, 1983's rootsy "Police in Helicopter," which both confirmed his re-emergence and redefined his image. Holt himself admitted that both his longevity and his past music had firmly cast him as a family entertainer; now he was acknowledging his Rastafarian beliefs by sprouting beard and dreads, and a harsh condemnation of the Jamaican government's recent militant crackdown on marijuana growing. "Police in Helicopter" was a massive hit, and his re-emergence was confirmed.

In 1984, Prince Jammy supervised the sterling "If You Were My Lover," before Holt reunited with Bunny Lee for Pure Gold (1985). He also cut a well-received album with Dennis Brown, an opening shot in the unnamed mid-1980s conspiracy of vocalists which vowed to flood the market with new material, to try and hold back the latest DJ boom. Remembering his role in launching the DJ phenomenon in the first place, back in 1970 with U-Roy, the irony was not, presumably, lost upon Holt himself.

Since that time, true to this mission, Holt has remained prolific and, if subsequent albums have been spotty, in terms of material, if not frequency, he remains a deeply respected force on the Jamaican scene. He also made triumphant returns to Sunsplash in 1990, 1991 and 1993–96.

The Paragons, too, have resurfaced as a Barrett/Evans duo. Both members relocated to New York after the band's break-up, with Evans resurfacing during the late 1970s with a handful of singles and the albums *For Lovers Only* and *Sings Bullwackie Style* for the Bullwackies label.

In 1981, the pair joined with Sly & Robbie to record a remarkable album (*Sly & Robbie Present the Paragons*) which offered Riddim Twins-powered remakes of a number of earlier hits. In 1996, a union with Yellowman (*Yellowman Meets the Paragons*) and their own *Heaven And Earth* offered further opportunities to prove that the heavenly harmonies which once powered the Paragons were still in business.

SELECTED DISCOGRAPHY

8 **A Love I Can Feel (Bamboo — UK) 1971**

Wrapping up the bulk of the newly solo Holt's work with Coxsone Dodd, including the hits "Stranger In Love," "My Heart Is Gone" and the title track, an early example of Holt's taste in American soul covers.

7 **Like a Bolt (Treasure Isle — JA) 1971**

Duke Reid's productions from the same period are highlighted by "Ali Baba," besides a host of lovely, romantic songs.

7 **Holt (Trojan — UK) 1973**
6 **Still in Chains (Trojan — UK) 1973**

Drifting between some excellent new material ("Mr TV Man," "Just Out of Reach"), the occasional revival ("Got To Get Away") and a smattering of covers ("Hey Jude," "Do You Love Me"), two albums demonstrate the ease with which Holt embraced — and possibly even co-created — the reggae-lite mood of the early 1970s. Both have since been packaged together onto one-CD (See for Miles — UK, 1999).

7 **Presenting the Fabulous John Holt (Magnet — UK) 1974**

Duke Reid produces a well-rounded selection of rootsy ballads.

8 **The Further You Look (Trojan — UK) 1974**
7 **Dusty Roads (Trojan — UK) 1974**
7 **Sings for I (Trojan — UK) 1974**

Three largely self-composed ballad sets that leave one wondering why Holt so frequently relies on covers. *Dusty Roads*,

incidentally, boasts an excruciatingly bad jacket. Intriguingly, all three have since been repackaged across two separate CD releases, with *The Further You Look* featuring on both (Trojan — UK).

6 **1000 Volts of Holt (Trojan — UK) 1974**

The first of several volumes (*2000 Volts*, *3000 Volts* inevitably followed). Throughout, producer Tony Ashfield leads Holt through pastures ranging from the movie theme "Alfie" to the Beatles' "I Will," a string of Motown classics and, ultimately, "Help Me Make It Through the Night." In the fondue party conscious 1970s, this was the music which allowed swinging 30-somethings to say, "I like reggae." A collection combining volumes two and three onto one disc was released in 1997.

8 **A Love I Can Feel (Attack — UK) 1974**

Excellent reunion with Coxsone Dodd offers an earthier sound than other Holt releases from this period, with "Tonight" and "Why Can't I Touch You" standing out.

8 **Time Is the Master (Cactus — UK) 1974**

String drenched and gently skanking, songs by Brook Benton ("Looking Back"), Ivory Joe Hunter ("It May Sound Silly") and producer Harry Mudie's own "Love Is Gone" posit a reflective mood perfectly in keeping with Holt's laid back vocals.

9 **Up Park Camp (Channel One — JA) 1976**

Very much a comeback album after his flirtation with UK pop success, Holt revisits some of his older classics, while showing he can still come up with new ones — as the title track brilliantly proves.

6 **Winter World of Love (Justice — UK) 1977**

A hit and miss selection drawn from the latter stages of Holt's partnership with Bunny Lee.

6 **Holt Goes Disco (Trojan — UK) 1977**

But how disco is it really? "I'll Never Fall in Love Again" would be a sweet ballad whatever backing it was saddled with, while Roger Whittaker's "Last Farewell" could never be anything but painfully mawkish. An eccentric album, rendered even weirder by the notions which went into its creation.

5 **Children of the World (VP) 1981**

Blandly pleasant set best distinguished by "This Old Heart Of Mine."

4 **Just the Two of Us (CSA — UK) 1982**

Holt's voice, of course, is faultless, but the material . . . oh, the material. "Let Your Love Flow," "Vaya Con Dios" and "This Masquerade" move things irrevocably into an early

70s AOR mode, a decade too late to be of any use, and Holt's own compositions seem happy to join them there.

8 Police in Helicopter (Greensleeves—UK) 1983

The best of Holt's later recordings, packed with realism-heavy Jamaican hit singles and expertly overseen by Junjo Lawes. The title track is the best known performance, "Chanting" and "I Got Caught" are supreme roots numbers, and even "Sugar and Spice" (a song which past Holt albums would have rendered intolerable) is a stand-out. Reissued in 2001 by Greensleeves (US).

6 Pure Gold (Vista Sounds—UK) 1985

A well constructed set, but the sharper eye for social commentary which marked out its predecessors is weakening, and too many tracks seem to lock Holt on cruise control. "TV Land," however, offers renewed hope for the future.

8 The John Holt Christmas Album (Trojan—UK) 1986

An absolute epic of unrepentant surrealism. Adapting half a dozen of the rock era's most successful/effective Christmas hits, then topping it up with five more traditional pop hits, Holt covers Greg Lake, Chris DeBurgh, Slade, Mud, John Lennon and George Michael, before sending us home with "Auld Lang Syne." A state of the art digital production adds to the weirdness.

7 Why I Care (Greensleeves—UK) 1989

Hugh "Redman" James produced set pushes Holt into an aggressive dance hall stance which works better than it might be imagined.

6 Reggae Hip House R&B Flavour ( ) 1993
6 Reggae Peacemaker (House of Reggae) 1996
6 All Night Long (MIL) 1997

With Johnny Clarke, Screwdriver and Latisha Vining among the guests, an enjoyable modernization of older hits, as usual thrown together with a handful of new songs. "Nightbird" and "Have Mercy" both raise the temperature, while a dubby "Tide [Is High] Jam" closes the disc in style.

7 New Horizon (VP) 1999

Producers Roy Francis and Computer Paul don't put a foot wrong guiding Holt through his best album of the 1990s . . . at least, it was, until someone hit upon remaking Holt's reggae-lite version of the 70s hit "Brandy."

JOHN HOLT & DENNIS BROWN
5 Wild Fire (Natty Congo—JA) 1986

Two of the most powerful voices, the sharpest pens and the keenest ears in Jamaica — and what do they do? "I'll Never Fall in Love Again." The album sounds lovely, but it could have been a lot more dangerous. Holt's "Oh Girl," a Brown single four years earlier, is an annoying omission.

JOHN HOLT & THE PARAGONS
9 On the Beach (Treasure Isle—JA) 1967

Any gathering of Paragons tracks amounts to a veritable greatest hits album, but the band's debut takes some beating. "The Tide Is High," of course, is here, alongside the less ubiquitous (and possibly infinitely preferable) "Happy Go Lucky Girl," "Village Girl," "Only a Smile" and more.

8 My Girl Wears a Crown (Trojan—UK) 1994

Far reaching hits collection which expands on the above to document the best of the band's 1966–68 output.

THE PARAGONS
8 Sly & Robbie Meet the Paragons (Island—UK) 1981

Largely a chance for the Riddim Twins to rework some of their own old favorites, with their adaptation of "Gotta Get Away," retitled "Indiana James" and a fiery essential.

SELECTED COMPILATIONS & ARCHIVE RELEASES
6 20 Golden Love Songs (Trojan—UK) 1980

Wandering starry-eyed around similar pastures to the *1000 Volts* repackage, a largely US-chart-ocentric gathering which sees Holt wrap honeyed tones around "Everybody's Talkin'," "Touch Me in the Morning," "Just the Way You Are" and further 70s-era MOR indignities.

7 20 Super Hits (Sonic Sounds—UK) 1990

Twenty super hits indeed, and if you need light dance hall flavored versions of "I Just Called to Say I Love You," "The Last Farewell" and "I'll Never Fall in Love Again," step right up. Though the album is drawn from a variety of Holt's Trojan label releases (including 1977's *Disco* album), "Sweetie Come Brush Me," a highlight of Holt's 1982 Sunsplash set, is also included, so that's alright.

9 Can't Keep Us Apart (Jamaican Gold—UK) 1999

Masterful recounting of Holt's work with Bunny Lee, 40 tracks divided neatly between original 45s and their dub versions. Some of Holt's finest solo recordings are included here, in a package (and packaging) which utterly outperforms any rival collection of the same material.

DE HUNTER

STYLE *calypso/soca*
BORN *Derrick St Rose De Hunter*

The biggest contemporary star on the island of Dominica, since his emergence on the calypso scene in 1988, De Hunter has done more than any other artist to introduce and popularize soca on the island. A police officer with the Dominican special unit, he first appeared at Mas Dominik in 1991. He put up a strong showing every year subsequently, until finally breaking through in 1997, when he collected his first title, the Caribbean Quest Music Award for Best New Calypso Artist. 1997 also brought the release of his first album, a pairing with 1995 Calypso Monarch de Scrunter, released under the name of the Brotherly Brothers.

The following year, De Hunter himself won Calypso Monarch at Mas Dominik, scoring a major smash with his first solo album *On de Road Again*. He repeated that triumph in 2000 with the infectious "Soca Lollipop" (also the title of his 2000 album). De Hunter's other Dominican hits have included the *What-A-Karnival* album (1999), and the singles "One People," "Take a Wine" and "Wom La (the Rum)," all produced by his wife and manager Marah St Rose. His backing band includes Martindale Olive and Fred Nicholas (guitars), Bing Casimir (trumpet), Norman Dorival (trombone), Norman Letang (sax), Cornell Phillip, Edmund Angel and Don Gabriel (keyboards, programming).

RECOMMENDED LISTENING

8 Soca Lollipop (—Dominica)

INNER CIRCLE

STYLE *reggae*
FORMED 1968 (Kingston, JA)
ORIGINAL LINE-UP *Stephen "Cat" Coore (guitar), Ian Lewis (guitar), Roger Lewis (bass), Michael "Ibo" Cooper (keyboards), William Stewart (drums), Irvin "Carrot" Jarrett (percussion)*

Alongside the Wailers and Third World, Inner Circle completed a triumvirate of roots reggae bands poised to go international during the early-mid 1970s — indeed, as late as 1978, and the legendary Peace Festival, Inner Circle were co-headlining the bill with the Wailers, with vocalist Jacob Miller an even more popular figure in his homeland than Bob Marley. Had Miller not perished in an auto accident in March, 1980, there is no telling what further triumphs his band might have accomplished.

Miller joined Inner Circle several years into the band's career. Originally formed as the Inner Circle Bond by brothers Roger and Ian Lewis — the self-styled Fatman Riddim Section — plus the formally trained Stephen Coore (then just 12 years old) and Michael Cooper, the band was completed by drummer William Stewart, percussionist Irvin Jarrett and singer William "Bunny" Clark in 1970, the latter newly returned to Jamaica after two years in New York.

In this form, the group cut a handful of singles, including the "Red Cherry" version of Dennis Alcapone's "Ripe Cherry" — itself a version of Eric Donaldson's "Cherry Oh Baby," which itself featured Inner Circle. They also recorded several other tracks as backing band for the Chosen Few vocal group.

Jarrett quit during 1972 to pursue an interest in film making; Clark followed later in the year, returning to New York, where he formed a new band, the Bluegrass Experience, with fellow expatriates Glen Adams, Eric Frater and Sparrow Martin. When that band broke up, he went back to Kingston to launch a solo career with producer Lee Perry.

(He eventually settled down as a member of Third World.)

He was replaced by Milton "Prilly" Hamilton; however, this new line-up fractured when Coore, Cooper and Hamilton all departed to form Third World in 1973.

New members Charles Farquharson (keyboards), Bernard Harvey (keyboards) and Calvin McKenzie (drums) were recruited, and Inner Circle became adept at playing the uptown clubs and hotels, while entering (and frequently winning) talent shows. With a repertoire comprised almost exclusively of smoothly executed reggae covers, they took the Best Band award on the *Johnny Golding Show*, and their first album, *Dread Reggae Hits* was a respectable seller.

They cut a handful of tracks with vocalist Funky Brown, including 1974's major hit "I See You" and "Song of the Swallow." However, the lack of a full time frontman continued to cause concern until, finally, Inner Circle invited Jacob "Killer" Miller (b 1955, JA) to join them.

Since bursting onto the recording scene in 1968, when he cut "Love Is a Message" for Coxsone Dodd, Miller had established himself at the forefront of the roots scene, recording such sufferer anthems as "Each One Teach One," "Keep on Knocking," "Hungry Town Skank" and "Girl Name Pat." The singer gained further recognition when the Augustus Pablo produced "Who Say Jah No Dread," "Baby I Love You So" and "False Rasta" were all featured on the acclaimed *King Tubby Meets the Rockers Uptown* dub album.

Nevertheless, he readily accepted Inner Circle's invitation, as much for the musical challenge it represented as for the visual spectacle which he knew would result — alongside the heavyweight Lewis brothers, Miller's own solid frame gave Inner Circle an imposing frontline which was second to none.

The union's earliest recordings did well to find a middle ground between Inner Circle's traditional sound and Miller's more forthright energies. A legacy of their North Shore hotel work, they were adept at reggae-fying current American soul hits ("Rock the Boat," "TSOP," "When Will I See You Again"), while they enjoyed a minor hit with a smooth lovers rock version of the Stylistics' "You Make Me Feel Brand New," rendered doubly remarkable by Miller's ability to match the original's falsetto lead.

Other popular material gathered on the band's early albums comprised similarly flawless covers of current reggae hits, including a remarkable adaptation of Rupie Edwards' "Irie Feelings," completely stripped of its original dub tones.

Miller's solo career continued simultaneously with his band work. He scored with "Girl Don't Come" (produced by Gussie Clarke, 1975) and "Forward Jah Jah Children," from which Augustus Pablo and King Tubby developed the sound system smash "Shakedown." (Inner Circle also made

Inner Circle, the heaviest heavyweights of all.

several attempts at this particular anthem.) Miller was elected Singer of the Year in a 1975 poll arranged by the Guinness Brewery.

Inner Circle's own first genuine success, the Miller/Roger Lewis produced "Tenement Yard," was also released under Miller's name alone, in 1976 ("Tired fe Lick Weed in a Bush" followed). The song's popularity, however, quickly improved the band's standing, and they were signed by Capitol Records soon after.

Inner Circle remained with the label for two albums, *Reggae Thing* and *Ready for the World*. By 1978, however, the group had moved to Island Records, already home to Bob Marley and Third World, and continued their rise from there, their career moving into overdrive in the aftermath of the Peace Concert.

The band did not lose its grassroots devotees. The aptly titled *Heavyweight Dub* album unleashed Prince Jammy upon some of the Inner Circle's best known material and reminded listeners that beneath the smooth confections which were the group's "popular" face, they remained a dangerous roots proposition.

Similarly, the band's role in the movie *Rockers* brought further acclaim to the party — taking an ironic potshot at their past, Inner Circle appear as the house band at an expensive hotel, baffling the tourists with an impassioned version of "Tenement Yard." "This isn't calypso, is it?" one bemused onlooker asks his companion. Miller himself also took an amusingly self-parodying acting role in the movie.

With Inner Circle alongside, Miller released a pair of nominally solo albums during 1978, *Killer Miller* (partnered by the *Killer Dub* companion) and the popular *Natty Christmas*. The group appeared at the inaugural Reggae Sunsplash festival that summer (they returned again twelve months later), while *Everything Is Great*, Inner Circle's Island debut album, spawned two UK Top 50 hit singles in early 1979, the title track and "Stop Breaking My Heart." Another 12-inch classic, "We a Rockers," became a club staple and, by the end of the year, the *New Age Music* album seemed poised to catapult the band to greater glory.

Miller's death in a car accident on March 23, 1980, then, stopped the group in its tracks. Inner Circle disbanded immediately, with Harvey and the Lewis brothers leaving Jamaica for Miami, where they opened their own recording studio.

Inner Circle reformed in 1986 with the same trio, joined by vocalist Carlton Coffie and drummer Lancelot Hall, and cut the *Black Roses* album. Live shows in the US were a success, and a second album, *One Way*, unveiled what became the new line-up's signature piece, the brooding "Bad Boys." After it was rerecorded for their next album, 1989's major label *Identified*, it was swiftly adopted as the theme to the Fox TV series *Cops*.

In 1990, Inner Circle were one of the highlights of the Reggae Sunsplash festival, their first showing at the event in over a decade. Meanwhile, their international acclaim continued to snowball.

A rap version of "Bad Boys" gave Inner Circle a US R&B chart hit in 1993 and subsequently earned the band a Grammy. Equally significantly, the *Bad to the Bone* album saw Inner Circle score hits on both sides of the Atlantic with "Sweat (A La La La La Long)," which reached #16 in the US and #3 in Britain. The success of *Bad to the Bone* itself, meanwhile, brought the group back into major label contention, earning a high profile reissue (retitled *Bad Boys*) on Atlantic in 1994.

A version of Joe South's "The Games People Play" introduced Inner Circle's next album, 1994's *Reggae Dancer*, with another major hit. However, Coffie's departure for a solo career took away some of the band's momentum, and close to three years passed before Inner Circle resurfaced, with new vocalist Kris Bentley. Subsequent albums have done little to suggest further monster successes are on the way, but Inner Circle's international reputation remains undisputed.

DISCOGRAPHY

2 Dread Reggae Hits (Top Ranking) 1973
3 Heavy Reggae (Top Ranking) 1974

One can try and look on the bright side, but to be honest, a lot of this stuff is really horrible. Stevie Wonder's "Blame It on the Sun," "Homely Girl," "I'm Going Home". . . no wonder the tourists kept coming back.

6 Blame It on the Sun (Trojan) 1975

Miller's Inner Circle debut introduces the future classic "Forward Jah Jah Children" to the proceedings, while still struggling with their appetite for slick covers — "Irie Feelings," Marley's "I Shot the Sheriff" and "Natty Dread," and Peter Tosh's "Burial" among them.

6 Rock the Boat (Trojan) 1975
7 Reggae Thing (Capitol) 1976
7 Ready for the World (Capitol) 1977

Across two vastly improved Capitol albums, Inner Circle's development is undeniable. A vastly punchier take on

"Forward . . ." surfaces, alongside "Tired fe Lick Weed in a Bush," "Roman Soldiers of Babylon," "80,000 Careless Ethiopians" and "I'm a Rastaman," as Miller and the band's own songwriting takes precedence.

8 Everything Is Great (Island) 1978

It is still easy to write Inner Circle off as a lightweight proposition — and many critics did. Suffice to say, another collection of E-Z Listening Sufferer Anthems (the disco-flavored "Music Machine") was always going to appeal to an audience now prepped for what the band themselves called the "Rastaman Melody" of the "Roots Rock Symphony." And Inner Circle weren't going to let a few purists stand in their way. So they threw them a dub bone, then got on with the show.

8 Killer Dub (Top Ranking — JA) 1978
8 Heavyweight Dub (Top Ranking — JA) 1979

In fact, both collections were based around vocalist Miller's *Killer Miller* and *Wanted* albums; the omnipresence of the Inner Circle axis, however, qualifies both as the band's own work. Respectively remixed by Prince Jammy and Maximilian, the pair are now available squeezed onto one-CD, credited to Inner Circle & The Fatman. (Blood & Fire — UK)

8 New Age Music (Island) 1979
7 Black Roses (RAS) 1986

A real surprise here. As the comeback slips effortlessly back into the same pleasing pop-shaped bag as the Miller era, and the modern dance hall overtones subvert the earlier roots sugar coating, it suddenly becomes apparent that the band's songwriting has improved immensely since the classic era.

7 One Way (RAS) 1987

Whoever could have predicted the way "Bad Boys" took off, all the more so since it was clearly overshadowed by half the other songs on the album, "Keep the Faith" and "Massive" most of all. Ah, but they weren't as catchy and as universally pertinent, and so the career takes a sharp turn towards the unexpected here.

6 Identified (WB) 1989

"Bad Boys" is back, of course, and again it sounds just a little out of place.

7 Bad to the Bone (RAS) 1992

Reissued in 1994 as *Bad Boys* (what else?), an album of extremes which wanders from the inner city belligerence of the title track through to the pure pop of "Sweat," but takes in some unexpected highs en route — Neil Young's "Down by the River" among them. Remixes of the two main attractions prop up the reissue.

5 Reggae Dancer (Big Beat) 1994

Coffie's farewell is actually a major step backwards for the band, lighter and blander than they've been for a while, with a few cuts which sound like they're trying to recreate "Bad Boys" again.

4 Da Bomb aka *Speak My Language* (Soundway) 1997

Despite possessing an excellent voice, new vocalist Bentley actually adds little else to the band, for whom the only way now appears to be down.

4 Jamika Me Crazy (Eureka) 1999
4 Big Tings (VP) 2000

Whoever wrote the reggae rules for the year 2000 insists that it wouldn't be a new album without a bucketload of guest appearances, and Inner Circle aren't about to disobey. Whether Mr Vegas, Beenie Man, Luciano and Anthony B bring much more than star power to the sessions is a moot point, however. Still one of the best live bands around, IC's studio work continues over-produced, under-written and almost painfully saccharine.

SELECTED COMPILATIONS & ARCHIVE RELEASES

8 The Best of Inner Circle (Mango) 1992

Handy round-up of the Island label albums, overcoming the absence of the band's best known (solo Miller) material with some excellent live versions. Also includes the band's fabulous assault on the pop heartbreaker "Delilah," meaning that song for song, it's actually a better purchase than either (or both) of the original albums.

7 The Best of Inner Circle (Capitol) 1993

Funny what a sudden hit can do — all of a sudden, all these best ofs, and a lot of very confused newcomers staring at the track listing and wondering why "Bad Boys" is missing. This none-too-generous set rounds up Inner Circle's Capitol label days with an eye for the harder-edged highlights — "Ghetto on Fire," "Careless Ethiopians," "Forward Jah Jah Children" etc.

6 Big in Jamaica (Music Club) 2000

15 track collection drawn from the pre-Capitol albums, highlighted by the original version of "Forward Jah Jah Children," but also illuminating their eye for covers — several Bob Marley songs, "Ire Feelings," "Some Guys Have All the Luck" and more. Also includes a smattering of pre-Miller tracks, just in case you need them.

CARLTON COFFIE

6 Scandal (Gator) 1998

Having spent the first years of his solo career recording movie soundtrack contributions (*Mega Man, Beverley Hills Cop III*), Coffie's debut album emerged a slick blend of self- compositions and unconventional covers — the Eagles' "Hotel California," Hot Chocolate's "You Sexy Thing" and Al Green's "Let's Stay Together." Odd.

4 Bad Boys 2000—Stop the Violence (Gator) 1999

Unnecessary remakes of his most famous compositions, "Bad Boys" and "Sweat," are joined by a virtual reprise of the *Scandal* album.

JACOB MILLER

8 Dread Dread (UA) 1978

Album features the epic "Tenement Yard," but delves elsewhere into similar reggae-lite territory to Inner Circle's own albums. Miller's "Dock of the Bay" is touching, however, and his gleeful take on War's "Why Can't We Be Friends" more than compensates for such unpalatable fluff as "Suzie Wong."

7 Killer Miller (Top Ranking—JA) 1978

Heavier set than *Dread Dread* (as the Inner Circle/Prince Jammy dub disc proves). Dylan's "I Shall Be Released" gets the dread treatment, but the album's real highlights are "80,000 Careless Ethiopians" and "Lambs Bread Collie."

6 Natty Christmas (Top Ranking—JA) 1978

In cohorts with DJ Ray I, Christmas goes Rasta with its tongue firmly burrowed into one cheek. "Natty No Santa Claus" indeed.

6 Wanted (Top Ranking—JA) 1979

"You Make Me Feel Brand New" resurfaces to provide a little light/lite relief among another distinctly darker collection than the mothership was want to offer.

SELECTED COMPILATIONS & ARCHIVE RELEASES

8 Greatest Hits (RAS) 1987

10 songs short, but certainly a valid round-up of Miller's better-known solo work, beginning (of course) with "Tenement Yard."

8 Who Say Jah No Dread (RAS) 1992

An essential gathering of Miller's fine early 45s, with both vocal and dub flips present, highlighting the manic inventiveness of those old King Tubby and Augustus Pablo manipulations.

3 Chapter a Day: The Jacob Miller Songbook (VP) 1999

Touchingly sincere tribute collection, 33 tracks see a variety of dance hall stars covering some of Miller's finest compositions. Luciano, Tony Rebel, Sanchez, General Degree and Red Rat are among the performers, most of whom temper their treatments with genuine affection. But really, if you want to listen to Miller, wouldn't you just play the originals?

I-ROY

STYLE *reggae (toasting/DJ)*
BORN *Roy Samuel Reid, 6/28/49 (St Thomas, JA); d 11/27/99.*

Roy Reid was working as a government accountant when he launched his Soul Bunny sound system in 1968, swiftly picking up a devoted audience with his dynamic and outspoken style. This audience accompanied him when he began working with the Spanish Town based Sons Junior system, which is where producer Harry Mudie discovered him.

Mindful of U-Roy's recent breakthrough at the head of the new wave of DJ superstars, Mudie rechristened Reid I-Roy and, in 1971, cut four tracks with him, collaborations with Dennis Walks ("The Drifter" and "Heart Don't Leap"), the Ebony Sisters (the sassy "Let Me Tell You Boy") and the toaster's solo debut 45, "Musical Pleasure."

The Mudie/Roy partnership broke up due to disagreements over a European tour and, by late 1971, the DJ was the prize attraction at King Tubby's Home Town Hi Fi (he also worked the Stereo, Ruddy's Supreme and V-Rocket set-ups). Lloyd Campbell took him into the studio to cut another single, "Hot Bomb" (with the Jumpers); Bunny Lee handled "Make Love," "Rose of Sharon" and "Who Cares."

Over the next two years, I-Roy became a veteran of sessions with Winston Blake ("Mood for Love"), Derrick Harriott ("Melinda"), Lloyd Daley ("Problems in Life," "Musical Drum Sound"), Jimmy Radway ("Sound Education"), Glen Brown ("Brother Toby Is a Movie from London," "Rasta on a Sunday," "Festive Season"), Lee Perry ("High Fashion," "Space Flight"), Ruddy Redwood ("Sidewalk Killer"), Byron Lee ("Dr Who"), Keith Hudson ("Silver Platter"), Clive Chin, Rupie Edwards and more.

His most productive sessions, however, were with Gussie Clarke. "Magnificent Seven" and "High Jacking" debuted their partnership on the chart; thereafter, the pair cut so many hit singles that, by the time I-Roy's debut album, *Presenting*, was released in 1973, it already doubled as a greatest hits album.

"Black Man Time," with its lengthy conversational intro, and "Tripe Girl" were both major smashes, while I-Roy's taste for potent commentary was evidenced by the pointed "Coxsone Affair," the cynical "Tourism Is My Business" and the dismissive "Screw Face," remarking upon the authorities' failure to clear up rising inner city crime rates.

Buoyed by the hits "Buck and the Preacher" (produced by Pete Weston, and discussing the 1971 movie of the same name) and "Monkey Fashion" (produced by Roy Cousins), a second album, the largely self-produced *Hell and Sorrow*, arrived before year's. It earned such praise in the UK, that in September, 1973, I-Roy relocated to London to help promote his forthcoming third album, *The Many Moods of I-Roy*.

He returned to Jamaica in June, 1974, taking up residence as unofficial house producer at Joe Gibbs and JoJo Hookim's newly opened Channel One studio. Though he was rarely credited in this capacity, I-Roy's sonic imprimatur can be detected across any number of period Channel One releases, including such seminal roots efforts as John Holt's "Up Park Camp," the Meditations' "Woman Is Like a Shadow" and more.

Among several Channel One innovations for which I-Roy is credited are the studio's use of an MCI high pass filter (the magic ingredient which gave King Tubby's dub mixes their distinctive feel), and persuading session drummer Sly Dunbar to perfect a clapping sound on his snare drum — a cornerstone of what subsequently emerged as the Sly & Robbie sound.

For close to eight months, I-Roy remained in the background, a period during which DJ-ing itself seemed to have passed from favor, finally crushed by the long standing opposition of the Jamaican Federation of Musicians (JFM). He re-emerged in February, 1975, to prove that the Federation's boasts simply were not true.

I-Roy launched his comeback with a single with Jackie Brown, "The Black Bullet." JoJo Hookim oversaw a string of Channel One releases, led by "I Man Time," "Welding," "Forward Yah!" and "Roots Man." But it was I-Roy's reunion with producer Bunny Lee which truly relaunched both his career, and that of so many other DJs.

Their first effort was "Straight to Jazzbo's Head," a vinyl assault on one of the many DJs to have tried on I-Roy's crown in recent months, Linval "Prince Jazzbo" Carter. Jazzbo, of course, responded in kind with "Straight to I-Roy's Head," and the ensuing feud became one of the year's most entertaining diversions.

"Jazzbo Have fe Run," which documented Jazzbo's recent (but thankfully, none too serious) encounter with the wheels of a moving bus, was met by "Gal Boy I-Roy," questioning I-Roy's manhood. That in turn provoked "Pad Lock," I-Roy's exquisitely entertaining attempt to wake up "Princess Jazzbo." Interestingly, the pair remained firm friends away from the microphone, and have recorded two albums together.

1975 brought additional recordings with Pete Weston ("Natty Down Deh," dedicated to JFM President, jazz-man Sonny Bradshaw, "Outformer Parker" and the *Truth & Rights* album) and Phil Pratt ("Ital Dish," "Musical Air Raid"). I-Roy also cut remarkable versions of the Melodians' "Rivers of Babylon" and the Paragons' "A Quiet Place," restructured as "A Noisy Place." In the space of just eight months, I-Roy placed 13 hits on the Jamaican chart.

In 1976, I-Roy was among the first Jamaican artists scooped up by Virgin Records. He swiftly proved himself to be among the most prolific artists on the label. Between 1976–79, Virgin and its subsidiaries Caroline and Front Line released eight I-Roy albums (including one under his real name, 1980's *Whap'n Bap'n*), even as the DJ continued to work for other producers and labels back in Jamaica.

Sessions in 1977 paired him with Niney Holness, for "Point Blank," "Rasta Pickney," "Jah Come Here" and "Zion Trip," a version of Dennis Brown's "Take a Trip to Zion" (all included on the Blood & Fire label's Niney compilation). Work with Alvin Ranglin evolved into the *Best of I-Roy* album, and in 1978, with Bunny Lee, he released "New York City" and *The Godfather* album. Further albums were cut with Joe Gibbs' *African Herbsman* and Harry J (*Hotter Yatta*) during 1979/80.

Unfortunately, this incredible burst of productivity appears to have exhausted the DJ. Sessions with Roderick "Blackbeard" Sinclair in 1984 were his weakest yet and, although I-Roy continued recording, subsequent releases were as spotty as they were sporadic.

Health problems suffered during the last years of his life were worsened by his financial situation. For much of this time, he was living rough, his only assistance coming from his mentally-challenged son; a second son was in prison, where he was killed in October, 1999. Four weeks later, I-Roy himself passed away at the Spanish Town hospital from heart problems.

DISCOGRAPHY

9 **Presenting (Trojan — UK) 1973**
The DJ's powerful debut threw up the shattering "Blackman Time," a deservedly massive hit built around the "Slaving" rhythm, but the rest of the album rarely slacks off from this height, and proclaims the arrival of I-Roy and his "food for thought" toasts.

9 **Hell & Sorrow (Trojan — UK) 1974**
"Medley Mood" includes, among other snips, stylized versions of "The Banana Boat Song" and "Baa Baa Black Sheep." Even with the amazingly high standard set by *Presenting*, this album still stands tall, including as it does a clutch of hits, among them "Monkey Fashion" and the Dennis Alcapone-ish "Buck and the Preacher," as well as equally strong new songs such as the DJ's version of "Sidewalk Killer," retitled "Dr Phibbs."

7 **The Many Moods Of (Trojan — UK) 1974**
8 **Truths & Rights (Grounation — UK) 1975**
Under-rated but ferocious set featuring the Lee Perry classic "Dread in the West," together with "Teapot," "Natty Down De" (dedicated to JFM head Sonny Bradshaw — "is easier for a camel to go through a needle's eye than for version to die"), another of I-Roy's always entertaining medleys, and a host of other hits from the year.

8 **Can't Conquer Rasta (Justice — UK) 1976**
Bunny Lee produced set heavy on dub and dark deliberation. In terms of matching wall-rattling sonics with potent imagery, this is the last truly essential I-Roy album — with just one exception (*10 Commandments*), subsequent sets offer either one or the other.

7 **Musical Shark Attack (Virgin — UK) 1976**
7 **Crisis Time (Caroline) 1976**
I-Roy turns down the madness a notch or two for the sake of his new international aspirations, but nevertheless slams solid roots straight into the heart of Babylon. Across the two albums, "Semi Classical Natty Dread," "Tribute to Marcus Garvey," "Holy Satta," replaying the Abyssinians' greatest hit, "African Herbsman" and "Hypocrite Blackout" are uniformly excellent.

6 **Dread Baldhead (Klik) 1976**
5 **The Best of I-Roy (GGs) 1977**
The title misleads — the ten tracks are all new and not especially great either. The best of the rhythms are drawn from Alton Ellis and the Heptones' Studio One days; I-Roy, meanwhile, sounds understated and generally uninspired.

10 **Ten Commandments (Front Line) 1977**
An astonishingly vibrant set, drawing its musical inspiration from Bob Marley's recent *Exodus* album, with each of the ten commandments set to one or the other of that album's rhythms.

7 **Heart of a Lion (Front Line) 1977**
I-Roy and Harry Johnson founder a little, as half a great album is matched with some distinctly throwaway cuts.

6 **The Godfather (Third World) 1977**
A set of Bunny Lee/Blackbeard sessions catching I-Roy's views on the mob, the law and his own DJ-ing prowess. What else?

7 **The General/Spider's Web (Front Line) 1977**
I-Roy's take on the standard "Killer Man Jaro" highlights *The General*, but the set was most notable for the bonus dub album included with early pressings — *Spider's Web* is as threatening as they come, with titles to match.

7 **World on Fire (Front Line) 1978**
Which came first — this album? Or Sly & Robbie's emergence from the shadows of Channel One? Either way, the immediate future is mapped out with graphic intensity.

6 **African Herbsman (Joe Gibbs — JA) 1978**
6 **Cancer (Front Line) 1979**
Another lesser album, its contents devoted in the main to either movie or musical icons (Andy Capp, Herbie Mann, Bruce Lee).

6 **Hotter Yatta (Harry J — JA) 1980**
6 **Whap'n Bap'n (Virgin) 1980**
Recorded in London with local hero Dennis Bovell, a subdued album which taps only the occasional high — "Alpha-

bet," "Jive Time" and "Conscious Argument" are the best cuts.

6 **I-Roy's Doctor Fish (Imperial — JA) 1981**
5 **Outer Limits (Intense — UK) 1983**

Initially impressive, but rather thin collection which finds I-Roy lifting as much from contemporary rap techniques as that artform borrowed from his own. "Girls School," "Street Chat" and "Mental Strain" are entertaining epics, but the old sharp wit is wilting.

6 **The Lyrics Man (Witty — JA) 1990**

I-ROY & PRINCE JAZZBO
7 **Step Forward Youth (Live & Love) 1975**
8 **Head to Head Clash (Ujama) 1990**

Bunny Lee produced this collected slew of knife twisting 45s, one of the funniest and most evenly matched battles since the heyday of Prince Buster's best-loved feuds.

I-ROY & JAH WOOSH
5 **We Chat You Rock (Trojan) 1987**

SELECTED COMPILATIONS & ARCHIVE RELEASES
6 **Crucial Cuts (Virgin) 1983**

Adequate collection drawn from the Front Line days, but one disc could never be sufficient to catch every deserving cut. A useful introduction, then, but you can't beat the original albums.

6 **Black Man Time (Jamaica Gold) 1994**

Bonus packed reissue of 1977's *The Best of I-Roy*, appended by three unissued cuts from the same sessions, plus four lackluster Blackbeard productions from 1984.

9 **Don't Check Me with No Lightweight Stuff (Blood & Fire) 1997**

Excellent trawl through I-Roy's 1972–75 output. Among so many distinguished masterpieces, "Holy Satta," "Ken Boothe Special," "Sidewalk Killer" and "Superfly" can all be singled out for high volume consumption — in every sense of the phrase.

8 **Touting I Self (Heartbeat) 2001**

Bunny Lee collection necessarily duplicates from of *Lightweight*, but fills in a lot of the gaps as well. Now, if only someone could start plugging all the others. . . .

GREGORY ISAACS

STYLE *reggae (lovers rock/roots)*
BORN *7/15/51 (Fletcher's Land, Kingston, JA)*

He has, and few deny it, the sweetest tones in reggae, an easing, smoothing, seducing voice which holds hearts captive long enough to reach into their soul, and captures souls for just enough time to make their hearts burst with its beauty. And neither time nor familiarity can ever dull its majesty. It is 20 years since Isaacs released the classic "Night Nurse," almost thirty since the immortal "All I Have Is Love," and they both still sound as fresh as they did the first time.

A talent contest veteran, the so-called Cool Ruler made his recording debut (a duet with Winston Sinclair) with 1968's "Another Heartache," recorded for Byron Lee at the WIRL studios. It went nowhere, and Isaacs next teamed up with two other vocalists, remembered today only as Penroe and Bramwell, as the Concords, part of Rupie Edwards' Success stable. "Buttoo" in 1969 and 1970's "Don't Let Me Suffer" led the band's short legacy. They also cut "(Out on the) Dancing Floor" with Prince Buster, to similarly muted applause.

The Concords broke up in 1970, and Isaacs relaunched his solo career. It got off to a slow start, and a handful of self-produced singles, including "While There Is Life," sold poorly. Further sessions with Rupie Edwards, too, were largely unproductive as "Too Late" and "Each Day" passed by during 1970. "Lonely Man," "Far Beyond the Valley," "Closer Together" and a melancholy cover of Greyhound's "Black and White" appeared in 1971, while the next few years brought the singles "I'm Coming Home," "Innocent People" and "Lonely Days." None of these made any more of an impact.

In 1973, Isaacs established his own African Museum label and record store in partnership with singer Errol Dunkley. Almost immediately he scored a massive hit with the self-produced "My Only Lover," arguably the first (and certainly the most influential) lovers rock record ever made. He further financed African Museum by continuing to record with other producers, maintaining a barrage of hits which defied belief, beginning in 1973 with "All I Have Is Love," produced by Phil Pratt.

Gussie Clarke oversaw "I Can't Believe," Pete Weston produced Isaacs' delicate revival of Dobbie Dobson's "Loving Pauper," and Clive Chin handled "Lonely Soldier" and "Do You Ever." Isaacs' own productions, meanwhile, were legion. Over the next three years, 1973–76, Isaacs was literally churning out material, ranging from the ballads for which he is best renowned, to the harder roots-edged material which deserves equal attention. Hits during this period include "Look Before You Leap," "Open the Door to Your Heart," "Promised Land," "Tumbling Tears," "Rasta Business," "Help Us Get Over," "Black a Kill Black" and "Extra Classic."

In 1974, Isaacs cut "Innocent People Cry" with producer Alvin Ranglin, the first in a string of hits which peaked with his first #1, "Love Is Overdue," that same year. "I Need Your Loving," "The Philistines" and "Don't Go" were further highlights from the same partnership, which also produced

Gregory Isaacs, the coolest ruler of all.

sufficient material to dominate what became Isaacs' first album, *In Person*.

Other hits during this time included recordings with Niney Holness ("Rock Away," "Bad Da"), Gussie Clarke (the up-beat "My Time," "Oh No I Can't Believe"), Prince Tony (the Paragons' "Fly Little Silver Bird"), Lloyd Campbell ("Slavemaster," "Promises"), Glen Brown ("One One Cocoa Fill Basket"), Harry Mudie ("Looking Back"), Roy Cousins ("Way of Life"), Bunny Wailer ("Sunday Morning") and Sidney Crooks ("Lonely Lover" and a remake of "All I Have Is Love," the seductive hit which titled Isaacs' next album. He also cut tracks with Dr. Alimantado, for the toaster's *Best Dressed Chicken in the Town*.

In the face of such prodigious output, by the late 1970s, Isaacs was arguably the biggest reggae performer in the world, up there alongside Dennis Brown (with whom he frequently toured and duetted) and Bob Marley in the estimation of the international audience, and outselling them both in the reggae market. Indeed, African Museum was itself responsible for releasing some of Brown's own greatest records, while Brown's DEB label released one of Isaacs' — 1977's *Mr Isaacs* album.

He became a regular at Joe Gibbs' Channel One, where he cut the epochal "Babylon too Rough," "The Sun Shines for Me" and several other tracks destined for 1979's *Meets Ronnie Davis* album. Lloyd Campbell oversaw the popular "Mr Know It All," while 1977–78 saw Isaacs release a stream of dynamic duets under the supervision of Alvin Ranglin: "I Will Never Love Again" with Ranking Barnabas, "Chunnie You Are My Number One" with Trinity, "The Border" with U-Brown. (Isaacs, Ranglin and Trinity continued recording together into the early 1980s.)

Isaacs signed with Virgin's Front Line label in 1978, a liaison which — coupled with a sterling performance in the movie *Rockers* (where he performed the hard-hitting "Slavedriver") — should have finally pushed him into the superstar bracket.

The albums *Cool Ruler* and *Soon Forward* failed to take off, however, while singles "Let's Dance," "John Public" and the Sly & Robbie produced "Soon Forward" (the first release on their Taxi label) did not register beyond Jamaica.

Further Sly & Robbie productions "Going Down Town" and "Motherless Children" led to 1980's acclaimed *Showcase* album, while Isaacs also scored with 1981's self-produced "What a Feeling" and 1982's "Don't Believe In Him" (prod Eli Immanuel). 1981 brought his first appearance at Reggae Sunsplash (he returned annually until 1991, then again at the final event in 1998.) He also appeared in American director's Alan Greenspan's documentary study of Bob Marley's funeral and its philosophical aftermath.

Isaacs joined the UK based Pre label for *The Lonely Lover* and *More Gregory* albums, and a string of well-promoted UK 45s — the dance hall classic "Tune In," "Front Door," "Permanent Lover," "Wailing Rudy" and "Tribute To Waddy."

It was "Night Nurse," the title track from Isaacs' 1982 debut for Island Records, which finally lifted his reputation into orbit. Although the record failed to chart in either the UK or US, it became one of the most memorable club and radio hits of the year, ironically at a time when Isaacs was least able to promote it. Mounting legal and personal problems (primarily involving drugs) saw him spend part of 1982 in prison in Kingston, celebrating his release with the exuberantly titled *Out Deh!*.

Financially straitened by his recent misfortunes, Isaacs was at the forefront of an unnamed, but extraordinarily effective movement to relaunch vocalists as a power in the land, at a time when sound system hits were almost exclusively instrumental, blank canvases upon which the DJs added their own individual stylings. Vowing to flood the marketplace with new product, the conspiracy's leaders included John Holt, Alton Ellis, Ken Boothe, Delroy Wilson, Leroy Sibbles, Freddie McGregor and Bunny Wailer. None, however, took the new resolution to heart with the same passion as Isaacs.

He launched into a period of blinding visibility. He not only recorded for whomever offered him the opportunity, he also commenced licensing his older material, again apparently without discrimination. It has been said, with only minor exaggeration that, throughout the late 1980s, not a week passed without some new Isaacs release hitting the stores — what is remarkable is that the quality of his work barely flickered.

Following 1984's self-redefining "Kool Ruler Come Again" single, Prince Jammy, Red Man, Bobby Digital, Tad Dawkins and Steely & Clevie all took Isaacs into the studio, the ensuing releases not only trading upon Isaacs' undisputed vocal talents, but also upon his reputation (fuelled, of course, by the prison stay) as the rudest rude boy in town.

It was veteran Gussie Clarke, however, who ensured both Isaac's biggest hit of the decade, and his role in the dramatic strides dance hall took into the latter half of the 1980s. They resumed working together in 1985 with "Private Beach Party," among others, before scoring a massive hit with the computerized ragga/roots hybrid "Rumours"/"More Rumours" in 1988. Follow-ups "Mind Yu Dis," "Rough Neck" (with the Mighty Diamonds), "Too Good to Be True" and "Report to Me," pursued it into legend. Clarke also masterminded Isaacs' 1989 studio reunion with Dennis Brown, and the popular *No Contest* album.

In 1990, Isaacs hit again with "I'm Your Lover Man," cut at the Black Scorpio studios. Clarke remained his producer of choice, however, with 1991's "John Law" proving a fascinating collision of old, new and newest as Isaacs, Freddie McGregor and Ninjaman lined up together for the song. Another remarkable collaboration saw him join forces with another of Clarke's proteges, JC (June) Lodge, for 1992's "Don Man Girl" single — three years earlier, Lodge's variation on the "Rumours" rhythm, "Telephone Love," gave the London born, Kingston raised singer her first US hit single.

Beres Hammond was Isaacs' next singing partner, on 1993's "One Good Turn," produced by Philip Burrell — the X-Terminator also oversaw 1994's *Midnight Confidential* album. "Thank You" (produced by Gussie Clarke), "Dapper Slapper" (King Jammy), a new version of the Front Line era "Universal Tribulation" (Musclehead) followed.

Since that time, Isaacs has remained startlingly prolific and, while his true glory days are probably now behind him, still he continues to turn out some genuinely sterling work. Meanwhile, a collaboration with his son, Kevin, suggests that an Isaacs dynasty might soon arise every bit as powerful as the Marleys and the Morgans.

For his own part, even in the face of several fairly poor 1990s titles, his interpretation of "House of the Rising Sun" in 1992 was the equal of any rock or folk revision of the same song, and it is that continuing ability to surprise and surpass which has kept his audience loyal, in the face of even the low points of his output.

DISCOGRAPHY

NOTE: There have been an estimated 400–500 Gregory Isaacs albums released in Jamaica, the US and UK over the past quarter century, many compilations, but many featuring new material too. The following represents the best, the best known and the most easily found sets currently in circulation.

7 In Person (Trojan) 1975

The Alvin Ranglin sessions were dominated by Isaacs' singles output, but there was also time to remake his less successful debut 45, "Another Heartache." Already, Isaacs' trademark smooth, soulful vocals are in place, although he has yet to tone the accompaniment down to match his delivery. The result can, occasionally, seem a little rough, but that adds to the appeal as well.

7 All I Have Is Love (Trojan) 1976

Sidney Crooks-produced set includes "Sinner Man," the Wailers' "Bend Down Low" and a clutch more Jamaican hits.

8 Best of Vol 1 (GGs — JA) 1977

Well titled, but by no means a simple compilation. Rather, producer Ranglin and the Revolutionaries pursue Isaacs through an album's worth of all new material ("Double Attack," "Look Before You Leap"), pausing only to pick up the recent hit "My Number One."

8 Extra Classic (African Museum — JA) 1977

One of Isaacs' rootsier sets, built around a string of recent 45s, many of which — "Mr Cop," "Black Against Black," "Loving Pauper" and "My Religion" — find him defiantly flaunting his dapper don image. Pete Weston and Lee Perry join Isaacs in the production credits.

9 Mr Isaacs (DEB — UK) 1977

In an album of brutal affirmation of his African roots, "Slavemaster" is crucial Isaacs (its "Paymaster" dub equivalent no less so), "Get Ready," "Hand Cuff" and "Sacrifice" run it a close second, while "Storm" proved its continuing popularity by the numerous times it was versioned.

9 Cool Ruler (Front Line) 1978

Despite "Let's Dance" having already scored as a Jamaican single, it actually emerges among the weaker tracks on the album. "Created By The Father," "Party in the Slum" and "John Public," on the other hand, are among the best Isaacs ever recorded. By rights, this album should have brought international success, but the eternally suffering Isaacs found the British public as fickle as his lyrical women.

8 Soon Forward (Front Line) 1979

"Universal Tribulation" has been called the greatest Isaacs song never to be released as a single. In fact, it is one of the few cuts on the album not to have spun at 45, although that does not dent the set's majesty in the slightest.

7 Slum: Gregory Isaacs in Dub (Burning Sounds — UK) 1978

Though Isaacs was universally revered as a crooner, he knew precisely what his audience wanted and, right now, they wanted roots. *Slum* is essentially versioned from *Cool Ruler*, highlighting the Revolutionaries, of course, and Ansell Collins' splendid keyboards, with Prince Jammy and producer Isaacs manipulating the mixes. Better dub albums abound, but still *Slum* has some revelations of its own.

8 Showcase (Taxi) 1980

Frequently reissued under various guises, but essentially a six (twelve with version b-sides) track recounting of classic 1979/80 period 45s, with both Isaacs and producers/rhythm section Sly & Robbie going hell for leather throughout. Legends are made of less than this.

7 The Lonely Lover (Pre) 1980

An album sharply drawn between three poles — the past lovers and roots rock styles Isaacs had already made his own, and the new dance hall future posited by "In Tune." "Poor Clean" and "Happy Anniversary" complete a patchy album's triumvirate of recent JA hits.

7 More Gregory (Pre) 1981

Retaining the Roots Radics from his last album, Isaacs turns in a set which doesn't deviate too far from that role model, while broadening its (and his own) appeal with fresh reworkings of the older "Fugitive" and "My Only Lover."

8 The Best of Gregory Isaacs Volume Two (GGs — UK) 1981

No less than volume one, an unequivocally titled Alvin Ranglin production which nevertheless lives up to its billing. "Village of the Under-Privileged" is dramatic docu-drama, while "A Riot" and "The Border" pack their own punch.

7 Night Nurse (Mango) 1982

Best known for his contributions to the *Countryman* soundtrack, electronics whizz Wally Badarou adds rock washed synths to the Isaacs sound, and creates what many regard as a masterpiece. In fact, the title track alone is classic Isaacs, but the same sensual drift dominates "Stranger in Town," "Objection Overruled," "Hot Stepper" — and that's just side one. Dispassionately, the fearlessly early-80s production ensures that the album does all begin to sound the same after a while, but if it's a sultry mood you're after, this is where to begin.

6 Out Deh! (Mango) 1983

With Errol Brown and Flabba Holt still behind the scenes, and Phillip Ramacon depping for Badarou's synths, a more natural sounding, but ultimately less cohesive set than *Night Nurse*, further scarred by the very real sense that almost every song is a rewrite.

6 Live at Reggae Sunsplash (Sunsplash) 1983
8 Live at the Academy Brixton (Rough Trade — UK) 1984

A red hot show, oft reissued (most recently as *Encore*), highlighting a decade's worth of hits and classics. "All I Have Is Love" falls comfortably amidships, "Night Nurse" closes the show.

7 Let's Go Dancing (— JA) 1984

Prince Jammy produced set includes "Dancing Time," "My Heart Is Aching" and "No Good Girl."

8 Private Beach Party (RAS) 1985

Carlene Davis proves one of Isaacs' most appealing duet partners on "Feeling Irie"; Dennis Brown one of his most reliable across "Let Off Supm." And of course there's the title track, a classic from every direction.

6 Live at Reggae Sunsplash with Third World (Sunsplash) 1985

6 Easy (Tads—JA) 1985

6 All I Have Is Love Love Love (Tads—JA) 1987

Precariously perched above the abyss of easy listening, Isaacs keeps his balance to deliver up two entertaining Tad Dawkins sets, each stuffed with smooth as silk songs, beautifully edged in rootsy arrangements. Neither is essential, but *Easy* restores Jacob Miller's "Tenement Yard" to its rightful place, and "Kool Ruler" is a welcome inclusion. Elsewhere, look out for further hits "Mi Come Again," "Bang Belly," "Musical Revenge," "Coronation Market" and the salutory "Hard Drugs."

4 Victim (VP) 1987

File alongside *Easy*. You'll want to hear it sometime, but there's plenty else to listen to first.

7 Red Rose for Gregory (RAS) 1988

Nothing, of course, matches the sheer visceral attack of "Rumours," but still *Red Rose* stands loudly amid Isaac's late 80s albums as one of those moments when producer and performer are as one, and the music — "Teacher's Plight," "Me No in a Dat," "Rough Neck" et al — cannot help but be borne along in their wake. Reissued 2001 by Greensleeves' newly launched US operation.

7 IOU (RAS) 1989

Gussie Clarke again produces, which is a recommendation in itself. Add Mutabaruka on the tremendous "Hard Road to Travel," and highlights the caliber of "Fatal Attraction" and "Break the Ice," and the album's strengths are apparent to all.

8 On the Dance Floor (Heartbeat) 1990

If the sheer quantity of latter-day Isaacs albums seem overwhelming, take a breath and start here. Niney is at the controls, which keeps even the most up-to-date digital techniques in check, while Isaacs sounds as assured as he ever has. (Subsequently rereleased as *Dancing Floor*.)

5 Call Me Collect (RAS) 1990

7 Come Again Dub (ROIR) 1991

Sly & Robbie return, alongside Clevie and producer Fatis, although the material doesn't always showcase its high profile progenitors. "Rude Boy" and "Smokey Head" stand out among the rent-a-ballad surroundings, while Clive Hunt's synths serve up a pleasing contemporary wash. The Dr Dread-led dub companion, meanwhile, summons up a threateningly brittle mix which gives the main album a whole new presence.

7 Set Me Free (Vine Yard—JA) 1991

Bobby Digital production fights hard to match the organic purity of Isaacs' approach with the electronics at the studio's disposal, and actually makes a good go of it.

4 No Intention (VP) 1991

4 Boom Shot (Shanachie) 1991

One of those albums which Isaacs probably knocks out before breakfast. Not unlistenable by any standards ("Rude Boy Saddam" is a laugh), but unless you simply have to hear everything, warmed-up rewrites of former glories are never going to set the pulse racing.

4 State of Shock (RAS) 1991

Again, nothing to get excited about, although "Freak of the Week" and "Night Flight" are as great as "Blouse and Skirt" and "Uptown Woman" are poor.

3 Past and Future (VP) 1991

With co-conspirators Sly & Robbie, Winston Riley, Boris Gardiner, JC Lodge and more, Isaacs flips through a few back pages ("Night Nurse," "Border," "Front Door"), a few new niceties, and comes up with a seamless, but soul-less, session.

7 Pardon Me! (RAS) 1992

A brutal rerecording of *Extra Classic*'s "Mr Cop" sets this album up best. Isaacs is in full scale sufferer mode, Dr Dread's production is both full and unobtrusive, and while Macka B's toast has dated badly, Isaacs' interpretation of "The House of the Rising Sun" is an absolute masterpiece.

4 Rudie Boo (Star Trail, JA) 1992

Overall a patchy release. Isaacs doesn't hit his stride until track four and producer Richard Bell's dance hall lite arrangements quickly become tiresome. But in places ("Yush" and "She Doesn't Want Me") it suddenly all comes together. Rereleased by Heartbeat under the title *My Poor Heart*.

6 Unattended (Pow Wow) 1993

It probably wasn't necessary to rerecord "Night Nurse," but its tenth anniversary did deserve to be celebrated, if only to prove how far Isaacs has come since then — suddenly the masterpiece of early 80s seduction sounds almost calculatedly calculating . . . like, who's gonna fall for that cheesy old line? Not when there's "Mr Sweetness" and "Footprints Across My Heart" to go home with. Gussie Clarke again produces.

5 Unlocked (RAS) 1993

Producers Jimi and Carlton Hines can't quite muster the sympathetic accompaniment which Clarke's work has accustomed us too, but the songs are strong ("Love and I Lost It," "Teacher inna Dis") and Dennis Brown is back for "Ready We Ready."

4 Midnight Confidential (Greensleeves—UK) 1994

"Not Because I Smile" is prototypical Isaacs unleashed, a lovely piece of work which dignifies an otherwise disappointing album.

6 Dreaming (Heartbeat) 1995

"Don't Dis the Dance Hall," growls Gregory on this album's best cut, and why would you? It engineered his continued relevance, a point proven by the similarly stand-out "Trench Town Comprehensive," and the sly "Men of Temptation."

6 Not a One Man Thing (RAS) 1995

"Don't Dis the Dance Hall" returns in new, and improved, Junior Reid-produced guise, kicking off an album which may not be the overall equal of its predecessor, but does pack a wider, better, selection of songs. "Rudeboy Brawl" and the lewd "Big Up Chest" are its well-placed poles.

3 Private Lesson (Heartbeat) 1996

A strangely fussy album, with weak songs and overdone arrangements. Revivals of "Mr Know It All" and "Slavemaster" will cater to the curious, but that's about it.

4 Mr Cool (VP) 1996

Bunny Gemini produced set characterized by very slick production, and remakes of "Rude Boy" and the "Dapper Slapper" single. A jungle mix of "Hop Off Mi Fender" misses the point, somehow.

6 Maximum Respect (House of Reggae) 1996

A triumphant return to latter-day form, growling through the anthemic "Murder in the Dance Hall" and storming, too, through "Me Nah Leggo" and the title track. Even more impressively, several years of increasingly diminished love and romance songs are turned around in an instant — "Promise to Be True," "No-One Is to Blame" and "My Heart Is Bleeding" are as precious as they come.

8 Hold Tight (Heartbeat) 1997

Producers Mafia and Fluxy gorge this with their warmest dubby roots rhythms, and Isaacs returns the favor with his most evocative performance in years. The title cut (a UK hit) is a classic, a rerecorded "Kill Them with Music" quivers with sheer joy, as does the celebratory "Thank You, Mr. Judge." The rest of the album is equally strong.

3 Hardcore Hits (Ikus) 1997

Deeply digital set produced by Elon Robinson . . . but not very well. The accompaniment completely overwhelms Isaacs, while a surfeit of slight songs ("Baby Come Back," "What Will Your Mama Say," "A fe Mek a Track" — so much for the album title!) does not help the cause in the slightest.

7 Live at Maritime Hall (Artists Only) 1998

Reviews were scathing, bewildered by the speed of the playing and the plethora of medleys — even "Night Nurse" is forced into a corner with "Private Secretary," while "Rumours" rubs choruses with "Not that Way" and "Mind You Dis." But it's a great show for all that, indicative not of Isaacs' stature, but of his continued growth.

4 Kingston 14 Denham Town (Jamaican Vibes) 1998

Hardnosed set blends some cynically soft love songs ("Miss Cutie Cutie") with the street smarts of the title track, "Food Clothes & Shelter" and "War." Self produced, and backed by the aptly named Computer Paul.

3 New Dance (Prestige World Music) 1999

Distressingly dire collection of heartache-by-numbers love songs.

5 Turn Down the Lights (Artists Only) 1999

A cliche the first time around, "Lady Of Your Calibre" (reprised from 1996's "Mr Cool") returns to prove a positive embarrassment. It is, however, a rare disappointment on a King Jammy led set which peaks with the latest of Isaac's rude boy anthems, "Rude Boy in a Penitentiary."

6 So Much Love (Joe Gibbs Music—JA) 2000

Third time lucky? "Lady of Your Calibre" is back, and this time she's looking pretty good. *Mr Cool*'s "Spend the Night," too, gets another crack of the whip and that's not half bad either. There again, with Joe Gibbs, Errol Thompson and Sidney Crooks on board, what did you expect? They know exactly what Isaacs is capable of — and they won't accept anything less.

3 Feature Attraction (VP) 2000

Or an entertaining b-movie. You choose.

GREGORY ISAACS & DENNIS BROWN
7 Two Bad Superstars Meet (Burning Sounds) 1984

Three tracks apiece, Isaacs' "My Time," "Loving Pauper" and "Never Be Ungrateful" arrive with dirty dub segues and hold up their end of the title bargain admirably.

6 Judge Not (Greensleeves—UK) 1985
7 No Contest (Greensleeves—UK) 1989

GREGORY ISAACS & RONNIE DAVIS
8 Gregory Isaacs Meets Ronnie Davis (Plant—UK) 1979

With Isaacs approaching the peak of his powers, Ossie Hibbert paired five of his recent recordings with five by Itals vocalist Davis, an intriguing combination with stand-outs found on both sides.

GREGORY ISAACS & JAH MEL
5 Double Explosive (Andy's) 1984

GREGORY ISAACS & SON
7 Father and Son (2B1) 2000

Kevin Isaacs is the star here; although dad duets on a handful of cuts, it's the younger Isaacs' writing and singing which marks the album out — even if the end result is not at all dissimilar to hearing an early Gregory reborn.

GREGORY ISAACS & SUGAR MINOTT
6 Double Dose (Blue Mountain) 1987

8 The Early Years (Trojan) 1981

At the time, a fair collection of early singles and album cuts, rushed out to meet the "Night Nurse." Still an adequate introduction, and it's impossible to complain about the track selection.

7 Lovers Rock (Pre—UK) 1982

Double album package recycling both of Isaacs' Pre releases (the pun was intended), again in the wake of his "Night Nurse" success.

7 The Sensational Gregory Isaacs (Vista Sounds 1982)

Five songs cut with Ossie Hibbert for the *Meets Ronnie Davis* album, alongside half a dozen Rupie Edwards productions. The time lapse between the two sets is noticeable, but Isaacs is on song throughout, and the Edwards material deserves to be heard.

8 Warning (Serious Business—UK) 1990

The dark sleeve and the opening "Long Sentence" place this album firmly outside Isaacs' customary battlegrounds of love and seduction—one reason, perhaps, for its belated release. Recorded in the mid-1980s, it did not appear until 1990, although its deep textures and digital dub forebodings were still ahead of their time, even then.

7 Once Ago (Caroline) 1990

If you already own *Lovers Rock*, this is as close to a complete reissue as you can get on one-CD—just two cuts are excised, "Happy Anniversary" and "Tune In" (from the *Lonely Lover* album), although the remastering is not all it could have been.

7 My Number One (Heartbeat) 1990
7 Love Is Overdue (Heartbeat) 1991

Across two discs, 27 cuts concentrate on Isaacs' work with Alvin Ranglin. The first adds rarities and extended mixes to a set already distinguished by "Border" and "Philistines"; the other features tracks remixed for modern tastes, although the changes are unobtrusive for the most part. The presence of U-Roy on a couple of tracks restores further long lost DJ versions to the marketplace. The Ranglin sessions story is completed by Heartbeat's single disc repackaging of the two *Best Of* volumes.

7 The Prime of Gregory Isaacs (Music Club) 1993

The liner notes describe Isaacs as the Jamaican Frank Sinatra, and quote an astrology book for insight. The album itself, however, swiftly settles into a 16 track overview of Isaac's 1973–76 period, drawing out the best of the hits and highlighting three dub b-sides as well.

8 Mr Love (Caroline) 1995

Well packed collection drawing from the Front Line and Pre albums.

9 Loving Pauper (Trojan) 1998

Okay, drop all those other Trojan/early comps; this is the only one you need. Opening with the original "Another Heartache" then skimming through the Concords, a solidly excellent 25 track set highlights Isaacs through the first half of the 1970s. Every key hit is here, together with choice album cuts and a few lesser-visited 45s.

4 Rasta Business (Exworks) 1999

Bizarrely compiled collection of titles drawn from the Ossie Hibbert, Pre Records and *Extra Classic* eras, serving up a patchy glimpse of Isaacs' late 70s/early 80s peak, but not necessarily in their original form. Beware of budget albums bearing well known song titles.

6 New Millennium (World) 1999

A generous hour of vocal and dub cuts reprises "Coronation Market" amid sundry other late 80s Bobby Digital cuts.

6 Greatest and Latest (Cult Records) 1999

Isaacs' studio records might be the ones which get talked about the most—and to keep the conversation going, there are four *Kingston 14* cuts included here. The remainder was recorded live, and on a better night than the Maritime Hall show.

8 Ultimate Collection (Hip-O) 2001

An excellent compilation gathers together African Museum label material dating back to 1975, odd cuts from the GGs, Taxi and Music Works catalogs and sundry other rarities. Most of the obvious standards are here – "Night Nurse," "Slavedriver," "Rumours" and "Love Is Overdue" included.

ISRAEL VIBRATION

STYLE *reggae (roots)*
FORMED *1976 (Kingston, JA)*
ORIGINAL LINE-UP *Cecil "Skeleton" Spence (b 1952 — vocals), Albert "Apple Gabriel" Craig (vocals), Lascelle "Wiss" Bulgin (b 1955 — vocals)*

The explosion of roots consciousness which hit the Jamaican scene in the mid-1970s was responsible for some of the finest, and longest lasting, bands in the island's history. Adapting the harmonious strains of the "classic" vocal groups of the 1960s—a route, of course, which was blazed by the Abyssinians—it was bands like the Congos, Culture, the Wailing Souls and the Prophets who finally gave Natty Dread the voice which spoke to listeners the whole world over, and not simply in those specialist enclaves where dub and the DJs held sway.

Israel Vibration slipped effortlessly into this category and, a quarter of a century later, remain one of the brightest beacons on any new listener's exploration of primal dread. Part of the credit for this must go to the American RAS label, which has systematically reissued the band's entire back catalog, and encouraged further, fresh recordings from the group. But Israel Vibration's own determination, too, played a major part in their survival, just as it did in their very birth.

The three members originally met at Kingston's Mona Rehabilitation Clinic, a residential facility for victims of the polio epidemics which periodically swept the Caribbean. The three were not together at the center for long, being constantly transferred to different institutions, but the connection was made.

Albert Craig spent some time at the Alpha Boys School, the Catholic nun-run establishment which has turned out some of Jamaica's best known musicians (several former Skatalites and DJ Yellowman were also graduates), but which he described as an abusive prison. Aged 14, he ran away and took to living on the streets.

Of the three youths, Cecil Spence appeared the most gifted. At age 12, he appeared on Jamaican television playing xylophone in a six piece youth group. He was also a member of the Hot Lickers, a band set up by the School of Music, and played in the Jamaican Wheelchair Basketball team, visiting Germany and New Zealand before he was dismissed from the set-up after converting to Rastafarianism in 1969. It was shortly after returning to Kingston that he met Craig again — he apparently found his friend living in a bush near a sports field.

Soon after, they hooked up again with Lascelle Bulgin, then working as a tailor. All three were Rastafarians, and they spent much of their time reading, talking and singing together. Having decided to form a vocal group, they originally called themselves Israel Vibration Israel Vibrates, but truncated the name soon after.

For some six years, the trio were homeless, surviving on the money they made singing in the streets. An attempt to launch themselves through the Channel One studio in 1975 fell through after just one song was cut, "Bad Intention" — produced by Ernest Hookim, but never released.

In 1976, Israel Vibration's religious beliefs brought them into contact with the Rastafarian sect the Twelve Tribes of Israel. They financed the trio's first recording session, at Treasure Isle in 1976, where the group cut the single "Why Worry" (backed with a new version of "Bad Intention") with producer U Booth. Released on the Twelve Tribe label, it was well-received and, as word spread, Israel Vibration were invited to open local shows for Dennis Brown, Bob Marley, Inner Circle and others.

In 1977, producer Tommy Cowan took Israel Vibration into the studio to cut their next single, "Same Song," for his Top Ranking label. Accompanied by the Revolutionaries, among other top session players, the project swiftly developed into a full album, also titled *Same Song*.

A dub version, *Israel Tafari* aka *Same Song Dub*, accompanied it, both sets proving so successful that, by the time

Israel Vibration came to cut their next album, Cowan had already arranged a UK deal for the band, through EMI's Harvest subsidiary. Spring, 1979, saw full British releases for the *Same Song* album and single; scant months later, *Unconquered People* appeared, alongside the well-received "Crisis" single (featuring Augustus Pablo on melodica).

Israel Vibration were a hit at Reggae Sunsplash in 1979; in 1981 they began work on their third album, *Why You So Craven*, with producer Junjo Lawes. It was a sound commercial decision, but from all accounts, a less than satisfactory artistic move. Indeed, after one dispute too many, Israel Vibration quit the studio with the album still incomplete; Lawes recruited the Tamlins to finish it.

Having played the 1982 Reggae Sunsplash (source of a fine live album split with the Gladiators), but otherwise dispirited by recent experiences, Israel Vibration relocated to New York, only to find the music industry utterly deaf to their sound. It was a time, after all, when "reggae," to the average American, meant white Englishmen called the Police or Eric Clapton's version of "I Shot The Sheriff." The group gigged occasionally, but slowly, Israel Vibration faded away.

All three members made tentative attempts at launching solo careers — Bulgin alone succeeded, cutting an album, *Mr Sunshine*, with the Freedom Fighters Band. Meanwhile, a best of Israel Vibration album kept the band's name alive and, in 1987, the trio decided to make one last attempt to relaunch their career.

They contacted the RAS label to inquire whether it was interested in an Israel Vibration reunion — all three band members had approached the label individually in the past, but had been turned down. This time, however, their enquiry met with success.

A meeting was set up with label head Gary Himelfarb aka Doctor Dread — only for the trio to simultaneously be offered a show in California. They accepted the gig, but neglected to tell Dread of the change in plans. It was another two weeks before the band got back in touch, but the meeting was a success and, within hours, Dread was supervising their first RAS recording, "Strength of My Life," with backing from Roots Radics.

An album of the same title followed, since when Israel Vibration have remained RAS artists (the label also picked up US release rights to the group's earlier albums), touring constantly, recording regularly, and establishing themselves among the venerable giants of the modern reggae scene.

Craig departed the group in 1997 to launch a solo career — he debuted with the album *Another Moses*, recorded with his own backing band, Zionists. Bulgin and Spence continued on as a duo, cutting the *Pay the Piper* and *Jericho* albums. In 2000, Israel Vibration's full career was the subject of the highly praised three-CD *Power of the Trinity* box set.

DISCOGRAPHY

9 The Same Song (Harvest—UK) 1978
9 Same Song Dub (Top Ranking—JA) 1978

Warm, heavy, brooding, but most of all inspirational, lyrically moving and musically impeccable, roots with soul and sufficient punch to deliver one of the era's finest dub albums. Both a rerecorded "Why Worry" and the hit title track are included, but the finest cut is the mantric "Lift Up Your Conscience." The two albums have since been paired onto one-CD (Culture Press—France).

8 Unconquered People (Harvest—UK) 1980

Apple's "We a de Rasta" remains a defiant chant of self affirmation, one of the finest songs of its ilk. The rest of the record is almost as strong.

6 Why You So Craven (Volcano—JA) 1981

A more abrasive backing than was probably necessary compounds the sense of unfulfillment surrounding this set. The title track is aimed at past producer Cowan and seethes suitably. A handful of Rastafarian devotions are very high quality, but the heart of the album is built around the insistent "Smack Right Jam."

7 Strength Of My Life (RAS) 1988

A hard, contemporary Roots Radics backing initially disorients, but Wiss's "Cool and Calm" takes the technology and tames it in a breath, while Apple's "Middle East" is as bright as any late period Marley pop classic, one of the band's better looks at current affairs. Also remarkable is the title track, a slow burning percussive chant.

6 Praises (RAS) 1990
7 Israel Dub (RAS) 1990
7 Dub Vibration (RAS) 1990

Solid dubs drawn from *Strength of My Life* and *Praises*, in places improving on the original models.

6 Forever (RAS) 1991

The utterly facetious "Reggae on the River" ("dis a dance hall stylee") and "Red Eyes," and the honking "Live in Jah Love" are highlights of an album which takes nothing seriously, including the band's own burgeoning status as elder statesmen.

8 Vibes Alive (RAS) 1992

Recorded in Santa Cruz, 10/2/91, an intense eleven track selection features the Roots Radics at their fieriest.

7 IV (RAS) 1993
7 IV Dub (RAS) 1993

The militant "Naw Give Up the Fight" could have emerged at any time in the last ten years of IV's development, but is especially welcome at a time when other roots survivors are embracing calmer concerns. Spence's

"Thank You Jah" features some of the band's most distinctive vocal harmonies, and borrows a little from "All Things Bright and Beautiful."

6 On the Rock (RAS) 1995
7 Dub the Rock (RAS) 1995

"Mr Consular Man" tells the tale of Bulgin's attempt to return to Jamaica after nine years away, a wry piece of observation which is one of several highlights—the almost rock steady swagger of "Rude Boy Shufflin'" is another.

5 Free to Move (RAS) 1996

The single "Feeling Irie" probably isn't the finest song Israel Vibration have ever cut, musically or lyrically, and this is by no means a classic album. But both impacted hard enough to raise their US profile sky high—and it is a catchy little devil.

7 Live Again (RAS) 1997

More than compensating for the lack of expected classics on *Vibes Alive*, a second live set features dramatic takes on "Same Old Song" and "Strength of My Life," plus an impassioned version of Marley's "War."

6 Pay the Piper (RAS) 1999
6 Jericho (RAS) 2000

Amid standard Vibration fare like "African Unification" and "Jammin'" (no relation to the Marley classic), "Gang Bang Slam" and "Thank God It's Friday" send the duo swooping off with joyous elan.

5 Dub Combo (RAS) 2000

The *Pay the Piper* and *Jericho* albums go through the echo machine. Some interesting textures, but the lack of stunning material on the parent albums proves an insurmountable obstacle.

ISRAEL VIBRATION & THE GLADIATORS
7 Live at Reggae Sunsplash (Sunsplash) 1983

SELECTED COMPILATIONS & ARCHIVE RELEASES
7 RAS Portraits (RAS) 1997

The previously unreleased "Livity in the Dub" and "Saviour in Your Dub" join excerpts from each of the band's studio albums to date.

9 Power of the Trinity (RAS) 2000

Limited edition three-CD box set devotes one disc to each member's greatest past compositions, with spoken introductions prefacing each track, and interview material at the end—sensibly, the spoken word tracks are separate, so they can be programmed out on the CD player. An excellent 100 page booklet completes an extremely worthwhile package, while almost every era of the band's career is amply profiled—sadly, the concept allows no room for dub cuts, leaving five tracks from the *RAS Portraits* set unduplicated.

KINDRED

STYLE *rhythm poetry/rapso*
FORMED *1992 (T&T)*
ORIGINAL LINE-UP *Nigel "Omari" Ashby (vocals), Akinde Gooding (vocals)*

Comprising two childhood friends whose musical tastes ranged from the Beatles and Bob Marley to Arrested Development and Public Enemy, Kindred was one of the first bands to pursue rapso pioneer Brother Resistance in creating an urban youth sound with a solid Caribbean feel — "New Conscious Dance Music," as they put it; dub poetry with a better beat, as less discerning ears preferred.

"Dis Trini Could Flow," the duo's first single, appeared in 1992. Self-composed and produced, it indicated the depth of talent within the duo — within five years, Omari was ensconced as house producer at the Rituals Music record label in Port of Spain, working with the up and coming Black Lyrics and the Point Fortin Engine Room.

Alongside fellow rapso acts Ataklan and 3 Canal, Kindred rapidly came to epitomize the next generation in soca/calypso's development (and, mourned an older generation, its shift towards mainstream Anglo-American tastes). Regular live shows opening for such visitors as Barrington Levy, Shabba Ranks, Maxi Priest, Ziggy Marley, Beres Hammond and Buju Banton were punctuated by further singles "Doh Stop" in 1993, "Freedom Jam" (1994) and "Get On" (1995).

With worldwide interest in the duo piqued by their appearance at the opening night of the MIDEM industry conference in Cannes, France, in January, 1996, Kindred's debut album, *Everything Is Everything* appeared later in the year. They also appeared at the 1996 POPKOMM music fair in Cologne, Germany.

The optimism surrounding Kindred was consolidated by the *Big Stone and Fire* compilation in 1998, a set rounding up past hits, unreleased material and Kindred's latest Carnival hits. These two sets were reissued for an American audience during 1999/2000; Kindred were also among the stars of the *Ultimate Jump Up* rapso anthology released in late 2000 (Rituals).

DISCOGRAPHY

7 **Everything Is Everything (Rituals) 1996**

A celebratory album whose positive imagery and problem solving did much to rid rapso of the slacker gunplay and crudity comparisons with which it had hitherto saddled. None of the band's best known earlier hits are included, although "Get Up," "On and On" and two versions of the impulsive "Yuh Never Know" offer ample compensation.

COMPILATION

8 **Big Stone and Fire (Rituals) 1998**

An hour long round-up of material that missed the first album, brought up to date by the inclusion of "Hotter Dan Fire" and "Hmmm," a collaboration with rising Jamaican star Ricky General. Aside from the early hits "Doh Stop" and "Call of de Wild" (both present as remixes), the oddly seductive "Come Be Mih Lady" is one of several tracks which indicate the breadth of the duo's vision; a reprise of "Das Trini" shows how far they've come.

JOHN KING

STYLE *soca*
BORN *5/10/64 (Birmingham, UK)*

The Barbados Pic-O-De-Crop Calypso Monarch for 1986 and 1994, and a regular finalist on either side of those victories, John King has also established himself among Barbados' most successful composers — his songs have been recorded by Alison Hinds ("Hold You in a Song"), Atlantik ("Bend Down," on their 1997 album, *Hot and Spicy*) and Traffik ("Leave It In," on the same year's *Wicked and Wild*).

Born in Britain, but emigrating to Barbados with his parents at age six, King trained as a social worker before launching himself into music. In 1982, appearing under the name Johnny Ma Boy, he became a founding member of the popular Conqueror's Tent at Crop Over, and made his recording debut with "Married Life," a cut on the tent's own compilation album, *Conquest 1*.

In November, 1982, King won the local St. Phillip's competition with the calypsos "Rosie" and "Senseless Killings" and, the next year, reached the Calypso Monarch finals for the first time with "Black Box," a song about the government's recent budget. 1984 brought "Cherie" and "Pamensy," a lyrical look at South African attempts to persuade West Indian cricketers to break the sporting boycott then in force against the apartheid regime.

In 1985, King became second runner-up at Crop Over with "I Want a Plantation" and "Queuing," before finally taking the crown in 1986 with "Tribute to the Skipper" — celebrating the recent re-election of Barbados' first Prime Minister, Errol Barrow — and "Congratulations."

King's debut album, *Different Strokes*, was released in 1987; his second, *Awesome*, followed the next year, as he made his first American tour. Hopes that he might retain his Crop Over title, however, were dashed when King changed his featured song apparently at the last minute. In the tent during the pre-season, he performed "Push It Back" and "Rocking Time," but in the finals, he unveiled the disappointing "I Am a Calypso." King was beaten into second place by Rita (Forester) — who, ironically, was performing two of his compositions. He was runner-up, too, at the 1988 Independence Calypso Monarch competition.

In 1989, having recorded his third album, *Massive: Unmistakably*, King joined the band Sygncha (pronounced "signature"), and embarked on a period of heavy touring, both in Barbados and abroad. They appeared at the 1991 Sunsplash, and cut one album, *Come Down Posse*, before King resumed his solo career in 1992.

He immediately scored a major hit when he and Square One vocalist Alison Hinds won that year's Barbados Song Contest with "Hold You in a Song." Another of his compositions, "Columbus Coming," came close to bringing Nicki V success at Crop Over, while King also joined singer Carolyn Leacock on an album of Christmas songs, to raise funds for the Barbados Cancer Society.

King spent much of 1993 working as an entertainer aboard the Norwegian cruise ship *Starward*. He returned to Barbados the following April, to record "Lift the Children Up" as a promotion for Child Month in May. That summer, he scored his second calypso Monarch crown, sweeping the board with the soca hit "Jump and Wave," and the self-explanatory "I'm Back," both taken from his new *Psyched* album.

In 1995, having finished second runner-up once again at Crop Over, King joined the band Spice & Co as lead vocalist. It was a brief liaison, and the next year King was celebrating the release of two separate solo albums, *Yard Style* in the US, and *Jegna* in Barbados. That latter then gave its name to his new band project, a collaboration with soca duo Nigel and Marvin Lewis. King's own follow up album was the self-explanatory *Crop Over Festival Classics: Tunes of the Crop Winners, 1979–1995*, while 1998 brought the critically acclaimed *Message from Beyond*.

King sat out Crop Over in 1999, although he maintained a strong presence at the event, as 17 year old singer Khiomal (a former Junior Monarch) finished third runner-up with his "Rise, Barbados Rise." At the same time, semi-finalists Natahlee and Ricky Stoute respectively performed his "Generation Next" and "Men in Crisis."

SELECTED DISCOGRAPHY

7 **Different Strokes (—BARB) 1987**
8 **Awesome (—BARB) 1988**
"Family Ties" and "Living a Lie," are the strong points here.

7 **Massive: Unmistakably (—BARB) 1989**
6 **Psyched (—BARB) 1994**
8 **Yard Style (Mesa) 1996**
7 **Jegna (—BARB) 1996**
9 **Crop Over Festival Classics: Tunes of the Crop Winners, 1979–1995 (—BARB) 1997**

King knows a winner when he hears one — he's written a few, after all, and been beaten out by a few more. His tribute to 26 years of Crop Over victors is remarkably true to the originals, although his pleasing vocals and ear for a smart arrangement offers a handful of improvements as well. This might not be the best album if you want to study his remarkable songwriting, but in terms of sheer enjoyment, it's hard to beat.

8 **Message from Beyond (—BARB) 1998**
King's most adventurous album, a calypso/soca heavy album shot through with a strong passion for folk music.

SYGNCHA
6 **Come Down Posse (—BARB) 1991**

KING SHORT SHIRT
STYLE *calypso*
BORN *McLean Emmanuel, 2/28/42 (St John's, ANT)*

The most successful calypsonian in Antiguan carnival prior to the emergence of Burning Flames, Short Shirt is blessed with a sharp sense of observation and a warm voice which conjures comparisons with the giants of a much earlier era.

Short Shirt first appeared in competition in 1962, but failed to make it past the elimination round. Just 12 months later, however, he finished second runner-up, and scored his first major hit with "Parasites." Third time lucky — 1964 brought Short Shirt the Calypso crown with "No Place Like Home" and "Heritage," a triumph which also ignited an intense rivalry with the island's other great performer, King Swallow.

Their feud was cultural as much as professional. While Short Shirt hailed from St John's notorious Point ghetto, Swallow was a child of the rural village of Willikies. Their two different backgrounds and startlingly different viewpoints sparked an enmity which was further exacerbated when Short Shirt proclaimed himself the Cassius Clay of Calypso, and pledged to rule for the next ten years.

He came close. He took the Calypso crown for the second time in 1965, and made it three in a row in 1966. Short Shirt was ultimately crowned 15 times in 33 years, setting a record which stands not only in Antigua, but across the Caribbean as a whole. Swallow, in contrast, took the title just four times.

One of the secrets of Short Shirt's success was his eye for topicality. His best known songs have included tributes to the Beatles ("Beatles MBE," written after the group was controversially given the honorary status of Members of the British Empire by Queen Elizabeth II), "Heart Transplant" (honoring the first successful operation by South African doctor Christian Barnard), "Martin Luther King" (written in the aftermath of the civil rights leader's assassination) and "Carnival on the Moon" (celebrating the 1969 moon landing). Later, during the 1970s, he commented on Jamaica's then prevalent Rastafarian roots movement with "Ital Dread."

Short Shirt was also a regular competitor at the T&T carnival, and in 1976, found himself at the center of a savage controversy during Road March. That year, his "Tourist Leggo" was widely proclaimed the most played song, but lost out to Lord Kitchener's "Flag Woman," because — in circumstances that were never satisfactorily explained — that was what the bands started playing every time they reached the judging points. Of course "Tourist Leggo" won the Antiguan Road March, one of Short Shirt's seven victories in that competition.

By the early 1980s, he had opened Shorty's Bar-B-Q bar and restaurant in Antigua's Halcyon Bay, with a fleet of glass bottomed boats to entertain the tourists. His popularity was such that his marriage to long time girlfriend Esther Barnes, in 1987, has been described among the most elaborate weddings ever seen in Antigua. Later, news of his retirement from carnival and calypso in 1994 dominated the island press for months. He bowed out with one final crown in 1992, with the aptly titled "Last J'Ouvert."

Short Shirt subsequently turned to performing gospel.

SELECTED DISCOGRAPHY

9 Ghetto Vibes (A&B—ANT) 1976

Widely proclaimed as one of the most exciting calypso albums of the decade, *Ghetto Vibes* is dominated by the deliriously free-flowing "Tourist Leggo," but peaks with "Viv Richards," a tribute to the cricketer of the same name. "Carnival 76," of course, is utterly self explanatory.

7 Press On (A&B—ANT) 1978
8 Hang On (A&B—ANT) 1983

Released midway through Short Shirt's least successful carnival spell ever (four years without a title), *Hang On* is contrarily one of his most exhilarating and outspoken efforts, from the droll "Party American Style," discussing the musical and cultural differences between local and New York carnivals, to "Iron Band," focussing on the wiles of petty officialdom. The uplifting "Buena Fiesta" is a stand-out, while there's also a fabulous ode to greed, disguised as a paean to the arcade game Pac Man, "eating everything in sight," complete with appropriate sound effects.

SELECTED COMPILATIONS & ARCHIVE RELEASES

8 Non Stop Dancing: #1 Calypsos (ParrotFish—ANT) 2000

Twelve tracks trace Short Shirt through some of his most memorable performances, including the farewell "Last J'Ouvert," "Iron Band," "Push" and the title track.

KING TUBBY

STYLE *reggae (dub)*
BORN *Osbourne Ruddock, 1/28/41 (Kingston, JA); d 2/6/89*

Osbourne Ruddock was working as a radio repairman when, one day in the late 1950s, a local (Waterhouse area) sound system operator approached him about fixing some of his equipment. Ruddock completed the job and soon found himself in regular demand from other operators.

Depending upon the scrupulousness of one's rivals, Kingston in the late 1950s could be a very dangerous place to run a system. Duke Reid, for one, used to employ a coterie of street villains to disrupt other dances by any means necessary. Slashed speakers, smashed amplifiers and torn cables were a way of life and, for Ruddock, they became a way of earning a living.

From fixing systems, the repairman began to consider improving them. Even at the humblest dance, the volume and tone of the sound system was often as important as the records being played, with the depth of the bass perhaps even more so. By the time Ruddock was ready to open his own sound system, Tubby's Home Town Hi Fi in 1968, he had spent the best part of a decade experimenting with the equipment's capabilities. Now all he needed were records which sounded as good as his system.

It was Reid who gave the newly dubbed King Tubby the opportunity he required, by employing him as a disc cutter at his Treasure Isle studio. There, Tubby began experimenting with the music as ruthlessly as he had the equipment, laying the foundations and the ground rules for what was soon termed dub.

Establishing his own studio on Drumlie Avenue, in 1971 Tubby purchased a four track mixer from Byron Lee's Dynamic Studios and began adding — or creating — new effects. Phasing, fading, delay and attack all became integral parts of his remixes and, by late 1971, producers Glen Brown, Augustus Pablo, Lee Perry and Prince Tony Robinson were all numbered among his most regular customers.

In his role as one of the most sympathetic producers any performer could ask for, Brown is generally credited as the first to physically credit King Tubby for his remixing, taking a Tubby mix of God Sons' (aka Tommy McCook and Rad Bryan) "Merry Up" and releasing it as "Tubby's at the Control." Prince Tony followed suit with "Tubby's in Full Swing," credited to Lloyd Robinson and Carey Johnson.

Although he was never less than a vociferous freelancer, working with any producer who wanted him, King Tubby nevertheless formed several long-lasting partnerships, around which much of his modern reputation still revolves.

Bunny Lee, in particular, used him ceaselessly. Throughout the early-mid 1970s, scarcely a record was made at Lee's Maxwell Avenue studio, which wasn't then delivered to King Tubby for a remix. Thus, this arrangement saw the studio maverick work with Owen Grey, Ronnie Davis, Horace Andy, John Holt, Delroy Wilson, Jackie Edwards, Derrick Morgan, Cornell Campbell, Linval Thompson, Johnny Clarke and many more, on some of their most important releases (The Linval Thompson compilation *Ride on Dreadlocks* features several spellbinding Tubby concoctions.)

Of course, the nature of the Jamaican music industry ensured that King Tubby dubbed many of these artists for other studios, too, but still the sheer weight of his Bunny Lee catalog is astounding.

Each of his remixes was eagerly awaited in the marketplace, so much so that in 1974, Lee Perry gathered together the best of King Tubby's Upsetters remixes as the *Black Board Jungle* album. Other sets followed, often in frighteningly limited editions. Many of the CD collections released under King Tubby's name in the past decade have returned these mixes to the marketplace for the first time in up to 30 years. It is a further indication of his individuality that few of them even bother to namecheck the original performer whose vocals may or may not be heard somewhere deep in the mix. It's King Tubby—that's all you need to know.

Another regular client was producer Vivian "Yabby You" Jackson, who first approached King Tubby in 1971 with a rhythm he'd recorded earlier in the year, and JA $50 to pay for the remixer's time. "Go to Zion," released in 1972 by the pseudonymous Brother Joe & The Rightful Brothers (actually Jackson, the Congos' Roydel Johnson and the Gladiators' Albert Griffiths), was a hit. Its follow-up, "Conquering Lion," providing Jackson with his new name—the song's refrain (and, indeed, opening line) is "be you, yabby yabby you." *Conquering Lion* also became the title of Yabby You's debut album in 1975, with King Tubby's dub remix of the entire set, *King Tubby's Prophecy of Dub* appearing in 1976. Yabby You's next set, 1977's *Walls of Jerusalem*, was split equally between songs and King Tubby dubs.

In 1973, King Tubby effectively doubled the size of his studio when he brought in a second four track, allowing him to record vocals as well. Roy Shirley's "Stepping Razor" was the first fruit of this new set-up, and King Tubby went on to handle some of the greatest DJ performances of the next few years. However, although such recordings became more common as time passed, still he remained best known for the visceral, uncluttered thump of his first love.

It was "Watergate Rock," King Tubby's dub version of Larry Marshall's 1974 hit "I Admire You," which gave him his own first major Jamaican hit. He went on to remix the rest of Marshall's album, also titled *I Admire You*, the singer's first since leaving the Studio One studios which made his name. Although the songs and performances had little in common with the sonic bruising most listeners expected from a King Tubby mix, his imprimatur is spread across the album.

1974 also saw Bunny Lee release his first King Tubby remix LP, *Dub from the Roots*. It was quickly succeeded by *Dubbing with the Observer*, an unimpeachable collision between the dub master and the equally experimental Niney Holness. Another crucial release was 1977's *King Tubby Meets the Rockers Uptown*, featuring a clutch of Augustus Pablo cuts, and widely credited as the album which established both men on the international scene. The title track was drawn from Tubby's reinvention of Jacob Miller's "Baby I Love You So."

By that time, however, King Tubby's own hands-on involvement with remixing had begun to slacken, as he turned his attention instead to training up and coming engineers and producers. Prince (later King) Jammy, Scientist and Prince Philip Smart would all take their first steps under his aegis. (Somewhat deceptively, a number of collections of their work have appeared under sundry *King Tubby's . . .* titles—the reference, of course, is to the studio, as opposed to the person.)

When Tubby did take control, the results were rarely less than superlative. Sylford Walker's *Lamb's Bread* album, produced by Glen Brown, was a late 1970s highlight. In 1981, King Tubby and Jah Screw remixed Ranking Joe and the Roots Radics for the *Dangerous Dub* album, an aptly titled project which also ranks among the last full-length projects he undertook.

King Tubby remained busy throughout the 1980s, re-equipping his now state of the art studio, and establishing his own labels, Firehouse, Kingston II, Waterhouse and Taurus. He recorded and mixed Jah Thomas' *Nah Fight Over Woman* album in 1983 and, two years later, stepped back into the main arena with singles by Sugar Minott ("Hard Rock Time"), Patrick Andy ("Love Me Forever") and Little John ("Tickle Me"). Anthony Red Rose's "Under Me Fat Ting" and "Tempo" followed and, over the next three years, King Tubby productions shook the dance halls as effectively as his dubs had rattled listeners a decade previous.

By 1988, rising DJ stars Pliers, Ninjaman, Courtney Melody and Pad Anthony had all recorded with him, alongside returning vocal veterans Cornell Campbell, Johnny Clarke and Gregory Isaacs. But King Tubby's new pre-eminence was to be tragically short-lived. On February 6, 1989, he was found shot to death outside his Waterhouse home. This apparent street robbery/homicide remains unsolved.

SELECTED DISCOGRAPHY

9 Blackboard Jungle Dub (Upsetter—JA) 1974

Credited jointly to Tubby and Lee Perry, this is the set which lay the ground rules for the dub album—no-one had done such a thing before, few (its makers notwithstanding) ever surpassed it. Junior Byles' "Fever" and "Place Called Africa" are especially phenomenal, while audiophiles will marvel at the album's greatest innovation—three mixes of each track playing simultaneously, one in each channel and the third across them both. Try it on headphones—dislocation is guaranteed. The album *King Tubby Meets the Upsetter at the Grass Roots of Dub* (Fay Music — 1975) also dates from this period.

8 Dub from the Roots (Total Sounds — JA) 1974

Bunny Lee productions, utterly reborn at Tubby's command — "Natty Dub," "Dub Magnificent," "Dub You Can Feel," "The Immortal Dub" — the titles are basic, but could scarcely say more. The later *Shalom Dub* (Klik — UK) was essentially a reprise of this album, with extra tracks ensuring an even weightier experience. Further crucial Bunny Lee dubs are featured on *King Tubby Meets the Aggrovators at Dub Station* (Live & Love) 1975.

10 Dubbing with the Observer (Trojan — UK) 1975

Niney was untouchable as a producer at this time, as imaginative as they come. Tubby was his match as a remixer, however, and the ensuing clash of rhythm and dub, peppered through such proven hits as "Rasta No Born Yah" (Sang Hugh), "Cassandra" (one of several Dennis Brown cuts), "Silver Words" (Ken Boothe) and more is obsessively earth-shattering.

8 Harry Mudie Meets King Tubby in Dub Conference Vol 1 (Mudies) 1975

Less well-known, but no less impressive, Tubby's collaborations with Mudie were eventually spread out over three volumes of *Dub Conference*.

9 King Tubby's Meets Larry Marshall (Java — JA) 1975

A master class in dub, in which King Tubby makes it seem so simple. The focus is obviously on the rhythms, as Tubby feeds the instruments in, flips on and off the reverb, and plays with the equalizer; the sound constantly shifts, morphing into new aural soundscapes, helped by Marshall's own excellent rhythms.

8 King Tubby Meets the Rockers Uptown (Clock Tower) 1976

Best known for Tubby's assaults on Augustus Pablo's instrumental hits, the set also includes three Jacob Miller tracks and "Say So," the Paul Whiteman/Blackman cut which was Pablo's first ever vocal production. Not that you'd know that once the dub-meister's finished with it. Further such shenanigans can be found on the compilation *Rockers Meet King Tubby in a Firehouse* (Yard Music — JA).

9 King Tubby's Prophecy of Dub (Prophet — JA) 1976

Yabby You in darkest dub territory, with Tubby's inspirational use of reverb and delay effects creating vast vistas of sound and glory on such classic cuts as "Jah Vengeance" and "Run Come Rally." A second Yabby You set, *Beware Dub* (Grove Music — 1978) divided dubs between Tubby and Prince Jammy.

6 Dangerous Dub: King Tubby Meets Roots Radics (Copasetic — JA) 1981

A companion to Ranking Joe's *Disco Skate* album, which Tubby and Jah Screw also mixed. In common with the bulk of Tubby's late 1970s/early 1980s work, many of the most pioneering developments had already taken place by now, and the dubs tended to either cruise through past territory or refine the odd rough edge. This set, while eminently listenable, does a little bit of both. Reissued on CD in 2001 by Greensleeves' newly launched US operation.

7 First, Second and Third Generations of Dub (KG Imperial — UK) 1981

Jammy and Scientist take co-credits on an album tracing the development of their dub techniques, but hamstrung by the lack of length at their disposal.

6 King Tubby the Dubmaster with the Waterhouse Posse (Vista Sounds — UK) 1983

Reuniting with Bunny Lee and the Aggrovators, some interesting sounds are floated, but the material is neither parties' finest.

6 Sly and Robbie Meet King Tubby (Vista Sounds — UK) 1985

A collision made in heaven actually turns out to be less than inspiring. The term "over-rated" comes to mind.

8 King Tubby's Presents Soundclash Dubplate Style (Taurus — JA) 1989

King Tubby's final release, drawing dubs from his late 80s dance hall hits, with spoken word intros from the artists concerned.

SELECTED COMPILATIONS & ARCHIVE RELEASES

6 King at the Controls (Vista Sounds — UK) 1984

Not an overly exciting collection of early 1980s Roots Radics dubs for Tad Dawkins.

8 Dubble Attack — The Original Pantomime DJ Collection 1972 – 74 (Greensleeves — UK) 1989

Excellent Glen Brown produced DJ set, featuring some of the best by Big Youth, I-Roy, U-Roy, Prince Jazzbo, Prince Hammer and more. Similar sets document the Pantomime vocal and instrumental catalogs, again with Tubby in the mix.

8 King Tubby's Special 1973 – 76 (Trojan) 1989

30 track collection blends the *Dubbing With The Observer* album with a choice selection of further Bunny Lee productions — dubs of Horace Andy's "Skylarking" and Cornell Campbell's "Dance In Greenwich Farm" hint at the range of expression which was Tubby's art at its best.

7 Dub Jackpot (Attack — UK) 1990

Bunny Lee again, with a host of lesser-known versions and dubs, including the "Straight To . . . Head" toast series.

8 If Deejay Was Your Trade — the Dreads at King Tubby's 1974 – 77 (Blood & Fire — UK) 1994

More Bunny Lee material, but with the vocals cut at Tubby's, the results are never less than dynamite. Dr Alimantado, I-Roy and Dillinger shine, but really there's not a dull moment in sight.

7 **Dub Gone Crazy: The Evolution of Dub at King Tubby's 1975–79 (Blood & Fire — UK) 1994**

Just two Tubby mixes, but his imprimatur is all over the rest of the set, as apprentices Prince Jammy, Phillip Smart and Scientist let rip with all he's ever taught them. A second volume was later released.

8 **Bunny Lee, King Tubby & the Aggrovators (Culture Press — France) 1995**

Tubby's disappointing assault on Dillinger's (similarly disappointing) "Marijuana in My Brain" makes a weak opener, but two discs stuffed with classic DJ cuts (Big Joe, Clint Eastwood, Trinity, U-Roy) and versions peak with excerpts from the I-Roy/Prince Jazzbo feud, and some choice Aggrovators instrumentals.

8 **King Tubby & Soul Syndicate — Freedom Sounds In Dub (Blood & Fire — UK) 1996**

A full-blooded set drawn from producer Bertram Brown's Freedom Sounds label archive, with Tubby unleashed upon late 70s roots epics Prince Alla's "Lot's Wife," Rod Taylor's "Ethiopian Kings," Philip Frazer's "Come Ethiopians" and more.

7 **Glen Brown & King Tubby — Termination Dub 1973–79 (Blood & Fire — UK) 1996**

The title is justified by just one cut from 1973, an unreleased mix of "Dirty Harry." The remainder, documenting Brown's roots-conscious South East Music label, dates from later in the decade, but finds Tubby in deadly form regardless.

7 **Rodigan's Dub Classics — Serious Selections Vol 1 (Grapevine — UK) 1996**

Spanning 1974–81, a label hopping selection featuring Tubby, Prince Jammy and Scientist. The deep tones of "Watergate Rock" offer a crucial introduction to the state of play in 1974.

6 **King Tubby Meets Scientist in a World of Dub (Burning Sounds — UK) 1996**

6 **King Tubby Meets Scientist at Dub Station (Burning Sounds — UK) 1996**

Across two separate discs, a virtual dub war between the King and one of his prize pupils, the pair throwing remixes at one another, topping and re-topping one another all the way. More a technical marvel than a musical experience, it's a rewarding listen all the same.

5 **King Tubby's in the House (ROIR) 1996**

Not a King Tubby album per se; rather, the work of his nephew and sometime protege, Digital K (Keith Ruddock), heavily influenced and enhanced by the master's memory.

5 **Heroes of Reggae in Dub (Guava Jelly) 1999**

Recorded over two months during the Skatalites' 1975 reunion, the dub version languished unreleased for another 24 years. Though the music is enjoyable enough, and Tubby unleashes his full arsenal of tricks, it is not hard to see why it took so long to emerge.

8 **The Sound of Channel One: King Tubby Connection (Guava Jelly) 2000**

Two-CD collection of Glen Darby produced remixes, dating from 1973–81. Dubs are accompanied by their vocal counterparts, several of which have eluded collectors for years — Desmond Irie's "Dub One" is an especial treasure. Other cuts highlight Delroy Wilson, Prince Pompidou, Calvin Stuart, Jim Brown and Badoo.

7 **King Dub: The Best of King Tubby (Music Club) 2000**

Of course no single disc budget compilation could ever live up to such a mighty title, although 15 tracks (all rare b-sides) drawn from the Bunny Lee days come close to fulfilling at least a fraction of the brief.

KROSFYAH

STYLE *soca*
FORMED 1989 (BARB)
ORIGINAL LINE-UP Edwin "General" Yearwood (vocals), Anthony Bailey (guitar), Felix Ford (bass — since replaced by Dwain Antrobus), Michael Agard (keyboards — since replaced by Elvis Edwards), Cameron "Doc" Quintyne (trumpet), Mark Husbands (trombone), Sherwin King (drums).

Asked once how Krosfyah rose from the Barbados tourist circuit of the early 1990s, to soca superstardom by the end of the decade, vocalist Edwin Yearwood admitted that he was as puzzled as anybody else. "We are just a bunch of island guys who love to play music," he said and that, perhaps, is the secret. Constant live work and a string of well-received albums (the group's worldwide sales top 300,000, without an ounce of assistance from any major label) have given Krosfyah an underground reputation second to none.

All seven members of the group came out of other bands, unknown concerns which plied either the hotel or the nightclub circuit to little avail. The line-up coalesced slowly, but by the late 1980s, Yearwood, Michael Agard, Felix Ford and Anthony Bailey were together as members of Higher Level, playing covers of popular hits for the tourist trade.

They metamorphosed into Crossfire in 1989, debuting at the Discovery Bay Hotel on New Year's eve. Continuing to build in popularity, in 1993 they were selected to star on a Tourist Board sponsored tour of the Caribbean, aimed at raising the profile of the annual Crop Over festival.

A performer since his early teens, when he won a talent contest performing Billy Preston's "You Are Everything to Me," Yearwood was constantly writing his own material throughout this period, but it was 1993, before Crossfire plucked up the courage to abandon their repertoire of covers and local folk songs, and utilize this impressive stockpile.

Changing their name to its now-familiar spelling, the band reinvented itself completely, throwing out the old songs, updating their image, and unleashing their debut single, "Hot Tempo." It was very well-received and, in 1994, Krosfyah released their debut album, *Ultimate Party* — a set which promptly propelled them to local stardom and won them the Barbados Band of the Year title.

In 1995, Krosfyah scored their first major hit, "Pump Me Up," a local smash which eventually (1997) went gold in Canada as well. The song was also instrumental in introducing the band to the American market via its inclusion on the Putamayo label's *Caribbean Party* compilation (1997). *Ultimate Party-Pump Me Up*, Krosfyah's second album, appeared that same year, as Yearwood stormed to an unprecedented triple crown at the 1995 Barbados Crop Over festival — he was named Party Monarch, Road Monarch Champion and Calypso King, the first artist ever to accomplish such a sweep.

1996 brought the *Aim High* album, home of the hit "Wet Me," a success across the Caribbean. The acclaimed *Fyah Riddims* appeared the next year, and Yearwood took the Party Monarch and Road March titles once again, performing the LP's "Road Block." Krosfyah immediately followed through with the festive *Fyahside Christmas* album, and ended 1997 with the Best Song of the Year award for "All Aboard."

Pausing to add a second vocalist, Ray "Papi Chulo" Armstrong (the reigning World Soca Monarch), Krosfyah's hectic release schedule continued into the new year with *Hot Zone*, while the success of the now three year old "Pump Me Up" enabled them to visit the US and Europe for a handful of summer festivals.

Back home in the new year, Yearwood was again elected Party Monarch at Crop Over, this time with "Agony," from Krosfyah's *Krosfyah Dot Com* album. The band were touring the US at the time of the carnival — Yearwood flew home from California, especially to appear. Further hits were scored with "Raga Beenie," "Forkin," "Be-sa-me" and "Sexy Body," while the group were among the best things in sight at the first World Beat Music Festival in T&T, in October, 1999.

The 2000 release of the compilation *The Best of Krosfyah* celebrated the band's first decade, and included two new

songs. Yearwood, meanwhile, cut his own debut solo album, *Influenced: The Good and Badd in Me*. Almost inevitably, a cut from the album, "Fiah Fiah," earned him his fourth Party Monarch title.

Christmas, 2000, saw Krosfyah touring the UK, afterwards they headed for New York for a handful of shows surrounding the new year celebrations.

SELECTED DISCOGRAPHY

7 Ultimate Party (Kalinago — BARB) 1994

8 Ultimate Party Pump Me Up (Kalinago — BARB) 1995
There's no escaping the brilliance of "Pump Me Up," the song which will epitomize Krossfyah's furious soca slam for all time. But "Crank It" and "Obadele" are its equal, and "Poom Poom" might even be more exciting still. Nicholas Brancker's production catches every last drop of sweat.

6 Aim High (Kalinago — BARB) 1996

7 Fyah Riddums (Kalinago — BARB) 1997

6 Fyahside Christmas (Krosfyah — BARB) 1997

8 Hot Zone (VP) 1998
14 tracks include the Road March sensation "No Behaviour" (it placed third), the bluesy ballad "Love Walks Alone" and new vocalist Armstrong's "Too Sexy" showcase.

7 Krosfyah Dot Com (Krosfyah — BARB) 1999
No matter how far Krosfyah range, that familiar loose bass remains, reassuring amid the rearranging and ensuring *Dot Com* at least comes close to matching its mega-predecessor. The bouyant "Deja Vu" and the dance hall "Don't Stop" are livid wonders, while "Agony," "Working" and "Sexy Body" live up to their titles with surprising ease.

SELECTED COMPILATIONS & ARCHIVE RELEASES

9 The Best Of (Krosfyah — BARB) 2000
Even without the ubiquitous "Pump Me Up," this would be a fabulous album, one of the finest regional collections of the decade, and a condemnation of the current Anglo-American obsession with marginalizing anything which doesn't fit into current taste brackets. Yes, they're a soca band, and no, there's probably not a slot for them in the local music supermarket. But they're also a better time than you're going to have with anything on the radio right now.

EDWIN YEARWOOD SOLO

8 Influenced: The Good And Badd In Me (BARB) 2000
Not too much of a departure from the main attraction, although the emphasis on Yearwood's lighter (and, as the title suggests, darker) sides post some intriguing notions for the future.

BYRON LEE & THE DRAGONAIRES

STYLE *reggae, soca*
BORN 6/27/35 (JA)

History has never treated Byron Lee kindly, generally relegating him to the ranks of the Jamaican artists whose greatest impact was felt in the hotels and ritzy resorts so far removed from the reality of Jamaican life, then adding to that indictment Lee's own powerfully developed business sense and political connections. Yet there is no doubt that without the Chinese-Jamaican Lee, and the Dragonaires band he has led for half a century, both the history and the development of modern Caribbean music would be very different indeed.

He himself describes his contribution as "midwifery," and that isn't far from the truth. In cohorts with music entrepreneur/politician Edward Seaga, Lee birthed ska (and, in its wake, reggae) as effectively as any of the better feted stars of the scene. And while he all but abandoned the music in the late 1970s, it was only to turn his attention to calypso and soca, further Caribbean causes in search of a fast route to international acclaim.

Lee and close friend Carl Brady launched the first incarnation of the Dragonaires around 1950; the band was actually named for the college soccer team the members played for, and gave its first shows in the common room to celebrate victories.

The Dragonaires' repertoire in these early years was straightforward mento, an unusual choice at a time when other local groups concentrated on big band productions. The first stirrings of American rock'n'roll, too, made their presence felt on the young Dragonaires—for Lee, one of the crucial discoveries of his youth was that musicians could play their instruments while standing up.

After some three years playing parties, birthdays and weddings, Lee took the decision to turn professional, much to his then employer's disdain. "Nobody in the Caribbean has ever left their work to take up music full time," he told him. "It's the biggest risk in the world." Lee decided to take the chance all the same.

By 1956, the Dragonaires were working what was then the still-fledgling Jamaican hotel circuit, both in their own right and as backing band and support act for such visiting American stars as Harry Belafonte and later, Chuck Berry, the Drifters, Sam Cooke and Fats Domino. Lee was, in fact, often also responsible for booking the tours in the first place, while his business empire expanded even further when he became the Jamaican head of distribution for the US label Atlantic Records.

Slick and self-contained musically and economically, the Dragonaires prided themselves in being able to play any music for anyone. In the nightclubs and bars, they specialized in sweet renditions of the latest American pop and R&B hits. As the first stirrings of ska crept into the mainstream consciousness, they turned their hands to that as well.

Recording at Edward Seaga's WIRL studios (he became the group's manager in the late 1950s), the Dragonaires cut their debut single, 1959's "Dumplin's," in a hybrid style which was guaranteed to appeal to each of their audiences. It was released in Jamaica on the band's own Dragon's Breath label; in the UK, it became the second ever release on the seminal Blue Beat label.

What gave "Dumplin's"—and, indeed, the Dragonaires' entire sound—its extraordinary bite were the electric organ and Fender bass which Lee purchased during a visit to the US in 1959. They were the first such instruments ever seen on the island, and Lee admitted their initial attraction was their portability.

Like Seaga, Lee was a firm believer in the importance of spreading Jamaican music, not worldwide initially, but simply across Jamaica. Three centuries of outside domination, from the colonizing British and the neighboring Americans, had seen the island's own heritage become as ghetto-ized as its population. Ska, both men knew, was the sound of that heritage finally breaking through the veneer of imported R&B which had hitherto dominated the stages and airwaves. But the enormous stand-up bass and piano which were the staples of the sound simply didn't lend themselves to any kind of sustained touring. These new instruments, on the other hand, were made for that lifestyle.

The difference they made to the Dragonaires' sound was astounding. Audiences accustomed to hearing the latest Jamaican hits on sound systems, often reacted to the artists' live performances with shock and disdain—where was the volume, where was the power? With Lee and the Dragonaires behind them, no singer need worry about such deficiencies again.

During the first years of the new decade, then, the Dragonaires accompanied virtually every performer of note on the island scene. Later, following the emergence of the Skatalites and sundry other purpose-built backing bands, their workload declined a little. But only a little.

The Dragonaires released a steady stream of singles during this period, both under their own name and as the Ska Kings. "Dumplin's" was succeeded by another Seaga produced hit, "Fireflies"; "Mash! Mr Lee," "Joy Ride" and a ska retread of "Over the Rainbow" appeared during 1961.

The Dragonaires scored their biggest break yet that same year, when they were cast as the hotel band in the first James Bond movie, Dr No. Island Records chief Chris Blackwell's mother's friendship with novelist Ian Fleming had landed Blackwell a job scouting Jamaican locations for the thriller. Fleming himself owned a summer home ("Goldeneye") in Oracabessa, Jamaica, and it was there that James Bond was created.

The movie score itself was composed by Monty Norman, but Blackwell was able to introduce several calypso/ska songs into the stew, to be performed on camera by Byron

Lee and co, although the actual recordings were made by guitarist Ernest Ranglin. "They gave me a whole soundtrack to be done in two weeks — I don't know how we did that!" he reflected, and in any case, "they didn't use all our stuff." However, sheet music for the Dragonaires' three songs, "Under The Mango Tree," "Three Blind Mice" and "Jamaica Jump Up" became best sellers, while the *Dr No* soundtrack itself remains one of the top-rated Bond spin-offs.

1964 saw the Dragonaires' international profile increase even further when they were selected as house band for the most ambitious attempt yet to draw Jamaican music onto the world stage.

Edward Seaga, now the government's head of Social Welfare and Economic Development, arranged for ska to have a presence at the 1964 World's Fair in New York, with sets from Jimmy Cliff, Prince Buster, Millie Small, Monty Morris and the Blues Brothers. It was not necessarily a sound decision in musical terms — although the Dragonaires had indeed backed the majority of the showcased acts in concert, they were nevertheless perceived as a hold-over from an earlier age; they could play ska, but they did not live it.

Culturally, too, there were differences. Lee and co were "uptown," apprenticed in the swank hotels, and accustomed to the high life. Their tour-mates, however, were "downtown," ghetto sufferers, rude boys and girls. When the excursion ended in acrimony and failure, this essential gulf between the musicians was widely singled out as one of the key reasons.

Lee himself appreciated these differences as much as anybody and, as early as 1963, he made the decision to forge a new identity, away from the requirements of the hardcore ska crowd. Inspired by recent releases by calypso stars Mighty Sparrow ("Dan Is the Man") and Lord Kitchener ("Road March"), the Dragonaires toured Trinidad & Tobago during 1963–64, with a repertoire which incorporated both ska and calypso. (Lee and Sparrow recorded together in 1969.)

Despite such ambitions, Lee was to remain a key figure on the Jamaican scene, as a musician, a producer (many of the Maytals' key rock steady sides were produced by him) and an entrepreneur. His Byron Lee's Spectacular Show road tour gave a number of Jamaican acts their first experience of an international audience, when they toured the Caribbean (the Maytals, again, were among the performers). Meanwhile, his relationship with Atlantic Records blossomed to the point where the label began releasing the Dragonaires' (and later, the Maytals') output in the US.

Two initial albums appeared, hoping to ride the wave of interest prompted by the World's Fair event, the group's own *Jump Up* and the remarkable various artists collection *Jamaican Ska*, produced by American R&B maestro Tom Dowd and combining the Dragonaires' instrumentals with various guest vocalists, the Blues Busters, the Charmers, the Maytals, Stranger Cole, Ken Boothe and Patsy Todd. The Dragonaires themselves were credited as Byron Lee and the Ska Kings. The Dragonaires also cut several albums firmly targeted at the international rock steady market — covers heavy collections like *Rock Steady Beat* and *Rock Steady '67*.

Lee's influence became even more pronounced after he purchased the WIRL Studios from Seaga. Rebuilding the studio following a fire and renaming it Dynamic Sounds, Lee set about maintaining its status among the best-equipped facilities in the entire Caribbean, attracting the cream of both local and international talent to the studio.

American singer Johnny Nash, resident in Jamaica since 1966, recorded his *Hold Me Tight* album there in 1968, and rewarded his adoptive homeland by taking the rock steady flavored title track into the US Top 5 that fall. Nash's own JAD label also released several of the Dragonaires' recent recordings internationally, including the minor classic "Every Day Will Be Like a Holiday." Further evidence of Dynamic's renown came when Paul Simon recorded his genre-crossing "Mother and Child Reunion" single there in 1971, and two years later, when the Rolling Stones cut their *Goat's Head Soup* album at the studio.

Lee himself also produced a number of excellent records, including Boris Gardiner's *Reggae Happening* (1970), Hopeton Lewis' *Grooving Out on Life* (1971) and the Slickers' seminal "Johnny Too Bad." Proof of how advanced Dynamic was arrived later that same year, when local dub producer King Tubby was looking to upgrade his own studio. His prize acquisition was a four track deck which Dynamic had declared redundant.

Of course Lee and the Dragonaires took full advantage of Dynamic's facilities, turning out a constant procession of exquisitely produced and performed albums during the late 1960s/early 1970s. Still concentrating on the day's biggest hits, generally rendered into smooth background music for the tourists to take home with their postcards and carved coconut monkeys, the *Reggay Blast Off* and *Reggay Splashdown* albums, titled in honor of the American moonshot, launched a string of up-tempo albums which pursued the "reggay" theme through the early 1970s.

The crucial moment in the Dragonaires' development came in 1974 when, having gigged with increasing regularity around T&T through the early 1970s, they played that island's Carnival for the first time. Since then, the group have become an integral part of the event, playing three nights a week during the first three weeks, continuing on with 16 consecutive shows at the carnival itself, then ending with two more on the road. (Since 1986, the group has also taken part in the street parade, first alongside Baila Baila; subsequently with Stephen Lee Heung.)

1974 also brought the *Carnival in Trinidad* album, followed a year later by the self-explanatory *Carnival '75*. For the remainder of the decade, "reggay" and "carnival" titles alternated through Lee's releases, while the Dragonaires' dexterity was highlighted by one of the most extraordinary albums in even Lee's canon, 1975's *Disco Reggae* — a set which actually found a full US release.

The Dragonaires appeared at Reggae Sunsplash in 1978 and 1979, and were one of the main backing bands at the 1982 event. The *Day One* event live album features their own "Mek We Jam," but sadly omits the highlight of their set, a scene-stealing ska medley. The group also appeared at the 1984 and 1990 events.

Still Lee's attentions were elsewhere. Beginning in 1979, however, the group's output switched almost exclusively to carnival — calypso, soca and mas (Lee's daughter, Julianne, leads her own mas band), interspersed with occasional sets devoted to nostalgia for past dance styles. Each year, the band journeyed to T&T to partake in carnival; then, the Dragonaires recorded an album of the year's most successful carnival songs, before setting out on tours of the Caribbean and North America.

In 1990, as part of that year's scheduled outing, Lee brought the same spirit (and music) back to his homeland with the first of the now annual Byron Lee Jamaica Carnivals, initially basing the event around the same songs that had scored in T&T, but increasingly introducing a more Jamaican flavor to the proceedings. Aiding this development throughout the 1990s, Lee and the Dragonaires contributed one sure fire hit a year to the Jamaican carnival. These include: 1990 — "Bacchanal in the City"; 1991 — "Lady Teaser"; 1992 — "Wine Down"; 1993 — "Dance Hall Soca"; 1994 — "Butterfly"; 1995 — "Tatie"; 1996 — "Ragga Soca"; 1997 — "Brassline"; 1998 — "Jump Up"; 1999 — "Soca Prang." The so-called ragga-soca explosion of the late 1990s was almost exclusively due to the Dragonaires' efforts, not least of all the hybrid hit "Dance Hall Soca," a collaboration with dance hall star Admiral Bailey which topped the Jamaican chart for four weeks. By 1997, an unabashed carnival culture in Jamaica finally solidified in the form of bands like the Revellers, Oak Ridge, Maestro and another Lee family enterprise, daughter Danielle's D Masqueraders.

The arrival of so much new talent allowed Lee, in 1997, to declare it was finally time to "pull back, to recharge batteries." The Dragonaires had never exactly rested on their laurels, but the 1990s in particular had seen them on the road for nine months a year, every year. But of course Lee was not absent for long — sitting out the 1998 carnival, he returned in 1999 for the event's tenth anniversary celebrations, and elsewhere, too, he continues on as relentlessly as ever.

SELECTED DISCOGRAPHY

7 **Come Fly with Lee** (Byron Lee/WIRL — JA) 1962
6 **The Sound of Jamaica** (Byron Lee/WIRL — JA) 1963
6 **First Class with Lee** (Byron Lee/WIRL — JA) 1964
6 **Caribbean Joyride** (Island — UK) 1964

There is little to choose between any of the Dragonaires' early albums, including the fact that they all cost a mint on the collectors market! The music is, without exception, polite ska, the same as could be heard played in any high class hotel on any night of the year. Overlook the lack of rough edges, however, and there's a proficiency on display which no other island act could compete with.

8 **Jump Up** (Atco) 1964

One of the seminal albums of 1960s Jamaica, if only because it was also one of the first to see an American release. Musically, it scarcely deviates from the Dragonaires' norm, which means possession of a copy is more a talking point than a listening experience.

6 **Christmas Party Time** (Byron Lee/WIRL — JA) 1966
7 **Rock Steady 67** (WIRL — JA) 1967
8 **Rock Steady Beat** (WIRL — JA) 1967

The so-called WIRL Recording Orchestra glides through a typical slice of the Dragonaires' contemporary repertoire, including current hits "Bend Down Low," "The Train Is Coming," a well-vocalized cover of the Impressions' "Keep on Pushing" and, oddly, the original version of Mighty Sparrow's "Obeah's Wedding" — which doesn't even pretend to have a rock steady beat!

6 **People Get Ready, This Is Rock Steady** (WIRL — JA) 1967

A similar set features "Girl I've Got a Date," "007" and "On the Beach" although, once again, the Dragonaires seldom let the excitement levels reach the originals' level.

7 **Rock Steady Intensified** (WIRL — JA) 1968

More of the above, only more up to date — "Napoleon Solo," "Ride Your Donkey," "Pup-a-Lick."

6 **Reggay with Byron Lee** (Trojan — UK) 1968
6 **The Many Moods of Lee** (Dynamic — JA) 1968
5 **Reggay Blast Off** (Dynamic — JA) 1969

Lloyd Terrell's "Birth Control" is the most ferocious beast tamed here, although "Monkey Man" and "Elizabethan Reggae," too, are translated to what was fast becoming a very square dance.

5 **Reggay Eyes** (Dynamic — JA) 1969

Typical Dragonaires fare, moving from current hits to lesser-known numbers, with so smooth renditions of "Long Shot Kick the Bucket" and "The Games People Play," alongside "Square from Cuba," "Musical Scorcher" and the somewhat dubiously titled "Pum Pum on a String."

5 Tighten Up (Dynamic—JA) 1969
5 Goin' Places (Dynamic—JA) 1970
5 Reggay Splash Down (Dynamic—JA) 1971
5 Reggay Hot Cool and Easy (Dynamic—JA) 1972
6 Reggae Roun' the World (Dynamic—JA) 1973
6 Reggae Fever (Polydor) 1974
5 Dancing Is Forever (Dynamic—JA) 1974
7 Carnival in Trinidad (Dynamic—JA) 1974
5 Carnival 75 (Dynamic—JA) 1975

Quite possibly the first genuinely committed album in the Dragonaires' catalog, in that their love of the music, and excitement to be playing it, is palpable. The band's latter day pre-eminence in calypso circles begins here.

8 Disco Reggae (Mercury) 1975

An absurdly delightful album, featuring everything from "The Reggae Hustle" (Van McCoy's disco "Hustle" with a reggae beat) to "The Reggae Stomp" (Bohannon's "Disco Stomp"...), plus a brace apiece by Bob Marley and Neville Hinds, the schoolboy sauciness of "Shaving Cream" and U-Roy's "Soldering," a recent US hit for Hall & Oates.

5 The Midas Touch (Dynamic—JA) 1975
6 Reggae International (Dynamic—JA) 1976
5 Six Million Dollar Man (Dynamic—JA) 1976
7 This Is Carnival (Dynamic—JA) 1976
7 Art Of Mas (Dynamic—JA) 1977

Another phenomenal album, open to accusations of dilettante-ism, of course, but so expertly executed that even the sourest grapes don't embitter the experience.

6 Jamaica's Golden Hits (Stylus) 1977

Smooth collection offering instrumental reminders of past ska glories — "My Boy Lollipop" and "Easy Snappin'" are the biggest hits in sight; "Oil in My Lamp" will reappear (as "Sing Hosanna") on 1999's *Jump & Wave for Jesus* album.

7 More Carnival (Dynamic—JA) 1978
5 Reggae Hits (Dynamic—JA) 1978
7 Carnival Experience (Dynamic—JA) 1979
8 Soca Carnival (Dynamic—JA) 1980
7 Carnival 81 (Dynamic—JA) 1981
7 Byron 1982 (Dynamic—JA) 1982
6 Soft Lee Vol 1 (Dynamic—JA) 1983

The first of six volumes (so far) of calypso flavored ballads, released at roughly two yearly intervals.

5 Soul Ska (Vista) 1983
6 Carnival City 83 (Dynamic—JA) 1983
7 Original Rock Steady Hits (Dynamic—JA) 1984

Credited to Byron Lee's All Stars, and produced by Alty East, a nostalgic journey back through the likes of "Girl I Got a Date," "On the Beach" (both familiar from past Lee albums), "CC Rider" and "Shoobe Doobe Doo."

7 Jamaica's Golden Hits Vol 2 (Dynamic—JA) 1984

More swinging remakes, moving into the rock steady era with suitably arranged versions of "Simmer Down," "Carry Go Bring Come," "Eastern Standard Time" and, perhaps oddly, "Puppet on a String." A third volume, addressing the birth of reggae offers similarly lightweight assaults on "007," "Girl I've Got a Date," "Cherry Oh Baby" and the Rolling Stones' "Satisfaction."

6 Heat in de Place (Dynamic—JA) 1984
7 Christmas in the Tropics (Dynamic—JA) 1984
6 Wine Miss Tiny (Creole—UK) 1985
6 Soca Girl (Dynamic—JA) 1986
5 De Music Hot Mama (Dynamic—JA) 1988
7 Soca Bacchannal in the City (Dynamic—JA) 1989
6 Wine Down (Dynamic—JA) 1992
6 Soca Thunder (Dynamic—JA) 1992
5 Soca Tatie (VP) 1995

With a jacket straight out of a 70s tourist brochure, a non-stop soca party . . . but how many times can you say that about Lee's 80s/90s albums?

7 Soca Engine (Dynamic—JA) 1996
6 Soca Greatest Hits (Dynamic—JA) 1997
6 Trinidad Tobago Carnival City (Dynamic—JA) 1997
4 Socarobics (VP) 1997
5 Soca Frenzy (VP) 1998
4 Soca Tremor (VP) 1999
5 Soca Fire inna Jamdown Stylee (Jamaican Vibes)
6 Jump And Wave for Jesus (Dynamic—JA) 1999

Joyous gospel collection which ranges through a musical history of Jamaican music, rendering hymns and other religious music in ska, rock steady, junkanoo, reggae and soca stylings — the calypso "Hallelujah Chorus" and ragga soca "Lord's Prayer" are highlights.

6 Soca Thriller (VP) 2000

There's something intriguingly kitsch about Lee's album covers these days — how many swimsuit clad females do we really need? And how many more variations on the same themes? A version of Burning Flames' "Magician (I Command You)" is enjoyable enough, while "Mambo #12" has its moments. But only #12? There have surely been many more than that.

BYRON LEE & MIGHTY SPARROW
7 Only a Fool (Dynamic—JA) 1969

T&T title: *Sparrow Meets Dragon*. Calypso easy listening with its ear firmly pointed towards Hollywood — the themes from *Born Free* and *Doctor Zhivago* are both given the treatment, alongside such staples as "Maria," "Try a Little Tenderness" and "Make the World Go Away."

6 Sparrow Dragon Again (Spalee—T&T) 1975

SELECTED COMPILATIONS & ARCHIVE RELEASES

7 Rock Steady Explosion (Trojan—UK) 1968

A neat summary of recent Jamaican releases. "The big Jamaican beat by the Good Guys" pledges the sleeve; "extra!! Illustrated rock steady steps on this album." And "Jamaica's & Caribbean's #1 band" are going to give you "music like dirt for days & days & E-X-T-R-A days."

6 Best of Soft Lee (Dynamic—JA) 1992

8 Play Dynamite Ska with the Jamaican All-Stars (Jamaican Gold) 1994

7 Rock Rock Steady (Jamaican Gold) 1994

A near-comprehensive round-up of the Dragonaires' mid-60s releases.

8 Reggae Hot Shots Vol 1 (Jamaican Gold) 1995

A "best of" the Dragonaires' 1970–71 output, highlighting both their good natured takes on current local hits ("Rivers of Babylon," "Johnny Too Bad") and stretching out over international smashes too—"My Sweet Lord," "I'll Be There" and "Satisfaction."

7 Reggae Hot Shots 1971–73 (Jamaican Gold) 1998

Lee's alleged aversion to Rastafarian culture apparently did not extend to the music—although neither "Message to a Black Man" nor "Maga Dog" retain too much of their original spirit here. Elsewhere, the O'Jays' "Backstabbers" and Cliff Richard's "Flying Machine" lend themselves nicely to the Dragonaires' experience.

BARRINGTON LEVY

STYLE *reggae (dance hall)*
BORN *1964 (Clarendon, JA)*

At the dawn of the 1980s, dance hall reigned supreme and the DJs were top of the pile. Then Barrington Levy came along, with a vocal range which reminded some listeners of Bob Andy, others of Jacob Miller, and prompted others still to rename him the "blue mountain yodeler," and almost singlehandedly brought singing back into style.

Equally impressively, he also kept faith with roots-based rhythms at a time when the rest of the scene was speeding away from such sounds. His hit single "Collie Weed" and album *Shine Eye Gal* were among the best selling releases of the early 1980s. Levy's renown slipped somewhat later in the decade, but successive releases retained the quality which had pushed him so far forward in the first place.

Having grown up around Clarendon, where he practiced his distinctive vocal tones in the local hillsides, Levy was 13 when he cut his first single, 1977's "My Black Girl," as a member of the Mighty Multitude, a band he formed with his cousin, Everton Dacres. The duo were regular performers on the sound system circuit, and when Levy first noticed people tape recording their performances, he was thrilled. Later it became a major concern, as these wholly unauthorized recordings began appearing as "legitimate" releases around the world, through labels he had never even heard of.

Levy went solo in 1978, cutting the single "A Long Long Time Since We Don't Have No Love." Over the next two years, a clutch of 45s followed, including "Call You on the Phone" (with Toyan), "Jumpy Girl," "Wicked Intention," "Sunday School" and the wry "Disco Music." Sessions with Alvin Ranglin, meanwhile, produced the oft-compiled "Never Tear My Love Apart," "When You're Young and in Love," "Jah" and "You Made Me So Happy." He also cut a tender version of Horace Andy's "Skylarking."

Working the dance hall circuit, in 1979 Levy met up with the then-unknown producers Junjo Lawes and Hyman "Jah Life" Wright. Recording at Channel One with the Roots Radics band, the partnership debuted with "Ah Yah We Deh." "Looking My Love," "Englishman" and "Wedding Ring Aside" followed, but it was "Collie Weed" which proved Levy's breakthrough. Its success was confirmed by the mighty "Shine Eye Gal," a Jah Whoosh composition more recently revitalized by Clint Eastwood, Ranking Joe and Black Uhuru. "Sister Debby" and "Moonlight Lover" then saw Levy team up with DJ Jah Thomas, and he also began a collaboration with Trinity, a pairing which produced "Lose Respect" (1979) and "I Need A Girl" (1980).

Aside from a pair of sensational Reggae Sunsplash appearances in 1980 and 1981, Levy never seemed to leave the studio during this period. The albums *Bounty Hunter* and *Englishman* were hits, while 1980 brought *Robin Hood*. These were accompanied by a host of singles; the Lawes-produced "Mary Long Tongue," "Crucifixion," "Even Tide Fire a Disaster," "Warm and Sunny Day" and "I Have a Problem" (produced by Karl Pitterson); "Too Poor" (Linval Thompson); and a new version of *Englishman*'s "Sister Carol," recorded with DJ Scorcher.

Even in the face of such prolificness, Levy's current output seemed in danger of being swamped beneath what he called "joke business" releases, recycled old singles, unreleased out-takes, and the one-off recordings he once made for sound system use. Albums such as *Doh Ray Me* (JB, 1980) and *Barrington Levy* (Clocktower, 1983) apparently made use of this material, while an otherwise impressive stream of Levy singles released over the next two years also included its fair share of unauthorized recordings.

The hits did not falter, whatever the source of the material. 1981 brought "You Have It," "I'm Not in Love," "Rob and Gorn"; 1982 continued with "Come On" and "To-morrow Is Another Day"; 1983 saw "Black Rose" and the deeply roots-based "Robberman," all four produced by Lawes and swiftly compiled onto the *Prison Oval Rock* album. There were also rewarding sessions with Joe Gibbs ("My Woman") and Alvin Ranglin; before Levy scored another monstrous hit with the George Phang produced "Money Move."

1984 delivered the self-produced "Love of Jah," "In the Dark" and "On Your Toe," and the John Carroll-overseen "Mini Bus." Other sharp recordings included "Revelation" with producer Lloyd Dennis and "MI6" with Pete Callendar. That same year also saw Levy visit the UK for the first time, to pick up the title of Best Vocalist at the UK Reggae Awards.

The disarming dread anthem "Under Mi Sensi," one of Levy's first recordings with producer Jah Screw (b Paul Love), became a major club hit in late 1984. In the new year, with London Records handling distribution, the rootsy-rapped title track from Levy's latest album, *Here I Come*, climbed to #41 in Britain, enthralling a nation with its declaration, "I'm broader than Broadway . . . extra size!"

Levy then lapsed into comparative silence (the ubiquitous oldies and reissues notwithstanding), before re-emerging at Sunsplash in 1987 (he would reappear every year until 1995) and, in 1988, with the *Love the Life You Live* album. He then opened the new decade with his most successful set in ten years, *Divine*. Signed now to Island Records' Mango subsidiary he also scored a Top 20 British hit with "Tribal Base," recorded with hardcore dance hall heroes Rebel MC and Tenor Fly.

Levy next linked with US major MCA, a short-lived affair which again made the mistake of trying to cross-over too quickly. Another minor UK hit, "Work," followed, but after just one album, the Lee Jaffe produced *Barrington*, Levy departed the label.

1994 brought two hit duets with fellow DJ Beenie Man, "Two Sounds" and a revival of "Under Mi Sensi" — both were swiftly remixed in jungle style, attracting even further attention. Jack Scorpio then paired Levy with Mega Banton for "She's Mine" and, pursuing this same course of action, Jah Screw took control of *Duets*, a set pairing Levy with a conveyor belt of hot DJs.

The opening track, the bouncy dance hall-flavored "Living Dangerously" (with Bounty Killer) was a major hit both in Jamaica and on the international dance charts; a second Bounty Killer cut, "Bad Talk," offered a fine follow-up and, four years later, this same team hit with "I'm Free."

DISCOGRAPHY

8 Bounty Hunter (Jah Life—JA) 1979
8 Shine Eye Gal (Burning Sounds—UK) 1979

Two variations on much the same album, but neither lacks for highlights — "Shine Eye Gal," "Shaolin Temple," "Collie Weed," "Ah Ya We Deh," are just a few of the hits featured on Levy's groundbreaking debut. The pairing of the singing DJ with the Roots Radics band initiated a major sea change in the island' music scene, as the blending of dance hall stylings and roots rhythms took hold on dancefloors across JA.

8 Englishman (Greensleeves—UK) 1979

Lawes, Scientist and Jammy combine to produce Levy's most consistent album, even if none of the songs (the title track notwithstanding) have the immediacy of his first hits. Nevertheless, *Englishman*'s rhythms were utilized for that so-cool *Scientist v Prince Jammy* album.

6 Robin Hood (Greensleeves—UK) 1980

Having been recording constantly for over a year, Levy hits his first career hiccup with an album whose production (Lawes again) places form far above content.

8 Lifestyle (GGs—JA) 1983

The risque "I Hold the Handle" and a cover of "You've Made Me So Very Happy" are the twin blades on this incisive set — Ranglin's characteristically taut production holds the Levy voice in just the right spot throughout, while the material is uniformly excellent.

8 Money Move (Powerhouse—JA) 1983

Levy's stint with producer George Phang was all but overlooked overseas, but nevertheless resulted in one of his biggest hits yet, in the title track. "Suffer the Little Children" is also majestic. Rhythms, incidentally, were taken from a stockpile Phang had acquired from Sly and Robbie some time earlier. One, "Mr Bassie," appears twice, while the title track draws from Phang's "One Step Beyond."

9 Here I Come (Greensleeves—UK) 1984

Now working with producer Jah Screw, Levy diversifies, moving into more urban stylings. The title track is an undisputed classic while the original mix of "Under Mi Sensi" is as strong as the more familiar jungle version. But the most remarkable moments are the smokey jazzclub "The Vibe Is Right," which continues to amaze long after the first hearings have passed into memory; and "Do the Dance," with its insidious melody line and a hook which hangs on the very edge of familiarity.

6 Love the Life You Live (Time—JA) 1988

Bob Andy's "Too Experienced" stands out as an example of the pupil showing the teacher what he's learned; it's as exquisite as Levy has ever sounded. But while this isn't a one song album, it's not an especially well-rounded one either.

8 Divine (Mango—UK) 1991

Turning his attention towards classic songs as well as classy performances, Levy delivers an album poised between past glory and future reinvention—Del Shannon's "Runaway" is glossy by any standards, and should have been a single (it would have scored so big). Another Bob Andy song, "My Time," Ken Boothe's "Silver Words" and John Holt's "Darling I Need Your Loving," however, convey all the old urgency.

7 Turning Point (Greensleeves—UK) 1992

Continuing the *Divine* reinvention with "Desperate Lover," "Why Can't I Touch You" and a joyous paean to Nelson Mandela, "Mandela You're Free."

7 Barrington (MCA) 1993

A reworking of "Under Mi Sensi," soon to be transformed beyond all recognition, bonus remixes of the opening "Murderer" and "Jeep," and a clutch of well-crafted, well-played and expertly delivered songs give *Barrington* a sheen which doesn't always sit comfortably with his natural emotion. As the key which will unlock the international heart, however, it's difficult to argue with its efficacy.

8 Duets (RAS) 1995

aka *DJ's Counter-actions* (Greensleeves — UK). Clever idea this, a Levy's greatest hits package featuring the hottest DJs toasting to the tracks. Standouts include Beenie Man's "Under Mi Sensi" and Bounty Killer's "Living Dangerously," the latter topped charts worldwide. Mega Banton, Lady Saw, Spragga Benz, Cutty Ranks, Fragga Ranks, Daddy Screw and Frisco Kid all appear, and while it does all get a little wearing, in short bursts the excitement is palpable.

7 Time Capsule (RAS) 1996

The excellent "Hypocrites" dominates an album which would be a bare eight tracks long were it not for five closing dubs. In the event, they are worth the price of admission alone.

6 Living Dangerously (Breakaway) 1998

Guest appearances from Snoop Doggy Dog, Betty Wright and the Long Beach Dub All Stars indicate the depth of respect in which Levy is held, and though this time, the album does go on too long (54 minutes), it can never truly be said to drag.

BARRINGTON LEVY & FRANKIE PAUL

5 Barrington Levy Meets Frankie Paul (Ariwa) 1984

Promising set which never truly delivers.

SELECTED COMPILATIONS & ARCHIVE RELEASES

7 Doh Ray Me (JB Music—UK) 1980

When Levy complained about too many albums appearing under his name, simply recycling old singles, out-takes and private sound system recordings, this is what he had in mind. However, "Call You on the Phone" is a great track, and others have their moments.

8 Hunter Man (Burning Sounds—UK) 1983

The singles-so-far includes all the early pace setters, plus "Sweet Reggae Music" with Jah Thomas, and the excellent "Shaolin Temple."

8 Broader than Broadway (Profile) 1990

A very sharp best of, issued by an American hip hop label which readily recognized the line of musical descent which Levy represented.

7 The Collection (Greensleeves—UK) 1991

Fairly straightforward set offers a good jumping off place for novices.

7 Prison Oval Rock (RAS) 1992

Tasty collection dominated by both regular and dub versions of the title track (which borrowed its heavy rhythm from the Wailers' "Firehouse Rock"). From the follow-up hit "Hammer" and the classic roots of "Robber Man," to the dubby tale of the trollop "Mary Long Tongue," another unforgettable updating of roots for the modern generation, engineered by Scientist and Sylvan Morris.

6 RAS Portrait (RAS) 1997

Up date of *Prison Oval Rock*, repeating the same highlights but replacing some cuts (the dub among them—shame) with highlights from *Divine* and *Time Capsule*.

LORD KITCHENER

STYLE *calypso*
BORN *Aldwyn Roberts, 4/18/22 (Arima, T&T) d 2/2000 (Port of Spain, T&T)*

The greatest calypsonian of the post-war age, and the most successful one as well, Lord Kitchener set the pace in so many different areas that it is impossible to isolate any single attribute as his greatest talent. His expressive performances, powerful voice and emotional compositions all revolutionized calypso in the 1940s–50s era, and continued doing so for the next 30 years. His early embrace of pan was crucial to that medium's development; in the late 1970s, his support of the new soca sound was equally instrumental in that style's acceptance.

In between times, Kitchener was responsible for some of the best-known and best-loved calypsos of the age, while his irrepressible humor and powers of observation saw him rise to near-superstar status even in lands where calypso had yet to take hold.

One of six children born to an Arima blacksmith, but orphaned at the age of 14, the grandmaster of calypso got his musical start playing guitar for Water Scheme laborers as they worked in the nearby San Fernando Valley. He

Lord Kitchener delivers another calypso too hot to handle.

wrote his own material from the beginning, and in 1938 saw one of his compositions, "Shops Close too Early," become something of a street anthem around Arima.

That same year, he served as a lead vocalist, or chanterelle, for the Sheriff Band, and also won the Arima Calypso King Title, from which he took the stagename "The Arima Champion." He retained the title for the next four years, but in 1943 he moved to Port of Spain.

There Roberts hitched up with the Roving Brigade, one of the loose aggregations of singers and performers who, as their name implies, spent carnival moving from place to place, rather than basing themselves in one tent. Their most frequent performances were at cinemas and it was one of these shows that entrepreneur Johnny Khan, who managed the Victory Tent, spotted the Arima Champion, performing "Mary I Am Tired and Disgusted."

Roberts was immediately invited along to the Victory tent, located at that time on Edward Street and home to some of the biggest names in calypso. There he was taken under the wing of the legendary Growling Tiger. Impressed by the young man's newly composed "Green Fig," Tiger rechristened the Arima Champion with the distinctive name he retained for the rest of his life, in honor of the World War One era British secretary of war.

Appropriately enough, in 1945, Lord Kitchener moved to the House of Lords tent alongside Lord Ziegfield and Lord Caresser, and received his first taste of controversy when his "Yankee Sufferers" was banned by Police Commissioner Angus Miller for fear of offending the vast American military presence then stationed on T&T. Nevertheless, Kitchener was invited to perform the less controversial "Green Fig" for President Harry Truman, when the American visited T&T that same year. Kitchener returned to the Victory Tent in 1946; it was there that he first performed "Tie Tongue Mopsy," a musical comedy sketch concerning a young woman with a speech impediment, trying to awaken her sleeping lover before her grandmother comes home. Together with the Road March champion "Lai Fung Lee (Chinee Never Had a VJ Day)," and ably supported by "Scandal in St Anns" and "Mount Olga," "Tie Tongue Mopsy" gave Kitchener his greatest carnival triumph yet.

Early the following year, Kitchener, manager Elias Moses and fellow Victory Tent regular Mighty Killer broke away to launch their own Young Brigade tent at 100 Vincent Street. Fellow stars Spoiler, Viking, Lord Ziegfield, Lord Pretender and Lord Melody were lured away from the House of Lords and together, this new band of upstarts set about revolutionizing the sound, the presentation and the very appeal of calypso.

Kitchener was also among the first men to recognize the value of the steelpan. In fact, 1946's "Beat of the Steel Band" is generally regarded as the first calypso ever to extol the virtues of this new musical force. But that was only the beginning of his reforms. Harder horns, wider-ranging rhythms and an uncompromisingly hostile attitude to the British government's continued hold on the island's politics were all thrown into an exciting, excitable brew.

The US troops based in T&T were especially enamored with the Young Brigade's antics and, encouraged by their support, Kitchener traveled to New York to appear alongside Houdini (the calypsonian, not the escapologist!), Sir Lancelot, Lord Invader, Lady Trinidad and others at the Golden Gate ballroom on 142nd and Lennox.

The trip was a success and Kitchener began to dream of spreading calypso even further afield. On May 24, 1948, Kitchener and his companion, Lord Beginner (b Egbert Moore) set sail for England, stopping off en route for performances in Curacao, Aruba and finally Jamaica (where "Kitch Come Go to Bed" — aka "Ah Bernice" — became a monster hit during 1948).

The pair traveled aboard the *Empire Windrush*, a converted troop carrier which, alongside the previous year's *Almazora*, was to spearhead one of the most remarkable experiments in British colonial history, the importation of thousands of West Indian migrants to assist in the reconstruction of the "Mother Country" following the ravages of World War Two. Some 500 West Indians paid a little over 28 pounds (one-third of the normal commercial rate) for berths aboard the *Empire Windrush*.

Over the next ten years, some 150,000 more followed them, opening the United Kingdom up to cultures (and, sadly, conflicts) unimaginable before the war. Many of these were highly skilled workers — estimates claim as much as 46%; almost a quarter more had professional or management experience; 5% were at least semi-skilled.

Nobody, however, seems to have considered how many, like Kitchener, were talented musicians; nor has their impact upon their new homeland ever been truly assessed. However, from the moment *Empire Windrush* docked at Tilbury, London, on June 22, 1948, Kitchener and all the other performers aboard the vessel discovered that not only could they rely upon the continuing support of the captive crowd which had traveled with them, there was also a vast audience already in place in Britain's biggest cities, anxiously awaiting a taste of the genuine Caribbean.

Kitchener made a splash the moment he set foot on British soil, breaking into the specially written "London Is the Place for Me," to the delight of the newsmen and passers-by who had gathered to watch the *Empire Windrush*'s arrival. His performance was even captured on a Pathe news reel and shown in cinemas the length and breadth of the country.

At first, Kitchener performed in pubs, battling to win over audiences who readily confessed they couldn't understand a word he said. However, the BBC were obviously intrigued and, by 1949, he was being regularly invited to perform on the radio. Soon he was playing two or three club engagements a night as well.

Kitchener hit the headlines again in 1950, following the West Indies cricket team's destruction of a highly fancied England team. The match was still underway when Kitchener leaped onto the Lords Cricket Ground pitch and commenced a war dance, while performing the impromptu calypso, "Walcott, Weekes & Worrell" — dedicated, of course, to three of the West Indian team's most popular players. A steel band joined in and, as the match ended, so the West Indian players and supporters, too, entered the parade, cavorting wildly through the streets of London to Piccadilly Circus. There, they brought central London to a grinding, but utterly joyful, standstill.

Kitchener signed to the EMI subsidiary label Parlophone (Decca in the USA) later in the year, cutting the 78 "Nora" with British jazz-man Denis Preston and backed by Cyril Blake's Calypso Serenaders — West Indian guitarist Blake had been working in London since the early 1920s, often with the Southern Syncopated Orchestra. (Lord Beginner's "Dollars And Pounds" appeared on the b-side of the 78.) It was a successful effort, but greater heights beckoned 18 months later, after he joined the Melodisc specialist label. He debuted with "Kitch" "Food from the West Indies," and a second 78, coupling the six year old "Tie Tongue Mopsy" with "Two Timing Josephine" followed later that year.

In 1953, Kitchener signed to the tiny (and even more Carib-centric) Lyragon label, itself hot from the success of Margaret Bryant's raucous "Don't Touch Me Tomato." His "Alec Bedser Calypso" eulogized the English cricket legend, hero of the 1953 test series against Australia. "Africa My Home," "Beware Tokyo" and "If You're Not White, You're Considered Black" followed that same year. Back in

T&T, meanwhile, his recordings were as popular as if he were still an island resident — "Mama Look a Band Passing" even won the 1954 Road March.

In 1955, Queen Elizabeth's sister, Princess Margaret, visited T&T and impressed her hosts with her knowledge of calypso in general, and Lord Kitchener in particular. Supposedly she purchased 100 copies of "Kitch Come to Bed" while she was there, as presents for friends. He repaid her favor when she attended one of his concerts at London's Chesterfield Club, several years later. According to recent news reports, the Princess had given her new-born nephew, Prince Andrew, a brown teddy bear named Nicky — Kitchener accordingly performed a new song called "Nicky the Brown Bear" in her honor.

Kitchener returned to Melodisc in 1955 for a run of 78s and 45s which extended into the mid-1960s. Working with arranger Rupert Nurse and seriously living up to his new self-styled nickname of "the Professor," Kitchener used London's studios to their limit, pioneering both harmony and rhythms on recordings like "Rock'n'Roll Calypso," "Black Puddin'," a reiteration of the earlier "If You're Not White" titled "If You're Brown (You're Not White)," "Nora and the Yankee," and "Ghana" — which was specially commissioned by the in-coming government of that newly independent African nation. Melodisc also issued a pair of his albums, two volumes of *Calypsos Too Hot to Handle*.

Kitchener himself opened a nightclub in the northern city of Manchester, while landing a phenomenally successful residency at London's jazz hotspot The Sunset, and returned to the US once again, playing New York and Washington DC to rapturous applause.

Even as he pushed the profile of international calypso towards new heights (only American-born Harry Belafonte was better known), however, Kitchener believed that his homeland's own scene was remaining static. In 1958, he attacked the newly emergent, but in his eyes, unimpressive Mighty Sparrow with "No More Calypso" and, in 1962, he decided it was finally time to go home and sort out the mess in person.

Immediately Kitchener had an impact. He promptly scored hit singles with "It Ain't Fair" and "The Captain Say," while "The Road" won the Road March in 1963. "Mama, dis Mama" took the same title the following year, narrowly beating out another Kitchener anthem, "Carnival." The risque "My Pussin" was victorious in 1965, "Sixty Seven" won in 1967, followed the next year by "Miss Tourist." In 1970, "Margie" took the title, in 1971, "Mas in Madison Square," in 1973, "Rain-O-Rama" (the name of his Diego Martin home), and in 1976, he won with "Flag Woman."

Kitchener also came to dominate the Panorama, the competition among steel bands. Winning titles over the next decade were: "Mama dis Is Mas" (1964), "67" (1967), "The Wrecker" (1968), "The Bull" (1969), "Margie" (1970), "Play Mas" (1971), "St Thomas" (1972), "Rain O Rama" (1973), "Jericho" (1974).

In 1975, Kitchener's "Tribute to Spree Simon," dedicated to the recently deceased father of the steel bands, earned him his first and, surprisingly, only Calypso King title. Uniquely, the song also took first, second and third place in the Panorama, performed respectively by the Maritime Hatters, Fonclaire and Carib Tokyo.

Further Panorama triumphs followed with "Pan in Harmony" (1976), "Crawford" (1977), "Pan Explosion" (1982) and "Sweet Pan" (1984). 1985 served up another unique first, as the WITCO Desperadoes and the Amoco Renegades tied for first place, with their own adaptations of Kitchener's "Pan Night and Day." "Iron Man" (1990), "Mystery Band" (1993) and "The Guitar Pan" (1997) round out Kitchener's record breaking Panorama victories.

Kitchener was also a prime mover behind perhaps the most successful tent in modern carnival history. The Calypso Revue was opened in 1964 at the Strand Cinema by International Recording Co head Leslie Lucky-Samarod and, that same year, it produced four Calypso King finalists — Kitchener, Nap Hepburn, Blakie and the eventual victor, Bomber. The following year, Sniper kept the Calypso King trophy at the tent.

That same year, however, saw Kitchener fall out with Samarod, and shift his loyalties to the Mighty Sparrow's Original Young Brigade tent — only to then break that contract and return to England instead. He remained there for a year before coming back to T&T to find the Calypso Revue now under the control of Lord Melody. Kitchener rejoined, and though Melody left following the 1968 season (his successors, Jazzy Pantin and Sonny Woodley remain in charge to this day), Kitchener himself stayed loyal to the tent for the remainder of his life.

Since that time, the Calypso Revue — with Kitchener a dedicated tutor — has helped groom some of the music's most important young talent, including Composer, three times Calypso Monarch Cro-Cro, Explainer, Iwer George, Merchant, Organizer, Penguin, Relator (1980 Calypso Monarch), Scrunter, Sniper, Valentino, Gypsy (1997 champion) and multiple monarch Black Stalin.

Neither would age dull Kitchener's enthusiasm for calypso's growth and development. As soca began moving into focus in the late 1970s, he was swift to sense its possibilities and, during the 1980s, he maintained a stream of albums reflecting both his support — and mastery — of the form. He also commenced overseeing the consolidation of his back catalog through the auspices of Eddy Grant's Ice label.

The 1990s, then, were a decade for Kitchener to sit back and accept — or reject — the accolades of his homeland. In

1993, a public petition to have him awarded the islands' highest civilian award, The Trinity Cross, was turned down by the government, who instead offered a lesser honor. Lord Kitchener proudly refused it.

The nation made amends somewhat three years later, when September 21, 1996, saw the debut of *The Musical Magic of Kitch*, an Honour Performance staged by the Patrons of Queen's Hall, St. Ann's. Directed by Rawle Gibbons and Noble Douglas, the production featured an assembly of orchestras which, through a variety of performing styles, explored every facet of Kitchener's music. Though Kitchener himself was too ill to perform that night, he did at least appear on stage towards the end of the show. Lord Kitchener died February 11, 2000.

SELECTED DISCOGRAPHY

9 **Calypso too Hot to Handle (Melodisc—UK) 1961**

9 **Calypso too Hot to Handle Volume Two (Melodisc—UK) 1962**

Collecting together the best of Kitchener's late 50s output, two albums which span the full breadth of his repertoire; one of the most expressive performers calypso had ever seen, Kitchener's writing traversed the gamut of human emotion, so if anyone ever tells you calypso all sounds the same. . . .

7 **67 Kitch (RCA) 1967**

7 **Carnival Fever (TR—T&T) 1975**

"No Streakers" is amazing, discussing that odd mid-70s taste for racing naked through a public place. The hits "Fever" and "Tribute to Spree" are both on board, but across all 10 tracks Kitchener is in fine form.

7 **Melodies of the 21st Century (Charlies—T&T) 1978**

An oddly adventurous album, as the track listing (and title) indicate — "Pan of the 21st Century" posits a fascinating future for steel drums . . . as fascinating, in fact, as the initial embrace with soca, "Soca Trinidad." There's also a distinctively personalized take on "Little Drummer Boy."

6 **Spirit of Carnival (Charlies—T&T) 1978**

"Pan Round the Neck," "Soca Millicent" and the tumultuous "Symphony in G" are the main attractions.

6 **Shooting with Kitch (Charlies—T&T) 1978**

Includes the sports favorite, "Netball Queen."

8 **Kitchener Goes Soca (Charlies—T&T) 1980**

Effortlessly, Kitchener cranks up the volume and the vivacity as well. Though his later work does pale in comparison with those earlier recordings, still there's an excitement here which is matched only by his experience.

7 **Simply Wonderful (Charlies—T&T) 1983**

"Tourist Elsie" must have set some after-vacation ears burning, while "Soca Corruption" just lit fires on the island.

6 **The Master at Work (Charlies—T&T) 1984**

Actually, not quite as masterful as it should have been, as "Break Dance," "Soca Misinterpretation" and "Last Year Bacchanal" all prove less than their titles deserve. But "Pan Night and Day" was so enormous, it's unlikely that anyone noticed.

7 **100% Kitch (Bs—T&T) 1988**

Kitch goes disco! Well, not quite, but there's certainly enough appropriate technology behind the frantic soca of the infidelity-hunting "The Last Dance." The best of Kitch's late 1980s albums features the incredible "Tobago Love Manohie," discussing the sexual habits of women from the neighboring island and the exhausting "Is the Pan in Me." He could have dropped "Mother's Day," though.

4 **Honey In The Kitchen (Wads—T&T) 1992**

Disappointing four song effort, but it does include the triumphant "Brooklyn Rock."

6 **Longevity (JW—T&T) 1993**

7 **Still Escalating (JW—T&T) 1994**

5 **Ah Have It Cock (JW—T&T) 1995**

Two mixes apiece of "Last Jump" and "Heavy Roller" detract somewhat from one of Kitchener's better 90s compositions, "Dance Hall King."

6 **Incredible Kitch (JW—T&T) 1995**

"Election Derby" and "Ah Stop Eating Now" catch the ear first, although the flow of the album is disrupted somewhat by a couple of heavy handed remixes.

6 **Reflections of a Legend (JW—T&T) 1997**

7 **Symphony in the Street (JW—T&T) 1998**

Two of Kitchener's final albums, each possessing their share of nostalgia, even closure . . . "Old Time Calypso" (from *Symphony*) and "Ash Wednesday Mas" (from *Legend*) are beautifully poignant.

8 **Vintage Kitch (JW—T&T) 1999**

Ignore the title! *Vintage* is almost brutally non-vintage, a raw and raucous raspberry blown at the fast passing years. A brilliant farewell.

LORD KITCHENER & MIGHTY SPARROW

8 **16 Carnival Hits (Ice—UK) 1993**

Killing two birds (well, one bird and one historical leader) with one stone, an excellent compilation of 60s/70s vintage calypsos by two of the undisputed masters.

SELECTED COMPILATIONS & ARCHIVE RELEASES

10 **Klassic Kitchener (four volumes) (Ice—UK) 1993–96**

Although other collections exist (most notably *Roots of Soca* (Charlies—1983) and *Master at Work* (Kalico—1987), this set—each volume available individually—tells the story best, tracing Kitchener through a lifetime of Road March and Panorama hits, interspersed with choice album cuts and singles. Volume one concentrates on the English 50s, with "Nora," "If You're Brown," "Chinee Never Had a VJ Day" and more. Volume Two marches through the 60s, with "My Pussin'," "67" and so forth. In all fairness, they're the most essential discs, but once you've started listening, you won't want to stop at two. You probably won't be able to, either.

LORD MELODY

STYLE *calypso*
BORN *Fitzroy Alexander, 1926 (T&T) d 1988 (T&T)*

One of the new wave of calypsonians who emerged in the wake (and, indeed, under the aegis) of Lord Kitchener, Lord Melody performed with a satirical savagery which swiftly set him up as one of carnival's most beloved sons. That his work retains its humor long after its topicality has been forgotten only emphasizes his brilliance.

Raised at an orphanage in Port of Spain, the young Melody was barely into his teens when he won his introduction to the world of professional calypso, after he relocated to Arima and met the area's own local champion, Aldwyn Roberts—the future Lord Kitchener.

Taken under his wing, Melody followed Kitchener back to Port of Spain and, over the next five years, swiftly established himself as one of the premier challengers for the older man's throne—all the more so after Kitchener departed for England in 1947. Early Melody classics included "Berlin on a Donkey," mocking the dead Adolf Hitler in a riotous combination of English and pidgin-German; and "Boo Boo Man" ("I wonder why nobody like me, is it because I'm ugly?") and "Creature from the Black Lagoon," discussing the supposed ugliness of most calypso singers, a popular subject among T&T comedians.

In 1954, Melody won his first Calypso crown with "Second Spring," and two years later came close to a second triumph with "Hurricane Janet," recalling the previous September's lethal storm. 1956 also saw him join American musicologist Emory Cook's eponymous record label.

Melody released his first album, *Lord Melody Sings Calypso*, in 1957, followed the next year by *Again!*. The singer's reputation took another major leap forward when Harry Belafonte took "Boo Boo Man" (as "Mama Look at Bubu") into the US Top 20 in March, 1957. The two men later toured together, and Belafonte went on to record several other Melody compositions.

Melody also earned considerable renown for a long running feud with the Mighty Sparrow, captured across searing (but very funny) recordings like "Picong Duel" and "Cowboy Sparrow" (and Sparrow's "Reply to Melody.")

While his Cook label single "Peddlars" hit in T&T, 1958 saw Melody's "Cricket, Lovely Cricket" become something of a family favorite on British radio waves and, that same year, Emil Shalit's Melodisc label began making his records available in Europe. "The Devil," "Robbery," "Do Able," "I Confess," the American folk song "Tom Dooley," "Romeo" and "Rock'n'Roll Calypso" were all hits with Britain's West Indian community during the late 1950s.

In 1960, Melody scored with "The Ice Man," composed by calypso entrepreneur (and Trinidadian diplomat) Tom Castagne. A succession of less-than-classic offerings subsequently saw his renown slip somewhat thereafter, although Melody bounced back sufficiently to see his "Melody Mas" win the panorama at Carnival in 1965, courtesy of the Cavaliers. Spectacularly, he was the only calypsonian to break Lord Kitchener and Mighty Sparrow's stranglehold on that competition all decade.

In the early 1970s, Melody was diagnosed with cancer and, although he remained a constant fixture on the T&T scene, illness increasingly restricted his activities. It was 1979 before he resurfaced internationally, with the release of *I Man*, embracing Rastafarian consciousness. He scored a pair of local hits around the same time with the similarly themed "Rastaman Be Careful" and "Brown Sugar." Three years later, he made the warm soca themed *Lola*, but his health was worsening. Lord Melody died in 1988, at the age of 62.

SELECTED DISCOGRAPHY

9 Lord Melody Sings Calypso (Cook) 1957

Several of Melody's best Cook recordings appeared on the *Jump Up Carnival* various artists album in 1956. However, "Cowboy Sparrow," accusing his fellow calypsonian of murder (!) and "Carnival Proclamation," in which the spirit of a Native American is invoked to cut down other of his enemies, certainly make this a worthwhile investment.

6 Again! (Cook) 1958

In a year which saw East Indian music finally impacting on the wider T&T scene, Melody hit with the almost swing-flavored "Come Go Calcutta," a call for even further acceptance between the two races. On an album which generally sags in comparison with its predecessor, this one song is worth far more than the price of admission.

8 Calypso Through the Looking Glass (Cook) 1959

aka *Melody's Top Ten*, an accurate summation of its contents. The call and bassy-response "Turn Back, Melody," the singer's musical reaction to the growing local problem of hooliganism (complete with another swipe at his greatest rival: "they think I stupid like Sparrow") is one of the finest.

7 Lord Melody (Cook) 1962
9 I Man (Charlies—T&T) 1979

Roots rock calypso? An intriguing album, one of the first to merge Rastafarian spirituality with the hedonism of calypso, and the fusion takes some getting used to. Persevere, and a magic emerges which may be a long way from what either discipline normally represents, but captures their hearts nonetheless.

7 Lola (Bs—T&T) 1982

SELECTED COMPILATIONS & ARCHIVE RELEASES

8 Precious Melodies (Ice—UK) 1994

20 track collection unearths treasures which should never have been buried (or, at least, lost) for so long. "Clay Vs Liston," "Radio Commercials," the robust "Spare Nose (St Lucian Women)" and the side splitting "Sparrow Melody Horse Race" date from the latter part of Melody's career, but show that he had lost little of his flair.

LORD TOKYO

STYLE *calypso*
BORN *Hayden Desiree (DOM)*

In 1967, Lord Tokyo became the first solo artist ever to make a record on the island of Dominica. His "De Man Doing de Pumpin'" was cut just weeks after the Swingin' Stars Orchestra debuted the island's recording industry with a cover of the Mighty Sparrow's "The Party." And, though both were barely heard outside the island, these were the first shots in what became one of the most vigorous markets in the entire Caribbean. Dominica itself is often overlooked by the compilers of the various "world music" guides on the market today, but it is safe to say that the nation has made as great a contribution to the modern flavor of the region as any of its neighbors. And Lord Tokyo has contributed just as much.

The winner of the 1969 Calypso King of Dominica competition, and composer of the 1970 Road March champion, "Tennis Shoe Scandal," Lord Tokyo is best known for his early 1970s collaboration with Lord Shorty, at a time when the Trinidadian was desperately seeking to revitalize calypso with new meaning and rhythms. Working with lyricist Chris Seraphine (of the Gaylords), the trio formulated a revolutionary fusion of calypso, cadence and Creole patois for the early 1970s hit "Ou Dee Moin Ou Petit Shorty" ("you told me you are small, Shorty"). It was through that hybrid, that Shorty went on to create what emerged as soca.

Lord Tokyo himself spent much of his career in the UK, US and Canada, performing regularly, but seldom recording. A visit to London in 1978, however, saw him cut the *Calypso Harmonies: Lord Tokyo Sings to the Nightingale* album for the local Caribana label.

In 1997, Lord Tokyo combined with the Mighty Sparrow's renowned Sparrow's Troubadours orchestra to cut a new version of "Tennis Shoe Scandal." Amazingly, it wasn't until the next year that Lord Tokyo released his first album

on CD, the festive *Merry Christmas and a Happy New Year*. The album's popularity can be gauged from the fact that, two years later, over Christmas 2000, Lord Tokyo placed four songs from the album in the Sensay Dominica Caribbean Top 20. Working with producer/programmer King Arthur Valmond, he followed through with *De Pumping Man*.

RECOMMENDED LISTENING

7 Merry Christmas and a Happy New Year (—Dominica) 1998

A joyful collection of traditional Caribbean Christmas melodies performed in a variety of regional musical styles — soca, bouyon, zouk and cadence among them.

9 De Pumping Man (—Dominica) 2000

A fine collection of old and new material updated for the 21st century. Mighty Sparrow guests on the reworked title track.

LOVERS ROCK

Though Lovers Rock was essentially a British media invention, a term coined in the mid–late 1970s to accommodate the wealth of artists who did not fall into the more culturally aware field of roots reggae, the genre itself had existed since the late 1960s saw Rastafarianism and social consciousness push themselves to the fore of the Jamaican scene, leaving all other concerns in their wake. Love songs naturally fell into this stylistic void.

Throughout the early 1970s, when the likes of Ken Boothe, Johnny Nash and John Holt scored massive international hits with their reggae-lite versions of established AOR classics, their silky smooth sounds were categorized as soft pop. Indeed, many of the Jamaican singles released in Europe at this time were purposefully arranged with precisely that audience in mind, with the more astute island producers deliberately leaving sufficient open spaces in their master tape for a British arranger to add strings, slow the tempo and smooth the rhythm out, to better blend in with the musical mood of the moment.

Back home, the performances often sounded substantially different to those being bought in droves in the UK. At the same time as these records were being brutally Euro-fied, however, other artists were releasing singles of similar smoothness, but packing undeniable power.

Beautiful recordings by Dennis Brown, Horace Andy and Gregory Isaacs unquestionably held the nascent (and still unnamed) lovers rock movement in their thrall, but continued releases from Susan Cadogan, Delroy Wilson, Errol Dunkley and many others also manipulated the discerning listener's affections with exquisite attention to detail. The only question exercising the self-consciously militant, but sentimentally drawn UK audience was, in which genre could these artists be placed?

Producer Dennis Bovell was among the men who had an answer. Born in Barbados in 1953, but raised in south London, Bovell's first band, Stonehenge, played hard psychedelic rock in the spirit of Jimi Hendrix — indeed, their devotion was such that when Hendrix died in 1970, the band broke up.

Bovell promptly formed a new group, Matumbi, this time with a largely self-composed diet of politically conscious ska and rock steady — the one cover in their repertoire was Hot Chocolate's "Brother Louie," a smoldering examination of the problems encountered by mixed racial couples. When Trojan Records picked the band up, predictably that was the label's first — and only — choice for a single; and, when Matumbi refused to record any more covers, the contract was terminated. (Subsequent Trojan sponsored *Best of Matumbi* type collections revolve around an album recorded for, but originally rejected by the label.)

Matumbi withdrew to regroup, eventually joining the DIP label, then flush from its success with Susan Cadogan's so sultry "Hurts So Good" single. There Bovell linked with producer John Kpiaye as assistant sound engineer. Although DIP was, at the time, best known for its connections with Lee Perry (a number of Upsetters related titles appeared in the UK through DIP during the mid-1970s), Kpiaye's own taste for romantic reggae soon came to dominate the label's output. 1976's *To Reggae for Lovers* compilation highlighted the best of his recent productions.

Kpiaye was not the only producer working in this direction; Larry Lawrence, Clem Bushay, Castro Brown and Delroy Witter were also cutting some deliciously smooth, smoochy reggae 45s. Meanwhile, in 1975, singer Louisa Mark recorded what was arguably the first successful homegrown response to the Jamaican masters, a succulent version of Bobby Parker's "Caught You in a Lie." Following her example, US soul hits remained a regular, and supremely successful, source for British lovers rock releases.

Kpiaye, Bovell and DIP label head Dennis Harris launched the Lovers Rock label in 1977, debuting with "I'm in Love with a Dreadlocks," by Brown Sugar, written and produced by Kpiaye, and featuring 15 year old vocalist Caron Wheeler (later of Soul II Soul). An immediate hit with the patrons of such London-based sound systems as Chicken Hi Fi, Success Sound and Soferno B, the single's success paved the way for a host of similar signings — Cassandra, Roland & Carolyn Catlin and TT Ross among them.

Success was immediate, for the Lover's Rock label and for what was fast coalescing into a genre in its own right. Guardian Angel and UK scene veteran Honey Boy both enjoyed major reggae hits during 1977, while singer Tim Chandell's debut album, 1977's *Loving Moods Of*, sold a staggering 50,000 copies without even being noticed outside of local reggae circles.

Other talents were swift to arrive on the scene. Guyanan born Neil "Mad Professor" Fraser debuted in 1979 with his Ariwa label, and sessions with Lovers Rock legend Deborahe Glasgow (b 1965; d 1/25/94); while Bovell was behind the biggest Lovers Rock record of them all, Janet Kay's 1979 #2 hit "Silly Games." (Kay had previously enjoyed club smashes with a superb cover of Minnie Ripperton's "Loving You," and "I Do Love You.")

The scene received another major boost in 1978, when Dennis Brown visited the UK to launch the European wing of his own DEB label. Among the first signings to the new company was 15–16–17, a Jamaican born, London raised female vocal trio whose name reflected their ages (they later changed it to 17–18–19).

DEB launched with 15–16–17's "Only 16" and "Emotion," while further label signings pursued both Jamaican and British-based lovers rock with effortless ease — Field Marshall Buckors, the Tamlins, Desi Roots, former Heptones frontman Leroy Sibbles, Black Harmony, Me and You, and Destiny all made well-received appearances on the label.

Despite the plethora of homegrown talent, Dennis Brown and Gregory Isaacs (also a DEB artist) epitomized Lovers Rock in the UK at the turn of the decade, their domination of the scene rivalled only by the newly emergent Sugar Minott. Both Brown and Minott scored genre-defining British hits during this period — Brown's "Money in My Pocket" reached #14 in March, 1979, Minott's "Good Thing Going" climbed ten places higher in March, 1981, with those dates neatly book-ending a period of unparalleled activity and creativity on the UK reggae scene.

The departure from British shores of these figureheads did much to lessen the overall impact of Lovers Rock domestically; it has, however, unquestionably continued to flourish in Britain, with the Fashion record label ascending to an immortality unmatched even by many of its Jamaican counterparts.

The Revue label, too, produced a number of fine titles. In 1986, Boris Gardiner scored his first British hit since 1970's "Elizabethan Reggae," when his distinctly lovers-inflected "I Want to Wake Up with You" topped the chart, while homegrown attractions have continued to sell well. Into the 1990s, names like Mike Anthony and Peter Hunningale have attained virtual superstar status, while British acts also proved a regular highlight at Reggae Sunsplash.

RECOMMENDED LISTENING

KEN BOOTHE 18 Classic Songs (Trojan — UK) 1991

For all his pre-eminence as a songwriter, Boothe's regular albums are often too sweet for continued listening. This collection of his best early 1970s work, however, pinpoints the sheer majesty of his songwriting ("Freedom Street," "Silver Words"), his vocals ("Come Softly to Me" and "Ain't No Sunshine," draped in the warmest baritone you can imagine) and his eye for a monster hit ("Everything I Own," "Crying Over You").

BERES HAMMOND A Love Affair (Penthouse—JA) 1992
The finest soul singer in modern reggae history, Hammond had a string of Lovers Rock triumphs to his name by the time he came to cut this set. It was thanks to him, after all, that dance hall embraced Lovers Rock with such avidity, and the new sense of rhythm and production innovations are epitomized by "Tempted to Touch," "Falling in Love Again" and "Love Me Hafe Get."

THE MEDITATIONS No More Friend (Greensleeves—UK) 1983
The trio aptly described this as their first dance album; powered by a rock steadyish tempo, it's perfect for couples to drift along to and for solo skankers to display their deftest gossamer moves, coupled with atmospheres that shift from exuberant to heavy, dub flecked roots.

DELROY WILSON Once Upon a Time (Trojan—UK) 1998
One latter-day Wilson compilation was titled, with a sure eye for its market, *Lovers Rock*. But when investigating the silkiest end of his catalog, this collection of 1967–74 material cannot be beat, including as it does a string of crucial Motown interpretations, together with the best of his work with producer Bunny Lee.

VARIOUS ARTISTS

Love All Nite (Music Club) 1999
Exploring the vaults of Britain's Fashion label, prime progenitors of lovers rock during 1985–97, and offering up cuts by Michael Gordon, Nerious Joseph, Peter Spence, Barry Boom, Philip Leo, Vivian Jones, Peter Hunningale, Neville Morrison and John McLean. Fashion's output can be an acquired taste in places, but it does repay perseverance.

VARIOUS ARTISTS

Lovers Box Set (Trojan—UK) 1999
A history lesson which doesn't necessarily stay on message, but sweeps up enough late 1960s/early 1970s Jamaican hits (50 tracks spread over three discs) to prove that Lovers Rock had been percolating for years before it was named. There are few surprises among the inclusions: Delroy Wilson, Jackie Edwards, Dennis Brown, Slim Smith, David Isaacs — hail hail, the gang's all here. Further romantic roots can be uncovered on the same label's *Touch Me in the Morning*, a 25 track collection featuring reggae covers of soul (mainly Motown) covers.

VARIOUS ARTISTS

Reggae Lasting Love Songs (VP) 2000
Lovely selection spanning several generations of reggae romancers, including Marcia Griffiths (Bunny Wailer's "Dreamland"), Doreen Schaeffer (Laurel Aitken's "Sugar Sugar"), the late Cynthia Schloss, Carlene Davis, Dobby Dobson and Boris Gardiner ("I Wanna Wake Up with You"). Again, it's not Lovers Rock in the strictest Anglo sense of the phrase, but it fits the mood regardless.

LUCIANO
STYLE *reggae (dance hall)*
BORN *Jepther McClymont, 12/20/74 (Davey Town, JA)*

Since his emergence in 1992, Luciano (Latin for "light and knowledge") has been widely feted among the most promising of all modern Jamaican songwriters. His deeply religious outlook (he was raised in a strict Adventist family) and profoundly spiritual lyricism reintroduced consciousness and humanity to the dance hall scene at a time when few among his contemporaries were even looking in that direction.

Indeed, Luciano himself has acknowledged that even as he prepared to enter the scene, he purposefully avoided listening to whatever other music was popular at the time, because he knew that it did not contain what he wanted to hear — and what he believed the audience needed as well.

But only with the emergence of the similarly inclined Garnett Silk during 1990–91 was Luciano emboldened to actually step forth, and even then he did so tentatively. His first release was a cover of Stevie Wonder's "Ebony and Ivory," cut with producer Herman Chin Loy under the name of Stepper John in 1992.

Changing his name to Lucian*a*, the singer next linked with producer Sky High for another clutch of songs, again predominantly covers, for inclusion on an album split with DJ Pressley, *Stuck on You*. Again it did not sell, although the material has since been included on any number of compilations.

1993 finally brought the newly renamed Luciano his first hit, the self-composed "Give Love a Try" (produced by Castro Brown). He enjoyed several further hits ("Slice of the Cake," "Jah Jah Never Fail I") with Brown before summer, 1993, saw him link with singer Freddie McGregor, owner of the Big Ship production company. The UK reggae chart-topper "Shake It Up" and "It's a Jungle Out There" sustained Luciano's burgeoning success and, over the next few months, he also worked with Blacka Dread ("Time Is the Master") and Sly & Robbie.

It was his meeting with Fatis Burrell, however, which finally determined Luciano's future direction. The pair immediately scored with "Chant Out" and "Poor and Simple," and an excellent album, *Moving Out*, before late 1993 saw Luciano announce he was taking a break from what had become an increasingly hectic schedule. In fact, it was an indication of the pressures and expectations heaped upon his head, that both the US and UK media commented at length upon what amounted to less than a year of silence.

Luciano returned in 1994 with "Programme fi Kill" and "Cool It Off," for producer Musclehead, and the excellent "Real Rastaman," cut with Louie Culture. (He also played Sunsplash.) He then reunited with Burrell for the stream of singles which in turn comprised the *One Away Ticket* album. Of these, "Ain't Giving Up," cut with DJ Charlie Chaplin, was Luciano's response to the rumors which surrounded his lay-off.

The following year, Island Records moved in for Luciano. *Where There Is Life*, also 1995, was very well received, spawning the silky smooth Jamaican #1 "It's Me Again, Jah" and the similarly hot "Who Could It Be." Twelve months later, Island released the acclaimed *The Messenger*, largely compiled from the previous year's-worth of hit singles, but no less powerful for all that. (Other recordings during this period included the singles "Rebel with a Cause," with Chaplin and Josey Wales, "This Is the Time" and "Peace My Brethren," with Dennis Howard, and a guest appearance on Mutabaruka's "Psalms 24.")

Another silence was broken by 1998's hits "Sweeping Over My Soul" and "Ulterior Motive," harbingers of 1999's *Sweeping Over My Soul* album. A collaboration with Sizzla and Anthony B, *Three Wise Men: Love Peace & Consciousness* followed in 1999, spawning the single "In this Time," while 2000 saw Luciano paired with Mikey General for *Wisdom, Knowledge & Overstanding*. Luciano's own next album was the excellent *Live*.

DISCOGRAPHY

6 Shake It Up Tonight (Big Ship) 1993
The McGregor sessions spawned Luciano's first major international hit (the title track), but little else matches the best of his Burrell recordings. The set has since reappeared as *After All*.

7 Moving Up (RAS) 1993
With Philip Burrell behind him, Luciano journeys from his own "Chant Out" to Jimmy Cliff's "Sitting in Limbo," on an extraordinarily confident set.

7 Back to Africa (Xterminator) 1994
8 One Way Ticket (Xterminator) 1995
"Chant Down Babylon," "Black Survivors" and "One Way Ticket" rate among Luciano's most militant lyrics, but the true razor-edge is deceptively cloaked beneath melody, production and an inspirational rootsiness.

8 Where There Is Life (Island) 1995
Often cited as Luciano's finest album (and at that point, it was), a tribute to Burrell's gentle production, as much as the drama of Luciano's performance. Anyone bemoaning

the still tentative toes being dipped into roots waters elsewhere would truly rejoice at hearing "Just Like the Wind," while the angels themselves must have acclaimed the soft beauty and deep spiritualism of the chart topping "It's Me Again Jah."

10 The Messenger (Xterminator) 1996
This is the masterpiece. Carrying on from *Life*, but adding so much more, *Messenger* continues down diversity's road, adding spirituality to a host of styles and genres — elements of Latin, pop, rock and big band ballads haunt the album, often in such fleeting bites that you don't even notice them till they've passed on by. Of course the lyrics remain the most uplifting focus, all delivered with eloquence and obvious passion. "Mama" is beautiful, and a showcase, too, for Luciano's astounding vocal abilities, while the majestic "Guess What's Happening" closes the album with such grandiosity that it's not worth resisting the impulse to just go back to the beginning and play the whole thing again.

8 Sweeping Over My Soul (VP) 1999
8 Live (VP) 2000
Suitably dramatic 16 song performance which hits all the right highs, and stands as an unimpeachable hits collection for anyone who's not been paying attention so far.

LUCIANO & PRESSLEY
5 Luciana Meets Pressley (Sky High) 1992

LUCIANO & SIZZLA, ANTHONY B
7 Three Wise Men: Love, Peace & Consciousness (J&D) 1999

LUCIANO & MIKEY GENERAL
7 Wisdom, Knowledge & Overstanding (J&D) 2000

SELECTED COMPILATIONS & ARCHIVE RELEASES
6 Don't Get Crazy (RAS) 1995
Awkward set features the young Luciano tackling "Satta Amasa Gana," a Bob Marley medley and other covers.

MACHEL MANTANO see XTATIK

BOB MARLEY & THE WAILERS
STYLE *reggae (roots)*
FORMED 1961 (Kingston, JA)
ORIGINAL LINE-UP *Bob Marley (b Nesta Robert Marley, 2/7/45, St Annes, JA, d 5/11/81 — vocals), Bunny Wailer (b Neville O'Riley Livingston, 4/10/47, Kingston, JA — vocals), Peter Tosh (b Winston Hubert McIntosh, 10/19/44, Grange Hill JA, d 9/11/87), Junior Braithwaite (vocals, b 1949; d 6/2/99), Cherry Green (backing vocals), Beverley Kelso (backing vocals)*

The first unassailable superstar of Jamaican music, a prime mover not simply in the worldwide explosion of reggae, but of interest in his country, his people and his religion as well, Bob Marley ranks among both the most popular and the most misunderstood figures in modern culture.

A devout Rastafarian, a strident rebel, a fearless campaigner, his best recordings (and, indeed, his life's objectives) burn with an affirmative fire which spread so far beyond the narrow parameters of 20th/21st century politics and correctness, that many of his original fans and supporters feel personally affronted by the fame which currently attends him, aware that it is as much a product of the Marley marketing machine, as it is a reflection of the man himself.

That the machine has utterly emasculated Marley is beyond doubt. Gone from the public record is the ghetto kid who dreamed of Che Guevara and the Black Panthers, and pinned their posters up in the Wailers' Soul Shack record store; who believed in freedom, and the fighting which it necessitated, and dressed the part on an early album sleeve; whose heroes were James Brown and Mohammed Ali; whose God was Ras Tafari and whose sacrament was marijuana.

Instead, the Bob Marley who surveys his kingdom today is smiling benevolence, a shining sun, a waving palm tree, and a string of hits which tumble out of polite radio like candy from a gumball machine. Of course it has assured his immortality. But it has also demeaned him beyond recognition. Bob Marley was worth far more.

EARLY YEARS: 1945–63

Bob Marley was born to a Jamaican mother and English father in 1945. Captain Norval Sinclair Marley was a low level government employee involved in overseeing the building of bridges and similar public works, and who never truly took to family life. Their young son spent most of his childhood living with his mother, Cedella, in the rural village of Nine Miles, and aside from a year spent in Kingston with the Captain when he was four, he barely saw his father.

By decade's end, Cedella and her son had moved to Kingston with another single parent family from the village, Toddy Livingston and his son, Neville, aka "Bunny." Together they settled in one of the subsidized housing projects, or government yards, in Kingston's Trench Town district, and the two boys swiftly slipped into the beat of city life, entering their teens just as the sound systems entered the Kingston bloodstream.

Marley began writing songs in his late teens, encouraged by both Livingston and another close friend, the young Desmond "Dekker" Dacres. He appeared regularly at talent contests — at one, he won a pound performing one of his earliest compositions, "Fancy Curls." In February, 1962, he approached Dekker's own record producer, Leslie Kong, with a clutch of his most recent compositions, "Judge Not," "Do You Still Love Me," "Terror" and "One Cup of Cof-

fee" among them. Kong conducted the "audition" in a room off his recording studio.

According to legend, Marley was no more than halfway through the first song, "Judge Not," when Kong told him to stop, led him into the studio, and recorded the songs on the spot. "Judge Not" was released under the pseudonym Bobby Martell just days later, with "One Cup of Coffee" following later in the year. It was a humble beginning, but it taught Marley his first lesson about the Jamaican music industry: it did not pay very well, if at all. Kong had given him twenty pounds for that first 45, but never a penny for the rest of the songs.

It was also obvious to Marley that Kong's attention was elsewhere. Desmond Dekker's career was nearing a peak, while Jackie Opel had also burst through with a string of irresistible hits. The young singer was determined to take his talent elsewhere.

Marley was apprenticed as a welder at the time, a choice of career which was already causing him some concern, even before an accident left him with slivers of steel embedded in his right eye. He now quit his apprenticeship and announced that he intended making music his life. He and Bunny Livingston had already talked about forming a group, and regularly attended the informal coaching sessions held by vocalist Joe Higgs (b 6/3/40; d 12/18/99) in one of the tenement yards on Third Street. It was there that they met Peter "Tosh" McIntosh and Junior Braithwaite, two more would-be singers, and two backing vocalists, Cherry Green and Beverley Kelso.

The group originally called themselves the Teenagers; over time, they changed to the Wailing Wailers, occasionally expanding to the Wailing Rudeboys or the Wailing Rude Boy Wailers, but eventually curtailed it to the Wailers alone. They played the Kingston circuit of talent shows and dances — their first ever live performances were at the Opportunity Knocks talent shows staged by promotor Joseph Verejohn at the Palace Theatre on South Camp Road. It was with these triumphs behind them that another of the group's friends, Rastafarian drummer Alvin Patterson, arranged for them to audition for producer Coxsone Dodd.

THE WAILERS AT STUDIO ONE: 1963–66

The audition took place in early December, 1963, and initially comprised four songs, "Straight and Narrow Way," "I'm Going Home," "Do You Remember" and "I Don't Need Your Love." Sensing that Dodd was not overly impressed, however, they then launched into a fifth, "Simmer Down," written by Livingston in response to the rising tide of rude boy violence on the streets of Kingston. Dodd told the band to return in a few days time.

With backing by the Skatalites, the Wailers cut their first single the following week — of course it was "Simmer

Down" ("Do You Remember" and "I Am Going Home" were also taped at this session) and, by the new year, the group had scored their first hit. "Simmer Down" topped the Jamaican chart for two months, selling 70,000 copies in the process. Its success was such that Dodd not only demanded an immediate follow-up, he also suggested an arrangement which was almost unheard of in Kingston at that time, an exclusive contract and a salary of three pounds a week. The Wailers accepted.

Dodd also became their de facto manager. Even as "Simmer Down" began its ascent, he was arranging for them to appear at the All Champion Night talent show at the Majestic Theater (they finished second, behind the Uniques). He even advanced them the money to buy stage clothes — gold lame outfits for the Majestic show, tight black suits at other engagements.

The Wailers' next single was Braithwaite's "It Hurts to Be Alone" — although Marley later claimed the younger member's high vocals made the group sound like the Jackson Five, Dodd thought Braithwaite's voice was the best in the band. It was followed by Marley/Livingston's "Lonesome Feeling" and, over the next year, the Wailers were seldom out of the Jamaican chart, both with their own material and with a string of adroitly chosen, if occasionally bizarre, covers.

Astutely aware of the volatility of the Jamaican marketplace, the fact that a familiar tune was often as important as a tight ska beat, Dodd encouraged the band to record any song that took their (or his) fancy — US hits like "On Broadway" (the Drifters), "Teenager in Love" (Dion & The Belmonts) and "Ten Commandments of Love" (Aaron Neville); spirituals "Swing Low Sweet Chariot," "Down by the Riverside," "Nobody Knows the Trouble I've Seen" and "Wings of a Dove"; show tunes and standards ("What's New Pussycat," "White Christmas").

The Wailers also went through a phase of favoring the collarless jackets popularized by the Beatles; Tosh, in particular, was utterly entranced by the new music coming out of Britain, the Beatles and the Rolling Stones most of all, and he lost no time in rearranging the former's "And I Love Her" for a 1965 single.

However, Dodd regarded the band as a cut above even the adept vocal quartet he had already seen in action. Sensing, in particular, Marley's restless curiosity, Dodd began playing the band new American R&B albums, then watching as those influences began to permeate the Wailers' own performances. Curtis Mayfield and the Impressions were a particular favorite, both lyrically and musically, and that band's impact can be heard all over the Wailers' 1964–65 era material.

The group were at their most dangerous, however, when their own influences and culture came to bear. Even before they found fame, Marley was known on the streets of Kingston as a hardened fighter — his nickname, Tuff Gong, said as much. He was, in the parlance of the day, a rude boy, a street hardened ghetto kid, as likely to use his fists as his mouth to win an argument and, as those streets continued to blaze with violence, that reputation strengthened. While other artists wrote rudie songs which echoed "Simmer Down"'s message of calm and restraint, the Wailers hit out with Livingston's "Let Him Go," suggesting that if anybody needed to loosen up, it was society and the authorities.

Following the rudies into the new preserve of rock steady, a dance which was fast superceding ska on the Kingston club scene, "Hooligan," "Jailhouse" and "Rude Boy" cemented the relationship, with defiant statements of rudie solidarity, whose very lyrics were a lexicon of rude boy terminology, slang and expressions. Even more impressive were a couple of Tosh compositions, "I'm the Toughest" and the leering, lunging "Stepping Razor," a song of such vitality that, almost 15 years later, it could accompany scenes in the *Rockers* movie without shedding an iota of its combat readiness.

In all, the Wailers recorded over 100 songs with Coxsone Dodd, (including several solo sides by Tosh and Livingston), with the core trio of Marley, Livingston and Tosh dominating to the extent that the departures of Green and Kelso during 1965 were barely noticed. Braithwaite was more of a loss — his range was unique among his fellow Wailers, and though Tosh, in particular, tried to duplicate Braithwaite's higher tones, the results were seldom satisfying. (Braithwaite never followed through on his early promise. He spent many years in the US before returning to Jamaica in the late 1980s, but plans to finally relaunch his career during 1999 ended when he was murdered on June 2nd that year.)

Many of the Wailers' Studio One recordings were major hits — many, too, so intrigued Island Records chief Chris Blackwell, that the UK label's mid-1960s catalog overflows with Wailers material, both under their own name and via the string of other acts with whom Dodd paired them.

They cut at least one song, "Where's Sammy Gone," with calypsonian Lord Brynner, but among their many other sessions, the most significant were the Soulettes, an all-female singing trio featuring Rita Anderson, her cousin Constantine "Dream" Walker and Marlene Gifford.

Beginning with the Soulettes' debut single, "I Love You Baby," and the Wailers' "One Love" (a song Marley returned to a decade later), the two groups regularly provided backing vocals on one another's releases. Marley also became the Soulettes' arranger, a role which brought him ever closer to Anderson. The pair married on February 10, 1966.

During 1965, the Wailers continued scoring hits. Marley, however, was growing increasingly restless. Although Dodd increased the band's salary on several occasions, his own earnings from their efforts remained many times the band's, a situation which was causing considerable friction.

Equally disruptive were the letters Marley was receiving from his mother, who had moved to Delaware in late 1964, and remarried. She wanted her son to join her, tempting him with details of the kind of work and — more importantly — paychecks he would find if he did. Finally, the day after his marriage, Marley left Jamaica for the US, vowing to return the moment he had saved enough money to launch his own record label. Rita remained in Kingston.

Marley's American sojourn was not a success. He found work first as a laboratory assistant at the DuPont Chemical Company, before joining the assembly line at the Chrysler car plant in Wilmington, DE, soul-destroying menial work which left him too much time for homesickness. Relations with his mother, meanwhile, soured when she learned that he had abandoned the family's Anglican beliefs for the Rastafarian faith of the ghettoes and tenements. And the promised land of the USA itself lost its allure when Marley applied for social security and was instead contacted by the draft board.

Once back in Kingston, Marley's first move was to sever the Wailers' association with Dodd. Then, using Marley's American savings, the group established their own record store, Soul Shack, and label, Wail'N Soul'M, inaugurating it with the singles "Bend Down Low" (featuring Marley's newly purchased electric guitar) and "Freedom Time." Both were recorded at Dodd's Studio One, using many of the same musicians who played on their earlier Wailers, including drummer Hugh Malcolm — later described by Livingston as "the man who bought the one drop to reggae music."

INTERREGNUM I: 1966–70

Initially, the band's success seemed set to continue. With the young Clancy Eccles installed as producer, the Wailers scored major dance hall hits with "Nice Time" and "Stir It Up." But it soon became apparent that such triumphs meant nothing in the world of radio — so crucial to scoring a bestselling record, but so utterly unconcerned with the actual quality of that record.

For the first time, the Wailers saw the one thing Dodd had brought to their relationship which couldn't be measured in terms of either cash or workload — the necessary industry contacts that ensured a record which left the pressing plant on Monday, would be blasting out of the radio on Tuesday. Although Wail'N Soul'M continued releasing singles into 1969, the Wailers themselves seemed unlikely to share its longevity.

In quick succession, all three members of the band were arrested — Tosh for taking part in an illegal demonstration against Rhodesian apartheid; Marley and Livingston on more serious charges involving marijuana, a drug whose illegality was as much an authoritarian blow against Rastafarianism, as it was a social or moral issue. Marley, whose crime was no more serious than sharing a car with a friend who was carrying the herb, received a month's imprisonment. Livingston, however, was caught with several pounds on his person, and was jailed for 14 months.

Just as Marley's absence in the US had not prevented the Wailers from continuing on without him, so Livingston's incarceration was not an insurmountable obstacle either. With Rita Marley moving into the frontline alongside Tosh and her husband, the Wailers organized a string of sessions during the spring and summer of 1968, either producing themselves or in tandem with Mortimer Planno, the Rastafarian elder of western Kingston.

That summer, too, the band entered a song for the national heats of the Pan-Caribbean cultural festival, Carifesta. The winning composition would represent Jamaica at the event, and Marley was convinced that "Don't Rock My Boat" had what it took to go all the way. In fact, the song didn't even make the top five, and it was another decade before his faith in it was borne out. Rerecorded for Marley's *Kaya* album, and retitled "Satisfy My Soul," the song which wasn't good enough for Jamaica, became a huge hit all around the world.

It was a chance encounter with American singer Johnny Nash at a Rastafarian grounation, which promised the greatest dividends, however. With his business partner Danny Sims, Nash had been living and recording in Kingston for several years at that point, initially regarding the city as nothing more than an inexpensive base while the partnership recovered from the collapse of its JODA record company, but gradually becoming entranced with both the culture and the music.

Set for release on a new co-owned label, JAD, Nash's own next album, *Hold Me Tight*, would have an inescapable rock steady flavor, while his meeting with Marley enflamed his enthusiasm even further. The Wailers signed with Nash and Sims' Cayman Music production company and, having imported a studio full of top American sessionmen, the pair set about recording the music which would, they believed, introduce the group to the American R&B market. Indeed, the build up to that breakthrough began in the studio itself — the group worked in full view of the top American label and studio heads who Nash and Sims had flown in for the occasion.

The tapes were then taken to New York to be overdubbed with all the strings, horns and accouterments which the US soul market then demanded, before an international record deal was sought out — which, unfortunately, is where the scheme went awry. Just one single was released from the sessions, a rerecording of "Bend Down Low" (c/w "Mellow

Mood"), credited to Bob Marley Plus Two in Jamaica (where WIRL handled the release) and "Bob, Rita & Peter" in the US and elsewhere (on JAD).

Other recordings, including remakes of such Coxsone-era classics as "How Many Times," "There She Goes" and "Put It On," remained unreleased for several years to come. However, the experience not only reinvigorated the Wailers, it also reshaped them. For the first time, they had recorded in an international fashion, subverting their natural rebelliousness (musical and cultural) for the sake of, if not a greater good, at least a more commercial one. Years later Chris Blackwell, still charting the band's development from his offices in London, drew upon that subversion as he bid to ensure Bob Marley's superstardom. In the meantime, however, the group still had one more set of hoops to jump through.

The Nash/Sims recordings were undoubtedly proficient, but they were also — by the Wailers' own standards — bland. Some of Marley's greatest love songs developed from those sessions, but they did so at the expense of the social, political and, increasingly, religious commentaries for which he was also renowned.

A song like "Selassie Is the Chapel," a Rastafarian variation on the country song "Crying in the Chapel" which the Wailers recorded with Mortimer Planno in summer, 1968, could never have been considered at the Nash/Sims sessions. Nor could the incredible treble-entendre of "Tread Oh," recorded in early 1969 with its composer, Livingston, now back on board. Livingston himself insists the song is a hymn to Jah. Others, however, can look at the lyrics and assign the song firmly to the stable of not-so-subtle sexual epics which were simultaneously so fashionable on the local scene.

The appearance of these songs within the Wailers' live set, and as one-off pressings for sound system use, reassured the group's audience that their true focus remained unchanged. So did the band's swiftly enacted awareness of the latest shift in the Jamaican musical climate, as rock steady shifted out of focus, to be supplanted by a new dance and discipline, the reggae.

Again, it was a development which Nash and Sims might never have comprehended, and it can be regarded as fortuitous indeed that, just as the Wailers themselves began to explore these areas, JAD Records began to scale back its operations. The group remained signed to the Cayman Music company, but they were given permission to record with whoever they wished, so long as the terms of the existing agreement were not broken.

Initially, the Wailers' ambition remained still-born. A November, 1969, session with Dutch-born producer Ted Prouder went nowhere; neither did a date with Errol Thompson. Attempts to produce themselves, too, were largely unproductive, although they did turn up "Trouble on the Road," recorded with a rhythm section comprising Lloyd Brevett (bass) and Hugh Malcolm (drums), and a version of the US band the Box Tops' US pop hit "The Letter," retitled (from its opening line) "Give Me a Ticket."

A brief liaison with Bunny Lee enabled a remake of the Studio One era "Mr Talkative," retitled "Mr Chatterbox" and dedicated to the rising star of Niney Holness. Another Lee production, "Hold onto this Feeling," debuted a new Wailers label, Tuff Gong, during summer, 1970 — although performed by the group, it was credited to "Bob & Rita."

The Wailers' next sessions paired them with producer Leslie Kong to cut a dozen songs, including another unlikely cover, the Archies' "Sugar Sugar," Tosh's "Stop the Train" and "Soon Come," the gospel number "Go Tell It on the Mountain" and "Soul Shakedown." The band then moved on, launching what became their most sustained, and certainly their most successful, relationship since the halcyon days at Studio One, when they teamed up with Lee "Scratch" Perry.

BOB MARLEY VS LEE "SCRATCH" PERRY

Shortly after wrapping up the Kong sessions, the Wailers linked with Perry's studio band, the Upsetters, to record "Black Progress," a heavily stylized version of James Brown's "(Say It Loud) I'm Black and I'm Proud." Marley himself produced, while the single also marked the first time the "classic" 1970s incarnation of the Wailers recorded together, as Tosh, Livingston and Marley were joined by the Upsetters' rhythm section of Aston and Carlton Barrett.

The single was a success, and in August, 1970, the group approached Perry about renewing a relationship which had first sparked half a decade earlier, when Scratch was an engineer at Studio One. Since that time, his career had moved ahead by leaps and bounds, most recently peaking with a UK hit single, "The Return of Django." The Wailers were now relying on Perry to share some of the magic — and he wasn't about to let them down.

Their first single together, "My Cup," was an enormous local hit, to be succeeded by an even bigger one, "Duppy Conqueror." "Mr Brown" followed, and "Kaya" — a song which Marley later rerecorded as the title track of his 1978 hit album.

Initial releases were split between Perry's Upsetter label and Tuff Gong — again, however, the quagmire politics of the Kingston music industry served to stifle the nascent enterprise. By the time the Wailers and Perry turned their attention to recording the group's first album together, 1970's *Soul Rebel*, the Upsetter label alone was pumping out the band's singles, at the rate of one every couple of months. Into 1971, the Wailer/Scratch machine kept on turning, a string of often stupendous 45s — "Small Axe," "Soul Shakedown Party," Tosh's "Downpresser"—together with a second album, the shattering, and provocatively jacketed *Soul Revolution*. (It was accompanied upon release by the limited edition *Volume Two* dub collection.)

Meanwhile, Leslie Kong was planning to release a Wailers album of his own, drawn from the sessions the previous summer. Ten songs were selected for inclusion on a set which he intended calling *The Best of the Wailers*. The band were horrified, with Livingston pointedly warning Kong that in no way did the album represent the best work that the Wailers would ever do. However, if Kong believed that the band were sending him their best, that meant he himself didn't have long left to live. Kong laughed, shrugged the admonishment off and titled the album as he saw fit. Just one week after its release, on August 9, 1971, he suffered a fatal heart attack. Few people ignored Livingston's warnings again.

It was at this point that Johnny Nash came back into the Wailers' lives. He and Sims had liquidated their JAD operation, but their faith in Marley remained unbroken. When Nash was invited to Sweden to score the movie *Love Is Not a Game*, he immediately offered the singer a piece of the action and, that summer, Marley scooped up his family and prepared to relocate.

Their first stop was Delaware, where Marley's mother was to house her daughter-in-law and three children—Rita found work as a nurse in a local hospital. Marley himself then traveled on to Europe to join Nash. One impromptu souvenir of this outing is preserved on the *Songs of Freedom* box set, an acoustic medley of songs recorded in Marley's Stockholm hotel room by Nash's musical director, John "Rabbit" Bundrick.

While Marley joined Nash on a Swedish tour through summer, 1971, Sims was working to interest CBS (to whom Nash was now also contracted) in picking up the Wailers for the international market. The label agreed to at least listen to the group and, that fall, Tosh, Livingston and the Barrett brothers were flown in from Jamaica (where they had continued working with Perry, among others) and booked into the CBS Studios in London's Soho Square. There they cut backing tracks for Nash's own next album, laying down a few songs of their own in between times, before returning to Kingston.

A new series of sessions effortlessly picked up where the Lee Perry adventure had ended. The band line-up had shifted once more, the now settled core of Marley, Tosh and Livingston augmented by the Barrett brothers, harmonica player Lee Jaffe and organist Tyrone Downie, coaxed away from the Youth Professionals (one of the groups Tosh and Livingston moonlighted with while Marley was in Europe).

With Lee Perry engineering, the Wailers tore through a succession of bold new songs, "Lively Up Yourself," "Craven Choke Puppy," "Screw Face" and "Lick Samba." But the real revelation was "Trench Town Rock," a triumphant affirmation of the spirit which bound together the ghettos with which the Wailers so identified, an alternative national anthem for an entire culture.

"Trench Town Rock" topped the Jamaican chart for the next five months, catapulting the Wailers to a level of stardom they had never dreamed possible. Immediately, plans which had lain in abeyance for years suddenly burst forth—the Marleys' humble Soul Shack record store was abandoned to be replaced by the grandiose Tuff Gong Records on Kingston's Parade street.

Tuff Gong Productions, too, swung into action, unleashing a tide of new Wailers singles to compliment the flood still pouring out of the Upsetter vaults. And Marley's political ambitions finally crystallized when he was introduced to Michael Manley, leader of the populist People's National Party, and a candidate for Prime Minister in the forthcoming Jamaican elections.

Manley had long fascinated Marley—it was he who arranged Haile Selassie's visit to Jamaica in 1966 (while Marley was in America), to affirm the Rastafarian faith at a time when more traditional political forces were doing their utmost to destroy it. Although many Rastafarians regarded politics with purist distrust, many more—Marley among them—acknowledged that Manley, at least, understood their life and lifestyle. When the electioneering PNP organized a Musical Bandwagon which blasted live music from the back of a flatbed truck as it drove through Jamaican neighborhoods, Bob and Rita Marley both came aboard.

The Wailers returned to London just as Nash's *I Can See Clearly Now* album was being prepared for release. Four Marley songs were included on the set—"Comma Comma," "Guava Jelly," "You Poured Sugar on Me" (co-written with Nash) and "Stir It Up," the latter in a flute-led mock-rock steady guise which lost no time in tearing up the UK charts.

The album's title track, too, was a major success, #5 in Britain and a quite unexpected #1 in the US, establishing the Wailers as the first Jamaican band ever to top the American chart (regardless of whether any of the record's purchasers were even aware of the fact). But even that was not enough to prompt CBS to pick up their own option on the group. The label released just one Wailers single, the Nash-produced "Reggae on Broadway."

The band accompanied Nash on a British tour during November/December, 1971, with the outing further highlighted by an unconventional 18 day mini-tour of British schools undertaken by Nash and Marley alone. Often visiting four establishments a day, the "show" featured 30 minutes of music and 30 more of a question and answer session.

The extraordinary bond which later developed between Marley and the British punk community of the mid-late 1970s, might well have had its roots in these early informal encounters.

The tour over, Nash traveled to the US to begin the promotional routine over again. The Wailers, however, remained in London, becoming increasingly desperate as the days passed. CBS had essentially washed their hands of the group and, with Danny Sims having joined Nash in New York, they did not even have the money to pay their airfare home.

Neither could they earn it — questions had arisen concerning their work permits (or lack thereof), meaning even occasional pub gigs were out of the question. There was also the matter of a large consignment of marijuana which had been intercepted by British customs en route from Jamaica. And just to compound the band's misery, it was the dead of winter.

THE ISLAND YEARS: 1972–73

Shortly before Christmas, 1971, Marley decided to pay Island Records chief Chris Blackwell a visit. The label's musical focus had long since shifted away from the imported ska and rock steady which once dominated its catalog, but Blackwell still commanded a great deal of respect in Jamaica. He was also the only person the Wailers knew, even by reputation, who might be able to help them out.

Marley had already prepared his introductory speech, intending to remind Blackwell that, though they had never met, their relationship dated back to 1962, when Island picked up the UK rights to both "Judge Not" and "One Cup of Coffee." In fact, Blackwell knew precisely who he was dealing with and, within days, had agreed not only to finance the band's return to Jamaica, he also advanced them eight thousand pounds to record an album for international release on Island.

In an arrangement hammered out some months later, Danny Sims (to whom the group was, of course, already contracted) received a further five thousand pounds, and the Wailers' publishing rights. Later in the decade, Sims rejoined Marley's inner circle as one of his most trusted advisers.

The group arrived home to find Kingston in turmoil. The general election was drawing closer, and Manley's PNP seemed certain to win — so much so that incumbent Prime Minister Hugh Shearer had instructed both the island's radio stations, JBC and RJR, to ban any record expressing even mild political sentiments, knowing full well that the music industry was solidly behind Manley, and was not shy of broadcasting that fact.

Delroy Wilson's "Better Must Come" had already been adopted as the PNP's campaign theme, while Clancy Eccles, Max Romeo and Junior Byles were only three of the many artists cutting unabashedly pro-Manley singles. Other bans lashed out at musicians who had shown support for Manley in other ways — the Wailers, tarred with the brush of the previous year's Musical Bandwagon, were naturally included.

The group responded by all but shutting down Tuff Gong, and not a single record was released on the label all year. Instead, the Wailers poured all their energies into their new album, and emerged with a disc of devastating power. Eleven songs were recorded for the set; nine were then sent to London for remixing and overdubbing by a group of English musicians captained by Rabbit Bundrick (from Johnny Nash's band). The remaining two songs, "High Tide or Low Tide" and "All Day All Night" remained unreleased until the mid-1990s.

Island's initial intention was to release the Wailers album on the Blue Mountain subsidiary, which had been maintaining a steady stream of reggae releases for the last two years. In the event, just one 45, "Baby Baby We've Got a Date," appeared on that label in early 1973. The main attraction, *Catch a Fire*, was switched to the parent label for release in the UK in December, 1972 (its US counterpart followed through Capitol in the new year).

From the moment of its release, *Catch a Fire* was heralded as the first genuine album in reggae history — a claim through which the Wailers were happy to allow pass unchallenged. Besides, in many ways, it was true. Island, after all, was firmly established among the very elite of UK record labels, in terms of both public and media perception. At least half a dozen of Britain's best-loved rock acts called the label home, while the company was almost addicted to high profile advertising and promotional campaigns. *Catch A Fire* might not have been the first reggae album ever released, but it was the first which the majority of people ever heard of, and, in the general marketplace, that amounted to much the same thing.

Tours of the UK and US were arranged, with the former kicking off in early spring; meanwhile, Island was calling for a second album to be launched upon the world that fall. Barely had they completed their debut, then, than the band was back in the studio working on the follow-up.

There was no shortage of material. All three founding Wailers were prolific writers, while they also had a decade long back-catalog which was all but unknown outside of their homeland. *Reincarnated Souls*, as the group intended titling this latest album, included revisions of "Put It On," "Duppy Conqueror" and "Small Axe" — reincarnations indeed.

The glue which held the album together, however, were those songs which, today, read like snapshots of Trench Town circa 1973, "Get Up Stand Up," co-written by Marley and Tosh; "Burnin' And Lootin'," from which the finished album took its eventual title of *Burnin'*, and "I Shot the Sheriff," the song which hastened Marley's superstardom without him having to lift another finger. Recorded with new keyboard player Earl "Wire" Lindo, *Burnin'* was completed less than a month before the band was scheduled to return to Britain.

The Wailers' first UK tour was a 90 day outing which ricochetted between London pubs, provincial theaters and West Indian dance halls, without even a road manager to ease the transition from a Kingston circuit one could walk around, to the rat's nest of highways and service stations through which the Wailers were expected to negotiate their hired van. The novelty of a new land swiftly wore off; the virtual impossibility of finding food they even recognized, let alone wanted to eat, compounded their dissatisfaction.

There were deeper problems, however. For a decade, the Wailers had been a three way split between its founding members. Each had his strengths, each had his weaknesses, but when they stood together, they were one. Now, however, that one-ness was shattering as the Wailers, who had already given so much to the rock marketplace, were now expected to make one more concession to their new audience, and provide it with a single, clear-cut frontman, a "band leader." And the audience had clearly decided who that was to be.

Already, if Island Records wanted a decision made by the group, it was Marley to whom they turned. Journalists, too, invariably sought him out as the focal and vocal point of the band. No longer the Wailers, suddenly they were Bob Marley *and* the Wailers.

Attempting to stem the tide, with which Marley himself felt as uncomfortable as his bandmates, the group insisted that the full band's portraits should appear on the jacket of their next album. Island conceded, but the victory was fleeting. No sooner had the Wailers returned to Kingston than Livingston announced that henceforth, he was a Wailer in Jamaica only. He would continue to record with the band and play local shows, but he would never tour again.

Joe Higgs, the tenement vocal coach who had been so instrumental in the Wailers' very formation, was recruited to replace Livingston for the American tour. It was a mixed affair, which alternated between audiences who knew exactly what they were in store for, and those who simply wanted a night out and didn't have a clue what was happening. But Boston loved them, and so did New York, where the Wailers opened for local hero Bruce Springsteen at Max's Kansas City and managed to tame even his fiercely partisan audience.

Their own club dates completed, the Wailers now set off on a 17 date tour opening for Sly & The Family Stone. Four days into the outing, in Las Vegas, they were sacked. Making their own way to San Francisco, the Wailers played the first of two final scheduled engagements, a KSAN radio broadcast which highlighted material from both *Catch a Fire* and the forthcoming *Burnin'*, then looked forward to songs earmarked for the future.

Higgs, horrified by the apparent disorganization of the outing, headed home immediately after, leaving the remaining Wailers to fly 1,000 miles in the opposite direction, to appear at an Ethiopian Famine Relief Fund benefit in Edmonton, Canada. Then they, too, returned home, before departing again for the UK in mid-November.

Set amid a bitter English winter, this was the Wailers' final tour. Just eleven dates out, in Northampton on November 30, the long simmering dispute over the band's direction and leadership finally burst into the open. Tosh and Marley came to blows, a battle which ended with Tosh announcing he was quitting the band on the spot. Earl Lindo, too, was leaving; he had recently been asked to join American bluesman Taj Mahal's band, and had decided to accept the invitation. The rest of the tour was cancelled, and the Wailers returned to Jamaica in shreds.

BREAKTHROUGH: 1974–75

Despite the apparent permanence of the split, the Marley, Livingston and Tosh reconvened just six months after the Northampton meltdown, opening for the visiting Marvin Gaye at Kingston's Carib Theater in May, 1974. The event was a fund raising benefit for a new sports center.

Hardly surprisingly, their set concentrated on familiar material, with just one new song on display. "Roadblock" was written in direct response to the nightmare which had descended upon Kingston in the first months of the year. The political divides which had scarred the country's government during the decade so far had now widened into a military divide and, as civil war loomed, so the ghettos became the most likely battleground.

The army patrolled Kingston enforcing a six P.M. curfew, emergency legislation promised life imprisonment to anybody found carrying an unlicensed gun, and and random roadblocks were established throughout Kingston and its environs. Marley himself was caught up in one just weeks after before the Carib show; "Roadblock" was his response. Timely and provocative, the song rewarded him with what looked like becoming his biggest hit since "Trench Town Rock."

Retitled "Rebel Music (3 O'Clock Roadblock)" was the first test of the new look Wailers. Marley had long since resolved to retain the band name, but this time, there was no question as to whose Wailers they were. "Roadblock" was recorded with the Barrett brothers and 16 year old organist Bernard Harvey alone, and was released by Tuff Gong in late May.

Strangely, at a time when even popular movies were banned from the theaters for fear of the trouble they might incite, "Roadblock" was not officially prohibited from radio play. Neither of Jamaica's radio stations, JBC and RJR, were willing to take a chance on playing it, however, and if Marley had not taken matters into his own hands, the most popular record of the year might have become the least heard.

Instead, he stopped by the JBC offices and, accompanied by two young juvenile offenders whom he introduced as convicted murderers he was trying to reform, he demanded a summit meeting with whichever disc jockeys were on the premises that day. Whether it was Marley's words, or his friends' bats and knives which had the greatest impact will never be known. But from that day on, "Roadblock" wasn't simply played, it saturated the airwaves, and wound up topping the Jamaican chart all summer long.

It was followed by "Knotty Dread," the projected title track of Marley's next album, and one of his most fulfilled compositions. The song was dedicated to the Rasta philosopher Countryman, a close friend of Marley's and the epitome of the jungle rasta, unkempt and wild, at one with nature and a bogeyman to smart city people, who were convinced he was waiting to make off with their children, to convert them into creatures just like him.

It was a role which Marley both respected and envied. From his hidden lair in the mountains, visions of Knotty haunted Babylon, his very existence an act of irrevocable psychic terrorism. It was a vision, however, which never reached his international audience — without Marley even being consulted on the matter, Island Records changed the album title to *Natty Dread*. The singer, however, did not raise a fuss. In London, as in Jamaica, the money men always got what they wanted in the end. (They got Countryman as well — in 1982, his lifestyle, at least, formed the basis for the excellent Chris Blackwell-produced movie *Countryman*.)

The bulk of the new Wailers album was recorded in Jamaica. It was completed, however, in London, with American funk rock guitarist Al Anderson completing the band line-up. Release was delayed as Marley and Island negotiated a new contract but, if there were any concerns that a year out of the spotlight had diminished the singer's star, the success of Eric Clapton's cover of "I Shot the Sheriff" swiftly dispelled them.

Taken from the rock legend's *461 Ocean Boulevard* comeback album, the song climbed to #9 in Britain and, like "I Can See Clearly Now" before it, #1 in America. But whereas Marley's involvement in Johnny Nash's hit had passed by unnoticed, this time his authorship created almost as many headlines as Clapton's performance itself. By the time a firm, early 1975, release date was set for *Natty Dread*, the anticipation was almost palpable.

SMILE JAMAICA: 1975-76

Everywhere one looked, Marley was gearing up for a major push forward. As part of his new arrangement with Island,

Tuff Gong had taken over the parent label's old headquarters in uptown Kingston. He had employed his first full-time manager, Don Taylor (b 2/10/43; d 11/1/99), who had been Marvin Gaye's road manager during the American's Jamaican visit the previous year. And he had confirmed the line-up of the Wailers — the rock solid backing of Al Anderson, the returning Tyrone Downie and the Barrett brothers, augmented by the soulful harmonies of the I-Threes — Rita Marley, Marcia Griffiths and Judy Mowatt. And he finally found a way around Jamaican radio's continued conservatism, by arranging for Tuff Gong itself to sponsor its own 15 minute show.

Marley also took on his first ever outside production job, when he agreed to work with white American rock singer Martha Velez on her *Escape from Babylon* album. Recorded with the full Wailers ensemble, including the I-Threes, Bernard Harvey and the Zap Pow Horns, and with Lee Perry earning a co-production credit, *Escape from Babylon* featured three Marley compositions — "Stand Alone" (retitled "There You Are"), "Bend Down Low," "Hurting Inside" (retitled "Happiness"), plus the Marley-Tosh classic "Get Up Stand Up," and a fifth song co-written with Velez, "Disco Night." The set was not a commercial success, but that was not necessarily the point of the exercise. Marley was already a proven singer-songwriter. Now he wanted to show the world everything else he was capable of.

The Wailers' US tour commenced in June, 1975. It, too, was a point of pride for Marley — the band had been invited to open the West Coast leg of the Rolling Stones latest tour, but turned the opportunity down, convinced it was better to tour the clubs as headliners, than to play arenas at the foot of the bill. The Stones respected the decision, too; when the Wailers played the LA Roxy, the group was there to see them perform.

From California, the Wailers flew to England, where *Natty Dread* had reached #43 on the chart. There, the second of their two London Lyceum shows was recorded for the *Live* album, and released just weeks later. It peaked at #38, while spinning off the epic "No Woman No Cry" single. That made #22 in September, 1975, pushed by a performance made all the more anthemic by the mass, and totally impromptu, audience sing-along which accompanied the band. In Jamaica, it was joined on the chart by "Jah Live," a heartfelt lament for the recently (August 22, 1975) deceased Haile Selassie. Released by Tuff Gong and credited to the mysterious Hugh Peart, there was no question that it was actually Marley and the Wailers.

In November, the original Wailers came together once more, this time at a benefit for the Jamaican Institute for the Blind, co-headlined by Stevie Wonder. Their performance was short, and little more than a prelude to a full set by the current incarnation of the Wailers, itself highlighted by the onstage appearance of Wonder for a jam through "Superstition" and "I Shot the Sheriff." The impact of the Marley-Tosh-Livingston act, however, could not and would not be suppressed — as the concert finally wound down at four A.M., the trio returned to the stage for what proved the very last time. Fittingly, they went with "Rude Boy."

Work on the next Wailers album continued across fall, 1975, and into the new year, as both the line-up and the sound were changed. Al Anderson had quit to join Peter Tosh's band, and was replaced by both rhythm guitarist Earl "Chinna" Smith, of Kingston sessions veterans the Soul Syndicate, and, in an hitherto unprecedented concession to the sonic requirements of a "rock" audience, American-born lead guitarist Don Kinsey, a member of Island label-mates White Lightning.

Kinsey joined the band in March, 1976, in Miami, where they were mixing the new album — not at all coincidentally the same studio (Criterion) that Eric Clapton had utilized for "I Shot the Sheriff." Kinsey added his searing rock leads to almost every track on the record, an unsettling intrusion for Marley (and reggae)'s hardcore fans, but the universal panacea which his backers required. Released in May, *Rastaman Vibration* peaked at #15 in the UK and #8 in America, where the single "Roots Rock Reggae" also climbed to #51.

Mammoth, massively over-subscribed tours of the US and Europe followed, further confirming the Wailers' status as the new heroes of the suddenly enlarged world of rock'n'roll. But when the group returned to Kingston in September, it was to plunge back into precisely the same seething cauldron they'd left behind six months earlier, except now there was another general election just around the corner.

Throughout the city, there were few doubts as to where Marley's political sympathies lay. He had, after all, ranked among the PNP's most visible supporters in 1972, and news that the Wailers intended staging a massive free concert in Kingston's National Heroes Park on December 5 made it apparent that his opinion had not changed since that time. Days after Marley's announcement, PM Manley confirmed that the election itself would take place on December 20, thus inexorably twinning the two events in the public mind.

In fact, Marley had no intention whatsoever of endorsing either candidate. Like the rest of Jamaica's Rastafarian community, he felt betrayed by Manley's failure to legalize marijuana, while he was also incensed by the continued censorship which dictated the nature of Jamaican radio — three of the Wailers' own recent singles had received radio bans, "War," "Rat Race" and "Who the Cap Fits." If the concert — dubbed "Smile Jamaica," and celebrated by a new Wailers single of the same name — had any political pur-

pose, it was to unify the warring parties on the streets. The question was, did the parties want to be unified?

On December 3, two days before the concert, two cars burst onto the grounds of the Wailers' Hope Road headquarters. One blocked the main gate, as the other pulled up in front of the house. Six armed men piled out, two stood guard, while their companions began shooting wildly into the house. Trying to escape with the children through a side door, a bullet grazed Rita Marley's head. Inside, manager Don Taylor was hit five times in the side and leg; Marley was hit once, by a bullet which grazed his sternum.

For two days, the fate of the concert hung in the balance. As the day itself dawned, nobody knew whether it would take place. The Wailers themselves were still in hiding, scattered across Kingston. Marley was deeply shaken; his wife lay in hospital with a bullet fragment lodged between her scalp and skull; his manager was airlifted to Miami and lay in intensive care with a bullet lodged in his spinal cord. The crowds which converged on the venue that day did so more out of a sense of solidarity, than any real hopes of seeing a show.

Peter Tosh, Bunny Wailer (as Bunny Livingston now called himself) and Burning Spear, all of whom had agreed to perform at Smile Jamaica, withdrew from the bill with just hours to go. When Third World, the afternoon's other scheduled performers, arrived at the park, it was to discover the entire place in chaos, a crowd of 80,000 people held in place only by the sandstorm of rumors descending upon them. On the spot, they decided to play a set, relaying reports on the crowd and their reception back to the still sequestered Marley. When he heard that the show had gone off without a hitch, he made his decision — the concert was on.

Still heavily bandaged, and with Rita still clad in her nightgown and hospital robe, Marley took the stage and announced they would play just one song, "War." In fact they played five, following through with "Trench Town Rock," "Rastaman Vibration," "Want More" and "So Jah Seh." The following morning, Marley left Jamaica for Chris Blackwell's home in Nassau, in the Bahamas. His family joined him the following day, his band the following week. They did not return to Jamaica for more than a year. The assailants, on the other hand, were never caught or even identified.

The PNP won the election.

EXODUS: 1977–78

The Wailers remained in Nassau for the next month, moving onto London in January, 1977, to begin work on their next album — the first time they had recorded outside of Jamaica since the Johnny Nash sessions six years earlier.

Don Kinsey had quit the band, returning to the US in

the aftermath of the shootings. He was replaced by Jamaican born and London raised guitarist Junior Marvin, leader of the blues rock band Hanson, but whose credits also included stints alongside Stevie Wonder, Billy Preston and T-Bone Walker. Like his predecessors in the Wailers, he came recommended by Chris Blackwell, unlike them, he played with a tight, economic style which lent itself perfectly to the new music fermenting in Marley's mind.

Exodus the album, but more crucially the song, grew directly out of the Wailers' recent experiences, both the personal nightmare of the shooting and the cultural horror of the homeland they had left behind. Throughout the album's gestation, too, the band listened closely to the music which continued to document Jamaica's suffering.

The previous year, Marley stated that his next album would be a dub set; that idea (sadly) never came to fruition. Even as he spoke those words, though, the Jamaican music scene was changing once again, regenerating itself, so that as one generation of bands — the Wailers, of course, but also Third World and Inner Circle — embraced the new sound of international reggae, another emerged from within the domestic cataclysm which their predecessors were escaping.

But it was a darker, heavier, angrier generation than its forebears had ever been, hallmarked by records like Culture's "Two Sevens Clash" and Junior Murvin's "Police And Thieves," heavy roots releases concerned with both an armageddon to come, and that which was already taking place. Even more remarkably, that same mood was translating on an international scale.

Britain, in 1977, was in the thrall of punk rock, a musical movement which valued militancy above any other attribute, and a cultural milieu whose hatred of the establishment was something which Marley identified with immediately — for what was the Babylon of Rastafarian lore if not that same establishment? The almost symbiotic link which later histories detected between punk and reggae was born from those two correlations and it was, indeed, no mere accident that the best of the UK punk acts, were those whose own musical educations had included a healthy immersion in the waters of the Caribbean.

Marley's own greatest contribution to the punky-reggae party was a song titled precisely that. Midway through the album sessions, Lee "Scratch" Perry arrived in London to produce the new single by one of the most fervent punk-reggae crossover acts, the Clash.

Entranced by their ideology and intrigued by their own fascination with the music (they had even recorded a version of "Police and Thieves," the original of which Perry produced) Scratch lost no time in relating his experiences to Marley, and the pair immediately went into the studio to record their own tribute. The marathon, ten minute "Punky

Reggae Party" featured backing from the British reggae band Aswad and the visiting Third World and, though it was to be several months more before an edited six minute version was released in Britain, Jamaican Tuff Gong pressings were on the streets of London within weeks.

More than twenty new songs were recorded for the new album — ten appeared there, while ten more were held back for the Wailers' next album, *Kaya*. Others still were salted away as b-sides (the spellbinding "Roots"), stockpiled for Jamaica-only 45s ("Rastaman Live Up," "Blackman Redemption" and Rita Marley's solo "A Jah Jah") or remained unreleased for years to come.

Introspection hung heavy over the sessions. "Natural Mystic," "One Love," "Satisfy My Soul," "Sun Is Shining," "Kaya" and "Keep on Moving" were all drawn from Marley's back catalog, while new songs dealt with the assassination attempt and Marley's refusal to be cowed by the bullies. But it was the title track, eight minutes of slow burning rhythm and a clarion call for Jah's people to reinherit their African homeland, which dominated, spiritually as much as musically.

Exodus was the Wailers' masterpiece, and was instantly proclaimed as such. When *Kaya* was released the following year, even the knowledge that it had been conceived in tandem with its predecessor did not prevent fans and critics alike from hammering it.

Exodus was not, after all, simply a musical triumph. Time and place, too, conspired with its genius. In Jamaica, it dominated the airwaves for much of the rest of the year; in Britain, it spawned three hit singles during 1977 alone (and a fourth in 1980), and broke the band into the Top 10 album chart for the first time; in the US, it readily consolidated *Rastaman Vibration*'s success. *Exodus* was the peak of the Wailers' development, now they needed only to consolidate it.

Tours of Europe and the US naturally followed the album's release, but early into the former, during an impromptu soccer match between the Wailers' crew and a team of French journalists, a rough tackle damaged a toe Marley had already injured once before, under similar circumstances in Trench Town. A French doctor examined the wound and recommended Marley stay off his feet for a few weeks, but of course that was not possible. The tour continued and so did the soccer games, and the wound simply refused to heal. Some nights, Marley took his right boot off to find his sock soaked through with blood and the toe livid with infection. Finally, with the pain now so acute that he could barely walk, he visited a foot specialist.

The diagnosis was appalling. Melanoma cancer cells were detected in the wound, and the only even halfway sure cure was amputation of the toe and part of the foot. An alternative course of action involved removing part of the toe and some adjacent flesh, and hoping that the disease had not spread further. Either option necessitated canceling the American tour.

Seeking a second opinion in the US, Marley then opted for the second course of treatment. The operation was carried out at Miami's Cedars of Lebanon hospital — the same hospital that saved Don Taylor's life following the shooting. Within two months, he had apparently made a full recovery, two months later, he was out playing soccer again.

Heavily remixed from the original London tapes, *Kaya* was released in March, 1978, towards the end of Marley's convalescence. He had finally returned to Jamaica that same month, and immediately threw himself into preparations for a concert intended both to compensate for the lost opportunity of Smile Jamaica, and to prove his still passionate belief that the island could find peace.

Indeed, the Peace Concert, as it became known, was even more important now than Smile Jamaica could ever have been. Kingston remained in a state of martial lawlessness. Neither curfews nor a renewed zero tolerance approach to unlicensed fire arms could prevent the carnage, while an official Peace Movement, established under the auspices of the Rastafarian Twelve Tribes organization, could offer little more than conciliatory rhetoric.

It was the Twelve Tribes who first approached Marley and, initially, he was uncertain how he could help. Convinced that the attempt of his life had been orchestrated from within the opposition JLP party; convinced, too, that they and the PNP existed for no reason other than to fight one another, his initial instinct was to stay out of the fray altogether. The involvement of the Twelve Tribes swayed him, however (Marley had been a member of the organization for several years). He agreed to headline the concert.

Officially billed as a commemoration of the twelfth anniversary of Haile Selassie's state visit to Jamaica, the concert took place April 22, 1978. The itinerary featured virtually every key act of the time: Althea & Donna, Dennis Brown, Culture, Dillinger, Bongo Herman, the Meditations, the Mighty Diamonds, LeRoy Smart, Trinity, Junior Tucker, Beresford Hammond, Inner Circle, Ras Michael & The Sons of Negus and Peter Tosh.

It was a triumphant show from the outset, but the finale exceeded anybody's expectations. Drawing their set largely from *Exodus*, but climaxing with an impassioned "War," Marley then launched into "One Love," and the invitation for Michael Manley and Edward Seaga to join him on stage.

Seaga appeared first — Manley, whose distrust of his opponents extended so far as to consider the Peace Movement itself a cynical JLP trick, moved more slowly. But finally he, too, appeared on the stage and, before the gaze not only of the enraptured audience, but TV and film cameras from around the world, Marley grabbed both mens' hands and held them above his head. Later, he is said to have told a friend that he should then have killed them both.

SURVIVAL: 1978–80

Despite its lukewarm critical welcome, *Kaya* never looked anything less than a major hit — it reached #4 in Britain in March, 1978, and topped the charts across Europe. The single "Is This Love," too, was enormous, its British #9 placing equalling 1977's "Jamming"'s career-best peak. "Satisfy My Soul," later in the summer, climbed to #21 and again, the accompanying tour sold out everywhere.

American record sales were less encouraging — the album stalled at #50 — but again, ticket sales were impressive, climaxing with a sell-out show at Madison Square Garden. It was the same story across Europe, where shows in London, Paris, Copenhagen and Amsterdam were recorded for a new live album, *Babylon By Bus*. (It replaced a previously scheduled LP taped in London in 1977.) Sessions with Lee Perry at Black Ark during a break in the touring itinerary, however, would not see the light of day for another two decades — "Who Colt the Game" and "I Know a Place" finally appeared on the 1998 Perry compilation *Lost Treasures of the Ark*.

Following the tour, Marley visited Ethiopia. He had been trying to obtain a visa since 1976, only to be stymied by the on-going war with Somalia — the difficulties were finally smoothed out by an old friend from Kingston, Alan Cole, now coach of the Ethiopian Olympic soccer team.

The visit was intended as both a religious and a cultural pilgrimage, but inevitably it became a political one as well, as Marley finally came face to face with the continental African homeland he had long dreamed of, as it continued to try and shake away the last remaining shreds of its colonial past.

"Zimbabwe," a song from Marley's next album, the provisionally titled *Black Survival*, was written during this trip, after Marley attended a massive rally in the Ethiopian capital, Addis Ababa, in support of the liberation movement whose land the minority white government still called Rhodesia. The song was swiftly adopted as an anthem by both the ZANLA and ZIPRA freedom fighters, and provoked cover versions from musicians across west Africa.

The Wailers' own first Jamaican single of 1979, "Ambush," meanwhile, described the nations where that liberation had already taken place, only for rival black parties to renew the fighting among themselves. A third song, "Africa Unite," called for those conflicts, too, to be resolved.

If Marley's outlook had been broadened by his African visit, elsewhere his attention seemed to become increasingly focused inward. His friends spoke of dark moods and a melancholy which they had never previously witnessed; his temper was short, and he seemed increasingly ready to use his fists.

There were, of course, any number of reasons for him to be feeling despondent. The Peace Concert had failed, and in parts of Kingston, the violence was worse than it had ever been. Friends were dying, or falling apart. The sessions for *Black Survival* (or *Survival* as it ultimately became) were taking longer than he wanted, with even the simplest tasks suddenly becoming mountainous problems.

The future itself loomed uncertain — Marley's Island Records contract was drawing close to its end, and it was by no means certain that he wanted to re-sign. His faith in manager Don Taylor was slipping, and more and more he was turning to Danny Sims, his publisher since the Johnny Nash days, for advice. But whatever was disturbing Marley's equilibrium seemed deeper seated than any of these things, to be welling up from deep within him. Friends thought it might be the cancer drugs he was still taking. They later realized that it was the cancer itself.

For the time being, Marley continued working. In July, 1979, the Wailers appeared at both Reggae Sunsplash and the Festival of Unity at Harvard University, a benefit for various African liberation forces. In October, with the ferociously militant *Survival* album finally on the streets (it made #20 in the UK, #70 in America), the band launched their latest US tour at the Harlem Apollo, playing 47 shows in 49 days. Marley spent much of the tour in a state of near-total exhaustion, however, often cancelling interviews because he simply didn't have the energy. By the time the tour reached San Francisco in late November, he was openly admitting that something was seriously wrong.

But still, his workload did not lighten. 1980 was set to bring another general election to Jamaica, and Marley intended to absent himself from the country for as much of the year as possible. He had already begun writing a new album, *Uprising*, which he intended recording in London. He now demanded a world tour which would truly cover the globe — Europe, Asia, North and South America, before closing in Africa.

In fact, the year opened on that continent too, as the Wailers flew to Gabon to perform for President Omar Bongo's birthday party, while the *Uprising* sessions, once they got underway, seemed intent on retaining the spirit of Africa. It was, perhaps, inevitable that when Rhodesia/Zimbabwe proclaimed its independence on April 17, the Wailers were invited to perform at the official ceremony.

Uprising was released in May, 1980; the following month the ambitiously scheduled and grandiosely titled Tuff Gong Uprising tour got underway in Zurich. By the time the European leg was complete, just six weeks later, the Wailers

had performed before one million people in twelve different countries.

That outing complete, Marley then flew to Miami to await the launch of the American dates. The remainder of the band returned to Jamaica for a time, but when Marley suggested joining them there, he was swiftly dissuaded. Danny Sims had learned, apparently from sources within the CIA, that conservative forces within Jamaican politics remained extremely hostile towards Marley, and that even the suggestion that the singer favored the PNP in the upcoming election would have dire consequences. Marley never saw Jamaica again.

The Wailers rejoined the singer in Miami, in August, to begin rehearsals for the American tour. They found him in high spirits — Stevie Wonder's latest single, "Master Blaster," was a blatant tribute to Marley, performed to a fiery reggae beat. But when the Master Blaster himself sat down to play one day, his breath rattled and he coughed continually. He admitted to a constant headache, and pain in his throat, but he also claimed he'd just had a complete physical check-up and came through with flying colors. The tour got underway as scheduled. Less than a week later on September 20, while jogging through New York's Central Park, Marley suffered a seizure and collapsed.

The following day, while the band flew on to the next show in Pittsburgh, Marley visited a New York neurologist. The diagnosis came back almost immediately. His collapse had been caused by a stroke; X-rays and a brain scan revealed an enormous brain tumor. Marley's response was to take the next flight out to Pittsburgh, to play the final show of his life. Indeed, he wanted the tour to continue until the bitter end, but Rita finally put her foot down. Two days after the Pittsburgh show, on September 23, the tour was officially cancelled. Marley, it was said, was suffering from exhaustion.

The last months of Marley's life were spent in treatment. Undergoing further tests in Miami, he discovered he was also suffering from lung cancer. Later, stomach cancer was added to his burden. Chemo-therapy stripped him of flesh and his hair; the brain tumor left him paralyzed from the waist down and on November 4, he was baptized into the Ethiopian Orthodox Church.

Against so many odds, Marley rallied. On November 9, he was admitted into the renowned Issels Clinic in the Bavarian Alps, certain to die within days. Instead, he fought back. THX, a drug prohibited in the US, but proven effective elsewhere around the world, helped him regain his strength. Spending hours on the telephone, he threw himself back into the Tuff Gong operation and, on February 2, celebrated his 36th birthday, surrounded by family, friends and bandmates. When, in early May, Dr Issel confided to Marley's mother that her son had no more than two weeks to live, Marley himself shrugged the news away and called the doctor a madman.

Nevertheless, he did not protest when he was flown back to Miami on May 9, nor did he complain over the next two days, before he slipped into unconsciousness for the last time. He died at 11:45 A.M. on May 11, 1981.

AFTERWARDS

With the government pledging a state funeral, Marley's body returned to Jamaica on May 19, two days beforehand. His body lay in state at the National Arena and, the following morning, the first funeral observances were held the following morning at the Ethiopian Orthodox Church on Maxfield Avenue. From there a massive motorcade returned the coffin to the National Arena.

A live presentation by the Wailers included performances by Marley's mother and half-sister Pearl Livingston and the I-Threes, before the funeral service itself began. His body was then driven the 55 miles to its final resting place at Nine Miles, a white mausoleum built alongside the house where Marley grew up. An estimated 12,000 people packed the Arena; many thousands more lined the route to St Ann.

Tributes to Marley piled up around the world. In Jamaica itself, Sunsplash was dedicated to his memory — 16 years later, the festival would itself end its days in St Ann's during Bob Marley Week, a festival established to observe what would have been the singer's birthday. That event was first celebrated in 1982, with a concert again featuring the Wailers, the I-Threes and Cedella Booker, plus Ziggy Marley and the Melody Makers.

Tuff Gong sprang back into operation, not only overseeing Rita and the Melody Makers' careers, but also organizing the first in a steady stream of authorized Bob Marley compilations; unauthorized ones, drawing in the main from the Leslie Kong/Lee Perry sessions, began appearing within weeks of his death. Of the Tuff Gong issues, the *Legend* hits collection is far and away the biggest selling album ever by a Jamaican artist.

The Wailers band, too, continued. With a core of the Barretts and Wire Lindo, they toured in support of *Legend* and have remained a going concern, even surviving the death of Carlton Barrett (murdered by his wife and her lover, 4/17/87). Coinciding with the 20th anniversary of Marley's death, their US tour in early spring, 2001, was as popular as any they have played.

In addition to music, Marley himself has been celebrated on several postage stamps — the first "pop" musician ever to be thus honored, while 2001 saw the opening of a temporary Bob Marley museum on the *Queen Mary* ocean liner, moored at Long Beach, CA.

ANNOTATED DISCOGRAPHY

7 Best of the Wailers (Beverley's — JA) 1971

Its ill-starred name, an uninspiring track listing and the redundant recycling of its contents over a thousand rip-off compilations have blackened this album's reputation enough. In its original form, strong performances, a number of excellent songs and some genuinely unexpected arrangements ("Sugar Sugar") conspire with a sparkling Kong production to all but vindicate the choice of title.

7 Soul Rebel (Trojan — UK) 1970
8 Soul Revolution (Upsetter — JA) 1972
8 Soul Revolution Part 2 (Upsetter — JA) 1972

The band's American influences shine vividly through both Perry-produced albums, with *Soul Revolution* just shading its predecessor in terms of all round brilliance. Amazingly, Trojan originally passed on the Wailers' second Perry album, ultimately picking it up in 1972 and retitling it *African Herbsman*, after the Ritchie Havens cover of the same name. Curtis Mayfield's "Keep on Moving" was also a highlight. But it was also a distinctly Jamaican album, far more so than either of its predecessors, an hypnotic roar of ghetto belligerence which hypnotized everyone who heard it. *Part Two* offers dub versions of the album. Again, these albums' contents have been recycled way too often, but in their original form, the future rings clear.

7 Catch a Fire (Island) 1973

The band's habit of constantly revisiting their past sees "Stir It Up" make an unnecessary reappearance; the heart of the album lies in the songs which would remain in the Wailers' live repertoire — "Concrete Jungle" and "Slave Driver." The mix and production are unerringly aimed at a rock cross-over market, and little about this album captures the sonic mood of its predecessors. However, a two-CD "definitive edition" in 2001 adds the original Jamaican mix of the album alongside the familiar overdubbed version, and the progression (not to mention a number of very telling sonic variations) is evident to all.

7 Burning (Island) 1973

Again the chaff outweighs the classics, although with three undisputed gems on board, *Burnin'* is a difficult album to dismiss. "Burnin' and Lootin'" and (over-rated though it may be) "I Shot the Sheriff" became band benchmarks, "Rastaman Chant" a symbol of their sincerity. But "Get Up Stand Up" stands so tall above the company, and will climb even higher still. Reissued, remastered in 2001.

6 Natty Dread (Island) 1975

Hindsight, and his subsequent deification insist Marley never made a bad album, and that may be so. But over-produced and over-played, this was certainly a weak link in the chain, with only "Rebel Music (3 O'Clock Roadblock)" and the curiously understated "Talkin' Blues" truly escaping the gloss. Reissued, remastered in 2001.

8 Live! (Island) 1975

The Wailers were best experienced live, and even in truncated form, their set that night in London remains magical. The definitive "No Woman No Cry," of course, is a standout, but so are "Trenchtown Rock" and "Lively Up Yourself," while "Get Up Stand Up" closes the set with Day of Judgement fervor. Reissued, remastered in 2001.

8 Rastaman Vibration (Island) 1976

The Wailers' most deliberately rock album, a feature which cannot be placed at guitarist Kinsey's door alone; nor can it be used to downplay the album's strengths. "War," "Johnny Was" and "Positive Vibration" epitomize everything Marley had been working towards, and even the bad times are pretty damned good. Reissued, remastered in 2001.

10 Exodus (Island) 1977

If the CD age has one crime to answer for, it's that albums can no longer be split into two sides, two moods, that exist absolutely independently of one another. *Exodus* is one of those albums which suffers immeasurably from its translation to CD, its natural divisions of (natural) mystic night and (one) love-soaked day utterly lost by the seamless transition between the eight minute grind of "Exodus," closing side one, and the jaunty groove of "Jamming" kicking in at the start of side two. (Or maybe that's what the pause button's for?) Reissued, remastered in 2001 with a second disc of alternate/unissued and live material.

6 Kaya (Island) 1978

Enough of the songs on this album had previously appeared in the pre-Island days that, within weeks of its release, utterly spurious "greatest hits" albums were appearing, each boasting the international smashes "Easy Skanking," "The Sun Is Shining," "Satisfy My Soul." Few of the reworked versions actually improve on the originals, and the flashy mix and production lessened their power even further. It's a nice album. But nice isn't necessarily a compliment. Reissued, remastered in 2001.

7 Babylon By Bus live (Island) 1978

First off, don't listen to popular wisdom's insistence that the first *Live* album is the only one you need. The mood here may be more celebratory, the tension between artist, song and audience distilled by the band's worldwide emergence. But the singalongs are just as lusty, the pace is just as hot (too hot, sometimes; "Exodus" races by like a Ferrari) and, even if none of the songs improve on their studio counterparts, this was the only CD source for "Punky Reggae Party" for years. (It has since been added to *Exodus*.) Reissued, remastered in 2001.

7 Survival (Island) 1979

The most heartfelt of Marley's later albums, but a very transitional one, as he tried to adjust himself to his fame, without losing sight of his own goals. "So Much Trouble in the World" is the catchiest number; others, even the hits "Zimbabwe" and "Africa Unite," take a little longer to absorb. Reissued, remastered in 2001.

6 Uprising (Island) 1980

Little about this album provoked a ticker-tape parade at the time — despite its truly contagious hook, "Could You Be Loved" was Marley-by-numbers, while both "Pimper's Paradise" and "Work" could have done with a longer gestation. But then you hit "Redemption Song". . . and even before Marley died; before the truth of his illness became that well known, the song struck a chord of such immeasurable sadness that all was readily forgiven. Reissued, remastered in 2001.

BOB MARLEY: THE REMASTERED EDITIONS

Of the myriad ways in which the twentieth anniversary of Bob Marley's death could be commemorated, the wholesale reissue of the Wailers' Island Records catalog was perhaps the biggest no-brainer of the year. The chain of albums which stretched from *Catch a Fire* (1972) to *Survival* (1979), then continued on through some surprisingly intelligent out-takes, rarities and hits packages, isn't simply the most essential in reggae history, it is also one of the most critically lauded in all of modern music. And the CD versions which have been on the shelves since the 1980s have long been crying out for revitalization.

They've got it . . . almost. Of the albums under the microscope, three — "deluxe editions of *Catch a Fire, Exodus* and the *Legend* hits package — have been remastered and expanded to two-CD sets. (Single disc editions are also available.) The remainder, meanwhile, were similarly remastered and granted a bonus track or three. Of the albums in the first batch of reissues, *Burning* is bolstered by the b-side "Reincarnated Soul," plus two unreleased cuts, Tosh's "No Sympathy" and Livingston's "The Oppressed Song"; *Natty Dread* gains the funky "Am a Do," *Live* captures the UK b-side "Kinky Reggae"; *Rastaman Vibration* gains "Jah Lives." Little which hasn't been heard before, of course, but if the choices initially left a few collectors mumbling darkly, the sound quality is so far beyond anything Wailers' fans have heard before, that all other complaints are rendered petty by comparison.

You need ears, not words, to appreciate the improvements. But *Rastaman Vibration*, hitherto the sonic runt of the studio litter, bristles with new electricity, while *Live* finally sheds the slightly muffled feel which had bedeviled every release since the original vinyl. A few imperfections do still come through — some distortion around Marley's vocals is the most pronounced — but otherwise, at last, an album which has long been ranked among the greatest live records ever released, finally sounds as great as it was meant to.

The "deluxe editions," meanwhile, live up to that lofty (and oft-over-used) title with a vengeance. *Catch a Fire* is restored to the Zippo lighter cover which adorned the album on its original release, with a 28 page booklet packed with lyrics, pictures and journalist Richard Williams' notes on the record's birth. But it is the music which is the revelation. The familiar version of the album was remixed and overdubbed in London after the Wailers delivered it to Island — that album consumes disc two of this package. Disc one, however, transports the listener back to Harry J's studio, as the Wailers put the finishing touches to their own vision of the record, then settled down for the playback. The whisperers were right. It's sensational.

The differences aren't direct. You notice the loss of the later frills, the steel guitar and the keyboard fills; you notice, too, a track order revised to incorporate two unfamiliar songs, "High Tide or Low Tide" and "All Day All Night." But most of all you notice the booming depth of the rhythms, the ragged edges around the vocals, the scratchy feel of Peter Tosh's guitar, and the absolute absence of any concessions to an audience which didn't bleed reggae from its very soul.

Compared to the released version, it sounds rough and unmixed, and that can take some getting used to. But that's how the Wailers themselves sounded then, and if you line the album up alongside first, its Lee Perry and Leslie Kong produced predecessors, and then the increasingly slick productions which Marley would go on to make, you realize for the first time just what an injustice has been perpetrated, both to fans and the band itself, by the long unavailability of these recordings. History records the Wailers making a light year leap in sound and substance as they raced in pursuit of the dangling dollars. Reality makes it apparent that they didn't give a damn. Not at the outset, anyway.

The second deluxe edition, *Exodus* is less revelatory, but even more impressive. The sheer prolific nature of the album sessions is well-documented — both *Exodus* and the following year's *Kaya* album were recorded during this single period, together with a clutch of songs which have scarcely been seen since their 1978 release.

Spread across disc two, and topping up disc one, some remarkable gems are now restored to their historical home: "Roots," a *Rastaman Vibration* out-take released on the b-side of the UK "Waiting in Vain" single; an alternate take of "Waiting in Vain" itself; 12-inch and/or instrumental versions of "Jamming" and "Exodus"; unreleased mixes of "Keep on Moving" and its dub counterpart; the full 9 minute-plus version of "Punky Reggae Party" (plus its version b-side) and, finally, excitingly, five tracks recorded at the London Rainbow on June 4, 1977 — a show which was scheduled to become the Wailers' second live album (with

a Christmas, 1977, release date), before Marley opted instead for the *Babylon by Bus* set. The overall package is less cohesive than *Catch a Fire*, but in terms of intensity, power and value *Exodus* is peerless.

The *Legend* deluxe edition is the least immediately impressive, simply adding a second disc of the 12-inch remixes commissioned around the time of the album's release. In fact, many of these remain as enjoyable as the original versions, a surprising discovery for purist collectors, but a rewarding one. Anyone seeking an alternate overview, meanwhile, is directed towards *One Love: The Very Best of Bob Marley & The Wailers*, a 20 track compilation drawn from the entire remastered collection, with a couple of bonuses on board to tempt the collector — a band version of "Redemption Song" and, for the first time in anything more than medium fidelity, the 1977 Lee Perry production "I Know a Place."

SELECTED COMPILATIONS & ARCHIVE RELEASES

With several hundred LPs and CDs currently available, many of them offering little more than duplication of the same material, the following has been divided into six chronological sections, each detailing releases conforming to significant eras in Marley and the Wailers' recorded career: (i) Studio One, (ii) sessions 1967–70, (iii) Lee Perry productions, (iv) sessions 1971–73, (v) Island Records-era compilations and posthumous releases, (vi) tributes and remix collections.

This discography is designed with the specialist collector in mind. Anybody seeking a simple one-stop guide to Marley's entire ouvre should seek out the *Songs of Freedom* box set (detailed in part five).

THE WAILERS AT STUDIO ONE

8 Birth of a Legend (Epic) 1990

Originally released across two LPs (*Early Music* and *Birth of a Legend* in 1977, and subsequently as *Trenchtown Days* (Sony Legacy, 2001), the best single CD documentary of the period. Although the Heartbeat collections (below) duplicate most (but not all) of the contents, the emphasis here is on quality, not rarity.

9 One Love—At Studio One (Heartbeat) 1991
8 Destiny: Rare Ska Sides from Studio One (Heartbeat) 1999
8 Climb the Ladder (Heartbeat) 2000

The Wailers recorded well over 100 tracks with producer Coxsone Dodd, a full and chronological accounting of which would indeed be a wonder to behold. Until then, one double CD set (*One Love*) and two single discs just about wrap everything up, adding alternate/unreleased cuts to the expected numbers, but swerving from year to year with little regard for the finer details. There is no quibbling with the quality within, however, with excellent sound and informative liner notes further bolstered by the use of original session tapes, as opposed to the subsequently overdubbed versions which are sometimes more familiar. *One Love* was subsequently reissued as two single discs, *Wailing Wailers at Studio One* and *Simmer Down at Studio One* (both Heartbeat — 1994).

8 The Wailers & Friends: Top Hits Sung by the Legends of Jamaican Ska (Heartbeat) 1999

In addition to their own recordings, the Wailers (individually and collectively) were involved in sessions with a number of other artists — Bob Andy, Delroy Wilson, Ken Boothe, Jackie Opel, calypso singer Lord Brynner and the young Lee Perry included. This set wraps up 18 of the most notable, including several Bob Marley/Bunny Livingston solo performances.

THE WAILERS: 1967–70

8 Selassie Is the Chapel (JAD) 1998

Excellent single disc collection of the Wailers' self-produced sessions from WIRL Studios (4/68), JBC (1969), Randy's (summer, 1970) and dates with producers Mortimer Planno (1968) and Ted Proud (1969).

7 Rock to the Rock (JAD) 1998

Not-quite-exhaustive round-up of material recorded with Nash and Jenkins during 1968–69, but a chance to hear at least a fraction of the material as its makers intended as opposed to the modern versions issued on the early 1980s LP *Chances Are*.

"Chances Are" itself is revealed as one of Marley's loveliest ever compositions, previously, it sounded like Phil Collins.

7 The Best of the Wailers (JAD) 1998

Titled for the 1970 Leslie Kong LP which it partially replicates, the set is completed by sessions that same year with Bunny Lee and Errol Thompson. The above three JAD titles are also available as the box set *The Complete Wailers 1967–72 Part 1*.

THE WAILERS AND LEE PERRY: 1970–71

NOTE: This period is responsible for well over 100 low quality, poorly detailed and generally disreputable compilations. Anybody interested in a basic introduction to the catalog is directed towards the following:

6 In the Beginning (Trojan — UK) 1988
7 African Herbsman (Trojan — UK) 1988
7 Rasta Revolution (Trojan — UK) 1988
6 Early Years 1969–73 (Trojan — UK) 1994

Each of the above also includes (non-Johnny Nash) material from the period 1967–71, but the Perry material dominates and avoids excessive duplication.

8 The Complete Bob Marley & The Wailers 1967–72 Part II (JAD) 1998

Box set distillation of the 1970–71 Lee Perry sessions, the three discs arranged chronologically according to the original *Soul Rebels* and *Soul Revolution* parts 1/2 album sessions, plus rarities and singles. Further Perry material was included in *Part III* of this series (see below).

8 1970–71: The Best of the Upsetter Years (Cleopatra) 1999

In terms of variety, one of the few non-Trojan releases to actually live up to its title.

7 13 Gold Dubs: Original Dubs & Riddims (Fine Tune) 2000

Two tracks duplicate cuts from Trojan's CD reissue of the *Soul Revolution Vol 2* dub album; otherwise, a solid introduction to the Wailers' Upsetter b-sides.

9 The Complete Upsetters Sessions (Trojan — UK) 2000

Ambitious and, if you really need such a thing, indispensable 113 song/six-CD box set containing every known recording from the Wailers' 1970–71 liaison with Lee Perry, including alternates, versions, dubs and collaborations. The additional inclusion of incomplete (no backing vocals) versions of 1978's "I Know a Place" and "Who Colt the Game" adds to the set's value, although there is something somewhat sordid about finding them packed unceremoniously away on the end of what is, after all, a budget-priced package — Perry's biographer, David Katz, describes them among the best work Perry did all year. The booklet accompanying the box, on the other hand, doesn't even acknowledge their importance or provenance. Throughout the set, sound quality is generally fine, although several tracks appear to have been mastered from vinyl or several-generation tapes.

SESSIONS: 1971–73

8 The Complete Wailers: 1967–72 Part III (JAD) 2000

While several Wailers sessions from this period are included among the Trojan and other compilations noted above, this represents the only serious attempt to document the band's immediate pre-Island era. Included are highlights of the 1971 Johnny Nash sessions, completing the restoration of the *Chances Are* material to its virgin state, plus the oft-compiled but rarely annotated "Craven Choke Puppy"/ "Guava Jelly"/"Screw Face"/"Trenchtown Rock"/"Lick Samba" sessions at Harry Js.

THE ISLAND YEARS

7 Confrontation (Tuff Gong) 1983

The first concerted burst of unreleased Marley music was highlighted by two *Exodus* era Tuff Gong singles, "Rastaman Live Up" and "Blackman Redemption," plus a heavily remixed version of the dub plate "Burn Down Babylon," transformed into "Chant Down Babylon." Another gem involved a rough King Sporty-produced demo of "Buffalo Soldier," cleaned up and completed. The remainder of the set lives up to its demos/out-takes origins, but holds up well. Reissued, remastered in 2001.

8 Legend (Tuff Gong) 1984

A straightforward greatest hits collection in the UK, with several tracks given a face-lifting, and generally acceptable, remix for the US market. Reissued, remastered in 2001 with a second disc of posthumous remixes. A companion volume, *Natural Mystic* (Tuff Gong — 1995) highlights lesser known but equally deserving album tracks.

8 Rebel Music (Tuff Gong) 1986

The non-album "Roots" is the prime bait for would-be purchasers, but an unexpected selection of album cuts also adds to the fun.

6 Talkin' Blues (Tuff Gong) 1991

Rough, but illuminating mixture featuring highlights from the Wailers' 1973 KSAN radio broadcast, plus a 1975 session and interview.

4 So Much Things to Say (RAS) 1992

Disappointing "live" album, the unreleased recordings blanketed by more interview material.

9 Songs of Freedom (Tuff Gong) 1994

Career spanning box set which, sadly, goes only some of the way towards fulfilling its potential. While the later Island years are covered with awesome detail, disc one certainly needs to be played in conjunction with the Heartbeat and JAD titles detailed above (cuts unavailable to the latter, incidentally, turn up here), while disc two just seems patchy. Nevertheless, a healthy smattering of genuine rarities and an excellent booklet do go a long way towards compensating.

5 Down South Miami (MVP — Japan) 1998

Subsequently released as *Reggae South* (RReMark — 2000), a previously bootleg-only snapshot of the 1977 Miami rehearsals, cursed by sub-standard sound (the bass seems to be auditioning for a very bad dub album), but featuring meaty versions of "Easy Skanking," "Crazy Baldheads" and "Roots."

6 Chicago Live 1975 (MVP — Japan) 1998
6 Live at the Lyceum in London 1975 (MVP — Japan) 1998
8 One Love Peace Concert 1978 (MVP — Japan) 1998
7 Rotterdam 1978 (MVP — Japan) 1998
6 Live at the Apollo Theatre 1979 (MVP — Japan) 1998
6 Live at Santa Barbara 1979 (MVP Japan) 1999
6 Live in Dortmund Germany 1980 (MVP Japan) 2000
7 Portland '78 (MVP Japan) 2000
5 Germany 1980 (MVP Japan) 2000

With mixed sound scarcely improved from sundry oft-circulated bootlegs, a crop of live albums nevertheless capture a handful of magical performances, and several more whose significance escapes even the most forgiving listener. For collectors only.

8 One Love: The Ultimate Bob Marley (Universal) 2001

Hits collection drawn from the remastered editions and including a full band version of "Redemption Song," from the *Uprising* remaster, and the 1978 Lee Perry production, "I Know a Place" — with sound quality which wipes the floor with past releases.

TRIBUTES AND TRAUMAS

3 Chances Are (Cotillion) 1981

A bizarre collection offering modern remixes of eight tracks from the 1968/69 Johnny Nash/Arthur Jenkins sessions. The actual material is fine, but the remixes so steadfastly refuse to let the Wailers speak for themselves that the end result sounds exactly like 40 minutes spent watching MTV *circa* 1982.

7 21st Century Dub (ROIR) 1993

Marley and Jah Pelikaho organized the 1980 sessions combining Jamaican (notably Sly & Robbie) and Japanese (Yellow Magic Orchestra cohorts) talent, and culminating in this dub spectacular.

1 Dreams of Freedom: Ambient Translations of Bob Marley in Dub (Island) 1997

Bill Laswell's redefinition of 11 Marley classics — dubbed up, to be sure, and the bass lines can be thunderous. But the singalong chorale is pregnant with niceness and a piano-led wash bleaches all soul from the rhythm, while the half-discerning listener assumes a sweat-soaked foetal position and begs for it to stop. At last, a rebel leader who even your granny can cuddle. Truly atrocious.

8 Jah Love: A Reggae Tribute to Bob Marley (Music Club) 1997

As opposed to . . . what? A punk tribute? It could be done, but in the meantime, Big Youth, former Tommorrow's Children vocalist Pluto Shervington, Dennis Brown, Ronnie Davis, Delroy Wilson and more reel out their best efforts, with Johnny Clarke's "No Woman No Cry" demanding your especial attention (and Inner Circle's "Rebel Music" surely defying the trade descriptions act).

3 Chant Down Babylon (Polygram) 1999

Well-intentioned, but musically misguided attempt to launch Marley towards the modern hip hop audience, by rewiring his work via Lauren Hill, the Lost Boyz, Krayzie Bone and, oddly, rocker Steve Tyler.

8 A Tribute to Bob Marley (Cleopatra) 1999

A plethora of JA superstars across the generations each take on a Marley/Wailers classic in their own inimitable styles. Bundling up 18 distinguished artists, highlights include U-Roy's DJ classic "Dreamland," Tappa Zukie's toaster take on "No Woman No Cry," Ken Boothe's soulful "African Lady," and the Heptones' harmony drenched "Hypocrite."

6 Tribute to Bob Marley (Trojan—UK) 2000

Three-CD box set comprising 50 Marley covers and tributes, the majority dating from the 1970s. The best was distilled onto the single disc above; one can certainly have way too much of a good thing.

7 Remixed Hits (Big Eye) 2001

An electro-gothic (!) tribute drives 11 Lee Perry era tracks through the often surprisingly sympathetic vision of such pacesetters as Astralasia, Sheep On Drugs, Love And Rockets and Fire House. Hit and miss elements abound, of course, but the overall mood is considerably tastier than other genre-bending assaults on the songbook.

ZIGGY MARLEY & THE MELODY MAKERS

STYLE *reggae (roots)*
FORMED *1979 (Kingston, JA)*
ORIGINAL LINE UP *David "Ziggy" Marley (b 10/17/68, Kingston, JA — vocals, guitar), Stephen Marley (vocals, guitar, drums), Cedella Marley (vocals), Sharon Marley (vocals)*

The first of four children born to Bob and Rita Marley, and the eldest of the ten eventually fathered by the singer, "Ziggy" Marley made his international public debut at age 8, when he danced onstage at the Tower Theater in Philadelphia on the opening night of the Wailers' 1976 American tour. (The boy's nickname developed from his love of rock artist David Bowie's Ziggy Stardust character.)

Ziggy appeared onstage at a number of other shows over the next four years, most famously the Wailers' Reggae Sunsplash II headliner in July, 1979, where he was joined by brother Stephen. He then made his recorded debut, alongside Stephen and sisters Cedella and Sharon, on "Children Playing in the Streets," a song written for them by their father four years earlier. Credited to the Melody Makers and released, of course, through the Marleys' Tuff Gong label, the single was also Bob Marley's gift to the United Nations' International Year of The Child — all royalties from the song went to the organization.

Ziggy and Stephen's next major public performance was at Marley's funeral on May 21, 1981, recreating the dance moves made famous by their father during a brief emotional set by the I-Threes and the Wailers. They also appeared at Sunsplash that summer. The following February, at a celebration of what would have been Marley's 37th birthday, the Melody Makers reconvened to perform a short set of his best-known songs.

A new Melody Makers single, "What a Plot" (Tuff Gong) hit in Jamaica that same year, while 1983 brought another Sunsplash performance. But it was 1984 before the quartet truly began to step out from behind their father's shadow, when they entered the studio with English producer Steve Levine. Although the sessions themselves were eventually scrapped, a single, "Lying in Bed," emerged that year and, in 1985, the Melody Makers (augmented by the Wailers' own Barrett brothers rhythm section) returned with their debut album, the pleasant pop-roots of *Play the Game Right*. They returned to Sunsplash that same year, and made subsequent appearance in 1987, 1989, 1991, 1994 and 1998.

1986 brought *Hey World*, credited this time to Ziggy Marley & The Melody Makers, and featuring both Ziggy and Stephen writing and taking lead vocals (roles they have retained ever since). Its release was supported by the group's first tour, headlining what amounted to a full scale Tuff Gong roadshow — the bill also featured Nadine Sutherland and the I-Threes. Ziggy also continued to reinforce his Jamaican popularity with a clutch of sound system specials, rerecording old Wailers' songs with new lyrics dedicated to the sound system itself.

In 1988, the Melody Makers signed with Virgin Records and released *Conscious Party*, produced by Chris Frantz and Tina Weymouth, members of the artsy new wave band Talking Heads. It was to prove the Melody Makers' long-prophesied breakthrough. While the group embarked on a phase of non-stop touring, both *Conscious Party* and its lead single, "Tomorrow People," were hits, with the album also winning the Best Reggae Grammy. Retaining the same producers, their follow up, 1989's *One Bright Day*, was similarly successful.

The group's fifth album, 1991's *Jahmekya*, brought the most enthusiastic reviews yet, without beginning to match its predecessors' success. A single, "Good Time," faltered at #85, while hopes of a third successive Grammy were shattered when Shabba Ranks' *As Raw as Ever* got the nod instead. The group left Virgin in 1993, following that year's *Joy and Blues*.

Launching their own Ghetto Youths United label, the Melody Makers moved to Elektra in 1994, releasing *Free Like We Want 2 B* the following year. Again sales were low compared to the group's late 1980s high, but against that was balanced the weight and acceptance of the group's reputation. When the United Nations appointed him a Goodwill Youth Ambassador, Ziggy Marley was arguably as popular as his father ever was and, to a younger generation, even more famous — an elder statesmen before he even hit his mid-30s.

Subsequent Melody Makers albums, then, have more than compensated for their less than stellar sales by maintaining both the band's profile and their reputation. 1997's *Fallen Is Babylon* brought a third Grammy; 1999's *Spirit of*

Ziggy Marley plays the game right.

Music proved one of the most powerful roots albums of the entire decade.

ZIGGY MARLEY & THE MELODY MAKERS DISCOGRAPHY

7 **Play the Game Right (EMI) 1985**

The band's youth is apparent in the rootsiness of their sound while also foreshadowing the hybrid stylings of the future. Interestingly, the weakest song is probably Bob's own "Children Playing in the Street." Ziggy's voice, meanwhile, is already a strident weapon, shaded with emotion and, if it has a superficial resemblance to his father's, he's hardly the first Jamaican singer to suffer that comparison.

6 **Hey World (EMI) 1986**

10 **Conscious Party (Virgin) 1988**

One listen and you knew this album was going to be enormous, and deservedly so. The scintillating production lands just on the pop side of dance hall, but the best songs are as thoughtful as they are buoyant, with deathless resonations. Among myriad highlights are the title track, "Have You Ever Been to Hell" and "Dreams of Home."

8 **One Bright Day (Virgin) 1989**

Still snapping with club-based beats, but now adding ever more styles to their sound, this album was obviously going to equal its predecessor. Dancefloor numbers, deep dread tracks, Afro-sounds, even funk and urban contemporary influences sneak in *One Bright Day* has it all, and then some, another monster of an album.

7 **Jahmekya (Virgin) 1991**

The group radically shifts their sound into the new urban contemporary world, fueling an album with funk, soul and modern R&B. There's still some reggae dance and roots pop numbers, and a wailing dancehall track, "Raw Riddim," but it's aimed at an older audience, and their pop fans are mostly out of luck.

8 **Joy & Blues: Ghetto Youths United (Virgin) 1993**

Changing direction somewhat, this was the Melody Makers' return to their reggae roots, its confidence marked by a strong revision of their father's "African Herbsman" and a return appearance from Wailers bassist Aston Barrett.

6 **Free Like We Want 2 B (Elektra) 1995**

A courageous rhythm-heavy album imbibes influences from

across the US R&B spectrum, most notably in the title track and the showcase "Hand to Mouth." "Water and Oil" is a sonic stand out; "In the Flow" an electronic conflagration cut through by haunted horns.

9 Fallen Is Babylon (Elektra) 1997

Unquestionably their best album since the late 1980s, and their most adventurous too. The urgent "I Remember" has an almost Bob Dylanish flavor to it, "Everyone Wants To Be" is an effortless roots R&B cover of a demented spaghetti western theme (complete with "The Good, the Bad & The Ugly" samples and a Wyclef Jean rap), while Curtis Mayfield's "People Get Ready" may reflect on one of Bob Marley's favorite artists, but is also a remarkable ragga reinvention in its own right.

7 Spirit of Music (Elektra) 1999
8 Live Volume One (Elektra) 2000

Twelve years after the *Conscious Party: Live* concert video demonstrated that the band's studio prowess readily translated to the live arena, an excellent set which not only hits the Melody Makers' most sensible peaks, but wraps up with a triumphant "People Get Ready," dad's "Could You Be Loved" and their own "I Know You Don't Care About Me."

SELECTED COMPILATIONS & ARCHIVE RELEASES

6 Time Has Come (EMI Manhattan) 1988

With only two under-performing albums to choose from, this attempt to ride the *Conscious Party* breakthrough really doesn't prove anything.

7 The Best Of: 1988–93 (Virgin) 1997

Odd compilation, generously stuffed with 17 tracks, but relying too much on singles and hit tracks to illustrate the massive strides the band made during a mere five years.

THE MAYTALS

STYLE *reggae*
FORMED 1962 *(Kingston, JA)*
ORIGINAL LINE-UP *Frederick "Toots" Hibbert (b 1945, Clarendon, JA — vocals), Nathaniel "Jerry Matthias" McCarthy (b 1939, Portland, JA — vocals), Henry "Raleigh" Gordon (b 1937, St Andrew, JA — vocals)*

If any band can claim to be the single thread which has united the Jamaican music scene over the past 40 years, it is Toots & The Maytals. It was they who, in 1962, crystallized the pumping, chopping ambitions of ska and fused it into a style which still thrives today. It was they who assisted at the birth of rock steady, as the dances slowed and the temperature rose; and it was they who introduced the word "reggae" to the international vocabulary in 1968.

From 1976, their *Reggae Got Soul* album is widely acclaimed as the first evidence that American R&B and its eccentric Caribbean cousin had more in common than a handful of rearranged cover versions; and when Bob Marley was asked who he credited with the vision which saw his Wailers rise to the top of the world, he had no hesitation in naming the Maytals.

Today, the Maytals' influence continues to permeate Jamaican music, whether in the vocal stylings of so many modern stars, or simply from the wealth of compilations and archive releases which have ensured their music has never faded away.

Toots Hibbert arrived in Kingston around 1958, from rural May Pen, Clarendon, where he had been singing with his seven siblings in church since childhood. Finding work at a barber shop, he regularly serenaded his customers, but his first attempt to break into the music scene was a failure. Accompanying himself on guitar, Hibbert auditioned for Derrick Morgan and Leslie Kong during 1961, and was turned down flat.

The following year he linked with Jerry Matthias and Raleigh Gordon as a vocal trio, dubbed the Maytals by Gordon. Of the three, Matthias alone had experience — he cut his first single, "Crazy Girl," with Duke Reid in 1958. The trio moved immediately onto the audition circuit, and soon found themselves able to choose which producer they wanted to work with — they settled on Coxsone Dodd and released their debut single, "Hallelujah," shortly after.

Nobody had heard anything like it. If Hibbert himself had any peer, it was James Brown — abandoned, evangelical, exploding with excitement from the moment he opened his mouth. The musicians behind him could not help but up their own performances to match, while endless rehearsals had already taught his fellow Maytals precisely what was expected of them. "Fever," the trio's second single, could not have been more appropriately named.

Over the next two years, the Maytals recorded some two dozen sides for Dodd, including the massive hit "Six and Seven Books of Moses" (actually produced by the young Lee Perry), "Marching On," the spirituals "He Will Provide" and "Shining Light," "I'll Never Grow Old," "Study War No More" (aka "Down by the Riverside"), "Matthew Mark," and "Helping Ages Past." Such was the quality of this material, in fact, that in 1964, Dodd took what was, by Jamaican standards, the virtually unprecedented decision to release a full length LP of Maytals material, *Presenting the Maytals*.

By the end of 1963, however, the group had broken away from their mentor in a dispute over payment — famously, Dodd was paying them no more than three pounds a song, while further subterfuge apparently surrounded his policy of licensing the band's material to the UK Island label under such alternative names as the Vikings and the Flames. When the Maytals visited the UK for a short tour that year, many of their shows were billed as the Vikings.

Touring the studios, the Maytals cut a handful of 45s with

various producers, including Deanne Daley, who oversaw "I Am in Love" and "Come into My Parlour"; Sonia Pottinger ("Joy and Jean," "Let's Jump"), Vincent Chin ("Someone Going to Bawl," "John & James," "He's the Greatest") and a now enthusiastic Leslie Kong ("Neither Silver or Gold," and "When I Get Home"). Kong also paired the group with Desmond Dekker for a pair of singles credited to Dekker and the Cherry Pies (and one of their own under that same pseudonym). But it was their liaison with Prince Buster which finally encouraged the band to work to its strengths.

Dodd, as was his wont, had recorded a number of ballads with the Maytals. Buster, however, demanded the jump-up frenzy which was the trio's true forte and, over the next few months the group turned out a seemingly endless stream of classics – "Dog War," "Bet You Lied," "He's Real," "Goodbye Jane," "My Old Flame," "You Got Me Spinning," "Pain in My Belly," "Domino" and more.

In late 1964, the Maytals joined forces with producer/entrepreneur Byron Lee and his partner Ronnie Nasralla, for a further deluge of classic 45s, beginning with "It's You," their first Jamaican chart topper. It was replaced at the top by its own b-side, "Daddy" and, thereafter, the band was seldom far from the top of the chart.

"Never You Change," "My Darling," "My New Name," "If You Act this Way," "So Mad in Love" and "Ain't Got No Tip" were all successful throughout 1965–66. Lee also arranged for the Maytals to record their second album, 1965's *The Sensational Maytals*, lending them the legendary American R&B producer Tom Dowd, who was in Jamaica to produce Lee & his Dragonaires' own *Jamaican Ska* album.

In 1966, the Maytals' "Bam Bam" ran out winner of the first ever Festival Song Competition, and became a major hit among the rude boys who were now emerging as the dominant force in the Jamaican musical audience. And, had circumstances been different, the Maytals could have run out the greatest rude boy band of them all. Their sound, their stance and most of all, their image certainly fed into the movement's iconography. As it turned out, however, "Bam Bam" was to be the Maytals' last single for almost two years. In 1966, Hibbert was found guilty of possessing marijuana and sentenced to 18 months imprisonment.

The Maytals did not even try to replace their frontman. McCarthy surfaced briefly as one half of the Ewam (McDermott) and Jerry duo, but the band itself remained moribund until Hibbert was released in 1968. Then they linked with Leslie Kong at Beverley's, and celebrated their return with two of the most memorable hits of the year.

The first, Hibbert's insistent "54–46 Was My Number," took its title from the singer's number in prison, and its theme from his belief that he was jailed not for his crime, but because of his Rastafarianism. The second was "Do the Reggay," the first single to actually identify and name the dance which had been slowly pushing rock steady out of the way since the beginning of the year.

Forming a full time backing band around Winston Wright, Hux Brown, Paul Douglas, Jackie Jackson and Dougie Bryan (better known as the Dynamics), the Maytals launched into a period of absolute indestructibility. They came very close to taking the Festival Song Competition again with "Bim Today (Bam Tomorrow)." The trio's "Desmond Dekker Came First" remembers the day — "the Techniques they came third, Clancy Eccles he runs fourth, Derrick Harriott he came fifth, so I came second."

"One Eyed Enos," "Schooldays" (a sequel to "Dog War"), "Don't Trouble Trouble," "Scare Him," "Struggle" and "We Shall Overcome" followed, each one confirming the group's street tough reputation, while "Sun Moon and Star" referenced Hibbert's Rastafarian faith. In 1970, the anthemic "Monkey Man" (dedicated, of course, to Kong) dented the UK Top 50. "Pressure Drop," a song later covered by Robert Palmer and the Clash (among others), the 1969 Festival winner "Sweet and Dandy" and "Peeping Tom" also figured within this stellar sequence, while Kong released two full albums by the band, *From the Roots* (1970) and *Monkey Man* (1971). This sequence of non-stop hits came to a halt when producer Kong died on August 9, 1971.

However, the group's international profile soared through their inclusion in the soundtrack to the movie *The Harder They Come* — the last project Kong oversaw before his death. Renaming themselves Toots & The Maytals, the trio now shifted their base of operations to Byron Lee's Dynamic Sounds, and cut 1972's *Slatyam Stoot* LP with Kong's former assistant, Warwick Lyn. That same year, they again won the Festival Song Competition, with "Pomp and Pride."

In 1973, Island records chief Chris Blackwell joined the band in the studio to co-produce (with Lyn and Dave Bloxham) the seminal *Funky Kingston* album. *In the Dark* followed, before the group signed directly to Island Records in 1975. Their first release was a revised version of the *Funky Kingston* album, followed by *Reggae Got Soul*, an album whose impact was so great that at least one reggae encyclopedia insists it made the UK chart. In fact it didn't, but it came close.

Hibbert spent much of 1977–78 establishing his own Righteous label, and unleashing a string of largely spiritual singles for Jamaican ears only — "Pass the Pipe on the Right Hand Side" and "Confess Your Sins" among them. Three years elapsed before the Maytals finally followed up *Reggae Got Soul* with 1979's *Pass that Pipe* and the following year's *Just Like That*.

The lay off had not slowed the band down, however. They were a hit at Reggae Sunsplash in July, 1979, and the following year Toots & The Maytals entered the *Guinness Book of Records*, courtesy of the fastest live album ever released. Recorded at the Hammersmith Palais, London, *Toots Live* was mastered, pressed, packaged and in the stores within 24 hours of the actual show.

Toots & The Maytals' final album, *Knockout* was released in 1981. The trio broke up soon after, bowing out with a revival of 1966's "Bam Bam" for inclusion on the *Countryman* movie soundtrack, and an appearance at the 1982 Reggae Sunsplash (subsequently released as a live album).

When Hibbert returned to the studio later that year, it was in the company of Sly and Robbie, Mikey Chung (guitar) and *Countryman* soundtrack composer Wally Badarou, a team debuted with tracks included on what was otherwise a straightforward Maytals greatest hits collection, *Reggae Greats*.

Over the next five years, Hibbert drifted in and out of reggae, as he experimented with other musical styles with mixed, but always fascinating, results. An album cut in 1986 with Irish producer Denny Cordell went unreleased; however, a return to his funky R&B roots, 1988's *Toots in Memphis*, was a phenomenal success as the singer came to grips with the classic Stax material which he had been rivalling back in the mid-1960s. The album earned a Grammy nomination.

Early in the 1990s, Hibbert convened a new generation of Maytals and launched into a decade of intensive live work. (They appeared at Reggae Sunsplash in 1993 and 1994.) He also formed a new label, Alla Son, releasing the *Recoup* and *Ska Father* collections of updated oldies and more recent material. Alla Son singles releases during 1998/99 include Hibbert's "Hard Road," "Fool for You," "More and More" and "When I Remember." In 2001, Toots contributed a track to the *Back to the Island: Reggae from Martha's Vineyard* album.

DISCOGRAPHY

8 Presenting the Maytals (Ska Beat) 1964

Despite the preponderance of singles, which render it a virtual greatest hits album, an unstoppable barrage which captures all the excitement of the original ska explosion. Producer Dodd reissued the album in 1966 as *Never Grow Old — Presenting the Maytals*; it has since been rereleased by Heartbeat.

7 The Sensational Maytals (WIRL) 1965

The Byron Lee sessions spawned two massive hits (the enjoyably mawkish "Daddy," the pounding "It's You"), plus the gruntingly insistent "Fever," "Never You Change" and "If You Act this Way." Without a drab moment in sight, a fabulous snapshot of a moment in time. The CD reissue (*Sensational Ska Explosion* — Jamaica Gold) appends eight bonus out-takes.

7 From the Roots (Beverley's—JA) 1970
6 Monkey Man (Beverley's—JA) 1971

So much of these albums have appeared across countless compilations and anthologies that it's easy to assign classic status to both. In fact, both albums are seriously weakened by the inclusion of sundry makeweight cuts — *Roots* dips with "Koo Koo" and "Know Me Good," *Monkey Man* with "Revival Reggae" and a barely recognizable cover of John Lennon's "Give Peace a Chance."

6 Slatyam Stoot (Dragon—JA) 1972
10 Funky Kingston (Dragon) 1973

From their slow skanking version of "Louie Louie" to a soulful, but utterly unexpected revival of "Daddy," and on to the exuberant "Pomp and Pride," Kingston goes to Memphis, but loses none of its own native qualities.

6 In the Dark (Dragon) 1974

And funky everywhere else. Toots gets eclectic, from Michael Jackson ("Got to Be There") to John Denver ("Take Me Home, Country Roads"), all delivered with a loving sincerity which surprised a lot of old devotees. "54–46 Was My Number" gets a welcome airing, but an unwelcome reappraisal.

8 Reggae Got Soul (Mango) 1976

If *Funky Kingston* set the stage for the Maytals next move, *Soul* sees them leaping over all expectations to deliver one of the key anthems of the mid-1970s, the self-defining (and self-explanatory) title track. Reveling in a crystal clear production, the downbeat "Rastaman" and the contrarily triumphant "Living in the Ghetto" are the other peaks and, while a ponderous remake of "Six & Seven Books" was probably an adaptation too far, still it's a mighty album.

6 Pass the Pipe (Mango) 1979

Jazz influences creep into the now solidly soulful brew, for an album which is high on soul and energy, but — the title track and the urgent "My Love Is So Strong" aside — a little low on content.

6 Just Like That (Mango) 1980
8 Toots Live (Mango) 1980

The immediacy of the album's release is conveyed by the music, a murderous assault on the senses which starts with a big hit ("Pressure Drop") and doesn't once let go. "54–46," "Sweet and Dandy," "Monkey Man" and "Funky Kingston" may not offer definitive retreads, but there's no arguing with the sparks.

6 Knockout (Mango) 1981
7 Toots in Memphis (Mango) 1988

After the experiments of the 70s, it was probably inevitable that the (now solo) Toots would go the whole soul hog at some point. But that doesn't alter the fact that his interpretations of some of the city's best-loved treasures ("Knock On Wood," Otis Redding's "Hard To Handle" and "Dreams To Remember") rank among the best those songs have ever seen.

7 Recoup (Alla Son — JA) 1997

8 Ska Father (Alla Son — JA) 1998

A lively set offers up sensational updates of "Broadway Jungle" and "Pressure Drop," and is also highlighted by the return of Matthias and the Dynamics.

6 Live in London (Trojan — UK) 1999

SELECTED COMPILATIONS & ARCHIVE RELEASES

8 Funky Kingston (Island) 1975

Hybrid collection drawn from the original *Funky Kingston* and *In the Dark* albums plus sundry 45s.

6 Live at Reggae Sunsplash (Sunsplash) 1983

Reasonable set pales in comparison with *Toots Live*, and winds up with a somber tribute to the late Bob Marley, which really goes on way too long.

9 Time Tough: The Anthology (Mango) 1996

It would take five discs at least to do true justice to the Maytals, and a booklet the size of Connecticut. Two discs and a few pages of impressions fill the void for the time being, but the 60s are dispensed with in just nine (well-chosen hits), and the 70s — *Funky Kingston* through *Live* — devour most of the rest. Rarities include the *Countryman* remake of "Bam Bam" and the unreleased Leslie Kong production "Desmond Dekker Came First"; unlooked for stand-outs include the buoyant "Chatty Chatty" (from *Just Like That*) and "Careless Ethiopians" (from *Knockout*). A tighter summary of the period covered by the first disc can be found on *The Very Best of Toots & the Maytals* (Music Club — 1997).

8 Never Grow Old (Heartbeat) 1997

Basically a reissue of the 31 year old Studio One collection, with bonus tracks drawn from the vaults.

7 Very Best of (Polygram) 2000

Single disc set largely recounts *Time Tough*, but makes a smooth one disc intro for anyone wanting more than the classic era hits deliver.

MENTO: JAMAICA'S OWN CALYPSO

What calypso is to T&T, mento (or mentor, the spelling preferred in early sources) is to Jamaica. A cacophony of disparate instruments ranging from penny whistles to pots and pans, from guitars and banjos to hand drums and thumb pianos, bamboo saxophones and home-made banjos, mento was local folk music at its purest. In the cities, it turned up on corners and in bars, cranked out by itinerant street performers busking for change. In the country, it was the staple fare at the local "bram," dances which attracted patrons from every rural hamlet in the region.

Like calypso, which it resembles in a number of ways, mento has no written tradition and few "classic" songs.

Rather, although melodies were often passed around and reused, the songs changed as frequently as a neighborhood newspaper — which is essentially what they were. Unlike calypso, neither the music industry nor the outside world ever paid much attention to the music, allowing it to develop with an insular purity which, today, ranks among its most precious attributes.

The most fundamental difference between mento and calypso lies, of course, in its origins. Throughout the Caribbean, whether one is speaking of the British, French or Spanish islands, the melodies often ultimately derived from Europe, while the rhythms were African. However, just as the European elements have their own distinct national characteristics (the folk songs of those three nations could never be confused!), so did the African.

All three colonial powers drew their slaves from different parts of western and north-western Africa, with the population of each individual island often drawn from very specific locales. Jamaica's African people have been traced almost exclusively to the Akan people of the Gold Coast, and mento derives in great part from their rhythmic traditions. The word "mento" itself is believed to be a corruption of "kromanti," a local 19th century term for Jamaican folk songs and itself a contraction of the Akan "koromantin."

Little else is known of mento's origins as a musical culture, beyond the standard line about it developing on the plantations during the days of slavery. Most slave-owners allowed their workers to devote Saturday nights to merry-making, and mento — like so many other Caribbean musical styles — doubtless did spring from those gatherings.

Like any other indigenous folk music it continued to grow over a period of decades, even generations, assuming the form most pleasing to each successive set of makers, but never standing still and certainly never reaching a "finished" state. However, it certainly existed in what we would now consider a recognizable form at the end of the 19th century, when one of T&T's leading calypso performers of that period, Richard Couer de Lion (Norman Le Blanc), adapted the mento song "Not a Cent" for his own audience.

During the 1930s, a Kingston street duo named Slim and Sam plied their trade so successfully that their names, at least, are still cited. Names, however, are all that even the most diligent musicologist has; names and, in rare cases, lyrics to some of their songs. There was no recording industry in Jamaica, and very little recording equipment either. But the more enterprising performers knew there was an audience for their work regardless, and printed up copies of their newest lyric to sell for a penny or two.

From the beginning, the most popular mento singers were those who could take the latest current affairs and set them to music; others sang of everyday life, bawdy romances and nights on the town, others still of their hopes, dreams and ambitions. The only binding rule was, they did it with humor.

Blunt and lascivious, mento was the irrepressibly good-natured sound of a people whose lot was, to lift a favorite saying from the island's colonial English overlords, to "grin and bear it." Whether it was a self-composed ditty or a ribald adaptation of an old English sea shanty, mento made people smile. Unless they were decent, God-fearing, church-going people. Then, they cringed at the very mention of the word and, when the first mento records began appearing in the 1950s, upright citizens prevailed upon store owners either to refuse to stock them, or to keep them under the counter where they might not offend innocent passers-by.

The development and history of mento is further distorted by Jamaica's proximity to T&T. Contemporary references to the first gramophone records cut in T&T in 1937 pointedly describe calypso as being far more popular in Jamaica than the native mento, unfortunately without leaving any clue as to precisely what criteria that determination was based upon. But by the time those aforementioned first mento records began appearing, the terms "calypso" and "mento" were all but interchangeable, even in Jamaica.

By then, after all, local musicians were just beginning to find work in the infant north shore tourist trade and it did not take a genius to figure out that visitors from abroad were far more likely to enjoy a musical form whose name they recognized, than one which even some of the locals were still unfamiliar with. To upper crust Jamaica, mento was the sound of beggars and the ghettos. Calypso, on the other hand, was even popular in America.

And so groups with names like Count Lasha's Calypso Quartet and Reynold's Calypso Clippers took to the stage and, so long as they ensured that their performance maintained the up-beat rhythms which characterized calypso, no-one was any the wiser. Back on the streets (or after hours, when only the fans remained), mento ran the gamut of tempos.

The first mento superstars, if such an oxymoron can exist, were Count Fly and Lord Flea, brilliant rivals in the Kingston clubs of the late 1940s. Flea, it is said, was the inspiration which drove Harry Belafonte to such great heights a few years later; Fly was the role model borrowed by Harold Robinson and the Ticklers, whose own fame was assured when they became the first mento band ever to make a record.

Stanley Motta, a Kingston sound system operator who also owned a number of electrical appliance stores, was the driving force behind that epochal moment. He had recently built a tiny recording studio and, in late 1951, arranged for Jamaican jazz-man Bertie King to produce Robinson and his band.

The absence of any mastering or pressing facilities in Jamaica saw the master tape sent to London, where Melodisc

Records head Emil Shallit oversaw the manufacturing process. The finished product—in the form of fragile 78rpm discs—was then shipped back to Jamaica for release the following summer as the debut release on Motta's own MRS label.

By the mid-1950s, two more labels dedicated to local music had emerged, Kalypso (a subsidiary of Federal, the island's largest label) and Caribou. Again using manufacturers as far afield as London and Florida, all three maintained a constant stream of new local releases, although by no means were they restricted to mento recordings alone.

The late 1950s were also the heyday of R&B in Jamaica, with local musicians and performers alike hastening to record their own variations on the exciting new American sound. They had no time for, and little interest in, the relaxed, old-fashioned sounds of their own heritage, and so the greatest market for mento moved abroad, back to Britain and the UK's ever-growing West Indian population.

Emil Shallit, once again, was swift to sense the potential of this otherwise culturally disenfranchised audience. The Melodisc label itself had been built upon appealing to minority markets, and in 1957, Shallit launched his own Kalypso label, licensing the most successful releases from all three leading Jamaican companies, MRB, Kalypso and Caribou.

The first major hit came as early as Kalypso's second release, Lord Power's now-legendary (and oft-revived) "Penny Reel." It did not receive any airplay—British radio was no keener on ladies who "shub" their "cushies" in 1957 than at any other time. But it dominated the West Indian enclaves of London and the British midlands and, when its appeal finally faded, listeners simply flipped it over and played "Chambolina" instead.

The following year, Lord Lebby's "Sweet Jamaica" proved another major hit, a heady taste of home for an increasingly homesick community. Further releases by Laro ("Jamaican Referendum Calypso"), Count Lasha ("Calypso Cha Cha Cha," "Slide Mongoose"), Count Boysie ("That Naughty Little Flea"), E Bedasse ("Big Boy and Teacher"), Laurel Aitken ("Sweet Chariot," "Aitken's Boogie," "Baba Kill Me Goat"), future Skatalites vocalist Lord Tanamo ("Blues Have Got Me Down") and Lord Daniel ("Small Island Girl") ensured Kalypso's continued success.

Other mento material appeared in Britain through Melodisc's distributor Decca, whose only marginally mistitled *Authentic Jamaican Calypsos* album was drawn from the handful of 10-inch albums released in Jamaica by MRS. Another UK label, Argo's Westminster subsidiary, released a collection of *Songs from Jamaica*, performed by Trinidadian folklorist Edric Connor, the album's liner notes commenting, "[while] the calypso of Trinidad has . . . become commercialized as a result of the development of the tourist industry . . . this has not yet been the fate of the Jamaican songs." The album itself included 30 songs, including "Sammy Dead Oh" and "Day-Oh" (both later covered by Prince Buster), "Chi Chi Bud Oh" (subsequently covered by Max Romeo), "Judy Drowned" and "Fyah Bun."

But no matter how much mento was recorded, much more was lost, songs performed a few times until their magic wore off, then discarded, unrecorded in every sense of the word. *Songs from Jamaica* remarks, "young educated Jamaicans are beginning to turn to their own music; many of them know something of the old songs, but when an attempt to sing them is made at any gathering it is nearly always found that only a few know the words of any particular song, and that each knows a different version of it, while the accompaniment is usually, at best, a gallant approximation."

Other songs survived, then, but they did so in that peculiar netherworld in which all "rediscovered" traditional music now languishes, where a single version of a song is recorded and is instantly proclaimed the "definitive" rendering — regardless of how many variations it may have passed through in the past, and how many more it might have undergone in the future. History is richer for the songs' preservation. But culture, perhaps, is a little poorer.

In strictly lineal terms, the emergence of ska around the dawn of the 1960s marked the end of mento as a developing genre, but also its rebirth as a commercial commodity. Ska was the sound of Jamaica rediscovering her musical past, creating a new form of folk music which wasn't merely unafraid to reach back into the heyday of mento for its inspiration, it positively thrived on doing so.

Prince Buster's production of the Folkes Brothers' "Oh Carolina" in 1961 was the spark which ignited the flame. Without it and Buster, ska would have remained the province of the Americanophiles, Coxsone Dodd and Duke Reid, with their regional variations on R&B and boogie, to have developed in who knows what direction.

Buster, however, tapped the spirit of mento at its core, and soon everybody was racing to emulate him. Phyllis Dillon's "Don't Touch Me Tomato" updated a typically risque mento song. Bob Marley's mother remembers her infant son delightedly singing it in the late 1940s, at which time it was already a golden oldie. Eric Morris' version of "Penny Reel," as produced by Duke Reid, was a hybrid cover of Lord Power's hit version and Monty Reynolds' "Long Time Girl I Never See You." Count Boysie's "Naughty Little Flea" was reborn under the aegis of the Maytals and producer Prince Buster as "Little Flea."

The Skatalites' Tommy McCook later acknowledged that his own band's music was forged via the "[combination of] the mento . . . type guitar and keyboards with a regular walking bass style." It was this combination, in the early 1960s, which ensured ska — in reality, simply a Jamaican approximation of American R&B — moved so far away from its role model.

Later, U-Roy took E Bedasse's "Big Boy and Teacher" for one of his early hits, while the early-1970s explosion of roots consciousness constantly looked back to mento folk tradition for both inspiration and material. The "country reggae" tag which attached itself to the purer roots acts was not arrived at by accident.

Elsewhere, the UK Melodisc Calypso label (the successor to Kalypso) was still releasing mento-flavored singles as late as 1964; others appeared into the late 1960s on the British Jump-Up label. And while many of the music's 1950s heroes (Aitken paramount among them) had long since moved on, new bands and musicians were emerging constantly. As late as 1987, bamboo saxophonist Sugar Belly was recording digital mento with producer Winston Riley, while mento is now a fixture in many Jamaican hotels — with and without its calypso camouflage.

The earlier traditions, too, live on. Of course mento has a strong presence at Jamaica's annual Independence Festival, while the music also survives in the form of the Jolly Boys, a mento band launched in the late 1940s by Moses Deans and still going strong today. Across four albums cut for the US Rykodisc label during the late 1980s/early 1990s, their vivid recreations of both the music and its moods have ensured an international appreciation and awareness which has been far too long in arriving.

MIGHTY DUKE

STYLE *calypso*
BORN *Kelvin Pope (Port Fortin, T&T)*

The first — and so far only — post-war performer ever to win the T&T Calypso Monarch title four years running, this former school teacher composed his first calypsos during the 1950s, basing his lyrical vision alternately on the wild, but so humorous bacchanals of his heroes the Mighty Cypher and the Mighty Spoiler, and pertinent political observation. His hometown, Port Fortin, lay at the center of T&T's oil industry, a magnet for poor immigrants in search of high wages, and their lives and culture, too, rubbed off on the young Duke.

Duke moved to Port of Spain in 1964, to launch his career as a professional singer and, four years later he was crowned Carnival King with "What Is Calypso?" and "Social Bacchanal." He retained his title the following year with "Black Is Beautiful" and "One Foot Visina," while 1970 brought a record-equalling third consecutive triumph with "Brotherhood of Man" and "See Through." Duke's unprecedented fourth straight victory came in 1971 with "Mathematical Formula" and "Melvie and Yvonne" — and only the Mighty Sparrow's immortal "Drunk and Disorderly" prevented him from making it five in a row in 1972.

Strangely, Duke never regained his throne, although there was no decline in the quality of his music. Throughout the 1970s and 1980s he maintained a constant stream of commentary — "How Many More Must Die," dedicated to the apartheid regime in South Africa, was a major hit; other Duke classics have included "Grenada Girl," "Mr Jarvis" and the racially themed "Black Skin" and "White Mask."

1987 saw Duke enter the soca arena with the tumultuous "Is Thunder," winner of that year's Road March. Albums from this period, barely available outside of T&T, included *Calypso Forever* (1983), *Poison* (1987), *Party for Yuh Life* (1988), *Total Disorder* (1990) and *Phung Uh Nung* (1992).

In 1993, Duke linked with Barbados-based producer Eddy Grant to record the critically acclaimed *Mask*; from the album, "Soca Have Meh Tu Tul Bey" became a strong challenger at carnival in 1994, but lost out to the suddenly ascendent De Lamo and Luta. Duke remains a regular competitor to this day.

SELECTED DISCOGRAPHY

8 Party For Yuh Life (JW Productions) 1988

"Face to Face" and "Jammin Time Again" both receive supersonic soca remixes, while the spikey "Yah hh HHH h" and "Ah Tired Do That" both thunder with abandon.

7 Mask (Ice) 1994

Certainly Duke's best sounding album so far, and one of his angriest. There's plenty of room for maneuver, though, with "Pretty Conchita" a squirming salsa-soaked Spanish soca, "The Baddest" and "Soca in Yuh Bam Bam" an especially kick-ass good time. But there's also room for social comment, via the downbeat "The World Today" and "Some People Never Satisfied" ("this world was meant to be a very very happy place").

8 The Spirit of Calypso (Ice) 1995

Enveloped again in Grant's rich, warm production, "Teach the Children" and "Anti-Social" are classic Duke compositions, but the highlight has to be the plaintive warning, "Don't Destroy Calypso."

6 Timbuktu (—T&T) 1997
8 Rebound (Ice) 1999

SELECTED COMPILATIONS & ARCHIVE RELEASES

7 Classics Collection (JW) 1991

Covering the period 1986–90 alone means it's slim pickings for anyone chasing the Duke's true 60s-70s classics. But his understanding of soca was second to none, while "Outrageous," "Tribal Wars," "South Africa Must Be Free" and, of course, "Is Thunder" certainly qualify among his finest latter-day recordings.

MIGHTY SPARROW

STYLE *calypso*
BORN *Slinger Francisco, 7/9/35 (Grandroy Bay, GREN)*

Born in Grenada, but raised in T&T, where his carpenter father relocated in early 1937, Sparrow was bitten by the calypso bug almost as soon as he could speak — and certainly as soon as he could sing. As a toddler, he entertained his mother singing the latest hits, accompanying himself on comb and paper.

Attending Newton Boys Catholic School, Sparrow's love of calypso was checked by the authorities' insistence that the music was an unhealthy distraction for young boys. He still performed at the weekly school concerts, however, usually trotting out a showstopping rendition of the ballad "Red River Valley." Only once did he break the calypso embargo, at a concert in front of a room full of parents and teachers, hitting the crowd with Lord Invader's "The Yankees Invade Trinidad" — and winning a standing ovation.

At 14, Sparrow participated in his first Carnival, as part of a neighborhood steel band. Leaving school, the teen found work at the government Control Board, but he quickly discovered calypso was a more lucrative pursuit, once promotor Holly Betaudier booked him into the famed Lotus club. He had already earned his distinctive nickname by this time — as he leaped around onstage, other performers compared him to an excitable little sparrow. The name stuck for a couple of years, before Sparrow swapped the Little prefix for the more impressive sounding Mighty.

At the Lotus, Sparrow and his accompanists, the Mough Band, became one of the club's biggest draws, their makeshift instrumentation (unable to afford proper instruments, the charismatic group improvised furiously) and Sparrow's unique vocal styling combining to create a calypso sound like none had heard before. Earthy as the old masters, but easy on the ear as well, unbeknownst to anyone, himself included, Sparrow was reinventing the very sound of calypso.

In 1954, Sparrow made his carnival debut as a singer at the Old Brigade tent on Port of Spain's South Quay, performing his own "The Parrot and the Monkey." It was a well-received performance, and he was back the following year with four songs, "Race Track," "The High Cost of Living," "The Missing Baby" and "Ode to Princess Margaret" (Queen Elizabeth II's sister had just completed a state visit to T&T.)

1955 also saw Sparrow undertake the first of the marathon tours for which he subsequently became renowned, heading off to Guyana, a country which was phenomenally loyal to calypso and carnival. Travelling by boat, truck and donkey cart, it was a gruelling outing, but one which unquestionably set Sparrow up for a career of remarkable longevity.

His residency at the Lotus ended when owner Betaudier refused to allow Sparrow time off to appear at Carnival 56. He attended the event regardless, and what could have proven an ill-starred venture took an even worse turn when

The Mighty Sparrow flies like an eagle.

he took the stage — the emcee introduced him as Lord Melody.

Utterly unflappable, Sparrow proceeded to perform every Melody song he knew, halting only when the ecstatic audience asked if he had any original material. He promptly launched into the infectious road march "Yankees Gone," celebrating the long-overdue departure of American troops from Trinidadian soil, and set himself on course for a phenomenal double triumph, taking both the Calypso King and the Road March crowns.

Sparrow made his recorded debut onstage at the Queens Club, Savannah on February 12, 1956, performing "Yankees Gone" (which subsequently became better known as "Jean and Dinah," under which title Harry Belafonte covered it). Broadcast on local radio that same evening, the song then appeared on the Emory Cook produced album *Jump Up Carnival in Trinidad.*

Despite his success, Sparrow went home utterly disgruntled by his experiences. His Calypso King triumph rewarded him with a grand prize of just $40 — by comparison, the winner of the Carnival Queen beauty contest received

$7,500). Immediately, Sparrow wrote the condemnatory "Carnival Boycott," and then matched actions to words by refusing to participate in the next year's festival. Instead, he made his mark during the pre-carnival season, taking over the Young Brigade Calypso Tent to record the four songs later released on the 1957 compilation *Calypso Kings and Pink Gin.*

Having scored further hits "Jack Palace" (1956), "No Doctor No" and "Sailor Man" (1957), Sparrow also launched into an amazing duel with Lord Melody. The first musical blows were exchanged in the Young Brigade tent at the 1957 pre-carnival event, a "Picong Duel" which, again, was captured on tape by Cook. Sparrow compares Melody's face to a crocodile's, Melody counters by claiming to have slept with his antagonist's mother, and Sparrow laughs because Melody is clearly unable to differentiate between a woman and a chimpanzee.

"Picong Duel" matched the two masters line for line, and set both up for a string of further assaults on one another. Melody unleashed "Cowboy Sparrow" (from his *Lord Melody Sings Calypso* album), accusing Sparrow of murder.

Sparrow hit back with the hilarious "Reply to Melody," suggesting that not only was Melody confusing his own sordid past with Sparrow's, he now had a face like a menagerie of wild animals and personal hygiene to match (*King Sparrow's Calypso Carnival*). This duel continued for several years to come.

Sparrow also cut his first album in late 1957, for release in the new year. *Calypso Carnival 58* was titled to amplify his non-appearance from that year's event as well, but wound up producing some of the event's most popular songs, regardless of his absence. Three of his compositions dominated the Road March competition — "PAYE" (a pro-Government song concerning the need to pay taxes), "Russian Satellite" (condemning the Soviets' launch of a dog into space) and "Theresa."

Sparrow was accompanied on the disc by The Boys, a band lining up as Poppo Arundel (guitar), Cyril Mitchell (piano), C Fitt (bass), Harold deFreitas, Sonny Dennis, Cyril Diaz, C Thompson and C Imlack (saxes) and Paul Oxley (trumpet). Released by the Balisier (and later, Cook) labels in Port of Spain, the album was subsequently issued in the UK, spread across three EPs by the Melodisc label's Kalypso subsidiary. A US release, similar to the original T&T pressing, appeared in 1958, just as Sparrow's next album, *This Is Sparrow*, was released.

A highly celebratory set, the album opened with a song which absolutely captured the sense of optimism then percolating through the region, as the islands of the British Caribbean embarked upon a new political venture, the West Indies Federation. Sparrow's "Federation" (aka "We All Is One") was his contribution to the festivities. (The union shattered in 1962.)

Once again, Sparrow boycotted the 1959 carnival, instead embarking on a series of marathon tours. The end of this self-exile was in sight, however. That same year saw the creation of the Carnival Development Committee, a body designed to assist and protect musicians.

1959 also brought the album *Sparrow in Hi Fi*, recorded with Sonny Denner and his Orchestra, before Sparrow signed with RCA that spring. His label debut, *Sparrow*, was recorded in Port of Spain in August, 1959, with DeFreitas, Diaz, Mitchell, Frankie Francis (alto sax), Errol Ince (trumpet), Arnold Bowen (bass) and Sonny Bain (drums). The set was released shortly before Sparrow returned to Carnival in 1960, an event which, predictably, he dominated with the effusive "May May."

1961 saw further Carnival triumphs with "Royal Jail" and "Ten to One Is Murder"; 1962 delivered "Model Nation" (celebrating T&T's newly attained independence) and "Sparrow Come Back Home"; 1963 brought "Dan Is the Man in the Van." Indeed, over the next decade, Sparrow

ran out Carnival King six times and Road March King five times, scooping both titles on three occasions.

It was this unique achievement which finally prompted Sparrow to retire from Carnival altogether in 1974, simply to give the younger generation a chance of glory. He returned from this self-imposed exile in 1992, to triumph with the aptly titled "Survival," but was defeated the following year by Chalkdust, who himself only narrowly made the show after his car broke down en route.

Sparrow also maintained a phenomenal barrage of new releases. Some 40 albums appeared during the 1960s and 1970s, with American political cuts like "Kennedy and Kruschev" and "Martin Luther King for President" acknowledging Sparrow's growing international following, even as he maintained a constant commentary on T&T's own government. Throughout the mid-1950s, he was a vociferous supporter of Eric Williams' independence-minded PNP party as it strove for election; and in the years leading up to the achievement of that goal, Sparrow continued to discuss Williams' policies in song.

In 1962, Sparrow departed RCA for National, where he remained for the next five years. His next album, *Sparrow Meets the Dragon*, was cut in Jamaica with band leader Byron Lee and his Dragonaires, validating the Jamaican veteran's own increasing flirtation with calypso. The pairing's version of "Only a Fool Breaks His Own Heart" earned a gold disc in the Netherlands.

Neither was the traffic purely one way. In 1967, Lee included Sparrow's "Obeah Wedding" on his *Rock Steady Beat* album — and that despite the song certainly not boasting anything of the sort. Two years later, Sparrow recorded his own version of Derrick Harriott's "John Jones," while several of his late 1960s/early 1970s albums were mixed and mastered at Byron Lee's Dynamic Studios.

Similarly, several UK ska and reggae labels entered Mighty Sparrow singles into their catalogs during the late 1960s — "Leading Calypsonians," "Clara Honey Bunch" and "Goaty" (1965), his last Melodisc releases, were followed by "The Village Ram" (1967), "Mr Walker" (1969), "I Don't Wanna Lose You" (1970) and "Maria" (1971).

Signing to Lennox Straker's eponymous label, the 1970s was the decade of Sparrow's greatest international success. It kicked off in 1971 with the *Best Of* album, recorded live in Brooklyn, NY. Three years later, marking his retirement from Carnival, Sparrow traveled to the legendary Criteria Studios in Miami to cut *Hot and Sweet*, his debut album for new label Warner Brothers.

1975 brought a reunion with Byron Lee for *Sparrow Dragon Again*, while 1977 saw Sparrow score a massive hit with "Crawford," a tribute to T&T's first ever Olympic gold medal winner, 100 meters runner Hasley Crawford. Other heroes honored by Sparrow during the late 1970s included Penny Commissiong, the first ever black Miss Universe (1978), Kerry Packer, the founder of an ill-fated "cricket circus" (1979), and the Shah of Iran (1980 — a song later covered by the Manhattan Transfer).

He toured west Africa during 1977 with the World Festival of Black Arts and Culture, during which outing he was awarded the honorary Yoruba title Chief Omo Wale of Ikoyi. In 1978, Sparrow was in London, recording another all covers collection, *Only a Fool*, for the Trojan label.

Proof that calypso was shifting was delivered by 1981's "Sexy Marajhin," Sparrow's first ever chutney composition. The following year's *Sweeter than Ever* album then ventured into the swirling soca waters via so-called "disco versions" of two tracks, "I Love New York" and "Rock Your Body." His continued stranglehold on the local scene, too, was reinforced when "Doh Back Back" won the 1984 Road March, and the next year, he agreed to appear at Carnival's King of Kings show.

Alongside fellow legends (and past Carnival Kings) Lord Kitchener, Lord Melody, Black Stalin and more, Sparrow effortlessly took the title and, this time, a first prize of $10,000. Further tribute to his vast contribution to Trinidadian music arrived when he was awarded an honorary Ph.D by the University of the West Indies. His recordings of the past three decades, after all, had been the subject of so many learned dissertations, that Sparrow was already a virtual doctorate course in his own right.

Although he has continued gigging, his output slowed during the 1990s. Following his return to carnival in 1992/93, and an unexpected reggae Sunsplash berth that same year, a union with Eddy Grant's Ice Records label saw new albums *Dancing Shoes* and *Hot Fire* released to great acclaim. Meanwhile, Sparrow also enjoyed a brief feud with Ras Shorty I, after the soca pioneer hit out at Sparrow's continued musical interest in sexual matters. Sparrow struck back with "The More the Merrier," reminding Shorty of his own youthful libido.

The mid-1990s also saw Ice launch a four volume series of compilations designed to continue acquainting the master to an entire new generation of pupils. Introductions complete, they would then be ready for the main feast, Sparrow's own forty-CD/600 song *The Anthology of Mighty Sparrow — The Millennium Series*.

DISCOGRAPHY

7 Calypso Carnival (Balisier — T&T) 1958

Wrapping up early hits "Theresa," "PAYE," "Russian Satellite" and, of course, "Reply to Melody."

6 This Is Sparrow (Balisier — T&T) 1958

"Federation" is the original version; following the political entity's disintegration in 1962, Sparrow cut a new "Feder-

ation," retitling the 1958 take "We All Is One." Elsewhere, "You Must Pay Tax" repeats the exhortations of "PAYE."

9 Sparrow in Hi Fi (Balisier — T&T) 1959

The best of Sparrow's early albums, especially "Harry in the Piggery," "The Gunslingers" and "Carlton Peeping at Me."

8 Sparrow (RCA) 1960

"May May" and "Leave the Damn Doctor," the hits of the 1960 carnival, are highlights of a delightfully boisterous album.

7 The Mighty Sparrow (RCA) 1960

8 Sparrow's Greatest Hits (RCA) 1960

8 More Sparrow's Greatest Hits (RCA) 1960

Two excellent sets featuring rerecordings (with the Joey Lewis and Errol Ince Orchestras) of material dating back to "Jean and Dinah."

6 Sparrow Calypso King (RCA) 1960

6 Sparrow the Conqueror (RCA) 1961

6 The Calypso King of Trinidad (RCA) 1961

6 Sparrow Come Back (RCA) 1962

6 Calypso Sparrow (RCA) 1963

Any of Sparrow's later RCA albums are representative, each one highlighted by that year's Carnival hits, but generally throwing in at least a couple of other gems.

6 The Slave (National — T&T) 1963

8 Sparrow at the Sheraton Kingston (National — T&T) 1963

Delightful in concert set includes the last album's "Kennedy & Kruschev," "Ten to One Is Murder," "Dan Is the Man" and a couple of his most riotously humorous routines, "English Society" and "Extemporaneous Singing."

7 Sparrow Sings Songs for Lovers (RCA) 1964

Possibly inspired by Harry Belafonte, but never hiding his calypso light under a bush, Sparrow brings those sonorous tones to bear on such standards as "Save the Last Dance for Me" and "The Great Pretender."

6 The Outcast (National — T&T) 1964

7 Christmas with Sparrow (National — T&T) 1964

"Frosty the Snowman" and "Rudolph the Red Nosed Reindeer" lead a joyful festive feast.

6 Congo Man (National — T&T) 1965

7 Sparrow's Calypso (National — T&T) 1965

7 Tattooed Lady (National — T&T) 1966

Cole Porter's "Under My Skin" gets an unlikely airing, alongside typical Sparrow fare "English Diplomacy," "Steering Wheel" and the traditional "Big Bamboo."

6 The Calypso Genius (National — T&T) 1966

6 Sparrow at the Hilton (Recording Artists — T&T) 1967

7 Spicy Sparrow (Recording Artists — T&T) 1967

7 Spicy Sparrow Revised Version (Recording Artists — T&T) 1968

The revisions actually mount to nothing more than a stereo mix, and the substitution of two ballads, "Who Can I Turn To" and "My Warm and Tender Heart," with "St Croix" and "Shake de Ting." In either case, a remake of 1965's "Congo Man" is the best cut.

8 Sparrow Calypso Carnival (Recording Artists — T&T) 1968

Strong set featuring another remake of "Jean & Dinah," plus "Sell the Pussy," "Royal Jail" and an odd "Theme from Romeo & Juliet." A reissue of this album with dubbed applause apparently appeared as *Sparrow in London* during the early 1970s.

8 More Sparrow More (Recording Artists — T&T) 1969

The original version of "Sparrow Dead" is the excellent opener; a lament for the recently deceased Martin Luther King a poignant highlight.

7 Bang Bang Lulu in New York (Recording Artists — T&T) 1969

6 Calypso Time (Recording Artists — T&T) 1970

6 Calypso a la King (Hilary — T&T) 1971

5 Live Volume Two (Hilary — T&T) 1971

Another odd release, largely compiling previously released material, but adding new vocals to the take. Just two new songs appear, "Blame It on Me" and "World on an Island." One also wonders where volume one/sides A and B got to — the sleeve and labels of this release are for sides C and D.

8 The Best Of (Strakers) 1971

Recorded live in Brooklyn, nine tracks include "May May," "Village Ram" and "Obeah Wedding," before a particularly enthused local audience.

6 Sparrow Power (Recording Artists — T&T) 1971

6 Moods of Sparrow (Bestway — T&T) 1972

7 Hotter than Ever (Recording Artists — T&T) 1972

Having recorded his last album in Canada, Sparrow thanks his hosts with "Toronto Mas," before launching into some of his most ribald songs in a while — "More Cock," "Wum Pum," "Drunk and Disorderly". . . .

6 Sparrow Spectacular (WIRL — JA) 1973

5 Knock Dem Down (Recording Artists — T&T) 1973

10 Hot and Sweet (Warner Bros) 1974

Modern rock studio, tight familiar band, Sparrow's best selling album by a long chalk serves up excellent revisions of some of his finest compositions — "Sparrow Dead," "More Cock," "Mr Walker," "English Diplomacy" and more.

6 Calypso Maestro (Recording Artists — T&T) 1974

7 Sparrow vs the Rest (Tysott — T&T) 1976

7 Boogie Beat 77 (Semp — T&T) 1977

The intriguing title suggests this might be Sparrow's disco album; it isn't, but only in as much as *Hot and Sweet* wasn't his rock album. There are definitely a few strands of international dance lurking beneath the traditional Sparrow arrangements, and the title track screams out for a disco ball remix.

6 Sparrow NYC Blackout (Charlie's — T&T) 1977

"King Kong," "Life Down in Hell," "Idi Amin" and "First Miss Black Universe" are the stand-outs; the title track is a wry walk through some scary streets.

6 Only a Fool (Trojan — UK) 1978

Updating the *Songs for Lovers* concept (and revisiting "Save the Last Dance for Me"), Sparrow strikes some surprising oil — Jimi Hendrix's "Angel" and Gilbert O'Sullivan's woeful "Alone Again (Naturally)" are not songs one instantly associates with the old bird.

6 Pussycat Party (SH — T&T) 1978

7 London Bridge (JAF — T&T) 1979

Sparrow's first double album includes "Rum Is Macho," "Mas in Caracas" and "Love African Style."

6 Latin Black (Sparrow — T&T) 1980

7 Sparrow Sanford (Charlies — T&T) 1981

6 Sweeter than Ever (Charlies — T&T) 1982

6 The Greatest (Charlies — T&T) 1983

7 Vanessa (B's) 1984

8 King of the World (B's) 1984

The best of Sparrow's early soca albums includes the superb "Grenada," cogently condemning the USA's recent invasion of his homeland; and "Marajhin Cousin," a delightfully sexual recipe for hot curry.

7 A Touch of Class (B's) 1986

6 One Love One Heart (— T&T) 1987

6 Dr Bird (— T&T) 1988

5 Hot Like Fire (Ice) 1992

6 Dancing Shoes (Ice) 1994

Sparrow's two Eddy Grant-led albums are both higher on good times vibes than the vibrancy of his best work, and revolve more around good time exhortations ("put on your dancing shoes!" "the more the merrier!!" "check me out!!!") than actual lyrics. Great party music, but it doesn't go much further.

6 The Supreme Serenader (AR) 1998

MIGHTY SPARROW & BYRON LEE

7 Sparrow Meets the Dragon (Spalee) 1968

Jamaican title *Only a Fool*

6 Sparrow Dragon Again (Spalee) 1975

9 Volume 1 (Ice) 1992
9 Volume 2 (Ice) 1993
8 Volume 3 (Ice) 1993
8 Volume 4 (Ice) 1994

There have been many earlier compilations, most on vinyl, the majority only released in T&T. This ambitious set is the first to cater for an international audience, highlighting Sparrow through the 1960s-early 1980s. There's also an abbreviated volume split with Lord Kitchener (*16 Carnival Hits* which is recommended for absolute beginners.

9 The Millennium Series (Mika Enterprises) 2000–2001

How much Sparrow is too much Sparrow? If you can't answer that, 40 discs (mercifully available individually) endeavor to make thematic and chronological sense of every extant Sparrow recording, some 600 songs. Titles in the series are:

A Mother's Love (Mika Enterprises) 2000
All the Girls (Mika Enterprises) 2000
Cassanova (Mika Enterprises) 2000
Christmas (Mika Enterprises) 2000
Cokie Eye Rooster (Mika Enterprises) 2000
Comikal (Mika Enterprises) 2001
Corruption (Mika Enterprises) 2001
Dance Party Gold (Mika Enterprises) 2000
Dirty Old Men (Mika Enterprises) 2001
Don't Touch Meh President (Mika Enterprises) 2000
Down Memory Lane (Mika Enterprises) 2000
Frenzy (Mika Enterprises) 2001
Guidance (Mika Enterprises) 2000
Heat Wave (Mika Enterprises) 2001
Humourous (Mika Enterprises) 2001
Jamboree (Mika Enterprises) 2001
Legend (Mika Enterprises) 2001
Rampage (Mika Enterprises) 2001
Renaissance (Mika Enterprises) 2000
Salvation with Soca Ballads (Mika Enterprises) 2000
Soca Jamback #2 (Mika Enterprises) 2000
Soca Lingo (Mika Enterprises) 2001
Soca Lover (Mika Enterprises) 2000
Street Dancing (Mika Enterprises) 2000
Supreme Serenader (Mika Enterprises) 2000
Sweet Soca Ballads (Mika Enterprises) 2000
Sweet Talk (Mika Enterprises) 2001
The Early Years (Mika Enterprises) 2001
Top Gun (Mika Enterprises) 2001
True Awakening (Mika Enterprises) 2001
Vigilance (Mika Enterprises) 2001
Zesty (Mika Enterprises) 2001

JACOB MILLER see INNER CIRCLE

SUGAR MINOTT

STYLE *reggae (dance hall)*
BORN *Lincoln Barrington Minott, 5/25/56 (Kingston, JA)*

Throughout the early 1980s, it would have been a foolhardy observer indeed who bet against Sugar Minott claiming the throne which Bob Marley's death had laid vacant. As both a writer and a vocalist, Minott had few peers even on a scene rich with new talent, while his international impact was assured as early as 1979 when, still considered a rising star in his homeland, he erupted onto the UK reggae charts with his British debut single, "Hard Time Pressure." The #4 hit "Good Thing Going" followed in 1981, and Minott's presence in Britain throughout this period was essential to the development of the country's indigenous Lovers Rock scene.

But Minott was also fiercely devoted to the talent being nurtured by his own Youth Promotion/Black Roots collective and, as the decade passed, so his refusal to advance his own career without taking at least some of his proteges with him began working against him. By the late 1980s, Minott was widely considered a spent force, and it was the middle of the next decade before he finally began to regain lost ground.

Having cut his performing teeth as selector on the Sound of Silence Keystone and his own Gathering of Youth sound systems, Minott first came to notice in 1969, as one third of the African Brothers, a hard-edged roots trio completed by Derrick Howard and Tony Tuff.

The group competed at a number of amateur talent contests, and first recorded for the Micron label, run by future Sunsplash figureheads Ronny Burke and Mick Johnson. Among the trio's releases over the next three years were "Hold on King Son," "Party Night" (produced by Duke Thelwell), "A di System" and "Gimme Gimme African Love," recorded with Jah Bunny, and the self-produced "Torturing." The African Brothers also launched their own Ital label, releasing "Youths of Today," "Righteous Kingdom," "Lead Us Father" and others.

Following a masterful collaboration with producer Rupie Edwards, "Mysterious Nature" (1974), the African Brothers wound up at Studio One, where they recorded "No Cup No Broke." The group broke up soon after, all three members opting for solo careers. Remaining at Studio One, Minott was instantly singled out as a potential star, both in his own right and as a session musician. Providing vocals, guitar and percussion to a succession of studio productions, he was soon cutting his own singles.

Studio head Coxsone Dodd was especially intrigued by Minott's ability to conjure new lyrics over existing rhythms, a time honored trick in the dance halls and sound systems, but still a largely untried skill in the studio. Soon, the singer was expertly voicing a host of archived backing tracks, scoring his first hit with "Vanity" in 1978. It was followed by "Mr DC," "House Is Not a Home," "Hang on Natty," "Wrong Doers" and "Is It True." The year also brought Minott's first album, *Live Loving*. Again largely comprising new lyrics to old tunes, the album went some way towards anticipating the dance hall explosion of the early 1980s.

Working extensively with producer Niney Holness, further Studio One singles included "Babylon," "No Vacancy" and "Give Thanks and Praise," while a second Studio One album, 1979's *Showcase* wrapped up the 45s which had not made the earlier set. Additional singles that year included "Give the People," "All Things Bright," "Lamb's Bread" (with Dillinger), "World of Sorrow," "Every Little Thing," "Every Day You Fight Rasta" and "Youthman Promotion"; while sessions cut with Prince Jammy at King Tubby's produced the hit "Never too Young" and a new album, *Bittersweet*.

In 1980, Minott launched his own Youth Promotion/ Black Roots label and production company, debuting it with the hit singles "Man Hungry," "River Jordan" and "51 Storm." He also appeared at Reggae Sunsplash, and by the end of the next year had issued the albums *Black Roots* (released in the US by Mango), *Roots Lovers* and *African Girl*. The key release, however, was *Ghetto-ology*, immaculately self-produced with backing from the Soul Syndicate, and a crucial dub remix by King Tubby.

It was this album which confirmed Minott's ascendancy, and the only person who didn't seem aware of that fact was the singer himself. Looking back on the occasion of the album's 2000 reissue, he mused, "I was so naive about being a star. I just wanted to play the music." The sleeve photograph was taken at the time of the album's recording, and Minott continued, "My girlfriend made me this shirt, Big Youth gave me this old guitar and I don't remember where I got this hat from. And this is, like, from here to boomin' on the streets of London a year later."

With the self-produced "Hard Time Pressure" introducing Minott to the UK, the singer relocated to that country in 1980, where he maintained a steady blast of new releases. "Not for Sale" (produced by Alvin Ranglin), "Steal Away Girl," "African Girl" (with Ranking Dread), "Run Come," "Mr Fisherman," "Hold On" and "Half of Love" (Linval Thompson) all appeared that year, with the Donovan Germain produced cover of Michael Jackson's "Good Thing Going" finally breaking him on the national chart.

Picked up for distribution by the RCA major, its success paved the way for an instant follow-up, "Never My Love," and a new album, *Good Thing Going*. Riding the Lovers Rock boom, Minott crowned himself its king with an in-

spired rewrite of David Gates' "Make It with You," retitled "Lovers Rock" and recorded in London with local superstar Carroll Thompson.

New singles continued to appear regularly: "Africa," "In a dis Ya Time," "How Could I Let You Go Away," "Is It True" and "Level Vibes." At the same time, however, a string of albums compiling earlier recordings hit the streets, so many that Minott himself did not release another album until 1983. Having returned to Jamaica, he concentrated his energies on Youth Promotion/Black Roots. (He announced his arrival with an excellent Sunsplash performance.) This devotion, compounded with his long absence from the dance halls during his period of greatest success, has often been cited for his failure to fully maximize his obvious popularity.

Nevertheless, Minott remained both active and successful. He appeared at Sunsplash in 1984, 1985 and 1986, performing alongside protege Abashanti at the latter two. He also set up the Youth Promotion sound system which took up residence in Maxfield Park, Kingston, with Jah Stitch leading the deejay team. Ranking Joe, Captain Sinbad and Ranking Dread all rose out of his outfit, while much of the Black Roots label's output was dictated by these performers, alongside 45s by Barry Brown, Tenor Saw, Michael Palmer (aka Palmer Dog), Junior Reid and one of the English performers Minott had discovered during his London sojourn, Trevor Hartley. Barrington Levy and Horace Andy also recorded sides for the label.

Following a stint with New York based producer Lloyd "Bullwackie" Barnes, and the *Wicked a Go Feel It* album, Minott linked with Sly & Robbie for 1984's "Rub a Dub Sound Style" single, a prototype for the ragga style which developed during the mid-1980s. An album recorded at that time, *Sugar and Spice* (featuring remakes of several *Ghetto-ology* tracks), did not appear until 1986. In the meantime, Sly & Robbie rhythms percolated through several subsequent Minott albums produced by George Phang, 1985's *Rydim* and *Time Longer than Rope*.

"Dance Hall We Deh," "All Day and Night" (produced by Errol Lewis/John Marshall), "We Have fi Live," "What a Feeling," "Mind Blowing Decisions," "Save Your Loving for Me" and the two part "Funking Song" (Gussie Clarke) maintained Minott's profile through the late 1980s, but unquestionably his standards had slipped somewhat since his peak. He had closed Black Roots and was now freelancing around the studios, frequently putting his name to work he wouldn't have touched a few years earlier.

Some releases, of course, were pure gold—*Showdown Volume Two*, a Joe Gibbs production which paired Minott with rising teenager Frankie Paul, showed class on both sides of the disc, while a duet with JC Lodge, "Since You Came into My Life," was also a marvel. A return engagement with Bullwackie Barnes in 1987 saw the *Jamming in the Streets* album achieve some success, while 1988's *Buy Out the Bar* album, a reunion with Phang, was titled for Minott's biggest hit single in several years.

Sunsplash appearances in 1989, 1992, 1995 and 1996 maintained his live profile, in the studio, however, Minott's best received work came in collaboration with the stars of the new decade. 1994's "Chow" paired him with Shaggy, 1996's "Wise Up" with Mutabaruka. He also teamed up with Youth Promotion prodigy Junior Reid to record 1992's "Wah Them a Do."

However, 1994's *Breaking Free* album, produced by Tappa Zukie, and 1996's *International*, with Scientist, both indicated that Minott was still firing on all cylinders, harnessing sufficient modern techniques to remain current, but not sacrificing any of his own original potency.

SELECTED DISCOGRAPHY

8 Live Loving (Studio One — JA) 1978

Studio One's response to the wholesale versioning of its rock steady/early reggae rhythms by the dance hall community. Over some of the label's most treasured classics, the sweet voiced Minott's new lyrics were a revelation, and his album debut is now almost unanimously credited among the crucial templates for the next decade.

7 Showcase (Studio One — JA) 1979

Basically a singles collection, twinning vocal and dub mixes, all heavy on the then-de rigueur syndrums.

7 Bittersweet (Ballistic — JA) 1979
8 Black Roots (Mango) 1980

Anybody coming to Minott from the sugary side should brace themselves now. Black and rootsy indeed, in the late 1970s this was just another deeply dread collection, albeit with a roster of notable musicians and backing singers. But time has bestowed a stately uniqueness to it, helped by such classic hits as "River Jordan" and "Hard Time Pressure."

7 Ghetto-ology (Trojan — UK) 1979

The last of Minott's unrepentant roots albums is marked out by the somber "People Got to Know," "Dreader Than Dread," "Never Gonna Give Jah Up" and the hymnal "Africa Is the Black Man's Home." "Strange Things," meanwhile, rewrites the MOR chestbeater "Those Were the Days" to classy effect. The 2000 reissue (Easy Street) appends the dub version to the original album.

7 Roots Lovers (Black Roots — JA) 1980

Minott's first unmistakably Lovers Rock album, showcasing those vocals with devastating accuracy.

8 African Girl (Black Roots) 1981
8 Good Thing Going (RCA) 1981

Minott's biggest seller and it's not hard to see why. The title track, a luscious Lovers Rock cover of the soul classic, remains timeless; Minott's take on "Walk on By" is positively majestic; and the rest of the set — seven originals and one more cover — follows them into smooth, heart-and soul-warming territory. Since reissued by Heartbeat.

7 Dance Hall Showcase (Black Roots) 1983
10 Herbman Hustling (Black Roots) 1984

The impeccable title track, the cheeky "Dance Hall Business" ("there's no business like . . ."), the temptations which awaited "Uptown Girl" and even an adaptation of the hymn "Rock of Ages" hallmark Minott's finest album, the happiest compromise of all between his rootsy roots and love of Lovers Rock. Since reissued by Heartbeat.

6 Slice of the Cake (Black Roots) 1984

Features the original, self-produced version of "Buy Out the Bar," together with the mighty "We a fi Live" and "Harbour Shark," although the highlight is "Inna Dance Hall Style" — which lives up to its title with a vengeance.

8 Wicked a Go Feel It (Wackies) 1984

Produced by Lloyd Barnes, *Wicked* covers cultural as well as lovers themes with equal aplomb. Consistently excellent, it also includes a notably different version of his UK hit "A Good Thing Going."

7 Leader of the Pack (Striker Lee) 1985
7 Rydim (Greensleeves — UK) 1985
6 Time Longer than Rope (Greensleeves — UK) 1985
9 Inna Reggae Dance Hall (Heartbeat) 1986

Roots goes ragga across a dozen crucial, hit heavy cuts, including frothing variations on "Rub a Dub," the sufferer's classic "Victim of Society," a taste of rock steady ragga-style ". . . Fashion," and pure dance hall a la "Four Wheel Wheelie."

8 Sugar & Spice (Taxi) 1986

Another hit filled album, and one of Minott's best, "Rub A Dub Style" with its fabulous rhythm and a remade "Herbman Hustling" are worth the price of entry alone.

7 Jamming in the Streets (Wackies) 1987
4 African Soldier (Heartbeat) 1988

Ostensibly a concept album, whose dozen tracks revolve mostly around the theme of Africa. It's heart (and vocals) are in the right place, but the synth heavy and effects-laden production popular in the day sucked the soul right out of it.

8 Buy Off de Bar (Sonic Sounds) 1988

Sly & Robbie may control the proceedings, but Minott's vocals conquer all; the rerecorded title track grabbed most of the attention, but the rest of the album is at least as strong.

7 Sugar Minott & Youth Promotion (NEC) 1988

6 Lovers Rock inna Dance hall (Youth Promotion — JA) 1988

8 Sufferers Choice (Heartbeat) 1988

Sly & Robbie and the Roots Radics provide the rhythms, Peter Chemist the mix, and the title track's a stand-out in dance hall roots. "Ghetto Life" offers some brilliantly scything social commentary, while "A Rough Ole Life (Babylon)" and "Lover's Race" were deserved UK hits, with the latter opening the Lovers Rock half of the album. And through it all, Minott's vocals and vision don't drop a cadence.

6 Ghetto Youth Dem Rising (Heartbeat) 1988

5 The Boss Is Back (RAS) 1989

7 Ghetto Child (Heartbeat) 1989

The roots may not be as deep as past discs, but even ominous tracks like "Danger Zone" have an overwhelming aura of optimism, with the title track a cry of defiance, Meanwhile, the lovers tracks bubble by with good-natured grace. The CD version appends dub mixes of all the tracks bar the final hymnal adaptation.

6 Smile (L&M - JA) 1990

6 A Touch of Class (Jammys — JA) 1991

6 Happy Together (Heartbeat) 1991

"This Reggae Feeling" adds an unexpected dose of funk, "My Girl She's Gone" introduces Motown to ragga, while the title track, a marvelously surreal cover of the The Turtles' hit, pulls a swing band into the dance hall. Diversity almost rules, but sadly the lightweight, pretty pop ends up predominating.

6 Run Things (VP) 1993

7 Breaking Free (RAS) 1994

Scratch the impossibly trite "Dance Hall Fever" out of the grooves and Minott's meeting with the masterful Zukie is flawless. "Sprinter Stayer" is quintessential Minott, layered over a typical Tappa rhythm attack, while "Heads of Conference" is a powerful condemnation of modern politics.

6 International (RAS) 1996

4 Musical Murder (VP) 1997

5 Easy Squeeze (World) 1999

SUGAR MINOTT & GREGORY ISAACS

6 Double Dose (Blue Mountain) 1987

SUGAR MINOTT & FRANKIE PAUL

8 Showdown Volume Two (Channel One — JA)

Up and comer Frankie Paul takes on the veteran Minott and fights him to a draw, aided by his debut hit single "Worries in the Dance" and mixes by the ever creative Scientist.

SUGAR MINOTT & LEROY SMART

7 Award Winners (Greensleeves — UK) 1985

SELECTED COMPILATIONS & ARCHIVE RELEASES

9 With Lots of Extra (Hitbound) 1983

Bundling up a clutch of Minott's Niney Holness produced hits, "Babylon" and "Give Thanks & Praise" included, then tossing in the extras that are all equally good.

7 Best of Vol 1 (Black Roots) 1988

7 Collectors Collection Vol 1 (Heartbeat) 1996

7 RAS Portrait (RAS) 1997

Fair representation drawn from three RAS albums, consistent with the concurrent *Breaking Free* and *International* (plus one cut from *Run Things*), but at its best in the earlier *Sugar and Spice* territory.

8 Sugar Minott's Hidden Treasures (Easy Street) 1999

Two volumes, but one killer collection, as the vaults of Minott's Black Roots throw up a powerful survey of the label's output, including both hits and unreleased cuts. Included are Barrington Levy, Horace Andy (a stunning "Ain't No Sunshine"), Garnett Silk, Ranking Joe, Yami Bolo, Junior Delgado and more, plus a real treasure in the form of the African Brothers' 1971 45 "Righteous Kingdom."

SUGAR MINOTT & THE AFRICAN BROTHERS

8 Collectors Item (Uptempo) 1987

Wicked selection of Minott's earliest work — not an easy disc to find, but it's worth the search. Not only was there life before Lovers Rock, it was pretty lively as well.

MUTABARUKA

STYLE *rhythm poetry/dub poetry*
BORN *Allan Hope, 12/26/56 (Rae Town, JA)*

Dub poet Mutabaruka is one of the founding fathers of the Caribbean rhythm poetry movement, itself a continuation of the oral traditions highlighted, at least for the postcolonial generation, by the work of Louise Bennett. He has also been credited, by literary sources hitherto utterly unfamiliar with "popular" musical forms, for creating an even fresher style, acceptable to mainstream literary critics, termed "meta-dub" — that is, dub poetry which is as effective on the printed page as it is in performance. That, indeed, is a rare talent.

Trained as an electrician, the young Allan Hope worked for the Jamaican Telephone Company before quitting in 1971.

Converting to Rastafarianism, Hope moved up to the Potosi hills, in the parish of St James, to concentrate on his poetry. He received considerable attention with "Wailin'," a 1974 dedication to Bob Marley constructed around Wailers' song titles. 1976 brought the widely acclaimed *Sun and*

Moon collection. His first poem was published by *Swing* magazine that July and, over the next three years, Hope became a regular contributor.

1973 saw him publish his first book of poems, *Outcry*, under the name Mutabaruka, a Rwandan phrase translating as "one who is always victorious."

Backed by his own band, Truth, Mutabaruka turned to live performance in 1977 and, the following year, he scored a Jamaican hit courtesy of Light of Saba's nyahbingi-inflected version of his 1973 poem "Outcry." Around the same time he began recording for Earl "Chinna" Smith's High Times label.

Having just published the *The Book: First Poems* collection, Mutabaruka finally burst onto the international scene with a well-received set at the 1981 Reggae Sunsplash. The success of that year's "Everytime a Ear de Soun'" single and 1983's *Check It* album added to his impact. (Mutabaruka returned to Sunsplash in 1982, 1983, 1985, 1987, 1988, 1991, and 1993–1996.) He also appeared in American director's Alan Greenspan's documentary study of Bob Marley's funeral and its philosophical aftermath.

In 1983, the US based Heartbeat label commissioned Mutabaruka to supervise a compilation of current dub poetry talent, *Word Sound 'Ave Power: Dub Poets & Dub*. A dub version, created by producer Scientist, and the *Womantalk* collection of female dub and rapso poets followed. Meanwhile, the Shanachie label picked up Mutabaruka's *The Mystery Unfolds* album, a mutually beneficial arrangement, which established the label among America's leading reggae outlets, at the same time as guaranteeing the artist an international audience.

Mutabaruka swiftly ensured his music packed sufficient textures to utterly decry the "militant poetry with a dub beat" summary beloved by sundry on- and off-line reference sources. Mutabaruka also drew a number of guests into play. Marcia Griffiths and Ini Kamosa feature on *The Mystery Unfolds*, while Kamosa returned alongside Sly and Robbie on *Melanin Man*. Among other most notable collaborations are "Hard Road to Travel," recorded with Gregory Isaacs, and 1990's "Great Kings of Africa" single, featuring Dennis Brown.

Elsewhere, "The People's Court," from 1991's *Blakk Wi Blakk . . . K . . . K . . .* album featured top Jamaican impressionist Gary Saddler taking the roles of politicians Michael Manley and Edward Seaga; Mutabaruka followed up in 1994 with "The People's Court Part Two." At the same time, tapes of his newly-launched, and never less than challenging IRIE-FM radio show became a hot underground commodity — all the more so after the station banned "People's Court" from its airwaves!

1996 brought major hits "Wise Up," recorded with Sugar Minott and "Psalm 24" with Luciano. Further evidence of Mutabaruka's dexterity was offered by 1998's *Gathering of the Spirits* album, recorded with the newly convened Roots All Stars band. A US tour in late 2000 indicated an imminent return to action.

DISCOGRAPHY

8 Check It (Alligator—JA) 1983

The rich atmospheres come courtesy of a coterie of Jamaica's best sessionmen, over which Mutabaruka eloquently explores culture, politics and identity. It's an amazingly haunting journey, from the ferocious "Everytime a Ear de Sound" to the lush lovers' rock of "Hard Time Loving," while the fiery "Angola Invasion" and cautionary "Witeman Country" are also highlights of an album that blazes from start to finish.

8 The Mystery Unfolds (Shanachie) 1984

"The revolutionaries have all gone to the art centers." In many ways, Mutabaruka's purest album, the accompaniment following his own rhymes and rhythms as opposed to later albums' more conciliatory compromise. "The Leaders Speak" is darkly thunderous, "Famine Injection" and the anti-imperialist "Old Cut Bruk" echo with spiteful scorn, while "Revolutionary Words" mourns everything that has gone wrong with precisely the revolution which Mutabaruka is trying to rekindle.

7 Out Cry (Shanachie) 1987
7 Any Which Way . . . Freedom (Shanachie) 1989

The powerful "H2 Worka," driving title track and ferocious "Drug Kulta" are the obvious points of entry, while the scathing "Letter from a Friend" is political skewering at its best, and "Skins" a wonder of wordplay, with the rest of the album just as biting.

8 Blakk Wi Blak. . . K . . . K . . . (Shanachie) 1991

A ferocious sound backs Mutabaruka's latest litany of complaints and assaults, but he's never sounded so menacing as "Ecology Poem," a hard rocking lesson which stands in terrifying contrast to the beautiful "Wind of Time" (a duet with Sharon Forrester), the sparse electronics of "Junk Food" and, of course, "The People's Court," an hysterical recapitulation of Buster's Judge Dread — now renamed Judge Better Must Come.

7 Melanin Man (Shanachie) 1994

"People's Court II" brings Judge Better Must Come back into chambers; what more could you want? History gets a beating on "Killin," scientists are brought down on "Bone Lies," while the eloquent title track opens up the theme of Black pride, which is further explored on the infectious "Garvey." "Dance" offers some yummy mind candy, on an otherwise nonstop provocative album.

5 Muta in Dub (Blackheart) 1998
8 Gathering of the Spirits (Shanachie) 1998

A colossal, crashing monster, quite possibly the last crucial superstar jam of the 20th century. Mutabaruka turns the time machine back to the late 1970s, to recreate the true spirit of roots before the dance hall dug them up. Musicians include Sly and Robbie (in distinctly retro mode), Leroy Sibbles and Earl "Chinna" Smith; while Justin Hinds, Big Youth, Judy Mowatt, Culture, the Mighty Diamonds and Marcia Griffiths are among the vocal talents. Not every track is crucial, and the intent does sometimes overcome the execution, but with songs like Marley's "Iron Lion Zion," Joseph Hill's "Black Man King" and a poem by the Native American Chief Seattle, overall, it's a stupendous album.

SELECTED COMPILATIONS & ARCHIVE RELEASES

8 The Ultimate Collection (Shanachie) 1996

16 track collection seeks out a handful of single-only rarities (including the Luciano and Sugar Minott sides), plus an eminently likeable selection of album cuts. Both installments of the wildly popular "Peoples Court" saga are present, together with "Johnny Drughead," a live "Witeman Country" and the electro-chant "Bun Dung Babylon."

NINEY THE OBSERVER

STYLE *reggae*

BORN *George Boswell aka Winston Holness, 1951 (Montego Bay, JA)*

Although Rastafarian themes and imagery had become increasingly prevalent and unimaginably complex in Jamaican music in the years since Count Ossie's drums powered Prince Buster's "Oh Carolina" in 1961, still it was another decade before they truly materialized on the international scene, when Trojan opened volume four of the seminal *Tighten Up* series with Niney the Observer's "Blood and Fire."

Over a bass driven rhythm which itself conjured up all the righteous wrath of mighty Jah, Niney invoked judgement in the form of all-consuming flames and it was, perhaps, only appropriate that he himself should have to spill blood and pass through fire before receiving his just reward.

Niney (so named after he lost a thumb in a workshop accident) was spinning the song's dub plate at Bunny Lee's record store, when musician Glen Adams accused him of having lifted part of the song from a Wailers song — and took the record to the Wailers' own headquarters to prove his point. In the ensuing melee, Niney was slashed across his left shoulder — he still bears the scar today — but his faith in "Blood and Fire" remained unshaken.

Borrowing money from producer Clancy Eccles, he pressed up 200 copies of the single at the Dynamic Records plant, and released it in late 1970 on his Destroyer label. The pressing sold out in record time, and Niney reissued it the following year on his newly formed Observer label. "Blood and Fire" went on to sell some 30,000 copies, and was named Jamaican Record of the Year. Just 19 years old,

and less than four years after he first appeared on the Kingston recording scene, Niney had arrived.

Niney's earliest work saw him employed as an engineer at KG Records, where his first productions included his own "Come on Baby," the single which inaugurated his Destroyer label. He moved on to Bunny Lee's set up in 1967 — ironically, Glen Adams was one of the musicians he recorded at that time. (Lee's All-Stars later recorded "Niney Hop" in his honor.)

From there, Niney joined Lynford Anderson's studio and, by 1968, he was part of Joe Gibbs' empire, replacing his friend, Lee Perry as Gibbs' chief sound engineer. His first major production was "Mr Brown" by the DJ team of Dennis Alcapone and Lizzy, and he also played a major role in launching Dennis Brown, who was just 15 at the time.

Niney's briefly revived his Destroyer label in 1970 as an outlet for his own productions and a handful of releases under his own name — "Blood and Fire" was joined by "Niney Special," "Honey No Money" and "Skankee" among others. Prompted by Lee Perry (who told him "I am the Upsetter, so you can't destroy me"), the label became Observer in early 1971.

With "Blood and Fire," Niney followed through with a succession of increasingly inventive singles under his own name and in cohorts with his studio group, the Observers (actually, the much used Soul Syndicate), featuring (among others) Tony Chin and Earl "Chinna" Smith (guitar), Leroy Wallace (drums), Glen Adams, Ossie Hibbert and Keith Sterling (keyboards). The hits "Brimstone & Fire" and "Lightning & Thunder" were both constructed around the "Blood and Fire" rhythm, while he also oversaw further versions by Tommy McCook ("Psalm 9 to Keep in Mind") and Big Youth ("Fire Bunn").

Niney's own recording career was maintained throughout 1971–72 via collaborations with DJs Max Romeo and Dennis Alcapone: "People Let Love Shine," "Message to the Ungodly," "You Must Believe," "The Red Sea," "Aily & Ailaloo," "In the Gutter" and a joyous Rastafarian adaptation of the gospel singalong "Down by the Riverside." Another prophetic masterpiece was delivered via the Observers' "Observing the Ave"/"Everyday Music" pairing, a DJ extravaganza built around a piano loop from Sly Stone's "Everyday People," with toasting which makes even Dave Barker's trademark yelping sound subdued.

This flurry of activity immeasurably raised Niney's profile as a producer. Delroy Wilson ("Rascal Man," "My Baby Is Gone"), the Heptones (whose "Keep on Pushing was credited to producer and band equally), Johnny Clarke, Slim Smith, Jacob Miller, Junior Delgado, Freddie McGregor and, of course, Dennis Brown all visited the Observer during the early 1970s, often emerging with the most crucial music of their careers so far.

As a producer, whether of other artists or his own material, Niney had no peers — sparse, seemingly simple, and utterly individualistic, he rivaled Lee Perry for innovation, and often eclipsed him. Cut with engineer Errol Thompson, 1971's "Ital Correction" — a musical dictionary translating, of all mundanities, Jamaican foodstuff from English into Rasta — ranks alongside Rupie Edwards' "Ire Feelings" among the most instantly and insistently dislocating pieces of music on the entire proto-dub scene. An album with King Tubby, 1975's *Dubbing with the Observer*, of course, only exacerbated the sensation.

Niney also worked extensively with Perry. Junior Byles' "Dreader Locks" (the dub version of 1974's "Curley Locks" hit) borrowed elements of its rhythm from Niney, while Perry, Niney and Max Romeo together co-wrote both "Babylon's Burning" (released on Upsetter Records) and "Rasta Bandwagon" (on the Observer label). The latter, famously, was a vicious swipe at the plethora of outsiders ("Chinee Rastamen" among them) seemingly hellbent on riding religion to reggae fame. The same rhythm fired another Niney dreadnought, "When Jah Speak," credited to Murt Turt and Purt, and updating the "Blood and Fire" imagery with even more foreboding.

Although Niney's personal output swiftly declined from its early 70s high, he continued unleashing some majestic 45s — 1975's "Zuki Zaki" among them. He also submitted to the will of another producer — Scientist oversaw "Love Comes and Goes." In the meantime, his client base continued to expand. Ken Boothe ("Silver Words"), Junior Byles ("King of Babylon"), Gregory Isaacs ("Rock Away," "Bad Da"), Horace Andy ("Nice and Easy," "I'm in Love"), I-Roy ("Point Blank," "Rasta Pickney," "Jah Come Here," "Zion Train"), Junior Delgado ("Everyday Natty," "Thinking") and Dillinger ("Flat Foot Hustling") all recorded with him

during the mid-1970s, while Niney was also instrumental in shaping what became Black Uhuru, when he cut Michael Rose's prototype version of "Guess Who's Coming to Dinner."

A reunion with the Heptones for 1975's *Better Days* album presaged some great work with Big Youth ("Four Sevens"), U-Roy, I-Roy, Trinity, UK reggae band The Cimarrons, Sugar Minott, Leonard Dillon and the Ethiopians. This flurry of late 1970s activity, however, was followed by several years of comparative silence as Niney traveled to Europe. In November, 1980, he produced American funk rock guitarist Danny Adler, overseeing a session which also featured Mikey Dread and Ansell Collins. He then resurfaced in Paris, France, in 1982 — his activities there included constructing the *Ital Observer Style* album.

Niney returned to Kingston shortly after and resumed recording at the Channel One studios, where he became house producer for the Hitbound label. He was one of the first producers to work with the youthful Beenie Man, for 1983's "Over the Sea." Holness' Observer label also remained high profile, releasing cuts by Sugar Minott ("Lover's Race"), Third World ("Roots with Quality") and others. Despite this success, the mid-1980s found Niney relocating to New York — there, he remixed a number of earlier King Tubby dubs for the *Space Flight Dub* collection. He returned to Kingston around 1988, producing landmark recordings by Yami Bolo, Frankie Paul, Andrew Tosh (the late Peter's son), the newly resurfaced Junior Byles and more — much of this material was collected on the *All Stars Turbo Charge* collection.

Linking with the American Heartbeat label, Niney supervised both the compilation of great swathes of his back catalog and a number of new recordings. He released a new solo album, 1992's *Freaks*, while that same year another reunion with Junior Byles ignited the "Little Fleego" 45. A 1993 collaboration with Dennis Brown produced the *Cosmic Force* album, and in 1997, he paired with Johnny Clarke for *Rock with Me*.

SELECTED DISCOGRAPHY

9 Dubbing With the Observer (Attack — UK) 1975
Famously the first pure dub album released in the UK, 13 slabs of primal Niney put through the King Tubby wringer to emerge with a health warning slapped to every distended bass depth charge. Essential.

7 Sledgehammer Dub (Observer — JA) 1976
Dynamite dub recounting of Dennis Brown's *Westbound Train* album.

7 Ital Observer Style (Jah Live — France) 1983
A powerful DJ collection featuring Niney's excursions over familiar Max Romeo cuts, alongside material by Dillinger, Big Youth, I-Roy and Jah Bop.

9 Freaks (Heartbeat) 1992

Unexpectedly brilliant return to solo action, cut with Steely and Clevie, Chinna Smith and others. The liner notes suggest a concept album analyzing the hell of modern urban life, and it might well be. Certainly there's a raw edge present which is absent from much of his recent production work, while material ranges from an oddly subdued (but effective nevertheless) remake of "Blood and Fire," and a snarling assault on Prince Buster's "Blackhead Chineman," to a handful of new compositions indicating Niney's grasp on sundry dance hall sensibilities.

SELECTED COMPILATIONS & ARCHIVE RELEASES

6 Space Flight Dub (ROIR)
10 Blood & Fire 1971–72 (Trojan) 1988

It's not totally apocalyptic, but there's more thunder and brimstone than you can shake a corrective rod at; 24 tracks of Niney numbers and productions from his best period, including a bucketful of "Blood & Fire" versions plus great tracks from Max Romeo, Delroy Wilson, The Heptones and Dennis Alcapone, all featuring some of Niney's most adventurous rhythms.

7 Bring the Couchie 1974–76 (Trojan) 1989

A singles collection from Niney's roots and dub period includes Max Romeo's title track, three versions of Dennis Brown's "Wolf & Leopard" and a pair of Horace Andy songs.

8 Observation Station (Heartbeat) 1990

Tracing the producer's gradual shift out of dread prophecy and into straightforward roots, this compilation features a host of seminal tracks, from Junior Byles' "Weeping" to the original recording of "Guess Who's Coming to Dinner," alongside cuts from Slim Smith, Ken Boothe, Delroy Wilson and a heavy dubwise version of Gregory Isaacs' "Paymaster."

7 Turbo Charge (Heartbeat) 1991

Heralded as Niney's comeback collection, 18 tracks cut during 1989–90 include Junior Byles' "Young Girl" — a performance which matches almost any of his 1970s material; fresh cuts by Ken Boothe and Big Youth; plus new talents Yami Bolo, Frankie Paul and Dignitary, and a handful of tough Observer All Stars dubs.

6 Niney the Producer (Heartbeat) 1992

Crucial for the inclusion of Junior Byles' "Little Fleego," this distinctly dance hall oriented set finds the Observer dividing his time between DJs, new stars and veterans.

8 Truth & Rights Observer Style (Heartbeat) 1994

More from the archives, the "Blood & Fire"-ish "Hail I" opens, before the set swings into a non-stop litany of crucial rarities: Niney's own "Mutiny (Confusion in a Babylon)," an extended version of Johnny Clarke's "Warrior," Sang

Hugh's "Last Call fe Blackman," the Heptones' "African Child" and Junior Delgado's "Long Way" (aka "Every Natty Wants to Go Home"). The mood of the album is fiercely judgmental.

8 Microphone Attack 1974–78 (Blood & Fire) 2001

Well-compiled study of Niney's DJ productions — U-Roy, Dillinger, Big Youth, I-Roy and more stars.

NYAHBINGI: THE ROOT OF ALL RHYTHMS

Nyahbingi lies at the foundation of all modern Jamaican music. Purely acoustic, purely organic, it is, as Bunny Wailer famously put it, "the root of all rhythms. That's where it begins." It is the sound of Rastafarian ceremony, the grounation, the relentless percussion and endless chant, which both dreams back to the peoples' African heritage, and looks forward to the day when they might return there. It is sacred music, best heard — as it is best performed — while musician and listener alike are shrouded in marijuana smoke, united in the hypnosis of the beat.

It is also fierce music. The word "nyahbingi" itself has been translated variously as "death to black and white oppressors," "death to the whites" and "death to the Europeans," a theme which dates back to 1935, when Italy justified her invasion of Ethiopia by painting Emperor Haile Selassie as the head of a secret racist African society pledged to overthrow white colonialism, the Nyahbingi Order.

It is likely that the Order itself was simply the product of a fertile Italian propaganda machine. No sooner were its name and aims published in the Jamaican press, however, than the Order sprang to life within Rastafarianism, with its goals apparently little changed from the Italian nightmare. When US President Reagan visited Jamaica in 1982, the interior of the island burned with nyahbingi as Rastafarians from all across Jamaica flocked to a week long grounation designed to ensnare the visitor in a death trap. (A recording of highlights of this ceremony was later released by Heartbeat Records as *Churchical Chants of the Nyahbingi*.)

Nyahbingi developed slowly as a musical force — the term is, after all, often used interchangeably with grounation, to describe any Rastafarian service. As late as the 1940s, grounations were as likely to incorporate suitably reworded Revivalist hymns and paeans to Marcus Garvey as they were unfettered drumming.

Even this early, however, fierce religious and class conflicts developed between Rastafarianism and the more conventional Christian cults of Pukumina and Zion. Pukumina, in particular, was a living religion, with a past, a future, and some very respectable relatives. Despite the supernatural overtones of the Jamaican faith, American Baptist ceremonies are not that far removed from Pukumina services.

It also has a culture and a literary heritage. One of the finest poems in the Jamaican canon, PM Sherlock's "Pocomania" (1949), describes a Pukumina ritual in terms and tones designed to entrance and defined by primeval fear: "Africa among the trees/Asia with her mysteries/Weaving white in flowing gown/Black Long Mountain looking down. . . ."

Rastafarianism had none of these things. It was an outlaw cult (even among its sympathizers, few termed it as a religion) built upon the shifting sands of selective Biblical interpretation, historical isolation and iconographical infatuation. It was the sound of the slums, of the ceaseless hub-bub spilling out of the urban squatter camps at Back A Wall and the Dungle. Nobody, it was said in polite quarters, could ever write such a beautiful poem about the Rastaman. So the Rastaman wrote it himself, on the drums.

During the late 1940s, Leonard Percival Howell, one of the founding fathers of Rastafarianism, championed the adoption of "kumina" drumming as the liturgical music of the new faith, agreeing with the musicologists who stated that kumina was the last surviving vestige of the peoples' west and central African heritage. It was an effective decision. Jamaican press reports of the first ever Rastafarian Universal Convention in March, 1958, made much menacing play of the "bearded brethren" dancing around a bonfire of old car tires to the beat of the drums.

If nyahbingi is the sound of seething, defiant revolution, however, it is also, as aforementioned, the bedrock of commercial Jamaican music. It was a nyahbingi ensemble which Prince Buster sought when he went up into the Wareika hills shortly before he commenced a recording session in 1961. He returned to Kingston with Count Ossie Williams (b 1928; d 10/18/76) and his four burro drummers, and it was their drumming which elevated the Folkes Brothers' "Oh Carolina" out of the realms of local R&B and mutated mento, and into a whole new sphere entirely.

The drummers subsequently featured on a clutch of further Buster productions, including hits by the Mellow Cats, Lascelles Perkins and Bunny & Skitter — whose "Chubby" represents one of the purest early nyahbingi recordings currently available. (Purer still, but unavailable, are tapes made by musicologist/anthropologist Professor George Simpson, in Kingston in December, 1953, described by author Peter Manuel in his book Caribbean Currents.)

Buster's efforts, of course, were despised by the old guard. The first time he and Ossie arrived at the Jamaica Broadcasting Company studios to record, Buster later recalled, "(rival producer) Duke Reid was there and he see Ossie with his lickle drum in his hand and he laughed. They were jazz people at heart, and here I was, coming up with what they thought was simple music."

In fact it was not. There are just three burra, or akete drums — the small, high-pitched repeater, the larger, flat, slack funde and the bass — but they weave around one another constantly. It was this dizzying snake dance which drove "Oh Carolina" to the top of the chart, not because listeners knew what they were hearing, but because those drums reminded them of what they were feeling and because, in so doing, they cracked the door on emotions which had been kept locked shut for generations.

Count Ossie was among the entertainers at the August, 1962, Independence celebrations, while he also cut several singles in his own right during the 1960s and early 1970s. But he was by no means the only practitioner on the scene. Skatalites Don Drummond and Johnny Moore also regularly attended grounations, there developing many of the musical techniques which they later employed on their own band's manifold sessions.

Nyahbingi also influenced some of the most distinctive hits of the late 1960s. The Royals' "Pick Up the Pieces," Carlton & His Shoes' "Happy Land," the Abyssinians' "Satta Amasa Ganna" and Burning Spear's "Door Peep" all utilized minor chord melodies, slow rhythms and chants drawn directly from cultural traditions. Affirmation of the music's eternal effectiveness, too, emerged in DJ Determine's 1995 "Kette Drum," a Bobby Digital production which swiftly spawned a host of versions, including Garnett Silk's "Silk Chant," Bounty Killer's "Seek God" and Cocoa Tea/Shabba Ranks' "Flag Flown High."

In more general terms, however, nyahbingi itself remained largely unknown (and certainly unheralded) until the early 1970s. Then, in 1973, Count Ossie led his grandiosely named Mystic Revelation of Rastafari through Grounation, historically recalled as the first triple album ever recorded and released in Jamaica. It did not sell especially well, but in a land where Rastafarianism itself was still regarded with more than a little suspicion and distrust, its very existence was a triumph.

Count Ossie recorded one further album, 1975's Tales of Mozambique, before his death, aged 56 (he also recorded a remarkable session with the band Culture, released 20 years later on their Trod On archive album). Already, however, other nyahbingi ensembles were emerging from the shadows, led by the long-running and vastly influential Ras Michael & the Sons of Negus, fronted by Ras Michael (born Michael George Henry.)

Again, the band was launched far from the hub of the Jamaican music industry, although — like Count Ossie's ensemble — their very existence proved a magnet of sorts to the Kingston cognoscenti. During the early-mid 1960s, the Wailers were regular guests at the Sons' meetings, while Ras Michael himself broke considerable ground when he was appointed host of Jamaican radio's first ever program dedicated to Rastafarianism, the spiritually inclined The Lion of Judah Time, in the wake of Haile Selassie's 1966 state visit.

In 1967, the group cut their first single, also titled "The Lion of Judah," for release on their own Zion Disc label. Several further 45s followed, before they scored a proxy hit when U-Roy and Peter Tosh utilized their "Ethiopian Na-tional Anthem" for the intro to their "(Earth's) Rightful Ruler" single.

Further boundaries shattered when Radio Jamaica DJ Philip Jackson, one of the few other Rastafarians on the "inside" of 1970s establishment Jamaica, took to airing both Count Ossie and Ras Michael — and beyond — on his own, strictly secular, show.

Working now with some of Jamaica's leading session mu-sicians, Ras Michael scored a hit of their own with "None a Jah Jah Children No Cry." Success begat success; soon demand for the music was so great that a new group, the Daughters of Negus, was launched alongside the Sons — future Black Uhuru vocalist Puma Jones was a member for a time, appearing on Ras Michael's *Movements* album in 1978.

The band's most notable feat, of course, was their ability to advance nyahbingi far beyond its own roots and into the commercial arena. For all the respect he eventually earned, Count Ossie was best remembered in Jamaica for perform-ing for Haile Selassie in 1966. His actual recordings passed utterly beneath the commercial radar, while Ras Michael's toyed with the best-seller lists.

Even the artwork was eye-catching — *Rastafari* designer Neville Garrick went on to become art director with the Wailers' Tuff Gong empire. The hybrid worked, however. If the most understanding reviews of Count Ossie's work were those which allied it to Nigerian band leader Fela Ran-some Kuti's similarly percussion and horn driven jams, Ras Michael & the Sons of Negus slipped effortlessly into main-stream reggae tastes.

Following swiftly in Ras Michael's footsteps were the Light of Saba, an aggregation which was similarly open to commercial influences, at the same time as remaining painstakingly true to their roots and beliefs — one of their finest tracks was a version of dub poet Mutabaruka's "Out-cry."

Formed in 1974 by horn player Cedric "Im" Brooks, the musical arranger at the *Grounation* sessions and a long-time veteran of Count Ossie's earlier material (they recorded to-gether as Im & Count Ossie), the group's debut album, that same year, *From Mento to Reggae to Third World Music* was credited to the Divine Light. As its title suggests, the record follows the full development of Jamaican music, but while it is fascinating from a musical point of view, the album was scarcely representative of the group's full force. That be-came apparent with the release of 1976's *The Light of Saba*.

Once again, the music allowed contemporary commer-cial sounds to merge, with covers of jazz-man Horace Sil-ver's "Song for My Father" (retitled "Words of Wisdom") and Tommy McCook's "Peanut Vendor." At the same time, however, the mood and movement of the album remained pure, which is as it should be. For what can never be over-looked is that it is nyahbingi's very lack of commerciality which has allowed it to retain both its purpose and its per-fection.

RECOMMENDED LISTENING

NYAHBINGI Churchical Chants of the Nyahbingi (Heartbeat) 1983

Recorded live at the Church of Jah Rastafari in Freeman's Hall, Trelawney, in April, 1982, and edited down from some seven days of ceremony, this album's main drawback is its length — ten chants run from three to six minutes, but never offer more than a fraction of the original performance. Which isn't to say the home listener particularly needs to sit through an hour long version of "Think I Never Know," but does acknowledge that the power of nyahbingi lies in the mantric ritual. Excuse that failing, and this emerges both a memorable and rewarding experience.

COUNT OSSIE & THE MYSTIC REVELATION OF RASTAFARI Grounation (Ashanti—UK) 1973

Sprawling three LP (83 minute) recreation of a grounation with all factors intact — lengthy percussion-driven chants are interspersed with oration by Brother Samuel Clayton, while careful listening unearths the myriad influences and musi-cal forebears which have been gathered into the nyahbingi canon. A version of "Oh Carolina" offers a reggae lifeline to anybody not transported by the rhythms, while "So Long" bears at least a stylistic similarity to the Wailers' "Rastaman Chant."

There are also "covers" of jazz-man Charles Lloyd's "Ma-brat" and the Jazz Crusaders' "Way Back Home," but al-ready the known world is slipping away, to leave you grounded within the 30 minute earthbeat of the title track, one of the few places on earth where old English folk songs and sea shanties can be united with African tribal lore to create a state akin to ecstasy. (A purported remix of the origi-nal album was released in 1976 (Vulcan — UK); the Ashanti release has since been reissued across two-CDs.)

LIGHT OF SABA The Light of Saba in Reggae (Total Sounds—JA) 1978

Anyone looking for the precise moment where nyahbingi stopped hanging around on the edges of Jamaican music and leaped right into its heart should begin here. The most conventional album released by any of nyahbingi's "big three," *In Reggae*'s cover of dub poet Mutabaruka's "Out-cry" is the best known track, as much for its success as a single as for its author's own latter-day pre-eminence. Other tracks, however, are of similar quality.

RAS MICHAEL & THE SONS OF NEGUS Dadawah Peace & Love (Tro-jan—UK) 1975

It is difficult to know where to begin with the longest run-ning and by far the most prolific band in the field; there are at least a dozen albums out there, including efforts featuring

Peter Tosh, Robbie Shakespeare, Geoffrey Chung and Lee Perry. None are utterly pure; from the outset, the band was clearly fascinated by the possibilities of fusing their own music with reggae, rock and jazz. This set is probably their most unique, however, with just four tracks, all constructed around traditional Rastafarian chant, with a sympathetic Lloyd Charmers production. It also occupies a middle ground between Count Ossie and Light of Saba, which is handy if you're just discovering this music.

RASTAFARI ELDERS Rastafari Elders (RAS) 1990

The aforementioned notwithstanding, the finest nyahbingi remains the handful of genuine field recordings made over the last 30 years, but rarely given more than a scholarly release. That is remedied by this album, recorded at a studio in Washington DC in 1990 and offering the closest thing to an authentic grounation atmosphere as such a set-up could ever permit.

VARIOUS ARTISTS

Grounation: The Indomitable Spirit of Rastafari (Music Club) 1999

The unlikely sight of a budget priced nyahbingi comp repays investigation by ranging across the Jamaican landscape, serving up cuts by Garnett Silk, Ronnie Davis, Nora Dean and Cynthia Richards, alongside the inevitable Count Ossie, Ras Michael and Rasta-jazz fusionists Negril. Margarita's magnificent "Woman a Come" makes an utterly unexpected appearance midway through, although it doesn't necessarily fit, while the absence of Prince Buster's early productions scuppers any hopes of an authoritative overview. Those are, however, the only wrong notes sounded on a remarkably ambitious and adventurous collection.

BILLY OCEAN
STYLE *pop/R&B*
BORN *Leslie Sebastian Charles, 1/21/50 (T&T)*

Although his reputation, and a vast part of his catalog, is rooted firmly in the Anglo-American pop/R&B tradition, Billy Ocean was, for many years, the biggest selling Caribbean artist on the international music scene.

He was also one of three Trinidadian acts to break into the UK chart during the mid-1970s — in 1975, the duo Mac & Katie Kissoon reached #3 with "Sugar Candy Kisses," the biggest of the five hits they enjoyed; in 1977, the Trinidad Oil Company steel band reached the Top 40 with "The Calendar Song." Neither, however, enjoyed anything like the success experienced by Ocean.

Ocean left his native land at age eight, when his family relocated to the UK. Upon leaving school, he worked as a tailor, while performing in clubs and pubs in the evenings. Taken by the youngster's enthusiasm, Ocean's boss lent him the money to buy his first piano.

Working with such bands as Shades of Midnight, the Go and Dry Ice, and performing solo under the aliases Sam Spade and Joshua, Ocean's repertoire was largely Motown soul based. Like the Jamaican born Carl ("Kung Fu Fighting") Douglas, then working the same circuit, and the somewhat more successful Guyanan born Eddy Grant, at that time a member of the Equals, Ocean was well aware that attempts to interest the UK music industry in the sounds of his homeland was, at that time, fruitless.

In 1974, Ocean joined the R&B band Scorched Earth, with whom he made his recording debut. The following year, solo again, he signed with the GTO label and released the single "Whose Little Girl Are You" that December. Produced by Ben Findon, the single (and accompanying, eponymous album) placed Ocean firmly in a disco-funk-lite vein, one which was mined with expert precision by the pair's next release, "Love Really Hurts Without You." It reached #2 in the UK (#22 US) during spring, 1976, and was followed by two further Top 20 singles that same year, "Love on Delivery" and "Stop Me (If You've Heard It All Before)."

Ocean scored another #2 in 1977 with "Red Light Spells Danger," after his own first choice for release, "Who's Gonna Rock You," was rejected by GTO. The song later became a hit for the singing group the Nolan Sisters. However, subsequent singles "American Hearts" and "Are You Ready" fared poorly, his sophomore album sank, and Ocean disappeared from view for several years.

He returned in 1980 as author of two tracks on LaToya Jackson's debut album and, having been dropped by GTO, relaunched his career in 1981 with the self-financed "Nights (Feel Like Getting Down)." Picked up by the Epic label, the disco single reached #7 on the US R&B chart and Ocean cut two albums for the label over the next two years. He then vanished once again, only to resurface in 1984 alongside fellow Trinidadian expatriate, producer Keith Diamond.

The duo's first collaboration, "European Queen," was released in May; it did little, until Ocean revised the lyric and title. As "Caribbean Queen," the song topped the US pop, dance and R&B charts, and made #6 in the UK, while its universality was proven when another version, "African Queen," took off across that continent. The song also earned Ocean a Grammy for best R&B Vocal.

With the *Suddenly* album in the Top 10 on both sides of the Atlantic, and his next single, "Loverboy," #2 in the US, Ocean embarked on a two month American tour in spring, 1985, his first live outing in a decade. He also appeared at Live Aid that May, and scored two further major hits, "Suddenly" and "Mystery Lady."

1986 saw Ocean supply the theme song to the Michael Douglas/Kathleen Turner movie *Jewel of the Nile*, "When the Going Gets Tough, the Tough Get Going" (coincidentally, fellow Caribbean superstar Eddy Grant had been approached to write the theme to the earlier *Romancing the Stone*). The song reached #2 in the US and #1 in the UK, positions which were reversed for his next release, the Grammy nominee "There'll Be Sad Songs." The *Love Zone* album, from which both singles were drawn, eventually sold two million in the US, and reached #6 (#2 in Britain). The year ended with "Love Is Forever" at #16 in America, with Ocean subsequently sweeping the American Music Awards, taking away the Best Single and Best Male Video titles.

Ocean was silent during 1987, bar a remix of his 12 year old debut smash, restyled to match "When the Going Gets Tough." He scored his last major successes in 1988, when the single "Get Outta My Dreams (Get into My Car)" gave him his third US chart topper (#3 UK). The *Tear Down These Walls* album reached #18 (#3 UK), while "The Colour of Love" single made #17 (#65 UK); Ocean also scored in Britain with "Calypso Crazy," a contagious nod to his homeland, which reached #35.

1989 brought Ocean's first hits collection, and the minor success "License to Chill." His musical tastes were now leaning towards hip hop, a discovery reinforced by his collaboration with the Fresh Prince & Mimi, "I Sleep Much Better (in Someone Else's Bed)" in early 1990.

In 1993, the now dreadlocked Ocean traveled to Jamaica to record with the renowned dance hall production team Steely & Clevie; the album *Time to Move On* spawned the single "Pressure," but achieved little else. Four years then elapsed before Ocean again resurfaced, with the *Love Is Forever* collection. In 1999, a remake of "When the Going Gets Tough," recorded by Irish teenybop idols Boyzone, topped the British chart.

SELECTED DISCOGRAPHY

⑤ Billy Ocean (GTO) 1975
⑥ City Limit (GTO) 1978
⑥ Nights (Feel Like Getting Down) (Epic) 1981
⑤ Inner Feelings (Epic) 1982
⑦ Suddenly (Jive) 1984
⑥ Love Zone (Jive) 1986
⑦ Tear Down These Walls (Jive) 1988
⑥ Time to Move On (Jive) 1993

SELECTED COMPILATIONS & ARCHIVE RELEASES

⑧ Greatest Hits (Jive) 1989
⑧ Love Is Forever (Jive) 1997

The often effervescent hits aside, Ocean's albums tend to underwhelm. Cut to the chase, then, with a set built around some of the most memorable pop-soul smashes of the decade, including the inevitable "Caribbean Queen," "There'll Be Sad Songs," "Loverboy" and "When the Going Gets Tough."

AUGUSTUS PABLO

STYLE *reggae (dub)*
BORN *Horace Swaby, 6/21/54, (St Andrew, JA), d 5/18/99*

Between 1970 and 1975, Augustus Pablo established himself as one of the most unrepentantly creative figures on the Jamaican music scene, the mastermind behind a clutch of tracks whose brilliance may not always have been recognized by the record buying public, but were avidly awaited by his fellow musicians and producers.

Pablo's use of the melodica as a key instrument in his recordings, of course, singled him out as unusual from the start — had such an instrument ever played more than a minor role in any artist's music before Pablo brought it to the fore? Certainly producer Herman Chin-Loy (Leslie Kong's cousin) did not think so, the day the 15 year old Horace Swaby walked into his Aquarius records store, intent on an audition. 24 hours later, Chin-Loy was producing the teen's first single, the insistent "Iggy Iggy."

It was Chin-Loy who renamed Swaby. Augustus Pablo was, in fact, a name common to many of Chin-Loy's productions, used by every keyboard player in the house band. This time, however, it stuck.

Based on a rhythm Chin-Loy purchased from Lee Perry, Pablo's next single, "East of the River Nile," was a vibrantly haunting duet for organ and melodica which launched the so-called Far East sound into fashion. Other Chin-Loy-produced sides included "The Mood," "Snowball & Pudding" and "Still Yet."

Following a brief stint as keyboard player with Mikey Chung's Now Generation band, Pablo next linked with producer Clive Chin. Together they cut 1971's classic "Java," the opening shot in a relationship which culminated with Pablo's massively influential *This Is Augustus Pablo* album in 1974 — among the numerous hit versions of the "Java" rhythm were Dennis Alcapone's immortal "Mava."

Pablo worked with a number of other producers during this early period, including Lee Perry ("Hot And Cold"), Leonard Chin ("Lover's Mood" and "Pablo in Dub," which launched Chin's Santic label), Gussie Clarke ("Born to Dub You," "No Entry"), and Bunny Lee ("The Great Pablo"). Of his other collaborations with Lee, "Pablo's Desire," a version of John Holt's "My Desire," was a major success in 1974. In addition, Pablo also turned his own hand to production. His first effort, during his time with Leonard Chin, was Paul Whiteman/Blackman's "Say So."

All the time, however, Pablo was chafing against the often ludicrously low financial returns he received from such partnerships. Thus, in 1972, he and brother Garth Swaby formed their own label, Rockers, named for the sound system they were also operating. (Subsequent Pablo labels included Hot Stuff, Pablo International, Rockers International and Message).

The earliest Rockers singles, by Pablo, included "Skanking Easy" and "Frozen Dub," both rerecorded and rearranged classic Studio One rhythms of a decade past. "Cassava Street," "Pablo's Theme Song," "Liberation," "Thunderbolt Lady," "Don Drummond" and "555 Crown Street" followed.

Pablo next launched a partnership with dubmeister King Tubby, whose mixes characterized many of Rockers' finest releases. Their first major collaboration was 1975's *Ital Dub* album, produced by Tommy Cowan and Warwick Lyn (former assistant to Leslie Kong), and featured deeply idiosyncratic versions of Bob Marley's "Road Block," Junior Byles' "Curly Locks" and Peter Tosh's "Funeral."

Pablo scored his first major hit as a producer that summer with Fred Locks' inestimable "Black Star Line." A reworking of an old New York jazz record, it was dedicated to Marcus Garvey's dream of launching a steamship company of that name to allow his people to compete with the white man's monopoly on trade and industry. (The company purchased just one vessel, an old cotton freighter which began trading between New York and Jamaica, before bankruptcy ended the enterprise.) Immediately upon release, "Black Star Line" moved 14,000 copies in Jamaica — Locks himself later estimated that another 10,000 sold just as quickly in the UK.

Flush with this success, Pablo handled sessions with Freddie McKay ("I'm a Freeman"), Big Joe ("Jah Guide"), Horace Andy ("Children of Israel," "Problems"), I-Roy ("Yamaha Ride"), Joe Higgs ("Creation") and Jacob Miller ("Each One Teach One," "Who Say Jah No Dread"). A number of Pablo's finest efforts were compiled as the legendary *King Tubby Meets Rockers Uptown* album, one of the crucial dub albums of the entire decade. The album's title track was drawn from the duo's devastating revision of another Jacob Miller cut, "Baby I Love You So."

1978 brought the acclaimed *East of the River Nile* album, cut at Lee Perry's Black Ark studio. The same year, Pablo produced 13 year old Hugh Mundell's "Let's All Unite," "Book of Life" and "My Mind" singles. He and Mundell also teamed up for 1979's *Africa Must Be Free by 1983* and *Time and Place* albums.

Sharing the fate of so many 1970s pioneers, Pablo spent the first half of the 1980s in a musical limbo of sorts, still recording heavily, but rarely recapturing either the spark or the critical attention his earlier work had taken for granted. Nevertheless, some vital work did emerge. The 1980 EP *Augustus Pablo Presents el Rockers Chapter I to IV* and 1986's *Rising Sun* album drew plaudits, before that later year saw him slam back into contention with his production of Junior Delgado's "Raggamuffin Year" single and album. (An equally stupendous dub version of the project appeared in 1990.)

In 1986, Rockers International launched a short-lived arrangement with Island Records, which saw several Pablo productions given a major label release, including 12-inch singles by Delgado, Carlton Hones, Delroy Wilson and Pablo himself ("Eastern Promise," "Sukiyaki"). The following year, he began touring internationally for the first time — 1991's *Live in Tokyo* captured one triumphant show.

Pablo continued producing fine records, including Dawn Penn's hit "Night and Day," and Yami Bolo's *Jah Made Them All* album. Further action revolved around Pablo's back catalog, an astonishingly vibrant trove of both released and unreleased material, which saw his reputation soar to new heights, and it was tragically ironic that he would not live to revel in the new recognition.

Dogged by health problems stemming from a nerve disorder through most of his life, Pablo died on May 18, 1999. He was remembered with a star studded tribute concert held on June 17, 2000, at the Countryside Lawn, Kingston — among the artists appearing were Sugar Minott, Junior Reid, saxophonist Dean Fraser and guitarist Earl "Chinna" Smith.

SELECTED DISCOGRAPHY

8 **Rebel Rock Reggae — This Is Augustus Pablo (Tropical — UK) 1974**

Clive Chin probably understood Pablo's vision better than anyone beyond Pablo himself at this stage, who himself turned in a sharp and well-rounded all-instrumental set. It's prejudiced only by the remakes of its highlights which a more ambitious Pablo (and others) would score with in the future. "Dub Organizer," incidentally, has more than a hint of Michael Rose's "Guess Who's Coming To Dinner" around its melody. Since reissued by Heartbeat.

7 **Thriller (Tropical — UK) 1975**
8 **Ital Dub (Trojan — UK) 1975**

History will not allow a word to be written against this album. Either you love every last reverb-drenched iota of it, or it reminds you of dinosaurs impersonating fax machines. Either way, it's unforgettable.

8 **King Tubby Meets Rockers Uptown (Clock Tower) 1976**
7 **East of the River Nile (Message — JA) 1978**

Almost po-faced in its thoughtfulness, and certainly not prone to leaping wildly around the mixing desk with phasers on stagger, an album of sonorous profundity ensures that anyone lured towards Pablo by the Tubby connection might well be wandering away quickly about now. Stick around, and you'll also want to hear *Let's Get Started* and *Eastman Dub*, respectively the vocal tracks and dub underbelly of the main attraction.

7 **Earth's Rightful Ruler (Message — UK) 1982**
7 **Rockers Meets King Tubby in a Fire House (Shanachie) 1982**

Tubby, Pablo and Jammy mixes of classic Rockers and cultural recordings, including a melodica version of Burt Bacharach's "A House Is Not a Home," alongside mixes of Hugh Mundell and Delroy Williams among others.

6 Rising Sun (Greensleeves—UK) 1986
7 Rockers Comes East (Greensleeves—UK) 1987

. . . and join the digital age, much to the surprise of the fans who almost universally condemned Pablo's progression. But his deep roots remain intact and, with rhythms taken from cuts like Junior Delgado's "Ragamuffin Year," the collision of past and present is occasionally spine-tingling.

8 Blowing with the Wind (Greensleeves—UK) 1990

Often cited as Pablo's comeback album, it's actually more of a reaffirmation—sounds have changed and fashion's gone flying, but Pablo is as Pablo does. And this time he does with some seminal nyahbingi drumming and trumpeter John Moore, for his most overall satisfying album in well over a decade.

7 Live in Tokyo (Rockers—JA) 1991
6 Dub Store 90s (RAS) 1993
6 Heartical Chant (RAS) 1993
7 Valley of Jehosophat (RAS) 1999

15 track album which is again heavy on the rhythms. Not classic Pablo by any standards, but remarkable in places.

AUGUSTUS PABLO & JUNIOR DELGADO

8 Ragamuffin Dub (Rockers International—JA) 1990
8 One Step Dub (Greensleeves—UK) 1991

Respectively, dub versions of Delgado's *Raggamuffin Year* and *One Step More* albums.

AUGUSTUS PABLO & HUGH MUNDELL

9 Africa Must Be Free by 1983 Dub (Greensleeves—UK) 1979

The staggering dub revision of the already exemplary debut by young Mundell.

AUGUSTUS PABLO & TETRACK

7 Augustus Pablo Presents Eastman Dub (Greensleeves—UK) 1988

Intriguing dub version of Tetrack's Pablo-produced *Let's Get Started*.

SELECTED COMPILATIONS & ARCHIVE RELEASES

9 Original Rockers (Greensleeves—UK) 1979

This classic compilation gathers up some of the greatest of Pablo's self-produced instrumentals from his early years—"Rockers Dub," "Up Wareika Hill," "Park Lane Special," "Tubby's Dub Song" and more.

6 King David's Melody (Message—JA) 1983

For fans only, featuring material from the late Seventies through the early Eighties, obviously not his strongest suit.

7 Presents Rockers International (Greensleeves—UK) 1991
7 Presents Rockers International 2 (Greensleeves—UK) 1991

Volume 2 is probably the stronger of the pair, featuring 15 different tracks exploring five different rhythms, while volume one gathers up four versions of "El Rockers," then tosses in some previously unreleased recordings that are nearly as good.

8 Golden Melodies (Rockers International—JA) 1992

And indeed they are, as well as rare. There's unreleased versions of "Satta Amasa Gana," the Gatherers' "Words of My Mouth" and Lloyd Parks' "Slaving," as well as a clutch of impossible to find cuts like "Islington Rock" and Vivian Jackson's "Conquering Lion."

8 Pablo & Friends (RAS) 1992

Bunny Lee productions, featuring U-Roy, Nora Dean (the intriguing "Scorpion in Her Underpants"), Prince Jazzbo, I-Roy, John Holt and others, alongside their Pablo-led b-side versions.

8 Classic Rockers (Island) 1995

Junior Delgado's "Blackman's Heart," Jacob Miller's "Baby I Love You So," Delroy Wilson's "Stop the Fighting" and Pablo's own "Eastern Promise" head up a strong compilation of both vocal and dub takes. The unreleased "Jah in the Hills" by Pablo and King Tubby is a welcome addition to the canon.

7 The Great Pablo (Music Club) 2000

A fine single disc overview tracing Pablo's development from "East of the River Nile" to *Ital Dub*, and stopping off at both "Java" and "Mava," "My Desire" and "The Great Pablo" en route.

8 El Rockers (Pressure Sounds—UK) 2000

17 tracks unearth out-takes and alternates from the *King Tubby Meets the Rockers Uptown* album. Most sound as solid as the released versions.

PAN: THE SOUND OF THE STEEL BAND

The steelband of today traces its origins back to the very roots of carnival, to a time when the festivities were accompanied by the sounds of stick fighting and the African drum. More specifically, however, it owes its genesis to the events of 1883, when the authorities banned both sticks and drums for fear of the effect they were having on the more excitable (and less law-abiding) segments of the populace.

That year's carnival had seen severe disturbances, some instigated by a motley gang of Englishmen known as the Newgates (they were out on bail at the time, and took their name from the notorious London prison), but also occasioned by other performers, who seemed to have purposefully set out to offend with a repertoire of obscene drum dances. Yet another group delighted in disturbing a nearby military barracks by playing their drums all night long.

The government initially favored outlawing carnival altogether — a measure which had been on the agenda for several years beforehand, and all the more so since the 1881 carnival ended in a riot of its own. Eventually they decided on a more prudent but, it was hoped, equally effective, course, passing a Musical Ordinance which prohibited the unlicensed playing of all percussion, stringed and woodwind instruments.

Adapting to the legislation, the next decade of carnival saw the emergence of the Tamboo Bamboo — literally, the sound of bamboo sticks being beaten rhythmically on the ground — to take the place of the drum and replace, symbolically at least, the stick fights. With time and practice, these bamboos themselves became finely tuned instruments — they were cut to three standard lengths, a five foot, low toned "boom"; the shorter "foule," for mid range sounds, and the hand held "cutter," which was smacked with a bottle. Other makeshift instruments included biscuit tins, bottles filled with varying amounts of water and hit with spoons, and so on.

Existing legislation kept these troupes down to no more than ten in number (other laws prohibited obscene words, transvestites and pierrots), but as the 20th century approached, carnival had already lost much of its original reputation for obscenity and lawlessness. The upper classes were, if not actually participating, at least enjoying the annual spectacle, and a fully costumed and choreographed tamboo bamboo band was nothing if not spectacular.

By the early 1910s, tamboo bamboo players were brazenly supplying percussion by banging their sticks together — creating the style known as qua-qua. 1914 saw a tamboo bamboo band captured on record for the first time, accompanying Jules Sims' performance of "Meet Me Round the Corner." Despite this burgeoning respectability, when a tentative attempt to relaunch carnival was made in 1919 following a two year hiatus occasioned by the Great War, the organizing *Aegis* newspaper's stringent rules included a ban on "bands using bamboos and bottles."

Again, the hypnotic effect of percussion had been singled out as a source for potential trouble and violence. The following year, however, with carnival officially restored to the calendar, the Port of Spain police force announced that they were well-prepared to deal with any trouble arising from the tamboo bamboo players. Indeed they were — shortly before carnival got underway, a reporter from the local *Guardian* newspaper was awakened at six A.M. by the sound of the sticks emanating from a nearby police barracks. He went over to investigate and discovered that the police themselves were the performers.

Tamboo bamboo remained an integral part of carnival throughout the 1920s and 1930s, but the situation — indeed, the very sound of carnival — was about to change quite dramatically.

In 1937, a band from Port of Spain's Big Yard area, Carlton Ford's Newtown (later Alexander's Ragtime Band), appeared at carnival armed with a battery of old cans, biscuit tins, dustbins, cooking pots and discarded oil drums as the principle percussion in their line-up, struck with an equally motley array of utensils and bottles. By 1940, almost every Tamboo Bamboo band in the city had replaced their bamboos with these new, supremely resonant instruments.

The outbreak of World War Two saw carnival severely curtailed (it was, in fact, officially banned from 1942, though it continued to be celebrated secretly), but behind the scenes, the development of percussion continued apace.

The man most commonly associated with innovating the steel drum was Winston "Spree" Simon, of the John John Band. According to legend, he was involved in a parade one day in spring, 1939, when a friend asked if he could take over on Spree Simon's kettle drum. By the time Spree Simon got his instrument back, it had been battered almost beyond recognition, so he set to work pounding it back into shape with a stone, noticing as he did so that different surfaces of the drum produced different sounds — which could, in turn, be manipulated into notes.

During the war years, Simon and others worked to perfect this discovery — history records the names Leonard Morris, Sonny Roach, Oscar Pyle, Dudley Smith, Randolph "Fisheye" Ollivierre and Wilfred Harrison among these pioneers. By 1943, sufficient progress had been made that local folklore expert Edric Connor was able to deliver a lecture on the history of the steel drums at the Prince's Building in Port of Spain, with accompaniment from a band called Gonzales.

The next major step came when a Woodbrook pan tuner named Ellie Mannette began experimenting with the massive 45 gallon metal drums discarded by the US military forces based on the island since 1941. Following Mannette's lead, skilled practitioners soon taught themselves how to "tune" them, carefully tempered with hammers and chisels. Added to Simon's newly tuned pots and pans, the steel band was now complete.

The new sound made its public debut, seemingly fully fledged, at the VE (Victory in Europe) and VJ (Victory in Japan) celebrations, which marked the end of World War Two in, respectively, May and August, 1945. At both events, bands emerged in all their glory — vast armies of steel and drumming with such resonant names as the Red Army, Sun Valley, Casablanca, the Invaders, the Renegades, the Rising Sun, Hell Yard, the Desperadoes and the Free French.

Their effect was immediate. Carnival 1946 was dominated by the new sound, and the more forward thinking calypsonians — Lord Kitchener paramount among them — began composing with the steelband foremost in mind. By 1950, the Road March seemingly featured nothing but steelbands, a vast army clattering and banging through the streets, performing the unstoppable hit of the year, "Last Train to San Fernando," a lament for the recently closed rail link between that city and Port of Spain.

Despite its popularity, the steelband's acceptance into polite society was still slow in coming. The renegade status which had attended drummers for so many years remained alive and well, all the more so since many of the players (and most of their followers) were drawn from the city slums and ghettoes. One band, the Dead End, not only named themselves after the juvenile tearaway heroes of the popular American movie series The Dead End Kids, they also styled themselves after those young ruffians.

And they were not the only offenders. Throughout carnival (and long after), rival bands and their supporters — "badjohns," in local street parlance — battled for physical, as well as musical, supremacy. It was, onlookers mused, the supreme irony — a music of such graceful beauty and precision, being played by hooligans, thugs and murderers.

In 1949, outraged by the violence, but sensibly aware of the music's value (tourists were already flocking to the pan yards, and apparently adored the drums), the government appointed a Steelband Committee specifically to look into the problem. Comprising president Sydney Gollop, solicitor Lennox Pierre, union leader Nathaniel Crichlow, together with several figures from the musical scene itself, the Committee was determined to find a peaceable solution.

Barbados born Lieutenant Nathaniel Joseph Griffith, a member of the Trinidad Police Band and a qualified musician, was seen as the ideal man to liaise with the bands themselves, and so it proved. Using his own contacts in the steelband community, Griffith brought 21 band leaders together in a summit held at the Teacher Training College in Port of Spain, all of whom were impressed enough by his arguments, that they promptly enrolled their bands in the newly formed Steelband Association.

Of these 21 leaders, eleven were then chosen to star in a new band, one which embodied the spirit of the Association — the Trinidad All Steel Percussion Orchestra. Theo Stephens was a member of San Fernando's Free French; Belgrave Bonaparte played with Southern Symphony; Andrew De La Bastide with Hill 60; Philmore Boots Davidson with the Syncopators; Orman Patsy Haynes with Casablanca; Dudley Smith with Rising Sun; Sterling Betancourt with Crossfire; Granville Sealey with Tropoli; and Anthony Williams with the North Stars. In addition, the band featured the very founding fathers of the steelband, Winston Spree Simon, of the band Tokyo and the Invaders' Ellie Mannette.

As a peace keeping gesture, it was an ambitious effort.

However, TASPO was to have far further reaching consequences than simply re-aligning a few hundred misguided street fighters. The band had barely formed when T&T governor Sir Hubert Rance suggested that they join calypsonian Roaring Lion as T&T's representatives at the Festival of Britain, a vast celebration of culture from all across the British Empire. Griffith agreed and, having replaced Sealey with Sun Valley's Sammy Roach, the group prepared for departure aboard the French ocean liner San Mateo.

Their first stop was Martinique, where they docked for five days. There, Roach fell ill and had to be left behind — it was hoped that he might rejoin the group once they arrived in Britain, but he never did.

The San Mateo berthed in her home port of Bordeaux, France on July 24, just two days before TASPO's first scheduled appearance at the South Bank exhibition grounds in London. Traveling by train and ferry, the group reached the city to discover that the long sea voyage had coated their instruments in rust. Their surprise, however, could have been nothing compared to that of the audience at that first show, who must have wondered what they had let themselves in for. Music from rusty cans? Whoever heard of such a thing?

Those questions were put to rest the moment the band started to play. They had rehearsed a repertoire which, opening with "Mambo Jambo," included Tosselli's Serenade, "After Johnny Drink Mih Rum," "Jamaican Rhumba," "Golden Earrings" and the closing "God Save the King," and they played it faultlessly.

In a month long stay, shows at St Pancras Town Hall in north London and the Savoy Hotel brought the band further acclaim. TASPO also played a benefit for the Jamaican relief fund set up in response to Hurricane Charlie, which had raged across the island for 24 hours, over August 17/18, leaving 30,000 homeless. The band's visit ended with a handful of shows in Paris, France.

TASPO arrived home to find their European successes had preceded them. Steelbands had been popular before they left, now, T&T was gripped by pan-mania, a fervor which reached into every corner of society. Groups formed in the classiest schools, bank managers and legal clerks became pan players and aficionados, and an all girl pan orchestra was formed. Soon a Steelband Music Festival was an integral part of the calendar, and when the first steelband LP records appeared, they took the market by storm.

Neither was the steelband to remain a phenomenon in T&T alone. Elsewhere around the Caribbean, local music was utterly transported by the sound, while its international impact was similarly profound. The first steelbands formed in Britain before TASPO had even left the country; now, groups appeared in Canada and the US (the American navy established one of the first). There was even a steelband in the tiny Venezuelan gold mining community of El Callao, formed by the descendants of West Indians who had been settling there since the 1870s. By the time a new TASPO line-up set out on an international tour in 1954, they were encountering steelbands at every stop.

The second generation of groups began emerging during the early 1960s, encouraged by the introduction in 1963 (the year after government sponsorship of Carnival commenced) of Panorama, a competition specific to steelbands, with the title awarded to the most creative arrangements of current popular hits. Many of carnival's most influential songwriters, again following Lord Kitchener's lead, began to compose specifically for the steelbands, to great acclaim and reward (see accompanying table).

The Hilanders, the Pan Am North Stars, the Guinness Cavaliers, the Silver-Stars and the Ebonites were all to prove successful at home and abroad, their names frequently reflecting the interests of the giant corporations who swiftly understood the benefits of sponsoring their own band. Today, almost every major (and minor) steelband has corporate sponsorship.

By the early 1970s, steelbands had begun to lose some of their domestic appeal, frequently fighting a losing battle at carnival with the more colorful and, certainly, more interactive mas bands. Internationally, however, they remained as popular as ever. In 1977, a steelband called the Trinidad Oil Company even scored a Top 40 hit in Britain, with the maddeningly infectious "Calendar Song," and it was towards these vast European and North American markets, that many groups now began focusing.

The modern orchestras of 200 or more players, as adept at classical as pop (known locally as "bomb") tunes, now became the norm — an ironic development as government funding for Panorama itself began to be slashed. Recent years have seen such cuts necessitate the truncation of the contest, and the loss or consolidation of several rounds of competition.

The sound of the pan remains integral to carnival across the Caribbean, however, with the pan yards, where the orchestras rehearse, one of the key stops on any musical tourist's visit.

PANORAMA CHAMPIONS: 1963–2001

1963

1 Pan Am North Stars: "Dan Is the Man" (wr: Sparrow/arr: Anthony Williams)
2 Sundowner: "Harry and Mama" (wr: Sparrow)
3 Coca Cola Gay Desperadoes: "The Road" (wr: Kitchener/arr: Beverly Griffith)

1964

1 North Stars: "Mama dis Is Mas" (wr: Kitchener/arr: Anthony Williams)
2 Desperadoes: "Mama dis Is Mas" (wr: Kitchener/arr: Beverly Griffith)
3 Starlift: "Mas in South" (wr: Kitchener/arr: Ray Holman)

1965

1 Cavaliers: "Melody Mas" (wr: Melody/arr: Bobby Mohammed)
2 North Stars: "Hold on to Your Man" (wr: Kitchener/arr: Anthony Williams)
3 Sun Jets: "Steering Wheel" (wr: Sparrow/arr: Herman 'Rock' Johnson)

1966

1 Desperadoes: "Obeah Wedding" (wr: Sparrow/arr: Beverly Griffith)
2 Cavaliers: "My Brother Your Sister" (wr: Kitchener/arr: Bobby Mohammed)
3 Hilanders: "Obeah Wedding" (wr: Sparrow/arr: Bertie Marshall)

1967

1 Cavaliers: "Sixty-Seven" (wr: Kitchener/arr: Bobby Mohammed)
2 Desperadoes: "Governor Ball" (wr: Sparrow/arr: Beverly Griffith)
3 Tropoli: "No Money No Love" (wr: Kitchener/arr: Hugh Borde)

1968

1 Harmonites: "Wrecker" (wr: Kitchener/arr: Earl Rodney)
2 Starlift "Jane" (wr: Sparrow/arr: Ray Holman)
3 Dixieland: "Miss Tourist" (wr: Kitchener/arr: Curtis Pierre)

1969

1 Starlift: "Bull" (wr: Kitchener/arr: Ray Holman)
2 Cavaliers: "Mas in Brooklyn" (wr: Sparrow/arr: Bobby Mohammed)
3 Harmonites: "Bongo" (wr: Sparrow/arr: Earl Rodney)

1970

1 Desperadoes: "Margie" (wr: Kitchener/arr: Clive Bradley)
2 Starlift: "Pan Man" (wr: Sparrow/arr: Ray Holman)
3 Silver Stars: "Simple Calypso"(wr: Blakie/arr: Junior Pouchet)
3 Invaders: "Margie" (wr: Kitchener/arr: Mackie Boyce)

1971

1 Harmonites: "Play Mas" (wr: Kitchener/arr: Earl Rodney)
1 Starlift: "Queen of the Bands" (wr: Sparrow/arr: Ray Holman)
3 Invaders: "Mas In Madison" (wr: Kitchener/arr: Mackie Boyce)

1972

1 Harmonites: "St. Thomas Girl" (wr: Kitchener/arr: Earl Rodney)
2 Tokyo: "Miss Harriman" (wr: Kitchener/arr: Gerald 'Belly' Charles)
3 Starlift: "Pan on the Move" (wr/arr: Ray Holman)

1973

1 Trinidad All Stars: "Rainorama" (wr: Kitchener/arr: Rudy Wells)
2 Tokyo: "My Connie" (wr: Sparrow/arr: Gerald 'Belly' Charles)
3 Harmonites: "Steel and Brass" (wr: Wellington/arr: Earl Rodney)

1974

1 Harmonites: "Jericho"(wr: Kitchener/arr: Earl Rodney)
2 Hatters: "20 to 1" (wr: Kitchener/arr: Steve Achaiba)
3 Antillean All Stars: "Bassman" (wr: Shadow/arr: Henry 'Bendix' Cumberbatch)

1975

1 Hatters: "Tribute to Spree Simon" (wr: Kitchener/arr: Steve Achaiba)

2 Fonclaire: "Tribute to Spree Simon" (wr: Kitchener/arr:—)

3 Tokyo: "Tribute to Spree Simon" (wr: Kitchener/arr: Gerald 'Belly' Charles)

1976

1 Desperadoes: "Pan in Harmony" (wr: Kitchener/arr: Clive Bradley)

2 Hatters: "Home for the Carnival" (wr: Kitchener/arr: Steve Achaiba)

3 Pandemonium: "We Kinda Music" (wr: Ray Holman, Sparrow/arr: Ray Holman)

1977

1 Desperadoes: "Crawford" (wr: Kitchener/arr: Clive Bradley)

2 Potential Symphony: "Tourist Leggo" (wr: Short Shirt/arr: Earl Brooks, Lawrence Guerra)

3 Pandemonium: "Panyard Vibration" (wr/arr: Ray Holman)

1978

1 Starlift: "Du Du Yemi" (wr: Sparrow/arr: Herschel Puckerin)

2 Desperadoes: "Pan in the 21st Century" (wr: Kitchener/arr: Clive Bradley)

3 Phase II Pan Groove: "Carnival Is Bacchanal" (wr/arr: Len "Boogsie" Sharpe)

1979 No Panorama

1980

1 Trinidad All Stars: "Woman on the Bass" (wr: Scrunter/arr: Leon "Smooth" Edwards)

2 Desperadoes: "No Pan" (wr: Kitchener/arr: Clive Bradley)

3 Renegades: "Jean the Netball Queen" (wr: Kitchener/arr: Jit Samaroo)

1981

1 Trinidad All Stars: "Unknown Band" (wr: Blue Boy/arr: Leon "Smooth" Edwards)

2 Renegades: "More Pan" (wr: Kitchener/arr: Jit Samaroo)

3 South Stars: "Mas in San Fernando" (wr: Francine/arr: Steve Achaiba)

1982

1 Renegades: "Pan Explosion" (wr: Kitchener/arr: Jit Samaroo)

2 Trinidad All Stars: "Heat" (wr: Kitchener/arr: Leon "Smooth" Edwards)

3 Desperadoes: "Party Tonight" (wr/arr: Clive Bradley)

1983

1 Desperadoes: "Rebecca" (wr: Blue Boy/arr: Clive Bradley)

2 Casablanca: "Ash Wednesday Jail" (wr: Chalkdust/arr: Henry 'Bendix' Cumberbatch)

3 Trinidad All Stars: "Rebecca" (wr: Blue Boy/arr: Leon "Smooth" Edwards)

1984

1 Renegades: "Sweet Pan" (wr: Kitchener/arr: Jit Samaroo)

2 Trinidad All Stars: "Don't Back Back" (wr: Sparrow/arr: Leon "Smooth" Edwards)

3 Casablanca: "Tourist Elsie" (wr: Kitchener/arr: Henry 'Bendix' Cumberbatch)

1985

1 Desperadoes: "Pan Night and Day" (wr: Kitchener/arr: Beverly Griffith)

1 Renegades: "Pan Night and Day" (wr: Kitchener/arr: Jit Samaroo)

3 Trinidad All Stars: "Soucouyant" (wr: Crazy/arr: Leon "Smooth" Edwards)

1986

1 Trinidad All Stars: "The Hammer" (wr: David Rudder/arr: Leon "Smooth" Edwards)

2 Phase II Pan Groove: "Pan Rising" (wr/arr: Len "Boogsie" Sharpe)

3 Fonclaire: "Pan Here to Stay" (wr: Kitchener/arr: Ken "Professor" Philmore)

1987

1 Phase II Pan Groove: "This Feeling Nice" (wr/arr: Len "Boogsie" Sharpe)

2 Renegades: "Pan in A Minor" (wr: Kitchener/arr: Jit Samaroo)

3 Desperadoes: "Pan in A Minor" (wr: Kitchener/arr: Beverly Griffith)

1988

1 Phase II Pan Groove: "Woman Is Boss" (wr/arr: Len "Boogsie" Sharpe)

2 Pandemonium: "Sailing" (wr: Trini/arr: Clive Bradley)

3 Desperadoes: "Panama" (wr: David Rudder/arr: Beverly Griffith)

1989

1 Renegades: "Somebody" (wr: Baron/arr: Jit Samaroo)

2 Fonclaire: "Fire Down Below" (wr: Len "Boogsie" Sharpe/arr: Ken "Professor" Philmore)

2 Phase II Pan Groove: "Fire Down Below" (wr/arr: Len "Boogsie" Sharpe)

1990

1 Renegades: "Iron Man" (wr: Kitchener/arr: Jit Samaroo)

2 Fonclaire: "Pan by Storm" (wr/arr: Ken "Professor" Philmore)

3 Phase II Pan Groove: "Breakdown" (wr/arr: Len "Boogsie" Sharpe)

1990

1 Desperadoes: "Musical Volcano" (wr/arr: Robert Greenidge)

2 Renegades: "Rant and Rave" (wr: Tambu/arr: Jit Samaroo)

2 Fonclaire: "Pan Ecstasy" (wr/arr: Ken "Professor" Philmore)

1992

1 Exodus: "Savannah Party" (wr: Pelham Goddard/arr: Pelham Goddard/Desmond Waithe)

2 Phase II Pan Groove: "Jam Meh Up" (wr/designer/arr: Len "Boogsie" Sharpe)

3 Renegades: "Bees Melody" (wr: Kitchener/arr: Jit Samaroo)

1993

1 Renegades: "Mystery Band" (wr: Kitchener/arr: Jit Samaroo)

2 Phase II Pan Groove: "Birthday Party" (wr: Len "Boogsie" Sharpe, Denise Plummer/arr: Len "Boogsie" Sharpe)

3 Exodus: "Dust in Yuh Face" (wr: David Rudder, Pelham Goddard/arr: Pelham Goddard)

3 Trinidad All Stars: "Dust in Yuh Face" (wr: Pelham Goddard, David Rudder/arr: Eddie Quarless)

1994

1 Desperadoes: "Fire Coming Down" (wr: Robert Greenidge, Superblue/arr: Robert Greenidge)

2 Trinidad All Stars: "Earthquake" (wr: Kitchener/arr: Eddie Quarless)

3 Renegades: "Earthquake" (wr: Kitchener/arr: Jit Samaroo)

1995

1 Renegades: "Laramania" (wr: Merchant, De Fosto/arr: Jit Samaroo)

2 Exodus: "Simple Thing" (wr/arr: Pelham Goddard)

3 Desperadoes: "Pan Parang" (wr: Robert Greenidge, Ronnie McIntosh/arr: Robert Greenidge)

1996

1 Renegades: "Pan in a Rage" (wr: Kitchener/arr: Jit Samaroo)

2 Phase II Pan Groove: "Mind Your Business" (wr: Len "Boogsie" Sharpe, Denise Plummer/arr: Len "Boogsie" Sharpe)

3 Desperadoes: "Blast Off" (wr: Robert Greenidge, Ronnie McIntosh/arr: Robert Greenidge)

3 Exodus: "The Disappearing Panyard" (wr: David Rudder/arr: Pelham Goddard)

1997

1 Renegades: "Guitar Pan" (wr: Kitchener/arr: Jit Samaroo)

2 Phase II Pan Groove: "Misbehave" (wr: Len Boogie Sharpe, Denise Plummer/arr: Len Boogie Sharpe)

3 Exodus: "Guitar Pan" (wr: Kitchener/arr: Pelham Goddard)

1998

1 Nu Tones: "High Mas" (wr: David Rudder/arr: Clive Bradley)

2 Exodus: "Pan Parade" (wr/arr: Pelham Goddard)

3 Trinidad All Stars: "Me & Meh Lady" (wr: Dustin Lawrence/arr —)

1999

1 Desperadoes: "In My House" (wr: Emanuel Synette/arr: Clive Bradley)

2 Exodus: "Play My Music" (wr/arr: Pelham Goddard)

3 Nu Tones: "Toco Band" (wr: Kitchener/arr: Clive Bradley)

2000

1 Desperadoes: "Picture on My Wall" (wr: Emanuel Synette/arr: Clive Bradley)

2 Exodus: "The Band Plays On" (wr: Alvin Daniel/arr: Pelham Goddard)

3 Petrotrin Phase II Pan Groove: "My Time" (wr: Denise Plummer, Len Boogie Sharpe/arr: Len Boogie Sharpe)

2001

1 Exodus: "A Happy Song"

2 Neal And Massy Trinidad All Stars: "Rain Melody"

3 WITCO Desperadoes: "Yuh Lookin' for Horn"

RECOMMENDED LISTENING

Pan compilations abound and are often distinguished as much by their contents as by the featured artists. That said, recordings by any of the annual Pan winners are worthy additions to any collection, while the following releases will certainly repay seeking out.

THE BARBADOS STEEL ORCHESTRA (aka THE AIR CANADA ALL STARS) Classics to Calypso (WIRL — BARB) 1973

An intriguing blend of classical staples and pop surprises ranges from "Eine Kleine Nachtmusik" to the Beatles'

"Something," and from "The House of the Rising Sun" to "Elizabethan Serenade" — of course, the barely disguised basis of Byron Lee's "Elizabethan Reggae" hit, but also a long-held favorite among steel orchestras.

THE WESTLAND STEEL BAND The Sound of the Sun (Nonesuch Explorer) 1965

Virtually every album in the Nonesuch Explorer catalog of world music is worthy of investigation, but this 12 track collection is one of the best. The sound quality is not the greatest, but across an album of primarily local compositions, cuts like "Love in the Mist," "Linstead Market" and "Co-Che-Oh-Co" reflect pan as a living tradition — as opposed to the sometimes populist repertoires and performances often found on US releases.

VARIOUS ARTISTS

The Heart of Steel — Featuring Steelbands of Trinidad and Tobago (Fly) 1990

The Amoco Renegades, Mat Securities Merrytones, the Catelli All Stars, the Samaroo Jets, Pamberi, and Birdsong recorded live in Port of Spain, performing classical and calypso hits. The Renegades' "Orpheus in the Underworld" and Birdsong's "Mr T" are stand-outs.

VARIOUS ARTISTS

Trinidad & Tobago Steelband Music Festival (RCA — T&T) 1963

Nine pan orchestras caught live in Port of Spain around 1962. The Desperadoes, Tropoli Steel Orchestra, West Side Symphony, Ellie Mannette's Shell Invaders, the Dixieharps, the Stereophonics, Wonderland, the Savoys and the Metronomes are featured highlighting one extract apiece from their classical repertoires. The audible presence of the audience throughout the performances adds an astonishingly rewarding ambience.

MUNGAL PATASAR

STYLE *pantar*

BORN *2/13/48 (La Plaisance, T&T)*

The son of a classical Indian singer, the young Mungal Patasar had mastered the traditional harmonium, dholak and dhantal by age eight. He also played clarinet in his school's military band, and took up mandolin after catching a performance by the popular East Indian band Mahendra Btansar, as they undertook one of the first ever visits to T&T by an Asian group.

By the early 1960s, the prodigy was a member of the BWIA (British West Indies Association) National Indian Orchestra, and had also launched his own band, playing at weddings and similar gatherings. Leaving school, Patasar worked briefly for the Post Office in San Fernando, where

Mungal Patasar & Pantar

new musical fusion which Patasar dubbed Pantar — "pan" for the steel drum, "tar" from the Hindi word meaning string.

Working the minor key calypsos of T&T's past into the purely Indian expressions of raga, this founding trio — themselves dubbed Pantar — were joined by Patasar's son, Prashant (tabla), Dawud Orr (sax), Albert Bushe (bass) and Earl Carnavon (keyboards). They debuted at the 1994 Panjazz Festival, but spent much of the 1990s refining their sound, and it was 1999 before Pantar finally released their debut album, *Nirvana*. Its success paved the way for Pantar to make a dynamic appearance at the 34th Montreaux Jazz festival in July, 2000.

Patasar has written and lectured extensively on Indian Classical Music and Indo-Calypso-Jazz, and is also the founder and director of the Caribbean School of Indian Music. With such a glowing career, he was a worthy recipient of the National Humming Bird (Gold) Medal Award, for his contributions to T&T culture.

SELECTED DISCOGRAPHY

10 Nirvana (Rituals) 1999

A blistering (and, until you've heard it) unimaginable fusion of raga, pan, calypso and reggae with no single instrument taking control, but all making their presence unmistakably known. The song titles suggest dominant themes — the sitar-led "Dreadlocks," the four part/10 minute "Vani Movement," "Ta Pan Jah," "Stay Conscious" — but there's room for deception even there.

Pulsating rhythms underpin every track, while the vocals (confined to the inspirational title track) tend towards the choral. Lord Kitchener's "Ole Lady" opens with utterly sun-drenched electronic pan, before the bass and sitar take over to follow the song's melody. Three mixes of "Dreadlocks" trace the song's evolution from dramatic raga to a dubby electro-dance thumper, and a reprise of the title track moves into unrestrained ragga territory. Raga ragga.

Occasional passages look towards easy listening for their inspiration ("Time Out" and "Ta Pan Jah" are especially guilty of this), but at its best, *Nirvana* is a death-defying achievement, influenced by much but beholden to absolutely nothing.

LEE PERRY

STYLE *reggae*
BORN *Rainford Hugh Perry, 3/28/36 (Hanover, JA)*

The most influential producer in Jamaican music; a legend not only for his work, but also for his uncompromising demeanor and larger-than-life persona, Lee Perry made his entrance into the Kingston music scene in the late 1950s.

A former teenaged dominoes and dance champion, he first approached Duke Reid, operator of the popular Trojan sound system, introducing himself as a singer-songwriter.

he met his wife. He then took up a post as music teacher at a Vedic (Hindu religious) school, at the same time as working in the Public Health department, a job which gave him the freedom he needed to pursue his musical ambitions.

He needed as much free time as he could get. At 17, a record by Pundit Ravi Qhankar encouraged him to start studying the sitar, a musical discipline which notoriously takes many years to master. In fact it was ten years before Patasar felt confident enough even to purchase his first sitar, and another eight before he was ready to perform in public.

In 1978, at the age of 35, Patasar appeared on the *Mastana Bahar* show and won with a performance which moved readily between strictly classical Indian music and the unique Indo-calypso jazz style which ultimately cemented his fame.

Encouraged by Scofield Pilgrim, music teacher at Queen's Royal College, Patasar joined with local jazz musicians Clive Zanda, Boogsie Qharpe and Toby Tobias, and fused their sound with his rhythms. Over the next four years, the quartet became one of the most popular on the T&T jazz circuit. In 1983, however, Patasar departed T&T for a five year stay in India, where he continued his sitar studies at Banaras Hindu University.

There, he practiced for upwards of eight hours a day, finally emerging with several academic degrees. Patasar also gained the glowing distinction of being only the second foreigner ever to earn the gold medal in the Master of Music exam set by Prayag Sangeet Samiti, one of Asia's most prestigious (and exacting) examining boards. The musician returned to T&T in 1990 and, in 1994, joined forces with jazz pannists Marlon Charles and Harold Headley. Pursuing his earlier experiments in Indo-Calypso-Jazz, the trio created a

Lee "Scratch" Perry—larger than life.

The relationship quickly splintered, apparently after the pair argued over some lyrics Perry had written, which Reid handed to Stranger Cole to sing after determining that Perry himself had no voice.

Perry then visited Coxsone Dodd's Downbeat system instead and was taken on as an errand boy. When Dodd began moving into record production, Perry was generally the one who transported Dodd's masters to the Federal pressing plant, picked up the finished product, then toured around Kingston, selling them. The then-unsung Prince Buster numbered among Perry's co-workers.

By 1959, Perry was Studio One's A&R man, supervising the weekly Sunday afternoon auditions held at Dodd's Orange Street store. Not surprisingly, one of his earliest "discoveries" was himself and, that same year, Dodd's Coxsone label released Perry's debut single, the self-composed and produced "Old for New." His second single, celebrating a newly fashionable dance called the "Chicken Scratch," was the source for the best-known of Perry's several nicknames.

By the early 1960s, Perry was an intrinsic part of the Studio One set-up. Working alongside organist Jackie Mittoo,

he produced and occasionally wrote songs for Delroy Wilson ("Spit in the Sky"), the Maytals ("Six and Seven Book of Moses"), Shenley Duffus, the Wailers and many more.

Recording under his own name and as King Perry, his distinctive vocal graced a slew of remarkable 45s during this period. "Prince in the Black," "Don't Copy," "Prince and Duke" (dedicated to Studio One arch-rivals Prince Buster and Duke Reid), "Mad Head" "Royalty," "Bad Minded People," "Chatty Chatty Woman" and "Roast Duck" were especially notable, while a union with Rita Marley's Soulettes saw him score with "Doctor Dick" and "Rub and Squeeze," two early entrants into Jamaican music's burgeoning fascination with lewdness and double-entendre.

THE UPSETTER: 1968–73

Perry broke with Studio One under less than amicable circumstances in 1966. He spent some time working as a freelance engineer around other studios — Prince Buster's "Ghost Dance," "Johnny Cool" and "Judge Dread" all involved him. Perry also contributed to productions by JJ Johnson and WIRL's Garnet Hargreaves and George Benson, in return for which he was given studio time on a "record now, pay later basis." Among the tracks recorded there were "Run for Cover," "Whup Whup Man" and "Set Them Free," an impassioned contribution to the then-ongoing saga of Prince Buster's Judge Dread.

Perry teamed up with Joe Gibbs in 1967. Charged with organizing Gibbs' Amalgamated label, he discovered the Versatiles, featuring the young Junior Byles, while also writing and producing for Errol Dunkley (the new label's debut hit, "Please Stop Your Lying"), Errol Brown and the Pioneers. His own most potent release became the source of his other best-known nickname: "The Upsetter" was written as an attack on Coxsone Dodd, and did its job so well, that Perry retained the name for his next few years' worth of projects.

Perry left Gibbs during 1968 (he was replaced by Niney Holness), incensed that the older producer refused to give him his creative due. Many of the Amalgamated label's early classics were not only produced by Perry, they were also written by him. He publicly aired his grievances on "People Funny Boy," which became the first hit on his own newly established Upsetter label, with sales of 60,000 + . Pointedly, the song's tune was lifted from the Pioneers' "Longshot," itself an uncredited Perry composition.

Upsetter Records was launched in tandem with engineers Lynford Anderson (b 7/8/41, Clarendon, JA) and Barry Lambert (producers Clive Chin and Errol Thompson also helped out), and a studio band built around Gladstone Anderson's renowned aggregation, Gladdy's All Stars. They were called, of course, the Upsetters.

Running his own label allowed Perry the freedom to try things no other producer would even have dreamed of unleashing. One early single, Burt Walters' "Honey Love," had for its b-side the mysterious "Evol Yenoh" — mysterious, that is, until you realized it was simply a reprise of "Honey Love," with the vocal track playing backwards over the rhythm. Another cut, "Noisy Village," comprised the rhythm of Tennors' "Ride Me Donkey" played at half speed, while Perry, Lambert and Anderson added a barrage of bizarre sound effects. Appropriately, the track was credited to The Engineers.

Perry scored his first international smash hit in October, 1969, when "Return of Django" reached #5 in the UK. He was promptly invited to tour Britain, piecing together a new generation of Upsetters to accompany him, as the existing line-up's commitments prevented them from joining him.

The new band, now regarded as the classic Upsetters line-up, was drawn from another popular studio team, Sonia Pottinger's Hippy Boys, featuring Glen Adams (organ), Alva Lewis (guitar) and future Wailers rhythm section Carlton and Aston Barrett (coincidentally, Perry would soon be producing the Wailers themselves, and the Barretts appear on many of the 100+ sides he cut with the group). This same coterie also worked with Bunny Lee at this time, as the Aggrovators and Bunny Lee's All Stars.

Perry and the Upsetters never followed up their UK hit, although in Jamaica, they were unstoppable. "Ten to Twelve," "Night Doctor" (one of the first records ever to feature drummer Sly Dunbar), "(Dangerous) Man from MI5" and "Medical Operation" were all local successes. At the same time, Perry's golden touch as a producer was confirmed by the seemingly endless barrage of singles exploding out of the Upsetter set-up, with such artists as Slim Smith (ex-the Techniques and Uniques), soul singer Busty Brown, Winston Jarrett (ex-Righteous Flames), David Isaacs, vocal groups the Silvertones and the Bleechers, Louis Armstrong impersonator Pat Satchmo, and Nora Dean.

Although Perry still used outside studios for recording — Randy's Studio 17 and Dynamic Sounds were his favorites — most of his planning took place at his Upsetter record store on Charles Street. The Bleechers' infectious "Check Him Out" single, released when the store first opened, is essentially an extended radio commercial for the shop.

The fruits of this activity are spread throughout the Upsetter label catalog. "Kill Them All," the first Upsetters release of 1970, was essentially a disconcerting medley of three separate rhythms, linked by Perry's growled vocal. Equally groundbreaking were the sides he cut with Dave Barker, one of the most distinctive singers — grunters, shouters, barkers indeed — on the contemporary scene.

Though Barker found his greatest fame elsewhere, with a UK chart-topping partnership with Ansell Collins, the singles he cut with Perry during 1969–70 included such triumphs as "Prisoner of Love," "Shocks of Mighty" and a frantic version of Blood Sweat & Tears' blues rock classic "Spinning Wheel." Indeed, the latter represented a feat of imagination so staggering that, years later, British DJ Kenny Everett ranked it among the *worst* records ever made!

Other Perry-produced covers of international hits were somewhat less contentious. The local practice of simply reggae-fying radio favorites was as rife on Upsetter as any other label, and so "Let It Be" (the Soulettes), "Leaving on a Jet Plane" (David Isaacs), "Melting Pot" (the Heaters), "Suspicious Minds" (Hugh Roy), "I'm a Believer" (British-based Denzil Dennis, a single recorded in Jamaica, then voiced in London) and "Na Na Hey Hey Kiss Him Goodbye" (the Upsetters themselves) all passed through the catalog during 1970–72.

1971 saw toasters Dennis Alcapone and Prince Winston Thompson (the future Dr Alimantado) record with Perry, while Junior Byles joined the Upsetter stable following the break-up of the Versatiles. Indeed, the label remained a force to be reckoned with for much of the next three years, commercially and in terms of innovation. Anybody looking to trace the origins of the hip hop practice of "scratching," for example, should search no further than Charlie Ace's "Cow Thief Skank," a 1973 Perry production which featured the vocal track leaping between two separate backing tracks.

Other excellent Perry/Upsetters releases included "Justice to the People" — a powerful cover of the Chi-Lites' "Give More Power to the People," "Kentucky Skank," "Cold Weather" and "Public Jestering," a Judge Dread type number credited to Judge Winchester. It was clear, however, that Perry's interests were moving away from simply churning out 45s and the occasional LP.

In 1973, Perry bought a house in the Washington Gardens suburb of Kingston and, over the next six months, converted the backyard of 5 Cardiff Crescent into what became one of the most legendary studios of the age, the Black Ark.

THE BLACK ARK: 1974–79

In terms of physical equipment, the Black Ark was a primitive set-up. A four track recorder, a mixing board and an Echoplex delay unit were the key ingredients — that, and the alchemical process by which Perry then converted the ensuing recordings to sonic gold.

Massive hits like Leo Grahams' "Black Candle," Junior Byles' "Curly Locks" and Susan Cadogan's "Hurts So Good"; cult masterpieces by Junior Murvin ("Police and Thieves") and Max Romeo ("War in a Babylon"); crucial cuts by Dillinger, I-Roy and Charlie Ace; earth-shaking collaborations with Niney Holness and King Tubby; and a string of majestic releases in his own right; all poured from Black Ark, establishing it overnight as THE happening studio of the day, a place of magic and mystery — and that despite it measuring no more than twelve feet square, with every available surface covered in the cheap rubber balls Perry collected.

"It doesn't look nothing like a studio until you hear it," Max Romeo said. "No-one knows what technique Perry used. Because he used those small track tape, and he seemed to get 16 tracks stuffed into that four track. It was a marvel." Perry agreed. "It was only four tracks on the machine. But I was picking up 20 from the extra-terrestrial squad."

Accompanied by the latest generation of the Upsetters — the brass quartet of Bobby Ellis, Richard Hall, Herman Marquis and Vin Gordon, drummer Michael Richards and bassist Boris Gardiner — Perry established a virtual open house at the studio, allowing people to wander in and out even at the height of a recording session. With the air thick with ganja and the walls reverberating to the sound of a non-stop party, Perry "produced" from his favorite chair, swinging back and forth, clapping his hands, shouting approval and instructions, and cleaning the tape heads with his T-shirt.

With its unbending allegiance to roots, Black Ark was at its peak from 1974–76. Singles like the Unforgettables' "Many a Call," Lee Locks' "What Can I Do," Bunny & Rickie's "Too Bad Bull" and Prince Jazzbo's "Penny Reel" were phenomenally successful, both in Jamaica and on the UK club circuit.

Perry's inventiveness hit further highs when he investigated the kung fu phenomenon across a pair of albums under his own name (*Return of Wax* and *Kung Fu Meets the Dragon*, while releasing 45s the quality of "Stay Dread," "Kiss Me Neck," "Rebels Train," "Dub a Pum Pum" (with the Silvertones), "Cane River Rock," "Black Belt Jones" and many more. Before long, Island Records looked to Perry for the bulk of their (non-Wailers) UK reggae catalog.

Unquestionably, they picked up some classic work, including recordings with the Heptones, Junior Dread, the Meditations, Errol Walker, Devon Irons, Mikey Dread and Augustus Pablo; and the ensuing widespread distribution sent Perry's name and reputation soaring.

Perry returned to Britain in 1977 to produce the Clash, a British punk band with a singular flair for reggae. They had already cut a dramatic version of Junior Murvin's "Police and Thieves"; Perry took the controls for their next single, "Complete Control." He celebrated the union by teaming up with Bob Marley — himself in London to record his *Exodus* album — for the joyous "Punky Reggae Party." (The Clash ended up remixing Perry's effort, to make it sound more like them.)

Back in Jamaica, 1977 saw Perry at the forefront of another innovation, when he released Carlton Jackson's "History," one of the first 12-inch singles the island had ever seen. Bob Marley rejoined him during 1978 to cut two songs, "Who Colt the Game" and "I Know a Place," while Black Ark also became the magnet for visiting white rockers.

John Martyn and Robert Palmer both recorded at the studio, while some of Perry's most idiosyncratic late 70s productions involved Beatle wife Linda McCartney, a fascinating version of "Sugartime" among them. Another project pregnant with promise was *Nyahbingi Slaughters the Dragon*, recorded, but never released, around 1978.

However, storm clouds were gathering. As Perry's workload increased, so did his consumption of alcohol and marijuana and, though the adventurous quality of his work certainly did not suffer, its commercial potential was perhaps waning. Certainly Island records thought so, not only rejecting what history now records as Perry's last bona fide classic, the Congos' seminal *Heart of The Congos* album, but also turning down two Perry solo albums, the skewered *Roast Fish Collie Weed and Cornbread* (the title track alone appeared as a single) and the dramatic *Return of Super Ape*.

Perry had maintained his own recording career throughout the 1970s although he increasingly viewed such releases — singles and albums alike — as little more than demonstrations of his genius, as opposed to genuine commercial recordings. However, he remained capable of some supremely majestic music, as 1976's *Super Ape* and its successor, *Return of the Super Ape*, proved. At the same time, disillusion was now setting in with unimaginable ferocity.

For some three years, Perry had allowed Black Ark to disintegrate. Inside, he smothered the walls in graffiti, paint and anything else he could affix to them. The roof began to leak, the furnishings to decay, and a handful of instruments lay in the rubble (master tapes and other equipment had been removed to the house). He would periodically hire workmen to try and fix the place up, but such resolutions rarely lasted long. Black Ark was ultimately leveled by a fire in the summer of 1983, but in fact, it had been destroyed years before.

Neither the truth nor the hand behind the fire was ever officially established. Perry was (and remains) most people's favorite suspect for setting it — one source claimed he did it in a fit of fury, after discovering his favorite rubber ball had been stolen from the mixing desk. In fact, the mixing desk was long gone, and the rubber balls with it.

Financial problems exacerbated by Island's recalcitrance have been suggested; but so have regular visits from masked gunmen demanding money and Wailers master-tapes from the producer. Perry himself was detained by the police for three days on suspicion of arson, but released due to lack of evidence.

THE LATER YEARS

Perry slipped now into a world where rumor, fact and wishful thinking all seem to have as much credence as one another. It is generally accepted that, in the months following the destruction of Black Ark, he lived amid the ruins, worshipping bananas and attempting to baptize visitors with his garden hose.

He remained musically active throughout these shadowy years, if increasingly ill-at-ease with his reputation. Around 1980, he began referring to himself as Pipecock Jackxon, in apparent homage to Michael Jackson, and cut one album under this name, 1981's *Return of Pipecock Jackxon*.

Relocating temporarily to the US during 1982, he produced the white reggae bands The Majestics and The Little Terrorists. Perry's own *Mystic Miracle Star* album was also recorded during this period (with the Majestics backing him), before he renewed his relationship with Island and delivered the *History, Mystery and Prophecy* album.

It was a fine recording, but the UK arm of the label passed on it, and Perry finally lost all patience with Island. He subsequently accused label head Chris Blackwell of vampirism (in the song "Judgement Inna Babylon") and, more seriously, held him responsible for Bob Marley's death.

In 1983, Perry moved to Britain, where a clutch of desultory Scratch-by-Numbers type albums were finally followed by partnerships with two of his most vociferous disciples, the Mad Professor and Adrian Sherwood. The 1987 album *Time Boom Z de Devil Dead* and "The Jungle" single, pairing Perry with Sherwood's Dub Syndicate, can be regarded as the dawn of Perry's critical rehabilitation. An extensive, decade-long sequence of albums cut with the Mad Professor, on the other hand, is often as enjoyable for its comic/lunacy quotient as for what's going on in the mix.

Briefly back in the US in 1988, Perry worked alongside Lloyd "Bullwackie" Barnes on *Satan Kicked the Bucket* and reunited with his old mentor Coxsone Dodd, also in New York, for what became the 1992 album *The Upsetter and the Beat*. A new single, "The Groove," inaugurated another reconciliation with Island in 1990 — the album *From a Secret Laboratory* followed. Perry also spent some time in the Netherlands before moving to Switzerland, where he married Swiss millionairess Mirielle Campbell. The ceremony took place in a Hare Krishna temple.

Although Perry has returned to Jamaica on occasion, even mooting the possibility of rebuilding the Black Ark, Zurich has remained his most permanent home, from whence he oversees what has become a virtual mini-industry of reissues and repackages. Together with his own former associates Bob Marley and King Tubby, Lee Perry dominates the reggae CD racks of today, with several hundred releases touching upon almost every era of his long career. The following discography, therefore, is extremely selective.

SELECTED DISCOGRAPHY

The vast majority of Perry's albums pre-*Return of Wax* were compilations of recent 45s and dubs, and credited either to Perry and/or the Upsetters. Although they can thus be considered compilations, they are collected together here to illustrate the continuity of Perry's career.

7 The Upsetter (Trojan — UK) 1969
8 The Return of Django (Trojan — UK) 1969
8 Clint Eastwood (Pama — UK) 1969

Bundling up a bumper crop of recent Perry/Upsetters' hit singles, including such classics as "Live Injection," "Night Doctor" and the irrepressible "Man from MI5," three albums highlight the sheer productivity which characterized Perry at this time. Not every cut is a gem, and most have been recycled ad nauseam on later compilations. But the individual platters each have many highlights.

7 The Many Moods of the Upsetters (Economy — UK) 1970
7 Scratch the Upsetter Again (Trojan — UK) 1970
6 Eastwood Rides Again (Trojan — UK) 1970

In as much as they round up a wealth of material not necessarily available on UK singles (alongside a lot that was), this sequence, too, was considered a veritable treasure trove by early collectors. Today they seem impossibly jumbled and, with much of the material again now available on sundry better-organized CDs, they are best regarded as curios from another age.

3 The Good, the Bad and the Upsetters (Trojan—UK) 1970

A lackluster collection largely recorded by the Upsetters band with English producer Bruce Anthony (aka promoters Tony Cousins and Bruce White), with little input or approval from Perry himself. He got his own back by pirating the sleeve for use with a Jamaica-only album of the same title but very different contents — unfortunately this extraordinarily limited edition has yet to resurface. (Highlights apparently included a DJ version of "Same Thing All Over" and a steel drum take of "Bum Ball".)

6 Africa's Blood (Upsetter—JA) 1972

A weak set, overloaded with too many similar sounding instrumental cuts, although the presence of Winston Prince's "Place Called Africa" goes a long way towards redeeming the entire package.

6 Rhythm Shower (Upsetter—JA) 1973

Brings the young Dillinger and the veteran Sir Lord Comic into focus, but again, there's a lot of inconsequential instrumental filler to wade through.

6 Cloak and Dagger (Upsetter) 1973

Widely referenced as one of the first ever dub albums, an instrumental set which gallops along with a mind of its own, but never really gets anywhere. Perry would take the same discipline a lot further in later years.

9 Double Seven (Trojan—UK) 1974

Perry's best album yet includes contributions from U-Roy, I-Roy and David Isaacs, with less reliance on the keyboard-sound-we've-heard-before, and more textures when it does turn up. Perry's own version of Isaac Hayes' "Soul Man" is sensational, the synthesizer-led "Long Sentence" has a squelchy feel all of its own, and "Cold Weather" is an ominously wacky toast. The closing "Waap You Wa," finally, is one of those proto-dub experiments you wish would go on forever.

8 Blackboard Jungle (Upsetter) 1973

The question is, with at least three different versions of this album on the streets, which one is the seminal monster which everybody goes on about? The true stereo Jamaican original? The alternate mix on Clocktower? The 1990 Coxsone label reissue with the wrong track listing? In fact, it's all of them, although any one will suffice for most listeners.

6 Return of Wax (DIP—UK) 1974

Following *Cloak & Dagger*'s instrumental ambitions into far more satisfying territory, *Wax* is a virtual concept album revolving around Perry's kung fu obsession via "Deadly Hands," "One Armed Boxer" and more.

7 DIP Presents the Upsetter (DIP) 1975

Excellent compilation of early 70s Perry productions, opening with the Upsetters' "Enter the Dragon," before unleashing sides by Sam Carty, King Burnett, the Gladiators, Leo Graham, the Gaylads, the Silvertones and Linval Spencer.

8 Kung Fu Meets the Dragon (DIP—UK) 1974

An early dub excursion from the Black Ark, again drawing its inspiration from the then pandemic obsession with the Martial Arts. Close your eyes and you can hear the death stars whirring through the mix.

9 Revolution Dub (Cactus) 1975

After so long spent on the cusp of dub, Perry finally goes for the golden ring, treating Junior Byles, Jimmy Riley and others to some truly dangerous textures, then splicing the plummy tones of English actor James Robertson Justice into the brew. In 1975, this album provoked widespread disconcerting delirium. Today, it still sounds fresh.

9 Colombia Colly (Mango) 1976

Credited to Jah Lion and sometimes overlooked by the CD shelf-stuffers, Perry picks up where his production of the first Congos album left off, delving deeper into darkest dread roots territory. Wild toast replaces tight harmony, but the entire experience is never less than essential.

7 Super Ape (Island—UK) 1976

Released with an alternate mix and rearranged tracks in Jamaica (as *Scratch the Super Ape*), a massively produced (some said over-produced) exploration of everything the Black Ark was capable of, an atmosphere-packed heavy dub excursion, but one which turned conventional dub technique on its head by adding to, rather than subtracting from, the tracks. Prince Jazzbo guests on "Croaking Lizard," but the real stars are the rhythms. "Dub it up blacker than dread!" roars the comic book cover, and they do.

5 Roast Fish Collie Weed and Cornbread (Lion of Judah—JA) 1978

The jazz-tinged "Soul Fire" and the spacey "Roast Fish and Cornbread" are the twin poles of a vocal excursion which ranks among Perry's most eccentric (read "self-indulgent") exercises.

10 Return of The Super Ape (Lion of Judah—JA) 1978

Some of the heaviest dubs of Perry's career, but also some of the most pop-inflected and simultaneously atmospheric music the Upsetters ever played, the precise point where earth rhythm and heavenly inspiration meet and melt together. The jazz riffs return, but so do a host of other sounds and notions — from Sly Stone to the Clash, from gospel harmony to sharp, barking breaks which take past Perry concepts back to home base before feeding them through the monstrous wringer of his sonic savagery. And, over it all, broods a palpable sense of unspoken menace, waiting, lurking, biding its time. A straightforward CD reissue is available through Cleopatra; another, *The Original Super Ape* (Jet Star — UK) adds five bonus tracks.

▣ Return of Pipecock Jackxon (Black Star) 1981
The word on the street was that Perry wasn't himself any longer. That's because he was Pipecock Jackxon, a restrained, refined and sometimes pitiful shadow of the Upsetting Scratch of old.

▣ Mystic Miracle Star (Heartbeat) 1982
Still at a loose end, Perry hitches up with the anonymous sounding Majestics and, while the 13 minute "Radication Squad" proves he's not entirely wiped out, the remainder of the set revolves around insubstantial tunes, lazy lyrics and leaden rhythms.

▣ History Mystery & Prophecy (Mango) 1983
Is this really Lee Perry? Weak reggae rhythms, trite lyrics (even the rude "Bed Jamming" sounds uncomfortable) and lackluster production. The UK and US pressings boast different mixes.

▣ Battle of Armagideon aka *Millionaire Liquidator* (Trojan — UK) 1986
The best thing about being renowned as a maverick madcap is knowing no-one dares tell you when you've gone too far. The hardest part is knowing in yourself where to stop. Too much of Perry's post Black Ark material sounds like unfinished experiments which he releases because he can. Here, however, everything comes together, including a distinctive cover of a Ray Charles song (reborn as "Show Me that River") and the multi-voice-tracked "Drum Song," while he addresses his reputation as well. "I Am a Madman" is the best indication yet that he probably isn't.

▣ Time Boom Z de Devil Dead (On-U — UK) 1987
Generally excessive dose of the weird stuff, roughly akin to spending an hour in the company of two people (Perry and Adrian Sherwood) who both think they're the most interesting men on earth. And they might well be, but it doesn't really come through on this album.

▣ Satan Kicked the Bucket (Bullwackies) 1988
A weak album better experienced via its dub counterpart, *Satan's Dub* (ROIR — 1990). For fanatical out-takes collectors, further Perry/Bullwackie meanderings appear on *The Dub Messenger* (Tassa — 1990) and *Message from the Yard* (Rohit — 1990); neither is especially worth hunting for.

▣ From the Secret Laboratory (Mango) 1990
Adrian Sherwood collaboration which emphasizes Perry's own awareness of his accomplishments, lyrically and musically. The Heptones' "Party Time" receives a great workout, while "African Hitch Hiker" might well be autobiographical.

▣ Spiritual Healing (Black Cat) 1990
Another of those albums which really wants to be more than it actually is. Co-producer Higi Heilinger is as far out of his depth as most of Perry's other collaborators. And Perry just sounds out of it.

▣ Lord God Musick (Network) 1991
Freakish dance hall meets dub experiment apparently aimed at predicting the end of the world, and threatening similar conclusions to sundry enemies. Probably Perry (and co-conspirator Niney Holness)'s least coherent offering, but that works to its advantage, with the self-indulgence salvaged by some hot rhythms, some great lyrics and some odd samples of past Upsetter cuts. "Colt the Game" is worth paying attention too, if only for Perry's potshots at Bunny Lee, inspired by Lee's licensing some old tapes to a dodgy reissue label, and haunted by the repeated demand "who shot King Tubby?" Since reissued by Heartbeat.

▣ The Upsetter & The Beat (Heartbeat) 1992
While producer Dodd unleashes some classic Studio One rhythms, Perry launches into a series of toasts which might well be ad libbed, and are certainly extemporized. Again, coherency is not the watchword here, but the album has its moments.

▣ Live at Maritime Hall (Maritime) 1997
The Mad Professor and his Robotiks are on hand to stamp their sound across the proceedings, but Perry's not paying too much attention. Armed with a toy horn, and with an awful lot to talk about (even with his between song raps excised, it's a wordy album), he turns in readily recognizable, but utterly unique renderings of "I Am a Madman," "Cornbread" and "Papa was a Rolling Stone."

▣ Technomajikal (ROIR) 1997
Collaboration with Dieter Meier, the Swiss mastermind behind 80s electro hero Yello. As such, it plays rather more to its makers' reputations than non-aficionados (of both) might want to hear, and spends a lot of time conducting pointless remixes of cuts which went on too long to begin with.

LEE PERRY & MAD PROFESSOR
▣ Mystic Warrior (Ariwa — UK) 1989
▣ Mystic Warrior Dub (Ariwa — UK) 1989
Mystic indeed, a journey back through some of the many tangents Perry has passed in his long career — "Kung Fu Fighting"! "Crazy Baldheads"! "Dub Reggae Soca"! From the sound of things, neither party took these albums too seriously — listeners would be advised to follow suit.

5 Black Ark Experryments (Ariwa—UK) 1995
5 Experryments at the Grass Roots of Dub (Ariwa—UK) 1995
4 Lee Perry Featuring Mad Professor, Dougie Digital & Juggler—Super Ape inna Jungle (Ariwa—UK) 1996

Another excuse to unleash the lunacy—if you liked the above, these'll tickle the same fancy; if you've not heard any of them, listen before you buy. Then listen a couple of times more. Some things don't get better (or funnier) the more you hear them.

6 Who Put the Voodoo pon Reggae (Ariwa—UK) 1996
6 Dub Take the Voodoo Out of Reggae (Ariwa—UK) 1996

High on rhythm, low on overt laughs, but shot through with clever nuances which remind you who you're listening to.

7 Dub Fire (Ariwa—UK) 1998
6 Dub in Fire (Ariwa—UK) 1998

The best of the otherwise maddening Professor sets, an assault on some of Perry's best loved oldies, rewrapped and occasionally speed-rapped with more instrumental restraint than might have been expected. Key revisions include "Doctor Dick," "People Funny Boy" and a handful of Wailers numbers. The dub version adds Junior Byles' "The Long Way," disguised as "I Won't Dub You."

5 Techno Party (Ariwa—UK) 2000

LEE PERRY & THE SCIENTIST
6 At the Blackheart Studio (Rhino) 1996

SELECTED COMPILATIONS & ARCHIVE RELEASES

This section comprises collections of archive material featuring Perry/Upsetters alone.

5 Chicken Scratch (Heartbeat) 1989

Epic recounting of Perry's Studio One days turns out to be considerably less epic than his subsequent reputation would have us believe. A handful of genuine gems ("Roast Duck," "Chicken Scratch") are balanced by way too much second rate ska and the fact is, it would be a few more years before Perry even began to shine. The sound quality is very shaky and, at a shade over 30 minutes, the disc itself is extraordinarily lightweight.

2 Smokin' (VP) 1994

Out-takes from sessions in New York in 1981 with producer Melvin Jackson. Apparently two albums worth of material was cut, although one *Pipecock Jackxon* was already more than enough.

5 The Upsetters a Go Go (Heartbeat) 1995

An odd collection, drawn from Perry's 1969–73 collaborations with Glen Adams, then remixed by the latter 20+ years later. While there's rarities a-plenty, odd excisions and the like do detract from its value. Keyboards fans will enjoy it the most.

5 On the Wire (Trojan) 2000

Cut in London in 1988 as the follow-up to *Battle of Armagideon*, Perry then salted the tapes away for another decade. Smart move. Had it appeared at the time, it would have added little to its predecessor. Arriving after a decade of under-achievement, it has been described as a lost classic . . . but isn't that always the way? (In fairness, "Born Funky" truly does merit such praise.)

LEE PERRY PRODUCTIONS (INDIVIDUAL ARTISTS)

DAVE BARKER
7 Prisoner of Love: Dave Barker Meets the Upsetters (Trojan—UK) 1970

At times, it seems as though Barker could not have been more aptly named if Perry had retitled him Yelp-Yowl-and-Holler. But he also possesses one of the sweetest singing voices around and this set allows both talents full rein. "Shocks of Mighty," "My Cup," "Prisoner of Love" and an outrageous "Blowing in the Wind" are included among the best-known tracks, but there's so much more here to recommend it.

THE SILVERTONES
7 Silver Bullets 1973

One of the finest vocal groups of the 1960s turn out to be not so shabby in the 1970s either. A restrained Perry production amplifies the sweetness, while songs like "Early in the Morning," "Souvenir of Mexico" and "Rejoice Jah Jah Children" are as well executed as they were well chosen.

VIN GORDON
7 Musical Bones (DIP—UK) 1975

PRINCE JAZZBO
6 Natty Passing Through (Black Wax—UK) 1976

JUNIOR MURVIN
8 Police and Thieves (Mango) 1977

The title track is such a classic that it's easy to forget there's a whole album of similar quality behind it—Max Romeo's *War in a Babylon* suffers from similar memory loss. Suffice to say, even without its cornerstone, this would be one of the crucial mid-70s roots albums, with "Lucifer," "Rescue Jah Children" and the seething nyahbingi "Working in a Cornfield" all the equal of the hit.

GEORGE FAITH
6 Super Eight (Black Art—JA) 1977
7 To Be a Lover (Black Swan—UK) 1977

Essentially the same album, but with some alternate tracks.

THE CONGOS
10 Heart of the Congos (Black Ark—JA) 1977

A masterpiece in its day, *Heart* has lost none of its power with the passage of time. The musicianship is simply superb, the backing vocalists (including the Meditations, a pair of Heptones and Gregory Isaacs) are sublime, while the Congos' own voices soar heavenward on the wings of Cedric Myton's angelic falsetto. Perry arguably does his best work ever here, revelling in the Congos rootsy style, fleshing out the sound with layers of dubby effects and electronic wizardry, but applying everything with a subtle touch that accentuates, never overshadows, the gorgeous vocals.

THE JOLLY BROTHERS
7 Conscious Man (Roots—UK) 1993

All good things . . . they say, and it's true. Recorded during 1977–78, but unreleased till now, a weighty Rasta manifesto built around the Jollies' 1978 UK Top 50 hit "Conscious Man." Band in-fighting saw this set shelved in favor of *Consciousness*, a lightweight collection of love songs recorded with Prince Jammy (of all people!) and the Jolly Brothers faded from view. Had they only gone with their initial instincts, they could have been bigger than the Congos.

See also entries for BOB MARLEY, JUNIOR BYLES, SUSAN CADOGAN, THE HEPTONES, MAX ROMEO, and THIRD WORLD.

LEE PERRY PRODUCTIONS (VARIOUS ARTISTS)
7 Battle Axe (Trojan—UK) 1973

Setting the scene for what would one day become a flood, a 14 track collection of recent 45s by both the Upsetters and an array of Perry's most sainted clients — Ras Dawkins, Andy Capp, Little Roy, Delroy Wilson and Junior Byles ("Place Called Africa" — you have to hear this song!).

7 Revolution Dub (Creole—UK) 1975

"Doctor on the Go," a dub take on Junior Byles' "The Long Way," is a wicked highlight on this collection covering Scratch versions dating between 1970–75. The set has since been reissued on CD (Orange Street — 1998).

8 Scratch on the Wire (Island) 1979

Superb compilation of 1976–78 material, including Perry's own "Big Neck Police Man" and "Soul Fire," Max Romeo's "War in a Babylon," a Jah Lion cut and others by Errol Walker, George Faith and the Meditations. A nice snapshot but, as with so many of Perry's pre-1990s collections, subsequent anthologies render it all but redundant.

4 Scratch and Company Chapter One (Clocktower) 1981

An intriguing track list drawing on lesser-known cuts recorded between 1967–76 is tempered by the knowledge that label owner Brad Osbourne remixed much of it for release. Since reissued on CD as *Scratch Attack* (alongside the remixed *Blackboard Jungle*) by RAS.

6 The Upsetter Collection (Trojan—UK) 1981

A well-conceived collection of 1969–73 material, includes Perry's "The Vampire," "Bucky Skank" and "Return Of Django," before jumping into the production archive for the Bleechers' "Check Him Out," Comic's "Django Shoots First" and the Gatherers' "Words of My Mouth."

6 Heart of the Ark Vols 1/2 (Seven Leaves—UK) 1982

The last days of the Black Ark saw a handful of genuine classics, and a lot of makeweight filler — as these sets prove. The rarity quotient is high — even long-time Perry collectors will be missing some of this album. But only Leroy Sibbles' "Rasta Fari" and Prodigals' whimsical "Four and Twenty Dreadlocks" (Volume One), and Lord Creator's "Such Is Life" (Volume Two) can be termed anything more than "interesting."

7 Excaliburman (Seven Leaves—UK) 1982

A further reaching set looks back to some overlooked mid-70s material, including Dillinger's "Dub Organiser" and Jah T's "Lick the Pipe." Again, however, the emphasis on later material will thrill collectors more than listeners — Jackie Bernard and Debra Keese are among the scarcest contenders. The same label's *Megaton Dub Vols 1/2* sets offer the other side of similar pieces.

7 Reggae Greats (Mango) 1984

Overlook the fact that there is no excuse on earth for not already owning the bulk of this set in one form or another, and there are few better introductions to the more sober side of Perry's genius. No surprises, either.

7 Some of the Best (Heartbeat) 1988

Basically, Perry's greatest hits 1968–74. "People Funny Boy," "Shocks of Mighty," "Duppy Conqueror," "The Thanks We Get" . . . the set leaps around a little disconcertingly and, at 13 tracks/40 minutes, it's maybe a little on the slim side. But there's not a dull moment in sight, and there's enough hard to find cuts to please most collectors.

9 Build the Ark (Trojan—UK) 1989

3LP/two-CD collection of 1972–76 productions, featuring both a- and b-side cuts. With the UK rights to more or less Perry's entire 1968–76 output, together with a lot of late decade material as well, Trojan have released a quite unfeasible number of Upsetter compilations, combining his own recordings and his best productions.

Others in this series include a second 3LP/two-CD box set, *The Upsetter Collection* (featuring the *Africa's Blood*, *Rhythm Shower* and *Double Seven* albums), and a number of single disc sets: *Chapter 2 of Words* (1972–73) *Dry Acid* (1968–73) *Give Me Power* (1969–73) *Open the Gate* (1974–76) *People Funny Boy* (1968–70) *Public Jestering* (1972–76) *Shocks of Mighty* (1969–74) *Upsetting the Nation* (1969–70) *Version Like Rain* (16 tracks drawn from just three basic rhythms — "Beat Down Babylon," "Fever" and "Musical Shower"). *Words of My Mouth* (1973–75).

A number of single artist collections also exist. All are

recommended as snapshots of Perry's power, often featuring both vocal and dub performances by some remarkable, and remarkably unknown, artists. But as with the above sequence, better annotation and organization is available elsewhere.

8 Soundz from the Hot-Line (Heartbeat) 1992

Heavier on songs than effects, unreleased gems and classic oldies make up this 13 track investigation of Perry's 1970s peak. 1978's "Bionic Rats" (the flip of the "City's too Hot" single) is a mighty opener, while the epic "Free Up the Prisoners" is extraordinary. The closing "Track 13" offers a snatch of knockabout entertainment based around Perry's Studio One era acetate "Joker [Brown Girl] in the Ring."

8 Voodooism (Pressure Sounds—UK) 1996

Yet another trawl through Perry's 1970s catalog, with the emphasis on excruciatingly rare 45s from James Booms, Errol Walker, Zap Pow, Leo Graham and more. Despite somewhat self-righteous liner notes, it is a dynamic collection, highlighting material which not only has never been compiled before . . . a lot of collectors had never even seen them before.

8 The Upsetter Shop Volume One (Heartbeat) 1997

Excellent deep dub set concentrating on the 1976–77 period, with 18 dynamite remixes of the Congos, Junior Murvin, Junior Delgado, Max Romeo, Junior Byles, Devon Russell and Perry's own output. Six previously unissued/alternate cuts are added to what are otherwise exclusively Jamaican b-sides.

9 Arkology (Island) 1997

Across three-CDs, the full genius of Perry's peak Black Ark work is revealed. The emphasis is on the period 1976–78, with a little overflow into 1979, with vocal and dub sides torn from a host of singles. Most of Perry's top line productions are represented — Max Romeo, Dillinger, the Congos, the Heptones, Junior Murvin and Augustus Pablo all feature, but lesser feted names Keith Rowe, George Faith, Devon Irons and Errol Walker also star.

8 Produced & Directed by the Upsetter (Pressure Sounds— UK) 1998

Great sounding early-mid 1970s Black Ark collection, featuring vocal and dub takes by future Congo King Burnett, Easton Clarke, the Flames, the Silvertones, Junior Murvin and more.

7 Ethiopia (Orange Street—UK) 1998

14 track collection scouring some of the lesser-visited corners of the Black Ark, featuring fine contributions from Aisha Morrison (the stupendous title track), Leo Graham, the Silvertones and Third World vocalist Bunny Clarke, plus several Perry/Upsetters cuts.

8 Lost Treasures of the Ark (Jet Star—UK) 1998

Rarities and out-takes set most immediately notable for the inclusion of demos for two "lost" Bob Marley songs from 1978, "Who Colt the Game" and "I Know a Place." Other material reaches back to 1968 sessions, in sometimes dubious sound quality, but there is no doubting both the scarcity and the invention behind the music.

6 Wizdom (Ascension) 1998

Another seemingly random round-up of 1971–75 era singles, again high on rarity while not necessarily watching the quality. I-Roy's "Doctor Who," Bobby Ellis' "Ska Baby," Jah Martin's "Kung Fu" and Dillinger's "Tighten Up Skank" are among the better tracks.

8 The Complete UK Upsetter Singles Collection Volumes 1–4 (Trojan—UK) 1998–2001

They are what they are, four two-CD collections rounding up every Upsetter a- and b-side. Most valid from an historical point of view, the sets provide a fascinating insight into one side of the Jamaican music industry which is often overlooked — there was a lot of rubbish released alongside the oft-compiled classics, and Perry was as guilty of it as anyone. (See also the UK SINGLES DIRECTORY entries 1969–72).

7 The Upsetter Shop Volume Two (Heartbeat) 1999

22 tracks that don't hit too many musical highlights, but do unearth some staggering rarities and unreleased recordings, including intriguing cuts by Dillinger, Eric Donaldson, Pat Satchmo, Carl Dawkins and The Wailers' version of the Temptations' "Cloud 9" and Dave Barker. Alternate takes, rehearsals and dub/DJ mixes are especially illuminating, while there's a ragged glory which gives the album the feel of one long, continuous session.

8 Essential Madness from the Scratch Files (Metro—UK) 2000

Although much of this set has appeared elsewhere, a well-structured 18 track collection runs through some of the most important milestones in Perry's career, opening with 1968's "The Upsetter," "Kimble" and "People Funny Boy"; closing with 1978's "City too Hot"/"Bionic Rats" coupling and, in between times visiting all the greatest Scratch obsessions. The tremendous "Public Jestering," adapting Horace Andy's "Skylarking" rhythm for a return to the days of Judge Dread, is a diamond inclusion.

7 Son of Thunder (Snapper—UK) 2000

Bonus price two-CD collection which wanders all over the place in search of titles which you probably have on some other compilation . . . but there's so many others to check through . . . ah it's cheap and I know I don't have "Words" (with Anthony "Sangie" Davis) . . . oh, whatever.

SUNDAR POPO

STYLE *chutney*

BORN *Sunilal Popo Bahora, 11/4/43 (Monkey Town, Barrackpore, T&T)/d 5/2/2000*

Of all the artists who pushed chutney to the forefront of first, the local scene and, ultimately, the international market, few can claim to have been so influential as Sundar Popo. His breakthrough hit "Nana and Nani" has been described among the most important single compositions in the history of East Indian music, while his willingness to experiment wildly within the hitherto narrow confines of his native sound was responsible for opening an entire culture up for musical investigation.

Sundar Popo had been singing since childhood, initially accompanying his parents (his mother was a fine vocalist, his father an accomplished tassa drummer) as they toured rural T&T. By his teens, he was also accompanying visiting orchestras, armed with a repertoire drawn equally from his own compositions, and the traditional favorites he remembered from his youth.

While employed as a watchman at a Barrackpore factory, Popo trained under Ustad (music guru) James Ramsawak. (1997 Soca Chutney Monarch Heeralal Rampartap was also one of Ramsawak's pupils, and many people hearing Rampartap's winning songs "Chutney Posse" and "Basmati" for the first time were convinced that they were, in fact, listening to Popo.)

Popo emerged from the slowly percolating Trinidadian East Indian music scene in 1969. He was performing at a mattikoor (the first night of a three-day Hindu wedding function) in Princes Town when he met radio host and promoter Moean Mohammed. Introducing himself, he then gave an impromptu performance of a song he had recently composed, "Nani and Nanu" — a remarkable piece which, uniquely, featured lyrics in both Hindi and English.

Suitably impressed, Mohammed booked Popo into a recording session at Television House, accompanied by the BWIA (British West Indies Association) National Indian Orchestra under Harry Mahabir. It was Mahabir who set the song's wry recitation of the activities of the archetypical Indian grandparents to the pulsating rhythmic beat, which combined dholak, dhantal, guitar and keyboards. The single's release revolutionized East Indian music in T&T.

Although he had been trained in India, Mahabir was nevertheless fascinated by western instruments, often preferring them to traditional Indian ones, and simplifying the naturally irregular Indian rhythms to meet his new requirements. Popo, too, saw music in those same terms of international co-operation. In 1971, he stormed *Mastana Bahar* with "Nana and Nani" — one of just five local compositions out of 88 competitors — and, although he did not win (and, amazingly, never would), he remains the show's most fa-

mous son. Later in the year, however, Popo did win the inaugural Road March at the St Kitts carnival with his "Play You Mas."

With Mohammed and Mahabir behind him, Popo followed through with an album combining Trinidadian folk songs with traditional Hindu material, setting the tempo for his work throughout the remainder of the 1970s, and confirming the popularity bestowed by his breakthrough hit. Among many other achievements, he won the Indian Cultural Pageant four times following its inauguration in 1975, a rate of success which ultimately forced the organizers to launch a separate competition for Popo's compositions alone!

His hits included "Oh My Lover," "Don't Fall in Love," "O Lover You Leave Me and Gone" and "Scorpion Girl," a vast repertoire which immediately came to the attention of the Bombay, India-based duo Babla and Kanchan, when they toured T&T in 1979. Over the next decade, they covered a number of Popo's songs for their own audience — one which was spread across five continents. Their version of his "Phulowarie Bin Chitney," in particular, was an enormous hit. Immediately after, Popo found himself in international demand, he visited the US and Europe, and released his albums worldwide.

The global explosion of interest in chutney in the early 1990s, as it fused with soca to create an entirely new exciting sound, was, in no small way, Popo's work, an achievement which the T&T government celebrated by awarding him the Humming Bird Medal (silver) in 1993. That same year, he also received a Sunshine Music Award for his contributions to music, and twelve months later, the Caribbean Music Award. Perhaps the greatest honor, however, came in 1995, when Black Stalin won the T&T Calypso Monarch title with his "Tribute to Sundar Popo."

Popo recorded incessantly throughout his career; under Moean Mohammed's supervision alone, he cut seven albums, five-CDs and 10 cassettes. Two further albums paired him with Guyanan performer Anand Yankharan, *Lovinda Baby* and *Sweet Sweet Guyana*, while the 1990s brought one album with JMC Triveni, together with *Screwdriver/Saas More Lage* and *Cool Yourself with Cool Water*, a set celebrating the 150th anniversary of East Indian settlement in T&T, and featuring the hits "Mother Love" and "Bolo GI."

He maintained his live workload, too, and with considerable success. Although he finished a lowly seventh in the 1997 Soca Chutney Monarch competition, still his performance was one of the day's best received.

Unfortunately, failing health and fading eyesight forced him to slow down. He made a sorrowful appearance at the 2000 Chutney Monarch competition, able to perform just one of the two songs he was scheduled to sing, and on April 1, he played his final concert, in Connecticut. His last recording saw him add backing vocals to Terry Gajraj's "Baka Bana."

In 1997, Popo built his dream home in Barrackpore, a million dollar bungalow styled after the suburban architecture of India. It was there that he died on May 2, 2000, of heart and kidney ailments brought on by a long battle with diabetes. He had been in New York until just three days before his death, flying home despite his American doctor's advice to the contrary. Among the many notable attendees of his wake was Trinidad & Tobago Prime Minister Basdeo Panday.

RECOMMENDED LISTENING

10 Come and Sing and Dance with the Champ
The most representative album, a sterling collection which includes "Nana and Nani," "Is that Spana She Want," "Hum Na Jaibay," "Phulowarie Bin Chitney," "Tears in My Eyes" and "A Mother's Love," songs which range the entire spectrum of Popo's repertoire.

PRINCE BUSTER

STYLE *reggae (ska/rock steady)*
BORN *Cecil Bustamente Campbell, 5/28/38 (JA)*

Prince Buster is one of the giants of ska, a name which everybody knows, a sound which everyone can identify. His specter haunts every great record of the Specials/Madness-fired 2-Tone era; his imagery lurks behind every new release from the modern American ska scene; and thirty years on from what even he would call his musical peak, he's still capable of taking the world by surprise. In spring, 1998, Buster landed a British Top 30 hit with an insistent update of his 1968 smash "Whine and Grind"; almost three years after that, he was filling halls throughout the UK on his latest tour.

The son of a railroad worker, the schoolboy Buster was a keen boxer and, upon graduating, began to make his way onto the professional circuit. He was also interested in music, however, leading an impromptu (or, locally, "spasm") band of like-minded friends, making music with tins, sticks and bottles.

Buster made his professional singing debut at club owner Tilly Blackman's Glass Bucket during the mid-1950s. He sang with a number of now forgotten bands, often working alongside his friend, session drummer Arkland "Drumbago" Parkes — it was Drumbago who introduced Buster to DJ Coxsone Dodd, who took him on as an odd-jobs man, employed to do whatever was necessary to ensure Dodd's continued survival on the cut-throat sound system circuit of the late 1950s.

Buster broke away from Dodd in 1959, and opened his own record store on Charles Street, Buster's Record Shack. He then launched a sound system to help bring his dream

closer, christening it, with typical panache, the Voice of the People.

From playing records, Buster began producing them in 1960 — his first ever recording was an instrumental titled "Little Honey," recorded with Jah Jerry (guitar), Rico Rodriguez (horns) and Drumbago (drums), and released under the name Buster's Group.

It was a none too remarkable debut, particularly in the light of Buster's actual intentions. Whereas other Jamaican musicians and DJs were content to simply work with, and cut records in imitation of, existing (usually American R&B) records, Buster dreamed of designing what he called "a new musical sound. A Jamaican sound." His efforts were despised by his jazz-loving contemporaries. But even they could not dispute the music's success.

Teaming up with singer Derrick Morgan, Buster convened his next studio sessions with singers Owen Gray and the brothers John, Mico and Junior Folkes, trombonist Rico Rodriguez and nyahbingi percussionists Count Ossie and His Wareikas, whom he brought down from the hills at a time when the very existence of Rastafarians was considered an affront to polite, or even conventional, Kingston society.

With Buster producing, the space of just one day saw this crew record 13 songs, each a future hit and every one a genuine classic. Led off by "Oh Carolina," which was released under the Folkes Brothers' name, the record was and an instant underground smash. It completely disavowed any hint of an imported heritage, and worked to create something new and daringly subversive of its own.

Backed by the seemingly tireless Buster's Group (now augmented by saxmen Stanley "Ribs" Notice, Val Bennett and Dennis Campbell, alongside sundry future Skatalites), during 1961–1962 Buster produced hits for Basil Gabbidon, Derrick Morgan, Eric Morris, Chuck & Dobbie, Rico Rodriguez and Owen Gray. He also launched his own performing career in 1962 with the singles "Time Longer than Rope," "Independence Song," "My Sound that Goes Around," "One Hand Wash the Other," "Cowboy Comes to Town," "Fake King," "They Got to Go," "These Are the Times" and "Wash Wash."

In 1963, Derrick Morgan departed the stable to link up with producer Leslie Kong. That alone infuriated Buster, but worse was to come. Morgan's first single for Kong's Beverley's label was "Forward March," soon to be followed by the monster hit "Housewife's Choice," and when Buster discerned one of his own instrumental breaks in one of those songs (reports seem unable to agree which one), he promptly launched a furious assault.

Buster's "Blackhead Chineman" single loudly condemned Morgan's perfidy. Morgan responded with the "Blazing Fire" riposte. Buster hit back with "Thirty Pieces of Silver." Morgan retaliated with "Praise Without Raise." And so it continued for months, with the two titans slugging it out on vinyl, while their fans echoed the battle with fists on the dance floor. Finally, the Jamaican government itself stepped in, arranging a truce between the two stars, followed by a highly publicized reconciliation. In terms of publicity, it was peerless. In terms of cementing Buster as a true man of *his* people, it was perfect.

By 1963, Buster was pumping out so many singles on Voice of the People that he had to launch two new imprints, Islam and Buster Wild Bells, to handle the overflow. He began releasing albums as well, simply to soak up the excess. His UK distributor, the Blue Beat label, had no alternative but to pump them out just as quickly in Britain, to keep ahead of both the vociferous bootleggers and a voracious import market.

On average, there were two new Buster singles appearing in the UK every month, and two of his productions on the street every week (in eight years, Blue Beat released over 600 Buster productions), and if some of them were simply filler, others remain amongst the greatest and, in political terms, the most volatile ska records ever made.

Buster's first unequivocal classic appeared amid the flood of singles he released in 1963 — although "The Ten Commandments of Man," a code of dress, behavior and morality aimed at Buster's womenfolk, would never make it past the P.C. police today. Weeks later, he followed through with "Madness" (covered 16 years later by the 2-Tone group of the same name), an allegorical tale of Rastafarian persecution which was as knowingly abstract as the (marginally) later "Sodom and Gomorrah" was incisive.

Despite his distinctly anti-authoritarian stance, 1964 saw

Buster included among Jamaica's cultural representatives at the New York World's Fair; he also visited the UK for the first time that year, a tour which opened Buster's eyes to an entire new musical world.

He appeared on *Ready Steady Go*, the bastion of British pop TV. He was also introduced to English R&B keyboardist Georgie Fame at the Flamingo Club, joining Fame and his Blue Flames band on stage, and then inviting the Englishman to join him for a session at Advision Studios. A remake of 1962's "Wash Wash" prominently features Fame's vocals and organ, together with Young Satchmo on trumpet, and the Les Dawson Blues Unit. More importantly, however, the song signposts the direction which ska itself would soon be taking, as the frenetic rhythms and juvenile energies of the sound were smoothed and cooled on the road to rock steady and the languorous dance steps preferred by the rude boys.

1964 saw no slackening of Buster's output, both as a producer and a performer. Hits that year included "ABC Ska," concerning the widespread illiteracy of Jamaica's poor, "Blue Beat Spirit," "Downbeat Burial," "Ska Day-O" (a stylized rendition of the traditional "Banana Boat Song"), "Eye for an Eye," "High Blood Pressure," "Solid as a Rock" and "Wings of a Dove." The following year, too, brought its share of future classics — "Wonderful Life," "Burke's Law," "Float Like a Butterfly," "Gun the Man Down," "Johnny Dollar," "One Step Beyond" and the calypso classic "Rum and Coca Cola."

Several of these songs have since become all but synonymous with Buster's brand of ska. But it was another of Buster's 1965 efforts which remains his best known recording, the driving "Al Capone," which reached #18 in the UK in February, 1967. Interestingly, the previous month had seen another oldie hand him his first (and only) American hit, when the four year old "10 Commandments of Man" spent seven weeks on the US *Cashbox* chart, climbing to #48.

Like the rest of Jamaica, Buster spent much of 1966 preoccupied with the rude boys movement which was creating chaos and carnage on the city streets. A number of his releases that year were unequivocally targeted at the rudie market — "Cincinnati Kid," "Hard Man fe Dead," "Rude Rude Rudie" (aka "Don't Throw Stones"), the mento "Sammy Dead Medley," "Shanty-Town" and "Under Arrest (but Officer)." Many outside observers complained, perhaps rightfully, that in sympathizing with (if not actively supporting) rude boy culture, artists like Buster were simply exacerbating an already volatile problem.

For the Prince was not alone in his rudie ruminations: the Wailers, the Rulers, the Spanishtonians, the Clarendonians, Desmond Dekker and the Pioneers all made similarly themed records, and on the streets, rudie ran riot. Until Buster's "Judge Dread" entered the scene. This iconoclastic magistrate meted out rough justice on record, with his draconian sentences outraging rudie sensibilities across the island, and even igniting a stream of anti-Dread singles from Buster's similarly affronted peers. All of Jamaica was held rapt by these courtroom dramas on 45 throughout the next year.

The other major theme of Buster's 1968–69 output was sex. With a lasciviousness which utterly predicted the slacker boom of two decades hence, Buster was responsible for some of *the* great lewd records of the era, including "Wreck a Pum Pum" (improbably set to the tune of "Little Drummer Boy"), "Rough Rider," "Pussy Cat Bite Me," "Pum Pum a Go Kill You" and "Big Five." Indeed, the latter in turn ignited one of the greatest success stories English reggae ever knew, when white DJ Alex Hughes renamed himself Judge Dread (of course!) and scored with "Big Six"... followed by "Big Seven"... and the inevitable "Big Eight"... and so on.

Buster's interest in the Beatles, meanwhile, saw him release covers of their "Hey Jude," "Ob-La-Di Ob-La-Da" and John Lennon's "Give Peace a Chance" during 1969–70. He also maintained a running commentary on the state of the nation, via "Taxation," "Rat Trap," and "Pharaoh House Crash." His output was clearly slowing, however, derailed by the gradual shift in musical focus of the early 1970s.

A Moslem since 1961, Buster was receptive to the now spreading tide of Rastafarianism, but scarcely able to participate in the roots movement which drew its very lifeblood from the cult. He released a handful of sympathetic singles during 1971–72, including "Police Trim Rasta Hair," "Sons of Zion" and a cover of the Abyssinians' "Satta Amasa Gana," but he was well aware that any attempts to take matters further were doomed to ridicule. Already the likes of Niney Holness and Max Romeo were commenting upon the fast rolling "Rasta Bandwagon"; Buster had no intention of being its next passenger.

He did dip a toe into the DJ waters, producing a number of successful sides for Dennis Alcapone ("Giant," "Dub Machine," "Let It Roll") and Big Youth ("Chi Chi Run" — the last record ever released on the UK Blue Beat imprint, in 1972); he cut a version of Augustus Pablo's 1971 hit "Java" with Pablove Black, while Dennis Brown, Alton Ellis, John Holt and the Heptones also enjoyed hits with his productions.

Buster's own releases, however, slowed to a trickle, with even the best of them — 1971's irrepressible "Black Organ," 1972's ribald "Bald Head Pum Pum" and "South of the Border" among them — now seeming desperately old-fashioned. By 1973, Buster was silent.

He was not idle, however. As sole owner of his vast back catalog, he had amassed a considerable fortune during his peak years, money which he wisely invested in record stores and juke box operations throughout the Caribbean.

Besides, even if he had no interest in competing with the new stars on musical terms, he was still able to maintain a running commentary on their activities, simply by periodically reminding the audience that he'd done almost everything first. Throughout the 1970s, Buster maintained a constant stream of reissues, often featuring purposefully provocative self-penned liner notes, decrying the declining standards and innovations of modern music.

By the time of the 2-Tone explosion in the late 1970s, Buster was already a figure of legend, to be invoked in tribute, cover and simply imitation. The screeching brakes which launch the Specials' "Gangsters" debut single were lifted from "Al Capone," the English Beat covered "Rough Rider," and the aforementioned Madness named themselves after one of his hits, recorded another ("One Step Beyond") and then paid homage with their own "The Prince."

Buster resumed regular live work in the late 1980s and, in 1992. began recording again. Having toured Japan with the reformed Skatalites behind him in 1990, he made a well-received appearance on their 1994 album *Hi Bop Ska*, while his own recordings saw him often in cohorts with Gaz Mayall, son of British blues legend John Mayall, and leader of the Trojans, one of the hottest 1990s British ska bands.

Reuniting once again with the Skatalites, this team contributed an excellent version of Jimmy Cliff's "King of Kings" to Island Records' 40th anniversary *Ska Island* compilation in 1997. The following year, another Briton, Tony Gad, produced the hit remake of "Wine and Grine."

DISCOGRAPHY

7 I Feel the Spirit (Blue Beat — UK) 1963

Combining recent 45s with other Buster productions, predominantly instrumentals, a stunning introduction into the world of the ska's most prolific producer. "Madness" and "Blackhead Chineman" are the headlining hits.

7 What a Hard Man fe Dead — Prince Buster Sings for the People (Blue Beat — UK) 1967

8 Prince Buster Sings His Hit Song Ten Commandments (RCA) 1967

Riding the US chart success of the title track, Buster's first and only US release goes for the lighter side of the sensation, with "Here Comes the Bride," "A Life Worth Living," "Wings of a Dove" and, co-headlined on the cover, "Ten Commandments from Woman to Man" by Buster "with his Princess."

8 On Tour (Blue Beat — UK) 1967

Surprisingly well-recorded for its age, and shockingly exciting even today, Buster before his Anglo acolytes on his first post-"Al Capone" tour, with a barrage of equally popular hits. Other acts of the era have great live reputations — here we hear how Buster earned his.

6 Judge Dread Rock Steady (Blue Beat—UK) 1967

The only source for the full Judge Dread saga, both then and now (the album has since been reissued by Jet Set — UK). "Ghost Dance" also dignifies the set; unfortunately, the remainder catches Buster is less than scintillating form.

7 Wreck a Pum Pum (Fab—UK) 1968
8 She Was a Rough Rider (Fab—UK) 1969

A rude reggae gem of a title track cohabits with some searing political material ("Taxation") and a handful of sweet soul covers, Sam Cooke's "You Send Me" the most unlikely recipient of Buster's honeyed tongue.

6 The Outlaw (Fab—UK) 1969
7 Big Five (Melodisc—UK) 1972

Anybody searching for the thrusting loins of reggae's late 60s fixation with sex might as well stop here. "Fishy Fishy," "Wash the Pum Pum," "Bald Head Pum Pum" and, of course, the title track are all couched in slang innuendo, but it doesn't take too much imagination to figure out what's going on.

PRINCE BUSTER [& HIS] ALL STARS
6 Ska Lip Soul (Blue Beat—UK) 1965

Fascinating set includes covers of the Beatles' "And I Love Her" and Aretha Franklin's "Respect," alongside such archetypical Caribbean pieces as "The Banana Boat Song," "Rum and Coca Cola," "Matilda" and "Oil in My Lamp." Scarcely the rough'n'tough Buster of repute, but a treat regardless.

SELECTED COMPILATIONS & ARCHIVE RELEASES
8 Fly Flying Ska (Blue Beat—UK) 1964
8 Pain in My Belly (Blue Beat—UK) 1965
8 It's Burke's Law—Jamaica Ska Explosion! (Blue Beat—UK) 1965

Solid collections of Buster productions, released while the songs were still fresh — spread across the three platters, treats include "River Jordan" (Owen Gray), "Dog War" (the Maytals) and driving instrumentals from Don Drummond and Roland Alphonso.

10 Fabulous Greatest Hits (Fab—UK) 1967

Since reissued on CD (Sequel — UK) with abundant bonus tracks, this was all the Prince Buster any self-respecting fan required for many years — and judging by the songs covered during the 2-Tone era, the only one that most of them had. It's still strong today — "Madness," "Al Capone," "10 Commandments," "Burke's Law," "Rough Rider," "Judge Dread," "Ghost Dance," "Shaking Up Orange Street". . . and that's not even the half of it. Indispensable.

8 The Original Golden Oldies Volume One (Prince Buster—JA) 1980s

10 track collection concentrating on the 1962–63 period, since reissued on CD (Jet Set — UK) alongside Volumes Two, featuring early Buster productions ("War Paint Baby," "Oh Carolina," "Humpty Dumpty") and Three, reissuing the *Judge Dread* album.

9 Prince Buster's Fabulous Greatest Hits (Jet Set—UK) 1998

If there was one valid complaint to be made about the Sequel CD above, it was that it omitted "The Barrister" and "Dance the Pardon," the concluding chapters in the Judge Dread saga. The good news, then, is that "Dance the Pardon" (oddly mistitled "Barrister Pardon") closes this 12 song set. The bad news is, 10 of the remaining 11 tracks are on the other album.

PRINCE FAR I

STYLE *reggae (roots)*
BORN *Michael James Williams, 1944 (Spanish Town, JA); d 9/15/83*

A former security guard at Joe Gibbs' studio (a profession from which he bore the scars for the rest of his life), and a DJ with the Sir Mike the Musical Dragon sound system, Michael Williams was employed as a bouncer at Coxsone Dodd's Studio One set up when he cut his first single, "Queen of the Minstrel," in 1970.

Studio One DJ King Stitt was scheduled to record that day, but failed to turn up. Rather than waste studio time, producer Dodd let Williams stand in, christening him King Cry Cry after observing how the performer habitually burst into tears whenever he became angry.

The Bunny Lee productions "I Had a Talk" and "The Great Booga Wooga" (over Lester Sterling's "Spring Fever") were minor hits in 1971. In 1973, "Simpleton Skank" was released as the dub DJ flip of the Cordells' "Simpleton," before another of his early producers, Enos McLeod, suggested King Cry Cry become Prince Far I — the Voice of Thunder. The name debuted on the single "Let Jah Arise."

Back with Coxsone Dodd, Far I scored a minor hit with "Natty Farmyard." He also self-produced a single on the Micron label, while another gem came courtesy of producer Winston Riley, who invited him to a Bobby & Tommy session to cut "Musical Rocket," a track featured on their 1973 *Green Mango* album. An even more spectacular partnership was forged with the Maytones in 1976, for the Alvin Ranglin produced "Creation Time."

Far I's debut album, *Psalms for I* was recorded with Lloydie Slim, in 1976, while a single, "Zion Call," also attracted attention. But it was not until Joe Gibbs began converting Far I's vision into rhythm, that he finally established himself as the sound of righteous apocalypse.

Over the rhythm of Naggo Morris' "Su Su pon Rasta," "Heavy Manners," recorded with Gibbs in 1977, was Far I's breakthrough. Documenting and damning the Jamaican government's recent imposition of near-martial law in an attempt to crackdown on rising violent crime, the single was instantly controversial. In fact, Jah Stitch promptly hit back with "Crazy Joe," a Bunny Lee/Clive Chin production which warned "We're gonna chase crazy Joe and his bald-head followers out of town."

Unperturbed, Far I and Gibbs followed through with 1977's *Under Heavy Manners* album, a Rastafarian manifesto paving the path for the final fall of Babylon. Alongside Culture's *Two Sevens Clash* album, released the previous year, no more powerfully portentous recordings escaped Jamaica during that crucial era. It was indeed a time when many Jamaicans believed the world was about to end, and Prince Far I, with his somber sermons and doomladen delivery, was perfectly placed to document armageddon.

If man was going to make it through the ensuing firestorm, he was going to need a lot more than a happy beat and a bagful of ganja — that was the knowledge which was instinctively inherent within Far I's unique vocal style, and the theme of his music. He didn't sing, he didn't talk, and he positively refused to be called a toaster. Far I was a chanter, the first and the best in reggae history, and behind him the Roots Radics band thundered some of the roughest, most claustrophobic rhythms imaginable — the only kind of accompaniment his lyrics could possibly have required.

Like an electric hellfire baptist preacher, Prince Far I saw the studio as a pulpit from which he seethed with righteous rage and warning. And though some Jamaican listeners were put off by his proselytizing, it was an explosion which found fertile ground in Britain. That country itself was undergoing the purging spiritual renaissance of punk and, in its parallel partnership with reggae, Prince Far I's rebel music shook the established order of things to their core.

His version of the country and western standard "Deck of Cards" was an especial hit on the London club scene — originally recorded by American Wink Martindale in the 1950s, the song had been reactivated just a couple of years before for a major hit single. Set to the rhythm track from the Mighty Two's version of the Abyssinians' "Satta Amasa Gana," Prince Far I's reappropriation of a cloyingly familiar song translated homily to devotion with devastating effect.

Neither did he stop there. With *Under Heavy Manners* a cult hit across Europe, Prince Far I signed with Virgin's Front Line subsidiary and cut two albums which, even today, are regarded among the very cornerstones upon which

modern reggae was erected, *Message from the King* and *Long Life*.

The label also paired him, unlikely as it sounds, with Gregory Isaacs for the 1979 single "Uncle Joe." Master tapes for an album, *Health and Strength*, featuring this track, plus Far I's fiery takes on Isaacs' "Handcuff" and "Sacrifice" rhythms, mysteriously went astray after arriving at the London label headquarters. It was another 20 years before even a cassette of the missing music surfaced.

Backed by the Roots Radics, masquerading under the alias of The Arabs, Far I also unleashed a quartet of dub albums, the *Cry Tuff Dub Encounter* series, named for his own Cry Tuff label. The set up was essentially devoted to artists who shared his own outlook; Junior Brown, Errol Holt, Carol Kalaphat and Bobby Melody all enjoyed releases on the label, several of which were remixed for release on the *Showcase in a Suitcase* compilation. Far I also issued a number of his own recordings on Cry Tuff, including a fiece reworking of I-Roy's "Tribal War," "No More War," and "Love to Everyone."

Far I's next crucial partnership was with English producer Adrian Sherwood. His Hit Run label built its very reputation around domestic releases for Cry Tuff 45s, and Far I and the Arabs. Sherwood himself mixed the first *Cry Tuff* dub collection, while the label was behind the Roots Encounter UK tour in April, 1979, featuring Far I and Hit Run labelmates Bim Sherman and Prince Hammer. When Front Line released the second volume of the *Cry Tuff Dub Encounter* collections while the tour was in full swing, Hit Run responded with the limited edition *Dub to Africa* set.

Of course, Far I continued to record elsewhere, completing his Virgin contract with one album for the Pre subsidiary, then cutting four sets for Trojan. However, the best of his work was alongside Sherwood and members of On-U superstars Creation Rebel and Singers And Players during 1979–81 — the Cry Tuff singles "Higher Field Marshall," "Frontline Speech" and "Quante Jubila," and the album *Prince Far I And Singers & Players*. (The Arabs' work for Sherwood generally appeared under the name of Dub Syndicate.)

Far I also readily joined Sherwood on the producer's then-newly formed, but now legendary On-U label — dedicated to what had apparently not been a happy time at the Front Line label, Far I's "Virgin" single was the new imprint's first 10-inch release.

Another rewarding collaboration saw Far I cut the "Wadada Magic" single with British roots band Sons of Arqa in early 1982. Touring the country later in the year, Far I and the Sons combined again for a stunning and, amazingly, completely unrehearsed show in Manchester on December 7. The performance was subsequently released as *Musical Revue*, and plans were laid for further work together. It was not to be. Having returned to Jamaica earlier in the year, Prince Far I was murdered during a burglary at his home on September 15, 1983.

Prince Far I lives on on record, of course — in 1991, Sherwood even sampled some of his vocals for Dub Syndicate's *Stoned Immaculate* album; and on stage as well — five years later, Dub Syndicate toured a live show where they provided accompaniment to a set comprised almost entirely of sampled Far I vocal lines.

PRINCE FAR I DISCOGRAPHY
7 Psalms for I (Carib Gems—UK) 1976

Nine psalms and the Lord's Prayer probably don't promise the best time on earth, but *Psalms for I* emerges a blueprint for future roots, and certainly a foreboding forebear of its immediate successors.

10 Under Heavy Manners (Joe Gibbs—JA) 1977

The title track, a scathing commentary of the government's anti-crime measures, sets the tone for this dread drenched album that adroitly shifts from religious to political themes.

8 Message from the King (Front Line—UK) 1978

Self produced epic which simply never lets up. "Moses Moses," "Armageddon" and "Blackman Land" are highlights.

7 Long Life (Front Line—UK) 1978

Oddly lacking the stellar "No More War" single, but otherwise another dramatic exploration of the Far I experience.

7 Dub to Africa (Hit Run—UK) 1979

Since reissued on CD by Pressure Sounds, an eight track dub set which anticipates dance hall in its militant moodiness, performed by Far I and the Originals, a scratch band featuring Flabba Holt (bass), Noel Bailey (guitar) and Lincoln Valentine Scott (guitar).

6 Livity (Pre—UK) 1979
7 Free from Sin (Trojan—UK) 1979

The most powerful of Far-I's later albums includes the blistered title track and "Call on I in Trouble," although it also descends towards self-parody with the trite "Reggae Music."

6 Jamaican Heroes (Trojan—UK) 1980

Despite the presence of a reworked, and possibly even more extraordinary "Deck of Cards," another slight album. "Jamaican Heroes" itself is extraordinary lightweight for Far I, although lyrically it packs the expected punch.

7 Voice of Thunder (Trojan) 1981

"Ten Commandments" is righteous wrath; while "Head of The Buccaneer," with a partial dedication to pirate Captain Morgan, comes complete with creaking decks and subsonic rhythms. Also worth checking is "Skinhead," Far I's invocation of the recent British riots.

6 Musical History (Trojan) 1983

An awkward album which catches Far I trying to maintain his customary defiant stance in the face of the band's shift towards dance hall.

PRINCE FAR I & SINGERS & PLAYERS
7 Prince Far I & Singers & Players (On-U—UK) 1981

PRINCE FAR I & THE SUNS OF ARQA
8 The Musical Revue (ROIR) 1983

The Suns' dense sound and slithering, shifting experiment stylings encourage Far I to similarly diversify his rap, treating the audience to a mini history of toasting as he enthusiastically moved from chanting to contemporary lyrical commentaries, a perfect counterpoint to the band's equally ferocious performance.

SELECTED COMPILATIONS & ARCHIVE RELEASES
8 Cry Tuff Dub Encounter (Front Line—UK) 1978
7 Cry Tuff Dub Encounter Vol 2 (Front Line—UK) 1979
7 Cry Tuff Dub Encounter Vol 3 (Daddy Kool—UK) 1980

Working with the toughened rhythms of Roots Radics, Prince Far I released record after record on his own label, with the flips nearly always featuring intriguing dub versions. Here they're handily bundled up in album form, heavy, metallic, skull crushing essays in bass, booming and echo with just enough shattered shards of melody trailing through the wreckage to remind the listener that it used to be a song. Vols 1 and 3 have since been reissued on CD (Pressure Sounds—UK).

6 Showcase in a Suitcase (Pre—UK) 1980

Collection comprising Cry Tuff (and other) excursions by Ashanti Roy Kongos, Wailing Souls and Naggo Morris, dramatically remixed by Prince Far I.

7 Cry Tuff Dub Encounter Vol 4 (Cry Tuff—JA) 1981

Further dub excursions through the Cry Tuff catalog, primarily drawing from version sides.

8 Black Man Land (Front Line) 1990
7 Dubwise (Front Line) 1991

Abbreviated encapsulation of the Front Line years, recommended for a handful of hard to find cuts.

9 Health & Strength (Pressure Sounds) 1998

Three decades after the original master tapes went missing en route to Virgin Records, a former Hit Run label staff member turned up a cassette he'd made all those years before. A lost classic? Indeed. Aside from the Gregory Isaacs collaborations/toasts, Cry Tuff singles "Frontline Speech" and "Weatherman Tam" surface, while DJ Blackskin Prophet guests on "When the King Comes to Earth." The overall outlook, then, is thunderous. File alongside *Under Heavy Manners*—Far I at his finest.

Somewhat scattershot selection includes the original "Heavy Manners," but lifts a lot (too much) from the later Trojan albums.

RAS SHORTY I

STYLE *calypso/soca*
BORN *Garfield Blackman, 10/6/41 (Barrackpore, T&T) d 7/12/2000 (T&T)*

Although there are many contenders for the title of the first ever soca record, there are few artists who can stake a similar claim of being the first ever soca performer. One of those who can — and with such conviction that few would want to argue with him — is Shorty . . . Lord Shorty . . . Ras Shorty I . . . three names which all belong to possibly the single most important innovator in modern calypso history. In 1978, Shorty's *Soca Explosion* album created just that, an explosion of artists intrigued and captivated by his absolute reinvention of traditional calypso, and racing to follow through with their own vision of the blend. From Eddy Grant to Lord Kitchener, from Byron Lee to Arrow, soca became the most powerful Caribbean musical force of the decade and beyond.

Born in the East Indian community of Barrackpore, surrounded by the rhythms and sounds of that community, Shorty's musical vision was unique from the start. As Lord Shorty (so named in ironic reference to his 6 foot 4 inch height), the man who turned calypso upside-down made his debut as a calypsonian in 1961, at the Victoria County Fair at Prince Town. He first appeared at carnival in 1963, performing "Cloak and Dagger" at the Original Young Brigade tent.

In 1966, "Indian Singers" became his debut single for the Telco label, the first of several 45s he released during the 1960s. He was a finalist in the 1968 Calypso King competition, and a semi-finalist in 1969. Always well-received, he won his first title, King of San Fernando, in 1970, when he beat Bomber and Black Stalin into second and third place respectively. He also reached the Calypso King finals that same year.

As the new decade progressed, Shorty became as well known for his work with other artists as for his own. He wrote material for Maestro, his cousin Baron and others, and also produced Baron's hit "Severe Licking" (aka "She Lick She"), the single which launched the latter's career. In 1973, he inaugurated his own Shorty label as an outlet for his own music, vocalist Ella Andell, and later, his eldest daughter Abbi Blackman. Blackman began singing calypso professionally in 1979, winning the Calypso Queen contest, and has since become a regular performer at carnival, reaching the finals in 1992.

Of his own recordings, "Sixteen Commandments" was a particular favorite, a boisterous calypso extension of ska star Prince Buster's already chauvinistic "10 Commandments of Man." Lord Shorty's other claims to fame included a reputation as a hard loving ladies man, embarking upon a self-described "orgy of the flesh." Among the hits testifying to, among other things, his sexual prowess were "Fat Pants Fathers," "Smart Country Girl" and, of course, the notorious "The Art of Love Making."

That latter was one of Shorty's 1973 carnival entrants ("Indrani" was the other), and took him into the finals of the Calypso King competition, as well as winning the South Calypso King competition. However, the song's explicit lyrics were not to everybody's taste, and Shorty was arrested for indecency, apparently on the instructions of Prime Minister Eric Williams. The charges were eventually dropped, but Shorty would respond with his own commentary, "PM Sex Probe."

Behind the scenes, meanwhile, the singer was experimenting wildly with his music. "Indrani" was dedicated to a childhood girlfriend, and featured an array of eastern instruments alongside traditional calypso sounds, borne along by the sinewy rhythms of a dholak drum. Years later, Shorty told *Caribbean* magazine, "I was trying to find something new. The talk was that calypso was dying and reggae was the thing. I felt it needed something brand new to hit everybody like a thunderbolt." "Indrani" was the earliest realization of this process, and it would have been so easy from there, he later acknowledged, to fall into the trap of simply raga-fying his sound, a route taken by many rock musicians during the late 1960s.

However, Shorty had no interest in simply creating a short-term fix. In tandem with Dominica's 1969 Calypso King, Lord Tokyo and Jamaican lyricist Chris Seraphine (of the Gaylords), his next single audaciously combined calypso, cadence and Creole patois for the hit "Ou Dee Moin Ou Petit Shorty" ("you told me you are small, Shorty"); while his debut album, *Love Man*, continued his restless search for new musical frontiers.

Two musicians were acknowledged as the "East Indian Influences" on the album, dholak player Robin Ramjitsingh and mandolinist Bisram Moonilal. Shorty, however, decided not to simply replace conventional instrumentation with esoteric eastern ones. It was the actual conventions he wanted to change, an innovation crystallized on 1975's *Endless Vibration* album. There he sang of the need to "change the musical structure . . . make it super sweeter . . . bring out that funky feeling."

Continuing to strike his own path, Shorty launched his own calypso tent, Professionals, at the NUGFW Hall on Frederick Street in 1976. Calypsonians Duke, Wellington, Gypsy, Brigo, Funny, Roaring Lion, Rio and All Rounder were among the tent's attractions, but despite some excellent performances (Shorty himself debuted "Sweet Music" and "Kim"), the tent was not a success and in 1977, Shorty returned to the Original Young Brigade.

It was 1978's *Soca Explosion* album which changed everything. It is fashionable to describe soca as, essentially, a hybrid of SOul and CAlypso. That, however, was never Shorty's aim. Rather, he saw the music — even before he had formulated it — as an wholly indigenous sound, one which bridged the three major ethnic groups living in Trinidad and Tobago and beyond, African, Creole and East Indian.

Soca, he explained, was the "Indianization of calypso" — and it wasn't meant to be called soca either. His own preferred name was Solka — SO from calypso, L from Creole and KA for the Indian influence. How it then made the transition to soca in time for his next album has never satisfactorily been explained. But it did, and he was stuck with it.

Shorty never expected the style to take off as it did. He certainly never dreamed that he had unleashed a monster which, even as it reinvigorated the calypso/carnival scene, was also responsible for cheapening it. Suddenly "soca" was everywhere, and everyone thought they could play it. Shorty's outrage was fuelled by more than musical disdain, however. He genuinely believed he had created a musical fusion which would advance calypso. Instead, he saw it reduced to a vehicle for the crassest sentiments and the most limited lyricism. He had never intended for that to happen.

Even more shattering, however, was the death of his friend Maestro in a car crash, shortly before the completion of the *Soca Explosion* album (it is the subject of the song "Higher World"). In his search for answers, Shorty turned towards Rastafarianism in the late 1970s. With wife Claudette and their 14 children, he retreated to the Piparo hills of Trinidad. He changed his name to Ras Shorty I in 1979 — Ras, of course, meaning Lord.

His music shifted with his beliefs. 1984's "Money Eh No Problem" and "Om Shanti" (a harbinger of the Chutney Soca movement, later covered by Bombay duo Babla & Kanchan) were his final recordings in the soca vein. Forming his family into a performing group, the Love Circle, Shorty set about inducing and introducing a new roots musical style which he dubbed jamoo (from Jah Music).

An obliging media swiftly appended this moniker with an irrelevant "-soca." Shorty responded by titling his next album *Jamoo: The Spirit of Soca*, and penning liner notes which proclaimed, "after the onslaught of the Spirit of Carnival upon the mind, Christ Jesus has sent us with healing in the wings of this music Jamoo to set the captives free. Jamoo is not a luxury. It is a necessity."

He maintained his place in the public eye too, releasing

a live album, *Watch My Children*, that same year. Its anthemic anti-drug title track was especially successful, topping the local chart for several weeks and later prompting T&T Prime Minster Panday to say, "it should be on the Syllabus of every school." The song has since been translated into ten different languages, while Singing Sandra has recently added it to her repertoire.

Of course, Shorty's new consciousness lyrics frequently saw him accused of both hypocrisy and sermonizing, particularly in the light of his own past. Still, he never failed to find his mark. "Latrine Singers" was a strong condemnation of the increased bad language and sex explicitness in modern soca songs — Iwer George responded with "Think It Over," suggesting that a new picong duel could be in the offing. Sadly, Shorty did not rise to the bait.

1993's "That's Eh Enough" also created a stir. The song hit out at Mighty Sparrow's continued musical obsession with sex, pointing out that such libidinousness was quite unbecoming for a man of his age. Sparrow, two years off his 60th birthday, promptly hit back with "The More the Merrier," an unforgiving memoir of the days when Shorty's own youthful nickname of "the Love Man" was being earned in bedrooms all over T&T.

1993 also saw Shorty score a hit with Rikki Jai's recording of his "Cry for Unity," a reply of sorts to Black Stalin's 14 year old "Caribbean Unity," calling for the region's East Indian and Chinese people, too, to "mix up cultures." Of course that was what soca had been trying to do all along — now, East Indian artists like Jai and Drupatee Ramgoonai were furthering the fusion.

It was Shorty's final gift to the world. In 1999, shortly after he and the Love Circle appeared at Brooklyn's Aristocrat Ballroom, he was diagnosed with multiple myeloma, a bone marrow cancer. Shorty passed away on July 12, 2000, aged 59.

SELECTED DISCOGRAPHY

8 **Love Man (Charlie's — T&T) 1974**

10 **Endless Vibration (Charlie's — T&T) 1975**

"How to Kill the Cat," "Is We Thing," and "High Faluting Lovers" were all hits, but it's the title track which points to the future, a smorgasbord of punchy horns, over which Shorty sounds almost as good as James Brown, and "Soul Calypso Music" which actually signposts the direction he will take.

6 **Sweet Music (Charlie's — T&T) 1976**

The carnival entrants "Sweet Music" offers more glances to the future; "Kim," on the other hand, proves that Shorty's brush with the law has not tamed his libido.

8 **Soca Explosion (Charlie's — T&T) 1978**

One of Shorty's loudest complaints about modern soca was that it replaced lyrics with catchphrases, and thoughtfulness with knee-jerk reactions. *Soca Explosion*, then, paints the music as he believed it should be. It would, of course, be unfair to expect the album to push boundaries from beginning to end. But it has its moments, bold and sensuous moments which offer a world where deep lyrics and deeper rhythms not only co-exist, they inspire one another.

7 Jamoo: The Spirit of Soca (—T&T) 1989
8 Watch My Children (—T&T) 1989
6 God's Calypsonian (JMC—T&T) 2000

Shorty's final album sees him return to a handful of his earlier songs, weeding out those whose lyrics now offended him, but turning in sterling updates of the survivors. Few of the performances match the originals, but the album is worth picking up.

SELECTED COMPILATIONS & ARCHIVE RELEASES

9 Greatest Hits (Charlie's—T&T)

Excellent collection highlights some of the most important songs in soca history and beyond. "Shanti Om" predicted chutney-soca by a full decade; the deeply spiritual "Who God Bless" and "Higher World" indicate Shorty's own future direction. Other crucial inclusions, drawn from the earlier albums, are "Endless Vibrations," "Sweet Music," "Soca Fever" and "Gone Are The Days."

REGGAE SUNSPLASH INTERNATIONAL

The most legendary reggae festival in the world, Reggae Sunsplash dominated the Jamaican concert scene for close to 20 years, between 1978 and 1998. Launched by Synergy Productions Ltd, a team set up by promoters Tony Johnson, Ronnie Burke, John Wakeling and Don Greene, the Sunsplash concept was originally very much a shot in the dark.

Only two previous attempts had been made at staging such a massive event in Jamaica. The first, the Smile Jamaica festival in December, 1976, was overshadowed by the shooting of Bob Marley. The second, the One Love event in April, 1978, was still so fresh in the memory that many observers doubted whether anybody would be interested in a repeat performance quite so soon. In any event, Sunsplash was a major success, and for two decades thereafter, the festival not only showcased virtually every significant act of the era, it also charted reggae's own development as both a musical and an international force.

That first Sunsplash was virtually ignored by the media outside of reggae's traditional foreign strongholds in the UK, New York and Canada; the last, staged as the climax of the first Bob Marley Week, attracted representatives from television and print media all across the world. In addition, Sunsplash became a focus for the Jamaican Tourist Board, with the 1980 event in particular rescuing what had hitherto been a disastrous tourist season.

Kingston was wracked by violence in the run-up to the next general election, and it was, perhaps, indicative of the strength and organization of Sunsplash, that the concert passed off without any reports of trouble whatsoever. Sunsplash 1981 launched a new pattern for the festival, being the first to be filmed and recorded — some 26 tons of equipment were flown in from the US for the occasion.

The ensuing Sunsplash Live album proved such a success, that every event thereafter was similarly preserved. Another very successful innovation, debuting in 1987, was a national sound system competition, climaxing in a Sound System Clash on the first day of the festival, slotted in immediately before the traditional opening event, the Sunsplash Beach Party. A second popular event subsequently added to the bill was a so-called oldies night, featuring some of the best-loved names from ska and reggae's past.

Sunsplash went international in 1984, with a one day show at London's Crystal Palace in July. The following March, a 30 city American tour, followed by more British, European and Japanese dates, took the name even further afield. These events, too, became a permanent part of the Sunsplash experience, while the festival's own make-up was similarly broadened in 1986, when Sunsplash opened its stage to artists from elsewhere around the Caribbean.

By 1991, this element had so grown in popularity that a "Caribbean Night" was introduced, showcasing top soca performers. The following year, a World Beat Night extended the focus.

Despite its vast musical successes, however, Sunsplash had suffered from financial problems from the outset. In early 1995, organizers Synergy finally gave up, selling the rights to the festival to Radobar Holdings Limited, who formed a new company, Reggae Sunsplash International.

Appreciating that one of the original festival's greatest problems lay in securing a permanent home, the company settled on a base in the St Ann district of Jamaica's north coast — famous as the birthplace of both Marcus Garvey and Bob Marley. Although the actual festival site would shift, from Dover in 1995 to Chukka Cove in 1996, and then to Ocho Rios, the general locale remained the same. However, while attendance figures among overseas visitors remained high, concern was growing that Jamaican audiences were no longer so enamored with Sunsplash.

Attempts to restructure the event saw the 1997 festival eventually postponed into early 1998, at which point Sunsplash was realigned to become the climax of a week long festival held from February 1–8, celebrating Bob Marley's birth. Despite plans being advanced for a similarly scheduled event the following year, that proved to be the final Sunsplash.

The event's mantel has instead been taken up by the summertime Sumfest.

INDEX OF REGGAE SUNSPLASH PERFORMERS: 1978–98

JUNE 23–30, 1978: JARRETT PARK, MONTEGO BAY

ALTHEA & DONNA
SUGAR BILLY
DENNIS BROWN
BURNING SPEAR
CORPORATION OF LOVE
CULTURE
BERES HAMMOND
HEAT INC
THE HEPTONES
JOE HIGGS
INNER CIRCLE
BYRON LEE & THE DRAGONAIRES
RAS MICHAEL & THE SONS OF NEGUS
LLOYD PARKS
SOUL SYNDICATE
THIRD WORLD
TOOTS & THE MAYTALS
TWELVE TRIBE BAND
U-ROY
BILLY VERNON & THE CELESTIALS
WAILING SOULS

JULY 3–7, 1979: JARRETT PARK, MONTEGO BAY

THE ABYSSINIANS
BURNING SPEAR
MICHAEL CAMPBELL
FAB FIVE INC
SHARON FORRESTER
HEAT INC
JOE HIGGS
INNER CIRCLE
ISRAEL VIBRATION
BYRON LEE & THE DRAGONAIRES
LONE RANGER
BOB MARLEY & THE WAILERS
RAS MICHAEL & THE SONS OF NEGUS
MIGHTY DIAMONDS
PAM & WOODY
LLOYD PARKS & WTP BAND
THE SHADES
SOUL TO SOUL DISCO
STAMMY & THE SOUNDS OF MO-BAY
TALLAWAH
THIRD WORLD
TOOTS & THE MAYTALS
JUNIOR TUCKER

JULY 2–5, 1980: RANNY WILLIAMS ENTERTAINMENT CENTER, KINGSTON

BOB ANDY
BLACK UHURU
KEN BOOTHE
DENNIS BROWN
BURNING SPEAR
CASUAL T
CULTURE
CARLENE DAVIS
BERES HAMMOND
BONGO HERMAN
I-KONG
KIDDUS—I
BARRINGTON LEVY
RAS MICHAEL & THE SONS OF NEGUS
MICHIGAN & SMILEY
MIGHTY DIAMONDS
SUGAR MINOTT
NATIVE
OLATUM
OKU ONUORA
LLOYD PARKS & WTP BAND
PRINCE EDWARDS
REVOLUTIONARIES
JIMMY RILEY
LEROY SIBBLES
THE TAMLINS
PETER TOSH
DELROY WILSON
WORD, SOUND & POWER
ZAP POW

AUGUST 4–8, 1981: JARRETT PARK, MONTEGO BAY

RICHARD ACES & SONS
BLACK UHURU
DENNIS BROWN
CHALICE
JIMMY CLIFF
CULTURE
CARLENE DAVIS
EEK-A-MOUSE
FUTURE WINDS
GODS CHILDREN BAND
MARCIA GRIFFITHS
SHEILA HYLTON
I-MAW
I-THREES
GREGORY ISAACS

THE ITALS
JAH ZULU
LOUIE LEPKE
BARRINGTON LEVY
LIGHT OF LOVE
LIGHT OF SABA
LONE RANGER
FREDDIE McGREGOR
ZIGGY MARLEY & THE MELODY MAKERS
MICHIGAN & SMILEY
THE MIGHTY DIAMONDS
PABLO MOSES
JUDY MOWATT
MUTABARUKA
ONE VIBE
LLOYD PARKS & WTP BAND
PRINCE EDWARDS
JIMMY RILEY
ERROL SCORCHER
SENA
LEROY SIBBLES
MICHAEL SMITH
WINSTON SMITH
SON OF THUNDER
SOUL VENDORS
STEEL PULSE
TINGA STEWART
NADINE SUTHERLAND
TAMLINS
ROD TAYLOR
THIRD WORLD
RUDDY THOMAS
TONY TUFF
THE WAILERS
STEVIE WONDER
TAPPA ZUKIE

AUGUST 3–7, 1982: JARRETT PARK, MONTEGO BAY

THE ASTRONAUTS
ASWAD
BIG YOUTH
AJ BROWN
BURNING SPEAR
CHALICE
CARLENE DAVIS
EEK-A-MOUSE
FUTURE WINDS
THE GLADIATORS BAND
MARCIA GRIFFITHS
JOHN HOLT
HOME-T-4

ISRAEL VIBRATION
BYRON LEE & THE DRAGONAIRES
MACAW
MICHIGAN & SMILEY
MUTABARUKA
NATIVE
JOHNNY OSBOURNE
GLEN RICKS
THE SAGITTARIUS BAND
ROY SHIRLEY
SISTER NANCY
SHEENA SPIRIT
STEEL PULSE
TAJ MAHAL
TOOTS & THE MAYTALS
TRINITY
TRUTHS & RIGHTS
TWINKLE BROTHERS
U-ROY
LEE VAN CLEEF
DENICE WILLIAMS
YELLOWMAN

JUNE 28—JULY 2, 1983: BOB MARLEY CENTRE, MONTEGO BAY

BANKIE BANKS
THE BARE ESSENTIALS
BIG YOUTH
BLACK UHURU
THE BLUE RIDDIM BAND
AJ BROWN
DENNIS BROWN
DON CARLOS
CHALICE
ALTON ELLIS
MARCIA GRIFFITHS
DERRICK HARRIOTT
GREGORY ISAACS
JONES GIRLS
RAS KARBI
KING SOUNDS
KOTCH
SHARON LITTLE
JC LODGE
RITA MARLEY
ZIGGY MARLEY & THE MELODY MAKERS
MASSIVE DREAD
FREDDIE McGREGOR
THE MELODIANS
MICHIGAN & SMILEY
SUGAR MINOTT
JUDY MOWATT

MUSICAL YOUTH
MUTABARUKA
TRISTON PALMER
LLOYD PARKS & WTP BAND
PRINCE EDWARDS
THE SAGITTARIUS BAND
SAM & FAY
GIL SCOTT-HERON
SEVENTH EXTENSION BAND
LEROY SIBBLES
THE SKATALITES
MIKE SMITH
STEEL PULSE
SUPERMAX
NADINE SUTHERLAND
THIRD WORLD
TONY TUFF
UNITED AFRICA
WADADA
DELROY WILSON
ORVILLE WOOD
YELLOWMAN

AUGUST 7–11, 1984: JARRETT PARK, MONTEGO BAY

AFRICAN WOMAN
ALPHA & OMEGA
BOB ANDY
ASWAD
BRIGADIER JERRY
DENNIS BROWN
BURNING SPEAR
CHARLIE CHAPLIN
CRAZY
CARLENE DAVIS
EEK-A-MOUSE
THE ELEMENTS
EDI FITZROY
ROBERT FFRENCH
MICHAEL HAMILTON
GREGORY ISAACS
JAH THOMAS
INI KAMOZE
KINGS SOUNDS
BYRON LEE & THE DRAGONAIRES
JC LODGE
FREDDIE McGREGOR
MEMORY OF JUSTICE
PETER METRO WITH TONTO METRO
THE MIGHTY DIAMONDS
SUGAR MINOTT
DERRICK MORGAN

THE MYSTIC REVEALERS
OKU ONUORA
MICHAEL PALMER
LLOYD PARKS & WTP BAND
FRANKIE PAUL
PRINCE EDWARDS
RAS MICHAEL & THE SON OF NEGUS
ROOTS ANABO
THE SAGITTARIUS BAND
SHERVINGTON
SISTER BREEZE
TYRONE TAYLOR
U-ROY
UMOJAH DANCE
JOSEY WALES
DELROY WILSON
YELLOWMAN
ZOUND SYSTEM

AUGUST 6–10, 1985: JARRETT PARK, MONTEGO BAY

BAMMY MAN
PAUL BLAKE & BLOOD FIRE POSSE
BRIGADIER JERRY
CHARLIE CHAPLIN
CULTURE
EARLY B
EBONY
FAB FIVE
FINNIGAN & JUNIOR RANKIN
PHILLIP FRASER
GENERAL TREES
CAROL GONZALES
HALF PINT
PAM HALL
JUSTIN HINDS
TONTO IRIE
GREGORY ISAACS & ROOTS RADICS
JAH MIA & UMOJA
KING SOUNDS & THE ISRAELITES
LITTLE JUNIOR TUCKER
LITTLE KIRK & WHITE MICE
ZIGGY MARLEY & THE MELODY MAKERS
MESSENJAH
PETER METRO WITH TONTO METRO
MICHIGAN & SMILEY
THE MIGHTY DIAMONDS
SUGAR MINOTT & ABASHANTI TENOR SAW
MUTABARUKA
THE MYSTIC REVEALERS
OSSIE D & STEVIE G
TRISTON PALMER

LLOYD PARKS & WTP
THE PEP BAND
THE PSYCH BAND & SISTER BREEZE
WINSTON REEDY
MICHAEL ROSE & GOVERNMENT BAND
THE SAGITTARIUS BAND
LEROY SMART
WAYNE SMITH
STEEL PULSE
NADINE SUTHERLAND
THIRD WORLD
U-ROY
JOSEY WALES WITH JOE LICKSHOP

AUGUST 26—30, 1986: JARRETT PARK, MONTEGO BAY

ADMIRAL BAILEY
BIG BAND
KEN BOOTHE
BRIGADIER JERRY
DENNIS BROWN
BURNING SPEAR
CHICKEN CHEST
CRUCIAL B
CULTURE
CARLENE DAVIS
EARLY B
EDUBE
ALTON ELLIS
EDI FITZROY
GENERAL TREES
MARCIA GRIFFITHS
HALF PINT
IJAHMAN & MADGE
GREGORY ISAACS
INI KAMOZE
LOVINDEER
FREDDIE McGREGOR
PETER METRO
THE MIGHTY DIAMONDS
ECHO MINOTT
SUGAR MINOTT & ABASHANTI
MONYAKA
JUDY MOWATT
JOHNNY OSBOURNE
LLOYD PARKS
THE RIDDIM KINGS BAND
JIMMY RILEY
THE SAGITTARIUS BAND
LEROY SIBBLES
SLY & ROBBIE
THE SOUL SYNDICATE

STUDIO ONE BAND
THE TAMLINS
THE WAILERS
WAILING SOULS
JOSEY WALES
MALLORY WILLIAMS
YELLOWMAN

AUGUST 18–22, 1987: BOB MARLEY CENTRE, MONTEGO BAY

ADMIRAL BAILEY
PATO BANTON & TIPPA IRIE
HUGO BARRINGTON
BIG YOUTH
PAUL BLAKE & BLOOD FIRE POSSE
DENNIS BROWN
BURNING SPEAR & BURNING BAND
CHALICE
COCOA TEA
CULTURE
809 BAND
GENERAL TREES
GWEN GUTHRIE
HALF PINT
DERRICK HARRIOTT
I-THREES
GREGORY ISAACS
KILLER BEES
BARRINGTON LEVY
LOVINDEER
MAKER
ZIGGY MARLEY & THE MELODY MAKERS
FREDDIE McGREGOR
SHIRLEY McLEAN
PETER METRO
THE MIGHTY DIAMONDS
ECHO MINOTT
MONTY MONTGOMERY
MUTABARUKA
LLOYD PARKS & WTP BAND
MAXI PRIEST
THE SAGITTARIUS BAND
SANDII & THE SUNSETZ
SHAKAMAN & SHAKEENA
SISTER CAROL
SISTER CHARMAINE
SLY & ROBBIE
TIGER
TONTO METRO
U-ROY
ET WEBSTER
YELLOWMAN

AUGUST 15–22, 1988: BOB MARLEY CENTRE, MONTEGO BAY

ADMIRAL BAILEY
AFRICAN SYMBLO DISCO
BOB ANDY
BLOOD FIRE POSSE
KEN BOOTHE
BRIGADIER
AJ BROWN
DENNIS BROWN
BUNNY & SCULLY
CHARLIE CHAPLIN
COCOA TEA
CRUCIAL BANKIE
CULTURE
DADDY LIZARD & FLOURGAN
CARLENE DAVIS
JUNIOR DELGADO
DOMINIC
ERIC DONALDSON
BRENT DOWE
THE DUPLICATE BAND
EBONY
809 BAND
ALTON ELLIS
EDI FITZROY
THE GAYLADS
SOPHIA GEORGE
LEROY GIBBONS
MARCIA GRIFFITHS
HALF PINT
BERES HAMMOND
THE HEPTONES
HIGH POWER KING SOUNDS
THE HOUSE OF ASSEMBLY
IDENTITY
GREGORY ISAACS
KING JAMMY'S
LADY ENGLISH & MISS LINDA
LADY G
LECTURER
TIPPA LEE & RAPPA ROBERT
BARRINGTON LEVY
LOVINDEER
LT STITCHIE
MAJOR MACKEREL
FREDDIE McGREGOR
COURTNEY MELODY
PETER METRO
JACKIE MITTOO
MUTABARUKA

NINJA FORCE BAND
NINJAMAN with TINGA STEWART
PAPA BIGGY
LLOYD PARKS & WTP BAND
LASCELLES PERKINS
PROFESSOR NUTS
RANKING TAXI
JUNIE RANKS
REBEL ROCKERS
RED CLOUD
RED DRAGON
RIDDIM KINGS BAND
THE SAGITTARIUS BAND
SAM & FAY
OLIVER SAMUELS
SANCHEZ
SCOTTY
SISTER CHARMAINE
SLY & ROBBIE
LEROY SMART
TINGA STEWART
STONE LOVE DISCO
STUDIO ONE BAND
NADINE SUTHERLAND
SWELELE
THE TAMLINS
TYRONE TAYLOR
U-ROY
THE WAILERS
JOSEY WALES
ERNEST WILSON
YELLOWMAN

AUGUST 14–19, 1989: BOB MARLEY CENTRE, MONTEGO BAY

A TEAM BAND
THE ABYSSINIANS
ADMIRAL BAILEY
ADMIRAL TIBET
HORACE ANDY
ATOMIC
BIGGA
KEN BOOTHE
DENNIS BROWN
CHARLIE CHAPLIN
CRUCIAL ROBBIE
CULTURE
DADDY LIZARD
DONOVAN
EBONY
ELECTRO FORCE DISCO
FLOURGAN

GENERAL TREES
GRINDSMAN
HALF PINT
HIGGS & TWINS
JUSTIN HINDS & THE DOMINOES
HONEY & SPICE
INNER CITY DISCO
CLEMENT IRIE
GREGORY ISAACS
KOTCH
JENNIFER LARA
BARRINGTON LEVY
JC LODGE
UU MADOO
ANTHONY MALVO
ZIGGY MARLEY & THE MELODY MAKERS
SHIRLEY McLEAN
SUGAR MINOTT
FRANKIE PAUL
SHABBA RANKS
SIXTH REVELATION
SANCHEZ
SHINEHEAD & A TEAM BAND
SISTER CHARMAINE
ERNIE SMITH
TREVOR SPARKS
STEEL PULSE
STUDS BAND
THE SWEAT BAND
THIRD WORLD
SHELLY THUNDER
TIGER
THE UNIQUE VISION BAND
WADADA
DELROY WILSON
ZYLAN

JULY 16–21, 1990: BOB MARLEY CENTRE, MONTEGO BAY

ADMIRAL TIBET
ASWAD
LASANA BANDELE
BIGGA
DENNIS BROWN
BURNING SPEAR
CAPTAIN BARKEY
CHALICE
COCOA TEA
COMMANDO SHAD
CHAKA DEMUS
THE DIAMOND BAND
BRENT DOWE

809 BAND
ELECTRO FORCE DISCO
ALTON ELLIS
5446
GEMINI DISCO
GHOST & CULTURE
MARCIA GRIFFITHS
HALF PINT
JOHN HOLT
INNER CIRCLE
INNER CITY DISCO
GREGORY ISAACS
PAT KELLY
KLASSIQUE DISCO
LADY G
BYRON LEE & THE DRAGONAIRES
BARRINGTON LEVY
HOPETON LINDO
LITTLE LENNY
LT STITCHIE
FREDDIE McGREGOR
PETER METRO
THE MIGHTY DIAMONDS
LEE MILO
JUDY MOWATT
LORNA NELSON
NINJAMAN
PAPA SAN
LLOYD PARKS & WTP BAND
MAXI PRIEST
PROFESSOR NUTS
SHABBA RANKS
THE RIDDIM KINGS BAND
ED ROBINSON
THE SAGITTARIUS BAND
SANCHEZ
SHINEHEAD
LEROY SIBBLES
THE SKATALITES
SLY & ROBBIE
SPANNER BANNER
SPLASH
RICHIE STEPHENS
THE STUDS BAND
SUPER CAT
THE SWEAT BAND
THE TAMLINS
THRILLER U
TIGER
U-ROY
WADADA
BUNNY WAILER
WILLIE ONE BLOOD

JULY 26–21, 1991: BOB MARLEY CENTRE, MONTEGO BAY

LASANA BANDELE
PATO BANTON
BLACK MUSIC DISCO
BLOODFIRE POSSE
BODY GUARD DISCO
DENNIS BROWN
CAPLETON
CAPTAIN BARKEY & WICKERMAN
JACKIE CHANG & SILVER FOX
CHARLIE CHAPLIN
COCOA TEA
CULTURE T
CARLENE DAVIS
DISCO SPICE & COMPANY
809 BAND
EDI FITZROY
CHEVELLE FRANKLYN
DOUG FRESH
BRIAN & TONY GOLD
BERES HAMMOND
JOHN HOLT
THE HOME T BAND
THE I-THREES
INDU
INNER CITY DISCO
GREGORY ISAACS
THE ITALS
JOHNNY P
BARRINGTON LEVY
LITTLE LENNY
LOVINDEER
LUCKY DUBE
MACKA B
MAJOR KNOWLEDGE
JULIAN MARLEY
ZIGGY MARLEY & THE MELODY MAKERS
FREDDIE McGREGOR
MICHIGAN & SMILEY
MUTABARUKA
NATIVE
OKU ONUORA
PANCHO
PAPA SAN
LLOYD PARKS
FRANKIE PAUL
PIECES DISCO
PINCHERS
PJ
PROFESSOR NUTS

CUTTY RANKS
JUNIE RANKS
NARDO RANKS
SHABBA RANKS
TONY REBEL
JUNIOR REID
THE RIDDIM KINGS BAND
ED ROBINSON
THE RUFF KUT BAND
SANCHEZ
SHEPHERDS
SHINEHEAD
SINGING MELODY
SISTER NANCY
SKY JUICE
SLY & ROBBIE/TAXI
SOUL SWINGER
RICHIE STEPHENS
REGGIE STEPPER
DEAN STEVENS
STONE LOVE DISCO
SUGAR D
SYGNACHA
THIRD WORLD
TIGER
ANDREW TOSH
THE UNIQUE VISION BAND
VISION
SABRINA WILLIAMS
WAYNE WONDER
ORVILLE WOOD
YELLOWMAN

AUGUST 3–8, 1992: BOB MARLEY CENTRE, MONTEGO BAY

THE ABYSSINIANS
ADMIRAL BAILEY
YASUS AFARI
ASWAD
AT KREW BAND
BUJU BANTON
BEENIE MAN
BIG YOUTH
BIGGA
BLAKK MUZIK DISCO
BODY GUARD DISCO
YAMI BOLO
KEN BOOTHE
CINDY BREAKSPEARE
DENNIS BROWN
BRUSHIE ONE STRING
CANDY MAN

CAPLETON
CHARLIE CHAPLIN
CITY HEAT BAND
THE CLARENDONIANS
COBRA
COCOA TEA
STRANGE JAH COLE
COUNTRY SPENG
CREUSHAL SUBSTANCE
CULTURE
CARLENE DAVIS
TONTON DAVIS
CHAKA DEMUS & PLIERS
DIRTSMAN
DOMINIC
DONOVAN
THE DREDS
ALTON ELLIS
FOUNDATION
GENERAL DEGREE
GENERAL TREES
BRIAN & TONY GOLD
DELLA GRANT
MARCIA GRIFFITHS
HALF PINT
BERES HAMMOND
DERRICK HARRIOTT
INSPECTOR LENNY
PAT KELLY
LADY G
BARRINGTON LEVY
LEXUS DISCO
LINK & CHAIN
LITTLE LENNY
PETER LLOYD
JC LODGE
LUCKY DUBE
MACKA B
MAJOR LLOYD
FREDDIE McGREGOR
THE MELODIANS
COURTNEY MELODY
PETER METRO
RAS MICHAEL & THE SONS OF NEGUS
THE MIGHTY DIAMONDS
MIGHTY SPARROW
SUGAR MINOTT
DENROY MORGAN
MORGAN HERITAGE
JUDY MOWATT
TANYA MULLINS
THE MYSTIC REVEALERS

NEGAS
CIDADE NEGRA
NINJAMAN
PAPA SAN
LLOYD PARKS & WTP BAND
FRANKIE PAUL
PIECES DISCO
PINCHERS
PROFESSOR NUTS
JACK RADICS
CUTTY RANKS
NARDO RANKS
TONY REBEL
JUNIOR REID
ED ROBINSON
MAX ROMEO
MICHAEL ROSE
RUMBLE
THE SAGITTARIUS BAND
THE SANE BAND
SCREWDRIVER
LEROY SIBBLES & THE HEPTONES
SIMPLETON
SINGING SANDRA
SISTER MARIE
THE SKOOL BAND
SLY & ROBBIE
LEROY SMART
SOUL SWINGER DISCO
THE SPLASH BAND
STEEL PULSE
SUPER CAT
THE TAMLINS
TIGER
JUNIOR TUCKER
THE WAILING SOULS
MAX WAYNE
DELROY WILSON
WAYNE WONDER

AUGUST 3–7, 1993: JAMWORLD, PORTMORE

THE ABYSSINIANS
ADMIRAL BAILEY
YASUS AFARI
LAUREL AITKEN
APACHE
BEETLE BAILEY
BUJU BANTON
MEGA BANTON & RICKY GENERAL
KEN BOOTHE
BORN JAMERICANS

BOUNTY KILLER
CINDY BREAKSPEARE
MORVIN BROOKS
DENNIS BROWN
BURNING SPEAR
CAPLETON
PETER CARTER
CHAKULA
CHALICE
THE CLARENDONIANS
COBRA
COCOA TEA
CRUCIAL SUBSTANCE
CULTURE
CARLENE DAVIS
DOBBIE DOBSON
EL GENERAL
ALTON ELLIS
EDI FITZROY
CHEVELLE FRANKLYN
TERRY GANZIE
GENERAL TREES
GHOST & CULTURE
BRIAN & TONY GOLD
JUNIOR GONG
OWEN GRAY
BERES HAMMOND
DERRICK HARRIOTT
DADDY HARRY & DON MIGUEL
GEORGIE HENRY
JOHN HOLT
LADY SAW
LE COUP
BARRINGTON LEVY
LITTLE LENNY
LOS PERICOS
LOVINDEER
MACARUFFIN
MAJOR MACKEREL
ANTHONY MALVO
HUGH MASAKELA
EILEEN MASCOLL
TRICIA McKAY
THE MELODIANS
PETER METRO
RAS MICHAEL
THE MIGHTY DIAMONDS
DERRICK MORGAN
COURTNEY MORRISON
MUTABARUKA
THE MYSTIC REVEALERS
NINJA KID

NINJAMAN
PAPA SAN
FRANKIE PAUL
PINCHERS
DENYSE PLUMMER
PROFESSOR NUTS
QUEEN PAULA
DOUGIE RANKS
RUMMIE RANKS
TONY REBEL
JIMMY RILEY
COLIN ROACH
ROUNDHEAD
SANCHEZ
ROY SHIRLEY
LEROY SIBBLES
LEROY SMART
ERNIE SMITH
SNAGGA PUSS
SNOW
SPRAGGA BENZ
STEEL PULSE
RICHIE STEPHENS
STRANGE JAH COLE
SUPER SASS & ITCHY RANKS
NADINE SUTHERLAND
THE TECHNIQUES
TIGER
TOOTS & THE MAYTALS
JUNIOR TUCKER
UNIVERSAL YOUTH
JOSEY WALES
DELROY WILSON
WAYNE WONDER

AUGUST 1–6, 1994: JAMWORLD, PORTMORE

LASANA BANDELE
BUJU BANTON
BEETLE BAILEY
BIG MOUNTAIN
EVERTON BLENDER
BOUNTY KILLER
DENNIS BROWN
BUCCANEER
THE CABLES
CAPLETON
JOHNNY CLARKE
COCOA TEA
LOUIS CULTURE
DADDY SCREW
CHAKA DEMUS & PLIERS

MANU DHANGO

FRISCO KID

GENERAL DEGREE

THE GLADIATORS

GRACY & THE HERBMAN BAND

JUSTIN HINDS & THE DOMINOES

JOHN HOLT

JAHPOSTLES BAND

LADY G

LADY SAW

LARRY & ALVIN

BARRINGTON LEVY

LIQUID LIGHT

LITTLE BEATER & APACHE

LITTLE LENNY

LOS PERICOS

LT STITCHIE

LUCIANO

MANDELA

ZIGGY MARLEY & THE MELODY MAKERS

HUGH MASAKELA

DERRICK MORGAN

MUTABARUKA

THE MYSTIC REVEALERS

PAPA SAN

PATRA

PINCHERS

PROFESSOR NUTS

QUEEN MAJEDA

JACK RADICS

ERNEST RANGLIN

DOUGIE RANKS

JUNIOR REID

SANCHEZ

SHAGGY

LEROY SIBBLES

GARNETT SILK

SISTER CAROL

KAREN SMITH

SPRAGGA BENZ

STANRYCK

RICHIE STEPHENS

NADINE SUTHERLAND

THE TECHNIQUES

TERROR FABULOUS

TOOTS & THE MAYTALS

TRINITY

JUNIOR TUCKER

JOSEY WALES

JOY WHITE

DELROY WILSON

WAYNE WONDER

WORL-A-GIRLS

DON YUTE

JULY 12–14, 1995: DOVER, ST ANN

ABBASANI

ADMIRAL BAILEY

BURO BANTON

BEENIE MAN

BIG MOUNTAIN

SUGAR BLACK & LEH-BANCHULAH

EVERTON BLENDER

YAMI BOLO

KEN BOOTHE

BOUNTY KILLER

DENNIS BROWN

CAPLETON

CAPT BARKEY & WICKERMAN

THE CLARENDONIANS

JOHNNY CLARKE

COCOA TEA

TONY CURTIS & JIGSY KING

DETERMINED

DOBBIE DOBSON

DOMINIC

BRENT DOWE

FABBY DALLY

FRISCO KID

JUNIOR GONG

UTON GREEN

BERES HAMMOND

DERRICK HARRIOTT

JUSTIN HINDS & THE DOMINOES

JOHN HOLT

ADINA HOWARD

IVAD

DIANA KING

LADY G

LADY SAW

BARRINGTON LEVY

LITTLE HERO

LITTLE KIRK

JULIAN MARLEY

MERCILESS

TONTO METRO

THE MIGHTY DIAMONDS

SUGAR MINOTT

DERRICK MORGAN

MR PECK

MUTABARUKA

JOHNNY NICE

PAPA SAN

FRANKIE PAUL

DAWN PENN

PINCHERS

PRESIDENT BROWN

PROFESSOR NUTS

TONY REBEL

DANNY RED

MICHAEL ROSE

SANCHEZ

SHAGGY

SHINEHEAD

SILVER CAT

SNAGGA PUSS

SPANNER BANNER

SPRAGGA BENZ

STANRYCK

RICHIE STEPHENS

NADINE SUTHERLAND

DON YUTE

AUGUST 1–4, 1996: CHUKKA COVE, ST ANN

ADMIRAL BAILEY

HORACE ANDY

MIKE ANTHONY

STARKY BANTON

BIG YOUTH

EVERTON BLENDER

KEN BOOTHE

BOUNTY KILLER

DENNIS BROWN

BUCCANEER

BURNING SPEAR

CAPT BARKEY & WICKERMAN

CELECIA

CHARLIE CHAPLIN

COCOA TEA

CULTURE

CARLENE DAVIS

JANET LEE DAVIS

CARL DAWKINS

ERIC DONALDSON

ALTON ELLIS

GENERAL B

GHOST

JOHN HOLT

PETER HUNNINGALE

ANGELIQUE KIDJO

KRUEZ

LECTURER

JC LODGE

LT STITCHIE

LUKEY D

MERCILESS
MICHIGAN & SMILEY
THE MIGHTY DIAMONDS
SUGAR MINOTT
PABLO MOSES
TANYA MULLINS
MUTABARUKA
BENJY MYAZ
NINJAMAN
JOHNNY OSBOURNE
PAPA SAN
FRANKIE PAUL
PINCHERS
PRESIDENT BROWN
TONY REBEL
ROBIN S
ROUNDHEAD
SANCHEZ
SCOTTY
SECOND IMIJ
LEROY SIBBLES
SISTER CHARMAINE
THE SKATALITES
THE SKOOL BAND
SLY & ROBBIE — TAXI CONNECTION
LEROY SMART
SPANNER BANNER
SPRAGGA BENZ
RICHIE STEPHENS
REGGIE STEPPER
SUPERCAT & CITY HEAT BAND
THE TAMLINS
ARTURO TAPPIN
THIRD WORLD
WORL-A-GIRLS

FEBRUARY 5–8, 1998: REGGAE PARK, ST ANN

YASUS AFARI
ALAZI
ALPANCHO
ANTHONY B
ARP
AXE OF JAHPOSTLES
BEENIE MAN

BLAKK SAFIYAH
THE BLAZE BAND
YAMI BOLO
BONGO
CEDELLA BOOKER
ANDRU BRANCH
DENNIS BROWN
BUSHMAN
CENTURION
CHAKULA
CHANGE
CHERRY NATURAL
COBRA
COYABALITES
CRISSY D
DADDYU
CARLENE DAVIS
CHAKA DEMUS & PLIERS
DJ MARSHALL
DOOM
DUTTY CUP
EL SENOR GRATTO
EMERGE
FAB 5
FAHRENHEIT
FOUNDATION
GENERAL DEGREE
GIBBY
GIRLZ TOWN BAND
GIZUM BAND
GOOFY
HAWKEYE
LAURYN HILL
I-THREES
THE INNOCENT CREW
GREGORY ISAACS
THE ISHAAN DANCERS
ITAL LEE
JAH MASON
JAHMALI
KIDDUS I
LADY G
LADY SAW
FLOYD LLOYD

LT STITCHIE
THE MACCABEE BAND
MARCUS
DAMIAN MARLEY
JULIAN MARLEY
ZIGGY MARLEY & MELODY MAKERS
MERCILESS
PABLO MOSES
JUDY MOWATT
MR VEGAS
THE MYSTIC REVEALERS
NECO FLEX
NOTCH
PAPA SAN
SEAN PAUL
PRESIDENT BROWN
RED RAT
REV ERROL HALL
RICH KID
THE RIDDIM KINGS BAND
JIMMY RILEY
THE RUFF KUT BAND
SAMPLE SHADE & CREW
GORDON SCOTT
SISTER CAROL
THE SONS & DAUGHTERS
ZIGGY SOUL
MICKEY SPICE
RICHIE SPICE
SPRAGGA BENZ
THE STAR TRAIL FAMILY
RICHIE STEPHENS
TANYA STEPHENS
THE TAMLINS
RUDDY THOMAS
GRACE THRILLERS
JUNIOR TUCKER
LOS TUMPOLOS
THE UPRISING BAND
WORD
BETTY WRIGHT
X-CALIBER
THE YARD BEAT BAND
YOGI

REGGAE SUNSPLASH ON RECORD: RECOMMENDED LISTENING

VARIOUS ARTISTS

Reggae Sunsplash '81: Tribute to Bob Marley (Elektra) 1981

History records the 1981 Sunsplash as a downbeat affair, overshadowed by Marley's death earlier in the year. In fact,

it offers up one of the best (and most lively) albums in the entire Sunsplash series.

British band Steel Pulse open things with four songs, two of which just happen to be the best they've ever recorded, the brooding "Ku Klux Klan" and "Handsworth Revolution," plus Marley's own "Smile Jamaica."

Rita Marley and the Wailers, and the still incredibly youthful Melody Makers get a song apiece, with the Wailers remaining onstage to back Eek-A-Mouse through a characteristically quirky "Wa-Do-Dem."

The Mighty Diamonds, Dennis Brown and Gregory Isaacs turn in typically joyous performances, and Third World, with a punchy "96 Degrees" and "Rock the World" close the disc in similar fashion.

But the true highlights are elsewhere, with Carlene Davis' dance hall style "The Harder They Come," two pulsing cuts from Black Uhuru (including the immortal "Guess Who's Coming to Dinner"), and Sheila Hylton's "The Bed's too Big Without You"—white reggae turned on its head and raised to quite unexpected heights.

Best of the Festival—Day One Live at Reggae Sunsplash 1982 (Sunsplash) 1983

Generally a sensational recounting of the day's highlights, opening with John Holt's amazing "Sweetie Come Brush Me," with expert accompaniment from Byron Lee & The Dragonaires—they also back up U-Roy (appropriately performing Holt's own "Wear You to the Ball") and Roy Shirley.

Big Youth's set was a revelation, best experienced on the live album released in his own name. The slow toast "I Pray Thee," an exemplary "Satta Amasa Gana" and a triumphant, jamming "Every Nigger Is a Star" complete his showing. Toots & The Maytals wrap the disc up with, again, a single excerpt from an entire album (and not the best one, either), the drab and over-long "(Marley's Gone) His Songs Live On."

Reggae Sunsplash Live (1992) (MCA) 1993

Even a triple album would be hard pressed to do justice to the multi-night festivities, so what hope is there with this particularly parsimonious CD—a mere 12 tracks and only 45 minutes long? Regardless, it at least gives the listener a flavor of the proceedings.

The magnificent Marcia Griffiths kicks off the groove with a mighty cover of Bob Andy and Jackie Mittoo's "Feel Like Jumping." Mystic Revelers arrive with a tune seemingly ripped right out of the hands of the latest boy band, but with lyrics torn straight out of the headlines. Its initial slickness is eventually roughed up by guest DJ Angie Angel.

Beres Hammond offers up the crowd pleasing "She Loves Me Now," before Ed Robinson brilliantly kicks off the album's dance hall section. The Dr'eds and Morgan Heritage keep the rootsy sound going but then Chaka Demus takes on the soca smash "Workie Workie" as part of a medley spit out at such speed that your ears can barely keep up, while Little Lenny wows the crowd with his always popular "Bum Flick."

But it's the young Buju Banton who virtually steals the show, not just from singer Wayne Wonder, whose stage he's sharing, but from every other DJ present. This leaves Ninjaman, next up, with little choice but to roust the growling teen in his opening number, the exuberant "Ready fi Dem," and throw out an invitation to clash that the competition all wisely declined.

Of course, Barrington Levy is a bigger man than that and, totally non-plussed by the boasting barrages around him, highlights his set with an unforgettable medley of his hits "Murderer" and "Black Roses."

From the contemporary stars, the album then returns to the older artists. Dennis Brown (with an evocative "Wolf & Leopard") and the always fabulous Freddie McGregor (showcasing his cultural classic "To Be Poor Is a Crime") prove yet again, that no matter how much fresh talent emerges on the island, the veterans' grip on Jamaican hearts will never loosen.

THE (BP) RENEGADES STEEL ORCHESTRA

STYLE *pan*
FORMED *1945 (T&T)*
CURRENT ARRANGER *Jit Sukha Samaroo (b 2/24/50, Surrey, T&T)*

One of the longest running of all steel bands, the Renegades Steel Orchestra was launched in early 1945, settling their name on the very morning of their first public performance, at Port of Spain's massive VE Day celebrations on May 8 (the official end of World War Two in Europe). The most familiar prefix to the band's name, Amoco, was added in 1970, after the Amoco Energy Company of Trinidad (formerly the Trinidad Oil Company) became the Renegades' official sponsors; beginning in 2001, the band came under the umbrella of British Petroleum (BP).

There was never a settled band line-up—at any given time, anywhere between 45 and 120 musicians performed with the Renegades, with the higher number, of course, being registered around the time of carnival. The group was also unusual in that much of their work was undertaken abroad—beginning in the early 1960s, the Renegades set about establishing themselves as the most traveled steel band in the world. Tours have taken them across South and Central America, the US, Europe, Africa and the Far East.

Despite their international success, the Renegades were constant under-achievers at the National Panorama Competition. They participated every year, but it wasn't until 1972 that they made any kind of impact, with an arrangement of Mighty Sparrow's "Soap." In 1976, they finally reached the "Big Yard"—the finals competition at the Queen's Park Savannah on carnival Saturday night, with Sparrow's "Statue" winning them second place.

The catalyst for the band's future carnival success was the arrival onto the scene of East Indian arranger Jit Samaroo. A pan enthusiast since his pre-teens, Samaroo was a former member of the Lever Brothers Camboulay Steel Orchestra, where band leader Lendeg White encouraged his talents as an arranger. He was also an accomplished soloist and, in 1972, came first in the Ping Pong (solo) category of the Steelband Music festival.

Samaroo was introduced to the Renegades around this same time by pan tuner Bertrand "Butch" Kellman, and his abilities soon came to bear on the band. Although the carnivals of 1977–79 proved as fallow as earlier years, in 1980 the Amoco Renegades entered a period of such success that carnival history still recalls it as the Renegades Era.

In that year they placed third in Panorama, with Samaroo's spirited arrangement of Lord Kitchener's "Jean the Netball Queen." Another Kitchener composition, "More Pan," saw them take runners-up honors in 1981 and, the following year, the group won with the same author's "Pan Explosion" — and that despite Samaroo near-simultaneously readying his own band, Samaroo's Jets, for a European tour with the Trinidad All Theatre Productions' play *J'Ouvert*. (The cast also included Crazy, Lord Relator and Lord Superior.)

1984 brought the Renegades' greatest triumph yet, when they swept Panorama by the highest margin ever recorded, 17.5 points, collecting 476 points out of 500 with yet another Kitchener melody, "Sweet Pan." Indeed, over the next 16 years, the Amoco Renegades performed Kitchener compositions every year bar five — 1989, 1991, 1995, 1996 and 1998. "Kitchener's unique chord progressions and rhythmic patterns are best suited to my style of arranging," explained Samaroo.

Accusations that the arranger was able only to work with Kitchener compositions, however, were silenced in 1989, when Samaroo reworked Devine's "Somebody" into a startling fusion of disco, soca, zouk, calypso, samba and merengue rhythms, and won Panorama once again. In total, the Renegades won Panorama nine times between 1982–1997, and never placed lower than sixth.

Consecutive victories occurred in 1984/85 and 1989/90. The mid-1990s then saw the Renegades take the crown three years running, with de Fosto's "Four Lara Four" (1995), and "Pan in a Rage" (1996), and Kitchener's "Guitar Pan" (1997). Samaroo was the first arranger in Panorama history to achieve this particular triumph.

Other Panorama hits for the Renegades have included: "50 Years of Steel" (1983 — 5th), "Pan Here to Stay" (1986 — 5th), "Pan in 'A' Minor" (1987 — 2nd), "The Pan in Me" (1988 — 6th), Tambu's "Rant and Rave" (1991 — 2nd), "The Bees' Melody" (1992 — 3rd), "Pan Earthquake"

(1994 — 3rd) and Shanqua's "Pan for Carnival" (1998 — 3rd).

Their domination of the competition is not wholly down to their choice of music, the Renegades have also proven one of the most innovative of modern steel bands. They demonstrated this most pertinently in 1993, performing Kitchener's "Mystery Man" with what most observers agreed was a mystery sound. Spies for other bands who ventured out to the Renegades pan yard at 17a Oxford Street, Port of Spain, returned utterly baffled by the bizarre rattling sounds which permeated the group's rehearsals.

It was only later, as the Renegades swept to victory once again, that they revealed their secret. The previous year, on a trip to the Indian Ocean island of Reunion, the band had been introduced to the sound of the kayamb, a native instrument with an absolutely distinctive rattle. They were so impressed that they returned home with 26 of them, which were immediately incorporated into the band's arsenal.

The Renegades are also regulars at the biannual Pan Is Beautiful festival, usually working under the baton of conductor Fr. John Sewell. In 1984, they received the highest marks for the test piece and placed second overall. Four years later, they received highest marks for the tune of choice, Sewell's daring adaptation of Gustav Holst's "Mars, the Bringer of War," and again placed second. On July 14, 1990, the Renegades performed at one of the largest outdoor concerts ever staged, appearing before an estimated 2.5 million strong crowd in the La Defense area of Paris, alongside composer Jean Michel Jarre. That same year, they also appeared as opening act at the Nelson Mandela Welcome Rally at Yankee Stadium, New York, and received a Sunshine Award.

Other honors accrued in the past two decades have included the Port of Spain City Corporation Award (1986), the Pan T&T award for Outstanding Contribution to the Development of the Steelband (1990) and the National Chaconia Gold Medal (1992). Samaroo alone received the Hummingbird Medal of Merit in 1987.

RECOMMENDED LISTENING

Panorama Saga: Tribute to Jit Samaroo (Delos) 1995

Seven tracks, most clocking in at around 10 minutes in length, show the sheer intricacies and magnificence of a steel band in full flight. All seven were Panorama entrants, all but one Lord Kitchener numbers ("Somebody" is the exception).

RHYTHM POETRY: RAPSO AND DUB

Although it is only within the last 25 years that the terms "dub poetry" and "rapso" have passed into the common musical lexicon, both forms arose perhaps 25 years earlier than that, in response to an extraordinary challenge thrown down to Caribbean artists by the intelligentsia — to prove that the "common man" could create uncommon art. It is a challenge which has been met so frequently, that today it is not even an issue.

Fundamentally, the two styles are parallel branches of the same tree, distinguished more by their musical accompaniment than by any variation in form. Dub poetry tends towards a reggae (but not necessarily dub)-based backing, rapso combines the "rap" with calypSO or, in the hands of more recent practitioners, SOca.

Both, too, draw upon the deepest traditions of Caribbean poetry, mindful as they are that those traditions are themselves of relatively recent vintage. The post-World War Two era saw a remarkable flowering of West Indian literature, as artists moved away from the rhapsodic declarations of devotion to motherland Britain which had hitherto passed as serious poetry, and began to embrace the islands' own strivings towards self-determination and independence, on the one hand, and an exploration of their deepest culture on the other.

Poets Claude McKay and HD Carberry mused upon the plight and the legacy of their enslaved forefathers, with a forcefulness and imagery which had never previously been seen. Others looked towards the future, and a time when laws would be passed by islanders for islanders, and not handed down by a remote assembly on the other side of the Atlantic. And one, Jamaican poetess Louise "Miss Lou" Bennett, emerged at the very dawn of this new era with a voice which is still heard today, in the work of the rhythm poets.

The contemporary Jamaican literati despised Bennett. She was not a poet, they swore, but a comedienne. It was not the content of her work which they objected to; indeed, Bennett attained a level of social consciousness and observation which remained above all reasonable criticism. Where Bennett "went wrong" was in her insistence on couching all her verse in a thick Jamaican patois — the language of the common people — at a time when speaking the King's English was regarded as the educated Jamaican's highest aspiration.

Bennett's popularity with the general public, too, conspired against her. Poetry was, after all, one of the highest arts, to be enjoyed by a silently seated, earnest audience who can appreciate its literary qualities. It was not something to be bellowed out at the common herd, by a woman whose diction and dialect was absolutely indistinguishable from the rabble to whom she was speaking. (One of her poems, 1966's "Jamaica Labrish," addresses this issue, welcoming home a local lad from a visit to the US, but frowning upon his failure to pick up even "a little twang" of accent: "yuh

mean yuh goh dah 'Merica . . . an' come back not a piece betta . . . bwoy, yuh noh shame?")

The titles of her published works summarize Bennett's perceived role in the arts of the era. *Jamaican Humour in Dialect* (1943), *Jamaica Dialect Poems* (1948, *Laugh with Louise* (1961). It took close to another 20 years before anybody realize that it was Louise who'd be laughing the loudest in the end.

In 1976, Big Youth wrote "Miss Lou Ring Ding" in Bennett's honor, and fellow DJ Trinity's "Miss Lou Rock" paid similar tribute. The early 1980s saw a massive resurgence of interest in her work, from a generation who might have had little time for pure poetry, but learned her verse almost as soon as they could read.

A new anthology of her work, *Selected Poems*, was published in Jamaica; she also launched a recording career which had hither to been confined to a handful of records released by scholastic US labels. Her influence, too, was palpable — in the late 1980s, dub poetess Jean Binta Breeze not only invoked the spirit of Bennett's work in her own heavily dialectal performance, she also acknowledged that the works of "Miss Lou" had been her constant companion since childhood, the staple of her repertoire "as a young child performing . . . on stages all over Jamaica."

Bennett, Breeze declared, "had not only drawn on the characters, experiences and language of the people. She had also managed to give the people's poetry back to them in a way that made the nation celebrate itself."

That celebration reached its climax in the early 1960s, as independence (or, at least, self-government) commenced its painstaking sweep across the West Indies. Jamaica and Trinidad & Tobago were granted their freedom in 1962, Montserrat and Barbados in 1966, the British Virgin Islands in 1967, the Cayman Islands in 1972, Bahamas in 1973, Grenada in 1974, Turks & Caicos in 1976, St Lucia in 1977, Dominica in 1978, St Vincent & The Grenadines in 1979. At last the islands could take their destiny into their own hands, and look their past in the face.

But freedom brought its own problems, socially, culturally and most of all politically, as successive governments (or would-be governments) struggled to find their own place in the world into which they had suddenly been projected. The conflicts of tradition and revolution arose across the region, devouring the islands' economy, debauching the existing infra-structure, devaluing the peoples' heritage. Voices began to rise, poets began to stir.

It was the late Lancelot "Kebu" Layne (d 7/28/90) who paved the way for what became the rapso and dub poetry movements, emerging on the T&T scene in the early 1970s with an act (and, specifically, a song — "Blow Away") designed solely to protest the darkening future, by reminding people of their deepest past.

Born in the poverty-stricken village of Gonzales, Layne showed how the traveling poets who once spread news around the villages of Africa, had become the chantuelle of the new world, and how the praise singers who led African religious ceremonies were now the calypsonians of the modern age. But most importantly, he spoke of the origins of the Creole people and the need, even in the modern era, never to forget them.

Single-handedly, he organized local Emancipation Days throughout the islands (at a time when such celebrations were officially frowned upon), working with and educating schoolchildren about their African heritage and the pride which that should instill in them.

Adapting the same linguistic approach as Louise Bennett, but delving even deeper into folk tradition, Layne's songs and performances invoked the imagery, the impact and most of all, the long-forgotten origins of such masquerade characters as the Chantuelle, the Pierrot and the fast talking, loudly boasting and witheringly witty Midnight Robber, to create a vibrant drum and chant driven sound which seamlessly melded tradition and modernity.

Layne traveled extensively, lecturing on local culture and giving pan demonstrations at universities throughout the world. And few who witnessed his displays ever forgot them. His homeland, however, all but ignored him. The early 1970s were tumultuous years, dominated in T&T by the rise of the Black Power movement, a battle which climaxed with bloody, open revolt in early 1970. That February, the radical National Joint Action Congress united with the islands' own (admittedly tiny) army, and began a campaign of terrorism and lawlessness which ended only when the still loyal coast guard began shelling the only road in and out of the army base.

In the ensuing climate of fear and distrust, anything even remotely resembling an attempt to reawaken black consciousness was either swept away or suppressed. Lancelot Layne's use of local dialects, street poetry, African rhythms and historical content was seen as an especially seditious political act, one which neither radio nor record companies could ever countenance. Layne released a number of notable singles, many of them on his own Jumbie Bead label: "Strike Song," composed for a local soccer team; "Get Off the Radio," mourning local broadcasters' preference for foreign music over domestic talents; "Dat Is Horrors," "Who Could Help Me," "Yo' Tink It Sorf" and, of course, the pioneering "Blow Away."

But he worked alone. It was the middle of the decade before any other performer even began to inspect Layne's legacy.

In 1976, T&T poet Cheryl Byron returned from several years in New York to perform at carnival, lining up at the Professionals Calypso Tent alongside the traditional delights of Lord Shorty, Duke, Cro-Cro and Gypsy, but with a far from traditional act.

Even with the hypnotic accompaniment of percussion and rhythm, she could not persuade anybody to listen. Like Bennett, she defied the conventions of poetry; like Layne, she was too weird for calypso. Byron returned to New York, her still unnamed medium ("a child is born before it's named," Byron reflected years later; "when people asked me 'what you call that?' I'd tell them it's a poem and a song") returned to the shadows.

Elsewhere, however, her notions were finding fertile ground. In London in 1974, Jamaican immigrant Linton Kwesi Johnson (b 1952, Chapeltown, JA) published *Voices of the Living and the Dead*, a slender collection of writings about life in black Britain, notable not only for its measured debate and livid consciousness, but also for its utilization of a local London-Jamaican patois which had never been placed in print before. Published in 1975, Johnson's second collection, *Dread Beat & Blood*, confirmed his impact, while his journalism appeared both in the music papers (he was reggae correspondent for the *New Musical Express* and *Black Music*) and in the cultural press (the *Race Today* co-operative newspaper).

Johnson was long accustomed to giving readings at parties, meetings and rallies; beginning in late 1976, he moved onto a wider stage, assembling a backing band and performing his poetry to music. Within a year, he was recording his first album, *Dread Beat an' Blood*, credited to Poet & The Roots (Island, 1977); within days of its release, what the music press hastened to term "dub poetry" was a reality.

For Johnson and those dub poets who emerged in the wake of his breakthrough (most notably Benjamin Zephaniah — born 1958, Birmingham, England; he first published in 1980, and released his *Dub Ranting* debut album in 1983), the road to both musical and literary acceptance was paved by the British West Indian community's own awareness of its importance, and the need to nurture its artists whatever mode of expression they chose.

Similar growth attended Mutabaruka, following his arrival on the Jamaican scene with his *Sun and Moon* poetry collection in 1976. After three years of increasingly adventurous experiments with a band, Mutabaruka was a runaway success at the 1981 Reggae Sunsplash. Indeed, within two years, he was proudly watching as his most promising protege, Jean Binta Breeze, graced the same stage in her own right.

Elsewhere, Oku Onuora (b Orlando Wong, 1952 — Kingston, JA) emerged from seven years in prison for armed robbery (where he first started writing poetry) in 1977, to cut the single "Reflections in Red" with the Wailers' rhythm section. A cynical study of the recent truce declared in the battle for Kingston's streets (Onuora performed the piece at the One Love Peace Concert the following year), it was the first shot in a volley of extraordinarily dramatic releases, both by Onuora and Mutabaruka, and a growing brigade of other young Jamaican poets.

But while Jamaica blazed with dub poetry, the same situation and, indeed, tolerance could not be said to flourish elsewhere in the West Indies. There, the prevalent attitude remained one of trying to "raise" the arts to Anglo-American standards, as opposed to encouraging an indigenous style of equal value.

It was an old problem. As far back as 1932, the publisher of the Trinidadian arts magazine *The Beacon* bemoaned the paucity of local authors willing to speak in their own voices, suggesting that "the average Trinidadian writer regards his fellow countrymen as his inferiors, an uninteresting people who are not worth his while. So [he peoples] [his stories] with creatures from other planets, American gangsters and English MPs."

Thirty-five years later, in 1968, calypsonian Mighty Chalkdust echoed similar concerns when he lambasted the government and media's constant carping about a so-called "Brain Drain" luring T&T's most gifted scholars and athletes to other lands, when the real drain was taking place under their own noses, and by their own tutelage. "Our children don't know what's B-flat in pan, while the US Army and all have Steelband," Chalkdust despaired. "We are living on Yankee sad song like bugs, while . . . parang and folk song going to the dogs. That is what I call Brain Drain."

The situation did not improve. In the late 1970s, the official view remained blinded to the artistry — or, more accurately, the offerings of the artistry — in its own backyard, insistent that local talents should not waste their time with provincial concerns. And condemning those that did as rebellious troublemakers.

Trinidadian Rasta Roy "Brother Resistance" Lewis certainly seemed to fit that description. He was already a familiar figure from the political rallies and picket lines of the 1970s; now he took the stage as frontman of the Network Riddum Band, an outfit which took a message borrowed from Lancelot Layne and a style derived from the dub poets, then slammed it onto the streets with raised fists and voices, amplifiers and instruments. It was still a poem and a song, but it was no longer accompanied by drums alone.

Resistance himself admitted to his music's precedents. Mutabaruka's Jamaican breakthrough certainly encouraged the Network Riddum Band, as did Linton Kwesi Johnson in Britain, and, of course, so did the emergent rap scene in North America. When people asked him what his noise was called, Resistance deliberately borrowed the American

term, then married it to T&T's other great musical obsession of the time, soca. It was called Rapso, and a more cynical inversion of the island's cultural snobbery could not be conceived.

But of course, rapso was so much more than a piece of clever word-play. Like Mutabaruka, like Johnson, it was the rapid-fire rattle of ghetto consciousness speaking out against oppression, with folklore, culture and impassioned honesty on its side. And, as such, it represented the spark which could ignite the one conflagration most calculated to strike fear in the authoritarian heart.

At a time when carnival and calypso were slipping into the hands of so many rapacious outsiders — government approval, corporate sponsorship, tourism and so on — the Network Riddum Band reminded people of the music's original subversion, its early superstition, and the anger which once fuelled the entire experience. And the establishment moved swiftly to suppress this new movement, hauling a 50 year old law out of mothballs, the Theatre & Dance Hall Ordinance, and scouring it for every provision which could be pressed into service against it.

Conceived back in the 1930s, the Ordinance was originally enacted to protect the public from the raucous obscenities and political slurs which no decent person could possibly want to hear. Now, in the 1980s, it could protect them from things they didn't *need* to hear. And when that didn't work, the government sent in the troops.

In a chilling (albeit much smaller scale) echo of the Nigerian government's heavy-handed assaults on the similarly disruptive Afrobeat pioneer Fela Kuti, June 27, 1983, saw the Network Riddum Band's offices — a complex which included rehearsal rooms, a performance area and a drug rehabilitation center — stormed by the police, uniquely accompanied by a demolition squad. The building was destroyed and the group's equipment confiscated.

The government's goal was to crush rapso. Instead they made it larger. Performers who had hitherto existed on the fringe of the music now stepped boldly into the ring to register their protest at such brutality. Watching developments from her base in the Big Apple, Cheryl Byron returned to Trinidad in 1983; then took rapso back to the streets of America as the leader of Something Positive, a 60+ member ensemble of New York based West Indian musicians, artists, poets and dancers.

Brother Book and Karega Mandela broke through with their own highly individual performing styles. Brother Resistance himself was offered a British tour, including a berth at the 1984 Commonwealth Festival staged at London's Royal Albert Hall.

Such honors, and so much activity, legitimized rapso. In 1990, Brother Resistance established a National Rapso Day of celebration in T&T, an event so popular that over the next decade it expanded first into National Rapso Week and, ultimately, National Rapso Month.

During the early 1990s, too, a whole new wave of rhythm poets emerged and, this time, the local music industry was ready for them. Performers like Adisa Andwele, Ataklan, 3canal and Kindred found willing homes at the Mad Bull and Rituals labels, while rapso's absorption into the mainstream saw Superblue, David Rudder and Machel Montano all experiment with the genre — Montano and Ataklan, in particular, have formed a rewarding partnership, frequently guesting at one another's shows.

This cross-fertilization perhaps reached its peak when Gabrielle Hosein, Queen of the *Mastana Bahar* 2000 festival lined up among the competitors at the Breaking New Ground all-comers event which is now a part of National Rapso Month.

The international audience, too, accepted rapso with rapture. In 1986, Cheryl Byron joined Breeze and Bennett, and the emergent Anita Stewart, Afua and Elaine Thomas on *Woman Talk: Caribbean Dub Poetry*, a compilation album produced by Mutabaruka for the US Heartbeat label. A less gender-specific companion volume, *Word Soun' 'Ave Power* also appeared.

In 1992, Brother Resistance was one of the attractions at the first International Dub Poetry Festival in Toronto, Canada (that city itself possesses a vibrant scene, highlighted by Michael St George and Anthony Bansfield). Then, in 1997, 3canal's *Blue* debut album created such a stir that the New York Sunshine Music Awards promptly instituted a new category for rapso alone.

No longer the now out-dated (but, according to many Anglo- American sensibilities, best understood) hybrids which their names suggest, both dub poetry and rapso burn today as vibrant fires in their own right, as relevant to the demands or, more accurately, requirements, of the modern musical age, as they remain aligned to the old time chantwells and the even older time African poets.

For that is where they sprang from, and that is where they hope to return. For there, as Brother Resistance himself explained, is "de power of de word in de riddum of de word." And that is an explanation which the fast talking, clean rhyming Midnight Robber would recognize immediately.

RECOMMENDED LISTENING

ATAKLAN Atanomical (—T&T) 1998
The marching song "Mastife" and the dance hall inflected ode to golf hero "Tiger Woods" offer the poles between which the rest of this exciting album exists — Ataklan's duets with Machel Montano, "Pananie" and "Rapso Blunt" (two versions, including a killer extended mix), are genre-busting stand-outs.

LOUISE BENNETT Miss Lou Live (Island) 1983

Bennett's second live album (following the earlier *Yes M'Dear*). It is difficult to say which area best suits the non-patois speaker, book or disc, but the concert environment is certainly the most indicative both of her popularity and humor, and of the sometimes manic form which she alone bestowed upon a later generation of rhythm poets.

[JEAN BINTA] BREEZE Tracks (LKJ—UK) 1992
Produced by Linton Kwesi Johnson and Dennis Bovell, following her relocation to the UK, Breeze's debut album succeeded two well-received books of poetry, *Riddym* (1988) and *Spring Cleaning* (1992). Her often deeply personal verse lacks some of the militant passion attending her *Woman Talk* contributions (see below); in fact, other earlier recordings had been rejected by several hitherto encouraging labels for that very reason. But as she herself said, "I allowed my pen its freedom when I realized that my politics had never been learned through the study or acceptance of any ideology. I have never read Marx totally and came to CLR James through my love of cricket."

CHERYL BYRON & SOMETHING POSITIVE Freedom Soon Come (Itopi Songs Unltd—T&T) 1993
Despite Byron's near veteran status, her debut album. "Ashe Maria," "Freedom" and "Ancestral Chant" are among the poems collected from over two decades worth of writings.

LINTON KWESI JOHNSON Poet & the Roots (Island) 1977
Although a two-CD anthology, *Independent Intravenshun* (Island, 1998) highlights the full range of Johnson's work, for sheer passion and innovation his debut remains his most overall satisfying effort.

OKU ONUORA Pressure Drop (Heartbeat) 1986
Accompanied by his AK7 (Armageddon Knights Column 7) band, *Pressure Drop* fulfills the promise of early singles "Reflections in Red" and "I a Tell," offering rootsy accompaniment to some dramatic visions. Later Onuora albums place more emphasis on dub than poetry.

MIKEY SMITH Mi C-Yaan Believe It (Mango—1982)
Stunning debut album overseen by Linton Kwesi Johnson and Dennis Bovell, readily comparable to the best of either Johnson or Mutabaruka. Unfortunately, Smith's death soon after the album's release leaves it more as a might-have-been than the definitive testament of an extraordinary talent.

3CANAL The Fire Next Time (Rituals) 1999
20 track set devoted to emphasizing rapso's versatility — rhythms draw from Latin, funk, R&B and electro fields, while never losing sight of the band's own origins.

VARIOUS ARTISTS

Word Soun' 'Ave Power (Heartbeat) 1983
Woman Talk: Caribbean Dub Poetry (Heartbeat) 1986

Two Mutabaruka-produced sets, rounding up a fair sampling of contemporary dub poetry and rapso artists. A number of crucial omissions scar the earlier set, and a companion dub volume (*Dub Poet Dub*, remixed by Scientist) adds nothing to the genre whatsoever.

ROARING LION

STYLE *calypso/soca*
BORN *Hubert Raphael Charles, 1909 (T&T) d July, 1999 (T&T)*

Almost a decade before his own death, at the age of 90 in 1999, Roaring Lion looked back on the generation of artists alongside whom he emerged, midway between the two world wars, and mourned, "All of them died except for me. I haven't decided to die yet."

Indeed, names like Chieftain Douglas, King Radio, Atilla the Hun, Lord Executor, Beginner, Invader, Lord Caresser, Tiger, Destroyer, Growler and Gorilla might well have been forgotten without Roaring Lion to both perpetuate and, through his own storehouse of memories, ensure that their deeds were recorded. But even in old age, Roaring Lion was so much more than a museum of ancient calypso history. He was also the music's first, and greatest, legend, an honor which death itself could not take away from him.

The son of a French trader and a maid of Afro-Indian descent, the young Hubert Charles was orphaned and ultimately raised by his mother's former employers. He left school and apprenticed as a pipe fitter, where he spent his spare time composing and singing calypsos.

In 1929 (some sources say 1927), a friend entered him in a talent contest at a small tent on Bedford Lane, Belmont. He intended singing the popular "Short Dresses," but forgot the lyrics when he took the stage. Instead he improvised wildly, and with such success that he was promptly hired for the season. Other regular sources of income included singing at a local gambling club and selling ice cream from a street cart.

Changing his name first to Raphael de Lion, he then adopted the name The Lion Flaps, before becoming Roaring Lion, allegedly (if somewhat inaccurately) taking it from his unique vocal style. A picture of sartorial elegance and charm he also swiftly earned another nickname, "The Beau Brummel of Calypso"—a role to which he adapted with suave aplomb.

Swinging the silver-topped cane which remained his trademark for the rest of his life, he was the smooth talking lover every woman dreamed of—and which, legend insists, many found. "I was good enough to leave my imprint wherever I went," he once remarked when asked about the many children he is said to have fathered, while anybody doubting his proclivity was simply referred to one of his greatest early

hits, the self-affirming "I Can Make More Love than Romeo."

Calypso, when the Lion first roared, was still an amateur affair, its champions decided on such merits as the ability to improvise new material, with its practitioners considered extraordinarily low on the social scale. "A calypsonian was a dog," Lord Iere reflected in 1972. During the early 1930s, however, commercial forces began to take an interest in the music, with the sharpest local operators opening the first professional calypso tents. Roaring Lion was recruited to the aptly-named Victory Tent in Port of Spain, using that as his base even as he strove to broaden his appeal across the Caribbean.

In 1930, Lion teamed with fellow performer Atilla The Hun to engineer several of the most original developments in modern calypso history. Atilla (born Raymond Quevedo, 3/24/1882; died 2/22/62) had already been on the scene for some 20 years at that point; he made his public singing debut in 1911, and by 1919 was a member of the Red Dragon Band. Lord Executor was an early mentor, but Atilla rapidly developed his own style, all the more so after he and Lion linked up. (The politically outspoken Atilla was elected a Port of Spain city councillor in 1946, eventually rising to deputy mayor. He was elected to Parliament in 1960.)

They pioneered the concept of calypso duets, then went a stage further by enacting entire dramas — mini soap operas with the singers each taking separate characters. Their first production, *The Divorce Case*, was staged at the Salada Tent during the 1933 carnival, and co-starred Chieftain Douglas, Lord Trafalgar, Inveigler, Lord Executor and King Radio.

Also in that year, Lion and Atilla were the moving force behind the first international calypso tour, leading a troupe featuring King Radio, Lord Beginner, clarinetist Willy West and his band and leading masqueraders around the Caribbean. In 1934, Lion and Atilla were in New York, the first Trinidadian calypsonians ever to record in that city.

The session for Brunswick Records producer Jack Kapp paid immediate dividends. Actor Rudy Vallee was visiting the studio at the time, and promptly booked Lion to perform his "Ugly Woman" calypso on the NMB radio broadcast, Fleishman's Variety Hour radio show on March 8. Vallee also arranged for Lion and Atilla to appear at his Hollywood Cafe; Lion alone then appeared before President Roosevelt in the Grand Ballroom of the Waldorf Astoria. The trip was later celebrated in Lion's "Guests of Rudy Vallee," recorded as a duet with Atilla in 1938.

In 1935, Lion was booked to entertain passengers on the US cruise ship SS *Scanpen*. He returned home to thrill the 1936 carnival with "Advantage Mussolini," a scathing attack on Italy's recent invasion of Ethiopia. He then returned to

New York to record, eventually cutting what was, in calypso terms, a record breaking 95 sides for Brunswick between 1934–41, including several field recordings in T&T.

His hits included the classics "War" (with Atilla, Lord Caresser and Lord Executor — 1937), "Death" (1939), "Poland, Poland" and "Mr Neville Chamberlain" (1940). Lion cut a total of 13 duets with Atilla, while the pair were also responsible for one of the first ever modern printed collections of calypsos, published during the 1940s. His annual visits to New York ended in 1941, after he was detained at Ellis Island, accused of, absurdly enough, being a spy. For the remainder of the war years, Decca recorded him in Trinidad.

His homeland fame, too, was vast. In 1933, Lion scored the first of five consecutive "Leggos," as the Road March competition was then called, with "Wanga" — he followed through with "Bamsi Lambay," "Woopsin," "Old Lady Run a Mile and a Half," and "Ask No Questions." Other Leggo triumphs included "Saga Boy," "Donkey," "Dorothy Went to Bathe" and, in 1937, the sexually controversial "Netty Netty," 4,000 copies of which were seized by local customs officials and, apparently, dumped in the harbor.

The record was banned elsewhere, too, but some copies did get through and, in May, the excursion boat SS *Trinidad* took over 100 Trinidadians to Grenada, to blast "Netty Netty" at full volume towards the shore. Lion himself then followed through with the calypso "Excursion to Grenada," attacking censorship in all its guises.

Lion became the first calypsonian ever to appear at Trinidad's super-elite Country Club and, again in 1937 he was appointed the "Official Entertainer" at Government House, in which role he entertained foreign dignitaries and heads of state as they visited T&T. Winner of the 1940 Calypso King crown, throughout World War Two Roaring Lion was constantly in demand to entertain the American troops stationed on the island. He also opened his own Calypsoville nightclub.

In 1943, he became the first Caribbean-based calypso singer ever to have a song, "Ugly Woman," featured in a Hollywood movie. Director Curtis Bernhardt had chosen T&T as the location for his *Happy Go Lucky*, and Rudy Vallee, one of the movie's co-stars (alongside Mary Martin, Dick Powell and Betty Hutton), was instrumental in the song's inclusion. Lion would not have the honor of performing it, though, that role went to Sir Lancelot, the New York/California based calypsonian who was now carving out a respectable movie career for himself.

1943 also saw Lion undertake a 14 day tour of British Guiana, accompanied by the Muttoo Brothers Band, who were Guianese natives. He then returned to New York in 1945, to appear at the Village Vanguard Club, established by Max Gordon and already renowned for its calypso entertainment. In 1939, Trinidadian bandleader Gerald Clark and his Caribbean Serenaders became the club's house band and, over the next five years, Gordon imported the likes of Houdini, Lord Invader and Lord Caresser, to perform alongside the Duke of Iron, MacBeth the Great and Sir Lancelot, Trinidadian born, but New York bred singers.

Lion slipped effortlessly into this new world, playing his own part in what became, over the next few years, a massive boom in calypso in the US. The Andrews Sisters covered Lord Invader's 1944 Leggo hit "Rum And Coca Cola," while a calypso show, Samuel Manning's *Caribbean Carnival*, ran on Broadway during 1947, starring the Duke of Iron. There was also a rash of homegrown calypsonians emerging during the late 1940s/early 1950s. (Among these, the Boston-based Charmer is better known today as Nation of Islam leader Louis Farrakhan. He turned professional in 1953 and recorded a number of calypsos for the Monogram label — the most prolific of several US-based calypso labels. He first encountered the Nation in the late 1950s, while appearing at Chicago's Calypso Follies.)

Meanwhile, no less a commentator than Walter Winchell was moved to review a number of Vanguard calypso shows, including at least one of Roaring Lion's. Society belle Peggy Hopkins Joyce, he noted, was "highly amused" by Lion's "Ugly Woman." (When Lion's Vanguard contract ended in 1945, he was replaced by Harry Belafonte — whose own repertoire include a number of Lion compositions.)

In 1945, Lion and Atilla broke away from Decca/Brunswick to record instead for Guild/Musicraft. Lion cut four numbers, including "Dorothy Went to Bathe" and "Mary Ann," the latter subsequently became a major US hit in 1957, after the folk group Terry Gilkyson and the Easy Riders adapted it.

In 1951, Roaring Lion cut his most controversial single yet, "The Lost Watch" (a carnival hit in 1948), released in both T&T and the UK by Port of Spain entrepreneur (and Decca Records' Caribbean agent) Eduardo Sa Gomes' eponymous label. Promptly banned by the local broadcast authorities in both countries, the song told the story of a young girl accused of stealing a watch, and the investigating police matron's struggle to find it. She knows the girl has it, she can hear it ticking. But the girl has no purse, no pockets, and it's not hidden in her hair. . . .

That same year, together with the Trinidad All Steel Percussion Orchestra, Lion traveled to London to represent T&T at the Festival of Britain. He cut his next 78 almost immediately upon arrival, linking with Cyril Blake's Calypso Serenaders for a version of the VJ Day celebration "Mary Ann," released through Parlophone that October. Another popular Lion recording was 1953's "Coronation of Queen Elizabeth II," cut for Melodisc.

The calypsonian remained in the UK until 1963, working as a performer, entrepreneur and a philanthropist. He established the Coloured People's Accommodation Bureau, dedicated to welcoming and helping to settle West Indian and African immigrants (similar organizations were established by Marcus Garvey's widow, Amy, and the future leader of the British Black Power movement, Michael deFreitas). He also launched his own cosmetics company, Rafael de Lion Beauty Products.

Returning to T&T in December, 1963, Lion appeared at the 1964 Calypso Revue. That same year he came second (behind Lord Brynner) in the TTT Television Calypso Competition. Thereafter, Lion continued performing and recording regularly, although he seldom bothered competing against the new wave of young talent rising up at carnival.

Rather, he preferred to reserve himself for "special" occasions. Towards the end of the 1960s he became a regular at the Calypso Theatre in Port of Spain, and in fall, 1970, he hosted a series of thirteen half hour radio shows on the history of calypso for Radio Trinidad. He participated in the 1972 Tenth Anniversary Independence competition, performing "Formula for Nationhood" and "Trinidad Carnival." Lion also served as president of the Calypsonian Association but, by the end of the decade, he had all but retired from the stage.

During 1981/82, Lion wrote a weekly column on calypso for the *Trinidad Evening News*, and in 1986 published the book *Calypso from France to Trinidad: 800 Years of History*, which grew out of his columns. It excited considerable controversy due to his insistence that calypso developed from European, rather than African roots.

In 1985, Lion was invited to perform a calypso greeting for Pope John Paul II when the Pontiff traveled to Trinidad. He didn't take the stage again until February 1991, when he made a guest appearance at Queen's Hall, as part of Rawle Gibbon's *Sing de Chorus* production, performing "Dorothy Went to Bathe" and "The Lost Watch." Two years later (the same year that his "Caroline" was featured in the hit movie *Captain Ron*), *Everybody's Magazine* presented Lion with its Lifetime Achievement Award.

That same year, 1993, Lion linked with Eddy Grant's Ice label, and recorded the album *Standing Proud* — among the featured musicians were David Rudder and guitarist Fitzroy Coleman, Lion's regular accompanist during the 1950s. Ice followed through with *Sacred 78s*, reissuing many of Lion's early recordings. In 1995, Lion scored a surprise hit at carnival with a soca-style re-recording of the classic "Papa Chunks." The song appeared on his final album, *Viva le King*.

Lion's health was failing, however, and he spent the last two years of his life out of sight. Lion roared for the final time in July, 1999.

SELECTED DISCOGRAPHY

◪ Roaring Loud, Standing Proud (Ice) 1993

Generally, the remakes simply add punch and a modern soca- esque sheen to some glorious oldies — "Nora Darling," "Dorothy Went to Bathe," "J'Ouvert," "Six Feet of Earth" and more. But it's worth picking up for a cheeky new production of "The Lost Watch."

◪ Viva Le King (Ice) 1995

More of the same, this time updating "Ugly Woman," "Papa Chunks," "All Women Are Beautiful" and "Man Centipede."

SELECTED COMPILATIONS & ARCHIVE RELEASES

◪ Sacred 78s (Ice) 1994

Absolutely crucial collection, 25 tracks recorded during Lion's Brunswick years and serving up the original (and, occasionally, authentically scratchy) sounds which captivated a nation. "Ugly Woman," "The Blue Tailed Fly," "More Love than Romeo" and "I Am Going to Buy a Bungalow" are as gleeful today as they were way back when, while "Royal Tour" and "Advantage Mussolini" are among the reminders of the world in which Roaring Lion prowled.

ROCK STEADY: RUDIES ALL ROUND

Ska was taking off in Britain and bubbling in America. So it was cripplingly ironic that just as its horizons broadened to span half the planet, ska in Jamaica was changing dramatically. Or, at least, its audience was, and in an industry which prided itself on listening to its customers, that amounted to much the same thing.

It was the spring of 1965 and kids no longer wanted to do "the ska," the fast, loose, punchy dance which had sustained the music industry for five years now, nor any of the countless variations which rose from the dance floor to sustain a handful of aptly named hits, then disappear again (the Jerk, popularized by the Wailers, Laurel Aitken and more, was one such.)

The rock steady was taking over, slower, more considered, more cool. Instead of honking horns and skipping rhythms, the bass now drove the song, and the heavier the better. The rhythm, the very pulse of the music, was fundamentally altered. Of course ska would continue to be made and enjoyed. But it was rock steady which now ruled the dance floors, and would continue to do so for the next three years.

Veteran band leader Lynn Taitt had been leading his Comets in something approaching this new direction for a couple of years, and musicologists have credited him with blueprinting this exciting, fresh music. Singer Hopeton

Lewis then formulated it, when he found the lyrics to his new "Take It Easy" single simply couldn't be fit over its original ska-style backing. And pianist Gladstone Anderson christened it at the same session, when he listened to the playback and remarked upon the new rhythm. It was, he said, "rock steady."

In the five years since ska's emergence, much had changed. The initial thrill of Jamaican independence had long since given way to weary acceptance, and the knowledge that freedom for the politicians did not, and would not, mean freedom for the people they governed.

Wages were still low, taxes were still high, but now there were no longer subsidies flooding in from a benevolent far off mother country to hold the wolves of international commerce at bay.

Jamaica was sinking into an economic hole which made even the poverty of past decades seem somehow luxurious. As is so often the case, the gap between rich and poor increased, and so did the lengths to which the latter were prepared to go in their attempts to bridge it.

Crime was soaring, and not only theft and burglary. Mindless violence, senseless hooliganism, unprovoked assaults were all on the rise. Gangs were forming, and the streets were their battleground—fermenting since the 1950s, the rude boys finally arrived, in suits as sharp as knives, and armed with ratchet blades honed sharper still.

This was the audience which killed ska, this was the audience which demanded rock steady—and this, with the Jamaican musician's keen eye for any topical issue to hang his next hit from, was to become the focus of some of the finest musical commentaries of the entire decade.

Ken Boothe, a long established singer whose roots lay back in the mento era, was relaunched as a rock steady balladeer. The Wailers, the group Morgan had rejected four years earlier, were already firmly entrenched within the rudie culture, there to be joined by a new wave of rude boy sympathizers.

Vocal trios like the Ethiopians, the Clarendonians, the Pioneers, the Gaylads and the Melodians moved to the fore. In fact, the rock steady era marks the apogee of the vocal group in the annals of Jamaican music, as influences which reached back to the doo wop age collided with the dreams and demands of a new generation, and unleashed some of the most sublimely beautiful music of the age.

The key figure in the early development of rock steady was Duke Reid. He had been out of the business for several months at this point, although he had enjoyed a major boom in the early 1960s, sponsoring his own radio show, *Treasure Isle Time*, to sell his wares, and operating a string of record labels which showcased his stable of bona fide stars. But over-expansion of his operation had, by 1964, all but removed the burly Duke from the picture—and half

the musicians in Jamaica breathed an involuntary sigh of relief. Too many of them saw their sessions interrupted by the producer suddenly deciding that somebody wasn't pulling their weight, and shooting holes in the studio wall where they stood.

Reid wasn't out of the way for long. In 1965, his wife won the football pools and reopened the studio with the proceeds. The talents inevitably followed. Dobby Dobson, the Paragons and Joya Landis all linked up with the Duke and they, too, confirmed rock steady's eminence.

The finest jewels in the Duke's crown, however, were the Techniques. Formed by Winston Riley, Franklyn White, Frederick Waite and the spectacularly voiced Keith "Slim" Smith in 1962, the Techniques, ironically, cut their first ever single for the British Columbia label, "No-one"/"Remember I Told You" in 1963. This was included on the period compilation *The Real Jamaican Ska*, alongside contributions from Lord Creator, Jimmy Cliff, the Charmers and Winston Samuel.

Despite this early success, the group waited close to three years before making their Jamaican debut, after Strange Cole introduced them to Duke Reid. It was a fortuitous union – Reid was as entranced by the new rock steady music as the most impressionable teen and, over the next year or so, he guided the Techniques towards sheer perfection, with records like "Don't Leave Me," "Little Did You Know" and "When You Are Wrong."

The original Techniques line-up shattered in 1966, at the peak of their powers. (Smith went onto the similarly scintillating Uniques.) Riley and the Techniques, however, continued on, replacing his errant bandmates and even finding somebody who could sing with at least as much distinction (if not, perhaps, emotional fragility) as Smith, Pat Kelly. In this form, the Techniques marched on, scoring with "Queen Majesty," "It's You I Love" and "Run Come Celebrate," together with cross-genre defining versions of Curtis Mayfield's "You'll Want Me Back" and the Temptations' "I Wish It Would Rain."

If the Techniques (and a handful of other acts, the Paragons and the implausibly juvenile Clarendonians paramount among them) represented the loving side of the rocksteady movement, other acts were concerned with less sensitive pursuits, their song titles leaping out with a resonance which countless past exhortations to "do the ska" never had. Records like the Soul Agents' "Get Ready, It's Rock Steady," of course, adhered to a tried and trusted gamut. But it was not the dance which fascinated the most perceptive songwriters now, it was the dancers and, in particular, their lifestyle.

The Maytals' "Bam Bam," winner of the first ever Independence Song Festival, Dandy Livingstone's "A Message to You, Rudie," the Rulers' "Don't Be a Rude Boy," Derrick Morgan's "Cool the Rudies" and a string of Alton Ellis singles attempted to introduce at least a soupcon of decency and morality to the situation — Ellis' "Dance Crasher" admonished the rudies who got their kicks from doing exactly that, crashing dances and causing trouble.

On the other side of the fence, however, rude boy society seemed impossibly exciting, implausibly romantic. England had her Robin Hood, Australia had Ned Kelly, the US had Bonnie & Clyde and Jamaica had the rude boys. Later, Jimmy Cliff would encapsulate the imagery and romance in the movie *The Harder They Come*.

Long before that hit the silver screen, however, the rude boy was already a legend of cinematic proportions, outlaw heroes who became the subject of records as disparate as Prince Buster's "Johnny Cool," detailing a veritable cross between Marlon Brando and Superman; Desmond Dekker's "007 (Shanty-Town)" — named for a youth camp and not, as is widely supposed, for James Bond (although he, too, was a Rude Boy hero); Peter Tosh's "I Am the Toughest"; and, the greatest of them all, the Skatalites' instrumental "Lawless Street." One of the Yap brothers finest ever productions was summed up by British journalist Johnny Copasetic as "'Heartbreak Hotel' and 'Desolation Row' in a nutshell."

The Spanishtonians weighed in with "Rudie Gets Plenty," Joe White with "Rudies All Around," Desmond Dekker (again) with "Rude Boy Train" and the Valentines with "Blam Blam Fever." But the greatest rude boy saga of them all was the unfolding drama of Judge Dread.

In January, 1967, Derrick Morgan released his single "Tougher than Tough," in which a quartet of rude boys are hauled up before the magistrate on the usual litany of delinquency charges — "ratchet-using," "gun-shooting" and, strangely, "bum-showing" (mooning). The rude boys, of course, are utterly unrepentant, sitting through the opening remarks, then responding, simply, "your honor . . . Rudies don't fear!"

The record was a massive success, the ultimate symbol of anti-authoritarian rebelliousness. But the rude boys would not be so cocky for long, as Prince Buster's "Judge Dread" stepped in where "Rougher than Rough" ended. Even rougher, even tougher, and proclaiming his presence with the announcement, "I am the rude boy now . . . and I DON'T CARE!", he then proceeded to live up to his nickname (and the song's subtitle) of Judge 400 Years, by sentencing everyone in sight to the most extended jail terms he could think of. Appeals for clemency were rewarded with an extra century in jail; and behind his harsh pronouncements, the barristers glumly chorused, "you're rough, you're tough. . . ."

It was only a record, but the real-life rudies were stunned.

They were the untouchables, above the law, beyond the law, and here was one of their own, the Prince himself, lyrically condemning them all to the slammer.

Immediately, other artists leaped to the defense of the Judge's victims. George Grabanflee, Adolphus James, Two Gun Tex and Zachariah Zakipon became instant folk heroes. Lee Perry appealed on their behalf with the plaintive "Set Them Free," Honeyboy Martin attacked the Judge with the magnificent "Dreader than Dread," while Derrick Morgan called for "The Retrial of Rudie." And Buster, astonished at the ludicrous uproar he created with one simple song, agreed to continue the saga himself with a new release, promisingly entitled "The Barrister," and credited to Appeal.

Few records, or real-life legal verdicts, come to that, were so eagerly awaited. The results of the rudies' pending appeal dominated street corner conversation, the wiles and ways of the rudie's defense team were conjectured in coffee bars, the imminent release of "the 400 Year Four" even made the radio news. But Buster had a surprise in store for everyone. Judge Dread wasn't about to be swayed by overwhelming public opinion. He jailed the barrister.

Again, the uproar was tremendous; more so, perhaps, than even Buster could stand. Or maybe he was simply bored with the whole surreal affair. Either way, a few weeks later he brought out the final installment in the drama, in which the Judge has a change of heart, summons the foursome back into court, turns on a record player, and they all dance the pardon. "Judge Dread Dance (the Pardon)" became one of Buster's biggest hits yet.

Once unleashed, however, the Judge himself was not going to prove so easy to escape from — if not for Buster, then certainly for the record buying public. Derrick Morgan even put Dread himself on trial in "Judge Dread in Court" during early summer, 1967, sentencing him to one million years imprisonment for impersonating a Judge.

Acting as judge, prosecutor and jury alike, Dread made an uncredited, but easily recognizable, appearance in Lloyd Dice and Mum's "Trial of Pama Dice" two years on, sentencing a rapist to a thousand years in jail. Almost a quarter of a century later, he reappeared on Mutabaruka's "People's Court," trying sundry local politicians for their crimes against humanity.

Young producers followed where the veterans led. Joe Gibbs, Bunny "Striker" Lee, former Skatalites road manager Ken Lack and Sonia Pottinger were names which came to dominate the late 1960s, as thoroughly as Reid and his rival Coxsone Dodd had the earlier years, all emerged as the rock steady boom flowered. Each had a stable of regular artists; each had personal techniques and visions which would power rock steady to even greater heights of success than ska.

Gibbs' work with the Pioneers, for example, is quintessential rock steady. Having knocked around the circuit for some five years before they met Gibbs and his then assistant Lee Perry, the group — at that time comprising Sidney Crooks and Jackie Robinson — scored an immediate #1 with the insistent "Gimme Some Loving." Other hits followed – "No Dope Me Pony," "Me Nah Go a Bellevue," "Catch the Beat" and "Mama Look Deh" (the rhythmic root of the Maytals' "Monkey Man") were all spectacular successes. But it was another of their earliest Gibbs efforts which set the stage for their greatest success, an ode to the champion racehorse Long Shot.

A Perry composition, "Long Shot" might have been forgotten had the horse himself not been tragically killed during a race meeting at Kingston's Caymanas Park. Now working with producer Leslie Kong, the Pioneers immediately mourned the horse's loss with "Long Shot Kick de Bucket," scoring a major hit both in Jamaica and the UK, and thrusting the rock steady beat into the headlines across Europe.

Yet rock steady's life was to prove even shorter than ska's. As early as spring, 1968, the first signs of a new dance began to rock the dance hall. Larry Marshall's "Nanny Goat," cut for Studio One, heralded the shift. Clancy Eccles and Lee Perry took it further with "Feel The Rhythm" and "Bangarang Crash." Now the Maytals were weighing in with a similar beat, but they had a name for it — the "reggay," and "Do the Reggay" became such a smash that within months, the new sensation had almost completely taken over.

Because reggay, or reggae, was more than a simple dance; more than a simple shift in the beat and the tempo — or, at least, it became more, which amounts to the same thing. Swiftly adopted as the generic name by which all past and future Jamaican musical forms would henceforth be grouped, reggae ushered in an era of unparalleled experimentation and untrammelled curiosity, an age in which the complex harmonies of one band and the jerking hyperactivity of another could fall side by side onto the turntable or off a compilation, and still be described by the same two syllables.

For much of the 1960s, through the protracted heyday of ska and the mercurial moment of rock steady, the studios had been churning out dance music. With the arrival of reggae, they started simply making music. The difference still shapes Jamaican music today.

Yet Jamaica's love affair with rock steady never really came to an end, even after reggae took hold of the island's affections. Veteran vocalists consistently revisited their old flames, escorting rocksteady classics back out on the town, garbed anew in the contemporary trappings of the day. But it was DJs who boomed in the Seventies, who had the most torrid relationship with the genre, toasting over the backing tracks from Treasure Isle jewels and Studio One gems. U-Roy, Big Youth, Dennis Alcapone, et al, all built their careers on rock steady classics. In the UK, Two Tone was equally enamored, while the third wave in the US spun off an entire sub-genre of trad bands, who pay homage to rock steady to this very day.

RECOMMENDED LISTENING

Jackpot of Hits/Explosive Rock Steady (Trojan—UK) 1997
Two classic Trojan label comps from 1967/68 on one CD, highlighting the best of Joe Gibbs' rock steady/reggae output. The Pioneers dominate, with Hugh Malcolm, the Versatiles, Roy Shirley and Cool Sticky picking up the slack, but there's really nothing wrong with that.

Rudies All Round (Trojan—UK) 1993
The ultimate rudies collection, rounding up 20 of the best records to even glance in that direction, from Alton Ellis to the Valentines, and two stray chapters (Derrick Morgan, Lee Perry) from the Judge Dread saga. The absence of Prince Buster (from this and virtually every other collection on earth) does compromise its authority somewhat, but there's enough else here to be getting on with.

Sir Lee's Rock Steady Party at Greenwich Farm (Jamaican Gold) 2000
Somewhat random, but generally satisfying selection of Bunny Lee's 1967–68 productions, avoiding many of the more obvious choices (the Uniques' "People Rock Steady" is an exception), but amply illustrating how the music was shifting again. Glen Adams' utterly infantile "S-H-I (I'm Shocking)" is a welcome find.

Top Rock Steady (Culture Press—France) 1992
Back to Treasure Isle for a 16 track collection of further Reid recordings, with backing this time by the Supersonics. The Melodians, the Techniques, the Paragons and the Silvertones are the star name attractions, but really, there's no need to play favorites.

The Trojan Tighten Up Box Set (Trojan) 2000
How many UK reggae fans got their first taste of action from the original vinyl *Tighten Up* albums? Between 1968–72, Trojan issued six volumes, this time charting both the hottest hits of the day and the way those hits were shifting the boundaries. Thus, though rock steady consumes a mere fraction of the total treat, anybody seeking a one-stop illustration of the shift into reggae will find *Tighten Up* a priceless purchase. Originally reissued across three separate CDs, and now available in a single box, the albums remain tiny time capsules, swinging from the sublime Nora Dean to ridiculous Beatles covers, and volumes 5 and 6 really aren't too exciting. The bulk of the rest, though, still sound sensational.

MAX ROMEO

STYLE *reggae (roots)*
BORN *Max Smith, 11/22/47 (St D'Acre, St James, JA)*

Max Romeo first came to international prominence with "Wet Dream" in May, 1969, a UK #10 hit which opened the floodgates for a veritable tide of rude reggae songs, despite being slapped with an absolute radio ban. Romeo himself denied any lyrical wrongdoing, insisting that the song documented his attempts to prop up a leaking roof while trying to convince a lady-friend that he didn't need any help ("lie down girl, let me push it up"). Few people were convinced.

Having left home when he was 14 to escape a disapproving step-mother, the young Max Smith was employed cleaning out the water canals in the sugar cane fields outside Clarendon, when he won a talent contest run by a local entrepreneur named Mr Denham. The teen promptly decided to try his luck in the music industry.

Moving to Kingston in 1965, he hooked up with singers Kenneth Knight and Lloyd Shakespeare as the Emotions. The trio undertook the usual tour of producers and studios, getting nowhere; meantime, Romeo found work as a record plugger for Ken "Calnek" Lack's Caltone label. With fairytale synchronicity, Lack then overheard Romeo singing to himself as he worked one day, and set up a full audition for the Emotions at WIRL Studios.

With the Lynn Taitt Band supplying inspired accompaniment, the session was a success — "(Buy You) a Rainbow," one of the songs recorded that day, became a national hit in 1966. Over the next two years, the Emotions maintained an impressive stream of 45s — "Rude Boy Confession," "I Don't Want to Let You Go" (credited to Romeo & The Emotions), "I Can't Do No More," "Heartbreaking Gypsy," "Careless Hands," "Soulful Music," "No Use to Cry," "Give Me Love," "Rum Baby" and "The Storm" among them.

Romeo quit the Emotions in 1968 (he was replaced by Milton Henry of the Leaders), around the same time as Caltone chief Lack emigrated to the US. The singer immediately began working with producer Bunny Lee at Studio One, cutting a sweet cover of "Twelfth of Never," the romantic "Walk into the Dawn" and "My One Girl," plus a song which, though none could have guessed at the time, was to predict the direction in which Romeo's career was most immediately set to move, the suggestive "Put Me in the Mood."

None of these was especially successful and, by the end of the year, Romeo had rejoined the Emotions. With producer Phil Pratt, another former Caltone artist, they cut further singles including "You Are the One," "Don't You Weep" and "Indeed I Love You."

Romeo also began working with the Hippy Boys, a Greenwich Farm-based band featuring members of the Gaylads singing group, plus Web Stewart (guitar) and the brothers Carlton and Aston Barrett. This line-up debuted on the Slim Smith single "Watch this Sound," a rendering of Buffalo Springfield's "For What It's Worth," before Stewart was replaced by Lorraine "Ronnie Bop" Williams and Alva Lewis. Organist Glen Adams also joined.

The group cut one single, "Dr No Go," for producer Sonia Pottinger. Before they could do much more, however, Romeo was suddenly diverted back to his solo career. (The remainder of the Hippy Boys went on to become Pottinger's house band, before joining Lee Perry's Upsetter clan. The Barretts subsequently joined the Wailers.)

In fact, Romeo's "big break" finally came courtesy of his day job, working as a record salesman for Bunny Lee. In late 1968, Romeo happened to be at the studio while Lee was trying to find a singer to voice a new lyric (which Romeo himself had written, but preferred not to sing) set to Derrick Morgan's "Hold You Jack" rhythm track. Morgan, John Holt and Slim Smith had already passed on it, and Lee finally called Romeo over and told him, in no uncertain terms, that if he didn't sing the song himself, he needn't come in for work the next day. The song was called "Wet Dream."

With the single climbing up the UK chart, and Romeo still denying it was in any way sexual (a plot he hatched with Equals guitarist Eddy Grant), the singer flew to London for a tour, only to find the controversy haunting him on the road as well. The Mecca chain of ballrooms banned him from appearing, and other clubs, too, balked at allowing him to sully their stages. Nevertheless, Romeo played a number of shows, accompanied by a local pick-up band, the Rudies, and ended up remaining in the UK for the next 18 months. (Towards the end of the visit, he replaced the Rudies with the fast rising Cimarrons.)

Once unleashed, Romeo's libido (or appetite for D-I-Y) knew no limits. He took the Beatles' "Sexy Sadie" title, but wrote an entirely new song, in which Sadie really is sexy. Recording with producer H Robinson, follow-ups to "Wet Dream" included "Mini Skirt Vision," "Fish in the Pot," "Belly Woman" and "Wine Her Goosie." Other tracks were recorded in London with Tony Pike — many of these were gathered up for the *A Dream* album.

Romeo returned to Jamaica in late 1970, launching his Romax label and sound system. The label folded after a mere handful of releases (Romeo sold it to Winston Riley) and, by mid-1971, he was working again with Bunny Lee. Utilizing some of the producer's best loved rock steady era rhythms, Romeo cut "Watch This Sound," "People Get Ready," "Fantastic Lover" and others. He also combined

Max Romeo, the master of rude reggae.

with Derrick Morgan for a fine version of the latter-day Emotions single, "Don't You Weep."

Over the next two years, recording with a variety of producers, Romeo's work represented some of the best roots on the scene — "Is It Really Over" and "Jordan River" (produced by Alvin Ranglin) and "Nobody's Child" (Winston Riley), "Pray for Me" (Sonia Pottinger), "Murder in the Place," the folk song "Chi Chi Bud," "Softie," "Words of Wisdom" and the outspoken "Maccabee Version," a Willie Francis-produced dismissal of the King James Bible, set to the mocking refrain of "Good King Wenceslas."

A fabulously productive union with Niney Holness saw Romeo cut "Beardman Feast," "The Coming of Jah" and the disparaging "Rasta Bandwagon," a commentary on the growing fashionableness, in musical circles, of a religious cult which had been virtually illegal a decade earlier. Another Niney-era track, "Babylon Burning," was co-written with both Holness and Lee Perry, and inaugurated what became Romeo's most significant relationship yet.

The strongest indication of Romeo's future intentions, however, was the Rastafarian spiritual "Let The Power Fall

on I," another Derrick Morgan production and one which utterly expunged the memory of "Wet Dream." As Jamaica braced itself for the upcoming (1972) general election and the firestorm of violence which would inevitably accompany it, "Let the Power Fall" was adopted as a campaign anthem by Michael Manley's socialist PNP party.

Romeo joined the PNP Musical Bandwagon, a traveling caravan of musicians which toured the countryside playing on the back of a flatbed truck (Bob and Rita Marley were also on-board). As the election loomed closer, Romeo's output was geared almost entirely towards his support of the party: "Press Along Joshua" (Manley's supporters' Old Testament name for the candidate), "Pharaoh" (targeted at the then incumbent Hugh Shearer of the conservative JLP party), "Rod of Correction" (Haile Selassie presented Manley with this very icon during his state visit to Jamaica in 1966), and the self-explanatory "Socialism Is Love."

Later in the year, following Manley's landslide victory, Romeo cut the admonitory "No Joshua No," a song reminding Manley not to forget the working class, ghetto and Rasta communities which had elected him — the politician later told Romeo that his entire social program of the next year was inspired by that song's advice.

Moving away from such overt politicism, Romeo maintained a stream of key 45s during 1973–76. "Word Sound Power" (produced by the soon-to-retire Prince Buster), "The Reverend" (Winston Riley) "Heads a Go Roll" (Azul), and "Cross Over the Bridge" (K Chin). A further string of intense 45s was also released via the fiercely roots-oriented Black World label, and were brought together in 1975 as the essential *Revelation Time* album.

A return to Bunny Lee saw the singles "We're Gonna Make It," "Natty Dread Take Over" and "Deacon Wife" released during 1975–76, but his most significant partnership debuted with 1975's "Three Blind Mice," recorded with Lee Perry.

"Sipple Out Deh," released in late 1975, prophesied war in Babylon — just weeks later, in January, 1976, Kingston burst into flame as the International Monetary Fund selected the city as the host for their annual meeting. From their high rise hotels in New Kingston, the delegates could see the ghettoes burn, while Prime Minister Manley, stunned at the ferocity of the rioting, convinced himself (not without reason) that the unrest was the handiwork of his political opponents. A seven P.M. curfew was established and troops were sent into the city. The police, however, pulled out, leaving great swathes of Kingston under mob rule.

Neither did the violence cease when the delegates left. With a general election looming, at which the current PNP government's socialist programs would be challenged by the JLP's increasingly bitter conservatism, Kingston burned for the remainder of the year, a conflagration which in turn fired further watchful Romeo singles, "One Step Forward" and "Fire fe the Vatican" and, most significantly of all, a remix of "Sipple Out Deh," succinctly retitled "War in a Babylon."

Later, Romeo revealed that he almost never got to record what became his biggest ever hit single. Bob Marley was visiting the Black Ark studio while Romeo and Perry were cutting the backing track, and was so taken by the song that he asked if he could have it for himself. In the liner notes to the Lee Perry box set *Arkology*, Romeo recalls, "I had to stand strong, otherwise it would become a Bob Marley song, even though it's mine."

[Finally] Scratch told him, 'give Max a break, let him keep it.' He could have taken it from me, I would have given it to him." Again according to Romeo, Marley contented himself by appropriating the rhythm for his own "3 Little Birds."

"War in a Babylon" became a massive hit; an album of the same title followed suit. But relations between Romeo and Perry crumbled soon after the album's release — they parted, prompting the producer to record "White Belly Rat" about his former friend, and inscribe the word "Judas" over a photograph of the singer which hung on the studio wall. Romeo, meanwhile, appeared at a loose end. He self-produced 1977's *Reconstruction* album, then departed Jamaica for the United States the next year.

Teaming with Michael Butler, producer of the stage show *Hair*, Romeo both wrote and appeared in a new, but short-lived Broadway musical, *Reggae*. He also encountered the Rolling Stones, joining them in the studio to add backing vocals to the song "Dance" on their 1979 *Emotional Rescue* album — Stones guitarist Keith Richard returned the favor by co-producing (with Geoffrey Chung and Earl Chin) Romeo's 1981 *Holding Out My Love to You* album.

Although he was one of the attractions at a Japanese reggae festival in 1984, Romeo drifted through much of the 1980s — at one point, he was working in an electronics store in New York. He did link with producer Lloyd Barnes to cut a pair of albums, but they passed by unnoticed. Finally Romeo returned to Jamaica in 1990, resumed touring and began recording more regularly. Visiting the UK in 1992, he linked with producer Jah Shaka for the albums *Far I Captain of My Ship* and *Our Rights*. Back in Jamaica, he recorded 1995's *Cross or the Gun* with Tappa Zukie, while 1999 saw British duo Mafia & Fluxy produce *Selassie I Forever*.

DISCOGRAPHY

6 A Dream (Trojan — UK) 1970

Unadulterated filth or schoolboyish humor, "Wet Dream" established Romeo as the king of rude reggae, a crown which this album does not dispute. His voice is already fully developed, sweet and tuneful and capable of imbibing the dumbest lyric with sincerity. But if you're approaching Romeo from his 70s peak, be ready for a shock.

8 Let the Power Fall (Dynamic — JA) 1972

His first classic, a politically charged collection which, remarkably, has lost none of its dread impact.

10 War in a Babylon (Island) 1976

One of producer Lee Perry's greatest achievements, the album is built around the smash hit title track, but other songs still hold their ground, "One Step Forward" and "Chase the Devil" amongst them. Unusually for Perry, it's Romeo's fabulous vocals that are allowed to dominate, not the producer's rhythms.

6 Reconstruction (Island) 1979
6 I Love My Music (Wackies) 1979
5 Rondos (King Kong — JA) 1980
6 Holding Out My Love for You (Shanachie) 1981

Sly & Robbie set the beat while Keith Richards flicks out the guitar licks (and co-produces) for this album of

"Nice'n'Easy" songs. There's few stand outs, but it's pleasant enough.

7 Far I Captain of My Ship (Jah Shaka — UK) 1992
7 Our Rights (Jah Shaka — UK) 1992

Shaka's production techniques don't suit all tastes, and his collaborations with Romeo fall beneath a similar caveat.

8 Cross or the Gun (Tappa Zukie) 1995

A superb return to form for Romeo, uniting with a producer who not only understands the singer's roots sensibilities, he's also capable of retrieving them. But this is no rootsy retro excursion — Zukie's comprehension of the modern studio is second to none, and *Cross or the Gun* ricochets with passion and punch.

7 Selassie I Forever (Mafia & Fluxy) 1999

SELECTED COMPILATIONS & ARCHIVE RELEASES

8 Revelation Time (Soundtrac — JA) 1975

An excellent round up of hits recorded between the slackness of "Wet Dreams" and the revolution of "War in a Babylon." A clutch of strong songs includes "Warning Warning," "Tacko" and the title track. Subsequently released in the US as *Open the Iron Gate*, within UA's ambitious Anthology of Reggae Collectors Series. The CD *Open the Iron Gate 1973–77* (Blood & Fire — UK, 1999) adds bonus tracks drawn from period singles. The 12-inch version of 1977's "Melt Away" is breathtaking.

6 Max Romeo Meets Owen Gray at King Tubby's Studio (Vista — UK) 1984

Mid-70s Bunny Lee productions divided one side apiece between Romeo and Gray.

7 The Many Moods of Max Romeo (Jamaica Gold — UK) 1991

20 track compilation drawing from 1967–71, with material ranging from an "extended" version of "Wet Dream," to more sedate selections — "Michael Row The Boat Ashore" and, incredibly, the Partridge Family's "I Woke Up in Love this Morning." Not the best work Romeo ever did, to be sure, but with a handful of Emotions cuts included, a representative sampling of his formative years.

8 Pray for Me: The Best of 1967–73 (Trojan — UK) 2000

Minimal duplication with the above means that two CDs essentially cover all the main bases from the period, with *Pray for Me* extending into the harder roots material of 1972–73. Fans of English reggae-punk band the Clash will find "Public Enemy #1" especially enlightening — the Brits' "Bank Robber" apparently took more than money.

ROOTS REGGAE

It was, and it remains, the heartbeat of reggae, the sound of Jamaica at her most militant, her most passionate and her most realistic. It was what Prince Buster was talking about when he christened his first sound system the Voice of the People; it was what Bob Marley was singing about when he wrote "Trench Town Rock"; it was the heartbeat which fired Sly & Robbie's earliest rhythm excursions and, throughout the 1970s, it was the sound, the lifestyle and the culture which Jamaica exported to the world — and by which, the world came to recognize the country.

Roots reggae is not a specific sound. Big Youth explained, "the people had had] enough of pure 'dibidibidabidoo' at the dances, without some alternative that represent how they feel" — feelings, Bob Marley continued, which emerged as "blessed reggae . . . when you deal with reality. You get more music, more anything. You feel dirt, the earth, and you play any way, you feel it different from just thinking about it."

It is an attitude, then, one which is informed by every aspect of the lives of its makers; the sound of the ghetto and, as such, its most common themes are rooted in either the struggle of the sufferers or in their aspirations. Rastafarianism, almost by definition the religion of the downtrodden, supplies the symbolism, but everyday life provides the mood and the momentum of the music. And when the two come together, there is not a power on earth which can hold them back.

That combination, of course, was as old as "modern" Jamaican music itself. Of all the flashpoints which determined the birth of ska, Prince Buster's recruitment of Rastafarian drummer Count Ossie Williams on the Folkes Brothers' seminal "Oh Carolina," in 1961, certainly ranks among the most shattering, not only for its musical importance, but for its cultural impact as well. Rastas were outcasts, wildmen who lived in the hills, practicing a religion which had no place in "modern" society. Of course their music was outcast too.

But Buster opened the door, and nobody was willing to close it again. By the time the Rastafarian figurehead, Ethiopian Emperor Haile Selassie, paid his state visit to Jamaica in 1966, both the religion and the criminally absurd lengths which the government went to repress it were out in the open. It is ironic, then, that the visit itself was intended to try and crush Rastafarianism — the government believed that if the Emperor himself told his followers that he was not immortal, they would disband. In fact, they simply ignored his declamation, both at the time and following his death a decade later.

During the second half of the 1960s, both the Rastafarian religion and the cultural stance which its adherents adopted were a common source of lyrical inspiration, without ever impacting upon the musical presentation itself. Ska, rock steady and the early days of reggae remained musical forms designed for the dances which named them, no matter what the content of the song itself.

When Coxsone Dodd refused to release the Abyssinians' "Satta Amasa Gana" after they recorded it in March, 1969, he was not reacting to its Rastafarian sentiments. He was simply obeying the commercial common sense which had guided him through ten years of recording success.

The new decade, however, unfolded around a wholly different landscape, one in which the music could be made of, and for, itself. For the first time, bands were forming who were not willing to remain beholden to the producers for their music, their ideas, their very identity; for the first time, autonomy was not another word for "don't forget to close the door on your way out." Not that every band who demanded artistic freedom was actually given it, of course — even the Wailers were ultimately bound to decisions made by executive producer Chris Blackwell. But, again for the first time, records were now being judged on their musical values, not how much sense they made on the dancefloor.

The then still-unreleased "Satta Amasa Gana" notwithstanding, the first record to truly open up the possibilities inherent in roots music was "Blood and Fire," the first hit for producer Niney "The Observer" Holness. Of course you could dance to it if you wanted, but how much better to listen to it, absorb it, and to lose oneself within its almost operatic panorama of armageddon. Blood and fire indeed.

"Blood and Fire" became one of the biggest hits of 1970 and, across a chain reaction of similarly themed dubs and versions, one of the most crucial of the entire decade. Likewise, Holness' work — as both producer and collaborator — with such artists as Dennis Alcapone, Max Romeo, Big Youth and Lee Perry ensured that further contributions to the theme from other performers found similarly fertile ground.

As early as 1972, Holness and Romeo were decrying the tidal wave of "false Rastas" suddenly sweeping the landscape. By 1976, even their most vociferous protests were swamped beneath a worldwide clicking of knitting needles (red, gold and green woollen hats a specialty) and the anguished twistings of blonde and ginger dreadlocks.

Yet, although Rastafarianism remained the outside world's most potent image of roots, by no means were the music's own greatest practitioners themselves practicing Rastas. Indeed, Vivian "Yabby You" Jackson, author of 1972's classic "Conquering Lion," was a Christian, militantly pointing out across a stream of truly dramatic records that many of the attributes and icons which Rastafarianism applied to Haile Selassie, were just as applicable to Jesus Christ.

Religion played a crucial role in roots music, of course. But simple consciousness was of considerably greater importance, an awareness of the iniquities of modern life, and a burning desire to see them changed. It is no coincidence that musicologists, at least, date the first stirrings of roots as a definable power to the early 1970s, and their peak to the middle of the decade. 1970 saw the Caribbean's inherited sense of law, order, decency and class utterly racked by the Black Power movement, with T&T in particular torn by rioting and terrorism.

Jamaica escaped the more vicious manifestations of the movement, largely through the ministrations of Michael Manley, leader of the opposition People's National Party, and son of Norman Manley, one of the founding fathers of an independent Jamaica. As the 1972 election campaign loomed, Manley went out of his way to appeal to the island's ghetto communities, a policy which helped assure his eventual victory, but which also led to scenes of frightening violence and street fighting as the campaign approached its climax.

These scenes were to be repeated during the run-up to the 1976 vote. Violent crime was rife, violent death was epidemic and, through it all, roots — indeed, the grassroots — maintained a perpetual soundtrack for what was happening on the streets: celebratory in 1972, as the upstart PNP swept to power on a tide of social reform; fearful in 1976 as Edward Seaga's JLP transformed ballots into battle.

It was in the last days of the 1976 election campaign that Bob Marley only narrowly escaped assassination, with his assailants almost certainly politically motivated. It was during that same period of fearful uncertainty that the roots band Culture debuted with the premonitory forebodings of "Two Sevens Clash," the record which, more than almost any other (Junior Murvin's "Police and Thieves" can also take a bow) finally alerted the outside world to what was happening.

The international attention paid to Marley and Peter Tosh furthered roots music's chokehold on the imagination. The sequence of Wailers albums book-ended by *Catch a Fire* and *Live*, then furthered by Tosh's *Legalise It*, was many listeners' first introduction to reggae — it became, therefore, the yardstick by which all subsequent acts would be measured.

Equally influential and, therefore, defining, was the emergent Anglo-American punk rock movement's almost familial identification with the roots scene. In London, the Clash did roots immeasurable service when they covered, in quick succession, Murvin's "Police and Thieves," the Maytals' "Pressure Drop" and Willie Williams' "Armagideon Time"; in New York, Patti Smith equated Tappa Zukie with James Brown, and gave his debut album a belated US outlet via her own Mer label.

Again in London, Rastafarian DJ Don Letts introduced an entire generation to his homeland's music when he began spinning at the punk mecca Roxy Club in January,

1977. No more than a handful of punk bands had actually released any records yet, so he played roots instead, sensing — as his audience would soon, similarly, sense — that though the musical styles were different, the sentiments behind them really weren't. Less than a year after the Roxy opened, Jamaican teens Althea and Donna scored a UK #1 hit with the sassy belligerence of "Uptown Top Ranking."

Similarly, just as Britain's skinhead culture had kept rock steady alive on those shores long after it was supplanted by reggae in Jamaica, so the punks enabled roots to exist even after the dance hall explosion of the late 1970s/early 1980s drew Jamaica's attention away — exist and thrive. By the early 1980s, the defiantly roots-based Black Uhuru were arguably as big as the Wailers had ever been, with the rhythm section of Sly & Robbie considered a guarantee of quality whoever they were working with.

Some bands, those with international record deals and a reputation to match, shifted their musical focus away from their homeland and made music which itself conformed to the international expectations of roots. Other, treading in the footsteps which those acts left behind them, relocated bodily to the US and Europe, there to acquaint themselves personally with an audience whose appetite for the music was still being whetted when Jamaica itself had decided to stop making it.

Some of these — Culture and Israel Vibration among them — became full time expatriates and devoted themselves to helping their adopted homeland's roots scene develop. Others — Wailing Souls, Horace Andy, Johnny Osbourne and Tappa Zukie among them — eventually returned to Jamaica, to find their passions were not so far removed from the local mainstream, after all.

Indeed, the rash of mid-1990s Rastafarian conversions which swept through the dance hall and ragga movements has since seen Buju Banton, Capleton and so many more espouse sentiments, and make music, which really is not that different from those their musical forebears had embraced, 15 years and so many musical convolutions before.

RECOMMENDED LISTENING

KEITH HUDSON Rasta Communication (Joint—JA) 1978

Moody, melancholic, yet still defiant, *Rasta* communicates via a deliciously atmospheric rockers style, with minor key melodies beautifully complementing Hudson's dark lyrics.

MIGHTY DIAMONDS Deeper Roots (Front Line—UK) 1979

Find the 1997 CD reissue, which appends the original album with its dub counterpart, cut from vinyl but still sounding amazing. The Diamonds' most commercial album is not necessarily their best; it does, however, sum up the state of roots at the end of the period, with the first hints of the latest instrumentation easing into the expected elements, while the Diamonds' ever enchanting voices float unfettered over the stew.

YABBY YOU Jesus Dread 1972–77 (Blood & Fire) 1997

47 tracks (two-CDs) spotlighting both Yabby You's own recordings and those he produced, a solid examination of one of the most extraordinary catalogs in the roots canon. You's personal philosophies are evident, but don't enter into the musical equation, which remains brain-charringly heavy, stirring, hard and combative. As the (excellent) liner notes proclaim, "one dread, who shall remain nameless, remarked at the time — 'this makes all the others sound like the Osmonds'."

VARIOUS ARTISTS

Countryman (Island) 1982

VARIOUS ARTISTS

Rockers (Island) 1979

The best contemporary summaries of the era available on single discs, these two soundtracks cover all the musical bases, from the lightweight pop of Inner Circle to the heavy roots of Junior Byles, the instrumental virtuosity of the Rockers All-Stars to the gorgeous harmonies of vocal trios the Maytones, the Maytals, the Heptones, and Justin Hinds and the Dominoes.

Countryman is extremely Bob Marley heavy, although its cherrypicking of different eras ensures a deeply spiritual vibe to go along with Wally Badarou's so-evocative theme — "Rastaman Chant," "Natural Mystic" and "Jah Lives" are especial highlights in this context. Other stand-outs include contributions by Britain's Steel Pulse and Aswad.

The *Rockers* movie's themes, meanwhile, are hammered home by Junior Murvin's "Police and Thieves," Jacob Miller's "Tenement Yard" and Gregory Isaacs' "Slave Master," while Burning Spear, Kiddus I's "Graduation in Zion" and Third World's take on "Satta Amasa Gana" promote the Rastafarian message. Finally Bunny Wailer's theme song and Peter Tosh's "Stepping Razor" are each worth the price of admission alone.

VARIOUS ARTISTS

Roots Reggae Essentials (Hip-O) 2000

Quite possibly, the closest to perfection any single disc could get. Of course it's a fairly obvious selection, but who wants obscure essentials? Third World, Black Uhuru, the Wailers, Johnny Clarke, the Abyssinians, Burning Spear, Max Romeo, the Congos, Dillinger, the Maytals, Junior Murvin — there's neither a misplaced act in sight nor a wrong song . . . okay, Jacob Miller's "Tenement Yard" may have the edge over the featured "Healing of the Nation," but hands up who thinks that the former is just a little bit too glib?

VARIOUS ARTISTS

Trojan Roots Box Set (Trojan—UK) 1999

Considering the Trojan label was out of action for much of the key roots period, this three-CD/50 track collection skips over the gap with admirable ease, reminding us just how much great roots was being made on either side of the mid-70s peak. Some surprising inclusions turn out to be well-chosen; some surprising omissions seem not to matter, and with almost every track drawn from either out of print 45s or compilations, it's well worth investigation.

MICHAEL ROSE see BLACK UHURU

DAVID RUDDER

STYLE *calypso/soca*
BORN 5/6/53 *(Belmont, T&T)*

A much loved actor—he starred in the TV series *Sugar Cane Arrows*; a respected artist—he has worked with some of T&T's most accomplished craftsmen, including Peter Minshall, a designer for the Barcelona and Atlanta Olympics; and one of T&T's most respected musicians; David Rudder has also positioned himself as one of calypso's most outspoken performers—who is, simultaneously, one of those who are most listened to.

Seriously concerned with T&T's place in the Caribbean, and the Caribbean's place in the wider world, Rudder has written and recorded some of the most ambitious music in the entire modern soca genre — admirers have compared his depth and honesty to such icons of rock'n'roll protest as Bob Dylan, Bruce Springsteen and U2 and, in his homeland, his popularity is at least equal to theirs.

One of nine children, Rudder discovered music at the age of 11, while attending parochial school, when he joined a band called the Solutions. A number of influences took hold of Rudder: the sound of the pan yards which dotted his childhood environs: the Shango Baptist church into which he was baptized by his grandmother (interestingly, Rudder was baptized three times, by his grandmother, as an Anglican by his mother, and as a Catholic by his school), and the jazz and African musics towards which his own listening habits gravitated. Still he did not move seriously into entertainment until his early 20s; in 1977, he joined the brass band Charlie's Roots, while serving as an apprentice to carnival craftsman Ken Morris.

Now working as an accountant for the Trinidad bus company, Rudder started singing back-up in Lord Kitchener's calypso tent in the early 1980s. He might have remained behind the scenes, too, had Charlie's Roots vocalist Christopher "Tambu" Herbert not fallen ill following a tour of Guyana. Herbert suggested that Rudder—already the band's regular songwriter—take the lead while he recuper-

ated, and the novice quickly developed such a presence and reputation that when Herbert returned, Rudder remained co-lead vocalist with the group. (Herbert went onto a trio of late 1980s Road March triumphs, before becoming a regular challenger in the Soca Monarch competition.) In 1985, Rudder's revision of the Mighty Killer's 1950 Road March champion, "In a Calabash" (retitled "Calabash") finished third in the Road March competition. The following year, he became one of the few artists ever to win Young King, Panorama and the overall Carnival Monarch titles in the same year.

His winning songs are now carnival mainstays—"The Hammer" was a tribute to the recently deceased Trinidadian pannist Rudolph Charles; "Bahia Girl," was the story of a Brazilian girl who brought the message of a shared musical heritage to T&T. Performing that song at the Queen's Park Savannah, Rudder brought the entire crowd to its feet—watching journalist Angela Fox of the local *Weekly Superstar* marveled, "not since 30,000 Trinis raised their hands chanting "We Pope" at the National Stadium has anyone received such an ovation."

Rudder's first album, also titled *The Hammer*, followed, and soon received further attention when "The Hammer" itself became the title track to American jazz-man Andy Narell's 1987 hit album. 1987 brought Rudder's *Calypso Music* album; the Desperadoes' arrangement of his "Panama" finished third at Panorama in 1988; and 1989 saw his US major label (Sire) debut, *Haiti*. It was 1991's *1990* which brought him his next major success, however; dedicated to the people of South Africa, the album was adjudged Best Calypso album of the year at the first annual Caribbean Music Awards held at the Apollo Theatre in New York. The song "1990," meanwhile, won Song of the Year at the Nafeita Awards.

Further triumphs awaited his follow-up, *Rough and Ready*, which scooped three Sunshine Awards; while 1992's *Frenzy* spawned "Knock Them Down," written as a light hearted commentary on the Gulf war, but swiftly adapted as the official theme song for the Cable & Wireless-sponsored International Cricket Competition. Another cut, "Hoosay," dealt with the attempted coup which shook T&T in 1990, and prompted University professor and calypso expert Gordon Rohlehr to describe Rudder as "a mighty poet of a shallow people in a savage time. In this calypso, Rudder is at his most metaphorical, his most oblique."

Rudder's success continued to grow. His next album *Ministry of Rhythm* emerged one of the biggest hits in years at carnival, and few could believe it when "Dust in Yuh Face" failed to sweep the Road March. It did, however, take third place at Panorama, thanks to spirited performances by both Exodus and the Trinidad All Stars.

1994's *Here Comes the West Indies* album was another major hit. But it was 1995's *Lyrics Man* which finally shattered the records Rudder had been gnawing at. The biggest selling carnival album of all time, it also unleashed one of the greatest hits ever, the vicious political satire "The Ballad of Hulsie X." Even more gratifyingly, the song looked to traditional calypso for its influence and impetus, rather than any of the newer strains and hybrids.

The concept album *Tales from a Strange Land* followed in 1996; it was Rudder's most ambitious set yet, but it was also to prove one of his most disillusioning. He had long since grown accustomed to local radio's penchant for playing just one or two songs from a new album, but had hoped that the elaborate tapestry woven into *Strange Land* might encourage DJs to investigate deeper.

Of course they didn't (although "The Disappearing Panyard" took third place at Panorama), so Rudder decided to take an wholly different course for his next release. *Wrapped in Plain Brown Paper* featured just five tracks. Radio obstinately concentrated on one, "The Strange Tale of Motilal and the Miami Mountain."

Recorded live over September 6–7, 1996, at the Jean Pierre Complex in Port of Spain, the triple CD *No Restriction* in 1997 returned Rudder to the world of grandiose gestures. Featuring guest appearances from the Lydian Singers, Ella Andall, Andre Tanker and the Mighty Shadow, the concert was an absolute spectacle, and the accompanying CD (and video) lost none of that glory.

No Restriction rounded out the first decade of Rudder's career; he launched the second with the transitional *Beloved*, before unveiling *International Chantuelle*. 1998 also saw Rudder's "High Mas" win the Panorama at Carnival.

2000 brought Rudders' *Zero* album, a set which ranged from Algerian rai to British-East Indian bhangra in search of textures, and he also produced Carol Jacobs' well-received *Family*. He embarked upon a US tour at year's end, then returned home to create his second concept set, *Autobiography of a Now*.

DISCOGRAPHY

7 The Hammer (—T&T) 1986

8 Calypso Music (—T&T) 1987

The sensational title track is joined by "Dedication," a tribute to the steelpan; the party pop groove "Madness" and "Song for a Lonely Soul," a longing slice of nostalgia written from the point of view of a homesick ex-pat, finally returning home.

6 Haiti (Sire) 1989

Despite its title, a study of T&T's own place in the modern Caribbean world, packed with hits—"Bacchanal Lady," "Engine Room" (a history of pan), "Rally Round the West Indies" (for the area cricket team) and a cover of Shadow's "One Love" were the fun side of things; "Haiti" castigated society for its refusal to offer more assistance to that island.

7 1990 (Sire) 1991

A companion to the similarly themed *New Day Dawning* set, which itself features alternate versions of several of the *1990* tracks, Rudder's first concept album traces the history and hoped-for repression of racism in South Africa, interspersed with a gloomy outlook for his own region (the initials "IMF" are hijacked for "Islands Must Fail"). Musically, it is just as thoughtful, combining calypso and Afrobeat to remarkably emotive effect.

6 Rough and Ready (Lypsoland—T&T) 1991

8 Frenzy (Lypsoland—T&T) 1992

"As much as I scream, the rock guitar dominates," Rudder announces in "Feeding Frenzy." But rock doesn't get a look in on his most spectacular album, a set which runs from the moody foreboding of "Hoosay" to the joyous "Long Time Past," a celebration of carnival's history.

9 Ministry of Rhythm (Lypsoland—T&T) 1992

Rudder's vision of the future, western pop clashing with its Caribbean counterparts in a fashion which went way beyond the shallow pronouncements of the world music crowd, exceeded, too, the briefs offered up by the practitioners of soca and ringbang. Espousing a truly universal sound, *Ministry of Rhythm* includes the awesome "Department of Percussive Energy," alongside "Caribbean Party," "Potato" and "LA."

7 Here Come the West Indies (Lypsoland—T&T) 1993

7 Lyrics Man (Lypsoland—T&T) 1994

8 Tales from a Strange Land (Ritual—T&T) 1995

Convoluted, but passionate, concept album, somewhere between a Sherlock Holmes novel ("The Case of the Disappearing Panyards") and weird existentialism ("The Secret Wife of Plants"), but all adding up to a broodingly kaleidoscopic examination of modern T&T society.

5 Wrapped in Plain Brown Paper (—T&T) 1996

9 No Restriction—The Concert (—T&T) 1997

If you only buy one Rudder album, this triple live set will do nicely. Utterly career spanning, and packed out with such extras as a lyric book, an interview (closing disc three) and every major song from a decade's worth of recording, it also serves as the model for what a Rudder box set should include. Spellbinding.

7 Beloved (JWP—T&T) 1998

8 International Chantuelle (JWP—T&T) 1998

A deeply Afrobeat flavored album which included Rudder's tributes to Nigerian band leader Fela Kuti, "I Remember Fela" and "Fela's Jam."

7 Zero (JWP—T&T) 2000

7 The Autobiography of the Now (JWP—T&T) 2001

Rudder returns to concept land, but if his last visit left him filled with wonder, the vista this time is vividly vicious, an urban hellscape where "Prelude To Chaos" is indeed the prelude to a filth-encrusted "Jerusalem," "41 Bullets," "Bigger Pimping". . . towards the end, however, "I'd Rather Be in Trinidad" doesn't quite convince the listener that he isn't already there.

SELECTED COMPILATIONS & ARCHIVE RELEASES

7 Greatest Hits (—T&T) 1990

Wrapping up the early years, through to 1990 itself. Rudder's vision remains formative, but hindsight marvels at his power.

7 Gilded Collection Vol 1 (CR—T&T) 1993

8 Gilded Collection Vol 2 (Rituals—T&T) 1996

Volume One reissues *Greatest Hits*; Volume Two brings the saga up to date. The emphasis remains on the carnival hits, of course, but Rudder has never been afraid to speak his mind, even at the height of a party.

GARNETT SILK

STYLE *reggae (dance hall)*

BORN *Garnett Damoin Smith, 4/2/66 (Manchester JA); d 12/9/94 (Mandeville, JA)*

Jamaica awoke on December 10, 1994, to the news that one of the island's most promising young stars, Garnett Silk, had died alongside his mother in an explosion at their home. It was a tragic end to a career which, though still in its infancy, had already seen the singer applauded with a passion unseen since the heyday of Bob Marley. That such a yardstick had, elsewhere around the world, become something of a cliche was immaterial — in Britain and the US, *any* successful new Jamaican would inevitably be compared to Marley. Jamaica, however, was more discerning.

Beginning as a 12-year-old going by the name Little Bimbo, Silk spent much of the 1980s DJ-ing for the sound systems Soul Remembrance, Pepper's Disco, Stereophonic and Destiny Outernational. It was there he first met fellow Manchester-born DJ Tony Rebel, along with such other notables as Uton Green, Culture Knox and Everton Blender.

Although Little Bimbo recorded at least one song in 1985, "Ram Dance Master," it was two years before he cut his first single, "Problem Everywhere," with producer Delroy Collins — an album's worth of material from this period subsequently appeared as *Journey*. The following year, he was scooped up by Sugar Minott's Youth Promotion label, for whom he cut "No Disrespect."

There he reunited with Tony Rebel, then the mouthpiece of the Youth Promotion sound system, and the pair began touring the dance halls together, Silk now billed as Bimbo alone. (It was Rebel and another close friend, dub poet Yasus Afari, who introduced the young DJ to Rastafarianism).

In 1989, veteran vocalist and producer Derrick Morgan suggested that Bimbo give up DJ-ing in favor of singing, taking the duo into Bunny Lee's studio, and recording a clutch of songs individually, as a team and in tandem with Anthony Selassie. Reverting to his given name, Garnett Smith, Silk cut a version of "Killing Me Softly" which singlehandedly justified Morgan's confidence in his abilities.

Silk moved on, working with producers King Tubby, Prince Jammy and Donovan Germain ("Lionheart") among others, before signing a two year contract with Steely & Clevie in 1990. It was they who changed his name to Garnett Silk, in reference, of course, to his voice; they, too, who captured Silk's natural resemblance to Horace Andy with his now legendary version of "Skylarking." Although an entire album was recorded, just one track actually found release, a duet with Chevelle Franklin, "We Can Be Together." By the end of the year, a disillusioned Silk had returned to his hometown.

He spent the next year writing, usually in partnership with childhood friend Anthony Rochester, before Tony Rebel resurfaced and introduced Silk to Courtney Cole, a producer and studio owner based in Ocho Rios. A clutch of singles followed, including "Mama," "Seven Spanish Angels" and a massive hit version of Johnny Nash's "I Can See Clearly Now."

In 1992, producer Bobby Digital brought Silk back to Kingston to record the album *It's Growing*, a powerful redefinition of roots music and one of the best selling albums of the year. He continued freelancing, of course, both solo and with Tony Rebel — 1992's "Christian Soldiers" was a major hit, while other sessions paired him with producers Richard "Bello" Bell ("Hey Mama Africa" — Silk's first international hit, which topped the UK reggae chart); King Jammy ("Fill Us with Your Mercy," "Lord Watch Over Our Shoulders"), and Black Scorpio ("Zion in a Vision").

Other releases during this period drew upon the stockpile of material he'd recorded three years earlier, a frustrating situation, but a gratifying one too. For a time, you could not turn on RJR without hearing Silk, while two compilation albums, *Gold* and *Nothing Can Divide Us*, offered new fans an exquisite glimpse into this new hero's past.

Silk, in the meantime, retreated again after being taken ill during a show at the New York Ritz. Rumors of drink and drug abuse abounded — in fact, he was suffering from low blood pressure and exhaustion. Cancelling all outstanding shows, including his Reggae Sumfest debut, he remained out of circulation for the next six months.

Silk re-emerged in early 1994, signed with the Ocho Rios-based Karlang Productions and, reunited with Steely and Clevie, hit the charts with "Love Is the Answer." "Fight Back," cut with Richie Stephens, followed and, that summer, he headlined both Reggae Sumfest and Reggae Sunsplash. The singer then signed with Atlantic Records for international distribution and began work on his second album with producer Errol Brown.

At least ten new songs were recorded with an all-star band including Aston Barrett (bass), Sly & Robbie, Tyrone Downie (keyboards), Earl "Chinna" Smith (guitar), and Uziah "Sticky" Thompson (percussion). The sessions, however, were never completed and the album remained unreleased until 2000.

According to reports in the Jamaican press, Silk's home had recently been burgled, and he borrowed two guns from his attorney as protection. While a friend was demonstrating how the weapons worked, one discharged accidentally, the bullet puncturing a nearby gas tank used for cooking. Flames erupted from the tank and, though Silk, his two brothers and two friends escaped, the singer returned to the burning building to rescue his mother. Both died.

Among the many tributes which followed, one of the finest saw Macka B and Mad Professor create the simple but touching "Tribute to Garnett Silk" on B's *Hold onto Your Culture* (1995).

DISCOGRAPHY

10 It's Growing (VP—US) 1992

This is it, the one and only. Who can say what Silk would have turned into, how far he could have gone . . . the Atlantic recordings (released years later) give a lot of hints, but the best taste of Silk's magic remains here, heard in the context which he intended, and tied to a time he understood. With such gems as "I Am Vex," "Bless Me," "Place in Your Heart," and a voice of supreme clarity and beauty, there's not a dull moment in sight.

SELECTED COMPILATIONS & ARCHIVE RELEASES

7 Gold (Charm—UK) 1993

Handy multi-producer set wraps up most of Silk's most important pre-Digital 45s plus "Nothing Can Divide Us."

6 Love is The Answer (VP) 1994

After four years in the vault, the Steely & Clevie tapes, including Silk's masterful interpretation of Horace Andy's "Skylarking."

6 Lord Watch Over Our Shoulders (Greensleeves—UK) 1994

"Babylon Be Still," "Zion in a Vision" and "Let Them Talk," cut with Frankie Paul, are the ones to watch for.

7 Tony Rebel Meets Garnett Silk in a Dance Hall Conference (Heartbeat) 1994

The perfect dance hall mash, the pair open with their own tracks, come together in the middle and then separate for more solos. Besides two versions of Silk's "Killing Me Softly," there's a clutch of slamming dance tracks, the inspirational duet of "Help the Poor and Needy," a pair of songs about girls and many more on cultural themes. Still sporting the clipped delivery of the dance hall, the glory of Silk's vocals are nevertheless self evident. Seven latter day dubs close the album.

7 Nothing Can Divide Us (VP) 1995

Rounding up Silk's earliest recordings for Courtney Cole's Roof International Label, the set includes a clutch of hit singles such as "Seven Spanish Angels" and "Mama," as well as the magnificent "Lord Watch Over Our Shoulders," all of which exhibited a maturity and style that portended his rise to stardom.

5 Journey (VP) 1996

Early Delroy Collins-produced DJ sides, fascinating from an historical point of view, but somewhat disconcerting if you're expecting him to sing for you. "Problems Everywhere," Silk's debut single, is included.

8 Live at Reggae Sunsplash 1994 (Tabou) 1999

With so many compilations around (this discography features less than half of them!), another greatest hits set is probably the last thing you need—right? Wrong. Live, Silk brings an entirely new complexion to even the most familiar songs, delivering one of the essential live albums of the last decade.

7 Garnett Silk Meets the Conquering Lion: A Dub Plate Selection (Conquering Lion) 2000

Raw and bleeding as only a great dub plate can be, cut for the Conquering Lion sound system in a galvanized metal studio in the Mandeville hills, this collection of exclusive recordings from the mid-late 1980s catches the formative Silk at his roughest.

8 The Definitive Garnett Silk (Atlantic) 2000

Two-CD set at last unveils the doomed second album, padded out with ten earlier hits. Highlighted by the low key "Your Time Has Expired," the ten Atlantic cuts, of course, are the main point of interest, and it is gratifying to discover that the majority pack all the vibrant energy and melody for which Silk was renowned (and his voice was intended). The production, on the other hand, is wholly a child of its early-mid 1990s time, meaning it's impossible to listen with the open, excited ears which would have greeted them then. Oddly, the CD is credited to a misspelled Garnet Silk.

SINGING SANDRA

STYLE *calypso/soca*
BORN *Sandra DesVignes (East Dry River, T&T)*

The teenaged Singing Sandra initially appeared on the international calypso scene with her victory in the 1987 National Calypso Queen competition. It was the first in a chain of honors (1992 Carifesta Monarch, 1992 Calypso Queen of the World, etc) which culminated in her being crowned Calypso Monarch at Carnival 1999, with "Song for Healing" and "Voices from the Ghetto."

The latter was a subject she was well qualified to sing about. Born in the East Dry River area, raised in Morvant, and schooled in Laventville, "real ghetto," as she put it, Sandra left school at 15 and took a number of low paying jobs just to keep the family afloat.

Her musical talents were apparent from childhood. A singer at Sunday school, she played the part of King Kong in a Best Village tribute to the Mighty Sparrow. Indeed, it was the Best Village competitions — designed to encourage rural communities to stage theatrical presentations — which gave Sandra her first professional opportunities. For three years running during her teens, she won the title of Best Actress and, while she also scooped Best Female Chantuelle and Best Calypsonian, her own early aspirations lay in acting.

That changed in 1984 when calypsonian Dr Zhivago contacted her with two songs which he wanted to be sung by a woman, "Pan for Independence" and "The Raper Man Comin'." The following year, she was recruited to the cast of the Mighty Sparrow's Young Brigade tent. It was Sparrow who told her she might not become the next Calypso Rose, but she was certainly going to run the queen mighty close, a prediction which was not long in bearing its first fruit, as Sandra's 1987 Calypso Queen title demonstrated.

Not that her triumph was without controversy. Although the likes of Baron, Mighty Sparrow and David Rudder have all turned to outside sources for new material on occasion (Winsford Devine and Gregory Ballantyne rank among calypso's best known non-performing writers), Sandra did not write any of her own material, relying instead upon Zhivago, Tobago Crusoe (the 1983 Calypso Monarch) and government attorney Christophe Quasar-Grant.

But while traditionalists insist that a truly great calypsonian must be able to produce self-composed material, all three of Sandra's writers agree that the partnership is truly collaborative. Quasar-Grant has called her the queen of the ad-libbers, acknowledging that though she might not change a word of the song, she brings an indefinable uniqueness to every performance, one which the writer could never have envisaged.

In 1992, Singing Sandra emerged a surprise highlight of Reggae Sunsplash, a triumph which she followed by forming the singing group United Sisters, with Lady B, Tigress and Marvellous Marva. Theirs' was an incredibly provocative act — for the calypso "Four Women to One Man," the quartet donned color co-ordinated lingerie, then leaped into the audience in search of suitable male partners. They also assaulted the traditions of carnival with the plaintive "Why Can't a Woman Win a Road March" and, in 1993, came close to proving that one could, with the party smash "Whoa Donkey." (It was beaten out by Superblue's "Bacchanal Time").

Sandra continued her solo career throughout this period, her militant stance and combat fatigues stagewear a stunning corollary to the Sisters' super-sexy routines, while calypsos such as "Sexy Employers" placed her firmly in the vanguard of carnival's feminist lobby — the song dealt with sexual harassment in the workplace. Her grasp on social concerns, meanwhile, was honored at Carnival 1997, when she received a $5,000 prize for "One Destiny One Heart," adjudged the Best Nation Building Song.

Beating out Sugar Aloes and Gypsy for the 1999 Calypso Monarch title was the peak of Sandra's career to date, her triumph coming with a moving rendition of Christopher Grant's "Voices from the Ghetto." According to news reports, she wept uncontrollably for 15 minutes after the results were announced.

Sandra was a firm favorite to retain her crown in 2000, she herself claimed that the only way she could fail was, if she didn't bother turning up. In the event, "True True Colors" and "Caribbean Man Part Two" (an extension of Black Stalin's "Caribbean Man") placed third behind Shadow and the unequivocally named Original De Fosto Himself. She finished fifth in 2001.

SELECTED DISCOGRAPHY

7 Voices from de Ghetto (—T&T) 1999

Includes the full 8 majestic minutes "Voices from the Ghetto," plus "Soca Boat" and "Oh Trinidad." The title track is the stand-out, although every track showcases a remarkable voice and an unexpected grasp of rapso ("Rapso Explosion").

SKA

Turf wars . . . stand aside.

In one corner, Ernest Ranglin, graying and well past retirement age, but still playing guitar like a-ringing-a-bell . . . recalling the shuffle boogie R&B records he was making in the early-mid 1950s, "and that's where the ska beat came in. With the shuffle rhythm we could formulate a ska beat from it. The second beat is much more emphasized."

In another corner, Prince Buster, a brash and brawny ex-boxer, remembering how Ranglin, Arthur "Duke" Reid and Clement "Sir Coxsone" Dodd were still messing around with American music, "So I had to design a new musical sound, something that was nothing to do with America.

They didn't think it was good music at all, they scorned it. They called it Buster's 'boop boop music.'"

And in a third, there's the Panamanian born Lorenzo "Laurel" Aitken and English entrepreneur Chris Blackwell, a partnership which came together in 1959 and recorded the song from which both Ranglin and Buster, and a bucketload more besides, took their cue — whether they knew it or not. "Boogie in My Bones" was a Jamaican #1 for 11 weeks and, whatever the claims from anywhere else, in the history of ska it remains Year Zero.

Jamaica throughout the 1950s was ripe for such an innovation. Enormous strides in the development of radio broadcasting saw the entire Caribbean swamped by the roar of American radio, blasting out of Miami, New Orleans and Nashville with a non-stop diet of big bands and be-bop, soul and swing. Before half of America was aware of what was happening on its own doorstep, Jamaica was in on the secret of these exciting new developments and, across the island, enterprising young men were picking up on the news.

It was the age of the sound systems, traveling DJs who set up on street corners or journeyed out into the countryside, to regale the locals with the latest hits. Jamaicans traveling to the US on business returned home with boxes of newly purchased R&B and blues records, to be sold to the disc jockeys, then played to the country, and the secret of success for any of them was to keep ahead of the competition.

With nothing more sophisticated than a rudimentary echo chamber, a microphone, a turntable, and a bank of speakers the size of the average house, stars arose from the streets faster than the records came in, sound system operators with names like Goodies, Count Nick the Champ, Count Jones, Tom the Great Sebastian with his legendary retinue of Duke Vin and Count Machuki. According to legend, Machuki was the first Jamaican disc jockey to toast, but before long, everyone was doing it. And so future legends like Whoopee, Winston "King Stitt" Sparkes, Sir Coxsone and more, piled down to Beat Street, the nicknamed heart of Kingston, and every night on the lawns outside the club and bar, they sparred for supremacy.

Duke Reid emerged into this fevered microverse in 1956, an ex-cop and champion marksman who ran a liquor store by day and a sound system by night. He auditioned disc jockeys in the store, in front of all his regular customers — if a performer met with their approval, then he was in with a chance. And if he didn't, but was big and tough enough anyway, there was always an opening among the Duke's enforcers, the army of heavies who ensured security at their employer's show, and breached it at his rivals'.

Insults were thrown, then stones, then punches and, if a rival still needed a lesson, the different operators weren't above sabotage. Sound system pioneer Count Vickram's entire collection of American R&B classics was shot full of holes by a jealous member of Reid's entourage. And he considered himself fortunate.

"Them were heavy days." Menser Manley, a sound system regular during the late 1950s, was caught in more battles than he can remember, and he can still pinpoint the source of the scars he bears — the bottle across the back of the head, hurled at one of Reid's rallies; the knife slash on one hand from a Vincent "King" Edwards show; and the one he's most proud of, the bullet-hole he won at one of Prince Buster's dances. Even Buster himself, whose skull still bears the ridge-shaped scars of a flying rock, could not top that.

Reid had already been in action for a few years when Coxsone Dodd arrived on the scene. His family, too, ran a liquor store, but the younger Dodd's interests lay exclusively in the sound systems. Soon, his Downbeat session was at least the equal of Reid's. But even as they battled it out on the streets, the sound systems themselves were fighting a losing battle. As radios and record players became more affordable, so the disc jockey's monopoly on American music began to weaken, beaten down by the rising availability of music from other sources.

From freely adapting existing records on stage, then, it was suddenly necessary to start creating new ones in the studio. At first, these were little more than pale reflections of the imported prototypes. In 1958–59, however, the first stirrings of a more individual sound began to be heard.

Pianist Theophilus Beckford's "Easy Snapping" became the first locally produced record to make a major splash on the sound systems, and with a smattering of other guinea pigs having proved what could be done, the Jamaican recording industry leaped into action.

Chris Blackwell was the catalyst which sparked the revolution. Born and schooled in Britain, but raised in Jamaica, his first job in the music industry came about completely by accident. Out swimming one afternoon, Blackwell found himself marooned on a coral reef. He was rescued by a bunch of passing Rastafarians, who offered him a job servicing jukeboxes all across the island, riding around on his moped with a box of singles strapped to the back.

It was hard work, but it was also illuminating, a lesson in record distribution which remained with Blackwell for years to come. The quality of the music was important, but the efficiency of its distribution and promotion was equally vital. Blackwell was already convinced that he could make great records. Now he knew how to get them heard as well.

In 1958, Blackwell decided to form a record label of his own. A number of record labels existed in Jamaica at the time, with Edward Seaga's WIRL (West Indies Records Limited) the best known, by virtue of Seaga's subsequent career in island politics. (He became Minister of Development for the governing Jamaican Labour Party in 1962;

Minister of Finance & Planning in 1967; party leader in 1972; Prime Minister in 1980; and has remained party leader, once the PNP returned to power.) Few of these companies, however, offered anything more than mento or indigenous recreations of existing American records. Blackwell wanted to capture the sound of modern Jamaica itself.

To this end, he launched two labels, R&B and Island, with his first release a live LP featuring Ernest Ranglin and pianist Lance Heywood, recorded at the Half Moon Hotel in Montego Bay. Ranglin also became a semi-regular member of Island's in-house band, the Caribs, and over the next year, as Blackwell's productions developed their own musical identity, Ranglin's trademark guitar sound proved equally important, bringing its own identifiable magic to a steady stream of new releases.

Ironically, the Caribs were actually a group of Australian musicians then living in Jamaica. But under Blackwell's direction, their authenticity was seldom questioned. It was they who accompanied Laurel Aitken on the double-sided "Boogie in My Bones"/"Little Sheila" single; they who joined Owen Gray on the classic *Owen Gray Sings* album; they who provided the backing on the more than thirty Jamaican singles which Blackwell released over the next two years.

The success of Blackwell's enterprise galvanized the sound system operators. Duke Reid held his first recording sessions in 1959, working with the Jiving Juniors, Eric Morris, Chuck and Dobby Dobson, Lord Power (the earthy "Penny Reel") and Derrick Morgan ("Lover Boy"), and creating at least one minor masterpiece with the insistent "Duke's Cookies," credited to Reid's own eponymous Group.

Coxsone Dodd followed. Indeed, within weeks of recording his live set for Blackwell, Ernest Ranglin and his double bassist, Cluett Johnson, were in Kingston, recording for Dodd as Clue J and the Blues Blasters (the hit "Shuffling Jug"), then backing Alton Ellis] and Eddy, Basil Gabbidon, Lascelles Perkins and Theo Beckford on further tunes.

It was at one of these sessions that the term "Ska" is first said to have originated, when Johnson, borrowing a catch phrase from jazz-man Slim Gaillard, told Ranglin to "play like ska, ska ska." Ranglin has since denied the tale ("Clue couldn't tell me what to play!"), but there is no doubt that an individual sound was certainly crystallizing, even if its roots were still heavily buried in American R&B and boogie.

Singer Derrick Harriott, who emerged in the late 1960s as one of the most prolific producers in Jamaica, recorded several crucial sides alongside his Jiving Juniors, working with both Dodd and Reid. The Juniors' "Lollipop Girl," rerecorded from a two year old demo, remains an indelible reminder of the sheer manic enthusiasm of this transitional period.

Yet even that was to pale in comparison with all that was going on over at Buster's Record Shack. Cecil Bustamente Campbell, "Buster" to everyone who knew him, was one of Dodd's crowd before he decided to go out on his own in 1959. His reasoning was simple. Dodd, Reid and George Edwards' King Edwards the Giant already had the R&B market sewn up, Reid pumping out the records which now dominated his Trojan sound system (named for the flatbed truck he drove it around on) at the Success Club on Wildman Street, Dodd's spinning on Downbeat at Forrester's Hall.

"I knew I couldn't compete with them," Buster reflected, "so I had to design a new musical sound. A Jamaican sound." And he wasn't referring to what was, at that time, universally regarded as the island's only indigenous music, the folky sounds of mento, bawdy, wry and utterly old-fashioned.

Tourists liked mento because it swayed like the palm trees in the gentlest breeze. But it was irrelevant to life beneath those deceptive fronds. When Buster christened his sound system the Voice of The People, that was what he wanted to create — and in very short order, that's what it became. It was still Jamaican music and his records would be performed in a Jamaican style, using Jamaican words. But mento — traditional mento, that is — barely got a look in.

What Buster dreamed of was a sound which had haunted him since childhood, the pounding of the military marching drum which he used to follow for miles, enthralled by the pageantry of the colonial army. "What I did was to transform it from the hand to the foot drum." With jazz drummer Arkland "Drumbago" Parkes by his side, guitarist Jah Jerry and tenor saxman Stanley "Ribs" Notice playing bap-bap-bap, "because that was still going with the marching beat," Buster knew he was onto a winner. "Because I knew how little boys would follow the march."

Coming together in fall, 1960, Buster's chief co-conspirator was Derrick Morgan, a 19 year old who had arrived in Kingston (from Stewarton) for an eye operation and never went home. He, too, had a long history on the embryonic scene — three years earlier, in 1957, Morgan became one of the new stars discovered at impresario Joseph Verejohn's Opportunity Show at the Palace Theater in Kingston, where his performance of Little Richard's "Jenny Jenny" and "Long Tall Sally" beat out entries from Owen Gray, Wilfred "Jackie" Edwards and Eric Morris.

Morgan then spent a year touring Jamaica with the comedy duo Bim and Bam, before returning to Kingston to record first with producer SL Smith (the hit "Fat Boy"), then with Duke Reid. He linked with Buster after meeting him walking up Orange Street — coincidentally, and unbeknownst to Morgan, Buster also lived next door to Morgan's singing partner, Patsy Todd.

Singers John, Junior and Mico Folkes, Owen Gray and trombonist Rico Rodriguez joined Buster and Morgan at their first ever session, recording 13 masterpieces. "Chubby," a 1961 hit for Bunny and Skitter, was first formulated at this session, over an insistently pounding percussion backing track recorded by the nyahbingi drummers Count Ossie and His Wareikas. So, even more significantly, was "Oh Carolina."

Released under the Folkes Brothers name in 1961, and an instant underground hit, "Oh Carolina" became a rallying cry for the ghetto Rastafarians who existed on the fringe of conventional Jamaican society (musical and otherwise), and all the more popular amongst them for being completely overlooked outside their community.

To them, as for countless subsequent historians, "Oh Carolina" took a step which even Chris Blackwell's recordings were still to accomplish, completely disavowing the music's American heritage, and working to create something new (yet simultaneously old — the drums were steeped in their African heritage), and daringly subversive, of its own.

Though it never even rippled the Jamaican mainstream, "Oh Carolina" had an immediate effect. According to Buster, Duke Reid — who hung around the studio throughout the entire recording — was trying to emulate the song's sound at a dance that very night. He failed, just as so many of his contemporaries failed over the next few years, because he lacked the one vital ingredient which Buster brought to the session — a vision of the future.

Jamaica had been a British colony for over 300 years. In the new world of post war determination, however, the Empire was crumbling, and Jamaica's own push for independence was as fierce as any other. It was alongside these political undercurrents that the new music marched. Hand in hand with the Rastafarian underground and the ghetto underbelly, the dreams of a bright new future were reflected in the new music's language and beats.

Ska's popularity took the island's existing musical hierarchy completely by surprise. In 1959, it didn't exist. In 1962 it was everywhere, and Kingston's studios were pumping out records as fast as they could be recorded — often utilizing the same pool of musicians for every one.

By 1964, the cream of this pool had coalesced as the Skatalites; by that time, however, innumerable permutations of the individual musicians had been playing together for close to five years. Every producer liked to give the impression that he had his own house band when, in fact, most of them simply had a name for their house band. Some permutation of Skatalites provided the actual musicians; it was up to the producer what he then called them — Buster's All Stars for Prince Buster, the Upcoming Willows for King Edwards and so on.

As the scene really heated up during 1963–64, both Duke Reid and Coxsone Dodd were almost completely out of the picture — Reid closed down operations while he sorted out some personal problems; Dodd was on an extended trip to the US. Both returned to reclaim their crowns, but in the meantime an entire new breed of producers arose to keep them warm.

Leslie Kong was one of several Chinese-Jamaican businessmen working on the fringe of the Jamaican music industry at this time, operating the Beverley label out of his family's ice cream parlor. Charlie Moo and Vincent "Randy" Chin, both of whom came into their own later in the decade, also got their start around this time.

In terms of vision and ability, however, Kong was streets ahead of his competitors, and what he missed, his newly acquired assistant Derrick Morgan, lured away from Buster's camp, inevitably caught. Morgan became Kong's de facto ears, auditioning new talent, then making the necessary introductions. He also proved Beverley's most reliable chart act. Revelling in his nickname of "The Hitmaker," at one point Morgan placed seven singles in the Jamaican top ten simultaneously, and even when he himself was between records, a number of his proteges were doing just as well.

Both Jimmy Cliff and Desmond Dekker were Morgan discoveries (so, although little came of it at the time, were Bob Marley and the Maytals). Interestingly, however, the first artist to take the logical next step and breach the international stage did not arise from any of the conventional Kingston studios. Rather, the endearingly squeaky-voiced Millie Small was a Chris Blackwell discovery — one which was unearthed *after* he left Jamaica to launch Island Records in London, but whose contagious ska version of Barbie Gaye's R&B classic "My Boy Lollipop" punctured both the UK and US chart.

The art of importing music from other genres, then skaifying it, was fundamental to the formation of the Jamaican music industry, and remained a common practice. Where "My Boy Lollipop" differed from most such recreations was in its determination not to simply skank up an existing song, but to create a whole new experience from it, a goal which Blackwell attained through his selection of participating players. There were only two Jamaican musicians on the session — trumpeter Pete Peterson and the ubiquitous Ernest Ranglin, brought to London the previous year by Blackwell and already a familiar face on the city's jazz and R&B circuit. The rest of the musicians were English, members of the R&B combo Jimmy Powell and the Dimensions, an aggregation best remembered today for their harmonica player, a young hopeful named Rod Stewart.

Back in Jamaica, Millie's British breakthrough was electrifying. Even though Blackwell himself predicted that she would enjoy no more than a couple of hits (he was right), simply seeing a ska record make the Top 10 in lands whose own releases traditionally dominated the Jamaican chart was enough to spark a revolution. To the watching musicians back in Kingston, Jamaica itself suddenly seemed very small. There really was an entire world out there, just waiting for Jamaica to sell it some hits.

RECOMMENDED LISTENING

VARIOUS ARTISTS

1959–64: The Ska's the Limit (Island) 1997

Welcome wrap up of Chris Blackwell/Island's crucial early years on and off Jamaica; "Boogie in My Bones" opens, "My Boy Lollipop" closes, the two book-ending a wealth of rare early riches from Derrick Morgan, the Maytals, Jimmy Cliff, Bob Marley and more.

Deep Ska (Proper—UK) 2000

Four-CD box set, budget priced and very well annotated, concentrating on the vast canon unleashed by Duke Reid and the Skatalites crew through the first half of the 1960s. Much of the music has been compiled elsewhere, and there is a strange random-ness to the selections that fall outside of that original remit (Byron Lee's version of "Oh Carolina"), but 80 songs pump past triumphantly, with more highlights than Penny Reel could keep track of.

Real Jamaica Ska (Sony Legacy) 2001

Reissuing a highly prized fall, 1964, compilation (with two bonus tracks from the Wailers), classic cuts by Lord Creator, Jimmy Cliff, Winston Samuel, the Charmers and the Techniques are united by the somewhat dubious claim that they were produced by American R&B legend Curtis Mayfield. Of course his influence on the scene (and, indeed, on several of the performers here) has never been disputed. But if he did visit Kingston during 1963 (when one of the Charmers cuts was first released) and 1964, history has kept that fact very much to itself. In fact Vincent Chin produced Lord Creator's "Don't Stay Out Late"; while Prince Buster is normally credited for the Charmers' "Time After Time," and Mayfield's role in any of this remains a mystery which the accompanying liner notes are as unable to solve as any other research.

Ska Bonanza: The Studio One Ska Years (Heartbeat) 1991

The other side of the studio coin, as Coxsone Dodd (and the Skatalites) rattle through their finest period pieces. Typically, the set has been compiled with an eye for rarity as much as anything else, although the great thing about Studio One at this time was, the quality normally went without saying.

The Original Golden Oldies Volume Two (Jet Set—UK) 1998

Reissuing a long out of print Jamaican LP, a short (10 tracks) but so sweet survey of early Prince Buster productions, fea-turing swathes of that so influential 1961 session ("Oh Carolina," "Chubby").

THE SKATALITES

STYLE *reggae (ska)*
FORMED *June, 1964 (Kingston, JA)*
ORIGINAL LINE-UP *Jerome "Jah Jerry" Hinds (guitar), Lloyd Brevett (bass), Donat Roy "Jackie" Mittoo (b 3/3/48, Browns Town, St Ann's JA; d 12/16/90 — piano), Tommy McCook (b Havana, Cuba, 3/3/27, d 5/5/98 — tenor sax), Lester Sterling (alto sax), Roland Alphonso (b Havana, Cuba, 1/12/31, d 11/20/98 — tenor sax), Don Drummond (b 1943; d 1969 — trombone), Johnnie "Dizzie" Moore (trumpet), Lloyd Knibbs (drms)*

Some people invented ska, some people developed it. But to thousands of fans around the world, the Skatalites *are* ska, and it isn't difficult to understand why they should believe that. Both individually and collectively, the band members played on — and made — so many of the records cut in Jamaica during the 1960s, that nobody has ever succeeded in tracking them all down. They worked with every major artist of the classic ska period; and possibly with every minor one as well.

Every studio in Kingston had at least one of the band permanently on call at some point during the 1960s; and while the vast majority of records rereleased in the Skatalites' name themselves involve no more than a handful of the featured players, still even they are indelibly stamped with the unmistakable imprimatur of the collective.

Neither can the fact that the Skatalites existed as a band for no more than 14 months be used against them when weighing up their contribution to Jamaican music. Again, the sheer ubiquity of their sound lived on years after the group itself collapsed, and if that sound lost its flavor during the latter part of the decade, the musicians themselves didn't.

The Skatalites' roots stretched back over two decades before they came together. Tommy McCook, Don Drummond, Lester Sterling and Johnny Moore were all pupils at the Alpha Boys' School on South Camp Road, Kingston, a Catholic nun-run academy for wayward boys which just happened to have a first class, and highly regarded, music department.

Boys were often offered a choice — chores or music; the vibrant Kingston jazz scene of the 1940s and 1950s testifies to how many picked the latter. (Other graduates of the school who would help build the Jamaican music industry of the 1950s include trombonist Rico Rodriguez, jazz-men Arthurlin Joe Harriot, Alphonse Reece, Dudley Farrier, Harold McNair, Wilton Gaynair, Joe Bennett, "Deadly" Headley Bennett and Eddie Thornton, trumpeter with English musician Georgie Fame's Blue Flames at that band's famous Prince Buster sessions.)

Like every other Jamaican musician of the period, the future Skatalites worked playing jazz and R&B for the hotel trade, disparagingly regarded today as a faceless circuit where one band was much the same as any other, and artistic expression and development were ruled out by the need to replicate the hits of the day. The disdain with which many hardcore ska and reggae fans treat Byron Lee & The Dragonaires' 1960s output is utterly symptomatic of this attitude.

In fact, the total opposite was true. Far more than musicians who have played one basic style of music their entire career, those recruited to the hotel bands not only needed to prove their adaptability, they were also required to keep an open mind about everything, and be willing to learn from it too.

When the Skatalites did come together in mid-1964, the aggregation which history records as the founding line-up was just one of perhaps a dozen different groupings who could arguably have played together just as well, and whose influence would have remained just as profound.

Guitarists Ernest Ranglin and Nearlin "Lynn" Taitt both vied with, and perhaps even surpassed Jerry Hines for the title of Jamaica's top guitarist; and, while it was two of Taitt's former bandmates, Jackie Mittoo and Lloyd Knibbs, who became the new group's keyboardist and drummer, producer Duke Reid invariably replaced Mittoo with Gladstone Anderson at his sessions. Lloyd Brevett was the Skatalites' official bassist, but he, too, was often supplanted by another Reid favorite, Lloyd Spence — renowned throughout Jamaica as the second musician to own an electric bass (Byron Lee was the first).

Drummers Arkland "Drumbago" Parks and Wackie Henry, double bassist Cluett "Clue J" Johnson, Rico Rodriguez (trombone), Aubrey Adams (keyboards), Theo Beckford (piano), Oswald "Baba" Brooks and Frank Anderson all could have been the Skatalites and, in many cases, they often were. Such was the demand for the individual musicians, such was the hectic schedule to which they all worked, that no producer thought twice about replacing one errant member with another instrumentalist, so long as the job was done correctly. And, of course, they had all played with one another so regularly in the past that it always would be.

Of the historical Skatalites line-up, Knibbs and Drummond arrived from Eric Dean's Band, where they played alongside Brooks, Ranglin and Brevett. That group toured constantly, traveling as far afield as British Honduras, Haiti and the Dominican Republic, but are best remembered today for the bolero "My Shawl," later adapted by Baba Brooks

for his ska hit "Guns Fever." Knibbs then joined the Sheiks alongside Mittoo and Moore — the band became the Cavaliers Orchestra in 1963.

Roland Alphonso had been recording since 1954, when he cut an acetate for sound system pioneer Stanley Motta. And Tommy McCook's recorded career dated back a year earlier than that; he made his debut on an acetate recorded for Jamaican radio station ZQ1 while a member of Don Hitchman's Group. In 1954, McCook left Jamaica to play jazz at the Zanzibar Club in Nassau; he returned to Kingston in 1962, and swiftly fell into session work, beginning with the Coxsone Dodd production *Jazz Jamaica From The Workshop*. It was there that he was introduced to Ranglin, Drummond and Alphonso, among others.

Although it was another Dodd session which officially inaugurated the Skatalites, Duke Reid's Treasure Isle studio was their home away from home during 1959–62. The compilation *Ska After Ska After Ska* (Heartbeat — 1999) does a sterling job in tracking down many of the earliest recorded permutations of the pre-Skatalite musicians.

This includes cuts credited to Drummond, Taitt, Brooks and Anderson, together with their contributions to hits by Eric Morris, Justin Hinds & The Dominos, the Silvertones, Wilburn "Stranger" Cole and more. Just two are credited to [Don Drummond] the Skatalites themselves — "Thoroughfare" (aka "Treasure Island") and "Street Corner"; in fact, both predate the formal naming of the band.

The Skatalites themselves date their actual formation to June, 1964. According to Ernest Ranglin, "I was working as an arranger for [Dodd], we got together to back a [Trinidadian] singer called Jackie Opel and, when the session was over, the trumpeter Johnny Moore said, 'well this is a nice group, we play well together, why let it go to waste?'" (Opel died in a car accident in the late 1960s.)

Another account credits the impetus to Lloyd Knibbs, who regularly visited McCook at the Courtleigh Manor Hotel where he was playing with pianist Aubrey Adams. Knibbs was keen to start a band with the saxophonist, and when McCook told him to find the musicians, Knibbs pointed out that he already had.

Whichever story is correct, a meeting was held at a local cinema, where one of the earliest points to settle was a name for the new group. With everybody adamant that they wanted something stronger than the usual "All-Stars" tag, calypso singer Joseph "Lord Tanamo" Gordon — already seconded as one of the band's vocalists — suggested the Orbits, presumably in deference to the world's then-on-going obsession with space travel. Somebody else offered up the Itallites — "ital" is a Jamaican term meaning "natural"; that became the Satellites, before finally Tommy McCook punned the *Ska*talites.

With Tanamo, Opel, Tony DaCosta and Doreen Schaeffer handling vocals, the band played their first ever gig under that name on June 27 at the Hi-Hat club in Rae Town. It was very nearly their last. Egos which co-existed quite happily in the privacy of the studio seemed to enlarge considerably on stage, every star apparently determined to outshine the other. Only the knowledge that there was enough room up there for everybody calmed the bruised egos and nerves and soon, the group had a three nights a week residency at the Bournemouth Beach Club in Eastern Kingston, and a regular Sunday show at the Orange Bowl on Orange Street.

With Dodd and Ken Lack (later head of the Caltone label) behind the scenes, overseeing the operational side of the band, the Skatalites were soon gigging all over the island, often in the company of other Studio One artists — aside from performing their own set, the group then accompanied the likes of Delroy Wilson, Lee Perry, the Blue Beats, the Wailers and many more.

They added neatly choreographed tricks to their routine and dancers to the show, exotic creatures with names like Pam Pam Gifford, Glory, Jabba, Persian the Cat and Madame Pussycat. Literally within weeks of coming together, the Skatalites established themselves — as if anybody could have doubted it — as the premier band on the island.

Indeed, when Jamaica's musical contribution to the New York World's Fair in August, 1964, ended in bitterness and recriminations, organizer Edward Seaga's decision to send his friend Byron Lee & his Dragonaires to the event rather than the Skatalites (whose Rastafarianism he frowned upon) was widely regarded as one of the chief causes. Members of the group, after all, were regularly playing with all the artists on the bill — Jimmy Cliff, Prince Buster, Monty Morris, Millie Small and the Blues Busters. Lee's band had slipped out of the movement several years earlier.

The Skatalites consoled themselves by recording with virtually every artist and producer then operating in Jamaica, not only providing backing for vocal tracks, but also executing some startling instrumentals as well. One especially wry effort was "World's Fair" itself, a Ken Boothe/Stranger Cole duet.

The bulk of the Skatalites' work was with Duke Reid and Coxsone Dodd, with Prince Buster and the brothers Duke and Justin Yap more or less an equal (if distant) third. Of this quartet, Dodd undoubtedly drew the best out of the band on the most consistent basis — "Timothy," "Beardman Ska," "Crime Wave," "Sudden Destruction," "Addis Ababa," "Tear Up," "Schooling the Duke," "Cleopatra," "Scandal" and "Looking Through the Window" were all cut with Dodd.

The Yaps, however, also had a magic touch where the group was concerned. Their very first session together produced "Marcus Junior," "Ringo," "Confucius," "Chinatown," "Phoenix City," "Ghost Town," "The Reburial" and "Smiling." And Prince Buster, of course, got "Al Capone," his first British hit and one of the most instantly recognizable, and most intoxicatingly original, performances in the Skatalites' entire repertoire.

Surprisingly few of these recordings actually credited the Skatalites with their performance. Even among the group's "own" records, the member who wrote the track invariably emerged the "featured" artist — "Crime Wave" and the 1967 UK hit single "Guns of Navarone," for example, were issued under Roland Alphonso's name; "Exodus," another Dodd production, was credited to Tommy McCook and so on. Other tracks were assigned according to the vocalist — Lord Tanamo released a number of fine 45s during 1964/65; Opel and Schaeffer likewise.

Duke Reid in particular adhered to this practice, actually naming the Skatalites on a mere handful of the dozens of singles they recorded for him. They are unmistakable, all the same, on Don Drummond's "Corner Stone," Tommy McCook's "Silver Dollar," Roland Alphonso's "Blackberry Brandy" and Roland Alphonso's "You Can Depend on Me" (also recorded for Dodd as "You're So Delightful").

Another fabulous Reid-produced performance from within the Skatalites immediate family was "Woman a Come," featuring Drummond's girlfriend Anita "Marguerita the Rhumba Queen" Mahfoud. Although by no means blessed with a conventional singing voice, Marguerita entwines with the band's almost African accompaniment to create an utterly unforgettable experience. It is ironic, then, that it was her death, at Drummond's hands, which brought about the final demise of the Skatalites.

The band was booked to end 1964 with a New Year's eve show at La Parisienne club in Harbour View, and were not overly perturbed when Drummond failed to turn up. All the members knew that he was under medical supervision at the time, suffering from a mental condition which had already seen him voluntarily commit himself to Bellevue Sanitarium on two past occasions.

Drummond, however, was incensed when he awoke in the early hours of January 1 and realized he'd missed the show. Earlier in the evening, Marguerita had given him his medication, but somehow the timing had been confused and the dose knocked him out. When she returned home from her own New Year's eve shows, at the Club Havana and Baby Grand, Drummond stabbed her to death with his pocket knife.

Although the police regarded it as an open and shut case, the band tried desperately to protect Drummond, even insisting that he had made the gig and was riding back to Kingston with them at the time the murder occurred. Their protests were in vain. Drummond was returned to Bellevue, where he remained for the next four years. He died there May 6, 1969.

The Skatalites continued working together for another six months following Drummond's incarceration, but although the quality of their work did not falter, their enthusiasm for it certainly did. On June 27, 1965, the Skatalites played their first anniversary show at the Glass Bucket Club — and according to many histories, it was the last show they ever played (there may have been one more, a police dance at the Runaway Bay Hotel in August).

The group shattered, although none of the members traveled too far. Alphonso, Brevett, Moore and Mittoo reunited as the Soul Brothers (later, the Soul Vendors), house band at Studio One throughout much of the 1960s. Alphonso and Mittoo also enjoyed solo careers during this period.

McCook decamped to Reid's Treasure Isle, where he formed a new band, the Supersonics, with alto sax player Herman Marquis; following Reid's death in 1976, he joined producer Bunny Lee's Aggrovators studio band. Lester Sterling recorded several strong singles with London-based producer "Sir" Clancy Collins; Johnny Moore worked with Lloyd "Matador" Daley; and so on.

Their paths, of course, continued to cross and, in 1975, the Skatalites reformed around a core of Brevett, McCook, Knibbs, Alphonso, Sterling and Mittoo, with guests including drummers Benbow and Leroy "Horsemouth" Wallace, Vin "Don D Junior" Gordon (trombone), Ernest Ranglin (guitar), and vocalists Tony and Ruth Brevett (respectively, Lloyd Brevett's brother and wife).

Working with producer Glen Darby (whose own early singles, cut as a 14 year old for Dodd, had featured the Skatalites as backing musicians) and mixer King Tubby, the sessions were originally conceived as a Lloyd Brevett solo album, *African Roots*. Working at Lee Perry's Black Ark studio, the album was built around swirling drums and percussion, through which Brevett's bass wound a sinewy course. Further sessions at Aquarius, however, prompted him to add some ska to the brew — and, as he himself has said, who better than his old bandmates?

Ten cuts made the final album, which was released in Jamaica in 1975 and the US in 1978. (Dub mixes from the sessions, unreleased for twenty years, finally appeared on the *Skatalites Meet King Tubby* album in 1998. Further tracks, including the legendary "Sealing Dub," were released as an EP by Motion Records in 2001.)

The band members continued freelancing elsewhere. A 1977 release, *Hot Lava*, credited to Tommy McCook & The Skatalites, is in fact a virtual McCook solo set cut for Bunny Lee, while a Coxsone Dodd produced Jackie Mittoo album, released in the US in 1978 as *Jackie Mittoo* (UA), is titled like a solo set, but actually features much of the band.

Also in 1978, Island Records chief Chris Blackwell suggested the group reform again, to cut an album for him. The ensuing album, *Big Guns*, was recorded in 1979, but was ultimately shelved, apparently following a disagreement between Blackwell and McCook. It finally surfaced as 1984's *Return of the Big Guns*, following the third Skatalites reunion at 1983's Reggae Sunsplash concerts in London and Montego Bay.

After Sunsplash, the band again went into the studio, this time with producer Bunny Lee and Sly & Robbie — the prosaically titled *Skatalites With Sly & Robbie & The Taxi Gang* album emerged from these sessions. Attempts to keep the Skatalites alive, however, foundered on the vast distances which separated the leading members. Alphonso and Sterling were now living in the US, the remainder of the band in Jamaica.

In September, 1985, however, McCook emigrated to America and immediately hooked up with Alphonso and Sterling. Brevett and Knibbs followed and, by mid-1986, the Skatalites were gigging on a regular basis. 1989 saw them back Bunny Wailer on his Liberation world tour; that same year, they toured Japan, backing the recently revitalized Prince Buster and a suddenly resurgent Lord Tanamo — in December, 1990, Tanamo hit the UK Top 60 with "I'm in the Mood for Love." Ironically, fellow founding member Jackie Mittoo died of cancer at his Toronto home that same month.

1990 found the Skatalites performing at Reggae Sunsplash, (they played again in 1996), and toured the US and the Far East with undisguised enthusiasm. The reborn group's first album, *Skavoovee*, finally appeared in 1993. A show-stopping performance on that fall's Skavoovie tour, on a bill otherwise dominated by the new breed of American ska bands, confirmed the Skatalites' ascendancy. The adulation of audiences (many of whom had never heard of ska before they encountered it on MTV) was matched only by the undisguised gratitude of the musicians, as they bathed in an international spotlight which years of laboring in the anonymity of sessionwork had never prepared them for.

Subtitled "the 30th Anniversary Recording," 1994's *Hi Bop Ska*, saw original vocalist Doreen Schaeffer joining the core line-up of Knibbs, Sterling, Brevett, Alphonso and McCook, with the group augmented by Devon James (guitar), Will Clark (trombone) and Nathan Breedlove (trumpet), plus a plethora of guests — Toots Hibbert, Prince Buster and Lester Bowie among them. The album brought the band their first ever Grammy nomination; 1996's *Greetings from Skamania* earned a second. Meanwhile, the band continued touring constantly, in their own right and with side projects such as Sterling's Ska Macka.

Sadly, however, whatever else this new fame brought the band members, it did not include time. In spring, 1995, two years short of his 70th birthday, McCook was forced off the road for a heart by-pass operation. He rejoined the group early the following year, but after just a few weeks on the road, health problems persuaded him to quit again. Aged 71, Tommy McCook passed away on May 5, 1998, from heart failure brought on by pneumonia — he had originally been hospitalized with a sinus problem.

The group carried on. They contributed three tracks to Island Records' 40th anniversary *Ska Island* compilation, including two cut with Prince Buster and Doreen Schaeffer. They also reworked some of their best known 60s numbers for 1998's *Ball of Fire* album with producer Trevor Wyatt, their first for Island Jazz Jamaica.

However, less than six months after McCook's death, Alphonso collapsed on stage at Hollywood's Key Club. He recovered quickly, but it was discovered that during his seizure, he had burst a blood vessel in his neck. Two weeks later, on November 17, a second burst and Alphonso slipped into a coma. He remained on life support for three days, before his family made the decision to disconnect the machine. He died on November 20, 1998.

The Skatalites, however, live on. The group's latest lineup of Brevett, Knibbs, Sterling, Schaeffer, former Count Ossie sideman Cedric IM Brooks, Will Clark, Devon James, Ken Stewart and Greg Glassman (trumpet) released a new album, *Bashaka*, in 2000.

SELECTED DISCOGRAPHY

7 **Ska Authentic (Studio One — JA) 1967**

A short, but definitive collection of instrumental and vocal cuts.

6 **African Roots (UA) 1978**

A heady mixture of jazz and reggae, with tinges of R&B and funk — the birth of the "modern" Skatalites sound.

6 **The Skatalites With Sly and Robbie and the Taxi Gang (Vista Sounds — UK) 1983**

13 instrumentals that don't really fit into either the Skatalites' nor the Riddim Twins' customary bag, but both sides emerge with credit for trying.

8 **Stretching Out (ROIR) 1984**

Jazz and jam heavy set drawn from the reformed band's rehearsals for Sunsplash, heavy going for acolytes of the band's original sound, but a remarkable indication of their true capabilities.

7 **Live at Reggae Sunsplash (Synergy — UK) 1986**
7 **Skavoovie (Shanachie) 1993**
7 **Hi Bop Ska (Shanachie) 1994**
8 **Greetings from Skamania (Shanachie) 1996**

The rhythm section and guitars fly the ska standard as the horns punctuate the songs with jazz solos, and everyone gets

down on dynamic remodels of "El Pussycat" and "Phoenix City."

6 **Balls of Fire (Island Jazz Jamaica) 1998**

The Skatalites posit an alternate universe in which they never had to stop playing jazz, but were given the same repertoire regardless. High on virtuosity, a little low on actual excitement, but a clutch of classics reinterpreted around the band members' own musical preferences.

7 **Bashaka (Marston) 2000**

SELECTED COMPILATIONS & ARCHIVE RELEASES

6 **Return of the Big Guns (Island) 1984**

Straightforward, if belated, release for the 1979 *Big Guns* album — not crucial Skatalites by any means, as they try to figure out quite what they (still) need to prove, but easygoing enough.

8 **Shuffle'n'Ska Time (Jamaica Gold — Neths) 1995**

Crucial compilation of pre-Skatalites material, with a very clean sound and lucid annotation drawn from first hand interviews. The emphasis is on Alphonso's work, but of course the rest of the gang are usually in attendance somewhere.

7 **Tribute to Jackie Mittoo (Heartbeat) 1995**

Two-CD Studio One collection seeks out some of what made Mittoo's contributions to the Skatalites so magical. The youngest member of the band was also the most adventurous, as "Hanging Tree" and "Killer Diller" prove, but the band is only part of the story — Mittoo's full Studio One repertoire is visited, through to 1971, all but two of them instrumentals. (Alton Ellis takes the lead on one.) Unreleased material also gets a look in.

8 **Skaravan — Top Sounds trom Top Deck (West Side) 1996 – 99**

It would probably take 10 stuffed CDs to sum up everything the Skatalites recorded with the Yap brothers . . . and this series has so far produced eight of them. Mixing sessions for the Avalons, the Angelic Brothers and so many more with the band's (and band members') own recordings, it's an incredible piece of skarchaeology.

9 **Foundation Ska (Heartbeat) 1997**

32 authentic ska hits, it says on the cover and truth in advertising finally prevails. The Skatalites may have recorded tighter, harder and heavier music elsewhere, but Studio One brought their playful side out, from the naked ambition of "Christine Keeler" to the Beatlemania of "Ringo's Theme." Even better, half a dozen Duke Reid productions ensure this emerges the be-all and end-all of classic Skatalites collections . . . at least for now.

7 **Hog in a Cocoa (Orange Street — UK) 1998**

High on quality, low on playing time, 14 primal slabs of Duke Reid productions which may have been repackaged a zillion times before and since (Marguerita, Maytals, Eric Morris, Stranger & Patsy, Justin Hinds), but do serve as a scintillating introduction to the group's session work.

9 Ska After Ska After Ska (Heartbeat) 1998

You'll never find every Skatalites track you want on one (or even a hundred) discs, but this collection of their Duke Reid period plucks most of the jewels from the Treasure Isle trove, covering both the band members' own releases, plus key sessions. Better still, it avoids (for the most part) duplicating the contents of any other compilation you may own.

7 Heroes of Reggae in Dub (Guava Jelly) 1999

After the completion of *African Roots* the tapes were handed to King Tubby to have a little dub magic spilled on them. Three of the ensuing cuts appeared on the finished record, the rest moldered, forgotten, until restored for this release. Far darker and much more brooding than the accompanying album, with the rhythms haunting and absolutely electrifying, an album that graces the Skatalites with a depth they'd never have attempted on their own.

8 Something Special: Roland Alphonso 1958–68 (Heartbeat) 1999

Supplementing *Shuffle'n'Ska Time* (above), a high energy trawl through Alphonso's work on either side of the Skatalites, drawn from the Studio One vaults. Rare singles and unreleased cuts make this a must-have.

8 Greatest Hits of the Skatalites Featuring Tommy McCook (Heartbeat) 1999

A collection of 18 McCook-led cuts, highlighting not only the saxophonist but also a number of tracks hitherto uncompiled. As with the Alphonso title above, not every song strictly dates from the Skatalites period — "The Answer" was first released on Dodd's *Jazz Jamaica from the Workshop* album, McCook's first recording with him; others were recorded with trumpeter Frank Anderson. Historically, then, it's a vital document but, even more importantly, it's exquisite listening as well.

9 Nucleus of Ska (Music Club) 2001

Long-awaited single disc compilation of the Skatalites' Justin Yap productions. 15 songs including the archetypes "Marcus Jr" and "Confucius," plus the scintillating "Lawless Street."

SLY & ROBBIE

STYLE *dub*
FORMED Kingston, 1975
ORIGINAL LINE-UP *Robbie Shakespeare (b 9/27/53, Kingston, JA — bass), Sly Dunbar (b Lowell Charles Dunbar, 5/10/52, Kingston, JA — drums)*

Although it was 1975 before the most famous rhythm section in modern Jamaican music first came together, the self-styled Riddim Twins had been already been a part of the Jamaican music landscape for a decade. Since that time, they have become positively ubiquitous, the most in-demand team since the Skatalites, and the most frequently used. A full documenting of every session the pair have played and produced would fill a phone book.

Both musicians served their apprenticeship in the studio bands of the late 1960s/early 1970s. Named for his love of American R&B star Sly Stone, Sly Dunbar was a member of RHT Invincibles, a group formed by Rastafarian baker Father Good'un, and also featuring Ansell Collins (keyboards), Lloyd Parks and Bertram McLean (guitars). The band cut no more than a handful of songs, including one, "Diplomat," sung by Dunbar.

Dunbar became one of Lee Perry's most favored drummers, making his debut on the Upsetters' 1969 cut "Night Doctor." He then moved onto the studio aggregation Skin Flesh & Bones, a slick reggae-disco band whose recording work was supplemented by a residency at the Tit for Tat club in Kingston.

Regularly playing just down the road at the Evil People Club, Robbie Shakespeare, meanwhile, was best known as a member of Bunny Lee's Aggrovators, with whom he, too, played alongside virtually every established star of the early 1970s. He was also among the musicians considered by the Wailers during 1972, contributing bass to "Concrete Jungle" on their *Catch a Fire* album.

Beginning in 1975, Shakespeare worked with JoJo Hookim's Revolutionaries outfit, joining around the same time as Dunbar came into the band. The pair knew each other from past meetings of course. Now they also discovered the musical chemistry they had spent their entire careers searching for.

The Revolutionaries released several records in their own right, while Shakespeare continued to play sessions with Bunny Lee — in 1977, Leroy Smart's *Super Star* album was released bearing the credit "backed by Robbie Shakespeare and the Aggrovators, Sly Dunbar and the Revolutionaries."

It was Sly & Robbie's work on Jimmy Cliff's 1975 *Follow My Mind* album which debuted them before the international arena, and later that year they undertook what remains one of their most bizarre assignments.

They were recruited to cut an album, *Aux Armes et Caetera*, with veteran French vocalist Serge Gainsbourg, an uneasy partnership which worsened when Gainsbourg asked if they knew any French music. Once the duo finished laughing, Dunbar acknowledged that they liked one song, an old instrumental with a woman groaning over the strings. It was Gainsbourg's own "Je T'aime." The sessions relaxed after that, and Sly & Robbie not only cut a second album with Gainsbourg, they also toured France with him.

In 1976, Sly & Robbie were behind Culture's *Two Sevens Clash*, and visited the UK with U-Roy (Sly alone appeared on the toaster's *Natty Rebel* album). The pair then joined Peter Tosh for his *Equal Rights* album, igniting a partnership which lasted for the next four years. As the heart of his Word, Sound & Power band, the duo accompanied the former Wailer not only at the 1978 One Love Peace Concert, but also on major tours of the US and Europe.

In 1978, having saved every cent they earned from that year's Tosh tour (apparently they lived on bread and water while on the road, in order to conserve their funds even further), Sly and Robbie launched their own Taxi label, lifting the name from a short-lived label operated by Dunbar and Skin Flesh & Bones bandmate Ranchie McLean in 1974. The original label released a mere handful of singles, including Skin Flesh & Bones' own "Bone Yard," plus cuts by Pat Davis, Joy White and McCrean himself, but closed within the year.

This time around, Taxi was built on firmer foundations. Sly & Robbie set up their own studio band, the Taxi All Stars/Roots Radics. Built around the musicians they'd worked with in the Revolutionaries, featured players included Ansell Collins and Winston Wright (keyboards), Rad Bryan (guitar) and Sticky Thompson (drums), the Taxi Gang would become one of the most trusted names in Jamaican music. But it was a mark of the Riddim Twins' preeminence that, even when the full Gang was present on a session, the simple credits "featuring/produced by Sly & Robbie" stated everything that most people needed to know.

The label debuted with Black Uhuru's "Observe Life" — the launchpad, this time, for a relationship which lasted until well into the next decade. Taxi scored its first hit with Gregory Isaacs' "Soon Forward" that same year, while other early Taxi releases saw Sly and Robbie alongside Junior Delgado, Bits'n'Pieces, Dennis Brown, Max Romeo, Prince Far I, the Wailing Souls, the Tamlins and ex-Uniques vocalist Jimmy Riley.

They remained readily available for other producers too. Jacob Miller, Ranking Dread, the Mighty Diamonds, Ronnie Davis, General Echo, Barrington Levy and Bunny Wailer all had albums fired by the pair during 1978–80. They also recorded an album with "Uptown Top Ranking" hitmakers Althea & Donna. Dunbar alone even released a handful of singles — including 1978's "A Who Say" and 1979's "Rasta Fiesta" — prior to unleashing the *Simple Sly Man* and *Sly, Wicked and Slick* solo albums through Virgin's Front Line subsidary.

Neither was the duo's reputation confined to Jamaican artists only. One fervent admirer was Island Records chief Chris Blackwell, who signed a distribution deal with Taxi in 1980, then paired Sly and Robbie with new wave funk singer Grace Jones (born in Spanishtown, JA, but resident in New York since 1964), to mastermind a funk-dub hybrid which dominated the new wave scene of the early 1980s.

Equally noteworthy was their pairing with English performer Ian Dury, for his 1981 *Lord Upminster* album. Other non-reggae artists to employ Sly & Robbie's talents over the next few years included Bob Dylan, Barry Reynolds, Joe Cocker, Robert Palmer, Herbie Hancock (on his US dance chart smash "Rockit") and Mick Jagger — whose own introduction to the duo came when Tosh signed to the Rolling Stones' own label in 1978.

Back in Jamaica, they worked with Natural Vibes, Johnny Osbourne (Prince Jammy's 1983 *Osbourne in Dub* album), Frankie Paul, Half Pint, Cornell Campbell, Patrick Andy, Charlie Chaplin, Michael Palmer and Sugar Minott, while they also cut a uniformly atypical album with the reformed Skatalites, released as *The Skatalites with Sly and Robbie and the Taxi Gang*.

Concentrating on devastatingly heavy dub, the duo began releasing records under both their own name and the Taxi Gang alias in 1981. The majority of tracks, of course, were drawn from sessions with others, frequently compiling instrumental and dub b-sides — the title of 1982's *Crucial Reggae Driven by Sly & Robbie* album says it all. Another release, 1985's *A Dub Experience*, drew from sources as far apart as Black Uhuru's "Chill Out" and Junior Moore's "Real Love," wryly retitled "Computer Malfunction."

Perhaps what marked Sly & Robbie out the furthest, however, was not so much what they played, but how they played it. Dunbar was one of the first drummers to take the newly-fashionable electronic syndrums and utilize them as an integral part of his kit, as opposed to simply a novel embellishment to an otherwise ordinary performance. Both Black Uhuru and Grace Jones benefitted immeasurably from this talent, as the duo created an almost other-worldly, and certainly futuristic, sounding rhythm behind them. Even as the digital age began to develop around the Kingston studios, Sly and Robbie had already drawn the blueprint.

Their awareness of the burgeoning dance hall scene saw them champion Ini Kamoze on the strength of nothing more than a six song demo tape recorded for Jimmy Cliff — Kamoze himself had never even performed in public at the time he began his partnership with the Riddim Twins in 1984. They were also involved with some of Bobby Digital's first productions, alongside Prince Jammy — Wayne Smith's masterful "Come Along" among them.

If there was any drawback to Sly & Robbie's prolificacy, it was just that — they were so prolific that even serious collectors are overwhelmed by the sheer weight of material released. Such was the cachet surrounding them that any session featuring their playing could — and often was — released with their names at least co-billed with the featured artist.

Sly Dunbar and Robbie Shakespeare, the world's best-known taxi drivers.

A number of Bunny Lee productions from the mid-1980s were guilty of this, but the situation reached its most absurd level in 1984, when the duo repaid a favor from producer George Phang with a stockpile of rhythms which graced his productions throughout much of the 1980s. Without Sly and Robbie themselves having any further input into the sessions, Sugar Minott's "Rydim," Barrington Levy's "Money Move," Frankie Paul's "Winsome," Michael Palmer's "Mr Booster," Tristan Palma's "Folly Rankin'" and many more were created from this particular treasure trove.

Other producers inextricably linked with Sly and Robbie's mid-late 1980s output include Clive Jarrett & Beswick "Bebo" Phillips (Carlton Livingstone, Al Campbell); Myrie Lewis & Erroll Marshall (Pad Anthony, Half Pint, Patrick Andy, Junior Reid); Augustus Clarke (Ruddy Thomas, Delroy Wilson, Larry & Alvin) and Philip "Fatis" Burrell, whose earliest (1987) digital hits featured the duo — Frankie Paul's "Warning," Sanchez's "Zim Bam Zim" and Pinchers' "Mass Out."

In 1988, Sly and Robbie were a vital component in the team which created Toots Hibbert's stellar *Toots in Mem-*phis album, while Marcia Griffiths' phenomenal take on "Fever" that same year was a joint production with Bunny Wailer. They also lay at the heart of New York sonics dilettante Bill Laswell's periodic excursions into the dub field — having guested on his 1985 *Language Barrier* project, he repaid the favor by producing 1987's *Rhythm Killers* album, featuring guest appearances from Shinehead and Bootsy Collins.

Their most crucial release from this period, however, was their own 1988 album *The Summit* — the last Sly and Robbie album to feature "live" drums, but the first to actually leave that fact open to question, so precise were the rhythms, and so adept had Dunbar become with programming.

As the raggamuffin boom gathered speed, a genre which relied almost wholly on computers, Sly and Robbie again found themselves at ground zero. In fact, 1989's *Silent Assassin* album anticipated much of what transpired in the early 1990s, not only rhythmically, but also through the duo's new-found interest in hip hop and rap. Queen Latifah, KRS-One and Young MC all guested on the album.

1992 saw Dunbar launch a new production partnership

with Peter Turner and Maureen Sheridan, handling such artists as Sabre and Junior Reid. A similar union with producers Redrose & Malvo brought him sessions with Mad Cobra, Snagga Puss, Jigsy King, Galaxy P and Spragga Benz, many accompanied by the unfamiliar "rhythms by Sly & Redrose" credit. (Dunbar has also been involved in the recording of a number of Revivalist-flavored religious tracks, again without Shakespeare.)

Sly and Robbie's own partnership, meanwhile, continued apace. Luciano, Chaka Demus & Pliers, Shabba Ranks and Beenie Man rank among their most notable 90s collaborations; while the duo's own release schedule remained prodigious, both through Taxi and via a wealth of licensing deals.

Their most noteworthy projects, then, tend to be the most unusual ones: the *Stripped to the Bone* DVD album, which paired 13 primal rhythms with 16 LA strippers; a *Taxi Christmas* selection of dubbed out festive tunes; Mutabaruka's Roots All Stars project; and a fascinating reunion with Black Uhuru vocalist Michael Rose, *X-Uhuru*. They have also remained an inexhaustible live act, both as backing musicians and in their own right, as stellar Sunsplash appearances in 1986–88, 1990–92 and 1996 testify.

DISCOGRAPHY

7 Simple Sly Man (Front Line — UK) 1979
7 Sly Wicked and Sly (Front Line — UK) 1979
Ostensibly solo Dunbar albums, both slip effortlessly into the roots framework of the late 1970s, with the dub-heavy instrumentals "Rasta Fiesta," "Dirty Harry" and "Sesame Street" as representative as any.

8 Sixties, Seventies + Eighties = Taxi (Island) 1981
Mikey Chung, Tyrone Downie and Uziah "Sticky" Thompson accompany the Riddim twins on a selection (largely) of covers drawn, indeed, from the 60s and 70s. The Beatles' "I Should Have Known Better," Herbie Hancock's "Watermelon Man" and Sam Cooke's "Only 16" are joined by a handful of Skatalites oldies, all executed with the duo's period panache.

6 Sly-Go-Ville (Island) 1982
7 Kings of Reggae (Keystone) 1983
3 Language Barrier (Island) 1985
Producer Laswell's inflexible attitude towards creativity — forget tune and rhythm, let's be CLEVER! — runs up against a wall whose entire fabric is built upon rhythm. So, the immovable meets the unstoppable and somewhere in the middle, there may be a purpose to all this. Or maybe not.

6 The Sting (Moving Target) 1986
7 Electro Reggae (Island) 1986
2 Rhythm Killers (Island) 1987

Another Laswell concoction, and an absolute disaster. The star of the album is Bootsy Collins and the best track is the Ohio Players' "Fire," but even that doesn't help. A pop-hop version of Allen Toussaint's "Yes We Can" (also released as a single) is utterly unlistenable, and still isn't the nadir.

6 Taxi Connection Live in London (Island) 1987
8 The Summit (Greensleeves — UK) 1988
Fatis Burrell produced set which anticipates and sets the stage for the digital meltdown to come. The best rhythms rank alongside the best of Sly and Robbie, but there's a distinct chill creeping in.

7 Silent Assassin (Island) 1989
Gripping dub-rap hybrid, recommended to fans of either genre. Among the highlights are Queen Latifah's "Woman for the Job," producer KRS-One's "Party Together" and a handful of contributions by the Shah of Brooklyn.

5 DJ Riot (Island) 1990
7 Remember Precious Times (RAS) 1992
Not quite the radioactive experience it ought to be with a roots-retro track listing like this, but still — cool takes on Leroy Sibbles' "I Love You," Unique Winston Riley's "My Conversation" and Willie Williams' "Armagideon Time."

7 Hail Up the Taxi (Island) 1996
A selective best from the past half decade's worth of productions and sessions, with Beenie Man, Michael Rose, Yami Bolo, Chaka Demus & Pliers and the seriously undervalued Gina Foster all pinpointing the duo's continued strengths.

2 Mysteries of Creation (Axiom) 1996
6 The Punishers (Island) 1996
7 Mambo Taxi (Island) 1997
Movie and TV themes dominate a collection of middling dubs and productions. Neville Hinds, Ansell Collins and Ambelique star, but the theme from *Mission Impossible* outshines them all.

7 Present Taxi Christmas (RAS) 1998
Festive offerings from the Tamlins and Beres Hammond are enjoyable, but the real meat is a 23 minute Taxi Gang medley, booming through "I Saw Mommy Kissing Santa Claus," "Little Drummer Boy," "Deck the Halls" and more. All you need for Xmas.

6 Babylon I Rebel (Exworks) 1998
6 Reggae Dance Hall (CAS) 1998
4 Friends (Elektra) 1998
A rather nasty little concoction as Simply Red's Mick Hucknall does dreadful things to "Night Nurse," and UB40 forget there was ever a day when they were considered one of Britain's finest reggae bands. Lionel Ritchie and the Rolling

Stones also get songs in, but it's the *Mission Impossible* theme which is the biggest attraction here. Again.

5 Strip to the Bone (Palm Pictures) 1999

If you can switch off the TV and just play the music, *Strip* is, at worst, a neat dub demonstration disc, and, at best, aural wallpaper for an earthquake zone. The "13 erotic music videos" alluded to on the cover, however, are somewhat less alluring—unless you really like dry ice, greasy poles and tassles. Lots of tassles.

5 Massive (NYC) 1999
5 Dub Fire (NYC) 2000

The suspicion that "experimental dub" is just another way of saying, "here's a bunch of rhythms we couldn't do anything else with," is cynical, insulting and horribly inaccurate. Probably.

4 Monty Meets Sly & Robbie (Telarc) 2000

Wasteful extended jam jazz collaboration with Monty Alexander.

SELECTED COMPILATIONS & ARCHIVE RELEASES

8 Present Taxi (Island) 1981

Excellent 12 song/10 artist round-up of early Taxi sides, featuring Gregory Isaacs, Dennis Brown and Junior Delgado, alongside harder to find performances by Wailing Souls, General Echo and Sheila Hylton, performing the Police's "The Bed's too Big Without You"—and proving the English band weren't as far off the point as reggae purists like to say! The Tamlins' take on the Undisputed Truth's funk hit "Smiling Faces Sometimes" is similarly appealing, while Sly's "Hot You're Hot" is a Black Uhuru dub in all but name.

6 Crucial Reggae Driven by Sly & Robbie (Mango) 1982

12 track compilation features eight Sly & Robbie productions, plus four others which simply feature them. Mighty Diamonds' "Pass the Kouchie" (a Gussie Clarke production), Jimmy Riley's steamy take on Marvin Gaye's "Sexual Healing" and Flabba Holt's "Danger Zone" are solidly excellent; the rest of the set, however, offers little in the way of must-haves.

7 Sly & Robbie & the Taxi Gang V Purpleman & Friends (Vista Sounds—UK) 1983

Eccentric Bunny Wailer production featuring remixes and restructuring of various sessions.

8 A Dub Extravaganza (CSA—UK) 1984

Excellent compilation pairing two of Prince Jammy's finest Sly & Robbie sets, the Black Uhuru and Johnny Osbourne dub albums. The set has since been reissued by UK label Snapper.

7 Sounds of Taxi Volume One (Taxi) 1984

The first of three volumes of label samplers released over the next three years, all sweeping up stray singles, b-sides and dubs.

6 A Dub Experience (Island) 1985

Eight dub mixes from past 45s, precise and pristine to be sure, but occasionally the ideas are more repetitive than remarkable ("Computer Malfunction" seems endless). The skittering exhilaration of "Joy Ride" and "Skull & Crossbones," however, more than redeem the show, while "Destination Unknown" (Uhuru's "Chill Out") is a remarkable reinvention.

7 Taxi Fare (Heartbeat) 1987

Luscious Taxi singles collection reaches its highest peaks with "Devil Pickney," "Fort Augustus" and "Triplet," with its melody line borrowed from new wavers Yaz's "Don't Go." Interestingly, the tracks with the most self-referential titles ("Taxi Connection," "Unmetered Taxi" and "Rock Music") are also the least enjoyable.

9 Hitbound! The Revolutionary Sound of Channel One (Heartbeat) 1989

Not a Sly & Robbie album per se; rather, an examination of the best output of Channel One during 1973–77, with the Revolutionaries of course the featured players. Hell & Fire, the Mighty Diamonds, Black Uhuru, Horace Andy, the Meditations and Junior Byles (the heavenly "Fade Away") pinpoint some of the studio's greatest triumphs, with a second volume, *The Mighty Two* (Heartbeat, 1992), picking up more of the same.

7 Two Rhythms Clash (RAS) 1989

Inventive compilation wrapping up recent work with Little John, Scarface, Half Pint and others.

6 Hits 1978–90 (Sonic Sounds) 1990
7 Dubs for Tubs (Rohit) 1990
8 Ragga pon Top (Pow Wow) 1993

Sides cut with Papa San, Cutty Ranks and General Degree are among Sly & Robbie's finest early 1990s work; a perfect latter-day primer.

7 Many Moods of (Sonic Sounds) 1994

Generous selection of mid-late 1980s dubs.

6 Duble Trouble (Artists Only) 1997

The lack of annotation is infuriating, but sonically this seems very early-mid 1980s, featuring dubs based around Peter Tosh's "Burial," John Holt's "Fancy Make-up" and Ken Boothe's "I'm Just a Man." None ever reach the heights the duo were capable of, but it's an enjoyable listen.

4 Gold Dubs: Ultimate Reggae Collection (Fine Tune) 2000

Low budget collection of dubious provenance. The dubs themselves are adequate, but the absence of any recording info means you could be listening to anyone.

9 **The Ultimate Collection: In Good Company (Universal) 2001**

17 tracks showcasing the duo's diversity, pulling from Taxi tracks and their work for other producers, and highlighting both their musical and studio genius. Amazingly, considering the material, the album holds together as a coherent whole, even while running riot across genres, from roots to disco, from dance hall to dub, Joe Cocker to Joan Armatrading, Grace Jones to Gregory Isaacs.

SOCA

The Trinidadian economic boom of the 1970s and early 1980s saw calypso spend the decade in a limbo of more-or-less absolute stagnation, drifting along in the same state of euphoric buoyancy as the populace. A mere handful of voices had spoken out against the island's sudden wealth and its attendant luxurious evils. Black Stalin, Chalkdust, Explainer and Maestro all took turns warning that the prosperity could not last forever, while Gypsy's "The Sinking Ship," in 1986, boldly prophesied the demise of the ruling PNP party itself, by pointing out all that had gone adrift since the death of Prime Minister Eric Williams in March, 1981. (Sure enough, the PNP was soundly defeated in that year's General Election.)

A few more calypsonians registered their protests in other ways, experimenting within the confines of calypso in the hope of finding new musical styles locked within its soul. But with a handful of exceptions — Lord Shorty's Indo-Caribbean hit "Indrani" (1973), Shadow's 1974 Road March winner "Bassman" and the later "De Hardis" — that's all they were, experiments.

In 1978, however, Shorty re-emerged with a sound which was not only defiantly different, it was also startlingly successful. His album *Soca Explosion* struck out at the very foundations of the genre. For the first time in calypso history, guitars, bass and synthesizers moved to the fore, altering the very fabric of the music. Suddenly louder and faster, bolder and brighter, soca was the sound of song being subverted by the senses, a passionate music which may still have had time for the lyricism of old, but offered the first time listener so much more. Dance now, pay attention later.

Soca swept the country and, as the hard times began to kick in, it rejuvenated it. Just as dance hall reinvigorated the Jamaican music industry with its return to the musical basics of abandon and freedom, so soca held out a similar promise and delivered accordingly. The difference was, there was no dark side to soca, no menacing slacker culture to push the lyrical and emotional envelope into ever deeper, darker recesses of socio-sexual drama.

If soca had any drawback, it was that it facilitated the opposite movement entirely, allowing the music access to areas where calypso had never previously ventured, where the lyric itself became a mere cog in the machine, and could

be reduced down to its barest catch-phrase simplicity. Shorty himself loathed that development, cursing the day he ever came up with the music, and abandoning it for a rebirth as the Rastafarian Ras Shorty I soon after.

But if he had not done it, somebody else would have. Some six months before Shorty's *Soca Explosion* album hit the streets, the Guyana-born, London-based musician Eddy Grant launched his debut solo album with the single, "Hello Africa" — itself close enough to Shorty's soca prototype to at least claim godparenthood. Elsewhere, the Montserrat-born Arrow, too, was becoming increasingly adventurous in his quest for a revolutionary fusion.

The speed with which soca took off is indicative of the need which it fulfilled. Within months, and certainly by the dawn of the 1980s, it seemed soca had all but pushed traditional calypso into a back-seat in its own back yard.

New talent exploded forth. Some artists — the majority — scored with one major anthem, then retreated back into obscurity. Others, however, were in it for the long haul. Arrow became renowned as soca's first superstar, and proceeded to clash soca with music from elsewhere around the region to create ever-more vibrant dance-friendly hybrids. David Rudder eschewed even the beguiling gimmickry of old by refusing to adopt a nickname, then produced calypso's first ever concept album. Lord Nelson delved into soca funk, Blue Boy toyed with the sounds of African spirituality.

Some of the doughtiest practitioners of the old music, Lord Kitchener, Roaring Lion and Jamaica's Byron Lee among them, were embracing the new sound with more enthusiasm than they had shown in years. Indeed, Kitchener himself described soca as the most exciting development in calypso history since his own Young Brigade shook the beast by the scruff of its neck thirty years before. And perhaps he, too, wondered why people weren't so quick to slap on new labels in those days.

Or maybe they were, and they just didn't believe the change was profound enough to merit one. Today, after all, a musician only needs to play in a slightly different key for the media to gaily festoon their bandwagon with yet another outlandishly meaningless generic title, and commentators enough have already mused that soca is simply calypso's current nom-de-plume.

Others, however, argue that soca has nothing more to do with true calypso than simple geography. In 1993, Chalkdust's "Kaiso In The Hospital" hit out at what he perceived to be a deluge of new songs, none of which seemed to demand the listener do anything more than jump up, jam and wine on a bumsie. "The young ran amok, they cursed in the worst way/drugs and sex they glorified/they called themselves rock, rap, zouk and reggae/and kaiso's house they occupied."

His words fell on fertile soil. Already, "old time" calypso

has threatened several comebacks, in T&T itself, but elsewhere around the world as well, where its roots and traditions may not be so actively cherished, but the appreciation is no less sincere.

There it rubs shoulders with the myriad other variations on a wealth of old themes which the modern age has seen fit to bless with sobriquets of various (and occasionally, extraordinarily dubious) relevance. And so we have jab-jab soca, named from the jab-jab, or devil, bands who once haunted early carnival, chasing evil spirits with a cacophony of hubcaps and biscuit tins. Then there's jamoo (from Jah Music)-soca, from Lord Shorty's Rasta-influenced spiritual sound, allying the consciousness of Dread with the abandon of his personal Frankenstein.

Chutney-soca notes the East Indian input into the fusion, while dance hall-soca and ragga-soca hail young T&T's interest in its Jamaican counterpart, and borrowing the Kingston studio practice of reusing the same rhythm for song after song. And beyond that there's rap-so(ca), for the poets who have returned the lyric to the forefront of the battleground. We even have boy band-soca, as an American DJ recently, stumblingly, summed up the Baha Men.

At the end of it all, though, what we really have is calypso. So many variations, so many disparate sounds. But just one single, common root. Calypso is the sound of carnival, and carnival is the world of calypso. And for as long as one prospers, the other has no alternative but to do likewise.

SOCA MONARCH

The most significant addition to carnival competition since Panorama, awarded in response to the worldwide explosion of interest in soca during the 1980s.

1994 "Flag Party"—Superblue

1995 "On the Road"—Ronnie McIntosh

1996 "Bounce"—Superblue

1997 (tie) "Barbara"—Superblue; "Ent"—Ronnie McIntosh

1998 "Ato Party"—Superblue

1999 "Dus Dem"—Kurt Allen

2000 "Pump Up"—Superblue

2001 —Shadow

RECOMMENDED LISTENING

Calypso Compilation (JWP) 1997–date
Calypsoca (JWP) 1998–date

Two of the best series rounding up the best of the current year's carnival crop.

Carnival 1994 (Ice—UK) 1994
Carnival 1995 (Ice—UK) 1994

Only two annual volumes appeared, both weighted, of course, in favor of Ice's own ringbang movement, but offering up some remarkable highlights from the years in question. The United Sisters (featuring Singing Sandra, 1994) and the Rude Girls' "Kaka Lala" (1995) are especial treats.

Champions of Our Music 1999 (JWP) 1999

You want winners? You got them. Wrapping up the 1999 victors, Singing Sandra, Blue Ventures, Bomber, De Fosto, the Exodus and Desperadoes Steel Orchestras, David Rudder and Kitchener.

De Young Ones (KDS) 1970s

Round-up of some of the lesser-known calypsonians of the mid 1970s, with contributions from Brother Ebony, Lady Gypsy, Kaiso-Quero, Zessman, Calypso Joe, Brother Ray and Manchild's "Pan in Crisis."

JW Raggasoca Hits (JWP) 1997-date

It's not always easy to differentiate between the myriad strands now flying out of soca, but this series helps.

Kaiso Gems 1998: Kitchener's Calypso Revue (JWP) 1998

Was it that long ago? Panther, Bomber, Organizer, Stinger, Brown Bo, Mudada, Prince, Brother Marvin, Soft Touch, Puppet Master and Prince Monique highlight one of the season's best troupes.

Kamalo Deem: Bacchanal Time (Pempalah International—T&T) 1978

Excitable round-up of 1978's most memorable carnival hits, opening with the double punch of Shadow's "Bacchanal Time" and Calypso Rose's "Heat in the Area," but also serving up smashes by Trinidadian Rio ("Scrunting Calypsonian" and "Kaiso Have Me"), Count Robin and the proto-chutney "Bacchanal Wedding" (Puniya Ramkissoon & the Gasparillo Ladies Group) and "Bacchanal Tassa" (S Ramlogan & the Dyer Village Tassa Group).

Rituals 99 (Rituals) 1999

Label sampler heavy on rapso, but sparing a thought for more delicate sensibilities: come on in for Kindred, Nikki Crosby, Brother Resistance, Sharlene Boodram and 3 Canal.

Soca Anthems (SJP) 2000

Soca is party music, and what do you want at a party? Variety. A dozen songs pinpoint many of the music's different strands, ranging from Crazy's "Nani Wine" to the KP Sunshine Band's "Hot Hot Hot," plus hits by Krosfyah, Taxi, Mighty Power and more. Not every inclusion packs name recognition, but when you get down to the music, there's few false steps.

Soca Gold various volumes (JWP) 1992–date

The full story, at least so far as the tumultuous 1990s go. Appearing annually since 1992, the *Soca Gold* series is the first place to look, and the last thing you need, when it comes to isolating the biggest, brightest and (generally) the best songs of the year in question. There's usually one or two omissions, just to keep you interested in other releases, but essentially, this is the grail.

Soca Switch (JWP) 1998–date
Multi disc series launched with three volumes telling the story of 1998's greatest soca smashes, and continuing equally ambitious since then.

Soca—The Next Generation (Hot Vinyl) 1998
A daring title, but one which the album more or less lives up to. Third Bass, Jump Up and the Soldier Ants certainly rank among the most gripping of recent new arrivals, while Kurt Allen wins points simply for coming up with a title (let alone a song) like "Snufferluphergus."

This Is Soca (Sire) 1987
Double album introduction to recent releases aimed at the US market, and featuring Scrunter, Baron, Natasha, Gypsy, Black Stalin and more.

This Is Soca (Music Club) 1998
Impressive hits heavy round up of mid-late 1990s carnival hits, including offerings from David Rudder and Superblue, rapso stars Kindred, and chutney-soca hero Ajala. The mood is unrelenting soca party—there's little room for nuance or subtlety among the selections, meaning this isn't the place to start if you're chasing the full spectrum of the music. But if you want 15 songs which never let up, here you go.

Wind Your Waist (Shanachie) 1991
Powerful wrap-up is highlighted by Drupatee's "Mr Bissessar," Arrow's "Long Time" and Burning Flames' "Workey Workey," but also includes sterling efforts from Spice, Shadow, Tambu, Organiser and the immortal Kitchener ("Parkway").

JOSEPH SPENCE
STYLE *Barbadian blues/gospel*
BORN *8/3/10 (Andros, BAHA); d 3/18/84*

He has been described as among the greatest and most influential guitar players in the world. Certainly, once one moves out of the narrow confines of the rock market, there are few players who have had the impact of Joseph Spence and, narrowing one's search even further, there are few single Caribbean artists, outside of Bob Marley, who can be said to have produced as indelible an effect on the international scene.

Spence never set out to become a "star"; neither did he become one. Rather, the son of a Bahamas pastor was content in his youth simply to play guitar in a band led by his great uncle, Tony Spence. Upon leaving school, he worked

as a sponge fisher. After marrying in the late 1930s, he found work as a stone mason and a carpenter, supplementing his income with regular trips to the American south aboard the tide of Caribbean crop cutters which landowners imported every year.

He kept up his guitar playing, of course, and his travels to the US broadened his repertoire considerably. Back home, he played for hours, often accompanying his sister, singer Edith Pinder, entertaining friends, passers-by or simply himself with stylish, and utterly unique, renderings of whatever came to mind, blues, calypsos, folk or sacred songs, and that was all he dreamed of doing.

It was in 1958 that Spence's life was changed. In that year, blues scholar Sam Charters paid a visit to the Bahamas, keen to follow up on the field recordings captured by American folk archivist Alan Lomax some two decades previous. One of the first sounds he and his accompanying fiance encountered were made by what Charters initially thought were two guitarists, duelling across "some of the most exuberant, spontaneous and uninhibited guitar playing we'd ever encountered." He was even more astonished when he discovered that the sounds were emanating from just one man, performing in a self-made style which Spence himself called "scramming."

Charters immediately set up his recording equipment and spent the rest of that day recording Spence as he ran through highlights of his entire repertoire. Then, back in the US, Charters delivered the tape to the Folkways label, to become the *Music of the Bahamas Volume One* album.

In 1964, former Jim Kweskin Jug Band mainstay Fritz Richmond came to Barbados, in search of the guitarist. With equipment supplied by the American Nonesuch label, Richmond recorded an entire album in Spence's living room, for release in Nonesuch's Explorer Series the following year as *Happy All the Time*.

"It was probably the best, the purest Explorer record of that time," Elektra's Paul Rothchild later remarked. "And it sold 93 copies." In fact, total sales were several thousand, with New York musician John Sebastian later exclaiming, "that album was radically different. For New York City finger pickers, it was required reading."

In June, 1965, another pair of American musicologists, Jody Stecher and Peter Siegel, paid their own visit to the Bahamas, again in search of Spence. "On our first day in Nassau we began our search," the pair recalled. "We asked everyone, and the response was uniform and predictable: 'sure mon, I know Spence'—until we arrived in his own neighborhood, [where] nobody knew of [him]."

Finally a neighbor determined that their motives were musical (they were initially mistaken for tax collectors) and made the necessary introductions. Under considerably more organized conditions than Charters had enjoyed, the pair captured a veritable superstar jam on tape—Spence was joined by Edith Pinder, her bassist husband Raymond and their daughter, Geneva.

The Americans recorded a number of performers during their visit—singer Frederick McQueen, the Swain family, Bruce Green and others—and compiled the best of the tapes, including five of the Spence/Pinder performances, as the album *The Real Bahamas Volume One*.

It caused an immediate stir—indeed, Spence's arrangement of "I Bid You Goodnight," a traditional wake song which Lomax had first captured on tape back in 1935, subsequently became the Grateful Dead's traditional show closer, and was recorded on their *Live/Dead* album in 1970. It has since provoked covers from Aaron Neville, Nicolette Larson and Ralph McTell. Despite this success, it was another 13 years before a second set of recordings from these same sessions appeared, as *The Real Bahamas Volume Two*; the 1978 album was highlighted by another three Spence performances, while five more surfaced in 1995 as *Kneelin' Down Inside the Gate*.

Spence toured the US following the release of *The Real Bahamas*, stopping off in New York to record the seven tracks incorporated (with further Siegel material) into the *Spring of Sixty Five* album. By the end of the decade, he had made several further visits to the US to perform and record. Spence never pursued his musical options, however, he was simply delighted to meet many of the American guitarists who cited him as an influence. He was reportedly stunned to learn that Ry Cooder (whom he met at a concert in Boston in 1971) knew all of his recordings by heart.

Spence died in 1984; a tribute album was subsequently compiled by the Green Linnet label, featuring Henry Kaiser, Taj Mahal, Martin Carthy and others. Bahamaian junkanoo star KB (Kirkland Bodie) has since recorded his own tribute to Spence, "Riddim and Rhyme," which itself features a sample of Spence's own "Victory Is Coming."

SELECTED DISCOGRAPHY

7 Happy All the Time (Carthage) 1964
8 Good Morning Mr Walker (Arhoolie) 1972

Widely regarded as Spence's most triumphant original recording, a showcase not only of his talent, but also of his taste in material. The CD reissue of *Mr Walker* surpasses everything ever said about its vinyl counterpart, adding eleven bonus tracks, including seven recorded live.

SELECTED COMPILATIONS & ARCHIVE RELEASES

8 The Complete Folkways Recordings (Folkways) 1958

Nine tracks were spread across the original Folkways Bahamas albums—here Spence's entire Charters ouvre is compiled in a set which is as loose as it is invaluable.

7 The Real Bahamas Vol 1 (Nonesuch) 1965
6 The Real Bahamas Vol 2 (Nonesuch) 1978

Informal, primitive, doors bang and bullfrogs croak, but get past the sonic imperfections and it's difficult not to be drawn in to the sheer simplicity and joy of the performances. Although a single disc recounting of Spence's contributions alone has yet to be released (five further cuts appear on *Kneelin' Down Inside the Gate* (Rounder—1995), both volumes here have been reissued on one CD (Nonesuch Explorer—1998).

7 Bahamian Guitarist (Arhoolie) 1972

Spence's acclaimed May 16, 1971 Boston show provides seven tracks, including "The Lord Is My Shepherd," "Yellow Bird" and "Sloop John B." The remainder offers home recordings from the 1970s.

8 Living on the Hallelujah Side (Rounder) 1980

Lively compilation of 1970s recordings, at home and in concert, ranging from hymns to Ledbelly ("Goodnight Irene") and a playful "Santa Claus Is Coming to Town." A short (30+ minutes) album, but an utterly delightful one.

7 Glory (Rounder—1990)

Informal sessions recorded with Guy Droussart during the 1970s, again with the Pinders in evidence.

8 Spring of Sixty Five (Rounder) 1992

Compilation of Siegel recordings from both Nassau and New York City.

SQUARE ONE

STYLE *soca*
FORMED 1986 *(BARB)*
ORIGINAL LINE-UP Andy *"Youngblood"* Armstrong *(vocals), Cecil "O Shaka" Riley (vocals), Paul Slater (bass), George Jones (keyboards), Winston Beckles (drums)*

Square One developed from a band first formed at Lodge Secondary School, where Mac Fingall, a popular local entertainer, was games master and a guiding influence for students with a musical talent. Under his aegis, Andy Armstrong, performing under the name Youngblood, began singing calypso in local competitions in 1983. The following year, Fingall recruited him to the Untouchables tent, and introduced him to Crop Over, two years later, Armstrong entered the history books as the youngest calypsonian to reach the finals of the Pic-O-De-Crop Calypso Monarch competition.

Square One officially formed, albeit without a name, in December, 1986, with co-vocalist Alison Hinds joining later the following year. Born in London, in 1971, she had spent much of her childhood vacationing in her parents' Barbados homeland, before returning to live there with her mother in 1981, following her parents' divorce.

She met Youngblood soon after, although it was Crop Over 1987 before they began working together, when Fingall brought Hinds into the Untouchables tent chorus. According to legend, Hinds was enlisted into Square One after singing a Stevie Wonder song over the telephone during a conversation with Youngblood. He also persuaded her to enter a Teen Talent competition organized by local impresario Richard Stoute. Hinds finished joint third.

The group became Square One at Fingall's insistence, after he tired of hearing them reject other suggestions and complaining, "looks like we're back to square one." From there, they progressed quickly. They released their first album, *Eat Drink and Be Merry* in 1988, the same year that they were voted the Musicians & Entertainers Guild of Barbados' Hotel Band of the Year. They retained that title in 1989, and in 1990—augmented by keyboard player and songwriter Terry Arthur—they took the first of three consecutive awards in the same category from the Barbados Tourism Authority. They also became regulars on the nightclub circuit and, by the end of the 1980s, Square One were the official backing band for the Untouchables tent, a remarkable achievement for a group so young.

Square One played their first European tour in 1990, with their sophomore album, *Special*, arriving two years later, after the band joined Eddy Grant's Ice label. Hinds—duetting with local singer-songwriter John King—furthered their appeal in 1992, when she won the Barbados Song Contest with "Hold You in a Song." The pair was also the first Barbados act to win the CBU Caribbean Song Contest in T&T. Meanwhile, Square One themselves then became the island's first representatives at the Caribbean Music Awards at the Harlem Apollo in 1993.

The *Square Roots* album followed that same year, while the group also contributed to Ice's *Ringbang Rebel Dance* compilation, alongside Adisa Andwele, Gillo, Grandmaster and Grynner. By 1995, however, they had quit the label, and were preparing—unbelievably—their tenth anniversary album, *4 Sides*.

The set immediately spun off a major hit, Terry Arthur's "Raggamuffin." "Ring Kiting" and "Black History" followed. In addition, Hinds became the first ever female to win Barbados' Road March at Crop Over that year. She repeated that triumph in 1997, along with victory in the Party Monarch competition, while Square One achieved another remarkable first when all three lead vocalists, Hinds, Youngblood and Cecil Riley appeared in the Crop Over Party Monarch finals.

1997 brought the *Sweetness* album, again the source of a string of hits—"Aye Aye Aye," "Turn It Around (the Plumber)," "Ju Ju" and "Sugar (Sweet)." Square One also won the Barbados Crop Over Road March with "In the Meantime," a song which was surprisingly omitted from *Sweetness*.

In Full Bloom, in 1998, only amplified its predecessors' success. The track "DJ Ride" topped St Lucia's Radio Caribbean chart for a month, until it was replaced by Square One's next single, a version of the traditional Surinamese song "Faluma." "Bandit Dance" reached #1 in Barbados, while the group placed an incredible eight tracks on the charts in Trinidad & Tobago: "DJ Ride," "Faluma," "Kitty Cat," "Electricity," "Mannequin," "Bandit Dance," "La La" and "25," celebrating the 25th anniversary of Crop Over. "Faluma" was also elected top song at the Miami Carnival.

1999's *Fast Forward* simply continued the group's rise, while Hinds received an unexpected honor when Trinidad calypsonian Cro-Cro made her the subject of his entry for the 1999 King of Kings calypso competition, "Tribute to Alison Hinds."

SELECTED DISCOGRAPHY

5 **Eat Drink and Be Merry (—BARB) 1988**
5 **Special (Ice) 1992**
5 **Square Roots (Ice) 1993**

Opening with a pair of raucous stabs at rapso from Armstrong, *Square Roots* remains the sound of a very young band, still seeking their own identity. A lot of "let me hear you whoa" type choruses go down great in concert, but the studio experience is wearing.

8 **4 Sides (—BARB) 1996**
7 **Sweetness (—BARB) 1997**
8 **In Full Bloom (—BARB) 1998**

The joyous "Faluma" is the sound of Square One demonstrating just how broad their abilities are, but there isn't a dull cut in sight, as the album's extraordinary chart performances would suggest.

9 **Fast Forward (—BARB) 1999**

Arthur has developed into one of the classiest songwriters in the region, dabbling in dub and hip hop ("Rescue"), zouk ("Can't Keep A Good Man Down") and cadance ("If You Really Want It"), without ever making it sound like he's simply switching styles for the sake of it. Hinds, meanwhile, is radiant on "Give You What You Want" and "Bazzody For Jour O'vert."

SUPERBLUE

STYLE *soca*
BORN *Austin Lyons, 5/25/56 (Point Fortin, T&T)*

The Artist Formerly Known As Blue Boy apparently appeared out of the blue in 1980 to win the Road March competition with the soca-soaked African spiritual "Soca Baptist." It was the first time this new musical styling had taken the title, but of course it would not be the last.

Blue Boy's musical roots lay in a childhood fascination with pan. He taught himself to both make and play steel drums and, by his mid-teens, he was leading his own band, the Apple Stars Steel Orchestra. When that project ended, he turned to singing, with his 1980 triumph proving the wisdom of his decision.

Blue Boy's debut album that same year, *Soca in the Shaolin Temple*, confirmed his arrival and, in 1981, he repeated his Road March success with "Ethell," and again in 1983 with "Rebecca." Impressively, the same two songs also took the National Panorama Competitions, in the hands of the All Stars and the WITCO Desperadoes, respectively. 1984 then saw him compose "Ain't Boung for You" for Crazy, a fellow competitor in that year's Calypso Monarch competition.

In 1986, Blue Boy launched his own calypso tent, Culture House, forming a record label to operate alongside it. It was a time-consuming enterprise, although his own career remained on track. His "Blue Fever" finished second at the Road March, while that summer saw him among the stars of London's Socalypso 86 festival. Blue Boy's third album, 1988's *Caribbean Magic*, preceded a brief retirement from the public eye, reportedly while he dealt with "personal problems." He returned in 1989 as co-writer of "Nani Wine," Crazy's 1979 Road March contender.

The following year, he relaunched his own career under the name of Superblue, and in February, 1991, "Get Something an' Wave" announced his return with another Road March triumph. Two months later, Superblue was appearing at the Jamaica carnival and, that August, he was back in London for Socalypso 91, while celebrating his first decade in the business with the album *10th Anniversary*.

The following year, a second successive Road March champion ("Jab Jab"—later proclaimed Calypso Record of the Year) was followed by a return engagement in Jamaica and a triumphant showing at a soca festival in Central Park, New York City. 1993 brought Superblue's third successive Road March victory, with "Bacchanal Time" (the title track from his latest album) running out the highest scoring winner in the competition's history. He took the title again in 1995 with "Signal for Lara."

In the meantime, a new competition had been inaugurated apparently for his pleasure alone. In 1993, Superblue became the inaugural Soca Monarch, again with "Bacchanal Time"—his performance was screened worldwide by CNN, the first time the carnival had been broadcast on international television.

Delays with Superblue's next album, *Flag Party* (his second for producer Eddy Grant's Ice label) saw it hit the streets too late for his latest crop of songs to be included in the Road March roster—and that despite Ice rush-releasing it in T&T in a plain white sleeve, with the self-explanatory title *The Late but Great 94 Album*.

Nevertheless, the title track made it two Soca Monarch crowns in a row, while Superblue repeated the feat in 1996, with "Bounce." 1997 then saw Superblue's "Barbara" tie for the crown with Ronnie Allen, the 1995 winner.

Victory with "Ato Party" in 1998 was followed by an unexpected defeat the following year, when Superblue's "Countdown" finished third (behind Kurt Allen and Iwer George) in a very closely fought contest—just three points separated first from third place. Superblue reclaimed the crown in 2000 with "Pump Up," with the song also taking the Road March title.

Also in 2000, Superblue joined with soca singer Andy Stephenson for the "Soca Jumblie" single. A new record deal with Rituals, meanwhile, brought the album *Soca Matrix*. Hopes that he might retain his carnival crowns in 2001, however, were dashed by the pre-eminence of Shadow.

SELECTED DISCOGRAPHY

BLUE BOY

5 **Soca in the Shaolin Temple (Remes) 1980**

The title track opens some interesting avenues, but the album as a whole is fairly one-dimensional, akin to repeated plays of "Ethel" at different volumes.

5 **Thundering Soca (Charlies—T&T) 1984**

5 **Caribbean Magic (Bs—T&T) 1988**

SUPERBLUE

6 **Poom Poom (Charlies—T&T) 1990**

5 **10th Anniversary (Charlies—T&T) 1991**

6 **In the Power (Charlies—T&T) 1992**

Compared to what he has since accomplished, Blue Boy/Superblue's early albums are more or less inter-changeable, punchy soca with great hooks and irresistible covers.

7 **Bacchanal Party (Ice) 1993**

Nothing could follow "Bacchanal Time," but Superblue works hard to keep up the excitement, tackling Bob Marley's "Redemption Song" and the Bee Gees' "To Love Somebody," before wrapping up with a reprise of his own "Jab Jab."

9 **Flag Party (Ice) 1994**

Slam past the opening carnival hits, and it might as well be an entirely different album. Swirling electronics remind one of some of producer Grant's better 1980s work, while the moody "If You Vex No Sex" and a rearrangement of Grant's own "Do You Feel My Love" are extraordinary. Elsewhere, Superblue turns the Beatles' "I Want to Hold Your Hand" into a seductive smooch, then transforms their "Yesterday" into a dance hall medley with "What a Ting."

8 **Happy Carnival (Ice) 1995**

The fascinating "Signal for Lara" is the key cut, but Superblue also demonstrates his dexterity with flavorsome covers of rock hit "Sylvia's Mother" and producer Eddy Grant's "Walking on Sunshine."

7 Extreme Blue (JMC) 1997

Like the following year's *Ato Party*, less an album, more a glorified 12-inch single. Disappointing length is remedied, however, by the infectious contents — "Billie Jean (Who Is de Daddy)" takes Michael Jackson into some very strange territory.

8 Soca Matrix (Rituals) 2000

Adding dance hall rapper General Grant to the zouk-ish "The Prayer" was a masterstroke, bringing the mood down from the jump up frenzy of "Jump for Joy" and "Pump Up," and ensuring *Matrix* remains as diverse as the best of Blue always ought.

SELECTED COMPILATIONS & ARCHIVE RELEASES

7 King of the Road March (Charlies—T&T) 1996

Collection tracing Superblue's development from the early days of Blue Boy, through to "Signal For Lara." The jumbled track selection makes no allowances for his stylistic changes, but neither does Road March, and most of the album was written for it.

7 Hooray (SJP) 1999

Another straightforward hits collection. Hooray.

THIRD WORLD

STYLE *reggae (roots)*
FORMED 1973 *(Kingston, JA)*
ORIGINAL LINE-UP *Milton "Prilly" Hamilton (vocals), Stephen "Cat" Coore (guitar), Richard Daley (bass), Michael "Ibo" Cooper (keyboards), Carl Barovier (drums), Irvin "Carrot" Jarrett (percussion)*

Although success and an eye for the poppier side of their music, have increasingly marginalized and minimized Third World's effect upon the modern reggae market, there can be little doubt that—alongside Inner Circle and the Wailers—the Kingston sextet were responsible for introducing an entire new audience to the sound of Jamaica, one which might otherwise have spent their lives believing that reggae meant Eric Clapton and the Police.

Third World's sheer longevity has not only marked them out as persevering, it has also seen them win the applause of Stevie Wonder, the Brecker Brothers and Stetasonic's Daddy O. The band's first international hit, 1978's "Now that We've Found Love," may have become a staple of American AOR radio, their blithe mix of the sweetest soul and the lightest roots may have alienated all but the staunch-est of the acolytes who greeted their debut album with rapturous cheers, but the group have still smashed musical boundaries without even appearing to raise their voices.

Third World formed in 1973, when Michael Cooper, Stephen Coore and Milton Hamilton quit the Inner Circle Band (as they were then called) partly because of their school exams, but also to pursue what they saw as a logical extension to Bob Marley's recent absorption of rock and soul influences into his music.

Their first recruit was bassist Richard Daley, ex-Ken Boothe's band and, subsequently, the Astronauts, the Hell's Angels and Tomorrow's Children (with whom he toured the US in 1972, opening for Toots & The Maytals). Drummer Carl Barovier and another Inner Circle graduate, percussionist Irvin "Carrot" Jarrett, followed and, early in 1974, the funk-reggae based Third World made their live debut.

Initial reaction to their hybrid was stunned astonishment; similar surprise greeted the band's resolute refusal to slip into the Kingston routine of freelancing around the studios until they found themselves a hit. They recorded some demos with Geoffrey Chung, but took the relationship no further, instead debuting with the self-produced "Railroad Track" 45 in 1974. They eschewed the dance halls in favor of the uptown circuit of hotels and nightclubs, and their reputation soared so swiftly that, when the Jackson Five performed at the Jamaican National Stadium, the still-infant Third World joined the veteran Wailers as the opening acts.

From there they traveled to the UK, where Island Records quickly snapped them up. By summer, Third World were touring Europe with the Wailers—they were opening act at the London Lyceum, the night the Wailers' breakthrough *Live* album was recorded.

Preceded by the single "Freedom Song," Third World's eponymous debut album followed in 1976. The album attracted warm interest from the specialist press, and reasonable sales. (Despite claims elsewhere, it was an entirely different Third World band which scored a US R&B hit that same year with "Disco Hop").

Early line-up changes saw the arrival of drummer Willie Stewart and singer/guitarist William "Bunny" Clark—another early member of Inner Circle (1970–72), but more recently a graduate of Lee Perry's Black Ark studio. Under Perry's supervision, Clark cut a number of tracks during 1972–74, including "What's the Use," "Kinky Fly" and versions of "Sweet Caroline," "Harry Hippy" and "To Love Somebody." (This material is included on the album, *To Love Somebody*, credited to Bunny & The Upsetters.) He now divided his time between recording in Jamaica and staying with his parents in New York. It was there that he met Third World.

With their new line-up settled, Third World prepared for what should have been the most exciting show of their career so far, the Wailers' Smile Jamaica festival at Kingston's National Heroes Park on December 5, 1976. Two days before the event, however, Marley was shot in an apparent assassination attempt. Although wounded, he refused to cancel the festival outright — rather, he announced he would decide at the last minute whether to go ahead.

When Third World arrived at the venue, it was to discover that they were the only scheduled act who had turned up — Peter Tosh, Bunny Wailer and Burning Spear had all dropped out, and it was left to Third World to gauge the mood of the audience alone. Their set, in front of a crowd of 80,000 people, was a success, prompting Marley and the Wailers to make their own way to the venue, for an abbreviated, and still heavily bandaged, set.

Third World's second album, *96 Degrees in the Shade* arrived in 1977, with its title track becoming a UK cult hit as one of the hottest summers on record dragged on. Among the other cuts, "Jah Glory" and a superb cover of Bunny Wailer's "Dreamland" confirmed the group members' Rastafarian beliefs. Again the band toured the UK — it was there that they encountered Marley once again, as he completed work on his *Exodus* album. Together with members of the British reggae band Aswad, Third World joined Marley in the studio with producer Lee Perry for a handful of sessions, cutting the seminal "Punky Reggae Party" and a new version of an original Wailers classic, "Keep on Moving."

Released as Third World became one of the stars of the inaugural Reggae Sunsplash festival, the band's third album, *Journey to Addis*, catapulted them to fame via a superb disco-reggae cover of the Gamble/Huff soul classic "Now that We've Found Love" and the title track, an adaptation of the late Don Drummond's "Confucius."

While the album made #30 in the UK, "Now that We've Found Love" reached #10, also climbing to #47 in the US during fall, 1978. A second single, "Cool Meditation," hit UK #17 in the new year, as Third World completed their next album, *The Story's Been Told*. A new single, "Talk to Me," reached #56, while Third World also appeared at the 1979 Reggae Sunsplash event. (The group returned to the festival in 1981, 1983, 1985, 1989, 1991 and 1997.)

Third World's fifth album appeared in 1980. *Arise in Harmony* sold poorly, despite good reviews, while a remarkably strong live album, *Prisoner in the Street*, was amazingly overlooked.

Everything turned around, however, in 1981. Having lost much of their original roots credibility over the course of their last three albums, Third World entered the studio with producer Niney Holness to cut a one-off single, the self-affirming — and so aptly titled "Roots with Quality." Then, newly signed to Columbia and with their *Rock the World* album having spawned another UK Top 10 hit, "Dancing on the Floor," Third World appeared at a Reggae Sunsplash utterly clouded by the death of Bob Marley just months earlier. There they turned in a dynamic, yet absolutely heartfelt set, closing with a special appearance from Stevie Wonder, performing his own tribute to Marley, "Master Blaster."

Wonder took the helm for Third World's next single, writing and producing "Try Jah Love," from 1982's *You've Got the Power* album, and contributing another track, the epic "You're Playing Us too Close." "Lagos Jump" and the album *All the Way Strong* followed in 1983, this time cut with another American funk legend, the Earth Wind & Fire horn section. 1985 brought *Strength of Purpose*, the band's first release as a five piece following the departure (due to "creative differences") of "Carrot" Jarrett.

Throughout much of this period, Third World's international profile was at an all-time low. Boasting remixes by American dancefloor specialist Shep Pettibone, "Sense of Purpose" and "One to One," from the *Strength of Purpose* album made the lower reaches of the American R&B chart. However, *Hold onto Love* (home of the Jamaican hit "Reggae Radio Station" — 1987) made no impression whatsoever outside of the island.

1989 saw the band back up to their original strength with the temporary arrival of Canadian-born multi-instrumentalist/producer Rupert Gypsy Bent III. Initially recruited for live work only, Bent co-wrote the band's next major hit, "Forbidden Love," from the *Serious Business* album, before departing again. Featuring Stetasonic's Daddy-O, "Forbidden Love" reached #17 on the American R&B chart, Third World's biggest US hit since "Now that We've Found Love," and one of the first ever reggae-rap crossover successes. "It's the Same Old Song" proved a reasonably successful follow-up later in the year.

With the band constantly touring, three years elapsed before Third World's next album, 1992's *Committed*, a set which included collaborations from either end of the historical spectrum — dance hall hero Terror Fabulous appeared on "Mi Legal," while Skatalites Tommy McCook and Roland Alphonso guested on "Give the People What They Need." Two years later, *Live It Up* continued their reggae rediscovery and included a radical version of the Temptations' "Papa Was a Rolling Stone" featuring dance hall superstar Beenie Man. The flip of the coin was their presence on the debut album by Sebastian, the cartoon crab in Disney's *The Little Mermaid* movie.

Live It Up reunited them with songwriter Rupert Bent — he joined Third World permanently in 1997, following the departure of founding member Cooper and drummer Stewart. Leroy Baarbe Romans (keyboards, flute — ex-Maxi Priest) and former Jimmy Cliff/Julian Marley drummer, Tony Ruption Williams were hastily recruited. Romans was later replaced, in March, 1999, by English born Mikel Wallace (ex-Chalice). Wallace was shot to death in Jamaica July 6, 1999; in his stead came Herbert Herbie Harris (also ex-Maxi Priest). This line-up debuted on 2000's Grammy nominated *Generation Coming*.

In the interim, Rugs released the solo albums *Talking to You* (1995) and the soul/R&B covers collection *On Soul* (2000). Cat Coore cut his own *Uptown Rebel* in 1997.

DISCOGRAPHY

7 **Third World (Island) 1976**
It's fashionable to call this the band's only true roots album, although a breezy cover of "Satta Amasa Gana" aside, all the ingredients of Third World's later convolutions are in place, including the pop masterpiece "Freedom Song."

8 **96 Degrees in the Shade (Island) 1977**
Again, there's one song (the title track) which promises a dread roots experience. Elsewhere, building on the foundation of their debut, the group hit new heights of reggae lite. It's very slick (especially "Third World Man"), but songs like "Human Market Place" are pure quality.

7 **Journey to Addis (Island) 1978**
With its now rampant pop flavor and nods to funk and jazz lite, *Addis* was an easy entry into reggae for those who like their lyrics upbeat and their music unchallenging. Cynics, unable to fault the band's conviction and musicianship, have since found this album guilty of laying the foundation for the worst excesses of world music . . . ah, but they've probably not heard the warm, smooth vibes of "Now that We've Found Love" and "Cool Meditation" for a while.

6 **The Story's Been Told (Island) 1979**
The funky title track takes the band firmly into Earth Wind & Fire territory, a mood which is pretty much relentless — even "Irie Ites" defies its title in favor of some tight disco riffs.

5 **Arise in Harmony (Island) 1980**
7 **Prisoner in the Street (Island) 1980**
Shrugging aside the smoother edges of their studio work, a powerful "greatest hits — live" set includes spellbinding versions of "96 in the Shade," "African Woman" and the title track. Further highlights from the same show appear on the *Reggae Ambassadors* anthology.

5 **Rock the World (Columbia) 1981**
4 **You've Got the Power (Columbia) 1982**
5 **All the Way Strong (Columbia) 1983**
5 **Sense of Purpose (Columbia) 1985**
4 **Hold onto Love (Columbia) 1987**
Occasional highlights leap out of each of the band's Columbia albums, but the 1993 *Best Of* wraps them up in repre-sentative style, and the group's blithe acceptance of US-style R&B, with just a hint of reggae beat, is little more than daytime radio fodder.

6 **Serious Business (Mercury) 1989**
A return to form of sorts, with "Reggae Ambassador" at least proving they can still dub out when they want to — Ibo's rap in the "DJ Ambassador" mirror is rather good, too.

6 **Committed (Mercury) 1992**
6 **Live It Up (Third World — JA) 1994**
6 **Generation Coming (Gator) 2000**

SELECTED COMPILATIONS & ARCHIVE RELEASES

6 **The Best of Third World (Columbia) 1993**
That's the best, minus anything recorded prior to 1980.

8 **Reggae Ambassadors (Island) 1993**
Two-CD anthology spanning the band's entire career and, while emphasizing their smoother side, at least acknowledging the roots sensibilities which continue to fire them. "Now that We've Found Love" is included in a hypnotic 8 minute, 12-inch, mix; while alternate versions of "Railroad Track" and "Mi Legal," unreleased live material and Niney's politely borderline cataclysmic "Roots with Quality" offer further highlights.

7 **The Ultimate Collection (Hip-O) 2001**
Well compiled set gathers together the best of the band's singles output.

TOASTING: THE ART OF THE DJ

Although it wasn't until the late 1960s that toasting made its mark on the Jamaican recording industry, the concept of disc jockeys talking — toasting or rapping — over the records they were playing is actually one of the oldest traditions in the island's modern musical history.

Barely had the first sound systems opened in the immediate post-World War Two era, than the more enterprising DJs were finding new ways of making their acts more exciting. At first, they were content simply to ensure that the selection of music at their disposal was wider and weirder than their rivals — every sound system that could afford it was employing agents, usually merchant seamen plying the waters between Jamaica and Florida, to scour US record stores in search of new tunes. When a ship docked, the harbor came alive with private enterprise as the sailors unloaded their vinyl cargo, and runners raced back to the DJs with the latest precious discs, to be slammed into action that same evening.

The biggest hits, which in turn often meant the ones which no other sound system had yet obtained, were worth their weight in gold, and DJs went to any lengths to safeguard that exclusivity. The modern "white label" pressings, manufactured for club DJs in the cut-throat world of discotheques and nightclubs, have their origins in the sound systems, as the operators painstakingly obliterated any identifying marks on a prized record's label.

A big dance hall hit — that is, a record so popular that audiences kept coming back to hear it — could make a DJ's reputation. More than one could assure at least fleeting immortality. The secret of true longevity, however, was to keep having the hits and, for those moments when a record simply wasn't getting the crowd moving, to have an act which itself captivated the audience.

Slowly the function of the DJ changed, from the simple disc spinner familiar to American and European audiences, to a performer in his own right. Soon, it was the "selector" who physically placed the record on the turntable, and the needle on the record. The DJ's job was to ensure that the record remained interesting.

Flamboyant names and outrageous clothing became a part of the game, so did verbal gimmicks and catch-phrases. Talking to the crowd, drawing them into the act (and the persona) was the next step; talking back to, or even over, the records, inter-acting with them while they played, naturally followed.

It is one of the musical tragedies of the age that none of the first DJs — or, at least, their performances — were ever recorded. Hearsay and memories alone survive today to tell us how, during the early 1950s, DJ Count Machuki was dropping jokes and wisecracks into the records he was playing; how, by the time he joined Coxsone Dodd's Downbeat system around 1956, he was incorporating his own lyrics into them; and how, within weeks, he was hearing about people buying records they'd heard at the dance hall, then returning them because they didn't sound the same. Of course they didn't — they didn't have Count Machuki on them.

Machuki is the first to admit that his style was rooted in the same fast-talking jive traditions which American DJs had been employing for years — both New Orleans and Miami boasted radio stations powerful enough to reach Jamaica. In the dance hall context, however, he was an absolute pioneer. Among the largest sound systems, both King Stitt and Sir Lord Comic were soon basing their acts on Count Machuki's, while smaller set-ups began staging regular talent contests as an entire generation of new DJs grew up in his tumultuous wake.

Although several early ska singles featured guest appearances (Count Machuki can be heard on Baba Brooks' "Alcatraz"; King Stitt appears on Lynford Anderson's "Pop a Top"), the first DJ to actually release a single was Sir Lord Comic, whose "Ska-ing West" appeared in 1966. King Stitt and Count Machuki followed him into the marketplace with Stitt, in particular, harnessing the then-new reggae rhythm for his own massively enjoyable, and wildly idiosyncratic, ends.

Born with a severe facial disfigurement, Stitt built his act around the fact that he *was* ugly, and his records followed suit, both overtly and otherwise. His biggest hit was the Clancy Eccles produced "Lee Van Cleef," dedicated to the western actor of the same name — and why? Because in the hit movie *The Good, the Bad & the Ugly*, Van Cleef took the latter role.

Throughout the 1960s, this trio ruled the DJ scene. As the new decade dawned, however, fresh talents began emerging. In very short succession, U-Roy, Dennis Alcapone, Big Youth and I-Roy broke through, a new generation of toasters, with a whole new sound of their own.

Among their predecessors, it had often been enough to simply jive talk over the rhythms. The new DJs went way beyond that. Sometimes sexual, often-times boastful, occasionally political but always worth listening to, they made records which transcended accepted musical boundaries, even as they adhered themselves to some of the best loved oldies which the studio could lay its hands on.

Nobody hearing U-Roy's rendering of the Paragons' "Wear You To The Ball" could have failed to recognize the song (and if they did, writer and original vocalist John Holt was on hand to jog their memory). But U-Roy completely restructured it and, in so doing, he not only launched his own career, he also launched those of all the DJs lined up behind him. His nickname of "the Originator" could not have been more accurate.

Each of U-Roy's first three singles topped the Jamaican charts, and Dennis Alcapone — equally unique, equally dramatic — pursued him to glory. Suddenly, every producer in Kingston had his own toasting prodigy and, suddenly, toasting itself was coming under scrutiny.

In an industry which had never paid its performers more than a handful of dollars for a recording; where such notions as copyright and royalties were unheard of; suddenly an awful lot of money was being made by having one guy shout over another guy's record — money which usually went straight to the third guy who produced both of them. Certainly neither the musicians nor the original composer of the song would see a cent, a woeful state of affairs which grew worse as the 1970s carried on.

The Jamaican Federation of Musicians (JMF) was especially incensed and, during the early 1970s, president Sonny Bradshaw led an increasingly outspoken campaign against the toasters. In 1974, he finally persuaded the two major national radio stations, JBC and RJF, to impose an unspoken ban on any DJ or dub record which didn't employ an original rhythm. Of course it was little more than a cosmetic gesture — it was the dance halls which made the hit records, not the radio — but it did turn the tide a little. More and more DJs and producers began working up original rhythms; either that, or veteran performers would be called into the studio to recreate their greatest hits. And the records just kept on selling.

U-Roy, I-Roy, Alcapone and Big Youth aside, few of the early 1970s DJ stars impacted beyond the Jamaican scene, although that is not to say that there were not plenty of gems to be found among the flood of hopefuls released during the peak of the toasting boom, 1970–74. Charlie Ace, Jah Lloyd, Jah Stitch, Big Joe and Mad Roy (aka session drummer and *Rockers* movie star Leroy Wallace) all cut excellent 45s, with Prince Jazzbo attaining a certain immortality via a well-received musical feud with I-Roy. Prince Glen also enjoyed some longevity, simply by reinventing himself as Trinity. It was his "Three Piece Suit" hit in 1977 which prompted the creation of one of Jamaica's biggest international hits of the decade, Althea & Donna's "Up Town Top Ranking."

The near-simultaneous advent of Dillinger, Tappa Zukie and Prince Far I during the mid-1970s reignited DJ fever, by allying it utterly with the now similarly explosive roots scene and cutting some of the most invigorating music of the age. Indeed, Zukie's "MPLA" and Far I's "Under Heavy Manners" traveled so far beyond the former boundaries of "toasting" that those earlier DJs who were still on the scene felt themselves duty-bound to follow in their footsteps — with I-Roy's *Ten Commandments*, reciting Biblical passages over the Wailers' *Exodus* album, ranking alongside the best of Far I in terms of apocalyptic dread.

The mid-1970s also saw the advent of Dr Alimantado. The self-styled Ital Doctor started DJing with the Lord Tippertone Hi Fi sound system in Kingston, recording a string of singles under such aliases as Winston Cool, Winston Prince and Youth Winston. He worked with Lee Perry for a time, and also with Bunny Lee, but his actual breakthrough came with the self-produced "The Best Dressed Chicken in Town," an utterly dynamic reworking of Bill Withers' "Ain't No Sunshine."

Utilizing much of what he learned from Perry and forming his own Ital and Vital Sounds labels, further singles "Chant to Jah," "Unitone Skank" and "Oil Crisis" (set to the "Best Dressed Chicken" rhythm) ensured his continued pre-eminence. Also popular was the topical "Poison Flour" (featuring backing vocals from Horace Andy), discussing a recent incident in rural Jamaica, where a shipment of contaminated flour led to a number of deaths.

In 1977, Alimantado was knocked down and almost killed by a bus in downtown Kingston. He recovered from his injuries and released the self-explanatory "Born for a Purpose" through Channel One in Jamaica, and on the tiny, newly formed Greensleeves label in Britain.

Weeks later in London, Sex Pistols frontman Johnny Rotten included the song among his all-time favorite records on a Capital Radio broadcast, and Alimantado's earlier specialist popularity exploded into de facto punk cultdom. UK sales of "Born for a Purpose" eventually exceeded 50,000, prompting Alimantado relocated to the UK, to become one of the guiding lights of that land's own reggae movement.

The dread DJs ruled supreme for five years, their consciousness messages hitting home as hard as any singer's. As the decade reached its close, however, the more perceptive of them noticed that the temperament of the dance halls was beginning to change.

They were not surprised; it had happened before, and it would happen again. They simply counted themselves fortunate to be given so much advance warning. It was the DJs, during the early 1960s ska years, who reported back when a new rhythm seemed particularly popular and, from these reports, both rock steady and reggae took wings, each displacing almost an entire generation of musicians and performers.

Now, in the late 1970s, it was the DJs who noticed how the floors began to clear when the latest roots record hit the turntable, then fill up again when something less weighty was spun. Again, it was time for a massive changing of the musical guard and, just as the first generation of toasters had moved aside when the roots crew stepped in, so they in turn were to be displaced as a third wave arose from the ringleaders of this latest shift. Dance hall, so named because that was where it began, had arrived.

It is impossible to over-estimate the importance of the DJ in Jamaican music. They stand, after all, at ground zero, the middle man, if you will, between consumer and supplier and, for any competent sound system owning producer, the conduit by which the audience's own demands reached the recording studio. A rousing success in the dance halls almost automatically ensures a similar hit in the record racks, but even before a record has been made, it is the DJ's sensitivity to, and awareness of, shifts in the audience's temperament which tells the producers what they should be doing next.

When Jamaica was swept by a passion for medleys in the late 1960s, it was because one DJ, in one dance hall, one night, seamlessly segued three records together and received the loudest roar of the evening. Fifteen years later, when the dance hall crowd embraced the religious revivalist sounds of the Pukumina church, it was because another (Lord Sassafrass, head DJ at the Black Scorpio sound system) cut the stamping, clapping, banging and cheering which hallmark the cult's services into his set, and was forced to keep playing them for the rest of the show.

It is to maintain a grip on this vibrant pulse that many of Jamaica's top producers still operate their own sound systems, long after other traditional reasons — promoting new releases, introducing new performers and so forth — had been rendered obsolete by the explosion of new communications and media technologies.

One of the greatest failures of the Anglo-American music industry in the past two decades has been its absolute withdrawal from the rhythm of the streets, and the consequential collapse of anything even remotely resembling musical consensus. In Jamaica, the opposite is true. Even at the high end of the local hierarchy, among those labels and producers whose own renown rivals that of any band or musician, the chain remains the same as it always has been. In modern America, the consumer is the last to know what is going to be deemed "popular" next month. In Jamaica, he has always been the first. The DJs are there to make sure the news gets through.

INDEX OF LEADING DJS/SOUND SYSTEMS

The following directories are not comprehensive. However, they do indicate both the leading Jamaican sound systems of the past 40 years, and a sampling of the principle DJs at each. It should be remembered that the nature of sound systems is such that the majority of the DJs below have appeared with many more than are noted here.

CHARLIE ACE (Valden Dixon)/Swing-A-Ling

ADMIRAL BAILEY (Glendon Bailey)/King Jammys, Roots Melody

AFRICAN/King Jammys

DENNIS ALCAPONE (Dennis Smith, b 8/6/47)/El Paso

DOCTOR ALIMANTADO (Winston Thompson)/Lord Tippertone

PATRICK ANDY (b 1965)/Gemini

DADDY ANTS/Youth Promotion

ARCHIE/Gemini

ASHMAN (R. Ashman)/Metro Media

BUJU BANTON (Mark Myrie, b 1973)/Rambo Mango, Sweet Love

BURO BANTON (b 1960)/Roots Unlimited, Gemini, Volcano

MEGA BANTON (Garth Williams, b 1973)/Black Scorpio

DAVE BARKER (David Collins, b 1952)

BEENIE MAN (Anthony Moses Davis, b 8/22/73)/Prince Jammy's, Volcano, Bunny Lee's Unlimmited

SPRAGGA BENZ (Carlton Grant, b 1975)

BIG JOE (Joe Spalding, b 1955)/Small Axe Hi Fi

BIG JOHN (d 11/22/90)/Echo Tone

BIG YOUTH (Manley Augustus Buchanan b 4/19/49)/Lord Tippertone

BINGIE (Reuben Dixon)

BIONIC STEVE "PIRATE" (M. Townsend, d 1996)

BLACKA T (Lindon A Robertson)/Youth Promotion

EVERTON BLENDER/Destiny Outerational

YAMI BOLO/Youth Promotion

BOUNTY KILLER (Rodney Basil Price, b 6/72)/Black Scorpio, Killamanjaro, Stereo Two, Metromedia

BILLY BOYO/Volcano

BRIGADIER JERRY (Robert Russell)/King Sturgav Hi-Fi, Jah Love, Jack Ruby's

BARRY BROWN (b 1962)/Black Roots

BUCCANEER (Andrew Bradford, b 1974)

BUSHMAN aka JUNIOR MELODY (Dwight Duncan, b 1973)/Black Star Line

BUTTERCUP/Sir George

BUDI BYE/Youth Promotion

AL CAMPBELL/Gemini

ICHO CANDY (Winston Evans, b 1964)/Jack Ruby's

CAPLETON (Clifton Bailey, b 1974)/African Star

CAPTAIN BARKEY (Johnson Hamilton)/Stereo One

CAPTAIN SINBAD (Carl Dwyer)/Sound of Silence, Black Roots

CATARACT/Black Roots

CHARLIE CHAPLIN (Richard Patric Benett)/King Stur Gav

CHICKEN CHEST (Alton O'Reilly, b 11/28/62)/Arrows

CITCHIE see LT STITCHIE

[MAD] COBRA (Ewart Everton Brown, b 1968)/Mighty Ruler, Climax, Stereo One, Inner City

COLOUR MAN (Fidel Hugh Henry, b 1965)/Cosmic Force, Ghetto International, Masterblaster, Cadett Hi Power, Gemini, Volcano, Youth Promotion

COOL STICKY (Uziah Thompson, b 8/1/36)/Sir Coxsone Down Beat, Treasure Isle

COMMANDER SHAD (Carl Barrett)/King Jammys

JOSEPH COTTON aka JAH WALTON (Silbert Walton, b 1957)

COUNT BENZ/President

COUNT MACHUKI (Winston Cooper, b 1939; d 12/94)/Voice of the People, Sir Coxsone Down Beat

COUNT PRINCE MILLER/Highlights

LOUIE CULTURE (Lewin Brown)

CULTURE KNOX/Destiny Outerational

CUTTINS/Duke Reid

CUTTY RANKS (Philip Thomas, b 2/12/65)/Feathertone, Stereomars, Killamanjaro, Arrows

DADDY BLUE (K.Walton)/Stereo One

DADDY LIZARD (Junior Bryan)

DADDY RINGS (Everald Dwyer, b 1972)/Black Cat, Oneness, Culture Shanti

DELANO Stone Love

CHAKA DEMUS aka NICODEMUS JR (John Taylor)/King Jammys, Supreme

DETERMINE (Rohan Bennett, b 1972)

DILLINGER (Lester Bullocks)/Prince Jackies, El Paso Hi Fi

DIRTSMAN (Patrick Thompson, b 1966; d 12/21/93)/Black Universe, Creation Rock Tower Sound

DOMINIC (Dominic Kenny)/King Jammys

DONNA P/Youth Promotion

DOUBLE UGLY (I) (D. Knight)

DOUBLE UGLY (II) see NINJAMAN

DANNY DREAD/Metro Media, Volcano

MIKEY DREAD (Michael Campbell)/Radio Jamaica Rediffusion

DUKE VIN/Tom the Great Sebastian

EARL SIXTEEN (Earl Daley, b 1958)/Black Roots

EARLY B (Earlando Neil, d 1997)/Killamanjaro

CLINT EASTWOOD (Robert Brammer)

EEK-A-MOUSE (Ripton Joseph Hilton, b 1957)/Papa Roots, Gemini, Jah Life, Black Scorpio, Virgo

FATHEAD (Vernon Rainford)

FLOURGON (Michael May)/Stone Love, Small Axe, Rambo Mango, Sweet Love, Africa Star

FLUX (d 11/22/90)/Echo Tone

FRISCO KID aka PARO KID (Steve Webley Wray, b 1970)/Exodus Nuclear

FUTURE TROUBLE (Rory Gladstone Williams)

RICKY GENERAL (Ricard Anderson)

GENERAL ECHO aka RANKING SLACKNESS (Earl Robinson, d 11/22/90)/Echo Tone, Stereophonic, Gemini, Ray Symbolic

GENERAL PLOUGH/Black Roots

GENERAL TREES (Amos Edward, b 1955)/Black Scorpio.

GOOFY (Chad Simpson, b 6/1/74)

GOSPEL FISH (Everald Thomas)/Happy Tone, Lightning, Nite Flight, Taurus

UTON GREEN/Destiny Outerational

HUGH GRIFFITHS Gemini

GRINDSMAN (Joseph Green)

HALF PINT (Lyndon Roberts, b 1962)/Gemini

LLOYD HEMMINGS/Youth Promotion

HIGGS & TWINS (Marcia Higgs)

RED HOPETON/King Edwards, Sir Coxsone Down Beat

I-ROY (Roy Reid, b 1949)/Soul Bunny, Sons Junior, Stereo, Ruddy's Supreme, V Rocket, King Tubbys, Viego

HORSEMAN see SASSAFRAS

INSPECTOR WILLIE/King Stur Gav

WELTON IRIE (b 1961)/Echo Tone, Gemini

DERRICK IRIS (Derrick Rowe)/King Tubbys

JACK/Metro Media

CARLTON JACKSON (b 1955)/Ethiopian Hi Fi

JAH LLOYD (aka Jah Lion)

JAH MIKE/Socialist Roots

JAH SCREW (Paul Love, b 1955)/Echo Bell, King Stur Gav, Prince Jammys, Ray Symbolic

JAH STITCH (Melborne James, b 1949)/Tippertone, Black Harmony, Youth Promotion

JAH STONE (Gladstone Fisher, b 1953)

JAH THOMAS (Nkrumah Thomas)

JAH WALTON see JOSEPH COTTON

JAH WISE/Lord Tippertone

JAH WOOSH (Neville Beckford, b 1952)/Prince Lloyd

JAPANESE/Metro Media

JESSIE JENDER/Xterminator

JOHNNY P (Johnny Morgan)

BASIL JOHNSON/Metro Media

JUNIOR CAT (Wayne Ricard Maragh)/Killamanjaro, Metro Media

JUNIOR DEMUS (Conrad McNish)

JUNIOR KONG see KING KONG

JUNIOR MELODY see BUSHMAN

JUNIOR METRO/Metro Media

JIGSY KING (Errol King, b 1970)

JUKSY KILLER/Travellers

KING CRY CRY aka PRINCE FAR I (Michael Williams b 1944; d 9/15/83)/Sir Mike the Musical Dragon, El Toro Hi Fi

KING KONG aka JUNIOR KONG (Dennis Anthony Thomas)/Tuff Gong, GT, Love Bunch

KING SPORTY (Noel Williams, b 1945)

KING STITT (Winston Spark)/Sir Coxsone #1 Set

LADY ANN (Barbara Smith)

LADY ANNE (Anne Smith, b 1960)

LADY G (Janice Fyffe, b 1974)/Black Scorpio

LADY JUNIE (Marcia Campbell)

LADY PATRA see PATRA

LADY SAW (Marion Hall)

LECTURER (Manley Martin Edward)

LUI LEPKI/Volcano

JACKIE LICK SHOT/Youth Promotion

LIEUTENANT STITCHIE aka RANKING NOSEWORTHY, CITCHIE, RANKING CITRUS (Cleveland Laing)/City Lights, Django, Lightning, Stereo One, Stone Love

TUMPA LION (Carlton Mason)

LITTLE BIMBO aka GARNETT SILK (Garnett Smith b 4/2/66; d 12/9/94)/Soul Re-membrance, Conquering Lion, Pepper's Disco, Stereophonic, Destiny Out-erational, Youth Promotion

LITTLE HARRY/Volcano

LITTLE JOHN (John McMorris, 1970)/Romantic, Killamanjaro, Gemini, Black Roots, Volcano

LITTLE LENNY (Nigel Grandison)

LITTLE ROY (Earl Lowe)

LITTLE TWITCH (R. Wright)/King Jammys

LIZZY/El Paso

LONE RANGER (Anthony Waldron)/Virgo

LORD SASSAFRAS (Michael Johnson)/Black Scorpio

LUKIE D (Michael Kennedy, 1972)/Stone Love

LYRICAL (Delroy Drecket)

MADOO/Stereophonic

MAJOR MACKEREL (Garfield Dixon)

MAJOR WORRIES (Wayne Jones, b 1966; d 1987)/King Jammys

MAMA LIZA (I) (Beverley Brown)/King Jammys

MAMA LIZA (II) (Jacqueline Boland)/King Jammys

JOE MANNIX (Rainford Foster)

HORACE MARTIN/Volcano

MERCILESS aka SUGAR DEMUS (Leonard Bartley)/Bass Odyssey

PETER METRO (Peter Clarke)/Metro Media

MICE see RED RAT

MICHIGAN & SMILEY (Anthony Fairclough & Errol Benett)

ECHO MINOTT/Black Scorpio, Gemini

SUGAR MINOTT (Lincoln Barrington Minott, b 5/25/56)/Sound of Silence Keystone, Gathering of Youth, Black Roots, Youth Promotion

NICODEMUS (Cecil Wellington b 1957; d 8/26/99)/King Stur Mar, Socialist Roots, Taurus

NIGGER KOJAK aka PRETTY BOY FLOYD (Floyd Anthony Perch, b 9/30/59)/King Jammys

NIGGER MIKEY (Michael Grant)

NINJAMAN aka DOUBLE UGLY, UGLYMAN (Desmond Ballantine)/Killamanjaro, Africa Star, Black Culture

NITTY GRITTY (Glen Holness, b 1957; d 6/24/91, NY)/Youth Promotion

AUGUSTUS PABLO (Horace Swaby b 1954; d 5/18/99) Rockers

TRISTAN PALMA (b 1962)/Black Roots, Gemini

MICHAEL PALMER (b 1964)/Echo Tone

PANHEAD (Anthony Johnson, b 1966; d 11/93)

PAPA BEETO (L. Anderson)

PAPA BIGGIE (C. Porteous)

PAPA SAN (Tyrone Thompson, b 1966)/People's Choice, Small Axe, Creation, Unlimmited, Metromedia

PAPA SKULL (Paul Bartley)

PARO KID see FRISCO KID

PATCHI I/Studio Mix

PATRA aka LADY PATRA (Dorothy Smith, b 11/22/71)

GREGORY PECK (Gregory Williamson)/King Jammys

PINCHERS/Youth Promotion

PLIERS (Everton Banner, b 1965)/Black Scorpio

POMPIDOU (Denzil Palmer)/King Jammys, Studio Mix

PRESIDENT BROWN (Fitzroy Cotterell)

PRETTY BOY FLOYD see NIGGER KOJAK

PRINCE BUSTER (Cecil Campbell, b 5/28/38)/Voice of the People

PRINCE FAR I (see KING CRY CRY)

PRINCE HAMMER (Beres Simpson, b 1962)

PRINCE JAZZBO (Linval Carter, b 1950)/The Whip

PRINCE MOHAMMED (George Nooks, b 1958)

PRINCE RUFF/Sir George

PROFESSOR NUTS (Carl Wellington)

JACK RADICS (Jordan Bailey)/New World

BLACKA RANKIN/Metro Media

DICKIE RANKING aka SNAGGA PUSS (Norman Supria)/Gemini, Youth Promotion

RANKING BARNABAS/Channel One

RANKING CITRUS see LT STITCHIE

RANKING DEVON (Devon Russell)

RANKING JOE aka LITTLE JOE (Joe Jackson, b 1960)/El Paso, King Stur Gav, Prince Jammys

RANKING NOSEWORTHY see LT STITCHIE

RANKING SLACKNESS see GENERAL ECHO

RANKING TOYAN/Volcano, Socialist Roots, Romantic Hi Fi

RANKING TREVOR/Socialist Roots

JUNIE RANKS (June Evans)

SHABBA RANKS (Rexton Gordon, 1965)/Roots Melody, King Jammys, Heatwave,

RAPPA ROBERT (Robert Wilson)

TONY REBEL (Patrick George Anthony Barrett)/Destiny Outerational, Youth Promotion

RED DRAGON (Leroy May)

RED RAT aka MICE (Allace Wilson, b 1/17/78)

BUNNY REMOS/El Toro Hi Fi

JOHNNY RINGO (b 1961)/Gemini, Unlimmited

RISTO BENJY/King Jammys

MAX ROMEO (Max Smith, b 11/22/47)/Romax

PUDDY ROOTS/Killamanjaro

RORY/Stone Love

SAMUEL THE FIRST/El Paso Hi Fi

SASSAFRAS aka THE HORSEMAN/Black Scorpio

ERROL SCORCHER (Errol Archer, b 1956)/King Jammys

SCOTTY (David Scott, b 1950)

APACHE SCRATCHIE (Raymond Hudson)

SCREETY DAN (Robert Stevens)

SHAGGY (Orville Richard Burrell, 10/22/68)

SHARK/Youth Promotion

SHORTY THE PRESIDENT (Derrick Thompson)

SHUKASHINE/Black Scorpio

SIMPLETON (Christopher Harrison, b 1975)

SINGIE SINGIE/Youth Promotion

SIR LORD COMIC/Admiral Deans, King Edwards

SISTER CAROL (Carol Theresa East, b 1959)

SISTER CHARMAINE (Charmaine Mckenzie)

SISTER NANCY (Nancy Russell)

SISTER VERNA/Metro Media

SIZZLA (Miguel Collins)/Caveman

SKY JUICE (Christopher Blake)/Metro Media

BILLY SLAUGHTER/Stone Love

SLUGGY (Andrew Gregory)

FRANKY SLY (Franklin Williams)

LEROY SMART/Gemini

DONOVAN SMITH/Black Roots

WAYNE SMITH (b 12/5/65)/King Jammys

SNAGGA PUSS see DICKIE RANKIN

SQUIDLY RANKIN (Paul Pauel)/Gemini

RICHIE STEPHENS/Bass Odyssey

REGGIE STEPPER (Reginald Williams)

RICKY STEREO (Richard Burde)/Stereo One

SUPER CAT (William Maragh, b 1966)/Soul Imperial, Killamanjaro, King Stur Mar

GARTH SWABY/Rockers

RAY SYMBOLIC/Prince Jammys, Ray Symbolic

TALL LIZZY/Prince Jammys

ROD TAYLOR/Black Roots

TENOR SAW (Clive Bright, b 1966; d 8/88)/Youth Promotion

TERROR FABULOUS (b 1974)

THRILLER/Youth Promotion

SHELLY THUNDER (Michelle Harrison)

TIGER (Norman Jackson, b 1960)/Black Star

TIPPA LEE & RAPPA ROBERT (A. Campbell, Robert Wilson)

TOM THE GREAT SEBASTIAN (Tom Wong)/Tom the Great Sebastian

TONTO IRIE/Black Star, King Jammys

TONTO METRO (Mark Wolfe)/Metro Media

TREVOR JUNIOR/Youth Promotion

TRINITY (Wade "Junior" Brammer, b 1954)

RICKY TROOPER/Killamanjaro

TUFFEST (Patric Main)

TULLO T (E Crawford)/King Jammys

TULUSI/Youth Promotion

TWIGGY (Mary Gitens)/54–46

U-BROWN (Huford Brown, b 1958)/Silver Bullet, King Tubby's, King Attorney, Socialist Roots, Channel One

U-ROY (Edward Beckford b 1942)/Dr Dickie's, Sir Mike the Musical Thunderstorm, Sir George the Atomic, King Tubbys, Coxsone's Down Beat, King Stur Gav

UGLYMAN see NINJAMAN

JOSEY WALES (Joseph Sterling)/Roots Unlimited, King Stur Gav, Volcano

ASHANTI WAUGH/Black Roots

CHRIS WAYNE/Youth Promotion

JOHN WAYNE (Norval Headley)/King Jammys

WEE POW/Stone Love

WICKERMAN (David Taylor)/Stereo One

YELLOWMAN (Winston Foster, b 1959)/Aces Disco, Gemini, Virgo

DON YUTE (Jason Andrew Williams, b 5/9/74)

TAPPA ZUKIE (David Sinclair, b 7/2/55)/I-Oses, Maccabees, Viego

PART TWO: SOUND SYSTEMS

The Sound System Association of Jamaica currently has around 150 members, although there are over 300 in operation throughout the island, a figure which has remained more or less constant since the mid-1980s. The following indexes the best known/most influential sound systems of the past 50 years — in which period, countless thousands of sound systems have passed across the scene.

Entries give sound system's name, primary period of operation, and performing name of leading DJs.

ACES DISCO (1980s) DJs: Yellowman

ADMIRAL DEAN'S SOUND (1950s) DJs: Sir Lord Comic (actually, dancer!)

AFRICA STAR (1980s) DJs: Capleton, Ninjaman, Anthony Malvo and Flourgon

ARROWS (1980s) DJs: Chicken Chest, Cutty Ranks

BASS ODYSSEY (1990s) DJs: Merciless, Richie Stephens

BLACK CAT (1980s) DJs: Daddy Rings

BLACK CULTURE (1980s) DJs: Ninjaman

BLACK HARMONY (1970s) DJs: Jah Stitch

BLACK ROOTS (1970s) DJs: Sugar Minott, Barry Brown, Tristan Palma, Captain Sinbad, Little John, Donovan Smith, Ashanti Waugh, Earl Sixteen, Rod Taylor, Cataract, General Plough

BLACK SCORPIO (1970s +) DJs: Mega Banton, Eek-A-Mouse, Lady G, Pliers, Bounty Killer, Shukashine, Sassafras, Echo Minott, General Trees

BLACK STAR LINE (1980s) DJs: Bushman, Tiger

BLACK UNIVERSE (1980s) DJs: Dirtsman

CADETT HI POWER (1980s) DJs: Colour Man

CAVEMAN (1990s) DJs: Sizzla

CHANNEL ONE (1970s) DJs: Ranking Barnabas, U Brown

CITY LIGHTS DISCO (1980s) DJs: Lt Stitchie

CLIMAX (1980s) DJs: Cobra

CONQUERING LION (1980s) DJs: Little Bimbo

COSMIC FORCE (1980s) DJs: Colour Man

COUNT NICK THE CHAMPION (1950s)

COUNT SMITH THE BLUES BLASTER (1950s)

CREATION ROCK TOWER SOUND (1980s) DJs: Dirtsman, Papa San

CULTURE SHANTI (1980s) DJs: Daddy Rings

DESTINY OUTERNATIONAL (1980s) DJs: Little Bimbo, Tony Rebel, Uton Green, Culture Knox and Everton Blender.

DJANGOS (1980s) DJs: Lt Stitchie

DOC'S THE THUNDERSTORM (1950s)

DOCTOR DICKIE'S (1960s) DJs: U-Roy DUKE REID THE TROJAN (1950s–60s) DJs: Cuttins

ECHO BELL (1980s) DJs: Jah Screw

ECHO TONE formerly BIG JOHN'S STEREOPHONIC SOUND DJs: General Echo, Big John, Flux, Michael Palmer, Welton Irie

EL PASO (1960s) DJs: Ranking Joe, Dennis Alcapone, Lizzy, Samuel The First, Dillinger

EL TORO HIFI (1960s) DJs: King Cry Cry, Prince Far-I, Bunny Remos

EMPEROR FAITH (1980s)

ETHIOPIAN HI FI DJs: Carlton Jackson

EXODUS NUCLEAR (1980s +) DJs: Frisco Kid

FEATHERTONE (1980s) DJs: Cutty Ranks

GATHERING OF YOUTH (1970s) DJs: Sugar Minott

GEMINI (1970S +) DJs: Buro Banton, Eek-A-Mouse, Yellowman, Ringo, Welton Irie, Dickie Ranking, Squiddly Rankin, Echo Minott, General Echo, Tristan Palma, Patric Andy, Colour Man, Leroy Smart, Hugh Griffiths, Al Campbell, Half Pint, Archie, Little John

GHETTO INTERNATIONAL (1980s) DJs: Colour Man

GT (1980s) DJs: King Kong

HAPPY TONE (1980s) DJs: Gospel Fish

HEATWAVE (1980s) DJs: Shabba Ranks

HIGHLIGHTS (1960s) DJs: Count Prince Miller

HOUSE OF JOY (1950s)

INNER CITY (1980s +) DJs: Cobra

I-OSES DISCOTECH (1970s) DJs: Tappa Zukie

JACK RUBY (1970s–80s) DJs: Brigadier Jerry, Icho Candy

JAH LIFE (1970s) DJs: Eek-A-Mouse

JAH LOVE (1980s +) DJs: Brigadier Jerry

JUNIOR SEBASTIAN (1950s)

KILLAMANJARO (1980s +) DJs: Early B, Super Cat, Puddy Roots, Ninjaman, Ricky Trooper, Bounty Killer, Cutty Ranks, Little John

KING ATTORNEY (1970s) DJs: U Brown

KING EDWARDS (1950s–60s) DJs: Red Hopeton, Sir Lord Comic

KING JAMMYS (1980s + previously PRINCE JAMMY'S) DJs: Shabba Ranks, John Wayne, Tonto Irie, Pompidou, Ranking Trevor, Wayne Smith, Nicodemus, Toots, Admiral Bailey, Chaka Demus, Major Worris, Shaba Ranks, Gregory Peck, Lecturer, Little Twitch, Risto Benjy, Tullo T, Collin Roach, Don Angelo, Admiral Bailey, Turbo Belly, Nigger Kojak, Mama Liza

KING STUR GAV (1970s–80s) DJs: U-Roy, Ranking Joe, Jah Screw, Charlie Chaplin, Josey Wales, Inspector Willie

KING STUR MAR (1980s) DJs: Nicodemus, Super Cat

KING TUBBY'S HOME TOWN HI FI DJs (1960s +): U-Roy, U-Brown, I-Roy

LIGHTNING SUPER MIX (1980s) DJs: Gospel Fish, Lt Stitchie

LORD KOOS OF THE UNIVERSE (1950s)

LORD TIPPERTONE (1960s–70s) DJs: Big Youth, Jah Wise, Jah Stitch, Dr Alimantado

LOVE BUNCH (1980s) DJs: King Kong

MACCABEES (1970s) DJs: Tappa Zukie

MASTERBLASTER (1980s) DJs: Colour Man

MELLOW CANARY (1950s)

METRO MEDIA (1980s+) DJs: Sister Verna, Peter Metro, Jack, Tonto Metro, Ashman, Blacka Rankin, Bounty Killer, Japanese, Danny Dread, Sky Juice, Jr Cat, Papa San

MIGHTY MERRITONE (1950s)

MIGHTY RULER (1980s) DJs: Cobra

NEW WORLD (1970s) DJs: Jack Radics

NICK THE CHAMP (1950s)

NITE FLITE (1980s) DJs: Gospel Fish

ONENESS (1980s) DJ: Daddy Rings

PEOPLE'S CHOICE (1980s) DJs: Papa San

PEPPER'S DISCO (1980s) DJs: Little Bimbo

PRESIDENT (1950s–60s) DJs: Count Benz

PRINCE JACKIES (1970s) DJs: Dillinger

PRINCE JAMMYS (1960s–70s; KING JAMMY'S thereafter) DJs: Beenie Man, Tall Lizzie, Ray Symbolic, Ranking Joe, Jah Screw

PRINCE LLOYD (1970s) DJs: Jah Woosh

RAMBO MANGO (1980s) DJs: Buju Banton, Flourgon

RAY SYMBOLIC (1970s–80s) DJs: General Echo, Ray Symbolic, Jah Screw

ROCKERS (1960s–70s) DJs: Augustus Pablo, Garth Swaby

ROMANTIC HI FI (1980s) DJs: Ranking Toyan, Little John

ROMAX (1970s) DJs: Max Romeo

ROOTS MELODY (1980s) DJs: Shabba Ranks, Admiral Bailey

ROOTS UNLIMITED (1970s) DJs: Buro Banton, Josey Wales

RUDDY'S SUPREME RULER OF SOUND (1960s) DJs: I-Roy

SILVER BULLET SOUND SYSTEM (1970s) DJs: U Brown

SIR COXSONE DOWN BEAT aka #1 SET (1950s–60s) DJs: King Stitt, Red Hopeton, Count Machuki, U-Roy, Cool Sticky

SIR GEORGE THE ATOMIC (1960s) DJs: Prince Ruff, Buttercup, U-Roy

SIR JESUS SOUNDS OF SHEPHERDS BUSH (1970s)

SIR MIKE THE MUSICAL DRAGON/THUNDERSTORM (1960s) DJs: King Cry Cry, U-Roy

SKY ROCKET (1950s)

SMALL AXE HI FI (1980s) DJs: Big Joe, Flourgon, Papa San

SOCIALIST ROOTS (1970s) DJs: Jah Mike, Ranking Trevor, U Brown, Nicodemus, Ranking Toyan

SON'S JUNIOR (1950s–60s) DJs: I-Roy

SOUL BUNNY (1960s) DJs: I-Roy

SOUL IMPERIAL (1970s) DJs: Super Cat

SOUL REMEMBRANCE (1980s) DJs: Little Bimbo

SOUND OF SILENCE KEYSTONE (1970s) DJs: Sugar Minott, Captain Sinbad

STEREO (1960s) DJs: I-Roy

STEREO ONE (1980s) DJs: Lt. Stitchie, Cobra, Captain Barkey, Daddy Blue, Ricky Stereo, Wickerman

STEREO TWO (1980s) DJs: Bounty Killer

STEREOMARS (1980s) DJs: Cutty Ranks

STEREOPHONIC (1970s) DJs: Little Bimbo, General Echo, Madoo

STONE LOVE (1980s) DJs: Wee Pow, Rory, Billy Slaughter, Lt. Stitchie, Luckie D, Delano, Flourgon

STUDIO MIX (1980s) DJs: Patchie I, Pompidou

SUPREME (1980s) DJs: Chaka Demus

SWEET LOVE (1980s) DJs: Buju Banton, Flourgon

SWING-A-LING (1960s) DJs: Charlie Ace

TAURUS (1970s–80s) DJs: Nicodemus, Gospel Fish

TOM THE GREAT SEBASTIAN (1950s–60s) DJs: Count Vin, Tom the Great Sebastian

TRAVELLERS (1980s) DJs: Juksy Killer

TREASURE ISLE (1950s, 1960s) DJs: Cool Sticky

TUFF GONG (1980s) DJs: King Kong

UNLIMMITED (1980s) DJs: Beenie Man, Papa San, Johnny Ringo

V ROCKET (1950s–60s) DJs: I-Roy

VIEGO (1970s) DJs: I-Roy, Tappa Zukie

VIRGO (1980s) DJs: Eek-A-Mouse, Lone Ranger, Yellowman

VOICE OF THE PEOPLE (1960s) DJs: Count Machuki, Prince Buster

VOLCANO (1980s) DJs: Buro Banton, Beenie Man, Colour Man, Ranking Toyan, Little John, Lui Lepki, Billy Boyo, Little Harry, Horace Martin, Josey Wales, Danny Dread

WHIP (1970s) DJs: Prince Jazzbo

YOUTH PROMOTION (1980s) DJs: Sugar Minott, Colour Man, Nitty Gritty, Trevor Junior, Tenor Saw, Thriller, Lloyd Hemmings, Singie Singie, Dickie Ranking, Yami Bolo, Donna P, Blacka T, Daddy Ants, Chris Wayne, Shark, Budi Bye, Pinchers, Jackie Lickshot, Jah Stitch, Tulusie, Tony Rebel, Little Bimbo

RECOMMENDED LISTENING

DR ALIMANTADO Sons of Thunder (Greensleeves — UK) 1981

A winning combination of warm familiarity and oddball dub, but never losing sight of Alimantado's innate tunefulness. "Marriage License" is appropriately lovely, the title track is suitably thunderous, and "Born for a Purpose" is reprised for the latecomers.

KING STITT Dance Hall '63 (Studio One — JA) 1994

The early 1990s saw a number of albums released purporting to transport the listener back to the halcyon days of ska, but in reality recorded in considerably more recent times. This is just one more in that sorry chain — the difference is, it really does do what it claims. Stitt's contribution to the fad is unbeatable, a virtual recreation of a classic 1963 set, with period hits augmented by precisely the same kind of DJ-ing act which made the Ugly One's fortune in the first place.

VARIOUS ARTISTS

From Chapter to Version (Jamaica Gold) 1998

20 tracks drawn from producer Alvin Ranglin's GG stable, the big stars Alcapone and U-Roy are joined by Charlie Ace, Cat Campbell, Samuel the First, Carey & Lloyd, Shorty Perry and Ranking Magnum on a set which is high on both energy and annotation — included within the liner notes is a song by song guide to the original versions of each track.

Trojan DJ Box Set (Trojan — UK) 1999

Another in the ongoing series of three-CD/50 track collections, their minimal packaging matching their budget price, but the contents repaying the purchase many times over. Concentrating wholly on the first flood of DJ-ing talent —

the good, the bad and the ugly (King Stitt is here) — the handful of obvious inclusions is more than obviated by a string of forgotten masterpieces: Blake Boy's "Cambodia," Scotty's "Riddle I This," Lloyd Young's "High Explosion" and "Place Called Africa" by Winston Prince — the young Dr Alimantado.

PETER TOSH

STYLE *reggae (roots)*
BORN *Winston Hubert McIntosh, 10/19/44 (Grange Hill, JA); d 9/11/87 (Kingston, JA)*

Brought up in rural western Jamaica by his mother and an aunt, Peter Tosh was 15 when he left home for Kingston. There he joined the handful of ghetto kids who flocked to vocalist Joe Higgs' informal singing lessons, held in one of the Third Street tenement yards; there, too, he met fellow aspirants Nesta "Bob" Marley, Neville "Bunny Wailer" Livingston and Junior Braithwaite. In late 1962, this quartet became the Wailers.

Marley, of course, dominated the Wailers' output, both as a singer and songwriter. Tosh and Livingston (and Braithwaite, before his early departure), however, made their presence felt, as accompanying vocalists, as frontmen when the occasion demanded and — in Tosh's case — as guitarist. His lead debuted on 1963's "I'm Going Home" and, though the band frequently called upon outside sessionmen (notably Ernest Ranglin), his work remains an exemplary component in the "classic" Wailers sound.

When Marley departed Jamaica for America, working in a car plant to raise money to launch the Wailers' own record label, it was Tosh and Livingston who kept the band alive with an impressive and seemingly unbreakable string of hits. During 1965–66, Coxsone Dodd produced singles of Tosh's "Hoot Nanny Roll," a cover of Sir Lancelot's calypso "Shame and Scandal in the Family," "The Jerk," "Making Love" and the rude boy anthem "I'm the Toughest," plus a duet with the newly wed Rita Marley, "It's Only Love." Rita also appeared on "Rasta Shook Them Up," Tosh's celebration of Haile Selassie's visit to Jamaica.

After Marley returned home, the Wailers duly launched the long dreamed of Wail'N Soul'M label — only for the line-up to be shattered once more, when Bunny Livingston was sentenced to 14 months imprisonment for marijuana possession. Rita Marley moved into the frontline and, with former Skatalites Tommy McCook and Johnny Moore behind them, the new-look Wailers cut Tosh's "Pound Get a Blow" — his first ever self-produced track, and the song often singled out as the true dawn of Tosh's solo career.

It was followed by "Fire Fire," subsequently covered by British band Simply Red but, more appropriately, also subject to a truly scintillating rendering by Niney Holness, Lee

Perry and Max Romeo ("Babylose Burning"). However, the Wail'N Soul'M experiment was not a success, and the Wailers returned to the freelance circuit.

The best known material from this period was cut with Lee Perry during 1969–71. Over 100 tracks were recorded, including several Tosh solo sides — notable here were "(Earth's) Rightful Ruler" in late 1970 (featuring contributions from Count Ossie and DJ star-in-waiting U-Roy), the booming "400 Years," "Brand New Second Hand," "Memphis," "No Sympathy" and a reworking of the Wailers' earlier "Sinner Man," retitled "Down Presser."

Other group collaborations were less productive. Sessions with Bunny Lee did not work out for the band, but Tosh himself got along well with the Striker, prompting a string of instrumental 45s during 1969–70. Many were released under the semi-pseudonym Peter Touch, and showcased Tosh's guitar and melodica playing) including "Crimson Pirate," "Ambitious Beggar," "Moon Dusk," "Romper Room," "Pepper Seed," "Selassie Serenade," "Sun Valley" and "The Return of Alcapone."

Despite this outlet, however, Tosh was deeply dissatisfied with life in the band, a discontent which surfaced in his lyrics for "Stop this Train," cut during the Wailers' liaison with producer Leslie Kong during 1970. In early 1971, Tosh became the first (and only) member of the Wailers ever to begin working completely outside of the hand, when he hitched up with Joe Gibbs to launch a separate, simultaneous solo career. Their first collaboration, a new version of the Wailers' "Maga Dog," proved a major hit (Tosh's first) and, while Gibbs maintained that song's profile via various DJ and instrumental versions, Tosh himself followed through with the impressive "Dem a fe Get a Beating."

Other Gibbs-produced gems included "Leave My Business," "Arise Blackman," "Black Dignity" and "Here Comes the Judge," in which God passes sentence on Christopher Columbus, Francis Drake and Vasco Da Gama for crimes against Africa. Tosh also leaped aboard the then-prevalent trend for oldies medleys with "Rudies Medley," a magical cut which combined Desmond Dekker's "Rude Boy Train" and "007 (Shanty Town)," with a reprise of his own "I'm the Toughest."

Although his period with Gibbs was very productive, it was to prove extremely brief. By late summer, 1971, Tosh had returned his solo efforts to the Wailers' Tuff Gong label, allegedly in retaliation for the lack of money he received for the smash hit "Maga Dog." Indeed, among his first Tuff Gong releases was "Once Bitten," a reworking of the "Maga Dog" rhythm with new lyrics apparently targeted directly at Gibbs. The song proved an even bigger hit this time around, so taking another leaf out of Gibbs book, Tosh followed through with "Dog Teeth," working the rhythm once again.

Peter Tosh—The true Steppin' Razor.

By this time, Tosh had launched his own record label, Intel Diplo HIM (Intelligent Diplomat for His Imperial Majesty); "Dog Teeth" was the label's first release — others included "Ketchy Shuby" (1971), "Can't Blame the Youth," "No Mercy" (1972) and "Mark of the Beast," "What You Gonna Do," "Foundation" and "Burial," a new version of the b-side to 1968's "Pound Get a Blow" (1973).

While Marley toured Sweden with Johnny Nash, Tosh and Livingston spent some months during summer, 1971, working alongside Upsetters Carlton and Aston Barrett and teenaged keyboard player Tyrone Downie, with a new band, the Youth Professionals. With Carl "Ras" Dawkins on lead vocals, this same aggregation recorded a single with Lee Perry, "The Sound of Thunder," opportunistically credited to Dawkins and the Wailers when it was released later in 1971.

The Wailers' own career finally took off in late 1971. The trio reassembled in London that fall to record with Nash, and while there signed to Island Records. Augmenting the vocal front line with the Aston and Carlton Barrett (b 12/17/50; d 4/17/87) rhythm section (ex-Upsetters), by late 1973, they had released two new albums, *Catch a Fire* and *Burnin'*, while tours had taken them across Europe, the UK and the US.

Unfortunately, restlessness, which had hitherto been suppressed by all three members' drive to succeed, was now surfacing. Livingston was first to depart, following a miserable British tour that spring. Tosh, who was still recovering from the Kingston highway accident which killed his girlfriend, followed him out at the end of the year, quitting the Wailers midway through their latest British outing.

Although the Wailers reunited for a one off concert just six months later, an era was over. Both Livingston and Tosh launched solo careers in earnest, with Tosh scoring an immediate hit with a new version of "Brand New Second Hand." The following year brought the herb anthem "Legalize It," a pointed reminder to Jamaican Prime Minister Michael Manley that the Rastafarian community which he'd rallied to his political cause was still waiting to receive something in return.

In Jamaica, the song fell on deaf ears — and was, in any case, banned from the radio. Elsewhere, however, it found fertile ground and, by the end of 1975, Tosh had signed with the US major label Columbia.

In November, 1975, the original Wailers came together once more, at a benefit for the Jamaican Institute for the Blind, co-headlined by Stevie Wonder. Their performance was short — they opened with "Rastaman Chant," from their last album together, then followed through with one song apiece from Livingston ("Arab Oil Weapon") and Tosh ("Mark of the Beast") before the current incarnation of the Wailers took the stage for a full set of their own. Tosh and Livingston reappeared for the encore, however, a triumphant "Rude Boy."

Tosh's first solo album, *Legalize It*, produced at Duke Reid's studio by Tosh and Wailers' harmonica player Lee Jaffe, was released in 1976, immediately creating a stir not only in Jamaica, but in Britain and the US too (the album *Live and Dangerous* was recorded during his first tour of the latter).

Shot through with virulent political and religious imagery, *Legalise It* blended effortlessly with the growing tide of Rastafarian militancy emerging from elsewhere on the Jamaican scene, even as its easy rhythms and open sound suggested that Tosh was as ready to step onto the international stage as erstwhile bandmate Marley.

Tosh, however, was never willing to take that step. Lyrically, he remained threatening, uncompromising, iconoclastic; and when you flipped over singles like "Babylon Queendom," "Dracula" and "Legalize It" itself, he was unleashing dubs as dark and dangerous as any of that genre's most notorious practitioners. *Equal Rights*, Tosh's second (and final) Columbia album, followed effortlessly in its predecessor's footsteps in 1977, but if any single event marked Tosh out as something more than simply an outspoken musician, it was his appearance at the One Love Concert in riot-torn Kingston, on April 22, 1978.

Tosh was initially hesitant about playing the show. Although it was officially billed as a commemoration of the twelfth anniversary of Haile Selassie's state visit to Jamaica, it swiftly took on far broader and, to Tosh's way of thinking, far more sinister connotations.

The headlining (and, in many ways, hijacked) Bob Marley aside, the entire event was being stage-managed by precisely the same people who were responsible for all the fighting and killing in the first place, the politicians who took their battles out of parliament and into the hands of street thugs, vigilantes and hired assassins. The only way to stop the fighting now, Tosh believed, was to stop the people who perpetuated it — preferably with a bullet in the head.

Tosh took the stage immediately before the headlining Wailers, with a band built around the same Word Sound & Power band responsible for his last two albums — former Wailer Al Anderson and Mikey Chung (guitars), Keith Sterling and Robbie Lynn (keyboards) and the formidable rhythm section of Sly Dunbar and Robbie Shakespeare.

Tosh himself appeared clad in a black and white striped karate suit and black beret, the epitome of the dread guerilla. But even his closest associates could never have predicted what Tosh wreaked that night, on a stage facing 30,000 fans, several hundred foreign journalists and cameramen, and the two most powerful men in Jamaican politics, Prime Minister Michael Manley and opposition leader Edward Seaga.

Tosh's set was drawn from his angriest songs — "400 Years," "Stepping Razor," "Burial," "Equal Rights," "Legalize It" and the Wailers' incendiary "Get Up Stand Up." But it was his words which tore the event to pieces and, with it, its sponsors. "Peace is the diploma you get in the cemetery," he told the crowd. "On top of your grave. . . ."

The following day, the Jamaican newspapers were unanimous in their condemnation of Tosh's words. With the entire world looking on, he had embarrassed the nation and her leaders. Neither would his victims forget what he had done. Less than five months after the show, Tosh was arrested for marijuana possession and, safely away from prying eyes, was almost beaten to death by the police. Indeed, as far as the officers were concerned, he was dead by the time they'd finished with him; as he lay virtually senseless on the ground, his skull and wrist both broken, he heard one of his assailants announce, "yes, he's dead." "Has anything changed since the Peace Concert?" Tosh was asked by a visiting journalist some time later. "Yes, more dead."

Some good did come out of the concert of course, even for the embattled Tosh. Shortly after the event, he was approached by Rolling Stones frontman Mick Jagger, who had attended the show and wanted to sign Tosh to the Stones' own, eponymous, record label. He was not, as has been claimed elsewhere, the label's first outside signing — that honor belongs to the barely remembered Kracker. But he was the first in six years, and the Stones seemed adamant that he would be granted every advantage their patronage could bring him.

That summer, Tosh was opening act on the Stones' North American tour, with Jagger joining him on stage on at least one occasion. The pair also appeared together on television's *Saturday Night Live*, performing what became Tosh's first release on the label, a revival of a Temptations' song which Tosh had recorded once before with the Wailers, "(You Gotta Walk and) Don't Look Back."

Elsewhere on the tour, Tosh leaped up on stage at Bob Marley's Starlite Amphitheater show in Burbank, CA, to perform "Get Up Stand Up." Mick Jagger, too, was in attendance, but Marley refused to allow him to join in — people had paid to see the Wailers, he said, not some English singer.

A #81 hit in America, #43 in the UK, "Don't Look Back" opened the door for Tosh's next album, *Bush Doctor*, itself a majestic set further highlighted by timely remakes of "I Am the Toughest" and "Them a fe Get a Beatin'," and further dignified by Tosh's recruitment of the Tamlins trio on backing vocals. They became an integral part of Tosh's show for the next four years.

1979 brought *Mystic Man* and another excellent single, "Buk-In-Hamm Palace"; "Steppin' Razor" was reprised for the soundtrack of the *Rockers* movie, an apposite choice which absolutely captured the mood of the film; and Tosh's latest US tour included massive shows in Toronto and New York's Central Park, before wrapping up at the Madison Square Garden No Nukes concert.

A triumphant Sunsplash performance notwithstanding, Tosh spent much of 1980 out of the spotlight. Although it was barely publicized at the time, the beating he had received two years earlier had left him severely weakened, a state exacerbated by the heavy workload of the previous twelve months. In Jamaica, the Intel Diplo HIM label was reactivated for the "Bumbo Klaat" single; his international following received "Nothing but Love," a duet with Gwen Guthrie.

Tosh bounced back in the new year with *Wanted Dread or Alive*, his first appearance on the US album chart (it reached #91), and tours of the US and Europe. He then took another year off, again for health reasons but also to escape the continued questions from the US media as to whether he considered himself the heir to the recently deceased Bob Marley's throne. "Every journalist come to me, always wants to say to I, 'now that you are the new king of reggae.'

[But] I don't want to be looked upon as no king . . . and I am not new. I am as old as the sun. . . ."

1983 gave Tosh his second hit single, when "Johnny B Goode" (from the forthcoming *Mama Africa* album reached #84 US, #48 UK. This album, too, charted in America (#59), while his 1983 tour proved his popularity to still be soaring. It was on this outing that Tosh introduced what became one of the most impressive images of his entire career, a guitar in the shape of an M-16 rifle.

Tosh played his first and, as it transpired, only African concert that year, in Swaziland; he also headlined the Reggae Superjam in Kingston — it was the last major concert he ever played. Announcing another sabbatical, he discharged his backing musicians and withdrew from the spotlight completely. An in-concert album, *Captured Live*, appeared the following year and, in 1985, Tosh's son Andrew (b 6/67; his mother is Bunny Livingston's sister, Shirley) launched his own career with the single "Vanity Love."

It was 1987 before Tosh senior resurfaced. That July, a new single "In My Song," appeared in both the UK and US, and in September, a new album *No Nuclear War* made its bow. Days later, on September 11, Tosh was murdered in his own home by a gang led by an old Wailers associate named Dennis Lobban—a man, local rumor insisted, who had taken the rap for Tosh himself in a murder case back in 1973.

Following his release, Lobban had actually spent some time living at the Tosh home, until he fell out with the singer's American girlfriend and manager, Marlene Brown. Days later, Lobban returned with two other men apparently intending only to menace the residents and rob the house. They found a small party underway and, though they initially kept to their plan, Lobban panicked when Brown began to scream.

All seven people in the room were shot in the head; Brown, former Soul Syndicate drummer Carlton "Santa" Davis and two friends survived; Tosh, JBC DJ and recording artist Jeff "Free I" Dixon and a third friend were killed. Lobban was subsequently sentenced to death. (Ironically, just five months before Tosh's death, fellow Wailer Carlton Barrett, too, was murdered in his home. His assailant has never been caught.)

DISCOGRAPHY

7 Legalize It (Virgin) 1976

The patchwork recording sessions were probably responsible for the patchy and occasionally unfocused feel of the album. Regardless, it remains memorable for a clutch of fervid anthems, the epic title track included.

9 Equal Rights (Virgin) 1977

Beginning work almost immediately upon completion of *Legalize It*, Tosh spits out his masterpiece. Both music and lyrics are infinitely harder hitting, with Sly & Robbie's heavy rhythms pulled to the front of the mix, and Tosh barely controlling his fury. By the time of the Peace Concert, of course, even that would be beyond him.

7 Bush Doctor (Rolling Stones Records) 1978

Taken under the wing of the Glimmer Twins, with the Riddim Twins still in tow, Tosh aims for international fame, with only the title track echoing the heavy hitting past. The rest rocks away in a funk lite mode to commercial success and mainstream acclaim.

7 Mystic Man (Rolling Stones Records) 1979

Another disappointment, although occasional flashes of his earlier self do shine through. "Jah Seh No" and "Rumours of War" are the best moments.

7 Wanted Dread and Alive (EMI America) 1981

6 Mama Africa (EMI America) 1983

Less thematically radical than its predecessors, but more musically adventurous. Tosh travels through the past, including a phenomenal cover of "Johnny B. Goode," visits the Afro-beat-meets-urban-sounds of the title track, and pulls out his bushwhacker for gunfire effects on the gloating "Peace Treaty."

7 Captured Live (EMI) 1984

A more determined performance than recent albums would have predicted, although the weariness which prompted his retreat is as evident in his vocals, as in the choice of material.

6 No Nuclear War (Capitol) 1987

At best, ponderous; at worst, dancehall done you wrong, this is Tosh's weakest album by far. Lyrically, it still bites, but musically it's totally at a loss, with "Vampire" alone returning to the roots of yore.

SELECTED COMPILATIONS & ARCHIVE RELEASES

9 The Toughest (Heartbeat)

19 track survey of Tosh's 1960s work with Coxsone Dodd (13 out of 15 known recordings) and Lee Perry (six songs). Tosh was often said to be a fish out of the Wailers' water, and this set doesn't contradict that notion — from the earlier sessions, "Maga Dog" and "The Toughest" set standards for the band which Tosh alone regularly met in the future, while his version of "Shame and Scandal" acknowledges the secret cross-pollination of calypso and ska louder than any academic paper. The Perry material, meanwhile, is uniformly fabulous — "400 Years" is a brooding predator; "Rightful Ruler" a triumphant storm, and worth even more than its traditional description (U-Roy's recorded debut) lets on.

7 Honorary Citizen (Columbia) 1997

Three-CD box set which really should have been a lot better. It's impossible to argue with disc one's retrieval of a host of generally obscure, Jamaica-only singles, running from 1967's "Pound Get a Blow," through the version sides of "Legalise It" and "Dracula" (1976–76) and on to 1980's "Bumbo Klaat." Essential stuff one and all. But a disc dedicated to late-in-the-day live is scarcely an improvement on *Captured Live*, while the third disc, a round-up of hits & classics, was promptly superceded by the following year's *Scrolls of the Prophet* compilation.

8 Arise Black Man (Trojan — UK) 2000

A companion to the Heartbeat collection, chasing down those startling sides cut with Bunny Lee, Lee Perry and Joe Gibbs, and including a number of version sides as well. Not everything is crucial Tosh, but the picture could scarcely be more complete.

10 Live at the One Love Peace Concert (JAD) 2000

Year zero, the holy grail and, if it wasn't for a few inopportune fades at the end of some songs, the most perfect Tosh album imaginable. Raw sound puts you on the edge of the bleachers; the incendiary speeches which divided a nation are presented in their entirety; while 18 minutes of "Legal-ize It"/"Get Up Stand Up" epitomize everything Tosh ever meant to anyone — passion and militancy are the mere tip of the iceberg.

8 Live & Dangerous: Boston 1976 (Columbia/Legacy) 2001

Recorded during the *Legalise It* tour, a sensational snapshot of the live experience is highlighted by a roiling six minute version of "Steppin' Razor," where a wah-wah-ish guitar goes funk, and R&B riffs sinuously twine round the arrangement. Most of the songs spin off into jams, where all genres bleed into one, and the rhythms throb in encouragement. Tosh's radical shift in styles is evident on the older song "Four Hundred Years," which resonates with new power, while the newer offerings shimmer with passion and innovation.

U-ROY

STYLE *reggae (toasting/DJ)*
BORN *Ewart Beckford, 1942 (Jones Town, JA)*

U-Roy was the first of the DJ superstars of the 1970s, the Originator, and, true to his nickname, he was indeed the first DJ superstar ever, at least in terms of making, as opposed to simply spinning, records. Following U-Roy's emergence in 1969, specialist charts around the world, not to mention Kingston's own studios, were soon over-flowing with new DJ-ing talent, taking their time-honored trade of toasting over existing rhythms and slapping them onto hot wax for all to hear. But U-Roy did it the best and those who followed in his wake, from Dennis Alcapone to Big Youth, from I-Roy to Scotty, freely acknowledged their debt to the master.

Initially christened by a young cousin who was unable to pronounce the name Ewart correctly, U-Roy began DJ-ing in 1961 for the Doctor Dickies/Dickies Dynamite sound system. He then enjoyed a stint with Sir Mike the Musical Thunderstorm, before hooking up with Sir George the Atomic's sound system around 1967.

That same year saw U-Roy encounter King Tubby, a disc cutter at Duke Reid's studio, who specialized in creating new versions of existing songs by manipulating the master tape and then adding effects of his own — the precursor, of course, of dub.

Normally no more than a handful of pressings of these special versions were made — most of King Tubby's work was carried out exclusively for a select few favored DJs, with U-Roy (now star turn at King Tubby's own sound system) one of the first to sense the possibilities laid bare by these dub plates. Soon, King Tubby dubs were an intrinsic part of his act.

In 1969, U-Roy was recruited to Coxsone Dodd's sound system, second billed to veteran DJ King Stitt. It was a short-lived liaison — second billing also meant he was given second choice of the music he could play (all drawn from

Redifusion) and JBC (Jamaican Broadcasting Corporation) radio charts.

Over the next year, U-Roy recorded 29 further tracks with Duke Reid, all drawing upon the Treasure Isle studio's rich archive of rhythms, the majority featuring former Skatalite Tommy McCook & The Supersonics. "Drive Her Home" was based upon Eric Morris' "Number One"; "Words of Wisdom" used Winston Wright's "Black Power," which itself was built upon the Silvertones' version of "In the Midnight Hour." None repeated the colossal impact of his debut hits, but still U-Roy was seldom out of the Jamaican chart, even after he and Reid parted company.

Freelancing around the Kingston scene during the early-mid 1970s, the DJ cut sides with Alvin Ranglin ("Way Down South," "Carolyn," "On Top of the Peak," "Hard Feeling," "Nana Banana," "Train from the West"), Glen Brown ("Number One in the World"), Lloyd Daley (who also recorded one of U-Roy's most devoted disciples, U-Roy Junior) and Niney Holness. There were also several self-produced singles released on U-Roy's own labels Del-Ma and Mego-Ann.

In 1975, U-Roy's international reputation received a major boost after the American duo Hall & Oates covered his "Soldering" for their eponymous fourth album. That same year, following sessions with Bunny Lee ("Heavy Duty Festival," "Gorgonwise," "Jump for Joy"), the DJ teamed up with Prince Tony Robinson, one of the architects behind the British based Virgin Records' move into the reggae market. The partnership debuted with the *Dread inna Babylon* album and "Runaway Girl" single.

Over the next three years, U-Roy released three further albums through Virgin's Front Line subsidiary, *Natty Dread*, *Rasta Ambassador* and *Jah Son of Africa*, all recorded with Robinson. In addition, a visit to London in August, 1976, saw the DJ and the Sly and Robbie-fired Revolutionaries headline the Lyceum, an event preserved in part on 1978's *Live* EP. Interestingly, while U-Roy was certainly a cult success in the UK, and remained of interest in Jamaica, his largest market was Africa. Sales of his late 1970s catalog on that continent were greater than the rest of his worldwide sales combined.

U-Roy launched his own sound system, Stur-Gav, in 1977, with DJs including Jah Screw and Ranking Joe. Unfortunately, the system was destroyed during the riots which shook Kingston in the run-up to the 1980 general election. Rebuilding it with new DJs Charlie Chaplin (b Richard Bennett) and Josey Wales (b Winston Sterling), 1983 saw U-Roy mastermind a pair of fascinating souvenirs of the system at its peak.

King Stur Gav Hi Fi Lee Unlimited offers a continuous live session with U-Roy, Josey Wales, Charlie Chaplin, Billy Boyo, Winston Hussey, Dillinger, Fathead, Ringo, Echo

Dodd's Studio One stockpile, of course) and, later that year, he quit and returned to King Tubby.

U-Roy's first recordings were with Keith Hudson, but the producer shelved the projected "Dynamic Fashion Way" single when he left for a visit to the US. U-Roy then fell in with Lee "Scratch" Perry and, in late 1969, the DJ cut his first single, duetting with the Wailers' Peter Tosh on the Scratch-produced "Selassie," a wild piece built around a turbulent Upsetters rhythm and Count Ossie's percussion, and credited to the Reggae Boys. The song was subsequently reissued as "(Earth's) Rightful Ruler" by Tosh and Hugh Roy, a name which the DJ continued using for several years to come.

A second Lee Perry production, the ultra-violent "OK Corral," followed; U-Roy then joined Lloyd Daley for "Scandal" and "Sound of the Wise" in October, 1969. Each of these records made waves on the underground scene, but it was his partnership with producer Duke Reid which truly set his recording career in motion, after singer John Holt caught his DJ set and recommended him to the producer. U-Roy was spinning Holt's own "Wear You to the Ball" at the time.

Two Reid-produced rhythms were selected for U-Roy's first Treasure Isle singles, Alton Ellis' "Girl I Got a Date" and the Techniques' "Love Is Not a Gamble" — they became, respectively, "Wake the Town" and "Rule the Nation" — meteoric Jamaican chart-toppers which were promptly followed by a third, a version of "Wear You to the Ball" which featured sufficient pieces of the original vocal that Reid marketed it as an actual duet between the DJ and Holt. For six weeks in early 1970, these three singles occupied the top three places on both the RJR (Radio Jamaica

Minott, Michael Irie, Dickie Ranking and Beenie Man, while *King Stur Gav Sounds Live at Clarendon JA*, credits U-Roy as selector only, and features DJs Charlie Chaplin and Inspector Willie.

Meanwhile, U-Roy's interest in recording was declining. Following 1980's disappointing *Love Is Not a Gamble* album, his only releases of significance over the next five years were singles, "Hustling," cut with Gussie Clarke in 1984, and "Get Ready" with Ossie Thomas. He also appeared at the 1982 Reggae Sunsplash, and is included on the *Best of the Festival — Day One* compilation. (U-Roy also performed at the festival in 1984, 1985, 1988 and 1990.)

U-Roy returned to action in 1986, teaming up with Tappa Zukie for *Line Up and Come*, followed immediately by the Prince Jazzbo produced *Music Addict*. Another lengthy silence was broken when he arrived in London in 1991 to headline a one-off show at the Hammersmith Palais. He also recorded a new album with the Mad Professor, *True Born African* — the title track (and first single) featured the DJ alongside singer Sister Audrey.

U-Roy's relationship with the Mad Professor has continued. In 1993, he guested on Nolan Irie's *Work So Hard* set and recorded a new album, *Smile a While*. Guests included Sandra Cross, Aisha, Yabby U and the recently revitalized Susan Cadogan — they appeared together on "The Hurt Is Good," a variation of her 1975 hit "Hurt So Good" and, three years later, remade that track as well. 1996 also saw U-Roy's own next album, *Babylon Kingdom Must Fall*.

Further duets marked U-Roy's 2000 album *Serious Matter* — Horace Andy, Gregory Isaacs, Israel Vibration and Third World all appeared, alongside Skatalite Johnny Moore.

DISCOGRAPHY

7 Dread inna Babylon (Virgin) 1975

"Subversive, spiritual, intra-offensive, impudent, psychedelic . . ." so announced a review of this album in the UK rock magazine *Street Life*. You might also add, revolutionary, war-like, sophisticated, stunning. Skin Flesh & Bones have never sounded so taut, while U-Roy himself calls up a storm.

8 Natty Rebel (Front Line) 1976

Rebel combines the rootsy rhythms of Lloyd Parks and Sly Dunbar with moods ranging from the exuberant hit "Babylon Burning," to the strolling "If You Should Leave Me," and cresting with the title track centerpiece, a roiling version of the Wailers' "Soul Rebel."

8 Rasta Ambassador (Front Line) 1977

Now backed by the likes of Sticky, Sly & Robbie, Ansell Collins and the Gladiators vocal trio, *Rasta* is true to its rootsy title, with rerecordings of "The Tide Is High" and

"Wear You to the Ball" featuring new fat rhythms, while cuts like "Evil Doers" and the Wailers' "Small Axe" pulse with deep dubby beats. U-Roy's laid back chats and Collins' keyboards then bring a piece of JA's pop past to reggae's present.

9 Jah Son of Africa (Front Line) 1978

Featuring a ten piece roots band and a host of vocalists, including the Gladiators and the inimitable Ken Boothe, U-Roy takes such classics as Bob Marley's "Africa" and the Paragons' "Got To Get Away" and makes them totally his own, a magnificent blend of spoken word, melody, rhythm and song.

5 Love Is Not a Gamble (Stateline) 1980
7 Line Up and Come (Tappa — JA) 1987

An unexpected return to form which did not receive anywhere near the exposure it deserved.

6 Music Addict (RAS) 1987

Prince Jazzbo production which warms up nicely over the first few cuts — "I Originate" and the title track — but peaks too early with a revived "King Tubby Skank." It's downhill thereafter.

6 True Born African (RAS) 1991
5 Smile Awhile (RAS) 1993
6 Babylon Kingdom Must Fall (Ariwa — UK) 1996
8 Serious Matter (Tabou) 2000

Reworked classics from some of the masters of the past mark out U-Roy's finest album in some years. Horace Andy, Dennis Brown, Third World, Israel Vibration and Gregory Isaacs are among the DJ's partners, with Ernest Wilson's "I Know Myself" and Beres Hammond's "Serious Matter" among the greatest highlights. There's also a sublime "Night Nurse," rapped over a Gregory Isaacs/Dennis Brown duet.

U-ROY & JOSEY WALES
6 Teacher Meets the Student (Sonic Sounds) 1992

SELECTED COMPILATIONS & ARCHIVE RELEASES
8 Version Galore (Trojan — UK) 1971

"The future is here my dear," the Melodians sonorously sing on the title track, and indeed it was, as this compilation of the Originator's early work proves. U-Roy arrived with Treasure Isle rock steady classics in hand and, while the vocal trios harmonized in the background, the DJ's exuberant yips, shouts and chatty, perceptive toasts melded perfectly with the original songs.

8 U-Roy (Attack — UK) 1974

UK release gathering up the majority of tracks recorded at Treasure Isle during 1969–70, since superseded by the Trojan compilations noted below. U-Roy rides the rhythms like a world class surfer, toasting mainly over instrumentals and stripped down rhythm tracks, while the vocal tracks that do appear (notably two Hopeton Lewis songs and an exquisite John Holt cut), allow the DJ to virtually duet with the singers.

7 With Words of Wisdom (Front Line) 1979

Released alongside a straightforward reissue of *Version Galore*, a compilation of further 1969–70 Duke Reid era material.

5 DJ Masterpieces (Vista Sounds) 1983

Credited to U-Roy and friends, shaky remixes of Bunny Lee sessions; I-Roy and Sir Lee are also featured.

8 With a Flick of My Musical Wrist (Trojan—UK) 1988

An excellent intro into the DJ world, where U-Roy is joined by Big Youth, I-Roy, Prince Jazzbo, and Kings Tony and Sporty.

6 Version of Wisdom (Front Line) 1990

Collection drawn from *Version Galore* and *With Words of Wisdom*.

8 Natty Rebel—Extra Version (Front Line) 1991

The *Rebel/Jah Son* albums are highlighted, but the real meat lies within the final four tracks, taken from a 12" single recorded live at London's Lyceum in 1976. An incredibly dubby "Runaway Girl" is joined by ". . . Ball" at its bounciest, an amazing version of The Techniques "Queen Majesty," and a romping "Babylon Burning."

8 Rock with I (RAS) 1992

With 1975's "Heavy Duty Festival" one of U-Roy's finest later cuts, this collection of Bunny Lee productions needs little further recommendation. An excellent summary, it includes his examination of his own reputation ("The Originator") and hauls out the immortal original "King Tubby's Skank." Much of the set was previously compiled as 1981's *The Originator* (Carib Gems—UK).

8 Original DJ (Caroline) 1995

Impressive track collection drawn from the Front Line releases, including the earlier material reissued during those crucial years. Jumbled together, the end result is a little disorienting—U-Roy advanced colossally between 1970–78, and the chronological gaps are noticeable. Nevertheless, there's no denying the classic quality of every cut in sight, with 16 of the 25 songs dating from those late 1970s masterpieces.

9 Your Ace from Space (Trojan) 1995

30 tracks serve up all but two of the tracks cut by U-Roy and Duke Reid between 1969–70, including both of the original Trojan compilation albums and a crop of singles. With that in mind, there's very little to add. This is the Originator at the peak of his originating. Nobody did it better.

BUNNY WAILER

STYLE *reggae (roots)*
BORN *Neville O'Riley Livingston, 4/10/47 (Kingston, JA)*

One of the founder members of the Wailers with Bob Marley and Peter Tosh, Bunny Livingston was seven when he first met Marley, after his father moved to the village of Nine Miles, St Ann's. The boys then relocated to Kingston, Marley with his mother, Livingston with his father and sister.

Together the pair attended the informal singing lessons offered by veteran vocalist Joe Higgs in one of the neighboring Third Street tenement yards and, following Marley's ill-fated attempt to launch a solo career in 1962, the pair formed their first band.

What became the Wailers originally lined up with fellow vocalists Peter Tosh and Junior Braithwaite, plus backing vocalists Cherry Green and Beverley Kelso. It was this outfit which recorded so many sides for Coxsone Dodd's Studio One set-up during the early-mid 1960s, including Livingston's classic "Simmer Down," the band's first major hit single.

By the time Marley left Jamaica to join his mother and her new husband in the US in 1965, however, the band was a classic vocal trio of Livingston, Tosh and Marley. All three members wrote material for the band, and Marley's departure did little to halt their momentum. Dodd had already stockpiled sufficient material to maintain their hectic release schedule, while the Soulettes' Constantine "Dream" Walker took Marley's place for live performances.

Livingston and Tosh also led the group through a number of new recordings ("Sinner Man," "Rude Boy," "Who Feels It Knows It" and "Dancing Shoes" among them) and, when Marley returned to Jamaica in October, 1966, it was to find their pre-eminence undiminished by his absence. Similarly, when Livingston was sentenced to 14 months in prison on marijuana charges in 1967, Tosh and Marley simply filled the gap with Marley's wife, singer Rita Anderson, and awaited his return.

Livingston's songwriting input diminished considerably over the years, although he continued to provide the band with some of their most spectacular songs—"What Am I Supposed to Do," from the last days at Studio One; the saucy spiritual "Tread Oh," from 1969; and "Riding High" and "Dreamland," recorded during their sojourn with Lee Perry, among them.

Livingston remained with the Wailers until 1973, and the very eve of the international breakthrough they had waited so long to achieve. There were any number of flashpoints, but the final straw was the group's experiences as they toured the UK for the first time, in the wake of the release of *Catch a Fire*, the band's debut album for Island records.

Traveling in a small van without even a road manager to lighten their load, the strictly Rastafarian Livingston was also destined to suffer from hunger throughout the entire tour. His religious beliefs forbade the consumption of processed food; the unwritten laws of a British tour in the early 1970s, on the other hand, forbade the consumption of anything but. By the time the Wailers returned to Jamaica, prior to the launching of an even longer American tour, Livingston had made up his mind to quit.

His initial intention was to remain on board as a singing and writing partner, and to appear in concert in Jamaica alone. In the event, Tosh's departure from the band at the end of the year ensured that never came to pass. Livingston made just two further appearances as a Wailer, at benefit shows in Kingston in May, 1974 and November, 1975; the last album to feature him was *Burning*, recorded immediately before that doomed UK tour and featuring his stately "Hallelujah Time" and "Pass It On."

Operating under his long-established stage name, Bunny Wailer, Livingston had already launched his own solo career prior to departing the Wailers, debuting his Solomonic label with the single "Searching for Love." 1974 brought four further singles, "Trod On," "Lifeline" and "Arabs Oil Weapon" (credited to the Wailers), followed by an alternate version of "Pass It On," all leading up to the 1976 release of his first album, *Blackheart Man*.

The set was recorded with Tosh and the Wailers' Barrett brothers rhythm section (Marley also appears on a remake of "Dreamland"), and spun off two further vital singles, "Battering Down Sentence" (aka "Fighting Against Conviction") and "Rasta Man."

With Solomonic now distributed by Island, and his releases critically feted without ever attaining the same heights as either of his erstwhile bandmates, Livingston followed through with *Protest* (again featuring a guest appearance from Tosh) and *Struggle* during 1977–78, and *In I Father's House* in 1980. Singles during this same period included "Bright Soul," "Free Jah Children" and "Rise and Shine."

1980 saw Livingston record the first of several Wailers tribute albums that have highlighted his career, the Studio One era heavy *Bunny Wailer Sings the Wailers*, backed by what became his regular group for the next few years, the Sly & Robbie powered Roots Radics. A second album from the same sessions, *Tribute*, appeared in Jamaica later in the year.

The success of these sets notwithstanding, it was becoming apparent that Livingston himself was largely content to remain an elder statesman of Jamaican music. 1981's *Rock'n'Groove* was an only partially successful attempt to embrace the new dance hall rhythms, while his dislike of touring saw him wait until December, 1982, before even setting foot on stage again. (His only other scheduled solo performance, at the 1976 Smile Jamaica festival, was cancelled after Marley was shot.)

Staged in Kingston, this live debut was recorded for release the following year as the *Live* album; another three years then elapsed before Livingston played his first show outside the island, on July 12, 1986, in Long Beach, CA. From the same tour, his New York appearance was recorded for the *In Concert* video.

In 1985, Solomonic landed US distribution through the Shanachie label, an arrangement debuted by the *Marketplace* album. American releases for several earlier Solomonic titles followed, together with 1987's *Roots Man Skanking* and *Rule Dance Hall* sets, hosts to a renewed — and this time emphatic — dance hall vibe. "Cool Runnings" and a rerecording of 1981's "Rock'n'Groove" were both major Jamaican hits, and 1989 brought Livingston's best received album in a decade, *Liberation*.

The singer finally undertook his first world tour in the wake of that album, with backing provided by the recently revitalized Skatalites; he also made his Sunsplash debut in 1990.

Another collection of Marley songs, *Time Will Tell*, earned Livingston a Grammy in 1991; Livingston's greatest tribute, however, was the two-CD *Hall of Fame* collection, released to mark what would have been Marley's 50th birthday in 1995 — and the recipient of another Grammy.

In addition to his musical career, Livingston has also become very active in youth politics, even forming his own party, the United Progressive Party (UPP), whose platforms include the decriminalization of marijuana and sweeping educational reforms.

DISCOGRAPHY

9 Black Heart Man (Island) 1976

Generally perceived as the greatest of his solo albums, and certainly on a par with anything he has done since his departure, Wailer's debut includes the classics "Rasta Man," "Armagideon" and "Fig Tree," together with a revamp of the old Wailers track "Dreamland" and a title track which can still raise hairs on the back of the neck.

8 Protest (Island) 1977

The old Marley/Tosh chestbeater "Get Up Stand Up" receives an unexpected airing, but fits easily into the dark militancy of an album which is all but the equal of its predecessor.

8 Struggle (Island) 1978

Completing a triumvirate of albums which really can be regarded as a single long playing statement.

7 In I Father's House (Solomonic—JA) 1980
7 Bunny Wailer Sings the Wailers (Mango) 1980
7 Tribute to the Hon Nesta Marley (Solomonic—JA) 1980

With Sly & Robbie nailing the old rhythms as effortlessly as they create new ones, Wailer wanders through a virtual Studio One days greatest hits collection, recreating many of his own favorite compositions, but adding strong interpretations of Marley's "Hypocrite" and Tosh's "I'm the Toughest."

6 Rock'n'Groove (Solomonic—JA) 1981

6 Hook Line & Sinker (Solomonic—JA) 1982

8 Live (Solomonic—JA) 1983

For a man who hated gigging, Wailer turns in a fabulous performance, as fiery and committed as his studio work, but with the added bonus of an audience which knows just how lucky it is.

5 Roots Radics Rockers Reggae (Solomonic—JA) 1984

5 Marketplace (Shanachie) 1985

The electro sheen and high tech production cannot be beat, but Wailer sounds uncomfortable, lapsing into a faintly absurd calypso-style vocal for the opening "Stay with the Reggae," and never really letting it go.

7 Roots Man Skanking (Shanachie) 1987

6 Rule Dance Hall (Shanachie) 1987

8 Liberation (Shanachie) 1989

The dance hall experiment is over, and *Liberation* lumbers back to the same territory (and almost the same magnificence) as his first solo sets.

7 Time Will Tell: A Tribute to Bob Marley (Shanachie) 1990

Ten well-chosen Marley compositions include a moving "Redemption Song," alongside strong takes on "I Shot the Sheriff," "No Woman No Cry," "Crazy Baldheads" and his adaptation of Haile Selassie's words, "War."

8 Gumption (Shanachie) 1991

More covers, and though there was no Grammy awaiting, in its own way this is the better album. Marley's "Bus Dem Shut" is joined by inspired attacks on the Johnny Clarke and Toots Hibbert's songbooks, with the latter's "Dog War" an especial jewel. Four fine originals end a set whose only pitfall is the synthesizers which really don't seem to know they're not needed.

5 Dance Massive (Shanachie) 1992

A return to the dance hall, with rhythms ruling and the songs slighter than he's let slip in for some time.

6 Just Be Nice (RAS) 1993

9 Hall of Fame: A Tribute to Bob Marley's 50th Anniversary (RAS) 1995

52 newly recorded tracks spread across two discs comprise Livingston's latest personal tribute to his former bandmate, with a track listing running from "Judge Not" to "Zion Train," and wonderfully warm interpretations of everything in between. Recorded with Sly & Robbie, early Wailers drummer Hugh Malcolm, later band members Junior Mar-

vin, Aston Barrett and more, Livingston's reinterpretations of material from his own era of the band serves to remind just what a contribution he made to the Wailers; songs composed following his departure let us know what we (and Marley) lost. The lyric booklet includes Livingston's own thoughts and recollections about the songs, including a few harsh corrections, while a truly unexpected gem is "Fancy Curls," an unrecorded Marley composition dating back to his earliest attempts at song writing. Another Grammy winner.

7 Communication (Solomonic/Tuff Gong) 2000

SELECTED COMPILATIONS & ARCHIVE RELEASES

7 Crucial! Roots Classics (Shanachie) 1994

Strong 1979–82 collection heavy on the darker political material.

8 Retrospective: Classic Tracks (Solomonic—JA) 1995

Comprehensive one disc examination of Bunny's 1980s, sensibly omitting the majority of dance hall excursions and ending with that warm "Redemption Song."

8 Dub D'Sco (RAS) 1998

Fascinating 17 track dub collection drawing from *Blackheart Man* and *Sings the Wailers*.

WAILING SOULS

STYLE *reggae (roots)*

FORMED *1966 (Kingston, JA)*

ORIGINAL LINE-UP *(as the Renegades) Winston "Pipe" Matthews, Lloyd "Bread" McDonald, George "Buddy" Haye (vocals)*

Although the Wailing Souls have never achieved the lasting commercial or critical acclaim which their long career deserves, their very longevity has marked them out among the most popular roots survivors on the current scene, a standing which has seen them enjoy major label attentions throughout the 1990s, and sell-out audiences whenever they visit the US.

Having graduated from the same tenement yard vocal classes as Bob Marley & the Wailers, held by singer Joe Higgs during the early 1960s, Winston "Pipe" Matthews was discovered by Prince Buster in 1963. As a member of the Schoolboys, he cut a string of singles during 1963–64, including "Little Dilly," "Little Boy Blue" and "Dream Lover." Then in 1965, he formed the Renegades with fellow Higgs graduates Lloyd "Bread" McDonald and George "Buddy" Haye.

The trio was frequently employed working alongside veteran guitarist Ernest Ranglin, and also cut a number of singles in their own right, debuting with "Lost Love." Recruited to Coxsone Dodd's Studio One, they followed

through with "Back Out with It," "Row Fisherman Row" and the foreboding-drenched "Mr Fire Coal Man," performed over the Silvertones' classic "Burning in My Soul."

Haye quit around 1968 and, following the recruitment of new members Oswald Downer and Norman Davis, the Renegades changed their name to the Wailing Souls. Releases from this period include the classic "Dungeon," "Pack Your Things," "Thou Shalt Not Steal" and early versions of songs which feature prominently in their later career, "You Should Have Known Better" (reborn as "Back Biter"), "Soul and Power" ("Feel the Spirit") and "Rock but Don't Fall" ("Walk the Chalk Line").

In 1970, the band cut "Gold Digger" with producer Lloyd Daley, released in the UK under the name the Little Roys. Other material appeared under the names the Classics, Atarra and Pipe and the Pipers, apparently to avoid confusion with the better known and established Wailers.

The Wailers themselves saw no conflict however, and by the end of the year, Wailing Souls had moved to that band's own Tuff Gong imprint. There they continued their success with "Harbour Shark," "Walk Walk Walk" and "You Should've Known Better," recorded with the Tuff Gong All Stars — the Wailers by any other name.

Downer and Davis quit in 1974, at which point founder member Haye rejoined, alongside their old mentor Joe Higgs. This reconstituted line-up had barely started moving, however, when Higgs accepted the offer of a US tour with Jimmy Cliff. He was replaced by Rudolph "Garth" Dennis, a founder member of Black Uhuru.

A union with producer JoJo Hookim now saw the Wailing Souls establish themselves among the Channel One studio's most reliable hit-makers. Paired with the Sly & Robbie led Revolutionaries, their mid-1970s output including the singles "Very Well," "Things and Time" (based on their earlier "Back Out with It"), revivals of "Back Out" and "Fire Coal Man," "Jah Jah Give Us Life," "War" (cut with DJ Ranking Trevor), "Back Biter" and "Joy Within Your Heart." An outtake from this period, "Lawless Society," gave the band another major hit some years later.

In 1977, Wailing Souls launched their own Massive label, finding immediate success with "Bredda Gravalicious" and "Feel the Spirit," and, two years later, Island Records picked up their *Wild Suspense* album for international distribution.

In 1980, the Wailing Souls placed Massive on hold and moved to Sly & Robbie's Taxi label, where "Old Broom" and "Sugar Plum Plum" proved major hits. Indeed, 1980–81 saw the group enter its most prolific spell ever. Recording at Channel One with the Roots Radics Band and producer Junjo Lawes, their output included the singles "Fire House Rock," "See Baba Joe," "Kingdom Rise Kingdom Fall," "A Day Will Come" and "Up Front."

The partnership also cut the albums, *Fire House Rock* and *Inch Pinchers*, while the group worked, too, with producers Cha Cha ("Grabbing and Running") and Linval Thompson, releasing 1981's "Rude Boy Say Him Bad" and "Who No Waan Come," and the *Wailing* album.

Also in 1981, Wailing Souls paid their first visit to the US, for a short California tour. They ended up staying in the country for much of the next three years, self-producing the singles "Take We Back" (with Ranking Trevor), "Take a Taste" (with Ringo), "They Don't Know Jah" and "Sticky Stay" (1982), and "War Deh Round a John Shop" (1984).

They also cut two albums, *On the Rocks* (1983) and *Stranded* (1984) — the latter taking its title from the wry, and not wholly exaggerated opening cut, "Stranded in LA," recounting the end of this line-up of the band. Garth Dennis quit, returning to Black Uhuru; so did Haye, who opted to remain in LA.

Matthews and McDonald returned to Jamaica and relaunched Wailing Souls, linking with producer Delroy Wright in 1986, for three albums, beginning with that year's *Lay It on the Line*. Sly & Robbie were recruited to lay down the backing on the following year's *Kingston 14* and the hit single "Full Moon." In 1988, they recorded *Reggae in a Firehouse*; unfortunately, it was not released at the time, but contentiously given a full international launch in 1991.

Wailing Souls next worked with King Jammy, a fortuitous decision which paved the way for the group's subsequent American pre-eminence. Although their first album together, 1989's *Stormy Night*, produced no hit singles and wasn't even released in Jamaica, it did astonishingly well elsewhere, and by 1991 the group had returned to the US.

There they recruited the singularly named vocalist Maisha and signed with US major label Sony's Chaos subsidiary for 1992's well-received *All Over the World* album. They became the first reggae band ever to appear on network TV's *The Tonight Show*, while the album itself was nominated for a Grammy.

They then made their debut appearance at Reggae Sunsplash, and only the unauthorized and unwelcome appearance of the four year old *Reggae in a Firehouse* disturbed the band's equilibrium. However, there is no evidence to suggest that it damaged their standing; in fact, it turned out to be of sufficient quality to only add to the excitement surrounding Wailing Souls.

The group's next album, 1994's *Live On*, two years later, was released on Sony's Zoo subsidiary. Although well-received, sadly it did not sell well, and by the time of 1997's *Tension*, Wailing Souls had returned to the independent sector. 1998's covers heavy *Psychedelic Souls* offered an entertaining diversion; 2000's *Equality* returned to basics with equal aplomb.

DISCOGRAPHY

9 Wild Suspense (Island—UK) 1979

Self-produced heavy roots featuring the band's three biggest 1970s hits, "Bredda Gravalicious," "Feel the Spirit" and "Very Well," and never failing to maintain those standards. The CD reissue features seven dub bonus cuts.

8 Firehouse Rock (Greensleeves—UK) 1980

A few minutes in the company of "Kingdom Rise Kingdom Fall" are enough to confirm this as one of the great roots albums of the late 1970s. Reissued in 2001 by Greensleeves' newly launched US operation.

6 Wailing (Jah Guidance) 1981

7 Inch Pinchers (Greensleeves—UK) 1982

Fine Lawes production moves sweetly into dance hall territory, featuring the favorites "Baby Come Rock," "Mass Charlie Ground" and "Infidels."

6 On the Rocks (Greensleeves—UK) 1983

6 Stranded (Greensleeves—UK) 1984

6 Lay It on the Line (Live & Learn) 1986

7 Kingston 14 (Live & Learn) 1987

The band's best in five years brings Sly & Robbie firmly to the fore, while never letting the studio steal the Souls' own spirit. One of their best sounding, and most organically textured, releases.

7 Stormy Night (Rohit) 1989

10 All Over the World (Chaos) 1992

Featuring a sound system party's worth of guest musicians, vocalists and rappers, *World* is a joyous musical celebration, stylistically diverse, with a big phat sound which crackles with energy. Although it certainly has its share of big-noise/no-content party fillers, "Shark Attack" and the seemingly autobiographical "Picky Picky Head" are among the more irresistible treats in store; U-Roy numbers among the rappers; while the band's increasingly eccentric taste in covers includes a Rolling Stones country number and a gem by French-Canadian folkies the McGarrigle Sisters.

6 Live On (Zoo) 1994

6 Tension (Big Ship) 1997

A reprise of "Fire Coal Man" doesn't necessarily fill one with enthusiasm, although once things get moving, the album at least lives up to its title.

7 Psychedelic Souls (Pow Wow) 1998

Curious set, totally enjoyable but strangely disturbing at the same time. Nevertheless, it continued Wailing Souls' ascent, a Sly & Robbie powered/Richard Feldman-produced assault on rock classics by the Doors, Bob Dylan, George Harrison, Jimi Hendrix and Procol Harum, among others.

7 Equality (Music Blitz) 2000

The purist complaints that Wailing Souls have gone too American are kicked into touch with a defiantly rootsy album sliced with both technological and musical strides forward. Sly & Robbie's work is exemplary, while songs range from the realism of "No Joy Ride" to the triumphant "Power and the Glory."

SELECTED COMPILATIONS & ARCHIVE RELEASES

7 The Wailing Souls (Studio One) 1976

8 Soul and Power (Studio One) 1984

Two collections of the group's earlier releases, cut during 1969–70 with producer Coxsone Dodd.

8 The Best Of (Empire—UK) 1984

Worthy collection of the Jojo Hookim/Channel One years, demonstrating both the immaculate harmonies which were the group's primary calling card, but also the early magic of Sly and Robbie.

7 The Very Best Of (Greensleeves—UK) 1987

Concentrating on the band's 1980s output, and work with Linval Thompson, Sly & Robbie and Junjo Lawes. "Bredda Gravalicious" slips in from the band's 1970s roots peak; "War deh Round a John Shop" (from *Stranded*) proves that the new decade occasionally sharpened their vision.

8 Reggae in a Firehouse (Live & Learn) 1991

Recorded in 1988. Sly and Robbie provide the powerhouse percussion to the heavy rootsy tracks, then lighten the load for the more Sixties-ish poppy numbers. Meanwhile, the

Wailing ones sing their souls out, all sweet, sweet vocals and shimmering, shifting harmonies, echoing back to the classic sounds of the early Seventies.

WINDSOR RECORDS

Launched in Trinidad in 1971 by pioneering East Indian producers/broadcasters Sham and Moean Mohammed, Windsor Records is the single most important source for pre- and proto-chutney recordings, alongside a wealth of other, more traditional native styles. The *Tent Singing* sub series is especially recommended, offering up performances by some of the giants of tan, caught in their most natural surroundings.

SELECT DISCOGRAPHY

03 Sharm Yankarran: *Gems of Yankarran/A Tribute to the Late . . .* (1971)

07 Yussuff Khan: *Haunting Melodies Of* (1971) 12 Henry Tooloom Dindial & Ramchaitar: *Memories of Masters* (1971)

21 Roy Cooper/Abdul "Kush" Razack: *Indian Classical Songs* (1972)

22 Isaac Yankarran: *We Remember* (1972)

23 Yussuff Khan: *Sings Again* (197-)

24 various: *Tent Singing by Our Classical Masters* (197-)

25 Sookdeo Sookhraj: *Tent Singing By* (197-)

26 Abdul "Kush" Razack: *Tent Singing By* (1977)

27 Dev Bansraj Ramkissoon: *Tent Singing By* (1977)

31 Yussuff Khan: *Tent Singing By* (1978)

32 Sharm Yankarran: *Tent Singing By* (1978)

33 Kung Beharry Singh: *Tent Singing By* (1978)

34 Haniff Mohammed: *The Best of Haniff* (1978)

52 Sam Boodram: *Favourite Hits Of* (1979)

53 Jameer Hosein: *Songs to Remember by Trinidad's Leading Vocalist* (1979)

73 Sam Boodram: *Joyful Songs Of* (1981)

76 various: *Stars of T&T* (1982)

79 Yussuff Khan/KB Singh: *A Battle of the Giants* (1982)

86 Lilly Ramcharan: *To My Dad Zoon, from Lilly with Love* (1982)

87 Leon Rampersad/Bansraj Ramkissoon: *Battle of the Giants* (1982)

XTATIK

STYLE *soca*

FORMED 1984 *(Port of Spain, T&T)*

ORIGINAL LINE-UP *Machel Montano (b 11/24/75, Port of Spain — vocals), Joseph Rivers (guitar), Vincent Rivers (bass), Derwin Vallie (keyboards), Sterling Paul (trombone), Oral Rodriguez (sax), Marlon Roach (trumpet), Rodney Daniel (trumpet), Gregory Pegus (drums), Darryl Henry (percussion)*

In 1982, Machel Montano was all of seven years old when he began performing, winning a local School Calypso Competition for Juniors and finished second overall — he came first the following year. In 1984, he took four Junior Calypso Monarch titles, performing the song "The Letter." That same year, he also linked with brother Marcus (aged 11)

and the Rivers brothers, Joseph (12) and Vincent (14) to form Pranasonic Express in May, 1984. The above line-up coalesced gradually — Marcus Montano left early on, Rodney Daniel joined in 1987, while the group itself became Xtatik in 1989.

Accompanied by studio musicians, Montano cut his first album in 1985, the not-too-aptly titled *Too Young to Soca*. The following year, the album's title track took him to third place in the Young Kings competition at carnival, the youngest performer ever to compete, and the next year he appeared on the American TV talent contest *Star Search*. His soca routine was middle America's first exposure to the sound and led to him being briefly saddled with the title "the Michael Jackson of soca."

In 1987, Montano became the first Trinidadian, and the youngest entertainer, ever to win the Caribbean Song Festival; the following year, Pranasonic Express bassist Vincent Rivers tasted carnival, playing with Shandileer and Charlie's Roots. (Xtatik percussionist Darryl Henry has also worked with the latter band; as has their current sound engineer, Sean Joseph.)

1988 brought the single "The Cry of Today's Youth," one of the young group's finest; Pranasonic Express also released three mini-albums, *Soca Earthquake*, *Dr Carnival* and *Catch Ya*. The development of the modern band, however, did not truly commence until 1990, following their renaming. *Breakin' Out* (1990) and *One Step Ahead* (1991) were both successful sets, and the group enjoyed hits with "In Time" and "Soca Santa"; 1991 also saw Montano win the Young Kings Competition.

That same year Xtatik arrived at what quickly proved a momentous decision. In the past, Montano recalled, the group's attempts to open for some of the heavyweight Jamaican and American artists visiting T&T had ended in despair. "We would open for big acts like Buju Banton and MC Hammer and we would play soca and get pelted with oranges, bottles and papers." Soca at that time, he reasoned, was hedonistic, humorous, party music. It had nothing to say about reality. Montano wanted to change that.

Declaring Xtatik to be "on a hectic mission" to modernize calypso, he began adding slang to his lyrics, "making it hip," while his bandmates, now augmented by guitarist Roger George, turned on a ferocious soca-dance hall fusion to match. It was an impressive move, and a successful one. "Over the years, we've seen a big change in the crowd's attitudes," Montano reflected later.

The single "First in de Party" served notice of the band's new direction. It was followed by the albums *X Amount ah Sweetness* (1992) and *Xtatik Soca Style*, cut in 1993 after Montano's graduation from Ohio's School of Recording Arts.

Overcoming the departure of Roger George, the following year brought "Xtatik By All Means," as the band claimed the road march titles at both Caribana and the Miami carnival in 1994. The group truly came of age with the following year's "Come Dig It," a soca-house fusion which defied belief. Montano's initial intention was to feature the song on the latest Xtatik album, in time for carnival 1995. Aware of the power and novelty of the production, however, he instead approached the American label Delicious Vinyl — and Xtatik were promptly offered the choice to cut it as a single. (Xtatik would be crowned Party Band for the year all the same.)

Accompanied by a video shot at Brooklyn's West Indian Day carnival, "Come Dig It" appeared in the US in mid-1996. It was followed by "Hot," "Outta de Boom Boom Family" and "Big Truck." The latter was pulled from the *Heavy Duty* album to become the 1997 Trinidad Road March winner for songwriter Montano (the youngest ever winner). Xtatik as a whole then followed through with the 1998 champion, "Footsteps."

Further evidence of the band's adventurousness was offered by 1998's *Machel Arts* album, whose highlights included "We Like It," updating calypsonian Lord Nelson's early 80s soca hit, with Nelson himself joining Machel on vocals.

That same year saw Xtatik joined by co-lead vocalist Peter C Lewis (b 1/3/72, T&T), a former member of the bands Massive Chandelier (1993–95) and Atlantik (1995–98) — he co-wrote the latter's hits "Showdown," "Left Foot Right Foot" and "We Sound." Lewis maintained a solo career outside of Xtatik, and in 2000, he scored hits with "Drag Yuh Bow," "Oh My Gosh" and "Five Types of Wine"; he also partnered Lexus and CL Smooth on the memorable "Kiki."

Atlantik guitarist Dean Williams followed Lewis into Xtatik in time for 1999's *Any Minute Now*, with the group's attack strengthened even further by the return of guitarist Roger George, who appeared on both Xtatik's 2000 offering *Here Comes the Band*, and Montano's own second solo album, the wryly titled *2000 Young to Soca*.

SELECTED DISCOGRAPHY

XTATIK

6 Breakin' Out (—T&T) 1990

5 One Step Ahead (—T&T) 1991

Formative renta-soca efforts, enjoyable in the context of the time, but swiftly laid hollow by the band's future accomplishments.

6 X Amount ah Sweetness (—T&T) 1992

Wild and in the streets, Xtatik sense their future and make an urgent lunge for it. Parts of the album are clumsily ill-focused, most notably the lyrics. But their heart is in the right place.

7 Xtatik Soca Style (—T&T) 1993

9 Loose Yuh Waist (Rainbow—T&T) 1995

Three versions of the title track are joined by the maddening "Soca World Dance" and "Fire in de Dance Hall," their titles offering explicit suggestions of what to expect. A fiery album which catches Xtatik in the first bloom of their violent reinvention.

8 Men at Work (X—T&T) 1996

The omission of the hit "Come Dig It" is disappointing, but the album shoots off in so many other directions that it's barely missed. "Wiper Dance," "Drop de Bum Bum" and "How Yuh Moving" all appear in two versions, but so much is going on that they reappear as old friends, as much as reprises.

6 Heavy Duty (JW Productions) 1997

Terry Gajraj's version of "Big Truck" is arguably the superior take, but there's no denying the horsepower unleashed here nor on the riotous "No Carnival." The rest of the album, sadly, does not live up to the same standards — *Heavy Duty* is actually heavy going in places.

7 Xtatik Live (JW Productions) 1997

Action packed live performance throws up few surprises, but is supplemented by some challenging remixes.

9 Charge aka Machel Arts (JW Productions) 1998

Versatile set includes the Spanish accented soca of "Toro Toro," featuring a guest appearance by Jamaican dance hall star Shaggy; the chutney smash "Harry Krishna," the reggae funk "Hardworking Dog" and the hip hop "De Vibz."

8 Any Minute Now (—T&T) 1999

Another star studded outing, this time involving Beenie Man ("Outa Space"), Burning Flames (the scintillating "Showdown—Band Meets Band") and Red Rat ("Rubber Waist"). Dwell on those cuts, though, and you may lose sight of the other gems — "Lo Riders," "Big Phat Fish" and "Mocking Meh," as Xtatik continue to veer across the stylistic scene.

8 Here Comes the Band (JW Productions) 2000

MACHEL MONTANO

5 Too Young to Soca (—T&T) 1985

7 2000 Young to Soca (JW Productions) 2000

Opens with a reprise of "Too Young to Soca," before spinning off on less of a tangent than the band are prone to, but still nothing that the *Star Search* viewers will recognize. "Love 2U 2Nite," "Pang Pang" and the gleefully foreboding "Y2K J'Ouvert" are the stars of this show.

TAPPA ZUKIE

STYLE *reggae (toasting/DJ)*
BORN *David Sinclair, 7/2/55 (JA)*

Possibly the finest DJ to emerge in the mid-1970s, Tappa Zukie was a magical wordsmith whose sense of timing has seldom been equalled. He also ranks among the most influential reggae artists of the last 25 years, not only as a performer but also as a producer. Since the mid-1980s, Zukie has coaxed career-best recordings from Dennis Brown, Gregory Isaacs, Michael Rose, Frankie Paul, Max Romeo, Yami Bolo and many more.

He is also firmly entrenched in the iconography of both British and American punk rock. In the early-1970s, Zukie was the first Jamaican DJ to take up residence in the UK, and thus was well placed to both witness and influence the rising tide of roots consciousness which enveloped the country later in the decade.

His records were firm favorites on British based sound systems of the time and, when New York punk poetess Patti Smith visited London in late 1976, Zukie joined her on stage for a colossal dub jam through her "Radio Ethiopia" song, further strengthening his ties with America's own punk community.

It was ironic, then, that Zukie never intended to make the UK his home—a rising 18 year old star on his homeland's DJ circuit, his mother sent him to stay with relatives in 1973, in an attempt to keep him out of trouble, a battle she had been fighting since he was tiny.

Even his nickname was drawn from his mischievous activities. The Zukies was the name of the juvenile gang which he led, while Tappa developed after his mother caught him stealing milk and called him a "pot-a-cat." His grandmother altered it to "top-a-cat," and familiarity reduced it further. There is, incidentally, absolutely no consistency to the spelling of this name—it appears as both "Tapper" and "Tappa" on Jamaican, UK and US releases alike, with Jamaican pressings of the *In Dub* and *Earth Running* albums utilizing both simultaneously.

Having debuted with the I-Oses Discotech, Zukie was working with the Maccabees sound system, and had come to the attention of producer Bunny Lee, when he learned he was being sent away. Faced with the imminent loss of a promising talent, Lee used his own British contacts to organize a live performance for the teen, within 24 hours of his arrival in London. Opening for the visiting U-Roy, Zukie performed one toast, over Slim Smith's "The Time Has Come."

That brought him to the attention of London-based producer Larry Lawrence. Zukie's debut single, "Jump and Twist," was released by Lawrence's Ethnic Records label in late 1973. The DJ also worked with producer Clem Bushay, but returned to Jamaica before their sessions were released.

Back home, he recorded "Judge I Oh Lord" with producer Lloydie Slim, following through with "Ira Lion" and "Viego" for Harry Mudie (the song was named for Mudie's

own sound system). He also worked with Yabby You during 1975, turning in a ferocious version of the producer's "Jah Vengeance" rhythm, "Natty Dread on the Mountain Top." You produced Zukie's "Don't Get Crazy" later that same year.

Now employed as Bunny Lee's bodyguard, Zukie then went into the studio with Lee himself to cut "Jah Is I Guiding Star," "Pontious Pilot" and 1975's classic "Natty Dread Don't Cry." However, the DJ was anxious to make his own way in the industry and the pair broke up—Lee's parting gift to Zukie was a clutch of rhythms to use as he saw fit.

With further rhythms supplied by producers JoJo Hookim and Ossie Hibbert, Zukie began work on his self-produced debut album. Booking his own session at King Tubby's studio, he recorded what became the *MPLA* album, a righteous blast of frustration and anger, shot through with some of the moodiest roots of the age.

Zukie intended releasing the album on his own label, once he got the financing together—Stars operated out of Bunny Lee's store at 101 Orange Street, but for now, he could afford only to release singles, beginning with his own "Marcus" (over a Horace Andy cut) and "Chalice to Chalice" (toasted over Johnny Clarke's version of Slim Smith's "Give Me Your Love").

He also began producing other artists, a sideline which has since utterly superceded his own recording career. His earliest sessions included stints with Errol Dunkley ("Enoch Power," disrespectfully dedicated to the right wing British politician, Enoch Powell), Ras Alla & the Spears ("Bosrah"), Junior Ross, Linford Newgend and ex-Itals vocalist Ronnie Davis. Other Stars label releases were handled by producer Glen Brown, including one by Zukie himself, "Wicked Can't Run Away."

Looking for a UK distributor for the label, Zukie returned to London in May, 1975. There he found the Clem Bushay sessions finally in the stores, packaged as the *Man a Warrior* album and selling up a storm for the tiny London-based Klik label. Zukie himself then licensed the company a single of "MPLA" in 1976.

Based around a radioactive Sly & Robbie rhythm, "MPLA" was an immediate reggae chart hit — although it was not, perhaps, the topical reference to the Angolan civil war which many contemporary listeners assumed. There, the MPLA was the Popular Movement for the Liberation of Angola, a Communist force partially financed by the Jamaican government. Zukie, however, preferred to think of it as "Members of the People's Liberation Army," with an at least partially autobiographical lyric, discussing the run-ins with the law which precipitated his teenaged departure to England.

With demand for more material soaring, Zukie followed up with "Ten Against One," "Natty Still Waiting" and "Pick Up the Rockers" (a prophetic warning to record collectors, about how old 45s would one day be extremely valuable, performed over one such golden oldie, the Royals' "Pick Up the Pieces"). The *MPLA* album, meanwhile, became Britain's biggest selling reggae release that Christmas. Combining cuts from the album with other Stars label material, an accompanying dub version followed in 1977 — the original Jamaican release, a limited edition of just 300 copies, had long since sold out.

Patti Smith's patronage added to the cachet surrounding Zukie's name. She booked him as opening act on her next tour, released *Man a Warrior* in the US on her own Mer label, and supplied laudatory sleeve notes for his next album, *Man from Bosrah*.

Earth Running followed during 1977, together with the single "New Star" and another acclaimed dub collection, *Escape from Hell*, while Zukie finally scored his first major Jamaican hits with "Oh Lord" (over Gregory Isaacs' "The Storm") and "She Wants a Phensic." By 1978, Stars had forged an alliance with Virgin's Front Line subsidiary for the *Peace in the Ghetto* and *Tappa Roots* albums; Front Line also reissued both *MPLA* and *In Dub* during 1979.

Now commuting regularly between Kingston and London, Zukie continued his production work, and regular live appearances (he played Sunsplash in 1981). He cut singles with Junior Ross and Horace Andy, the remarkable "Natty Dread a Weh She Want," and also discovered the teenaged Trench Town band Knowledge, signing them to the A&M major in 1981. Unfortunately, (as several other Jamaican recruits discovered), that label's understanding of the reggae

market was essentially based around their experiences with the Police, and Knowledge's debut album, *Word Sound and Power* was quickly lost.

In 1983, still based in London, he mixed Militant Barry's acclaimed *Green Valley* album, from tapes sent over from Kingston by producer Keith Hudson; remembering his own career, he also released the *People Are You Ready?* album that same year.

Zukie returned to Jamaica soon after. A new album in 1986, *Ragamuffin*, took its title from a track first included on *Earth Running* a decade earlier, and essentially marked the end of Zukie's recording career, until 1996 brought a comeback with *Deep Roots*.

His production work, however, has maintained him in both the public eye and the critical spotlight. Among Zukie's best-loved productions have been albums by veterans Ken Boothe, Cornell Campbell, Jackie Edwards, the Heptones, the Mighty Diamonds, Sugar Minott, Frankie Paul, Max Romeo and U-Roy. He has also masterminded a wealth of fascinating compilation albums, including the self-deprecatingly named *Old Time DJ Come Back Again*, highlighting both current and classic toasters, including Dillinger, U-Roy, Jah Stitch, Prince Jazzbo and Zukie himself.

His whimsically logoed Tappa label has unleashed further hits by JC Lodge, Brigadier Jerry, Courtney Melody, Saint & Campbell, GG Wayne, Malcolm X, Simpleton & Jakki James, Beres Hammond and Sly Dunbar. Zukie himself often takes the instrumental b-sides.

SELECTED DISCOGRAPHY

LPs

7 **Man a Warrior (— UK) 1975**

Although it never gained the popularity of later albums, this Clement Bushay production, recorded while Zukie was in the UK, remains a powerful debut and a showcase for the young DJ's toasting.

10 **MPLA (Klik — UK) 1976**

Rough and tumble reggae heavy with dub overtones and rocker guitar provides the perfect props for Zukie's always enjoyable toasts. Despite disappointing on any number of political levels — most pertinently the intentions of the title track — *MPLA* ranks among the watershed albums of 1976 — a year which provided so many!

8 **Man from Bosrah (Stars — JA) 1977**
8 **Earth Running (Stars — JA) 1977**

Zukie's vocal versatility captures the shifting stylings of the age, singing, chanting and toasting his way across such crucial cuts as "The General" and "Raggamuffin," with the remaining tracks just as strong.

7 Escape From Hell (Stars—JA) 1977
9 In Dub (Stars—JA) 1977

A crucial compilation of Zukie productions, brought to new heights by the mixing wizardry of Philip Smart. The set includes Zukie's own "MPLA," Junior Ross' "Judgement Time" and Ras Alla's "Bosrah," among other dance floor delighting dubs.

8 Peace in the Ghetto (Front Line) 1978
8 Tappa Roots (Front Line) 1978

"Green Bay Murder" offers the most overt commentary on an album of simmering rage; the government sponsored massacre of so-called Rasta revolutionaries ignited a firestorm which none could have predicted.

6 Black Man (Stars—JA) 1979
6 Raggy Joey Boy (Stars—JA)

Joe Gibbs productions.

7 People Are You Ready (Stars—JA) 1983
6 Ragamuffin (World Enterprise) 1986

It's not that he's past caring, but little about *Ragamuffin* exemplifies the values which Zukie once espoused—primarily because his attention is now focused on making other people's records.

7 Deep Roots (RAS) 1996

A bright return featuring the mini-classics "Yagga Yagga" and "Everybody Bawling," plus Zukie's own take on "Satta Amasa Gana."

SELECTED COMPILATIONS & ARCHIVE RELEASES

8 From the Archive (RAS) 1995

An *MPLA* heavy retrospective—eight tracks in all culled from that set, plus the girls-in-shorts shout of "Oh Lord," "Pick Up The Rockers" and the ahead of its time slacker anthem, "Bum."

PART THREE: THE PRODUCERS

What the record company is to the American and European music industry, the record producer is to the Jamaican. There are no "major" record labels on the island, at least in a form that a US audience would recognize. What there are, are major record producers, a coterie of ever shifting size and dynamics which is personally responsible for every record released on the island.

Some of them operate from tiny premises, renting out recording studios on an as needed basis, pressing up singles in limited quantities, and hoping that one of them, one day, will make a sizeable splash. Others are as old as the Jamaican industry itself, have watched and nurtured the music through four decades of constant change and evolution, and turn out hit records today because that is the only job they know. All, however, have one thing in common. They believe that theirs is the ear which can predict what the dance halls will be playing next.

During the 1950s, the first record producers on the island were the sound system operators, for whom cutting acetates of original music was merely the next stage in the battle to ensure their system had music which their rivals would never find.

Prior to this, the operators relied on singles imported from elsewhere (usually the US), and the more obscure the better. That, too, was a serious business. Veterans still talk about the day Duke Reid finally got his hands on a copy of Coxsone Dodd's so-called "Coxsone's Hop," a full seven years after Dodd first brought a copy into the country, scratched out the original label and matrix number, and built his very reputation on the raucous instrumental disc's exclusivity. Once Reid got his hands on a copy, though, "Later for 'Gator" by American R&B saxophonist Willis Jackson never sounded the same again.

Stanley Motta was the first Jamaican sound system man to cut records on the island, in 1951, his interests almost purely mento-driven. It was 1957 before any of the major operators took an interest, with Duke Reid the first to enter a studio. Although the majority of early recordings were intended for sound system use only, it was Reid, who set the precedents by which the next generation of record producers would be judged.

The producer booked the studio (in those instances where he didn't already operate one of his own), he picked the performers, he chose the songs and he paid the bills. And at the end of the day, he owned the record. It wasn't until the 1990s that anything approaching a modern copyright law was put in place in Jamaica — for more than 30 years before that, the person who "produced" the session

was the person who owned the performance, to do with as he would.

If he wanted to strip off the vocals and release an instrumental version, he could. If he wanted to re-use the rhythm and rewrite the lyric, he could. Neither the original musicians nor even the song's composer had any further rights to their work once they'd been paid for the original session — and with the rates of pay often seeming derisory compared to the potential profits, it was a situation which eventually led to much ill-feeling.

The flip side of the coin, of course, was that artists were seldom bound to any one producer. Many, of course, would form a partnership which, whether through friendship or success, lasted over a period of months or even years. But few did so before they had first recorded with virtually every other producer in town, and few, even at the height of success, recorded exclusively for one at a time. At one point in the 1980s, singer Dennis Brown was said to spend his entire day simply making the rounds of the studios, cutting a few sides with one producer, a few with another and so on, until he came back around to the first one. Then the cycle would begin again.

Similarly, had the system more heavily favored the artists, fewer would have been recorded. And even for that elite, the benefits would have been ephemeral, for one wrong step or a change in fashion, would have ended their careers. The sheer breath of talent and wealth of music which flooded out of Jamaica, during the 1960s in particular, was almost exclusively down to the fact that producers could afford to take chances, especially with new artists and forgotten veterans. More importantly, artist development itself would have been stifled, because how many producers would be willing to invest large sums of money in an act, unless they believed they were going to keep them long enough to recoup?

It may not have been perfect, but the producer system gave many hundreds of artists regular work and recording time, freedom to work with whomever they so desired, and kept a constant ear to the street. It also allowed for the most massive flowering of music, talent and records anywhere in the world. And it began with Duke Reid's first session, in 1957.

In fact, that initial session produced little of lasting value — a handful of raw R&B instrumentals, plus a new version of another of Coxsone Dodd's old favorites, "Lollipop Girl," by Derrick Harriott and Claudie Sang. (The original, by the same artists, was recorded the previous year by Stanley Motta, for Dodd's exclusive use. Reid had his own pirate copy of it within hours of its debut, at which point, Dodd abandoned the record altogether and left it to his rival.)

However, the recordings sowed a seed which soon come to flower. Reid returned to the studio in 1959; Dodd followed before the end of the year, with Prince Buster making his production debut in 1960. There was similar activity, too, from Chris Blackwell, head of the Island record label, and Edward Seaga, a half-Syrian, Harvard educated anthropologist, who owned the WIRL studios. With Ken Khouri's Federal Studios also in operation, plus the Indo-Jamaican Tuari family's Caribbean Records pressing plant, the Jamaican music industry was ready to burst into action.

Reid was very much a hand's-off producer. Although he certainly listened in to the majority of sessions conducted under his aegis, he was aware enough of his own musical limitations, to restrict his actual involvement to barking out opinions on the quality of the performance, while leaving the technical business to other hirelings. Dodd, too, frequently allowed his staff to oversee sessions — Lee Perry got his start with Dodd, as de facto producer of many of the Studio One set-up's most important recordings.

Prince Buster, on the other hand, was involved in so many aspects of the recording, that it is often difficult to ascertain where his performance ends and the actual performers' begins. As the 1960s progressed, this was the role model which the majority of new producers followed. Perry, Niney the Observer, Bunny Lee and Keith Hudson all developed extraordinarily individual sounds which were theirs and theirs alone — at least until another producer figured out how it was done, at which point, it was a free for all.

King Tubby's dub experiments, while confirming his reputation more as a remixer than a producer, were popular enough that they actually engendered a whole new musical genre. Bunny Lee's "flying cymbals" sound of the early 1970s came close to doing likewise. A decade later, Prince (later King) Jammy's "sleng teng" rhythm sent the whole of Kingston scampering out to buy Casio rhythm boxes, to see what other treats lay programmed within.

Indeed, whereas most of the music's most dramatic stylistic shifts (ska to rock steady, to reggae, to roots) evolved from the grassroots dance hall audience on up, the greatest movement of the last 15 years, ragga, was wholly the creation of the producers, working within the seemingly limitless confines of the very latest technology. Their forebears, needless to say, considered themselves lucky if they could outfit their studios with even semi-outdated equipment.

The fact that the likes of Buster, Perry, Tubby, Lee, Niney and Rupie Edwards (to name but a handful of the music's greatest innovators) were then able to shape the sound of the future with the cast-offs of the past, only increases one's admiration of their work. Famously, Tubby created many of his greatest dubs using a four track mixing desk which the Dynamic Studios (formerly WIRL) had long since declared obsolete, while Perry was still cleaning his tape heads with his T-shirt years after other studios decided that even looking at the equipment the wrong way could knock it fatally out of alignment.

Of course, making (or, at least, financing) a record is only the first part of the producer's job. It then has to be marketed.

Again, with no major record companies releasing records, it was the producers who put them out, on imprints which, in many cases, became as well-known as the artists who appeared on them (and, in some cases, more so).

A label became a trademark of quality — if you bought a Treasure Isle single, you knew you were buying something that had the Duke Reid seal of approval. The Studio One label offered the best that Coxsone Dodd had to offer. Voice of the People spoke for Buster's latest taste. Today, Taxi (Sly & Robbie), Xterminator ("Fatis" Burrell), Madhouse (Dave Kelly), Penthouse (Donovan Germain), Digital B (Bobby Digital), Roof International (Courtney Cole) and so on make similar guarantees on the behalf of the modern producer.

In the early days, many producers also owned storefronts — Buster had his Record Shack, Vincent Chin had Randy's, Lee Perry had Upsetter Records. Leslie Kong sold his productions out of his Beverley's ice cream parlor, Coxsone Dodd and Duke Reid via their liquor stores, Glen Brown out of a used car lot in Caledonia Place.

These were the hubs of activity, whether you were looking to buy the latest hot sound, or thought you could offer an even hotter one. Reid notoriously pushed young hopefuls to audition right there in the liquor store, in front of his regular customers. If a singer could impress them, he was probably worth taking a chance on.

Other, independent, retail outlets existed. As soon as a record was off the press, runners loaded up their bikes with boxes, then took off around the neighborhoods, hoping to offload them on local stores and merchants, or even set up "shop" on a convenient corner, selling them to passers-by on the street. It was a rudimentary system by any standards, but few producers cared how much finesse went into selling the record. The main thing was selling it.

The sound systems were the chief vehicle for actually promoting a new release. At least into the late 1960s, radio paid so little attention to local music, that few producers even bothered servicing the stations with the majority of their output. Neither were the charts considered any kind of reliable barometer of a record's popularity. Both major radio stations, JBC (the Jamaican Broadcasting Corporation, a BBC-sponsored and influenced set up) and RJR (Radio Jamaica Rediffusion) compiled their own weekly listings of the most popular songs, but popularity was gauged from their own playlists. The true test of a record's strength was its longevity on the dance floor — and again, that still holds true today.

Indeed, for all the vast advances which have been made in the recording, manufacture, distribution, marketing (and copyrighting) of Jamaican music, in many ways it has barely changed one iota from the day when Duke Reid first walked into Federal Studios in 1957, looked around the room and then back at the musicians accompanying him, and told them, "Okay. Let's make a record."

DIRECTORY OF LEADING JAMAICAN RECORD PRODUCERS

GLEN ADAMS

b 1950 (JA). Adams was organist with the Pioneers, Hippy Boys and the Upsetters, and a mix engineer for Lee Perry at the Wailers sessions 1970–71. He relocated to Brooklyn, NY, around 1972, forming the band Bluegrass Experience with fellow expatriates Eric Frater (guitar), Sparrow Martin (drums) and Bunny Clarke (vocals — ex-Inner Circle).

He launched his own Capo label around 1974, but later in the decade worked with the New York area Clocktower and Bullwackies (see Lloyd Barnes) labels. However, as the 1980s progressed, Adams became more involved in the R&B and rap scenes, producing hip hop artist T Ski Valley. He has also worked with Shaggy, and remixed a CD of unreleased Upsetters material, *Upsetters A Go Go* for Heartbeat, 1996.

LLOYD BARNES

b 1948 (JA). A Prince Buster protege, Barnes recorded several singles during the 1960s, but became better known as a producer following his relocation to New York in the 1970s. There he set up one of America's first dedicated reggae studios, working with many visiting Jamaican stars.

Establishing the now-legendary Bullwackies and Wackies labels (other imprints include Senrab, Hamma and Senta), among Barnes' best-known productions during the late 1970s/early 1980s are sets by Horace Andy, Sugar Minott, Junior Byles, Roland Alphonso, Tyrone Evans (ex-Paragons) and Lee Perry. The late 1980s brought albums by Mortie Butler, Mikey Jarrett, Jerry Johnson, Maxine Miller, Robert Minott and the Skatalites' Jackie Mittoo.

RICHARD BELL

b (JA). Bell launched the Star Trail label in partnership with Garnet Dally around 1989, with releases by Beres Hammond and Hugh Griffith. Its greatest successes, however, came in 1992 with Garnett Silk's "Hello Africa," Yami Bolo's "Non Stop Loving" and cuts by General Degree and Leroy Smart. Later releases have included hits by Everton Blender, Capleton, Sizzla and Mykal Rose. Bell has also produced Anthony B, Everton Blender, Fleshy Ranks, Gregory Isaacs, Nardo Ranks, Jack Radics and Screwdriver.

MICHAEL BENNETT and PATRICK LINDSAY

The Two Friends team formed after Bennett departed Gussie Clarke's set-up (where he was vocal arranger) in the early 1990s. Shabba Ranks, Cutty Ranks, Hopeton Lindo, Brian & Tony Gold, Gregory Isaacs and Dennis Brown are included among their greatest triumphs.

CHRIS BLACKWELL

b 6/22/37 (London, UK). A distant relative of the founder of the Crosse & Blackwell condiments company, Blackwell cut his first records in Jamaica in the late 1950s. He launched the Island label on the island, before transplanting it to London in 1962. In 1964, his production of Millie's "My Boy Lollipop" became ska's first ever international hit.

In later years, Blackwell became better known as an executive producer than for his actual studio work. Nevertheless he had considerable influence on the multitude of seminal records released by his label throughout the 1960s-80s, including sets by the Maytals, the Wailers, Third World, Inner Circle and more. He sold Island to the Polygram major in 1989, but purchased Island Jamaica back from them in 1994.

DENNIS BOVELL

b 1953 (St Peter, BARB). Brought up in the UK, Bovell was a member of Matumbi, one of the first British reggae bands of note, and also an engineer at Dip Records, the precursor of the Lovers Rock label (and genre) of the late 1970s. As comfortable working on the fringes of dub (British punk acts the Slits and Pop Group) as the heart of lovers rock (Marie Pierre, Janet Kay), he formed several lasting relationships of vital importance to the UK scene, including a co-production team with dub poet Linton Kwesi Johnson. He has also produced Rico Rodriguez, the late Michael Smith (d 1980), I-Roy and rhythm poetess Jean Binta Breeze.

BERTRAM BROWN

b (JA). Producer whose Freedom Sounds label is best associated with some excellent roots material from Prince Allah, Phillip Frazer, Earl Zero and Rod Taylor.

GLEN BROWN

b Glenmore Lloyd Brown (JA). Vocalist with Sonny Bradshaw's jazz band; he pursued a solo career during the 1960s, then re-emerged in the 1970s as a producer. His Pantomime label assisted in the rise of Augustus Pablo; other key recordings were made with DJs I-Roy, U-Roy, Big Youth and Prince Jazzbo, while the roots period saw him peak alongside Gregory Isaacs. Active during the early dance hall period, when he produced several of Sylford Walker's best 45s (plus cuts with Welton Irie and Joseph Cotton), the 1990s have seen him take a back seat, dividing his time between Kingston, London and New York.

RECOMMENDED LISTENING: Boat To Progress 1970–74 (Greensleeves — UK)

DANNY BROWNE

b (JA). Browne's Main Street label was one of the many to record Garnett Silk during the early 1990s — his "Oh Me Oh My" was a strong seller. General Degree, Lt Stitchie, Junior Tucker and Red Rat have also recorded with Browne, but his most memorable triumph was probably Buccaneer's "Man Thief Sonata" in 1997.

PHILLIP "FATIS" BURRELL

b (JA). Burrell emerged on the scene in 1984, when his Kings & Lions label launched with the latest 45 by Sugar Minott. Over the next five years, Burrell continued expanding, debuting the Vena label in 1986, and launching the careers of Sanchez, Pinchers and Thriller U, while also recording Gregory Isaacs, Frankie Paul, Charlie Chaplin and others.

Burrell launched the Exterminator/Xterminator set up at the end of the decade (the latter name was inspired by the movie *Malcolm X*), and released singles by Cocoa Tea, Admiral Tibet, Beres Hammond, Ninjaman and Capleton, who offered the label its first undoubted superstars. Since that time, the label has come to dominate the scene, largely thanks to Burrell's tremendous work with Luciano, Sizzla, Ras Shiloh and Everton Blender.

CLEMENT BUSHAY

One of the UK Trojan label's first domestic producers, Bushay came to greatest prominence in the late 1970s as one of the prime movers in the lovers' rock movement (Louise Marks' "Keep it Like it Is" was a Bushay production). He also worked with visiting Jamaicans Owen Gray, Rico, Gregory Isaacs, Dave Barker, Dillinger and Trinity, while running his own Burning Sounds and Bushays labels. However, his best known work remains alongside homegrown stars Marks, Junior English and Janet Kay.

LLOYD CHARMERS

b Lloyd Tyrrel, 1938 (JA). An active recording artist throughout the 1960s, with the Charmers, Conscious Minds, the Uniques, the Messengers and solo, Charmers turned to production in the early 1970s, generally releasing material through his own Splash, Soul Beat and Wildflower labels.

Like Derrick Harriott, he had a keen appreciation of the then current American/Philadelphia soul sounds, exemplified by his greatest hit, Ken Boothe's "Everything I Own" in 1974. That said, he also handled Ras Michael's groundbreaking *Dadawah Peace and Love Wadadasow*, in 1975. Charmers has also scored with sides by Bob Andy, Dennis Brown and Marcia Griffiths, while continuing to record under his own name.

CLIVE CHIN and VINCENT CHIN

b (JA). During the early 1960s, the Chins' retail outlet, Randy's, was the best known record store in Kingston. Vincent was the first to move into record production, cutting sides with Lord Creator, Jackie Opel, Alton Ellis, the Skatalites and Rico Rodriguez.

Brother Clive is best remembered for his early 1970s recordings with Augustus Pablo, Dennis Brown and Carl Malcolm, whose 1975 hit "Fattie Bum Bum" made the UK Top 10. He subsequently relocated to New York, where the Chin family launched the VP label.

GEOFFREY CHUNG

b (JA). Guitarist with the Now Generation and Lee Perry's Upsetters, among other session line-ups. His Edge Productions was established around 1974, and worked with Sharron Forrester, the Abyssinians, the Heptones, Marcia Griffiths and more. Resident engineer at Dynamic during the early 1980s, Chung mixed several Peter Tosh albums and co-produced Frankie Paul (with Freddie McGregor), then established his own studio in Miami, in the late 1980s. He died of kidney failure 11/95.

GUSSIE CLARKE

b Augustus Clarke, 1953 (Kingston, JA). Having made his production debut with U-Roy's "The Higher the Mountain" in 1972, Clarke established himself as a giant on the DJ scene, producing Big Youth's *Screaming Target* and I-Roy's *Presenting*. His chief interests, however, lay in dub, and subsequent productions, while classy, were sporadic — distinctive sides by Dennis Brown, Big Youth, Gregory Isaacs and the Mighty Diamonds rank among his greatest. (The latter's "Pass the Kouchie," a Clarke production, was later covered by English juveniles Musical Youth, as "Pass the Dutchie," a UK #1 in 1982.)

Launching his own Music Works Studio in 1988, Clarke immediately scored with further hits by Isaacs (the landmark "Rumours"), Eek-A-Mouse, Dean Fraser, English singer Deborahe Glasgow and JC Lodge ("Telephone Love"). He remained highly visible during the early 1990s, working with Shabba Ranks, Gregory Isaacs, Maxi Priest, Cocoa Tea, General Levy, Daddy Rings, Tony Green and more.

RECOMMENDED LISTENING: *Gussie Clarke Presents Music Works vols 1/2* (Music Works — JA) 1996

COURTNEY COLE

b (JA). Ocho Rios-based Cole's Roof International studio was placed on the map via his late 1980s association with Garnett Silk and, later, Capleton and Stanrick.

COUNT SHELLY

b (JA). During the 1970s, the Count's sporadic productions included work with Dennis Alcapone, Errol Dunkley and Horace Andy.

ROY COUSINS

b 1945 (Cockburn Pen, JA). A former member of the Royals singing group, Cousins turned to production in 1972.

Initially, his Tamoki label concentrated on his own recordings, until his breakthrough production of Gregory Isaacs' "Way Of Life." Launching his Wambesi label in 1974, Cousins again maintained a stream of his own recordings, including a Royals reunion in 1978. He also produced several tracks on the Gaylads' 1979 reunion set. 1980s and 1990s productions have included Prince Far I, the Meditations, Charlie Chaplin and Cornell Campbell.

RECOMMENDED LISTENING: *History Of Tamoki Wambesi* (Tamoki — JA)

TOMMY COWAN

b 1950 (Kingston, JA). A member of the Jamaicans, winners of Jamaica's 1967 Independence Festival Song Competition (with "Baba Boom"), Cowan launched his own Top Ranking label in the early 1970s, following a spell as engineer at Dynamic. His most renowned production work was with Jacob Miller and Inner Circle, whom he managed. He has also produced Junior Tucker, Dean Stone, John Holt, Israel Vibration, Dobby Dobson, Toots Hibbert and Jack Radics, while wife Carlene Davis scored a 1988 Jamaican #1 with the Cowan-produced "Dial My Number." Among Cowan's other achievements, is a lengthy career as a concert MC — he worked the One Love Peace Concert, Bob Marley's 1980 Zimbabwe tour and several Reggae Sunsplash festivals.

LLOYD COXSONE

b Lloyd Blackwood (JA). Blackwood relocated to London in 1962, and spent most of the 1960s on sound systems (his adopted surname was cheekily borrowed from Coxsone Dodd, to draw attention to Blackwood's own Coxsone Sound set-up). He moved into production during the early 1970s, scoring his first success with the lovers rock pioneer "Caught You in a Lie" by Louisa Mark. Coxsone launched his own Tribesman and Outernational labels during the late 1970s, releasing both self-productions and licensed cuts.

SIDNEY CROOKS

b 2/24/45 (Westmoreland, JA). Founder member of the vocal group The Pioneers, Crook turned to production in 1973, working with Dennis Alcapone, Dennis Brown and Gregory Isaacs.

In the 1980s, he also produced the revitalized Justin Hinds, Owen Gray and Marcia Griffiths.

LLOYD DALEY

b (JA). Operator of the famed Lloyd The Matador sound system, until it was broken up by the police in 1966, Daley launched a label of the same name, with two singles by the Overtakers in 1965. He went on to produce some excellent 45s during the rock steady era for both Matador and a second label, Mystic, several of which then provided the basis for some equally remarkable DJ sides by U-Roy, U-Roy Jr, Big Joe, I-Roy and Sir Lord Comic.

Daley scored his first hit, in 1968, with the Scorchers' "Uglyman." Further successes included Little Roy, Lloyd Charmers, Lloyd Robinson, the Caribbeans, Dennis Brown and the Abyssinians. He faded from the music industry during the late 1970s, returning to his first love, electronic engineering.

RECOMMENDED LISTENING: *Matador Productions 1968–72* (Heartbeat)

EVERTON DASILVA

Based in New York, from the mid-1970s until his murder in 1979, Hungry Town label founder DaSilva is best remembered for producing Horace Andy's *In the Light* masterpiece. However, he also cut an excellent dub set with Augustus Pablo, *Chanting Dub with the Help of the Fathers*.

LLOYD DENNIS

b (JA). Dennis' Pickout label was a major player during the late 1980s, releasing hits by Pliers, Gregory Isaacs, Wayne Wonder and Dillinger (the sensational "Gun Ark"), and Ninjaman and Tinga Stewart — their "Cover Me" remains a period classic.

BOBBY DIGITAL

b Robert Dixon (Kingston, JA). A protege of Prince/King Jammy, where he was among the pioneers of the digital scene, Digital launched his own Heatwave studio in 1988. His Digital B label debuted that same year with Cocoa Tea's "Lonesome Side" and Shabba Ranks' "Peanie Peanie."

Both swiftly established Digital at the forefront of the digital/ragga movement, fostering a reputation which grew via his overseeing of seminal sides by Garnett Silk (his debut album), Shabba Ranks ("Wicked in a Bed"), Sanchez, Chaka Demus & Pliers, Ninjaman, Cobra and Tony Rebel, among a multitude of others.

As such, his influence on the last decade is without peer, while Digital productions can also be given credit for some of the finest recent releases by Gregory Isaacs, Sugar Minott and Garnett Silk. Morgan Heritage's second album, their first to be recorded in Jamaica, was a Digital production.

COXSONE DODD

b Clement Seymour Dodd, 1/26/32 (JA). With Duke Reid and Prince Buster, one of the so-called Big Three who launched the age of ska. Like them, he worked with every key artist of the era, releasing the majority of his productions on the Worldisc and Studio One labels. (The latter has since become an umbrella title for all Dodd's production work).

Furiously active throughout the 1960s, the changing face of reggae during the 1970s and 1980s barely affected his workload. Indeed, he often contributed to the changes; it was at Studio One that Sugar Minott first began cutting new songs over old rhythms, precipitating the dance hall age. Dodd was also responsible during the mid 1970s for a string of "disco mix" remixes of older hits.

Dodd relocated to New York during the late 1980s, from where he oversaw the anthologizing of his past productions through the Heartbeat label, making periodic forays back into the studio for new material. He returned to Jamaica in 1998, following the death of his mother.

RECOMMENDED LISTENING: Heartbeat's on-going, multiple volume Studio One series.

BLACKER DREAD

London based graduate of Lloyd Coxsone's Tribesman set-up, emerged in the late 1980s and has produced Fred Locks, Sugar Minott, Frankie Paul, Michael Palmer and more.

DR DREAD

b Gary Himelfarb. The charismatic head of the US label RAS, Dread has produced (or co-produced) many of the company's releases since its launch in the early 1980s. Included are efforts by Peter Broggs, Don Carlos, Charlie Chaplin, Israel Vibration, Brigadier Jerry and Michigan & Smiley.

CLANCY ECCLES

b 12/19/40 (St Mary's, JA). Having launched his career as a vocalist with Coxsone Dodd, Eccles turned to production in 1967, with Monty Morris' "Say What You're Saying." The best of Eccles' early work favored either lewd self-productions ("Fatty Fatty," "Open Up") or excitable DJs — King Stitt's earliest recordings were Eccles productions.

However, he was also instrumental in the shift from rock steady to reggae, via his "Feel the Rhythm" (cut with Lee Perry) and "Bangarang Crash." It was Eccles, too, who helped both Lee Perry and Niney Holness set up on their own, even advancing Holness the money to press the first copies of the seminal "Blood and Fire."

His Clandisc and New Beat labels, meanwhile, were responsible for some great sides by Alton Ellis, Busty Brown and Cynthia Richards, among many others. However, Eccles' interest in music was balanced by a keen political mind and, in 1972, he was appointed an adviser on the music industry to Michael Manley's ruling PNP party, the first step in a career which has since all but removed him from production work.

RECOMMENDED LISTENING: Kingston Town: 18 Reggae Hits (Heartbeat)

RUPIE EDWARDS

see entry on page 103.

PAT FRANCIS

b (JA)/d 1999. The alter-ego of DJ Jah Lloyd was a respected, but none too prolific, mid-1970s producer.

DONOVAN GERMAIN

b (JA). Germain began producing while living in New York, where he ran a record store during the 1970s, and headed the Revolutionary Sounds label from the early 1980s.

Interestingly, his actual studio work took place in Kingston, where he cut hits with Sugar Minott and Cultural Roots.

Germain returned to Kingston in 1987, to establish his Penthouse Studios and label, the former swiftly establishing itself (alongside Gussie Clarke's Music Works) as the city's key studio.

Early recordings with Freddie McGregor, Tenor Saw, Marcia Griffiths and Delroy Wilson barely served notice of the deluge to come. Hits with Buju Banton, Cobra, Cutty Ranks, Morgan Heritage and Wayne Wonder, and the continued success of veterans Beres Hammond and Dobby Dobson are simply the tip of the Penthouse success story.

JOE GIBBS

b Joel Gibbs, 1945 (Montego Bay, JA). A former TV repairman, Gibbs moved into production in 1966, scoring immediately with the rock steady anthem "Hold Them" by Roy Shirley. His Amalgamated label, launched in 1968, was distinguished first by the presence of Lee Perry, and then by his replacement, Niney Holness; a wealth of talent which ensured that Amalgamated had one of the highest hits-to-releases ratios in Jamaica.

Gibbs opened his own first studio in 1969, a two track set up at the back of his Joe Gibbs Record Mart. By 1975, he was running the 16 track Record Globe studio on Retirement Crescent, where he and engineer Erroll Thompson forged one of the most successful production teams in Jamaican history, the Mighty Two (see below).

Gibbs retired in 1983, although he continues to work with his back catalog, with son (and occasional co-producer) Rocky.

RECOMMENDED LISTENING: *Explosive Rock Steady: Joe Gibbs' Amalgamated Label* — Heartbeat)

DENNIS HALES

b (JA). Beginning in 1988, Hales' Dennis Star label released singles by Sanchez, Mikey Melody, Dean Fraser, Charlie Chaplin, a pre-Chaka Demus Pliers and Richie Stephens.

DERRICK HARRIOTT

b 1942 (Kingston, JA). Harriott was originally one half of a vocal duo with Claude Sang, reaching the finals of the Verejohn Opportunity Hour. The pair formed the Jiving Juniors around 1959. Following a string of hits, Harriott quit the group in 1962, to launch a similarly successful solo career, while simultaneously working with the Mighty Vikings from 1965–69.

Harriott also turned to production as owner of the Crystal, Derrick and Move'n Groove labels. Noel Brown, Keith & Tex, the Kingstonians and Rudy Mills rank among his best known early clients, later ones include Dennis Brown (the stellar *Super Reggae & Soul Hits* album), the Chosen Few, the Ethiopians, Scotty and Junior Soul (Murvin). An early patron of dub pioneer King Tubby, he made the transition to both roots and dance hall, and remains one of Jamaica's most potent survivors.

RECOMMENDED LISTENING: *Ride the Musical Chariot* (Heartbeat)

NINEY "THE OBSERVER" HOLNESS

see entry on page 194.

ERNEST and JOSEPH "JOJO" HOOKIM

With siblings Paul and Kenneth, the Hookim brothers ran a successful slot machine business, before being forced to find a new career after the Jamaican government outlawed gaming machines in 1970. The following year, they opened Channel One studios on Maxfield Avenue, a fairly minor concern which finally hit the headlines in 1976, following the Hookims' discovery of the Mighty Diamonds.

With the house band, the Revolutionaries (featuring Sly & Robbie), perfecting a roots-heavy sound which became the envy of the island, Channel One's Hitbound label also pioneered the plundering of old Studio One rhythms for new recordings. This practice initially earned a great deal of criticism, but ultimately helped fire the dance hall revolution.

Other Hookim innovations included the release of the first Jamaican 12-inch singles and a series of early-mid 1980s "clash" albums, shared one side apiece by two leading artists. By the end of the decade, however, Channel One had closed down, and the Hookims had retired from the industry.

RECOMMENDED LISTENING: *Well-Charged, Channel One* (Pressure Sounds)

KEITH HUDSON

b 1946 (Kingston, JA)/d 11/14/1984 (NY). Hudson produced his first record in 1960, an instrumental featuring several future Skatalites. It lay unreleased until 1968, by which time, Hudson had completed an apprenticeship in dentistry, and launched his own record label, Inbidimts.

Over the next four years, Hudson was responsible for such hits as Delroy Wilson's "Run Run," Dennis Alcapone's "Shades of Hudson" (which versioned that original 1960 recording) and Big Youth's "S90 Skank." He relaunched his own solo career in 1972, concentrating thereafter on that. He was diagnosed with lung cancer in August, 1984, and died just three months later.

RECOMMENDED LISTENING: *Studio Kinda Cloudy* (Trojan — UK)

CLIVE AZUL HUNT

b (JA). Hunt received major acclaim as the producer of the Abyssinians' debut album in 1976. Sessions with Lizzard and Max Romeo followed, before he relocated to New York as a member of the Wackies session team (productions include Wayne Jarrett). Hunt worked with Joe Gibbs on Dennis Brown's 1981 A&M album, and has also recorded Al Campbell, Danny Red, Loose Caboose, Pablo Moses, Dawn Penn, Maxi Priest and Bunny Clarke.

HARRY J

b Harry Johnson, 1945 (Kingston, JA). J began producing in 1966, before launching his Harry J label in 1968, debuting with the Beltones' hit "No More Heartache." Forming the Harry J All-Stars from among the era's top sessionmen, J scored a major UK hit with "The Liquidator" in 1969, while maintaining a successful barrage of singles similarly targeted towards that country's skinhead audience. He also oversaw Bob & Marcia's UK hit career in 1970/71.

In 1972, he sold his record store and sank all his UK earnings into a new 16 track studio on Kingston's Roosevelt Avenue. Bob Marley & the Wailers recorded their first four Island records albums there; Burning Spear, Augustus Pablo and the Heptones also cut successful albums. The early 1980s found J concentrating on cutting DJ records for local sound systems; he returned to the international scene in 1983 with Sheila Hylton's hit "The Bed's too big without You."

Since that time, however, he has concentrated on overseeing the studio's operation and the distribution network which it also encompasses — the Harry J, 10 Roosevelt Ave, Sunset and Henry Lawes' Junjo labels all operate from there.

RECOMMENDED LISTENING: Return of the Liquidator: 30 Skinhead Classics 1968–70 (Trojan — UK)

SIGGY JACKSON

b (UK). Jackson was house producer at Britain's legendary Melodisc/Blue Beat labels during the 1950s/60s. His earliest productions were calypso; during the 1960s, he worked with Laurel Aitken, Blue Rivers & The Maroons and others.

JAH SCREW

b Paul Love, 1955 (Kingston, JA). Originally a DJ with U-Roy's Stur Gav sound system, Screw's first productions, in 1982, were alongside fellow DJ Ranking Joe, for their own Sharp Axe label. In 1984, operating under his given name, Screw oversaw Barrington Levy's "Under mi Sensi"; a number of subsequent hits developed from the same pairing, while Screw also launched the Time One production company. Since that time, he has executed successful recordings with Dennis Brown, Chaka Demus, Beenie Man, Cutty Ranks, Bounty Killer and more.

JAH SHAKA

The UK based producer emerged from Mad Professor's stable in the early 1980s to work with Johnny Clarke, Horace Andy, Icho Candy, the Disciples, Dread & Fred, Vivian Jones and others.

JAH THOMAS

b Nkrumah Thomas, 1955 (Kingston, JA). A DJ who launched his own label, Midnight Rock, following his first #1 (also titled "Midnight Rock," produced by Alvin Ranglin) in 1976.

Thomas did not begin producing other artists until the late 1970s — Midnight Rock's first 45, Junior Keeting's "Watch What You Do," was released in 1979. He went on to handle hits for Early B, Ranking Toyan, Barrington Levy, Barry Brown, Little John, Sugar Minott and Tristan Palma.

HUGH "REDMAN" JAMES

b (JA). Hits by Admiral Tibet, Conroy Smith and Carl Meeks launched Redman in 1988, followed by ones from Courtney Melody, Frankie Paul, Horace Martin, Sugar Minott and revitalized veterans Johnny Osbourne and John Holt. By the early 1990s, however, James had all but retired

from music, though he has since returned at the helm of his own sound system.

TREVOR JAMES

b (JA). Prince/King Jammy's brother, James first came to attention with Cocoa Tea's "Uptight Saturday Night" variation on Frankie Paul's "I Know the Score."

CLIVE JARRETT and BESWICK "BEBO" PHILLIPS

Dance hall partnership whose Dynamite label was launched on a string of Sly & Robbie rhythms, most notably the version of Derrick Harriott's "Solomon" which became Carlton Livingstone's "Rumours." They have also recorded Leroy Smart, Michael Palmer, Peter Metro, Welton Irie and Lone Ranger.

JJ JOHNSON

b Carl Johnson (JA). A former jukebox distributor on Kingston's Orange Street, Johnson's JJ (later Sir JJ) label was responsible for mid-1960s releases by Carl Dawkins, the Ethiopians, the Kingstonians, etc.

MAURICE JOHNSON aka JACK SCORPIO

b (JA). Owner of the dance hall staple Black Scorpio sound system, and responsible for launching DJs Sassafras and General Trees, as well as sides by Admiral Bailey, Barrington Levy, Earl Sixteen, Culture Lee, Echo Minott and most of General Tree's best work. He also cut some crucial 45s with Capleton during the early 1990s, together with efforts by Dennis Brown, Horace Andy, Johnny Osbourne, Chaka Demus, Barrington Levy, Audrey Mann, Echo Minott, Garnett Silk, Mega Banton and Junior Reid.

DAVE "RUDE BOY" KELLY

b (JA). Formerly producer/engineer at Donovan Germain's Penthouse empire, Kelly broke away in 1993 to open his own Boxx studio and the Madhouse label. From there, he pioneered one of the most intriguing developments of the 1990s, taking the established "one rhythm" album concept, whereby a dozen or so variations of the same song were lined up alongside one another, and seguing them together into one continuous piece — 1994's *Pepper Seed Jam* album is a superb example. Cobra, Terror Fabulous, Beenie Man, Louie Culture, Spragga Benz, Buju Banton and Baby Cham rank among Kelly's best-known artists.

KEN KHOURI

b (JA). Owner of the Federal studio and record label, Khouri was one of the pioneers of mento recording during the 1950s.

PAUL KHOURI

The son of Ken Khouri, Paul's earliest productions were alongside his father (Hopeton Lewis). Alone, Khouri has worked with Dobby Dobson, Bob Andy, Lord Laro, Eddie Lovette, Ernie Smith, Ernest Ranglin. His brother Richard Khouri also produces.

KING EDWARDS

b (JA). Though Edwards' primary interest lay in cutting sound system specials (limited runs and acetates which remained exclusive to his system), he did handle some remarkable sides by Lord Tanamo, Bobby Aitken, Shenley Duffus and others.

Edwards retired from music in 1964.

KING JAMMY

b Lloyd James (Kingston, JA). Best known as King Tubby's most promising apprentice throughout the 1970s, where he replaced Phillip Smart as chief engineer (and earned the title Prince Jammy), Jammy launched his own Jammy label in 1976.

He came to international attention as the producer of the first Black Uhuru album in 1977.

Jammy brought Half Pint to fame in 1983, and also scored hits with Admiral Bailey, Junior Reid and Johnny Osbourne. Still, he remained best known (particularly in the UK and US) as a dub remixer, until 1985 brought his production of Wayne Smith's "Under mi Sleng Teng," the most resounding blow yet in the burgeoning digital revolution.

Since that time, he has ruled supreme, adopting the King Jammy title following Tubby's death, and establishing himself as the most successful and influential producer of the digital age. He is responsible, too, for bringing his own acolytes to the forefront — Bobby Digital was one of his discoveries.

RECOMMENDED LISTENING: *A Man & His Music* (RAS)

KING TUBBY

see entry on page 138.

LESLIE KONG

b 1933 (JA); d 8/8/71. Chinese-Jamaican producer who launched Jimmy Cliff and Desmond Dekker to fame in the early 1960s, his eye for fresh talent was originally aided by Derrick Morgan.

Initially based out of the family-owned Beverley's ice cream parlor, Kong proved one of the most consistent and prolific producers of the 1960s, at the same time as basing his reputation on just a handful of acts. Cliff and Dekker remained at his side throughout the decade, while he also cut important records with the Pioneers, the Melodians, the Maytals and both a solo Bob Marley (1963) and the Wailers (1970). He died from a heart attack in 1971.

RECOMMENDED LISTENING: *Leslie Kong's Connection* (Jet Star — UK)

KEN LACK

b (JA). The Skatalites' road manager launched his own label, Caltone, in 1965, cutting excellent rock steady sides with the Clarendonians and the Tartans. He was also instrumental in launching the Pioneers and the Emotions (featuring Max Romeo).

HENRY "JUNJO" LAWES

b 1948 (JA)/d 6/14/99. Formerly a vocalist with the group Grooving Locks, Junjo Lawes' first success as a producer came with Barrington Levy in 1979. He oversaw several of Levy's early hits and also produced the singer's *Bounty Hunter* album, one of the blueprints for the dance hall revolution.

Junjo launched his Volcano and Arrival labels with a plethora of similarly incisive recordings by Little John, Michael Prophet, Josey Wales, Eek-A-Mouse, Yellowman, Little Harry and more, and was responsible for many of the live dance hall/sound system albums which appeared during the early 1980s. He also assisted in relaunching several struggling veteran careers, including John Holt, Alton Ellis and the Wailing Souls.

Lawes relocated to New York in 1985, remaining there until 1991 (his visit including a spell in prison), thus effectively missing the chance to make his mark on the digital movement. Upon his return to Jamaica, his best work was with up and coming talent, including Ninjaman and Shaka Shamba.

Lawes was murdered during a visit to London in 1999.

BUNNY LEE

b Edward O'Sullivan Lee, 8/23/41 (JA). Bunny Lee was originally a record plugger for Duke Reid, to whom he was introduced by Derrick Morgan in 1962. From there, he moved to former Skatalites road manager Ken Lack's Caltone label, again originally in an administrative role, before graduating to the studio.

In 1967, Lee launched his own Lee's label with Lloyd Jackson's "Listen to the Beat," and a hit with Roy Shirley's "Music Field," followed. By the end of the year, Lee was running his own eponymous label, with his biggest successes coming via Slim Smith, Pat Kelly and the Uniques.

Lee was at his peak during the mid-1970s, however, when his "flying cymbals" sound dominated reggae radio, even as he joined Lee Perry and King Tubby in exploring the possibilities of dub. Rarely mentioned in that capacity, Lee was nevertheless one of dub's most fearless adventurers, at the same time as maintaining a solid stream of commercial recordings. His output slowed during the 1980s, even after his purchase of Joe Gibbs' former set-up. Like many of his contemporaries, he appears content to oversee operations, while arranging the reissue of his immense back catalog.

BYRON LEE

see entry on page 142.

ERROL "MYRIE" LEWIS and ERROL "JOHN" MARSHALL

Lewis & Marshall are remembered as the first producers to work with Half Pint in 1982, and also the masterminds behind his greatest hit, "Winsome." With their efforts backed by some fine Sly & Robbie rhythms, the duo's Sun Set label also scored with Patrick Andy and Junior Reid.

RECOMMENDED LISTENING: Waterhouse Revisited (High Tone)

WILLIE LINDO

b (JA). Co-producer (with Joe Gibbs) of Marcia Aitken's *Reggae Impact* in 1981, and albums by Dennis Brown (1982). Lindo went on to work with Barbara Jones (1984), Sophie George, JC Lodge, Maxi Priest, BB Seaton, Beres Hammond, Ricky Chaplin, Carlene Davis, Dean Fraser and others. He also produced Boris Gardiner's UK #1 "I Want to Wake up with You."

ROBERT LIVINGSTON

New York based producer who brought Shaggy to fame in the early 1990s. He has also recorded Frankie Paul, Maxi Priest, Rayvon, Beres Hammond and others. Livingston's Wild Apache label is part-owned by DJ Super Cat.

WINSTON LOWE

b (Greenwich Town, JA). A friend of Bunny Lee's, Lowe enjoyed a short, but extraordinarily fulfilling, production career, handling several of the Uniques' early, crucial, recordings for his own Tramp label.

HERMAN CHIN LOY

A cousin and employee of producer Leslie Kong, Chin Loy launched his Aquarius record store and label in 1969, with releases by the Hippy Boys and the Now Generation. Augustus Pablo's debut recordings were Chin Loy productions; other hits were scored with Dennis Brown, Alton Ellis, Bruce Ruffin and Ernest Wilson. His output, however, is patchy; aside from a flurry of hit-making activity during 1979–80, Chin Loy has produced little of note, although he continues operating his own studio (concentrating on non-reggae artists).

MAD PROFESSOR

b (Guyana). Based in London, UK, where his Ariwa label was one of the first punk-era D-I-Y type companies to specialize in reggae, Mad Professor and his studio band, the Sane Inmates, began attracting attention in the early 1980s, with the *Dub Me Crazy* album series. Well respected on the alternative dance scene (an audience he shares with fellow London dub pioneer Adrian Sherwood), Mad Professor has also worked extensively with a number of visiting Jamaican

artists, including Lee Perry, Horace Andy, Susan Cadogan, U-Roy and Dennis Alcapone.

MAFIA & FLUXY

British-born brothers Leroy "Mafia" and David "Fluxy" Heywood were members of the 1980s north London based lovers rock band The Instigators. Later they established themselves as an in-demand rhythm section in both London and Kingston, which they visited for the first time in 1987, cutting rhythm tracks for Bunny Lee, Phillip Burrell, King Jammy and others. The pair launched their own eponymous label that same year, and have produced Sugar Minott, Billy Melody, Beenie Man, Private Collection, Cobra, Cutty Ranks, Chaka Demus & Pliers and more.

DON MAIS

b Errol Mais (JA). Mais launched his career as singer Jah Bible, before launching his Roots Tradition label in 1976, with the backing band Roots Radics as his ace in the hole.

Widely acclaimed, alongside the Channel One team, for rediscovering the Studio One rhythms which became the bed rock of dance hall, Mais also nurtured the nine year old Little John to fame. Other important productions include sides by Brigadier Jerry, Sammy Dread, Pliers, Frankie Paul, Phillip Frazer, Michael Prophet, Ranking Toyan and Rod Taylor.

FREDDIE MCGREGOR

b 1955 (Clarendon, JA). Former child star vocalist with the Clarendonians, and a session singer/drummer at Studio One during the 1970s, McGregor's successful solo career was further supplemented during the late 1970s when he turned to production, launching his own Big Ship label in 1984. Big Youth and Luciano rank among his greatest successes.

ENOS MCLEOD

b 1946 (Trenchtown, JA). McLeod's sporadic output as a producer has seen him established simultaneously among the most overlooked, and the most collected, of them all. Trained by Studio One engineer Syd Bucknor, McLeod's first hit production was Lloyd Clarke's "Young Love" in 1968. He also recorded Prince Far I, while the latter still traded as King Cry Cry, and by the mid-1970s, he was resident at Joe Gibbs' studio, alongside engineer Errol Thompson. Interestingly, Gibbs originally hired McLeod in his former capacity as a boxer, to handle security at the studio. Present at the recording of many late 1970s Gibbs classics, McLeod has since faded from public view.

THE MIGHTY TWO

Formed by Joe Gibbs and Erroll Thompson in 1975, following the opening of Gibbs' new studio on Retirement

Crescent. The pair turned out hits by Junior Byles, Dillinger, Gregory Isaacs, Dennis Brown, Althea & Donna, Sylford Walker and, perhaps most memorably, Prince Far I. They were also instrumental in the rise of Eek-A-Mouse in the early 1980s, but broke apart in 1983, when Gibbs relocated to Miami following a legal battle concerning royalties for JC Lodge's "Someone Loves You Honey." He sold his studio to Bunny Lee.

RECOMMENDED LISTENING: The Mighty Two — Heartbeat 1992)

SUGAR MINOTT

see entry on page 189.

SYLVAN MORRIS

b (JA). Having apprenticed at Studio One, Morris was an in-demand engineer throughout the 1970s, working on such albums as John Holt's *Time is the Master*, the Royal Rasses' *Humanity* and sets by Junior Delgado, Dennis Brown, the Ethiopians, Gregory Isaacs etc. Studio engineer at Harry Js for some years, he moved on to Channel One, and worked extensively with Junjo Lawes in the early 1980s (Yellowman, Frankie Paul, etc). In the early 1990s, he oversaw the digital transfer of innumerable Dynamic Studios classics in readiness for their CD debuts. He was producer of African Star's 1992 *Days in Creation*, and also recorded the Clarendonians, I-Roy and Larry Marshall.

MORWELLS

A production duo comprising Morris "Blacka" Wellington (b 1950 (JA)/d 10/12/2000) and guitarist Eric "Bingi Bunny" Lamont (b 1955 (JA)/d 12/31/93). Founder members of the band the Morwells, alongside Louis Davis (ex-Versatiles); the group cut several singles on their own Morwells Esq label from 1974, before Wellington left to become engineer at Joe Gibbs studio.

He then reunited with Lamont as the production team Morwells.

Working in both Kingston and New York, Morwells was responsible for cutting some fine sides with Davis' fellow Versatile Junior Byles in 1978, and Horace Andy in 1979. Other Morwells productions include Prince Hammer and Jah Lloyd The Black Lion.

After the duo broke up in 1981, Lamont returned to session work. Wellington continued in production as Blacka Morwell, recording Robert Minott, Trump Jack All Stars and others.

STANLEY MOTTA

b 10/5/15 (JA). Sound system operator and owner of a chain of electrical supply stores, Motta's Hanover Street studio opened in 1951, and was responsible for many of the earliest mento recordings. Much of his material was subsequently released in the UK through the Melodisc/Kalypso labels.

HARRY MUDIE

b 1940 (Spanishtown, JA). Mudie's first production was Count Ossie and Wilton Gaynair's "Babylon Gone" in 1962. However, he spent much of the 1960s operating his Scaramouch Garden Amusement Center in Spanishtown. He did not return to active production until the late 1960s, when he launched his Moodisc label with a string of classy singles by Winston Wright, Winston Shand, Lloyd Jones, Count Ossie and the then-unsung I-Roy.

Mudie also pioneered the use of strings in reggae, with John Holt's *Time is the Master* album in 1973, and cut several excellent dub albums with King Tubby. At his peak, during the mid-late 1970s, he recorded Gregory Isaacs, Joe White, Prince Heron and more. Mudie relocated to Florida during the 1980s and has been rarely sighted since.

RECOMMENDED LISTENING: Let Me Tell You Boy (Trojan — UK)

MUSCLEHEAD

b (JA). The singularly named Musclehead originally launched his Saxon label around 1983, recording Sanchez, Pinchers and Phillip Fraser. After several years hiatus, the label relaunched in 1994, and scored immediately with Luciano's "Programme fi Kill." Other hits have included cuts by Frankie Paul, Dennis Brown, Jack Radics, Gregory Isaacs, British singer Peter Hunningale, Tenor Fly and Leroy Sibbles.

RECOMMENDED LISTENING: The Best of Saxon (Saxon – two volumes)

BRAD OSBORNE

Osborne's Clocktower label was responsible for a clutch of now collectible albums released in the US during the mid-late 1980s, including titles by Johnny Clarke, Horace Andy, Dennis Brown, Barrington Levy, Dillinger, Lee Perry, Linval Thompson and others.

AUGUSTUS PABLO

see entry on page 200.

LEE PERRY

see entry on page 208.

GEORGE PHANG

b (JA). Phang's Powerhouse label was another of those whose early success was built upon Sly & Robbie — indeed, the duo presented him with a veritable goldmine of unused rhythms, in return for a favor Phang once did them. Beginning in 1984, Powerhouse ruled the dance halls with hits like Sugar Minott's "Buy off the Bar," Barrington Levy's "Money Move," Frankie Paul's "Tidal Wave," Little John's "True Confession" and the greatest of them all, Half Pint's "Greetings."

Phang also worked well with Admiral Bailey, Josey Wales, Charlie Chaplin, Yellowman and General Echo — his *Friends Live at Skateland* live album is an especially powerful document of the scene. Phang also cut an excellent single with the Tamlins, "Smiling Faces." Powerhouse faded around the end of the 1980s.

KARL PITTERSON

b (JA). Under-rated producer whose work during the late 1970s included albums with Althea & Donna, Rico Rodriguez, Mighty Diamonds, Babylon Warriors, Burning Spear and UK reggae band Steel Pulse. He was also responsible for a 1990 dub remix of the Abyssinians' early material.

LINDON POTTINGER

b (JA). Former husband of the better known Sonia, Pottinger recorded with Winston Samuels and Jimmy James, among others during the early-mid 1960s.

SONIA POTTINGER

b 1943 (JA). The first, and still the most successful, woman producer in Jamaican music, Pottinger opened her Tip Top record store in 1965, moving into production the following year with Joe White & Chuck's "Every Night." At her best during the rock steady era, Pottinger's Gay Feet, Tip Top, Rainbow and High Note labels were responsible for major hits by the Ethiopians, the Conquerors, the Melodians, Delano Stewart, the oft-overlooked Gaylads and more.

She then lapsed into comparative inactivity before re-emerging in 1974 at the head of the late Duke Reid's Treasure Isle business (dub sides of her productions at Treasure Isle were provided by Errol Brown, one of Reid's nephews). Her greatest 1970s productions were undoubtedly her work with Culture, although she also recorded Marcia Griffiths, Ken Boothe and Bob Andy, among others. The dance hall era saw her cut Archie & Lynn's classic "Rat in the Centre" over Michigan & Smiley's recent "Nice up the Dance" rhythm. Pottinger retired in 1985.

RECOMMENDED LISTENING: Musical Feast (Heartbeat)

PHIL PRATT

b George Phillips, 1942 (Kingston, JA). A box loader for Coxsone Dodd, Pratt moved to the UK in the early 1960s, but returned to Kingston in 1965.

As a vocalist, he cut a single for Coxsone Dodd, "Safe Travel." It went unreleased, and Pratt turned to production in his own right, cutting sides with Ken Boothe and the then-unknown Horace Andy. Many of his productions appeared on the Caltone, Wiggle Spoon and WIRL labels, before Pratt launched his own John Tom label.

One of the new wave of producers who emerged in the very early 1970s, largely buoyed by the DJ explosion — his

recordings with Big Youth at the outset of the latter's career were especially highly-regarded. That led to further collaborations with U-Roy, I-Roy, Dennis Alcapone and Dillinger, as well as some excellent work with vocalists Dennis Brown, John Holt (including the notorious *Disco* album) and Pat Kelly.

In 1985, Pratt produced the entertaining *Clash of the Andys* set featuring Horace and Patrick Andy; but again seemed happier working within the DJ scene.

RECOMMENDED LISTENING: DJ Legends of the 60s and 80s (Angella)

PRINCE BUSTER

see entry on page 219.

JIMMY RADWAY

b (JA). "One Foot" Radway was active during the mid-1970s, cutting hits with Tommy Cowan, Errol Dunkley, Desmond Young, Leroy Smart and others.

ALVIN RANGLIN

b (JA). A former electrician, Ranglin sang in an early incarnation of the Maytones before moving into songwriting and publishing. Around 1969, he took over the Gloria label, owned by another family member, and moved into production — his first hit was the Maytones' "Loving Reggae" that same year.

Ranglin's GG, Hit and Typhoon labels are among the most fondly remembered (and actively collected) of all late 1960s Kingston imprints, not only for the wealth of artists whose best early work appeared thereon (Gregory Isaacs, U-Roy, Max Romeo), but also for Ranglin's own tight production, a sound which borrowed much from his love of mento, and would in turn have considerable influence on the roots of the future.

Isaacs' "Love is Overdue" proved a massive hit for him in 1974. Later in the decade, Ranglin produced the Maytones' "Holy Ground," and cuts by Freddie McKay, Starlights, Delroy Wilson, I-Roy and Big Youth. Into the 1980s, Ranglin was behind the Lone Ranger's hits "Barnabus Collins" and "Fort X."

RECOMMENDED LISTENING: Holy Ground (Heartbeat)

DUKE REID

b Arthur Reid, 1915 (JA)/d 1974. A former police officer, sound system operator Reid made several forays into the studio during the late 1950s, before turning to full-time record production in 1962. A year long break around 1964 notwithstanding, his Treasure Isle label (named for the liquor store he ran) was one of the dominant forces on the ska scene. Indeed, alongside Coxsone Dodd and Prince Buster, Reid can be ranked among the forces which shaped the entire Jamaican music industry of the 1960s and 1970s.

Treasure Isle reached its true peak during the later rock steady era, with Reid — again alongside Dodd — responsible for so many now classic recordings, that even the mass re-issues of the CD age have scarcely scratched the surface of his output.

Though his star could never truly be said to have fallen, Reid did undergo a period of low visibility in the late 1960s, but re-emerged as the producer behind toaster U-Roy in 1970. The roots scene, however, did not interest him in the slightest, and the last years of his life again saw Reid take a back seat.

RECOMMENDED LISTENING: Heartbeat's on-going, multiple volume Treasure Isle series.

WINSTON RILEY

b (JA). A founder member of the Techniques, Riley quit in 1968, to launch his own Techniques label. It became home to Johnny Osbourne and the Sensations, Alton and Hortense Ellis, Rad Bryan and, most successfully of all, Dave & Ansell Collins.

Riley's production of their "Double Barrel" was a UK #1 in 1971.

Active throughout the 1970s, Riley next impacted on an international level in 1979, as producer of General Echo's epochal *The Slackest* album. Subsequent triumphs have included the launch of Sister Nancy, the first lastingly successful female DJ (and sibling of Brigadier Jerry), Buju Banton, Cutty Ranks, Lone Ranger and singer Frankie Paul. Riley was also present at the birth of the digital boom, via recordings by Super Cat, Junie Ranks and Red Dragon.

RECOMMENDED LISTENING: Best of the Best (RAS)

LEEWARD ROBINSON

b (JA). Robinson was responsible for one of the Gladiators' earliest recordings, "The Train is Coming Back," in 1967.

TONY ROBINSON

b (JA). "Prince" Tony Robinson was owner of a record store on Slipe Road, Kingston, when he launched the High School label. He concentrated on the DJ scene, and Dennis Alcapone, Winston Scotland and Lloyd Young all made fine early 45s with him. Later in the 1970s, Robinson was one of the key players in the Virgin Front Line label's swoop for the cream of the toasters, and produced albums by all of their key signings — Big Youth, the Gladiators and U-Roy. He also produced sides by Owen Gray.

SCIENTIST

b Overton Brown (JA). First noted as an engineer at Studio One, Scientist shot to widescale attention working alongside Prince/King Jammy at King Tubby's studio, where his dubs were frequently placed on a par with the masters. His mixes of Barrington Levy's early work introduced him to Junjo Lawes, who organized the release of several Scientist vs Jammy dub clash albums.

In 1982, Scientist moved to Channel One, working alongside Niney Holness, where his wild dub experiments continued. He subsequently relocated to New York, but remains in high demand.

Among his best-received titles have been dub collaborations with Yabby You, Culture, Jah Thomas, Mad Professor, Sugar Minott and a slew of albums under his own name.

RECOMMENDED LISTENING: Scientist Rids the World of the Evil Curse of the Vampires (Greensleeves)

EDWARD SEAGA

b (JA). Although Seaga's career has been in politics, which took him to the highest offices in Jamaican and regional politics (he was elected Prime Minister in 1980), the Harvard-educated anthropologist was also a powerful force in the early Jamaican recording industry. He launched the WIRL studios and label as an outlet for mento, R&B and later, ska recordings — Joe Higgs was among the artists Seaga regularly recorded.

His production of Byron Lee & The Dragonaires was instrumental in that band's rise and, when Seaga's political activities became too time consuming, it was to Lee that he sold the studio (it was subsequently renamed Dynamic). Paramount among WIRL's attributes, incidentally, was its availability — it was a favorite for freelance producers who had yet to set up their own studio.

ADRIAN SHERWOOD

b Adrian Maxwell, 1958 (London, UK). A former employee at the UK reggae labels Pama and Vulcan, Sherwood co-founded the London based label Carib Gems in 1975. He immediately came to prominence through early releases by Black Uhuru, Bim Sherman and Prince Far I. Three years later, Sherwood launched a new label, Hitrun, and produced Creation Rebel's *Dub From Creation* album. Other releases included Far I's "Higher Field Marshall" 12-inch and *Cry Tuff Dub Encounter* album.

Indeed, much of Far I's better later work was recorded with Sherwood.

Sherwood and photographer Kishi Yamamoto launched On-U Sounds in 1980, with Sherwood-produced releases by the New Age Steppers, London Underground and Mark Stewart (of the Pop Group). Over the next three years his revolutionary dub deconstructions graced a string of ostensibly rock releases by Judy Nylon, the Fall, Depeche Mode and many others. He has also worked with Lee Perry, Dennis Alcapone and Junior Delgado.

SHOCKING VIBES

b (JA). Producer Patrick Roberts' Shocking Vibes crew have been responsible for some of the most scintillating 1990s DJ cuts, including efforts from Beenie Man, Mad Cobra, Little Kirk and Little Lenny.

SLY & ROBBIE

see entry on page 267.

BYRON SMITH

b (JA). Oft-overlooked early 1970s producer, whose excellent work included singles by Dennis Alcapone and U-Roy.

SL SMITH

b (JA). In 1959/60, High Lite haberdashery store-owner Smith was one of the earliest non-sound system owners to see the possibilities within the new born Jamaican recording industry.

His Hi-Lite label was responsible for early releases by Derrick Morgan, Keith & Enid, Eric Morris and others.

STEELY & CLEVIE

Wycliffe "Steely" Johnson b (JA) and Cleveland "Clevie" Browne b (JA) were long-standing veterans of the session scene (most notably with Prince/King Jammy), before they launched their own Steely & Clevie label in 1986.

Initially favoring the "combination style" of matching veteran DJs with newly arrived singers, the label's debut release (and first hit) was Leroy Gibbons & Dillinger's "Bruk Camera." In much the same manner as Sly & Robbie, the duo were a living rhythm machine. Their drum and (increasingly, keyboard) bass underpinned further hits by Tiger ("Windscreen"), Ninjaman, Cutty Ranks, Garnett Silk, Foxy Brown, JC Lodge, Shabba Ranks and Dawn Penn (the 1994 US Top 60 hit "You Don't Love Me").

RECOMMENDED LISTENING: *Play Studio One Vintage* (Heartbeat) 1992

OSSIE THOMAS

b (JA). The Black Solidarity label owned by Thomas and singer Tristan Palma was responsible for some of the toughest early dance hall singles (Little John, Frankie Paul, Sugar Minott, Lone Ranger, Peter Metro), as well as some dynamite revivals — U-Roy and the Mighty Diamonds both resurfaced under Thomas' aegis.

ERROL THOMPSON

b (JA). Although Thompson's reputation is as an engineer, he has also proved himself a breathtakingly visionary producer. After apprenticing at Studio One, under the aegis of engineer Sylvan Morris, Thompson's first engineering project was Max Romeo's "Wet Dream," for producer Bunny Lee. He then moved on to the Chin family's Randy's studio, where he worked alongside Lee Perry and Niney Holness, before linking up with Joe Gibbs as the Mighty Two (see above).

LINVAL THOMPSON

b 1959 (Kingston, JA). Raised in Queens, NY, where he launched his recording career as a vocalist, Thompson spent much of the 1970s shifting between the US and Jamaica, before turning to production in the late 1970s.

During the early 1980s, his Thompson Sounds label released material by the Wailing Souls, Tappa Zukie, Freddie McGregor, Eek-A-Mouse, Cornell Campbell, Trinity and Barrington Levy.

Thompson also gave Henry Lawes his first ever co-production credit, on the *Aces International* dance hall clash album (1983).

RECOMMENDED LISTENING: *Jah Jah Dreader than Dread* (Munich)

BABA TUARI

East Indian who established the Caribou label in 1955 as an outlet for mento and R&B releases. Laurel Aitken recorded several sides for him before Tuari moved into record manufacturing (Caribbean Records) around 1959.

WITTY

b (JA). A dance hall producer who emerged in the late 1970s working with David Isaacs. His greatest triumphs, however, have included mid-late 1980s work by Tenor Saw & Cocoa Tea, Shelly Thunder, Chaka Demus, Hugo Barrington, Dean Fraser, I-Roy, Barrington Levy, Sugar Minott, Ninjaman, Nitty Gritty and Tony Tuff.

YABBY YOU

b Vivian Jackson, 8/14/46 (Kingston, JA). A former backing vocalist with Ras Michael & The Sons Of Negus, before forming his own band, the Prophets, Yabby You was one of the most individual characters in the early days of the roots scene, all the more so after it became known that he was a devout, if perhaps unconventional, Christian. He cut a string of classic 45s in the name of Jesus Dread ("Conquering Lion," "Jah Vengeance," "Judgement on the Land," "Fire in Kingston"). His own unusual name was taken from the vocal refrain which opens "Conquering Lion."

An active and reliable producer, Yabby You launched his own Prophet label in 1972, working with Willie Williams, Patrick Andy, Michael Prophet, Tony Tuff, Trinity, Dillinger, Tappa Zukie and others. Ill health forced him into virtual retirement during the mid-1980s. He resurfaced in 1993 alongside the Mad Professor, and also began working with new talent. 1997 brought a fresh Yabby You album, *Jah Will Be Done.*

RECOMMENDED LISTENING: *Yabby You Jesus Dread 1972–77* (Blood & Fire)

TAPPA ZUKIE

see entry on page 301.

PART FOUR: DIRECTORY OF SINGLES

Throughout the 1950–1960s, the West Indian music industry was driven by 45s. Albums released during this period were few and far between and, in any case, rarely offered more than a gathering of past singles hits. The situation was no different in the UK, the largest and most important foreign market for Caribbean — primarily Jamaican — artists, where a number of labels had been established to cater exclusively to the calypso and ska/rock steady audience. It wasn't until the very late 1960s, and a corresponding boom in LPs for the rock market, that albums began appearing in any appreciable numbers; and it was only with the international rise of the Wailers, that artists finally looked beyond the 7-inch single as their medium of choice.

Many of the UK labels were formed around exclusive (or thereabouts) deals with individual producers. Others, however, ranged across the spectrum of new releases, ensuring that by 1960 few 45s of any significance passed an English audience by.

Attempts to catalog this vast corpus of material, however, are destined to end in frustration. Neither the British music press nor the music industry's own trade publications felt duty bound to document the near-Biblical flood of new releases unleashed on a twice-weekly basis by upwards of 50 different, largely independent, record labels, while the labels themselves were notoriously lax when it came to promoting their wares.

No less than their counterparts back in Jamaica and Trinidad, labels relied upon word of mouth to promote new releases. This began both in the dance clubs, where a grassroots base of fans and DJs made sure that every record received at least one spin, and the specialist stores and market-stalls which dotted the country, where regular Tuesday and Friday deliveries were met by a rush of loyal customers. It is these original UK pressings which are most frequently encountered by fans and collectors today; while the vast majority of both currently and historically available compilations also derive from Britain.

The following catalogs approximately 5,000 Jamaican/West Indian 45s as released in the UK between 1957–72. They are arranged chronologically by year (and alphabetically by artist thereafter), providing an intimately detailed study of the manner in which the music — particularly in Jamaica — evolved during this period, from the R&B boogie shuffles at the dawn of the period; through the incorporation of various mento and folk elements which created ska in its purest sense; into the rock steady era and the music's ultimate emergence as reggae at the end of the decade. Therein, too, can be traced the evolution of the version b-sides, dub, toasting, and other sub-genres.

Although it is by no means complete, it does include near-comprehensive directories of releases of all of the era's most collected record labels, while reviews and historical data have been added for many of the most important and, via those aforementioned compilations, frequently encountered tracks. In addition, introductory pieces highlight crucial events on the overall UK scene, noting the launch and motives of many of the leading record labels.

In addition, this section serves as a reference for many key and semi-key artists omitted from other sections of this book.

Within each year's catalog, the information is presented as follows:

ARTIST NAME: Biographical information, including other recorded appearances and pseudonyms used, appears for first year of inclusion only. (X) indicates other singles in current year (noted as flip of other artist release).

LABEL/CATALOG # A-SIDE TITLE /B-SIDE TITLE: Producer. (a) a-side review/(b) b-side review. In general, session musician credits are given in lower case, principle artists referenced elsewhere are given in upper case.

NOTE: No attempt has been made to provide production credits for every release.

1957–59: THE CALYPSO YEARS

In 1954, Jamaican disc jockey Count Suckle opened the first Caribbean sound system ever seen in Britain, based out of the west London neighborhood of Ladbroke Grove. The center of London's West Indian community, the Grove and neighboring Notting Hill were home to almost 7,000 West Indian immigrants, close to 60% of the area's entire population, and they made it their own.

All night at the Apollo pub on All Saints Road and in the basement of the Bajay coffee house on Talbot Road, all day at the Fortess cafe on Blenheim Crescent, and nonstop at the impromptu "shebeen" parties which every other house seemed to host, Jamaican music blared out and Jamaican voices blared within. Michael de Freitas, later to find media fame as the leader of British Black Power movement, regularly held deafening parties in his basement apartment and, a few houses down the block, someone else would be hosting another in theirs.

It was the noise which attracted Count Suckle, and the handful of sound systems which followed him. Duke Vin, whose Tickler sound system joined Suckle in England in August, 1956, remembered, "we used to have very good times. And all these people used to follow the sound. If we went to Birmingham, they used to come from London. We used to play all over the country — Birmingham, Manchester, Reading, you name it. People were so glad to know there was a sound system here, because of what they were used to in Jamaica."

Suckle and Vin inspired others to follow in their footsteps, but they remained top of the pile for a good couple of years. In 1956 and again in 1957, Vin won the newly instituted (but soon to become annual) Sound Systems Battle at Lambeth Town Hall in south east London. And the following year, when Notting Hill exploded in the worst race riots England had ever seen, Suckle was in the thick of it, DJ-ing the Blechynden Street party which was the flash-point of the fighting.

For four days at the height of August, an entire inner city neighborhood was reduced to a no-go area by stone and bomb throwing white youths, knife and axe waving Blacks, while the police stood paralyzed by the unprecedented vistas of carnage. Years later, King Dick, the party host, could still remember what was playing on the turntable when the first stones started flying. It was a calypso number called "Oriental Ball."

In recording terms, the 1950s were the golden age of calypso in Britain, some 15 years after a similar peak in the United States. Records like "Oriental Ball" and hundreds more besides, were flooding into the country, in the luggage of the newly arrived immigrants or in regular mailings from family back home. Sometimes, fans didn't even need to look back to the Caribbean for a taste of the newest local hits. Lords Beginner, Kitchener and Melody, and Roaring Lion were all resident in the UK during this period, with sufficient popularity to maintain a stream of recordings for British labels.

The primary domestic outlet for this material was Melodisc, a specialist record label formed in 1950 by Emil E Shallit, an entrepreneur of Serbo-Croat parentage, whose past careers included a period working as an Allied spy in occupied Yugoslavia during World War II.

Melodisc catered exclusively to the audiences which the major labels — at that time, EMI, Decca, Pye and Philips — overlooked. American jazz, blues, and country were popular lines (Ledbelly and Bill Haley both enjoyed Melodisc releases), while the label also handled a number of foreign language courses (Shallit himself was reported to be extraordinarily multi-lingual).

Despite considerable success in these areas, Shallit's primary interest lay in what modern marketers term World Music — European, African (Sierra Leone's Ali Ganda and Tejan Sie both cut popular sides) and, most importantly, Caribbean acts. Beginning in 1948, the UK actively encouraged immigrants from her West Indian colonies, with some 150,000 arriving, mainly from Jamaica, over the next decade. They brought with them their culture, their dialect and their cooking. They also brought their love of music, and that was the niche into which Shallit moved.

It was a fascination which eventually saw Shallit presiding over around a dozen different labels, including that most beloved of UK ska imprints, Blue Beat. In the meantime, Melodisc set about cornering the market in calypso and mento, the folk musics of Trinidad and Jamaica respectively.

In 1950, Lord Beginner and the Mighty Terror became Melodisc's first high profile calypsonians, with Beginner proving especially prolific. Over the next four years, he released at least ten singles for the label, including "Joe Louis Calypso," "Victory Test Match Calypso," "Family Scandal," "Jamaica Hurricane," and "Sir Winston Churchill Calypso." (Terror's first release was "The Queen Is In"). Lord Kitchener followed in 1952; with his Melodisc debut, "Kitch."

Soon, Melodisc releases were appearing in Trinidad itself and, by the end of the decade, Lord Melody, King (Mighty) Sparrow, Azie Lawrence, the FitzVaughan Bryan Orchestra, and Jamaican R&B/mento singer Laurel Aitken were all part of the Melodisc family. Finally, in 1958, Shallit launched a new label to cater exclusively for their output. Forthright as always, he named it Kalypso.

1957

BEN BOWERS ACOMPANIED BY BERTIE KING'S ROYAL JAMAICANS

Veteran Jamaican balladeer Bower and saxophonist King arrived in the UK in 1954.

PYE NEP 24069 Not Me EP

a) "Not Me" is better known as "Man Smart, Woman Smarter."

THE KINGS OF THE CARIBBEAN STEEL BAND

A number of steel band recordings were issued in the UK following the triumphant TASPO tour in 1951 (including several sides by the Trinidad Steel Band).

MELODISC 1429 Rock'n'Roll Susie/Down in Soho

(a) "Rock'n'Roll Susie" with a rock'n'roll beat — pan style. One wonders quite what the band were trying to achieve here — a novelty cross-over hit, perhaps?

LORD FLEA & HIS CALYPSONIANS

b Norman Thomas (JA). One of the most popular 1940s era calypso stars on the New York circuit, and regularly appeared at venues in Miami and Las Vegas. According to his own publicity material, he was crowned the 1951 calypso king of Jamaica. Flea also starred in the movies *Calypso Joe* and *Bop Girl Goes Calypso*. His band included drummer ALVIN PATTERSON, who later introduced BOB MARLEY & THE WAILERS to COXSONE DODD.

CAPITOL 14704 The Naughty Little Flea/Shake Shake Senora
Produced by Stanley Motta.

LORD POWER

KALYPSO 02 Penny-Reel/Chambolina
Produced by Duke Reid. (a) Reid's first ever release. The soon-to-be-infamous "Penny-Reel" makes one of her first recorded appearances: "gal you owe me a little money, and you no have it back fi gimme, I beg you shub your chushu gimme, and let me rub out me money." Enough said!

1958

KING SPARROW
aka MIGHTY SPARROW (some releases as SPARROW only). See MIGHTY SPARROW entry on page 184.

MELODISC 1447 Leading Calypsonians/BILLY MOORE: Love Is Everywhere
(a) With the CARIBBEAN ALL STARS aka THREE CALYPSONIANS. Reissued as CALYPSO 15.

MELODISC 1475 Family-Size Cokes/Clara Honey Bunch
With the CARIBBEAN ALL STARS aka THREE CALYPSONIANS. Reissued as CALYPSO 17.

LORD LEBBY

KALYPSO 05 Sweet Jamaica/Mama Want No Rice No Peas
Produced by Stanley Motta.

LORD MELODY
See LORD MELODY entry on page 154.

MELODISC 1440 The Devil/No No
MELODISC 1449 Robbery/Men Company
MELODISC 1474 Do Able/Happy Holiday
Reissued as CALYPSO 16.

LORD POWER

MARACAS 20001 Special Mamba Calypso/Mambo La La

MIGHTY TERROR & HIS CALYPSONIANS
b Fitzgerald Henry (T&T). Having relocated to the UK around 1954, Terror recorded for both Melodisc and Pye Nixa — favorites included "Patricia Gone with Millicent" and the tribute "Kitch Cavalcade."

PYE NEP 24086 TV Calypso EP

1959

AZIE LAWRENCE

MEZZOTONE 7001/2 West Indians in England/Jump Up
reissued as STARLITE 022.

MEZZOTONE 7004 Love in Every Land/No Dice

LORD INVADER & HIS CALYPSO RHYTHM BOYS
b Rupert Grant (T&T). One of the big stars of the 1940s New York calypso boom, and a member of the RAF Syndicate vaudeville act which played Trinidad during the war years.

PYE 7N 15162 Teddy Boy Calypso/Reincarnation (The Bed Bug)
(a) Old-timer Invader leaps aboard the then prevalent UK youth bandwagon with a questioning examination of rock'n'roll's most fervent followers.

LORD KITCHENER
See LORD KITCHENER entry on page 149.

MELODISC 1498 Black Puddin'/Piccadilly Folk
MELODISC 1538 If You're Brown/Come Back in the Morning

LORD MELODY

MELODISC 1491 I Confess/MIGHTY SPARROW: Goaty
(b) aka "John & Goat." Reissued as CALYPSO 18.

MELODISC 1503 Tom Dooley/Jealous Woman
MELODISC 1504 Romeo/Knock on any Door

MIGHTY TERROR & HIS CALYPSONIANS

PYE 7N 15177 Women Police in England/Patricia Gone with Millicent
PYE 7N 15178 Brown Skin Gal/Kitch Cavalcade

1960–64: EVERYTHING'S GONE SKA
"They started to press up 45s in Jamaica in 1958 or 1959," London sound system owner Count Vin reflected. "The first Jamaican produced record I remember playing [in Britain] was [Laurel Aitken's] 'Boogie in My Bones.' The other one was Owen Gray's 'Please Let Me Go.'" And then the new releases started coming so thick and fast that Vin could barely keep up with them, from Emil Shallit at Melodisc/Kalypso, from Prince Buster, Duke Reid, and Coxsone Dodd in Kingston, and from Chris Blackwell.

Exporting records to Britain's West Indian immigrant community, but seldom pushing them far beyond that, Blackwell's reasons for wanting to break blue beat in his homeland were not purely altruistic. In Jamaica, competition in the marketplace was fierce. Aside from the big three producers, smaller concerns had erupted all over as producers left gasping by Prince Buster's 1961 landmark "Oh Carolina" finally began to catch up, poaching musicians from one another as they chased the elusive ska sound and, more often than not, getting it right.

Britain, however, was an untapped market, and one which was ripe for the picking. Rita Issels and Benny King's R&B Records shop in Stoke Newington and Sonny Roberts' Orbitone Records store in Willesden (the first black-owned record store in the whole of London), both branched into promoting concerts and releasing records which they flew in from Jamaica. The first release on the R&B label, "Do the Ska," by Clive and Gloria, was a devastating statement of the Kings' intent.

But only one company, Emil Shallit's Melodisc, was anything more than a shoestring concern, and actively catered to the West Indian community. In early 1960, then, Blackwell finalized a licensing deal with Starlite Records, a subsidiary of the Esquire jazz label, and announced that Shallit had competition at last. That June saw the British release of Laurel Aitken's "Boogie in My Bones," and Blackwell was off and running.

So was Aitken. The same month as "Boogie in My Bones" came out, Melodisc released an Aitken single of its own, "Lonesome Lover," and while the Starlite release sold respectably enough, the Melodisc record went through the roof. "Lonesome Lover" shifted an estimated 80,000 copies in 1960–61, a staggering quantity for a minority release, and one which sent Emil Shallit jumping the next plane to Jamaica, to search out follow-up material. According to legend, he spent his time in Kingston walking around with his briefcase painted with the warning, "Danger: Explosives," an insurance against being mugged on the street.

"Siggy" Jackson, one of the Melodisc directors, recalled, "I [made] some calypso recordings and we had a lot of hits." In the aftermath of "Lonesome Lover," however, "[We] got some Jamaican releases, which were then called Jamaican blues, which [were] released on a new label. . . called Blue Beat." The first Blue Beat releases set the flavor for the label's output, as Shallit set about covering every musical base he could.

Aitken's "Boogie Rock," a Jamaican hit for Sir Coxsone's Downbeat label, catered for the hardcore youth; Byron Lee's "Dumplin's" and Joe Higgs & Delroy Wilson's "Manny Oh" were licensed from WIRL, intended for the gentler, showband-loving crowd. The label also put the word out for "local," British, talent, and was rewarded with the discovery of Bobby Muir, a young immigrant whose "Baby What You Done Me Wrong" (recorded with the Blue Beats) bears the distinction of being the first ska record ever recorded in Britain. By 1961, Melodisc was operating three more blue beat labels, Chek, Duke, and Dice, and scoring with every one.

Yet Blackwell's Starlite operation was to prove no less successful and, by the end of the year, he relocated to London to launch his own British-based label. Island Records was relaunched in early 1962, its debut coinciding, with sanguine serendipity, with the declaration of Jamaica's independence. The label's second ever release was Trinidadian Lord Creator's smooth "Independant [sic] Jamaica Calypso." (In fact, the record was intended to be Island's very first release, as its catalog number, WI 001, insists. So quickly did the company fall into place, however, that WI 002, Owen Gray's "Patricia," reached the stores a few weeks earlier.)

With the Jamaican studios literally pumping the singles out, and a voracious British market sucking them all up, by the end of 1962, the Island Records' catalog exploded across 33 singles, sold almost exclusively through a chain of 40 or 50 independent specialist record stores. Some of these singles, of course, were forgettable. Others, however, were to have an indelible effect on the British market—Derrick Morgan and Patsy Todd's "Housewife's Choice"; Eric Morris' rekindling of Lord Creator's "Penny-Reel" mento; Jimmy Cliff's "King of Kings" included. A deal with producer Leslie Kong ensured a hot line to Jamaica's biggest hits; now, other producers too were flocking to do business with Chris Blackwell and, by 1963, the Island catalog boasted some of the most important names in Jamaican music. Island itself was now a name to be reckoned with.

Everybody Blackwell knew pitched in. When Island put out a Keith and Enid album, but were unable to find a photograph of the duo for the jacket, Blackwell's girlfriend Esther and a friend named Winston Stonor posed instead. Jackie Edwards, one of Blackwell's favorite recording artists, frequently helped out with distribution, traveling by bus with a box of records under each arm. Both Blackwell's landlord, Jamaican born accountant Lee Gopthal, and his downstairs neighbor, Sonny Roberts, helped sell Island product, Gopthal through his newly formed Beat & Commercial (B&C) distribution company, Roberts from his Orbitone Records shop.

Indeed, Roberts was an especially valuable ally. Aside from the store, Roberts also operated the Sway and Planetone record labels (early releases included sides by such newly transplanted Jamaican performers as Dandy Livingstone and Mike Elliott) and a house band, the Planets (led by another recent immigrant, trombonist Rico Rodriguez). He even ran his own basement recording studio, lined with egg cartons and infested by rats. Blackwell put everything to use and, by late 1963, was strong enough to launch two new subsidiary labels, Black Swan (christened by, and largely an outlet for, guitarist Ernest Ranglin) and Jump Up, dedicated to calypso and mento. Elsewhere, too, fresh concerns were emerging.

Melodisc closed Kalypso in 1963, only to relaunch it as the reissues-heavy Melodisc Calypso later that same year. Carnival Records got underway, spearheading its drive with the blue beat/blues pianist Errol Dixon. Headed by Graeme Goodall, an Australian studio engineer who'd spent many years working in Jamaica (including several as Coxsone Dodd's engineer), Rio Records was flourishing with a catalog devoted almost exclusively to Laurel Aitken, and the occasional Prince Buster production (Dawn Penn's "Long Days Short Nights," Errol Dunkley's "Love Me Forever"). By 1964, Rita Issels and Benny King's newly launched Ska Beat label was enjoying a radio hit with "Girl's Town Ska" by trumpeter/orchestra leader Baba Brooks.

The biggest hit of all, however, turned the spotlight back on Blackwell. In 1964, his production of 14-year-old Millicent "Millie" Small's "My Boy Lollipop" charted in both the UK (on the Fontana major) and the US (through Smash), a monster hit which catapulted ska — or blue-beat as British fans habitually termed it — into the international spotlight. The record rocketed to #2 in both countries and, while Millie enjoyed no more than a modicum of subsequent success ("Sweet William" was a trans-Atlantic hit in June, "Bloodshot Eyes" scraped the UK chart almost 18 months later), the point was made. Ska was breaking through.

Immediately, Blackwell set about persuading Jimmy Cliff to relocate to London, confident that his presence on the live circuit would break his career wide open. Cliff remained in London for three years, working with everybody from Millie Small to the Spencer Davis Group, an English R&B band who would soon score a chart-topper of their own with Jackie Edwards' "Keep on Running."

Across town, Blue Beat's perseverance was also paying dividends, and in a far more cohesive manner than even Island were managing. For a while Chris Blackwell appeared to be ranging at will across Jamaican music, licensing anything he wanted from anyone he met (by 1964, Sir Coxsone and Duke Reid were both leasing material to him), but still Island was simply building a catalog. Blue Beat, however, was building a career. Prince Buster's.

The first person to play a Buster record in Britain was Count Suckle, three years after he so unwittingly provided the soundtrack to the Notting Hill riots. 1961's "Oh Carolina" was an instant hit on the British sound systems, so instant, in fact, that pirate copies of Suckle's personal acetate were soon circulating all over town, and inevitably pricking up ears in high places.

Siggy Jackson, over at Melodisc/Blue Beat (and host, every Thursday, of the regular West Indian nights staged at the Flamingo club in the west end's Wardour Street) was especially impressed by the track and, unaware that the tape was a bootleg, he leased "Oh Carolina" for release in the UK He had, after all, dealt with the Prince once before, when he picked up "Little Honey" by Buster's Group and released it backed by a Rico Rodriguez instrumental. He was accustomed, then, to dealing with passing intermediaries, and was horrified when he discovered what really happened. Contacting Buster himself, Jackson offered the producer a full British deal. Buster accepted, and in 1964, he visited the UK on his first-ever tour.

Flying over with Derrick Morgan, Buster arrived in London with newspaper and television reports of the Notting Hill riots still burning in his mind. Six long years may have passed since that time, but memories are even longer; Buster hit Britain convinced that he was walking into a powder-keg of prejudice. He certainly didn't expect to see any white faces in his audience. Instead, he was blown away by his reception. "There was this same bunch of kids at every show. White kids. I first saw them in London, then in Birmingham, Manchester, Nottingham."

He visited the Ram Jam Club in Brixton, and received a heroes' welcome. He went to the Marquee, and the cheers drowned out the P.A. "Everywhere I went, [white kids] would go and make sure everything was alright, and would be around me like my bodyguards. They'd ride along all around my car on their scooters, like I was royalty." Prince Buster had met the Mods, the latest British youth cult obsession and, by its own reckoning, the closest thing to Kingston's rude boy society this side of the Spanish Main. Buster was stunned to discover the standard rude boy uniform of sharp suits and pork-pie hats was as common in London as it was in Kingston. And so was the Mods' devotion to the music.

In 1972, journalist Johnny Copasetic nailed the reasons why blue beat was so popular with this audience. It was because it defied convention. "The records were issued in excessive numbers and were often badly made. The music was pretty wildly unacceptable. The heavy offbeat made it sound like a parody of the crudest rock and roll, the words were often unintelligible. To the populace as a whole, it was rather revolting." How could it go wrong? Prince Buster epitomized all of these qualities. So what if his message went right over the heads of his Anglo Mod audience? They heard it nonetheless and, picking up on the casual phrases with which Buster so effortlessly peppered his lyrics, they perpetuated it within their own culture.

Other highlights of that UK tour included an appearance on British television's *Ready Steady Go*, and recording sessions with English R&B performer Georgie Fame — Buster cut "Wash Wash," Derrick Morgan recorded "Telephone." But the pair's London visit was also notable for a piece of business which eventually landed Emil Shallit in front of the Jamaican government.

Because both Island and Blue Beat (not to mention all the lesser concerns) dealt with their Jamaican sources on a release-by-release basis, there was considerable label hopping among the artists they recorded, and often a great deal of confusion. The Maytals, for example, were known as a Blue Beat combo, but their material regularly appeared on Island, credited either to the Vikings or the Flames. According to the trio's "Toots" Hibbert, it was several royalty-less years before the Maytals themselves discovered what was going on, by which time such staples as "Hallelujah!," "Six and Seven Books of Moses," and "Never Grow Old" had already disappeared under those pseudonymous credits.

The subterfuge was finally unveiled in early 1964 when Prince Buster, having already leased a Vikings song to Island as the Vikings' "Broadway Jungle," then handed it to Blue Beat as the Maytals' "Dog War." To try and prevent a similar faux pas from reoccurring, Shallit proposed that both Buster and Derrick Morgan sign exclusively to Blue Beat. They did, but Morgan had barely returned to Jamaica before he petitioned against the contract's perceived restraint of trade. Minister of Trade Edward Seaga agreed, and the contract was declared invalid.

Buster, however, remained loyal to Blue Beat, aware that of all the acts on the label, he was synonymous with the famous blue and silver label logo. He continued to lease out productions, of course, but his own records had but one home. And Blue Beat rewarded him for his loyalty in 1967, when the brake-screeching, gun rattling, belligerent insistence of the two year old "Al Capone" catapulted out of the clubs and into the British chart.

1960

LAUREL AITKEN

b 1927 (Cuba). Versatile vocalist who has turned his talents to every prevalent musical form, from mento and R&B in the 1950s, to dancehall in the 1990s, and even 2-Tone in Britain in the late 1970s. Much of his career was spent in the UK, where he first relocated in 1960, following the success of these earliest releases. He was rewarded with immense popularity on both the West Indian and white skinhead circuits of the late 1960s and, in 1980, he scored a UK hit with "Rudi Got Married." Recorded as a duo with OWEN GRAY.

BLUE BEAT 1 Boogie Rock/Heavenly Angel

Produced by Stanley Motta. (a) One of the first boogie rock shuffles recorded in Jamaica, and one of the finest, too. A driving beat powers the song, while Aitken has clearly waited a long time to let rip like this.

BLUE BEAT 10 Jeannie Is Back/It's Money You Need

BLUE BEAT 14 Judgement Day/Yes Yea Baby

Produced by Duke Reid. (a) Aitken deserts wine and women for this gospel-inspired offering. Regardless of the upcoming apocalypse, however, the overall mood is decidedly upbeat, with just a hint of boogie.

BLUE BEAT 22 Railroad Track/Tell Me Darling

BLUE BEAT 25 More Whisky/LLOYD CLARKE: Parapinto Boogie

Produced by Duke Reid. (a) A solid boogie which probably sounded as great in the wily producer's liquor store as it would on the dance floor.

KALYPSO 15 Sweet Chariot/Nebuchadnezzar

Produced by Laurel Aitken. (a) Lilting mento stylings mark out this sweet cover of "Swing Low, Sweet Chariot." Years later, rock guitarist Eric Clapton would utilize a similar arrangement for his own version of the song.

KALYPSO 16 Aitken's Boogie/Sweet Chariot

Produced by Laurel Aitken.

KALYPSO 19 Baba Kill Me Goat/Tribute to Collie Smith

Produced by Laurel Aitken. (b) Mento dedicated to "the Mighty Mouse," Jamaican born cricketer who died, age 24, following a car accident 9/59.

STARLITE 011 Boogie in My Bones/Little Sheila

Produced by Chris Blackwell. (a) Recorded in 1958, it was debuts all around on "Bones," for club singer Aitken, producer Blackwell and his new label, Island Records. True to its title, the song boogied its way straight into the bones of JA record buyers, who sent it dancing up to the top of the chart. Interestingly, most of the band consisted of visiting white musicians./(b) A distinctive R&B belter. Reissued as ISLAND 198.

STARLITE 014 Honey Girl/Drinkin' Whisky

Produced by Chris Blackwell.

ALTON & EDDY

Vocal duo comprising ALTON ELLIS and EDDY PARKINS of CARLOS MALCOLM'S AFRO-CARIBS.

BLUE BEAT 17 Muriel/CLUE J & HIS BLUES BLASTERS: Silky

Produced by Coxsone Dodd. (a/b) Cut at Federal in 1959, at Coxsone Dodd's first commercial recording session — earlier Dodd recordings had been intended for sound system use only.

CHOY AMING & ORCHESTRA

Indo-Trinidadian performer, best known for the island hit "Blue Danube Calypso."

KAY 528 Shabeen/ERROL INCE & HIS BAND: Midnight Man

KAY 529 Tina/The Joker

KAY 530 Lovers Lullaby/The Scratcher

THEO BECKFORD

b Theophilus Beckford, 1935 (Kingston, JA). Highly influential pianist as R&B was displaced by ska. He headed his own Kingston-based label, King Pioneer, for a time, but was best regarded as a session man.

BLUE BEAT 15 Easy Snapping/Goin' Home

Produced by Coxsone Dodd. (a) with bassist CLUE J & HIS BLUES BLASTERS, A 1959 RECORDING CUT (ALONGSIDE ALTON & EDDY's "Muriel") at Dodd's first commercial session. "Easy Snappin'" remains one of the most aptly titled records of all time, a cool, finger-poppin' boogie, which resurfaced in 1992 as the accompaniment to a Levi's commercial. Reissued as NU-BEAT 009.

THE BLUE BEATS

The first ska single ever cut in Britain. Fronted by singer BOBBY MUIR, the Blue Beats band featured on many early Blue Beat label 45s. They also recorded extensively with LAUREL AITKEN.

BLUE BEAT 20 Baby What You Done Me Wrong/Go Pretty Baby O
Produced by Siggy Jackson.

THE BLUES BUSTERS

Long-running vocal duo comprising PHILIP JAMES and LLOYD CAMPBELL, launched on the north shore cabaret circuit, from which they were plucked as support for Sam Cooke on a short Jamaican tour. Over a decade later, they recorded an entire album in tribute to him. The duo enjoyed many minor hits throughout a 25-year career.

LIMBO 101 Little Vilma/Early One Morning

FITZVAUGHN BRYAN'S ORCHESTRA

Bryan was among the players featured on the Cook Records album *Belly to Belly*, recorded live in Trinidad during 1960.

MELODISC 1560 Evening News/Hold Your Head Up & Smile
Produced by Fitzvaughn Bryan.

THE CARIBS

The Australian-Jamaican backing band recruited by CHRIS BLACKWELL as backing musicians on many early Jamaican releases on the Island label.

STARLITE 012 Taboo/Mathilda Cha Cha Cha
Produced by Chris Blackwell.

CHUCK & DOBBY

Vocal duo, CHUCK JOSEPHS and DOBBY DOBSON. Duo also known as CHUCK & DARBY.

BLUE BEAT 19 Til the End of Time/DUKE REID & GROUP: What Makes Honey
Produced by Duke Reid. (b) The Duke's tribute to the musical past, this enthusiastic instrumental freely blends swing styles and melodies with early rock'n'roll rhythms and sounds. Recorded at Reid's second session, in 1959.

BLUE BEAT 23 Cool School/DUKE REID & HIS GROUP: The Joker
Produced by Duke Reid. (b) This bustling boogie instrumental includes not only spectacular brass solos, but a bass line sure to curl your toes. Recorded at Reid's second ever session, in 1959.

LLOYD CLARKE

One half of duo DERRICK & LLOYD. (X) ALTON ELLIS

ERROL DIXON

Also recorded as a duo with WINSTON STEWART and GAYNOR.

BLUE BEAT 27 Midnight Train/Anytime Anywhere

DUKE REID & HIS GROUP

Producer Reid and musicians from the SKATALITES axis. Also known as DUKE REID'S ALL STARS. (X) CHUCK & DOBBY, JIVING JUNIORS

WILFRED (JACKIE) EDWARDS

b 1938 (JA)/d. 8/15/92. "The Original Cool Ruler" was a key player in the early days of Island Records, following its London launch. Although Edwards' solo career did little, he wrote two consecutive UK #1s for British R&B band Spencer Davis Group and remained an influential figure behind the scenes. Also recorded as a duo with PATSY TODD.

STARLITE 016 We're Gonna Love/Your Eyes Are Dreaming
Produced by Chris Blackwell. (a) There's a bit of the Four Seasons about this single, which is probably due to the falsetto vocal elements. Otherwise, it's a mid-tempo soulful number, with Edwards showboating his most passionate vocals.

STARLITE 026 I Know/Tell Me Darling
Produced by Chris Blackwell.

OWEN GRAY

b 7/5/39 (JA). Long-standing veteran who scored a wealth of Jamaican hits during the early-mid 1960s, before emigrating to the UK and maintaining his domination from there. Also recorded as a duo with LAUREL AITKEN, DANDY LIVINGSTONE, MILLIE SMALL, DENNIS.

STARLITE 015 Please Let Me Go/Far Love
Produced by Chris Blackwell. (a) A jumped up beat, a trademark ERNEST RANGLIN rockabilly guitar break, jazzy horns, and Gray's inimitable vocals. What more could you ask for?

STARLITE 019 Jenny Lee/The Plea
Produced by Chris Blackwell. (a) A gripping indication of where Jamaican musical tastes were then situated, straight to the soul of Little Richard.

BLUE BEAT 8 Cutest Little Woman/Running Around
(a/b) Recorded with the KEN RICHARDS BAND.

HIGGS & WILSON & KEN RICHARDS & HIS COMETS

Vocal duo comprising JOE HIGGS and DELROY WILSON.

BLUE BEAT 3 Manny Oh/When You Tell Me Baby
(a) Produced by Edward Seaga at WIRL Studios in 1958.

LYNN HOPE

BLUE BEAT 21 Shockin'/Blue & Sentimental

ERROL INCE & HIS BAND

(X) CHOY AMING & HIS ORCHESTRA

CLUE J & HIS BLUES BLASTERS

Session band led by CLUETT JOHNSON (double bass) frequently featuring KEITH STODDART and ERNEST RANGLIN (guitar), AUBREY ADAMS (keyboards), RICO RODRIGUEZ (trombone), KEN WILLIAMS (drums). Recorded exclusively with COXSONE DODD. (X) ALTON & EDDY, THEO BECKFORD

THE JIVING JUNIORS

Vocal group comprising DERRICK HARRIOTT, MAURICE WINTER, CLAUDE "HERMAN" SANG, EUGENE DWYER.

BLUE BEAT 4 Lollipop Girl/Dearest Darling

Produced by Duke Reid. (a) Mid-tempo smoocher which reflects on the doo-wop roots shared by all contemporary vocal trios.

BLUE BEAT 5 My Heart's Desire/I Love You

Produced by Duke Reid.

BLUE BEAT 24 I Wanna Love/DUKE REID & HIS GROUP: Duke's Cookies

Produced by Duke Reid. (b) Cut at Reid's second recording session, a driving R&B instrumental which at least nods in the direction of ska. It's so infectious, that by the time the sax takes its solo, the rest of the band are shouting out in excitement.

STARLITE 028 Lovers' Line/Tu Woo Up Tu Woo

Produced by Coxsone Dodd.

KEITH & ENID

Vocal duo comprising KEITH STEWART and ENID CUMBERLAND.

BLUE BEAT 6 Worried Over You/Everything Will Be Alright

Produced by SL Smith. (a) Romantic croon which famously became one of the fastest selling "ethnic" singles in British music history.

BLUE BEAT 11 Send Me/TRENTON SPENCE & HIS GROUP: People Will Say We're in Love

(a) Produced by SL Smith.

LARO

KALYPSO 21 Jamaican Referendum Calypso/Wrong Impressions of a Soldier

BYRON LEE & THE DRAGONAIRES

See BYRON LEE entry on page 142.

BLUE BEAT 2 Dumplin's/Kissin' Gal

Produced by Edward Seaga.

LORD LEBBY

STARLITE 018 Caldonia/One Kiss for My Baby

LORD MELODY

KALYPSO 14 Rock'n'Roll Calypso/Bo Bo Man

(b) Melody responds to Harry Belafonte's hit version with a rerecording of his own original, one of the funniest pieces of self-mockery ever recorded.

LORD TANAMO

See entry for the SKATALITES on page 262.

KALYPSO 20 Blues Have Got Me Down/Sweet Dreaming

THE MAGIC NOTES

BLUE BEAT 9 Album of Memory/Why Did You Leave Me

THE MELLOW LARKS

Vocal group featuring BASIL GABBIDON.

BLUE BEAT 16 Time to Pray/Love You Baby

Produced by Coxsone Dodd. Recorded at Dodd's first ever session, in 1959.

MIGHTY SPARROW

KALYPSO 10 Carnival Boycott/Gloria

With the CARIBBEAN ALL-STARS.

KALYPSO 17 The Sack/Round & Round

Both cuts taken from the *This Is Sparrow* LP.

KALYPSO 22 Mr Herbert/Simpson

KALYPSO EP 1 This Is Sparrow EP

Includes the tracks Jean and Dinah/Queen's Canary/Everybody Go Get (aka "Sparrow's Dream")/Mango Wood (aka "No Doctor No"). Accompanied by CYRIL DIAZ & ORCHESTRA.

KALYPSO EP 2 Man Dig this Is Sparrow EP

Includes the tracks They Washing They Mouth on Me/Sparrow Is a Bird/Explorer.

DERRICK MORGAN

b 3/40 (Stewarton, JA). Prolific performer whose talent spotting was also integral to the early success of PRINCE BUSTER (with whom he recorded as a duo) and LESLIE KONG. His output declined considerably during the 1980s and 1990s, largely a consequence of worsening vision problems. However, his immortality was assured not only by his famous feud with Prince Buster, but also his contributions to the Judge Dread soap opera. Also recorded as a duo with JENNIFER, LLOYD CLARKE, NAOMI CAMPBELL, PATSY TODD, PAULETTE WILLIAMS, MARTIN RILEY, PAULINE MORGAN, YVONNE (ADAMS), and trio MONTY, DERRICK, & PATSY.

BLUE BEAT 7 Fat Man/I'm Gonna Leave You

Produced by SL Smith.

BLUE BEAT 12 Don't Cry/I Pray for You

Produced by Prince Buster. Recorded with THE EBONIES.

BLUE BEAT 18 Lover Boy/Oh My!

Produced by Duke Reid. (a) The singing sensation's Jamaican debut single (but third UK release) is a pure delight, with the band's creative take on boogie playing off perfectly against the teenager's passionate vocals. After all that, the killer sax solo is just cream on top. The performance was such a hit at King Edwards' sound system that it also became known as "S Corner Rock," after the system's most familiar location.

THE PALMETTO KINGS

STARLITE 021 10 Rum Bottles/Home Cookin' Mama

KEN RICHARDS

Band leader whose COMETS featured several future SKATALITES during the late 1950s/early 1960s. (X) OWEN GRAY, HIGGS & WILSON

BERESFORD RICKETTS

One-half of duo RICKETTS & ROWE.

STARLITE 025 Cherry Baby/I Want to Know

STARLITE 029 Baby Baby/When I Woke Up

THE SKYLARKERS STEEL BAND

KAY 535 If You Love Me/I'll Gather Lilacs

KAY 536 Cara Mia/O Promise Me

TRENTON SPENCE & HIS GROUP

(X) KEITH & ENID

THE SYMPHONETTES STEEL BAND CALYPSO

KAY 532 Bless This House/Because

1961

AUBREY ADAMS & HIS DU DROPPERS

Pianist Adams (d 1990) often worked with SKATALITES founder member TOMMY MCCOOK. His own band featured several other in-demand session musicians. GLADSTONE ANDERSON is his nephew. (X) CHUCK & DOBBY

LAUREL AITKEN

BLUE BEAT 40 Hey Bar Tender/Mash People

Produced by Ken Khouri. (a) Aitken gives a performance worthy of a year's free beer on this classic R&B style single; drinks all around, and this time the audience is buying.

BLUE BEAT 52 Bouncing Woman/Nursery Rhyme Boogie

BLUE BEAT 70 Mighty Redeemer/Please Don't Leave Me

Produced by Duke Reid. (a) One of the first openly Rastafarian recordings ever, and certainly the first by a major artist.

MELODISC 1570 Mary Lee/Lonesome Lover

STARLITE 034 Love Me Baby/Stars Were Made

(a) A smooth boogie with an R&B twist built around an infectious melody. Aitken brings a sense of fun to the lyrics, while the sax hugs the corners with caressing style.

ROLAND ALPHONSO

See also entry for THE SKATALITES on page 262. (X) DERRICK & PATSY, MELLOW LARKS, MONTY & ROY.

BLUE BEAT 58 Blackberry Brandy/ALVIN & CECIL: Marjorie

Produced by Duke Reid. (a) As sweet and smooth as the liqueur it's titled after. The band swings, the bassist soft-steps around R&B, while the horns heat up the drink with a touch of jazz.

ALVIN & CECIL

(X) ROLAND ALPHONSO

THEO BECKFORD

BLUE BEAT 33 Jack & Jill Shuffle/Little Lady

Produced by Coxsone Dodd. Credited to Beckford & CLUE J & HIS BLUES BLASTERS.

BLUE BEAT 50 Georgie & the Old Shoe/That's Me

Produced by Coxsone Dodd. Credited to Beckford & THE CITY SLICKERS.

THE BLUES BUSTERS

BLUE BEAT 55 Donna/You're Driving Me Crazy

Produced by Coxsone Dodd.

KENT BROWN

Vocalist, also recorded as a duo with DIMPLE HINDS and JEANNIE, and THE RAINBOWS. (X) SIR D'S GROUP.

C BYRD

BLUE BEAT 49 Baa Baa Black Sheep/LLOYD & CECIL: Come Over Here

THE CHARMERS

Vocal duo comprising ROY WILLIS and LLOYD TYRELL aka LLOYD TERRELL aka LLOYD CHARMERS, later of CONSCIOUS MINDS, THE UNIQUES.

BLUE BEAT 42 Lonely Boy/I Am Going Back Home

CHUCK & DOBBY

BLUE BEAT 39 I Love My Teacher/Do Du Wap

Recorded with AUBREY ADAMS & HIS DU DROPPERS. (b) Doo Wop, Jamaican style! The band swings joyfully along, while the duo deliver up the delightfully catchy lyrics.

BLUE BEAT 59 Oh Fanny/Running Around

BLUE BEAT 69 I Was Wrong/BASIL GABBIDON & BUSTER'S GROUP: War Paint Baby

Produced by Prince Buster. (b)The band boogies its best for this jazzy/R&B tubthumper, as Gabbidon rather languorously encourages his girl to get ready for a big night out.

STARLITE 043 Sad Over You/Sweeter than Honey

Produced by Edward Seaga.

STARLITE 044 Lovey Dovey/Sitting Square

Produced by Edward Seaga.

FITZROY COLEMAN

STARLITE 064 Lucille/Caribbean Sunset

COUNT OSSIE

b OSSIE WILLIAMS, 1928/d 10/18/76. Rastafarian father of modern nyahbingi drumming, his early work with PRINCE BUSTER revolutionized Jamaican music. Recorded with THE WAREIKAS, named for their hill home, and as a duo with IM. Later formed MYSTIC REVELATION. (X) JACKIE ESTICK.

DERRICK & PATSY

Vocal duo comprising DERRICK MORGAN and PATSY TODD.

BLUE BEAT 57 Feel So Fine/ROLAND ALPHONSO & GROUP: Mean to Me

Produced by Duke Reid.

BLUE BEAT 65 Let the Good Times Roll/Baby Please Don't Leave Me

Produced by Duke Reid. Recorded with DRUMBAGO & HIS HARMONISERS.

ERROL DIXON

BLUE BEAT 46 Mama Shut Your Door/Too Much Whisky

CLANCY ECCLES

See entry in DIRECTORY OF PRODUCERS. Also recorded with his eponymous ALL STARS/SET and KING STITT.

BLUE BEAT 34 River Jordan/I Live & I Love
Produced by Coxsone Dodd. (a) Dodd paired Eccles with HERMAN HERSANG'S CITY SLICKERS to paint an awesome musical soundscape. The bass and keyboards conjure up a swirling watery atmosphere, the percussion and handclaps add a revivalist tinge and the superb brass section takes turns soloing, while Eccles and his female backing vocalists give a simple melody a singalong urgency.

BLUE BEAT 67 Freedom/More Proof
Produced by Coxsone Dodd. Both songs were cut soon after Dodd "discovered" Eccles at a November, 1959, talent contest. (a) "Freedom" was co-opted by the JLP as part of their drive for Jamaican political independence.

WILFRED (JACKIE) EDWARDS

STARLITE 046 Whenever There's Moonlight/Heaven Just Knows
Produced by Chris Blackwell.

STARLITE 062 More than Words Can Say/I Love You No More
Produced by Chris Blackwell.

NEVILLE ESSON

BLUE BEAT 37 Lovers Jive/Wicked & Dreadful
Produced by Coxsone Dodd. Recorded with CLUE J & HIS BLUES BLASTERS.

JACKIE ESTICK

R&B vocalist whose earliest recordings were for Coxsone Dodd's Worldisc label.

BLUE BEAT 64 Boss Girl/COUNT OSSIE & HIS GROUP: Cassavubu
Produced by Coxsone Dodd.

FOLKES BROTHERS

Vocal trio of JOHN, MICO and JUNIOR FOLKES.

BLUE BEAT 30 Oh Carolina/I Met a Man
Produced by Prince Buster. (a) Recorded at RJR studios in Kingston, the Folkes Brothers were less folky than doo-wopish, but it was the up-front tribal beat, courtesy of COUNT OSSIE, that put this single into a genre all its own.

BASIL GABBIDON

Veteran studio singer and member of THE MELLOW LARKS, who recorded extensively with Coxsone Dodd during the early 1960s. A namesake co-founded UK reggae band Steel Pulse in 1975. (X) CHUCK & DOBBY.

GIRL SATCHMO

BLUE BEAT 45 Satchmo's Mash Potato/Darling

OWEN GRAY

BLUE BEAT 43 Sinners Weep/Get Drunk
Produced by Coxsone Dodd. (a) A powerful early invocation of Rastafarian imagery recorded with HERMAN HERSANG & HIS CITY SLICKERS.

STARLITE 032 Mash It Up (parts 1/2)

HIGGS & WILSON

STARLITE 035 Pretty Baby/I Long for the Day

STARLITE 036 Lover's Song/It Is a Day

STARLITE 042 Come on Home/The Robe
Produced by Edward Seaga. (b) Excellent gospel performance highlighting two of the sweetest voices around.

STARLITE 053 Sha Ba Ba/Change of Mind

CLUE J & HIS BLUES BLASTERS

BLUE BEAT 60 Little Willie/Pine Juice
Produced by Coxsone Dodd.

THE JIVING JUNIORS

BLUE BEAT 36 Over the River/Hip Rub
Produced by Coxsone Dodd/recorded with HERMAN HERSANG & HIS CITY SLICKERS. (a) A pulsing bass line, flash guitar, and steaming horns combine to make this a musical treat, while the call and response vocals add a gospel edge.

STARLITE 049 Slop & Mash/My Sweet Angel
Produced by Derrick Harriott.

KEITH & ENID

STARLITE 067 You're Gonna Break My Heart/What Have I Done?

STARLITE 047 Never Leave My Throne/Only a Pity

BOBBY KINGDOM & THE BLUE BEATS

Kingdom aka BOBBY MUIR.

BLUE BEAT 44 Honey Please/That's My Girl

AZIE LAWRENCE

BLUE BEAT 71 So Far Apart/Palms of Victory
Recorded with the MELLOWBEATS.

MELODISC 1563 Jamaica Blues/Come Rumble & Tumble with Me

MELODISC 1572 You Didn't Want to Know

STARLITE 041 No Dice/Love in Every Land

BYRON LEE & HIS DRAGONAIRES

BLUE BEAT 28 Mash! Mr Lee/Help Me Forget
Produced by Edward Seaga.

STARLITE 045 Joy Ride/Over the Rainbow
Produced by Edward Seaga.

LLOYD & CECIL

(X) C BYRD

THE MAGIC NOTES

BLUE BEAT 51 Rosabel/I'm Not Worthy

THE MELLOW LARKS

BLUE BEAT 38 No More Wedding/Lite of My Life

BLUE BEAT 54 Another Moses/ROLAND ALPHONSO & THE ALLEY CATS: Hully Gully Rock

BLUE BEAT 68 Rock a an Soul/MONTY & THE CYCLONES: Lazy Lou
Recorded with COUNT OSSIE & THE WAREIKAS.

MIGHTY SPARROW

KALYPSO EP 3 A Party with Sparrow EP

KALYPSO EP 4 This Is the Sparrow Again EP
Includes the tracks Federation/The Base.

KALYPSO EP 5 Greetings from Sparrow EP
Includes the tracks No More Rocking and Rolling/Country Girl/Dorothy/Postcard to Sparrow.

MONTY & THE CYCLONES

(X) MELLO LARKS

MONTY & ROY

Vocal duo comprising ERIC "MONTY" MORRIS AND ROY PANTON.

BLUE BEAT 61 In & out the Window/Tra La La Boogie
Produced by Duke Reid. (a) A #1 hit composed by STRANGER COLE. Following its success, Reid invited Cole in to make his own recording debut.

BLUE BEAT 63 Sweetie Pie/ROLAND ALPHONSO'S GROUP: Green Door
Produced by Duke Reid.

DERRICK MORGAN

BLUE BEAT 31 Now We Know/Nights Are Lonely
Recorded with tenor saxophonist TRENTON SPENCE and his orchestra and featuring ERIC MORRIS on shared vocals—the single was actually released under Morris' name in Jamaica.

BLUE BEAT 35 Leave Earth/Wigger wee Shuffle
Produced by Coxsone Dodd. (a) A violent boogie recorded with CLUE J & HIS BLUES BLASTERS, a serious shot in the growing competition between Dodd and DUKE REID's sound systems.

BLUE BEAT 48 Times Are Going/I Love You Baby
Produced by Prince Buster. Credited to MARTIN (RILEY) & DERRICK.

BLUE BEAT 62 Shake a Leg/Golden Rule
Produced by Prince Buster. Recorded with DRUMBAGO ALL-STARS.

ERIC "MONTY" MORRIS

Inspired to record by the success of his friend DERRICK MORGAN, Morris proved one of the 1960s most enduring vocalists. Also recorded as a duo with ROY PANTON, and a trio with DERRICK MORGAN & PATSY TODD, and with THE CYCLONES. (X) BUSTER'S GROUP, MONTY & ROY

BLUE BEAT 53 Humpty Dumpty/Cornbread & Butter
Produced by Prince Buster. (a) Laid back sax and nursery rhyme lyrics contributed to the monster success of producer Buster's first major hit. Recorded with the DRUMBAGO ALL-STARS, it is another cut from Buster's maiden recording session.

MOSSMAN & ZEDDSE

(X) SIR D'S GROUP

LASCELLES PERKINS

Sentimental balladeer best remembered for his early 60s work with Coxsone Dodd. A member of CARLOS MALCOLM's AFRO-CARIBS, also recorded as a duo with HORTENSE ELLIS, YVONNE (ADAMS).

BLUE BEAT 41 Creation/Lonely Robin
Produced by Coxsone Dodd. (b) Perkins is given ample room for his smoothest, most passionate vocals via the charming melody, with the piano providing a sip of champagne music and the sax a whiff of a smokey lounge setting.

(PRINCE) BUSTER'S GROUP

Prince Buster's band, frequently featuring VAL BENNETT, DENNIS CAMPBELL (sax), also various SKATALITES. Subsequently known as BUSTER'S BAND, BUSTER'S ALL STARS/ PRINCE BUSTER'S ALL STARS. Frequently backed other artists.

BLUE BEAT 56 Little Honey/RICO RODRIGUES: Luke Lane Shuffle
Produced by Prince Buster. (a) Buster's first-ever production, featuring Jah JERRY, DRUMBAGO and RICO RODRIGUEZ. (b) A jaunty little shuffle whose laid back beat is further emphasized by the trombonist's exciting, yet never overly showy, solo.

STARLITE 052 Buster's Shack/ERIC MORRIS: Search the World
Produced by Prince Buster. (a) A pumping instrumental titled after Buster's own record store.

THE RHYTHM ACES

Vocal group featuring DELANO STEWART, RICHARD MOSS, RICHARD ACE and BORIS GARDINER.

STARLITE 066 Please Don't Go Away/Oh My Darling
Produced by Chris Blackwell.

STARLITE 061 A Thousand Teardrops/Wherever You May Go
Produced by Chris Blackwell.

RICKETTS & ROWE

Vocal duo BERESFORD RICKETTS & KEITH ROWE.

STARLITE 048 Hold Me Tight/Dream Girl

RICO RODRIGUEZ

b Emmanuel "Rico" Rodriguez, 10/17/34 (Kingston, JA). The trombonist relocated to the UK in 1962, where he became a guiding force on the local ska scene. Re-emerged in the late 1970s to take a similar pole position in the 2-Tone movement. (X) BUSTER'S GROUP.

SHENLEY & ANNETTE

Vocal duo featuring SHENLEY DUFFUS and ANNETTE (of ROY. . .).

BLUE BEAT 72 Million Dollar Baby/The First Time I Met You

JIMMY SINCLAIR & TRENTON SPENCE ORCHESTRA

BLUE BEAT 47 Verona/To Prove My Love

SIR D'S GROUP

BLUE BEAT 66 Hey Diddle Diddle/Pocket Money
Produced by Coxsone Dodd. (a) With KENT BROWN (b) With MOSSMAN & ZEDDSE.

THE WIGGANS

BLUE BEAT 29 Rock Baby/Let's Sing the Blues

1962

BOBBY AITKEN

Guitarist brother of LAUREL AITKEN. Led THE CARIB BEATS with CYNTHIA RICHARDS.

BLUE BEAT 93 Never Never/Isabella

ISLAND 028 Baby Baby/Lonely Boy

LAUREL AITKEN

BLUE BEAT 84 Brother David/Back to New Orleans

Produced by Ken Khouri.

BLUE BEAT 109 Lucille/I Love You More Everyday

Produced by Siggy Jackson.

BLUE BEAT 120 Sixty Days & Sixty Nights/Going to Kansas City

Produced by Siggy Jackson.

BLUE BEAT 142 Jenny Jenny/Weary Wanderer

(a) Recorded with BANDITS WITH RUDDY & SKETTO.

DICE 1 Mabel/You Got Me Rockin'

ROLAND ALPHONSO

BLUE BEAT 112 4 Corners of the World/THE SHINERS: Romantic Shuffle

Recorded with THE ALLEYCATS.

ALTON & EDDY

ISLAND 009 My Love Divine/Let Me Dream

ANDY & JOEY

Vocal duo featuring BOB ANDY and JOEY DENNIS, sister of BLACK UHURU's Garth.

ISLAND 056 Have You Ever/Cross My Heart

CLIVE BAILEY & RICO'S BLUES GROUP

RICO is RICO RODRIGUEZ.

BLUE BEAT 92 Evening Train/Going Home

THEO BECKFORD

BLUE BEAT 87 Walking Down King Street/The Clock

(a) Beckford has such a wonderful time on his stroll that you'll have no hesitation joining him. U-ROY later revamped this track as "Earthquake."

BELL'S GROUP

(X) DERRICK MORGAN

THE BLUE BEATS

(X) JIMMY CLIFF

THE BLUES BUSTERS

BLUE BEAT 73 There's Always Sunshine/You Had It Wrong

BLUE BEAT 102 Tell Me Why/I've Done You Wrong

ISLAND 023 Behold!/Oh Baby

Produced by Byron Lee. (a) A perfect representation of American pop, all sublime silky vocals and pretty harmo-

nies, with only the rhythm and horns giving away the duo's true location.

BUNNY & SKITTER

Vocal duo featuring ARTHUR "BUNNY" ROBINSON and NOEL "SCULLY" SIMMS, later of the SUPERSONICS. (X) EMMANUEL RODRIGUES ORKESTRA.

BLUE BEAT 132 Bringing in the Sheep/Run Away

ISLAND 026 I Don't Want You/Seven Long Years

BUSTY & COOL

Duo featuring BUSTY BROWN.

BLUE BEAT 144 Mr Policeman/What a World

THE CHARMERS

BLUE BEAT 114 Crying Over You/Now You Want to Cry

LLOYD CLARKE

BLUE BEAT 99 Good Morning/Now I Know a Reason

Produced by SL Smith.

BLUE BEAT 104 Fool's Day/You're a Cheat

(a) Recorded with RECO'S ALL-STARS.

ISLAND 007 Love You the Most/LLOYD ROBINSON: You Said You Loved Me

JIMMY CLIFF

See JIMMY CLIFF entry on page 76.

BLUE BEAT 78 I'm Sorry/THE BLUE BEATS: Roarin'

Produced by Sir Cavalier. Recorded with CAVALIERS COMBO.

ISLAND 012 Hurricane Hattie/Dearest Beverley

Produced by Leslie Kong. (a) The eighth tropical storm in a murderously active fall, 1961, season, Hattie hit British Honduras (modern Belize) with such force that one town, Stann City, was utterly destroyed — to be rebuilt as Hattieville.

ISLAND 016 Miss Jamaica/Gold Digger

Produced by Leslie Kong. (a) Independence brought a host of new experiences to the island, not just in government, but in almost every facet of life. The prolific Cliff was quick to see the possibilities, and swiftly penned this simple, but pretty, ode to the island's first national beauty contest, delivered with genuine conviction.

ISLAND 025 Since Lately/I'm Free

Produced by Leslie Kong.

THE CONTINENTALS

ISLAND 010 Going Crazy/Give Me All Your Love

COSMO & DENNIS

Vocal duo of FRANK COSMO and DENZIL DENNIS.

BLUE BEAT 145 Bed of Roses/Tonight & Evermore

Produced by Duke Reid.

COUNT LASHER

KALYPSO 100 Calypso Cha Cha Cha/Perseverance

Produced by Stanley Motta.

KALYPSO 105 Slide Mongoose/Miss Constance
Produced by Stanley Motta. (a) aka "Sly Mongoose," a Jamaican mento popular in Trinidad since the turn of the century. Guyana-born vaudevillian Phil Madison cut it in 1923, Lionel Belasco recorded it around 1925; the song itself describes a liaison between a newspaper reporter (the mongoose) and a preacher's daughter.

COUNT OSSIE

(X) WINSTON & ROY

DERRICK & LLOYD

Vocal duo comprising DERRICK MORGAN and LLOYD CLARKE.

BLUE BEAT 135 Love & Leave Me/Merry Twist

DERRICK & PATSY

BLUE BEAT 97 Love Not to Brag/Duck Soup
Produced by Duke Reid.

BLUE BEAT 106 Oh Shirley/BASIL GABBIDON'S GROUP: Sam the Fisherman
Produced by Vincent Chin. (a) Recorded with DRUMBAGO ALL-STARS.

BLUE BEAT 110 Are You Going to Marry Me?/Trouble

BLUE BEAT 121 Crying in the Chapel/Come Back My Love

BLUE BEAT 123 Oh! My Love/Let's Go to the Party

ISLAND 018 Housewife's Choice/Gypsy Woman
Produced by Leslie Kong. (a) This hit was originally called "You Don't Know," but the upbeat love duet received so many requests from women radio listeners, that it was swiftly retitled. "Choice" became the first of many chart toppers for singer Derrick Morgan; it is also one of several records credited with igniting Morgan's feud with PRINCE BUSTER, who believed "Choice"'s sax solo was lifted from his "They Got to Go."

DERRICK & YVONNE

Vocal duo featuring DERRICK MORGAN and YVONNE ADAMS, sister of keyboard player GLEN ADAMS. She also recorded with SONNY BURKE, ROY PANTON, LASCELLES PERKINS.

BLUE BEAT 94 Meekly Wait/Day In & Day Out

ERROL DIXON & HIS BACK BEATS

BLUE BEAT 86 Bad Bad Woman/Early this Morning

ISLAND 017 Morning Train/Lonely Heart

DON DRUMMOND ORCHESTRA

See the SKATALITES entry on page 262.

(X) RHYTHM ACES

ISLAND 021 Schooling the Duke/SHENLEY DUFFUS: Bitter Rose
Produced by Coxsone Dodd.

SHENLEY DUFFUS

b Chenley Duffus, 2/10/38 (Roland Field, JA). Vocalist who cut his first tracks with SL SMITH in 1958. Also recorded as a duo with ANNETTE, HYACINTH, LITTLE LUMAN.

(X) DON DRUMMOND ORCHESTRA

DUKE REID & HIS GROUP

BLUE BEAT 119 12 Minutes to Go/HORTENSE ELLIS: Midnight Train
Produced by Duke Reid. (a) The SKATALITES, of course. Even with time running out, this instrumental has a relaxed air, fed by the steady-as-she-goes rhythm, topped by the typically suave brass.

THE ECHOES & THE CELESTIALS

BLUE BEAT 89 Are You Mine/I'll Love You Forever

WILFRED/JACKIE EDWARDS

DECCA F11547 Lonely Game/Suddenly
Produced by Chris Blackwell.

STARLITE 076 Little Bitty Girl/Never Go Away
Produced by Chris Blackwell.

ISLAND 008 All My Days/Hear Me Cry
Produced by Chris Blackwell.

ISLAND 019 One More Week/Tears Like Rain
Produced by Chris Blackwell.

RUPERT EDWARDS & SMITHIE'S SEXTET

See entry for RUPIE EDWARDS on page 103.

BLUE BEAT 90 Guilty Convict/Just Because
Produced by SL Smith.

ALTON ELLIS

b 1944 (Kingston, JA). Started his career as one-half of the ALTON & EDDY duo; also recorded with his sister as HORTENSE & ALTON. Ellis ultimately emerged as one of the all-time greatest rock steady vocalists, ably backed by his FLAMES. He recorded regularly throughout the remainder of the decade, and relocated to the UK in 1972, where his proteges included JANET KAY. (X) ERIC MORRIS

HORTENSE ELLIS

b 1941 (Trenchtown, JA), d 10/19/2000. Sister of singer ALTON ELLIS, with whom she recorded as HORTENSE & ALTON. Also recorded as a duo with DELROY WILSON, JACKIE OPEL, STRANGER COLE, and PETER. Voted Jamaica's top female vocalist in 1964, she later recorded with BYRON LEE & THE DRAGONAIRES. During the 1970s she worked regularly with producer BUNNY LEE, occasionally under the name QUEEN TINEY — her "Down Town Ting" was a clever response to Althea & Donna's "Uptown Top Ranking," which itself utilized the rhythm to brother Alton's "I'm Still in Love with You." She died age 59 of a stomach infection.

(X) DUKE REID GROUP

THE FACELLS

KALYPSO 116 So Fine/If You Love Me

LLOYD FLOWERS & RICO'S RHYTHM GROUP

Flowers later became one-half of the FLOWERS & ALVIN duo.

BLUE BEAT 88 I'm Going Home/Lovers' Town

BASIL GABBIDON

(X) DERRICK & PATSY, DERRICK MORGAN

BLUE BEAT 111 Iverene/Lover Man

BLUE BEAT 124 Independent Blues/For My Love

BLUE BEAT 129 Our Melody/Going Back to JA

Produced by Vincent Chin.

ISLAND 033 I Found My Baby/No Fault of Mine

GIRL SATCHMO & KARL ROWE & THE BLUE BEATS

BLUE BEAT 79 Twist Around Town/My New Honey

TOP GRANT

(X) RHYTHM ACES

OWEN GRAY

BLUE BEAT 75 Rocking in My Feet/Nobody Else

Recorded with THE JETS.

BLUE BEAT 91 Millie Girl/DERRICK MORGAN: Headache

Produced by Prince Buster. (a) Gray passionately declares his love on this scorcher, equally notable for its strong ska beat and R&B edge.

BLUE BEAT 103 Lonely Days/No Good Woman

Recorded with SONNY BRADSHAW QUARTET.

BLUE BEAT 108 Keep It in Mind/Do You Want to Jump

Recorded with LES DAWSON COMBO.

BLUE BEAT 113 Best Twist/Grandma Grandpa

BLUE BEAT 127 Pretty Girl/Twist So Fine

BLUE BEAT 136 They Got to Move/I Love Her

BLUE BEAT 139 Tree in the Meadow/Lizabella

Produced by Prince Buster.

DICE 3 On the Beach/Young Lover

Produced by Coxsone Dodd. (a) From 1959, a rollicking R&B number celebrating producer Coxsone Dodd's Downbeat sound system's recent visit to the Gold Coast beach.

ISLAND 002 Patricia/Twist Baby

Produced by Coxsone Dodd. (a) There's a nostalgic air of the old big band sound here, with Gray's vocals a silky delight.

ISLAND 014 Sugar Plum/Jezebel

Produced by Coxsone Dodd. (b) Gray hits the perfect note of righteous indignation, while the band's bubbling, boogiefied swing comes to the defense of the hussy.

ISLAND 020 Audrey/Dolly Baby

Produced by Coxsone Dodd. (a/b) recorded with ERNEST RANGLIN ORCHESTRA.

ISLAND 030 Midnight Track/Time Will Tell

Produced by Chris Blackwell. (a) Despite its late UK release date, Gray's recording debut. An up-tempo boogie with attitude, Gray smoothly knocks out the vocals with all the aplomb of a superstar, which is precisely what he became.

STARLITE 078 I Feel Good/Someone to Help Me

STARLITE 088 Let Me Go Free/In My Dreams

DERRICK HARRIOTT & THE VAGABONDS

See entry in DIRECTORY OF PRODUCERS. Also a member of THE JIVING JUNIORS, MIGHTY VIKINGS.

BLUE BEAT 131 I Are/Have Faith in Me

Produced by Derrick Harriott.

THE HI-TONES

ISLAND 029 Goin' Steady/Darlin' Elaine

HIGGS & WILSON

BLUE BEAT 95 How Can I Be Sure/Mighty Man

JIMMY JAMES

b Michael James, 9/13/40. US-born, but raised in JA, James subsequently moved to the UK where he relaunched himself as a soul musician, leading the band the Vagabonds.

DICE 4 Bewildered & Blue/I Don't Want to Cry

Produced by Lindon Pottinger.

THE JIVING JUNIORS

ISLAND 003 Sugar Dandy/Valerie

Produced by Derrick Harriott.(a) Cut in New York with R&B star Chuck Jackson's former producer, Teacher Wiltshire, and sax legend Buddy Lucas. It's Lucas' riff which leads into (and underpins) another of the Juniors' note- and style-perfect recreations of American doo-wop, falsetto-fronted and sweet as, indeed, sugar. Reissued as ISLAND 129.

ISLAND 027 Andrea/Don't Leave Me

Produced by Derrick Harriott.

AL T JOE & THE CELESTIALS

Widely regarded as north Jamaica's premier touring band, THE CELESTIALS featured BILLY VERNON and E T WEBSTER.

BLUE BEAT 126 You Cheated on Me/This Heart of Mine

JOSH & HERBIE

KALYPSO 107 I'm Nobody's Child/How Can I Believe in You

KEITH & ENID

BLUE BEAT 125 When It's Spring/True Love

Credited to K&E with the SONNY BRADSHAW ORCHESTRA.

KENT & JEANIE WITH THE CITY SLICKERS

Vocal duo featuring KENT BROWN.

BLUE BEAT 98 Daddy/Hello Love

BOBBY KINGDOM & THE BLUE BEATS

BLUE BEAT 77 Brand New Automobile/Spanish Town Twist

LEON & OWEN WITH DRUMBAGO ALL-STARS

Vocal duo comprising brothers OWEN and LEON SILVERA. (X) OWEN & LEON.

BLUE BEAT 117 Murder/ROY PANTON: Forty Four

LORD CREATOR

b Kentrick Patrick (T&T). Creator scored his first Jamaican hit in 1959 with "Evening News," relocating to Kingston in its aftermath. Frequently recording with producer Vincent Chin, he also recorded under his given name, and performed as a duo with NORMA FRAZIER, PATRICK & GEORGE.

ISLAND 001 Independent Jamaica Calypso/Remember

Produced by Vincent Chin. (a) "Evening News" may have been his biggest hit, but "Independent Jamaica" comes a close second. Lyrically a wordy optimistic editorial on the coming joys of independence, musically a potpourri of Caribbean styles and big band swing.

MIGHTY SPARROW

KALYPSO EP 6 Sparrow the Conqueror EP

Includes the tracks Short Little Shorts/Eve/PAYE.

MONTY & THE CYCLONES

Featuring ERIC MORRIS. (X) DERRICK MORGAN

DERRICK MORGAN

(X) OWEN GRAY

BLUE BEAT 76 Sunday Monday/Be Still

Produced by Leslie Kong. (a) Before Leslie Kong's Beverley label was even up and running, the wily producer had poached Morgan away from PRINCE BUSTER's stable, slamming him straight into Federal studios, on Marcus Garvey Drive, and unleashing his "Be Still" as the new label's own debut release.

BLUE BEAT 82 Don't You Know Little Girl/BASIL GABBIDON: Hully Gully Miss Molly

Produced by Prince Buster.

BLUE BEAT 85 Come on Over/Come Back My Darling

Produced by Prince Buster.

BLUE BEAT 100 In My Heart/BELL'S GROUP: Kingston 13

Produced by Prince Buster.

BLUE BEAT 130 Should Be Ashamed/Marjorie

Produced by Prince Buster.

BLUE BEAT 141 Joybells/Going Down to Canaan

Produced by Duke Reid.

ISLAND 004 Travel On/Teach Me Baby

Produced by Leslie Kong.

ISLAND 006 The Hop/Tell It to Me

Produced by Leslie Kong. (a) Breezy performance as notable for the chirping harmonica, jaunty brass parts and sax solo as for the singer's sublime vocals.

ISLAND 011 Forward March/Please Don't Talk About Me

Produced by Leslie Kong. (a) A celebration, of course, of Jamaican independence, perfectly capturing the optimism and joy surrounding the moment. A passing similarity to some of PRINCE BUSTER's recent work, however, helped ignited a conflict which eventually demanded the Jamaican government's intervention.

ISLAND 013 Cherry Home/See & Blind

Produced by Leslie Kong.

DERRICK MORGAN & MARTIN RILEY

Vocal duo featuring DERRICK MORGAN and MARTIN RILEY (later of THE UNIQUES).

ISLAND 024 Come On/MONTY & THE CYCLONES: Organisation

Produced by Leslie Kong.

ERIC MORRIS

BLUE BEAT 74 My Forty Five/I've Tried Everything

Produced by Prince Buster.

BLUE BEAT 81 Sinners Repent & Pray/Now & Forever More

Produced by Prince Buster.

BLUE BEAT 83 Money Can't Buy Life/ALTON ELLIS: True Love

Produced by Prince Buster.

BLUE BEAT 105 Pack up Your Troubles/Oh What a Smile Can Do

Produced by Prince Buster. Recorded with D COSMO WITH DRUMBAGO ALL- STARS.

BLUE BEAT 115 GI Lady/Going to the River

Produced by Prince Buster.

BLUE BEAT 128 Over the Hills/Lazy Women

Produced by Prince Buster.

BLUE BEAT 137 Miss Peggy's Grandmother/BUSTER'S GROUP: Megaton

Produced by Prince Buster.

BLUE BEAT 140 Seven Long Years/For Your Love

Produced by Prince Buster.

OWEN & MILLIE SMALL

Vocal duo of OWEN GRAY and future solo star MILLIE SMALL.

BLUE BEAT 96 Sit & Cry/Do You Know

ROY PANTON

Vocalist, also recorded as a duo with MONTY MORRIS, ANNETTE, ENID CUMBERLAND, MILLIE SMALL, PATSY TODD, PAULETTE WILLIAMS, YVONNE (ADAMS); also with DUKE ALL STARS. (X) LEON & OWEN

PRINCE BUSTER

See PRINCE BUSTER entry on page 219.

BLUE BEAT 101 They Got to Go/My Sound that Goes Around

Produced by Prince Buster. (a) Recorded at Buster's first recording session, this two-pronged attack is aimed at the rich in general and more specifically at Coxsone Dodd and Duke Reid, as the young producer slams his way into the music industry. Cowritten with Derrick Morgan, after the two men's falling out Buster recycled the rhythm as "They Got to Come" and Morgan recut it as his scathing retort "Blazing Fire" before the Prince recorded the definitive version as "Madness."

BLUE BEAT 116 Independence Song/RICO & BLUEBEATS: August 1962

Produced by Prince Buster.

BLUE BEAT 133 Time Longer than Rope/Fake King

Produced by Prince Buster.

BLUE BEAT 138 One Hand Washes the Other/Cowboy Comes to Town

Produced by Prince Buster.

(PRINCE) BUSTER'S GROUP

(X) ERIC MORRIS

ERNEST RANGLIN ORCHESTRA

b 1932 (Manchester, JA). Guitarist Ranglin was one of Jamaica's most ubiquitous sessionmen.

ISLAND 015 Harmonica Twist/Mitty Gritty

THE RHYTHM ACES

ISLAND 032 Christmas/TOP GRANT: A Christmas Drink
Produced by Chris Blackwell.

BLUE BEAT 134 I'll Be There/DON DRUMMOND: Dew Drops

BERESFORD RICKETTS

BLUE BEAT 107 You Better Be Gone/I've Been Walking
Recorded with THE BLUE BEATS.

STARLITE 079 I'm Going to Cry/Waiting for Me

RICO (RODRIGUEZ)

(X) CLIVE BAILEY, LLOYD FLOWERS, PRINCE BUSTER, EMMANUEL RODRIGUES

PLANETONE 1 London Here I Come/Midnight in Ethiopia
(a) One of several "farewells" to Jamaica cut by Rodriguez before he relocated to the UK.

PLANETONE 4 Planet Rock/You Win

PLANETONE 5 Youth Boogie/Western Serenade

LLOYD ROBINSON

Member of THE TARTANS. Also recorded as a duo with GLEN BROWN, DEVON RUSSELL, ZOOT SIMMS. (X) LLOYD CLARKE

BLUE BEAT 122 Give Me a Chance/When You Walk

EMMANUEL RODRIGUES ORKESTRA

See RICO.

ISLAND 022 Rico Special/BUNNY & SKITTER: A Little Mashin'

ROY & MILLIE

Vocal duo comprising ROY PANTON and MILLIE SMALL.

ISLAND 005 We'll Meet/ROLAND ALPHONSO: Back Beat
Produced by Roy Robinson. (a) Those unmistakably strident, squeaky vocals belong to a young Millie Small, paired with the dulcet tones of Roy Panton on this jumped up, jazz-pop duet.

ROY & PATSY

Vocal duo comprising ROY PANTON and PATSY TODD.

BLUE BEAT 118 My Happy Home/In Your Arms Dear
Recorded with HERMAN HERSANG & HIS COMBO.

RUDDY & SKETTO & RECO'S ALL-STARS

Vocal duo featuring SKETTO RICH.

DICE 5 Summer Is Just Around the Corner/Nothing Like Time

DEVON RUSSELL

d 6/18/92. Vocalist with the TARTANS. Also recorded as a duo with LLOYD ROBINSON, CEDRIC MYTON. Subsequently relaunched his career as DJ RANKING DEVON.

THE SHINERS

(X) ROLAND ALPHONSO

SIMMS & ROBINSON

Vocal duo featuring ZOOT SIMMS and LLOYD ROBINSON.

BLUE BEAT 143 White Christmas/Searching

WINSTON & ROY

Vocal duo featuring WINSTON STEWART and ROY ROBINSON.

BLUE BEAT 80 Babylon Gone/COUNT OSSIE ON AFRICAN DRUMS: First Gone
Produced by Harry Mudie.

1963

THE AFRO ENCHANTERS

ISLAND 071 Peace & Love/Wayward African

BOBBY AITKEN

(X) LAUREL AITKEN

BLUE BEAT 146 Don't Leave Me/Mom & Dad
Recorded with TINSE.

RIO 14 I've Told You/Please Go Back

RIO 15 It Takes a Friend/LAUREL AITKEN: Sunshine

LAUREL AITKEN

(X) BOBBY AITKEN

BLACK SWAN 401 Lion of Judah/Remember My Darling

BLACK SWAN 411 The Saint/Go Gal Go

BLUE BEAT 164 Zion City/Swing Low Sweet Chariot
Produced by Duke Reid. (a) A boogie with a gospel theme, its exuberance heightened by the jazzy brass.

BLUE BEAT 194 Little Girl/Daniel Saw the Stone

DICE 12 Oh Jean/Rivers of Tears

DICE 13 Sweet Jamaica/Bossa Nova Hop

DUKE 1002 Low Down Dirty Girl/DUKE REID & HIS GROUP: Pink Lane Shuffle
Produced by Duke Reid.

ISLAND 092 I Shall Remove/We Got to Move
Produced by Leslie Kong.

ISLAND 095 What a Weeping/Zion City Wall
Produced by Leslie Kong.

ISLAND 099 In My Soul/One More River to Cross
Produced by Leslie Kong.

RIO 11 Adam & Eve/BOBBY AITKEN: Devil Woman
Produced by Graeme Goodall.

RIO 12 Mary/Hometown
Produced by Graeme Goodall.

RIO 13 Bad Minded Woman/Life

Produced by Graeme Goodall. (a) Aitken tells a gossiping woman just where to go (home, actually) on this classic R&B laced song, delivered with passion and jazzed up by the backing musicians.

RIO 17 Devil or Angel/Fire

Produced by Graeme Goodall.

RIO 18 Freedom Train/Peace Perfect Peace

Produced by Graeme Goodall.

ROLAND ALPHONSO

(X) CORNELL CAMPBELL, THE CHARMERS

THEO BECKFORD

ISLAND 106 Boiler Man/Daphne

BILLY & BOBBY

(X) BABA BROOKS

THE BLUES MASTERS

Featuring BABA BROOKS.

ISLAND 078 5 o'Clock Whistle/African Blood

Produced by Justin & Duke Yap.

BONNIE & SKITTO

Duo featuring BONNIE FRANKSON and SKETTO RICH.

ISLAND 122 Get Ready/DON DRUMMOND: The Rocket

Produced by Coxsone Dodd. (a) actually performed by THE MAYTALS.

SONNY BRADSHAW

Veteran JA jazz-man, later head of the Jamaican musicians' union. His band included HERBIE GRAY.

DUKE 1003 Yellow Birds/Festival Jump Up

Produced by Duke Reid.

BABA BROOKS

b Oswald Brooks, 1935 (Kingston, JA). One of the key trumpeters of the early ska-rock steady period, appears on many more records than he is credited for here. (X) HIGGS & WILSON.

ISLAND 096 Bank to Bank (parts 1/2)

Produced by Duke Reid. (a) Brooks adapts the old mento nugget "River to the Bank," modernizing it with jazz flourishes and a crashing, syncopated beat.

ISLAND 127 Three Blind Mice/BILLY & BOBBY: We Ain't Got Nothing

R&B 125 Watermelon Man/STRANGER COLE: Things Come to Those Who Wait

(a) American jazz-man Herbie Hancock wrote the perfect showcase for Brooks' brass, the syncopated beat powering the song, while the horns interlace, grab the spotlight, and join together to blast out the hook.

MARIE BRYANT

KALYPSO 28 Don't Touch My Nylon/Little Boy

BUBBLES

DUKE 1001 Bopping in the Barnyard/The Wasp

Produced by Duke Reid.

CORNELL CAMPBELL

b 1948 (JA). Campbell's striking falsetto led THE SENSATIONS and THE ETERNALS; also recorded as a duo with ROY PANTON, ROY SHIRLEY. His sister CECILE was a latter-day member of the SOULETTES.

ISLAND 039 Rosabelle/Turndown Date

(b) The young singer shines on this endearing ska single, giving an emotive performance on the stood-up theme, ably assisted by the tight backing band.

ISLAND 083 Each Lonely Night/ROLAND ALPHONSO: Streamline

THE CHARMERS

BLUE BEAT 157 Time After Time/Done Me Wrong

Produced by Prince Buster.

R&B 118 Angel Love/My Heart

R&B 121 Oh Why Baby/ROLAND ALPHONSO: Perhaps

LLOYD CLARKE

ISLAND 045 Japanese Girl/He's Coming

(a) The intro and outro are the only nods to the east on this swinging R&B laced boogie, where the sax controls the room, while Clarke handles lyrical duties with aplomb.

RIO 16 Love Me/Half as Much

JIMMY CLIFF

BLACK SWAN 403 The Man/You Are Never too Old

Produced by Leslie Kong.

ISLAND 062 My Lucky Day/One-Eyed Jacks

Produced by Leslie Kong.

ISLAND 070 King of Kings/SIR PERCY: Oh Yeah

Produced by Leslie Kong.

ISLAND 112 Miss Universe/The Prodigal

Produced by Leslie Kong.

CLIVE & GLORIA

R&B 113 Change of Plan/Little Gloria

STRANGER COLE

b Wilburn Theodore Cole, 1945 (JA). He was nicknamed Stranger by his family, after they noticed he did not resemble any of his kin. Also recorded as a duo with GLADSTONE ANDERSON, KEN BOOTHE, CLAUDETTE, HORTENSE ELLIS, PATSY TODD. Still active, he is now known as STRANGE JAH COLE. (X) BABA BROOKS, RICHARD BROTHERS

BLUE BEAT 165 Rough and Tough/The Mood I Am In

Produced by Duke Reid. (a) According to JOE HIGGS, LEE PERRY wrote the lyric; Reid co-opted it for Cole after deciding Perry's voice was not good enough, and apparently, Perry's objections were met by Reid's fist. As for the song, it may not be particularly catchy, but Cole makes everything he sings sound good, aided by the slow, stomping beat, and the punchy musical break.

BLUE BEAT 195 Miss Dreamer/RICO & HIS BLUES BAND: Blues from the Hills

ISLAND 110 Stranger at the Door/Conqueror

ISLAND 114 Last Love/STRANGER & KEN: Hush Baby

ISLAND 126 We Are Rolling/Millie Maw

R&B 129 Morning Star/Beat Up Your Gum

THE COLLEGE BOYS

BLUE BEAT 202 Love Is a Treasure/Someone Will Be There

FRANK COSMO

aka COSMO; of COSMO & DENNIS DUO.

ISLAND 058 Revenge/Laughin' at You

ISLAND 073 Dear Dreams/Go Go Go

ISLAND 100 Merry Christmas/Greetings from Beverleys

R&B 119 I Love You/DON DRUMMOND: Close of Play

BLUE BEAT 175 Gypsy Woman/Do unto Others

(LORD) CREATOR & NORMA (FRAZIER)

Vocal duo comprising LORD CREATOR and NORMA FRAZIER.

ISLAND 105 We Will Be Lovers/Come on Pretty Baby

DESMOND DEKKER (aka DECKER, DEKKAR)

See entry for DESMOND DEKKER on page 90.

ISLAND 054 Honour Your Mother & Father/Madgie

Produced by Leslie Kong. (a) Recorded with BEVERLEY'S ALL STARS. Thankfully Dekker was a persistent young man, as it took several attempts before he finally auditioned for producer Leslie Kong (with whom he recorded exclusively until the producer's death in 1971). Much to both men's amazement, and the delight of parents across the island, Desmond's self penned debut, arranged by THEOPHILUS BECKFORD, shot to the top of the JA chart.

ISLAND 111 Parents/Labour for Learning

Produced by Leslie Kong. (a) A blatant attempt to follow-up his earlier hit, thematically and musically.

DENZIL

Vocalist DENZIL DENNIS. b 10/13/45 (Manchester, JA). His elder cousin is producer LLOYD DALEY. Recorded as a duo with FRANK COSMO, before relocating to UK, where he recorded with LAUREL AITKEN under his own name; also recorded a number of singles as ALAN MARTIN. Next joined DANDY LIVINGSTONE and PAT RHODEN as the BROTHER DAN ALL STARS, also recording as a duo with Rhoden, before relaunching solo career as DD DENNIS and DENNIS, and forming new duo with MILTON HAMILTON, aka THE CLASSICS.

BLUE BEAT 181 Seven Nights in Rome/Love Is for Fools

Produced by Laurel Aitken. (a/b) Featuring English jazz musicians Red Price and Ronnie Scott.

DERRICK & PATSY

BLUE BEAT 152 Little Brown Girl/Mow Sen Wa

Produced by Duke Reid.

BLUE BEAT 160 Trying to Make You Mine/Hold Me

Produced by Duke Reid.

ISLAND 055 Sea Wave/Look Before You Leap

Produced by Duke Reid. (b) A word of warning from the effervescent Morgan and his inimitable cohort, with a chorus guaranteed to be rattling round your head for days.

ERROL DIXON

CARNIVAL 7001 Oo Wee Baby/Twisting & Shaking

CARNIVAL 7004 Mean & Evil Woman/Tutti Frutti

ISLAND 069 I Love You/Tell Me More

DRUMBAGO

b Arkland Parkes. Vintage session drummer also a renowned fife player, who continued performing even when semi-invalided.

ISLAND 085 I Am Drunk/Sea Breeze

DON DRUMMOND

(X) BONNIE & SKITTO, FRANK COSMO, ROY & MILLIE, STRANGER & PATSY

BLACK SWAN 406 Scrap Iron/DRAGONAIRES: Prevention

Produced by Coxsone Dodd.

BLUE BEAT 179 Reload/Far East

Produced by Coxsone Dodd.

ISLAND 094 Scandal/My Ideal

Produced by Coxsone Dodd. (a) A reveille trumpet kicks off this swinging instrumental, wrapped around a solid ska beat and the trombonist's upbeat melody.

R&B 103 Royal Flush/MAYTALS: Matthew Mark

Produced by Coxsone Dodd. (b) With a coterie of SKATALITES skanking in the background, TOOTS HIBBERT passionately testifies about his religious beliefs, accompanied by affirming "Hallelujah"s from MATHIAS and GORDON.

R&B 105 The Shock/TONETTES: Tell Me You're Mine

R&B 123 Rock Away/HI-TONES: You Hold the Key

(a) The musicians don't really rock, but title aside, this is a tight variation on TOMMY MCCOOK's "Bond Street" musical theme.

SHENLEY DUFFUS

ISLAND 036 Give to Get/What You Gonna Do

ISLAND 063 Fret Man Fret/Doreen

Produced by Coxsone Dodd. (a) LEE PERRY wrote the lyrics and later claimed this was his only Studio One era composition to actually credit him on the label.

ISLAND 093 What a Disaster/I Am Rich

Produced by Coxsone Dodd. (a) Duffus' debut recording for Dodd was intended by lyricist LEE PERRY to salve the then-ongoing feud between PRINCE BUSTER and DERRICK MORGAN.

ISLAND 115 Know the Lord/TOMMY MCCOOK: Ska Ba

Produced by Coxsone Dodd. (b) One of the first tunes TOMMY MCCOOK wrote after returning to Jamaica in 1962, a pleasing instrumental with FRANK ANDERSON leading on trumpet.

ISLAND 125 Easy Squeal/Things Ain't Going Right

DUKE REID'S GROUP

(X) LAUREL AITKEN

CLANCY ECCLES

ISLAND 044 Judgement/Baby Please
Produced by Coxsone Dodd.

ISLAND 098 Glory Hallelujah/Hot Rod
Produced by Coxsone Dodd.

WILFRED JACKIE EDWARDS

BLACK SWAN 404 Why Make Believe/Do You Want Me Again
Produced by Chris Blackwell.

EDWARDS GROUP

ISLAND 082 He Gave You to Me/Kings Priests & Prophets

HORTENSE ELLIS

R&B 101 I'll Come Softly/I'm in Love
The male vocals are provided by brother Alton.

JACKIE ESTICK

ISLAND 042 Since You've Been Gone/Daisy I Love You

JACKIE FOSTER

One of the earliest of London entrepreneur Sonny Roberts' UK- based artists.

PLANETONE 13 Oh Leona/I Fell in Love

BASIL GABBIDON

BLUE BEAT 155 Ena Mena/Since You Are Gone
BLUE BEAT 161 I'll Find Love/MELLOW LARKS: What You Gonna Do
ISLAND 076 I Bet You Don't Know/3 x 7
ISLAND 089 St Louis Woman/Get on the Ball

GIRL SATCHMO

BLUE BEAT 156 Don't Be Sad/Brother Joe

RONNIE GORDON

R&B 127 Shake Some Time/Comin' Home

TOP GRANT

ISLAND 034 Searching/David & Goliath
ISLAND 052 Suzie/Jenny
ISLAND 072 Riverbank Coberley/Nancy
ISLAND 074 Money Money Money/Have Mercy on Me
ISLAND 077 War in Africa/The Birds

OWEN GRAY

BLUE BEAT 147 Big Mabel/Don't Come Knocking
BLUE BEAT 188 Call Me My Pet/Give Me Your Love
BLUE BEAT 201 Snow Falling/Oowee Baby
Credited to OWEN GRAY & HIS BIG BROTHER.
CHEK 101 Come on Baby/My One Desire
ISLAND 048 I'm Still Waiting/Last Night

DERRICK HARRIOTT

BLUE BEAT 178 Be True/I Won't Cry
Produced by Derrick Harriott.

THE HI TONES

(X) DON DRUMMOND
ISLAND 086 Ten Virgins/Too Young to Love

HIGGS & WILSON

BLUE BEAT 190 If You Want a Pardon/BABA BROOKS BAND: Musical Communion
Produced by Duke Reid. (b) The trumpeter adds a jaunty note to this ska instrumental in a religious mood.

ISLAND 081 Last Saturday Morning/Praise the Lord
R&B 109 Let Me Know/Bye & Bye

JOHN HOLT

See entry for JOHN HOLT on page 117. Also a member of THE PARAGONS.

ISLAND 041 I Cried a Tear/Forever I'll Stay
Produced by Leslie Kong.

JIMMY JAMES

R&B 112 Jump Children/Tell Me
Produced by Lindon Pottinger.

AL T JOE

BLUE BEAT 166 Goodbye Dreamboat/Please Forgive Me
BLUE BEAT 169 Fatso/Slow Boat
DICE 9 Rise Jamaica/I'm on My Own

KEITH & ENID

DICE 14 Sacred Vow/My Dreams
DICE 20 Just a Closer Walk/Don't Yield to Temptation

KENT & DIMPLES

Vocal duo featuring KENT BROWN and DIMPLE HINDS.
ISLAND 046 Day Is Done/Linger a While

LAUREL & OWEN

Vocal duo featuring LAUREL AITKEN and OWEN GRAY.
BLUE BEAT 149 She's Going to Napoli/Have Mercy Mr Percy

BYRON LEE & THE DRAGONAIRES

(X) DON DRUMMOND

JOE LIGES

Liges was a pseudonym for DELROY WILSON.
BLUE BEAT 172 Spit in the Sky/Tell Me What
Produced by Coxsone Dodd.

LITTLE WILLIE

b Wilbert Francis.
BLUE BEAT 151 Settle Down/I'm Ashamed

LORD BEGINNER

CALYPSO 1 Victory Test Match—Calypso/Sgt Brown
Originally released in 1950, revived to launch Melodisc's new specialist label.

LORD CREATOR

KALYPSO 24 Peeping Tom/Second Hand Piano

LORD DANIEL

KALYPSO 26 Small Island Gal/?

LORD KITCHENER

CALYPSO 2 Kitch/Rebound Wife

CALYPSO 3 Muriel & the Bug/Nora & the Yankee

CALYPSO 4 Kitch Take It Easy/Redhead

CALYPSO 5 Drink a Rum/Your Wife

CALYPSO 6 Too Late Itch/Saxophone #2

CALYPSO 7 Wife & Mother/Mango Tree

MELODISC 1577 Jamaica Turkey/Edna What You Want

LORD NELSON

STATESIDE 189 I Got an Itch/Problems on My Mind

LORD ROSE

KALYPSO 25 Independent Jamaica/Twistin' Uncle

LORD TANAMO

ISLAND 108 Come Down/I Am Holding On

Produced by Lindon Pottinger. (a) The SKATALITES' vocalist cuttingly puts a braggart in his place, as the band instrumentally boast of their own devastating talent.

ROBERT MARLEY

See entry for BOB MARLEY & THE WAILERS on page 158.

ISLAND 088 Judge Not/Do You Still Love Me

Produced by Leslie Kong. (a) A very young Marley belts out this song's message of "don't throw stones." Adding a recorder is a clever touch, taking the edge off what could otherwise have been a rather strident song.

ISLAND 128 One Cup of Coffee/ERNEST RANGLIN: Exodus

Produced by Leslie Kong. (a) A punchy SKATALITES rhythm underpins Marley's sad tale of a final break-up between husband and wife: "I've bought the money like the lawyer said to do." (b) Ranglin and his band give the theme song from the movie a ska beat, a touch of jazz, some lovely guitar work, and magnificent brass.

ALAN MARTIN

aka DENZIL DENNIS.

RIO 3 The Party/Indeed

RIO 6 You Came Late/Dreaming

RIO 9 Secretly/Fame & Fortune

RIO 10 Mother Brother/Tell Me

THE MARVELS

BLUE BEAT 176 Hallelujah/Helping Ages Past

BLUE BEAT 191 Sonia/The More We Are Together

THE MAYTALS

See MAYTALS entry on page 178. aka THE VIKINGS, THE FLAMES/ALTON ELLIS & THE FLAMES. (X) DON DRUMMOND, TOMMY MCCOOK.

TOMMY MCCOOK

See the entry for THE SKATALITES on page 262.

ISLAND 102 Adam's Apple/MAYTALS: Every Time

Produced by Coxsone Dodd. (a) aka "Don't Bother Me No More," a runaway instrumental with the horns dancing all over one another.

ISLAND 118 Below Zero/LEE PERRY: Never Get Weary

Produced by Coxsone Dodd.

ISLAND 124 Junior Jive/HORACE "BB" SEATON: Power

Produced by Coxsone Dodd. (a) A bit of a leaden plod this, with only McCook appearing to care what happens at the end. Sweet melody, but barely essential.

THE MELLOW LARKS

(X) BASIL GABBIDON

THE MELODY ENCHANTERS

Vocal group featuring KINGSLEY DAVID, BASIL MARTIN and ANTHONY DAVIS, formed 1959, breaking up around 1962. Davis formed THE GATHERERS.

BLACK SWAN 408 Oh Ma Oh Pa/TOP GRANT: Coronation Street

Produced by Chris Blackwell.

ISLAND 049 Enchanter's Ball (aka Crusader's Ball)/I'll Be True

Produced by Chris Blackwell.

R&B 117 Gone Gone/Blueberry Hill

Produced by Chris Blackwell.

MILLIE

b Millie Small, 10/8/48 (JA). Also recorded as a duo with OWEN GRAY, JACKIE EDWARDS, ROY PANTON.

FONTANA 425 Don't You Know/Until You're Mine

Produced by Chris Blackwell. (a)/(b) Setting the pace for Millie's immediate career, horn-driven pop with the hint of something tropical in the background — but Millie's signature vocals notwithstanding, scarcely distinguishable from any other British Invasion girl singer single of the era.

THE MOONLIGHTERS

ISLAND 043 Going Out/Hold My Hands

DERRICK MORGAN

BLACK SWAN 402 Street Girl/Edmarine

BLUE BEAT 148 Jezebel/Burnette

Produced by Charlie Moo.

BLUE BEAT 177 Patricia My Dear/The Girl I Left Behind

BLUE BEAT 187 Tears on My Pillow/You Should Have Known

BLUE BEAT 196 Telephone/Life Is Tough

Produced by Prince Buster.

ISLAND 037 Dorothy/Leave Her Alone

Produced by Leslie Kong.

ISLAND 051 Blazing Fire/DERRICK & PATSY: I'm in a Jam

Produced by Leslie Kong.

ISLAND 053 No Raise No Praise/Loving Baby

Produced by Leslie Kong. (a) Morgan's scathing retort to PRINCE BUSTER's public tantrums over borrowed melody lines and breaks. The line "once a man, twice a child, my friend" alone was cutting enough that Buster would have to record yet another derogatory reply.

ISLAND 080 Angel with Blue Eyes/Corner Stone

Produced by Duke Reid.

ISLAND 091 Sendin' this Message/L LAWRENCE: Garden of Eden

RIO 1 Blazing Fire/Edmarine

Produced by Leslie Kong. (a) Morgan hits back at PRINCE BUSTER's "Black Chineman," (a searing indictment of the singer and his producer Leslie Kong) with lyrics equally insulting. Wrapping them in the "They Got to Go" melody which he co-wrote with Buster, just adds further injury.

ERIC MORRIS

(X) ZOOT SIMMS

BLUE BEAT 184 Sweet Love/(PRINCE) BUSTER, DERRICK (MORGAN), ERIC (MORRIS): Country Girl

Produced by Prince Buster.

JACKIE OPEL

See entry for THE SKATALITES on page 262. Also recorded as a duos DOREEN & JACKIE, HORTENSE & JACKIE.

JUMP-UP 512 TV in Jamaica/Worrell's Captaincy

(b) 1963 saw the West Indies cricket team lash the English once again, in a game made all the more significant by the retirement of Barbados-born captain Frank MM Worrell.

ROY PANTON

BLUE BEAT 182 Mighty Ruler/Run Old Man

KENTRICK PATRICK

aka LORD CREATOR.

ISLAND 066 Man to Man/ROLAND ALPHONSO: Blockade

ISLAND 079 Don't Stay out Late/Forever & Ever

(a) Early 60s MOR pop goes ska. The horn solo salvages it from total commercial meltdown, although few could quarrel with Patrick's smooth vocal ability. UK band Reggae Regular scored a mini-hit with a cover of the song in 1980.

ISLAND 104 The End of the World/Little Princess

The band creates a wonderfully smokey, moody atmosphere for the balladeer's passionate delivery on this cover of Skeeter Davis' lovelorn epic.

ISLAND 119 Golden Love/Beyond

PAULETTE & DELROY

Vocal duo featuring DELROY WILSON and PAULETTE WILLIAMS.

ISLAND 120 Little Lover/Lovin' Baby

LASCELLES PERKINS & YVONNE (ADAMS)

Vocal duo. YVONNE also recorded with SONNY BURKE, DERRICK MORGAN, ROY PANTON.

ISLAND 038 Tango Lips/DENNIS SINDREY: Rub Up

LEE PERRY

See entry for LEE PERRY on page 208.

R&B 102 Prince in the Black/Don't Copy

Produced by Coxsone Dodd. (a/b) Lee Perry's first ever international release (other sources erroneously credit "Old for New").

R&B 104 Old for New/Prince & Duke

Produced by Coxsone Dodd. (a/b) Not content with jabbing PRINCE BUSTER once again with "Old And New," Perry adds DUKE REID to his list of targets on the flip.

R&B 106 Mad Head/Man & Wife

Produced by Coxsone Dodd. (a) A very deliberate parody of PRINCE BUSTER's "Madness." (b) A tale of marital infidelity, as a man discovers his wife and brother are lovers.

PRINCE BUSTER

(X) THE SCHOOLBOYS

BLUE BEAT 150 Run Man Run/Danny, Dane & Lorraine

Produced by Prince Buster.

BLUE BEAT 153 Oh We/ERIC MORRIS: Lonely Blue Boy

Produced by Prince Buster.

BLUE BEAT 158 Open Up Bartender/Enjoy It

Produced by Prince Buster.

BLUE BEAT 163 King Duke Sir/See Them in My Sight

Produced by Prince Buster.

BLUE BEAT 167 10 Commandments of Man/Buster's Welcome

Produced by Prince Buster. (a) Today best described as the male chauvinist book of rules, the Prince addresses women on appropriate conduct when in his royal presence. Sternly spoken over a repeated snatch of melody, it's hard to take this song seriously now, and it was probably equally laughed about in its day. Behind His Highness' back, of course. Reissued as BLUE BEAT 334, also PHILIPS BF1552.

BLUE BEAT 170 Madness/Toothache

Produced by Prince Buster. (a) Musically Buster turned ska inside out on this classic single, utilizing not just the rhythm section, but the brass players to pump up the syncopated beat. A thinly veiled tale of Rastafarian persecution, the single's power extended both across the ocean and generations, heavily influencing the original UK rudies and their 2-Tone progeny. The rhythm is lifted from Buster's earlier "They Got to Go."

BLUE BEAT 173 Burning Creation/Boop

Produced by Prince Buster.

BLUE BEAT 180 3 More Rivers to Cross/RAYMOND HARPER & PRINCE BUSTER ALL-STARS: African Blood

Produced by Prince Buster. (b) Led by trumpeter Harper (later of THE SUPERSONICS), the big band brass sound of the past is beautifully revisited on this slow, swing song with a syncopated beat.

BLUE BEAT 186 Fowl Thief/Remember Me

Produced by Prince Buster.

BLUE BEAT 189 Watch It Blackhead/Hello My Dear

Produced by Prince Buster.

BLUE BEAT 192 Rollin' Stone/RICO & HIS BLUES BAND: His Day
Produced by Prince Buster. (a) Credited to PRINCE BUSTER & CHARMERS.

BLUE BEAT 197 Window Shopping/Sodom & Gomorrah
Produced by Prince Buster.

BLUE BEAT 199 Spider & Fly/Three Blind Mice
Produced by Prince Buster.

BLUE BEAT 200 Wash All Your Troubles Away/RICO & THE BLUE BEATS: Soul of Africa
Produced by Prince Buster. (b) Though trombonist Rodriguez would spend much of his career in London, he was also responsible for some of the early overtly Rastafarian-themed singles released in Jamaica. "Soul of Africa" itself was inspired in part by the spell Rodriguez spent living in COUNT OSSIE's commune in the Wareika hills in the early 1950s. Reissued as BLUE BEAT 210.

DICE 6 They Got to Come/These Are the Times
Produced by Prince Buster. A revision of the earlier "They Got to Go."

DICE 11 Blackhead Chineman/You Ask
Produced by Prince Buster. (a) Buster's vitriolic assault on DERRICK MORGAN's newly consummated partnership with producer LESLIE KONG.

DICE 18 World Peace/The Lion Roars
Produced by Prince Buster. Credited to PRINCE BUSTER & HAZEL.

PRINCE BUSTER'S ALL-STARS
(X) ZOOT SIMMS

ERNEST RANGLIN
(X) BOB MARLEY

THE RICHARD BROS
ISLAND 060 I Need a Girl/Desperate Lover
ISLAND 109 I Shall Wear a Crown/BABA BROOKS: Robin Hood

RICO
(X) STRANGER COLE, PRINCE BUSTER

LLOYD ROBINSON
BLUE BEAT 159 I Need Your Love/You Told Me

ROY & ANNETTE
Vocal duo featuring ROY PANTON & ANNETTE (of SHENLEY . . .).
R&B 107 My Baby/Go Your Ways
Produced by Coxsone Dodd.
R&B 111 I Mean It/LESTER STERLING: Air Raid Shelter
Produced by Coxsone Dodd.

ROY & MILLIE
BLACK SWAN 409 Cherry I Love You/You're the Only One
BLACK SWAN 410 Oh Merna/DON DRUMMOND: Dog War Bossa Nova
BLUE BEAT 154 Over & Over/I'll Go

ISLAND 090 There'll Come a Day/I Don't Want You
ISLAND 050 This World/Never Say Goodbye

ROY & PAULETTE
Vocal duo featuring ROY PANTON and PAULETTE WILLIAMS.
ISLAND 067 Have You Seen My Baby/Since You're Gone

RUDDY & SKETTO
BLUE BEAT 198 Was It Me/Minna Don't Deceive Me
DICE 7 Little Schoolgirl/Hush Baby
Recorded with BARON TWIST & HIS KNIGHTS.
DICE 10 Mr Postman/Christmas Blues
Produced by Laurel Aitken.
DICE 16 Hold the Fire/Good Morning Mr Jones
DICE 19 Never Set You Free/Brothers & Sisters

THE SCHOOLBOYS
Featuring vocalist Winston Matthews. See entry for THE WAILING SOULS on page 297.
BLUE BEAT 162 Little Boy Blue/PRINCE BUSTER: Money
Produced by Prince Buster.
BLUE BEAT 174 Little Dilly/The Joker
Produced by Prince Buster.

THE SCHOOLGIRLS
BLUE BEAT 168 Love Another Love/Little Keithie
Produced by Prince Buster.
BLUE BEAT 185 Live Up to Justice/Give Up
Produced by Prince Buster.

HORACE "BB" SEATON
b Harris Lloyd Seaton, 9/3/44 (Kingston, JA). aka BIBBY, BB SEATON, a member of THE ASTRONAUTS, CONSCIOUS MINDS, THE GAYLADS, THE MESSENGERS.
ISLAND 123 I'm So Glad/Tell Me

ZOOT SIMMS
Not to be confused with the US jazz-man. Also recorded as a duo with LLOYD ROBINSON and ELMOND.
BLUE BEAT 183 Press Along/PRINCE BUSTER ALL-STARS: 100 Ton Megaton
Produced by Prince Buster.
BLUE BEAT 193 Golden Pen/ERIC MORRIS: So You Shot Reds
Produced by Prince Buster.

SIR PERCY
(X) JIMMY CLIFF

ADAM SMITH
ISLAND 057 I Wonder Why/My Prayer

LESTER STERLING
See the entry for the SKATALITES on page 262. (X) ROY & ANNETTE.
ISLAND 121 Clean the City/Long Walk Home
R&B 115 Gravy Cool/WINSTON & BIBBY: Lover Lover Man

STRANGER & KEN

Vocal duo featuring STRANGER COLE and KEN BOOTHE. (X) STRANGER COLE

R&B 120 Thick in Love/All Your Friends

STRANGER & PATSY

Vocal duo featuring STRANGER COLE and PATSY TODD.

BLUE BEAT 171 When You Call My Name/Take My Heart

Produced by Duke Reid. (a) The lovebirds deliver up an upbeat romantic chart-topper, featuring some nice work by members of the SKATALITES (as the DUKE REID ALL STARS).

ISLAND 113 Senor & Senorita/DON DRUMMOND: Snowboy

SUGAR & DANDY

London based vocal duo featuring TITO SIMONE and DANDY LIVINGSTONE.

CARNIVAL 7006 One Man Went to Mow/Cryin'

TONY TOMAS

(X) TONY & LOUISE

THE TONETTES

Vocal group featuring MARLENE WEBBER. (X) DON DRUMMOND

ISLAND 064 Love that Is Real/Pretty Baby

TONY & LOUISE

Vocal duo. (X) TONY WASHINGTON

ISLAND 059 Ups & Downs/TONY TOMAS: Brixton Lewisham

THE VIKINGS

aka THE MAYTALS.

ISLAND 035 Maggie Don't Leave Me/Henchman

Produced by Coxsone Dodd.

ISLAND 065 Hallelujah/Helpin' Ages

Produced by Coxsone Dodd. (a) The Maytals' first release for Coxsone Dodd, and their first #1. There's so much going on here that it's hard to keep track—a jiving ska beat, a throbbing bass rhythm, a punchy piano, brassy flares and solos (all courtesy of the SKATALITES), and the magnificent trio engaged in a singing spelling lesson.

ISLAND 075 6 & 7 Books of Moses/Zacions

Produced by Coxsone Dodd. (a) Penned by TOOTS HIBBERT himself, this song is all over the place as the ska beat, Hibbert's spiritual-inspired lead vocal, a happy harmonica and a horn solo all vie loudly for attention. But above this confusion, the harmonies still stand out, helping place the Maytals at the forefront of the explosion of vocal trios.

ISLAND 101 Never Grow Old/Irene

Produced by Coxsone Dodd. (a) The Maytals joyously embrace eternal life through love of the Lord, as the SKATALITES enthusiastically join the festivities.

ISLAND 107 Just Got to Be/You Make Me Do

Produced by Coxsone Dodd. (a) A flurry of close harmonies punctuate this love song set to a ska beat, with the SKATALITES adding further musical excitement.

ISLAND 117 Fever/Cheer Up

Produced by Coxsone Dodd. (a) The Maytals' second single . . . and second #1.

TONY WASHINGTON

ISLAND 068 Something Gotta Be Done/TONY & LOUISE: I Have Said

DUKE WHITE

ISLAND 084 It's Over/Forever

DELROY WILSON

b 1948 (Kingston, JA)/d 3/6/95. Released one UK 45 as JOE LIGES. Also recorded as a duo with CLIVE WILSON, PAULETTE WILLIAMS, HORTENSE ELLIS, KING SPORTY, DANDY LIVINGSTONE; and with THE TENNORS. Ska pioneer who readily adapted to rock steady, and remained in great demand during the early DJ period, recording with DENNIS ALCAPONE, LIZZY, & U-ROY.

BLACK SWAN 405 Spit in the Sky/Voodoo Man

Produced by Coxsone Dodd. (a) Co-written by LEE PERRY and BB SEATON, "Spit In The Sky" was Dodd's response to PRINCE BUSTER's growing success, and the first shots in a sound clash between the two producers.

ISLAND 097 Naughty People/I Shall Not Remove

Produced by Coxsone Dodd. (b) Co-written by LEE PERRY, and another attack on PRINCE BUSTER.

ISLAND 103 One Two Three/Back Biter

Produced by Coxsone Dodd.

ISLAND 116 You Bend My Love/Can't You See

Produced by Coxsone Dodd.

R&B 108 Lion of Judah/Joe Lieges

Produced by Coxsone Dodd. (a) Co-written by LEE PERRY, a cleverly camouflaged espousal of Rastafarian solidarity which somehow escaped the fiercely disapproving Dodd's attention. (b) Co-written by LEE PERRY in response to PRINCE BUSTER's "Bad Minded People," accusing the latter of trying to steal Dodd's glory ("lieges"). The song was so successful in the UK that "Spit in the Sky" (Black Swan 405) was also released there under the name JOE LIGES.

R&B 128 Prince Pharaoh/Don't Believe Him

Produced by Coxsone Dodd. (a) Dodd's most stinging riposte against the increasingly barbed PRINCE BUSTER, and also the only known recording of the producer's spoken voice.

WINSTON & BIBBY

Vocal duo featuring WINSTON STEWART and BB SEATON. (X) LESTER STERLING

1964

BOBBY AITKEN

BLACK SWAN 441 Jericho/LESTER STERLING: Lunch Time

RIO 34 Rolling Stone/LESTER STERLING'S GROUP: Man about Train

RIO 40 Garden of Eden/Whiplash

RIO 50 Little Girl/Together

LAUREL AITKEN

BLUE BEAT 249 This Great Day/I May Never See My Baby

JNAC 1 West Indian Cricket Test/Three Cheers for Worrell

R&B 170 Pick Up Your Bundle/Let My People Go

R&B 167 Yes Indeed/You Can't Stop Me from Loving You

R&B 171 Bachelor Life/You Was Up

RIO 36 Leave Me Standing/Bug a Boo

RIO 37 John Saw Them Coming/Jericho

RIO 35 Rock of Ages/The Mule

VERNON ALLEN

One-half of the duo ALLEN & MILTON.

R&B 169 Fari Come/Babylon

ROLAND ALPHONSO

(X) LITTLE LUMAN, MAYTALS, OWEN & LEON, JOE WHITE

ANDY & JOEY

PORT O'JAM 4009 I Want to Know/My Love Has Gone
Produced by Coxsone Dodd.

SKA-BEAT 162 You're Wondering Now/You'll Never
Produced by Coxsone Dodd.

BARBARA & WINSTON

Vocal duo featuring WINSTON STEWART.

BLACK SWAN 418 The Dream/I Love You

LLOYD BARNES

See entry: DIRECTORY OF PRODUCERS. (X) PRINCE BUSTER'S ALL STARS

THEO BECKFORD

BLACK SWAN 449 Ungrateful People/BEVERLEY'S ALL-STARS: Go Home

BLACK SWAN 452 Take Your Time/STRANGER COLE: Happy Go Lucky

BLUE BEAT 250 She's Gone/Old Flame
Produced by Prince Buster.

BLUE BEAT 256 Glamour Girl/BUSTER'S ALL-STARS: Down Beat Burial
Produced by Prince Buster. (b) A honking ska instrumental celebrating a memorable sound system victory.

BLUE BEAT 257 Don't Worry to Cry/Love Me or Leave Me
Produced by Prince Buster.

BEVERLEY'S ALL STARS

Session band for producer LESLIE KONG. (X) THEO BECKFORD

BIG CHARLIE

aka CHARLES ORGANAIRE.

BLUE BEAT 241 Red Sea/You May Not Believe

THE BLUE BEATS

BLUE BEAT 209 Blue Beats Over (The White Cliffs of Dover)/Kiss the Baby

(a) As the search for UK recognition grew keener, so the net was cast wider for suitable material to skank up. Wartime songstress Vera Lynn's rousing promise of brighter, bluebird infested tomorrows was, with hindsight, a sitting target.

THE BLUES BLENDERS

Vocal group featuring KEN PARKER.

RIO 93 Girl Next Door/?
Produced by King Edwards.

BRIDGITTE BOND

BLUE BEAT 212 Blue Beat Baby/Oh Yeah Baby

LLOYD BREVETT

See entry for THE SKATALITES on page 262 . (X) WINSTON SAMUELS

BABA BROOKS

(X) STRANGER COLE, LORD BRISCO

BLACK SWAN 412 Jelly Beans/ERIC MORRIS: Samson
Produced by Duke Reid. (b) Morris discovers that times don't change and women still put men in their place — even big strong chaps like Samson. But judging by his tone, and the SKATALITES' perky accompaniment, it probably served him right.

BLACK SWAN 434 Spider/Melody Jamboree

BLACK SWAN 438 Cork Foot/HERMAN HERSANG COMBO: BBC Channel 2

BLACK SWAN 442 Musical Workshop/DUKE WHITE: Be Wise

BLACK SWAN 444 Bus Strike/DUKE WHITE: Sow Good Seeds

BLACK SWAN 451 Ethiopia/ARCHIBALD TROTT: Promised Land

BLACK SWAN 453 Take Five/VINELY GAYLE: Go On

BLACK SWAN 456 Dreadnought/PLAYGIRLS: Looks Are Deceiving

BLACK SWAN 466 Baby Elephant Walk/DON DRUMMOND: Don's Special
Produced by Vincent Chin.

R&B 131 Maybe Once/Tell Me You're Mine
Credited to JOEY SMITH & BABA BROOKS BAND.

CARL BRYAN ORCHESTRA

Fronted by saxophonist BRYAN. (X) SHENLEY DUFFUS

SONNY BURKE

Also recorded as duo SONNY & YVONNE.

BLACK SWAN 457 I Love You Still/It's Always a Pleasure

BLACK SWAN 458 City in the Sky/Everyday I Love You More

BLACK SWAN 469 Glad/Jeanie

BLACK SWAN 470 Dance with Me/My Girl Can't Cook

BLACK SWAN 471 Wicked People/Good Heaven Knows

ISLAND 155 Live & Let Live/Our Love Is True

ISLAND 156 Write Your Name/It Means So Much

THE TOMMY BURTON COMBO

BLUE BEAT 237 Lavender Blue/I'm Walking

CORNELL CAMPBELL

(X) STRANGER & PATSY

PORT O'JAM 4008 Jericho Road/DON DRUMMOND GROUP: Roll on Sweet Don

Produced by Coxsone Dodd. (b) The talented trombonist rolls on across this atmospheric minor key skanker.

RIO 38 Gloria/I'll Be True

THE CHAMPS

BLUE BEAT 267 Walk Between Your Enemies/Do What I Say

THE CHARMERS

BLUE BEAT 204 I'm Back/It's a Dream

BLUE BEAT 238 You Are My Sunshine/Waiting for You

BLUE BEAT 251 Dig Then Prince/Girl of My Dreams

R&B 151 What's the Use/I Am Through

R&B 156 In My Soul/Beware

THE CHARMS

ISLAND 154 Carry Go Bring Come/Hill & Gully Ride

Produced by Duke Reid. (a) A classic example of the erroneous credits which dog many early Jamaican singles; the a-side, of course, is by JUSTIN HINDS & THE DOMINOES (b) And the b-side appears to be by the L REID GROUP, which in turn points the finger towards the Duke. A tumultuous mento number based on an early LORD COMPOSER recording, it features all the ups and downs which its title implies, with some great honking horns along for the journey.

THE CHERRY PIES

aka THE MAYTALS.

BLACK SWAN 448 Do You Keep on Dreaming/Sweeter than Cherry Pie

CHUCK & DOBBY

BLUE BEAT 246 Tell Me/I'm Going Home

CHUCK & JOE WHITE

Vocal duo CHUCK JOSEPHS & JOE WHITE. aka JOE WHITE & CHUCK. JOSEPHS also of CHUCK & DOBBY.

SKA-BEAT 180 Punch You Down/TOMMY MCCOOK: Cotton Tree

(b) The great ska beat seems just on the verge of boiling over, but the saxophonist and his coworkers refuse to let go, and the tree never really takes root.

LLOYD CLARKE

RIO 23 Stop Your Talking/A Penny

RIO 24 Fellow Jamaican/PATRICK & GEORGE: My Love

JIMMY CLIFF

STATESIDE 342 One Eyed Jacks/King of Kings

Produced by Leslie Kong.

CLIVE & GLORIA

KING 1004 Do the Ska/You Made Me Cry

R&B 173 Money Money Money/Have I Told You Lately

CLIVE & WILSON

Vocal duo featuring DELROY WILSON & CLIVE WILSON.

R&B 144 Mango Tree/Midnight in Chicago

STRANGER COLE

(X) THEO BECKFORD

BLACK SWAN 413 Uno Dos Tres/Look

(a) Cole and KEN BOOTHE duet on this love lost song, with the former taking lead, but the latter still stamping his vocal imprint all over the grooves. Further backing comes from GLEN ADAMS.

BLACK SWAN 415 Summer Day/Loving You Always

BLACK SWAN 435 Boy Blue/ERIC MORRIS: Words of Wisdom

ISLAND 133 Til My Dying Days/STRANGER & PATSY: I Need You

ISLAND 137 Goodbye Peggy/BABA BROOKS: Portrait of My Love

Produced by Vincent Chin.

R&B 133 Out of Many/Nothing Tried

Produced by Duke Reid.

BILLY COOKE

(X) GAYLADS

(FRANK) COSMO

BLACK SWAN 446 Alone/Beautiful Book

BLUE BEAT 244 Oh God/BUSTER'S ALL-STARS: Prince Royal

BLUE BEAT 269 Rice & Badgee/BUSTER'S ALL-STARS: The Tickler

ISLAND 135 Better Get Right/Ameletia

COUNTRY BOY

BLUE BEAT 236 I'm a Lonely Boy/EDWARDS' ALL-STARS: He's Gone Ska

Produced by Rupie Edwards.

CYNTHIA & ARCHIE

Vocal duo featuring CYNTHIA RICHARDS.

R&B 168 Every Beat/DELROY WILSON: Sammy Dead

DANDY

b Robert Livingstone Thompson, 1944, (Kingston,JA). Vocalist DANDY LIVINGSTONE also recorded as a duo with SUGAR SIMONE/THE JETLINERS (aka TITO SIMON), OWEN GRAY, BARBARA, DELROY WILSON, LEE PERRY, CHARLIE GRIFFITHS, DON MARTIN, LITTLE SAL, AUDREY HALL, JACKIE. His band THE SUPERBOYS backed him on many releases. As a producer in London he formed the BROTHER DAN ALL-STARS with PAT RHODEN and DENZIL DENNIS; Livingstone himself recorded as BROTHER DAN. He came close to a hit with the popular "Reggae in Your Jeggae" in 1969, eventually breaking through in 1972 with "Suzanne Beware of the Devil" and "Big City."

DICE 21 Rudie Don't Go/It's Just Got to Be

DESMOND DEKKER

BLACK SWAN 455 Dracula/DON DRUMMOND: Spitfire
Produced by Leslie Kong.
ISLAND 158 Jeserine/King of Ska
Produced by Leslie Kong. (b) Paired with the MAYTALS, Dekker gleefully celebrates both the musical form and his own enthusiastic embrace of it, as the brass blares in approval.

DERRICK & PATSY

BLUE BEAT 247 Troubles/Right
BLUE BEAT 207 Lover Boy/The Moon
BLUE BEAT 224 Steal Away/Money

DOTTY & BONNIE

Duo featuring BONNIE FRANKSON of BONNIE & SKITTO duo.
ISLAND 143 Your Kisses/Why Worry
ISLAND 148 Dearest/Tears Are Falling
(a) The duo beautifully harmonize on a love ballad taken out to sea by the exceptional surf guitar, then returning to shore on the muted notes of the brass.
ISLAND 161 Bunch of Roses/SKATALITES: Trip to Mars
RIO 43 I'm So Glad/DOUGLAS BROS: Got You on My Mind

DON DRUMMOND

(X) BABA BROOKS, CORNELL CAMPBELL, DESMOND DEKKER, SHENLEY DUFFUS, STRANGER & PATSY
ISLAND 149 Eastern Standard Time/DOTTY & BONNIE: Sun Rises
Produced by Duke Reid. (a) This instrumental is a brilliant example of the (pre-AUGUSTUS PABLO) Far East style that raged across JA's scene at the time, a gem of a song with a truly haunting minor key melody. (b) The sax solo almost steals the show, but the duo give an illustrious performance, easily overcoming the juvenile, pedestrian lyrics they're working with.
ISLAND 153 Musical Storeroom/STRANGER COLE: He Who Feels
Produced by Duke Reid. (a) Not so much a storeroom as a marching band, the up-tempo beat, heavy on the cymbals, clatters away while the SKATALITES (augmented by FRANK ANDERSON) breezily blaze along.
ISLAND 162 Garden of Love/STRANGER COLE: Cherry May
Produced by Duke Reid. (a) This instrumental finds the trombonist abetted by a studio of star talents with all the musical flair you'd expect. But while the melody is pleasant, it's nothing to get passionate about.
SKA-BEAT 178 Silver Dollar/TOMMY MCCOOK: My Business
Produced by Duke Reid. (a) Eschewing the obvious (ie making this into a ska-ified Western), the SKATALITES go for subtlety, turning out a jazzy instrumental with a supple melody, while the galloping hoof-like rhythms acknowledges the Western influence.

SHENLEY DUFFUS

BLACK SWAN 440 Digging a Ditch/He's Coming Down
BLACK SWAN 443 Gather Them In/Crucifixion
R&B 134 No More Wedding Bells/Let Them Fret
R&B 146 Big Mouth/FRANK ANDERSON: Peanut Vendor
Produced by Coxsone Dodd. (b) One of Anderson and TOMMY MCCOOK's most distinctive performances on an adaptation of a Mongo Santamaria cut, so beguiling it could sell accents to Englishmen.
R&B 152 Christopher Columbus/CARL BRYAN ORCHESTRA: Barber Chair
R&B 154 Mother in Law/DON DRUMMOND: Festival
Produced by Coxsone Dodd. (a) LEE PERRY also recorded a version of this Ernie Doe US hit.
RIO 41 I Will Be Glad/Heariso

DUKE WHITE

(X) BABA BROOKS

(WILFRED) JACKIE EDWARDS

BLACK SWAN 416 The Things You Do/Little Smile
Produced by Chris Blackwell.
FONTANA 465 Sea Cruise/Little Princess
Produced by Chris Blackwell.
SUE 329 Stagger Lee/Pretty Girl
Produced by Chris Blackwell.

EDWARDS' ALL-STARS

(X) COUNTRY BOY, LITTLE GEORGE

THE FLAMES

aka THE MAYTALS.
BLUE BEAT 205 Helena Darling/My Darling
Produced by Prince Buster.
ISLAND 130 He's the Greatest/Someone's Going to Bawl
Produced by Vincent Chin.
ISLAND 136 Little Flea/Good Idea
Produced by Prince Buster.
ISLAND 138 When I Get Home/Neither Silver nor Gold
Produced by Leslie Kong.
ISLAND 139 Broadway Jungle/Beat Lied
Produced by Prince Buster. (a) A scorching Maytals performance, best described as a tent revival held in an uncivilized corner of the world. TOOTS HIBBERT leads the choir, whose perfect call and response are a joy to behold, accompanied by an ape-like yipping which adds an extra punch of exuberance to an already exhilarating song. The same performance subsequently appeared as "Dog War," under the Maytals' own name.

THE FREE SOULS

BLUE BEAT 264 I Want to Be Free/Angel

THE GAYLADS

vocal group featuring BB SEATON (b 1944), MAURICE ROBERTS (b 1945) and WINSTON STEWART (b 1947). Also recorded as the GAYLORDS and were founder members of THE HIPPY BOYS.

R&B 159 There'll Come a Day/BILLY COOKE: Iron Bar
R&B 165 What Is Wrong with Me?/Whap Whap

VINELY GAYLE

(X) BABA BROOKS

GIRL SATCHMO

BLUE BEAT 227 Rhythm of the New Beat/Blue Beat Chariot

OSBOURNE GRAHAM

(X) LORD TANAMO

OWEN GRAY

BLUE BEAT 217 Draw Me Nearer/Daddy's Girl

DERRICK HARRIOTT

ISLAND 157 What Can I Do/Leona
Produced by Derrick Harriott. (a/b) Donnie Elbert compositions.

HERMAN HERSANG COMBO

Hersang's CITY SLICKERS and the later COMBO were one of the leading session bands of the R&B/early ska scene. (X) BABA BROOKS

HIGGS & WILSON

RIO 29 Love Is Not for Me/Gone Is Yesterday

JUSTIN HINDS aka HINES

b 7 May, 1942 (Steertown, JA). Elder cousin of singer Horace Hinds aka Horace Andy. Led THE DOMINOES, vocal group comprising DENNIS SINCLAIR and JUNIOR DIXON.
SKA-BEAT 176 King Samuel/River Jordan
Produced by Duke Reid. (b) The SKATALITES are particularly punchy over this upbeat song, while Hinds and The Dominoes create an atmosphere somewhere between a church revival and a campside sing-along.

HORTENSE & JACKY

Vocal duo featuring HORTENSE ELLIS and JACKIE OPEL.
R&B 138 Stand by Me/JACKIE OPEL: Solid Rock

THE OSSIE IRVING SIX

(X) DAVE MARTIN

JAMAICA'S OWN VAGABONDS

DECCA DFE8588 Behold EP

JIMMY JAMES

BLACK SWAN 437 Thinking of You/Shirley

JOE & ANN

BLACK SWAN 468 Gee Baby/Wherever You May Be

JOHNNY & THE BLUE BEATS

BLUE BEAT 229 Shame/Ball & Chain

KEITH & ENID

BLACK SWAN 429 Lost My Love/I Cried

ROY KILDARE

BLUE BEAT 226 I Won't Leave/What About It

KINGSTON JOE

BLUE BEAT 253 Time Is on My Friend/Wear & Tear

AZIE LAWRENCE

BLUE BEAT 222 Perripelem/Lovers Understand

BYRON LEE & THE DRAGONAIRES

MGM 1256 Night Train from Jamaica/Ska Dee Wah
Produced by Byron Lee.
PARLOPHONE R5124 River Bank/Musical Communion
Produced by Byron Lee.
PARLOPHONE R5125 Sour Apples/Hanging Up My Heart
Produced by Byron Lee.
PARLOPHONE R5140 Sammy Dead/Say Bye Bye
Produced by Byron Lee.
PARLOPHONE R5177 Beautiful Garden/Too Late
Produced by Byron Lee.
PARLOPHONE R5182 Come Back/Jamaica Ska
Produced by Byron Lee.

LITTLE GEORGE

RIO 45 Mary Anne/EDWARDS ALL-STARS: Blue Night

LITTLE JOYCE

(X) C SYLVESTER & THE PLANETS

LITTLE LUMAN

Also recorded as a duo with SHENLEY DUFFUS.
RIO 44 Hurry Hurry/R ALPHONSO: Hucklebuck

LORD BRISCO

BLACK SWAN 447 Spiritual Mambo/BABA BROOKS: Fly Right
BLACK SWAN 450 My Love Has Come/BABA BROOKS: Sweet Eileen
BLACK SWAN 454 Trojan/I Am the Least
ISLAND 131 Praise for I/Tell You the Story

LORD CREATOR NATIONAL

CALYPSO 2001 Drive with Care/Sweet Jamaica
PORT O'JAM 4005 Rhythm of the Blues/Simple Things
Produced by Coxsone Dodd.
PORT O'JAM 4019 Jamaica's Anniversary/Mother's Love
Produced by Coxsone Dodd.

LORD KITCHENER

CALYPSO 10 Kitch Mambo Calypso/Ghana
CALYPSO 11 Life Begins at 40/Short SkirtsCALYPSO 12 Romeo/
    Kitch Calypso Medley
CALYPSO 14 Federation/Alfonso in Town
CALYPSO 19 Black Pudding/Piccadilly
CALYPSO 21 Come Back in the Morning/If You Brown
CALYPSO 22 Jamaica Turkey/Edna What You Want
CALYPSO 23 Carnival/More Rice

LORD NELSON

STATESIDE 281 It's Delinquency/Proud West Indian

STATESIDE SE 1024 Proud West Indian EP

LORD RIGBY

KALYPSO 29 The Milkman/Old Veterans

LORD TANAMO

RIO 21 I Had a Dream/OSBOURNE GRAHAM: Be There

SKA-BEAT 177 Night Food Ska/THE SKATALITES: Latin Goes Ska

Produced by Duke Reid. (b) The title sums up this jazzy instrumental!

MARGUERITA

b Marguerita Mahfood, d 1/1/65. Professional dancer who was also one of the most distinctive vocalists of the era. Murdered by boyfriend DON DRUMMOND of the SKATALITES.

BLACK SWAN 431 Woman a Come/ERIC MORRIS: Number One

Produced by Duke Reid. (a) Marguerita's dedication to boyfriend DON DRUMMOND—the king of ace from outer space," recorded with BABA BROOKS and TOMMY MCCOOK. Marguerita's own title for the song was "Ungu Malungu Man"; Duke Reid retitled it, but even he couldn't disguise the song's furiously tribal instincts, pounding percussion with Marguerita's sensual yowl rising high above the chaos. GLEN ADAMS was responsible for the distinctive arrangements.

DAVE MARTIN

PORT O'JAM 4112 Let Them Fight/OSSIE IRVING SIX: Why I Love You

Produced by Coxsone Dodd.

PORT O'JAM 4115 All My Dreams/Take Your Belongings

Produced by Coxsone Dodd.

THE MARVELS

BLUE BEAT 221 Millie/Saturday

MARVIN & JOHNNY

BLACK SWAN 467 Cherry Pie/Ain't that Right

THE MAYTALS

BLACK SWAN 463 My Little Ruby/LORD CREATOR: Wicked Lady

BLACK SWAN 464 John & James/THEO BECKFORD: Sailing On

Produced by Leslie Kong. (a) This remarkable single showcases some great jazzy horns (the SKATALITES, of course), over which the trio's vocals reach new heights. A sublime cross between gospel harmonies and a R&B mood.

BLUE BEAT 215 He Is Real/Domino

Produced by Prince Buster.

BLUE BEAT 220 Pain in My Belly/BUSTER'S ALL-STARS: City Riot

Produced by Prince Buster.

BLUE BEAT 231 Dog War/RICO & CREATORS: I'll Be Home

Produced by Prince Buster.

BLUE BEAT 245 Little Flea/Don't Talk

Produced by Prince Buster.

BLUE BEAT 255 Judgment Day/Goodbye Jane

Produced by Prince Buster.

BLUE BEAT 270 You Got Me Spinning/Lovely Walking

Produced by Prince Buster.

R&B 130 Hurry Up/Love Divide

Produced by Coxsone Dodd.

R&B 141 Another Chance/FRANKIE ANDERSON: Always on a Sunday

Produced by Coxsone Dodd. (b) This swing-style instrumental is merely an excuse for the brass to show off, with an arrangement so loose that you can hear the musicians stepping on each others' toes.

R&B 150 Marching On/LESTER STERLING: Hot Cargo

Produced by Coxsone Dodd. (b) A STERLING composition, featuring solos by MCCOOK and ALPHONSO.

R&B 153 Give Me Your Love/He Will Provide

Produced by Coxsone Dodd.

R&B 155 Shining Light/LESTER STERLING & HIS GROUP: Baskin' Hop

Produced by Coxsone Dodd.

R&B 164 Hello Honey/ROLAND ALPHONSO: Crime Wave

Produced by Coxsone Dodd.

R&B 174 Christmas Feelings/Let's Kiss

Produced by Coxsone Dodd.

TOMMY MCCOOK

BLACK SWAN 422 Two for One/LASCELLES PERKINS: I Don't Know

Produced by Coxsone Dodd. (a) The barrel-house piano promises a little more than this straightforward honking instrumental eventually delivers. Underneath, however, there lurks a pumping R&B classic just dying to get out.

PORT O'JAM 4001 Exodus/LEE PERRY: Help the Weak

Produced by Coxsone Dodd. (a) Recorded in November, 1963, at Dodd's recently opened Studio One, an stirring adaptation of the movie theme, featuring solos by FRANK ANDERSON and McCook, starring on his first ever ska recording.

R&B 139 Samson/ROY & ANNETTE: My Arms Are Waiting

R&B 163 Bridge View/NAOMI & CO: What Can I Do?

(a) Adapted from a Mongo Santamaria cut, the excellent solos are shared between trombone and sax on an instrumental which trots along to a perfect swinging ska groove.

THE MELLODITIES

R&B 179 Vacation/TOMMY MCCOOK: Music Is My Occupation

THE MELODY ENCHANTERS

BLACK SWAN 432 Enchanted Ball/Sailor Boy

MILLIE

FONTANA 449 My Boy Lollipop/Something's Gotta Be Done

Produced by Chris Blackwell. (a) Ludicrously catchy, "Lollipop" put producer Blackwell on the map, rocketing to #2 in the UK and selling seven million copies worldwide. The original was an R&B hit for Barbie Gaye, but Millie's tremulous, adenoidal vocals, ERNEST RANGLIN's orchestration, and the insistent ska beat wiped the floor with its predecessor.

FONTANA 479 Sweet William/Oh Henry
Produced by Chris Blackwell. (a)/(b) Two cuts from Millie's *The Blue Beat Girl* album, haunted by Ms Small's astonishing range (high and higher), a fire-cracker exploding around the punchy pop backing.

FONTANA 502 I Love the Way You Love/Bring It on Home to Me
Produced by Chris Blackwell.

DERRICK MORGAN

BLACK SWAN 425 Cherry Pie/BOB ALLS: Beware
BLUE BEAT 261 Soldier Man/BUSTER'S ALL-STARS: Jet 707
Produced by Prince Buster.
BLUE BEAT 268 Katy Katy/Call on Me
BLUE BEAT 239 Miss Lulu/She's So Young
BLUE BEAT 233 Let Them Talk/Sleeping

ERIC MORRIS

(X) BABA BROOKS, STRANGER COLE, MARGUERITA
BLACK SWAN 414 Solomon Grundie/BABA BROOKS: Key to the City
Produced by Leslie Kong. (a) Only Morris could take an old children's rhyme and convincingly turn it into a delicious ska single, puffed up by the jumping beat and horn solo.
BLACK SWAN 433 Supper in the Gutter/Words of My Mouth
BLACK SWAN 439 River Come Down/Seek & You Will Find
BLACK SWAN 445 Home Sweet Home/LESTER STERLING: 64 Special
BLUE BEAT 218 Love Can Break a Man/Worried People
BLUE BEAT 273 Stitch in Time/For Ever
ISLAND 142 Penny-Reel/DUKE REID'S GROUP: Darling When
Produced by Duke Reid. (a) An old mento fave (one wonders how many impressionable youngsters tried similar methods of debt collection in its aftermath), this song was covered time and time again, but Morris' fabulous vocals (with STRANGER COLE alongside), and the SKATALITES' sterling musicianship makes this version a stand out.
ISLAND 147 Mama No Fret/FRANKIE ANDERSON: Santa Lucia
Produced by Duke Reid.
ISLAND 150 Drop Your Sword/Catch a Fire
Produced by Duke Reid.
ISLAND 151 What a Man Doeth/DUKE REID'S GROUP: Rude Boy
Produced by Duke Reid. (a) Or, as the lyrics explains, "what you sow, that's what you will reap," a message Morris conveys with great conviction, while various SKATALITES give it all an upbeat, optimistic edge. (b) No glorification or words of warning here, just a great instrumental aimed straight at the title's market. A magnificent pumping beat, and plenty of room for Reid's group of musical greats to strut their stuff.
PORT O'JAM 4006 Oh My Dear/Lena Belle
Produced by Coxsone Dodd.

RIO 39 Little District/True & Just
RIO 48 Live as a Man/Man Will Rule

SANDRA MURRAY

(X) ROLAND SYLVESTER

JACKIE OPEL

(X) HORTENSE & JACKIE
BLACK SWAN 421 You're No Good/King Liges
R&B 160 Pity the Fool/The Day Will Come

CHARLES ORGANAIRE

aka BIG CHARLIE.
R&B 149 Little Village/It Happens on a Holiday
Also released as RIO 28.

OWEN LEON

aka LEON & OWEN.
ISLAND 146 Next Door Neighbour/ROLAND ALPHONSO: Feeling Fine
Produced by Duke Reid. (a) Bar the beat, this single wouldn't have seemed out of place on Your Hit Parade circa, say, 1960. The pair play up the sweet romance to the hilt, while the SKATALITES take a trip down memory lane. (b) A celebratory instrumental, perfect for a graduation march or even a New Orleans' funeral.
ISLAND 163 My Love for You/How Many Times
ISLAND 164 The Fits Is on Me/SKATALITES: Good News
ISLAND 165 Running Around/SKATALITES: Around the World
Produced by SL Smith.

ROY PANTON

BLUE BEAT 219 Good from the Bad/Hell Gate
RIO 19 Cherita/Seek & You Will Find
RIO 33 You Don't Know Me/KING EDWARD'S ALL-STARS: Doctor No

KENTRICK PATRICK

ISLAND 132 Take Me to the Party/I'm Sorry
ISLAND 140 I Am Wasting Time/RANDY'S GROUP: Royal Charley

PATRICK & GEORGE

Vocal duo featuring KENTRICK PATRICK/LORD CREATOR.
(X) LLOYD CLARKE

LASCELLES PERKINS

R&B 175 I Am so Grateful/When I Survey

LEE PERRY

PORT O'JAM 4003 Bad Minded People/TOMMY MCCOOK & HIS GROUP: Jam Rock
Produced by Coxsone Dodd.
PORT O'JAM 4010 Chatty Chatty Woman/TOMMY MCCOOK & HIS GROUP: Road Block
Produced by Coxsone Dodd. (b) The first song McCook wrote after he returned to Jamaica, featuring the unusual sound of violin, courtesy of a veteran quadrille player named Raymond.
R&B 135 Royalty/Can't Be Wrong

THE PLAYGIRLS

(X) BABA BROOKS

THE PLUMMERS

BLUE BEAT 260 Johnny/Little Stars

PRINCE BUSTER

BLUE BEAT 211 Bluebeat Spirit/Beggars Are No Choosers
Produced by Prince Buster.

BLUE BEAT 216 You're Mine/Tongue Will Tell
Produced by Prince Buster.

BLUE BEAT 225 Three Blind Mice/I Know
Produced by Prince Buster.

BLUE BEAT 232 Sheep on Top/Midnight
Produced by Prince Buster.

BLUE BEAT 234 She Loves You/Healing
Produced by Prince Buster.

BLUE BEAT 243 Jealous/Buster's Ska
Produced by Prince Buster.

BLUE BEAT 248 30 Pieces of Silver/Everybody Ska
Produced by Prince Buster. (a) Ostensibly about a charming rogue, this cracking number is powered by a pounding up-tempo beat, and spiffing horn, and harmonica solos. And although neither protagonist is named, it doesn't take much imagination to realize this was yet another salvo against MORGAN and KONG. Reissued as STATESIDE 335, UNITY 522.

BLUE BEAT 254 Wings of a Dove/MAYTALS: Sweet Love
Produced by Prince Buster.

BLUE BEAT 262 Old Lady/Dayo Ska
Produced by Prince Buster.

BLUE BEAT 271 No Knowledge in College/The Middle of the Night
Produced by Prince Buster.

BLUE BEAT 274 I May Never Love You Again/Hey Little Girl
Produced by Prince Buster.

(PRINCE) BUSTER'S ALL STARS

(X) THEO BECKFORD, FRANK COSMO, MAYTALS, DERRICK MORGAN, SCHOOLGIRLS, WINSTON STEWART

BLUE BEAT 235 Reincarnation/LLOYD BARNES: Time Is Hard
Produced by Prince Buster.

BLUE BEAT 266 Dallas Texas/PRIEST HERMAN: We Are Praying
Produced by Prince Buster. (a) A raw, honking ska instrumental, one of Buster's first UK club hits.

ERNEST RANGLIN & THE GBS

BLACK SWAN 417 Swing a Ling (parts 1/2)
Recorded in London, shortly after Ranglin's relocation.

THE RICHARD BROTHERS

(X) JOE WHITE

LLOYD RICHARDS

PORT O'JAM 4004 Be Good/I Need You
Produced by Coxsone Dodd.

RICO

(X) THE MAYTALS, PRINCE BUSTER

RIFF

BLUE BEAT 242 Primitive Man/Oh What a Feeling

M ROBINSON

PORT O'JAM 4114 Who Are You/Follow you
Produced by Coxsone Dodd.

ROY & MILLIE

BLACK SWAN 427 Oh Shirley/Marie
Produced by Leslie Kong.

ROY & YVONNE

Vocal duo featuring ROY PANTON, YVONNE ADAMS.

BLACK SWAN 436 Two Roads/Join Together

BLUE BEAT 258 Little Girl/No More

THE ROYALS

Vocal group originally comprising ROY COUSINS, BERTRAM JOHNSON, KEITH (SLIM) SMITH, and ERROL WILSON—Cousins (see entry in DIRECTORY OF PRODUCERS) was the only permanent member.

BLUE BEAT 259 Save Mama/Out de Fire

RUDDY & SKETTO

BLUE BEAT 208 Show Me the Way to Go Home/Let Me Dream

BLUE BEAT 230 10,000 Miles From Home/I Need Someone

BLUE BEAT 252 I Love You/If Only Tomorrow

WINSTON SAMUELS

BLACK SWAN 419 Luck Will Come My Way/LLOYD BREVETT: One More Time

BLACK SWAN 426 You Are the One/Gloria Love

COLUMBIA DB7405 You Are the One/Angela

RIO 26 Follow/I'm So Glad

RICHARD SAUNDERS

(X) STRANGER & KEN

THE SCHOOLBOYS

PORT O'JAM 4000 Dream Lover/I Want to Know
Produced by Coxsone Dodd.

THE SCHOOLGIRLS

BLUE BEAT 214 Sing & Shout/Last Time
Produced by Prince Buster.

BLUE BEAT 263 Never Let You Go/BUSTER'S ALL-STARS: Supercharge
Produced by Prince Buster.

HORACE "BB" SEATON

R&B 143 Hold On/LESTER STERLING: Peace & Love

SIMMS & ROBINSON

PORT O'JAM 4007 Please Don't Do It/Don't Do It
Produced by Coxsone Dodd.

THE SKATALITES

See entry for THE SKATALITES on page 262. (X) LORD TANAMO, OWEN & LEON, JOE WHITE

SONNY & YVONNE

Duo featuring SONNY BURKE and YVONNE ADAMS.

BLACK SWAN 461 Night After Night/SONNY BURKE: Here We Go
  Again

ISLAND 134 Life without Fun/SONNY BURKE GROUP: Mount
  Vesuvius

LESTER STERLING

(X) BOBBY AITKEN, HORACE SEATON, STRANGER &
PATSY

WINSTON STEWART

b Winston Delano Stewart, 1/5/47. A member of THE GAYLADS, also recorded as a duo with ROY ROBINSON, BIBBY, BARBARA, ERROL DIXON.

PORT O'JAM 4002 All of My Life/How Many Times

Produced by Coxsone Dodd.

R&B 147 But I Do/MAYTALS: Four Seasons

Produced by Coxsone Dodd. (b) The Maytals celebrate the seasons with typical style on this breezy single. The SKATALITES bring their usual panache to the proceedings.

STRANGER & KEN

BLACK SWAN 465 I Want to Go Home/RICHARD SAUNDERS: Sign of
  the Times

STRANGER & PATSY

(X) STRANGER COLE

BLACK SWAN 462 Hey Little Girl/CORNELL CAMPBELL: Make Hay

Produced by Duke Reid.

ISLAND 141 Oh Oh I Need You/DON DRUMMOND: JFK's Memory

Produced by Duke Reid.

ISLAND 144 Tom Dick & Harry/We Two, Happy People

Produced by Duke Reid. (b) Stranger Cole and Patsy Todd are, indeed, two happy people on this bubbling single that just can't stop swinging. The jazzy horns are fabulous, but the spotlight shines on the great surf guitar.

ISLAND 152 Yeah Yeah Baby/BABA BROOKS: Boat Ride

Produced by Duke Reid. (a) A perky pop-lite charmer with that surf guitar making a welcome return.

ISLAND 160 Miss B/Things Come to Those Who Wait

Produced by Duke Reid.

R&B 172 I'll Forgive You/LESTER STERLING & HIS GROUP: Indian
  Summer

Produced by Duke Reid.

SUGAR & DANDY

CARNIVAL 7009 Oh Dear What Can the Matter Be/Tra La La

CARNIVAL 7015 What a Life/Time & Tide

CARNIVAL 7016 I'm Not Crying Now/Blues Got a Hold on Me

SYKO & THE CARIBS

BLUE BEAT 213 Do the Dog/Jenny

BLUE BEAT 223 Big Boy/Sugar Baby

C SYLVESTER & THE PLANETS

BLUE BEAT 206 Going South/LITTLE JOYCE: Oh Daddy

ROLAND SYLVESTER

CARNIVAL 7018 Grandfather's Clock/SANDRA MURRAY: Nervous

TREVOR & THE CARIBS

Featuring TREVOR WILSON.

BLUE BEAT 228 Down in Virginia/Hey Little Schoolgirl

THE VIKINGS

aka THE MAYTALS. The band shared its name with one of Kingston's most notorious gangs.

BLACK SWAN 423 Down by the Riverside/This Way

Produced by Coxsone Dodd. (a) Turning the anti-war classic into a spiritual, The Maytals deliver up some of their best harmonies, while the SKATALITES have a picnic.

BLACK SWAN 428 Treat Me Bad/Sitting on Top

Produced by Coxsone Dodd. (a) There's a wondrous (if inexplicable) tinge of Britbeat percolating across this single. But while the SKATALITES shine, the Maytals are almost lost in the mix. Almost.

BLACK SWAN 430 Come into My Parlour/I Am in Love

Produced by Deanne Daley.

ISLAND 167 Daddy/It's You

Produced by Ronnie Nasralla and Byron Lee. (a) Producer Ronnie Nasralla later described "Daddy" as "the worst song we recorded," originally placing it on the Jamaican 45's b-side because, "we didn't want to waste two good tunes on one single." But its haunting guitar and horn duet, and TOOTS HIBBERT's impassioned ode to his mother (communicated through daddy) struck a heartbreaking chord throughout Jamaica. "It's You" did well, but "Daddy" did better. (b) The beat may be straightforward, but the vocal parts are surprisingly complex, turning a simple love song into a masterpiece. Searing horn solos add to the fun.

THE WILF TODD COMBO

BLUE BEAT 240 He Took Her Away/Have You Ever Been Lonely

ARCHIBALD TROTT

(X) BABA BROOKS

TONY WASHINGTON & HIS DCS

BLACK SWAN 459 But I Do/Night Train

BLACK SWAN 460 Dilly Dilly/But I Do

JOE WHITE

Also recorded as duo CHUCK & JOE WHITE.

ISLAND 145 When You Are Young/Wanna Go Home

ISLAND 159 Hog in a Co-Co/SKATALITES: Sandy Gully

(b) Arguably the closest ROLAND ALPHONSO and his cohorts ever get to dreamy, an instrumental in a mutedly cheerful mood.

ISLAND 166 Downtown Girl/RICHARD BROS: You Are My Sunshine
R&B 137 Sinners/ROLAND ALPHONSO: King Solomon

Produced by Coxsone Dodd. (a) Recorded with THE MAY-TALS (b) Adapting a merengue which Alphonso recalled from his days with the ERIC DEAN band, "King Solomon" features solos by TOMMY MCCOOK and FRANK ANDERSON.

DELROY WILSON

BLACK SWAN 420 Goodbye/Treat Me Right
R&B 132 Squeeze Your Toe/Sugar Pie
R&B 148 Lover Mouth/Every Mouth Must Be Fed

WINSTON & FAY

Vocal duo featuring WINSTON STEWART.

BLUE BEAT 272 Fay Is Gone/THE MONARCHS: Sauce & Tea

Produced by Prince Buster. (a) Well, if Fay is gone, who's that singing her praises with Winston? It's Prince Buster, of course.

1965–67: The Rocksteady Beat

"My Boy Lollipop" did more than launch the ska sound onto the international scene. It created a scene of its own, as musicians across the UK (America was somewhat slower) hastened to make their own mark in this exciting new world. R&B singer Chris Farlowe and the Beazers landed a club smash with "The Blue Beat"; the Migil Five went to #10 with the ska flavored "Mockingbird Hill"; while showband leader Ross McManus (better known today as Elvis Costello's father) created one of the most convincing white ska records of the era with 1965's pounding "Patsy Girl."

In north London, a schoolboy outfit called the Soul Survivors were rehearsing with visiting Jamaican star Owen Gray; vocalist Steve Ellis recalls, "[He] came down with his big herb cigarettes — we didn't know what they were. We did a cover of Prince Buster's 'Ten Commandments'." Soul Survivor later became "Everlasting Love" hit makers Love Affair.

Simply to absorb the wealth of talent emerging from home quarters, Island launched another subsidiary, Brit, with the intention of turning it over at least partially to homemade ska. In the event, of Brit's five releases, only Millie's "My Street" was even remotely appropriate, with the most interesting releases eventually being siphoned onto a second imprint, Aladdin. Jackie Edwards, Owen Gray, and calypso superstar Lord Kitchener all appeared within Aladdin's 12 single catalog.

The demand for ska continued to grow, however. 1966 brought an enterprising new label called Dr Bird, established by Rio label chief Graeme Goodall. Within a year, the Bird was flying high with Skatalite Roland Alphonso's immortal "Phoenix City." Indeed, 1967 would see a host of Jamaican ska singles either break into, or bubble under, the lower reaches of the British chart.

The first, perhaps inevitably, was by Prince Buster. Already two years old, but still as fresh as newly-discharged cordite, "Al Capone" reached #18 in February. It is impossible to overstate the significance of that hit. In purely material terms, it meant that after close to seven years of trying, and a myriad releases on a variety of labels, a Jamaican single released through a tiny independent company had finally proved capable of challenging the "big boys" — the Beatles and the Stones, EMI and Decca. In cultural terms, however, it meant far, far more than that. Over the next three years, the doors which "Al Capone's" guns blasted open would swing wide to admit a host of Buster's countrymen.

No matter that in Jamaica, the tempo (and therefore the majority of records being exported to Britain) was now shifting into the rock steady beat. "Ska" and "Blue beat" nights sprang up all over the country and, alongside them, hosts who became as well-known as the records they played. And just as they had during the heyday of the Kingston sound systems, they utilized every sonic trick at their disposal, anything to gain an edge on the competition.

Sir Neville the Enchanter, at the Ska Bar in Woolwich, created the most unique sound around by turning the treble up full, scything the rhythm guitar through the mix in a way which other sound systems, long accustomed to letting the bass do the work, could only marvel at.

Of course it did not take them long to figure out how it was done and, soon, Sir Fanso at the Islington Sunset, Count Shelley at the 007 in Dalston, and lesser set-ups everywhere else, were all employing the same technique, rewriting the production rulebook before the producers themselves knew what was going on. So the producers came over to see for themselves. In 1968, Coxsone Dodd decamped to London, to guest on the resident sound system at the Ram Jam club in Brixton.

The Ram Jam's importance to the British ska underground can never be overestimated. It was there that English and West Indians alike heard for the first time such future classics as Alton Ellis' "Rock Steady," Derrick Morgan's "Kill Me Dead," Lester Sterling's ground-breaking "Sir Collins' Special," and the Hamlins' "Soul and Inspiration" — records which might not appear on domestic British, vinyl for months to come, if ever.

Sir Coxsone maintained this tradition, previewing records (his own productions, naturally) on the dancefloor, and then launching a lucrative sideline by selling limited pre-release acetates at suitably expensive pre-release prices. And as the competition warmed up and other venues imported their own resident disc jockeys, so the pre-release gap grew longer and longer — until in some cases acetates being played at a nightclub in 1968 wouldn't actually become available in Britain until the same scratchy discs were unearthed for CD compilations a quarter of a century later.

For a time, Sir Coxsone had the field to himself. Late in 1968, however, the Blue Ribbon in Peckham dropped the bombshell they'd been hoping to detonate for six long months. Duke Reid was coming.

The loss, even temporarily, of its two best known producers did not, of course, affect either the quantity or the quality of the music being produced in Jamaica. If anything, it opened the door to even further talents, with singer Derrick Harriott one of the first to grasp the new opportunities. Very swiftly, he established himself amongst the most prolific producers on Island Records' books — so much so that the label was soon able to compile two "Best Of" collections without even flipping one single over! Indeed, Island eventually presented Harriott with his own subsidiary label, Song Bird, and over the next four years, 1969–73, Harriott rewarded them with 90 self-produced singles, including the Kingstonians' much loved "Singer Man."

Both at home and in the UK, rock steady burned briefly, but so brightly. It was a golden era, during which time Coxsone Dodd reintroduced Blackwell to the Wailing Wailers; Justin Hinds followed up the Jamaican success of the innuendo charged "Penny Reel O" with the equally risque "Rub Up Push Up"; and the moribund Skatalites were rejuvenated when Roland Alphonso and the Studio One Orchestra's blue beat-ified rearrangement of "The Guns Of Navarone" movie theme was released in the UK under the old, familiar brand name, reaching #36 in April.

Even as ska finally broke into the British mainstream, however, the fathers of the genre's emergence were stepping out of the limelight. Blue Beat folded in 1967, after some 400 singles (but just nine albums, all either by Buster, or featuring his productions), and Siggy Jackson moved over to EMI to form the Columbia Bluebeat specialist label, although it was to be a short-lived enterprise.

So were subsequent attempts by Emil Shallit to rejuvenate Melodisc's fortunes. The Fab label, an attempt to branch into mainstream pop music, and Rainbow, dedicated to soul, both failed to take off and, by the end of the decade, Melodisc's Jamaican output was confined primarily to Prince Buster reissues.

Island, too, was steering away from ska. Chris Blackwell started looking towards rock'n'roll as early as 1965 and his success with the Spencer Davis Group, and the following year, he launched his first attempt at a pop label, Aladdin. In 1967, he decided to try another, realigning Island Records towards the newly emergent progressive rock scene, with just Jimmy Cliff remaining to fly the old island flag.

Even as they left the room, however, both Shallit and Blackwell knew that their baby was in good hands. The Locomotives scored with the infectious "Rudi's in Love." The Ethiopians gave Graeme Goodall's Rio label its first hit when they rode the "Last Train to Skaville" into the Top 40.

The President label launched the Pyramids, whose "Train Tour to Rainbow City" travelled just as far. And Pyramid, a Graeme Goodall imprint established to cater for Leslie Kong's continued output, scored with a #14 placing for Desmond Dekker's "007 (Shanty-Town)." Pama, formed in 1967 by the three brothers who ran Harlesden's Club West Indies, Harry, Carl, and Geoffrey Palmer, was also to enjoy considerable success.

But the most important of them all was Trojan, headed up by Chris Blackwell's old landlord, Lee Gopthal, and the man upon whose shoulders devolved all of Island's proud traditions. Island label executive David Betteridge explained, "Gopthal had a company called Beat and Commercial (B&C). . . Island and B&C decided to form a joint company for Jamaican music between ourselves," creating an umbrella identity which would not only fill the streets with the sound of contemporary Kingston, it would feel like it as well. Every individual producer this new company contracted with was granted their own separate label identity, just as they were at home. They began carefully, with Duke Reid's Treasure Isle, Coxsone Dodd's Coxsone and Studio One, and Ken Lack's Caltone. But within a year, Betteridge laughed, "we had labels coming out of our ears."

1965

BOBBY AITKEN

RIO 52 Rain Came Tumbling Down/SHENLEY & LUMAN: Something Is on Your Mind

RIO 64 Mr Judge/BINZ: Times Have Changed

LAUREL AITKEN

DICE 28 Jamaica/Don't Want No More
Produced by Laurel Aitken.

DICE 31 We Shall Overcome/You Left Me Standing
Produced by Laurel Aitken.

RIO 53 Mary Don't You Weep/I Believe
Produced by Laurel Aitken.

RIO 54 Mary Lou/Jump & Shout
Produced by Laurel Aitken.

RIO 56 One More Time/Ring Don't Mean a Thing
Produced by Laurel Aitken.

RIO 65 Let's Be Lovers/I Need You
Produced by Laurel Aitken.

ROLAND ALPHONSO

(X) DOTTY & BONNIE, LEE PERRY

BLUE BEAT 286 Roland Plays Prince/GAYNOR & ERROL: My Queen
Produced by Prince Buster.

ISLAND 217 El Pussy Cat/LORD BRYNNER: Tiger in Your Tank
(a) This slow tempo instrumental strolls along behind Alphonso's yowling sax, while a chorus of motley cats meow across the room.

RIO 58 Jazz Ska/HYACINTH: Oh Gee

SKA-BEAT 216 Nuclear Weapon/STRANGER COLE: Love thy Neighbour

Produced by Duke Reid.

SKA-BEAT 210 Nimble Foot/ANDY & JOEY: Love Is Stronger

Produced by Coxsone Dodd. (a) The SKATALITE beat's built for fancy footwork, while the jazzy melody stirs the blood.

ANDY & CLYDE

RIO 62 Never Be a Slave/Magic Is Love

RIO 69 I'm So Lonesome/WINSTON STEWART: Day After Day

RIO 71 We All Have to Part/UPSETTERS: Scandalizing

ANDY & JOEY

(X) ROLAND ALPHONSO

THEO BECKFORD

BLUE BEAT 287 On Your Knees/Now You're Gone

ISLAND 238 Trench Town People/THE PIONEERS: Sometimes

ISLAND 243 You Are the One Girl/Grudgeful People

ISLAND 246 If Life Was a Thing/L CLARKE: Parro Saw the Light

ISLAND 248 What a Whoe/Bajan Girl

BIBBY

aka BB SEATON.

BLUE BEAT 289 Rub It Down/Wicked Man

BINZ

(X) BOBBY AITKEN

THE BLUES BUSTERS

ISLAND 214 How Sweet It Is/I Had a Dream

ISLAND 222 Wings of a Dove/BYRON LEE & THE DRAGONAIRES: Dan Is the Man in the Van

Produced by Byron Lee. (b) Lee launches into a pleasing rendition of MIGHTY SPARROW's 1963 Calypso King triumph, a condemnation of the (post-)colonial education system, wondering why a child is regarded as stupid because he hasn't committed Brer Rabbit to memory.

LLOYD BREVETT

(X) WINSTON SAMUELS

BABA BROOKS

(X) LORD TANAMO, OWEN & LEON, DERRICK MORGAN, ERIC MORRIS, THE RIOTS

BIG SHOT 444 Bus Strike/DUKE WHITE: Sow Good Seeds

ISLAND 229 Guns Fever/DOTTY & BONNIE: Don't Do It

Produced by Duke Reid. (a) The trumpeter and his cowhands ride in with this jazzy instrumental with a western flare, as the guns fire wildly across the grooves, and DERRICK MORGAN rousts the cowboys to action.

ISLAND 233 Independent Ska/STRANGER & CLAUDETTE: Seven Days

Produced by Duke Reid.

ISLAND 235 Duck Soup/ZODIACS: Renegade

Produced by Duke Reid. (a) Weak instrumental which never quite comes together, although the honking melody has potential.

ISLAND 239 Vitamin A/ALTON ELLIS & THE FLAMES: Dance Crasher

Produced by Duke Reid. (b) Ellis pulls out some of his best soulful vocals here, ably assisted by the obvious enthusiasm of The Flames, add a great melody and shimmering musicianship for a notable single.

ISLAND 241 Teenage Ska/ALTON ELLIS: You Are Not to Blame

RIO 61 Skank J Sheck/SHENLEY & HYACINTH: Set Me Free

SKA-BEAT 220 One Eyed Giant/THE DYNAMITES: Walk Out on Me

(a) Regardless of the suggestive title (it doesn't refer to Cyclops), this is another classic Brooks' instrumental, cum dance floor workout, whose jazzy undertones are virtually overwhelmed by the pounding, syncopated beat. Also released as SKA-BEAT 268.

SONNY BURKE

ISLAND 221 Grandpa/KEITH PATTERSON: Deep in My Heart

VIC BROWN'S COMBO

(X) ALAN MARTIN

THE CARNATIONS

BLUE BEAT 285 Mighty Man/What Are You Selling

THE CHARMERS

(X) DOUGLAS BROTHERS

BLUE BEAT 279 Nobody Takes My Baby/BUSTER'S ALL-STARS: Mules Mules

Produced by Prince Buster.

BLUE BEAT 293 Agua Fumar/Long Winter

Produced by Prince Buster.

THE CHECKMATES

Vocal group aka OSSIE & THE UPSETTERS. (X) WINSTON & THE TONETTES

CHUBBY & THE HONEYSUCKERS

RIO 75 Emergency Ward/LEN & THE HONEYSUCKERS: One More River

CHUCK & JOE WHITE

ISLAND 201 Low Minded People/JOE WHITE: Irene

THE CLARENDONIANS

Originally a vocal duo featuring juveniles FITZROY "ERNEST" WILSON and PETER AUSTIN, later augmented by FREDDIE MCGREGOR. Solo activities consumed much of the member's time, with McGregor in particular becoming far better established on his own. (X) FOUR ACES

SKA-BEAT 219 Mey Bien/You Are a Fool

LLOYD CLARKE

(X) THEO BECKFORD

CLIVE & NAOMI

Duo featuring CLIVE WILSON and NAOMI CAMPBELL.

R&B 181 You Are Mine/Open the Door

Produced by Duke Reid. (b) One of the all-time great duets. Turning the traditional "I love you and you love me" ethic utterly upside down, the pair stand on either side of a well-bolted door, screaming the odds at one another and threatening violence or worse with every breath. The smart money's on Naomi — she sounds especially vexed.

STRANGER COLE

(X) ROLAND ALPHONSO, PRINCE BUSTER, PRINCE BUSTER'S ALL STARS

BLUE BEAT 322 When the Party Is Over/BUSTER'S ALL-STARS: Happy Independence 65

Produced by Prince Buster.

ISLAND 169 Koo Koo Doo/GLORIA & THE DREAMLETTS: Stay Where You Are

ISLAND 177 Run Joe/Make Believe

Produced by Duke Reid. (a) Credited to Cole & BABA BROOKS. The warm harmonies of the TECHNIQUES — SLIM SMITH, JIMMY RILEY AND LLOYD CHARMERS — and a variety of SKATALITES provide a great backdrop as the inimitable Cole offers encouragement to a hapless Joe, who's being chased down the street. It's all a little laid back considering the theme, but a fine sounding song regardless.

SKA-BEAT 192 Pussy Cat/MAYTALS: Sweet Sweet Jenny

Produced by Coxsone Dodd. (b) Party time in a priory (the call and response vocals are a treat). The customary aggregate of future SKATALITES provide the jumped up accompaniment, while the Maytals sing out their love to the departing Jenny.

COSMO & DENNIS

BLUE BEAT 296 Sweet Rosemarie/Lollipop I'm in Love

Produced by Duke Reid.

BLUE BEAT 312 Come on Come On/I Don't Want You

Produced by Duke Reid.

DANDY

BLUE BEAT 308 To Love You/I'm Looking for Love

BLUE BEAT 327 My Baby/I'm Gonna Stop Loving You

DICE 29 The Operation/A Little More Ska

DANDY & BARBARA

Vocal duo featuring DANDY LIVINGSTONE.

DICE 24 You Got to Pray/I Got to Have You

DANDY & DEL

Vocal duo comprising DANDY LIVINGSTONE and DELROY WILSON.

BLUE BEAT 319 Hey Girl Hey Boy/So Long Baby

DESMOND DEKKER

(X) DERRICK & PATSY, DON DRUMMOND

ISLAND 181 Get Up Edina/PATSY & DESMOND: Be Mine Forever

Produced by Leslie Kong. (a) With its triumphant horns and dancefloor friendly beat, never has a reprimand (directed at a lazy girl) boasted such a sense of celebration.

ISLAND 202 This Woman/OSSIE & THE UPSETTERS: Si Senora

Produced by Leslie Kong.

THE DELTAS

(X) THE SKATALITES

SUSAN DENNY

MELODISC 1596 Don't Touch Me/Johnny

DERRICK & NAOMI

Vocal duo featuring DERRICK MORGAN and NAOMI CAMPBELL. (X) DON DRUMMOND

SKA-BEAT 185 Heart of Stone/DERRICK MORGAN: Let Me Go

SKA-BEAT 188 I Wish I Were an Apple/DERRICK MORGAN: Around the Corner

The disparate duo. Derrick smooth as glass, Naomi capable of breaking a pane with a single well-chosen note, trading lines of love on this jazzy, upbeat single.

DERRICK & PATSY

BLUE BEAT 291 You I Love/Let Me Hold Your Hand

BLUE BEAT 318 Eternity/Want My Baby

ISLAND 224 National Dance/DESMOND DEKKER: Mount Zion

Produced by Leslie Kong.

DOBBY DOBSON & THE DELTAS

Vocalist DOBSON. b Highland Dobson, 1942. His distinctive singing style (and an early hit) earned him the name "the Loving Pauper." A member of THE VIRTUES, THE SHEIKS (with JACKIE MITTOO), he also recorded as the duo CHUCK & DOBBY, but did not give up his day job as a proofreader at Jamaica's oldest newspaper, the *Gleaner*, until 1971's "That Wonderful World" gave him a massive hit. He subsequently turned to production, but, by the late 1970s, had relocated to New York and retired from the music business. Periodic comebacks are restricted to the nostalgia circuit — he was a favorite at oldies night at Sunsplash.

BLUE BEAT 265 Georgia/The Party

KING 1008 Cry the Cry/Diamonds & Pearls

Produced by Lindon Pottinger.

DOREEN & JACKIE

Vocal duo comprising DOREEN SCHAEFFER and JACKIE OPEL.

SKA-BEAT 208 Welcome Home/You & I

Produced by Coxsone Dodd.

SKA-BEAT 209 Adorable You/The Vow

Produced by Coxsone Dodd and credited to JACKIE & DOREEN. (b) A live highlight at SKATALITES show, this lively ballad floats over a brooding rhythm and gives Opel, in particular, a chance to really stretch his voice.

DOTTY & BONNIE

(X) BABA BROOKS

SKA-BEAT 183 Foul Play/ROLAND ALPHONSO GROUP: Yard Broom
Produced by Duke Reid. (a) This particularly infectious single is built on an unquenchable beat, a jazzy sax, and the duo's understated vocals. (b) The brass goes for that great jazzy sound, while the bassist plucks out a perfect R&B groove, but the saxophonist still grabs centerstage on this swinging instrumental.

DOUGLAS BROTHERS

RIO 57 Valley of Tears/CHARMERS: Where Do I Turn
RIO 63 Down & Out/RONALD WILSON: Lonely Man

THE DREAMLETTS

Featuring GLORIA CRAWFORD and CONSTANTINE WALKER (later SOULETTES). (X) SKATALITES.

DON DRUMMOND

(X) JUSTIN HINDS, ERIC MORRIS

ISLAND 175 Dragon Weapon/DESMOND DEKKER: It Was Only a Dream
Produced by Leslie Kong. (a) A peculiarly muted song considering its title, shuffling along oblivious to the danger, while Drummond's mellow solos offer no threat either to the giant firebreather.

ISLAND 192 Stampede/JUSTIN HINDS & THE DOMINOES: Come Bail Me
Credited to Drummond & DRUMBAGO.

ISLAND 204 Coolie Boy/LORD ANTICS: You May Stray

ISLAND 208 Man in the Street/RITA & BENNY: You Are My Only Love
Produced by Coxsone Dodd. (a) A stirring showcase with its jumping ska beat, jazz inflected brass, and plenty of room for Drummond to blare his best.

ISLAND 231 Cool Smoke/TECHNIQUES: Little Did You Know
Produced by Duke Reid. (b) The cloppity percussion gallops off with the brass solo soaring by its side, while the lead Technique attempts to imprint soul into the grooves, and his cohorts brand their signature harmonies on the song before it rides by. Rock steady won't arrive a minute too soon for this group.

ISLAND 242 University Goes Ska/DERRICK & NAOMI: Pain in My Heart

SKA-BEAT 191 Don de Lion/MOVERS: Jo-Anne
Produced by Duke Reid. (a) A Drummond composed buru, inspired by his favorite Cuban radio station. He and LLOYD KNIBB alone appear on the track, but the trombonist pulls out some of his best work on an instrumental driven by the cymbals and carried away by the horns.

SHENLEY DUFFUS

ISLAND 184 You Are Mine/UPCOMING WILLOWS: Red China
ISLAND 186 Rukumbine/One Morning

Produced by Duke Reid. (a) An up-tempo beat and the swinging sounds of the SKATALITES gives a powerful push to this punchy number. Duffas' slender vocal talents are overcome by his sheer exuberance, and with a range of about five notes, he doesn't so much sing as toast—years before anyone else had the same idea!

DUKE WHITE

(X) BABA BROOKS

THE DYNAMITES

Although the name was also used by a Studio One backing vocals duo, the Dynamites was the brand name producer CLANCY ECCLES applied to the session musicians working with him at any given session. Regulars included HUX BROWN (guitar), JACKIE JACKSON (bass), BORIS GARDINER (bass), BOBBY ELLIS (trumpet), GLADSTONE ANDERSON (keyboards), WINSTON WRIGHT (keyboards), WINSTON GRENNAN (drums), PAUL DOUGLAS (drums), BONGO LES (percussion), BONGO HERMAN (percussion)—aka THE AGGROVATORS, ALL STARS, THE CRYSTALITES, THE SUPERSONICS, LYNN TAITT'S COMETS/BOYS/JETS, THE UPSETTERS, ETC. (X) BABA BROOKS

CLANCY ECCLES

SKA-BEAT 194 Sammy No Dead/Roam Jerusalem
Produced by Coxsone Dodd. (a) "Sammy Dead," a traditional mento, charted three times with three different artists (ERIC MORRIS, DELROY WILSON, and BYRON LEE) in 1964 alone. Eccles cleverly adapted the melody, changed the lyrics and took it back into the charts yet again. In JA, a catchy tune takes on a life of its own!

SKA-BEAT 198 Miss Ida/KING ROCKY: What Is Katty

JACKIE EDWARDS

ALADDIN 601 He'll Have to Go/Gotta Learn Again
Produced by Chris Blackwell. (a) Aladdin was set up as a pop label, Edwards had already scored on the pop chart (as songwriter behind the Spencer Davis Group), and his ska records really weren't selling that well. The sweetest voice in skanked-up soul turns his hand to a Jim Reeves standard with pleasant, but distinctly MOR results.

ALADDIN 605 Hush/Am I in Love with You No More
Produced by Chris Blackwell.

ALADDIN 611 The Same One/I Don't Know
Produced by Chris Blackwell.

ISLAND 255 White Christmas/My Love & I
Produced by Chris Blackwell. (a) A straightforward rendering, "classic" pop in a very mid-1960s way, but you can't help thinking Edwards is wasting his time and talent.

ALTON ELLIS

(X) BABA BROOKS

HORTENSE ELLIS

BLUE BEAT 295 I've Been a Fool/Hold Me Tenderly

ERROL & HIS GROUP

Featuring ERROL DUNKLEY and ROY SHIRLEY.

BLUE BEAT 284 Gypsy/Miss May

THE FOUR ACES

Vocal group featuring brothers BARRY, CARL, CLIVE, and PATRICK HOWARD. Later became DESMOND DEKKER's regular backing vocalists, THE ACES, after he heard them perform and introduced them to producer Leslie Kong. It was 1970 before the group — by now a duo of Carl and Barry only — scored their own first hit, "Mademoiselle Ninette," and the Aces continued recording into the early 1980s.

ISLAND 178 Hoochy Koochy Kai Po/River Bank Coberley Again

Produced by Leslie Kong.

ISLAND 179 Sweet Chariot/Peace & Love

Produced by Leslie Kong.

ISLAND 180 Little Girl/CLARENDONIANS: Day Will Come

Produced by Leslie Kong.

B FRANCIS

SKA-BEAT 193 Judy Crowned/Who Crunch

NORMA FRAZIER

Also recorded as a duo CREATOR & NORMA.

SKA-BEAT 223 Heartaches/Everybody Loves A Lover

BASIL GABBIDON

BLUE BEAT 288 Tick Tock/Streets of Glory

BLUE BEAT 303 Dig the Dig/Don't Let Me Cry No More

GAYNOR & ERROL

Vocal duo featuring ERROL DIXON. (X) ROLAND ALPHONSO

GLORIA & THE DREAMLETTS

Featuring GLORIA CRAWFORD. (X) STRANGER COLE, SKATALITES

OWEN GRAY

(X) THE SURVIVORS

ALADDIN 603 Gonna Work Out/Dolly Baby

Produced by Prince Buster.

ALADDIN 607 Can I Get a Witness/Linda Lu

BLUE BEAT 290 Daddy's Gone/BUSTER'S ALL-STARS: Johnny Dark

Produced by Prince Buster.

ISLAND 252 Shook Shimmy & Shake/I'm Going Back

ISLAND 258 You Don't Know Like I Do/Take Me Serious

DERRICK HARRIOTT

ISLAND 170 I Am Only Human/ROY PANTON: Good Man

Produced by Derrick Harriott.

ISLAND 237 My Three Loves/The Jerk

Produced by Derrick Harriott.

ISLAND 245 Together/Mama Didn't Lie

Produced by Derrick Harriott. (b) Sharp version of a Curtis Mayfield song.

SKA-BEAT 199 Monkey Ska/Derrick!

Produced by Derrick Harriott. (a) Working from the old adage, monkey see, monkey do, Harriott takes the tale to its obvious dancing conclusion, while leaving listeners to decide for themselves whether this catchy song merely refers to monkeys or other primates as well. (b) It's the unforgettable cries of "Derrick!" (think of the old pig call, "suuueeee") that overwhelms. . . the song itself is pleasantly upbeat, with Harriott obviously enjoying himself to the hilt.

JOE HAYWOOD

ISLAND 218 Warm & Tender Love/I Would if I Could

HIGGS & WILSON

(X) PRINCE BUSTER'S ALL STARS

JUSTIN HINDS (aka HINES) & THE DOMINOES

(X) DON DRUMMOND

ISLAND 171 Botheration/Satan

Produced by Duke Reid. (a) The staccato beat adds tension to Hinds' sing-along ode to the social turmoil rolling across the island.

ISLAND 174 Jump Out of Frying Pan/Holy Dove

Produced by Duke Reid.

ISLAND 194 Rub Up Push Up/The Ark

Produced by Duke Reid. (a) The lyrics belie the risque title, with Hinds and the Dominoes having a marvelous time telling off a girl who's offering affection in lieu of an apology; the vocal parts are simply wonderful and the melody is brilliant. (b) With lyrics ripped straight from the Old Testament, this is one of Hind's most overtly religious numbers. However, with its driving beat and celebratory sax, it's far removed from the spiritual end of songwriting.

ISLAND 232 Turn Them Back/TOMMY MCCOOK: Rocket Ship

Produced by Duke Reid.

ISLAND 236 Peace & Love/Skalarama

Produced by Duke Reid.

SKA-BEAT 187 Mother Banner/DON DRUMMOND & HIS GROUP: Ally Pang

Produced by Duke Reid. (b) "Ally Pang" is dedicated to the diminutive (three foot) Annie Palmer, the white witch of Rose Hall, with honking solos by Don Drummond and ROLANDO ALPHONSO.

THE HONEY DUCKERS

(X) ALAN MARTIN

HORTENSE & ALTON

Vocal duo HORTENSE ELLIS and ALTON ELLIS.

ISLAND 230 Don't Gamble with Love/Something You Got

HYACINTH

Also recorded as a duo with SHENLEY DUFFUS. (X) ROLAND ALPHONSO, BABA BROOKS

C HYMAN

SKA-BEAT 200 The Ska Rhythm/The Ska Is Moving On

JACKIE & MILLIE

Vocal duo JACKIE EDWARDS and MILLIE SMALL.

ISLAND 253 This Is the Story/SOUND SYSTEM: Never Again

JAMAICA'S GREATEST

BLUE BEAT 309 Here Comes the Bride/It's Burke's Law

Produced by Prince Buster. (b) Another okra Western instrumental, slowing towards rock steady but still delivering a powerful punch, aided by Buster's unusual oin-oinga vocals, a template for Eek-A-Mouse's similarly bizarre performances.

BLUE BEAT 313 Everybody Yeah Yeah/BUSTER'S ALL-STARS: Gun the Man Down

Produced by Prince Buster.

BLUE BEAT 317 Come Home/I Thank You

Produced by Prince Buster.

PHILIP JAMES & THE BLUES BUSTERS

Alongside LLOYD CAMPBELL, JAMES was vocalist with the Blues Busters. (X) THE MAYTALS

THE KHANDARS

(X) PRINCE BUSTER'S ALL STARS

KING JOE FRANCIS

aka JOE FRANCIS.

BLUE BEAT 323 Wicked Woman/King Joe's Ska

KING ROCKY

aka ANTHONY "ROCKY" ELLIS. Recorded as a duo with LEROY SIBBLES and LITTLE ROY. (X) CLANCY ECCLES

KEN LAZARUS & THE BYRON LEE ORCHESTRA

Lazarus was vocalist with CARLOS MALCOLM'S AFRO-CARIBS and BYRON LEE & THE DRAGONAIRES. He later recorded with TOMORROW'S CHILDREN.

ISLAND 220 Funny/BYRON LEE ORCHESTRA: Walk Like a Dragon

Produced by Byron Lee.

BYRON LEE & THE DRAGONAIRES

(X) BLUES BUSTERS

THE BYRON LEE ORCHESTRA

(X) KEN LAZARUS

BYRON LEE'S SKA KINGS

aka BYRON LEE & THE DRAGONAIRES.

ATLANTIC 6014 Ska Time EP

Produced by Byron Lee.

LEN & THE HONEYSUCKERS

(X) CHUBBY & THE HONEYSUCKERS

LIGES

JOE LIGES aka DELROY WILSON. (X) THE SLANES

LITTLE DARLING

(X) PRINCE BUSTER'S ALL STARS

LITTLE JOE & BUSTER'S ALL STARS

No relation to the later El Paso Sound DJ of the same name (who subsequently became RANKING JOE), although both were named after the character on TV's Bonanza. (X) SEXY GIRLS

LORD ANTICS

(X) DON DRUMMOND

LORD BRISCO

ISLAND 187 Jonah/Mr Cleveland

LORD BRYNNER

(X) ROLAND ALPHONSO

LORD CREATOR

BLUE BEAT 292 Evening News/Good for Creator

(a) One of several ska-style remakes of his greatest hit, recorded during the mid-1960s. The story of a young boy forced to earn a living selling newspapers on the street fed easily into the rude boy iconography — many of them had shared the protagonist's lot.

LORD TANAMO

SKA-BEAT 217 Mattie Rag/BABA BROOKS BAND: Mattie Rag

(a) Lord Tanamo at his plaintive best, although the SKATALITES' jazzy upbeat arrangement somewhat undermines the melancholy mood.

SKA-BEAT 224 I'm in the Mood for Ska/You Never Know

A ska-ified version of the old chestnut "I'm in the Mood for Love," with a smoking band and Tanamo flitting between pop and soul. The singer would return the song to its original title for a 1990 UK hit single.

CARLOS MALCOLM & THE AFRO CARIBS

One of the founders of the Jamaican Broadcasting Corporation, trombonist MALCOLM's band members included vocalists JOE HIGGS, KEN LAZARUS, EDDIE PARKINS (of ALTON & EDDIE), LASCELLES PERKINS and BORIS GARDINER (also bass), WINSTON MARTIN (drums), KARL BRYAN (sax), KART MCDONALD (congas).

ISLAND 173 Bonanza Ska/Papa Luiga

Produced by Carlos Malcolm, (a) The epitome of the novelty single, "Ska" took the TV theme song to its ultimate island limits before melting into a medley of other classics. The perfectly in-sync horns are a wonder, the Rasta cowboys shout in delight and, most amazingly, a blaring horn sounds exactly like a whinnying horse. From this same period, the band's sole album, Skamania is well worth seeking out by fans of tough jazz/mento flavored ska.

ALAN MARTIN

RIO 66 Must Know I Love You/VIC BROWN'S COMBO: Rio Special

RIO 68 Why Must I Cry/Shirley I Love You

RIO 67 Sweet Rosemarie/HONEY DUCKERS: Banjo Man

RIO 74 Since I Married Dorothy/You Promised Me

THE MAYTALS

(X) STRANGER COLE

BLUE BEAT 281 Looking Down the Street/PRINCE BUSTER: Blues Market

Produced by Prince Buster.

BLUE BEAT 299 The Light of the World/Lovely Walking

Produced by Prince Buster.

BLUE BEAT 306 Ska War/SKATALITES: Perhaps

Produced by Prince Buster.

ISLAND 200 Never You Change/What's on Your Mind

Produced by Ronnie Nasralla/Byron Lee. (a) A perfect up-tempo beat (echoed by the brass) curls around the exquisite harmonies and sublime guitars, while TOOTS HIBBERT sings his heart out. (b) One of the all-time classic Maytals hits, a compulsive rhythm with the group's doo-wop roots showing proudly.

ISLAND 213 My New Name/It's No Use

Produced by Ronnie Nasralla/Byron Lee.

ISLAND 219 Tell Me the Reason/PHILIP JAMES & THE BLUES BUSTERS: Wide Awake in a Dream

Produced by Ronnie Nasralla/Byron Lee.

SKA-BEAT 202 Let's Jump/Joy & Jean

Produced by Sonia Pottinger. (a) By the time the trio are done, everyone in the room must have been jumping along to this jiving single — a piano boogie with a powerful stand up bass line and scorching horns, with the musicians carried away by the Maytals' own enthusiasm.

TOMMY MCCOOK

(X) JUSTIN HINDS

MILLIE

BRIT 1002 My Street/Mixed Up, Fickle, Moody, Self Centered, Spoiled Kind of Boy

Produced by Chris Blackwell. Also released as FONTANA 591.

FONTANA 515 I've Fallen in Love with a Snowman/What Am I Living For

Produced by Chris Blackwell. This must have made a lot of sense, exported back to Jamaica. Millie wraps her tonsils around one of the 1950s' cutest kiddy Christmas songs, with predictably cloying results.

FONTANA 529 See You Later Alligator/Chilly Kisses

Produced by Chris Blackwell. Desperate for a hit, a lightly (very lightly) skanked version of the old Bill Haley corker, raucous in all the right places, but the alligator went home hours ago.

FONTANA 617 Bloodshot Eyes/Tongue Tied

Produced by Chris Blackwell.

MONTY, DERRICK & PATSY

Vocal trio featuring ERIC MORRIS, DERRICK MORGAN and PATSY TODD.

BLUE BEAT 280 Stir the Pot/Mercy

Produced by Prince Buster.

DERRICK MORGAN

BLUE BEAT 276 Weep No More/I Want a Girl

BLUE BEAT 283 Johnny Grave/BUSTER'S ALL-STARS: Yeah Yeah

BLUE BEAT 311 Throw Them Away/Baby Face

ISLAND 193 Two of a Kind/I Want a Lover

ISLAND 225 Starvation/I Am a Blackhead Again

SKA-BEAT 218 Don't Call Me Daddy/BABA BROOKS BAND: Girl's Town Ska

(a) The "Billie Jean" of its day as Morgan eloquently demands "don't call me Daddy." He puts up a fine defense, too; it indeed seems unlikely that the singer was responsible for this Black mother's Chinese baby. "This woman is crazy," Morgan declares, and we're forced to agree. (b) The trumpeter and his band kick it down in Girl's Town — obviously the place to be, as the cheery melody buttressed by percolating rhythms prove.

DERRICK MORGAN WITH PRINCE BUSTER

Self-explanatory duo.

BLUE BEAT 329 Sweeter Than Honey/You Never Know

Produced by Prince Buster.

ERIC MORRIS

BLUE BEAT 298 Those Teardrops/DON DRUMMOND: Ska Town

Produced by Prince Buster.

ISLAND 183 Love Can Make a Mansion/Ungodly People

ISLAND 185 Suddenly/Many Long Years

ISLAND 199 Fast Mouth/The Harder They Come

ISLAND 234 Children of Today/BABA BROOKS: Greenfield Ska

RIO 72 By the Sea/I Wasn't Around

THE MOVERS

(X) DON DRUMMOND

TERRY NELSON & THE FIREBALLS

BLUE BEAT 326 Help/PRINCE BUSTER: Johnny Dollar

Produced by Prince Buster.

DICE 23 Run Run Baby/Bonita

DICE 25 Bulldog Push/Pretty Little Girl

DICE 27 Tomorrow Will Soon Be Here/My Blue Eyed Baby

JACKIE OPEL

ISLAND 203 Wipe those Tears/Don't Take Your Love

ISLAND 209 Go Whey/Shelter the Storm

ISLAND 227 Old Rockin' Chair/SKATALITES: Song of Love

(a) The SKATALITES stand behind Opel, of course, while ERNEST RANGLIN turns in a characteristic solo.

KING 1011 Cry Me a River/Eternal Love

The Julie London tearjerker, with a light jazz-ska backing only mildly detracting from the lyrics' absolute desolation.

SKA-BEAT 190 More Wood in the Fire/Done with a Friend
An infectious melody, a sing-along chorus, suggestive lyrics and Opel's exuberant delivery render this an unforgettable experience.

SKA-BEAT 227 A Little More/The Lord Is with Thee

OWEN & LEON

SKA-BEAT 189 Woman/BABA BROOKS WITH DON DRUMMOND: Doctor Decker
(b) Drummond leads the tight rhythm section and upbeat saxes through an infectious instrumental, with a signature SKATELITES' melody.

ROY PANTON

(X) DERRICK HARRIOTT

PATSY & DESMOND

Vocal duo featuring PATSY TODD and DESMOND DEKKER.
(X) DESMOND DEKKER

KEITH PATTERSON

(X) SONNY BURKE

LEE PERRY

(X) DESMOND DEKKER

ISLAND 210 Please Don't Go/Bye St Peter
Produced by Coxsone Dodd. (a) Oddly, in light of his later reputation, the bulk of Perry's earliest recordings were convention personified. This one's no different, although the SOULETTES' harmonies are sweet and the snatch of chatter towards the end adds a certain club ambience to the proceedings. (b) The SKATALITES' stately intro is undone by a fairly mundane song, the SOULETTES' echo of Perry's vocal rapidly growing grating.

SKA-BEAT 201 Roast Duck/Hand to Hand, Man to Man
Produced by Coxsone Dodd. (a) There's a hint of Motown to the bass line, and the SOULETTES are unmistakable in the background. Unsurprisingly, the lyric itself revolves around a girlfriend's demands for roast duck. Naturally, she doesn't *really* want a duck. (b) A defiant slice of fighting talk, with the angelic-sounding WAILERS egging Perry on to "defeat dem one by one."

SKA-BEAT 203 Trails & Crosses/Jon Om
Produced by Coxsone Dodd.

SKA-BEAT 212 Wishes of the Wicked/Hold Down
Produced by Coxsone Dodd.

SKA-BEAT 215 Open Up/ROLAND ALPHONSO: Twin Double
Produced by Coxsone Dodd. (b) Claude King's "Wolverton Mountain" goes ska.

THE PERSONALITIES

DICE 30 I Remember/Suffering

THE PIONEERS

Formed in 1962 as a vocal trio comprising WINSTON HEWITT and brothers DERRICK and SIDNEY "LUDDY" CROOKS, in which form they self-financed/produced "Good Nanny" for the Caltone label. Band split when Derrick emigrated to Canada, reforming as a duo of Sidney Crooks and JACKIE ROBINSON, aka THE SOUL MATES (1967). Joined by GEORGE DEKKER, half-brother of DESMOND, in 1968, they recorded as THE PIONEERS, SIDNEY GEORGE & JACKIE, and THE SLICKERS. A tight and lovely sounding group, their early career has been utterly overshadowed by the hit "Long Shot Kick de Bucket"; their later releases distorted by it. The group broke up around 1973, with Crooks moving into production (see entry in DIRECTORY OF PRODUCERS), while Dekker returned to his solo career. (X) THEO BECKFORD.

PRINCE BUSTER

(X) THE MAYTALS, TERRY NELSON & THE FIREBALLS

BLUE BEAT 278 Blood Pressure/Islam
Produced by Prince Buster.

BLUE BEAT 282 Big Fight/Red Dress
Produced by Prince Buster.

BLUE BEAT 302 Ling Tong Tong/Walk Along
Produced by Prince Buster.

BLUE BEAT 307 Bonanza/Wonderful Life
Produced by Prince Buster.

BLUE BEAT 314 Float Like a Butterfly/Haunted Room
Produced by Prince Buster.

BLUE BEAT 316 Sugar Pop/Feel Up
Produced by Prince Buster. Credited to Buster & JAMAICA'S GREATEST

BLUE BEAT 321 My Girl/The Fugitive
Produced by Prince Buster.

BLUE BEAT 324 Al Capone/One Step Beyond
Produced by Prince Buster. (a) From the opening squeal of burning rubber, this song had hit written all over it. Its insistent, pounding beat, jazzy brass, and trademark chigga-chigga provided by the SKATALITES (disguised as the ALL STARS) made it a rude boy fave, as did the gangster's name-check which passes within for lyrics. The devastating sax lines were supplied by VAL BENNETT and future SOUL BROTHERS mainstay DENNIS CAMPBELL.

BLUE BEAT 328 Ambition/Ryging
Produced by Prince Buster.

BLUE BEAT 330 Rum & Coca Cola/I Love Her
Produced by Prince Buster. (a) Driving cover of the wartime LORD INVADER calypso.

BLUE BEAT 335 Respect/Virginia
Produced by Prince Buster.

(PRINCE) BUSTER'S ALL STARS

(X) THE CHARMERS, STRANGER COLE, OWEN GRAY, JAMAICA'S GREATEST, DERRICK MORGAN

BLUE BEAT 277 Going West/(JOE) HIGGS & (ROY) WILSON: Pain in My Heart
Produced by Prince Buster.

BLUE BEAT 294 Eye for Eye/South Virginia
Produced by Prince Buster.

BLUE BEAT 325 Congo Revolution/LITTLE DARLING: No-One
Produced by Prince Buster.

BLUE BEAT 331 Vera Cruz/SPANISH BOYS: I Am Alone
Produced by Prince Buster.

BLUE BEAT 332 Skara/KHANDARS: Don't Dig a Hole for Me
Produced by Prince Buster.

BLUE BEAT 333 Captain Burke/STRANGER COLE: Matilda
Produced by Prince Buster.

P REID

SKA-BEAT 197 Redeemed/Goodbye World

THE RIOTS

ISLAND 176 Telling Lies/Don't Leave Me

ISLAND 195 You Don't Know/DON DRUMMOND & DRUMBAGO: Treasure Island
Produced by Duke Reid.

ISLAND 197 I Am in Love/When You're Wrong

ISLAND 247 Yeah Yeah/BABA BROOKS: Virginia Ska
(a) The tambourine mixed way up front certainly gives this instrumental a unique sound, while the brass swings in the usual jazzy way.

RITA & BENNY

RITA ISSELS and BENNY KING were the owners of London's R&B store and record label. (X) DON DRUMMOND

THE RUB A DUBS WITH DANDY

Featuring DANDY LIVINGSTONE.

BLUE BEAT 304 Without Love/I Know

RUDDY & SKETTO

BLUE BEAT 297 See What You Done/Heart's Desire

BLUE BEAT 310 Oh Dolly/You're Mine

WINSTON SAMUELS

SKA-BEAT 196 Be Prepared/Jericho Wall

SKA-BEAT 213 My Bride to Be/LLOYD BREVETT: Wayward Ska
(a) With a melody vaguely reminiscent of DERRICK MORGAN's "No Raise No Praise," Samuels' cheeriness is unquenchable, helped by a particularly exuberant sax. (b) The bassist sets the rhythm, while the horns inject a sprightly instrumental with an almost oom-pah punch.

SKA-BEAT 214 Never Again/My Angel

RUDY SEEDORF

ISLAND 189 One Million Stars/Mr Blue

THE SEXY GIRLS

DICE 100 Pom Pom Song/LITTLE JOE & BUSTER'S ALL-STARS: Hi There
Produced by Prince Buster. Reissued as FAB 100.

SHENLEY & HYACINTH

Vocal duo featuring SHENLEY DUFFUS. (X) BABA BROOKS

SHENLEY & LUMAN

Vocal duo featuring SHENLEY DUFFUS and LITTLE LUMAN. (X) BOBBY AITKEN

LIONEL SIMPSON

aka LEO SIMPSON.

SKA-BEAT 205 Tell Me What You Want/Love Is a Game

SKA-BEAT 221 Red River Valley/Eight People

THE SKA CHAMPIONS

BLUE BEAT 305 My Tears/Yesterday's Dreams

THE SKATALITES

(X) MAYTALS, JACKIE OPEL

BLUE BEAT 275 Hanging the Beam/THE DELTAS: The Visitor
Produced by Coxsone Dodd.

ISLAND 168 Guns of Navarone/Marcus Garvey
Produced by Coxsone Dodd. (a) Perhaps the best-known song from the Skatalites' copious catalogue, and certainly the most typical. The mighty instrumentalists take a rather bland war movie theme and turn it into a Caribbean classic, egged on by the yips and shouts of LEE PERRY.

ISLAND 191 Dr Kildare/Sucu Sucu
Produced by Coxsone Dodd. (a) Another of the multitude of instrumentals adapted from movie/TV themes. The musicianship is excellent, but the song itself withers beneath the Caribbean sun and hot jazz adaptation. (b) ROLAND ALPHONSO takes center stage on this swinging ska instrumental in a festival mood.

ISLAND 207 Ball of Fire/LINVAL SPENCER: Can't Go On

ISLAND 226 Dick Tracy/RITA & THE SOULETTES: One More Chance
Produced by Coxsone Dodd. (a) ALPHONSO, MOORE, and DRUMMOND handle the solos on this fiery secret agent theme.

ISLAND 228 Beardsman Ska/RONNIE & RITA: Bless You
Produced by Coxsone Dodd. (a) Based on a piece the Skatalites used to jam with COUNT OSSIE, "Beardsman Ska" was originally titled "Beardsman Shuffle." In 1997, BEENIE MAN used the rhythm for his "Foundation" single and topped the chart for seven weeks.

ISLAND 244 Lucky Seven/JUSTIN HINDS & THE DOMINOES: Never Too Young
Produced by Duke Reid. (a) There's a cloppity sense of the Magnificent Seven in the beat and the vocal "pick it up" lines, but that's the only nod to the West on this upbeat, jazzy instrumental.

SKA-BEAT 182 Street Corner/THE DREAMLETTS: Really Now
Produced by Duke Reid. (a) It starts like a party, then turns down a few notches to settle into a mid-tempo groove. The highlight is the sax part in the second half of the song, which will reappear for years after, both among the band's own membership and scores of their imitators. (b) The trio take on a perky love song and acquit themselves well, although it's not really a stand-out.

SKA-BEAT 206 Timothy/KING SCRATCH & THE DYNAMITES: Gumma

Produced by Coxsone Dodd. (a) Kicking ska instrumental powered by ROLAND ALPHONSO, but driven by the scat vocals, hissing and hiccuping along with the beat.

THE SLANES

BLUE BEAT 300 It Takes Time/LIGES: Have Mercy Baby

THE SOULETTES

Vocal trio comprising RITA MARLEY (b Alpharita Anderson, Cuba), CONSTANTINE "DREAM" (aka "VISION") WALKER (ex-DREAMLETTS), and MARLENE "PRECIOUS" GIFFORD. Frequently accompanied by Rita's husband BOB MARLEY (the trio's musical director) and THE WAILERS. Original group broke up around 1967, but Rita reformed it with HORTENSE LEWIS and CECILE CAMPBELL (sister of CORNELL) for sessions with LEE PERRY in 1970. (X) THE SKATALITES

SKA-BEAT 204 Opportunity/DIZZY JOHNNY & THE STUDIO 1 ORCHESTRA: Sudden Destruction

Produced by Coxsone Dodd. (b) This punchy instrumental blends a tinge of Western with a hint of surf; listening to the horns you'll understand precisely how "Dizzy" Mr Moore got his nickname.

THE SPANISH BOYS

(X) PRINCE BUSTER'S ALL STARS

THE SPANISHTOWN SKA-BEATS

BLUE BEAT 315 Oh My Baby/Stop that Train

Produced by Prince Buster.

BLUE BEAT 320 King Solomon/BUSTER'S ALL-STARS: Devil's Daffodil

Produced by Prince Buster.

LINVAL SPENCER

(X) SKATALITES

WINSTON STEWART

(X) ANDY & CLYDE

STRANGER & CLAUDETTE

Vocal duo featuring STRANGER COLE. (X) BABA BROOKS

SUFFERER

aka FRANK COSMO. (X) TWO KINGS

SUGAR & DANDY

CARNIVAL 7023 Let's Ska/Only Heaven Knows

Also released as PAGE ONE 044.

CARNIVAL 7024 I'm into Something Good/Crazy for You

CARNIVAL 7027 Think of the Good Times/Girl Come See

CARNIVAL 7029 I Want to Be Your Lover/I Don't Know What I'm Going to Do Now

SUNNY & THE HI JUMPERS

CARNIVAL 7022 Tarry Til You're Better/Dance Til You're Better

CARNIVAL 7025 Going to Damascus/Sweet Potatoes

THE SURVIVORS

RIO 55 Take Charge/Ska-ology

RIO 70 Rawhide Ska/OWEN GRAY: Girl I Want You

THE TECHNIQUES

One of the all-time greatest vocal groups, originally featuring WINSTON RILEY, SLIM SMITH, FRANKLYN WHITE, and FREDERICK WAITE. White and Smith left for THE UNIQUES during 1966; they were replaced by PAT KELLY before Riley left to form his own Techniques label (and TECHNIQUES ALL STARS) in 1968. Subsequent band members included LLOYD PARKS (THE TERMITES), DAVE BARKER, MORVIN BROOKS, BRUCE RUFFIN. Riley continues producing; Waite moved to the UK and managed "Pass The Dutchie" hitmakers Musical Youth. (X) DON DRUMMOND

PETER TOUCH

aka PETER TOSH. See entry on page 288.

ISLAND 211 Hoot Nanny Hoot/WAILERS: Do You Remember

Produced by Coxsone Dodd. (a) Excellent skanker introducing a new dance which even Tosh admits "I just don't know how to do. . . ." The riff parodies a traditional American folk theme — the hootenanny, of course. (b) aka "How Many Times." A mantric horn riff underpins a yearning boy meets girl type song, a kind of Kingston answer to *American Graffiti*.

ISLAND 215 Shame & Scandal/WAILERS: The Jerk

Produced by Coxsone Dodd. (a) Over a seething rhythm, an adaptation of the SIR LANCELOT calypso where boy meets girl, and things just go haywire from there. (b) The Wailers adapt the Larkers' dance craze hit "The Jerk" to a ska beat, then toss Jr. Walker & The All Stars' "Shotgun" and the "ooh ah"s from Sam Cooke's "Chain Gang" into the mix. The jazzy horn solo still manages to throw the song for a loop, though.

THE TWO KINGS

ISLAND 240 Rolling Stone/SUFFERER: Tomorrow Morning

ISLAND 249 Hit You Let You Feel It/Honey I Love You

THE UPCOMING WILLOWS

Studio band for KING EDWARDS. (X) SHENLEY DUFFUS

ISLAND 182 Jones Town Special/SHENLEY DUFFUS: La La La

THE UPSETTERS

Not the Lee Perry band!

ISLAND 223 Country Girl/Strange Country

THE VIRTUES

Shortlived trio best remembered for its membership — the original line-up included RUPIE EDWARDS (keyboards), ERIC FRATER (guitar), and JUNIOR MENZ (THE PARAGONS). DOBBY DOBSON was also involved.

ISLAND 196 Your Wife & Mother/Amen

Produced by Harry J.

THE WAILERS

(X) PETER TOUCH.

ISLAND 188 It Hurts to Be Alone/Mr Talkative

Produced by Coxsone Dodd. (a) A gorgeous ballad with vocals by JUNIOR BRAITHWAITE (his last recording with the band) and a slow burning ERNEST RANGLIN guitar. An alternative take appears on the *Simmer Down At Studio One* compilation. (b) Cut at the Wailers' second Studio One session, a singalong chorus sticks it to the chattering title character, all wrapped around an unstoppable ska beat. The group would later rerecord the song for LEE PERRY under the title "Mr Chatterbox."

ISLAND 206 Play Boy/Your Love

Produced by Coxsone Dodd. (a) The SKATALITES play as suavely as the title suggests, on a ska-fired infectious adaptation of the Contours' hit "Do You Love Me." (b) A fast ska featuring an exuberant BUNNY/BRAITHWAITE/KELSO chorus behind MARLEY's lead, with JOE HIGGS stepping in for the deep bass parts.

ISLAND 212 Hooligan/Maga Dog

Produced by Coxsone Dodd. (a) Written in direct response to the rude-boy rioting which was mashing up the ska revues, lovely harmonies blend across a hook ridden chorus and an infectious ska beat, but cannot disguise the warning to the rude boys. (b) TOSH's first unequivocal classic, barking mad rhythms and a vicious bite as well. "Maga" is slang for scrawny, and the dog certainly sounds deserving of Tosh's pity.

ISLAND 216 Don't Ever Leave Me/Donna

Produced by Coxsone Dodd. (a) BRAITHWAITE takes a breathlessly angelic lead on a fairly drab MARLEY composition, while ERNEST RANGLIN (guitar), RICHARD ACE (piano), and LLOYD SPENCE (bass) throw in some instrumental flourishes which remind us just how heavily the British Invasion impacted upon Jamaica. The bass, indeed, seems literally to have just walked out of a London studio.

ISLAND 254 What's New Pussycat/Where Will I Find

Produced by Coxsone Dodd. (a) Of course, not everything the Wailers did turned to gold, although Dodd was happy enough with their ska'd-up, but otherwise straightforward, rendition of the Tom Jones movie theme hit.

SKA-BEAT 186 Simmer Down/I Don't Need Your Love

Produced by Coxsone Dodd. (a) The Wailers' first release and first hit. Featuring a killer solo from SKATALITE TOMMY MCCOOK, a beat that won't quit and a melody and harmonies worth fighting for, a musical reprimand to rambunctious rude boys which, of course, merely prompted them to party harder.

SKA-BEAT 211 Lonesome Feelings/There She Goes

Produced by Coxsone Dodd. (a) Doo-wop meets R&B, accompanied by the de rigueur jazzy horn solo. Cut soon after BRAITHWAITE's departure, MARLEY sounds like Elvis gone Stax, while TOSH, LIVINGSTON, KELSO, and GREEN harmonize high and sweet in the background. The MIGHTY VIKINGS do the instrumental honors. (b) The Wailers' doo-wop with the best of them on this cover of the old Jerry Wallace hit, again cut with the MIGHTY VIKINGS. BUNNY LIVINGSTON reaches new heights of soulful passion, with the cheesy organ adding to the chest thumping over-the-top emotion of it all.

SKA-BEAT 226 I Made a Mistake/SOUL BROTHERS: Train to Skaville

Produced by Coxsone Dodd.

JOE WHITE

(X) CHUCK & JOE WHITE

WILFRED & MILLICENT

Vocal duo featuring JACKIE EDWARDS and MILLIE SMALL.

ISLAND 190 The Vow/I'll Never Believe in You

Produced by Chris Blackwell.

DELROY WILSON

ISLAND 205 Pick up the Pieces/Oppression

Produced by Coxsone Dodd.

RONALD WILSON

(X) DOUGLAS BROTHERS

TREVOR WILSON

CARIBS vocalist, aka TREVOR.

SKA-BEAT 207 You Couldn't Believe/You Told Me You Care

WINSTON & THE TONETTES

SKA-BEAT 225 You Make Me Cry/CHECKMATES: Invisible Ska

Produced by Coxsone Dodd.

ROYCE WONG

BLUE BEAT 301 Everything's Gonna Be Alright/Hang Your Head & Cry

THE ZODIACS

(X) BABA BROOKS

1966

LLOYD ADAMS

(X) THE CREEPERS

BOBBY AITKEN

SKA-BEAT 252 Thunderball/ORIGINATORS: Chelip Chelip
BLUE BEAT 369 Shame & Scandal/Coconut Women

LAUREL AITKEN

BLUE BEAT 340 Clementine/Bongo Jerk
RAINBOW 101 Don't Break Your Promises/Last Night
RAINBOW 106 Voodoo Woman/Bewildered & Blue
RIO 91 How Can I Forget You/Weeping & Crying
RIO 92 Baby Don't Do It/That Girl
RIO 97 We Shall Overcome/Street of Glory
RIO 99 Clap Your Hands/Revival
SKA-BEAT 232 Jumbie Jamboree/Looking for My Baby

SKA-BEAT 236 Propaganda/Shake

SKA-BEAT 239 Green Banana/Darling

ALLEN & MILTON

Vocal duo comprising VERNON ALLEN and MILTON HAMILTON.

BLUE BEAT 348 It Is I/Baby What's More

BLUE BEAT 353 You're the Angel/Someone Like You

ROLAND ALPHONSO

(X) JACKIE OPEL, THE WAILERS

DR BIRD 1008 VC 10/LARRY MARSHALL: Snake in the Grass

Produced by Justin & Duke Yap.

DR BIRD 1005 Miss Ska-Culation/JACK SPARROW: Ice Water

Produced by Coxsone Dodd. Also released as DR BIRD 1027. (b) One of four songs cut by ETHIOPIANS' singer LEONARD DILLON under this alias, but the only one issued in the UK.

DR BIRD 1010 From Russia with Love/Cleopatra

Produced by Coxsone Dodd. (a) The James Bond movie theme delivered with clinical style. (b) A steamy and occasionally eastern flavored instrumental titled from, but not covering, the 1963 Elizabeth Taylor movie.

DR BIRD 1011 Sufferer's Choice/SOULETTES: I Want to Be

Produced by Coxsone Dodd.

DR BIRD 1017 Sugar & Spice/Get Out of My Life

Produced by Coxsone Dodd.

DR BIRD 1020 Phoenix City/DEACONS: Men Alone

Produced by Coxsone Dodd. (a) Another instrumental winner from the SKATALITE mainstay, this one's jazz lite with a great chigga chigga beat and horn solos that will leave you breathless. Phoenix City itself was the name of one of Kingston's most notorious gangs.

DR BIRD 1023 Dr Ring a Ding/FREDDIE & THE HEARTACHES: Here Is My Heart

Produced by Coxsone Dodd.

DR BIRD 1039 Ska with Ringo/THE WAILERS Put It On

Produced by Coxsone Dodd. (a) Credited to ROLAND AL & THE SOUL BROTHERS, "Ska With Ringo" is another in the SKATALITES' Beatles "tributes."

ALTON & THE FLAMES

Vocal group originally comprising ALTON ELLIS and THE MAYTALS, before a new Flames lineup was built around WINSTON JARRETT.

BLUE BEAT 356 Just a Little Closer/Jericho Chain

DR BIRD 1049 The Preacher/LYNN TAITT & THE COMETS: Tender Loving Care

(a) Ellis delivers up some of his most soulful vocals over a slow simmering beat, to detail the tale of a preacher who doesn't approve of rude boys. (b) More upbeat than you'd expect from the title, TAITT & THE COMETS don't provide so much TLC on this instrumental, as perky pecks on the cheek.

ISLAND 259 James Bond/LEE PERRY & THE DYNAMITES: Just Keep It Up

Produced by Coxsone Dodd. (b) Straightforward love song with pumping horns and the SKATALITES on autopilot.

SKA-BEAT 231 Rinky Dink/SCRATCH & DYNAMITES: Deacon Johnson

REUBEN ANDERSON

DR BIRD 1045 Christmas Time Again/DESMOND TUCKER: Oh Holy Night

THE ASTRONAUTS

Original lineup featured vocalist "BIBBY" (BB) SEATON, WEB STEWART (guitar).

HALA GALA 9 Before You Leave/Syncopate.

Produced by Justin & Duke Yap. Also released as ISLAND 3065.

THE AVALONS

ISLAND 263 Everyday/I Love You

DESMOND BAKER & THE CLARENDONIANS

ISLAND 295 Rude Boy Gonna Jail/SHARKS: Don't Fool Me

Produced by Coxsone Dodd.

THE BLUES BUSTERS

DR BIRD 1030 I've Been Trying/Pretty Girls

KEN BOOTHE

b 1948 (Kingston, JA). Launching his career as one-half of a duo with STRANGER COLE, Boothe truly broke through in the rock steady era, before the early 1970s reinvented him as a smoothly orchestrated balladeer. He scored major UK hits in 1974/75 with "Everything I Own" and "Crying over You," both produced by LLOYD CHARMERS. He also recorded as a duo with ROY SHIRLEY, and was a founder member of CONSCIOUS MINDS and THE MESSENGERS.

SKA-BEAT 248 You're No Good/SOULETTES: I Don't Care What the People Say

Produced by Coxsone Dodd. (a) A late-in-the-day ska number, inadvertently caught in the middle of major studio politics — according to Coxsone, the BRENTFORD ROCKERS backing band's horn section was "kicking up," so their bandmates cut them loose to prove they could have a hit without horns. In truth, the song sounds a little bare without them, but Boothe carries the day.

ERNEL BRAHAM

RIO 79 Musical Fight/EDWARDS ALL-STARS: Pipeline

Produced by Rupie Edwards. (b) Fronted by RONALD WILSON and ROLAND ALPHONSO, the All-Stars turn in a fiery version of the surf hit.

BABA BROOKS

(X) JOE WHITE

DR BIRD 1001 First Session/CHUCK & JOE WHITE: Every Night

DR BIRD 1009 King Size/SAINTS: Brown Eyes

DR BIRD 1042 The Clock/LYNN TAITT & COMETS & SILVERTONES: Raindrops

Produced by Duke Reid. (a)The rhythm section ticks with metronomic precision, while the brass and guitar soothingly plays above. It's a little upbeat for a lullaby, but that's the mood regardless. (b) The vocal group recreate the doo-wop sound of the early 60s for this cover of the Dee Clark hit, while TAITT & co provide a sympathetic accompaniment.

DR BIRD 1046 Jam Session/CONQUERORS: What a Agony

SONNY BURKE

BLUE BEAT 363 Blue Island/You Came & Left

DION CAMERON & THE THREE TOPS

RIO 111 Lord Have Mercy/Get Ready

CORNELL CAMPBELL & ROY PANTON

(X) THE CHARMERS

THE CARIB BEATS

Featuring BOBBY AITKEN (guitar), CYNTHIA RICHARDS (vocals), ANSELL COLLINS (vocals, later keyboards), WINSTON GRENNAN (drums). Band disbanded in mid-1960s, Grennan formed the MEDITATORS with ROLAND ALPHONSO, then the ALL STARS.

SKA-BEAT 246 Bells of St Mary's/WINSTON RICHARDS: Loki

THE CASTLE SISTERS

SKA-BEAT 257 Stop Your Lying/Don't Be a Fool

THE CHARMS

RIO 98 Everybody Say Yeah/This World Is Yours

THE CHARMERS

BLUE BEAT 345 Oh My Baby/STRANGER COLE: When the Party Is Over

RIO 78 You Don't Know/CORNELL CAMPBELL & ROY PANTON: Sweetest Girl

SKA-BEAT 237 Best Friend/MAYTALS: My Darling

Produced by Ronnie Nasralla/Byron Lee.

CHUCK & JOE WHITE

(X) BABA BROOKS

THE CITY SLICKERS

HERMAN HERSANG's regular combo. (X) THE WAILERS

THE CLARENDONIANS

(X) DESMOND BAKER

ISLAND 284 Try Me One More Time/Can't Keep a Good Man Down

Produced by Coxsone Dodd. Also released as STUDIO ONE 2007.

ISLAND 3005 I'll Never Change/Rules of Life

Produced by Coxsone Dodd.

RIO 112 Rudie Bam Bam/Be Bop Boy

Produced by Coxsone Dodd. (a) The Clarendonians deliver up the morality tale of a rudie who finally gets his come-uppance. No matter how many of his mates later dance the

pardon, here's one rude boy who will never see the light of day again.

RIO 115 Musical Train/Lowdown Girl

Produced by Coxsone Dodd.

SKA-BEAT 261 Doing the Jerk/You Won't See Me

Produced by Coxsone Dodd.

JIMMY CLIFF

FONTANA 641 Call on Me/Pride & Passion

Produced by Leslie Kong.

STRANGER COLE

DR BIRD 1025 We Shall Overcome/Do You Really Love Me

DR BIRD 1040 Drop the Ratchet/Oh Yee Mahee

(a) Cole eloquently pleads with the bad boys to leave their weapons at home as "the ratchet will do you no good," on this scorching single which kicks off slow and steady, but picks up pace and emotion by the end.

THE CONQUERORS

Duo featuring ASTOR CAMPBELL. (X) BABA BROOKS

GLORIA CRAWFORD

Vocalist with THE DREAMLETTS. (X) LESTER STERLING

THE CREEPERS

BLUE BEAT 366 Best of My Soul/LLOYD ADAMS: I Wish Your Picture Was You

CALVIN DAFOS

BLUE BEAT 347 Brown Sugar/I'm Gone

DAKOTA JIM

BLUE BEAT 358 Only Soul Can Tell/DAKOTA'S ALL-STARS: Call Me Master

DANDY

BLUE BEAT 336 I Found Love/You Got Something Nice

SKA-BEAT 247 The Fight/Do You Know

HORREL DAWKINS

SKA-BEAT 240 Cling to Me/Butterfly

(b) Dawkins does his best, but this single still sounds outright amateurish. As the band nonchalantly powers along, the harmonica carries the tune better than the singer, whose slightly off-key delivery might strike some as charming, but can also be termed annoying.

THE DEACONS

(X) ROLAND ALPHONSO

DERRICK & PATSY

ISLAND 288 I Found a Queen/It's True My Darling

ERROL DIXON

BLUE BEAT 337 Heavy Shuffle/Gloria

BLUE BEAT 344 You're No Good/Midnight Bus

FAB 1 I Need Someone to Love/I Want

Also released as RAINBOW 104.

DON DRUMMOND

(X) SOUL BROTHERS

ERROL DUNKLEY

RIO 109 Love Me Forever/VIETNAM ALL-STARS: The Toughest
Produced by Prince Buster.

THE EAGLES

Featuring CARLTON BROWN and PAT FRANCIS (b 8/29/47, St Catherine, JA). Francis later of THE MEDITATORS and solo. (X) ROY RICHARDS

JACKIE EDWARDS

ISLAND 270 Sometimes/Come On Home
Produced by Chris Blackwell. (b) Edwards sings his heart out on this soul-influenced number with a barely syncopated beat, wrapped in a Motown arrangement and production.

ISLAND 274 Love/What's Your Name
Produced by Chris Blackwell.

ISLAND 287 Think Twice/Oh Mary
Produced by Chris Blackwell.

ISLAND 3006 I Feel So Bad/I Don't Want to Be Made a Fool Of
Produced by Chris Blackwell.

ST MARY'S 701 Sacred Hymns Volume One EP
ST MARY'S 702 Sacred Hymns Volume Two EP
Two staggeringly rare releases catch Edwards delivering exactly what is promised. And if you think his last few releases are stretching the ska limits a little, you've not heard anything yet. Lovely voice, though.

ALTON ELLIS

DR BIRD 1044 Blessings of Love/Nothing Sweeter
Produced by Duke Reid. (a) The great Alton Ellis promotes peace. After all, if rudie's really and truly in love, isn't it time that he "stop the shootings, no more killings"?

DR BIRD 1055 Shake It/THE SILVERTONES: Whoo Baby
Produced by Duke Reid.

THE EMOTIONS

See entry for MAX ROMEO on page 248. Original line-up featured ROMEO, KENNETH KNIGHT, and LLOYD SHAKESPEARE. LEROY BROWN (HIPPY BOYS) was also a member. MILTON HENRY (ex-THE LEADERS, THE PROGRESSIONS) replaced Romeo during 1969, and appears on the band's High Note label recordings.

SKA-BEAT 263 Rude Boy Confession/Heartbreaking Gypsy
Produced by Ken Lack.

BERTRAM ENNIS COMBO

(X) LORD CREATOR

JACKIE ESTICK

SKA-BEAT 256 The Ska/Daisy I Love You
(a) The smooth singer introduces today's sound to the people, just as it was pushed into yesterday by rock steady./(b)

The brass section delivers a punchy brashness, in what would otherwise be a pleasant, if typical, upbeat love song.

THE ETHIOPIANS

Original line up: LEONARD "SPARROW" DILLON aka JACK SPARROW (b 12/42, Portland, JA), ASTON MORRIS, STEPHEN TAYLOR (b 1944, St Mary, JA/d 1975). Morris departed in late 1966 and the band continued as a duo. Following Taylor's death, Dillon carried on alone. PETER TOSH and BUNNY LIVINGSTON of THE WAILERS frequently appeared as backing vocalists on the group's early COXSONE DODD productions.

ISLAND 3015 I Am Free/SOUL BROTHERS: Shanty-Town
Produced by Coxsone Dodd. (a) This rootsy gem swings from moody to bright, and minor to major keys, as the Ethiopians' lovely harmonies drive home the message of freedom.

RIO 110 Owe Me No Pay Me/SHARKS: I Wouldn't Baby
Produced by Lloyd Charmers.

RIO 114 I'm Gonna Take Over Now/JACKIE MITTOO: Home Made
Produced by Coxsone Dodd.

SKA-BEAT 260 Live Good/SOUL BROTHERS: Soho
Produced by Coxsone Dodd.

FITZ & FREDDY

aka FREDDIE MCGREGOR and ERNEST WILSON of THE CLARENDONIANS. (X) ROY RICHARDS

HELEN FLEMING

BLUE BEAT 341 Eve's Ten Commandments/Don't Take Your Love Away
Produced by Prince Buster. (a) Swift and stern response to PRINCE BUSTER's "10 Commandments of Man."

JOE FRANCIS & RICKY LOGAN & SNOWBALLS

SKA-BEAT 262 Scarborough Ska/I Got a Scar

NORMA FRAZIER

(X) TOMMY MCCOOK

FREDDIE & THE HEARTACHES

(X) ROLAND ALPHONSO

THE GAYLADS

DR BIRD 1014 Lady with the Red Dress/Dinner for Two
DR BIRD 1031 You Should Never Do That/WINSTON STEWART: I Don't Know Why I Love You
(b) A pleasant solo outing from Gaylad Stewart.

ISLAND 281 Goodbye Daddy/Your Eyes
ISLAND 291 You Never Leave Him/Message to My Girl
ISLAND 3002 Stop Making Love/They Call Her Dawn
Produced by Coxsone Dodd. (a) Exuberant production based around the Motown hit "Same Old Song." The vocal trio deliver it up in appropriate Detroit fashion, while the sonics and rhythm are set firmly in Kingston.

RYMSKA 104 You Should Never Do That/TECHNIQUES: So Many Times

THE GAYLORDS
aka THE GAYLADS.

ISLAND 269 Chipmunk Ska/What Is Wrong
Produced by Coxsone Dodd.

GIRL SATCHMO
(X) THE JETLINERS

GIRL WONDER
DR BIRD 1015 Mommy out the Light/Cutting Wood

GLEN & LLOYD
Vocal duo comprising GLEN BROWN and LLOYD ROBIN-SON. aka LLOYD & GLEN.

SKA-BEAT 250 Live & Let Others Die/Too Late
(b) The duo belt out the vocals in their most soulful Stax fashion, although the flashy rag-time piano and powerful brass section clarify the song's true geographical origins.

OWEN GRAY
BLUE BEAT 365 I'm Gonna Say So Long/The Days I'm Living
ISLAND 267 Paradise/Bye Bye Love

TONY GREGORY
DR BIRD 1007 Baby Come on Home/Marie Lena
DR BIRD 1016 Give Me One More Chance/I've Lost My Love

MARCIA GRIFFITHS
b 11/51 (Kingston JA). A child star discovered by Phillip James of the BLUES BUSTERS; at age 12, she performed with BYRON LEE & THE DRAGONAIRES and shared his management. Also recorded as a duo with BOB ANDY and JEFF DIXON. She later became a mainstay of the I-THREES, while maintaining a solidly enjoyable solo career. (X) ROY RI-CHARDS, SOUL BROTHERS

ISLAND 285 Funny/KING SPARROW: Beggars Have No Choice

THE HARMONIZING FOUR
aka THE CHARMS.

RYMSKA 102 Who Knows/Heart of Stone

DERRICK HARRIOTT
DR BIRD 1002 Jon Om/AUDREY WILLIAMS: Solas Market
Produced by Derrick Harriott.

THE HEPTONES
See entry on page 114.

RIO 104 Gunmen Coming to Town/TOMMY MCCOOK & THE SUPERSONICS: Riverton City
Produced by Ken Lack. (a) Snatches of the William Tell Overture slice through this driving saga of looming desperados, raising the temperature and distinguishing what would, otherwise, be a somewhat one-dimensional melody.

JUSTIN HINDS
DR BIRD 1048 The Higher the Monkey Climbs/Fight for Your Right

Produced by Duke Reid. (a) The SKATALITES provide the musical backing on this old adage come to musical life, a slow skanker perfect for the dulcet tones of Hinds and the Dominoes.

HORTENSE & DELROY
Vocal duo comprising HORTENSE ELLIS and DELROY WIL-SON. (X) THE SOUL BROTHERS

PATRICK HYTTON
(X) JACKIE MITTOO

DAVID ISAACS
b 6/9/46. Vocalist and frontman of THE RACE FANS (and later, THE ITALS), later became one of LEE PERRY's favorite collaborators, after being introduced by CLANCY ECCLES.

ISLAND 261 I'd Rather Be Lonely/See that Man
Produced by Ronnie Nasralla.

SAMMY ISMAY
(X) JOE WHITE

JACKIE & MILLIE
ISLAND 265 My Desire/MILLIE: That's How Strong My Love Is
Produced by Coxsone Dodd.

JAMAICA FATS
BLUE BEAT 368 Jacqueline/Please Come Home

JIMMY JAMES
SKA-BEAT 242 Your Love/Someday

THE JETLINERS
aka SUGAR & DANDY.

BLUE BEAT 367 Meditation/GIRL SATCHMO: Nature of Love

B JUNIOR
BLUE BEAT 361 Just to Keep You/You Only Want My Money

KING JOE FRANCIS & THE HIGHJACKERS
RIO 90 Have My Body/Everybody's Got to Know

KING PERRY
aka LEE PERRY.

ISLAND 292 Doctor Dick/SOUL BROTHERS: Magic Star
Produced by Coxsone Dodd. (a) Perry barely contains himself on this naughty number, although the accompanying SOULETTES don't appear to be in on the joke. The catchy melody must have really infuriated the prudes, as it's hard not to sing along. (b) Why nobody ever cut a ska version of "Ride of the Valkyries" is a mystery which might never be solved. But if you ever need to know what it would have sounded like, there's more than a hint playing around this bright instrumental.

ISLAND 298 Rub & Squeeze/SOUL BROTHERS: Here Comes the Minx
Produced by Coxsone Dodd. (a) Perry's high vocals and the DYNAMITES' soaring backing take some of the tension out of another innuendo-laced number. The bassist in contrast,

has taken Perry's "take it easy" lyric to heart, and found a smooth groove all his own.

KING SPARROW

aka MIGHTY SPARROW. (X) MARCIA GRIFFITHS

BYRON LEE & THE DRAGONAIRES

(X) MIGHTY AVENGERS

DR BIRD 1003 Sloopy/Gold Finger

Produced by Byron Lee. Reissued as PYRAMID 6015.

BEN LEVY

SKA-BEAT 245 Doreen/Never Knew Love

SKA-BEAT 255 I'll Make You Glad/Keep Smiling

LORD BRYNNER & THE SHEIKS

THE SHEIKS featured vocalist DOBBY DOBSON and pianist JACKIE MITTOO.

ISLAND 266 Congo War/Teach Me to Ska

(a) Succinct summary of the situation in the African Congo, listing most of the major players involved (except for the one "whose name is to long to remember"). It's all a bit of an oddity, but it packs a jazzy flair.

LORD CREATOR

DR BIRD 1029 Obeah Wedding/BERTRAM ENNIS COMBO: Part 2

LORD TANAMO

SKA-BEAT 243 Mother's Love/Downtown Gal

MAJAMOOD

DR BIRD 1052 Two Hundred Million Red Ants/Faces Amassed

RITA MARLEY

b Rita Anderson. Vocalist with THE SOULETTES, later the I-THREES. Married BOB MARLEY in 1966. (X) SOUL BROTHERS

RIO 108 Pied Piper/It's Alright

Produced by Coxsone Dodd. (a) A cover of the recent Crispian St Peter hit.

LARRY MARSHALL

b Fitzroy Marshall, 17 Dec, 1941 — WAILERS ASTON and CARLTON BARRETT are his cousins. Also recorded as a duo with ALVIN LESLIE and ENID CUMBERLAND. It was in the mid-1970s that Marshall truly found fame, with his "I Admire You" single and album, and an accompanying AUGUSTUS PABLO dub mix. A decade later, GUSSIE CLARKE produced a hit remake of the song. (X) ROLAND ALPHONSO

ALAN MARTIN

RIO 94 Days Are Lonely/My Baby

The inimitable Martin (DENZIL DENNIS, of course) is at his crooning best on this weepy single, with the up-tempo band playing the blues for all they're worth.

RIO 96 Rome Wasn't Built in a Day/I'm Hurt

MARTINE

(X) SOUL BROTHERS

THE MAYTALS

(X) THE CHARMERS

DR BIRD 1019 If You Act this Way/SIR LORD COMIC & HIS COWBOYS: Ska-ing West

Produced by Ronnie Nasralla/Byron Lee.

DR BIRD 1038 Bam Bam/So Mad in Love

Produced by Ronnie Nasralla/Byron Lee. (a) Rudie runs riot and still manages to win the first Festival Song Competition in 1966. A truly captivating rock steady rhythm leads TOOTS HIBBERT through one of his most menacing performances ever.

TOMMY MCCOOK & THE SUPERSONICS

Following the Skatalites' demise, McCook formed the SUPERSONICS as the house band at TREASURE ISLE studios. Line-up varied between sessions, but principle players included ROLAND ALPHONSO (tenor), VAL BENNETT, LENNOX BROWN (alto), HERMAN MARQUIS (baritone), RAYMOND HARPER, LESTER STERLING (trumpet), DANNY SIMMS, VIN GORDON (trombone), GLADSTONE ANDERSON (piano), WINSTON WRIGHT (organ), LYNFORD "HUX" BROWN, LYNN TAITT, LORRAINE "RONNIE/RANNY BOP" WILLIAMS (GUITAR), LLOYD BREVETT, JACKIE JACKSON (bass), ARKLAND "DRUMBAGO" PARKS, HUGH MALCOLM, LLOYD KNIBBS (drums), NOEL "SCULLY" SIMMS, HUGH "STICKY" THOMPSON, LARRY MCDONALD (PERCUSSION). Many of these players AKA THE AGGROVATORS, ALL STARS, THE CRYSTALITES, THE DYNAMITES, LYNN TAITT'S COMETS/JETS/BOYS, etc. (X) SHENLEY DUFFUS, THE HEPTONES, THE SILVERTONES

RIO 100 Jerk Time/THE UNIQUES: The Journey

RIO 101 Out of Space/THE UNIQUES: Do Me Good

(a) Out of space? More like outer space, as McCook rockets this instrumental into the stratosphere and beyond with a series of soaring, dizzying brass solos; Houston, we've achieved liftoff.

RIO 103 Ska Jam/Smooth Sailing

(a) The Supersonics celebrate ska in all its glory, in a bouncy instrumental where the clattering percussion vies for attention with McCook and co's exuberant brass.

DR BIRD 1032 Naked City/NORMA FRAZIER: Heartaches

Produced by Coxsone Dodd. (a) Lugubrious shuffle horns open in two minds — is this another spy theme or is everything going to go the Duane Eddy route? In the end, the song settles down into a fairly stock Skatalites instrumental groove, but the drums are well worth keeping an ear out for.

DR BIRD 1047 Spanish Eyes/STRANGER (COLE) & HORTENSE (ELLIS): Loving Wine

Produced by Duke Reid. (a) credited to McCook & LYNN TAITT, a moody twang-infested rendition of the Al Martino smoker.

DR BIRD 1051 A Little Bit of Heaven/LLOYD WILLIAMS: Sad World

Produced by Duke Reid. (a) Crashing duet between McCook and BABA BROOKS.

DR BIRD 1053 Indian Love Call/OWEN & LEON: How Would You Feel

Produced by Duke Reid.

DR BIRD 1056 Danger Man/ERIC MORRIS: If I Didn't Love You

Produced by Duke Reid. (b) The female backing vocals hark back to the early '60s, but the Hammond organ gives it a modern touch, while ERIC MORRIS gives the whole song a soulful air.

THE MELODIANS

Vocal trio comprising BRENT DOWE, TREVOR MCNAUGHTON, TONY BREVETT, plus songwriter ROBERT COGLE. After six years of sweeping the talent contest circuit, the Melodians found their niche with rock steady, cutting some spectacular 45s for DODD, POTTINGER, and KONG. They broke up in 1974, launched shortlived solo careers, then reformed two years later to rerecord their greatest hits. Since then they have made sporadic reappearances.

ISLAND 3014 Lay It On/Meet Me

THE MERRYMEN

DR BIRD 1004 Big Bamboo/Island Woman

THE MIGHTY AVENGERS

aka BYRON LEE & THE DRAGONAIRES.

RYMSKA 101 Scatter Shot/BYRON LEE: Like You Do

Produced by Byron Lee.

GLEN MILLER & HONEYBOY MARTIN

Duo featuring future rude boy apologist Honeyboy ("Dreader Than Dread"), but not, obviously, the deceased American band leader! (X) LYNN TAITT & THE COMETS

MILLIE

(X) JACKIE & MILLIE

JACKIE MITTOO

See entry for THE SKATALITES on page 262. Keyboard wizard Mittoo was a member of THE RIVALS and THE SHEIKS alongside DOBBY DOBSON. (X) THE ETHIOPIANS, JACKIE OPEL

ISLAND 293 Killer Diller/PATRICK HYTTON: Oh Lady

Produced by Coxsone Dodd. (a) A big band tune recharged by Mittoo, with some dangerous guitar cutting through the almost Booker T keyboards.

DERRICK MORGAN

ISLAND 277 It's Alright/I Need Someone

Produced by Leslie Kong.

ISLAND 289 Ameletia/Don't You Worry

ISLAND 3010 Gather Together Now/Soft Hand

RIO 122 Cool Off Rudies/Take It Easy

(a) The indomitable Morgan wades into rock steady waters with this suave yet insistent demand of a song. The singer gives it all he's got, tied to some nice guitar work and a slow beat.

ERIC MORRIS

(X) TOMMY MCCOOK

BLUE BEAT 349 I'm the Greatest/BUSTER'S ALL-STARS: Picket Line

Produced by Prince Buster.

TERRY NELSON

HALA GALA 19 That True Love Must Be Me/Bulldog Walk

JACKIE OPEL

ISLAND 264 A Love to Share/ROLAND ALPHONSO: Devoted to You

RIO 117 I Am What I Am/JACKIE MITTOO & THE SKATALITES: Devil's Bug

THE ORIGINATORS

(X) BOBBY AITKEN

OSSIE & THE UPSETTERS

At least one source claims this to be a collaboration between LEE PERRY and COUNT OSSIE. In fact it's a vocal group aka THE CHECKMATES, who recorded for COXSONE DODD and, later, LESLIE KONG. Another UPSETTERS active in the early 1960s was led by SKATALITE-to-be ROLAND ALPHONSO.

DR BIRD 1018 Turn Me On/True Love

Produced by Coxsone Dodd.

OWEN & LEON

(X) TOMMY MCCOOK

PAT & MARIE

UK based vocal duo featuring PAT RHODEN.

SKA-BEAT 234 I Try Not to Tell You/PAT RHODEN: Don't Blame It on Me

SKA-BEAT 235 You're Really Leaving/PAT RHODEN: Broken Heart

DAWN PENN

b 1952 (Kingston, JA). Backing vocalist with Johnny Nash during the early 1970s.

RIO 113 Long Days Short Night/Are You There

Produced by Prince Buster.

LEE PERRY

(X) ALTON & THE FLAMES

SKA-BEAT 251 The Woodman/Give Me Justice

Produced by JJ Johnson. (a) A moody melody, heightened by horns and an intriguingly out of tune piano. Perry sounds as impassioned as the subject matter (infidelity) demands, but the backing vocalists' incessant "yeah yeah"-ing does get a bit tedious. (b) Actually stronger than the a-side, with an infectious melody, more interesting harmonies, and a stronger lyrical theme—hammering COXSONE DODD for not giving him credit for the songs he wrote and produced during his years at Studio One.

THE PERSONALITIES

BLUE BEAT 354 Push It Down/BUSTER'S ALL-STARS: Blues Market
Produced by Prince Buster.

PETER & PAUL

BLUE BEAT 364 Hosana/Schoolgirl

THE PIONEERS

RIO 102 Good Nannie/Doreen Girl
Produced by the Pioneers. (a) Financed by SIDNEY CROOKS' mother, recorded at Treasure Isle, and featuring AL & THE VIBRATORS as backing band.

RIO 106 Too Late/Give It Up
Produced by the Pioneers.

PRINCE BUSTER

BLUE BEAT 338 Big Fight/Adios Senorita
Produced by Prince Buster.

BLUE BEAT 339 Under Arrest/Say Boss Man
Produced by Prince Buster.

BLUE BEAT 343 Don't Throw Stones/Prince of Peace
Produced by Prince Buster.

BLUE BEAT 352 Day of Light/It's too Late
Produced by Prince Buster.

BLUE BEAT 355 Sunshine with My Girl/Answer Your Name
Produced by Prince Buster.

BLUE BEAT 357 I Won't Let You Cry/Hard Man fe Ded
Produced by Prince Buster. (b) "Hard Man" is a rude boy anthem if ever there was one, the Prince's tale of a tough guy who just won't die has all the kick of a New Orleans' send-off—a perfect shuffling beat, a slew of gleeful horn solos, and an exuberant melody in a melancholy key.

BLUE BEAT 359 The Prophet/Lion of Judah
Produced by Prince Buster.

BLUE BEAT 362 To Be Loved/Set Me Free
Produced by Prince Buster.

RAINBOW 107 Your Turn/If You Leave Me
Produced by Prince Buster.

PRINCE BUSTER'S ALL-STARS

(X) ERIC MORRIS, THE PERSONALITIES

BLUE BEAT 342 Cincinnati Kid/Sammy Dead
Produced by Prince Buster. (a) Another of the driving instrumentals which Buster apparently knocked out by the dozen. (b) One of the many covers of the ever popular traditional West Indian song, this version features an interesting musical arrangement with some nice brass accents, a solo harmonica, and a brash beat, while ERIC MORRIS nonchalantly sings along.

PRINCE BUSTER JNR WITH NAT FRANCIS & THE SUNSETS

BLUE BEAT 346 Tra La La/Mama Kiss Him Goodnight
Produced by Prince Buster.

CARLTON REID

SKA-BEAT 254 Funny/Turn on the Lights

PAT RHODEN

b WINSTON PATRICK RHODEN, 1950 (JA). Left Jamaica in 1963 to pursue his career in the UK, and later launched his own Jama label. Recorded under his birth name, as a duo with MARIE and DENZIL DENNIS, and a member of the BROTHER DAN ALL STARS. (X) PAT & MARIE

WINSTON RHODEN

aka PAT RHODEN.

BLUE BEAT 360 Send Your Love/Make Believe

ROY RICHARDS

DR BIRD 1012 Contact/Maureen
(a) The perfect parade piece, with a joyous harmonica leading the way, and the insistent rhythms in marching form.

ISLAND 283 Double Trouble/FITZ & FREDDY: Why Did You Do It
ISLAND 297 Green Collie/MARCIA GRIFFITHS: You No Good
ISLAND 299 Western Standard Time/THE EAGLES: What a Agony
Produced by Coxsone Dodd.

ISLAND 3000 South Viet Nam/You Must Be Sorry

BERESFORD RICKETTS

BLUE BEAT 350 Jailer Bring Me Water/Careless Love

JACKIE RIDING & IMESON SOUND

FAB 4 Don't Wanna Leave/The Wave

THE RIO GRANDES

PYRAMID 6001 Soldiers Take Over/Moses
(a) Almost hymnal in delivery, the rock steady spiritual aura is belied by the lyrical theme of the imposition of martial law to combat the growing violence percolating across the island.

ROY & CORNELL

Vocal duo comprising ROY SHIRLEY (b 1948) & CORNELL CAMPBELL. (X) SHENLEY & HYACINTH

ROY & KEN

Vocal duo comprising ROY SHIRLEY and KEN BOOTHE.

SKA-BEAT 253 Paradise/Calling
(a) A lovely celebration of religious salvation.

THE RULERS

RIO 105 Don't be A Rude Boy/Be Good
(a) Flying in the face of the rising youth culture, this vocal trio proclaims they "don't want to be no rude boy, I want to be a good boy," attempting to rehabilitate the rudies via the sweet vocals and rock steady rhythms which the bad boys preferred.

RIO 107 Copasetic/Too Late
(a) Actually it was NOT copasetic, as the vocal trio point out in a succinct and condemnatory summary of the events leading up to the Jamaican government's declaration of a state of emergency.

THE SAINTS

(X) BABA BROOKS

WINSTON SAMUELS

SKA-BEAT 238 What Have I Done/Broken Hearted

SKA-BEAT 241 Ups & Downs/Come What May

SKA-BEAT 244 Time Will Tell/I'm Sorry

SCRATCH & THE DYNAMITES

aka LEE PERRY. (X) ALTON & THE FLAMES

THE SHARKS

(X) DESMOND BAKER, THE ETHIOPIANS

SHENLEY & HYACINTH

RIO 80 The World Is on a Wheel/ROY & CORNELL: Salvation

THE SILVERTONES

Vocal group comprising KEITH COLEY (b 3/7/44, St Elizabeth, JA), DELROY DENTON, CARL aka GILMORE GRANT (b 7/11/43, Kingston, JA). Also recorded as THE MUSKYTEERS. Most active during the 1970s, when they cut the hit *Silver Bullets* album (1975) and voiced the BRENTFORD ROCKERS' "Come Forward" (1979). (X) ALTON ELLIS

DR BIRD 1028 True Confession/TOMMY MCCOOK & THE
   SUPERSONICS: More Love

Produced by Duke Reid. (a) A snappy beat gets the Silvertones on their feet and over to their writing desk, where they knock out this scandalous tale of a man who's done his woman wrong by lying and cheating and other mean things; a letter to the editor is apparently a lot easier than a personal apology. Later versioned by U-ROY.

DR BIRD 1041 It's Real/LYNN TAITT & THE BOYS: Storm Warning

Produced by Duke Reid. (a) The vocal group eagerly assert that their love is real on this exuberant number, with the snappy ska arrangement provided by LYN TAITT & THE BOYS. (b) As ominous as its title, this instrumental has a swirling dark undercurrent, all threatening clouds, with the brass blowing like a stiff breeze to herald the oncoming deluge.

RYMSKA 105 True Confession/GRANVILLE WILLIAMS ORCHESTRA:
   Honky Tonk Ska

Produced by Duke Reid. (b) Jumping on the ska bandwagon, the orchestra combine two rather disparate genres and make them sound made for each other.

LEO SIMMO

BLUE BEAT 351 I Love Her So/Good to Be Seen

SUGAR SIMONE

b KEITH FOSTER, 1948 (St Marys, JA). aka TITO SIMON. Also recorded as the duo SUGAR & DANDY, THE JETLINERS.

RAINBOW 103 Is It Because/I Want to Know

LIONEL SIMPSON

SKA-BEAT 233 Give Over/Never Before

SIR LORD COMIC & HIS COWBOYS

Early sound systems DJ whose "Ska-ing West" is widely regarded the first DJ single — coincidentally, he also cut what many call the last ever ska record, "The Great Wuga Wuga."

(X) THE MAYTALS

THE SKATALITES

(X) THE WAILERS

MILLIE SMALL

FONTANA 740 Killer Joe/Carry Go Bring Come

(a) Out of the mouths of babes. . . . Teenybop toddler Little Jimmy Osmond later recorded his own version of "Killer Joe."

THE SONS OF SOUL

DR BIRD 1037 Yeah Yeah Baby/So Ashamed

THE SOUL BROTHERS

See entry for THE SKATALITES on page 262. Band formed by ROLAND ALPHONSO and JACKIE MITTOO following the demise of THE SKATALITES as house band at Studio One. As such, they took over the earlier group's role as one of Jamaica's most ubiquitous backing bands. Other members included BOBBY ELLIS and HUX BROWN (DYNAMITES, CRYSTALITES, MIGHTY VIKINGS, etc). Following their performance on the FRANK ANDERSON hit "Peanut Vendor," they changed their name to the SOUL VENDORS for a UK tour, retaining that title thereafter. (X) THE ETHIOPIANS, LEE PERRY, WAILERS, DELROY WILSON

ISLAND 282 Green Moon/E Gal OK

Produced by Coxsone Dodd.

ISLAND 294 Ska-Bostello/DON DRUMMOND: Looking through the
   Window

Produced by Coxsone Dodd.

ISLAND 296 Sound One/MARTINE: Grandfather's Clock

Produced by Coxsone Dodd.

ISLAND 3016 Mr Flint/Too Young to Love

Produced by Coxsone Dodd.

RIO 118 Crawfish/RITA MARLEY: You Lied

Produced by Coxsone Dodd.

RIO 119 Ska Shuffle/HORTENSE & DELROY: We're Gonna Make It

Produced by Coxsone Dodd.

RIO 121 Mr TNT/MARCIA GRIFFITHS: Mr Everything

Produced by Coxsone Dodd.

SKA-BEAT 258 James Bond Girl/SUMMERTAIRES: My Heart Cries
   Out

Produced by Coxsone Dodd.

THE SOULETTES

(X) ROLAND ALPHONSO, KEN BOOTHE

JACK SPARROW

aka LEONARD DILLON of THE ETHIOPIANS. (X) ROLAND ALPHONSO

LESTER STERLING

DR BIRD 1057 Inez/GLORIA CRAWFORD: Sad Movies
Produced by Duke Reid. (a) The laid-back rhythm sets the tone for this airy number, the saxophone solos (by Sterling and TOMMY MCCOOK) add some heat, while the flute floats the song into the breeze.

WINSTON STEWART

(X) THE GAYLADS

STRANGER & HORTENSE

Vocal duo featuring STRANGER COLE and HORTENSE ELLIS. (X) TOMMY MCCOOK

STRANGER & PATSY

DR BIRD 1050 Give Me the Right/Tonight
RIO 81 Give Me One More Chance/Fire in Cornfield

SUGAR & DANDY

See THE JETLINERS.

THE SUMMERTAIRES

(X) SOUL BROTHERS

LYNN TAITT & THE COMETS

b Nerlynn Taitt, (San Fernando, T&T). Taitt launched his career as a steel pan player in Trinidad. He learned guitar during the late 1950s and, recording for Emory Cook, formed the NERLYNN TAITT ORCHESTRA in 1960. In 1962, Taitt was booked to back LORD MELODY at Jamaica's Independence celebrations and remained on the island until 1968, when he departed for Canada. THE COMETS aka THE JETS, THE BOYS.

He led a number of live bands, before finally launching his own recording career in 1966. Members of his groups at various times have included HEADLEY BENNETT (sax), HOPETON LEWIS (vocals), HUX BROWN (guitar), JACKIE JACKSON (bass), BORIS GARDINER (bass), BOBBY ELLIS (trumpet), GLADSTONE ANDERSON (keyboards), WINSTON WRIGHT (keyboards), WINSTON GRENNAN (drums), PAUL DOUGLAS (drums), BONGO LES (percussion), BONGO HERMAN (percussion) — aka THE AGGROVATORS, ALL STARS, THE CRYSTALITES, THE DYNAMITES, THE SUPERSONICS, THE UPSETTERS, etc. (X) ALTON & THE FLAMES, BABA BROOKS, TOMMY MCCOOK, SILVERTONES

DR BIRD 1006 Vilma's Jump Up/GLEN MILLER & HONEYBOY MARTIN: Dad Is Home

THE TECHNIQUES

(X) THE GAYLADS

LLANS THELWELL & HIS CELESTIALS

Vocal group featuring BUSTY BROWN.
ISLAND 262 Choo Choo Ska/Lonely Night

DESMOND TUCKER

(X) REUBEN ANDERSON

MEL TURNER

ISLAND 276 Welcome Home Little Darlin'/C'est L'Amour

THE UNIQUES

Vocal group originally formed by SLIM SMITH, FRANKLYN WHITE (ex-TECHNIQUES), and ROY SHIRLEY. Following a handful of hits for KEN LACK and JJ JOHNSON, Smith went solo, relaunching a new Uniques line-up in 1967 with MARTIN RILEY and LLOYD CHARMERS. The group folded for good in 1969. (X) TOMMY MCCOOK

THE UPSETTERS

DR BIRD 1034 Wildcat/I Love You So

THE VIBRATORS

Band fronted by bassist LINVAL "AL" MARTIN. Among other sessions, they accompanied the PIONEERS on their 1965 debut single.
DR BIRD 1036 Sloop John B/Amour

THE VIETNAM ALL STARS

(X) ERROL DIXON

THE WAILERS

DR BIRD 1013 Rude Boy/ROLAND AL & THE SOUL BROTHERS: Ringo's Theme
Produced by Coxsone Dodd. (a) "Why, why," the Wailers disappointedly query on this rock steady smash thematic follow up to "Hooligan." The group cleverly utilize a snatch of The Impressions'"Keep on Moving" to capture the flavor of the rude boy now on the run from the law. Oddly, the Wailers also make reference to a ska quadrille, possibly an attempt to reintroduce this once-popular intricate dance of the past. (b) Though the tune itself is the Beatles' "This Boy," the original "Ringo's Theme" was an instrumental arrangement of the song, included in the *Hard Day's Night* movie.

DR BIRD 1021 Good Good Rudie/CITY SLICKERS: Oceans II
Produced by Coxsone Dodd. (a) Completing the rude boy quartet commenced with "Simmer Down," this rock steady classic features a New Orleansesque piano. Lyrically the message is obvious, but it still impacts. (b) Swing returns with a vengeance on this fabulous instrumental. ROLAND ALPHONSO handles the solos with aplomb enough to make hepcats weep, while CECIL LLOYD's keyboards are equally awe inspiring.

ISLAND 260 Jumbie Jamboree/SKATALITES: Independent Anniversary Ska
Produced by Coxsone Dodd. (a) Excellent PETER TOSH composition inspired by a recent show in Kingston where the power went out and the audience rioted. "Jumbie," like "duppy," is a local term meaning a ghost, or a soul-less person. (b) Adapted from the Beatles' "I Should Have Known Better" (under which title it is generally reissued), the Skatalites first played "Independent Anniversary Ska," fittingly,

at the Independence Day parade, riding on the Cable & Wireless float.

ISLAND 268 Put It On/Love Won't Be Mine

Produced by Coxsone Dodd. (a) Recorded with Dwight Pinkney's Sharks, the beat is pure Jamaican, the guitar's California surf and the lyrics are deeply religious. One of the Wailers' best, "Put It On" was apparently played non-stop at BOB and RITA MARLEY's wedding.

ISLAND 3001 He Who Feels It Knows It/Sunday Morning

Produced by Coxsone Dodd. (a) With MARLEY abroad, his wife RITA, NORMA FRASER, and CONSTANTINE WALKER beautifully filled out the vocal ranks for this quiet, yet emotive LIVINGSTON jewel. It borrows a melodic line from JUSTIN HIND's "Save A Bread," but has also been ranked among the first songs to use the seminal phrase "I and I."

ISLAND 3009 Let Him Go/Sinner Man

Produced by Coxsone Dodd. (a) LIVINGSTON now exhibits second thoughts about the jailing of the Wailer's rude boy anti-hero, prompted perhaps by the clutch of "rudie gone a jail" themed rock steady songs hitting the charts elsewhere. This, then is an emotive plea for his release, although the line "remember he is young, and will live long," could also be read as an anti-authoritarian threat. (b) One of the first recordings made by TOSH and LIVINGSTON after MARLEY left for the US, their take on the much covered religious number (initially a hit for Trini Lopez) is an intriguing blend of sweet and soulful vocals, with the riff from the Motown classic "Money" tossed wryly in for good measure.

RIO 116 Dancing Shoes/Don't Look Back

Produced by Coxsone Dodd. (a) The Wailers search for a dance partner and love on this flawless piece of rock steady. It was later versioned by DENNIS ALCAPONE. (b) The flawless original version of what would become PETER TOSH's greatest solo hit, a slow-burning cover of the Temptations' standard. BUNNY LIVINGSTON and "DREAM" WALKER provide the harmonies . . . years later, Mick Jagger would fulfill the same function.

SKA-BEAT 228 Love & Affection/Teenager in Love

Produced by Coxsone Dodd. (a) Unremarkable repetitive rock steady number into which a doo-wop backing vocalist unexpectedly wanders. ROLAND ALPHONSO's sax is a less surprising star. (b) It was no secret that the Wailers were heavily influenced by 1950s American doo-wop bands, and their cover of "Teenager In Love" is precisely what you would expect. PETER TOSH handles the falsetto.

SKA-BEAT 230 And I Love Her/Do It Right

Produced by Coxsone Dodd. (a) Straightforward, if overly doo-woppy cover of the Beatles ballad. Horns replace the guitar lines on the original, while the ghost of an organ line haunts the background. (b) The clattering percussion is producer Dodd playing beer bottles with a piece of metal; the

hissing rhythm is TOSH and LIVINGSTON breathing heavily. The song itself rattles along in typical Wailers' fast mode.

SKA-BEAT 249 Lonesome Tracks/Sinner Man

Produced by Coxsone Dodd.

KARL WALKER & THE ALL-STARS

RYMSKA 103 One Minute to Zero/Don't Come Back

JOE WHITE

DR BIRD 1024 My Love for You/SAMMY ISMAY & BABA BROOKS & HIS BAND: Cocktails for Two

DR BIRD 1043 So Close/BABA BROOKS & HIS BAND: Eighth Games

Produced by Sonia Pottinger.

AUDREY WILLIAMS

(X) DERRICK HARRIOTT

GRANVILLE WILLIAMS

(X) THE SILVERTONES

LLOYD WILLIAMS

(X) TOMMY MCCOOK

DELROY WILSON

DR BIRD 1022 Give Me a Chance/It's Impossible

Produced by Coxsone Dodd.

ISLAND 3013 Dancing Mood/SOUL BROTHERS: More & More

Produced by Coxsone Dodd. (a) A superb cover of the Tams' soul hit. JACKIE MITTOO's piano intriguingly carries not just the melody, but the syncopated beat, while Wilson's soulful, pensive vocal totally redefines the song's mood.

WINSTON & GEORGE

PYRAMID 6002 Denham Town/Keep the Pressure On

(a) The pair scored a British hit with this rock steady ode to rude boys, with the message that Crime Doesn't Pay neatly wrapped up in a simple harmony laced, slow skanking package.

1967

RICHARD ACE

COXSONE 7031 Don't Let the Sun Catch You Crying/VICEROYS: Magadown

Produced by Coxsone Dodd.

STUDIO ONE 2022 I Need You/SOUL VENDORS: Cool Shade

Produced by Coxsone Dodd.

GLEN ADAMS

b 1950 (JA). A founder member of THE HEPTONES and THE PIONEERS. Cousin HERBIE GRAY was a member of SONNY BRADSHAW's band, sister YVONNE a popular duettist. Subsequently became a leading session musician, working with the HIPPY BOYS, THE REGGAE BOYS and the UPSETTERS. Relocated to the US in 1975 and later recorded with rapper T Ski Valley.

ISLAND 3072 Silent Lover/I Remember

Produced by Coxsone Dodd. (b) Recorded with KEN

BOOTHE, "I Remember" placed second at the 1966 Festival Song Competition.

ISLAND 3083 He/SONNY BURKE: Some Other Time

BOBBY AITKEN

(X) LLOYD & GLEN

DR BIRD 1072 Let Them Have a Home/Temptation

DR BIRD 1077 Sweets for My Sweet/How Sweet It Is

GIANT 11 What a Fool/Curfew

(b) A wonderfully slow, soulful number that highlights Aitken's superb vocals, as he demands that rude boys change their ways before the soldiers take over the streets again.

ISLAND 3028 Kiss Bam Bam/CYNTHIA RICHARDS: How Could I

LAUREL AITKEN

COLUMBIA BLUE BEAT 102 Rock Steady/Blowin' in the Wind

(a) Not to be confused with the ALTON ELLIS hit of the same name, the lyrical come-on of "let's do the rock steady" is all the two have in common, with Aitken's take on the new style so soulful it smokes, all cool grooves and dizzying muted horns.

COLUMBIA BLUE BEAT 106 I'm Still in Love with You Girl/Blue Rhythm

FAB 5 Never Hurt You/I Need You

(a) Another soulful classic, seemingly tailor made for Jackie Wilson or even James Brown. The organ provides that cool 60s flavor, the horns cook, and the vocals are belted out with a style worthy of Chicago's best, while a taste of the Far East just makes it even hipper.

RAINBOW 111 Sweet Precious Love/I Want to Love You Forever

AL & THE VIBRATORS

Al is bassist LINVAL MARTIN.

DR BIRD 1085 Move Up/One Lover

CARLTON ALPHONSO

PAMA 700 Where in this World/Peacemakers

ROLAND ALPHONSO

(X) KEN BOOTHE, DESMOND DEKKER, DUKE REID'S ALL STARS, HOPETON LEWIS, DERRICK MORGAN, PRINCE BUSTER

PYRAMID 6005 Women of the World/SPANISHTONIANS: Kisses

PYRAMID 6007 Jungle Bit/NORMAN GRANT: Somebody Please Help Me

PYRAMID 6009 Guatanamera Ska/SPANISHTONIANS: Suffer Me Not

PYRAMID 6016 Stream of Life/AUSTIN FAITHFUL: I'm in a Rocking Mood

PYRAMID 6018 Sock It to Me/SPANISHTONIANS: Rudie Gets Plenty

(b) "Shanty town get scanty, rudie get plenty," the Spanishtonians accurately note, but, in the end, "rudie, you're only hurting yourself." As always, the group coat their rock steady lecture in sweet harmonies, gently admonishing the bad boys like a loving parent.

PYRAMID 6022 Whiter Shade of Pale/On the Move

(a) The Procol Harum hit gets the most melodic Alphonso treatment.

PYRAMID 6023 Peace & Love/JOHNNY MELODY: Govern Your Mouth

BOB ANDY

b Keith Anderson, 1944. Founder member of THE PARAGONS who went on to record a string of solo classics at Studio 1. Also recorded as a duo with JOEY DENNIS and, most successfully, MARCIA GRIFFITHS, while also maintaining a successful career in acting.

ISLAND 3040 I've Got to Get Back Home/SONNY BURKE: Rudy Girl

Produced by Coxsone Dodd. (a) For the homesick everywhere, Andy's yearning vocals are backed by gorgeous harmonies, and saved from total depression by the upbeat brass solo.

ASTON & YEN

Duo featuring ASTON CAMPBELL. (X) BABA BROOKS

BALDHEAD GROWLER

JUMP-UP 531 Sausage/Bingo Woman

DAVE BARKER

b David Crooks, 1948 (Kingston, JA). An occasional member of THE TECHNIQUES, also recorded as DAVE COLLINS and as a duo with GLEN BROWN, MEL and ANSELL COLLINS, with whom he voiced the UK chart topper "Double Barrel." Equally highly regarded for his work with LEE PERRY during the late 1960s and early 1970s; later in that decade he turned to soul, forming the band Chain Reaction.

THE BASSIES

(X) KEITH MCCARTHY

COXSONE 7030 River Jordan /SOUL VENDORS: Swing Easy

Produced by Coxsone Dodd.

THE BEES

Vocal group formed from the PRINCE BUSTER'S ALL STARS stable.

BLUE BEAT 386 Jesse James Rides Again/The Girl in My Dreams

Produced by Prince Buster. (a) Predominantly instrumental, gunshots ring out, the horses' hooves clippity-clop, and the Bees wind up the crowd with a Western flair. Also released as COLUMBIA BLUE BEAT 101.

JO JO BENNETT

Former trumpeter with BIG RELATIONS, featuring CARL MALCOLM. Also leader of THE FUGITIVES.

DR BIRD 1097 The Lecture/Canteloupe Rock

DR BIRD 1116 Rock Steady/Real Gone Loser

BLUE RIVERS & MAROONS

COLUMBIA BLUE BEAT 103 Witchcraft Man/Searching for You Baby

Produced by Siggy Jackson. (a) An unusual melding of ska and pop. The basic elements are all here, from the perfect syncopated beats to the happily blaring horns — in fact, the only thing missing is a decent production.

THE BLUES BUSTERS

DR BIRD 1078 There's Always Sunshine/Lover's Reward
Produced by Byron Lee/WIRL.

JOYCE BOND

AIRBORNE 0011 It's Alright/Mrs Soul
ISLAND 3019 Tell Me What It's All About/Tell Me Right Now
ISLAND 6010 Do the Teasy/Sugar
ISLAND 6018 This Train/Not So with Me

KEN BOOTHE

CALTONE 107 The One I Love/You Left the Water Running
Produced by Phil Pratt.
COXSONE 7006 Lonely Teardrops/Oowee Baby
Produced by Coxsone Dodd.
COXSONE 7020 Home Home Home/SOUL BROTHERS: Hey Windell
Produced by Coxsone Dodd.
DR BIRD 1110 Say You/LYNN TAITT & THE JETS: Smokey Places
Produced by Sonia Pottinger. (a) A lovely ballad showcases Boothe's voice at its very best, from the little quiver he brings to the long notes, to the snatches of falsetto he throws in around the rhythm. The bass line is also worth following.
ISLAND 3020 This Train Is Coming/This Is Me
Produced by Coxsone Dodd. (a) This slowly building single chugs along at virtual half-speed but gradually gains momentum, urged along by Boothe's smooth, sweet vocals. The WAILERS line up behind him.
ISLAND 3035 I Don't Want to See You Cry/Baby I Need You
Produced by Coxsone Dodd.(a) A gorgeous BOB ANDY composition is given sterling treatment by the ever-soulful sounding Boothe. JOHN HOLT and DENNIS ALCAPONE would later make it theirs as well, but Boothe's might be the definitive rendering.
STUDIO ONE 2000 Feel Good/Mustang Sally
Produced by Coxsone Dodd. (a) An archetypal Boothe performance, reworking ROY SHIRLEY's "Hold Them." (b) Boothe shows off both his roots and his influences with an excellent reworking of the Wilson Pickett classic.
STUDIO ONE 2012 Puppet on a String/ROLAND ALPHONSO: Look Away
Produced by Coxsone Dodd. (a) Points for trying, but rushing out a rock steady version of Sandy Shaw's Eurovision Song Contest winner was not Boothe and Dodd's brightest idea. Boothe later cut a superior version with Bunny Lee.
STUDIO ONE 2026 Why Did You Leave/Don't Try to Reach Me
Produced by Coxsone Dodd.
Vocal quartet featuring the singularly named BOP, plus TREVOR SHIELD, HAL LEWINSON, and LEON BROWN. Following Bop's departure the band continued on as the BELTONES, before becoming the FANTELLS during the early 1970s. (X) PETER TOUCH

COXSONE 7007 Smile Like an Angel/SOUL AGENTS: Get Ready, It's Rock Steady
Produced by Coxsone Dodd.
COXSONE 7028 Love/SOUL VENDORS: You Troubled Me
Produced by Coxsone Dodd.

BABA BROOKS

DR BIRD 1064 Party Time/ASTON & YEN: Skillamy
DR BIRD 1065 The Scratch/VALENTINES: Blam Blam Fever
(b) The vocal group tries to make sense of the epidemic of violence raging across the island. A rock steady classic hung on a great hook, and featuring a baritone which could scour the sea bed.

SONNY BURKE

(X) GLEN ADAMS, BOB ANDY, GAYLADS, KEN PARKER
BLUE BEAT 371 Look in Her Eyes/LLOYD CLARKE: Love Is Strange

LESLIE BUTLER

(X) THE FUGITIVES
DR BIRD 1083 Winchester Rock Steady/ASTON CAMPBELL & CONQUERORS: Ramona
ISLAND 3069 Hornpipe Rock Steady/You Don't Have to Say You Love Me

RAY CAMERON

ISLAND 6003 Doin' My Time/Getaway Getaway Car

ASTON CAMPBELL & THE CONQUERORS

(X) LESLIE BUTLER

FITZROY CAMPBELL

(X) PRINCE BUSTER

THE CARIB BEATS

DOUBLE D 101 Highway 300/I Think of You
DOUBLE D 103 I'll Try/If I Did Look

CAROL & TOMMY MCCOOK

(X) THE PARAGONS

LLOYD CHARMERS

See entry in DIRECTORY OF PRODUCERS. aka LLOYD TYRELL. Also of THE CHARMERS, CONSCIOUS MINDS, THE UNIQUES, THE MESSENGERS, recorded as a duo with JOHNNY MELODY. (X) TONY GREGORY

THE CLANCY SET

Studio act formed by CLANCY ECCLES. aka CLANCY ALL STARS.
PAMA 703 Western Organ/Mother's Advice
Produced by Clancy Eccles.

THE CLARENDONIANS

(X) GAYLADS
ISLAND 3032 Shoo Be Doo Be/Sweet Heart of Beauty
ISLAND 3041 You Can't Be Happy/Goodbye Forever
STUDIO ONE 2004 The Tables Going to Turn/I Can't Go On
Produced by Coxsone Dodd.

LLOYD CLARKE

(X) SONNY BURKE

JIMMY CLIFF

ISLAND 6004 Aim & Ambition/Give & Take
Produced by Leslie Kong.

ISLAND 6011 I Got a Feeling/Hard Road to Travel
Produced by Leslie Kong.

ISLAND 6024 That's the Way Life Goes/Thank You
Produced by Leslie Kong.

STRANGER COLE

DR BIRD 1066 You Took My Love/FUGITIVES: Living Soul

THE CONNECTIONS

(X) DON MARTIN & DANDY

THE CONQUERORS

DR BIRD 1119 Won't You Come Home Now?/Oh that Day
Produced by Sonia Pottinger. (a) JO JO BENNETT'S FUGI-TIVES provide the backing on a minor epic of heartfelt pleading. DELROY WILSON, SLIM SMITH, and TEDDY would later turn in hit cover versions.

COOL SPOON

COXSONE 7032 Yakety Yak/SOUL VENDORS: Drum Song
Produced by Coxsone Dodd.

THE CREATIONS

RIO 133 Meet Me at Eight/Searching

THE DALTONS

(X) THE RIGHTEOUS FLAMES

DANDY

SKA-BEAT 269 One Scotch One Bourbon One Beer/Maximum Pressure

SKA-BEAT 273 Rudie, a Message to You/Til Death Us Do Part
(a) Dandy Livingstone gives a smooth as silk admonition to the rudies, wrapped in a beat to fill the dancefloor, a melody to sing along with, and some classic horn solos. The Specials made it their own years later, but the original still stands up.

SKA-BEAT 279 You're No Hustler/No No

DANDY & THE SUPERBOYS

(X) HONEYBOY MARTIN

GIANT 3 My Time Now/East of Suez

GIANT 7 We Are Still Rude/Let's Do Rock Steady

GIANT 15 There Is a Mountain/This Music Got Soul

CARL DAWKINS

b 8/1/48 (St Catherine, JA). Son of drummer JOE DAWKINS (SONNY BRADSHAW, BABA MOTTA), aka RAS DAWKINS. His early career was interrupted by a jail term for marijuana possession. Following his release, he recorded for LEE PERRY and led the YOUTH PROFESSIONALS, a band featuring PETER TOSH, BUNNY WAILER, and the CARLTON/AS-TON BARRETT rhythm section. (X) THE RULERS

RIO 136 All of a Sudden/Running Shoes
Produced by JJ Johnson.

RIO 137 Baby I Love You/Hard Time
Produced by JJ Johnson. (a) This rock steady gem was just one of a stream of UK club hits Dawkins racked up starting in 1967. His strong, clear tenor was a glory to behold and, even on a simple love song like this, his emotive vocals turned it into something special.

THE DEFENDERS

aka LEE PERRY.

DR BIRD 1104 Set Them Free/Don't Blame The Children
Produced by Lee Perry. (a) Perry rides the Judge Dread rude-boys-on-trial bandwagon in the guise of the singing solicitor Barrister Lord Defend. "No education, no qualification, so they are driven to desperation," he pleads, and never has the rude boy culture had such an eloquent and well-conceived defense. Both sides utilize the same rhythm, from Perry's "Run For Cover."

DESMOND DEKKER

PYRAMID 6003 Wise Man/ROLAND ALPHONSO: Middle East
Produced by Leslie Kong. (a) Emperor Haile Selassie's Jamaican visit touched off a wave of spirituality that washed across the island. "Wise Man" was just one of scores of songs with a religious theme subsequently released. The emphasis is firmly on the vocals and harmonies, with the strong beat giving the lyrics further urgency.

PYRAMID 6004 007 (Shanty-Town)/ROLAND ALPHONSO: El Torro
Produced by Leslie Kong. (a) The song that defined the summer of '67, Dekker's break-out hit was aimed straight at the rude boy crowd and fired point- blank. The rudies ignored the implicit lyrical warning within and dubbed Dekker one of their own. (b) Jazz goes to Juarez on this simmering instrumental, with enough Latin coloring to justify its Spanish title.

PYRAMID 6006 It's a Shame/ROLAND ALPHONSO: On the Move
Produced by Leslie Kong. (b) A moody, darkly atmospheric instrumental, the saxophonist seems to be casually strolling down late night streets, as the smoky mists swirl round.

PYRAMID 6008 Rudy Got Soul/ROLAND ALPHONSO: The Cat
Produced by Leslie Kong. (a) The down-tempo shuffling beat is perfect for slow dancing, Dekker is as soulful as the title promises, and is superbly backed by the ACES in their mellowest mood—an atmosphere echoed by the sublime sax solo.

PYRAMID 6011 Rude Boy Train/ROLAND ALPHONSO: Nothing for Nothing
Produced by Leslie Kong. (a) One of a triptych of Dekker rude boy classics that made their way into the UK club charts (alongside "007" and "Rudy Got Soul"), this rock steady gem simmers beneath lovely vocal harmonies, as well as again name-checking Britain's greatest fictional spy.

PYRAMID 6012 Mother's Young Girl/SOUL BROTHERS: Confucius

Produced by Leslie Kong. (a) In contrast to Dekker's rude boy tributes, this slow, soulful number reminds naive young women to beware charming young men.

PYRAMID 6017 Unity/Sweet Music

Produced by Leslie Kong. (a) With a sharp eye for rear-rangement, the backing singers are given the song's hook, a nice touch that works a charm. The arrangement and production are nigh on perfect, completing a sweet-but-never-saccharine melodic complexity which still sounds fabulous.

PYRAMID 6020 Sabotage/Pretty Africa

Produced by Leslie Kong. (a) By now, Dekker was capable of tossing out hits the way most people do cigarette butts. Stylistically, this one leans towards the popular vocal trio mood, with producer Kong keeping the perky rhythm section front and center. (b) Another one written following Emperor Haile Selassie's Jamaican visit, Dekker's heartfelt plea of "take me back to Africa," makes this one the earliest and, indeed, most beautiful repatriation songs ever recorded.

PYRAMID 6026 It Pays/Young Generation

Produced by Leslie Kong. (a) The harmonies here are truly inspiring, with Dekker kept virtually on the sidelines. However with its marvelous melody, and simple, but effective lyrics, "It Pays" is also an exhibition of the artist's sublime songwriting talent.

THE DEWDROPS

BLUE BEAT 381 Somebody's Knocking/By & By

PHYLLIS DILLON

b 1948 (Kingston, JA). Spent much of her early career in New York, but returned occasionally to JA to record.

DR BIRD 1061 Don't Stay Away/TOMMY MCCOOK: What Now

Produced by Duke Reid. (a) The perfect JA answer to American girl groups, Dillon's crystalline vocals emote just the right amount of sincerity and disingenuousness. CHARLIE CAMERON's harmonica adds a nice touch of jazz, while TOMMY MCCOOK and Duke Reid keeps everything simple. Later versioned by U-ROY.

TREASURE ISLE 7003 This Is a Lovely Way/Thing of the Past

Produced by Duke Reid. (b) A bittersweet gem whose mournful lyrics, beautifully delivered, are tempered by the mid-tempo beat and brass accents. Also released as TROJAN 006.

TREASURE ISLE 7015 Perfidia/Rockin' Time

Produced by Duke Reid. (a) The old classic rendered remarkably faithfully, with a tight rock steady rhythm buoying Dillon's occasionally uncertain vocal. Her "sock it to me" is pregnant with promise, though, and a spoken word interlude offers a dynamic interruption.

DION & THE THREE TOPS

DR BIRD 1101 Miserable Friday/This World Has Feeling

THE DIPLOMATS

(X) LLOYD & THE GROOVERS

ERROL DIXON

DIRECT 5002 I Don't Want/The Hoop

SKA-BEAT 271 Midnight Party/Makes No Difference

JEFF DIXON

b Jeff Samuel Dixon 3/31/46 (Davyton, JA). d 9/11/87. Immensely popular JBC disc jockey aka SOUL SAM, BIGGER D, FREE I. Also recorded as a duo with MARCIA GRIFFITHS. Was murdered alongside PETER TOSH.

COXSONE 7015 The Roll/HAMBOYS: Harder on the Rock

Produced by Coxsone Dodd.

DOBBY DOBSON

(X) TOMMY MCCOOK

DOREEN & THE ALL-STARS

aka DOREEN SCHAEFFER and sundry SKATALITES.

RAINBOW 113 Rude Girls/Please Stay

DOTTY & BONNIE

SKA-BEAT 274 I'll Know/Love Is Great

DON DRUMMOND JUNIOR

aka trombonist VIN GORDON, a Studio One session player.

CALTONE 104 Sir Pratt Special/HEMSLEY MORRIS: Love Is Strange

Produced by Ken Lack.

DUKE REID'S ALL-STARS

MASTER'S TIME 003 Religious Service at Bond Street Gospel Hall/ Continued

Produced by Duke Reid.

TROJAN 001 Judge Sympathy/ROLAND ALPHONSO: Never to Be Mine

Produced by Duke Reid. (a) The first release for what was to become the greatest reggae label in British history was not especially grandiose — a middling song performed by the SUPERSONICS and the FREEDOM SINGERS.

ERROL DUNKLEY

b 1951 (Denham Town, Kingston, JA) Also recorded as a duo with ROY SHIRLEY, JUNIOR ENGLISH. Having recorded first with PRINCE BUSTER, Jamaica's second child star was touted as the next DELROY WILSON (he being Jamaica's first). His "Please Stop Your Lying" (produced by LEE PERRY, whose "I Am The Upsetter" featured on the flip) was one of the debut releases on Joe Gibbs' Amalgamated label and was the company's first hit. Maintained a fairly low profile through the 1970s, recording for various producers, before 1979 brought a version of JOHN HOLT's "OK Fred," a UK #11 hit. Its success prompted Dunkley to relocate to Britain, where he continues to enjoy a fruitful career.

RIO 131 You're Gonna Need Me/Seek & You'll Find

Produced by Joe Gibbs. (a) The young Dunkley has the voice of an angel, but a maturity of delivery far beyond his tender years. This performance sizzles with his passionate reworking of the old Gloria Lynn R&B hit.

THE DYNAMITES

(X) BABA BROOKS, ROY SHIRLEY

CLANCY ECCLES

PAMA 701 What Will Your Mama Say/Darling Don't Do That
Produced by Clancy Eccles.

JACKIE EDWARDS

ISLAND 3018 Royal Telephone/It's No Secret
Produced by Chris Blackwell.

ISLAND 3030 Only a Fool Breaks His Own Heart/The End
Produced by Chris Blackwell.

ISLAND 6008 Come Back Girl/Tell Him You Lied
Produced by Chris Blackwell.

ALTON ELLIS

(X) ROY RICHARDS

DR BIRD 1059 Girl I've Got a Date/LYNN TAITT & TOMMY MCCOOK: The Yellow Basket
Produced by Duke Reid. (a) The song that sealed Ellis fame. The singer took this pretty, self-penned number to soaring heights with soulful, emotive vocals, and established himself as a superstar talent.

ISLAND 3046 Cry Tough/TOMMY MCCOOK: Mr Solo
Produced by Duke Reid. (a) Occasionally Ellis moved beyond relationships and, on this classic song, he takes on the problems of old age in a tough world, with the aid of a pair of sublime backing vocalists. The pensive melody, exceptional arrangement, and superb performances by all involved make this one of Ellis' best.

STUDIO ONE 2028 I Am Just a Guy/SOUL VENDORS: Just a Little Bit of Soul
Produced by Coxsone Dodd. (a) One of Ellis' biggest hits ever, he recorded several versions including one tremendous performance with the magnificent PHYLLIS DILLON (produced by DUKE REID), their vocals beautifully intertwining as they warn each other against betraying their love.

STUDIO ONE 2033 Only 16/Baby
Produced by Coxsone Dodd.

STUDIO ONE 2037 Live & Learn/HEPTONES: Cry Baby Cry
Produced by Coxsone Dodd.

TREASURE ISLE 7004 Rock Steady/TOMMY MCCOOK & THE SUPERSONICS: Wall Street Shuffle
Produced by Duke Reid. (a) Devastating, a masterpiece of melody, sweet backing vocals, and a self-defining beat which defies you not to sway along.

TREASURE ISLE 7010 Duke of Earl/All My Tears Come Rolling
Produced by Duke Reid. (a) The old doo-wop hit, performed with reasonable flair but not too much passion. (b) The upbeat melody and perky beat seem at odds with the title, but Ellis is crying because he's in love, not because

he's lost it. And every girl in JA wishes it was her he was singing so soulfully about.

TREASURE ISLE 7016 Ain't that Loving You/TOMMY MCCOOK & THE SUPERSONICS: Tommy's Rock Steady
Produced by Duke Reid. (a) Ellis could be just as passionate as soulful, as he shows on this cover of the R&B classic, with the SUPERSONICS' rock steady rhythm and bluesy horns adding to the beauty of the mood. U-ROY later versioned the performance. Also released as TROJAN 004.

TROJAN 009 Why Birds Follow Spring/TOMMY MCCOOK & THE SUPERSONICS: Soul Rock
Produced by Duke Reid. (a) This classic crooner was a strong platform for Ellis to strut his vocal stuff, allowing him to play with moods (thoughtful to exhilarating) and styles (soft pop to soul).

BOBBY ELLIS

Trumpeter with BUNNY LEE'S AGGROVATORS, CLANCY ECCLES' DYNAMITES, DERRICK HARRIOTT'S MIGHTY VIKINGS and CRYSTALITES, etc. (X) DERRICK HARRIOTT, KEITH & TEX, RUDY MILLS

HORTENSE ELLIS

FAB 20 Somebody Help Me/BUSTER'S ALL-STARS: Rock & Shake

EL RECO, SIR COLLINS & J SATCH

(X) OWEN GRAY

THE EMOTIONS

CALTONE 100 A Rainbow/TONY & DOREEN: Just You & I
Produced by Ken Lack.

THE ETHIOPIANS

COXSONE 7022 Let's Get Together/THE HAMLINS: Soul and Inspiration
Produced by Coxsone Dodd.

DR BIRD 1092 I Need You/Do It Sweet
Produced by Coxsone Dodd.

DR BIRD 1096 The Whip/Cool It, Amigo
Produced by Coxsone Dodd.(a) Notable for its percussive effects (possibly played on a glass bottle), great guitar riffs, and muted horns plying the melody, The Ethiopians' angelic harmonies sing out snatches of verse with dislocating precision.

DR BIRD 1103 Stay Loose, Mama/The World Goes Ska
Produced by Coxsone Dodd.

ISLAND 3036 For You/SOUL VENDORS: Sound Pressure
Produced by Coxsone Dodd.

RIO 123 What to Do /JACKIE MITTOO: Got My Bugaloo
Produced by Coxsone Dodd.

RIO 126 Dun Dead A'Ready/Stay in My Lonely Eyes
Produced by Coxsone Dodd.

RIO 130 Train to Skaville/You Are the Girl
Produced by Coxsone Dodd. (a) Perfect down to its last note, the rhythm section rattles along, the horns echo and

re-echo the song's hook, while the Ethiopians harmonies are exquisite. Plus, there's a toaster to turn up the heat.

STUDIO ONE 2035 Leave My Business/SOUL VENDORS: Pupa Lick
Produced by Coxsone Dodd.

EWAN & JERRY

Vocal duo featuring EWAN MCDERMOTT and JERRY JONES.

BLUE BEAT 385 Oh Babe/Dance with Me

GIANT 5 The Right Track/We Got to Be the One

GIANT 10 Rock Steady Train/My Baby Is Gone

GIANT 14 Tennessee Waltz/You've Got Something

GIANT 17 I Want You So Bad/ERIC MCDERMOTT: I'm Gonna Love You

AUSTIN FAITHFUL

(X) ROLAND ALPHONSO

FITZI & FREDDY

(X) WINSTON SAMUELS

J FRANCIS & PRINCE BUSTER ALL-STARS

BLUE BEAT 379 Warn the People/THE SWINGERS: Simpleton
Produced by Prince Buster.

J FRANCIS & RICO'S BOYS

RAINBOW 114 My Granny/Pull It Out

NAT FRANCIS

BLUE BEAT 376 Seven Nights of Love/Feeling Blue

WILBERT FRANCIS & VIBRATORS

FRANCIS aka LITTLE WILLIE.

SKA-BEAT 267 Memories of You/CHUCK JACQUES: Now that You're Gone

NORMA FRAZIER

(X) THE VICEROYS

COXSONE 7017 First Cut Is the Deepest/BUMPS OAKLEY: Rag Doll
Produced by Coxsone Dodd. (a) Rock steady remake of the Cat Stevens composition, a little faster than the song is comfortable with, but buoyant on Frazier's sweet, clear vocal.

STUDIO ONE 2024 Come by Here/WAILERS: I Stand Predominate
Produced by Coxsone Dodd. (b) Again featuring the vocal talents of RITA MARLEY, Norma Fraser, and CONSTANTINE WALKER, this BUNNY LIVINGSTON composition was one of the last the group cut with Coxsone Dodd. He originally envisioned it as a successor to past WAILERS rude boy statements, but he also wanted a record which would sound great on his sound system. He succeeded on both counts, conjuring up a masterful ode to both Rastafarianism and ethnic pride.

THE FREEDOM SINGERS

(X) SLIM SMITH

STUDIO ONE 2010 Have Faith/Work Crazy
Produced by Coxsone Dodd.

THE FUGITIVES

One of the rock steady era's most successful session bands, led by trumpeter JO JO BENNETT. (X) STRANGER COLE

DR BIRD 1082 Musical Pressure/LESLIE BUTLER & THE FUGITIVES: Winchester Rock Steady

THE GAYLADS

(X) JACKIE MITTOO

COXSONE 7002 Sound of Silence/JACKIE MITTOO: Somebody Help Me
Produced by Coxsone Dodd.

ISLAND 3022 Don't Say No/SONNY BURKE: You Rule My Heart

ISLAND 3025 You No Good Girl/Yes Girl

RIO 125 Put on Your Style/SOUL BROTHERS: Soul Serenade
Produced by Coxsone Dodd.

STUDIO ONE 2002 Tears from My Eyes/Never Let Your Country Down
Produced by Coxsone Dodd.

STUDIO ONE 2017 Love with Me with All Your Heart/CLARENDONIANS: Love Don't Mean Much to Me
Produced by Coxsone Dodd. (a) An energetic rock steady groove with an infectious chorus ("wake me, shake me!") and a drive which subsequently lent itself perfectly to a late 1970s Studio One remix.

STUDIO ONE 2034 Africa/SOUL VENDORS: Hot Rod
Produced by Coxsone Dodd.

STUDIO ONE 2038 I'm Free/SOUL VENDORS: Psychedelic Rock
Produced by Coxsone Dodd. (b) Actually it's not psychedelic at all, but a thunderous horn-led instrumental with a stirring DJ introduction. "Coming from the top. . . ."

THE GLADIATORS

Original line-up: ALBERT GRIFFITHS, CLINTON FEARON, and DAVID WEBBER (brother of MARLENE and JOYCE). Fine exponents of the rock steady style, the Gladiators became better known a decade later, as one of the first signings to Front Line, the UK roots label which helped shape British reggae tastes of the late 1970s.

DR BIRD 1114 The Train Is Coming/So Fine
Produced by Leeward Robinson. (a) Great sounding single which really isn't that far removed from the sound of the trio's later triumphs.

HUGH GODFREY

(X) MARCIA GRIFFITHS

COXSONE 7001 A Dey pon Dem/SOUL BROTHERS: Take Ten
Produced by Coxsone Dodd.

NORMAN GRANT

Member of THE TWINKLE BROTHERS. (X) ROLAND ALPHONSO

OWEN GRAY

COLLINS DOWNBEAT 003 Collins Greetings/Rock It Down

COLLINS DOWNBEAT 004 I'm So Lonely/EL RECO, SIR COLLINS & J
  SATCH: Shock Steady

TONY GREGORY

COXSONE 7013 Only a Fool/Pure Soul
Produced by Coxsone Dodd.

COXSONE 7023 I Sit by the Shore/LLOYD CHARMERS: Time Is
  Getting Hard
Produced by Coxsone Dodd.

ISLAND 3029 Get Out of My Life/SOUL BROTHERS: Sugar Cane
Produced by Coxsone Dodd.

MARCIA GRIFFITHS

(X) PETER TOUCH

COXSONE 7029 Call to Me/SOUL VENDORS: Fat Fish
Produced by Coxsone Dodd.

STUDIO ONE 2008 Hound Dog/HUGH GODFREY: My Time
Produced by Coxsone Dodd.

STUDIO ONE 2015 After Laughter/HUGH GODFREY: Go Tell Him
Produced by Coxsone Dodd.

THE GROOVERS

Featuring LLOYD YOUNG. (X) ALVA LEWIS

THE HAMBOYS

(X) JEFF DIXON

MILTON HAMILTON

One-half of the duo ALLEN & MILTON.

SKA-BEAT 265 Something Gotta Ring/DENNIS LYNWARD & HIS
  GROUP: Jazz Session

THE HAMLINS

(X) ETHIOPIANS, THE MINSTRELS, WAILERS

DERRICK HARRIOTT

ISLAND 3063 The Loser/Bless You
Produced by Derrick Harriott. (a) Arguably Harriott's best
performance (and composition), the falsetto backing vocals
are otherworldly, the delivery superb, the piano break perfect, and the song's mood as fragile as Venetian glass.

ISLAND 3064 Happy Times/You Are Everything
Produced by Derrick Harriott.

ISLAND 3077 Walk the Streets/BOBBY ELLIS: Step Softly
Produced by Derrick Harriott. (a) Harriott's poignant song
of lost love is a mid-tempo heart string puller, with the guitar
handing round the hankies.

ISLAND 3089 Solomon/BOBBY ELLIS: The Emperor
Produced by Derrick Harriott. (a) Harriott boasts he's wiser
than Solomon, at least in regards to women, and the backing
vocalists enthusiastically back him up. Even better, the
singer delivers these outrageous claims as understated fact,
without a hint of arrogance. Quite a feat!

YVONNE HARRISON

CALTONE 102 The Chase/Take My Hand
Produced by Ken Lack.

HAZEL & THE JOLLY BOYS

Featuring HAZEL WRIGHT.

DR BIRD 1063 Stop Them/Deep Down

HEMSLEY MORRIS

(X) DON DRUMMOND JNR

HENRY III

(X) THE UNIQUES

ISLAND 3078 Thank You Girl/Take Me Back

ISLAND 3081 I'll Reach the End/Won't Go Away

THE HEPTONES

(X) ALTON ELLIS

CALTONE 105 Schoolgirls/Ain't that Bad?
Produced by Ken Lack. (a)/(b) A weak coupling emphasizing the Heptones' balladeering strengths, but not really giving them strong ballads to do it with.

SKA-BEAT 266 We've Got Love/I Am Lonely
Produced by Ken Lack. (b) Slow, squeaking ballad with
LEROY SIBBLES' best heartbroken tones sobbing over the
lonely trombone.

STUDIO ONE 2005 A Change Is Gonna Come/Nobody Knows
Produced by Coxsone Dodd.

STUDIO ONE 2014 Fat Girl/DELROY WILSON: Mother Word
Produced by Coxsone Dodd. (a) aka "Fatty Fatty."

STUDIO ONE 2021 If I Knew/Festival Day
Produced by Coxsone Dodd.

STUDIO ONE 2027 Why Must I?/SLIM SMITH: Try Again
Produced by Coxsone Dodd.

LENNIE HIBBERT & COUNT OSSIE BAND

Vibraphone maestro HIBBERT was bandmaster at the Alpha
school. Frequently worked with SOUND DIMENSION.

DR BIRD 1113 Pure Sole/PATSY: A Man Is Two Faced
(a) An exhilarating instrumental collision between Hibbert's
trademark vibraphone and Ossie's nyahbingi percussion.

JOE HIGGS

b 6/3/40 (Kingston, JA). Veteran vocalist famed for coaching
THE WAILERS and WAILING SOULS, both of whom he sub-
sequently toured with. He also worked with JIMMY CLIFF,
but is best regarded for a long and thoughtful solo career.
Half of duo HIGGS & WILSON, also performed with CAR-
LOS MALCOLM'S AFRO-CARIBS. (X) THE WAILERS

COXSONE 7004 Neighbour Neighbour/MELODIANS: I Should Have
  Made It Up
Produced by Coxsone Dodd.

ISLAND 3026 I Am the Song/Worry No More
Produced by Coxsone Dodd.

STUDIO ONE 2018 Change of Plans/SOUL VENDORS: Rocking Sweet
  Pea
Produced by Coxsone Dodd.

JUSTIN HINDS & THE DOMINOES

ISLAND 3048 On a Saturday Night/Save a Bread

Produced by Duke Reid. (b) "Save" features some of the group's most sublime vocal work, a stripped down arrangement shining the spotlight on the singers, with Hinds obligingly sharing vocals throughout the verses. Also released as TREASURE ISLE 7014.

TREASURE ISLE 7002 Here I Stand/No Good Rudie

Produced by Duke Reid. (a) Hinds stands all alone looking for love (with just his ever superb backing singers for company), on this yearning, soulful number, which features one of the singer's most emotive vocals. (b) Hinds and co-weigh into the rude boy rage with this rock steady offering, a response to the WAILERS' recent "Good Good Rudie" hit. But forget the trite lyrics ("crime doesn't pay"), and concentrate on their always spectacular vocals instead.

TREASURE ISLE 7005 Carry Go Bring Come/Fight Too Much

Produced by Duke Reid. (a) Reissue of the song which carried Hinds' career into the big-time, a perfect blend of mid-tempo beat, light harmonies, and Hinds' sharp as a bell signature vocals.

TREASURE ISLE 7017 Once a Man/TOMMY MCCOOK & THE SUPERSONICS: Persian Cat

Produced by Duke Reid.

HORTENSE & ALTON

(X) MR FOUNDATION

THE INVADERS

COLUMBIA BLUE BEAT 105 Limbo Girl/Soul of the Jungle

Produced by Laurel Aitken. (b) The Invaders invite RICO RODRIGUEZ, LAUREL AITKEN, and the EQUALS' EDDIE THORNTON in for this instrumental expedition, the bongos give it a jungle feel, but the song is really a musical showcase for all involved.

THE ITALS

Vocal group featuring KEITH PORTER (WESTMORELITES, FUTURE GENERATION, SOUL HERMITS), RONNIE DAVIS, LLOYD RICKETTS (THE TENNORS), and later DAVID ISAACS.

GIANT 8 New Loving/I Told You Little Girl

GIANT 12 Don't Throw It Away/Make up Your Mind

CHUCK JACQUES

(X) WILBERT FRANCIS

SKA-BEAT 264 Dial 909/THE VIBRATORS & TOMMY MCCOOK & THE COMETS: Wait for Me

(a) The unmistakable rock steady of LYNN TAITT & THE COMETS.

THE JAMAICAN SHADOWS

COXSONE 7005 Have Mercy/Blending Love

Produced by Coxsone Dodd.

THE JAMAICANS

Vocal group featuring TOMMY COWAN.

D BIRD 1109 Cool Night/Ma & Pa

TREASURE ISLE 7007 Things You Say You Love/I've Got a Pain

Produced by Duke Reid. (a) The close harmonies are heavenly, with the bouncy horns slightly lightening the lyrical warnings of the danger of throwing away love. Later versioned to great effect by U-ROY.

TREASURE ISLE 7012 Ba-Ba Boom/TOMMY MCCOOK & THE SUPERSONICS: Real Cool

Produced by Duke Reid. (a) It's not hard to see why this song won the 1967 Festival Song Competition. A sultry melody, gorgeous vocals, and the crowd pleasing plea to "come do the rock steady" were a guaranteed winner.

TROJAN 007 Dedicated to You/Things I Said to You

Produced by Duke Reid. (a) Exquisitely sweet harmonies and a light as a feather lead vocal. It's the Jamaicans — what else would you expect?

JOHNNY & THE ATTRACTIONS

(X) DUDLEY WILLIAMSON

SHIRLEY KAYE

TROJAN 015 Make Me Yours/We Have Happiness

KEITH & TEX

Vocal duo comprising KEITH ROWE, ex-RICKETTS & ROWE, and TEX DIXON.

ISLAND 3085 Tonight/LYNN TAITT & THE JETS: You Have Caught Me

Produced by Derrick Harriott. (a) Keith and Tex surpass themselves on this moody R&B-esque number, with a Western twang and a simply sublime bass line.

ISLAND 3091 Stop that Train/BOBBY ELLIS: Feeling Peckish

Produced by Derrick Harriott. (a) Harriott revitalizes "Tonight's" sinuous bass line to propel a surly version of the SPANISHTONIANS favorite, where the Far East meets Country & Western. Vanilla Ice later covered the song.

KING FIGHTER

Popular calypsonian from British Guyana.

JUMP-UP 518 People Will Talk/Same Thing

KING ROCK & WILLOWS

(X) ALVA LEWIS

TEDDY KING & BUSTER'S ALL-STARS

FAB 27 Mexican Divorce/SOUL TOPS: Baby I Got News

Produced by Prince Buster.

KINGSTON PETE & BUSTER'S ALL-STARS

BLUE BEAT 403 Little Boy Blue/I'm a Lover Try Me

Produced by Prince Buster.

THE KINGSTONIANS

Featuring vocalist JACKIE BERNARD.

RIO 140 Winey Winey/I Don't Care

Produced by Derrick Harriott. (a) "You wine, you winey, too much," and by the time this is over, you'll agree. The bland, repetitive beat and the interminable chorus conspire to make this song a real irritant.

DIANE LAWRENCE
DR BIRD 1075 I Won't Hang Around Like a Hound Dog/Read It Over

GENE LAWRENCE
JUMP-UP 505 Longest Day Meringue/Bachelor Boy
JUMP-UP 510 Meringue Triniana/Devil Woman

BOBBY LEE
(X) THE SENSATIONS

DON TONY LEE
b Don Antonio Lee, brother of producer BUNNY LEE and a store manager at WIRL Studios. (X) LLOYD & THE GROOVERS

ALVA LEWIS
aka HIPPY BOYS/REGGAE BOYS/UPSETTERS guitarist REGGIE LEWIS.
CALTONE 111 Return Home /KING ROCK & WILLOW: You Are the One
Produced by Ken Lack.
DR BIRD 1107 Revelation/LESTER STERLING: Soul Voyage
ISLAND 3080 I'm Indebted/THE GROOVERS: You've Got to Cry

HOPETON LEWIS
Vocalist with LYNN TAIT's stable, later with BYRON LEE & THE DRAGONAIRES. Also recorded as a duo with PRIMO, GLENMORE BROWN, U-ROY. Jamaica was dominated by Lewis' "Take It Easy," a soft-as-silk WINSTON BLAKE production which sold 10,000 copies in a single weekend. It titled Lewis' first UK album, and helped give rise to the whole rock steady boom. But it never made it out on a British 45.
ISLAND 3054 Rock Steady/Cool Collie
ISLAND 3055 Finders Keepers/ROLAND ALPHONSO: Shanty-Town Curfew
ISLAND 3056 Let Me Come on Home/Hardships of Life
ISLAND 3057 Run Down/Pick Yourself Up
ISLAND 3059 Let the Little Girl Dance/This Music Got Soul
ISLAND 3068 Rock a Shacka/I Don't Want Trouble
ISLAND 3076 Everybody Rocking/Stars Shining So Brightly

LITTLE JOHN
No relation to the dance hall DJ of the same name!
PAMA 702 Let's Get Married/Around the World

LLOYD & GLEN
Vocal duo comprising LLOYD ROBINSON and GLEN BROWN; aka GLEN & LLOYD.
COXSONE 7011 That Girl/You Got Me Wrong
Produced by Derrick Harriott. (a) Hey, check out that girl, the sweet one walking down the street! If we sing really loud,

act really jaunty, and pull out our best falsetto harmonies, maybe she'll look at our way. Oh my god, it worked!
DR BIRD 1099 Feel Good Now/What You've Got
DR BIRD 1058 Jezebel/TOMMY MCCOOK & THE SUPERSONICS: Jam Session
(a) Picking up the theme of the notorious Biblical temptress, "Jezebel" struts across an upbeat, if somewhat musically (and lyrically) repetitive, single.
DR BIRD 1071 Keep on Pushing/BOBBY AITKEN: You Won't Regret It

LLOYD & THE GROOVERS
Featuring LLOYD YOUNG.
CALTONE 108 Do It to Me Baby/DIPLOMATS: Meet at the Corner
Produced by Bunny Lee.
CALTONE 109 My Heart My Soul/DIPLOMATS WITH TOMMY MCCOOK & THE SUPERSONICS: Going Along
Produced by Bunny Lee.
DR BIRD 1106 My Heart & Soul/DON TONY LEE: Lee's Special
Produced by Bunny Lee.

LORD CREATOR
JUMP-UP 503 Jamaica Jump Up/Laziest Man
(a) A cover of the Monty Norman composed hit from Dr No.
JUMP-UP 524 Big Bamboo/Marjorie & Harry

LORD CRISTO
JUMP-UP 515 Dumb Boy & The Parrot/General Hospital
JUMP-UP 517 Election War Zone/Bad Luck Man

LORD KITCHENER
ALADDIN 612 Dr Kitch/Come Back Home Meh Boy
Produced by Chris Blackwell. Reissued as JUMP-UP 511.
JUMP-UP 504 Love in the Cemetery/Jamaica Woman
Produced by Chris Blackwell.
JUMP-UP 506 The Road/Neighbour
Produced by Chris Blackwell. (a) The big band sound lives on with all the lushness of a Hollywood musical, while Lord Kitchener — with a knowing nod and a conspiratorial wink — belts out a commentary on the latest local news.
JUMP-UP 530 Kitch You So Sweet/Ain't that Fun
Produced by Chris Blackwell.

EARL LOWE
b 2/25/53 (Whitfield Town, JA). Renamed LITTLE ROY during later sessions with PRINCE BUSTER. Also recorded as a duo with KING ROCKY, JOY.
STUDIO ONE 2013 I Am Going to Cool It/MELODIANS: Let's Join Together
Produced by Coxsone Dodd. (a) Song composed by Lowe's brother Campbell, released erroneously credited to the GAYLADS.

DERMOTT LYNCH
DR BIRD 1115 Adults Only/Cool It

DENNIS LYNWARD & HIS GROUP

(X) MILTON HAMILTON

THE LYRICS

Trio formed by one S. ELLIOT, who re-emerged a decade later as FRED LOCKS.

COXSONE 7003 A Get It/KEN PARKER: How Strong
Produced by Coxsone Dodd.

COXSONE 7026 Money Lover/JACKIE MITTOO: Something Stupid
Produced by Coxsone Dodd.

RITA MARLEY

ISLAND 3052 Come to Me/SOUL BOYS: Blood Pressure
Produced by Coxsone Dodd.

LARRY MARSHALL

BLUE BEAT 374 Move Your Feet/Find a New Baby

BLUE BEAT 380 Suspicion/Broken Heart

DON MARTIN & DANDY

Dandy is DANDY LIVINGSTONE.

GIANT 6 Got a Feeling/CONNECTIONS: At the Junction

HONEYBOY MARTIN

CALTONE 103 Dreader than Dread/DANDY: In the Mood
Produced by Bunny Lee.(a) A fiery response to PRINCE BUSTER's notorious Judge Dread. Martin takes up the "tougher than tough" refrain from DERRICK MORGAN's earlier courtroom drama, then declares himself "dreader than [Judge] Dread." But unlike the wailing defendants appearing before Prince Buster's magistrate, this rude boy's delivery is so provocatively nonchalant, that it inevitably turned up the temperature of the simmering soap opera, and cried out for (yet another) judicial response.

KEITH MCCARTHY

COXSONE 7014 Everybody Rude Now/BASSIES: Beware
Produced by Coxsone Dodd.

FREDERICK MCCLEAN

(X) DERRICK MORGAN

TOMMY MCCOOK & THE SUPERSONICS

(X) PHYLLIS DILLON, JUSTIN HINDS, JAMAICANS, CHUCK JACQUES, LLOYD & GLEN, LLOYD & THE GROOVERS, MELODIANS, PARAGONS, SILVERTONES, TECHNIQUES

ISLAND 3047 One Two Three Kick/TREASURE ISLE BOYS: What a Fool
Produced by Duke Reid.

ISLAND 3049 Saboo/MOVING BROTHERS: Darling I Love You
Produced by Duke Reid. Also released as TREASURE ISLE 7018.

TROJAN 002 Starry Night/TONY & DENNIS: Folk Song
Produced by Duke Reid. (b) The duo's close harmonies are the highlight of this rock steady single, the piano intro/outro adds a nice Far Eastern touch.

TROJAN 010 Zazuka/TREASURE BOY: Love Is a Treasure
Produced by Duke Reid.

TROJAN 011 Sir Don/DOBBY DOBSON: Loving Pauper
Produced by Duke Reid. (b) Sweet harmonies, a steady rock solid beat, lyrical love conquering poverty and Dobson's emotive vocals were all the ingredients necessary for another Duke Reid success.

ERIC MCDERMOTT

(X) EWAN & JERRY

THE MELODIANS

(X) GAYLADS, JOE HIGGS

TREASURE ISLE 7006 You Don't Need Me/I'll Get Along Without You
Produced by Duke Reid. (a) The trio at their most soulful and passionate, on a song that combines a bittersweet melody with an up-tempo beat./(b) The infectious, upbeat chorus coupled with a shimmering melody highlights this number, accompanied by a bright horn solo and some sublime guitar work.

TREASURE ISLE 7022 You Have Caught Me/I Know Just How She Feels
Produced by Duke Reid. (a) Now that the girl's caught them, all the Melodians can do is sweetly croon their happiness on this classic, romantic, rock steady single. U-ROY utilized this rhythm for his "Versions Galore."

TREASURE ISLE 7023 Last Train to Expo 67/TOMMY MCCOOK & THE SUPERSONICS: Expo
Produced by Duke Reid. (a) The Melodians' plaintively harmonize on this lovely rock steady cut, afire with yearning and just a hint of the ETHIOPIANS "Train to Skaville." U-ROY would revive this song under the title "Super Boss."

JOHNNY MELODY

b Johnny Jones. Also recorded with LLOYD TYRELL and CANNONBALL BRYAN. (X) ROLAND ALPHONSO

MIGHTY DOUGLAS

JUMP-UP 501 Laziest Man/Dance Me Lover

JUMP-UP 509 Ugliness/My Wicked Boy Child

JUMP-UP 508 Teacher Teacher/Split Me in Two

MIGHTY POWER

JUMP-UP 513 You're Wasting Your Time/Smart Barbaran

MIGHTY SPARROW

JUMP-UP 523 Village Ram/Pull Pistle Gang

THE MIGHTY VIKINGS

DERRICK HARRIOTT joined the Vikings in 1965 as vocalist and MC. BOBBY ELLIS was band leader and trumpeter; other members included LYNFORD "HUX" BROWN (b 12/4/44, Port Antonio, JA), DESMOND MILES (bass), HEADLEY BENNETT (sax), LEROY "HORSEMOUTH" WALLACE (drums). They toured extensively; Harriott remained a member until 1969.

ISLAND 3060 Do Re Mi/The Sound of Music

Produced by Derrick Harriott.

ISLAND 3074 Rockitty Fockitty/Give Me Back Me Gal

Produced by Derrick Harriott.

GLEN MILLER

DR BIRD 1089 Where Is the Love/Funky Broadway

RUDY MILLS

ISLAND 3092 A Long Story/BOBBY ELLIS: Now We Know

Produced by Derrick Harriott. (a) It may well be a long story, but in short, it's simply another tale of heartache, set to a jaunty beat. Thankfully, Mills is good enough to get the heartbreak across.

THE MINSTRELS

STUDIO ONE 2036 People Get Ready/HAMLINS: Everyone's Got to Be There

Produced by Coxsone Dodd.

JACKIE MITTOO

(X) ETHIOPIANS, GAYLADS, LYRICS, SLIM SMITH, SUMMERTAIRES

JOHNNY MOORE

See entry for THE SKATALITES on page 262. (X) ROY SHIRLEY

DERRICK MORGAN

ISLAND 3079 Someone/Do You Love Me

PYRAMID 6010 Tougher than Tough/ROLAND ALPHONSO: Song for My Father

Produced by Leslie Kong. (a) Rude boys DESMOND and GEORGE DEKKER face the music, appearing in court before Magistrate Morgan. "Rudies don't fear," they sing in their own defense, being "rougher than rough, tougher than tough." Their sweet harmonies sways the judge into letting these knife wielding, gun toting, mooning miscreants go to sin another day. The forces of law and order will have their revenge though, when PRINCE BUSTER dons the Judge's robes in response.

PYRAMID 6013 Greedy Gal/SOUL BROTHERS: Marcus Junior

PYRAMID 6014 Court Dismiss/FREDERICK MCCLEAN: Fine Fine Fine

PYRAMID 6019 Judge Dread in Court/Last Chance

(a) In an hilarious turn of events, the now notorious Dread appears before Morgan's own magistrate, accused of impersonating a judge. He is found guilty and, to his shouts of dismay, is sentenced to a million years in prison. This remains one of the funniest offerings of the ouvre, but only when your laughing stops can you fully appreciate its perfect rock steady beat, sweet melody and exquisite harmonies.

PYRAMID 6021 Kill Me Dead/Don't Be a Fool

PYRAMID 6025 Do the Bang Bang/Revenge

PYRAMID 6024 No Dice/I Mean It

MONTY MORRIS

aka ERIC MORRIS.

DR BIRD 1067 Play It Cool/BABA BROOKS BAND: Open the Door

DR BIRD 1081 Put on Your Red Dress/BABA BROOKS: Faberge

THE MOVING BROTHERS

(X) TOMMY MCCOOK

MR FOUNDATION

STUDIO ONE 2001 Have a Good Time/KEN PARKER: See Them a Come

Produced by Coxsone Dodd.

STUDIO ONE 2003 All Rudies in Jail/HORTENSE & ALTON: Easy Squeeze

Produced by Coxsone Dodd.

BUMPS OAKLEY

aka GLENROY OAKLEY, later of GREYHOUND. (X) NORMA FRAZIER

THE PARAGONS

See entry for JOHN HOLT on page 117. Members included BOB ANDY, JOHN HOLT, GARTH EVANS, LEROY STAMP, JUNIOR MENZ, and HOWARD BARRETT.

DR BIRD 1060 Happy Go Lucky Girl/Love Brings Pain

Produced by Duke Reid. (a) It was with singles like this that Reid established himself as the ruler of rock steady. Paragon JOHN HOLT penned the song, TOMMY MCCOOK and the SUPERSONICS set the mood, while the trio's sweet, emotive vocals are absolutely delicious. U-ROY later versioned this gem of a song.

ISLAND 3045 On the Beach/CAROL & TOMMY MCCOOK: Sweet & Gentle

Produced by Duke Reid. (a) JOHN HOLT at his smoothest, his compatriots at their most exquisite, this lilting, wistful song perfectly conjures up those happy summer days at the shore.

ISLAND 3067 Talking Love/If I Were You

Produced by Duke Reid.

ISLAND 3093 So Depressed/We Were Meant to Be

Produced by Duke Reid.

TREASURE ISLE 7009 Only a Smile/The Tide Is High

Produced by Duke Reid. (a) The Paragons try to smile through their tears in this lost love weepie. JOHN HOLT's emotional delivery is heartrending, the backing vocals croon softly in comfort. U-ROY, in contrast, would by "Flashing My Whip" across a later version. (b) This charming ballad would later be revived by Blondie (who'd take it into both the US and UK charts). The Paragons' original has a yearning quality, with the focus, obviously, on Holt's lead vocal and the harmonies.

TREASURE ISLE 7011 Mercy Mercy Mercy/Riding on a High & Windy Day

Produced by Duke Reid. (b) The melancholy melody is

given depth by a rootsy arrangement, accentuated by the Paragons' moody vocals in a minor key.

TREASURE ISLE 7013 The Same Song/TOMMY MCCOOK & THE SUPERSONICS: Soul Serenade

Produced by Duke Reid. (a) The close harmonies are as exquisite as ever, and the melody is as pretty as we've come to expect. The horns add the perfect touch of melancholy to this bittersweet single.

TREASURE ISLE 7025 Wear You to the Ball/You Mean the World to Me

Produced by Duke Reid. (a) Another unforgettable Holt number, driven by the trio's rich harmonies and a simple melody that sticks. Three years later, HOLT and U-ROY would take this song back into the charts.

KEN PARKER

b 1948. Founder member BLUES BLENDERS. (X) THE LYRICS, MR FOUNDATION

ISLAND 3082 How Could I/SONNY BURKE: Choo Choo Train

PATSY

b Millicent Todd. JA's favorite duettist! Recorded alongside DERRICK MORGAN, ERIC MORRIS, ROY PANTON, STRANGER COLE, DESMOND DEKKER, PEGGY, before launching a solo career. (X) LENNIE HIBBERT & COUNT OSSIE BAND

ISLAND 271 Disappointed Bride/EARL BOSTIC: Honeymoon Night

DAWN PENN

STUDIO ONE 2030 No No No/SOUL VENDORS: Portobello Road

Produced by Coxsone Dodd. (a) "No No No" arrived in Jamaica during the 1950s, a blues chestbeater originally titled "You Don't Love Me." Penn retitled it for her greatest hit, then revisited the song again in 1994, with producers STEELY & CLEVIE.

LEE PERRY

(X) ROY SHIRLEY

DR BIRD 1073 Run for Cover/Something You've Got

Produced by Lee Perry. (a) Cut at WIRL, another attack on COXSONE DODD, with sweet harmonies from the Sensations. Lynn Taitt's guitar is sublime. (b) A cover of a Chris Kenner R&B hit.

DR BIRD 1098 Whop Whop Man/Wind Up Doll

Produced by Lee Perry. (a/b) Recorded at the same session as "Run for Cover."

PETER & HORTENSE

Vocal duo featuring HORTENSE ELLIS. (X) DELROY WILSON

PRIMO & HOPETON

Vocal duo featuring HOPETON LEWIS.

RIO 139 Your Safekeep/Loving & Kind

PRINCE BUSTER

BLUE BEAT 370 Shanty-Town/Duppy Seven

Produced by Prince Buster.

BLUE BEAT 373 Knock on Wood/And I Love Her

Produced by Prince Buster.

BLUE BEAT 377 Dark End of the Street/Love Oh Love

Produced by Prince Buster.

BLUE BEAT 382 Sit & Wonder/ROLAND ALPHONSO: Sunrise in Kingston

Produced by Prince Buster.

BLUE BEAT 387 Judge Dread/FITZROY CAMPBELL & PRINCE BUSTER'S ALL-STARS: Waiting for My Rude Girl

Produced by Prince Buster. (a) The judge lives up to his name, by handing out draconian thousand year sentences to the hapless rude boys unfortunate enough to appear before him. Backing vocals have been credited alternately to LEE PERRY and Buster's brother Fitzroy, and to LARRY MARSHALL and SUPERSONICS percussionists HUGH THOMPSON and NOEL "SCULLY" SIMMS.

BLUE BEAT 388 Dance Cleopatra/All in My Mind

Produced by Prince Buster.

BLUE BEAT 389 Ghost Dance/SWEETHEARTS: Sit Down & Cry

Produced by Prince Buster. (a) Composed while on a tour of Britain, "Dance" follows a long line of Caribbean poets by adopting the form of a letter home, only the friends he's addressing are all "duppies" (ghosts) in the boneyard! Nevertheless, Buster inquires about the latest news, sends regards to friends and acquaintances, speaking softly over a rock steady beat and a haunting backing vocal from LEE PERRY. But is that a belch over the intro?

BLUE BEAT 390 Soul Serenade/Too Hot

Produced by Prince Buster. (b) This glorification of the rude boy has all the impetus of a careening train, even though the beat never picks up one iota of speed. The underlying tension is so intense, and the song so remarkably restrained, that it virtually bursts from the grooves in frustration, which of course was the point. A decade later, the Specials finally freed it from its bonds.

BLUE BEAT 391 Land of Imagination/The Appeal

Produced by Prince Buster. (b) Ah, the appeal. That was a good idea. "Hey Judge Dread! Don't be so harsh on my clients!" And that's 400 years for their lawyer as well, while the "Judge Dread" rhythm plays merrily in the background.

BLUE BEAT 393 Johnny Dollar/Rude Boys Rule

Produced by Prince Buster.

BLUE BEAT 400 All in My Mind/Judge Dread Dance the Pardon

Produced by Prince Buster. (b) Again utilizing the "Judge Dread" rhythm, "700 letters" have descended upon the Judge, demanding that he offer the rudies some clemency. But contradicting the title, they're not actually pardoned, but paroled with stiff conditions, and the further threat that, if they ever come back, Dread doesn't know what he'll do to them next.

BLUE BEAT 402 Vagabond/Come Get Me

Produced by Prince Buster.

FAB 10 Shakin' Up Orange Street/Black Girl

Produced by Prince Buster. (a) A real charmer this. A throbbing, pulsing rhythm, subtle organ flourishes, a dizzy horn, lovely harmonies, and one of Buster's sweetest deliveries — all in honor of Kingston's musical mecca, Orange Street, home to JA's greatest recording studios, his own included.

FAB 11 Johnny Cool (Parts 1/2)

Produced by Prince Buster. (a/b) A Buster/LEE PERRY collaboration in which Judge turns vigilante and takes to the streets to clean up the rude boys on their own turf. "I'm a ice box man, Johnny Cool." Cleverly, a medley of favorite rude boy hits ("Ba Ba Boom," "Minstrel and Queen") filters through the scenario.

FAB 16 Bye Bye Baby/Human

Produced by Prince Buster.

FAB 25 Train to Girl's Town/Give Love a Try

Produced by Prince Buster.

FAB 26 Going to the River/PRINCE BUSTER'S ALL-STARS: Julie on My Mind

Produced by Prince Buster. (b) A lovely ballad, inoffensive and loving, with guitars that sound like they've just got back from Hawaii and Buster bemoaning the girl who doesn't quite love him the way that he loves her. Indeed, it's all so sweet that you can't help but wonder whether Buster's really as sincere as he sounds?

PRINCE BUSTER'S ALL STARS

(X) HORTENSE ELLIS, J FRANCIS, TEDDY KING, KINGSTON PETE, PRINCE BUSTER, PROTOGUE

BLUE BEAT 372 Sounds & Pressure/My Darling

Produced by Prince Buster.

BLUE BEAT 375 Rock Steady/SHIRLEY & THE RUDE BOYS: Gently Set Me Free

Produced by Prince Buster.

BLUE BEAT 378 Drunkard Psalm/7 Wonders of the World

Produced by Prince Buster.

BLUE BEAT 383 Sharing You/You'll Be on the Lonely Train

Produced by Prince Buster.

BLUE BEAT 384 Take It Easy/Why Must I Cry

Produced by Prince Buster. (a) As slow and smooth as its title, "Easy"'s steadying beat, soothing melody, calming lyrics and Buster's serene vocals were the perfect antidote for the stressed or distracted.

BLUE BEAT 395 This Gun for Hire/Yes Daddy

Produced by Prince Buster.

PROTOGUE & PRINCE BUSTER'S ALL-STARS

BLUE BEAT 398 Fowl Dance/This Is It

Produced by Prince Buster.

THE PYRAMIDS

UK based group formed by RAY ELLIS, JOSH ROBERTS, RAY KNIGHT, ROY BARRINGTON, MONTY NAISMITH, FRANK PITTER, and MICK THOMAS, regularly backed PRINCE BUSTER on UK tours, and were usually produced by EDDY GRANT. Naismith, Thomas, and Ellis also recorded as the near-anagrammatical SYMARIP.

PRESIDENT 161 Train Tour to Rainbow City/John Chewey

Produced by Eddy Grant. (a) written by Eddy Grant.

CYNTHIA RICHARDS

Vocalist with THE CARIB BEATS and, later, SKIN FLESH & BONES. Also recorded with duo CYNTHIA & ARCHIE.

(X) BOBBY AITKEN.

ROY RICHARDS

(X) DELROY WILSON

ISLAND 3027 Rub a Dub/THE SHARKS: Baby Come Home

Produced by Coxsone Dodd.

STUDIO ONE 2020 Hanky Panky/ALTON ELLIS: I Am Still in Love

Produced by Coxsone Dodd.

WINSTON RICHARDS

RIO 124 Studio Blitz/Don't Up

RICO WITH HIS BOYS

Rico is RICO RODRIGUEZ.

FAB 12 Jingle Bells/Silent Night

A festive offering, stylishly played, but scarcely a major accomplishment.

THE RIGHTEOUS FLAMES

Formerly ALTON ELLIS' backing band THE FLAMES, led by WINSTON JARRETT. Restyled as RIGHTEOUS FLAMES with JARRETT, JUNIOR GREEN, and EGGA GARDNER. Later became WINSTON JARRETT & THE FLAMES. DANNY CLARKE and LLOYD FORRESTER of THE HURRICANES were occasional members later in the decade.

FAB 17 Need to Be Loved/I Am Going Home

FAB 18 Gimme Some Sign Girl/Let's Go to the dance

FAB 30 When a Girl Loves a Boy/THE DALTONS: Never Kiss You Again

THE ROCK STEADYS

GIANT 2 Squeeze & Freeze/JUNIOR SMITH: I'm a Good Boy

ROMEO & THE EMOTIONS

CALTONE 106 Don't Want to Let You Go/I Can't Do No More

Produced by Ken Lack. (a) With Max the Romeo leading the parade, the Emotions are particularly true to their name on this mid-tempo single.

KEN ROSE

(X) THE UNIQUES

THE RUDE BOYS

ISLAND 3088 Rock Steady/Massachusetts/Going Home

THE RULERS

RIO 132 Wrong Embryo/Why Don't You Change

Produced by JJ Johnson.(a) Opening with an adaptation of "Stagger Lee," "Wrong" then totally shifts gears into a snail-paced R&B number showcasing The Rulers' fabulous vocals. The Clash heard the possibilities, and revised it into the punk powered "Wrong 'Em Boyo."

RIO 135 Well Covered/CARL DAWKINS: Help Time

Produced by JJ Johnson.

RIO 138 Be Mine/CARL DAWKINS: Hot & Sticky

Produced by JJ Johnson.

WINSTON SAMUELS

ISLAND 3053 I Won't Be Discouraged/FITZI & FREDDY: Why Did My Little Girl Cry

Produced by Coxsone Dodd.

ISLAND 3051 The Greatest/FITZI & FREDDY: Truth Hurts

Produced by Coxsone Dodd.

THE SENSATIONS

Fronted by JIMMY aka MARTIN RILEY, later a member of THE UNIQUES. Band also featured CORNELL CAMPBELL, AARON "BOBBY" DAVIS, BUSTER RILEY (brother of the TECHNIQUES' WINSTON RILEY). Following Martin Riley's departure, the band recorded briefly as a trio before the arrival of JACKIE PARIS.

DR BIRD 1074 A Thing Called Soul/BOBBY LEE & THE SENSATIONS: I Was Born a Loser

DR BIRD 1100 Right on Time/Lonely Lover

DR BIRD 1102 Born to Love You/Your Sweet Love

THE SHADROCKS

ISLAND 3061 Go Go Special/Count Down

Studio One session band led by Dwight Pinkney, supposedly named in emulation of the WAILERS ("Whalers"). (X) ROY RICHARDS

ROY SHIRLEY

Founder member of THE UNIQUES. Also recorded as a duo with CORNELL CAMPBELL, ERROL DUNKLEY, ALTYMAN REID, KEN BOOTHE, SLIM SMITH.

CALTONE 101 Get on the Ball /JOHNNY MOORE: Sound & Soul

Produced by Ken Lack. (a) A slow swing boogie featuring a slew of showy solos, from sax to harmonica, while Shirley's smooth vocals are equally sure to please.

DR BIRD 1068 Hold Them/Be Good

Produced by Joe Gibbs. (a) "Hold Them" was originally offered to COXSONE DODD, who rejected it because he didn't think Shirley's voice was strong enough (he subsequently recorded a version of the song with KEN BOOTHE). Gibbs was more enthusiastic and was rewarded with one of Shirley's best ever performances. The voice is odd, but it carries the melody on quavering passion, entwined around the rock steady beats.

DR BIRD 1079 I'm a Winner/Sleeping Beauty

Produced by Lee Perry. (a) An earlier version cut with BUNNY LEE was apparently ruined at acetate stage.

DR BIRD 1088 Prophet/What to Do

DR BIRD 1093 Musical Field/LEE PERRY & THE DYNAMITES: Trial & Crosses

Produced by Lee Perry.

DR BIRD 1108 Thank You/Touch Them

(a) Probably the closest Shirley gets to a soul-pop song, aided by a tight brass section and an upbeat rhythm. Also released as ISLAND 3098.

ISLAND 3070 People Rock Steady/Trying to Find a Home

(a) A melody (and lyrics) that slip in and out of "I'm in the Mood for Love," nice singing and a great beat.

ISLAND 3071 Musical War/Soul Voice

SHIRLEY & THE RUDE BOYS

Shirley is ROY SHIRLEY. (X) PRINCE BUSTER'S ALL STARS

DUDLEY SIBLEY

COXSONE 7010 Run Boy Run/Message of Old

Produced by Coxsone Dodd.

ISLAND 3034 Gun Man/Monkey Speaks His Mind

THE SILVERTONES

TREASURE ISLE 7020 Cool Down/TOMMY MCCOOK: Shadow of Your Smile

Produced by Duke Reid. (b) An instrumental cover of the theme from *The Sandpiper* (a hit for Tony Bennett in '65), McCook's tenor sax is the obvious focal point with the song given a somewhat more upbeat feel than the original.

SUGAR SIMONE

RAINBOW 115 I Love My Baby/I'll Keep You Satisfied

SUE 4029 Suddenly/King Without a Throne

JEANETTE SIMPSON

GIANT 16 Rain/Whatcha Gonna Do About It

SIR LORD COMIC

(X) THE THREE TOPS

MILLIE SMALL

FONTANA 796 Chicken Feed/Wings of a Dove

DAVE SMITH & THE ASTRONAUTS

COLUMBIA BLUE BEAT 104 A Lover Like You/Cup ff Love

JUNIOR SMITH

(X) THE ROCK STEADYS

GIANT 1 Cool Down Your Temper/I'm Groovin'

SLIM SMITH

b Keith Smith, 1948/d 10/9/72. Former member of VICTORS YOUTH BAND, later of THE ROYALS, THE TECHNIQUES, THE UNIQUES, also recorded as a duo with ROY SHIRLEY and U-ROY. Passionate and soulful, his was one of the greatest voices to chime through the 1960s and his records remained remarkable even after personal problems started to mount. Having quit the Uniques for a solo career in 1969, he and producer BUNNY LEE quickly scored with "Everybody Needs Love" but, in 1972, Smith was committed to Belleview asylum. He committed suicide at his parents' home the following year. (X) THE HEPTONES

COXSONE 7009 Mercy Mercy Mercy/JACKIE MITTOO: Ba Ba Boom
Produced by Coxsone Dodd.

COXSONE 7016 Hip Hug/FREEDOM SINGERS: I Want Money
Produced by Coxsone Dodd.

ISLAND 3023 I've Got Your Number/The New Boss
Produced by Coxsone Dodd. (a) "Please be true," Smith pleads on this masterful showcase, as he slides from soulful proclamations of love, sweet yearning begging, and heartbreaking nostalgia of romance past; so many emotions, so short a song. (b) The singer pulls out his best soul-man vocals for this sublime song of promise. "Boss" features a cymbal heavy beat, and a subtle melody which gives Smith the perfect opportunity to showcase his superb vocal skills.

THE SOUL AGENTS

(X) SUMMERTAIRES

COXSONE 7024 One Stop/TENNORS: Pressure & Slide
Produced by Coxsone Dodd.

COXSONE 7027 Lecture/SOUL BOYS: Blood Pressure
Produced by Coxsone Dodd.

THE SOUL BOYS

(X) RITA MARLEY, SOUL AGENTS

THE SOUL BROTHERS

(X) KEN BOOTHE, DESMOND DEKKER, ALTON ELLIS, GAYLADS, HUGH GODFREY, TONY GREGORY, DERRICK MORGAN, TERMITES, VICEROYS, DELROY WILSON

THE SOUL LEADERS

RIO 134 Pour on the Sauce/Beauty Is Only Skin Deep

THE SOUL TOPS

(X) TEDDY KING

THE SOUL VENDORS

aka THE SOUL BROTHERS. Having scored a club hit with TOMMY MCCOOK/FRANKIE ANDERSON's "Peanut Vendor," the group was renamed for a UK tour backing ALTON ELLIS and KEN BOOTHE, retaining the name thereafter. (X) RICHARD ACE, BASSIES, BOP & THE BELTONES, COOL SPOON, ALTON ELLIS, ETHIOPIANS, GAYLADS, MARCIA GRIFFITHS, JOE HIGGS, JACKIE MITTOO, DAWN PENN, DELROY WILSON, ERNEST WILSON

JUNIOR SOUL

b 1949 (Port Antonio, JA). Later known as JUNIOR MURVIN and, as such, the man who gave us "Police and Thieves."

DR BIRD 1112 Miss Cushie/LYNN TAITT: Doctor Paul
Produced by Sonia Pottinger.

THE SOULETTES

(X) THE UNIQUES

THE SPANISHTONIANS

(X) ROLAND ALPHONSO

OLIVER ST PATRICK & THE DIAMONDS

TROJAN 005 I Want to Be Loved by You/Tulipa

LESTER STERLING

(X) ALVA LEWIS COLLINS

DOWNBEAT 001 Sir Collins Special/Lester Sterling 67

STRANGER & PATSY

DR BIRD 1084 Tell It to Me/Your Photograph
Produced by Sonia Pottinger.

DR BIRD 1087 Down the Trainlines/Sing & Pray
Produced by Sonia Pottinger. (a) DENZELL LAING's nyahbingi-style drumming drives this sublimely moody, gloriously stately number along, while Cole and Todd sail above with characteristic grace.

THE STUDIO ONE ALL-STARS

aka SOUND DIMENSIONS.

ISLAND 3038 Sherry Out of My Mind/
Produced by Coxsone Dodd.

THE SUMMERTAIRES

(X) THE TERMITES

COXSONE 7018 Tell Me/SOUL AGENTS: For Your Education
Produced by Coxsone Dodd.

COXSONE 7019 You're Gonna Leave/JACKIE MITTOO: Ram Jam
Produced by Coxsone Dodd.

THE SWEETHEARTS

(X) PRINCE BUSTER

LYNN TAITT & THE JETS

(X) KEN BOOTHE, ALTON ELLIS, CHUCK JACQUES, JUNIOR SOUL, KEITH & TEX

ISLAND 3066 Something Stupid/Blue Tuesday

ISLAND 3075 I Don't Want to Make You Cry/Nice Time

THE TARTANS

Vocal group comprising DEVON RUSSELL aka DEVON IRONS, PRINCE LINCOLN THOMPSON (d 1/23/99), LINDBERGH "PREPS" LEWIS, CEDRIC MYTON. LLOYD ROBINSON was also a member. Myton subsequently joined THE CONGOS. Russell and Myton, Russell and Robinson also recorded as a duos.

ISLAND 3058 Dance All Night/What Can I Do
Produced by Ken Khouri. (b) A lovely melody and sublime harmonies unite on this song aimed straight at the hearts of the rude boys. Yet another gorgeous musical plea for peace goes unanswered.

VIC TAYLOR

TREASURE ISLE 7021 Heartaches/When It Comes to Loving You

Produced by Duke Reid. (a) The title tells you this is a real weepy, and Taylor plays it for all it's worth; rock steady at its most heartbreaking.

THE TECHNIQUES

TREASURE ISLE 7001 You Don't Care/TOMMY MCCOOK & THE SUPERSONICS: Down on Bond Street

Produced by Duke Reid. (a) There's just a hint of Motown to the melody, which the Techniques emphasize with their harmonies. The inimitable SLIM SMITH's high vocals float overhead on this lovely rock steady gem. U-ROY would turn the performance into one of his biggest hits, "Rule the Nation." (b) The saxophonist and his Supersonics take a stroll on this jaunty, yet haunting, instrumental in a minor key.

TREASURE ISLE 7019 Queen Majesty/Fighting for the Right

Produced by Duke Reid. (a) The Impressions must have turned green with envy after hearing this adaptation of their "Minstrel & Queen." PAT KELLY expertly handles the lead (he'd depart the trio soon after), and Reid made sure that his vocals and the Techniques' exquisite harmonies took center stage. The song was later versioned by DENNIS ALCAPONE on "My Voice Is Insured for Half a Million Dollars."

TREASURE ISLE 7026 Love Is Not a Gamble/Bad Minded People

Produced by Duke Reid. (a) The Techniques make a hit record seem like simplicity itself. All it takes is a subtle, solid rock steady rhythm, instrumentation that accents the beat and pretty melody, and the group's own oh-so-sublime harmonies.

THE TENNORS

(X) THE SOUL AGENTS

THE TERMITES

Vocal duo featuring LLOYD PARKS (b 1949, Walton, JA) and WENTWORTH VERNAL (b 1945, Kingston JA). Parks later joined THE TECHNIQUES, SKIN FLESH & BONES, THE REVOLUTIONARIES, THE PROFESSIONALS, and WE THE PEOPLE.

COXSONE 7008 Sign Up/DELROY WILSON: Troubled Man

Produced by Coxsone Dodd.

COXSONE 7025 Do It Right Now/SUMMERTAIRES: Stay

Produced by Coxsone Dodd.

STUDIO ONE 2006 Mercy Mr Percy/SOUL BROTHERS: Hot & Cold

Produced by Coxsone Dodd. (a) It's the first of the month, the landlord's knocking at the door, and you're a bit short. What do you do? Well, if you're the Termites, you plead sonorously for another day. Was Mr. Percy charmed by their dulcet tones? Perhaps, but more likely he commented on their exquisite harmonies, a sure sign that the pair were spending more time on their music than looking for work.

STUDIO ONE 2029 It Takes Two to Make Love/Beach Boy

Produced by Coxsone Dodd.

MIKE THOMPSON JUNIOR

ISLAND 3090 Rock Steady Wedding/Flower Pot Bloomers

THE THREE TOPS

DR BIRD 1070 Feel So Lonesome/SIR LORD COMIC: The Great Wuga Wuga

STUDIO ONE 2023 Moving to Progress/Love & Inspiration

Produced by Coxsone Dodd.

TREASURE ISLE 7008 Do It Right/You Should Have Known

Produced by Duke Reid. (a) This rock steady gem finds the trio at their best, gracing the charming melody and simple lyrics with an air of total sincerity.

TROJAN 003 It's Raining/Sound of Music

Produced by Duke Reid. (a) Offering up the sunny possibilities for an otherwise rainy day life, the trio's delivery glows with so much soul there could be four Tops, not three.

TOMORROW'S CHILDREN

Rock influenced band fronted by KEN LAZARUS.

ISLAND 3073 Bang Bang Rock Steady/Rain Rock Steady

TONY & DENNIS

(X) TOMMY MCCOOK

TONY & DOREEN

Duo featuring DOREEN SCHAEFFER. (X) EMOTIONS

PETER TOUCH & THE WAILERS

COXSONE 7012 Dancing Time/BOP & THE BELTONES: Treat Me Good

Produced by Coxsone Dodd. (b) The artist credit (on both the UK and Jamaican releases) long disguised what turned out to be a lost TOSH/WAILERS cut—albeit a fairly inconsequential one.

ISLAND 3042 I'm the Toughest/MARCIA GRIFFITHS: No Faith

Produced by Coxsone Dodd. (a) Tosh spits out a swaggering slice of rude boy punk, one of the most unequivocally menacing records of the era and that despite "DREAM" WALKER's light harmonies echoing in the background. An invocation/impersonation of the recently murdered Zachariah Palm, a JLP gunman and Kingston gang leader, turns the heat up further during the instrumental break.

TREASURE BOY

aka THE TREASURE ISLE BOYS, another pseudonym for the SUPERSONICS. (X) TOMMY MCCOOK

THE UNIQUES

COLLINS DOWNBEAT 002 Dry the Water/I'm a Fool for You

ISLAND 3084 Gypsy Woman/KEN ROSE: Wall Flower

Produced by Bunny Lee.

ISLAND 3087 Never Let Me Go/HENRY III: Won't Go Away

ISLAND 3086 Let Me Go Girl/SOULETTES: Dum Dum

Produced by Coxsone Dodd.

THE VALENTINES

(X) BABA BROOKS

THE VIBRATORS

(X) CHUCK JACQUES

THE VICEROYS

aka THE VOICEROYS. Vocal group fronted by WESLEY TINGLIN (b 1947, Kingston, JA), LINVAL WILLIAMS (b 1950, St Mary's, JA), DANIEL BERNARD (b 1949, Westmoreland, JA). The band remained active into the mid-1970s as THE INTURNS. (X) RICHARD ACE

STUDIO ONE 2016 Lose & Gain/SOUL BROTHERS: Honeypot

Produced by Coxsone Dodd.

STUDIO ONE 2025 Shake Up/NORMA FRAZIER: Telling Me Lies

Produced by Coxsone Dodd.

THE WAILERS

(X) NORMA FRAZIER, PETER TOUCH

COXSONE 7021 Oh Darling/THE HAMLINS: Trying to Keep a Good Man Down

Produced by Coxsone Dodd.

DR BIRD 1091 Nice Time/Hypocrite

Produced by Clancy Eccles. (a) Jazzy horns vie with the R&B guitar while the Wailers entice us to have, indeed, a nice time, by rocking steady of course. (b) An excitable rock steady gem that sweeps along on the back of a wonderful rhythm, puffed on its way by the brass, while the Wailers' vocals sail sweetly over the melody. Also released as FAB 37.

ISLAND 3043 Bend Down Low/Freedom Time

Produced by Coxsone Dodd. (a) The first song recorded by the Wailers following BOB MARLEY's return from the US, and their first for their own Wail'n Soul'm imprint. The riff, played on Marley's newly purchased electric guitar, rules the roost, but the Wailers' spiritual vocals and airiest harmonies carry this song to heaven. (b) The pretty piano melody sets the stage for this optimistic herald of the coming days of freedom. Perhaps a little more understated than the militant lyric demands, but there's a lovely hint of spirituality around the vocals.

JOE WHITE

DR BIRD 1069 Rudies All Round/Bad Man

(a) This infectious celebration of rude boy-dom is a rock steady classic, showcasing White's smooth, effecting vocals, ably assisted by the backing singers.

DR BIRD 1080 Lonely Nights/I Need You

DR BIRD 1090 I Need a Woman/Hot Hops

GRANVILLE WILLIAMS ORCHESTRA

ISLAND 3062 Hi Life/More

Produced by Granville Williams.

DUDLEY WILLIAMSON

DR BIRD 1117 Coming on the Scene/Anything You Want

DR BIRD 1118 I'm Moving On/JOHNNY & THE ATTRACTIONS: Young Wings Can Fly

(b) A moody melody and a slow pulsing rhythm provide the foundation for this optimistic love song, delivered with appropriate passion.

DELROY WILSON

THE HEPTONES, THE TERMITES

ISLAND 3033 Riding for a Fall/Got to Change Your Ways

Produced by Coxsone Dodd.

ISLAND 3037 Ungrateful Baby/ROY RICHARDS: Hopeful Village Ska

Produced by Coxsone Dodd.

ISLAND 3039 Close to Me/SOUL BROTHERS: Hi Life

Produced by Coxsone Dodd.

ISLAND 3050 Get Ready/ROY RICHARDS: Port O' Jamaica

Produced by Coxsone Dodd.

STUDIO ONE 2009 Won't You Come Home Baby/PETER & HORTENSE: I've Been Lonely

Produced by Coxsone Dodd.

STUDIO ONE 2019 Never Conquer/Run for Your Life

Produced by Coxsone Dodd. (b) You better run, because Wilson is after you, and when he catches up, he's going to . . . cover you in his smooth, loving tones. DENNIS ALCAPONE will chase after you with this same version later.

STUDIO ONE 2031 I'm Not a King/SOUL VENDORS: Take Me

Produced by Coxsone Dodd.

ERNEST WILSON

The first member of THE CLARENDONIANS to go solo.

STUDIO ONE 2032 Money Worries/SOUL VENDORS: Pe da Pa

Produced by Coxsone Dodd.

1968–72: Reggae Everywhere

Trojan continued to expand. A deal with Joe Gibbs brought the likes of Lee Perry, the Pioneers, the Destroyers, and a solo Peter Tosh to the Amalgamated and Pressure Beat subsidiaries. Another with Clancy Eccles created the Clandisc label. Gayfeet and High Note catered for Sonia Pottinger's output; Big handled Rupie Edwards'. Other labels simply picked up whatever they were offered — Big Shot, Blue Cat and Duke (originally formed for Duke Reid, of course, but quickly branching out). Homegrown concerns went with J Dan and Downtown, both specializing in Dandy Livingstone's output as both a vocalist and a producer. Bunny Lee was gifted with Jackpot and, as if to remind the English of the labyrinthine politics of the Kingston music industry, he promptly leased the label's first release, Derrick Morgan's "Seven Letters," to the Palmer brothers' Pama set-up in north London.

They, too, presided over a mini-empire. Having started out as a soul label, the brothers — Carl, Harry, and Jeff —

moved onto the Jamaican scene around 1967, signing Norman T Washington, Joyce Bond, the Marvels, and others. Licensing deals with Bunny Lee, Rupie Edwards, Clancy Eccles, and Lee Perry soon followed, while Pama also formed a house band, the all-white Inner Mind, to accompany visiting Jamaican artists.

Soon, Pama was presiding over a dozen labels: Pama itself, Nu-Beat, to deal with British productions; Bullet, Unity, Camel, Crab, Ocean, Punch, Success, Supreme, Escort, and Gas, and their output, too, plucked the cream of the Kingston crop, often via the same producers as Trojan boasted. Success was dominated by Edwards, Escort by Harry J, and Unity by Bunny Lee, who gave the company its first major hit when Max Romeo's "Wet Dream" soared into the UK chart in 1969.

Elsewhere, Graeme Goodall's Pyramid launched JJ and Attack. But still it was Trojan who dominated the market. As other producers emerged and proved their worth, Gopthal gave them a label. Joe Mansano ran Joe; Harry Mudie ran Moodisc. Lee Perry went solo and offered up his output; Trojan presented him with Upsetter, while one of Perry's proteges, Melanie Jonas, was given Spinning Wheel, named after a Perry produced 45 for Jonas and Dave Barker. The list goes on. Coxsone Dodd struck out alone and formed Bamboo, and soon added Ackee and Banana to the family.

Winston Riley fronted Techniques, Alvin Ranglin took GG, Keith Hudson ran Green Door, Byron Lee had Dynamic. Other thriving concerns included Randy's, Summit, Explosion, Ashanti, Sacred, CSP, Smash, Action, Grape, Bread, Hot Rod, and Horse.

Not every label remained exclusive to one producer — Spinning Wheel, for example, began diversifying after barely a handful of Jonas' own productions, and it wasn't alone. Nor was every label a success — some survived for just a handful of singles. Nevertheless, with over 40 different subsidiaries, Trojan's empire seemed endless, and so was the litany of success which it conjured up. "We were extremely successful," David Betteridge reflected. "At one stage we had four records in the [British] Top Twenty."

Jimmy Cliff became Trojan's first star, when his "Wonderful World, Beautiful People" made #6 in 1969. Following his London sojourn, Cliff returned to Jamaica in 1968, reunited with Leslie Kong, and recorded his critically acclaimed debut platter, *Hard Road to Travel*. Further hits "Viet-Nam" and a cover of Cat Stevens' "Wild World" followed, while Cliff's own compositions were covered by Desmond Dekker ("You Can Get It if You Really Want") and the Pioneers ("Let Your Yeah Be Yeah"). They, too, made the UK chart.

Few of Trojan's best remembered acts actually enjoyed lengthy careers in Britain. Rather, the one hit wonder was the rule — Jimmy Cliff aside, only Desmond Dekker comprehensively bucked the trend. He hit #1 in 1969 with "The

Israelites," following on from "007 (Shanty-Town)," and preceding the mighty "It Mek," "Pickney Girl" and "You Can Get It," a statistical supremacy which remained unchallenged until the emergence of home-grown rude reggae specialist Judge Dread in 1972.

Mainstream chart hits, however, were no gauge of success and, even if they were, so many one-offs themselves boasted a cohesion which remains tangible, a combination of simple chronology (the period 1969–71) and subsequent familiarity — all shot through with their irrevocable association with the latest twist in British youth culture fashion, the skinhead movement.

Monster hits like "Return of Django" (the Upsetters with Dave Barker — #5 in 1969), "Liquidator" (Harry J — #9 in 1969), and "Long Shot Kick de Bucket" (the Pioneers' ode to a legendary Jamaican racehorse — #21, 1969) all started their British life in the clubs and discotheques which grew up on the sites of the original West Indian clubs, in London, Manchester, Birmingham, Leeds, any place where there was a heavy concentration of working class Black and white kids. It just so happened that the majority of those white kids seemed to be skins.

To outsiders, the co-mingling of what is widely regarded as a racist white cult and an ethnic community remains a baffling phenomenon. Indeed, when journalist Pete Fowler confronted the issue in 1972, he, too, found it "crazily illogical" that, while the skinheads he studied professed to hate Blacks, they not only maintained friendships with West Indians, they also allowed them into their gangs.

By Blacks, however, Fowler swiftly realized that the skins meant Pakistanis and Indians, the clannish Asian communities which closed ranks against any kind of interaction with their white neighbors. "The West Indian kids are mixing . . . they are beginning to see [Britain] as their home. They get drunk, they like dancing, they like dressing up in Skingear. [They] are more 'normal.'. . ."

These observations dealt a mortal blow to any number of over-riding stereotypes, even as they confirmed the sociological belief that the Skins themselves were the direct descendants of the ska-loving Mods of half a decade before. They came from the same streets, they fought the same battles, and they liked the same music. It was as though the rudies never went away and Jamaican musicians were to embrace the new breed as wholeheartedly as they had their predecessors.

Indeed, Tony Cousins of the Creole booking agency (and one half of the pseudonymous UK production team Bruce Anthony) was able to trace the genesis of this new cult directly to a Jamaican prototype. "When we brought Desmond Dekker over [in 1967] we gave him a suit, but he insisted that the bottom six inches of the trousers should be cut off. Then the kids began to follow him, they rolled up their trousers and had their hair cut short." The most distinctive icons of the Skinhead cult fell into place there and then.

In terms of appealing to this audience, Derrick Morgan was the first Jamaican artist off the mark, when he adapted the old Sam and Dave shouter, "I Thank You," for the anthemic "Moonhop." Produced by Bunny Lee (now Morgan's brother-in-law), "Moonhop" was nothing less than an outright declaration of skinhead solidarity and a guaranteed smash hit. Certainly Pama's Crab subsidiary thought so as they prepared it for release and, over at Trojan, Lee Gopthal obviously thought so too. He ordered an immediate "spoiler" version, a spot-on cover which would detract from, and maybe even shoot down, Morgan's original.

Disguising themselves as Simaryp, it was the Pyramids (who had, in fact, backed Morgan on his recent UK visit) who came up with the goods, the mighty "Skinhead Moonstomp." Not only that, they also managed to squeeze an entire album out of the concept, topping off such de rigueur soundalikes as "Skinhead Girl" and "Skinhead Jamboree," with a positively inspired version of "These Boots Are Made for Walking."

Certainly they walked all over Derrick Morgan's "Moonhop," and they continued walking over the skin storm which followed in "Moonstomp"'s wake: Laurel Aitken's "Skinhead Train"; the Hot Rod All-Stars' "Skinhead Speaks His Mind," "Skinhead Moondust" and "Skinheads Don't Fear"; Desmond Riley's "A Message to You, Skinhead" (rewriting, of course, Dandy Livingstone's rude boy anthem "Rudie, a Message to You"); the Mohawks' "Skinhead Shuffle."

None of these cash-ins sold in any appreciable quantities; few of them actually involved even second-generation Jamaican musicians, as Laurel Aitken complained when he discovered he was often the only Black in the studio during his own recording sessions.

But authentic or otherwise, hit parade fodder or not, by 1969–70 their popularity had reached epic proportions in Britain. Dances, specialist stores, and the maze of booming record players at the far end of ethnic street markets may have been the only source of new releases, and those records which did eventually hit the charts may have done so only after weeks, even months, of cult exposure. But still they got heard.

The Specials, Madness, UB40, the English Beat, Bad Manners, Selecter, the very cream of the 2-Tone movement of a decade hence, cut their own musical teeth on the skinhead sounds, a debt they repaid in full by incorporating a well-stocked sound system's worth of covers into their own early live sets. "Guns of Navarone," "Monkey Man," "Too Hot," "Skinhead Moonstomp," would all be reborn in the late 1970s, shaking off a decade's worth of dust to prove they were just as powerful in this new age, as they ever had been back then.

And they were powerful back then. Records like the Maytals' "Decimal Money," the Uniques' "Too Proud to Beg," the Pioneers "Mama Look Deh," and Prince Buster's "Rough Rider" appealed not because they were "good" music (in fact, the UK music press and DJs of the time were adamant that they weren't), but because they were so immediate: easy to dance to, easy to understand.

Back in Jamaica, the music was already moving toward the more mystic Rasta angle which became world famous as reggae in the 1970s, but in Britain, the beat remained simple and the lyrics straightforward. Indeed it is worth noting that only a couple of Rastafarian-flavored records can be said to have found even basic acceptance among the skins, Laurel Aitken's atypical "Haile Selassie" and Niney's dread apocalypse "Blood and Fire."

"[Skinhead] musical tastes are strictly ska and soul [although] even soul is regarded as a little passe now," journalist Chris Welch told *Melody Maker* readers in mid-1969. "Blue beat, reggay, rock steady . . . are the kind of beats best to be seen clomping boots too."

Yet massive hits by Dave and Ansell Collins, Greyhound, and Bob and Marcia were as familiar in the kitchens of suburbia as the dance halls of the cities, while the now legendary (and supremely budget priced) *Tighten Up* series of compilations was as avidly purchased by bank clerks as by "Bovver Boys."

Indeed, "Tighten Up" (any volume) remains the most representative cross-section of Trojan's output, a combination of bona fide hits, excruciating misses (Joyce Bond's version of the Beatles' own blue beat led "Ob-La-Di Ob-La-Da"); and the infectiously, but irredeemably batty (Nora Dean's "Barbed Wire").

Released between 1968–72, all six volumes of *Tighten Up* sold prodigiously, although only one (volume four) actually made the British chart, proof that despite blue beat's increasing chart presence, it remained a distinctly underground phenomenon. The music press, after all, paid no real attention to even "serious" reggae until 1973, and the first stirrings of the Bob Marley cult; radio ignored it until it hit the chart; record stores simply scratched their heads at the mention of it.

But its popularity was undeniable all the same. Early in 1970, the self-proclaimed Biggest Reggae Package in the World arrived in Britain for a four-week tour, headlined by Desmond Dekker, Jimmy Cliff, the Pioneers, the Upsetters, Max Romeo, and Harry J's All Stars. Scant months later, a similarly Brobdingnagian gathering appeared at the Caribbean Music Festival at Wembley—Dekker, the Pyramids, the Pioneers, Prince Buster, Bob and Marcia, Black Faith, Junior Lincoln, and John Holt. Media coverage of the events was minimal, but both outings sold out in record time, with the Wembley event unleashing upwards of 8,000 skins on a succession of acts who had never received, or even dreamed of receiving, such a welcome in their lives.

1971 proved even more exciting. Dave and Ansell Collins' "Double Barrel" and "Monkey Spanner" astonished even seasoned reggae watchers, not only commercially, but also for the skillful way in which they so effortlessly combined elements both of traditional ska/rock steady and modern reggae. On the one hand, the records' distinctive organ sound dominated an increasing number of records over the past couple of years; on the other, the vocals provided a foretaste of the toasting style which was only just coming into vogue in Jamaica itself, via the emergent talents of U-Roy, I-Roy, Big Youth, and Dennis Alcapone. Maybe Sir Collins and King Stitt had already pointed the way with club hits back in 1967–68, but still this double smash package was remarkable.

They were also, however, the end of an era. Although the next few years would see any number of records emerge which could, in style if not execution, be lumped into what local reporters still termed the blue beat bag — hits by Nicky Thomas, Ken Boothe, John Holt and, from 1974, Lee Perry and Susan Cadogan's timeless "Hurts So Good," still the days when any number of labels could turn up any number of instant classics were over.

By 1972, reggae had taken over, as a dancestyle, as a musical style, as a lifestyle and Laurel Aitken, for one, mourned the move. "Reggae and ska are the same thing, except it's just a change of drum beat or a different drop of the bass." But one was now hip, and the other was old. And the new generation of Jamaican musicians, he insisted, "want to play reggae." They wanted to be hip.

JUDGE DREAD

The single most important figure in the history of British ska was a 250 lb former debt collector and wrestler (the Masked Executioner!), who not only kept the music alive and kicking through the fallow years of the Seventies, he also made sure that it retained its libido. Retained it, and waved it around as much as possible.

Born in 1945, Hughes discovered Jamaican music as a white teenager lodging in a west Indian household in Brixton, south London. During the late 1950s and 1960s, he was forever to be found on the fringes of Britain's ska community, as a doorman at Brixton's Ram Jam Club and bodyguard for such visiting stars as Coxsone Dodd, Duke Reid, and Prince Buster. It was in honor of one of Buster's greatest hits, "Judge Dread," that Hughes renamed himself in 1972, when he released his first single, "Big Six."

Based upon Verne & Son's "Little Boy Blue" backing track, over which Dread recited a string of suggestive nursery rhymes, "Big Six" was originally recorded for Dread's own sound system. He was cutting it at Trojan's studios when label head Lee Gopthal walked in. According to Dread,

Gopthal announced, "that's great — is it one of ours?" And when Dread said no, he replied, "it is now." Dread was signed on the spot to the Big Shot label. (He later transferred to Cactus.)

Promptly banned by the BBC, "Big Six" made the Top 20 regardless, selling over 300,000 copies and even making the Jamaican chart, the first time a reggae record by a British artist had ever scored that distinction. Indeed, when Dread visited Kingston later in the year, many people assumed he was simply one of the star's entourage — they certainly couldn't believe this hot new toaster was white.

Dread then unzipped with "Big Seven," whose own success naturally paved the way for a string of similarly sanctioned follow-ups of ever more impression dimensions — "Big Eight," "Big Nine," "Big Ten." Not one of them flopped. Indeed, by the end of the 1970s, Dread had run up eleven UK hits without receiving any airplay whatsoever. By comparison, Bob Marley scored just seven, with all the airplay in the world.

Dread wasn't simply a rude joke machine, however. He wrote one of the last songs Elvis Presley ever intended recording; the king meant to cut "A Child's Prayer" as a Christmas gift for his daughter Lisa Marie.

More importantly, Dread's passion for ska laid much of the groundwork for the 2-Tone explosion of 1979–80 and, though his own hits dried up, he continued recording and gigging, literally until the end of his life. Suffering a massive heart attack as he left the stage at Canterbury's Penny Club on March 13, 1998, Dread's final words were "let's hear it for the band."

1968

RICHARD ACE

STUDIO ONE 2072 More Reggae/GLADIATORS: Hello Carol
Produced by Coxsone Dodd.

GLEN ADAMS

(X) OWEN GRAY, ROY SHIRLEY, UNIQUES, DELROY WILSON

BLUE CAT 126 She Is Leaving/UNIQUES: Girls Like Dirt
COLLINS DOWNBEAT 006 Cool Cool Rock Steady/OWEN GRAY: Girl I Will Be Leaving
ISLAND 3100 Hold Down Miss Winey/VIN GORDON: Sounds & Soul
Produced by Bunny Lee. Recorded with LYNN TAITT's band. (a) Adams turns his keyboards off and picks up a mike, to reprimand Miss Winey for . . . well, for whining.

ISLAND 3120 She's So Fine/ROY SHIRLEY: Girlie
Produced by Bunny Lee. (a) Adams doesn't have the vocal range to pull this song off, but his heartfelt delivery ensures that hardly matters. Add a charming melody, a tight backing band, and some lovely horn parts, and you've got a winning combination.

TROJAN 621 Rent too High/Every Time

LAUREL AITKEN

DR BIRD 1160 Mr Lee/Birmingham Girl
Produced by Laurel Aitken.

DR BIRD 1161 La La La (Means I Love You)/DETOURS: Sunnyside
Produced by Laurel Aitken.

FAB 45 For Sentimental Reasons/Last Waltz
Produced by Laurel Aitken.

AL & THE VIBRATORS

(X) PATSY TODD

ALFRED & MELMOTH

Duo featuring ALFRED "AL" BROWN.

ISLAND 3130 I Want Someone/ALFRED BROWN: One Scotch One Bourbon One Beer

CARLTON ALPHONSO

(X) FREDERICK BELL

ROLAND ALPHONSO

(X) THE CONSUMMATES, AUSTIN FAITHFUL, THE MAYTALS, DERRICK MORGAN

COXSONE 7077 Reggae in the Grass/ROY RICHARDS: Get Smart
Produced by Coxsone Dodd.

THE ALPINES

DOUBLE D 110 Get Ready/CARIB BEATS: Come Back Charlie

ANDERSON'S ALL-STARS

BLUE CAT 132 Intensified Girls/Jump & Shout

BOB ANDY

COXSONE 7074 Born a Man/MARCIA GRIFFITHS: Mark My Word
Produced by Coxsone Dodd.

STUDIO ONE 2063 Too Experienced/Let Them Stay
Produced by Coxsone Dodd.

THE ANGLOS

ISLAND 6061 Incense/You're Fooling Me

ERIC BARNET

GAS 100 The Horse/Action Line

THE BASSIES

STUDIO ONE 2056 I Don't Mind/JACKIE MITTOO: Race Track
Produced by Coxsone Dodd. (b) Set to a beat built for the popular John Crow skank, the rhythm rules, with JACKIE MITTOO'S organ trading musical passages and flourishes with the flash sax.

THE BEAS

PAMA 744 Dr Goldfoot & His Bikini Machine/Where Do I Go From You

LYN BECKFORD

aka KEELING BECKFORD.

ISLAND 3144 Combination/Hey Little Girl
Produced by Lee Perry.

FREDERICK BELL

NU-BEAT 004 Rock Steady Cool/CARLTON ALPHONSO: I Have Changed

THE BELTONES

TROJAN 628 No More Heartaches/I'll Follow You
Produced by Harry J. (a) This was the Beltones' (formerly Bop & The Beltones) biggest hit ever, and launched producer J to similar success (in Jamaica, it debuted his eponymous label). The vocal trio were at their best here, but it was the up-tempo new beat that made the song a classic, often considered the first reggae record to be released.

ROY BENNETT

(X) DEE SET

VAL BENNETT

Saxophonist best remembered for his contributions to PRINCE BUSTER's "Al Capone." (X) LLOYD CLARKE, MELLOTONES, DERRICK MORGAN, KEN PARKER, GEORGE A PENNY, MAX ROMEO, ROY SHIRLEY, THE UNIQUES

ISLAND 3146 The Russians Are Coming/LESTER STERLING: Sir Lee's Whip
Produced by Bunny Lee. (a) A reggae-fied version of Dave Brubeck Quartet's 1961 hit "Take Five," titling it after the hit movie gave it a contemporary feel it would otherwise have lacked. Also released as TROJAN 640.

BEVERLEY'S ALL STARS

(X) DESMOND DEKKER, PAT KELLY, MAYTALS, MELLOTONES, DERRICK MORGAN, PIONEERS

KEITH BLAKE

b 1950 (Kingston, JA), aka PRINCE ALLA. Member of THE LEADERS. (X) OVERTAKERS, THE UNIQUES

BLUE CAT 102 Musically/I'm Moving On

RALPH BLAKE

(X) ROY & ENID

BLUE & FERRIS

BLUE CAT 147 You Stole My Money/Tell Me the Reason

BLUE RIVERS & THE MAROONS

SPECTRUM 105 Take It or Leave It/I've Been Pushed Around

JOYCE BOND

ISLAND 6051 Ob-La-Di Ob-La-Da/Robin Hood Rides Again
Produced by Les Carter. (a) Inevitably the drunken high-point of many parties at the time, Bond belts out Paul McCartney's silliest lyrics while the band split their time between Oktoberfest oom-pah and a New Orleans Mardi Gras, with the producer adding ludicrous sound effects to an already over the top melange.

PAMA 718 Back to School/They Wish

KEN BOOTHE

(X) THE CHARMERS

COXSONE 7041 Everybody Knows/GAYLADS: I'm Free

Produced by Coxsone Dodd.

FAB 63 I Remember Someone/Can't You See?

(b) A touch of American pop permeates this brooding, percolating song, with Boothe's emotive vocals a paragon of heartbreak.

HIGH NOTE 003 Lady with the Starlight/LESLIE BUTLER & COUNT OSSIE: Gay Drums

Produced by Sonia Pottinger. (a) An old Nat King Cole number, featuring a relatively straightforward Boothe vocal — which, of course, means it's as perfect as it should be.

STUDIO ONE 2039 When I Fall in Love/HEPTONES: Christmas Time

Produced by Coxsone Dodd.

STUDIO ONE 2041 The Girl I Left Behind/TERMITES: My Last Love

Produced by Coxsone Dodd. (b) A ragged rock steady pinned down by the duo's so distinctive style — not quite duetting, not quite fighting for supremacy, the chorus lines still fall over themselves in their struggle to be heard. Majestic.

STUDIO ONE 2053 Tomorrow/Moving Away

Produced by Coxsone Dodd. (a) An old Manfred Mann number, restructured to a beefy rock steady beat. (b) A Kenny Lynch song featuring a powerful SOUL VENDORS backing — JACKIE MITTOO's newly purchased Farfisa dominates the hook, while Boothe sings with all his customary confidence.

MILTON BOOTHE

(X) THE PIONEERS

BOP & THE BELTONES

COXSONE 7046 Not for a Moment/JACKIE MITTOO: Man pon Shot

THE BOYS

(X) HERBIE CARTER

BROTHER DAN ALL-STARS

Featuring DENZIL DENNIS, PAT RHODEN, and DANDY LIVINGSTONE.

TROJAN 601 Donkey Returns/

Produced by Dandy Livingstone. (a) This mellow reggae single is highlighted by the harmonica which carries the melody, while the vocals are almost lost beneath the guitar riff and rhythm section.

TROJAN 609 Follow that Donkey/Raver's Serenade

Produced by Dandy Livingstone.

ALFRED "AL" BROWN

Kingston born vocalist, ex-VOLCANOES with CARL MALCOLM, also SKIN FLESH & BONES. (X) ALFRED & MELMOTH

BUSTY BROWN

b Clive Smith, aka COUNT BUSTY and BUSTY JAMES. Former dancer and a member of LLANS THELWELL AND THE CELESTIALS, UPSETTER PILGRIMS, and THE MESS-

ENGERS, also recorded as a duo BUSTY & COOL. Best known for his time with LEE PERRY in the late 1960s, Brown turned to self-production for the Tramp label in 1971, then formed his Mo Bay label in 1971. Subsequently joined THE CHOSEN FEW.

DR BIRD 1158 Here Comes the Night/Don't Look Back

Produced by Clancy Eccles.

DAVID BROWN

(X) ROY WILSON

(X) THE CONSUMMATES

GLEN BROWN

See entry: DIRECTORY OF PRODUCERS. Also recorded as a duo with HOPETON LEWIS, DAVE BARKER, RICHARD MCDONALD, LLOYD ROBINSON.

BLUE CAT 131 Way of Life/CARL BRYAN & LYNN TAITT: I'm So Proud

GLENMORE BROWN & HOPETON LEWIS

FAB 42 Girl You're Cold/Soul Man

KENT BROWN & THE RAINBOWS

FAB 53 When You Going to Show Me How/Come Ya Come Ya

MARK BROWN

(X) DAWN PENN

NOEL BROWN

Member of THE CHOSEN FEW.

ISLAND 3149 Man's Temptation/Heartbreak Girl

CANNONBALL BRYAN

Saxophonist CARL BRYAN, backed by LYNN TAITT & THE JETS. (X) HUGH MALCOLM, THE ROYALS

COXSONE 7050 You're My Everything/JACKIE MITTOO: Napoleon Solo

Produced by Coxsone Dodd.

CARL BRYAN & LYNN TAITT

(X) GLEN BROWN, JOE WHITE

BUNNY & RUDDY

Vocal duo featuring BUNNY (ARTHUR ROBINSON) and RUDDY, both of past duos with SKETTO/SKITTO RICH.

NU-BEAT 011 On the Town/MONTY MORRIS: Simple Simon

LESLIE BUTLER

(X) KEN BOOTHE, GAYLADS, WEBBER SISTERS

THE BUTTERCUPS

PAMA 742 If I Love You/Loving You

THE CABLES

Group comprising KEEBLE DRUMMOND (vocals), VINCE STODDART, and ELBERT STEWART (sax).

COXSONE 7072 What Kind of World/My Broken Heart

Produced by Coxsone Dodd. (a) If you didn't know any better, you'd think it was "Spanish Harlem" coming through the speakers. It isn't, but "What Kind of World' is a classic regardless, a low-key showcase for some of the most under-rated vocals of the age.

STUDIO ONE 2060 Baby Why?/Be a Man

Produced by Coxsone Dodd. (a) A delicate rock steady bal-lad, its falsetto harmonies and lead drifting over the beat, and the ghost of a tune playing around the edges. Dodd kept the record on the sound system for four months before releasing it, guaranteeing a massive demand.

STUDIO ONE 2071 Love Is a Pleasure/Cheer Up

Produced by Coxsone Dodd.

THE CARIB BEATS

(X) THE ALPINES

CARLTON & HIS SHOES

Vocal group comprising CARLTON MANNING, DONALD MANNING, LYNFORD MANNING. (X) ROY & ENID

COXSONE 7065 Love Me Forever/Happy Land

Produced by Coxsone Dodd. (a) The Shoes' Studio One debut is as romantic as it gets, with a warm production draw-ing every nuance of sweetness out of the harmonies. Later versioned by DENNIS ALCAPONE. (b) Popularly described as the inspiration behind the ABYSSINIANS' "Satta Amasa Gana."

STUDIO ONE 2062 This Feeling/You & Me

Produced by Coxsone Dodd.

HERBIE CARTER

DUKE 4 Happy Time/BOYS: Smashville

TEDDY CHAMES

BLUE CAT 141 I Want It Girl/She Is Gone

THE CHARMERS

COXSONE 7043 Things Going Wrong/KEN BOOTHE: You Keep Me Hanging On

Produced by Coxsone Dodd. (b) Boothe effects a straight-forward cover of the Motown classic.

TREASURE ISLE 7036 Keep on Going/SILVERTONES: Don't Say No

Produced by Duke Reid.

CINDERELLA

(X) V VINSTRICK & THE JJ ALL-STARS

CLANCY'S ALL-STARS

PAMA 722 CN Express (parts 1/2)

Produced by Clancy Eccles. (a/b) Manic variation on the ECCLES/LEE PERRY "Say What You're Saying" rhythm, fea-turing train impersonations, clattering bottles, and an emi-gration rap by DJ COOL STICKY.

THE CLARENDONIANS

CALTONE 114 Baby Baby/Bye Bye Bye

LLOYD CLARKE

(X) THE UNIQUES

BLUE CAT 136 Young Love/UNTOUCHABLES: Wall Flower

Produced by Enos McLeod.

ISLAND 3116 Summertime/VAL BENNETT: Soul Survivor

Produced by Bunny Lee. (a) A reggae cover of the Gershwin standard, featuring a stroppy rhythm, a moody sax, and Clarke's sweet, languid delivery, lovingly accompanied by the high-pitched backing vocalists.

JIMMY CLIFF

ISLAND 6039 Waterfall/Reward

Produced by Leslie Kong.

CLIVE ALL STARS

(X) THE TENNORS

STRANGER COLE

ISLAND 3154 Jeboza Macoo/Now I Know

STRANGER COLE & GLADSTONE ANDERSON

AMALGAMATED 801 Just Like a River/LEADERS: Hope Someday

Produced by Joe Gibbs. (a) Anderson leaves his keyboards behind for this emotive duet with Cole, and the pair are swept along by the rock steady rhythms and lush melody.

THE CONQUERORS

TREASURE ISLE 7035 Lonely Street/I Fell in Love

Produced by Duke Reid. (a) The vocal group are searching for Lonely Street after they were caught cheating by their girl. Obviously, the chirpy organist feels no pity either.

THE CONSUMMATES

COXSONE 7054 What Is It/ROLAND ALPHONSO: Musical Happiness

Produced by Coxsone Dodd.

ISLAND 3103 Do It Now/FRANK BROWN: Some Come Some Go

THE COOL CATS

JOLLY 007 What Kind of Man/HEMSLEY MORRIS: Little Things

COOL STICKY

b Uziah "Sticky" Thompson, 8/1/36 (Mannings Mountain, JA). Originally a DJ with COXSONE DODD's Down Beat, he also voiced the intro to the SKATALITES' "Ball Of Fire" for DUKE REID and became a regular at Treasure Isle Sound. Sticky later became one of Jamaica's top session drummers.

AMALGAMATED 825 Train to Soulsville/MONTY MORRIS: Cinderella

Produced by Joe Gibbs. (a) A rock steady take on the ETHIO-PIANS' classic "Train to Skaville," with Sticky playing a split role of DJ/conductor.

COUNT BUSTY & THE RUDIES

aka BUSTY BROWN.

MELODY 003 You Like It/The Reggay

THE CREATIONS

AMALGAMATED 818 Holding Out/Get on Up

Produced by Joe Gibbs. (a) Rock goes to JA on this single, the rhythms are syncopated and the brass used in ways that

US/UK bands would never consider, but the guitar and melody is pure pop-rock.

THE CREATORS

(X) THE PIONEERS

THE CROWNS

PAMA 725 I Know It's Alright/I Surrender
PAMA 736 Jerking the Dog/Keep Me Going
PAMA 745 She Ain't Gonna Do Right/I Need Your Loving
PAMA 759 Since You Been Gone/Call Me

BASIL DALEY

(X) THE HEPTONES

DALTONS

(X) PRINCE BUSTER

DANDY

COLUMBIA BLUE BEAT 112 Play It Cool/Rude with Me
Produced by Dandy Livingstone.
DOWNTOWN 401 Move Your Mule/Reggae Me This
Produced by Dandy Livingstone.
TROJAN 618 The Toast/Kicks Out
Produced by Dandy Livingstone.

DANDY & CHARLIE GRIFFITHS

Vocal duo featuring DANDY LIVINGSTONE.
GIANT 20 Charlie Brown/Groovin' at the Cue
Produced by Dandy Livingstone.

DANDY & LEE

Vocal pairing, DANDY LIVINGSTONE and LEE PERRY.
TROJAN 629 Sentence/LEE PERRY: You Crummy
Produced by Lee Perry. (b) Remake of "People Funny Boy," this time directed at CLANCY ECCLES, notable for a calypso-inspired organ part.

DANDY & THE SUPERBOYS

GIANT 27 Sweet Ride/Up the Hill
Produced by Dandy Livingstone.
GIANT 30 Tears on My Pillow/Mad Them
Produced by Dandy Livingstone.
GIANT 36 I'm Back with a Bang Bang/Jungle Walk
Produced by Dandy Livingstone.

CARL DAWKINS

BLUE CAT 114 I Love the Way You Are/DERMOTT LYNCH: I Can't Stand It
Produced by JJ Johnson.
DUKE 3 I'll Make It Up/JJ ALL-STARS: One Dollar Of Music
Produced by JJ Johnson.

THE DEE SET

BLUE CAT 146 I Know a Place/ROY BENNETT: I Dangerous

ANTHONY DEELEY

PAMA 728 Anytime Man/Don't Change Your Mind About Me

DESMOND DEKKER

(X) MAYTALS

PYRAMID 6031 Beautiful & Dangerous/I Got the Blues
Produced by Leslie Kong. (a) It was songs like this that kept Dekker at the head of the island pack. "Beautiful" is true to its title, all pulsing beat and simmering, moody melody. Its perfect arrangement and production are equalled by the sparkling musicianship and echoed in the exquisite vocals.

PYRAMID 6035 Bongo Gal/Shing a Ling
Produced by Leslie Kong. (a) A chirpy serenade to the "unforgettable" Matilda, the bongo gal of every guy's dreams. (b) A jumped-up beat, high harmonies and peppy vocals are pursued around the grooves by the horns and piano.

PYRAMID 6037 To Sir with Love/Fu Manchu
Produced by Leslie Kong.

PYRAMID 6044 Mother Pepper/Don't Blame Me
Produced by Leslie Kong.

PYRAMID 6047 Hey Grandma/Young Generation
Produced by Leslie Kong.

PYRAMID 6051 Music Like Dirt/Coconut Water
Produced by Leslie Kong. (a) Dekker and the Aces won the Festival Song Competition in 1968 with this number. The hints of calypso and Latino flavor helped, but its pure perkiness and spectacular vocals and harmonies were what sold the crowd.

PYRAMID 6054 It Mek/Writing on the Wall
Produced by Leslie Kong. (a) Unsuccessful first time around in the UK, a rock steady groove is lit up by Dekker's obvious grinning exasperation with his mischievous sister, the lyrical inspiration for this song. (b) This singer showcase features Dekker at his most emotive, surrounded by shimmering harmonies bouncing between high and low, all powered by a slowly pulsing beat.

PYRAMID 6058 The Israelites/BEVERLEY'S ALL-STARS: The Man
Produced by Leslie Kong and Desmond Dekker. (a) JA's first international chart-topper. A contagious beat, Dekker's emotive delivery, and the baritone backing vocal were all unforgettable and, while the lyric drew direct parallels between the toil of the Biblical Israelites and present-day Jamaicans, it had a universal quality that is timeless and knows no borders.

PYRAMID 6059 Christmas Day/I've Got the Blues
Produced by Leslie Kong.

THE DELTA CATS

(X) THE THRILLERS

DENZIL DENNIS

TROJAN 614 Donkey Train/Down by the Riverside
Produced by Dandy Livingstone.
TROJAN 615 Me Nah Worry/Hush Don't You Cry
Produced by Dandy Livingstone.

DERRICK & PATSY

NU-BEAT 008 Hey Boy Hey Girl/Music Is the Food of Life

THE DETOURS

(X) LAUREL AITKEN

PHYLLIS DILLON

TREASURE ISLE 7041 I Wear this Ring/Don't Touch Me Tomato
Produced by Duke Reid. (b) A classic mento. The girls get in on the slack act, as Dillon suggestively allows you to touch her here, there, everywhere but . . . . Now you know why the boys in *Animal House* found the produce aisle so sexually stimulating.

DOBBY DOBSON

COXSONE 7058 Seems to Me I'm Losing You/GAYLADS: Red Rose
Produced by Coxsone Dodd.

STUDIO ONE 2068 Walking in the Footsteps/SOUL VENDORS: Studio Rock
Produced by Coxsone Dodd.

ROY DOCKER

DOMAIN 3 Mellow Moonlight/MUSIC THROUGH SIX: Riff Raff

PAMA 750 When/Go

PAMA 756 I'm an Outcast/Everyday I'll Be a Holiday

THE DOMINOES

Vocal group comprising DENNIS SINCLAIR and JUNIOR DIXON, also recorded with JUSTIN HINDS.

MELODY 002 A Tribute/Hooray

DON & DANDY & THE SUPERBOYS

Featuring DANDY LIVINGSTONE and DON MARTIN.

GIANT 24 Keep on Fighting/Rock Steady Boogie

DRUMBAGO

(X) DENNIS WALKS

BLUE CAT 145 Reggae Jeggae/TYRONE TAYLOR: Delilah

DON DRUMMOND JUNIOR

(X) THE PIONEERS

CALTONE 124 Dirty Dozen/PHIL PRATT: Reach Out
Produced by Phil Pratt.

THE DUKE ALL-STARS

BLUE CAT 11 Letter to Mummy & Daddy (Parts 1/2)

ERROL DUNKLEY

(X) KEN PARKER

AMALGAMATED 800 Please Stop Your Lying/Feel So FineFine
Produced by Joe Gibbs.

AMALGAMATED 805 I'm Going Home/I'm Not Your Man
Produced by Joe Gibbs.

AMALGAMATED 807 The Scorcher/Do It Right Tonight
Produced by Joe Gibbs. (a) This slow, brooding number has a wondrously dark, almost ominous atmosphere shrouding Dunkley's threatening lyrics.

AMALGAMATED 820 Love Brother/I Spy
Produced by Joe Gibbs. (a) Even without the soaring falsetto, Dunkley's vocals are still lovely, and this unity themed song encouraged the teenager to sing with conviction and passion.

BIG SHOT 504 The Clamp Is On/DON TONY LEE: It's Reggae Time
(b) Lee introduces the hip beat on this showcase of the new genre, chatting up the crowd in support while, in-between times, we're treated to harmonica solos. Also released as Island 3160.

ISLAND 3150 Once More/I'm Not Your Man

THE DYNAMICS

BLUE CAT 104 My Friends/NEVILLE IRONS: Soul Glide

CLANCY ECCLES

DR BIRD 1156 Feel The Rhythm/Easy Snapping
Produced by Clancy Eccles. (a) Astonishing performance in which Eccles and co-conspirator LEE PERRY not only seem to have discovered a new rhythm, they spend most of the song extolling its virtues. ERNEST RANGLIN is the featured guitarist, and has since described this (and MONTY MORRIS' similarly styled "Say What You're Saying") as the first ever reggae record. Eccles himself credits his own "Bangarang Crash."

NU-BEAT 006 Festival 68/I Really Love You

PAMA 712 The Fight/Great

JACKIE EDWARDS

ISLAND 3157 You're My Girl/Heaven Only Knows
Produced by Chris Blackwell.

ISLAND 6026 Julie on My Mind/If this Is Heaven
Produced by Chris Blackwell.

JACKIE EDWARDS & JIMMY CLIFF

ISLAND 6036 Set Me Free/Here I Come
Produced by Leslie Kong.

ISLAND 6042 You're My Girl/Heaven Only Knows
Produced by Leslie Kong.

RUPIE EDWARDS

(X) THE VIRTUES

DR BIRD 1163 I Can't Forget/I'm Writing Again
Produced by Rupie Edwards.

ALTON ELLIS

COXSONE 7071 A Fool/SOUL VENDORS West of the Sun
Produced by Coxsone Dodd. (b) JACKIE MITTOO shines on this brash little instrumental, carrying the jaunty melody with flair and just the right amount of flourish.

NU-BEAT 010 I Can't Stand It/Tonight
Produced by Duke Reid. (a) A bad girlfriend gives Ellis and co-vocalist LLOYD WILLIAMS the perfect opportunity for a defiant display of emotion and soul, while the saxophonist

bleatingly commiserates on this simmering, soul-esque number.

NU-BEAT 013 Bye Bye Love/MONTY MORRIS: My Lonely Days

Produced by Clancy Eccles. (a) What could have been a straightforward cover of the old Everly Brothers hit takes a turn for the unexpected, courtesy of a superbly loose rhythm, an exemplary Ellis vocal, and a cowbell striking in some unexpected places. (b) Steel drums bring a totally alien mood to the proceedings, and make you wonder why more people didn't use them. The song is not spectacular, but Morris' voice is a revelation, with such a casual air that some of his harmonies even sound like off-mike asides.

NU-BEAT 014 La La Means I Love You/Give Me Your Love

Produced by Duke Reid. (a) Great idea Duke, get Jamaica's definitive soul singer to cover the defiantly lightweight Delfonics' hit, then add a bubbly arrangement to further twist the knife. Oh the indignity of it all.

PAMA 707 The Message/Some Talk

PAMA 717 My Time Is the Right Time/JOHNNY MOORE: Tribute to Sir Alex

TREASURE ISLE 7030 Oowee Baby/How Can I

Produced by Duke Reid. (b) Ellis is at his most gloriously romantic on this passionate ballad, with the backing vocalists adding a doo-wop styling to the proceedings.

TREASURE ISLE 7044 Willow Tree/I Can't Stop Now

Produced by Duke Reid. (a) A cover of an Ivy League hit, the lack of strong melody actually coaxes a sublime soul performance from Ellis — forget the song, just enjoy the delivery. The rhythm was later used for I-ROY's "Weeping Widow." (b) A slow reggae beat wraps itself around this song, with Ellis, enmeshed in a web of love gone wrong, by turns vulnerable, defiant, plaintive, and positively heartbreaking.

ALTON ELLIS & LLOYD WILLIAMS

TROJAN 630 Can't Stand It/Trying to Reach My Girl
Produced by Duke Reid.

BOBBY ELLIS & THE CRYSTALITES

ISLAND 3136 Dollar a Head/RUDY MILLS: I'm Trapped
Produced by Derrick Harriott.

HORTENSE ELLIS

(X) THE THREE TOPS

EMOTIONS

CALTONE 118 Soulful Music/No Use to Cry

CALTONE 129 Careless Hands/TOMMY MCCOOK & SUPERSONICS: Caltone Special
Produced by Ken Lack. (a) A slow, soulful cover of the Des O'Connor ballad, which the Emotions handle with aplomb, as warm as a lullaby, with the twangy guitar break counterpointing the mood beautifully.

ENFORCERS

STUDIO ONE 2051 Forgive Me/JEFF DIXON: Tickle Me
Produced by Coxsone Dodd.

ENOS & SHEILA

Vocal duo featuring ENOS MCLEOD.

BLUE CAT 135 La La La Bamba/ENOS MCLEOD: You Can Never Get Away

BLUE CAT 138 Tonight You're Mine/UNTOUCHABLES: Your Love

MINNIE EPPERSON

ACTION 4503 Grab Your Clothes/No Love at All

THE ETHIOPIANS

CRAB 2 Fire a Muss Trail/Blacker Black
Produced by H Robinson.

CRAB 4 Reggae Hit the Town/Ding Dong Bell
Produced by H Robinson. (a) Reggae hit the town and no-one was more excited about it than The Ethiopians, who sing (and talk) about the new sound, while the musicians showcase the new style with equal enthusiasm.

DR BIRD 1141 Come on Now/Sh'Boom
(a) Even this early in the proceedings, the Ethiopians already featured the stirrings of their signature rootsy sound. This simmering performance features a powerful melody, flashy piano, and some very effective brass, plus the fabulous vocals of course.

DR BIRD 1147 Engine 54/Give Me Your Love
Produced by JJ Johnson. (a) The trio's tribute to the Kingston-to-Spanishtown train (which served the countryside), perfectly recapturing that chugging feeling, from the whoosh of the brakes to the hoot of the whistle.

DR BIRD 1148 Train to Glory/You Got the Dough
Produced by JJ Johnson.

DR BIRD 1169 Everything Crash/I'm Not Losing You
Produced by JJ Johnson. (a) The trio adapt THE PIONEERS' "Long Shot Kick de Bucket" for this update on JA's woeful economic state, the sweet harmonies taking some of the sting out of the crisis.

LLOYD EVANS

(X) ALBERT TOMLINSON

AUSTIN FAITHFUL

BLUE CAT 140 Uncle Joe/Can't Understand

PYRAMID 6028 Eternal Love/ROLAND ALPHONSO: Goodnight My Love

PYRAMID 6042 Ain't that Peculiar?/Miss Anti-Social

FEDERALS

Vocal group formed by DAVID "SCOTTY" SCOTT.

ISLAND 3126 Penny for Your Song/I've Passed this Way Before

ISLAND 3152 Shocking Love/By the River
(a) With a melody as delicate as a butterfly wing, the lead vocal and backing harmonies deftly capture the winsome

mood, delivering the subtlest, yet most overpowering come-on ever.

FITZ & COOLERS

Featuring ERNEST WILSON of THE CLARENDONIANS. COOLERS was a pair of Waterhouse area vocalists who CLANCY ECCLES knew — "Coolers" was actually their nickname for him, before he gave it back to them.

NU-BEAT 003 Cover Me/Darling

BOBBY FRANCIS

DR BIRD 1153 Chain Gang/Venus

BONNIE FRANKSON

Also recorded as duo DOTTY & BONNIE.

COLUMBIA BLUE BEAT 114 Dearest/London City

NORMA FRAZIER

(X) RIGHTEOUS FLAMES

COXSONE 7060 Respect/Time

Produced by Coxsone Dodd.

GAYLADS

(X) KEN BOOTHE, DOBBY DOBSON

BLUE CAT 110 Go Away/SOUL VENDORS: Julie on Your Mind

COXSONE 7040 Most Peculiar Man/JACKIE MITTOO: Norwegian Wood

Produced by Coxsone Dodd.

DR BIRD 1124 It's Hard to Confess/I Need Your Loving

Produced by Sonia Pottinger. (a) The Gaylads' silky vocals are the focus of this charmer, often cited among the finest early reggae songs ever cut. There's a snatch of early Beatles around the melody, which just adds to the fun.

DR BIRD 1145 She Want It/Joy in the Morning

FAB 62 Looking for a Girl/Aren't You the Guy

HIGH NOTE 001 ABC Rock Steady/LESLIE BUTLER & COUNT OSSIE: Soul Drums

Produced by Sonia Pottinger. (a) True to their name, this carefree trio makes even school sound like fun and, once past counting and the alphabet, they slip gaily into a series of nursery rhymes. It seems a little twee today, but was inevitably charming in its time.

HIGH NOTE 009 Over the Rainbow's End/LESLIE BUTLER: Revival

Produced by Sonia Pottinger. (a) The Lads are in a mellow mood on this bittersweet romantic number, although the twangy guitar break seems incongruous in a song that would otherwise just melt in your mouth.

GAYLETS

Trio formed by BERYL LAWSON, MERLE CLEMENSON and DAWN HANCHARD. Hanchard quit and the group fell into abeyance until dancer JUDY MOWATT came in during 1967.

BIG SHOT 502 If You Can't Be Good to Me/Something About My Man

Produced by Lynford Anderson.

ISLAND 3129 Silent River Runs Deep/You're My Kind of Man

Produced by Lynford Anderson. (a) Taking their cue from sundry American girl groups, the Gayletts let loose with this mid-tempo scorcher — Martha & The Vandelas with a syncopated beat.

ISLAND 3141 I Like Your World/Lonely Feeling

Produced by Lynford Anderson.

PAMA 740 How Come/MR MILLER: Oh My Lover

Produced by Lee Perry. (a) Mysteriously credited to LLOYD TYRELL upon its UK release. An incredibly saucy rock steady duet between Perry and JUDY MOWATT, featuring breathy sighs and squeaking doors.

THE GLADIATORS

(X) RICHARD ACE

VIN GORDON

b Vincent Gordon. Trombonist Gordon was one of the top session musicians. He also recorded as DON DRUMMOND JUNIOR. (X) GLEN ADAMS

THE GRAY BROTHERS

BLUE CAT 124 Always/Big Man

HERBIE GRAY

A member of SONNY BRADSHAW's band. Cousin of GLEN ADAMS.

GIANT 38 We're Staying Here/Life Ska

OWEN GRAY

(X) GLEN ADAMS

BLUE CAT 123 These Foolish Things/This I Promise

COLLINS DOWNBEAT 007 Am Satisfy/BOB STACKIE & SIR COLLINS & BAND: Sweet Music

COLLINS DOWNBEAT 010 I'm Gonna Take You Back/GLEN ADAMS: King Sized

COXSONE 7047 Give Me a Little Sign/Ain't Nobody Home

Produced by Coxsone Dodd.

COXSONE 7053 Give It to Me/Isn't It So

Produced by Coxsone Dodd.

TROJAN 632 Lovey Dovey/Grooving

ROOSEVELT GRIER

ACTION 4515 People Make the World/Hard to Forget

MARCIA GRIFFITHS

(X) BOB ANDY

COXSONE 7035 Mojo Girl/HAMLINS: Tell Me that You Love Me

Produced by Coxsone Dodd.

COXSONE 7055 Feel Like Jumping/HORACE TAYLOR: Thunderous Vibrations

Produced by Coxsone Dodd. (a) An infectious performance whose rhythm would be revisited for the MAYTALS' "54–46 Was My Number."

COXSONE 7062 Hold Me Tight/BASSIES: Home Sweet Home

Produced by Coxsone Dodd.

STUDIO ONE 2059 Truly/SIMMS & ROBINSON: Drought

Produced by Coxsone Dodd.

THE GROOVERS

(X) DENNIS WALKS

THE HAMLINS

BLUE CAT 115 Sugar & Spice/SOUL VENDORS: Mercy Mercy Mercy

COXSONE 7048 Sentimental Reasons/SOUL VENDORS: Last Waltz

Produced by Coxsone Dodd.

DERRICK HARRIOTT

ISLAND 3135 Do I Worry/BOBBY ELLIS & THE CRYSTALITES: Shuntin'

Produced by Derrick Harriott. (a) Way ahead of its time, with its rockers guitar and a rootsy aura, deft guitar vies with the flashy piano, but both are eventually topped by Harriott on this sensational Tams cover.

ISLAND 3147 Born to Love You/BOBBY ELLIS & THE CRYSTALITES: Alfred Hitchcock

Produced by Derrick Harriott. (a) With the musical arrangement stripped to a simple riffing guitar, subtle bass, and understated drums, Harriott's shimmering falsetto is the highlight of this affirmation of love, bolstered by the soaring backing vocalists. (b) Yet another in a ludicrously long line of inappropriately titled instrumentals. "Hitchcock" contains none of the director's ominous air, just a laid back reggae beat to provide the backdrops for the muted choral horns, with just a touch of Tijuana Brass.

ISLAND 3153 Tang Tang Festival Song/CRYSTALITES: James Ray

Produced by Derrick Harriott. (b) The fat bass line makes it all worthwhile, the horns are no slackers either, but the inconsequential melody lets the side down.

YVONNE HARRISON

(X) CLAUDETTE THOMAS

THE HEPTONES

(X) KEN BOOTHE

COXSONE 7038 If You Knew/THE SOUL VENDORS: Whipping the Prince

Produced by Coxsone Dodd.

COXSONE 7052 Love Won't Come Easy/Gee Wee

Produced by Coxsone Dodd. (a) The trio bravely fight for love, with the simple arrangement giving them plenty of room to state their case.

COXSONE 7068 Equal Rights/Ting a Ling

Produced by Coxsone Dodd. (b) The tinkling piano and lush arrangement are the perfect backdrop for the Heptones at their most vulnerable, fearful of losing love and gently vocalizing their concern in a harmonic tour de force.

COXSONE 7075 Giddy Up/JACKIE MITTOO: Mission Impossible

Produced by Coxsone Dodd. (b) Don't be deceived by the TV show title. This is actually a happy Hammond cover of

"Old Man River" set to a beat that bounces along as high as a superball.

STUDIO ONE 2049 Cry Baby Cry/Mama

Produced by Coxsone Dodd.

STUDIO ONE 2052 Dock of the Bay/KING ROCKY: The Ruler

Produced by Coxsone Dodd. (a) Sweet recapitulation of the recently deceased Otis Redding's greatest hit.

STUDIO ONE 2054 I Got a Feeling/BASIL DALEY: Hold Me Baby

Produced by Coxsone Dodd.

STUDIO ONE 2055 Party Time/Oil in Your Lamp

Produced by Coxsone Dodd. (a) LEROY SIBBLES' vocals are so well echoed by his bandmates that he could be singing into a tunnel, a delicious effect which adds power to what was otherwise a fairly thin song.

JOE HIGGS

ISLAND 3131 You Hurt My Soul/LYNN TAITT: Why Am I Treated So Bad

ELDRIDGE HOLMES

PAMA 746 Beverly/Wait for Me Baby

JOHN HOLT

TROJAN 643 Tonight/Oh How It Hurts

Produced by Bunny Lee. (a) A bubbly reggae rhythm underpins an emotive ballad, which Holt delivers with passionate conviction. But the mood is broken by the brass solos.

HORACE & THE IMPERIALS

NU-BEAT 012 Young Love/Days Like These

IKE B & THE CRYSTALITES

ISLAND 3134 Ilya Kurayakin/BOBBY ELLIS & THE CRYSTALITES: Anne Marie

Produced by Derrick Harriott.(a) The UNCLE agent's secret decoding device quickly untangles this deceit — in actuality, this is a cover of the theme from A Summer Place, with mere nods towards the TV show. Great organ and horns though.

ISLAND 3151 Try a Little Merriness/Patricia

Produced by Derrick Harriott.

THE INVADERS

COLUMBIA BLUE BEAT 109 Stop Teasing/Invaders at the Carnival

Produced by Laurel Aitken. (b) Trombonist RICO joins forces with the Invaders, and ropes in LAUREL AITKEN on piano, a real festival of musical talent.

STUDIO ONE 2044 Soulful Music/SOUL VENDORS: Happy Organ

Produced by Coxsone Dodd.

NEVILLE IRONS

(X) DYNAMICS

DAVID ISAACS

TROJAN 616 A Place in the Sun/UPSETTER ALL-STARS: Handy-Cap

Produced by Lee Perry. (a) A cover of the movie theme, previously a hit for Stevie Wonder. Isaacs' delivery is aptly passionate, while the tinkling keyboard solo lifts the serious mood somewhat.

JAMAICAN ACTIONS

COXSONE 7070 Catch the Quinella/JACKIE MITTOO: Songbird
Produced by Coxsone Dodd.

JAMAICAN FOUNDATIONS

COXSONE 7036 Take It Cool/VICEROYS: Try Hard to Leave
Produced by Coxsone Dodd.

THE JAMAICANS

TREASURE ISLE 7037 Peace & Love/Woman Gone Home
Produced by Duke Reid. (a) Sweet, close harmonies grace this pretty antiwar song, with just a touch of gospel around the edges. U-ROY would later add his own distinctive vocals to this performance.

TONY JAMES

JOLLY 002 Treat Me Right/Me Donkey's Dead

JAY & JOYA

Vocal duo featuring JOYA LANDIS.

TROJAN 633 I'll Be Lonely/SUPERSONICS: Second Fiddle

THE JIVERS

TROJAN 604 Wear My Crown/Down on the Beach

JJ ALL STARS

Studio band for producer JJ JOHNSON. (X) CARL DAWKINS

BOBBY KALPHAT

NU-BEAT 007 Rhythm & Soul/BUNNY & RUDDY: True Romance

KEITH & TEX

ISLAND 3137 Hypnotizing Eyes/Lonely Man
Produced by Derrick Harriott. (a) The duo's characteristic twang permeates the lovelorn lyrics, delivered with just the right blend of yearning soulfulness.

CHARLIE KELLEY

(X) STRANGER & GLADDY

PAT KELLY

Vocalist with THE TECHNIQUES, THE UNIQUES. In 1969, the Beatles offered to sign him to their Apple label, but Kelly's existing UK contract would not allow them.

GIANT 37 Little Boy Blue/You Are Not Mine
Credited to Kelly & THE UNIQUES, one of his first recordings after quitting the Techniques.

ISLAND 3121 Somebody's Baby/BEVERLEY SIMMONS: Please Don't Leave Me
(a) The clattering percussion perks up this yearning for love song, with Kelly hitting the just the right note of winsomeness, without descending into sap.

THE KILOWATTS

DR BIRD 1140 Bring It on Home/What a Wonderful World
(a/b) Double-sided Sam Cooke tribute.

KING CANNONBALL

TROJAN 636 Thunderstorm/BURT WALTERS: Honey Love
Produced by Lee Perry. (b) "Honey Love" is better known for its Jamaican b-side, Lee Perry's "Evol Yenoh," featuring Walter's original vocal played backwards over the rhythm.

KING ROCKY

STUDIO ONE 2045 The King Is Back/THREE TOPS: Vex Till Yuh Buss
Produced by Coxsone Dodd.

PETER KING

CRAB 3 Reggae Limbo/DERRICK MORGAN: River to the Bank
Produced by Derrick Morgan.

THE KINGSTONIANS

COXSONE 7066 Mother Miserable/I Make a Woman
Produced by Coxsone Dodd.

DR BIRD 1120 Put Down Your Fire/Girls Like Dirt
DR BIRD 1123 Mummy & Daddy/False Witness
DR BIRD 1126 Fun Galore/Crime Don't Pay
TROJAN 627 Mix It Up/I'll Be Around
(a) This brash little number was aimed straight up the dancefloor, with a driving beat, riffing guitars, and the vocal trio urging the band and crowd to "pick it up, pick it up, that's the way I like it."

THE KNIGHTS OF THE ROUND TABLE

PAMA 734 Lament to Bobby Kennedy/If You Were My Girl

JOYA LANDIS

Also recorded as a duo JAY & JOYA.

TROJAN 620 Kansas City/Out the Light
Produced by Duke Reid. (a) Landis has a lark with this breezy C&W tinged version of the much covered R&B classic, adding a slight twang to her vocals to complement the clopping beat.

DIANA LANDOR

PAMA 726 Afro Blue/Empty Little Shadow

LARRY & ALVIN

Vocal duo comprising LARRY MARSHALL and ALVIN LESLIE.

STUDIO ONE 2065 Nanny Goat/Smell You Creep
Produced by Coxsone Dodd. (a) Stunning performance later pinpointed as another of the first "reggae" records ever. The bubbling keyboards set the scene and, though there's a definite hint of "Wear You to the Ball Tonight" hanging around, you can still imagine the impact this must have had at the time.

STUDIO ONE 2067 Can't You Understand/Hush Up
Produced by Coxsone Dodd.

BETTY LAVETTE

PAMA 748 Only Your Love Can Save Me/I Feel Good All Over

DIANE LAWRENCE

JOLLY 005 Treat Me Nice/I'll Be Loving You

THE LEADERS

Featuring MILTON MORRIS and KEITH BLAKE. (X) STRANGER COLE & GLADSTONE ANDERSON, THE PIONEERS, THE VERSATILES

AMALGAMATED 804 Tit for Tat/MARVETTS: You Take too Long
Produced by Joe Gibbs.

BYRON LEE & THE DRAGONAIRES

TROJAN 624 Soul Limbo/The Whistling Song
Produced by Byron Lee. (a) Booker T & the MGs took this song into the US Top 20 the same year as Lee's version was blasting from radios across JA. Not surprisingly, Lee gave it a calypso-esque feel, with the cowbells adding even more punch.

TROJAN 631 Mr Walker/Sunset Jump Up
Produced by Byron Lee.

DON TONY LEE

(X) ERROL DUNKLEY

LEROY & ROCKY

Vocal duo featuring LEROY SIBBLES (THE HEPTONES) and KING ROCKY.

STUDIO ONE 2042 Love Me Girl/WRIGGLERS: Reel Up
Produced by Coxsone Dodd.

ALVA LEWIS

(X) WEBBER SISTERS

HOPETON LEWIS

FAB 43 Skinny Leg Girl/Live Like a King

LITTLE BEVERLEY

PAMA 731 What a Guy/You're Mine

LITTLE FREDDIE

aka FREDDIE MCGREGOR of THE CLARENDONIANS. (X) ERNEST WILSON

LITTLE SAL WITH DANDY & THE SUPERBOYS

Featuring DANDY LIVINGSTONE.
GIANT 19 I'm in the Mood/I'm a Lover

LLOYD & THE GROOVERS

CALTONE 112 Listen to the Music/DIPLOMATS: Strong Man
Produced by Bunny Lee.

LLOYD & JOHNNY MELODY

Featuring LLOYD TYRELL and GLEN ADAMS.
ISLAND 3158 My Argument/JOHNNY MELODY: Foey Man

FITZROY D LONG & BUSTER'S ALL-STARS

FAB 32 Get a New Girl/BUSTER'S ALL-STARS: Come & Do It with Me

LORD NELSON

DIRECTION 58−3909 Michael/No Hot Summer

LORD SALMONS

(X) THE PIONEERS

LOVELETTES

(X) LEROY REID

DERMOTT LYNCH

(X) CARL DAWKINS

BLUE CAT 101 Hot Shot/I've Got Your Number
BLUE CAT 122 I Got Everything/Echo
BLUE CAT 129 Something Is Worrying Me/TREVOR: Tender Arms
BLUE CAT 130 You Went Away/TREVOR: Pretty Girl

THE LYRICS

COXSONE 7067 Music Like Dirt/TONETTES: I Give It to You
Produced by Coxsone Dodd. (a) Great rock steady rhythm which was reused for BOB ANDY's "Desperate lover." The three Lyrics chirrup like a less experienced WAILERS, and there's a cool keyboard break.

THE MAGPIES

DR BIRD 1129 Lulu/I Must Be Lonely
DR BIRD 1132 Blue Boy/I Guess I'm Crazy

HUGH MALCOLM

A fine baritone vocalist who also cut several 45s for Coxsone Dodd, MALCOLM was better known as a drummer, and a regular member of TOMMY MCCOOK's SUPERSONICS. (X) LYNN TAITT & THE JETS

AMALGAMATED 829 Mortgage/CANNONBALL BRYAN TRIO: Man About Town
Produced by Joe Gibbs.

MARCIA & JEFF

Featuring MARCIA GRIFFITHS and JEFF DIXON.
STUDIO ONE 2047 Words/SHARKS: How Could I Live
Produced by Coxsone Dodd.

LARRY MARSHALL

CALTONE 126 No-one to Give Me Love/PHIL PRATT: Safe Travel
Produced by Phil Pratt.

MARTIN

COXSONE 7056 I Second that Emotion/ROY TOMLINSON: I Stand for I
Produced by Coxsone Dodd.

RON MARTIN & THE JUBILEE STOMPERS

DR BIRD 1151 Give Your Love to Me/I Cry My Heart

MAXIMUM BAND

FAB 51 Cupid/Hold Me Tight

THE MAYTALS

PYRAMID 6030 54−46 That's My Number/ROLAND ALPHONSO: Dreamland

Produced by Leslie Kong. (a) TOOTS HIBBERT's paean to prison life; the song is powered both by BEVERLEY'S ALL-STAR rhythm section (reworking MARCIA GRIFFITHS' "Feel Like Jumping" rhythm) and the singer's exuberant delivery. The churchy call-and-responses drive the performance to even greater heights, and Hibbert's sheer joy at freedom bleeds through every note.

PYRAMID 6043 Struggle/ROLAND ALPHONSO: Steam of Life
Produced by Leslie Kong.

PYRAMID 6048 Just Tell Me/Reborn
Produced by Leslie Kong. (a) This uplifting love song is delivered with all the dash that the Maytals were famed for. TOOTS HIBBERT delivers the emotional punch, while his companions provide uplift. And check out that great guitar in the background.

PYRAMID 6050 Bim Today Bam Tomorrow/Hold On
Produced by Leslie Kong.

PYRAMID 6052 We Shall Overcome/DESMOND DEKKER & THE ACES: Fu Manchu
Produced by Leslie Kong.

PYRAMID 6055 Schooldays/Big Man
Produced by Leslie Kong.

PYRAMID 6057 Do the Reggay/BEVERLEY'S ALL-STARS: Double Action
Produced by Leslie Kong. (a) With TOOTS HIBBERT leading the call, it was hard to avoid joining in with the latest dance craze. The horns blow jazz, the guitars have an almost surf feel, while Hibbert's vocals are pure soul, a heady concoction of styles that still sets feet tapping today.

PYRAMID 6064 Scare Him/In My Heart
Produced by Leslie Kong.

PYRAMID 6066 Don't Trouble Trouble/BEVERLEY'S ALL-STARS: Express
Produced by Leslie Kong.

TOMMY MCCOOK & THE SUPERSONICS
(X) EMOTIONS, MELODIANS, SILVERTONES, LLOYD WILLIAMS

TREASURE ISLE 7032 Venus/Music Is My Occupation
Produced by Duke Reid.

TOMMY MCKENZIE

PAMA 720 Fiddlesticks/HEMSLEY MORRIS: Please Stay
Produced by Clancy Eccles.

ENOS MCLEOD
b 1946 (Trench Town, JA). Producer who cut a handful of his own sides. Also recorded as a duo with SHEILA. (X) ENOS & SHEILA

THE MELLOTONES
Featuring vocalist WINSTON FRANCIS and Sammy of the BLEECHERS.

AMALGAMATED 812 Fat Girl in Red/VERSATILES: Trust the Book
Produced by Joe Gibbs. (b) Powered by a great bass line, "Trust" chugs along like a freight train, with the percussion and brass adding to the feeling. The Versatiles' harmonies, too, are reminiscent in places of a train whistle.

AMALGAMATED 817 Feel Good/Soulful Mood
Produced by Joe Gibbs. (a) Maybe it's the powerful, driving beat or the passionate delivery, but this single simply quivers with sexual desire, even if the band itself never falls into the throes of orgasmic excess.

DR BIRD 1136 None Such/VAL BENNETT: Popeye on the Shore
Produced by Lee Perry. (a) An estranged cousin to the PIONEERS' own race track epics.

PYRAMID 6060 Let's Join Together/BEVERLEY ALL-STARS: I Don't Know
Produced by Leslie Kong.

TROJAN 612 Uncle Charlie/What a Botheration
Produced by Lee Perry. (a) The sad tale of a drunkard uncle, set to a suitably dissolute rhythm. (b) Equally tragic, Christmas, no money, no food, and not a decent pair of pants in sight.

MELODIANS

DR BIRD 1125 Little Nut Tree/You Are My Only Love
Produced by Sonia Pottinger. (a) The Melodians bring a tinge of spirituality to everything they sing, even to this moody boy meets girl number. TONY BREVETT takes the lead.

DR BIRD 1139 Swing And Dine/I Could Be King
Produced by Sonia Pottinger. (a) Rock steady rhythms were the perfect format for the trio's melodious talents. Here, the backing vocals — part sung, part hummed — provide quiet inspiration, while TONY BREVETT's lead vocal is as sweet as it's conniving.

FAB 61 Sweet Rose/It Comes & It Goes

TREASURE ISLE 7028 Come on Little Girl/TOMMY MCCOOK & THE SUPERSONICS: Got Your Soul
Produced by Duke Reid. (a) The harmonies are so subtle they could be in another room, while the song doubtless made more sense booming on the dance floor than squeaking out of the home hi-fi. Still, it's compulsive rhythm epitomizes rock steady, and the keyboards have an edge all of their own.

MIGHTY SPARROW

NEMS 563558 Mr Walker/Carnival in 68

GLEN MILLER

DR BIRD 1128 Rock Steady Party/Book of Memories

MILLIE

FONTANA 948 When I Dance with You/Hey Mr Love

THE MILWAUKEE COASTERS

PAMA 733 Treat Me Nice/Sick & Tired

THE MINSTRELS

STUDIO ONE 2050 Miss Highty Tighty/WESTMORELITES: Let Me Be Yours Until Tomorrow

Produced by Coxsone Dodd.

MISS JANE

PAMA 704 Bad Mind People/My Heart Is Aching

JACKIE MITTOO

(X) BASES, BOP & THE BELTONES, CANNONBALL BRYAN, GAYLADS, HEPTONES

COXSONE 7042 Sure Shot/THE OCTAVES: The Bottle

Produced by Coxsone Dodd.

STUDIO ONE 2043 Put It On/SOUL VENDORS: Chinese Chicken

Produced by Coxsone Dodd.

THE MOHAWKS

PAMA 719 The Champ/Sound of the Witchdoctors

PAMA 739 Baby Hold On (Parts 1/2)

PAMA 751 Sweet Soul Music/Hip Jigger

PAMA 757 Monty Monty/Pepsi

PAMA 758 Ride Your Pony/Western Promise

AMEIL MOODIE

BLUE CAT 143 Mello Reggae/Lifeline

JOHNNY MOORE

(X) ALTON ELLIS

THE MOPEDS

COLUMBIA BLUE BEAT 108 Whisky & Soda/Do It

(a) The suave pulsing bass line is the stand-out on this great instrumental, over which the saxophonist gently spars with the organist.

DERRICK MORGAN

(X) PETER KING

AMALGAMATED 824 I Want to Go Home/JACKIE ROBINSON: Let the Little Girl Dance

Produced by Joe Gibbs. (a) A proper depth and reverence characterizes the longing religious theme via an overt spiritual delivery.

ISLAND 3094 Conquering Ruler/LLOYD & DEVON: Red Rum Ball

(a) Apparently being a Judge just wasn't enough for the singer, and he now returns as the "ace from space, the conquering ruler." Thankfully, the all-powerful Morgan seems as benign a ruler as he was a magistrate although, once past the humorous concept, the song is pretty forgettable.

ISLAND 3101 Gimme Back/THE VICEROYS: Send Requests

ISLAND 3159 Hold You Jack/One Morning in May

Produced by Bunny Lee. (a) Featuring the HIPPY BOYS.

NU-BEAT 016 I Love You/JUNIOR SMITH: Searching

PYRAMID 6029 I Am the Ruler/I Mean It

Produced by Leslie Kong.

PYRAMID 6039 Woman a Grumble/Don't Be a Fool

Produced by Leslie Kong.

PYRAMID 6040 Want More/ROLAND ALPHONSO: Goodnight My Love

Produced by Leslie Kong.

PYRAMID 6045 Try Me/DERRICK MORGAN & PAULINE: Last Chance

Produced by Leslie Kong.

PYRAMID 6053 Me Naw Give Up/BEVERLEY'S ALL-STARS: Dreadnought

Produced by Leslie Kong.

PYRAMID 6056 Ben Johnson Day/MAYTALS: Ain't Got No Tip

Produced by Leslie Kong.

PYRAMID 6061 What's Your Grouse/BEVERLEY'S ALL-STARS: I Don't Know

Produced by Leslie Kong.

TROJAN 626 Fat Man/VAL BENNETT: South Parkway Rock

(a) Morgan initially recorded this song as a single way back in 1960, then resurrected it as this skankified reggae hit in 1968 (he tossed it out again in 1970). The soulful vocals and moody melody made it a consistent favorite. (b) The tenor saxman heads up the highway on this mid-tempo instrumental, tootling along nicely, but never in danger of running anyone off the road.

DERRICK MORGAN & PAULINE

PYRAMID 6027 You Never Miss Your Water/DERRICK MORGAN: Got You on My Mind

Produced by Leslie Kong.

PYRAMID 6046 King for Tonight/Last Chance

Produced by Leslie Kong.

PYRAMID 6063 Don't Say/DERRICK MORGAN: Johnny Pram Pram

Produced by Leslie Kong.

HEMSLEY MORRIS

(X) COOL CATS, TOMMY MCKENZIE

MONTY MORRIS

(X) THEO BECKFORD, BUNNY & RUDDY, COOL STICKY, ALTON ELLIS

AMALGAMATED 813 Now I'm Alone/Rise & Fall

Produced by Joe Gibbs.

DR BIRD 1162 Last Laugh/You Really Got a Hold on Me

PAMA 721 Say What You're Saying/Tears in Your Eyes

Produced by Clancy Eccles.

MR FOUNDATION

STUDIO ONE 2061 Time Oh/DUDLEY SIBLEY & PETER AUSTIN: Hole in Your Soul

Produced by Coxsone Dodd.

STUDIO ONE 2069 Reggae Rumble/MARCIA GRIFFITHS: You Keep Me on the Move

Produced by Coxsone Dodd.

MR MILLER

(X) LLOYD TYRELL

MUSIC THROUGH SIX

(X) ROY DOCKER

ED NANGLE

BLUE CAT 120 Good Girl/ENFORCERS: Musical Fever

THE NATIVES

ISLAND 3143 Live It Up/Never Break My Heart

(a) The call and response chorus and the close harmonies present the Natives at their best. The cheery guitar riff and powerful rhythm section are an added bonus.

THE OCTAVES

(X) JACKIE MITTOO, THE VICEROYS

THE OVERTAKERS

Rock steady band featuring LEO GRAHAM (b 12/15/41, Trelawny, JA).

AMALGAMATED 803 That's the Way You Like It/The Big Take Over

Produced by Joe Gibbs. (a) This plaintiff number captures the vocal trio at their most emotive. The guitar riff tries to turn the mood upbeat, but the Overtakers ensure the sadness shines through.

AMALGAMATED 809 Girl You Ruff/KEITH BLAKE: Woo Oh Oh

Produced by Joe Gibbs.

GENE PANCHO

GIANT 21 I Like Sweet Music/Seven Days

THE PARAGONS

DUKE 7 Left with a Broken Heart/I've Got to Get Away

Produced by Duke Reid. (a) The Paragons are downhearted, but still optimistic in their heartbreak. Besides the always superb vocals, check out the rootsy arrangement. (b) aka "Man Next Door." The Paragons reach politically incorrect heights in their response to the domestic abuse next door. However, no one can fault the melancholy melody and yearning for peace and quiet that the trio so eloquently express.

ISLAND 3138 Memories by the Score/The Number One for Me

Produced by Duke Reid. (a) JOHN HOLT plays it straight, even while the lush backing vocalists virtually sing him down. But it's the musical arrangement that's particularly disconcerting, which from the first note seemingly parodies champagne stylings.

TREASURE ISLE 7034 Silver Bird/My Best Girl

Produced by Duke Reid. (b) A fine gem this — a subtle reggae beat, a bouncy organ, some of the sharpest horns around, a supple little melody, and JOHN HOLT singing the praises of his best girl to the harmonious accompaniment of the rest of the Paragons. Perfect.

KEN PARKER

GIANT 34 Change Is Gonna Come/VAL BENNETT: Jumping with Val

ISLAND 3096 Down Low/Sad Mood

ISLAND 3105 Lonely Man/ERROL DUNKLEY: I Am Going Home

BOBBY PATTERSON & THE MUSTANGS

PAMA 735 Broadway Ain't Funky No More/I Met My Match

PAMA 743 The Good Ol' Days/Don't Be So Mean

PAMA 754 Busy Busy Bee/Sweet Taste of Love

DAWN PENN

(X) MAX ROMEO, THE VICEROYS

ISLAND 3097 I'll Never Let You Go/MARK BROWN: Brown Low Special

GEORGE A PENNY

TROJAN 625 Win Your Love/VAL BENNETT: All in the Game

(a) Taking on a Sam Cooke song is just asking for trouble, and Penny, while giving a passionate performance, inevitably pales in comparison. The overly busy and upbeat reggae rhythm doesn't help either.

PAT PERRIN

(X) LLOYD TYRELL

LEE PERRY

(X) DANDY & LEE

AMALGAMATED 808 The Upsetter/Thank You Baby

Produced by Joe Gibbs (actually Perry). (a) Perry's delivery is pretty pedestrian, but the message to his former employer, the "gravelicious" COXSONE DODD is clear and Perry takes this simple song to great musical heights via an arrangement showcasing the individual talents of the band — listen carefully and LYNN TAITT is playing two guitars simultaneously (the wonders of double tracking!). (b) This is arguably one of Perry's best singles, its pretty, simple melody was perfect for his admittedly limited vocal range, with the doo-wopish backing singers expanding the sound and charm, a flashy surf-style guitar counterpoints, and a solid beat filled in the gaps.

DR BIRD 1146 People Funny Boy/BURT WALTERS: Blowing in the Wind

Produced by Lee Perry. (a) How to make friends and influence people. Having already assaulted one former employer, Perry now takes a poke at another (JOE GIBBS), although if you hadn't read that some place, you'd never know from the lyrics. A tight rhythm teases the PIONEERS' Long Shot," and sets the stage for the musical upsetting to come. After so many years of waiting, Perry finally steps out of his creative chrysalis. (b) Shoeless Burt Walters manfully dispatches Dylan's anti-war classic, while Perry sets off a wind machine for emphasis.

THE PIONEERS

AMALGAMATED 811 Give Me a Little Loving/This Is Soul

Produced by Joe Gibbs. (a) CROOKS intended recording this song solo — indeed, he was about to voice the track alone when he noticed a youngster watching outside and asked him if he could sing. It was JACKIE ROBINSON, and he could. The Pioneers' breakout UK club hit features fabulous toe curling falsetto backing harmonies, a solid rock steady rhythm, and the catchiest chorus since the flu.

AMALGAMATED 814 Long Shot/Dip & Fall Back
Produced by Joe Gibbs. (a) The CROOKS/ROBINSON duo kick off the story of the now famous "Long Shot," with this racing report set to a rock steady rhythm. "He gallop and he gallop, but he couldn't bust the tape," the Pioneers melodiously moan, while the guitarist twangs away unconcernedly . . . obviously he didn't have money riding on this loser.

AMALGAMATED 821 Jackpot/THE CREATORS: Kimble
Produced by Joe Gibbs. (a) From the opening horn blast, you know this is another race-track song. The melody borrows heavily from "Long Shot," but this time the Pioneers' pick wins, and it's smiles all round. (b) The Creators, of course, is LEE PERRY, chatting merrily about his favorite character in *The Fugitive* TV series, and emphasizing his points with breaking glass and whip cracks.

AMALGAMATED 823 No Dope Me Pony/LORD SALMONS: Great Great In 68
Produced by Joe Gibbs. (a) No, not another song about Long Shot, but an entertaining single nonetheless. "Hold on to your donkey," the Pioneers sing, because apparently he's as keen to do the rock steady as every one else.

AMALGAMATED 826 Tickle Me for Days/THE VERSATILES: The Time Has Come
Produced by Joe Gibbs. (b) This celebration of unity with political overtones was a perfect party piece, a hint of calypso, an exhilarating string section, and a dance friendly tempo. LEE PERRY actually oversaw the session, LYNN TAITT's band provide accompaniment.

AMALGAMATED 828 Catch the Beat/SIR GIBBS' ALL-STARS: Jana
Produced by Joe Gibbs.

AMALGAMATED 830 Sweet Dreams/DON DRUMMOND JUNIOR: Caterpillar Rock
Produced by Joe Gibbs. (a) The Pioneers go country on this much-covered classic (Patsy Cline's version is probably the definitive rendering). However, the clattering rhythm section, jazzy horn flourishes, and overly busy musical arrangement were more likely to bring on nightmares.

BLUE CAT 100 Shake It Up/Rudies Are the Greatest
Produced by Joe Gibbs. (b) The hit group rallies round the rudies . . . well better late than never. Not one of their best, the backing vocals are just repetitive accents, and the saving grace is the guitar.

BLUE CAT 103 Give It to Me/THE LEADERS: Someday Someway
Produced by Joe Gibbs.

BLUE CAT 105 Whip Them/Having a Bawl

Produced by Joe Gibbs. (b) A big, fat bass groove, an insolent, choppy guitar and the Pioneers drolly comment on a brawl between rude boys and the police. A slow, melodic scorcher.

BLUE CAT 139 Reggae Beat/Miss Eva
Produced by Joe Gibbs. (a) This upbeat number has a calypso flair and a perfect holiday-in-the-sun feel, an extravaganza atmosphere that perfectly encompasses the carnival theme.

CALTONE 119 I Love No Other Girl/MILTON BOOTHE: I Used To Be a Fool

PYRAMID 6062 Easy Come Easy Go/BEVERLEY'S ALL-STARS: Only a Smile
Produced by Leslie Kong.

PYRAMID 6065 Pee Pee Cluck Cluck/BEVERLEY'S ALL-STARS: Exclusively
Produced by Leslie Kong.

PHIL PRATT
See entry in DIRECTORY OF PRODUCERS. (X) DON DRUMMOND JUNIOR, LARRY MARSHALL

PRIMO & HOPETON
PAMA 753 Peace on Earth/SCHOOLBOYS: Love Is a Message

PRINCE BUSTER
FAB 31 Kings of Old/Sweet Inspiration
Produced by Prince Buster.

FAB 35 Try a Little Tenderness/All My Loving
Produced by Prince Buster.

FAB 36 South of the Border/Version
Produced by Prince Buster. Also released as PRINCE BUSTER 36.

FAB 38 Free Love/DALTONS: All Over the World
Produced by Prince Buster. (a) The ponderous bass intro threatens a more significant song than actually seems to be delivered. But slowly, a bland love'n unity lyric slides into a more militant, questioning demand, which winds up at utter odds to the unflappable harmonies mouthing the title.

FAB 40 Rough Rider/127 Orange Street
Produced by Prince Buster. (a) Less lyrically clumsy than most of the sexploitation singles flooding the streets, if only because even the most prurient listener has to appreciate the strong melody, catchy bass line, and bubbly organ. Years later, when the English Beat resurrected the song, it didn't raise a single eyebrow.

FAB 47 Going to Ethiopia/PRINCE BUSTER'S ALL-STARS: Shakin' Up Orange Street
Produced by Prince Buster.

FAB 49 Glory of Love/WAILERS: Mellow Mood
(a) Produced by Prince Buster. (b) Produced by the Wailers.

FAB 56 Intensified Dirt/Don't You Know I Love You
Produced by Prince Buster.

FAB 64 Cool Stroker/It's You I Love

Produced by Prince Buster. (b) Featuring EARL LOWE on vocals.

FAB 80 Hypocrite/New Dance

Produced by Prince Buster.

FAB 81 Wine & Grind/The Scorcher

Produced by Prince Buster. (a) A relatively insignificant song which nevertheless made its way into the charts three times — in JA, upon its initial release; in the UK when the English Beat included a version on their smash debut album; and again in 1998, when Prince Buster took a rerecorded "Wine" back to the top after it featured in a UK Levi's ad. Made for the dance floor this exhilarating song is all contagious beat, happy-go-lucky Hammond, and irrepressible double entendres. Also released as FAB 108.

PRINCE BUSTER'S ALL-STARS

(X) FITZROY D LONG

FAB 37 This Is a Hold Up/Julie on My Mind

Produced by Prince Buster. (a) Opening with a cavalcade of gunfire, this okra Western features members of the inimitable SKATALITES, all chigga chiggas, jazzy horn solos, and Western flare, a brilliant melding of disparate styles.

FAB 57 Green Green Grass of Home/SOUL MAKERS: Girls Like You

Produced by Prince Buster.

FAB 58 We Shall Overcome/Keep the Faith

Produced by Prince Buster.

PRINCE BUSTER & TEDDY KING

FAB 41 Shepherd Beng Beng/TENNORS: Ride Me Donkey

Produced by Prince Buster. (b) The rhythm later provided the foundation for the ENGINEERS' "Noisy Village," an early LEE PERRY experiment in special effects and overdubbing.

THE PYRAMIDS

COLUMBIA BLUE BEAT 111 Prisoner from Alcatatraz/THE RUDE BOYS: The Ska's the Limit

(a) An adaptation of the the Sam Cooke hit "Chain Gang" and you can feel the sweat dripping off the toiling bodies as the Pyramids convey the sheer drudgery and hopelessness of prison life. (b) Also released credited to the BEES, this instrumental's got it all — a chugging beat, a smokey melody, an upbeat tinkling piano, and the moodiest horn solo you've ever heard.

PRESIDENT 177 Wedding in Peyton Place/Girls Girls Girls

PRESIDENT 195 All Change on the Bakerloo Line/Playing Games

PRESIDENT 206 Mexican Moonlight/Mule

PRESIDENT 225 Tisko My Darling/Movement All Round

THE RACE FANS

Featuring vocalist DAVID ISAACS.

TROJAN 610 Bookie Man/UNIQUES: More Love

Produced by Lynford Anderson.

ERNEST RANGLIN

PAMA 711 Heart Beat/Birds of the Air

EDWARD RAPHAEL

(X) THE UNTOUCHABLES

LEROY REID

BLUE CAT 125 The Fiddler/LOVELETTES: Shook

BLUE CAT 127 Great Surprise/TENNORS: Khaki

(b) "When I was a little laddy, I used to watch mummy and daddy." A gently rocking paean to masturbation.

NEHMIAH REID

ISLAND 3102 Family War/Give Me that Love

PAT RHODEN

TROJAN 606 Woman Is Greedy/Endlessly

ROY RICHARDS

(X) ROLAND ALPHONSO

COXSONE 7037 Warm & Tender Ska/SOUL VENDORS: Grooving Steady

Produced by Coxsone Dodd.

COXSONE 7049 I Was Born to Be Loved/NORMA FRAZIER: Heartaches

Produced by Coxsone Dodd.

COXSONE 7061 Summertime/RIGHTEOUS FLAMES: You Don't Know

Produced by Coxsone Dodd.

THE RIGHTEOUS FLAMES

(X) ROY RICHARDS

BLUE CAT 112 Seven Letters/SOUL VENDORS: To Sir with Love

Produced by Coxsone Dodd. (b) A skankified version of the movie theme, ROLAND ALPHONSO plays the brass off against the flashy surf guitar for a version which winds up more interesting than the usual cover fodder.

STUDIO ONE 2048 Ease Up/SOUL VENDORS: Evening Time

Produced by Coxsone Dodd.

JACKIE ROBINSON

From 1967, a member of THE PIONEERS.

AMALGAMATED 819 Over & Over/Woman of Samaria

Produced by Joe Gibbs.

LLOYD ROBINSON

DUKE 5 Cuss Cuss/Lavender Blue

Produced by Harry J. (a) Superbly swaggering number by one of the most underrated vocalists of the era.

RICO RODRIGUEZ

(X) THE RUDIES

NU-BEAT 015 Blue Socks/Solas Market

PAMA 706 Soul Man/It's Not Unusual

PAMA 715 Tender Foot/Ska Memories

MAX ROMEO

Of THE EMOTIONS. Also recorded as a duo with DENNIS ALCAPONE. See entry on page 19.

ISLAND 3104 Put Me in the Mood/My One Girl

Produced by Bunny Lee. (a) Never has slackness sounded so sweet on this slow, heated single. (b) Romeo at his most endearing, gently rhapsodizing his true love with passion and conviction.

ISLAND 3124 Twelfth of Never/VAL BENNETT: Caledonia

Produced by Bunny Lee.

ISLAND 3111 Walk into the Dawn/DAWN PENN: I'll Get You

Produced by Bunny Lee.

GENE RONDO

b WINSTON LARA, 5/43 (Kingston, JA)/d 6/94. Moved to the UK in 1962 and conducted his career from there. Member of band THE UNDIVIDED.

GIANT 39 Ben Nevis/Grey Lies

JOLLY 004 Mary Mary/Baby Baby

ROY & DUKE ALL-STARS

ROY PANTON fronts Duke Reid's studio band.

BLUE CAT 113 Pretty Blue Eyes (parts 1/2)

Produced by Duke Reid.

BLUE CAT 117 The Train (parts 1/2)

Produced by Duke Reid.

ROY & ENID

Vocal duo comprising ROY PANTON and ENID CUMBERLAND.

COXSONE 7063 Rocking Time/RALPH BLAKE: High Blood Pressure

Produced by Coxsone Dodd.

COXSONE 7069 He'll Have to Go/CARLTON & THE SHOES: Love Is a Treasure

Produced by Coxsone Dodd.

THE ROYALS

AMALGAMATED 831 Never See Come See/CANNONBALL BRYAN TRIO: Jumping Jack

Produced by Joe Gibbs. (a) The fabulous Royals wade in with their own contribution to the Long Shot saga, surging along like a racehorse on the final stretch, with an infectious chorus you'll be humming the rest of the week. It was also a Joe Gibbs composed jab at THE PIONEERS, following their departure for LESLIE KONG's Beverley stable. (b) A fairly high octane instrumental, featuring Bryan's jazzy alto sax, a spiffy little melody, and a beat that won't quit.

THE RUBAIYATS

ACTION 4516 Omar Khayan/Tomorrow

THE RUDE BOYS

(X) THE PYRAMIDS

THE RUDIES

Featuring FREDDIE NOTES and DANNY SMITH. Band later became hitmakers GREYHOUND.

BLUE CAT 107 The 7–11 Go to the Go Go Club (parts 1/2)

BLUE CAT 109 Cupid/RICO'S ALL-STARS: Wise Message

FAB 46 I Wanna Go Home/La Mer

NU-BEAT 001 Train to Vietnam/Skaville to Rainbow City

NU-BEAT 005 Engine 59/My Girl

THE RUDIES FANATICS

FAB 70 Give Me the Rights/I Do Love You

FAB 71 Mighty Meaty/Go

THE SCHOOLBOYS

(X) PRIMO & HOPETON

THE SENSATIONS

DUKE 2 Those Guys/I'll Never Fall in Love

Produced by Duke Reid. (a) The perfect slow smoocher this, as the Sensations try to win back their girl with some of their sweetest, most sincere acclamations of devotion. (b) Popular theme, popular song; the Sensations wrap their version up in a cascade of harmonies and a winsome lead falsetto, the daintily airy band seem to believe that this is all a cause for muted festivities.

ISLAND 3110 Long Time Me No See You Girl/ROY SHIRLEY: Million Dollar Baby

ROY SHIRLEY

(X) GLEN ADAMS, SENSATIONS, STRANGER & GLADDY, THE UNIQUES, THE UNTOUCHABLES

AMALGAMATED 815 The World Needs Love/Dance The A

Produced by Joe Gibbs.

DR BIRD 1165 Hush a Bye/Musical Dinner

DR BIRD 1168 Dance the Reggae/The Agreement

GIANT 32 Dance Arena/Musical Train

(a) Featuring BOBBY AITKEN and the CARIB-BEATS. Shirley struts his favorite vocal quirks, which reach almost operatic proportions on this up-tempo song.

GIANT 33 Warming Up the Scene/GLEN ADAMS: Lonely Girl

(a) GLEN ADAMS and SLIM SMITH provide backing vocals, providing a nice counterpoint to Shirley's emotive delivery, while the cheery keyboard gives it that great mid-60's sound.

FAB 54 Think About the Future/Golden Festival

ISLAND 3108 Move All Day/Rollin' Rollin'

ISLAND 3113 Keep Your Eyes on the Road/VAL BENNETT: Jumping with Mr Lee

Produced by Bunny Lee.

ISLAND 3118 Good Is Better than Bad/Fantastic Lover

Produced by Bunny Lee.

ISLAND 3119 Facts of Life/Lead Us Not into Temptation

Produced by Bunny Lee. Credited to Shirley & THE UNIQUES.

ISLAND 3125 If I Did Know/Good Ambition

Produced by Bunny Lee. (a) Shirley remains an acquired taste, and this ballad finds him at his most passionately histrionic. Detractors will find him ludicrous, fans will find his heartrending delivery awesome.

TROJAN 611 If I Did Know/VAL BENNETT: Spanish Harlem

Produced by Bunny Lee. (b) An instrumental version of the much-covered classic, with the saxophonist taking the melody line and improvising wonderfully around it.

DUDLEY SIBLEY & PETER AUSTIN

Vocal duo featuring Austin of THE CLARENDONIANS. (X) MR FOUNDATION.

SILVER & THE MAGNETS

JOLLY 006 Baby Oh Yeah/Rock Steady Is Here to Stay

THE SILVERTONES

(X) THE CHARMERS

TREASURE ISLE 7027 In the Midnight Hour/TOMMY MCCOOK: Soul for Sale

Produced by Duke Reid. (a) Wilson Pickett's monster hit undergoes a radical transformation, softened by the sweet harmonies and island-fied arrangement, it's more like four A.M. than midnight. None of which stopped U-ROY from borrowing the rhythm and tarting it up.

TREASURE ISLE 7039 Old Man River/TOMMY MCCOOK: Our Man Flint

Produced by Duke Reid.

TREASURE ISLE 7042 Slow & Easy/TOMMY MCCOOK: Moving

Produced by Duke Reid.

DAN SIMMONDS

(X) BOB STACKIE

BEVERLEY SIMMONS

PAMA 716 Mr Pitiful/That's How Strong My Love Is

ZOOT SIMMS

BLUE CAT 118 Bye Bye Baby/AL & THE THRILLERS: Heart for Sale

SUGAR SIMONE

CBS 3250 The Vow/Spinning Wheel

GO 11409 It's Alright/Take It Easy

JEANETTE SIMPSON

GIANT 29 My Baby Just Cares for Me/Don't Let Me Cry No More

Produced by Dandy Livingstone.

GIANT 35 Through Loving You/Send Me Some Lovin'

Produced by Dandy Livingstone.

SIR COLLINS BAND

COLLINS DOWNBEAT 005 Sock It Softly/LESTER STERLING, SIR COLLINS & BAND: Three Wise Men

Produced by Sir Collins.

COLLINS DOWNBEAT 011 Collins & The Boys/Bob Stackie in Soho

Produced by Sir Collins.

COLLINS DOWNBEAT 017 Bob Stackie in Soho/LORD CHARLES & HIS BAND: Jamaican Bits & Pieces

Produced by Sir Collins. Credited to band & BOB STACKIE.

SIR GIBBS

Joe Gibbs put his name to one of the most phenomenal gatherings of talent around. His ALL-STARS, backing band on most of the Amalgamated label releases included LYNN TAITT (guitar), JACKIE JACKSON (bass), CARL BRYAN, and TOMMY MCCOOK (sax), while the actual production duties fell first to LEE PERRY, then NINEY HOLNESS. Engineer was Errol Thompson. (X) THE PIONEERS

AMALGAMATED 822 People Grudgeful/Pan Ya Machet

Produced by Joe Gibbs. (a) THE PIONEERS at their most plaintive and irritated, asking the musical question "why, why people grudgeful, why?" A variation on LEE PERRY's anti-Gibbs tirade "People Funny Boy," the noisy arrangement plays up the exasperated feel for all it's worth. (b) Another pop at Perry, with a whining puppy dog for added emphasis.

THE SLICKERS

aka THE PIONEERS.

BLUE CAT 133 Wala Wala/LESTER STERLING: Super Special

(b) No matter what the current style, Sterling leaves his imprint on it. Here we find the trumpeter blasting his best to a rock steady-ish rhythm.

BLUE CAT 134 Nana/MARTIN RILEY: I May Never See My Baby Anymore

JUNIOR SMITH

GAS 101 Gimme Little/Trip to Warland

Reissued as GAS 132.

GIANT 18 I'm Gonna Leave You Girl/I Love You I Love You

GIANT 25 Come Cure Me/I Want Your Loving

SLIM SMITH

COXSONE 7034 Rougher Yet/I'll Never Let Go

Produced by Coxsone Dodd. (a) Smith's vocals leant themselves best to emotion-drenched lost love songs, but his passion extended beyond relationships, as on this moving plea to God to help people through the rough times ahead. Besides featuring the singer's toughest ever vocals, the sublime beat became a favorite for versioning. (b) Keeping with the a-side's tough delivery, Jamaica's most hopeless romantic now exhibits surprising defiance. "I will never let go, I'll always try, I've got so much soul, . . ." he proudly exclaims, a theme that works well for any unhappy situation.

TROJAN 619 Watch this Sound/Out of Love

Produced by Lloyd Tyrell, credited to Smith & THE UNIQUES. (a) One of the most embarrassing covers of all time, the UNIQUES and the HIPPY BOYS attempt to bend Buffalo Springfield's already mawkishly over-wrought "For What It's Worth" to their own signature style. This is so wrong on just about every conceivable level, but it was also future WAILER FAMILY MAN BARRETT's recorded debut. Amazingly, rumor insists that it was the bass sound on this record which first caught BOB MARLEY's attention. (b) Lovely Smith composition which wouldn't have looked wrong on a Motown compilation! DEVON RUSSELL later unveiled a decidedly meaty interpretation, but the delicate original remains the best.

THE SOUL MAKERS

(X) PRINCE BUSTER'S ALL-STARS

THE SOUL TOPS

NU-BEAT 102 Rain and Thunder/Swing Baby Swing

THE SOUL VENDORS

(X) DOBBY DOBSON, ALTON ELLIS, GAYLADS, HAMLINS, HEPTONES, INVADERS, JACKIE MITTOO, ROY RICHARDS, RIGHTEOUS FLAMES, ERNEST WILSON

COXSONE 7057 Real Rock/AL CAMPBELL: Don't Run Away
Produced by Coxsone Dodd.

STUDIO ONE 2066 Soul Joint/Soul Limbo
Produced by Coxsone Dodd.

STUDIO ONE 2070 Captain Cojoe/JACKIE MITTOO: Drum Song
Produced by Coxsone Dodd. (b) Mittoo's organ weeps the sultry melody, the brass mutedly add their own heartbreak to the mix, and underpinning it all, the tribal drums murmur sympathetically.

HORATIO SOUL

ISLAND 3132 Ten White Horses/Angela

JUNIOR SOUL

BIG SHOT 503 Chatty Chatty/Magic Touch
Produced by Derrick Harriott.

BOB STACKIE

(X) OWEN GRAY

COLLINS DOWNBEAT 009 Grab It Hold It Feel It/DAN SIMMONDS: Way Out Sound
Produced by Sir Collins.

CINDY STARR

COLUMBIA BLUE BEAT 107 Pain of Love/CINDY STARR & THE RUDE BOYS: Hippy Ska

THE STEAM SHOVEL

TROJAN 635 Rudi the Red Nosed Reindeer/White Christmas

FITZROY STERLING

GAS 102 Got to Play It Cool/Jezebel

LESTER STERLING

(X) VAL BENNETT, SIR COLLINS BAND, THE SLICKERS, THE UNIQUES

BLUE CAT 116 Zigaloo/Wiser than Solomon

DELANO STEWART

aka WINSTON STEWART.

DR BIRD 1138 That's Life/Tell Me Baby
Produced by Sonia Pottinger. (a) A determined lyric and a pulsing LYNN TAITT accompaniment, with Stewart's vocal matching both qualities.

HIGH NOTE 004 Let's Have Some Fun/Dance with Me
Produced by Sonia Pottinger.

ROMEO STEWART

(X) THE TENNORS

STRANGER & GLADDY

aka STRANGER COLE & GLADSTONE ANDERSON.

AMALGAMATED 806 Seeing Is Knowing/ROY SHIRLEY: Music Is the Key
Produced by Stranger & Gladdy. (a) A gorgeous showcase for the pair's most soulful and emotive vocals.

ISLAND 3128 Love Me Today/Over Again
Produced by Stranger & Gladdy.

ISLAND 3155 Over Again/CHARLIE KELLEY: So Nice Like Rice
Produced by Stranger & Gladdy.

THE SUPERBOYS

DANDY LIVINGSTONE's backing band.

GIANT 22 Ain't that a Shame/Do It Right Now
Produced by Dandy Livingstone.

GIANT 31 You're Hurtin' Me/Funky Soul
Produced by Dandy Livingstone.

LYNN TAITT & THE JETS

(X) THE TARTANS, JOE WHITE

AMALGAMATED 810 El Casino Royale/Dee's Special
Produced by Joe Gibbs. (a) The burbling Hammond sets the happy-go-lucky mood, the rhythm section places the movie theme in the islands and the DJ rousts the crowd.

AMALGAMATED 827 Sleepy Judy/HUGH MALCOLM: Good Time Rock
Produced by Joe Gibbs. (b) The bongos rule the roost on this spiritually based single; indeed, the preacher/choir vocals are mixed so far down as to be just one of a multitude of sounds.

ISLAND 3139 Napoleon Solo/Pressure & Slide
(a) This has as much to do with the U.N.C.L.E. spy as THE CRYSTALITES' "Ilya K" (ie: nothing), but at least Taitt wrote his own spiffing, dapperish melody. It might have made more sense if he retitled the song "Mr. Steed."

PAMA 723 Soul Food/Music Flames

THE TARTANS

CALTONE 115 Awake the Town/LYNN TAITT & THE JETS: The Brush

CALTONE 117 Coming on Strong/It's Alright

TYRONE TAYLOR

(X) DRUMBAGO

THE TECHNIQUES

DUKE 1 I Wish It Would Rain/There Comes a Time
Produced by Duke Reid. (a) An unexpectedly original take on the Motown classic (a hit for both the Temptations and Gladys Knight & The Pips). The Techniques eschew an emotional downpour in favor of a surprisingly breezy version, that literally whips by.

DUKE 6 A Man of My Word/The Time Has Come

Produced by Duke Reid. (b) SLIM SMITH ventures away from his usual passionate fare to sing about larger issues, bringing equal conviction to this anti-violence song, while his Techniques provide sporadic backup.

TREASURE ISLE 7038 Bless You/Devoted

Produced by Duke Reid. (a) What should have been a magnificent confirmation of love is undermined by the showboating organist whose Hammond keeps hogging the spotlight.

TREASURE ISLE 7031 My Girl/Drink Wine

Produced by Duke Reid. (a) Not a cover of the Temptations' hit, but Motown-esque nonetheless. The harmonies are a dream and the vocals thick with sweet yearning. A version by U-ROY would later turn the love theme on its head. (b) The brass vies for center stage with the vocals on this mutedly upbeat single that's light as a summer breeze.

TREASURE ISLE 7040 Travelling Man/It's You I Love

Produced by Duke Reid. (a) Rock steady masterpiece featuring some of the trio's most heavenly harmonies, accompanied by the group's favorite fragile and delicately emotive lead vocals. (b) Classic rock steady in a romantic mood, with a bass pulse that throbs like a heartbeat, the perfect counterpoint to the the glittering falsetto vocals that etch this song like Waterford crystal.

THE TENNORS

Featuring RONNIE DAVIS, LLOYD RICKETTS (THE ITALS). (X) LEROY REID

BIG SHOT 501 Reggae Girl/CLIVE ALL-STARS: Donkey Trot

DR BIRD 1152 Massy Massa/CLIVE ALL-STARS: San Sebastian

FAB 50 Let Go Yah Donkey/ROMEO STEWART: While I Was Walking

ISLAND 3133 Ride Your Donkey/I've Got to Get You off My Mind

(a) The Tennors obviously had a fondness for the four-footed beast, and here they reminisce of happy childhood days spent on one, a simple song that shines with a touch of folksiness, but is fired by a powerful slow reggaefied beat.

ISLAND 3140 Copy Me Donkey/The Stage

ISLAND 3156 Grampa/ROMEO STEWART: While I Was Walking

THE TERMITES

(X) KEN BOOTHE

COXSONE 7039 Mama Didn't Know/I Made a Mistake

Produced by Coxsone Dodd.

PAMA 729 Push It Up/Two of a Kind

(a) Well, there's no mixing metaphors here. An utterly insistent reggae rhythm, a full-bodied falsetto chorus, while the Termites leap in with their demands right from the start — "rub it and a push it up" is an ear-catching opening line in any language.

PAMA 738 Show Me the Way/What Can I Do

CLAUDETTE THOMAS

CALTONE 116 Roses Are Red My Love/YVONNE HARRISON: Near to You

THE THREE TOPS

COXSONE 7033 A Man of Chances/HORTENSE ELLIS: A Groovy Kind of Love

Produced by Coxsone Dodd.

COXSONE 7051 Great Train in 68/You Should Have Known

Produced by Coxsone Dodd.

THE THRILLERS

BLUE CAT 128 The Last Dance/DELTA CATS: Unworthy Baby

PATSY TODD

DR BIRD 1122 Little Flea/The Return Song

HIGH NOTE 007 Fire in Your Wire/AL & THE VIBRATORS: Move Up Calypso

Produced by Sonia Pottinger.

ALBERT TOMLINSON

GIANT 28 Don't Wait for Me/LLOYD EVANS: Losing You

ROY TOMLINSON

(X) MARTIN

THE TONETTES

(X) THE LYRICS

TREVOR

(X) DERMOTT LYNCH

LLOYD TYRELL

aka LLOYD CHARMERS. Also of THE CHARMERS, CONSCIOUS MINDS, THE UNIQUES, THE MESSENGERS, recorded as a duo with JOHNNY MELODY.

ISLAND 3115 Lost Without You/PAT PERRIN: Over You

PAMA 710 Bang Bang Lulu/MR MILLER: I Never Knew

PAMA 752 Lulu Returns/MR MILLER: I Never Knew

THE UNIQUES

(X) GLEN ADAMS, RACE DANS, PAT KELLY, ROY SHIRLEY, SLIM SMITH

ISLAND 3106 Speak No Evil/GLEN ADAMS: That New Girl

Produced by Bunny Lee.

ISLAND 3107 Lesson of Love/DELROY WILSON: Til I Die

Produced by Bunny Lee.

ISLAND 3114 Build My World Around You/LLOYD CLARKE: I'll Never Change

Produced by Bunny Lee. (a) Not instantly catchy, but The Unique's fabulous harmonies and SLIM SMITH's fragile lead takes the group to new soulful heights.

ISLAND 3117 Give Me Some More Of Your Loving/VAL BENNETT: Lovell's Special

Produced by Bunny Lee. (a) The harmonies are even more breathtakingly delicate than usual, while SLIM SMITH's vocals are so filled with passion and conviction you expect him to collapse before the song finishes. A vocal masterpiece from everyone involved.

ISLAND 3122 My Conversation/SLIM SMITH: Love One Another

Produced by Bunny Lee. (a) SLIM SMITH's smooth, sweet as sugar vocals wind across the customary exquisite melody, abetted by LLOYD CHARMERS' warm backing harmony. The CARIB BEATS provided the rhythms, while a tinkling piano accent further sweetened the mix.

ISLAND 3123 The Beatitude/KEITH BLAKE: Time on the River

Produced by Bunny Lee.

ISLAND 3145 Girl of My Dreams/LESTER STERLING: Tribute to King Scratch

Produced by Bunny Lee. (b) Sterling's saxophone is a revelation, while never appearing to showboat.

THE UNTOUCHABLES

Vocal duo featuring JIMMY LONDON (aka TREVOR SHAW) and BILLY DYCE (aka RANSFORD WHITE). Duo also recorded as THE INSPIRATIONS. (X) LLOYD CLARKE, ENOS & SHEILA

BLUE CAT 137 Prisoner in Love/EDWARD RAPHAEL: True Love

TROJAN 613 Tighten Up/ROY SHIRLEY: Good Ambition

Produced by Lee Perry.

THE VERSATILES

Featuring JUNIOR BYLES, BEN "LOUIS" DAVIS, EARL DUDLEY. See entry for JUNIOR BYLES on page 54. (X) MELLOTONES, PIONEERS

AMALGAMATED 802 Just Can't Win/THE LEADERS: Sometimes I Sit Down & Cry

Produced by Joe Gibbs. (a) JUNIOR BYLES' passionate vocals are the highlight of this plaintive single, ably assisted by the rest of the trio's sublime harmonies.

CRAB 1 Children Get Ready/Someone to Love

Produced by Lee Perry.

CRAB 5 Spread Your Bed/Worries a Yard

Produced by Joe Gibbs.

ISLAND 3142 Teardrops Falling/Someone to Love

Produced by Lee Perry. (a) The versatile trio wrap their dulcet tones around this rather perky rock steady-esque song, driven by the guitar riff and led by the ever-stupendous BYLES.

THE VICEROYS

BLUE CAT 121 Fat Fish/THE OCTAVES: You're Gonna Lose

ISLAND 3095 Lip & Tongue/DAWN PENN: When Am I Gonna Be Free

STUDIO ONE 2064 Last Night/Ya Ho

Produced by Coxsone Dodd.

V VINSTRICK & THE JJ ALL-STARS

DR BIRD 1167 Love Is Not a Game/CINDERELLA: The Way I See You

Produced by JJ Johnson.

THE VIRTUES

DR BIRD 1164 High Tide/RUPIE EDWARDS & THE VIRTUES: Burning Love

Produced by Rupie Edwards.

THE VOLUMES

PAMA 755 I Just Can't Help Myself/One Way Lover

THE WAILERS

(X) PRINCE BUSTER

FAB 34 Pound Get a Pound/Funeral

Produced by the Wailers.

TROJAN 617 Stir It Up/This Train

(a) Produced by Clancy Eccles. (b) Produced by the Wailers. (a) The backing Wailers doo-wop in harmony, while MARLEY stirs it up in best rock steady fashion. But the trio just can't stick to one genre and eventually break into a call and response in best gospel fashion. The possibilities for this song were obvious, right from the start. (b) The Wailers go "whooo" and the guitar rattles along the tracks, TOSH practices his deep bass doo-wop and the SOULETTES add a genuinely gospel-like hook. The song is all over the place (have we mentioned the barrelhouse piano, yet?), but it's astonishingly likeable.

DENNIS WALKS

Vocalist best remembered for mid-70s hit "Sad Sweet Dreamer." Also recorded as a duo with I-ROY.

AMALGAMATED 816 Having a Party/GROOVERS: Day by Day

Produced by Joe Gibbs.

BLUE CAT 144 Belly Lick/DRUMBAGO & THE BLENDERS: The Game Song

BURT WALTERS

Perry allegedly discovered Walters singing barefoot in East Kingston. Sensibly, he spent the payment for his first session on a pair of shoes. (X) KING CANNONBALL, LEE PERRY

NORMAN T WASHINGTON

PAMA 730 Same Thing All Over/You've Been Cheating

PAMA 741 Tip Toe/Don't Hang Around

PAMA 749 Jumping Jack Flash/You've Got Me Spinning

THE WEBBER SISTERS

Vocal duo featuring MARLENE WEBBER of THE TONETTES and JOYCE WEBBER. Brother DAVID was a member of THE GLADIATORS.

HIGH NOTE 008 Stars Above/LESLIE BUTLER: Top Cat

Produced by Sonia Pottinger.

ISLAND 3109 My World/ALVA LEWIS: Lonely Still

THE WEST INDIANS

Vocal group formed by ERIC DONALDSON, LESLIE BURKE, HECTOR BROOKS. Subsequently became the KILOWATTS before breaking up in 1970.

DR BIRD 1121 Right on Time/Hokey Pokey
Produced by JJ Johnson.
DR BIRD 1127 Falling in Love/I Mean It
Produced by JJ Johnson.

THE WESTMORELITES
Featuring KEITH PORTER (THE ITALS). (X) THE MINSTRELS

WHISTLING WILLIE
DUKE 8 Penny Reel/Soul Tonic
Produced by Duke Reid.

JOE WHITE
BLUE CAT 108 Way of Life/I'm So Proud
BLUE CAT 119 Try a Little Tenderness/LYNN TAITT & CARL BRYAN: Tender Arms

LLOYD WILLIAMS
DR BIRD 1135 Wonderful World/TOMMY MCCOOK & THE SUPERSONICS: Mad Mad World
Produced by Duke Reid.
TREASURE ISLE 7029 Funky Beat/Goodbye Baby
Produced by Duke Reid.

MARSHALL WILLIAMS
(X) DELROY WILSON

DELROY WILSON
(X) THE UNIQUES
COXSONE 7064 True Believer/MARSHALL WILLIAMS: College Girl
Produced by Coxsone Dodd.
ISLAND 3099 This Old Heart of Mine/GLEN ADAMS: Grab a Girl
Produced by Bunny Lee. (a) A gorgeous cover of the Isley Brothers' classic, with Wilson delivering up his sweetest and most passionate vocals.
ISLAND 3127 Once Upon a Time/I Want to Love You
Produced by Bunny Lee. (a) The emotive vocals sold this song, a cover of the Marvin Gaye and Mary Wells' hit. Otherwise the overly emphasized link between vocal sections is so repetitively annoying it would have killed a lesser performance. (b) This cheery little number is nigh on flawless — the slowly simmering rhythm, sweet melody, infectious hook, soaring backing vocals (probably STRANGER COLE), and pretty piano, combine with Wilson's vocals to make this unforgettable.
STUDIO ONE 2040 Mr DJ/Tripe Girl
Produced by Coxsone Dodd. (b) Wilson and THE TERMITES unite for a rootsy cover of the MAYTALS' song, with the muted horns adding further atmosphere to the moody close harmonies.
STUDIO ONE 2046 Rain from the Skies/How Can I Love Someone
Produced by Coxsone Dodd.
STUDIO ONE 2057 Feel Good All Over/I Like the Way You Walk

ERNEST WILSON
COXSONE 7059 Undying Love/SOUL VENDORS: Tropic Isle
Produced by Coxsone Dodd.

COXSONE 7044 Storybook Children/LITTLE FREDDIE: After Laughter
Produced by Coxsone Dodd.
STUDIO ONE 2058 If I Were a Carpenter/SOUL VENDORS: Frozen Soul
Produced by Coxsone Dodd.

ROY WILSON
Occasional saxophonist with the HIPPY BOYS.
ISLAND 3112 Dread Saras/DAVID BROWN: All My Life
(a) After a false start, the harmonica unusually takes center-stage and plays for all it's worth, on this light hearted instrumental set to a reggae rhythm.

WINSTON & PAT
TROJAN 605 Pony Ride/Baby You Send Me

THE WRIGGLERS
BLUE CAT 106 Get Right/If I Did Look
GIANT 26 The Cooler/You Cannot Know

1969

RICHARD ACE
TROJAN 654 Hang 'Em High/BLACK & GEORGE: Candy Lady
Produced by Harry J.

GLEN ADAMS
(X) DERRICK MORGAN, PETER TOSH, ERNEST WILSON
ESCORT 804 Rich in Love/WOODPECKERS: Zumbelly

AFRO-TONES
(X) BELTONES, DELROY WILSON
DUKE 19 Freedom Sounds/THE BOYS: Easy Sound
TROJAN 655 Things I Love/ERIC FATTER: Since You've Been Gone

LAUREL AITKEN
(X) GIRLIE
DR BIRD 1187 Fire in Your Wire/Quando Quando
Produced by Laurel Aitken.
DR BIRD 1190 Rice & Peas/CLASSICS Worried Over Me
Produced by Laurel Aitken.
DR BIRD 1196 Reggae Prayer/Deliverance Will Come
Produced by Laurel Aitken.
DR BIRD/JJ 1197 The Rise & Fall of Laurel Aitken/If You're Not Black
Produced by Laurel Aitken.
DR BIRD 1202 Haile Haile/SEVEN LETTERS: Call Collect
Produced by Laurel Aitken.
DR BIRD 1203 Carolina/Kingston Town
Produced by Laurel Aitken.
JUNIOR 105 Think Me No Know/RICO: Trombone Man
Produced by Laurel Aitken.
NU-BEAT 024 Woppi King/Mr Soul
Produced by Laurel Aitken.
NU-BEAT 025 Suffering Still/Reggae 69
Produced by Laurel Aitken.

NU-BEAT 032 Haile Selassie/Blues Dance
Produced by Laurel Aitken.

NU-BEAT 033 Lawd Doctor/Big Fight in Hell Stadium
Produced by Laurel Aitken.

NU-BEAT 035 Run Powell Run/RICO RODRIGUEZ: A Message to You
Produced by Laurel Aitken.

NUBEAT 039 Save the Last Dance/Walk Right Back
Produced by Laurel Aitken.

NU-BEAT 040 Don't Be Cruel/John B
Produced by Laurel Aitken. (a/b) Unimaginative covers of Elvis Presley and the Beach Boys respectively.

NU-BEAT 043 Shoo Be Doo/Babylon Gone
Produced by Laurel Aitken.

NU-BEAT 044 Landlords & Tenants/Everybody Sufferin'
Produced by Laurel Aitken.

NU-BEAT 045 Jesse James/Freedom
Produced by Laurel Aitken.

NU-BEAT 046 Pussy Price Gone Up/Gimme Back Me Dollar
Produced by Laurel Aitken. (a) British journalist Carl Gayle described this as "one of the most directly rude records ever, more offensive even than 'Fire in Your Wire' and 'The Rise and Fall of Laurel Aitken'." And he's right, it is, a chronicle of how "pussy price" has soared from 30 cents to the equivalent of your rent.

NU-BEAT 047 Skinhead Train/Kent People

UNITY 506 Donkey Man /TOMMY MCCOOK: The Avengers

AL & THE VIBRATORS
(X) LORD POWER

CARLTON ALPHONSO
GRAPE 3000 Belittle Me/Keep Your Love
Produced by Bunny Lee. (a) Proof that "Wet Dream" was a great song, no matter the lyrics.

CLYDE ALPHONSO
STUDIO ONE 2076 Good Enough/Let the Music Play
Produced by Coxsone Dodd.

ROLAND ALPHONSO
(X) PRINCE BUSTER
GAS 112 A Thousand Tons of Megatons/Musical Resurrection

THE AMBLINGS
(X) THE CARIBBEANS

GLADSTONE ANDERSON
b 6/18/34 (Jones Town, JA). Leading session pianist throughout the 1960s. Nephew of band leader AUBREY ADAMS, led own band GLADDY'S ALL STARS (aka THE AGGROVATORS, THE CRYSTALITES, THE DYNAMITES, LYNN TAITT'S COMETS/BOYS/JETS) and was a founder member of LEE PERRY'S UPSETTERS. Also recorded as a duo with STRANGER COLE.
BLUE CAT 172 Judas/The World Come to an End

BOB ANDY
DR BIRD 1183 The Way I Feel/ETHIOPIANS: Long Time Now
STUDIO ONE 2075 I'm Going Home/SOUND DIMENSION: Straight Flush
Produced by Coxsone Dodd.

ANONYMOUSLY YOURS
DUKE 40 Organism/Itch
TROJAN 680 Get Back/ERNIE SMITH: Not for Sale
TROJAN 681 It's Your Thing/69

BRUCE ANTHONY
(X) KINGSTONIANS

THE ARABIS
DR BIRD 1204 Jump High Jump Low/TONY SHABAZZ: Stool Pigeon

AUDREY
Vocalist AUDREY HALL. (X) DANDY
DOWNTOWN 414 Love Me Tonight/BROTHER DAN ALL-STARS: Show Them Amigo
Produced by Dandy Livingstone.

DOWNTOWN 418 Lover's Concerto/BROTHER DAN ALL-STARS: Along Came You
Produced by Dandy Livingstone.

DOWNTOWN 436 You'll Lose a Good Thing/DESMOND RILEY: If I Had Wings
Produced by Dandy Livingstone.

KEITH BALFOUR
STUDIO ONE 2079 Dreaming/Tired of Waiting
Produced by Coxsone Dodd.

THE BAND OF MERCY & SALVATION
DUKE 20 Suffering Stink/BOB MELODY: The Break

DAVE BARKER
PUNCH 20 Prisoner of Love/BUSTY & THE UPSETTERS: Soul Juice
Produced by Lee Perry. (a) In an emotional maelstrom pinioned between passion and pain, Barker delivers up one of his most powerful singing (as compared to DJ-ing) performances, all set to a typically bubbly Perry arrangement.

ERIC BARNET
CRAB 37 Quaker City/Double Up
GAS 106 Te Ta Toe/MILTON BOOTHE: Lonely & Blue

ASTON "FAMILY MAN" BARRETT
Sessions bassist best known for stint with LEE PERRY's UPSETTERS, HIPPY BOYS and, later, BOB MARLEY's WAILERS. Brother was drummer CARLTON BARRETT. (X) ERROLL WALLACE

BILLY BASS
PAMA 761 I Need Your Love So Bad/I'm Coming To

KEELING BECKFORD

b 6/13/54 (Kingston, JA). Nephew of pianist THEO BECK-FORD.

BIG SHOT 521 Suzie Wong/SWINGING KINGS: Deebo

LYN BECKFORD

JACKPOT 707 Kiss Me Quick/MR MILLER: Feel It

Produced by Bunny Lee.

THEO BECKFORD

CRAB 26 Brother Ram Goat/STARLIGHTS: What a Condition

THE BELTONES

DUKE 17 Home Without You/Why Pretend

HIGH NOTE 017 Mary Mary/Going Away

Produced by Sonia Pottinger.

HIGH NOTE 023 A Broken Heart/AFRO-TONES: All for One

Produced by Sonia Pottinger.

BRUCE BENNETT

UPSETTER 319 Who to Tell/BUSTY BROWN: I Can't See Myself Cry About You

Produced by Lee Perry. (a) An unexpected twist to the typical Lee Perry formula with the inclusion of a horn section, it's a pleasant change of pace, and Bennett belts out the vocals in approving fashion. (b) Brown delivers up one of his greatest performances, accompanied by a superb blues guitar and a melancholy keyboard.

HEDLEY BENNETT

(X) REGGAE BOYS, PETER TOSH

VAL BENNETT

(X) CLANCY ECCLES, DERRICK MORGAN, THE VERSA-TILES

CRAB 6 Reggae City/KING CANNON: Mellow Trumpet

CAMEL 24 Midnight Spin/SOUL CATS: Money Money

UPSETTER 321 Stranger on the Shore/UPSETTERS Drugs & Poison

Produced by Lee Perry. (a) Originally issued as "Popeye on the Shore" (Dr Bird 1136), the UPSETTERS' take on the much-covered 60s classic is as reggaefied as you'd expect, with some great cheesy keyboards. But it's Bennett's superb alto sax which obviously takes center stage. (b) The UPSETTERS' ode to the recently deceased DON DRUMMOND, this is a celebratory single in the upbeat Skatalite sound style, featuring Bennett's impassioned, jazzy sax.

BEVERLEY'S ALL-STARS

(X) MAYTALS, PIONEERS

TROJAN 683 Double Shot/Gimme Gimme Gal

Produced by Leslie Kong. (a) The fabulous bass line comes courtesy of the PIONEERS' "Long Shot," but you'll be weeping and a wailing after hearing the abuse it's put to, unless you're a big fan of harmonicas.

THE BIG L

(X) THE FAMILY CIRCLE

SONNY "SS" BINNS

Keyboard player with the UK-based band THE CIMARRONS.

DOWNTOWN 420 The Untouchables/Lazy Boy

Produced by Dandy Livingstone.

DOWNTOWN 424 Wheels/Night Train

Produced by Dandy Livingstone.

ESCORT 818 Boss a Moon/BUNNY LEE ALL STARS: Brotherly Love

BLACK & GEORGE

(X) RICHARD ACE

WINSTON BLAKE

b 11/19/40 (Morant Bay, JA). Operator of the Mighty Merritone sound system, which he inherited from his father. Also recorded as BLAKE BOY.

CRAB 40 Big Thing/RUPIE EDWARDS: Exclusively Yours

Produced by Rupie Edwards.

PUNCH 13 The Bigger Way/THE ITALS: Chatty Chatty

Produced by Rupie Edwards.

PUNCH 15 Herbert Splifington/THE ITALS: Oh Lord, Why Lord

Produced by Rupie Edwards.

THE BLEECHERS

Vocal trio featuring LEO GRAHAM (ex-OVERTAKERS), WESLEY MARTIN, and former MELLOTONES member SAMMY. The band's name is local slang for people who stay up all night partying. The trio split in 1971, and Graham went solo. (X) BUSTY BROWN, UPSETTERS

TROJAN 679 Ease Up/You're Gonna Feel It

Produced by Byron Lee. (a/b) Recorded at Dynamic; Lee Perry was the actual (uncredited) producer.

UPSETTER 314 Come into My Parlour/MELLOTONES: Dry Up Your Tears

Produced by Lee Perry. (a) Graham has a tinge of Sam Cooke to his vocals, the organ burbles cheerfully along, while the rhythm section seems to be having a great private party of their own; all in all a simmering little single. (b) Not one of their best, the fault lies more with the song, perhaps, than the Mellotones. The melody just doesn't support the vocals, although the singers attempt multi-part harmonies to cover this fact, while the band plink along totally unaware behind them.

THE BLENDERS

(X) THE PIONEERS

BOB & ANDY

(X) LARRY & ALVIN

BOB & TYRONE

Duo featuring BOB ANDY and GARTH EVANS of THE PARAGONS.

COXSONE 7086 I Don't Care/LASCELLES PERKINS: Little Green Apples

Produced by Coxsone Dodd.

JOYCE BOND

PAMA 771 Mr Pitiful/Let's Get Married

KEN BOOTHE

(X) KEITH HUDSON

BAMBOO 4 Pleading/SOUND DIMENSION: Call 1143
Produced by Coxsone Dodd.

BAMBOO 8 Be Yourself/SOUND DIMENSION: Rathid
Produced by Coxsone Dodd.

COXSONE 7094 Sherry/I've Got You
Produced by Coxsone Dodd.

STUDIO ONE 2073 You're on My Mind/RICHARD ACE: Love to Cherish
Produced by Coxsone Dodd. (a) An impossibly catchy keyboard opens the song, before Boothe slides into one of his most heartfelt vocals.

MILTON BOOTHE

(X) ERIC BARNET

THE BOYS

(X) THE AFRO-TONES

BABA BROOKS

(X) HIPPY BOYS

BROTHER DAN ALL-STARS

(X) AUDREY

BUSTY BROWN

(X) DAVE BARKER, BRUCE BENNETT, PAT SATCHMO

PUNCH 10 Broken Heart/Tribute to a King
Produced by Lee Perry.

UPSETTER 304 What a Price/How Can I Forget
Produced by Lee Perry. (a) Those deep, booming, soul vocals are unmistakable. Here the singer works himself into quite a lather over the price he's had to pay for love, while the UPSETTERS bubble potently in the background. (b) Brown takes on a hit by the mighty Marvin Gaye and delivers a vocal tour-de-force. The band wisely keep out of the way, simmering appreciatively in the background.

UPSETTER 308 To Love Somebody/BLEECHERS: Farmers in the Den
Produced by Lee Perry. (a) Brown turns the Bee Gees hit on its head. The upbeat arrangement, all keyboard and guitar flourishes, staccato rhythms, and palpitating bass line makes the song barely recognizable, but the singer's delivery is no less soulful. (b) Ludicrously enough, this is a cover of the old children's song "Farmer in the Dell," appropriately quick tempoed with a reggae beat.

GLEN BROWN & DAVE BARKER

STUDIO ONE 2078 Lady Lovelight/DON DRUMMOND JUNIOR: Heavenless
Produced by Coxsone Dodd.

LENNOX BROWN

(X) NOEL BROWN, PETER TOSH

SONGBIRD 1012 By the Time I Get to Phoenix/Heartbreak Girl
Produced by Derrick Harriott. Also released as BULLET 423.

CARL "CANNONBALL" BRYAN

CAMEL 22 Run for Your Life/TWO SPARKS: When We Were Young

DR BIRD 1180 Reggae this Reggae/JOHNNY MOORE: Big Big Boss

DUKE 13 Soul Pipe/Over Proof
Produced by Duke Reid.

TROJAN 673 Red Ash/SILVERTONES: Bluebirds Flying Over
Produced by Duke Reid.

THE BUTTERCUPS

PAMA 760 Come Put My Life in Order/If I Love You

THE CABLES

(X) ALTON ELLIS

BAMBOO 12 So Long/PRESSURE BOYS: More Love
Produced by Coxsone Dodd.

STUDIO ONE 2085 Got to Find Someone/ALEXANDER HENRY: Please Be True
Produced by Coxsone Dodd.

THE CALEDONIANS

(X) PRINCE BUSTER

FAB 103 Funny Way of Laughing/Don't Please

CALYPSO JOE

ESCORT 800 Adults Only/Calalue
(a) There's no calypso in sight, just a ramshackle vaudevillian beat to power Joe's warnings to young men contemplating matrimony.

NOLA CAMPBELL

GAS 107 Pictures of You/Searching for My Baby

CANNONBALL & JOHNNY MELODY

Featuring CARL BRYAN.

BIG SHOT 518 Parapinto/Cool Hand Luke

CANNONBALL KING

CAMEL 14 Danny Boy/Reggae Happiness

THE CARIBBEANS

CRAB 14 Please Please/MATADORS: Destroyer

DR BIRD 1181 Let Me Walk By/AMBLINGS: Tell Me Why
Produced by Lloyd Charmers. (a) A fairly pedestrian cut by Charmers' usual standards, with the lyric largely comprising the title phrase, and only a keyboard solo to lift things out of the morass.

CECIL & JACKIE

Vocal duo comprising CECIL THOMAS and JACKIE MITTOO.

COXSONE 7083 Breaking Up/SOUND DIMENSION: Scorcia
Produced by Coxsone Dodd.

LLOYD CHARMERS

(X) MARTIN RILEY

CAMEL 30 Confidential/TOMMY COWAN: House in Session

DUKE 25 5 to 5/SOUL STIRRERS: Come See About Me

DUKE 36 Safari/Last Laugh

ESCORT 820 Soul of England/Shanghai

EXPLOSION 2001 Death a Come/Zylon

Produced by Lloyd Charmers. (a) Charmers meets death with a grin on his face, as the keyboardist showcases his flashy talents on this cheery instrumental. (b) A jaunty instrumental which actually became more popular than the a-side both in Jamaica and the UK.

SONGBIRD 1001 Ling Ting Tong/LLOYD ROBINSON: Sweet Sweet

Produced by Derrick Harriott.

SONGBIRD 1007 Duckey Luckey/In the Spirit

Produced by Derrick Harriott. (b) The organ conjures up a reflective mood, the rhythm is unstoppable and the DJ doesn't so much rap as become a crucial instrument in the sound.

THE CHUCKLES

BULLET 416 Run Nigel Run/Come Home

THE CIMARRONS

Britain's first homegrown reggae band. Members have included WINSTON REID (vocals), LOCKSLEY GICHIE (guitar), FRANKLYN DUNN (bass), SONNY BINNS (keyboards). (X) WINSTON GROOVEY

THE CLARENDONIANS

(X) DENNIS WALKS

TREVOR CLARKE

(X) JACKIE MITTOO

THE CLASSICS

Duo featuring DENZIL DENNIS, MILTON HAMILTON. (X) LAUREL AITKEN

CLAUDETTE

JACKPOT 712 Let's Fall in Love/PROPHETS: Purple Moon

Produced by Bunny Lee.

JIMMY CLIFF

TROJAN 690 Wonderful World Beautiful People/Hard Road to Travel

Produced by Jimmy Cliff and Leslie Kong.

THE CLIQUE

(X) LESTER STERLING

THE COBBS

(X) KEN PARKER

AMALGAMATED 845 Hot Buttered Corn/COUNT MACHUKI: It Is I

Produced by Joe Gibbs. (b) The veteran DJ enlivens this jazzy instrumental with a reggae beat.

AMALGAMATED 849 Space Daughter/LLOYD & DEVON: Reggae Baby

Produced by Joe Gibbs.

STRANGER COLE

(X) LESTER STERLING, DELROY WILSON, ERNEST WILSON

AMALGAMATED 838 What Mama Na Want She Get/We Two

Produced by Joe Gibbs.

DUKE 27 Glad You're Living/Help Wanted

(b) Not one of his best. The band gurgles along, but there doesn't seem to actually be a melody. Cole tries to cover this up, but ends up just sounding strident.

ESCORT 810 Pretty Cottage/To Me

ESCORT 819 Leana Leana/Na Na Na

UNITY 501 Last Flight to Reggae City/JUNIOR SMITH: Watch Dem Go

Credited to Cole & TOMMY MCCOOK & THE SUPERSONICS.

UNITY 514 When I Get My Freedom/Life Can Be Beautiful

ANSELL COLLINS

b 4/16/48 (Kingston, JA). A vocalist who debuted at Verejohn's talent show in 1960, Collins joined THE CARIBBEATS, where band-mate BOBBY ELLIS prompted him to learn keyboards. First session was SLIM SMITH's "My Beatitude" for BUNNY LEE. Also a member of RHT INVINCIBLES, featuring singing drummer SLY DUNBAR. Heavily used session organist, scored major UK hits in partnership with DAVE BARKER. (X) ETHIOPIANS, IMMORTALS

TROJAN 699 Night of Love/DERRICK MORGAN: Copy Cat

(b) Ansell Collins steals the show here, as Morgan's smooth delivery actually slows down what could have been an exuberant single. The band are grooving, but the singer just won't join the party.

THE CONCORDS

Vocal group featuring GREGORY ISAACS.

BLUE CAT 170 Buttoo/I Need Your Loving

Produced by Rupie Edwards.

THE CONQUERORS

AMALGAMATED 832 Secret Weapon/Jumpy Jumpy Girl

Produced by Joe Gibbs.

HIGH NOTE 016 If You Can't Beat Them/Anywhere You Want to Go

Produced by Sonia Pottinger.

HIGH NOTE 025 National Dish/Mr DJ

Produced by Sonia Pottinger.

CONROY CANNON MISSION

PAMA 769 Oh Happy Day/I Can't Get Along Without You

THE COOL CATS

BULLET 419 Copy Cat/BUNNY LEE ALL-STARS: Hot Lead

Produced by Bunny Lee.

JOLLY 009 Hold Your Love/ALVA LEWIS: Hang My Head & Cry

COUNT MACHUKI

A professional DJ since 1950, Machuki's domination of the

dance halls was confirmed when he became the first DJ to regularly talk — toast — over records. (X) THE COBBS

TOMMY COWAN

Vocalist with THE JAMAICANS. (X) LLOYD CHARMERS

THE CRASHERS

AMALGAMATED 834 Hurry Come Up/Off Track
Produced by Joe Gibbs. (a) Beholden to THE PIONEERS "Long Shot Kick de Bucket," with the Crashers doing a fair impression of the superstars. Changing the lyrics and the arrangement would only fool the totally ignorant.

THE CREATIONS

(X) LITTLE ROY
PUNCH 2 Mix Up Girl/Qua Kue Shut

THE CRYSTALITES

Convened by producer DERRICK HARRIOTT, the Crystalites was the name applied to the session musicians working with him at any given session. Regulars included HUX BROWN (guitar), JACKIE JACKSON (bass), BORIS GARDINER (bass), GLADSTONE ANDERSON (keyboards), BOBBY ELLIS (trumpet), WINSTON WRIGHT (keyboards), WINSTON GRENNAN (drums), PAUL DOUGLAS (drums), BONGO LES (percussion), BONGO HERMAN (percussion) — aka THE AGGROVATORS, THE ALL STARS, THE DYNAMITES, THE SUPERSONICS, LYNN TAITT'S COMETS/JETS/BOYS, THE UPSETTERS, ETC.

BIG SHOT 510 Biafra/Drop Pan
Produced by Derrick Harriott.

EXPLOSION 2002 Dr Who (parts 1/2)
Produced by Derrick Harriott.

EXPLOSION 2003 Barefoot Brigade/Slippery
Produced by Derrick Harriott. (b) The sax skitters along, the guitar twangs, the organ pipes out and the beat grooves along on this dreamy number in a minor key.

EXPLOSION 2005 Bombshell/Bag a Wire
Produced by Derrick Harriott. (a) This breezily, nonchalant instrumental seems a bit incongruous with its title, but if you're into denial, it's the perfect tune to play when the air raid warning sounds.

EXPLOSION 2006 A Fistful of Dollars/Emperor
Produced by Derrick Harriott.

NU-BEAT 036 Splash Down/Finders Keepers
Produced by Derrick Harriott.

CLIFFORD CURRY

ACTION 4549 She Shot a Hole in My Soul/We're Gonna Hate Ourselves in the Morning

CALVIN DAFOS

DR BIRD 1174 Lash Them/Medicine Master

DANDY

DOWNTOWN 402 Come Back Girl/Shake Me Wake Me
Produced by Dandy Livingstone.

DOWNTOWN 404 Tell Me Darling/Cool Hand Luke
Produced by Dandy Livingstone.

DOWNTOWN 406 Doctor Sure Shot/Put on Your Dancing Shoes
Produced by Dandy Livingstone.

DOWNTOWN 410 Reggae in Your Jeggae/DREAMERS: Reggae Shuffle
Produced by Dandy Livingstone. (a) An unapologetic skinhead fave, perfect to snap your suspenders to, and just fast enough to show off the latest stomp.

DOWNTOWN 415 Rock Steady Gone/Walking Down
Produced by Dandy Livingstone.

DOWNTOWN 416 I'm Your Puppet/Water Boy
Produced by Dandy Livingstone.

DOWNTOWN 421 Games People Play/AUDREY: One Fine Day
Produced by Dandy Livingstone.

DOWNTOWN 429 People Get Ready/RUDIES: Near East
Produced by Dandy Livingstone.

DOWNTOWN 434 Be Natural, Be Proud/Who Do You Want to Run To
Produced by Dandy Livingstone.

DOWNTOWN 437 Come on Home/Love Is All You Need
Produced by Dandy Livingstone.

DOWNTOWN 442 Everybody Loves a Winner/Try Me One More Time
Produced by Dandy Livingstone. (a) The Doris Day chestbeater.

DOWNTOWN 445 Let's Come Together/JAKE WADE: Music Fever
Produced by Dandy Livingstone. (a) Credited to Dandy & THE ISRAELITES.

DANDY WITH AUDREY

(X) Vocal duo featuring DANDY LIVINGSTONE and AUDREY HALL.

DOWNTOWN 411 You Don't Care/Tryer
Produced by Dandy Livingstone.

MELVIN DAVIS

ACTION 4531 Save It/This Love Was Meant to Be

CARL DAWKINS

(X) DENNIS WALKS, WEST INDIANS, WINSTON WRIGHT
NU-BEAT 030 Rodney's History/DYNAMITES: Tribute to Drumbago

NORA DEAN

b 1952, JA. A former member of THE EBONY SISTERS, aka KAY SARAH.

UPSETTER 322 The Same Thing that You Gave to Daddy/ UPSETTER PILGRIMS: A Testimony
Produced by Lee Perry. (a) The percussion provides a touch of calypso flair, and what starts as a sweet lullaby, then turns into innuendos of incest. Lock this song up now. (b) Can I get a witness? The Pilgrims are testifying in their most righteous and soulful manner, "glory, hallelujah," with the brass

capturing the exuberance of the moment, on a song that brings a revivalist tent straight into the studio.

DESMOND DEKKER

PYRAMID 6068 It Mek/Problems

Produced by Leslie Kong. (a) A remix of the earlier Jamaican hit, this punchy version places the emphasis on the beat (while retaining the pretty harmonies) and is further propelled by the blasting brass. (b) Arguably the epitome of Dekker's songwriting, "Problems" combined his vocal talents with the backing singers' and, like a game of tag, they chase each other around the song, in and out, high and low, catching up, breaking away, winding their way across the infectious melody and its gently optimistic lyrics.

THE DELTA CATS

BAMBOO 3 I Can't Relive/I've Been Hurt

Produced by Coxsone Dodd.

THE DEMONS

BIG SHOT 523 You Belong to My Heart/Bless You

DENZIL DENNIS

JOLLY 011 Oh Carol/Where Has My Little Girl Gone

Produced by Dandy Livingstone.

DENZIL & PAT

Vocal duo featuring DENZIL DENNIS and PAT RHODEN of the J- DAN ALL-STARS.

DOWNTOWN 403 Dream/Sincerely

Produced by Dandy Livingstone.

DERRICK & PAULETTE

Vocal duo featuring DERRICK MORGAN and PAULETTE WILLIAMS (EBONY SISTERS).

NU-BEAT 027 I'll Do It/Give You My Love

DEVON & CEDRIC

Vocal duo comprising DEVON RUSSELL and CEDRIC MYTON of THE TARTANS.

BLUE CAT 158 What a Sin Thing/Short Up Dress

DEVON & THE TARTANS

Featuring DEVON RUSSELL.

NU-BEAT 021 Let's Have Some Fun/Making Love

THE DIALS

DUKE 48 Bye Bye Love/It's Love

DUKE 49 Love Is a Treasure/DIAMONDS: I Want to Be

THE DIAMONDS

(X) THE DIALS, SIR COLLINS BAND

DICE THE BOSS

Outfit fronted by UK-based producer JOE MANSANO.

DUKE 51 Gun the Man Down/JOE MANSANO: The Thief

Produced by Joe Mansano.

DUKE 52 But Officer/JOE'S ALL-STARS: Reggae on the Shore

Produced by Joe Mansano.

DUKE 57 Your Boss DJ/TITO SIMON: Read the News

Produced by Joe Mansano.

PAMA DICE

JOE MANSANO project. (X) KING HORROR

JACKPOT 715 Honky Tonk Popcorn/Bongo Man

Produced by Joe Mansano.

JACKPOT 716 Sin Sun & Sex/Reggae Popcorn

Produced by Joe Mansano.

PHYLLIS DILLON

TROJAN 651 Love Is All I Had/Boys & Girls Reggae

Produced by Duke Reid.

TROJAN 671 The Right Track/TOMMY MCCOOK: Moonshot

Produced by Duke Reid. (a) A reggae-lite love song gets the star treatment from the dulcet Dillon, with HOPETON LEWIS curling his own smooth vocals sinuously around her.

TROJAN 686 Lipstick on Your Collar/TOMMY MCCOOK: Tribute to Ramases

Produced by Duke Reid. (a) Dillon takes the Connie Francis hit way too seriously, although the surf guitar and airy flute go someway towards salvaging the song.

BABA DISE

GAS 118 Wanted/SENSATIONS: I'll Always Love You

ERROL DIXON

DR BIRD 1197 Why Hurt Yourself/She Started to Scream

DOBBY DOBSON

BLUE CAT 171 Strange/Your New Love

Also released as PUNCH 4.

PUNCH 12 The Masquerade Is Over/Love for Ambition

DODD'S ALL-STARS

Coxsone Dodd's studio band under another guise.

COXSONE 7096 Mother Aitken/What a Love

Produced by Coxsone Dodd.

ERIC DONALDSON

b 6/11/47 (JA). Ex-WEST INDIANS. The most successful ever performer in the Festival Song Competition — following his best-remembered victory in 1971 ("Cherry Oh Baby"), further victories followed in 1977, 1978, 1984, 1993, and 1997.
(X) PAT SATCHMO

LLOYD DOUGLAS

(X) DAVID ISAACS

THE DOWNTOWN ALL-STARS

Session band for DANDY LIVINGSTONE's Downtown label.

DOWNTOWN 426 Everybody Feels Good/RUDIES: Downtown Jump

Produced by Dandy Livingstone.

THE DREAMERS

(X) DANDY

DOWNTOWN 407 Sweet Chariot/Let's Go Downtown

Produced by Dandy Livingstone.

DOWNTOWN 408 I Second that Emotion/Dear Love
Produced by Dandy Livingstone.

DRUMBAGO

(X) CLANCY ECCLES

DON DRUMMOND JUNIOR

(X) GLEN BROWN & DAVE BARKER, JOHN HOLT, THE TOBIES

DUKE MORGAN

(X) ALTON ELLIS

ERROL DUNKLEY

(X) MR VERSATILE

FAB 117 I'll Take You in My Arms/KING CANNON: Daphney Reggae

THE DYNAMICS

PUNCH 1 The Burner/Juckie Juckie

THE DYNAMITES

(X) CARL DAWKINS, CLANCY ECCLES, KING STITT

THE EAGLES

SONGBIRD 1006 Rudam Bam/Prodigal Boy
Produced by Derrick Harriott.

THE EARTHQUAKES

DUKE 56 Earthquake/Simmering

DUKE 54 Pair of Wings/I Can't Stop Loving You

THE EBONY SISTERS

Featuring PAULETTE & GEE WILLIAMS; NORA DEAN is also believed to have been a member. May also have recorded as THE SOUL SISTERS.

BULLET 401 Let Me Tell You/RHYTHM RULERS: Mannix

CLANCY ECCLES

(X) KING STITT

DUKE 30 Fire Corner/THE DYNAMITES: John Public
Produced by Clancy Eccles. (a) The organ wades in with flourishes of melody, but this rhythm/riff heavy single is just a showcase for DJ KING STITT, making his recorded debut by shouting the title and generally exhorting the audience to their feet.

CLANDISC 201 The World Needs Loving/DYNAMITES: Dollar Train
Produced by Clancy Eccles.

DUKE 9 Auntie Lulu/SLICKERS: Bag a Boo
Produced by Clancy Eccles.

DUKE 31 Shoo Be Do /THE DYNAMITES: I Don't Care
Produced by Clancy Eccles.

TROJAN 638 China Man/DRUMBAGO: Dulcemania
Produced by Clancy Eccles.

TROJAN 639 Sweet Africa/Let Us Be Lovers
Produced by Clancy Eccles.

TROJAN 647 Bangarang Crash/DYNAMITES: Rathid
Produced by Clancy Eccles. (a) Eccles has a grand time with this punchy number, driven by the pulsing bass, ALVA LEWIS' signature guitar and GLEN ADAMS' keyboards, with the backing vocalists joining in enthusiastically. Lewis and Eccles both rate this the first ever "reggae" record. (b) Carnival-esque in mood, this bright instrumental is all light-hearted horns and flowery flute, fueled by a compulsive beat.

TROJAN 648 Constantinople/Deacon Sun
Produced by Clancy Eccles.

TROJAN 649 Demonstration/VAL BENNETT: My Girl
Produced by Clancy Eccles.

TROJAN 658 Fattie Fattie/SILVERSTARS: Last Call
Produced by Clancy Eccles. (a) Forgetting the question of why, if he really loved the lady, he interminably refers to her as "fattie fattie," Eccles was still onto a winner here. A great bass line vies with the catchy melody, with the infectious chorus just puts it over the edge. The English 2-Tone band Bad Manners would build their career on this number. (b) This instrumental epitomizes the good time song, from the individual musicians that make the most of their 15 seconds in the spotlight, down to its clopping beat, all encased in a beerily grinning melody.

JACKIE EDWARDS

DIRECTION 4096 Why Must I Be Alone/I'm Gonna Make You Cry

DIRECTION 4402 Too Experienced/Someone to Love

DIRECTION 4630 Oh Manio/Here We Go Again

RUPIE EDWARDS

(X) WINSTON BLAKE

BLUE CAT 169 Long Lost Love/SOUL KINGS: The Magnificent Seven
Produced by Rupie Edwards.

CRAB 35 Long Lost Love/Uncertain Love
Produced by Rupie Edwards.

SAMUEL EDWARDS

BLUE CAT 159 Want It Want It/SPARKERS: Israel

ALTON ELLIS

BAMBOO 2 Better Example/DUKE MORGAN: Lick It Back
Produced by Coxsone Dodd.

DUKE 14 Diana/Some Talk
Produced by Duke Reid. Also released as GAS 105.

DUKE REID 2501 What Does It Take to Win Our Love/TOMMY MCCOOK: Reggae Meringue
Produced by Duke Reid. (a) Surprisingly, this doesn't hold a candle to the Jr. Walker original, sabotaged as it is by the reggae-pop-lite arrangement. Still, Ellis is in great form.

STUDIO ONE 2084 Change of Plans/CABLES: He'll Break Your Heart
Produced by Coxsone Dodd.

THE EMOTIONS

DOWNTOWN 446 Give Me Love/HORACE FAITH: Daddy's Home
Produced by Ken Lack.

HIGH NOTE 018 The Storm/Easy Squeeze
Produced by Sonia Pottinger.

HIGH NOTE 026 Rum Baby/PATSY: Find Someone
Produced by Sonia Pottinger.

EMPEROR
PAMA 786 Karate/I've Got to Have Her

JUNIOR ENGLISH
b Lindal Beresford English, 1951 (Kingston, JA). Launched his career in the UK, as a member of THE MAGNETS.
CAMEL 35 Nobody Knows/TONY SEXTON: Somewhere

THE ETERNALS
Fronted by CORNELL CAMPBELL.
COXSONE 7091 Queen of the Minstrels/Stars
Produced by Coxsone Dodd.

THE ETHIOPIANS
(X) BOB ANDY
CRAB 7 I Am a King/What a Big Surprise
DR BIRD 1172 Not Me/Cut Down
Produced by Lee Perry.
DR BIRD 1185 Hong Kong Flu/Clap Your Hands
Produced by JJ Johnson.
DR BIRD 1186 What a Fire/You
Produced by JJ Johnson.
DR BIRD 1199 Everyday Talking/Sharing You
Produced by JJ Johnson.
DUKE 35 My Girl/ANSELL COLLINS: Bigger Boss
(b) DJ SIR HARRY roasts the crowd as organist Collins runs lightly across the keys, on this light-hearted, dance friendly number.
NU-BEAT 031 My Testimony/JJ ALL-STARS: One Dollar of Soul
Produced by JJ Johnson.
NU-BEAT 038 Buss Your Mouth/REGGAE BOYS: Rough Away Ahead
TROJAN 666 Woman Capture Man/One
TROJAN 697 Well Red/JJ ALL-STARS: One Dollar of Soul
Produced by JJ Johnson.

THE FABIONS
BULLET 410 V Rocket/Smile

HORACE FAITH
(X) THE EMOTIONS
B&C 104 Spinning Wheel/Like I Used to Do

THE FAMILY CIRCLE
ATTACK 8001 Phoenix Reggae/BIG L: Music Box
ATTACK 8004 By The Time I Get to Phoenix/BIG L: Hungry Man
ATTACK 8005 Stagger Back/BIG L: The Show Boat

ERIC FATTER
(X) THE AFRO-TONES
CAMEL 20 Since You've Been Gone/WINSTON HINES: Cool Down

THE FEDERALS
HIGH NOTE 024 Wailing Festival/Me & My Baby
Produced by Sonia Pottinger.

THE FLAMES
NU-BEAT 028 You've Lost Your Love/Little Girl

LESLIE FOSTER
JOLLY 022 Muriel/Nowhere to Hide

VINCENT FOSTER
ESCORT 803 Shine Eye Gal/Who Nest

WILLIE FRANCIS
Later moved into production, remembered for cutting the first ever single by COCOA TEA, "Searching in the Hills" (1974, under the name CALVIN SCOTT).
BULLET 415 Motherless Children/I Am Not Afraid

WINSTON FRANCIS
Vocalist with THE MELLOTONES.
BAMBOO 10 The Same Old Song/SOUND DIMENSION: Rattle On
Produced by Coxsone Dodd.
COXSONE 7089 Reggae & Cry/FREEDOM SINGERS: Easy Come Easy Go
Produced by Coxsone Dodd.
PUNCH 5 Too Experienced/JACKIE MITTOO: Mule Jerk
Produced by Coxsone Dodd.
STUDIO ONE 2086 The Games People Play/ALBERT GRIFFITHS: The Kicks
Produced by Coxsone Dodd.

BONNIE FRANKSON
JOLLY 014 Loving You/Shoo Be Do
JOLLY 021 London City/Dearest

NORMA FRAZIER
BAMBOO 13 Working/SOUND DIMENSION: Whoopee
Produced by Coxsone Dodd.

THE FREEDOM SINGERS
(X) WINSTON FRANCIS

BORIS GARDINER
b 1/13/46. Renowned session vocalist and bassist, ex-CARLOS MALCOLM & THE AFRO CARIBS, also performed with RHYTHM ACES, BYRON LEE & THE DRAGONAIRES. Played the tourist circuit during much of the 1960s, before joining the Kingston session scene; was a regular with THE AGGROVATORS, CRYSTALITES, etc. Scored UK hits with "Elizabethan Reggae" (1969), "I Want to Wake Up with You" and "You're Everything to Me" (1986).
DR BIRD 1205 Elizabethan Reggae/Hooked on a Feeling
Produced by Byron Lee. (a) This fast-paced hit was as light as a feather and virtually spun off the dancefloor, the delicate flute and tinkling piano giving it just a touch of baroque.
DUKE 21 Never My Love/The Old One
HIGH NOTE 010 Lucky Is the Boy/Bobby Sox to Stockings
Produced by Sonia Pottinger.

THE GAYLADS

TROJAN 688 You Had Your Chance/Wha' She Do Now

UPSETTER 323 The Same Things/I Wear My Slanders

Produced by Lee Perry. (a) Originally cut for Randys as "Room for Rent," the Gaylads go bubblerock with a reggae beat. It's an interesting change of pace and what the song lacks in a strong hook, it makes up for with charming harmonies. (b) A tinkling keyboard highlights this single about not judging a book by its cover, with an unexceptional melody, but lovely vocal delivery.

THE GAYLETS

BIG SHOT 516 Son of a Preacher Man/That's How Strong My Love Is

Produced by Lynford Anderson.

THE GAYTONES

(X) DELANO STEWART

BILL GENTLES

Treasure Isle protege later recorded for BUNNY LEE, before relocating to the UK and becoming producer in his own right. Died in the early 1990s.

GAS 104 Long Life/SCHOOLBOYS: O Tell Me

(a) This celebratory single showcases a particularly hammy Hammond, a roiling rhythm, and Gentles' upbeat religious message.

GG RHYTHM SECTION

Session band for producer ALVIN RANGLIN. aka GG ALL STARS. (X) MAYTONES, VERNE & ALVIN

GIRL SATCHMO

FAB 111 Take You for a Ride/I'm Coming Home

Also released as TROJAN 676.

GIRLIE

BULLET 400 Madama Straggae/LAUREL AITKEN: Stupid Married Man

GIRLIE & JUNIOR

DUKE 42 African Meeting/JOSH: Higher & Higher

THE GLADIATORS

BAMBOO 7 Anywhere/SOUND DIMENSION: Baby Face

Produced by Coxsone Dodd.

DUKE 58 My Girl/You Were to Be

GLEN & DAVE

(X) KING CANNON

TROJAN 675 La La Always Stays the Same/HARRY J ALL STARS: LIQUIDATOR

Produced by Harry J. (b) Originally a version variation on Tony Scott's "What Am I to Do?," Harry J oversaw his All-Stars (actually the HIPPY BOYS) for this instrumental masterpiece, driven by a bass line borrowed from the Staple Singers' "I'll Take You There," and revved up by WINSTON

WRIGHT's masterful, bubbling organ and VAL BENNET's superb tenor sax.

VIN GORDON

COXSONE 7085 Soul Trombone (Suffering Stink)/LARRY & ALVIN: Your Cheating Heart

Produced by Coxsone Dodd.

CRAB 16 Walking By/VICEROYS: Promises Promises

DUKE 37 Everybody Bawlin'/SILVERTONES: Come Look Here

Produced by Duke Reid.

HERBIE GRAY & THE RUDIES

(X) OWEN GRAY, OWEN & DANDY, TONY TRIBE

OWEN GRAY

BLUE CAT 156 I Can't Stop Loving You/Tell Me Darling

CAMEL 25 Girl What You Doing to Me/Woman a Grumble

CAMEL 34 Don't Take Your Love Away/Two Lovers

CAMEL 37 Every Beat of My Heart/Don't Cry

DOWNTOWN 423 Groovin'/HERBIE GRAY & THE RUDIES: Kitty Wait

DUKE 12 Reggae Dance/I Know

Produced by Duke Reid. (a) The veteran vocalist takes on the new style, but does he go tough or sweet? Undecided on what's required, Gray goes soul on the chorus and smooth on the verse.

DUKE 33 Seven Lonely Days/He Don't Love You Like I Do

Produced by Duke Reid.

FAB 90 Three Coins in the Fountain/Tennessee Waltz

FAB 96 Ay Ay Ay/Let It Be Me

FAB 120 Understand My Love/Apollo 12

TROJAN 650 I Can't Stop Loving You/Tell Me Darling

TROJAN 670 Too Experienced/I Really Loved You Baby

ROOSEVELT GRIER

PAMA 774 Who's Got the Ball (Parts 1/2)

PAMA 784 C'mon Cupid/High Society Woman

ALBERT GRIFFITHS

Member of THE GLADIATORS. (X) WINSTON FRANCIS

MARCIA GRIFFITHS

ESCORT 808 Don't Let Me Down/REGGAEITES: Romper Room

GAS 111 Tell Me Now/STAN HOPE: The Weight

(a) Another smash from BOB ANDY's irrepressible pen, performed by the era's finest female vocalist. An irresistible combination.

HIGH NOTE 029 Talk (Parts 1/2)

Produced by Sonia Pottinger.

TROJAN 693 Put a Little Love in Your Heart/J BOYS: Jay Fever

JOE GRINNE

COXSONE 7098 Mr Editor/How I Feel

Produced by Coxsone Dodd.

WINSTON GROOVEY

b Winston Tucker, 1946 (JA). Relocated to UK in 1972. (X) KING HORROR

GRAPE 3005 Leaving Me Standing/Little Girl
GRAPE 3008 Merry Xmas/I Am Lonely
JACKPOT 708 Funky Chicken/CIMARRONS: Pt. 2
JACKPOT 709 Funny/CIMARRONS: Version
NU-BEAT 041 Island in the Sun/Work It Up

(a) With the Paragons as his blueprint, Groovy turns the old Harry Belafonte hit into a rock steady classic, all lush vocals ringing with passion and a touch of spirituality.

NU-BEAT 042 Josephine/Champagne & Wine

GROSSETT
CRAB 10GG Run Girl Run/DENNIS WALKS: The Drifter
Produced by Alvin Ranglin.
CRAB 34GG Greater Sounds/Live the Life I Love
Produced by Alvin Ranglin.

LANCE HANNIBAL
BLUE CAT 148 Read the News/RICO & THE RHYTHM ACES: Return of the Bullet

THE HARMONIANS
(X) WINSTON SHAN, TONY

THE HARMONISERS
DUKE 32 Mother Hen/WINSTON SINCLAIR: Chastise Them

DERRICK HARRIOTT
BIG SHOT 505 Standing In/Bumble Bee
Produced by Derrick Harriott.
BIG SHOT 511 Another Lonely Night/Been So Long
Produced by Derrick Harriott.

HARRY & RADCLIFFE
CAMEL 26 History/Just Be Alone
Also released as PUNCH 8.

ALEXANDER HENRY
(X) THE CABLES

THE HEPTONES
BAMBOO 11 I Shall Be Released/Love Me Always
Produced by Coxsone Dodd. (a) Great in theory, less so in reality. The trio give the Dylan classic their spiritual best, but the band boogieing in the background have obviously confused a Sunday service with a Saturday night party. The rhythm was later utilized by I-ROY for his classic "Black Man Time." Also released as STUDIO ONE 2083.
COXSONE 7082 Soul Power/Love Me Always
Produced by Coxsone Dodd.
COXSONE 7092 Sweet Talking/Ob-La Di
Produced by Coxsone Dodd. (a) Dodd kept things simple here—a driving, but not overpowering beat married to a keyboard that merely keeps the time, allowing LEROY SIBBLES plenty of space to unleash his most emotive and seductive vocals.

LENNIE HIBBERT
COXSONE 7093 Village Soul/SOUND DIMENSION: More Scorcia
Produced by Coxsone Dodd.

HIGGS & WILSON
(X) KING STITT

JUSTIN HINDS
TROJAN 652 You Should've Known Better/TOMMY MCCOOK & THE SUPERSONICS: Third Figure
Produced by Duke Reid.

WINSTON HINES
(X) ERIC FATTER

THE HIPPY BOYS
Early line-ups featured MAX ROMEO and LEROY BROWN of THE EMOTIONS, plus THE GAYLADS (BB SEATON, DELANO STEWART, MAURICE ROBERTS), WEB STEWART (guitar—ex-THE ASTRONAUTS), ASTON, and CARLTON BARRETT (bass/drums). Web departed; subsequent members included LORRAINE "RONNIE/RANNY BOP" WILLIAMS and ALVA LEWIS (guitar), GLEN ADAMS (keyboards). Sessioned as HARRY J'S ALL STARS, also with Bunny Lee, Lloyd Daley, Sonia Pottinger. When GLADDY'S ALL STARS were unable to tour the UK with LEE PERRY in late 1969, Lewis, Barrett, and Glen Adams became the next generation of UPSETTERS. (X) TONY KING, THE PIONEERS, RONNY WILLIAMS
BULLET 412 Hog in a Me Minte/Lorna Run
BULLET 413 What's Your Excuse/Tell Me Tell
CAMEL 29 Cat Nip/Cooyah
HIGH NOTE 021 Doctor No Go/Sailing
Produced by Sonia Pottinger.
HIGH NOTE 030 Chicken Lickin'/BABA BROOKS: Old Man Flint
Produced by Sonia Pottinger.
TROJAN 668 Love/The Whole Family
TROJAN 669 Michael Row the Boat Ashore/Who Is Coming to Dinner
UNITY 528 Dreams to Remember/Peace Maker

JOHN HOLT
TROJAN 653 I Want You Closer/DANNY SIMPSON: Outa Sight
TROJAN 661 Ali Baba/I'm Your Man
TROJAN 674 What You Gonna Do/Have You Ever Been to Heaven
TROJAN 678 Darling I Love You/DON DRUMMOND JUNIOR: Memory of Don
TROJAN 694 Have Sympathy/HARRY J ALL-STARS: Spryone
Produced by Harry J.

STAN HOPE
(X) MARCIA GRIFFITHS

THE HOT ROD ALL-STARS
DUKE 59 Lick a Pop/Treasure

KEITH HUDSON

See entry: DIRECTORY OF PRODUCERS. Also recorded as a duo with DENNIS ALCAPONE, CHUCKLES.

BIG SHOT 528 Tambourine Man/KEN BOOTHE: Old Fashioned Way

Produced by Keith Hudson. (b) A Ken Boothe composition and Hudson's first Jamaican hit as a producer. (It actually debuted his Inbidimts label.) This soulful rocker was driven by a street wise rhythm, a memorable melody, a tight arrangement, and Boothe himself at his most exciting.

DELLA HUMPHREY

ACTION 4525 Don't Make the Good Girls Go Bad/Your Love Is All I Need

THE IMMORTALS

AMALGAMATED 851 Bonjo Jah/ANSELL COLLINS: My Last Waltz

Produced by Joe Gibbs.

THE IMPERIALS

BULLET 417 Black Is Soul/Always with You

THE IMPERSONATORS

BIG SHOT 524 Make It Easy on Yourself/I've Tried Before

(a) Ah, but who are they impersonating? Certainly not the American vocal group the Walker Brothers, who turned in the definitive rendering of this heart-stopping big ballad.

THE INSPIRATIONS

Vocal duo featuring TREVOR SHAW and RANSFORD WHITE. Duo also worked under aliases JIMMY LONDON (Shaw) and BILLY DYCE (White) as THE UNTOUCHABLES. (X) LEE PERRY

CAMEL 11 Down in the Park/Love Oh Love

CAMEL 21 Wonder of Love/Cinderella

DAVID ISAACS

PUNCH 6 I Can't Take It Anymore/LLOYD DOUGLAS: Anyway

Produced by Lee Perry. (a) Isaacs delicate vocals are just about overwhelmed by the band. A slower tempo and muted musicians might have helped.

UPSETTER 302 Good Father/SLIM SMITH: What a Situation

Produced by Lee Perry. (a) Isaacs waxes eloquently about the perfect pater, while the band stampedes happily by. Yet another odd coupling of reggae masters meet heartthrob. (b) There's no hook, the melody is barely noticeable, but the mighty Smith doesn't care. It's all in the delivery and here, he gives a performance so powerful it'll curl your toes.

UPSETTER 305 I've Got Memories/Leaving on a Jet Plane

Produced by Lee Perry. (a) Isaacs goes soul for this driving, upbeat number, with the sax, organ, and guitar combining to emphasize the beat and add some stirring flourishes. (b) Yes, indeed it's a cover of the Peter, Paul, and Mary hit, the band (Studio One's SOUND DIMENSION) take a light hearted view of it all, but Isaacs doesn't seem to get the joke, more's the pity.

UPSETTER 311 He'll Have to Go/Since You Are Gone

Produced by Lee Perry. (a) This version of the much covered Jim Reeves' hit might have been tolerable, as Isaacs's vocals are heartfelt and the band simmers suitably in the background, but the off-key backing singers ruin it. (b) The happy Hammond, upbeat rhythm and brightly strumming guitar are pretty incongruous for this heart breaker of a song, although Isaacs delivers with aplomb.

THE ISRAELITES

DOWNTOWN 413 Moma Moma/Melody for Two

Produced by Dandy Livingstone.

DOWNTOWN 433 Seven Books/Chaka Beat

Produced by Dandy Livingstone.

THE ITALS

(X) WINSTON BLAKE

HARRY J ALL-STARS

House band for producer HARRY J. (X) GLEN & DAVE, JOHN HOLT

JACK & THE BEANSTALKS

SUPREME 203 Work It Up/Chatty Chatty

THE JAMAICANS

ESCORT 806 Early in the Morning/Mr Lovely

WINSTON JARRETT

9/14/40 (St Anne, JA). Leader of THE RIGHTEOUS FLAMES. (X) MAD LADS

UPSETTER 306 Mini Dress (aka Where the Lights Are Low)/LEE PERRY: Mad House

Produced by Lee Perry. (a) Never quite coming together, at times the UPSETTERS seem to be loudly playing an entirely different song. Too much instrumentation, not enough melody. (b) The BARRETT brothers groove along unconcernedly as Perry shouts madly, the sax blares obligingly along, and a metal sheet is clattered to add to the insanity.

THE JAY BOYS

(X) TREVOR SHIELD

JJ ALL-STARS

(X) THE ETHIOPIANS

TROJAN 691 Memphis Underground (Parts 1/2)

(a/b) A fancy free flute skipping gaily along is the light-hearted focus of this instrumental, carried on its way by the percolating beat and muted accents of the rest of the band.

JOE'S ALL-STARS

Outfit fronted by UK-based producer JOE MANSANO. (X) DICE THE BOSS, KING HORROR, PATTI LADONNE

DUKE 24 Hey Jude/Musical Feet

Produced by Joe Mansano.

DUKE 28 Battle Cry of Biafra/Funky Reggae Part One

Produced by Joe Mansano.

DUKE 50 Brixton Cat/Solitude
Produced by Joe Mansano.

LYDON JOHNS
DOWNTOWN 444 Don't Gamble with Love/Songbird
Produced by Dandy Livingstone.
DOWNTOWN 451 Oh Mama Oh Papa/Bring Back the Night
Produced by Dandy Livingstone.

SAMMY JONES
(X) HONEYBOY MARTIN

JOSH
(X) GIRLIE & JUNIOR
DUKE 41 Judge/RON: Soul of Joemel

KEITH & TEX
EXPLOSION 2008 Tighten Up Your Gird/Look to the Sky

PAT KELLY
(X) WONDER BOY
GAS 110 The Workman Song/Never Give Up
Produced by Bunny Lee.
GAS 115 How Long/Try to Remember
Produced by Bunny Lee.(a) The BARRETT brothers created the hypnotic rhythm for this yearning love song, penned by the former TECHNIQUE. Kelly delivers a tour de force with a hint of Sam Cooke in his passionate vocals, while pianist CHARMERS lives up to his name.
GAS 124 Festival Time (Parts 1/2)
Produced by Bunny Lee.
GAS 125 If It Don't Work Out/I Am Coming Home
Produced by Bunny Lee.

KID GUNGO
ESCORT 801 Hold the Pussy/KING CANNON: Wh-a-pen

KING CANNON
(X) VAL BENNETT, ERROL DUNKLEY, KID GUNGO, MAX ROMEO, TREVOR SHIELD
UNITY 517 Five Card Stud/LESTER STERLING: 1000 Tons of Megaton
TROJAN 663 Soul Scorcher/GLEN & DAVE: Lucky Boy
Produced by Harry J. (a) A truly disturbing amalgamation of moody blues, BENNETT's bright sax, and a pulsing bass that somehow all comes together on this searing single.

KING HORROR
Entertaining and risque in equal proportions, this UK artist was one of the few 1960s-era British reggae performers whose work was successfully exported back to Jamaica.
DUKE 34 Dracula Prince of Darkness/ JOE'S ALL-STARS: Honky
Produced by Joe Mansano.
JACKPOT 713 Wood in the Fire/The Naked City
Produced by Laurel Aitken.
JACKPOT 714 Police/PAMA DICE: Honky Tonk Popcorn
Produced by Laurel Aitken.

GRAPE 3003 Cutting Blade/Vampire
Produced by Laurel Aitken.
GRAPE 3006 The Hole/WINSTON GROOVEY: Lover Come Back
Produced by Laurel Aitken.
GRAPE 3007 Loch Ness Monster/VISIONS: Zion I
Produced by Laurel Aitken.

KING STITT
A star at Coxsone Dodd's Number One set sound system, a pioneering disc jockey best associated with CLANCY ECCLES. (X) CYNTHIA RICHARDS
CLANDISC 200 Who Yeah/DYNAMITES: Mr Midnight
Produced by Clancy Eccles.
CLANDISC 202 Vigorton Two/In the Street
Produced by Clancy Eccles. (a) Arranged by Eccles and LEE PERRY, a DJ classic set to an infectious reggae beat, enhanced by a catchy keyboard melody, with the great Stitt exclaiming over it all.
CLANDISC 206 The Ugly One/CLANCY ECCLES: The Dance Beat
Produced by Clancy Eccles.

KING STITT & ANDY
CLANDISC 207 Herbsman Shuffle/HIGGS & WILSON: Don't Mind Me
Produced by Clancy Eccles. (a) King Stitt tempts the audience with his signature DJ style over a solid riff and infectious organ. "Take a drag," he offers over and over again, then takes a long, loud toke as further temptation. (b) Two of the best voices of the 60s entwine again, on a cool, soulful rocker.

TONY KING & THE HIPPY BOYS
TROJAN 667 Proud Mary/My Devotion

THE KINGSTONIANS
BIG SHOT 508 Sufferer/Kiss a Little Finger
(a) Contrary to its suffering title and despondent lyrics, this song is ludicrously bright and cheery sounding, a feeling abetted by a happy Hammond, an up-tempo beat and the bright melody and harmonies. One of the Kingstonians' better efforts.
BIG SHOT 526 Nice Nice/I'll Be Around
BULLET 409 I Am Just a Minstrel/Yesterday
CRAB 20 Hold Down/BARRY YORK: Who Will She Be
SONGBIRD 1011 The Clip/BRUCE ANTHONY: Little Miss Muffett
Produced by Derrick Harriott.

PATTIE LADONNE
DUKE 23 Friends & Lovers/JOE'S ALL-STARS: Hot Line
Produced by Joe Mansano.

DENZIL LAING
(X) SOUL VENDORS

JOYA LANDIS
TROJAN 641 Moonlight Lover/I Love You True

Produced by Duke Reid. (a) Landis pulled out all the emotional stops for this ballad. The accompaniment is a little overly busy and noisy, but the singer's vocals are strong enough to take control regardless.

LARRY & ALVIN

Vocal duo comprising LARRY MARSHALL and ALVIN LESLIE. (X) VIN GORDON, JACK SPRATT

COXSONE 7081 Love Got Me/BOB & ANDY: Lady with the Bright Light
Produced by Coxsone Dodd.

STUDIO ONE 2080 Lonely Room/You Mean to Me
Produced by Coxsone Dodd.

LAXTON & OLIVER

BLUE CAT 168 Wickeder/Stay in My Arms

BUNNY LEE ALL STARS

Producer BUNNY LEE's studio band. (X) SS BINNS, COOL CATS

BYRON LEE & THE DRAGONAIRES

DUKE 39 Elizabethan Reggae/Soul Serenade
Produced by Byron Lee. (a) Apparently, Lee learned to love this classical piece at carnival in Trinidad, where it had long been a staple of the steel band repertoire. Lee cut two versions, one credited to BORIS GARDINER, which became a major UK hit, and this slower paced one. It's majestic either way, though, as the stately mood- swinging keyboard spins the melody round the floor, but when the guitarist tries to cut in, he is quickly elbowed away.

MAJOR MINOR MM615 Every Day Will Be Like a Holiday/Oh What a Feeling
Produced by Byron Lee.

DON TONY LEE

UNITY 519 Peyton Place/Red Gal in The Ring
Produced by Bunny Lee.

GEORGE LEE

(X) DESMOND RILEY

DOWNTOWN 443 Talking Boss/Jungle Fever
Produced by Dandy Livingstone.

WARREN LEE

PAMA 762 Underdog Backstreet/Come Put My Life in Order

LEONIE & THE JOE NOLAN BAND

JOLLY 015 Move & Groove/Don't Let Me Do It

ALVA LEWIS

(X) COOL CATS

LITTLE BOY BLUE

(X) MR VERSATILE

LITTLE ROY

aka EARL LOWE.

CAMEL 36 Bongo Nyah/CREATIONS: Bad Name

Produced by Lloyd Daley. (a) "Baa Baa Black Sheep" meets its maker, a nursery rhyme with distinctly apocalyptic overtones.

CRAB 39 Without My Love/WINSTON SAMUELS: Here I Come Again
Produced by Lloyd Daley.

LLOYD & DEVON

Vocal duo comprising LLOYD ROBINSON and DEVON RUSSELL of THE TARTANS. (X) THE COBBS

BLUE CAT 151 Out of the Fire/Can't Understand

PUNCH 14 Love Is the Key/VIRTUES: High Tide
Produced by Rupie Edwards.

LLOYD'S ALL-STARS

(X) THE UNIQUES

LORD POWER

COXSONE 7079 Temptation/AL & THE VIBRATORS: Change Everything
Produced by Coxsone Dodd.

EDDIE LOVETTE

BIG SHOT 519 You're My Girl/Let Them Say

THE LYRICS

(X) THE VICEROYS

THE MAD LADS

COXSONE 7099 Losing You/WINSTON JARRETT: Peck Up a Pagan
Produced by Coxsone Dodd.

STAVELY MAKEPEACE

PYRAMID 6072 Mad Dog/Greasy Haired Woman

PYRAMID 6082 Tarzan Harvey/Reggae Denny

JOE MANSANO

UK record producer, responsible for a host of skinhead reggae cult classics often credited to and revolving around the misadventures of the miscreant Pama Dice. (X) DICE THE BOSS

BLUE CAT 150 Life on Reggae Planet/RICO & THE RHYTHM ACES: ZZ Beat
Produced by Joe Mansano.

C MARSHALL

(X) JACKIE MITTOO & THE SOUND DIMENSION

BAMBOO 9 I Need Your Loving/SOUND DIMENSION: Jamaica Rag
Produced by Coxsone Dodd.

LARRY MARSHALL

(X) MAX ROMEO

HONEYBOY MARTIN

GAS 123 Unchained Melody/SAMMY JONES: You're My Girl

MATADOR ALL-STARS

Studio band for producer LLOYD DALEY. (X) JACKIE MITTOO, VICEROYS

THE MATADORS

(X) THE CARIBBEANS

THE MAX GROUP

FAB 110 Abraham Vision/My Heart Was Breaking

THE MAYTALS

PYRAMID 6070 Aldina/Hold On

Produced by Leslie Kong.

PYRAMID 6073 Pressure Drop/BEVERLEY'S ALL-STARS: Express

Produced by Leslie Kong. (a) Not only would this searing serenade to ghetto existence turn up on the *The Harder They Come* soundtrack, it reappeared again on the trio's own *Funky Kingston* album. Arguably the Maytals' finest single, it absolutely quivers with TOOTS HIBBERT's heartfelt emotion, the harmonies are gorgeous, the beat compulsive, and the melody unforgettable.

PYRAMID 6074 Sweet and Dandy/Oh Yeah

Produced by Leslie Kong. (a) Winner of the 1969 Festival Song Competition a full three years before it was included on the *The Harder They Come* soundtrack. As always, HIBBERT's vocals are sublime, but it's MATHIAS' backing falsetto, echoed by GORDON's deep tenor, that made this song a classic. (b) The grandiloquent soulful refrain is the hook which holds a petulant lyric together.

TROJAN 7808 54–46 Was My Number/BEVERLEY'S ALL-STARS: Version

Produced by Leslie Kong.

THE MAYTONES

Originally a vocal trio comprising ALVIN RANGLIN, VERNON BUCKLEY, and GLADSTONE GRANT. Buckley and Ranglin also recorded as a duo. Ranglin subsequently quit to concentrate on production. Buckley and Grant continued on through a string of underground hits, before returning to Ranglin in the mid-1970s with a new roots sound. Renamed the MIGHTY MAYTONES, the duo continued on into the late 1970s.

BLUE CAT 149 Billy Goat/Call You Up

Produced by Alvin Ranglin.

BLUE CAT 152 Loving Reggae/Musical Beat

Produced by Alvin Ranglin.

BLUE CAT 165 Botheration/GG RHYTHM SECTION: TNT

Produced by Alvin Ranglin.

BLUE CAT 166 Copper Girl/Love

Produced by Alvin Ranglin.

BLUE CAT 173 We Nah Tek You Lick/Dig Away de Money

Produced by Alvin Ranglin.

CAMEL 27 Sentimental Reason/Lover Girl

Produced by Alvin Ranglin. Reissued as EXPLOSION 2013.

SONGBIRD 1009 I've Been Loving You/Memphis Reggae

Produced by Derrick Harriott.

SONGBIRD 1010 Gin Gan Goolie/I'm Thirsty

Produced by Derrick Harriott.

VINCENT MCCLEOD

JACKPOT 711 Too Late/SIR COLLINS: Late Night

TOMMY MCCOOK

(X) LAUREL AITKEN, PHYLLIS DILLON, ALTON ELLIS, JUSTIN HINDS, MELODIANS, LESTER STERLING, TENORS

TROJAN 642 Breaking Up/Party Time

TROJAN 657 When the Saints Go Marching In/SOUL OF ROUS: Ease Me Up Officer

UNITY 534 Dream Boat/Tommy's Dream

UNITY 535 Peanut Vendor/100,000 Tons of Rock

THE MEDITATORS

Featuring PAT FRANCIS (ex-EAGLES) and PAUL ASTON JENNINGS.

BULLET 403 Duba Duba/CECIL THOMAS: Running Alone

THE MELLOTONES

(X) THE BLEECHERS

CAMEL 18 Facts of Life/TERMITES: I'll Be Waiting

Produced by Lee Perry. (b) Motown meets Mobile on this dance friendly single. The Termites sweet, soulful vocals work a charm, as the UPSETTERS steam along to a reggae beat.

THE MELODIANS

CRAB 15 When There Is You/UNIQUES: My Woman's Love

(b) The Uniques reverse the gender role from Carla Thomas' original R&B hit, delivering up their undying love and "do anything for you" sentiments with sweet, harmonious sincerity.

GAS 108 Ring of Gold/You've Got It

(a) A simple love song takes on a religious aura in the trio's hands. The band is mere window dressing, as the vocalists take on total melodic duties.

GAS 116 Personally Speaking/LLOYD ROBINSON: Trouble Trouble

TROJAN 660 Everybody Bawlin'/TOMMY MCCOOK: Kilowatt

Produced by Duke Reid. (a) No matter how many times the Melodians utter the word "love," it never sounds less than convincing, one of the secrets of the group's success. Gently uplifting melody, a soothing rock steady beat, and gorgeous harmonies were the rest. U-ROY would revisit this song to much effect.

TROJAN 695 Sweet Sensation/It's My Delight

Produced by Leslie Kong.

BOB MELODY

(X) BAND OF MERCY & SALVATION

MIGHTY SPARROW

FAB 116 Mr Walker/Jane

MILLIE

DECCA F12948 Readin' Writin' Arithmatic/I Want You Never to Stop

PYRAMID 6080 My Love & I/Tell Me About Yourself

RUDY MILLS

BIG SHOT 509 John Jones/A Place Called Happiness

(a) The band powers along, while Mills indignantly belts out the story of the rough-and-ready title character.

CRAB 21 Tears on My Pillow/I'm Trapped

CRAB 25 A Heavy Load/Wholesale Love

EXPLOSION 2007 Lemi Li/Goody Goody

MISTER MOST

DOWNTOWN 409 Reggae Train/Pushwood

Produced by Dandy Livingstone.

JACKIE MITTOO

(X) WINSTON FRANCIS

DR BIRD 1177 Dark of the Sun/MATADOR ALL-STARS: Bridge View

STUDIO ONE 2082 Hi Jack/TREVOR CLARKE: Sufferer

Produced by Coxsone Dodd.

JACKIE MITTO & THE SOUND DIMENSION

BAMBOO 6 Our Thing/C MARSHALL: Tra La La Sweet 69

Produced by Coxsone Dodd.

BAMBOO 15 Clean Up/Spring Time

Produced by Coxsone Dodd.

THE MOHAWKS

SUPREME 204 Let It Be/Looking Back

AMEIL MOODIE

BLUE CAT 164 Ratchet Knife/Bend the Tree

THE MOON BOYS

AMALGAMATED 846 Apollo 11/PIONEERS: Love Love Everyday

Produced by Joe Gibbs. (b) Another glittering jewel, the trio's vocals sparkle, the melody is infectious, and the band bubbles happily along.

JOHNNY MOORE

(X) CARL "CANNONBALL" BRYON

DERRICK MORGAN

(X) ANSELL COLLINS

BIG SHOT 506 Shower of Rain/VAL BENNETT: It Might as Well Be Spring

CRAB 8 Seven Letters/TARTANS: Lonely Heartaches

Produced by Bunny Lee.

CRAB 11 My First Taste of Love/TARTANS: Dance All Night

CRAB 19 Don't Play that Song/How Can I Forget You?

CRAB 23 Mek It Tan Deah/Gimme Back

CRAB 24 Send Me Some Loving/Come What May

CRAB 29 Hard Time/ROY RICHARDS: Death Rides a Horse

CRAB 31 Man pon Spot/What a Thing

CRAB 32 Moon Hop/Harris Wheel

JACKPOT 700 Seven Letters/Too Bad

Produced by Bunny Lee.

UNITY 540 Derrick—Pop the Pop/GLEN ADAMS: Capone's Revenge

Produced by Bunny Lee.

MILTON MORRIS

aka MILTON HENRY, frontman with THE LEADERS, later of THE PROGRESSIONS, EMOTIONS. (X) UPSETTERS

MONTY MORRIS

BIG SHOT 513 Deportation/Say I'm Back

CAMEL 12 Can't Get No Peace/UPSETTERS: For a Few Dollars More

Produced by Lee Perry. (b) It may be 1969, but this song has Carnaby Street Mod scrawled all over it, from that great cheesy organ to the garage R&B guitar, and fueled by those jerking beats the Upsetters are renowned for.

CAMEL 28 No More Teardrops/Love Me or Leave Me

DR BIRD 1176 Same Face/A Little Bit of This

BILL MOSS

PAMA 765 Sock It to 'Em Soul Brother (Parts 1/2)

MR FOUNDATION

SUPREME 201 Time to Pray/Young Budd

SUPREME 202 Maga Dog/SOUND DIMENSION: More Games

Produced by Coxsone Dodd.

MR MILLER

(X) LYN BECKFORD

MR VERSATILE

JACKPOT 701 Apple Blossom/LITTLE BOY BLUE: Dark End of the Street

Produced by Bunny Lee.

JACKPOT 702 Devil's Disciples/ERROL DUNKLEY: Having a Party

Produced by Bunny Lee.

THE MUSIC DOCTORS

Studio band for producer DANDY LIVINGSTONE's Downtown label. (X) PRINCE OF DARKNESS, DESMOND RILEY

DOWNTOWN 447 Music Doctor (Parts 1/2)

Produced by Dandy Livingstone.

THE MUSKYTEERS

aka THE SILVERTONES. (X) CARL BRYAN, VIN GORDON

UPSETTER 309 Kiddyo/Endlessly

Produced by Lee Perry. (a) An unusual musical arrangement is the highlight of this cover of the Brook Benton hit. GLEN ADAMS finds some unique organ flourishes, the beat eschews the usual guitar heavy riffing, and the Silvertones add a doo-woppy sound to the harmonies. (b) The Muskyteers add a country twang to their vocals for this cover of another Brook Benton hit. THE UPSETTERS, however, play it reggae straight, although more muted than usual.

JOE NOLAN & HIS BAND

JOLLY 013 Cool It with Reggae/Reggae with Me

JOLLY 016 Confidential/Poison Reggae

FREDDIE NOTES & THE RUDIES

NOTES was lead vocalist with THE RUDIES.

DOWNTOWN 427 I Don't Wanna Lose that Girl/Train from Vietnam
Produced by Dandy Livingstone.

GRAPE 3010 Guns of Navarone/Yester-Me Yester-You Yester-Day

GRAPE 3011 Babylon Girl/Girl I've Got a Date

JOHNNY ORGAN

(X) THE SENSATIONS

THE OTHER BROTHERS

PAMA 785 Let's Get Together/Little Girl

OWEN & DANDY

Vocal duo comprising OWEN GRAY and DANDY LIVING-STONE.

DOWNTOWN 428 Lovey Dovey/HERBIE GRAY & THE RUDIES: Kitty Wait
Produced by Dandy Livingstone.

THE PARAGONS

(X) LESTER STERLING

CRAB 13 Take Your Hand from My Neck/Equality & Justice

STUDIO ONE 2081 Have You Ever Been in Love/Change Your Style
Produced by Coxsone Dodd.

KEN PARKER

AMALGAMATED 847 It's Alright/COBBS: One One
Produced by Joe Gibbs. (b) The rhythm section power this dance friendly number, with the riffing guitar providing a sense of melody, over which the jazzy horns blow away.

AMALGAMATED 853 Only Yesterday/COBBS: Joe Gibbs Mood
Produced by Joe Gibbs. (b) The Cobbs groove contentedly in the background as keyboardist ANSELL COLLINS takes the instrumental's spotlight, creating a series of shimmering, ever-shifting melodic moods.

BAMBOO 1 My Whole World Is Falling Down/The Chokin' Kind

BOBBY PATTERSON & THE MUSTANGS

PAMA 763 TCB or TYA/What a Wonderful Night for Love

PAMA 773 My Thing Is Your Thing/Keep It in the Family

PAULETTE & THE LOVERS

Featuring PAULETTE WILLIAMS of THE EBONY SISTERS.
(X) MAX ROMEO

LASCELLES PERKINS

(X) BOB & TYRONE

LEE PERRY & THE UPSETTERS

(X) WINSTON JARRETT

TROJAN 644 Uncle Desmond/Bronco
Produced by Lee Perry. Featuring THE MELLOTONES, a reply to "Uncle Charlie," in which the accused angrily de-

nies all the earlier slurs, through a barrage of coughs and slurred splutters.

UPSETTER 300 Eight for Eight/INSPIRATIONS: You Know What I Mean
Produced by Lee Perry. (a) A feel-good instrumental, with a hint of mod, plenty of cheesy keyboards, and a rumbling little beat, while the ever intractable Perry hisses out the title. (b) A chirpy melody, enthusiastic vocals, a deft sax, and a bouncy, reggae beat all combine on this knock out number. Also released as DUKE 11.

UPSETTER 324 Yakety Yak/The Tackro
Produced by Lee Perry. (a) The old Coaster's classic is deconstructed into the most eccentric shape imaginable, all staccato beat driven by a cowbell. The horns appear to be playing snatches of "When the Saints Come Marching In," while DAVE BARKER and Lee Perry chant the lyrics. (b) An even weirder, dub version of "Yakety Yak." The sound-effects were pretty fresh at the time, but it's not danceable, barely listenable, and, as the obvious successor to "Clint Eastwood," only of interest to electro-mavens.

THE PERSIANS

PAMA 772 I Only Have Eyes for You/?

THE PIONEERS

(X) MOON BOYS

AMALGAMATED 833 Don't You Know/Me Naw Go a Believe
Produced by Joe Gibbs.

AMALGAMATED 835 Mama Look Deh/THE BLENDERS: Decimal Currency
Produced by Joe Gibbs. (a) Released in Jamaica as the REGGAE BOYS. A thumping bass drum sets the mid-tempo beat, a riotous riffing guitar fuels the excitement and the Pioneers set the pace, carried by the baritone. TOOTS & THE MAYTALS would revisit the melody for their 1970 hit "Monkey Man." (b) One of a number of songs cashing in on Jamaica's currency decimalization, the Blenders' instrumental is a spiffing number driven by a good-humored Hammond and the flashy R&B-esque guitar.

AMALGAMATED 840 Who the Cap Fits/I'm Moving On
Produced by Joe Gibbs. (b) The line "some movin' here, some moving there, some even rockin' steady" was sure to make the rude boys shout, a superbly simmering single.

AMALGAMATED 850 Alli Button/HIPPY BOYS: Death Rides
Produced by Joe Gibbs. (a) With its repeated title refrain, this single had all the infectious charm of a nursery rhyme or skipping song. The rhythm section fires the song, while the Pioneers harmonize beautifully on top. Sometimes simple is best.

TROJAN 672 Long Shot Kick de Bucket/RICO: Jumping the Gun
Produced by Leslie Kong. (a) Secretariat may be more famous, but never has a race horse been so honored as Long

Shot, a gamblers' favorite who died during a Caymanas Park race earlier in the year. Another horse, Combat, also succumbed in the accident, but does not seem to have struck the same chord. This gorgeous slow-tempo classic's bass line is as sleek as an Arab, the percussion as sure-footed as a steeplechaser and The Pioneers as wondrous as a Lippizane. The Specials would turn the song into a derby in 1979, but it was strong enough to survive any indignity.

TROJAN 685 Black Bud/Too Late

TROJAN 698 Poor Ramases/BEVERLEY'S ALL-STARS: In Orbit
Produced by Leslie Kong.

ROLO POLEY

JACKPOT 704 Zapatoo the Tiger/Music House

PHIL PRATT

JOLLY 008 Sweet Song for My Baby/THRILLERS: I'm Restless

THE PRESSURE BOYS

(X) THE CABLES

THE PRIME-MATES

ACTION 4530 Hot Tamales/Version

PRINCE BUSTER

FAB 82 Dr Rodney/Taxation
Produced by Prince Buster.

FAB 92 Pharaoh House Crash/Ob-La-Di Ob-La-Da
Produced by Prince Buster. (a) Buster's strong delivery and the lovely harmonies make this song a stand-out, aided by the brash militaristic beat. The lyrics are a modern adaptation of the plagues visited upon the Biblical Egyptians. (b) The Beatles' own take on ska is returned to ground zero.

FAB 93 Ob-La Di Ob-La-Da/Wreck a Pum Pum
Produced by Prince Buster. (b) When Christmas songs turn bad. "Little Drummer Boy" heads out for a night on the town.

FAB 94 Hey Jude/Django Fever
Produced by Prince Buster.

FAB 102 Black Soul/CALEDONIANS: Oh Baby
Produced by Prince Buster.

FAB 118 Bull Buck/ROLAND ALPHONSO: One Heart
Produced by Prince Buster.

FAB 119 Let Her Go/Tie the Donkey's Tail
Produced by Prince Buster.

FAB 122 Stand Up/Happy Reggae
Produced by Prince Buster.

(PRINCE) BUSTER'S ALL STARS

FAB 101 Pum Pum a Go Kill/Oh Lady Oh
Produced by Prince Buster.

PRINCE CHARLIE

COXSONE 7101 Hit & Run/Darling There I Stand
Produced by Coxsone Dodd.

PRINCE OF DARKNESS

aka DANDY LIVINGSTONE.

DOWNTOWN 441 Burial of Long Shot/MUSIC DOCTORS: Version
Produced by Dandy Livingstone.

DOWNTOWN 448 Meeting Over Yonder/MUSIC DOCTORS: Ghost Rider
Produced by Dandy Livingstone.

THE PROPHETS

See YABBY YOU entry in the DIRECTORY OF PRODUCERS.

(X) CLAUDETTE

THE PYRAMIDS

DR BIRD 1307 Stay with Him/Chicken Mary

PRESIDENT 243 Do Re Mi/I'm Outraged

PRESIDENT 274 I'm a Man/Dragon Fly

CLAIRE RAINE

JOLLY 010 La La La/I Want You

THE RAVERS

(X) UPSETTERS

THE RAVING RAVERS

(X) LESTER STERLING

THE REGGAE BOYS

Featuring ALVA LEWIS and GLEN ADAMS of the HIPPY BOYS. In 1998, the band's name would be reborn for the Jamaican soccer team, as they marched into the World Cup finals for the first time. (X) THE ETHIOPIANS, UPSETTERS

AMALGAMATED 841 Me No Born Ya/The Wicked Must Survive
Produced by Joe Gibbs. (a) "Ai, yi, ya-ya," yip the Boys as they launch into another anthemic single. The mellow horn feeds the party feel, the band grooves along, and the enthusiastic vocals ratchet up the excitement.

AMALGAMATED 843 The Reggae Train/Dolly House on Fire
Produced by Joe Gibbs.

GAS 122 Phrases/Give Me Faith

UNITY 530 What You Gonna Do/HEDLEY BENNETT: Hot Coffee

THE REGGAE GIRLS

NU-BEAT 029 Rescue Me/Unity Is Strength

THE REGGAEITES

(X) MARCIA GRIFFITHS

AL REID

(X) MAX ROMEO

CARLTON REID

BLUE CAT 162 Leave Me to Cry/Warning

THE RHYTHM FLAMES

(X) ROLAND RUSSELL

THE RHYTHM RULERS

Session band featuring TONY CHIN (drums) and GEORGE FULLWOOD (bass). (X) EBONY SISTERS

CYNTHIA RICHARDS

CLANDISC 203 Foolish King/KING STITT: On the Street
Produced by Clancy Eccles.

ROY RICHARDS

(X) DERRICK MORGAN

RICO

aka RICO RODRIGUEZ. (X) LAUREL AITKEN, LANCE HANNIBAL, JOE MANSANO, THE PIONEERS, TONY TRIBE
BLUE CAT 160 The Bullet/Rhythm In
BULLET 407 Tribute to Don Drummond/Japanese Invasion
DR BIRD 1302 Baby Face/THE RUDIES: News
(a) Credited to RICO & THE RUDIES.
DOWNTOWN 417 Quando Quando/Reg a Jag
Produced by Dandy Livingstone. (a/b) RICO & THE RUDIES.

THE RIGHTEOUS TWINS

BLUE CAT 174 If I Could Hear My Master/Satan Can't Prevail

DESMOND RILEY

(X) AUDREY
DOWNTOWN 432 Tear Them/GEORGE LEE & THE RUDIES: Chaka Ground
Produced by Dandy Livingstone.
DOWNTOWN 435 Tears on My Pillow/THE RUDIES: Man pon Spot
Produced by Dandy Livingstone.
DOWNTOWN 438 Out Your Fire/No Return
Produced by Dandy Livingstone.
DOWNTOWN 450 Skinhead, a Message to You/MUSIC DOCTORS: Going Strong
Produced by Dandy Livingstone.

MARTIN RILEY

aka JIMMY RILEY. Brother of THE TECHNIQUES' WINSTON RILEY. Member of THE SENSATIONS, THE UNIQUES, also recorded as a duo with DERRICK MORGAN and FAY BENNETT.
GAS 114 Walking Proud/LLOYD CHARMERS: Why Baby
Produced by Martin Riley.
PUNCH 7 Trying to Be Free/I've Got It Bad
Produced by Martin Riley.

LLOYD ROBINSON

(X) THE CHARMERS, MELODIANS

MAX ROMEO

BLUE CAT 161 Me Want Man/AL REID: Vietcong
BLUE CAT 163 It's Not the Way/AL REID: Darling
NU-BEAT 022 Blowing in the Wind/LARRY MARSHALL: Money Girl
TROJAN 656 Sweet Chariot/Far Far Away
UNITY 503 Wet Dream/She's but a Little Girl
Produced by Bunny Lee. (a) Lee initially wanted DERRICK MORGAN to voice this sticky-sheet gem, but it was composer Romeo who eventually took the mike. Despite a lovely, lilting melody, only a toddler could misconstrue the lyric and, not surprisingly, the British BBC banned it. They were rewarded by the sight of it soaring up the chart, ensuring a string of equally bawdy follow-ups. A DJ version by DAVE BARKER brings things to a suitably explosive climax.
UNITY 507 Belly Woman/PAULETT & THE LOVERS: Please Stay
Produced by H Robinson.
UNITY 511 Twelfth of Never/TARTANS: Solid as a Rock
Produced by Bunny Lee.
UNITY 516 Wine Her Goosie/KING CANNON: Fire Ball
Produced by H Robinson.
UNITY 532 Mini Skirt Vision/Far Far Away
Produced by H Robinson.

GENE RONDO

DOWNTOWN 422 A Lover's Question/HERBIE GRAY & THE RUDIES: Blue Moon
Produced by Dandy Livingstone.
DOWNTOWN 431 Sentimental Reasons/Then You Can Tell Me Goodbye
Produced by Dandy Livingstone.

ROY & ENID

COXSONE 7088 Reggae for Days/SOUND DIMENSION: Holy Moses
Produced by Coxsone Dodd.

THE ROYALS

CAMEL 17 100lbs of Clay/THE SCORCHERS: Hold on Tight
(b) The Scorchers second and final 45.
DUKE 29 Never Gonna Give You Up/Don't Mix Me Up
TROJAN 662 Pick Out Me Eye/Think You too Bad

THE RUDIES

British-based band. (X) DANDY, DOWNTOWN ALL-STARS, HERBIE GRAY, OWEN GRAY, OWEN & LEON, RICO, DESMOND RILEY, GENE RONDO, SUGAR SIMONE, ERNIE SMITH, TONY TRIBE
DR BIRD 1301 Sin Thing/What's Your Name
FAB 104 Brixton Market/Rudie's Joy

BRUCE RUFFIN & THE TEMPTATIONS

Ruffin was a member of THE TECHNIQUES and not in any way related to American soulman David Ruffin, not at all coincidentally a member of that country's own Temptations.
SONGBIRD 1002 Long About Now/Come See About Me
Produced by Derrick Harriott.

THE RULERS

TROJAN 696 Got to Be Free/Situation

ROLAND RUSSELL

NU-BEAT 019 Rhythm Hips/RHYTHM FLAMES: Deltone Special

THE SAINTS

BIG SHOT 522 Windy (Parts 1/2)

WINSTON SAMUELS

(X) LITTLE ROY

PAT SANDY

ATTACK 8000 Gentle on My Mind/BIG L: Soulful

PAT SATCHMO

PUNCH 9 Hello Dolly/ERIC DONALDSON: Never Get Away
Produced by Lee Perry.

UPSETTER 316 Hello Dolly/BUSTY BROWN: King of the Trombone
Produced by Lee Perry. (a) A far from serious cover of the stageshow stopper, with Satchmo doing a great imitation of his famous namesake, while a guitar strums along nonchalantly and the sax shows off just as you'd expect. (b) Brown's tribute to the late, great DON DRUMMOND, the lyrics are particularly heartfelt and the singer delivers them with passion, while a brass section pays homage to the SKATALITE sound.

DOREEN SCHAEFFER

See entry for THE SKATALITES on page 262. Also recorded as a duo with TONY, JACKIE OPEL.

UNITY 536 No Matter What/Walk Through this World

UNITY 538 How Much Is that Doggy in the Window/As Long as He Needs Me

THE SCHOOLBOYS

(X) BILL GENTLE

SCIENTIST

AMALGAMATED 848 Professor in Action/THE SUPERSONICS: Reflections of Don D
Produced by Joe Gibbs. (b) Surprisingly bright and cheery for a tribute, but that's obviously the point. Lovingly incorporates snatches from the trombonist's best loved songs, JOHNNY MOORE's instrumental is a celebration of fellow Skatalite DON DRUMMOND's life, not his tragic end.

THE SCORCHERS

Vocal group featuring GLEN DARBY plus GEORGE AND DENNIS. Darby of Syrian/Indian extraction; his father was a concert promotor, six uncles were jazz and calypso musicians. (X) THE ROYALS, THE VIBRATORS

DR BIRD 1170 Uglyman/Whip Cracker
Produced by Lloyd Daley. (a) Swaggering number dominated by its sing-song refrain and Darby's extraordinarily expressive vocal. CARLTON and ASTON BARRETT appear on the session.

TONY SCOTT

ESCORT 805 What Am I to Do/Bring Back that Smile
Produced by Harry J. (a) Featuring the HIPPY BOYS, this borrows the bass line from the Staple Singers' "I'll Take You There," and creates the rhythm which would soon buoy up his own "Liquidator."

ESCORT 816 Darling If You Love Me/Saturday Night
Produced by Harry J.

THE SENSATIONS

(X) BABA DISE

CAMEL 31 The Warrior/JOHNNY ORGAN: Don Juan

THE SEVEN LETTERS

(X) LAUREL AITKEN

DR BIRD 1189 People Get Ready/The Fit

DR BIRD 1194 Please Stay/Special Beat

DR BIRD 1195 Flour Dumpling/Equality

DR BIRD 1206 Mama Me Want Girl/Sentry

DR BIRD 1207 Soul Crash/Throw Me Things

DR BIRD 1208 There Goes My Heart/Wish

DR BIRD 1209 Bam Bam Baji/Hold Him Joe

TONY SEXTON

(X) JUNIOR ENGLISH

TONY SHABAZZ

(X) ARABIS

THE SHADES

GAS 119 Never Gonna Give You Up/Let Me Remind You

THE SHADOWS

Featuring BOBBY AITKEN, who is also believed to have produced their Upsetter 45.

UPSETTER 320 Dirty Dozen/Crying too Long
Produced by Lee Perry. (a) Surprisingly this is not a cover of the movie theme song — or, if it is, it's utterly concealed beneath the clattering percussion, sinuous bass line, and blaring horns. Sadly though, the Shadows' bland delivery brings down this song about a gang of bad girls. (b) There's just a hint of C&W to the instrumentation, while the band's delivery is pure soulful melancholy, with the horns mournfully echoing the melody.

SAM SHAM

BLUE CAT 157 Drumbago's Dead/SPARTERS: Song of the Year

WINSTON SHAN

BULLET 399 Throw Me Corn/Darling Remember

BULLET 411 Matilda/HARMONIANS: Come to Me

TREVOR SHIELD

TROJAN 665 Please/JAY BOYS: Splendour Splash

ROY SHIRLEY

DUKE 18 Life/I Like Your Smile
(b) Shirley's clenched, quavery vocals are at their most emotion-torn majestic.

THE SHOWMEN

PAMA 767 Action/What Would It Take

THE SILHOUETTES

SSY 103 In Times Like These/Version

SILVER

JOLLY 012 Things/Sweet Lovin'

JOLLY 017 I Need a Girl/Lost & Found

THE SILVERSTARS

(X) CLANCY ECCLES

TROJAN 646 Old Man Say/Promises
(a) Reggae perfect beat with an island flair, which the Stars wrap their silvery vocals around. (b) The Silverstars don't believe in promises, and on their plea for love, they add just the right amount of desperation to their tones.

SIMMS & ELMOND

Duo featuring ZOOT SIMMS.

COXSONE 7095 Tit for Tat/We Can Talk It Over
Produced by Coxsone Dodd.

TITO SIMON

aka SUGAR SIMONE. (X) DICE THE BOSS

SUGAR SIMONE

DR BIRD 1192 Black Is Gold/The Invitation
DR BIRD 1193 The Squeeze Is On/Tell Me
DR BIRD 1201 Come & Try/Don't Listen to What They Say
FAB 106 Boom Biddy Boom/THE RUDIES: What Can I Do
FAB 107 I Need a Witness/Johnny Guitar
UPFRONT 1 Turns on the Heatwave/Crying Blues

DANNY SIMPSON

(X) JOHN HOLT

WINSTON SINCLAIR

(X) THE HARMONISERS

NUBEAT 026 Another Heartache/Come on Little Girl

SIR COLLINS BAND

(X) VINCENT MCCLEOD

DUKE 46 Black Panther/I Want to Be Loved
Produced by Sir Collins.

DUKE 47 Black Diamonds/THE DIAMONDS: I Remember
Produced by Sir Collins.

DUKE 55 Brother Moses/Funny Familiar Feeling
Produced by Sir Collins.

THE SLICKERS

(X) CLANCY ECCLES

AMALGAMATED 852 Man Beware/Matty Matty
Produced by Joe Gibbs. (a) A slowly rocking beat, a tight band, and the incognito PIONEERS' marvelous vocals make this song a stand-out, even with its simple melody and repetitive lyrics.

BLUE CAT 154 Frying Pan/RARFIELD WILLIAMS: Code It

ERNIE SMITH

(X) ANONYMOUSLY YOURS

JUNIOR SMITH

(X) STRANGER COLE, SLIM SMITH

CRYSTAL 7002 Put on the Pressure/I Don't Know

ROY SMITH

(X) TERRY, CARL & DERRICK

SLIM SMITH

(X) DAVID ISAACS

JACKPOT 703 If It Don't Work Out/Love Power
Produced by Bunny Lee. (a) Smith's take on the much covered Casino hit "Then You Can Tell Me Goodbye," features an unusually powerful delivery, awash in sweet conviction. This song was also covered the same year by PAT KELLY.

UNITY 504 Everybody Needs Love/JUNIOR SMITH: Come Back Girl
Produced by Bunny Lee. (a) The UNIQUES' vocalist is even more emotive than usual on Gladys Knight's soft pop skanker.

UNITY 508 For Once in My Life/Burning Desire
UNITY 510 Zip a Dee Doo Dah/On Broadway
UNITY 513 Let It Be Me/Love Makes You Do Foolish Things
UNITY 515 Somebody to Love/Confusion
UNITY 520 Slip Away/Spanish Harlem
UNITY 524 Sunny Side of the Sea/A Place in the Sun
UNITY 527 Blessed Are the Meek/Conversation
UNITY 537 Keep that Light Shining/Build My World Around You
Produced by Coxsone Dodd. (a) Smith's a bit overwrought on this spiritually uplifting song, but perhaps that's just so he can be heard above the busy reggae arrangement. As in the ska days, his fragile vocals can be easily swamped by the band and, without sympathetic production, he was a goner. This performance is just on the edge of that.

UNITY 539 Love Me Tender/This Feeling
UNITY 542 Honey/There's a Light

THE SOUL CATS

(X) VAL BENNETT

CAMEL 23 Keep It Moving/Your Sweet Love
GAS 109 Choo Choo Train/The Load

THE SOUL FLAMES

NU-BEAT 020 Mini Really Fit Dem/Soul Train

THE SOUL KINGS

(X) RUPIE EDWARDS

THE SOUL MATES

Studio outfit featuring THE PIONEERS' SIDNEY CROOKS and JACKIE ROBINSON, plus GLEN ADAMS.

AMALGAMATED 836 Them a Laugh & a Ki Ki/The Hippys Are Here
Produced by Joe Gibbs. (a) With a title like this, you know the mood is going to be pretty exuberant. The Soul Mates' strong lead and melodious harmonies set the tone, the organ bubbles enthusiastically along, and the rhythm section finds the perfect groove.

AMALGAMATED 842 On the Move/Jump It Up
Produced by Joe Gibbs.

CAMEL 33 Beware of Bad Dogs/Short Cut

THE SOUL OF ROUS

(X) TOMMY MCCOOK

THE SOUL PARTNERS

PAMA 766 Walk on Judge/Lose the One You Love

THE SOUL RHYTHMS

BULLET 404 Work Boy Work/CECIL THOMAS: Girl Lonesome Fever

GAS 113 Soul Call/Musical Gate

Produced by Coxsone Dodd. (a) The perky reggae beat underpins this instrumental, the sax adds soul, with JACKIE MITTOO's organ providing a bouncy and atmospheric edge.

HIGH NOTE 013 National Lottery/Round Seven

Produced by Sonia Pottinger.

THE SOUL SET

(X) LESTER STERLING

THE SOUL SISTERS

JOE GIBBS conceived act, widely assumed to be the EBONY SISTERS.

AMALGAMATED 839 Wreck a Buddy/THE VERSATILES: Push It In

Produced by Joe Gibbs. (a) The Soul Sisters' reply to PRINCE BUSTER's "Wreck a Pum Pum" is still based on the Christmas classic "The Little Drummer Boy," and built around an up-tempo reggae beat. But the slack lyrics are not going to endear these sisters to Santa. (b) Lead vocalist JUNIOR BYLES can barely contain himself on this ribald number, so he barely even tries. The best bits are when he loses control completely, and launches into almost operatic arias, while the rest of the trio sigh contentedly along.

THE SOUL STIRRERS

(X) LLOYD CHARMERS

THE SOUL VENDORS

COXSONE 7084 Sixth Figure/DENZIL LAING: Man Payaba

Produced by Coxsone Dodd.

HORATIO SOUL

CRYSTAL 7006 Nobody's Gonna Sleep Tonight/Turn Around Baby

JUNIOR SOUL

BIG SHOT 527 Hustler/Big Touch

Produced by Derrick Harriott.

THE SOUND DIMENSION

House band at Studio One, featuring JACKIE MITTOO (keyboards), ERIC FRATER (guitar), LEROY SIBBLES (HEPTONES — bass), BUNNY WILLIAMS (drums), and others. The band was named for Frater's echo box. (X) BOB ANDY, KEN BOOTHE, CECIL & JACKIE, WINSTON FRANCIS, NORMA FRAZIER, GLADIATORS, LENNIE HIBBERT, C MARSHALL, JACKIE MITTOO, MR FOUNDATION, ROY & ENID

BAMBOO 5 Doctor Sappa Too/Soul Eruption

Produced by Coxsone Dodd.

BAMBOO 14 Black Onion/Bitter Blood

Produced by Coxsone Dodd.

COXSONE 7090 Soulful Strut/Breaking Up

Produced by Coxsone Dodd.

THE SPARKERS

(X) SAMUEL EDWARDS

BLUE CAT 155 Dig It Up/DELROY WILSON: This Life Makes Me Wonder

(b) Not one of Wilson's catchiest efforts, but the upbeat reggae rhythm clatters along, the backing vocalists harmonize sweetly in the background and the singer's sincerity still bleeds across the grooves.

THE SPARTERS

(X) SAM SHAM

JACK SPRATT & LEROY SIBBLES & THE HEPTONES

COXSONE 7100 Give Me Your Love/LARRY & ALVIN: Magic Moments

Produced by Coxsone Dodd.

SPRONG & NYAH SHUFFLE

GRAPE 3001 Moonwalk/Think

THE STARLIGHTS

(X) THEO BECKFORD

LESTER STERLING

(X) VAL BENNETT, KING CANNON

BIG SHOT 507 Forest Gate Rock/RAVING RAVERS: Rock Rock & Cry

(a) The saxophonist takes center stage on this instrumental. The melody might be minimal, but the beat and musicianship carry it through.

COXSONE 7080 Africkaan Beat/THE PARAGONS: My Satisfaction

Produced by Coxsone Dodd.

GAS 103 Reggae in the Wind/SOUL SET: Try Me One More Time

UNITY 502 Bangarang/STRANGER COLE: If We Should Ever Meet

Produced by Bunny Lee. (a) An adaptation of Kenny Graham's 1950s UK jazz song "Bongo Chant," Sterling had already rearranged the music when Stranger Cole stopped by the Treasure Isle studio. The result is a fabulous blend of Caribbean beats and jazz inflected musicianship.

UNITY 505 Reggae on Broadway/CLIQUE: Love Can Be Wonderful

UNITY 509 Spoogy/TOMMY MCCOOK: Monkey Fiddle

UNITY 512 Regina/Bright as a Rose

UNITY 518 Man About Town/Man at the Door

UNITY 531 Lonesome Feeling/Bright as a Rose

DELANO STEWART

HIGH NOTE 014 Rocking Sensation/GAYTONES: One Look

Produced by Sonia Pottinger.

HIGH NOTE 027 Got to Come Back/Don't Believe in Him

Produced by Sonia Pottinger.

STRANGER & PATSY

ESCORT 807 My Love/SWEET CONFUSION: Windsor Castle

ESCORT 811 Why Did You/Do You Remember

THE SUPERSONICS

(X) SCIENTIST

SWEET CONFUSION

(X) STRANGER & PATSY

ESCORT 809 Elizabethan Serenade/Don at Rest

ESCORT 812 Hotter Scorcher/Conquer Lion

THE SWINGING KINGS

(X) KEELING BECKFORD

SYMARIP

UK-based band formed by THE PYRAMIDS' NAISMITH, THOMAS AND ELLIS. The name, of course, is near-anagrammatical.

DR BIRD 1306 Fung Sure/Tomorrow at Sundown

Produced by Duke Reid.

TREASURE ISLE 7050 Skinhead Moonstomp/Must Catch a Train

Produced by Duke Reid. (a) The most anthemic mock-Jamaican song ever recorded. Driven by the pulsating bass and persistently infectious guitar riff, it is then overpowered by the scratchy lead guitar, pummelled by the fashionable checklist, then finally brought to the ground by the "yeah, yeah, yeah" refrain, which really puts the boot in. A previously unissued JUDGE DREAD cover version was unearthed for the toaster's posthumous *Big Tin* compilation.

THE TADPOLES

HIGH NOTE 032 Rasta/Like Dirt

Produced by Sonia Pottinger.

THE TARTANS

(X) DERRICK MORGAN, MAX ROMEO

THE TECHNIQUES

CAMEL 10 Who You Gonna Run To/Hi There

CAMEL 19 Everywhere Everyone/Find Yourself Another Fool

DUKE 22 What Am I to Do/You're My Everything

(a) The vocal trio musically express their total devotion, with the lovely melody bolstered by the gorgeous, sighing harmonies. As usual.

DUKE 60 Where Were You/Just One Smile

THE TENDER TONES

CRAB 38 Devil Woman/Nobody Cares

THE TENNORS

BIG SHOT 514 You're No Good/Do the Reggae

BIG SHOT 517 Another Scorcher/My Baby

BULLET 406 Greatest Scorcher/Making Love

CRAB 27 Baff Boom/Feel Bad

CRAB 30 True Brothers/Sign of the Time

CRAB 36 I Want Everything/Cherry

DR BIRD 1175 Sufferer/Little Things

DUKE REID 2502 Hopeful Village/TOMMY MCCOOK: The Village

THE TERMITES

(X) MELLOTONES, UPSETTERS

NU-BEAT 017 Push Push/Girls

TERRY, CARL & DERRICK

GRAPE 3012 True Love/ROY SMITH: Another Saturday Night

CECIL THOMAS

(X) MEDITATORS, SOUL RHYTHMS

THE THRILLERS

(X) PHIL PRATT

TINGA & ERNIE

Featuring TINGA STEWART and ERNIE SMITH.

EXPLOSION 2009 She's Gone/Old Old Song

THE TOBIES

JACKPOT 710 Resting /DON DRUMMOND JUNIOR: Memory of Don Drummond

Produced by Bunny Lee.

PATSY TODD

(X) THE EMOTIONS

HIGH NOTE 012 We Were Lovers/Give Me a Chance

Produced by Sonia Pottinger.

TONY

GAS 121 Janet/THE HARMONIANS: Believe Me

(a) With THE HIPPY BOYS.

GRAPE 3004 Casa Boo Boo/My Girl

PETER TOSH

BULLET 414 Selassie Serenade/GLEN ADAMS: Cat Woman

Produced by Bunny Lee. (a) Igniting a clutch of instrumentals designed by Tosh and Lee around one single backing track. All are sprightly enough, with sufficient variation to keep them interesting, albeit with the occasional caveat along the way. . . .

JACKPOT 706 The Crimson Pirate/Moon Dust

Produced by Bunny Lee. (a) An entire album could be filled with this song's peppy beat, just from Tosh versions alone. Here it's accompanied by an overly enthusiastic and irritatingly simplistic melodica flourishes. (b) And here it is again, with its annoying organ friend, but this time a visiting California guitar riff joins the party.

UNITY 525 The Return of Al Capone/LENNOX BROWN: O Club

Produced by Bunny Lee. (a) More like return of "The Crimson Pirate," but at least the gangster has silenced the swashbuckler's more annoying melodica excesses.

UNITY 529 Sun Valley/HEDLEY BENNETT: Drums of Fu Manchu

Produced by Bunny Lee. (a) The "Pirate" beat is back (again), this time wed to a melody based (very) loosely on a melding of "I'm in the Mood for Love" and "Blue Moon," with the melodica finally showing a bit of restraint.

TREVOR

aka TREVOR SHIELD.

BLUE CAT 153 Everyday Is Like a Holiday/Have You Time

TONY TRIBE

DOWNTOWN 419 Red Red Wine/RICO & THE RUDIES: Blues

Produced by Dandy Livingstone. (a) An upbeat reggaefied cover of the Neil Diamond song which made #46 in the UK, paving the way for UB40's subsequent abomination.

DOWNTOWN 439 Gonna Give You All The Love/HERBIE GREY: Why Wait

Produced by Dandy Livingstone.

THE TWO SPARKS

(X) CARL BRYAN, WINSTON WRIGHT

LLOYD TYRELL

DUKE 15 Cooyah/UNIQUES: Forever

DUKE 16 Follow this Sound/Why Pretend

NU-BEAT 023 Mr Rhya/After Dark

(a) Love conquers all . . . or, fourth time lucky. The story of a woman who believes that no man can satisfy her, and the first three times, she simply laughs at Rhya's exertions ("he tried it again, she said 'you're worse than a hen'"). But Rhya gets there in the end, and Tyrell's warm, conspiratorial voice eggs him on all the way.

THE UNIQUES

(X) MELODIANS, LLOYD TYRELL

DR BIRD 1178 Secretly/LLOYD'S ALL STARS: Love Kiss Blue

(b) Trumpeter JOHNNY MOORE and altoist CARL BRYAN sparkle through an instrumental reading of the Hamlins' "I Don't Care At All."

GAS 117 Too Proud to Beg/Love & Devotion

NU-BEAT 034 Crimson & Clover/What a Situation

Produced by Bunny Lee. (b) Composed by LEE PERRY, who was also present at the session.

NU-BEAT 037 I'll Make You Love Me/Lover's Prayer

(a) And who could resist this passionate declaration of love, delivered in sweet harmony by the backing pair, and with chest thumping sincerity by SLIM SMITH.

TROJAN 645 A-Yuh/Just a Mirage

UNITY 527 The Beatitude/My Conversation

Produced by Bunny Lee.

THE UPSETTER PILGRIMS

Studio choir featuring LEE PERRY, NORA DEAN, BUSTY BROWN. (X) NORA DEAN

THE UPSETTERS

Lee Perry's long running backing band. Regulars included HUX BROWN (guitar), JACKIE JACKSON (bass), BORIS GARDINER (bass), BOBBY ELLIS (trumpet), GLADSTONE ANDERSON (keyboards), WINSTON WRIGHT (keyboards), WINSTON GRENNAN (drums), PAUL DOUGLAS (drums), BONGO LES (percussion), BONGO HERMAN (percussion) — aka THE AGGROVATORS, ALL STARS, THE CRYSTALITES, THE DYNAMITES, THE SUPERSONICS, LYNN TAITT'S COMETS/JETS/BOYS, ETC. (X) ANDY & CLYDE, VAL BENNETT, DESMOND DEKKER, MONTY MORRIS, LEE PERRY

CAMEL 13 Taste of Killing/My Mob

Produced by Lee Perry.

PUNCH 18 Return of the Ugly/I've Caught You

Produced by Lee Perry.

PUNCH 19 Dry Acid/REGGAE BOYS: Selassie

Produced by Lee Perry.

PUNCH 21 Clint Eastwood/Lennox Mood

Produced by Lee Perry. (a) Perry's tribute to the movie hero is all juttering rhythms and no melody to speak of. But it was the perfect cut for DJs to toast over.

UPSETTER 301 Return of Django/Dollar in the Teeth

Produced by Lee Perry. (a) "Django" features some of the best bleating, squeaking horns ever, starring VAL BENNETT's sax, all wrapped around that unforgettable melody line, lifted from the earlier "Sick And Tired." (b) An intriguing amalgamation of sounds and styles, featuring a great mid-60ish sounding organ, a stunningly complex beat that feeds across the bass, percussionists, and hooting trombone, and snatches of great sax work.

UPSETTER 303 Ten to Twelve/LEE PERRY: People Funny fi True

Produced by Lee Perry. (a) "It's ten to twelve, the bewitching hour," Lee Perry announces, so what's with the crowing rooster? The rhythm section plows happily through the old standard "Moonlight Bay," but the rest of the band seems unclear if it's day or night and switch parts and moods at will, from brightly brash to moodier dreamtime. (b) Perry makes the distinctive stop-start rhythm the focal point — which is probably for the best, given his truly atrocious vocal delivery, as he lays into new-found rival CLANCY ECCLES once again. Only the backing singers offer a hint of melody.

UPSETTER 307 Night Doctor/TERMITES: I'll Be Waiting

(a) Produced by Ansell Collins, (b) Produced by Lee Perry. (a) Immaculately performed by the RHT INVINCIBLES, featuring an already metronomic SLY DUNBAR (drums), LLOYD PARKS (guitar), and BERTRAM MACLEAN (guitar), while ANSELL COLLINS keeps the medic alert with a showcase of his most exquisite keyboards. (b) A quirky little piece set, for no apparent reason, in Paris.

UPSETTER 310 Man from MI5/WEST INDIANS: Oh Lord

Produced by Lee Perry. (a) "A dangerous man from M.I.5," Lee Perry intones. And perhaps he is, but this is much more poppy than your typical spy theme, as ANSELL COLLINS unveils his best atmospheric organ sounds. (b) A showcase for ERIC DONALDSON's heartfelt and powerful lead vocals, as the other Indians harmonize softly in the background for this religiously themed, but upbeat, performance.

UPSETTER 312 Medical Operation/RAVERS: Badam Bam

Produced by Lee Perry. (a) Covering the Meters' "Sophisticated Sissy," the wonderfully twangy guitar steals the show, while the sublimely subtle keyboard plays a definite second fiddle. The rhythm section pumps away, and this operation is a total musical success. The first recording Perry made with the next generation of Upsetters, the HIPPY BOYS. (b) A breezy little number on which the band steam cheerily along, and the Ravers chirp their sweet, mellow vocal lines.

UPSETTER 313 Live Injection/BLEECHERS: Everything for Fun

Produced by Lee Perry. (a) Over the RAVERS' "Badam Bam," WINSTON WRIGHT's piercing organ wails away, the rhythm section simmers below, the arrangement and mix flips focus between the two. What more could you ask for? (b) The Upsetters conjure up a hint of carnival with a particularly bouncy keyboard, while the Bleechers sing cheekily about the delights of their favorite girl.

UPSETTER 315 Cold Sweat/BLEECHERS: Pound Get a Blow

Produced by Lee Perry. (a) Having originally tried to cut a vocal by WATTY BURNETT, titled "Little Suzy," Perry had GLEN ADAMS showboat his organ, a one-sided duet with a piano. The rest of the Upsetters (the newly installed HIPPY BOYS) stay out of the way, but keep the mid-tempo beat going strong. (b) Actually cut by the SOUL TWINS, who harmonize about the latest economic crisis, changes which forced Jamaica to switch currencies from the pound to the dollar. The choppy rhythms and burbling organ fit the mood perfectly. The song placed third at the Festival Song Competition.

UPSETTER 317 Vampire/BLEECHERS: Check Him Out

Produced by Lee Perry. (a) Lee Perry ominously announces at the beginning of this mid-temp instrumental, "You're the witch doctor, but I'm the vampire" . . . and GLEN ADAMS is the keyboardist unconcernedly sitting center stage, playing a cheery little melody. A fascinating scenario unfolds. (b) Why spend a fortune at a Madison Ave ad agency, when the Bleechers will cost a mere fraction of the price? Lee Perry found the perfect way to advertise his new store, simply sliding its name, address and directions into the lyric.

UPSETTER 318 Soulful I/MILTON MORRIS: No Bread and Butter

Produced by Lee Perry. (a) An instrumental cover of the DAVID ISAACS hit "Since You Are Gone" (also covered by PAT KELLY) but, considering the song's soulful nature, the keyboards' swing from bubbly to strident is a bit over the top. (b) A typical Perry production of the period — bouncy beat, a riffing rhythm guitar, and GLEN ADAMS' bubbly keyboards initially counterpointing the melody, then taking a solo spin, over which the vocalist unleashes a tempestuous chest thumper.

VERN & ALVIN

Duo featuring producer ALVIN RANGLIN and VERNON BUCKLEY (THE MAYTONES).

BIG SHOT 525 Old Man Dead/GG RHYTHM SECTION: Reggae Me

Produced by Alvin Ranglin.

BLUE CAT 167 Everybody Reggae/Another Fool

Produced by Alvin Ranglin.

THE VERSATILES

(X) SOUL SISTERS

AMALGAMATED 854 Lu Lu Bell/Long Long Time

Produced by Joe Gibbs. (a) Engineer LEE PERRY took this kiddies' counting song and gave it a power packed rhythm, while JUNIOR BYLES interspersed the numbers game with religious adages. (b) A fast-paced piece, over which the sublime Versatiles effortlessly stream across the call-and-response parts, then break into the vibrant harmonies. Byles, of course, supplies the sublime lead.

BIG SHOT 520 Worries a Yard/VAL BENNETT: Hound Dog Special

Produced by Joe Gibbs.

CRAB 17 The Horse/Hot Line

Also released as NU-BEAT 018.

THE VIBRATORS

DUKE 26 Live Life/THE SCORCHERS: Hear Ya

THE VICEROYS

(X) VIN GORDON

CRAB 12 Work It/You Mean So Much to Me

CRAB 28 Death a Come/MATADOR ALL-STARS: The Sword

PUNCH 3 Jump in a Fire/Give to Get

STUDIO ONE 2077 Things A-Come to Bump/THE LYRICS: Old Man Say

Produced by Coxsone Dodd.

THE VICTORS

HIGH NOTE 019 Reggae Buddy/Easy Squeeze

Produced by Sonia Pottinger. (b) The harmonies bunch together with a claustrophobic fire, and the rhythm doesn't let up for a moment.

THE VIRTUES

(X) LLOYD & DEVON

THE VISIONS

(X) KING HORROR

GRAPE 3009 Captain Hook/The Girl

JAKE WADE

(X) DANDY

ANNA WALKER & THE CROWNETTES

PAMA 768 You Don't Know/Billy Joe

DENNIS WALKS

(X) GROSSETT

BULLET 402 Heart Don't Leap/THE CLARENDONIANS: I Am Sorry

BULLET 408 Love of My Life/Under the Shady Tree

ERROL WALLACE

ESCORT 817 Bandit/ASTON BARRETT: Family Man Mood

NORMAN T WASHINGTON

PUNCH 11 Oh Happy Day/Spinning

THE WEBBER SISTERS

(X) DELROY WILSON

THE WEST INDIANS

(X) UPSETTERS

CAMEL 16 Strange Whisperings/CARL DAWKINS: Hard to Handle
Produced by Lee Perry.

GEORGE WILLIAMS

BULLET 405 No Business of Yours/Mash It Up

RANNY WILLIAMS

Guitarist LORRAINE WILLIAMS, aka RONNIE BOP, RANNY BOP, was a leading session guitarist turned producer.

UNITY 526 Ambitious Beggar/Pepper Seed

RARFIELD WILLIAMS

(X) THE SLICKERS

RONNY WILLIAMS

GAS 120 Throw Me Corn/HIPPY BOYS: Temptation

SYLVIAN WILLIAMS

BIG SHOT 532 Sweeter than Honey/Son of Reggae
BIG SHOT 533 This Old Man/When Morning Comes

DELROY WILSON

(X) THE SPARKERS

CAMEL 15 Sad Mood/STRANGER COLE: Give It to Me
HIGH NOTE 011 Put Yourself in My Place/It Hurts

Produced by Sonia Pottinger. (a) This soul-lite song was originally a hit for the Elgins, and is bolstered by Wilson's heartfelt Sam Cook-ing delivery, the insistent up-tempo beats, and a memorable chorus. (b) A cover of the Tams' hit. Considering the theme, it's a remarkably upbeat, breezy number, perfect for the dancefloor; perhaps the star is actually enjoying the emotional torment.

HIGH NOTE 015 I'm the One Who Loves You/AFRO-TONES: If I'm in a Corner

Produced by Sonia Pottinger. (a) The dreamy atmosphere is created by the keyboards and driven by the percolating rhythms, while Wilson gives a beautifully delicate vocal performance.

HIGH NOTE 022 Your Number One/I've Tried My Best

(a) The simmering rhythm and upbeat keyboard provides the perfect springboard for Wilson's sublime soulful vocals. (b) It could have been a classic, if only producer Pottinger had put her foot down and not allowed Wilson to break into the wretched choruses of "nyah, nyah, nyah."

HIGH NOTE 028 Good to Me/What Do You Want Me to Do
Produced by Sonia Pottinger.

STUDIO ONE 2074 Easy Snappin'/WEBBER SISTERS: Come On
Produced by Coxsone Dodd.

ERNEST WILSON

AMALGAMATED 837 Private Number/GLEN ADAMS: She's So Fine
Produced by Joe Gibbs.

CRAB 9 Private Number/Another Chance
Produced by Lee Perry.

CRAB 18 Freedom-Train/STRANGER COLE: You Should Never Have to Come
Produced by Lee Perry. (a) One of the first Jamaican singles ever to be released in stereo.

CRAB 22 Just Once in My Life/GLEN ADAMS: Mighty Organ
Produced by Lee Perry.

WONDER BOY

JACKPOT 705 Love Power/PAT KELLY: Since You Are Gone
Produced by Bunny Lee. (b) Actually produced by LEE PERRY.

THE WOODPECKERS

(X) GLEN ADAMS

OTIS WRIGHT

HIGH NOTE 033 Man of Galilee/Take Up the Cross
Produced by Sonia Pottinger.

WINSTON WRIGHT

b 1944; d 1993. Prolific session keyboard player.

CAMEL 32 Power Pack/TWO SPARKS: Throwing Stones
DR BIRD 1308 Five Miles High/CARL DAWKINS: Only Girl
Produced by JJ Johnson.

DUKE 10 Poppy Cock/CARL DAWKINS: This World & Me
Produced by JJ Johnson.

BARRY YORK

(X) KINGSTONIANS

1970

CHARLIE ACE

b Valden Dixon, 12/27/45 (Cascade, JA). DJ who later became producer and road manager of the YOUTH PROFESSIONALS. Also recorded with GARY WILSON, THE MAYTONES.

PUNCH 49 Silver & Gold/PHIL PRATT ALL-STARS: Bump & Bore
Produced by Lee Perry.

PUNCH 53 Book of Books/WINSTON HARRIS: Musical Dove
Produced by Lee Perry.

RICHARD ACE

SUGAR 104 Sound of the Reggae/Got to Build a Wall

GLEN ADAMS

GAS 135 Power Cut/REGGAE BOYS: Ba Ba (aka What Is This)
Produced by Lee Perry. (a) Actually the UPSETTERS' "Cold Sweat," without LEE PERRY's spoken intro.

GAS 141 Leaving on a Jet Plane/REGGAE BOYS: Phrases
Produced by Lee Perry.

THE AGGROVATORS

Name applied to the musicians working with producer BUNNY LEE at any given session. Regulars included HUX

BROWN (guitar), BORIS GARDINER (bass), JACKIE JACKSON (bass), BOBBY ELLIS (trumpet), GLADSTONE ANDERSON (keyboards), WINSTON WRIGHT (keyboards), WINSTON GRENNAN (drums), PAUL DOUGLAS (drums), BONGO LES (percussion), BONGO HERMAN (percussion) — aka THE ALL STARS, THE CRYSTALITES, THE DYNAMITES, THE SUPERSONICS, LYNN TAITT'S JETS, THE UPSETTERS, etc.

JACKPOT 751 Sex Machine/You Left Me & Gone
Produced by Bunny Lee.

LAUREL AITKEN

ACKEE 104 Pussy Got Thirteen Life/Single Man

ACKEE 106 Sin pon You/Everynight

BAMBOO 16 Moon Rock/Cut Up Munno

NU-BEAT 048 Skinhead Invasion/Benwood Dick
Produced by Laurel Aitken.

NU-BEAT 049 I've Got Your Love/GRUVY BEATS: Blue Mink
Produced by Laurel Aitken.

NU-BEAT 050 Scandal in Brixton Market/Soul Grinder
Produced by Laurel Aitken.

NU-BEAT 054 Nobody But Me/Baby Please Don't Go
Produced by Laurel Aitken.

NU-BEAT 056 I'll Never Love Any Girl/The Best I Can
Produced by Laurel Aitken.

NU-BEAT 057 Reggae Popcorn/Take Me Back
Produced by Laurel Aitken.

NU-BEAT 063 Baby I Need Your Loving/Think It Over
Produced by Laurel Aitken.

NU-BEAT 065 Sex Machine/Since You Left
Produced by Laurel Aitken.

NU-BEAT 072 Pachanga/Version
Produced by Laurel Aitken.

PAMA 818 Mary's Boy Child/RUPIE EDWARDS ALL-STARS: Version
Produced by Rupie Edwards.

PAMA SUPREME 300 Why Can't I Touch You/Can't Turn Your Back on Me

DENNIS ALCAPONE

See entry on page 19. Also recorded as a duo with JOHN HOLT, KEITH HUDSON, MAX ROMEO, LEE PERRY, DELROY WILSON.

EXPLOSION 2039 Revelation Version/Marka Version
Produced by Keith Hudson.

ROLAND ALPHONSO

PUNCH 39 Roll On/CARL DAWKINS: True Love
Produced by Lee Perry

RITA ALSTON

TROJAN 7751 Popcorn Funky Reggae/NAT COLE: My Love

AMOR VIVI

BIG SHOT 534 Dirty Dog/Round & Round the Moon

BARBARA ANDREWS

ESCORT 838 Lonesome Feeling/RANNY BOP: Hopscotch

BOB ANDY

(X) BOB & MARCIA

HARRY J 6612 Peace of Mind/Weep
Produced by Harry J.

AUDREY

DOWNTOWN 454 Oh I Was Wrong/Let's Try It Again
Produced by Dandy Livingstone.

DOWNTOWN 457 Someday We'll Be Together/MUSIC DOCTORS: Sunset Rock
Produced by Dandy Livingstone. (a) Audrey's passion-filled vocals are the focus, but the accompanying trio set this well apart from the Supremes' Motown prototype, ably assisted by the bubbling band's reggafied rhythms.

DOWNTOWN 452 Sweeter than Sugar/The Way You Move
Produced by Dandy Livingstone.

DOWNTOWN 463 How Glad I Am/DANDY & AUDREY: I'm So Glad
Produced by Dandy Livingstone.

TREND 006 Getting Ready for Heartache/MYOB: Leave Me Alone

PETER AUSTIN

Member of THE CLARENDONIANS. (X) LITTLE FREDDY

PETER AUSTIN & HORTENSE

Vocal duo featuring THE CLARENDONIANS' Austin and HORTENSE ELLIS. (X) BIM & BAM

DAVE BARKER

(X) NORMAN GRANT, LESTER STERLING

DUKE 74 Funky Reggae/TOMMY MCCOOK & THE SKATALITES: I Love You My Baby
Produced by Duke Reid. (a) The band lay down the reggae beat, and Barker yelps out in best funk fashion. However, if you want more than that, look elsewhere.

HIGH NOTE 049 She Want It/FIRST GENERATION: Give Him Up
Produced by Sonia Pottinger.

JACKPOT 742 Wet Version/I Got to Get Away
Produced by Bunny Lee. (b) THE PARAGONS' "I've Got to Get Away" (aka "Man Next Door") takes on an even more heated sense of urgency when accompanied by Barker's sheer desperation.

JACKPOT 745 Girl of My Dreams/On Broadway
Produced by Bunny Lee.

PUNCH 22 You Betray Me/Will You Still Love Me Tomorrow

PUNCH 25 Shocks of Mighty (Parts 1/2)
Produced by Lee Perry. (a) With a rhythm lifted from the INSPIRATIONS' "Bhutto Girl," the instrumental version of Barker's "Set Me Free" is riven by the UPSETTERS' soft, yet persistent beat and bass line, with a muted organ tinkling in the background. Barker's yelping is the powerhouse behind this number.

PUNCH 42 Reggae Meeting/RUPIE MARTIN ALL-STARS: Soul Bone
Produced by Martin Riley.

RANDY'S 503 October/RANDY'S ALL-STARS: Time Out
Produced by Randy's.

UNITY 567 Blessed Are the Meek/JEFF BARNES & THE UNIQUES: The People's Voice

UPSETTER 331 Set Me Free/Shocks of Mighty

(a) A simmering mix of soul, UPSETTER backup (and lyrics lifted from SLIM SMITH's "Born To Love"), Barker's unexpectedly sweet, uncommonly passionate vocals are enough to melt the coldest heart, while the band, led by the muted clopping beat, simmer along in appreciation.

UPSETTER 344 Some Sympathy/THE UNTOUCHABLES: Tender Love

(a) Barker reaches new soul heights on this cover of a song originally a hit for The Bobettes and later for James Brown. The horns give it that Stax feel, but the rhythms are obviously a Perry special.

UPSETTER 347 Sound Underground/DAVE BARKER & THE WAILERS: Don't Let the Sun Catch You Crying

(a) Dave Barker works it out underground on this simmering track which is all rhythm, bar a riffing guitar and muted keyboard, which provide the barest sense of melody. (b) Barker again at his sweetest, with The WAILERS adding gorgeous harmonies for a lovely cover of the Gerry & The Pacemakers hit. The vocals are the focus, with musical backup kept to a minimum.

UPSETTER 349 Upsetting Station/THE UPSETTERS: Dig Your Grave
Produced by Lee Perry. (a) This version of THE WAILERS' "Duppy Conqueror" rhythm features a languorous Upsetter beat and Barker playing DJ for the night. (b) The trumpeter digs his own grave, then blares forth from six feet under. The rhythm section kicks happily away, while the keyboardist floats above, sprinkling down bits of melody and touches of atmosphere.

JEFF BARNES

(X) DAVE BARKER, JOHN HOLT, BILL GENTLES

JACKPOT 735 Get in the Groove/JOHN HOLT: A Little Tear
Produced by Bunny Lee.

PAMA 802 Jeff Barnes Thing/LENNOX BROWN: Lover's Mood

UNITY 568 1000 Tons of Version/Wake the Nation

ERIC BARNET

GAS 130 Pink Shark/Swing Free

GAS 147 Bumper to Bumper/Fat Turkey

THE BARONS

(X) NORA DEAN, WINSTON WRIGHT

ASTON BARRETT

(X) PETE WESTON

BUNNY BARRETT

(X) SOUL TONES

UB BARRETT

CRAB 51 Thinking About My Baby/I Wonder

BARRY & THE AFFECTIONS

(X) CLANCY ECCLES

AL BARRY

DR BIRD 1502 Morning Sun/MARKONIANS: Over & Over

DUKE 81 Ooh Wee/Hold It Baby

KEELING BECKFORD

(X) THE MAYTONES

JO JO BENNETT

EXPLOSION 2029 Groovy Jo Jo/Ten Steps to Soul

TROJAN 7774 Leaving Rome/In the Nude

VAL BENNETT

(X) LLOYD TYRELL

BEVERLEY'S ALL STARS

(X) KEN BOOTHE, GLEN BROWN, CLARENDONIANS, ANSELL COLLINS, GAYLADS, MAYTALS, MELODIANS, PIONEERS, ROCKSTONES, BRUCE RUFFIN, WAILERS, DELROY WILSON

BIGGIE

(X) THE SLICKERS, THE VICEROYS

BARRY BIGGS

b 1953 (St Andrews, JA). Former Studio One/Treasure Isle backing vocalist, also a member of THE CRYSTALITES and a producer/arranger at Dynamic studios. Scored a major UK hit, "Sideshow," in 1976.

DYNAMIC 401 Got to Be Mellow/Love Grows
Produced by Byron Lee.

BIM & BAM

(X) PETE WESTON

CRAB 48 The Pill/TOMMY MCCOOK: Spring Fever

CRAB 49 Immigrant Plight/PETER AUSTIN & HORTENSE: Bang Shangalang

BIM, BAM & CLOVER

TROJAN 7754 Party Time (Parts 1/2)

SONNY BINNS

(X) NAT COLE

SONNY BINNS & RITA

Featuring RITA ALSTON. (X) NAT COLE

THE BLACK BEATLES

PAMA 804 Reggae & Shout/LENNOX BROWN: Green Hornet

BLACK GEORGE

(X) JACKIE MITTOO

WINSTON BLAKE

(X) MAX ROMEO

THE BLEECHERS

COLUMBIA BLUE BEAT 118 Send Me the Pillow/Adam & Eve

BOBBY BLUE

DUKE 86 Going in Circles/Doggone Right
(b) A cover of the Miracles' hit, Blue gives it a burnished smooth delivery, aided by the deft backing vocalists. The beat's up-tempo and the guitar riff's a delight.

BOB & MARCIA

Vocal duo comprising BOB ANDY & MARCIA GRIFFITHS.

BAMBOO 40 Always Together/BOB ANDY: Desperate Lover
Produced by Coxsone Dodd. (a) A beautiful ballad blends the two voices together like coffee and cream. It is a frequently remarked upon irony that, despite the duo scoring a number of international hits, their finest performance failed to register anywhere outside Jamaica. (b) Since covered by Taj Mahal, one of Andy's most impassioned vocals dignifies what is already a memorable song.

ESCORT 824 Young Gifted & Black/BARRINGTON BRIGGS: My Cheri Amour
Produced by Harry J. (a) The duo give their all on this version of the Nina Simone song. This is the original production, unadorned by British orchestration.

HARRY J 6605 Young Gifted & Black/THE JAY BOYS: Young, Gifted & Black (Instrumental)
Produced by Harry J. (a) And this is it as remodelled for a European audience. The lush orchestration sounds particularly dated today, but it worked a charm at the time.

HARRY J 6615 We Got to Get Ourselves Together/JAY BOYS: Festival Spirit
Produced by Harry J.

JOYCE BOND

UPFRONT 5 Wind of Change/First in Line

KEN BOOTHE

JACKPOT 748 You Left the Water Running/PHIL PRATT ALL-STARS: Cut Throat

PUNCH 30 Artibella/Version
Produced by Coxsone Dodd. (a) STRANGER COLE joins Boothe in chastising the faithless Artibella — "I saw you with a fellow." The breathless accompaniment further fuels their rage.

PUNCH 33 Morning/Version

TROJAN 7716 Why Baby Why/Keep My Love from Fading
(a) Boothe brings the ring of emotional truthfulness to every song he sings, and this yearning lament, with a surprisingly perky beat, is no exception. (b) Boothe belts out another winner, as his excitable vocals swing from strong and soulful to passionately sweet, aided by the equally expressive backing singers.

TROJAN 7756 Freedom Street/BEVERLEY'S ALL-STARS: Version
Produced by Leslie Kong. (a) Boothe's passionate, soulful take on the unity theme, aided by the enthusiastic backing vocalists and some intriguing echoing bass.

TROJAN 7772 It's Gonna Take a Miracle/Now I Know

TROJAN 7780 Drums of Freedom/BEVERLEY'S ALL-STARS: Version
Produced by Leslie Kong.

RANNY BOP

(X) BARBARA ANDREWS

GAS 155 Pipe Dream/Suck Suck

BOSS ALL STARS

JOE MANSANO-led outfit. (X) DICE & THE BARRISTER, LLOYD, DELROY WILSON

THE BOSS SOUNDS

Featuring JOE MANSANO. (X) HOT ROD ALL-STARS

BOTHERATION

(X) SOUND DIMENSION

THE BOVVER BOYS

TORPEDO 22 A.G.G.R.O./ERROL ENGLISH: Sha La La Lee

THE BOYS

(X) YOUNG SATCH

BOYSIE

(X) WINSTON LARO

THE BRENTFORD ALL STARS

Coxsone Dodd/Studio One session band named for the studio's location on Brentford Road, Kingston. (X) JACKIE MITTOO, MARLENE WEBBER

BARRINGTON BRIGGS

(X) BOB & MARCIA

D BROOKS

BIG 304 Oh Me Oh My/ANSELL COLLINS: Staccato
Reissued as BIG 307.

BUSTY BROWN

(X) JOHN HOLT

ESCORT 822 Fight for Your Right/Soul Fight

GAS 154 I Love You Madly/Greatest Love
Also released as PUNCH 38.

HIGH NOTE 048 Ten to One/Another Version
Produced by Sonia Pottinger.

DENNIS BROWN

See entry on page 43.

BAMBOO 56 Love Grows/SOUND DIMENSION: Less Problem
Produced by Coxsone Dodd. (a) A bubblegum hit in Britain (for Edison Lighthouse), Brown brings some quite surprising drama to the song, without ever losing sight of its innate poppiness.

GLEN BROWN

SONGBIRD 1021 Love I/CRYSTALITES Heavy Load
Produced by Derrick Harriott.

SUMMIT 8502 Collie & Wine/BEVERLEY'S ALL-STARS: Version
Produced by Leslie Kong.

IRVING BROWN

BAMBOO 36 Today/SOUND DIMENSION: Young Gifted & Black Version

Produced by Coxsone Dodd.

BAMBOO 58 I'm Still Around/Run Come

Produced by Coxsone Dodd.

BAMBOO 61 Let's Make It Up/BURNING SPEAR: We Are Free

Produced by Coxsone Dodd.

LENNOX BROWN

Saxophonist BROWN best known for work with TOMMY MCCOOK's SUPERSONICS. (X) JEFF BARNES, BLACK BEATLES, YOUNG FREDDIE

PAMELA BROWN

JOE'S 8 People Are Running/CRITICS: School Days

TEDDY BROWN

TROJAN 7793 What Greater Love/Lady Love

VINCENT BROWN

GAS 128 Look What You're Going to Do/Hold on to What You Have Got

CARL BRYAN

GAS 133 Stagger Back/The Creeper

GAS 134 Walking the Dead/TREVOR & KEITH: Got What You Want

BURNING SPEAR

See entry on page 51. (X) IRVING BROWN

THE CABLES

BAMBOO 19 How Can I Trust You?/SOUND DIMENSIONS: Version

Produced by Coxsone Dodd.

HARRY J 6614 Didn't I/JAY BOYS: Tilly

Produced by Harry J. (b) A pretty instrumental with an uptempo beat and a charming piano melody, deftly played.

HARRY J 6620 Feel All Right/Equal Rights

TROJAN 7792 Salt of the Earth/Ring a Bell

Produced by Harry J.

TUBAL CAINE & THE CIMARRONS

ATTACK 8023 I'm a Drifter/Version

CANDY

GRAPE 3017 Ace of Hearts/BILLY JACK: Bet Yer Life I Do

CANNONBALL

(X) TECHNIQUES ALL STARS

ANDY CAPP

b Lynford Anderson, 1948 (Kingston, JA). Engineer and producer, alone and in tandem with LEE PERRY, CLANCY ECCLES. Also recorded with BYRON LEE & THE DRAGONAIRES.

DUKE 69 The Law (Parts 1/2)

Produced by Lynford Anderson. (a) Very much a stylistic recapitulation of PRINCE BUSTER's "Al Capone," bubbling with enthused percussion and wild ejaculations, Capp insists that "this is the law" — but never gets around to explaining precisely what "this" is.

DUKE 71 Poppy Show/Pop a Top Part 2

Produced by Lynford Anderson.

TREASURE ISLE 7052 Pop a Top/RICO: The Lion Speaks

Produced by Lynford Anderson. (a) LLOYD CHARMERS plays keyboards, the GAYLETS harmonize, and the lyric is based on a Canada Dry commercial.

THE CARIBOES

BULLET 479 Let It Be Me/All I Have to Do Is Dream

THE CHAMPIONS

(X) ERROL ENGLISH, DOMINO JOHNSON, LARRY LAWRENCE, MCBEAN SCOTT, TONY & THE CHAMPIONS

CHARLIE & THE MELODIANS

HIGH NOTE 051 Creation/GAYTONES: Version III

Produced by Sonia Pottinger.

THE CHARMERS

DUKE 87 Colour Him Father/Version

EXPLOSION 2026 Can I Get Next to You/Big Five

EXPLOSION 2035 Sweet Back/Music Talk

TROJAN 7773 Sweeter She Is/Fire Fire

LLOYD CHARMERS

(X) HIPPY BOYS

BULLET 435 Dollars & Bonds/Sounds Familiar

Produced by Bunny Lee.

BULLET 442 Reggae a Bye Bye/Dr Jekyll

Produced by Bunny Lee.

ESCORT 836 Hi Shan/Soul at Large

Produced by Bunny Lee.

EXPLOSION 2032 Vengeance/Look a Py Py

Produced by Bunny Lee. (a) With the HIPPY BOYS offering a seething backdrop, Charmers warns LEE PERRY and NINEY HOLNESS that the Bunny's coming to steal their thrones.

EXPLOSION 2034 Ready Talk/There Is Something About You

Produced by Bunny Lee.

SMASH 2302 Big Red Ball (Part One)/BUNNY LEE ALL-STARS (Part Two)

Produced by Bunny Lee.

TROJAN 7788 Oh Me Oh My/I Did It

Produced by Bunny Lee.

THE CHOSEN FEW

Vocal group formed by FRANKLIN SPENCE and ex-FEDERALS vocalist DAVID "SCOTTY" SCOTT, later joined by NOEL BROWN and RICHARD MCDONALD. Scotty was later replaced by BUSTY BROWN.

SONGBIRD 1031 Time Is Hard/CRYSTALITES: Part Two

Produced by Derrick Harriott.

SONGBIRD 1032 Going Back Home/CRYSTALITES: Part Two

Produced by Derrick Harriott.

SONGBIRD 1046 Why Can't I Touch You/INNER CIRCLE BAND:
Version

Produced by Derrick Harriott.

CHUCK JUNIOR

(X) THE UPSETTERS

SPINNING WHEEL 102 Penny Wise/THE UPSETTERS: The Chokin'
Kind

Produced by Melanie Jonas.

THE CIMARRONS

(X) CARL LEVY, PEGGY, PRODIGAL SONS, REACTION, THERESA & CATHERINE

HOT ROD 105 Grandfather Clock/Kick Me or I Kick You

THE CIMARRONS WITH THE CIMARRON KID

REGGAE 3003 Bad Day at Black Rock/Fragile

THE CLAN

BULLET 430 Na Na Hey Hey/KING SUTCH: Musical Bop

CLANCY & STITT

DJ KING STITT with producer CLANCY ECCLES. (X) CYNTHIA RICHARDS

THE CLARENDONIANS

(X) KEN PARKS

DUKE 97 Come Along/Try to Be Happy

GAS 131 When I Am Gone/She Brings Me Joy

TROJAN 7714 Lick It Back/BEVERLEY'S ALL-STARS: Busy Bee

Produced by Leslie Kong. (a) The vocal trio are exuberant about the state of the nation circa 1969, "Jamaica is on the move," they enthuse and, even though the melody isn't that catchy, you'll still want to join in. (b) A little too bloated to be that busy, the horns have a great, fat sound, and the middling tempo just adds to the weight. Imagine a stuffed sparrow trying to achieve lift off.

TROJAN 7719 Baby Don't Do It/BEVERLEY'S ALL-STARS: Touch
Down

Produced by Leslie Kong.

LLOYD CLARKE

ESCORT 849 Chicken Thief/STRANGER COLE: Tomorrow

THE CLASSICS

NU-BEAT 061 Same Old Feeling/So Much Love

Produced by Laurel Aitken.

NU-BEAT 071 History of Africa/Honeybee

Produced by Laurel Aitken.

CLAUDETTE & THE CORPORATION

GRAPE 3020 Skinheads a Bash Them/CORPORATION: Walkin' Thru
Jerusalem

JIMMY CLIFF

ISLAND 6087 Wild World/Be Aware

Produced by Cat Stevens. (a) The Cat Stevens number, given a righteous once over and impressed with far more power than the songwriter himself wrung out of it.

ISLAND 6097 Synthetic World/I Go to Pieces

Produced by Jimmy Cliff and Leslie Kong.

TROJAN 7722 Vietnam/She Does It Right

Produced by Jimmy Cliff and Leslie Kong. (a) Over a pounding beat which is as reggae as you want it to be, one of the strongest anti-war protests of the era, and certainly one of the smartest. The gospel backing vocals add an initially celebratory, but ultimately hollow ring, to Cliff's tale of a serviceman who'll be coming home soon — or would have, if he wasn't killed in the second verse.

TROJAN 7745 Those Good Good Old Days/Pack Up Hang Ups

Produced by Jimmy Cliff and Leslie Kong. (a) Cliff's genius was that he was able to dispense with the overt reggae sound almost entirely, but still retain the mood, the sound and the thrill. This nostalgic look back at days when skies were blue and fields were green is slight but sweet, powered by the passion of his vocal more than anything else.

TROJAN 7767 You Can Get It if You Really Want/Be Aware

Produced by Jimmy Cliff.

NAT COLE

(X) RITA ALSTON

CREOLE 1002 Me & My Life/Version

EXPLOSION 2022 In the Summertime/Apollo Moon Walk

JACKPOT 717 Pack of Cards/RITA & NAT COLE: Spread Joy

JACKPOT 718 Love Making/SONNY BINNS & RITA: My Love

JACKPOT 722 Sugar Sugar/SONNY BINNS: Sign Off

STRANGER COLE

(X) LLOYD CLARKE

CAMEL 54 Everyday Tomorrow/Lift Your Head Up High

ESCORT 826 Loneliness/Remember

ESCORT 830 Little Things/Til the Well Runs Dry

ESCORT 831 Everything with You/Pictures on the wall

ESCORT 832 Pussy/Let Me In

GAS 152 Lift Your Head Up High/Every Day Tomorrow Version

PAMA 790 Come Dance with Me/Dance with Me

ANSELL COLLINS

(X) D BROOKS, PAM BROOKS

J-DAN 4401 Cock Robin/KING DENNIS: Seven Zero

TECHNIQUES 907 Top Secret/Crazy Rhythm

Produced by Winston Riley. (a) The secret, of course, is Collins' piano, which tinkles gaily along, while the rhythm section grooves and the guitarist riffs away. A stronger melody, however, would have helped make it more memorable.

TROJAN 7712 Cotton Dandy/CARL DAWKINS: Don't Get Weary

TROJAN 7729 Moon Dust/Fat Cat

TROJAN 7730 Monkey/Version

THE COLOURED RAISINS

TROJAN 7700 One Way Love/No More Heartaches

THE COMBINATIONS

PUNCH 99 123 ABC/Version

THE CONCORDS

ATTACK 8020 Let Me Out/I Belong to You
Produced by Rupie Edwards.

SUCCESS 904 Don't Let Me Suffer/U-ROY & HENRY: Red Sun Rise
Produced by Rupie Edwards.

DON CORNELL & THE ETERNALS

MOODISC 3506 Christmas Joy/Now the Days Are Gone

THE CORPORATION

(X) CLAUDETTE

GRAPE 3022 Sweet Musille/Walkin' Thru' Jerusalem
(a) This lightweight, lighthearted instrumental focuses on the rhythm and strumming guitar, with just a tinge of organ to add some depth and flourishes.

THE CORSAIRS

UNITY 558 Goodnight My Love/Lover Girl

TOMMY COWAN

(X) NORRIS WEIR

THE CRITICS

(X) PAMELA BROWN

THE CRITICS & NYAH SHUFFLE

JOE'S 1 Behold/SEXY FRANKIE: Tea Patty Sex & Ganja
Produced by Joe Mansano.

THE CRYSTALITES

(X) GLEN BROWN, CHOSEN FEW, ETHIOPIANS, DERRICK HARRIOTT, BONGO HERMAN, KINGSTONIANS, PAT SATCHMO, SCOTTY

BULLET 424 A Fistful of Dollars/BOBBY ELLIS: Crystal
EXPLOSION 2010 The Bad/Version
Produced by Derrick Harriott. Ripping another page from the Clint Eastwood saga, we now get "The Bad." The rhythm is lifted from the KINGSTONIANS' "Winey Winey," with the obligatory silly spoken introduction a la LEE PERRY.

SONGBIRD 1015 The Undertaker/Stop that Man
Produced by Derrick Harriott. (b) A steaming instrumental cover of the SPANISHTONIANS hit "Stop that Train," the Crystalites punch up the beat and add some fabulous Far Eastern guitar . . . that man must be trying to board the Orient Express.

SONGBIRD 1020 Lady Madonna/Ghost Rider
Produced by Derrick Harriott.

SONGBIRD 1024 Isies/Version
Produced by Derrick Harriott.

SONGBIRD 1025 Stranger in Town/Version
Produced by Derrick Harriott.

SONGBIRD 1030 Sic Him Rover/Drop Pon
Produced by Derrick Harriott.

SONGBIRD 1034 Overtaker V1/V2
Produced by Derrick Harriott.

SONGBIRD 1035 Undertaker's Burial/Ghost Rider
Produced by Derrick Harriott.

RUPERT CUNNINGHAM

DUKE 98 Funky/Sugar Cane

CLIFFORD CURRY

PAMA 793 You Turn Out the Light/Good Humour Man

PAMA 797 I Can't Get a Hold of Myself/Ain't No Danger

THE CYBERMEN

PUNCH 40 It's Party Time/Peace & Love

DANDY

DOWNTOWN 453 Won't You Come Home/Baby Make It Soon
Produced by Dandy Livingstone.

DOWNTOWN 456 Raining in My Heart/First Note
Produced by Dandy Livingstone. (a) Bordeaux Bryant's weepy ballad showcases Dandy's sweet, emotive vocals.

DOWNTOWN 458 Build Your Love/Let's Talk It Over
Produced by Dandy Livingstone.

TROJAN 7800 Take a Letter Maria/You're Coming Back
Produced by Dandy Livingstone.

DANDY & AUDREY

(X) AUDREY

DOWNTOWN 462 Morning Side of the Mountain/AUDREY: Show Me Baby
Produced by Dandy Livingstone.

DANDY & SHANDY

CAMEL 68 Rice and Peas/All the While
Produced by Dandy Livingstone.

DANIEL IN THE LION'S DEN

TROJAN 7797 Dancing in the Sun/LION'S DEN: Chick a Bow

DAVE & ANSELL COLLINS

Duo comprising DAVE BARKER (vocals) and ANSELL COLLINS (keyboards).

TECHNIQUES 901 Double Barrel/Version
Produced by Winston Riley. (a) A tangy musical cocktail driven by a great beat and stunning bass, over which vocalist Barker delivers a series of impassioned exhortations in impressive James Brown style. Collins' piano tinkles below and the Hammond organ melts with just the right amount of period style. An utterly unexpected UK #1 for Barker's fellow ex-TECHNIQUE WINSTON RILEY, producer; drums by SLY DUNBAR.

SILKIE DAVIS

English artist, also recorded as a duo with LES FOSTER.

TORPEDO 2 Conversations/**TWIZZLE & THE HOT ROD ALL-STARS:** Peace & Tranquility

Produced by Lambert Briscoe.

TORPEDO 12 When I Was a Little Girl/I'm So Lonely

CARL DAWKINS

(X) ROLAND ALPHONSO, ANSELL COLLINS

DUKE 93 Get Together/**FAMILY MAN:** Installment Plan

TROJAN 7765 Satisfaction/Things a Get Bad to Worse

NORA DEAN

(X) U-ROY

HIGH NOTE 050 Must Get a Man/The Valet

Produced by Sonia Pottinger.

TROJAN 7735 Barbed Wire/**BARONS:** Calypso Mama

Produced by Byron Smith. (a) Taking THE TECHNIQUES' "You Don't Care," Dean's vocals shift between just this side of shrill to throaty on this infectious slacker paean to a forward boy. Or maybe he has other reasons for wanting to get his pants off so quickly.

PAULA DEAN & NYAH SHUFFLE

JOE'S 2 Since I Met You Baby/Jug Head

Produced by Joe Mansano.

DESMOND DEKKER

TROJAN 7777 You Can Get It if You Really Want/Perseverance

Produced by Leslie Kong. (a) It was Kong who pressured Dekker into recording a cover of the JIMMY CLIFF hit. Although Dekker's delivery can't equal Cliff's own conviction, the Brits loved it regardless, sending it to #2 in the charts.

TROJAN 7802 The Song We Used to Sing/Get Up Little Suzie

Produced by Leslie Kong.

DENNIS

(X) LES & SILKIE

CRAB 61DD Having a Party/Man with Ambition

Produced by Laurel Aitken.

PAMA SUPREME 301DD My Way/Happy Days

Produced by Laurel Aitken.

PAMA SUPREME 304 Painful Situation/Nothing Has Changed

Produced by Laurel Aitken.

DENNIS &LIZZY

CAMEL 56 Everybody Bawlin'/Mr Brown

DERRICK & JENNIFER

Duo featuring DERRICK MORGAN and JENNIFER JONES.

CRAB 47 Need To Belong/Let's Have Some Fun

CRAB 55 Rocking Good Way/Wipe these Tears

DES ALL STARS

GRAPE 3014 Night Food Reggae/Walk with Dee

GRAPE 3015 If I Had a Hammer/Hammer Reggae

GRAPE 3016 Henry the Great/Black Scorcher

THE DESECTORS

GAS 137 King Kong/Please Stay

THE DESTROYERS

(X) JOE GIBBS, NINEY, SOUL DESTROYERS, NICKY THOMAS

PRESSURE BEAT 5505 Pressure Tonic/Machuki's Cooking

DICE & CUMMIE

JOE MANSANO project. (X) TREVOR LLOYD

DICE THE BOSS

JOE MANSANO project.

EXPLOSION 2017 Funky Monkey/**JOE'S ALL-STARS:** Version

EXPLOSION 2020 Funky Duck/Dunkier than Duck

DICE THE MAN

JOE MANSANO project.

JOE'S 17 The Informer/Cool It

PAMA DICE

JOE MANSANO project. (X) WINSTON GROOVEY, RAY MARTELL

REGGAE 3001 Brixton Fight/**OPENING:** Tea House

PHYLLIS DILLON

DUKE 76 Walk Through this World /**TOMMY MCCOOK:** The Rooster

(b) There's a hint of Far East dark melody here, chased away by the chirpy saxes, but the title must have come from the DJ's crowing.

DUKE REID 2508 This Is Me/Skabuvie

DIRTY HARRY

UNITY 573 Big Hair/**YOUNG DOUG:** Skank in Skank

ERROL DIXON

GAS 148 Something on Your Mind/I Need Love

TEX DIXON

Vocalist ex-KEITH & TEX.

ACKEE 111 Funky Trombone/Crying Horn

ACKEE 112 My Ring/Here I Am

DOBBY DOBSON

BIG 303 That Wonderful Sound/I Wasn't Born Yesterday

BIG 310 Halfway to Paradise/Utopia

SUCCESS 906 Crazy/**RUPIE EDWARDS ALL-STARS:** Your New Love

Produced by Rupie Edwards.

DONNA & THE FREEDOM SINGERS

BAMBOO 53 Oh Me Oh My/**JACKIE MITTOO:** Goldmine

Produced by Coxsone Dodd. (b) Instrumental version of the Casinos' "Then You Can Tell Me Goodbye."

DON DRUMMOND

(X) WINSTON WRIGHT

DELROY DUNKLEY

HOT ROD 109 I Wish You Well/**TONY & DELROY:** Impossible Love

Produced by Lambert Briscoe.

ERROL DUNKLEY

BANANA 302 Satisfaction/CECIL LOCKE: Sing Out Loud
Produced by Coxsone Dodd.

THE DYNAMITES

(X) CLANCY ECCLES, JOE HIGGS, CYNTHIA RICHARDS

CLANDISC 219 Sha La La La/Pop It Up

THE EBONY SISTERS

BULLET 420 Each Time/BUNNY LEE ALL-STARS: Boss Walk
Produced by Bunny Lee.

CAMEL 63 Hold On/THE MAYTONES: Cleanliness

CLANCY ECCLES

(X) WESTMORELITES

CLANDISC 209 Open Up/HIGGS & WILSON: Agane
Produced by Clancy Eccles. (a) A suitably grinding rhythm accompanies Eccles' lascivious cries, compliments, and instructions. And as for other artists' complaints that "pussy price too high . . . if it reaches the moon, I'll just learn to fly."

CLANDISC 212 Black Beret/BARRY & THE AFFECTIONS: Love Me
    Tender
Produced by Clancy Eccles.

CLANDISC 213 Phantom/Skank Me
Produced by Clancy Eccles.

CLANDISC 214 Africa (Parts 1/2)
Produced by Clancy Eccles.

CLANDISC 221 Unite Tonight/Uncle Joe
Produced by Clancy Eccles. (a) The strings give this single that turn of the decade lushness, furthered by the female backing vocalists. But while Eccles handles the vocals with aplomb, this remains a typical MOR overly-slick offering.

CLANDISC 227 Credit Squeeze/DYNAMITES: Version
Produced by Clancy Eccles.

JACKIE EDWARDS

CBS 5147 Tell Me Why Say Goodbye/Walter Walter

RUPIE EDWARDS

CRAB 41 Sharp Pan Ya Machete/Redemption
Produced by Rupie Edwards.

EXPLOSION 2030 Full Moon/Baby
Produced by Rupie Edwards.

EXPLOSION 2031 Love at First Sight/I Need Your Care
Produced by Rupie Edwards.

SUCCESS 905 Handicap/If You Can't Beat Them
Produced by Rupie Edwards.

SUCCESS 911 Census Taker/Souling Way Out
Produced by Rupie Edwards.

RUPIE EDWARDS ALL-STARS

House band for producer RUPIE EDWARDS featuring HUX BROWN (guitar), JACKIE JACKSON (bass), GLADSTONE ANDERSON (piano), WINSTON WRIGHT and TYRONE DOWNIE (organ), TOMMY MCCOOK (tenor sax), STANLEY RIBBS (baritone sax), and CARLTON DAVIS (drums). (X) LAUREL AITKEN, DOBBY DOBSON, JOHN HOLT, KINGSTONIANS, MEDITATORS, JOE WHITE

CRAB 42 Never Miss/Redemption

SUCCESS 902 Promotor's Grouse/Grandfather's Clock
Produced by Rupie Edwards.

SUCCESS 910 Return of Herbert Splifington/Version
Produced by Rupie Edwards.

THE ELDORADOS

BULLET 428 Savage Colt/The Clea Hog

ALTON ELLIS

BAMBOO 29 Tumbling Tears/SOUND DIMENSION: Today Version
Produced by Coxsone Dodd.

DUKE 72 Remember that Sunday/TOMMY MCCOOK: Last Lick
Produced by Duke Reid. (a) Why waste a great talent on throwaway pop twaddle like this? Ellis, always the professional, does his best, but it's like asking Mozart to play Chopsticks.

DUKE REID 2512 You Make Me So Very Happy/TOMMY MCCOOK:
    Continental
Produced by Duke Reid. (a) The lyrics have resonance, but there's no getting around the pop-lite melody, and while Ellis has a go, it's pretty hopeless. There again, it's still preferable to Blood, Sweat & Tears' US hit version.

GAS 151 Suzie/Life Is Down in Denver

TECHNIQUES 903 It's Your Thing/TECHNIQUES ALL-STARS: Get Left
Produced by Winston Riley.

TECHNIQUES 905 I'll Be Waiting/TECHNIQUES ALL-STARS: Version
Produced by Winston Riley. A remake of an earlier Studio One hit, as downbeat as Ellis' best work should be.

BOBBY ELLIS

(X) CRYSTALITES

HORTENSE ELLIS

BULLET 427 Last Date/PAT SATCHMO: Cherry Pink

TECHNIQUES 908 To the Other Man/TECHNIQUES ALL-STARS:
    Version
Produced by Winston Riley.

THE EMOTIONS

SUPREME 209 Hallelujah/MATADOR ALL-STARS: Boat of Joy
Produced by Lloyd Daley.

ERROL ENGLISH

(X) BOVVER BOYS

BIG SHOT 547 I Don't Want to Love You/Love Is Pure

BIG SHOT 548 Once in My Life/Rabbit in a Cottage

TORPEDO 8 Open the Door to Your Heart/That Will Do
Produced by Larry Lawrence.

TORPEDO 9 Where You Lead Me/Hitchin' a Ride
Produced by Eddy Grant.

TORPEDO 16 Sad Girl/Welcome You Back Home

ERROL ENGLISH & THE CHAMPIONS

JACKPOT 732 Lonely Boy/Da Boo

JACKPOT 738 Lonely Boy/TONY & THE CHAMPIONS: All of My Life

THE EPICS

BAMBOO 37 Your Love/Driving Me Crazy

THE ESCORTS

BIG SHOT 535 I'm So Afraid/Mother Nature

THE ETHIOPIANS

BAMBOO 26 Walkie Talkie/SOUND DIMENSION: Moan & Groan
Produced by Coxsone Dodd.

BAMBOO 38 You'll Want to Come Back/JACKIE MITTOO: Baby Why
Produced by Coxsone Dodd. (a) One of those deceptively catchy numbers which were the Ethiopians' specialty at this time, the sort which burbles in the background while the vocals hang high above it, then once it's over and you're off somewhere else . . . "any-anywhere you want to go, I know that you will want to come back." It'll haunt you for days.

DUKE 61 Mek You Go On/WINSTON WRIGHT & JJ ALL-STARS: Neck Tie
Produced by Winston Wright.

DUKE REID 2507 Mother's Tender Care/TOMMY MCCOOK: Soldier Man
Produced by Duke Reid. (a) Even the tenderest Mom can't soothe away all the troubles then prevalent, so the Ethiopians reverently pray for the Lord's help. Unfortunately, a cloppity beat and twangy guitar rather make a nonsense of it all.

GAS 142 Satan Girl/MATADORS: The Pum
(a) Fairly undistinguished contribution to both the Ethiopians' canon and the annals of rude reggae.

HIGH NOTE 042 Praise for I/GAYTONES: Charrie (Pt 2)
Produced by Sonia Pottinger.

JJ 3302 Wreck It Up/Don't Go

JJ 3303 Hong Kong Flu/Everything Crash

SONGBIRD 1040 No Baptism/CRYSTALITES: Version
Produced by Derrick Harriott. (a) The melody's reminiscent of "Solomon," the organ and rhythm section are inordinately perky, but the Ethiopians are as impassioned as ever on this spiritually themed performance.

SONGBIRD 1047 Good Ambition/CRYSTALITES: Version
Produced by Derrick Harriott. (a) The Hammond sets a jaunty mood, but the Ethiopians have a hint of pensiveness about them, an aura heightened by the lost love lyrics, bittersweet at its best.

THE FABULOUS FLAMES

Singing dance troupe engaged by BYRON LEE & THE DRAGONAIRES, COMPRISING LLOYD LOVINDEER, OSWALD DOUGLAS, KIRK SALMON. Canadian GLEN RICKS subsequently joined; Rick and Lovindeer then became THE FABULOUS FIVE INC.

CLANDISC 224 Holly Holy/LORD CREATOR: Kingston Town
Produced by Clancy Eccles. (a) The piping keyboard intro and the deeply soulful vocal chorus are utterly at odds with the reggae backing, but it's a tight, versatile performance with one of the most memorable melody lines around.

HORACE FAITH

A&M 817 Shame & Scandal in the Family/REGGAE STRINGS: Reggae Strings

TROJAN 7766 Susie Is Sorrow/DERRICK PEPPER: Don't Go

TROJAN 7790 Black Pearl/Help Me Help Myself
(a) The Checkmates hit is given the appropriate slick Stateside production with lush instrumentation. If not for the reggae light beat, you'd think you were listening to an American Holiday Inn cover band.

FAMILY MAN

aka ASTON BARRETT. (X) CARL DAWKINS

ESCORT 834 Midnight Sunshine/GREGORY & STICKY: You Are My Sunshine

THE FEDERALS

CAMEL 40 In this World/You Better Call on Me

FERDINAND & DILL

PAMA 805 Take Back Your Nicklet/Blueberry Hill

JANET FERRON

(X) WINSTON JAMES

THE FIRST GENERATION

(X) DAVE BARKER

HIGH NOTE 045 When/Chapter
Produced by Sonia Pottinger.

FITZROY ALL STARS

Studio band led by FITZROY STERLING. (X) FITZROY STERLING

FITZROY & HARRY

(X) Duo featuring FITZROY STERLING.

BULLET 439 Freedom Street/Version
Also released as BULLET 438.

ESCORT 827 Pop a Top Train/Doing the Moonwalk

FLECE & LIVE SHOCKS

(X) FREEDOM SINGERS

BOBBY FOSTER

BREAD 1101 Tell Me Why You Say Goodbye/YOUTH: I'll Make Him Believe in You

LARRY FOSTER

FAB 130 Boom Biddy Boom/Next to Me

LES FOSTER

English artist. Also recorded as a duo with SILKIE DAVIS.

TORPEDO 7 Run Like a Thief/Nobody's Fool
Produced by Eddy Grant.

WINSTON FRANCIS

BAMBOO 46 Turn Back the Hands of Time/Soul Bowl
Produced by Coxsone Dodd.

BAMBOO 48 California Dreaming/JACKIE MITTOO: Soul Stew
Produced by Coxsone Dodd.

THE FREEDOM SINGERS

(X) THE VERSATILES

BAMBOO 21 Give Peace a Chance/SOUND DIMENSION: In Cold Blood
Produced by Coxsone Dodd.

NU-BEAT 059 Election/FLECE & LIVE SHOCKS: Tomorrow's World

FRENZ

SUGAR 101 Mee Lee Moi/I Hear Music

THE FRUIT GUMS

FAB 138 Sweet Pork/Crying All Night

BASIL GAIL

BULLET 454 I Wish/Black Is Black

BORIS GARDINER

BIG SHOT 537 Sweet Soul Special/Memories of Love
(b) A strong mid-tempo beat lays the groundwork for the enthusiastic Hammond to wail over on this perky instrumental.

BIG SHOT 538 Darkness/Watch this Music

BIG SHOT 539 Hot Shot/Watch this Music

DYNAMIC 404 Commanding Wife/Band of Gold
Produced by Byron Lee.

TREASURE ISLE 7056 Hooked on a Feeling/MESSAGE: Turn Around Twice
Produced by Duke Reid.

TROJAN 7753 Dynamic Pressure/Reggae Me dis Reggae Me Dat

THE GAYLADS

TROJAN 7703 There's a Fire/Last Time

TROJAN 7738 That's What Love Will Do/This Time I Won't Hurt You
(a) Curtis Mayfield cover.

TROJAN 7743 Young Gifted & Black/BEVERLEY'S ALL-STARS: Moon Glow
Produced by Leslie Kong.

TROJAN 7763 Tell the Children the Truth/Something Is Wrong Somewhere
Produced by Leslie Kong.

TROJAN 7771 Soul Sister/BEVERLEY'S ALL-STARS: Version
Produced by Leslie Kong.

TROJAN 7782 It's All in the Game/BEVERLEY'S ALL-STARS: Version
Produced by Leslie Kong.

TROJAN 7799 Fire & Rain/Cold & Lonely Night
Produced by Leslie Kong.

THE GAYTONES

(X) CHARLIE & THE MELODIANS, ETHIOPIANS, NAOMI, RIGHTEOUS FLAMES

HIGH NOTE 037 Target/PATSY: Find Someone
Produced by Sonia Pottinger

ROY GEE

J-DAN 4412 Consider Me/You Walked Away

J-DAN 4413 Try to Understand/I'd Rather Go Blind

THE GENTILES

HIGH NOTE 046 Your Destiny/Lock Love Away
Produced by Sonia Pottinger. (b) Performed by THE MELODIANS.

BILL GENTLES

PAMA 801 What a Woman/Sleepy Cat

PAMA 809 True True Train/JEFF BARNES: Give & Take

PUNCH 54 Fight the Good Fight/Fight Beat

SMASH 2307 Stop Then/MAXINE: I Don't Care

GG ALL STARS

(X) MAYTONES, MONTY MORRIS, PAULETTE & GEE.

ESCORT 835 African Melody/Man from Carolina
Produced by Alvin Ranglin. (b) Once past the rather irritating laughing intro, this instrumental take on the FOLKES BROTHERS' "Oh Carolina" riffs along, powered by the Hammond organ. LEE PERRY contributed the intro.

EXPLOSION 2023 Man from Carolina/Gold on Your Dress
Produced by Alvin Ranglin.

EXPLOSION 2024 African Melody/Serious Love
Produced by Alvin Ranglin.

EXPLOSION 2025 Ganja Plane/Deep River
Produced by Alvin Ranglin.

GAS 153 So Alive/Mercy Mr DJ
Produced by Alvin Ranglin.

GG 4501 Music Keep on Playing/Version
Produced by Alvin Ranglin.

GG 4505 I Don't Like to Interfere/Version
Produced by Alvin Ranglin.

CALY GIBBS

AMALGAMATED 870 Seeing Is Believing/JOE GIBBS ALL-STARS: Ghost Capturer
Produced by Joe Gibbs. (a) DJ Gibbs toasts over, under and in-between the STRANGER COLE and GLADSTONE ANDERSON hit "Seeing Is Knowing."

CARLTON GIBBS

AMALGAMATED 872 Ghost Walk/Joy Stick
Produced by Joe Gibbs.

JOE GIBBS

See entry in DIRECTORY OF PRODUCERS. (X) CALY GIBBS, LIZZY, REGGAE BOYS, NICKY THOMAS, DESI YOUNG

AMALGAMATED 855 Nevada Joe/Straight to the Head

Produced by Joe Gibbs. (a) Johnny Lover gives the echo heavy intro to this instrumental. It's too upbeat to be called dub, but so filled with echoing effects that it certainly comes close.

AMALGAMATED 858 Franco Nero/Version

Produced by Joe Gibbs.

AMALGAMATED 859 Rock the Clock/Version

Produced by Joe Gibbs.

AMALGAMATED 860 Let It Be/Turn Back the Hands of Time

Produced by Joe Gibbs.

AMALGAMATED 865 Hijacked/Life Is Down in Denver

Produced by Joe Gibbs.

AMALGAMATED 867 Movements/Caesar

Produced by Joe Gibbs. (a) Here's one that's got everything—a rootsy instrumental with a driving beat, a superb melody carried by the marvelous organ, a fat bass line, and the fervid DJ COUNT MACHUKI to further enliven the proceedings.

AMALGAMATED 868 Gift of God/The Rapper

Produced by Joe Gibbs.

GIRLIE

TREASURE ISLE 7053 Boss Cocky/LOVE SHOCKS: Musical True

Produced by Duke Reid.

GIRLIE & JOE

JOE'S 7 Small Change/Mind Your Business

GLEN & ROY

(X) HIGGS & WILSON

GLORIA'S ALL STARS

Featuring GLORIA CRAWFORD. (X) MAYTONES.

CAMEL 48 News Room/Jumping Dick

THE GOOD GUYS

DUKE 82 Death Rides/Destruction

DUKE 83 Wreck It Up/Dynamic Groove

DUKE 84 Happiness/Latissimo

NORMAN GRANT

JACKPOT 736 Bloodshot Eyes/DAVE BARKER: Fastest Man Alive

OWEN GRAY

(X) DERRICK MORGAN

ACKEE 102 No More/Don't Leave Me

Produced by Coxsone Dodd. Credited to Gray & OMEN.

BAMBOO 47 I Can Feel It/I Don't Want

Produced by Coxsone Dodd.

CAMEL 50 Don't Sign the Paper/Packing Up Loneliness

CAMEL 51 Bring Back Your Love/Got to Come Back

FAB 126 Swing Low/Release Me

PAMA 810 Sugar Dumpling/I Don't Know Why

PAMA SUPREME 299 I Am in Love Again/RANNY WILLIAMS: Version

PAMA SUPREME 302 Candida/When Will I Find My Way

SUPREME 206 Surfin'/All My Love

UPFRONT 3 Dream Lover/Mudda Granma Reggae

GREGORY & STICKY

(X) FAMILY MAN

MARCIA GRIFFITHS

BAMBOO 59 Shimmering Star/SOUND DIMENSION: Mun Dun Gu

Produced by Coxsone Dodd.

HARRY J 6613 Put a Little Love in Your Heart/JAY BOYS: Bah Oop Ah

Produced by Harry J. (a) The seminal singer takes on the Jackie De Shannon hit and, even though you can't get much lighter weight than this song, the arrangement and Griffiths' vocals give it some depth.

HARRY J 6623 Band of Gold/JAY BOYS: Cowboy Version

Produced by Harry J.

VICTOR GRIFFITHS

PUNCH 29 I'm Proud of You /KING VICTOR ALL-STARS: Version

WINSTON GROOVEY

ATTACK 8019 You Can't Turn Your Back on Me/PAMA DICE: The Worm

CRAB 63 I Like the Way/Tell Me Why

NU-BEAT 053 Standing at the Corner/You End Me

NU-BEAT 055 Yellow Bird/For Your Love

NU-BEAT 058 Here Is My Heart/Birds & Flowers

NU-BEAT 066 Groovin'/Sugar Mama

NU-BEAT 073 Tennessee Waltz/Old Man Trouble

TORPEDO 11 Please Don't Make Me Cry/Motion on the Ocean

THE GRUVY BEATS

(X) LAUREL AITKEN

NEILL HALL

SPINNING WHEEL 103 This Man/THE UPSETTERS: Land of Kinks

Produced by Lee Perry.

THE HAMMERS

(X) JOAN ROSS

THE HARMONIANS

ACKEE 107 Music Street/Group of Girls

DERRICK HARRIOTT

SONGBIRD 1013 Riding for a Fall/I'm Not Begging

Produced by Derrick Harriott. (a) An exquisitely moody cover of the DELROY WILSON hit, punctuated by the muted horn solos and Harriott's heartfelt vocals.

SONGBIRD 1014 Sitting on Top/You Were Meant for Me

Produced by Derrick Harriott.

SONGBIRD 1022 Go Bye Bye/Laugh It Off
Produced by Derrick Harriott.

SONGBIRD 1028 Message from a Black Man/Version
Produced by Derrick Harriott.

SONGBIRD 1029 Psychedelic Train/Part 2
Produced by Derrick Harriott.

SONGBIRD 1033 No Man Is an Island/CRYSTALITES: Part 2
Produced by Derrick Harriott.

SONGBIRD 1042 Groovy Situation/CRYSTALITES: The Crystal Groove
Produced by Derrick Harriott. (a) A straightforward recounting of the Gene Chandler hit which a lot of people seem to remember being called "That Girl, Gonna Make Her Mine if It Takes All Night (Can You Dig It)." But it wasn't.

SONGBIRD 1043 Psychedelic Train Chapter 3/CRYSTALITES: Groovy Situation Version
Produced by Derrick Harriott.

WINSTON HARRIS

(X) CHARLIE ACE

THE HEATERS

UPSETTER 329 Melting Pot/UPSETTERS: Kinky Mood
Produced by Lee Perry. (a) A cover of Blue Mink's ode to multi-culturalism, which actually betters the rather bland original. A chirpy Lee Perry and MELANIE JONAS succinctly sum up the ethnic elements that make up a melting pot population. (b) A staccato, dub version, with the emphasis on the tight drumming and pulsing bass, with the guitar and keyboards swooped in and out for that cool whooshing effect.

HENRY

aka MILTON MORRIS (THE LEADERS). (X) U-ROY

HENRY III

DYNAMIC 402 Out of Time/VICEROYS: Love for Everyone
Produced by Byron Lee.

THE HEPTONES

BANANA 311 Be a Man/U-ROY: Shock Attack
Produced by Coxsone Dodd. (a) In other hands this would be a call to revolution, although the Heptones' harmonious declaration of Black empowerment is just as strong in its understated way.

BAMBOO 28 Young Gifted & Black/SOUND DIMENSION: Joyland
Produced by Coxsone Dodd. (a) The Heptones use the BOB & MARCIA hit as a showcase for their harmonies. Not as strident as the original, and much sweeter.

BAMBOO 39 Young Generation/You Turned Away
Produced by Coxsone Dodd.

BAMBOO 43 Message from a Blackman/SOUND DIMENSION: Jamaica Underground
Produced by Coxsone Dodd.

BONGO HERMAN WITH LES & THE CRYSTALITES

HERMAN and BONGO LES were percussionists with THE CRYSTALITES, DYNAMITES etc.

SONGBIRD 1018 True Grit/Version
Produced by Derrick Harriott.

JOE HIGGS

CLANDISC 208 Mademoiselle/DYNAMITES: Lion
Produced by Clancy Eccles.

HIGGS & WILSON

(X) CLANCY ECCLES

CLANDISC 218 Don't Mind Me/GLEN & ROY: Angel
Produced by Clancy Eccles.

JUSTIN HINDS

DUKE 67 Drink Milk/Everywhere I Go

DUKE REID 2511 Say Me Say/I Want It
Produced by Duke Reid.

NEVILLE HINDS

Producer/performer. (X) LLOYD ROBINSON

CAMEL 44 London Bridge/SCORCHERS: Things & Time

DUKE REID 2503 Sunday Gravy/JOHN HOLT: Write Her a Letter
Produced by Duke Reid.

GAS 126 I Who Have Nothing/You Send Me

SUCCESS 907 Conjunction/Love Is a Wonderful Wicked Thing

THE HIPPY BOYS

(X) MAX ROMEO

DUKE 92 Cloud Burst/LLOYD CHARMERS: Message from a Black Man

HIGH NOTE 038 Piccadilly Hop/Nigeria
Produced by Sonia Pottinger.

HIGH NOTE 035 Reggae Pressure/SOUL RHYTHMS: It Hurts
Produced by Sonia Pottinger.

JOHN HOLT

(X) JEFF BARNES, NEVILLE HINDS, TOMMY MCCOOK, U-ROY, WAILERS

BAMBOO 44 A Love I Can Feel/JOHNNY LAST: Long Liver Man
Produced by Coxsone Dodd. (a) A roiling reggae beat pumps across the grooves while the brass kicks back. An excellent performance and DENNIS ALCAPONE subsequently had an equally good time with it.

BAMBOO 62 Holly Holy/Do You Love Me?
Produced by Coxsone Dodd. (a) A Neil Diamond song which was also a hit for the FABULOUS FLAMES. Holt's utterly understated vocal perfectly fits the song's own mood of reverential somberness.

BANANA 314 Why Can't I Touch You/SOUND DIMENSION Version
Produced by Coxsone Dodd.

DUKE REID 2506 Come Out of My Bed/WINSTON WRIGHT: Hide & Seek
Produced by Duke Reid.

DUKE 73 Stealing Stealing/WINSTON WRIGHT: Stealing Stealing Version
Produced by Duke Reid.
JACKPOT 753 A Little Tear/JEFF BARNES: Get in the Groove
Produced by Bunny Wailer.
PUNCH 48 My Heart Is Gone/PRATT ALL-STARS: Version
Produced by Phil Pratt. Also released as SMASH 2303.
SMASH 2305 I Had a Talk with My Woman/MAXINE: Life Is Not the Same Anymore
SUCCESS 903 Fat Girl Sexy Girl/RUPIE EDWARDS ALL-STARS: Man & Woman
Produced by Rupie Edwards.
TROJAN 7702 Wooden Heart/All My Life
UNITY 548 Sometimes/BUNNY LEE ALL-STARS: Lash La Rue
Produced by Bunny Lee.
UNITY 549 Sea Cruise/BUNNY LEE'S ALL-STARS: Niney's Hop
Produced by Bunny Lee.
UNITY 552 Walking Along/BUNNY LEE'S ALL-STARS: Warfare
Produced by Bunny Lee.
UNITY 556 Give Her All the Love/BUSTY BROWN: Nobody But You
Produced by Bunny Lee.

HORTENSE
CRAB 50 Immigrant Flight/Bang Shang a Lang

THE HOT ROD ALL-STARS
Studio band for UK producer LAMBERT BRISCOE. (X) MERRITS, BETTY SINCLAIR, TWIZZLE
DUKE 66 Return of the Bad Man/Kaisoe Reggae
Produced by Lambert Briscoe.
HOT ROD 104 Skinhead Speaks His Mind/CARL LEVY: Carnaby Street
Produced by Lambert Briscoe.
HOT ROD 107 Strictly Invitational/PATSY & PEGGY: Dog Your Woman
Produced by Lambert Briscoe.
HOT ROD 108 Beautiful Woman/Shocks of a Drugs Man
Produced by Lambert Briscoe.
TORPEDO 1 Pussy Got Nine Life/BOSS SOUNDS: Lick It Back
Produced by Lambert Briscoe.
TORPEDO 5 Skinheads Don't Fear/10 Commandments from the Devil
Produced by Lambert Briscoe.
TORPEDO 10 Moonhop in London/Skinhead Moondust
Produced by Lambert Briscoe.
TORPEDO 14 Control Your Doggy/Follow the Stars
Produced by Lambert Briscoe.
TROJAN 7732 Strong Man/Sentimental
Produced by Lambert Briscoe.
TROJAN 7733 Virgin Soldier/Brixton Reggae Festival
Produced by Lambert Briscoe.(a) An almost militaristic, marching beat fuels this instrumental, with the organ taking center stage and abetted by a sublime guitar riff.

HUBCAP & WHEELS
DYNAMIC 403 One Pound Weight/VICEROYS: Come Dance
Produced by Byron Lee.

KEITH HUDSON
SMASH 2311 Don't Get Me Confused/DENNIS SMITH: Ball of Confusion
Produced by Keith Hudson.

IM
b CEDRIC BROOKS, 1943 (Kingston, JA). Ex-VAGABONDS, GRANVILLE WILLIAMS saxophonist and a former Alpha Catholic Schoolboy. Alongside DAVID MADDEN, he cut several instrumentals for COXSONE DODD, before teaming up with COUNT OSSIE. Brooks was musical director of Ossie's seminal *Grounation* album in 1973, before forming his own LIGHT OF SABA/DIVINE LIGHT band. Subsequently returned to solo work. (X) JERRY & THE FREEDOM FIGHTERS

IM & DAVID
Featuring CEDRIC "IM" BROOKS AND ZAP POW trumpeter DAVID MADDEN.
BAMBOO 57 Candid Eye/SOUND DIMENSION: Federated Backdrop
Produced by Coxsone Dodd.

THE IMPERSONATORS
(X) MOFFATS

THE INNER CIRCLE BAND
See entry on page 121. (X) THE CHOSEN FEW

THE INNER MINDS
House band at Pama Records. The members were all white, but the group played a number of well-received shows backing ALTON ELLIS and other visitors.
NU-BEAT 067 Witchcraft Man/Night in Cairo
NU-BEAT 069 Pum Pum Girl/Freedom

THE INSPIRATIONS
(X) NINEY
AMALGAMATED 857 Take Back Your Duck/Nothing for Nothing
Produced by Joe Gibbs.
AMALGAMATED 861 La La/Reggae Fever
Produced by Joe Gibbs.
AMALGAMATED 862 The Train Is Coming/Man Oh Man
Produced by Joe Gibbs.

THE INTERNS
JACKPOT 729 See You at Sunrise/LITTLE WONDER: Out of Reach

GREGORY ISAACS
See entry on page 127. Ex-CONCORDS.
ESCORT 833 While There Is Life/HARRY YOUNG: Come on Over
Produced by Gregory Isaacs.

SUCCESS 914 Too Late/KINGSTONIANS: You Can't Wine
Produced by Rupie Edwards.

THE ISRAELITES

(X) MUSIC DOCTORS

J-DAN 4410 Can't Help from Crying/Can't Get Used to Losing You
Produced by Dandy Livingstone.

HARRY J ALL STARS

HARRY J 6601 The Big Three/Lavender
Produced by Harry J.

HARRY J 6608 Reach for the Sky/Interrogator
Produced by Harry J.

HARRY J 6610 Je T'Aime/JAY BOYS: It Ain't Me Baby
Produced by Harry J. (a) The Serge Gainsbourg/Jane Birken original was steamy orchestral sex. Well, it's still orchestral.

HARRY J 6619 Cambodia/JAY BOYS: Cambodia
Produced by Harry J. (a) BLAKE BOY's scattershot toasting approach encompasses everything from anti-war sentiment to DJ catchphrases.

HARRY J 6621 Return of the Liquidator/All Day
Produced by Harry J.

BILLY JACK

(X) CANDY

BIG SHOT 558 Once a Man/Soul Mood

GRAPE 3018 Let's Work Together/CORPORATION: Jam Monkey

THE JAMAICANS

HARRY J 6604 Fire (Parts 1/2)
Produced by Harry J.

BOBBY JAMES

(X) WINSTON WILLIAMS

BUSTY JAMES

aka BUSTY BROWN.

UPSETTER 328 Consider Me/Version
Produced by Lee Perry. (a) A cover of the recent Eddie Floyd R&B hit. Brown gives an emotive performance on the classic, ably accompanied by the supple guitar and a palpitating rhythm. (b) Instrumental cut which established this as the first UK Upsetter 45 to feature a version b-side.

WINSTON JAMES

(X) TONY NASH

HOT ROD 106 Prison Sentence/JANET FERRON: Darling I Need You
Produced by Lambert Briscoe.

TORPEDO 4 Gal You Think You Nice/White Silver Sands

TORPEDO 6 I May Never/The Longest Day

THE JAY BOYS

(X) BOB & MARCIA, THE CABLES, MARCIA GRIFFITHS, HARRY J ALL STARS

HARRY J 6602 The Dog (Parts 1/2)
Produced by Harry J.

HARRY J 6607 Jack the Ripper/Don't Let Me Down
Produced by Harry J.

HARRY J 6609 Jay Moon Walk/Elcong
Produced by Harry J.

HARRY J 6617 Del Gago/Killer Version
Produced by Harry J.

HARRY J 6618 Can't Get Next to You/(Part two)
Produced by Harry J. (a/b) The Jay Boys do their best Temptations' impression, while the band do everything in their power to sound the opposite, tossing out the original's soul/funk power in favor of a poppy reggae feel. Very disconcerting.

JERRY & THE FREEDOM SINGERS

(X) OWEN WRIGHT

BANANA 308 It's All in the Game/IM: The Way to My Heart
Produced by Coxsone Dodd.

JJ ALL STARS

(X) ETHIOPIANS

DUKE 94 Collecting Coins/Cabbage Leaf
Produced by JJ Johnson.

DUKE 95 This Land/Land Version
Produced by JJ Johnson.

ESCORT 821 Mango Tree/The Removers
Produced by JJ Johnson.

JOE

aka JOE MANSANO. (X) LLOYD, DICE & HIS MUM

JOE THE BOSS

aka JOE MANSANO. (X) JOE'S ALL STARS

JOE'S 6 Son of Al Capone/All My Enemies
Produced by Joe Mansano.

JOE'S 10 If Life Was a Thing/LLOYD KINGPIN: Daisy Bothering
Produced by Joe Mansano

AL T JOE

DUKE 70 It's a Shame/Desertion

JOE'S ALL STARS

Outfit fronted by JOE MANSANO. (X) DICE THE BOSS

JOE'S 9 Tony B's Theme/JOE THE BOSS: Skinhead Revolt
Produced by Joe Mansano.

DOMINO JOHNSON & THE CHAMPIONS

DUKE 89 You Broke My Heart/TONY & THE CHAMPIONS: Tell Me the Reason

PETE JOHNSON

(X) RICO & SATCH

THE JOLLY BOYS

MOODISC 3504 On the Water/MUDIE'S ALL-STARS: Cash Register
Produced by Harry Mudie.

JENNIFER JONES

Also recorded as a duo with DERRICK MORGAN.

CRAB 56 Tenants/RICO: Western Standard Time

JERRY JONES

BANANA 316 Still Waters/SOUND DIMENSION: Wig Wam

Produced by Coxsone Dodd. Also released as BAMBOO 65.

KEN JONES

(X) SYLVIN JONES

LLOYD JONES

BULLET 429 Rome/RHYTHM RULERS: Version

SAMMY JONES

b Samson Jones, 1945 (Dominican Republic). Relocated to UK where he later formed mid-70s band BRIMSTONE. (X) RUPIE MARTIN'S ALL STARS

SOLOMON JONES

BULLET 452 Be Strong/Version

PAMA 812 Here Comes the Night/RICO RODRIGUEZ: Jaded Rumble

THE JUBILEE STOMPERS

TROJAN 7725 Luciana/I Really Like It

PAT KELLY

GAS 144 Tammy/I Am Not Your Guy

GAS 145 Striving for the Right/When a Boy Fall in Love

GAS 157 I Just Don't Know What to Do with Myself/What's He Got that I Ain't Got

JACKPOT 734 I Just Don't Know What to Do with Myself/Lorna

KING CHUBBY

aka JUNIOR BYLES.

PAMA SUPREME 297 What's the World Coming To/Live as One

Produced by Lee Perry. (a) Recorded in Jamaica, the tape was then shipped to London for full pop-reggae orchestration by arranger Tony Hartley. The strings are a little sickly, but they cannot disguise the power of Byles' voice and delivery.

KING DENNIS

(X) ANSELL COLLINS, MUSIC DOCTORS

KING HORROR

NU-BEAT 051 Frankenstein/WINSTON GROOVEY: I Can't Stand It

KING SPORTY

b NOEL WILLIAMS, 1945 (JA). One of the first DJs to record, he relocated to Miami in early 1970s. COCOA TEA scored a 1997 hit reviving Sporty's "I'm Not A King." Also recorded as a duo with DELROY WILSON.

PUNCH 44 For Our Desire/WINSTON WRIGHT & TOMMY MCCOOK: Version

KING STITT

(X) KURASS

CLANDISC 223 King of Kings/DYNAMITES: Reggaedelic

Produced by Clancy Eccles.

KING SUTCH

(X) THE CLAN

KING VICTOR ALL STARS

(X) VICTOR GRIFFITHS

THE DAVE KING REGGAE BAND

ATTACK 8014 Hey Little Girl/Why Don't You Try Me

TONY KING

GAS 156 Daddy Daddy Don't Cry/I Like It

LLOYD KINGPIN

A member of JOE MANSANO's studio crew. Also recorded as a duo with DICE. (X) JOE THE BOSS

THE KINGSTONIANS

(X) GREGORY ISAACS

DUKE 88 You Can't Wine/RUPIE EDWARDS ALL-STARS: Bee Sting

Produced by Rupie Edwards.

SONGBIRD 1019 Singer Man/CRYSTALITES: Version

Produced by Derrick Harriott. (a) The Kingstonians take on a more soulful air for this single. It wasn't one of their better moves, especially as the melody is nothing to get excited about.

SONGBIRD 1041 Rumble Rumble/CRYSTALITES Version

Produced by Derrick Harriott.

SONGBIRD 1045 Out There/CRYSTALITES: Version

Produced by Derrick Harriott.

TROJAN 7708 I'll Need You Tomorrow/I'm Gonna Make It

(a) Enthusiastic delivery, chirpy backing singers, and a peppy band fuels this upbeat reggae-fied number.

KURASS

ESCORT 825 Stampede/KING STITT: You Were Meant for Me

Produced by Clancy Eccles. (b) Utilizes a rhythm first designed by Eccles and LEE PERRY for MONTY MORRIS' "Say What You're Saying."

ESCORT 840 Do It/MOOSE: Engine #9

JOEL LACE

NU-BEAT 062 Nobody but You/Version

WINSTON LARO

DOWNTOWN 461 Goodnight My Love/BOYSIE: I Don't Want to Be Hurt

Produced by Dandy Livingstone.

JOHNNY LAST

(X) JOHN HOLT

LARRY LAWRENCE

UK-based producer. (X) MCBEAN SCOTT

KEN LAZARUS & CREW

LONDON HLJ10301 Monkey Man/Bongo Nyah

BUNNY LEE'S ALL STARS

(X) LLOYD CHARMERS, EBONY SISTERS, JOHN HOLT

CAMEL 39 The Three Stooges/Isle of Love

Produced by Bunny Lee.

PAMA 803 Annie Pama/Mr Magoo
Produced by Bunny Lee.
SMASH 2304 Stanley (Parts 1/2)
Produced by Bunny Lee.

BYRON LEE & THE DRAGONAIRES

DUKE 91 Cashbox/WINSTON WRIGHT: Strolling Through the Park
Produced by Byron Lee.
DYNAMIC 405 Hitching a Ride/Version
Produced by Byron Lee.
TROJAN 7731 Squeeze Up (Parts 1/2)
Produced by Byron Lee.
TROJAN 7736 Birth Control/Love at First Sight
Produced by Byron Lee.
TROJAN 7747 Bond in Bliss/Musical Scorcher
Produced by Byron Lee.
TROJAN 7761 Julianne/We Five
Produced by Byron Lee.

GEORGE LEE & THE MUSIC DOCTORS

J-DAN 4407 Johnny Dollar/Tough of Poison
Produced by Dandy Livingstone.

JOHN LENNON & THE BLEECHERS

No relation to the Beatle of the same name. Obviously.
PUNCH 23 Ram You Hard/THE UPSETTERS: Soul Stew
Produced by Lee Perry.

LES & SILKIE

Duo featuring SILKIE DAVIS and LES FOSTER.
TORPEDO 13 I Don't Want to Tell You/DENNIS: Come on In
Produced by Eddy Grant.

CARL LEVY

(X) HOT ROD ALL STARS, PEGGY
HOT ROD 100 Walk the Hot Street/PEGGY & THE CIMARRONS: You Say You Don't Love Me
Produced by Lambert Briscoe.
HOT ROD 101 Remember Easter Monday/PEGGY & JIMMY: Pum Pum Lover
Produced by Lambert Briscoe.

HOPETON LEWIS

DUKE REID 2505 Boom Shacka Lacka/TOMMY MCCOOK QUINTET: Dynamite
Produced by Duke Reid. (a) The winner of the 1970 Festival Song Competition opens with a ragged guitar, plinking piano and Lewis' sweet voice buoyant over the CHOSEN FEW's bassy recounting of the title. '50s doo-wop reborn.

EARL LINDO

(X) U-ROY & JOHN HOLT

THE LION'S DEN

(X) DANIEL IN THE LION'S DEN

LITTLE BROTHER GRANT & ZAPATTA SCHMIDT

Featuring EDDY GRANT. See entry on page 111.
TORPEDO 28 Let's Do It Together/Hey Man, Why
Produced by Eddy Grant.

LITTLE DES

J-DAN 4400 Somebody's Baby/Spy Man
Produced by Joe Mansano.

LITTLE FREDDIE

UNITY 551 Why Did My Little Girl Cry/PETER AUSTIN: Change Partners

LITTLE GRANT

aka EDDY GRANT. See entry on page 111.
TORPEDO 27 Baby Don't Let Me Down/Brother Strong Man
Produced by Eddy Grant.

LITTLE JOE

TORPEDO 15 Bad Blood/The Maxi-Mini War
Produced by Torpedo.

LITTLE ROY

BULLET 445 Keep Trying/MATADORS: Version
Produced by Lloyd Daley.
CAMEL 42 Gold Digger/MATADORS: The Mine
Produced by Lloyd Daley.
CAMEL 43 Scrooge/The Days of Old
Produced by Lloyd Daley.
CAMEL 46 You Run Come/Skank King
Produced by Lloyd Daley.
CAMEL 52 Fight Them/Dreadlock
Produced by Lloyd Daley.
CAMEL 57 Selassie Want Us Back/ROY & JOY: Make It with You
Produced by Lloyd Daley.

LITTLE WONDER

(X) THE INTERNS

LIZZY

One of the pioneers of the toasting scene, but swiftly eclipsed by DENNIS ALCAPONE, U-ROY, etc. Also recorded as a duo with DENNIS ALCAPONE, TONY BOP, THE PARAGONS, DELROY WILSON.
HARRY J 6625 More Heartaches/HARRY J ALL-STARS: More Heartaches Version
Produced by Harry J.
PRESSURE BEAT 5508 Ten Feet Tall/JOE GIBBS & THE DESTROYERS: Chapter
Produced by Joe Gibbs.

LLOYD & CLAUDETTE

BIG SHOT 546 Queen of the World/PROPHETS: Top of fhe World
(a) Lloyd acts as sonorous consort to Claudette's dulcet queen, celebrating the latest dance craze. Simple, catchy

lyrics, a solid rhythm section, and the persistent riffing guitar made this a dance floor fave.

LLOYD, DICE & THE BARRISTER

Featuring JOE MANSANO and LLOYD KINGPIN.

JOE'S 14: Appeal of Pama Dice/BOSS ALL-STARS: Young & Strong

Produced by Joe Mansano. (a) Would you let him off? (see below!)

LLOYD, DICE & HIS MUM

Featuring JOE MANSANO and LLOYD KINGPIN

JOE'S 5 Trial of Pama Dice/JOE: Jughead Returns

Produced by Joe Mansano. (a) A shocker even by the apparently lax moral standards enjoyed by rude reggae's target audience, as Pama Dice goes up before the court, accused by "Mum" of "pushing me and hitting me and starting to, you know, wreck the pum-pum." Thankfully, the magistrate hearing the case is none other than a variation on a certain Dread, and acts as Judge, Prosecution and Jury. Dice doesn't even get to speak.

LLOYD & ROBIN

(X) WINSTON WRIGHT

LLOYD & THE PROPHETS

BIG SHOT 553 Bush Beat/PATRICK & THE PROPHETS: Please Come Come

BIG SHOT 556 Jaco/Soul Reggae

TREVOR LLOYD

EXPLOSION 2018 Chinee Brush/DICE & CUMMIE: Real Colley

EXPLOSION 2019 Give Me Back Your Love/Hold Me

CECIL LOCKE

(X) ERROL DUNKLEY

LORD CREATOR

(X) FABULOUS FLAMES

LORD SPOON

ESCORT 839 Woman a Love in the Night/World on a Wheel

LOVE SHOCKS

(X) GIRLIE

JOHNNY LOVER

AMALGAMATED 871 Pumpkin Eater/Version

Produced by Joe Gibbs.

AMALGAMATED 873 Two Edged Sword/Version

Produced by Joe Gibbs.

DENNIS LOWE

DOWNTOWN 465 What's Your Name/MUSIC DOCTORS: Mr Locabe

Produced by Dandy Livingstone.

THE LYRICS

RANDY'S 504 Give Thanks & Praises/TOMMY McCOOK: Get Ready

Produced by Randy's.

JOHNNY MACK

COLUMBIA BLUE BEAT 116 Reggae All Night Long/A Million Marvellous Feelings

THE MACKENZIE JET COMBO

TORPEDO 18 The Milkman's Theme (Caysoe)/The Capadulah Recipe (Caysoe)

THE MARKONIANS

(X) AL BARRY

LARRY MARSHALL

(X) JACKIE MITTOO

BAMBOO 22 Girl of My Dreams/SOUL DIMENSION: Give It Away

Produced by Coxsone Dodd.

LARRY MARSHALL & ENID CUMBERLAND

CUMBERLAND also recorded as a duo with KEITH STEWART, ROY PANTON.

BAMBOO 52 Man from Galilee/Give It Away

Produced by Coxsone Dodd.

WILLIE MARSHALL

TORPEDO 20 Loosen Up Strong Man/Strong Man

RAY MARTELL

ATTACK 8015 Loving Lover/Cora

DR BIRD 1503 This Little Light/Lover

JOE'S 3 She Caught the Train/PAMA DICE: Tea House From Emperor Rosko

Produced by Joe Mansano. (b) Jaunty organ and horn-led skanker based on RICO's "The Bullet," although the toast is a little stale by the time the record's over.

TROJAN 7787 This Little Light/Lover

RUPIE MARTIN ALL STARS

(X) DAVE BARKER

PUNCH 43 Death in the Arena/SAMMY JONES: Julia Caesar

Produced by Rupie Martin.

TORPEDO 24 Last Flight/Super Lotus

Produced by Rupie Martin.

TORPEDO 26 Musical Container (Parts 1/2)

Produced by Rupie Martin.

THE MARVELS

GAS 138 Sail Away/Fight a Broke

GAS 139 Someday We'll Be Together/MORGAN'S ALL-STARS: Instrumental

PAMA 813 Love One Another/Falling Rain

PAMA 817 Don't Let Him Take Your Love from Me/A Little Smile

JOEL MARVIN

EXPLOSION 2028 Too Late/Each Day

MATADOR ALL STARS

(X) EMOTIONS

THE MATADORS

(X) ETHIOPIANS, LITTLE ROY, LASCELLES PERKINS

CAMEL 45 Dark of the Sun/Dreader than Dread
Produced by Lloyd Daley.

MAXINE

(X) JOHN HOLT, BILL GENTLES
SMASH 2301 My Boy Lollipop/Everybody Needs Love

THE MAYTALS

SUMMIT 8510 Peeping Tom/BEVERLEY'S ALL-STARS: Version
Produced by Leslie Kong. (a) The lyrics are totally at odds with the churchy call and responses integral to this hit. Kong deserves much credit for amalgamating the vocals, a stomping beat, and an almost nursery rhyme melody into a coherent whole.

TROJAN 7709 Pressure Drop/BEVERLEY'S ALL-STARS: Smoke Screen
Produced by Leslie Kong. (b) This barely qualifies as a song. It's merely two minutes of repetitive beats and guitar riffs — perhaps the engineer forgot to add the rest of the tracks.

TROJAN 7711 Monkey Man/Night & Day
Produced by Leslie Kong. (a) The song that brought the Maytals into the UK charts for the first time, and later revived by 2-Tone heroes the Specials. While the latter's version was anarcho-ska at its best, the Maytal's original is slower, more controlled and smoother, but buoyed by an overwhelming joie de vive.

TROJAN 7741 Bla Bla Bla/Reborn
Produced by Leslie Kong.

TROJAN 7757 Water Melon/She's My Scorcher
Produced by Leslie Kong. (b) Steel drums add a nice touch to this single, with the trio's strong vocal delivery taking a rather forgettable melody and making it special.

TROJAN 7726 Sweet & Dandy/54–46 That's My Number
Produced by Leslie Kong. (a/b) Reissues.

TROJAN 7786 Dr Lester/Sun Moon & Star
Produced by Leslie Kong.

THE MAYTONES

(X) EBONY SISTERS, SISTER
BULLET 446 I Don't Like to Interfere/Preaching Love
CAMEL 47 Black & White/GLORIA'S ALL-STARS: Jumbo Jet
CAMEL 49 Since You Left/GLORIA'S ALL-STARS: Bird Wing
EXPLOSION 2012 Funny Man/GG ALL-STARS: Champion
Produced by Alvin Ranglin. (b) Stripping down to the forceful rhythms and guitar strums, the driving "Champion" leaves plenty of space for the DJ to excite the audience.

EXPLOSION 2014 Barrabus/GG ALL-STARS: Part 2
Produced by Alvin Ranglin.

EXPLOSION 2027 Cecilia/Chariot Without Horse
EXPLOSION 2033 Another Festival/Happy Time
GG 4503 Searching for You
Produced by Alvin Ranglin.

PUNCH 35 Serious Love/KEELING BECKFORD: Musical Combination

TOMMY MCCOOK

(X) DAVE BARKER, BIM & BAM, ALTON ELLIS, ETHIOPIANS, KING SPORTY, HOPETON LEWIS, LYRICS, KEN PARKER, BOB ROBERTS, U-ROY
DUKE 77 Open Jaw/JOHN HOLT: The Working Kind
Produced by Duke Reid.

DUKE 78 Key to the City/DOROTHY REID: Give It to Me
TROJAN 7706 Black Coffee/VIC TAYLOR: Heartaches
Produced by Duke Reid.

THE MEDITATORS

(X) PAT SATCHMO
BIG 302 When You Go to a Party/Good Morning Mother Cuba
Produced by Rupie Edwards.

BIG 305 Music Alone Shall Live/RUPIE EDWARDS ALL-STARS: Version
Produced by Rupie Edwards.

SUCCESS 901 Look Who a Bust (Parts 1/2)
Produced by Rupie Edwards.

SUPREME 210 When You Go to a Party/RUPIE EDWARDS ALL-STARS: Stop the Party
Produced by Rupie Edwards.

THE MEGATONS

(X) REVELATION
DOWNTOWN 464 Take It Easy/Funk the Beat
Produced by Dandy Livingstone.

MEL & DAVE

Featuring MELANIE JONAS and DAVE BARKER. Jonas later became a producer in her own right, launching the Spinning Wheel label under LEE PERRY's aegis.

UPSETTER 330 Spinning Wheel/Version
Produced by Lee Perry. (a) A cover of the Blood, Sweat & Tears hit, with Barker's vocals the model of controlled passion — which perhaps explains Jonas' over-excitement./(b) With the focus now moved to the keyboards, you notice just how annoying the rhythm is becoming.

THE MELODIANS

HIGH NOTE 044 Love Is a Good Thing/No Nola
Produced by Sonia Pottinger.

SUMMIT 8505 Walking in the Rain/Rivers of Babylon
Produced by Leslie Kong. (b) Based on Psalm 137, this deeply spiritual single combines religious lyrics with sublime harmonies, delivered with the fervor of true conviction. The vocals are the focal point, but the insistent rhythms and twangy guitar parts aren't neglected.

SUMMIT 8508 Rivers of Babylon/BEVERLEY'S ALL-STARS Version
Produced by Leslie Kong.

TROJAN 7720 A Day Seems So Long/BEVERLEY'S ALL-STARS: Project
Produced by Leslie Kong.

TROJAN 7764 Say Darling Say/Come Rock It to Me
Produced by Leslie Kong.

THE MERRITS

HOT ROD 113 I Don't Want To/HOT ROD ALL-STARS Version
Produced by Lambert Briscoe.

TROJAN 7707 Little Drummer Boy/Mary's Boy Child

THE MESSAGE

(X) BORIS GARDINER

MIGHTY SPARROW

FAB 147 I Don't Wanna Lose You/The Truth

MILLIE

PRESIDENT 306 We're All in a Zoo/Pickaninny Man

TROJAN 7744 Enoch Power/Mayfair

She's not a little girl any more. Millie delivers a powerful, irony laden commentary on the right wing English politician whose racist views proved so outrageous that they probably did more to help race relations than any number of his liberal opponents.

TROJAN 7801 Honey Hush/Sunday Morning

MILTON & DENZIL

Featuring MILTON HAMILTON and DENZIL DENNIS. Also recorded as THE CLASSICS. (X) PAT RHODEN

THE MINNA BOYS

(X) TREVOR & KEITH

JACKIE MITTOO

(X) DONNA & THE FREEDOM SINGERS, WINSTON FRANCIS, ETHIOPIANS

BAMBOO 17 Dark of the Moon/Moon Walk
Produced by Coxsone Dodd.

BAMBOO 20 Gold Dust/THE SUPERTONES: Real Gone Loser
Produced by Coxsone Dodd.

BAMBOO 31 Can I Change My Mind/BRENTFORD ALL-STARS: Early Duckling
Produced by Coxsone Dodd.

BAMBOO 51 Dancing Groove/BLACK GEORGE: Peanut Butter
Produced by Coxsone Dodd. (a) DELROY WILSON's "Dancing Mood," reinterpreted for Mittoo's organ.

BANANA 315 Holly Holy/LARRY MARSHALL: I've Got to Take It
Produced by Coxsone Dodd.

THE MODIFIES

PUNCH 45 Bye Bye Happiness/Sufferation We Must Bear

THE MOFFAT ALL STARS

JACKPOT 719 Riot/IMPERSONATORS: Girls & Boys

THE MOHAWKS

PAMA 798 Skinhead Shuffle/RICO RODRIGUES: Red Cow

SUPREME 207 Give Me Some/Version

THE MOOD REACTION

GAS 136 Too Much Loving/Roaring 20s

GAS 143 Change of Heart/Runaway Man

MOOSE

(X) KURASS

DERRICK MORGAN

CRAB 44 A Night of Sin/Telephone
Also released as CRAB 45.

CRAB 52 I Wish I Was an Apple/The Story

CRAB 53 Take a Letter Maria/OWEN GRAY: Just a Little Loving

CRAB 58 My Dickie/Brixton Hop

CRAB 59 I Can't Stand It No Longer/Beyond the Wall

CRAB 60 Endlessly/Who's Making Love

CRAB 63 Hurt/Julia

UNITY 546 Return of Jack Slade/Fat Man

UNITY 569 The Conquering Ruler/Bedweight

SAMMY MORGAN

BULLET 455 Get Out of this Land/SIDNEY ALL-STARS: Landmark
Produced by Sidney Crooks. Also released as PUNCH 57.

MORGAN'S ALL STARS

(X) THE MARVELS

MONTY MORRIS

(X) TWINKLE BROTHERS

EXPLOSION 2016 Higher than the Highest Mountain/GG ALL-STARS: Musical Shot
Produced by Alvin Ranglin.

UNITY 557 Do It My Way/Where in the World

BILL MOSS

PAMA 796 Number One/?

THE MOTHERS SONS

J-DAN 4415 Underground Man/?

MUDIE'S ALL STARS

House band for producer HARRY MUDIE. (X) GG RUSSELL, JOLLY BOYS

THE MUSIC DOCTORS

(X) AUDREY, GEORGE LEE, DENNIS LOWE, GENE RONDO

J-DAN 4402 Electric Shock/KING DENNIS: Black Robin
Produced by Dandy.

J-DAN 4403 Bush Doctor/Lick Your Stick
(a) A glorious mix of piano, a fat bass line, organ accents, and just a hint of Afro-beats.

J-DAN 4411 The Wild Bunch/ISRAELITES: Born to Be Strong

J-DAN 4414 In the Summertime/Foundation Track

MYOB

(X) AUDREY

NAOMI

Vocalist NAOMI CAMPBELL. Also recorded as a duo with DERRICK MORGAN, CLIVE WILSON.

HIGH NOTE 047 Natural Woman/GAYTONES: Woman Version
Produced by Sonia Pottinger. (a) Naomi was never going to improve on her performance (with Wilson) on "Open the Door," and the feminist anthem "Natural Woman" simply isn't the place to try.

TONY NASH
HOT ROD 110 Keep on Trying/WINSTON JAMES: Just Can't Do Without Your Love
Produced by Lambert Briscoe.

JAMES NEPHEW

NINEY & THE DESTROYERS
Producer WINSTON "NINEY THE OBSERVER" HOLNESS; See entry on page 194.
AMALGAMATED 856 Niney Special/Danger Zone
Produced by Joe Gibbs (actually Niney Holness).
PRESSURE BEAT 5501 Honey No Money/INSPIRATIONS: This Message to You
Produced by Niney Holness.
UNITY 563 Skankee/Version
Produced by Niney Holness.

NOEL & THE FIREBALLS
PAMA 808 Can't Turn You Loose/Skinny Legs

FREDDIE NOTES & THE RUDIES
B&C 125 It Came Out the Sky/Well Oh Well
BULLET 421 The Feeling Is Fine/Girl You're Killing Me
DUKE 63 The Bull/River Ben Come Up
DUKE 68 Chicken Inn/Chicken Scratch
Produced by Duke Reid.
TROJAN 7713 Shanghai/Rome Wasn't Built in a Day
TROJAN 7724 Rocco/Don't Tell Your Mama
TROJAN 7734 Down on the Farm/Easy Street
TROJAN 7791 Montego Bay/RUDIES: Blue Mountain
(a) Taking the calypso classic that was an international hit earlier in the year, Notes and his Rudies toughens it up, giving it a street sound far removed from the resorts and 5-star hotels where it remains a favorite.

NYAH EARTH
ATTACK 8016 Nyah Bingy/Message
ATTACK 8017 Dual Heat/Night of the Long Knives
GRAPE 3021 Sting Ray/Paradise

THE OPENING
(X) PAMA DICE

JOHNNY OSBOURNE
b 1948 (JA). Vocalist with THE WILDCATS. Later relocated to Canada with new band, THE ISHAN PEOPLE.
BIG SHOT 549 See & Blind/TECHNIQUES: Scar Face
Produced by Winston Riley.

THE PACESETTERS
BIG CHIEF 101 Cool Coffee/Israelites
ESCORT 829 Bits & Pieces/Nimrod Leap

ROY PANTON
HARRY J 6624 The Same Old Life/JAY BOYS: Life Version
Produced by Harry J.

PAULA PARFITT
UPFRONT 4 Peace of Mind/Baby You Give Me a Song to Sing

KEN PARKER
DUKE 79 I Can't Hide/TOMMY MCCOOK: Kansas City
DUKE REID 2504 Sugar Pantie/TOMMY MCCOOK: All Afire
UNITY 553 When You Were Mine/CLARENDONIANS: The Angels

LLOYD PARKS
Parks was ex-THE TERMITES and THE TECHNIQUES. Also recorded as a duo with PATRICK.
HARRY J 6603 Feel a Little Better/I'll Be Your Man
Produced by Harry J.

PATRICK & LLOYD
Vocal duo featuring LLOYD PARKS.
BIG SHOT 550 Return of the Pollock/PROPHETS: Concorde

PATSY
(X) GAYTONES

PATSY & PEGGY
(X) HOT ROD ALL STARS

EUGENE PAUL
PAMA SUPREME 303 Don't Let the Tears Fall/Another Saturday Night
PAMA SUPREME 305 I Found a Man in My Bed/So Many Things
TORPEDO 17 Sugar Dumpling/I May Dwell
Produced by Larry Lawrence.

PAULETTE & GEE
Vocal duo featuring PAULETTE WILLIAMS and GEE WILLIAMS OF THE EBONY SISTERS. (X) WINSTON WRIGHT
GG 4506 Hold on Tight/GG ALL-STARS: Version
Produced by Alvin Ranglin.

PEGGY
HOT ROD 103 I Shall Follow the Star/CARL LEVY: Gifted at the Top
Produced by Lambert Briscoe.
TROJAN 7752 All Kinds of Everything/CARL LEVY: Version

PEGGY & THE CIMARRONS
(X) CARL LEVY

PEGGY & JIMMY
(X) CARL LEVY

DERRICK PEPPER
(X) HORACE FAITH

LASCELLES PERKINS

ESCORT 814 Please Stay/MATADORS: Voyage from the Moon
Produced by Lloyd Daley.

BARBARA PERRY

PAMA 795 Say You Need Me/Unloved

LEE PERRY

UPSETTER 325 Kill 'em All/THE UPSETTERS: Soul Walk
Produced by Lee Perry. (a) Another nod to Clint Eastwood, "Kill" re-uses the UPSETTERS' "Yakety Yak" rhythm, starting off at a trotting pace, then shifting gears into pure reggae, with the keyboards giving this instrumental the veneer of a real song. (b) The magnificently cheesy keyboard takes centerstage with a moody melody and a nod to Motown soul, while the rhythm section keeps a sharp, tight beat.

UPSETTER 327 Do You Like It/THE UPSETTERS: Touch of Fire
Produced by Lee Perry. (a) A spiffing rhythm and poppy keyboard overture set the stage for Perry and NORA DEAN's innuendo laced lyric, "I'll make it scratchy," interlaced with various grunts and groans a la DAVE BARKER. (b) Saxophonist VAL BENNETT adds a touch of fire to this instrumental, while the melody is carried deep in the keyboard's bass range. And it just gets more interesting from there.

THE PIONEERS

TROJAN 7710 Samfie Man/Mother Rittie
Produced by Leslie Kong.

TROJAN 7723 Boss Festival/Lucky Slide
Produced by Leslie Kong.

TROJAN 7739 Driven Back/Trouble Dey a Bush
Produced by Leslie Kong.

TROJAN 7746 Simmer Down Quashie/Caranapo
Produced by Leslie Kong.

TROJAN 7760 Battle of the Giants/Message to Maria
Produced by Leslie Kong.

TROJAN 7781 Money Day/BEVERLEY ALL-STARS: Ska Ba Do
Produced by Leslie Kong.

TROJAN 7795 I Need Your Sweet Inspiration/Everything Is Nice
Produced by Leslie Kong.(a) Straight out of Motown, the horns and harmonies gallop over a generously jerking rhythm.

PHIL PRATT ALL STARS

House band for producer PHIL PRATT. (X) CHARLIE ACE, KEN BOOTHE, JOHN HOLT

THE PRESSURE BEAT

CAMEL 67 Heavy Load/Version

PRINCE BUSTER

FAB 127 Young Gifted & Black/PRINCE BUSTER'S ALL-STARS: The Rebel
Produced by Prince Buster.

FAB 131 That's All/The Preaching
Produced by Prince Buster.

FAB 132 Ganja Plant/Creation
Produced by Prince Buster.

FAB 140 Hit Me Back/Give Peace a Chance
Produced by Prince Buster.

FAB 150 Big Five/Musical College
Produced by Prince Buster. (a) The lush organ-led rendition of "Rainy Night in Georgia" is the only hint of decency on this post-innuendo laden slow stomper . . . that and the horn which obscures at least one of the obscenities. "Big Five" is often credited as the song which kicked off a host of imitators, each more bawdy and less veiled than the last, pushing the limits of both reality and trouser until JUDGE DREAD's "Big Twelve" finally tore them both. In fact, it leaves less to the imagination than any of them. (b) Once more around for the "Judge Dread" rhythm, except this time the Justice is giving singing lessons. He's not bad, either, although it's a shame the song fades just as he hits his stride and starts discussing the penalties for truancy. . . . Also released as PRINCE BUSTER 1.

PRINCE BUSTER'S ALL STARS

(X) PRINCE BUSTER

FAB 124 The Rebel/The Preacher
Produced by Prince Buster.

THE PRODIGAL SONS WITH THE CIMARRONS

ATTACK 8021 Get Lost Boss/THERESA & CATHERINE WITH THE CIMARRONS—I'll Be There

THE PROPHETS

(X) LLOYD & CLAUDETTE, LLOYD & THE PROPHETS, PATRICK & LLOYD

BIG SHOT 554 Crystal Blue Persuasion (Parts 1/2)

BIG SHOT 555 Tumble Time (Parts 1/2)

BIG SHOT 557 Revenge of Eastwood/Version

THE PRUNES

SONGBIRD 1023 Come a Little Closer/Version
Produced by Derrick Harriott.

THE PUNCHERS

(X) THE UPSETTERS

THE PYRAMIDS

DUKE 80 Geronimo/Feel Alright

TROJAN 7755 Feel Alright/Telstar

TROJAN 7770 To Sir with Love/Reggae Shuffle

RANDY'S ALL STARS

House band for VINCENT and CLIVE CHIN at Randy's. (X) DAVE BARKER

RANDY'S 500 I'm the One You're the One/End Us
Produced by Randy's.

RANDY'S 501 Pepper Pot/Same Thing
Produced by Randy's.

RANDY'S 502 Dixie/Five Cents
Produced by Randy's.
RANDY'S 506 Blue Danube Waltz/Together
Produced by Randy's.
RANDY'S 507 Bridge Over Troubled Water/Waterfall
Produced by Randy's.
RANDY'S 505 Emperor Waltz/War
Produced by Randy's.

THE RATIO
BIG CHIEF 102 Let There Be Peace in the World/Pharaohs Walk

THE REACTION
ATTACK 8022 Yes Yes You/CIMARRONS: Be There
COLUMBIA BLUE BEAT 119 Oh Me Oh My/RICO: It's Love

THE REBELS
BULLET 440 Nice Grind/SIDNEY ALL-STARS: Version
Produced by Sidney Crooks.
TROJAN 7779 It's All in the Game/Easy Come
Produced by Sidney Crooks.

KIRK REDDING
PAMA 799 Close Shave/THE UNTOUCHABLES: Prisoner of Love

THE REGGAE BOYS
(X) GLEN ADAMS
BULLET 431 Pupa Live on Eye Top/Give Me Faith
PRESSURE BEAT 5503 Walk by Day Fly by Night/JOE GIBBS:
  Unknown Tongue
Produced by Joe Gibbs.

THE REGGAE STRINGS
(X) HORACE FAITH

DOROTHY REID
(X) TOMMY MCCOOK

NEHEMIAH REID'S ALL STARS
HOT SHOT 03 Hot Pepper/Seawave
TORPEDO 23 Mafia/H.E.L.L. 5

THE REVELATION
TROJAN 7727 Suffering/MEGATONS: Crazy Elephant

ELI REYNOLDS
PUNCH 37 Mr. Carman/Chiney Man

PAT RHODEN
MARY LYN 101 Time Is Tight/MILTON & DENZIL: I Like It Like That
PAMA 811 Maybe the Next Time/Got to See You
PAMA SUPREME 298 Do What You Gotta Do/Crying Won't Help
  You

THE RHYTHM RULERS
(X) LLOYD JONES, WINSTON WRIGHT
BULLET 447 Second Pressure/Sammy Dead

SKETTO RICH
PAMA 806 Hound Dog/Black Girl

CYNTHIA RICHARDS
(X) SIR LORD COMIC
CLANDISC 210 Conversation/DYNAMITES: Version
Produced by Clancy Eccles.
CLANDISC 216 Can't Wait/Promises
Produced by Clancy Eccles.
CLANDISC 220 Foolish Fool/CLANCY & STITT: Dance Beat
Produced by Clancy Eccles.

RICO
(X) ANDY CAPP, JENNIFER JONES, SOLOMON JONES, MO-
HAWKS, REACTIONS

RICO & SATCH
Duo comprising PAT SATCHMO and RICO RODRIGUEZ.
DUKE 96 Surprise Package/PETE JOHNSON: I'm Sorry

THE RIGHTEOUS FLAMES
HIGH NOTE 052 Run to the Rock/GAYTONES: Run to the Rock
  Version
Produced by Sonia Pottinger.

MARTIN RILEY
(X) SLIM SMITH
CAMEL 53 Catch this Sound/Suspense
Produced by Martin Riley.
ESCORT 823 It Grows/We Had a Good Thing Going
Produced by Martin Riley.

MARTIN RILEY & FAY BENNETT
RILEY of THE SENSATIONS, THE UNIQUES; FAY BENNETT
daughter of saxophonist VAL BENNETT. (X) MARTIN RILEY
UPSETTER 336 Self Control/The Pill
Produced by Martin Riley. (a) Utilizing the same rhythm as
LLOYD TYRELL's "Birth Control," Riley works himself into
a suggestive lather while Bennett moans and groans in uni-
son . . . and the band grooves along nonchalantly in the
background. Bennett can be heard to similar effect on the
supremely suggestive "Mr Whittaker," one of DJ CHARLIE
ACE's finest moments. (b) The UPSETTERS' instrumental
version of "Self Control," with the keyboard now taking control. This was the only UK Upsetter 45 not to feature a
PERRY production on either side.

RITA & NAT COLE
(X) NAT COLE

BOB ROBERTS
EXPLOSION 2021 Stick by Me/TOMMY MCCOOK: The Designer

HUGH ROBERTS
EXPLOSION 2041 California Dreaming/One Woman

J ROBERTS
BAMBOO 30 Some Day We'll Be Together/SOUND DIMENSION:
  Everyday People
Produced by Coxsone Dodd.

JACKIE ROBINSON

PUNCH 50 Heart Made of Stone/BOB TAYLOR: I May Never See My Baby Anymore

LLOYD ROBINSON

CAMEL 41 The Worm/NEVILLE HINDS: Afro

THE ROCKSTONES

SUMMIT 8501 Everything Is Beautiful/BEVERLEY'S ALL-STARS: Give Up

Produced by Leslie Kong.

TROJAN 7762 ABC Reggae/BEVERLEY'S ALL-STARS: Be Yours

Produced by Leslie Kong. (b) Champagne music with a reggaefied beat, it might be a little too upbeat for the five star restaurants, but it's perfect for after-dinner dancing.

MAX ROMEO

CAMEL 66 Black Equality/WINSTON BLAKE: Big Thing

UNITY 545 Clap Clap/Death Rides a Horse

UNITY 547 What a Cute Man/Buy You a Rainbow

UNITY 560 Fish in the Pot/Feel It

Produced by H Robinson.

UNITY 571 Maccabee Version/SOUL SYNDICATE: Music book

Produced by Willie Francis. (a) The tinkling organ solos with "Good King Wenceslas," the rhythm section plays "Aily And Ailaloo," and Romeo sings an entirely different song altogether, a passionate defense in favor of the Maccabee version of the Bible and a condemnation of the more popular King James version.

GENE RONDO

DOWNTOWN 459 Spreading Peace/MUSIC DOCTORS: Guitar Riff

Produced by Dandy Livingstone.

THE ROOT BOYS

COLUMBIA BLUE BEAT 115 Please Don't Stop the Wedding/Your Love Your Love

ROSKO

UK disc jockey MICHAEL "EMPEROR ROSKO" PASTERNAK.

TROJAN 7758 Al Capone/Kaiser Bill

JOAN ROSS

CRAB 62 Band of Gold/THE HAMMERS: Midnight Sunshine

ROY & JOY

Duo featuring LITTLE ROY. (X) LITTLE ROY

THE RUDIES

PAMA 789 Give Peace a Chance/Theme from She

TROJAN 7798 Patches/Split

BRUCE RUFFIN

SUMMIT 8509 O-o-h Child/Bitterness of Life

TROJAN 7704 Dry Up Your Tears/BEVERLEY'S ALL-STARS: One Way Street

Produced by Leslie Kong.

TROJAN 7737 I'm the One/Who's Gonna Be Your Man?

Produced by Leslie Kong.

TROJAN 7776 Cecilia/BEVERLEY'S ALL-STARS: Stand Up

Produced by Leslie Kong.

RADCLIFF RUFFIN

(X) WINSTON WRIGHT

GG RUSSELL

MOODISC 3503 Wha Who Wha/MUDIE'S ALL-STARS: Version

CLAUDE SANG

SUGAR 105 I'm in Love Again/You'll Never Fool Me Again

PAT SATCHMO

(X) HORTENSE ELLIS

PUNCH 24 Wonderful World/THE MEDITATORS: Purple Mast

SONGBIRD 1039 A Handful of Friends/CRYSTALITES: Version

Produced by Derrick Harriott.

DOREEN SCHAEFFER

(X) THE SOUL MATES, THE WAILERS

THE SCORCHERS

(X) NEVILLE HINDS

MCBEAN SCOTT & THE CHAMPIONS

JACKPOT 744 Top of the World/THE CHAMPIONS: Everybody Reggae

Produced by Larry Lawrence.

SCOTTY

DJ aka DAVID SCOTT of THE FEDERALS, THE CHOSEN FEW. Also recorded as a duo with UX BROWN.

SONGBIRD 1044 Sesame Street/CRYSTALITES: Version

Produced by Derrick Harriott.

THE SENSATIONS

(X) WINSTON WRIGHT

TECHNIQUES 902 War Boat/Mr Blue

Produced by Winston Riley.

THE SETTERS

DUKE 65 Paint Your Wagon/Organ Man

TROJAN 7738 Virgin Soldier/Brixton Reggae Festival

SEXY FRANKIE

(X) CRITICS & NYAH SHUFFLE

WINSTON SHAN

MOODISC 3505 I'll Run Away/Time Is the Master

THE SHOW BOYS

GAS 129 People Are Wondering/Long Time

SID, JOE & THE MOHAWKS

PAMA 800 Down on the Corner/Who Is that Stranger

THE SIDNEY ALL STARS

Backing group formed by THE PIONEERS' SIDNEY CROOKS for his production work, following his relocation to the UK.

(X) SAMMY MORGAN, THE REBELS, THE VICEROYS

BULLET 436 The Return of Batman/In Action

BULLET 437 Outer Space/Full Moon

SILVER

COLUMBIA BLUE BEAT 117 Love Me Forever/SILVER & NOREEN: Sugar Sugar

SILVER & NOREEN

(X) SILVER

THE SILVERTONES

TROJAN 7705 Intensified Change/Marie

SUGAR SIMONE

BEACON 156 Keep on Trying/Only the Lonely

BEACON 174 Why Can't I Touch You/Gotta Get It off My Mind

BETTY SINCLAIR

TORPEDO 19 Why Why Why/HOT ROD ALL-STARS: A Fistful of Dollars

Produced by Lambert Briscoe. (a) Sinclair's strong, melodic vocals are the focus of this up-tempo song, on which she asks the musical question "why do coffee prices never rise at all?" Certainly an odd one.

SIR HARRY

(X) ERNEST WILSON

SIR LORD COMIC

PRESSURE BEAT 5507 Jack of My Trade/CYNTHIA RICHARDS: United We Stand

(a) Judging by his name, you'd expect a stand-up routine. Instead you're left with a few really moldy jokes, as Comic lazily toasts, boasts, and tears apart the competition across a repetitive backing track.

UPSETTER 326 Bronco/THE UPSETTERS: One Punch

Produced by Lee Perry. (a) Originally released in Jamaica in 1968. The guitar and clopping beat hold up the Western end, while the keyboard takes off for the greener pastures of a 60s pop variation on "Old Man River." Sir Lord Comic is left to round up the doggies with squeals, as Lee Perry intones the title over and over again. Perry would reissue the performance for a third time as "Django Shoots First," on 1973's *Rhythm Shower* album. (b) DERRICK MORGAN's "Hey Boy Hey Girl" rhythm. And one punch would be all it would take to knock out that annoying one finger keyboard. Sadly the tight beat isn't quite up to the task.

SIR WASHINGTON

BIG CHIEF 100 Apollo 13/Space

SISTER

CAMEL 55 Feel It/THE MAYTONES: Serious

THE SLICKERS

(X) THE VICEROYS

AMALGAMATED 866 Money Reaper/Man Beware

Produced by Joe Gibbs.

BULLET 449 Coolie Girl/BIGGIE: Bawling Baby

TROJAN 7718 Run Fattie/Hoola Bulla

DENNIS SMITH

(X) KEITH HUDSON

PUNCH 36 Ball of Confusion/Oh My Darlin'

Produced by Keith Hudson.

RAY SMITH

JACKPOT 723 The Wedding/Air Balloon

ROY SMITH

GRAPE 3013 See Through Craze/TERRY, CARL & DERRICK: I'm the One

SLIM SMITH

(X) WINSTON WILLIAMS

BANANA 304 Do Dang Do/JACKIE MITTOO & THE SOUND DIMENSION: Hot Milk

Produced by Coxsone Dodd.

GAS 132 The Vow/JAMES NEPHEW: Why Don't You Say

GAS 150 What Kind of Life/MARTIN RILEY: It's All in the Game

Produced by Martin Riley.

UNITY 570 Jenny/The Race

THE SOUL BROTHERS

PRESSURE BEAT 5506 Pussy Catch a Fire/THE DESTROYERS: Follow this Beat

(a) A lot of what we term rude reggae relies, indeed, on its rudeness for its impact, with the music a distinctly secondary concern. "Pussy," however, has an endearingly amateur quality to both the vocals and the execution, being primarily a discussion on how pussy caught a-fire, while the chorus simply laments that it has. A plodding piano and a screaming fire engine add to the carnage.

THE SOUL DIMENSION

(X) LARRY MARSHALL

THE SOUL DIRECTIONS

ATTACK 8011 Su Su Su/Better Hearing

Produced by Coxsone Dodd.

THE SOUL EXPLOSION

DOWNTOWN 455 Let's Try It Again/Gumpton Rock

Produced by Dandy Livingstone.

J-DAN 4405 My Mothers Eyes/Gum Pot

Produced by Dandy Livingstone.

THE SOUL MATES

UNITY 555 10 Cent/DOREEN SCHAEFFER: Stay with Me Forever

THE SOUL RHYTHMS

(X) HIPPY BOYS

THE SOUL SYNDICATE

Originally the RHYTHM RAIDERS, Greenwich Farm based session band first discovered by BUNNY LEE. Core members included GEORGE FULLWOOD (bass), TONY CHIN (guitar), KEITH STERLING (keyboards — brother of LESTER STERLING), EARL "CHINNA" SMITH (vocals, guitar), CARLTON "SANTA" DAVIS (drums). Temporary members included LEROY "HORSEMOUTH" WALLACE (drums), CLEON DOUGLAS (guitar), EARL LINDO (keyboards), TYRONE DOWNEY (keyboards), and others. (X) MAX ROMEO

THE SOUL TONES

PAMA 791 Dancing Time/BUNNY BARRETT: Love Locked Out

THE SOUL TWINS

Duo formed by DERRICK BURNETT and JIMMY NELSON. Rejected by DUKE REID, they cut "Pound Get a Blow" with LEE PERRY — credited to the BLEECHERS in the UK.

HIGH NOTE 043 Little Suzie/Cherrie

Produced by Sonia Pottinger.

THE SOULETTES

UPSETTER 337 Let It Be/THE UPSETTERS: Big Dog Bloxie

Produced by Lee Perry. (a) Just what the world needed, a chirpy reggae cover of the Beatles' most boring single. But the new-look Soulettes' lovely harmonies make it just about bearable. (b) No dog day afternoon this, "Bloxie" trots along on the laid back "Let It Be" beat, wagging his tail to a now-cheery melody.

THE SOUND DIMENSION

DENNIS BROWN, IRVING BROWN, THE CABLES, ALTON ELLIS, ETHIOPIANS, WINSTON FRANCIS, MARCIA GRIFFITHS, HEPTONES, JOHN HOLT, IM & DAVID, JERRY JONES, JACKIE MITTOO, J ROBERTS

BAMBOO 18 Poison Ivy/BOTHERATION Version

Produced by Coxsone Dodd.

BANANA 313 In the Summertime/Version

Produced by Coxsone Dodd.

FITZROY STERLING

BULLET 422 That's My Life/Queen of Hearts

LESTER STERLING

UNITY 562 Slip Up/DAVE BARKER: On Broadway

DELANO STEWART

HIGH NOTE 034 Hallelujah/I Wish It Could Last

Produced by Sonia Pottinger.

HIGH NOTE 039 Wherever I Lay My Hat/Don't Believe Him

Produced by Sonia Pottinger. (a) The band stay well in the background for this showcase of the popular singer's most impassioned vocals, on a Marvin Gaye song that white soul singer Paul Young would later take to the top of the UK chart.

HIGH NOTE 041 Stay a Little Bit Longer/Piano Version

Produced by Sonia Pottinger. (a) And how could you leave, with Stewart's sweet, sweet vocals echoing in your ears? At least, that's what the song seems to be hoping. One isn't quite sure what to make about the "hold on I'm coming" line, though.

THE SUGARPLUMS

FAB 160 Red River Reggae/Too Much

THE SUPERTONES

(X) JACKIE MITTOO

BANANA 312 Freedom Blues/First Time I Met You

Produced by Coxsone Dodd.

SYLVIN & GLENROY

TORPEDO 25 What You Gonna Do 'Bout It/KEN JONES: Sad Mood

SYMARIP

ATTACK 8013 I'm a Puppet/Vindication

TREASURE ISLE 7054 Parson's Corner/Redeem

Produced by Duke Reid.

TREASURE ISLE 7055 La Bella Jig/Holidays by the Sea

Produced by Duke Reid.

BOB TAYLOR

(X) JACKIE ROBINSON

VIC TAYLOR

(X) TOMMY MCCOOK

THE TECHNIQUES

(X) JOHNNY OSBOURNE, TECHNIQUES ALL STARS

BIG SHOT 536 He Who Keepeth His Mouth/One Day

Produced by Winston Riley. Also released as TREASURE ISLE 7054.

BIG SHOT 543 Come Back Darling/Move Over

Produced by Winston Riley.

TECHNIQUES 904 Lonely Man/I Feel Alive

Produced by Winston Riley.

TECHNIQUES 906 Feel a Little Better/You'll Get Left

Produced by Winston Riley.

THE TECHNIQUES ALL-STARS

Techniques label house band led by WINSTON RILEY, ex-TECHNIQUES. (X) ALTON ELLIS, HORTENSE ELLIS

BIG SHOT 545 Elfrego Bacca/TECHNIQUES: Iron Joe

Produced by Winston Riley.

TECHNIQUES 900 Something Tender/CANNONBALL: Bewitched

Produced by Winston Riley.

TROJAN 7728 Eldora/TECHNIQUES: If It's Not True

Produced by Winston Riley.

TERRY, CARL & DERRICK

(X) ROY SMITH

THERESA & CATHERINE WITH THE CIMARRONS

(X) PRODIGAL SONS WITH THE CIMARRONS

THE THIRD DIMENSION
UNITY 566 Peace & Love/Version
NICKY THOMAS
b Cecil Nicholas Thomas, 1949 (Portland, JA).
AMALGAMATED 863 Danzella/JOE GIBBS ALL-STARS: Kingstonians
  Reggae
Produced by Joe Gibbs. (a) Thomas sings soulfully over the busy backing band, all riffing guitar, stop and start rhythms, and percolating bass. In other words, yet another example of taking a perfectly good reggae arrangement and stiffing it with an emotive, R&B song.
TROJAN 7750 Love of the Common People/THE DESTROYERS:
  Compass
Produced by Joe Gibbs. (a) The Winstons' hit goes reggae light. Thomas tries to give it an urban feel, by virtually toasting the lyrics, but the instrumentation (and the references to the decidedly non-Caribbean phenomenon of snow) makes it clear this is destined for the overseas market, where it did very nicely indeed.
TROJAN 7796 God Bless the Children/Red Eye
Produced by Joe Gibbs.
TIGER
UK-based performer.
NU-BEAT 052 Soul of Africa/Dallas Texas
Produced by Laurel Aitken.
NU-BEAT 064 Musical Scorcher/Three Dogs Night
Produced by Laurel Aitken.
TOMMY & THE UPSETTERS
TROJAN 7717 Lock Jaw/YARDBROOMS: My Desire
Produced by Lee Perry. (a) DJed by DAVE BARKER.
TONY & DELROY
Vocal duo featuring DELROY DUNKLEY. (X) DELROY DUNKLEY
TONY & THE CHAMPIONS
(X) ERROL ENGLISH & THE CHAMPIONS
DUKE 90 Eye for an Eye/THE CHAMPIONS: Broke My Heart Version
TREVOR & KEITH
(X) CARL BRYAN
PUNCH 41 The Ark/MINNA BOYS: False Reader
THE TWINKLE BROTHERS
Original line-up: NORMAN GRANT (vocals, drums), RALSTON GRANT (vocals, guitar), ERIC BARNARD (vocals, guitar), KARL HYATT (percussion), ALBERT GREEN (percussion). One of the giants of the mid-late 1970s roots scene, the Twinkles broke up around 1980, although Grant — now based in the UK — continues to use the name for sporadic recordings and live work.
JACKPOT 731 You Can Do It Too/Enemies Beware
JACKPOT 740 Miss World/Take What You've Got

JACKPOT 741 Sweet Young Thing/Grandma
TWIZZLE & THE HOT ROD ALL-STARS
(X) SILKIE DAVIS
TORPEDO 3 Jook Jook/Graduate
Produced by Lambert Briscoe.
LLOYD TYRELL
BULLET 434 Exposure/Baby Huey
PAMA 792 Birth Control/VAL BENNETT: Return To Peace
(a) "Meeow Doris, the pussy dirty . . . go right in that bathroom and wash the pussy now." The backing track isn't all that special, but once you've figured out that it's not a record about bathing the cat, there's a lascivious smirk to be drawn from the lyric.
U-ROY
aka HUGH-ROY. See entry on page 292. Also recorded as a duo with HENRY, JOHN HOLT, HOPETON LEWIS, TOMMY MCCOOK, SLIM SMITH. (X) HEPTONES, YOUNG FREDDY
DUKE REID 2509 Wake the Town/Big Boy & Teacher
Produced by Duke Reid. (a) Stripping down the old ALTON ELLIS classic "Girl I've Got A Date" to its basic beats and organ flourishes so U-Roy can wake the town and tell the people. . . . (b) The original "What Is Katy" was innuendo laden to begin with, and U-Roy has a ball chasing the lyrics to their logical conclusions, as he sings and chats his way across the cut.
DUKE REID 2510 Rule the Nation/NORA DEAN: Ay Ay Ay
Produced by Duke Reid. (a) The TECHNIQUES' hit "You Don't Care" provided the rock steady rhythm and melody but, with the vocal track stripped away, U-Roy ruled the song, exhorting listeners to "make a move." And they did . . . directly to the stores, to buy up this single in massive numbers. (b) Another completely overlooked masterpiece. Rolling percussion and jungle cries dominate a deeply atmospheric chant, part erotic missive, part spiritual exaltation.
DUKE REID 2514 You'll Never Get Away/TOMMY MCCOOK: Rock
  Away
Produced by Duke Reid.
DUKE REID 2515 Versions Galore/TOMMY MCCOOK: Nehru
Produced by Duke Reid. (a) "Versions galore, you can hear them by the score," U-Roy exclaims, and The MELODIANS' reply, "We going to have good times together" — an astute summing up of rock steady's new musical role as backdrop to the toasters. This classic cut (of "You Have Caught Me") cemented the explosive rise of the DJ.
EXPLOSION 2040 Whisper a Little Prayer/Rain a Fall
PUNCH 34 Scandal/U-ROY & JOHN HOLT: Son of the Wise
Produced by Lloyd Daley.
U-ROY & HENRY
(X) CONCORDS

U-ROY & JOHN HOLT

(X) U-ROY

DUKE REID 2513 Wear You to the Ball/EARL LINDO: The Ball

Produced by Duke Reid. (a) Over the PARAGONS' hit of the same title, U-Roy throws down the musical gauntlet, "I'm tougher than tough, and that is no bluff, maybe because I've got the musical stuff," encouraging not just a host of imitators but an entire generation of chatterers to grab the mike and try to best him. (b) Jaunty organ-led instrumental version of the a-side.

THE UNTOUCHABLES

(X) DAVE BARKER, KIRK REDDING

UPSETTER 345 UNTOUCHABLES: Same Thing All Over/It's Over

Produced by Lee Perry. (a) The Untouchables do a fine job imitating the best of American R&B a la Sam Cooke, but the musical arrangement is pure Perry, with the horns adding a nice emphasis to the vocalists' soulful delivery. (b) A radical reworking of the old hit. The absence of drums surprises, but the rhythm is set by the slow, pulsing bass and, with just a hint of subtle keyboards behind them, the vocalists are left to sing virtually a cappella. A staggering performance.

THE UPSETTERS

(X) DAVE BARKER, NEILL HALL, THE HEATERS, JOHN LENNON, CHUCK JUNIOR, LEE PERRY, SIR LORD COMIC, SOULETTES, TOMMY

PUNCH 27 The Result/Feel the Spirit

Produced by Lee Perry.

PUNCH 46 Son Of Thunder/PUNCHERS: Do It Madly

Produced by Lee Perry. (a) Perry, in his guise of the almighty "Son Of Thunder" displays his wrath, hurling lightning bolts and threats across a track designed to make you quake, proving "you should never upset The Upsetter." Maybe he can do something about those keyboards, then.

SPINNING WHEEL 100 Haunted House/Double Wheel

Produced by Melanie Jonas.

SPINNING WHEEL 101 The Miser/CHUCK JUNIOR: Do It Madly

Produced by Melanie Jonas. (b) The clattering band almost overpowers Chuck, but so focused is he on his soul light vocals, that he just pulls this single out of the trash.

TROJAN 7748 Family Man/Mellow Mood

Produced by Lee Perry.

TROJAN 7749 Apo/Mama Look

Produced by Lee Perry.

UPSETTER 332 Na Na Hey Hey (Kiss Him Goodbye)/Pick Folk Kinkiest

Produced by Lee Perry. (a) A rather irreverent version of the Steam smash, with a punctuated rhythm and some great wah-wah keyboards. The chorus is delivered at breakneck pace. (b) "I am the kinkiest," Perry announces, and it's hard to argue when the producer knocks out rhythm and effects riven tracks like this.

UPSETTER 333 Granny Show (Parts 1/2)

Produced by Lee Perry. (a) There's a hint of the racecourse about this upbeat instrumental. The racing rhythm is the centerpiece, with the staccato keyboards adding a fun day at the fairground feel. (b) This version adds a flamboyant organ on top of the flipside.

UPSETTER 334 Fire Fire/The Jumper

Produced by Lee Perry. (a) A solid mid-tempo instrumental that wants to set the world alight, but the keyboard's too restrained for that. More flamboyance, for once, would have helped. (b) GLEN ADAMS obviously saved his keyboard excitement for this hopping track. The beat slams up and down like a toddler screaming for ice cream — all together now: pogo, pogo, pogo, pogo.

UPSETTER 335 The Pillow/Grooving

Produced by Lee Perry. (a) A twangy lullaby meets "Save the Last Dance for Me." (b) A lackadaisical rhythm is punctuated by keyboard flourishes, and segments where the organ has an acid flashback and the guitars churn in a psychedelic haze. And then it's back into the groove.

UPSETTER 338 Fresh Up/Toothache

Produced by Lee Perry. (a) The band is off on a lark for this breezy instrumental. The bongos add to the walk in the local park feel, while the keyboards create a touch of dreaminess, like lying back and staring at the clouds. (b) The Upsetters' dentist must use some mighty magic gas. Why else would the group sound so upbeat? Even when the organ buzzes like a drill, the rhythm keeps loping happily along.

UPSETTER 339 Thanks We Get/Hurry Up

Produced by Lee Perry. (a) THE VERSATILES take the lead, their hard-done-by anger seeps across the single, emphasized by the jerking rhythms. Later, Perry would create an even harder hitting version by adapting the rhythms for "Beat Down Babylon," a single featuring JUNIOR BYLES alone. (b) The restrained, insistent beat prods this infectious song into action, while the VERSATILES beautifully declare their urgency in harmony "no time to waste, I'm just going my way."

UPSETTER 341 Thunder Version/Blood Poison

Produced by Lee Perry. (a) Without Perry's magnificent oracle, "Son Of Thunder" just doesn't sound anywhere near as threatening as its vocal counterpart. (b) An almost languid instrumental, the organ melody slowly flowing by, but the rhythm section keeps it all pumping.

UPSETTER 342 Dreamland/Version of Cup

Produced by Lee Perry. (a) An instrumental version of the WAILERS' song, with the organ taking BUNNY LIVINGSTON's vocal lines. (b) The instrumental version of the WAILERS' "My Cup."

UPSETTER 346 Bigger Joke/Return of the Vampire
Produced by Lee Perry. (a) The rhythm section blithely plays away, while keyboardist ADAMS reluctantly follows along. . . . But what's the offbeat hammering going on in the background? No, it's not a "knock-knock" gag, but it's just as inexplicable. (b) This time the vampire needs no introduction, but it's now left to the sax player to take the melodic lead, which leaves the old bloodsucker seeming just as pleasant as last time, but not quite as ludicrously cheerful.

UPSETTER 343 Sipreano/Ferry Boat
Produced by Lee Perry. (a) The rhythm does all the expected things, but the melody is a nod to a moody "The Liquidator," with The Upsetter taking on the role of toaster to mash up the nation. (b) This boat is apparently ferrying a herd of mustangs to judge by its clopping beat. And perhaps the repetitive keyboard lines are meant to remind us of waves, which would explain why it never really arrives anywhere.

THE URBAN CLEARWAY

TORPEDO 21 Open Up Wide (Parts 1/2)
Produced by Eddy Grant.

THE VERSATILES

NU-BEAT 060 Pick My Pocket/THE FREEDOM SINGERS: Freedom
Produced by Joe Gibbs.

THE VICEROYS

(X) HENRY III, HUBCAP & WHEELS
BULLET 441 Chariot Coming/SIDNEY ALL-STARS: Stackata
Produced by Sidney Crooks.
BULLET 444 Power Control/THE SLICKERS: Dip Dip
Produced by Sidney Crooks.
BULLET 450 Come on Over/SIDNEY ALL-STARS: Version
Produced by Sidney Crooks.
BULLET 453 Fancy Clothes/BIGGIE: Jack & Jill
Produced by Sidney Crooks.

THE WAILERS

(X) DAVE BARKER, LEE PERRY
BAMBOO 55 Jailhouse/JOHN HOLT: A Stranger in Love
Produced by Coxsone Dodd. (a) Reissued and retitled from 1965's "Good Good Rudie."
ESCORT 842 Run for Cover/To the Rescue
Produced by the Wailers.
JACKPOT 730 Mr Chatterbox/DOREEN SCHAEFFER: Walk Thru this World
Produced by Bunny Lee. (a) The Wailers dismiss the mighty NINEY in the intro to this revised version of "Mr Talkative."
TROJAN 7759 Soul Shakedown Party/BEVERLEY ALL STARS: version
Produced by Leslie Kong. (a) The perfect accompaniment to those British Northern soul parties, "Shakedown" encompasses a hint of Motown around the harmonies, some per-

fect cheeky keyboards, a tinge of funky soul to the beat, and an exuberant melody.

UPSETTER 348 Duppy Conqueror/UPSETTERS: Justice
Produced by Lee Perry. (a) The juttering beat's a Perry classic, while LIVINGSTON and TOSH's backing vocals are at their most delicate (at times they actually twitter like tiny songbirds). An exquisite proto-roots recording, a showcase for MARLEY at his most outspoken and rebellious. This was the accompanying SOUL SYNDICATE's second Wailers session, following "The Sun Is Shining." (b) An instrumental version of "Give Me Justice" with the sax just as demanding as Perry's vocals. Also released as UNITY 562.

UPSETTER 340 My Cup/LEE PERRY & THE WAILERS: Son of Thunder
Produced by Lee Perry. (a) The first Wailers track cut in what would prove a fabulously productive relationship. Perry pulls out a suitably sinuous bass rhythm, while the Wailers belt out the lyrics in their most soulful vocals.

THE WAILING SOULS

BANANA 305 Row Fisherman Row/Thou Shalt Not Steal
Produced by Coxsone Dodd.
BANANA 307 Back Out/Pack Your Things
Produced by Coxsone Dodd.

WALTERS ALL STARS

(X) DELROY WILSON

THE WANDERERS

TROJAN 7721 Wiggle Waggle/Jaga Jaga War

NORMAN T WASHINGTON

PUNCH 26 Sweeter than Honey/1000 Pearls
PUNCH 31 Last Goodbye/Mother's Pride
A Pama Records Production.

MARLENE WEBBER

b 1952. Member of THE TONETTES, WEBBER SISTERS.
BAMBOO 33 My Baby/BRENTFORD ALL-STARS: You Gonna Hold Me Version
Produced by Coxsone Dodd.

NORRIS WEIR & THE JAMAICANS

DUKE 85 Hard on Me/TOMMY COWAN & THE JAMAICANS: Please Stop the Wedding

THE WESTMORELITES

CLANDISC 217 Zion/CLANCY ECCLES & THE DYNAMITES: Revival
Produced by Clancy Eccles.

PETE WESTON BAND

GAS 146 Something Sweet/BIM & BAM: Love Letters
PUNCH 28 In the Mood/ASTON BARRETT: Slide Mongoose

JOE WHITE

BIG 301 This Is the Time/The Other Day
BIG 309 Baby I Care/Ain't Misbehavin'
SUGAR 103 Yesterday/I Am Free

SUGAR 102 My Guiding Star/If I Needed Someone
TROJAN 7742 So Much Love/Maybe Now
(a) The overly busy band roadblocks White throughout this tortured torch song.
TROJAN 7768 I'm Going to Get There/RUPIE EDWARDS ALL-STARS: Kinky Funky Reggae
Produced by Rupie Edwards. (a) A rather disconcerting amalgamation of social consciousness twinned with a plea for a good woman, but White's heartfelt passion bleeds through regardless. (b) Kinky maybe, funky not at all; a rather tedious up-tempo reggaefied instrumental, with just a touch of oddness about it all.

SPENCER WIGGINS

PAMA 794 I'm a Poor Man's Son/That's How Much I Love You

LLOYD WILLIAMS

BAMBOO 41 I'm in Love with You/Little Girl

RANNY WILLIAMS

(X) OWEN GRAY
BULLET 426 Summer Place/Big Boy
PUNCH 32 Smile/Musical ID
Produced by Ranny Williams.

WINSTON WILLIAMS

JACKPOT 733 DJ Choice/SLIM SMITH: Can't Do Without It
Produced by Bunny Lee. (a) Williams boastfully toasts over a stripped down rhythm track with just a whiff of melody to keep it going.
JACKPOT 743 The People's Choice/BOBBY JAMES: Let Me Go Girl

LLOYD WILLIS

Producer aka GITSY.
PRESSURE BEAT 5502 Mad Rooster/As Far as I Can See
UNITY 543 Ivan Hitler the Conqueror/The Splice

DELROY WILSON

CAMEL 69 Be My Wife/WALTER'S ALL STARS: Hit Me Honey
JOE'S 11 Don't Play that Song/BOSS ALL-STARS: Just One Look
Produced by Joe Mansano.
SUMMIT 8503 Got to Get Away/BEVERLEY'S ALL-STARS: Version
Produced by Leslie Kong. (a) A twangy guitar gives this old chestnut a Western tinge; the organ adds just the right topping of ebullience, while Wilson's soulful vocals hit just the perfect note of panic.
TROJAN 7740 Show Me the Way/BEVERLEY'S ALL-STARS: Version
Produced by Leslie Kong.(a) Wilson explores the theme of betterment on this optimistic song, which features one of the producer's subtler rhythms.
TROJAN 7769 Gave You My Love/BEVERLEY'S ALL-STARS: Version
Produced by Leslie Kong. (a) The breezy keyboard melody is a delight, Wilson's delivery is beautifully understated and the harmonies add further fizz.
UNITY 559 Drink Wine Everybody/Someone to Call My Own

ERNEST WILSON

CRAB 43 Elusive Dream/SIR HARRY: Hi Cup

ERNEST WILSON & FREDDY

Vocal duo featuring CLARENDONIANS WILSON and FREDDIE MCGREGOR.
CRAB 46 Sentimental Man/It's a Lie
UNITY 564 Love Makes the World Go Round/Version

WINSTON & CECIL

BANANA 306 United We Stand/SOUND DIMENSION: Sweet Message
Produced by Coxsone Dodd.

WINSTON & RUPERT

BULLET 425 Come by Here/Somebody

OWEN WRIGHT

BANANA 310 Wala Wala/JERRY & THE FREEDOM SINGERS: Got to Be Sure
Produced by Coxsone Dodd.

WINSTON WRIGHT

(X) ETHIOPIANS, JOHN HOLT, KING SPORTY, BYRON LEE
BAMBOO 60 Reggae Feet/DON DRUMMOND: Royal Flush
EXPLOSION 2011 Flight 404/LLOYD & ROBIN: Gawling Come Down
Produced by Alvin Ranglin.
EXPLOSION 2015 Funny Girl/Version
GG 4504 It's Been a Long Time/PAULETTE & GEE: Feel It More & More
Produced by Alvin Ranglin.
HIGH NOTE 040 Soul Pressure/Seed You Sow
Produced by Sonia Pottinger.
MOODISC 3501 Musically Red/RHYTHM RULERS: Bratah
TROJAN 7701 Moonlight Groover/SENSATIONS: Everyday Is Just a Holiday
Produced by Duke Reid (b) A suggestion of the ABYSSINIANS' "Satta Amasa Gana" lends this lovely ballad a powerfully rootsy sensation.
TROJAN 7715 Moon Invader/RADCLIFF RUFFIN: You Got to Love Me
TROJAN 7775 Meshwire/THE BARONS: Darling Please Return
(b) The lead Baron croons and the backing vocalists "ooh" and "aah." And then the band wakes up. Yet another tragic twinning of a perfectly decent torch song to upbeat, reggaefied rhythms.

THE YARDBROOMS

(X) TOMMY & THE UPSETTERS

YOUNG DOUG

(X) DIRTY HARRY

YOUNG FREDDIE

aka FREDDIE MCGREGOR of THE CLARENDONIANS.
CAMEL 38 Drink & Gamble/LENNOX BROWN & U-ROY: King of the Road

YOUNG SATCH

BLACK SWAN 1401 Bongo Bongo/BOYS: Ramba

DESI YOUNG

PRESSURE BEAT 5504 News Flash/JOE GIBBS: Version

HARRY YOUNG

(X) GREGORY ISAACS

YOUTH

(X) BOBBY FOSTER

1971

CHARLIE ACE

GG 4507 Ontarius/GG ALL-STARS: Ontarius Version

Produced by Alvin Ranglin.

GG 4518 Do Something/MAYTONES: Groove Me

Produced by Byron Smith. (a) Ace toasts over THE MAY-
TONES' "Groove Me," winding up the audience to a limber
beat in BIG YOUTH-like fashion. Also released as PUNCH 67.

SMASH 2325 Need No Whip/Grine Grine

UPSETTER 359 The Creeper/Version

Produced by Lee Perry.

GLEN ADAMS

(X) MAXIE & GLEN

BIG 321 Weary/TONY BREVETT: Hills & Valleys

EXPLOSION 2048 Never Fall in Love/JET SCENE: Jet 747

(b) An instrumental version of "I'll Never Fall in Love
Again," with the sublime sax handling the melody and the
backing singers giving the song even more power.

AFRO

PUNCH 89 Lonely World/ALTON ELLIS ALL-STARS: Put It On

THE AGGROS

(X) BOBBY JAMES & DAVE

PUNCH 56 What Do You Fall in Love For/SLICKERS: Too Much

THE AGGROVATORS

(X) DENNIS ALCAPONE, JOHN HOLT, DELROY WILSON

SMASH 2312 One More Bottle of Beer/Version

Produced by Bunny Lee.

LAUREL AITKEN

BIG SHOT 595 Dancing with My Baby/Do the Boogaloo

Produced by Laurel Aitken.

BLACK SWAN 1408 If It's Hell Below/Just a Little Bit of Love

Produced by Laurel Aitken.

NU-BEAT 078 True Love/The Best I Can

Produced by Laurel Aitken.

NU-BEAT 089 I Can't Stop Loving You/El Paso

Produced by Laurel Aitken.

TROJAN 7826 It's Too Late/Slow Rock

Produced by Laurel Aitken.(a) Over a tentative rhythm, Aitken's emotional lyrics are lightened by the cheery melody.

AL & EWAN

Featuring EWAN MCDERMOTT.

MOODISC 107 Let's Talk It Over/Set Me Free

Produced by Harry Mudie.

DENNIS ALCAPONE

(X) STRANGER COLE, KEITH HUDSON

BANANA 341 Forever Version/I Don't Want to See You Cry

Produced by Coxsone Dodd. (a) Over the rhythm of CARL-
TON AND THE SHOES' "Love Me Forever," the DJ rousts
and rocks upon the theme of versions, riding the waves of
harmony and beats like a rodeo star.

CAMEL 74 This a Butter/PHIL PRATT ALL-STARS: Version

Produced by Phil Pratt. (a) The DJ tries to enliven the proceedings, but the riff and lyrical snatch are so repetitive that
even Alcapone can't rouse them from their slumbers.

DUKE 125 Medley/Version

Produced by Duke Reid.

DYNAMIC 421 Horse & Buggy/ROLAND ALPHONSO & DENZIL LAING:
    Buggy & Horse

Produced by Bunny Lee. (a) The hop-along rhythm, Western guitar twang, screechy organ and cries of "Mule Train"
fuel the cut, while Alcapone's vocals are like a whip to a
steer and spurs to the horses.

DYNAMIC 422 Ripe Cherry/INNER CIRCLE: Red Cherry

Produced by Bunny Lee. (a) ERIC DONALDSON's "Cherry
Oh Baby" provides the background for Alcapone to sing and
boast to, while tossing in his nursery-like rhymes.

DYNAMIC 427 Alcapone's Guns Don't Argue/Version

Produced by Bunny Lee. (a) But they do take a bow, as the
DJ debuts munitions into his patter, and once here, they'll
rarely leave the dancehall again.

GG 4526 King of Kings/GG ALL-STARS: Rod of Righteousness

Produced by Alvin Ranglin. (a) Alcapone sets aside his usual
rhymes to preach the Rastafarian word, with MAX ROMEO
and GLEN ADAM's beautiful duet "Jordan River" providing
the perfect backdrop.

JACKPOT 776 Tell It Like It Is/Come Along

Produced by Bunny Lee.

SUPREME 214 You Must Believe Me/RUPIE EDWARDS ALL-STARS:
    Funk the Funk

Produced by Rupie Edwards.

TREASURE ISLE 7069 The Great Woggie/TOMMY MCCOOK:
    Buttercup Version

Produced by Duke Reid. (a) PRINCE TONY ROBINSON was
behind the CHOSEN FEW's "You Don't Care," a brashly
reggaefied cover of the TECHNIQUES classic; now the DJ
chants his musical rhymes over it, a combination which
works perfectly.

TREASURE ISLE 7074 Wake Up Jamaica/TOMMY MCCOOK: version

Produced by Duke Reid.

TROPICAL 003 False Prophet/MAX ROMEO: Rude Medley
Produced by Niney Holness. (a) Alcapone is righteously indignant in this soulful song about a thieving preacher.

UPSETTER 373 Well Dread/UPSETTERS:Dread Version
Produced by Lee Perry. (b) Featuring trombonist VIN "DON DRUMMOND JR" GORDON, and utilizing the same rhythm as Alcapone's recent "Ripe Cherry" 45.

UPSETTER 377 Alpha & Omega/JUNIOR BYLES: Beat Down Babylon
Produced by Lee Perry.

DENNIS ALCAPONE & JOHN HOLT
JACKPOT 773 Jumping Jack/THE AGGROVATORS: King of the Track
Produced by Bunny Lee.

JACKPOT 775 Togetherness/?
Produced by Bunny Lee.

DENNIS ALCAPONE & MAX ROMEO
PRINCE BUSTER 12 Let It Roll/ANSELL COLLINS: Clear Blue
Produced by Prince Buster.

DENNIS ALCAPONE & DELROY WILSON
(X) STRANGER COLE

URIE ALDRIDGE
(X) JOHN HOLT

HARRY J 6634 Set Me Free/Version
Produced by Harry J.

ROLAND ALPHONSO
(X) MAYTALS, NINEY, THE SLICKERS

BANANA 327 Shelly Belly/MAD ROY: Universal Love
Produced by Coxsone Dodd.

ROLAND ALPHONSO & DENZIL LAING
(X) DENNIS ALCAPONE

BOB ANDY
TROJAN 7809 Green Green Valley/Peace of Mind
TROJAN 7821 One Woman/You Don't Know
The former PARAGON takes on the Johnny Rivers' hit for a MOR vocal showcase that oozes lush strings and sweet female backing singers. But one wonders why he bothered, considering his own songwriting genius. Also released as TROJAN 7840.

HORACE ANDY
See entry on page 22. (X) JUNCUNO SINGERS

ANDY'S ALL STARS
(X) NORA DEAN

THE AQUARIANS/AQUARIUS SOUL BAND
Studio band at Aquarius for producer HERMAN CHIN-LOY. aka AQUARIUS SOUL BAND. (X) HERMAN, AUGUSTUS PABLO

ACKEE 135 Circy Cap/Version
Produced by Herman Chin-Loy.

ACKEE 137 Rebel/Invasion Version
Produced by Herman Chin-Loy.

JOHNNY ARTHEY ORCHESTRA
(X) FREDDIE NOTES

HERON ATTAR
(X) TWINKLE BROTHERS

DAVE BARKER
(X) BUSTY BROWN, LIZZY & THE PARAGONS

ACKEE 113 Johnny Dollar/Version
ACKEE 119 Life of a Millionaire/Version
DOWNTOWN 482 Only the Strong Survive/Version
PUNCH 69 What a Confusion/WAILERS: Small Axe
Produced by Lee Perry.

SUPREME 228 Double Heavy/Johnny Dollar
TROJAN 7851 Sex Machine/You Left Me & Gone
UPSETTER 358 Shocks 71/HURRICANES: You've Got to Be Mine
Produced by Lee Perry.

UPSETTER 362 Groove Me/UPSETTERS: Screwdriver
Produced by Lee Perry. (a) Cover of the King Floyd blues.

UPSETTER 364 What a Confusion/UPSETTERS Version
Produced by Lee Perry.

JEFF BARNES
(X) DARKER SHADE OF BLACK, DELROY WILSON

SMASH 2313 Wake the Nation/1000 Tons of Version

KEELING BECKFORD
GG 4514 Groove Me/Groove Version
Produced by Alvin Ranglin.

THE BELTONES
(X) WILLIAM BROWN

BRUCE BENNETT
BIG 311 If You Don't Mind/Lenore

JO JO BENNETT
(X) I-ROY

MOODISC 104 Snowbird/The Drifter
Produced by Harry Mudie.

MOODISC 108 Poison Ivy/Ivy Poison
Produced by Harry Mudie.

MOODISC 3514 Snowbird/Change the Tide
Produced by Harry Mudie.

VAL BENNETT
(X) GG ALL STARS

BEVERLEY'S ALL STARS
(X) KEN BOOTHE, BRENT DOWE, BRUCE DOWNER, GAYLADS, MAYTALS, MELODIANS, PIONEERS, SAMUEL THE FIRST

BIGGER D
aka JEFF DIXON. (X) MAD ROY

TONY BINNS
EXPLOSION 2044 Love I Madly/Musical Shower
EXPLOSION 2046 Humpty Dumpty/I Got to Get a Message

WINSTON BLAKE & M SQUAD

GREEN DOOR 4003 Carroll Street/ANSELL COLLINS & M SQUAD: Version

THE BLEECHERS

DUKE 118 Put It Good/JJ ALL-STARS: Good Good Version
Produced by JJ Johnson.

THE BLUES BUSTERS

DYNAMIC 408 Each One Teach One/Thinking of You
Produced by Byron Lee. (a) From the album of the same name, grisly over-produced tourist-trapping sap, benighted by lounge club arrangements and dog-whistle backing vocals. There are worse cuts on the full album ("To Love Somebody"), but the single is cursed enough. (b) Ditto.

BOB & MARCIA

TROJAN 7818 Pied Piper/Save Me
Produced by Harry J.

BOBBY & DAVE

(X) LIZZY & DENNIS
ACKEE 116 Build My World Around You/LIZZY & TONY BOP: Sammy Version

LEE BOGLE

BLACK SWAN 1406 Tomorrow's Dreams/SWANS: Hot Pants Reggae

JOYCE BOND

TROJAN 7837 Help Me Make It Through the Night/Reconsider Our Love

KEN BOOTHE

BANANA 352 Original Six (Parts 1/2)
Produced by Coxsone Dodd.

BIG SHOT 590 So Nice/Version

DYNAMIC 411 Hallelujah/Trying to Reach
Produced by Byron Lee.

GAS 169 Give It Me/Why

GREEN DOOR 4002 Medley Version/Medley Version

PUNCH 70 Stop Your Crying/CONSCIOUS MINDS: Suffering Through the Nation

SUMMIT 8518 I Wish It Could Be Peaceful Again/BEVERLEY'S ALL-STARS: Version
Produced by Leslie Kong.

SUMMIT 8519 Your Feeling & Mine/BEVERLEY'S ALL-STARS: Version
Produced by Leslie Kong.

SUMMIT 8523 Now I Know/JAMES CHAMBERS: Bongo Man
(a) Everything comes together perfectly here, the band simmer along, the backing trio are heavenly, and Boothe is all sweet passion.

BOY FRIDAY

(X) DANNY RAYMOND
DOWNTOWN 470 Version Girl/Grumble Man
Produced by Dandy Livingstone.

DOWNTOWN 471 Music So Good/Right Track
Produced by Dandy Livingstone.

DOWNTOWN 472 Sounds I Remember/JOAN LONG: Reconsider Our Love
Produced by Dandy Livingstone.

DOWNTOWN 473 Take a Message Ruby/Sunshine Track
Produced by Dandy Livingstone.

DOWNTOWN 476 There'll Always Be Sunshine/Sunshine Track
Produced by Dandy Livingstone.

DOWNTOWN 477 Hot Pants Girl/Raunchy
Produced by Dandy Livingstone.

DOWNTOWN 481 El Raunchy/Conversation
Produced by Dandy Livingstone.

J-DAN 4416 I Don't Want No War/Third Note Swing
Produced by Dandy Livingstone.

J-DAN 4418 Situation Version/OUR BAND: Keep Tracking
Produced by Dandy Livingstone.

BOY WONDER

(X) TWINKLE BROTHERS

SONNY BRADSHAW & YOUNG JAMAICA

BIG SHOT 576 Wig Wam/Peace & Love

TONY BREVETT

A member of THE MELODIANS. (X) GLEN ADAMS
SUPREME 224 Don't Get Weary/BREVETT ALL-STARS: Version

BREVETT ALL STARS

(X) TONY BREVETT

AL BROWN

(X) JOHN HOLT
BANANA 360 No Soul Today/RUFFIANS: Where Did I Go Wrong
Produced by Leslie Kong.

BUSTY BROWN

ESCORT 845 Man Short/DAVE BARKER: She Want It
(b) Barker barks his usual brand of wild whoops and exhortations, encouraging a friend to give the girl what she wants. "Don't be SHY! Sock it to HER!! Give her LOVE!!!"

PUNCH 72 You Inspire Me/Version

DENNIS BROWN

BAMBOO 309 No Man Is an Island/SOUL SISTERS: Another Night
Produced by Coxsone Dodd.

BAMBOO 336 Never Fall in Love/Make It with You
Produced by Coxsone Dodd.

BANANA 338 Silky/SOUND DIMENSION: My Sweet Lord
Produced by Coxsone Dodd.

OCEAN 001 Little Green Apples/SOUND DIMENSION: Version
Produced by Coxsone Dodd.

JACKIE BROWN

HIGH NOTE 057 One Night of Sin/GAYTONES: Version
Produced by Sonia Pottinger.

JAMES BROWN

PUNCH 76 Don't Say/TRANS AM ALL-STARS: Version

TEDDY BROWN

TROJAN 7827 Walk the World Away/Senorita Blue

TREVOR BROWN

(X) MAYTONES

WILLIAM BROWN

ACKEE 128 I'm Alone/BELTONES: Soul People

Produced by Coxsone Dodd. (b) Heavy on the harmonies, the Beltones' creamy vocals lift a fairly mediocre song towards the skies — the "la la la la" refrain is utterly contagious.

CARL BRYAN

(X) ALTON ELLIS

DES BRYAN

(X) THE DELTONES

RAD BRYAN

b Radcliff Bryan. One of Jamaica's leading session guitarists; in the mid-1970s a member of the REVOLUTIONARIES and later SLY & ROBBIE'S TAXI GANG.

BIG SHOT 559 Just Do the Right Thing/Corporal Jones

BIG SHOT 591 I'll Be Right There/Hot Pants Rock

BIG SHOT 592 My Best Girl/Version

BULLET 463 Shock Attack/Cuban Waltz

TECHNIQUES 909 Jumping Jack/ANSELL COLLINS: Point Blank

Produced by Winston Riley.

BUNNY & KEIMANAIRIES

GG 4521 Devil's Angel/Version

Produced by Alvin Ranglin.

BURNING SPEAR

(X) KING CRY CRY

JUNIOR BYLES

See entry on page 54. Member of THE VERSATILES. Also recorded as KING CHUBBY. (X) DENNIS ALCAPONE, THE WAILERS

UPSETTER 365 Place Called Africa/THE UPSETTERS: Earthquake

Produced by Lee Perry. (a) One of the most passionate repatriation songs ever released, Byles' vocals vividly express pure yearning for the lost homeland. The bittersweet melody further enhances the mood, while the instrumentation gives the song an overall dreamy quality.

THE CABLES

(X) DINGLE BROS

BIG SHOT 598 A Sometime Girl/Version

THE CAMBODIANS

DUKE 101 Coolie Man/JJ ALL-STARS: Coolie Version

Produced by JJ Johnson.

BILL & PETE CAMPBELL

DUKE 123 Come on Home/You Are Mine

CANDY & THE CIMARRONS

(X) BILLY JACKS

JAMES CHAMBERS

(X) KEN BOOTHE

CHARLES, PAULETTE & GEE

Vocal trio featuring PAULETTE and GEE WILLIAMS (THE EBONY SISTERS).

GG 4515 Shock & Shake/WINSTON WRIGHT: Roll On

Produced by Alvin Ranglin.

CHARLEY & ALTON

(X) CHARLEY & LLOYD

CHARLEY & LLOYD

PUNCH 62 Love I Madly/CHARLEY & ALTON: Especially for You

LLOYD CHARMERS

(X) ERIC DONALDSON, LLOYD TYRELL

EXPLOSION 2045 Skinhead Train/TONY & CHARMERS: Everstrong

EXPLOSION 2055 Reggae in Wonderland/Version

GREEN DOOR 4000 Rasta Never Fails/Version

GREEN DOOR 4001 One Big Unhappy Family/CONSCIOUS MINDS: Africa Is Paradise

PAMA SUPREME 339 Shaft/Harry's Mood

PAMA SUPREME 340 Red Head Duck/Jingle Jangle

SUPREME 220 Just My Imagination/Got to Get a Message to You

THE CHOSEN FEW

SONGBIRD 1061 Shaft/Version

Produced by Derrick Harriott. (a) Starts off as a note perfect cover, then goes all rootsy with the funk erased and replaced by fat bass, bubbling organ, and riffing guitar. No one told the vocalists, though.

SONGBIRD 1067 Everybody Just a Stall/Version

Produced by Derrick Harriott.

THE CIMARRONS

BIG SHOT 562 Funky Fight/You Turned Me Down

DOWNTOWN 486 Oh Mammy Blue/Version

Produced by Dandy Livingstone.

DOWNTOWN 487 Holy Christmas/Silent Night/White Christmas

Produced by Dandy Livingstone.

SPINNING WHEEL 107 Soul for Sale/Bogus-ism

CLANCY'S ALL STARS

(X) OWEN GRAY

THE CLARENDONIANS

GREEN DOOR 4009 Seven in One (Parts 1/2)

LLOYD CLARKE

(X) SOULETTES, DELROY WILSON

THE CLASSICS

PAMA 830 Sex Education/POWER: Soul Flash
Produced by Laurel Aitken.

PUNCH 79 Cheerio Baby/Civilisation
Produced by Lee Perry. (a) Based on ERIC DONALDSON's "Cherry Oh Baby" and recorded in London, although producer Perry cut the rhythm track (in Jamaica) at the same time as that of "I'm A Believer," a single he produced for vocalist DENZIL DENNIS during the same trip. (b) Credited to the CLASSICS, but clearly featuring entirely different (unknown) vocalists.

JIMMY CLIFF

ISLAND 6100 Sitting in Limbo/The Bigger They Come
Produced by Jimmy Cliff. (a) Mini-epic showcasing Cliff's most delicate vocals. The breathtaking arrangement starts with acoustic guitars and ends in a glorious shower of horns, organ and soulful backing singers.

ISLAND 6103 Goodbye Yesterday/Breakdown
Produced by Jimmy Cliff.

CLIFF & THE ORGANIZERS

(X) JAN FENDER

KEITH COLE

BIG 315 Musical Attack/RUPIE EDWARDS ALL-STARS: Shack Attack
Produced by Rupie Edwards.

BIG 316 KEITH COLE: Music Alone/RUPIE EDWARDS ALL-STARS: Behold Another Version
Produced by Rupie Edwards.

STRANGER COLE

CAMEL 72 Crying Every Night/DENNIS ALCAPONE & DELROY WILSON: It Must Come
(b) Delroy Wilson's "Better Must Come" gives the DJ not just a great theme, but a score of rhymes to work off — a shock attack indeed.

ANSELL COLLINS

(X) DENNIS ALCAPONE, WINSTON BLAKE, RAD BRYAN, PRINCE BUSTER

TECHNIQUES 913 Nuclear Weapon/TECHNIQUES ALL-STARS La La La
Produced by Winston Riley.

COLLINS ALL STARS

(X) MARLENE WEBBER, DELROY WILSON

THE CONSCIOUS MINDS

Studio vocal group comprising LLOYD CHARMERS, KEN BOOTHE, and BB SEATON, backed by MIKEY CHUNG & THE NOW GENERATION. (X) KEN BOOTHE, LLOYD CHARMERS, JAMAICANS

ACKEE 141 Paul Marcus & Norman/Version

BIG 318 Jamaican Boy/Brainwash

ESCORT 857 Peace Treaty/Brainwash

PUNCH 97 Paul Marcus & Norman/Conscious Mind: Version
Produced by BB Seaton.

PAUL COOKE

ACKEE 129 That Girl Was Mine/No Harm

COUNT OSSIE & ALTON ELLIS

(X) LITTLE ROY

COUNT OSSIE & HIS MYSTIC REVELATION

MOODISC 105 Whispering Drums/SLIM SMITH & THE UNIQUES Give Me Some More Loving
Produced by Harry Mudie. Also released as MOODISC 3515.

COUNT PRINCE MILLER

BREAD 1110 Bewildered/JACKIE'S BOYS: Cum-Ba-Laa
Produced by Jackie Edwards.

COXSONE'S ALL STARS

(X) LESTER STERLING

JOAN CREARY

FAB 181 Your Best Friend/Version

DAVE CROOKS

JACKPOT 759 I Won't Hold It Against You/BOBBY JAMES: King of Hearts

THE CRYSTALITES

(X) ETHIOPIANS, DERRICK HARRIOTT, BONGO HERMAN, DENZIL LAING, SCOTTY, TINGA STEWART

SONGBIRD 1057 Earthly Sounds/Version
Produced by Derrick Harriott.

DANDY

DOWNTOWN 483 Could It Be True/DANDY & JACKIE: Your Eyes Are Dreaming
Produced by Dandy Livingstone.

DOWNTOWN 484 Daddy's Home/Everyman
Produced by Dandy Livingstone.

TROJAN 7816 Same Old Fashioned Way/Out of Many, One People
Produced by Dandy Livingstone.

DANDY & JACKIE

Vocal duo featuring DANDY LIVINGSTONE. (X) DANDY

THE DARKER SHADE OF BLACK

JACKPOT 758 War/JEFF BARNES: People's Version

DAVE & ANSELL COLLINS

TECHNIQUES 914 Monkey Spanner (Parts 1/2)
Produced by Winston Riley. (a) It certainly was "a heavy, heavy monster sound." The burbling melody loops in and out, Collins' Hammond flourishes fill in the gaps, while Barker intersperses snatches of singing between the yelps; once heard, never forgotten. (b) Surprisingly weaker than the original, it just goes to show Barker's inimitable contribution to the duo. For full details, think of all those Moog-

fired pop covers released during the late 1960s, then add maracas.

BOBBY DAVIS

(X) BARBARA DUNKLEY

BANANA 344 Return Your Love/RILEY'S ALL-STARS Version
Produced by Martin Riley.

DEL DAVIS

BREAD 1105 Baby Don't Wake Me/-
Produced by Jackie Edwards.

CARL DAWKINS

(X) THE UNTOUCHABLES

BIG SHOT 570 Perseverance/JJ ALL-STARS: Version
Produced by JJ Johnson.

EXPLOSION 2051 I Feel Good/JJ ALL-STARS Version
Produced by JJ Johnson.

EXPLOSION 2059 Make It Great/STONE: What a Day
Produced by JJ Johnson.

NU-BEAT 086 Walk a Little Prouder/YOUTH PROFESSIONALS: Version

CARL DAWKINS & THE WAILERS

Featuring PETER TOSH and BUNNY WAILER.
UPSETTER 368 Picture on the Wall/UPSETTERS: Version
Produced by Lee Perry.

THE DAYTRIPPERS

TROJAN 7839 The Birds & the Bees/My Family

NORA DEAN

BULLET 472 Peace Begins Within/THE SLICKERS: Go Back Home
GAS 165 Greedy Boy/KEITH: Please Stay
RANDY'S 508 Want Man/ANDY'S ALL-STARS: Man

DESMOND DEKKER

TROJAN 7847 Lightning Stick/Troubles & Miseries
Produced by Leslie Kong.

DELROY & SPORTY

Duo featuring KING SPORTY and DELROY WILSON. (X) DUDLEY SIBLEY

DELROY & THE TENNORS

Featuring DELROY WILSON.
CAMEL 62 Donkey Shank/MURPHY'S ALL-STARS Donkey Track

THE DELTONES

GREEN DOOR 4010 Chopsticks/DES BRYAN: Belmont Street

DENNIS

PAMA SUPREME 330DD I'm a Believer/I'll Make the Way Easier
Produced by Lee Perry. (a) The vocals were recorded in London, and it's one of Perry's few concessions to the UK fascination with lashing strings over a reggae beat. Perry cut the rhythm track for this single in Jamaica at the same time as that of "Cheerio Baby," cut with Dennis's CLASSICS duo during the same trip.

PUNCH 93DD Christmas Message/Cool It Girl
Produced by Noel Blake.

PHYLLIS DILLON

TREASURE ISLE 7058 One Life to Live/TOMMY MCCOOK: My Best Dress
Produced by Duke Reid.

TREASURE ISLE 7070 Midnight Confession/TOMMY MCCOOK: Version
Produced by Duke Reid.

THE DINGLE BROS

DYNAMIC 418 You Don't Know/CABLES: Rich Man Poor Man

DOBBY DOBSON

(X) ERNEST WILSON

DYNAMIC 426 Carry that Weight/More Weight

ERIC DONALDSON

DYNAMIC 420 Cherry Oh Baby/LLOYD CHARMERS: Sir Charmers Special
Produced by Bunny Lee. The former WEST INDIANS' vocalist captured the 1971 Festival Song Competition, with a lilting number which remains a perennial covers' fave. INNER CIRCLE provided the insistent rhythm, while Donaldson showboats his incredible vocal talent.

DYNAMIC 423 Love of the Common People/DRAGONAIRES: The Dragon's Net

DYNAMIC 425 Just Can't (Happen this Way)/Version

MIKE DORANE & THE CIMARRONS

UK keyboard player Dorane later joined mid-70s reggae band MERGER.
ACKEE 144 Penguin Funk/Ad Lib

BRENT DOWE

Dowe was a member of THE MELODIANS.
SUMMIT 8521 Knock Three Times/GAYLADS: This Time I Won't Hurt You
SUMMIT 8525 Put Your Hand in the Hand/Miracle
SUMMIT 8530 Freedom Train/BEVERLEY'S ALL-STARS: Version

DOWN TO EARTH

DOWNTOWN 485 Under the Boardwalk/Version
Produced by Dandy Livingstone.

BRUCE DOWNER

SUMMIT 8524 Free the People/BEVERLEY'S ALL-STARS Version

THE DREADLOCK ALL STARS

(X) UPSETTING BROTHERS

BARBARA DUNKLEY

BANANA 342 We'll Cry Together/BOBBY DAVIS: Got to Get Away
Produced by Coxsone Dodd.

ERROL DUNKLEY

BIG 324 Deep Meditation/RUPIE EDWARDS ALL-STARS Version
Produced by Rupie Edwards.

BIG 327 Three in One/RUPIE EDWARDS ALL-STARS: One in Three

Produced by Rupie Edwards. (a) His voice may have broken, but it's still just as sweet and strong, as Dunkley proves on this charming medley of three of his earlier hits ("You're Gonna Need Me," Please Stop Your Lying," and "I'm Going Home"). Also released as NU-BEAT 091.

EXPLOSION 2053 O Lord/KEITH WITH IMPACT ALL-STARS: Raindrops

THE DYMONDS

BIG 326 Girl You Are too Young/RUPIE EDWARDS ALL-STARS: Version

Produced by Rupie Edwards.

THE DYNAMIC BOYS

(X) AUSTIN FAITHFUL

THE DYNAMIC GANG

MOODISC 3511 I'll Never Believe in You/Black Attack

THE DYNAMITES

(X) CLANCY ECCLES, CYNTHIA RICHARDS, SILVERTONES, STRANGER & GLADDY

CLANDISC 237 Hello Mother/FABULOUS FLAMES: Hi De Ho

Produced by Clancy Eccles. (a) Cut specially for anyone who's ever felt the need for a lush, reggaefied instrumental cover of Allan Sherman's early '60s novelty smash "Hello Mudduh, Hello Faddah!" (The SKATALITES did a ska one, after all!)

CLANCY ECCLES

(X) MARLENE WEBBER

CLANDISC 231 Sweet Jamaica/DYNAMITES: Going Up West

Produced by Clancy Eccles. (a) The best of Eccles' self-productions sound like he really wasn't intending to sing them himself, but banged them out anyway, just to see what would happen. "Sweet Jamaica" is an extraordinarily slight song, but Eccles' uncertain lead (and the hesitant backing vocals) give it a charm which a touch more polish would have completely thrown away.

CLANDISC 232 Rod of Correction/Version

Produced by Clancy Eccles. (a) The rod itself was given to PNP leader Michael Manley by Haile Selassie in 1966. Eccles takes an old song about a 1920s preacher, adds a host of Biblical unfortunates (Sodom and Gomorrah, the Pharaoh, et al.) to the lyric, then licks 'em all with the rod. And it's all set to a virtual nursery rhyme melody, pepped up by the beat.

CLANDISC 235 John Crow Skank/KING STITT: Merry Rhythm

Produced by Clancy Eccles.

CLANDISC 236 Power for the People/DYNAMITES: Version

Produced by Clancy Eccles.

PAMA SUPREME 332 What Will Your Mama Say/TIGER: United We Stand

Produced by Lee Perry.

ECCLES & NEVILLE

Featuring CLANCY ECCLES. (X) RIGHTEOUS SOULS

JACKIE EDWARDS

BREAD 1107 Johnny Gunman (Parts 1/2)

BREAD 1108 I Do Love You/Who Told You So

(b) A solid reggae rhythm section, fleshed out with some subtle piano, accompanies the singer on this mellow number. The lovely backing vocalists provide the hook.

HORSE 1 I Must Go Back/Baby I Want to Be Near You

TROJAN 7833 In Paradise/Take Me as I Am

(a) The duetting backing singer helps Edwards give this love song a soulful edge. The delivery of both is exceptional, conjuring an early hint of Lovers Rock.

RUPIE EDWARDS

BIG 320 Soulful Stew/Version

Produced by Rupie Edwards.

NU-BEAT 082 Black Man/Tell the People

Produced by Rupie Edwards.

RUPIE EDWARDS ALL-STARS

(X) DENNIS ALCAPONE, KEITH COLE, ERROL DUNKLEY, DYMONDS, ETHIOPIANS, GAYLADS, JOE HIGGS, GREGORY ISAACS, ITALS, DAVE MCCLAREN, FROGGIE RAY, HUGH ROY JUNIOR

SUPREME 213 Musical Attack/Music Alone

Produced by Rupie Edwards.

EL PASO

BIG SHOT 572 Out de Light Baby/Mosquito

PUNCH 61 Mosquito One/Out de Light

Produced by Byron Smith.

ELIJAH

ACKEE 121 Selassie High/Mount Zion

ALTON ELLIS

ACKEE 145 Oppression/Version

Produced by Coxsone Dodd.

BANANA 318 Sunday Coming/CARL BRYAN: Version

Produced by Coxsone Dodd. (a) A smoking reggae beat, gorgeous harmonies, and the inimitable Ellis combine on this charming single, which was later versioned by DENNIS ALCAPONE.

BANANA 330 Bam Bye/Keep on Yearning

Produced by Coxsone Dodd.

BANANA 347 Hey World/Harder than Harder

Produced by Coxsone Dodd.

BIG SHOT 589 Be True/Version

BULLET 466 Black Man's Pride/LEROY PALMER: Groove With It

Produced by Coxsone Dodd. (a) JACKIE MITTOO's organ forms the backdrop for this fierce performance.

BULLET 485 Don't Care/True Born Africa

FAB 165 Good Good Loving/Since I Fell for You

GAS 161 Deliver Us/NEVILLE HINDS: Originator
GAS 164 Back to Africa/NEVILLE HINDS: Originator
Produced by Lloyd Charmers. (a) Ellis' clipped vocals catch the mood of the era with razor sharp precision — "going back to Africa because I'm black . . . and that's a fact." Chirpy backing vocals add to the optimistic buoyancy of one of the veteran's finest recording.
SMASH 2319 A Little Loving/Version
SMASH 2320 I'll Be There/ITALS: Rude Boy Train

ALTON ELLIS ALL STARS

(X) AFRO

HORTENSE ELLIS

GAS 160 To the Other Man/MUSIC BLENDERS: Raindrops

ERROL ENGLISH

DUKE 99 Sometimes/Sugar Cane

JUNIOR ENGLISH

PAMA 828 Jesamine/SIDNEY ALL-STARS: The Flash
Produced by Sidney Crooks.

THE ETERNALS

MOODISC 3507 Push Me in the Corner/MUDIE'S ALL-STARS: Mudie's Madness
Produced by Harry Mudie.
MOODISC 3508 Keep on Dancing/HAZEL WRIGHT: My Jealous Eyes
Produced by Harry Mudie.

THE ETHIOPIANS

BIG 330 Solid as a Rock/RUPIE EDWARDS ALL-STARS: Version
Produced by Rupie Edwards.
BIG SHOT 569 He's Not a Rebel/JJ ALL-STARS: Version — Produced by JJ Johnson.
BIG SHOT 574 Selah/Don't Let Me Go
Produced by JJ Johnson. (a) The bass line is mixed a bit too up front, but even it can't upstage the vocal trio on this beautiful spiritual, as they passionately sing of their desire to leave Babylon and return home.
DUKE 102 Drop Him/JJ ALL-STARS: Version
Produced by JJ Johnson.
DUKE 108 Rim Bim Bam/RANDY'S ALL-STARS: Version
Produced by Randy's.
EXPLOSION 2050 Starvation/TROJAN ALL-STARS: Version
FAB 180 Donkey Money/Version
GG 4519 Love Bug/Sound of Our Forefathers
Produced by Alvin Ranglin. Also released as SUPREME 221.
PUNCH 96 Solid as a Rock/RUPIE EDWARDS ALL-STARS: Rock Version
Produced by Rupie Edwards.
RANDY'S 509 Mi Want Girl/RANDY'S ALL-STARS: Version
Produced by Randy's.

RANDY'S 510 True Man, Free Man/RANDY'S ALL-STARS Version
Produced by Randy's.
RANDY'S 512 Mr Tom/Sad News
Produced by Randy's. (b) The Ethiopians plead with the listener to discover the whereabouts of their departed girlfriend, comforted only by the fabulous riffing guitar on this sweet tearjerker.
SONGBIRD 1059 What a Pain/CRYSTALITES: Version
Produced by Derrick Harriott.
SONGBIRD 1062 Lot's Wife/DERRICK HARRIOTT: Slave
Produced by Derrick Harriott.
SONGBIRD 1064 Best of Five (Parts 1/2)
Produced by Derrick Harriott.
SUPREME 226 Starvation/MAXIE & GLEN: Jordan River
(b) Max Romeo and Glen Adams pull out their sweetest vocals on this beautiful religious offering.
TREASURE ISLE 7067 Pirate/TOMMY MCCOOK & THE SOUL SYNDICATE: Depth Charge
Produced by Duke Reid. (a) Choppily dynamite rhythms and an unrelenting air of righteous disdain completely belay the laid-back performance. One of the Ethiopians' finest.

EXODUS

DUKE 103 Pharaoh's Walk/Little Caesar
SIOUX 001 Pharaoh's Walk #9/SAMMY JONES: Worried Over You

THE FABULOUS FLAMES

(X) DYNAMITES, LARRY MCDONALD & DENZIL LAING
TROJAN 7822 Growing Up/Lovitis

AUSTIN FAITHFUL

DYNAMIC 407 "634 5789"/DYNAMIC BOYS: Warm & Tender Love

JAN FENDER

FAB 164 Sweet P/CLIFF & ORGANIZERS: Mr Brown
Produced by Prince Buster.
FAB 166 Holly Holy/Old Kentrone Version
Produced by Prince Buster.
PRINCE BUSTER 5 Sea of Love/Heaven Help Us All
Produced by Prince Buster.

GEORGE FERRIS

ACKEE 117 With Every Dream/Diana

WILLIE FRANCIS

(X) MARTIN RILEY
ESCORT 848 Burn Them/Poor Boy
PAMA 829 Oh What a Mini/Version

THE FREEDOM SINGERS

NU-BEAT 074 Your Testimony/Train Coming

PAUL FREEMAN

PUNCH 82 Don't Give Up/UPSETTERS: Version
Produced by Lee Perry.

THE FUD CHRISTIAN ALL-STARS

(X) LINKERS

BIG SHOT 571 Never Fall in Love/Version

THE GAYLADS

(X) BRENT DOWE

ACKEE 142 Accept My Apologies/My Version

Produced by Coxsone Dodd.

BIG 319 Can't Hide the Feeling/RUPIE EDWARDS ALL-STARS: Version

Produced by Rupie Edwards.

BULLET 462 My Love/Stranger Love

CAMEL 79 Seven in One Medley (Parts 1/2)

SUMMIT 8514 My Jamaican Girl/BEVERLEY'S ALL-STARS: Version4

Produced by Leslie Kong. (a) The Gaylads proudly proclaim the superiority of Jamaican women. It's not as catchy or lyrically clever as say "California Girls," but they do make some good points.

THE GAYTONES

(X) JACKIE BROWN, JEAN & THE GAYTONES, TEDDY, UXBROWN & SCOTTY

GREEN DOOR 4016 Jamaican Hilite (Parts 1/2)

HIGH NOTE 055 Heart of the Knights/One Toke Over the Line

Produced by Sonia Pottinger.

BILL GENTLES

ESCORT 853 Bachelor Boy/SCORPIONS: Colour Rites

GG ALL STARS

(X) CHARLIE ACE, DENNIS ALCAPONE, MAYTONES

GG 4510 Rocking on the GG Beat/Version

Produced by Alvin Ranglin.

GG 4511 Lonely Nights/MAYTONES: Let the Version Play

Produced by Alvin Ranglin.

GG 4513 All One Nation/VAL BENNETT: Judgement Warrant

Produced by Alvin Ranglin.

GI GI

PAMA SUPREME 335 Daddy Love/Version

JOE GIBBS

(X) THIRD & FOURTH GENERATION

GIRLIE & PAUL

ACKEE 124 Decimalization/Version

THE GLADIATORS

(X) WILLIE & LLOYD

GRANT & RICHARDS

(X) SHEILA

OWEN GRAY

ACKEE 123 Whispering Bells/CLANCY'S ALL-STARS: Whiplash

Produced by Clancy Eccles.

CAMEL 60 Groove Me/No Other One

Produced by Sidney Crooks.

CAMEL 73 Nothing Can Separate Us/Girl I Want You to Understand

PAMA SUPREME 310 You Gonna Miss Me/I Hear You Knocking

PAMA SUPREME 325 Summer Sand/Something to Remind Me

PUNCH 87 Sincerely/Hold On I'm Coming

TONY GREGORY

HORSE 3 Bouncing All Over the World/Tell Me

GREYHOUND

aka THE RUDIES. GLENROY OAKLEY replaced FREDDIE NOTES in 1971.

TROJAN 7820 Black & White/Sand in Your Shoes

(a) An overblown cover of the Three Dog Night ditty, where the vocalist gets hot and sweaty amongst the string section.

TROJAN 7834 Follow the Leader/Funky Jamaica

TROJAN 7848 Moon River/I've Been Trying/The Pressure Is Coming On

(a) Compulsive but, when overplayed, lifeless recounting of *Breakfast at Tiffanies* queerest tear-jerker.

THE GROOVERS

(X) ZIMM & DEE DEE

CAMEL 83 Put Me Down Easy/I Want to Go Back Home

ESCORT 863 Bend Down Low/The Burning Feeling

WINSTON GROOVEY

BULLET 471 I Wanna Be Loved/Get Back Together

CRAB 64 I've Got to Find a Way to Win Mary Back/Wanna Be There

PAMA 827 Don't Break My Heart/How Long Will this Go On

PAMA SUPREME 323 Free the People/Not Now

THE HAMMERS

GAS 162 Hotter than Scorcher/Someday Could See You

HARDY

ACKEE 131 Glorious Morning/Hearing's Not Seeing

DERRICK HARRIOTT

(X) ETHIOPIANS

SONGBIRD 1052 Candy/CRYSTALITES: Version

Produced by Derrick Harriott.

SONGBIRD 1055 Lollipop Girl/CRYSTALITES: Version

Produced by Derrick Harriott.

SONGBIRD 1063 Medley in 5 (Parts 1/2)

Produced by Derrick Harriott.

SONGBIRD 1065 Have You Seen Her/CRYSTALITES: Version

Produced by Derrick Harriott. (a) Harriott provides some of his most effective falsetto on this cover of the Chi-Lites' hit and, even better, pulls off the cheesy spoken word sections with aplomb.

THE HEPTONES

BANANA 325 Suspicious Minds/Haven't You Any Fight Left?

Produced by Coxsone Dodd. (a) Elvis Presley's is arguably the definitive version, Dee Dee Warwick gave it soul and the Fine Young Cannibals made it sound quite hip. But the Heptones are certainly the sweetest and most upbeat.

BANANA 349 Freedom Line/SOUND DIMENSION: Version

Produced by Coxsone Dodd.

HERMAN

aka HERMAN CHIN LOY, cousin of LESLIE KONG. DJ and owner of the Aquarius record store when he moved into production, using THE HIPPY BOYS as his studio band. (X) AUGUSTUS PABLO

ACKEE 133 Dunce Cap/AQUARIANS: Version

Produced by Herman Chin-Loy.

ACKEE 140 Youth Man/AQUARIANS: Version

Produced by Herman Chin-Loy.

BIG SHOT 573 El Fishy/HERMAN'S ALL-STARS: Nightmare

Produced by Herman Chin-Loy.

BIG SHOT 577 Tar Baby/TOMMY MCCOOK: Archie

Produced by Herman Chin-Loy.

BIG SHOT 578 New Love/AUGUSTUS PABLO: The Mood

Produced by Herman Chin-Loy.

DUKE 107 To the Field/HERMAN'S MEN: Version

Produced by Bunny Lee. (a) DJ Herman is evidently so enjoying this exuberant instrumental he doesn't actually say a word for half the the song. Finally somebody prods him, and he jumps in with some catchphrases to see the single out.

ESCORT 854 Love Brother/Version

Produced by Herman Chin-Loy.

EXPLOSION 2049 Love Brother/Uganda

(a) The backing singers add a touch of spirituality, as Herman preaches directly from Bible quotes. The incongruous flute alone deprives the song of a rootsier bend. (b) A nursery rhyme plays around the edges, but this is really nothing more than a stripped-down rhythm track, with occasional snippets of melody.

PUNCH 55 Hold The Ghost/AQUARIUS SOUL BAND: Duppy Dance

Produced by Herman Chin-Loy.

PUNCH 58 Listen to the Beat/AQUARIANS: Sounds Only

Produced by Herman Chin-Loy.

BONGO HERMAN & LES & BUNNY

Featuring guitarist ERIC "BINGY BUNNY" LAMONT (d 12/31/93) and fellow DYNAMITES' percussionist BONGO LES.

SONGBIRD 1060 Know Far-I/CRYSTALITES: Version

Produced by Derrick Harriott. (a) Faintly reminiscent of the MELODIANS' "Rivers of Babylon," it's just as spiritual and musically sparse, with a similar focus on the lyrics.

SONGBIRD 1066 Salaam (Peace)/CRYSTALITES: Scraper

Produced by Derrick Harriott.

HERMAN'S ALL STARS

Studio band for HERMAN CHIN-LOY. (X) HERMAN

HERMAN'S MEN

Studio band for HERMAN CHIN-LOY. (X) HERMAN

WINSTON HEYWOOD

CAMEL 64 I Will Never Fall in Love Again/LA FUD DIL ALL-STARS: La Fud Dil

(a) This slow ballad showcases Heywood's dulcet tenor tones, while the backing singers add that old rock steady feel.

DYNAMIC 424 Am Sa Bo/Version

JOE HIGGS

BIG 312 Burning Fire/RUPIE EDWARDS ALL-STARS: Version

Produced by Rupie Edwards.

NU-BEAT 087 Mother Radio/DAWN SHARON: Little Deeds

SUPREME 215 Burning Fire/RUPIE EDWARDS ALL-STARS: Push & Pull

Produced by Rupie Edwards.

JUSTIN HINDS

TREASURE ISLE 7063 Botheration/VINCENT HINDS: Mouth Trombone

Produced by Duke Reid.

TREASURE ISLE 7068 Mighty Redeemer (Parts 1/2)

Produced by Duke Reid.

NEVILLE HINDS

(X) ALTON ELLIS, THE MARVELS

EXPLOSION 2043 Delivered/Specially for You

VINCENT HINDS

(X) JUSTIN HINDS

THE HIPPY BOYS

(X) CYNTHIA RICHARDS

BIG SHOT 580 Voodoo/LITTLE ROY: Hard Fighter

Produced by Lloyd Daley.

JOHN HOLT

ASHANTI 401 Again/MUDIE'S ALL-STARS: 10 Steps to Soul Version

Produced by Harry Mudie.

BANANA 340 OK Fred/Fancy Make-Up

Produced by Coxsone Dodd.

BANANA 345 Build Our Dreams/LEROY SIBBLES: Love in Our Nation

Produced by Coxsone Dodd.

CAMEL 78 Linger a While/Version

ESCORT 847 Knock on Your Door/URIEL ALDRIDGE: Set Me Free

JACKPOT 772 Stick by Me/It's a Pleasure

Produced by Bunny Lee. (a) Lee slams out another John Crow Skank masterpiece, this time with a version of an old hit by Shep & The Limelites. A simple song, with a pleasant enough melody, the rhythms and Holt's impassioned delivery turned it into a classic.

JACKPOT 774 It's a Jam in the Streets/A Man Needs a Woman

Produced by Bunny Lee.

JACKPOT 784 Any More/ Lost Love

Produced by Bunny Lee.

MOODISC 3513 It May Sound Silly/MUDIE ALL-STARS: Instrumental

Produced by Harry Mudie. (a) A masterful revision of Ivory Joe Hunter's US hit.

PUNCH 60 Strange Thing/WINSTON WRIGHT: Want Money

Produced by Coxsone Dodd. (a) A moody rumination of the "strange things" which happen on a Friday night, "lots of hugging and kissing" included. But Holt's not part of the party and the vocal captures all his frustration.

SMASH 2324 Mother & Father Love/AGGROVATORS: Version

Produced by Bunny Lee.

SUPREME 212 Share My Rest/AL BROWN: Always

TREASURE ISLE 7061 Let's Build Our Dreams/TOMMY MCCOOK & THE SUPERSONICS: Testify Version—Produced by Duke Reid.

TREASURE ISLE 7065 Sister's Big Stuff/TOMMY MCCOOK & THE SUPERSONICS: Black River

Produced by Duke Reid.

TREASURE ISLE 7066 Paragons Medley/TOMMY MCCOOK & THE SUPERSONICS: Version

Produced by Duke Reid.

HONEYBOY

aka HONEYBOY MARTIN.

TROJAN 7835 Jamaica/ITALS: Sea Wave

KEITH HUDSON

SMASH 2326 Light of Day/I Thought You Knew

KEITH HUDSON & DENNIS ALCAPONE

BIG SHOT 565 Shades of Hudson/Spanish Amigo

Produced by Keith Hudson. (a) The first piece of music Hudson ever produced, as a 14-year-old in 1960, and featuring several future SKATALITES. A white label of the unadorned track was released in 1968; here, Alcapone adds his own special magic. (b) KEN BOOTHE's "Old Fashioned Way" storms away in the background, while Alcapone beautifully sing-songs along, commenting and elaborating on the lyrics.

THE HURRICANES

Featuring vocalists DANNY CLARKE (b 8/7/53) and LLOYD FORESTER, both ex-RIGHTEOUS FLAMES. Clarke later formed THE MEDITATIONS. (X) DAVE BARKER, DONALD SMYTHE

UPSETTER 363 Got to Be Mine/UPSETTERS: Version

Produced by Lee Perry.

I-ROY

See entry on page 124. Also recorded as a duo with DENNIS WALKS, and EBONY SISTERS

MOODISC 3509 Musical Pleasure/JO JO BENNETT: Hot Pop

Produced by Harry Mudie.

I-ROY & THE EBONY SISTERS

MOODISC 3512 Let Me Tell You Boy/MUDIE'S ALL-STARS: Version

Produced by Harry Mudie.

I-ROY & DENNIS WALKS

(X) JO JO BENNETT

MOODISC 3510 Heart Don't Leap/DENNIS WALKS & MUDIE'S ALL-STARS: Snow Bird

Produced by Harry Mudie.

THE IMPACT ALL STARS

Studio band at Randy's studio. (X) JIMMY LONDON

BULLET 483 Dandy Shandy/Go Back

Produced by Randy's.

RANDY'S 519 Go Back/Version

Produced by Randy's. Also released as SUPREME 223.

THE IN CROWD

SPINNING WHEEL 105 Bush Jacket/Soul Face

THE INN KEEPERS

(X) WINSTON MATTHEWS

BANANA 328 Duppy Serenade/Sunshine Version

THE INNER CIRCLE

(X) DENNIS ALCAPONE

THE INNER MINDS

BULLET 465 Arawak Version/Cuffy Cuffy

THE INVADERS

GG 4527 Got to Go Home/PAULETTE & GEE: How Long Will You Stay

Produced by Alvin Ranglin.

THE INVITATIONS

CRAB 66 Birmingham Cat/Now You're on Your Own

DAVID ISAACS

BULLET 459 Just Enough/ROY PATIN: Standing

PUNCH 84 You'll Be Sorry/Knock Three Times

Produced by Lee Perry.

TROPICAL 006 Love Has Joined Us/MAX ROMEO: Cross Over the Bridge

UPSETTER 370 You'll Be Sorry/THE UPSETTERS: Dark Moon

Produced by Lee Perry.

GREGORY ISAACS

BIG SHOT 584 Lonely Man/RUPIE EDWARDS ALL-STARS: Version

Produced by Rupie Edwards.

THE ITALS

(X) ALTON ELLIS, HONEYBOY

BIG 325 Ba Da Doo Ba Dey/RUPIE EDWARDS ALL-STARS: Version

Produced by Rupie Edwards.

BLACK SWAN 1404 Dawn Patrol/Whisky Bonga

BLACK SWAN 1407 Judgement Rock/Night West

BILLY JACK

BIG SHOT 559 Bet Your Life I Do/CANDY & THE CIMARRONS: Ace of Hearts

JACKIE'S BOYS

(X) COUNT PRINCE MILLER

BREAD 1104 Cum-Ba-Laa/I Want You Beside Me

LLOYD JACKSON

PAMA SUPREME 308 Cracklin' Rosie/Little Deeds of Kindness

THE JAMAICANS

DYNAMIC 410 Love Uprising/My Love for You

(a) Mellowy upbeat, this song was never going to start a revolution. But the vocal trio sound wonderfully soulful, and the melody is charming enough.

DYNAMIC 417 Mary/CONSCIOUS MINDS: Soldier Boy

(a) The jaunty tale of a sailor boy who falls in love with a pretty servant girl. . . and that's pretty much it. Much passing of notes and singing of names, but it's also rather inconsequential. (b) Largely instrumental version, but with sufficient snatches of lyric intact to leave you hoping something might happen on this side. But it doesn't. Also released as NU-BEAT 084.

BOBBY JAMES

(X) DAVE CROOKS

BOBBY JAMES & DAVE

SMASH 2314 You Said It/AGGRO BAND: Hot Sauce

JIMMY JAMES & THE VAGABONDS

BAMBOO 67 Riverboat Jenny/If I Wasn't Black

TROJAN 7806 Help Yourself/Why

THE JAY BOYS

HARRY J 6628 The Arcade Walk/Version
Produced by Harry J.

THE JAY LADS

PUNCH 95 Royal Cord/Soul Beat

JEAN & THE GAYTONES

JEAN was JUDY MOWATT, of the GAYLETS, later of the I-THREES. Also recorded as JULIEN & THE GAYTONES.

TROJAN 7817 I Shall Sing/GAYTONES: Target

Produced by Sonia Pottinger. (a) The reggae rhythm, and upbeat brass juice up a joyous affirmation, while Mowatt's strong, clear vocals ring with triumphand zeal. The harmonies—from producer Pottinger herself—add further spice.

THE JESTERS

(X) RAPHAEL STEWART

PUNCH 65 Cholera/LLOYD ALL-STARS: Black Bird

Produced by Lloyd Charmers. (a) Another of those records which so accurately pinpointed the mood of the impending roots movement, all understated rhythm, and vocals just on the bright side of world-weariness.

THE JET SCENE

(X) GLEN ADAMS

JIMBILIN

BAMBOO 68 Human Race/Let Love In

JJ ALL-STARS

(X) BLEECHERS, CAMBODIANS, CARL DAWKINS, ETHIOPIANS

BARBARA JONES

GG 4520 Have a Good Time
Produced by Alvin Ranglin.

SAMMY JONES

(X) EXODUS

JULIEN & THE CHOSEN FEW

Julien was JUDY MOWATT.

HIGH NOTE 054 Joy to the World/Version

Produced by Sonia Pottinger. (a) A slowed-down, reggae cover of The Three Dog Night hit, Mowatt belts out the lyric, the backing vocalists add some interest, but all in all it still falls flat.

THE JUNCUNO SINGERS

BAMBOO 69 Love Is a Stranger/When We Were Children
Produced by Coxsone Dodd.

BANANA 361 The End/HORACE ANDY: See a Man's Face
Produced by Coxsone Dodd.

KEITH

(X) NORA DEAN

KEITH & THE IMPACT ALL STARS

(X) ERROL DUNKLEY

RANDY'S 515 Down by the Riverside/Version
Produced by Randy's.

PAT KELLY

CAMEL 65 Talk About Love/PHIL PRATT ALL-STARS: Version
Produced by Phil Pratt.

GAS 171 Love/With All Your Heart

PUNCH 88 Soulful Love/U-ROY: One for All

Produced by Phil Pratt. (a) Aptly titled, Kelly's vocals are just wonderful, as soulful as the title (and twice as sweet) on this cover of the Curtis Mayfield song.

TONY KING

(X) MAYTONES

KING CANNON

HILLCREST 2 Reggay Got Soul/SOUL CATS: Land of Love

MOODISC 109 Raw Deal/MUDIE'S ALL-STARS: Shirley's Hide Out
Produced by Harry Mudie.

KING CRY CRY

The future PRINCE FAR I: see entry on page 222.

BANANA 356 I Had a Talk/BURNING SPEAR: Zion Higher

(a) Produced by Bunny Lee (b) Produced by Coxsone Dodd. (a/b) Forget what it sounds like, what a remarkable coupling this is, Prince Far I on one side, Burning Spear on the other. And neither of them meant a jot at the time.

KING SPORTY

(X) WAILING SOULS

BANANA 321 Inspiration/Choice of Music

BANANA 323 DJ Special/RICHARD & MAD: Creation Version

KING STITT

(X) CLANCY ECCLES, VEGETABLES

BANANA 334 Rhyming Time/Reality

Produced by Coxsone Dodd.

THE KINGSTONIANS

DUKE 126 Lion's Den/Version

LA FUD DIL ALL STARS

(X) WINSTON HEYWOOD

DENZIL LAING

SONGBIRD 1054 Medicine Stick/CRYSTALITES: Short Cut

Produced by Derrick Harriott.

JOYA LANDIS

(X) U-ROY

LARRY & ALVIN

(X) SONNY

LARRY'S ALL STARS

(X) THE SENSATIONS, THE TEARDROPS

ACKEE 130 Pre-Fight/The Prayer

KEN LAZARUS & CREW

EXPLOSION 2056 Girl/TOMORROW'S CHILDREN: Sister Big Stuff

BYRON LEE & THE DRAGONAIRES

(X) ERIC DONALDSON, HOPETON LEWIS

DYNAMIC 409 My Sweet Lord/Shock Attack

Produced by Byron Lee.

DYNAMIC 414 Way Back Home/Version

Produced by Byron Lee.

DONALD LEE

GAS 163 Work Out/Too Long

BUNNY LEE'S ALL STARS

(X) LLOYD & DOREEN

B LEGGS

GREEN DOOR 4004 Drums of Passion/Love & Emotion Version

CARL LEWIN

BULLET 456 Knock Three Times/SIDNEY ALL-STARS: The Whealing Mouse

Produced by Sidney Crooks.

HOPETON LEWIS

DUKE 112 Grooving Out on Life/BYRON LEE & THE DRAGONAIRES: Fire Fire

Produced by Byron Lee. (a) Lewis tackles the Newbeats' hit, taking the lightweight song and giving it a powerful soul flavor, further fueled by a strong reggae beat and punchy brass solo.

TREASURE ISLE 7060 To the Other Man/TOMMY MCCOOK: Stampede

Produced by Duke Reid.

TREASURE ISLE 7071 Judgement Day/EARL LINDO: Version

Produced by Duke Reid.

HOPETON LEWIS & U-ROY

DUKE REID 2517 Tom Drunk/TOMMY MCCOOK: Waiting

Produced by Duke Reid. (a) A simply steaming version of "Tom Hark," a traditional drinking song featuring the vocals of the sadly neglected Hopeton Lewis. U-Roy toasts encouragement, and almost acts as backing vocalist for the singer.

EARL LINDO

(X) HOPETON LEWIS

THE LINKERS

BIG SHOT 567 Bongo Man/FUD CHRISTIAN ALL-STARS: Creation Version

(a) Afro-lite beats fuel this mid-tempo single, with the Linkers taking the opportunity to show off their most melodically soulful vocals.

LITTLE ROY

(X) HIPPY BOYS

ESCORT 850 Yester-Me Yester-You Yesterday/MATADOR ALL-STARS: Yes Sir

Produced by Lloyd Daley.

PUNCH 75 Hard Fighter/COUNT OSSIE & ALTON ELLIS: Back To Africa Version

Produced by Lloyd Daley.

LIZZY & TONY BOP

(X) BOBBY & DAVE

LIZZY & DELROY WILSON

JACKPOT 771 Double Attack/AGGROVATORS: The Sniper

Produced by Bunny Lee.

LIZZY & DENNIS

ACKEE 114 Happy Go Lucky Girl/BOBBY & DAVE: Sammy

LIZZY & THE PARAGONS

ACKEE 118 On the Beach/DAVE BARKER: Maria

Produced by Coxsone Dodd.

LLOYD & DOREEN

JACKPOT 762 Midnight/BUNNY LEE'S ALL-STARS: Midnight Version

Produced by Bunny Lee.

LLOYD & JOY

EXPLOSION 2047 Back to Africa/Born to Lose

LLOYD & LARRY

NU-BEAT 080 Monkey Spanner/LLOYD & LARRY'S ALL-STARS:
  Version

LLOYD & LARRY'S ALL STARS

(X) LLOYD & LARRY

JAH LLOYD & FREDDIE MCKAY

GG 4517 War Is Over/Version
Produced by Alvin Ranglin.

LLOYD'S ALL STARS

House band for producer LLOYD CAMPBELL (ex-BLUES
BUSTERS). (X) DON RECO, JUSTINS, RUBY & GLORIA, THE
VICTORS.

JIMMY LONDON

aka TREVOR SHAW of THE INSPIRATIONS, THE UNTOUCH-
ABLES.

RANDY'S 514 Shake a Hand/CARL MURPHY: Lick I Pipe
Produced by Randy's.

RANDY'S 517 Bridge Over Troubled Waters/RANDY'S ALL-STARS:
  War
Produced by Randy's. (a) A reggaefied beat and muted brass
provide the backdrop for London to croon this cover of the
Simon & Garfunkle hit.

RANDY'S 518 Hip Hip Hooray/IMPACT ALL-STARS: Version
Produced by Randy's.

RANDY'S 520 A Little Love/IMPACT ALL-STARS: Version
Produced by Randy's.

JOAN LONG

(X) BOY FRIDAY

LORD COMIC

aka SIR LORD COMIC.

BAMBOO 66 Rhythm Rebellion/ROY RICHARDS: Reggae Children

LORD KITCHENER

DUKE 115 Dr Kitch/Love in the Cemetery

LORD TANAMO

BANANA 319 Keep on Moving/JACKIE MITTOO: Totally Together
Produced by Coxsone Dodd.

LORENZO

NU-BEAT 094 I Will Never Let You Down/This Magic Moment

DENNIS LOWE

DOWNTOWN 468 Stand Up for the Sound/OWEN & DENNIS: Old
  Man Trouble
Produced by Dandy Livingstone.

THE LYRICS

RANDY'S 511 Give Thanks/RANDY'S ALL-STARS: Version
Produced by Randy's.

MAD ROY

aka LEROY "HORSEMOUTH" WALLACE (b 1947, Kingston,
JA). One of Jamaica's top session drummers, played with
SOUL SYNDICATE, MIGHTY VIKINGS, THE UPSETTERS,
BURNING SPEAR, etc. Also starred in the movie *Rockers*. (X)
ROLAND ALPHONSO

BANANA 324 Nannie Version/BIGGER D: Freedom Version
Produced by Coxsone Dodd.

BANANA 326 Home Version/SOUND DIMENSION: One Time
Produced by Coxsone Dodd.

TEDDY MAGNUS

GREEN DOOR 4008 Flying Machine/VERSION BOYS: Machine Version

HERMAN MARQUIS

Saxophonist Marquis was a regular member of TOMMY
MCCOOK's SUPERSONICS. (X) TOMMY MCCOOK

KEN MARSHALL

TREASURE ISLE 7073 Help Me Make It Through the Night/TOMMY
  MCCOOK & THE ALL-STARS: Version
Produced by Duke Reid. (a) JOHN HOLT would record the
definitive reggae-lite version of the soulful ballad, but Marshall's prototype lacks only the orchestration and Holt's own
brand of emotion to equal it.

LARRY MARSHALL

BAMBOO 300 Stay a Little Longer/MAYTALS: He'll Provide
BAMBOO 364 Maga Dog/OSSIE ROBINSON: Economical Heatwave

THE MARVELS

NU-BEAT 081 Co Co/Hey Girl Don't Bother Me
PAMA 819 Oh Lord Why Lord/NEVILLE HINDS: Love Letter
PAMA SUPREME 338 Rock Steady/Be My Baby

THE MATADOR ALL STARS

(X) LITTLE ROY

THE MATADORS

(X) ROBINSONS

BIG SHOT 594 Nyah Festival/Brixton Serenade
GREEN DOOR 4017 I'm Sorry/RHYTHM RULERS: Version

WINSTON MATTHEWS

BANANA 329 Sun Is Shining/INN KEEPERS: My Friend

MAXIE & GLEN

(X) ETHIOPIANS

GG 4520 Jordan River/GLEN ADAMS: Version 2
Produced by Alvin Ranglin.

THE MAYTALS

(X) LARRY MARSHALL

BANANA 339 Marching On/ROLAND ALPHONSO: Mellow Mood
Produced by Leslie Kong.

SUMMIT 8513 Monkey Girl/BEVERLEY'S ALL-STARS: Version
Produced by Leslie Kong.

SUMMIT 8520 One Eye Enos/BEVERLEY'S ALL-STARS: Version

Produced by Leslie Kong. (a) It says much about the trio's standing that even a song like this could chart — a repetitive, if solid beat, equally simplistic (and obviously suggestive) lyrics, and not much else to salvage it. But at least Kong made it sound vaguely interesting.

SUMMIT 8527 It's You/BEVERLEY'S ALL-STARS: Version

Produced by Leslie Kong.

SUMMIT 8529 Walk with Love/BEVERLEY'S ALL-STARS: Version

Produced by Leslie Kong.

SUMMIT 8533 Never You Change/BEVERLEY'S ALL-STARS: Version

Produced by Leslie Kong.

TROJAN 7849 Johnny Cool Man/BEVERLEY'S ALL-STARS: Version

Produced by Leslie Kong.

THE MAYTONES

(X) CHARLIE ACE, GG ALL STARS, CYNTHIA RICHARDS

DUKE 116 Babylon a Fall/TONY KING: Version Buggy

CAMEL 61 Judas/Mi Nah Tek

GG 4508 Cleanliness/GG ALL STARS: Cleanliness Version

Produced by Alvin Ranglin.

GG 4522 Black & White/TREVOR BROWN: Mr Brown

Produced by Alvin Ranglin.

GG 4525 Bongo Man Rise/ROY & BIM: Remember

Produced by Alvin Ranglin.

DAVE MCCLAREN

BIG 323 Love Is What I Bring/RUPIE EDWARDS ALL-STARS: Version

Produced by Rupie Edwards.

TOMMY MCCOOK

DENNIS ALCAPONE, PHYLLIS DILLON, ETHIOPIANS, HERMAN, JOHN HOLT, HOPETON LEWIS, KEN MARSHALL, AUGUSTUS PABLO, U-ROY

BIG SHOT 585 Psalms 9 to Keep in Mind/Mood of Observers

Produced by Niney Holness. (a) The instrumental version of "Blood and Fire" is less apocalyptic than optimistic, with McCook's saxophone ringing to the heavens in eager anticipation of world's end. (b) Another "Blood & Fire" version.

SPINNING WHEEL 109 Crying Everynight/HERMAN MARQUIS: Tom's Version

SPINNING WHEEL 110 Stupid Doctor/ROB WALKER: Grooving in Style

LARRY MCDONALD & DENZIL LAING

Percussionist MCDONALD a regular member of TOMMY MCCOOK's SUPERSONICS.

CLANDISC 228 Name of the Game/FABULOUS FLAMES: Holly Version

Produced by Clancy Eccles.

FREDDIE MCKAY

b 1947 (St Catherine, JA).

BANANA 348 Picture on the Wall/SOUND DIMENSION: Version

Produced by Coxsone Dodd. (a) Cut so firmly in the mold of a period US Stax single, it wouldn't be hard to imagine Otis Redding singing the same song. But McKay's distinctive vocals ensure there's no mistaking him.

BANANA 358 Sweet You Sour You/High School Dance

Produced by Coxsone Dodd. (b) Peeling keyboards ride the rhythm, while McKay nails down a slice of low-key adolescent romance.

MOODISC 110 Old Joe/Too Much Fore

Produced by Harry Moodie.

TOMMY MCKENZIE

PAMA SUPREME 327 Eastern Promise/Fiddlesticks

NANA MCLEAN

BANANA 355 A Little Love/SOUND DIMENSION: Heavy Beat

Produced by Coxsone Dodd.

GERALD MCLEASH

GG 4516 False Reaper/Version

Produced by Alvin Ranglin.

THE MEGATONS

DOWNTOWN 469 Militant Man/MUSIC DOCTORS: Reggae Jeggae Version

Produced by Dandy Livingstone.

THE MELLOTONES

ESCORT 844 Work It/SOUL MAN: Good Lover

THE MELODIANS

DUKE 128 The Sensational Melodians (Parts 1/2)

SUMMIT 8512 It Took a Miracle/BEVERLEY'S ALL-STARS: Version

Produced by Leslie Kong.

SUMMIT 8522 Come Ethiopians Come/BEVERLEY'S ALL-STARS: Version

Produced by Leslie Kong.

SUMMIT 8532 My Love My Life/Version

Produced by Leslie Kong.

THE MERRYMEN

DUKE 113 Big Bamboo/King Ja Ja

THE MESSAGE

SONGBIRD 1503 Rum Bum a Loo/Drummer Boy

Produced by Derrick Harriott.

MIGHTY SPARROW

DUKE 114 Maria/Only a Fool

Produced by Byron Lee/Slinger Francisco.

JUMP-UP 541 Mr Walker/Mae Mae

Produced by Harold De Freitas/Robert Nicol.

JAMES MILLER

TROJAN 7804 You Got to Me/2001

JACKIE MITTOO

(X) LORD TANAMO

BANANA 320 Peenie Wallie/ROY RICHARDS: Can't Go On

MONSOON

TROJAN 7831 Hot Honolulu Night/Come Back Jane

DERRICK MORGAN

BULLET 467 Nobody's Business/Standing By

CAMEL 84 I Am Just a Sufferer/We Want to Know

CRAB 67 Searching So Long/MORGAN'S ALL-STARS: Drums of Passion

PAMA 822 Love Bug/My Dickie

MORGAN'S ALL STARS

(X) DERRICK MORGAN

CAMEL 76 I Love You the Most/Version

MR CALYPSO

JUMP-UP 540 Mohammed Ali/SAMSON DE LARK: Undemocratic Rhodesia

MUDIE'S ALL STARS

(X) JO JO BENNETT, ETERNALS, JOHN HOLT, I-ROY, KING CANNON, NINEY

CARL MURPHY

(X) JIMMY LONDON

MURPHY'S ALL STARS

(X) DELROY & THE TENNORS, HUGH ROY JUNIOR, SCOTTY

THE MUSIC BLENDERS

(X) HORTENSE ELLIS

THE MUSIC DOCTORS

(X) MEGATONS, PRINCE OF DARKNESS

DOWNTOWN 479 The Pliers (Parts 1/2)

Produced by Dandy Livingstone.

NEVILLE

EXPLOSION 2057 I Love Jamaica/Marry Me Marie

THE NEW RELIGION

BAMBOO 70 In the Black Caribbean/Black Is Black

NINEY

BIG 317 You Must Believe/Version

Produced by Niney Holness. (a) THE OBSERVERS are at their smoothest for this cover of the Impressions' hit, with DENNIS ALCAPONE at his suavely, rousting best.

BIG SHOT 568 Blood & Fire/Mud & Water

Produced by Niney Holness. (a) This is it, one of the greatest records ever made. Niney stormed the Jamaican chart over Christmas, 1970, with this revolutionary offering, all radical rasta message wrapped in a perfect reggae beat. Deservedly, it captured Record of the Year. (b) Pretty much the same as the flip, but with the odd vocal lines and harmonies stripped out.

BIG SHOT 575 Brimstone & Fire/Lightning & Thunder

Produced by Niney Holness. (a) A dubbier version of "Blood & Fire," featuring some neat electronic effects and an even more dread atmosphere. (b) Another instrumental version,

this time featuring a cheerfully psychotic organ.

BIG SHOT 586 Message to the Ungodly/Version

Produced by Niney Holness. (a) Niney tries another tack, this time preaching not of the end of the world, but of God's love — at least until the last verse, when fire and brimstone rain down again. The rhythms are incredibly juttery, but the backing singer's harmonies soften their impact.

GAS 167 Blood & Fire/ROLAND ALPHONSO: 33 66

Produced by Niney Holness.

MOODISC 111 People Let Love Shine/MUDIE ALL-STARS: Too Much

FREDDIE NOTES & THE RUDIES

TROJAN 7810 Walk a Mile in My Shoes/JOHNNY ARTHEY ORCHESTRA: Reggae Rouser

THE OBSERVERS

Studio band behind NINEY HOLNESS.

BIG SHOT 588 Keep Pushing/Hot Tip

ORGAN D

(X) SIR HARRY

OUR BAND

(X) BOY FRIDAY

OWEN & DENNIS

Vocal duo comprising OWEN GRAY and DENNIS LOWE. (X) DENNIS LOWE

AUGUSTUS PABLO

See entry on page 200. (X) HERMAN

ACKEE 134 Still Yet/AQUARIANS: Version

Produced by Herman Chin-Loy.

ACKEE 138 Snowball & Pudding/AQUARIANS: Version

Produced by Herman Chin-Loy.

BIG SHOT 579 East of the River Nile/HERMAN CHIN-LOY: Version

Produced by Herman Chin-Loy. (a) The song that launched Pablo's Far East style. A showcase for Pablo's melodica and GLEN ADAMS' organ, the melody has an Arabesque aura, while the jagged rhythms (purchased by Chin-Loy from LEE PERRY) add to an unsettling atmosphere where ghostly caravans shimmer in the distance, dark back alleys beckon, and the delights of Eastern entrepots have a foreboding air.

CREOLE 1004 405/Duck It Up

Produced by Herman Chin-Loy.

DUKE 122 Reggae in the Fields/TOMMY MCCOOK: Love Brother

Produced by Herman Chin-Loy.

PAT

GAS 158 Teach Me/RHYTHM RULERS: Sea Breeze

ROY PATIN

(X) DAVID ISAACS

MANLEY PATTERSON

PAMA SUPREME 337 I Stayed Away too Long/Country Boy

EUGENE PAUL

PAMA SUPREME 317 Farewell My Darling/Whole Lot of Woman

PAMA SUPREME 329 Somebody's Changing My Sweet Baby's Mind/Hard Minded Neighbour

PAULETTE & GEE

(X) THE INVADERS

LASCELLES PERKINS

BANANA 317 Tell It All Brothers/SOUND DIMENSION: Polkadots
Produced by Coxsone Dodd.

LEE PERRY

BULLET 461 All Combine (Parts 1/2)
Produced by Lee Perry. (a/b) Preposterous easy-listening style medley, horns and keyboards over vague approximations of the rhythms "Yakety Yak," "Pop a Top," "Maccabee Version," "Solomon," "Holly Holy," "Mr Brown," "Duppy Conqueror," and "The Sun Is Shining."

THE PIONEERS

SUMMIT 8511 Starvation/BEVERLEY'S ALL-STARS: Version
Produced by Leslie Kong. (a) A rock guitar opens this socially conscious song, the rhythm section has an almost funk feel, while the organ and guitars give it that real 70s sound. But the vocals harken back to an earlier era.

SUMMIT 8517 Get Ready/Version
Produced by Leslie Kong.

SUMMIT 8528 Land of Complexion/No Sad Song
Produced by Leslie Kong.

TROJAN 7825 Let Your Yeah Be Yeah/More Love
Produced by Leslie Kong. (a) A slick production and a string and brass section elbow out whatever charm and dignity the Pioneers have left, but the saddest part is that the lead is now accompanied by a chorus. Once upon a time, all that was needed was a backing vocalist or two.

THE PLAYBOYS

TROPICAL 007 Change Change/TROPICAL ALL-STARS: Version

POWER

(X) THE CLASSICS

PHIL PRATT ALL STARS

(X) DENNIS ALCAPONE, PAT KELLY
PUNCH 94 Winey Winey/There Is a Place
Produced by Phil Pratt.

PRINCE BUSTER

FAB 176 Police Trim Rasta/Smooth
Produced by Prince Buster.

PRINCE BUSTER 2 Rat Trap/Black Organ
Produced by Prince Buster.

PRINCE BUSTER 4 Fishey/More Fishey
Produced by Prince Buster.

PRINCE BUSTER 7 I Wish Your Picture Was You/PRINCE BUSTER ALL- STARS: It Mash Up Version
Produced by Prince Buster.

PRINCE BUSTER 8 Sons of Zion/ANSELL COLLINS: Short Circuit
Produced by Prince Buster.

PRINCE BUSTER 9 My Happiness/Human
Produced by Prince Buster. (a) A crooning love song with the ALL STARS at their muted, melodic best.

PRINCE BUSTER'S ALL STARS

(X) PRINCE BUSTER

PRINCE OF DARKNESS

DOWNTOWN 467 Sound of Today/MUSIC DOCTORS: Red Red Wine Version
Produced by Dandy Livingstone.

THE PYRAMIDS

(X) BRUCE RUFFIN

CREOLE 1003 Mosquito Bite/Mother's Bath

CREOLE 1006 Can't Leave Now/Teardrops

TROJAN 7803 All for You/Version

RAMON & THE CRYSTALITES

SONGBIRD 1053 Golden Chickens/Stranger Version
Produced by Derrick Harriott.

RANDY'S ALL STARS

(X) ETHIOPIANS, JIMMY LONDON, DENNIS LOWE, LYRICS
EXPLOSION 2052 Hold on Girl/Version

FROGGIE RAY

BIG 313 Uncle Charlie/Party Version
Produced by Rupie Edwards.

BIG 314 Half Moon/RUPIE EDWARDS ALL-STARS: Full Moon
Produced by Rupie Edwards.

DANNY RAYMOND

BIG SHOT 587 Sister Big Stuff/BOY FRIDAY: Free Man

THE REBELLIOUS SUBJECTS

(X) WEST INDIANS

DON RECO

BIG SHOT 597 Waterloo Rock/LLOYD'S ALL-STARS: Walls Soul

THE RED RIVER BAND

BANANA 35 I'm Gonna Use What I've Got/Shame Shame

THE RHYTHM RULERS

(X) MATADORS, PAT

RICHARD & MAD

(X) KING SPORTY

CYNTHIA RICHARDS

BIG SHOT 581 I'm Moving On/HIPPY BOYS: Version

CLANDISC 229 Stand by Your Man/DYNAMITES: Version
Produced by Clancy Eccles.

ESCORT 861 Love & Unity/MAYTONES: Jah Not Dead

GG 4528 Place in My Heart/You've Got a Friend
Produced by Alvin Ranglin.

ROY RICHARDS

(X) LORD COMIC, JACKIE MITTOO

RICO

(X) SLIM SMITH

THE RIGHTEOUS FLAMES

NU-BEAT 083 Love & Emotion/Version

THE RIGHTEOUS SOULS

SUPREME 217 Mount Zion/ECCLE & NEVILLE: All Over

Produced by Perry Marvin (actually LEE PERRY). (a) The writing credits erroneously give this moving repatriation song to the Righteous *Brothers*. (b) Jamaican releases of this song (as "Once a Man") credit MILTON HENRY as the artist.

MARTIN RILEY

CAMEL 77 When Will We Be Paid/WILLIE FRANCIS: He's Got the Whole World in His Hands

Produced by Martin Riley.

RILEY'S ALL STARS

Fronted by MARTIN RILEY. (X) BOBBY DAVIS, THE TECHNIQUES

BANANA 343 Glory of Love/We'll Cry Together Version

Produced by Martin Riley.

RIP'N'LAW

CRAB 65 In the Ghetto/Something Sweet

(a) Elvis Presley's recent chart-topper, lightly reggae-fied but little more than a blueprint for SUSAN CADOGAN's definitive reading.

ROBI'S ALL STARS

(X) TARTANS

IAN ROBINSON

(X) MAHALIA SAUNDERS

OSSIE ROBINSON

(X) LARRY MARSHALL

THE ROBINSONS

PUNCH 66 Come Ethiopians/THE MATADORS: Zion Gate

Produced by Lloyd Daley.

ROCKIN' HORSE

CAMEL 75 Running Back Home/SOUL SYNDICATE: Version

MAX ROMEO

(X) DENNIS ALCAPONE, DAVID ISAACS

BULLET 478 Mother Oh Mother/Dreams of Passion

CAMEL 82 The Coming of Jah/Watch & Pray

Produced by Niney Holness. (a) A bouncy single with a strong melody and a catchy harmony-drenched chorus. Even the convoluted rhythm can't slow down this number, as Romeo delivers up some of his sweetest vocals.

PAMA SUPREME 306 Let the Power Fall on I/The Raid

Produced by Derrick Morgan. (a) Morgan recycled the rhythms from NINEY's "In The Gutter" for this spiritual, where the beat sets the disjointed pace and Romeo and his backing vocalists carry the melody virtually a cappella.

PAMA SUPREME 318 Don't You Weep/Version

Produced by Derrick Morgan. (a) Morgan opts for a subtler rhythms for this call and response gospel song. Romeo's lead is magnificently backed by the high/low backing vocals.

PAMA SUPREME 328 Ginal Ship/UPSETTERS: Version

Produced by Lee Perry. (a) A straight forward upbeat reggae rhythm sparks this brash single, accented by the brash brass section and Romeo's light, lilting vocals.

PRINCE BUSTER 11 River Jordan/Words Sound & Power

Produced by Prince Buster.

PUNCH 73 Chi Chi Bud/Version

ROY & BIM

(X) MAYTONES

HUGH ROY JUNIOR

aka FROGGY.

BIG 329 Papcito/RUPIE EDWARDS ALL-STARS: I'm Gonna Live Some Life

Produced by Rupie Edwards.

SUPREME 211 Double Attack/MURPHY'S ALL-STARS: Puzzle

RUBY & GLORIA

Duo featuring GLORIA CRAWFORD.

BIG SHOT 583 Worried Over You/Version

BLACK SWAN 1409 Talk to Me Baby/LLOYD'S ALL-STARS: Version

RUDDY & SKETTO

SUPREME 218 Every Night/Ethiopia

THE RUDIES

SPINNING WHEEL 106 My Sweet Lord/Devil's Lead Soup

THE RUFFIANS

(X) AL BROWN, THE SENSATIONS

BANANA 359 Room Full of Tears/Black Soul

BRUCE RUFFIN

SUMMIT 8516 Candida/Are You Ready

TROJAN 7814 Rain/THE PYRAMIDS: Geronimo

TROJAN 7832 One Big Happy Family (Parts 1/2)

SAMSON DI LARK

(X) MR CALYPSO

SAMUEL THE FIRST

b Phillip Samuels, DJ.

SUMMIT 8515 Sounds of Babylon/BEVERLEY'S ALL-STARS: Second Babylon Version

Produced by Leslie Kong.

MAHALIA SAUNDERS

MOODISC 112 Down the Aisle/IAN ROBINSON: Three for One

Produced by Harry Mudie.

UPSETTER 374 Pieces of My Heart/UPSETTERS: Version
Produced by Lee Perry.

THE SCORPIONS

(X) BILL GENTLES

SCOTTY

DUKE 106 Donkey Skank/MURPHY'S ALL-STARS: Version

SONGBIRD 1049 Riddle I This/Musical Chariot

Produced by Derrick Harriott. (a) After all the boasts he made on "Solomon," Harriott had it coming. And Scotty makes sure he gets it, by chanting nursery rhymes over his old hit.

SONGBIRD 1051 Jam Rock Style/Version
Produced by Derrick Harriott.

SONGBIRD 1056 Penny for Your Song/CRYSTALITES: Version
Produced by Derrick Harriott.

THE SELECTED FEW

BANANA 351 Selection Train/SOUND DIMENSION: Version
Produced by Coxsone Dodd. (a) A tight skank over electric rhythms, that even the thinness of the vocals are unable to detract.

THE SENSATIONS

DUKE 120 Remember/LARRY'S ALL-STARS: Madhouse

DUKE 121 What Are You Doing Sunday/THE RUFFIANS: Sweet Dream

DAWN SHARON

(X) JOE HIGGS

SHEILA

NU-BEAT 079 Only Heaven Knows/GRANT & RICHARDS: Freedom Psalm

ROY SHIRLEY

NU-BEAT 090 Hold Them/One Two Three Four
Produced by Joe Gibbs.

ROY SHIRLEY & SLIM SMITH

(X) RON SIG

SHOUT

EXPLOSION 2058 Life Is Rough/Version

LEROY SIBBLES

b 1949 (JA). HEPTONES vocalist. (X) JOHN HOLT

DUDLEY SIBLEY

BANANA 322 Having a Party/DELROY & SPORTY: Lovers Version

SIDNEY ALL STARS

(X) JUNIOR ENGLISH, CARL LEWIS, SAMMY MORGAN

RON SIG

CAMEL 58 1970s/Version

CAMEL 59 You Girl/ROY SHIRLEY & SLIM SMITH: Facts of Life

SILVER & MAGENTA

FAB 163 Change Has Got to Come/Magnet Stomp

THE SILVERTONES

CLANDISC 234 Tear Drops Will Fall/THE DYNAMITES: Version
Produced by Clancy Eccles.

SIR HARRY

DUKE 127 Last Call/ORGAN D: Hot Organ

THE SLICKERS

(X) AGGROS, NORA DEAN

DYNAMIC 419 You Can't Win/Don't Fight the Law

DYNAMIC 406 Johnny too Bad/ROLAND ALPHONSO: Saucy Hoarde

GG 4524 Oh My Baby/WINSTON WRIGHT: Change of Lover Version
Produced by Alvin Ranglin.

PUNCH 59 Johnny too Bad/Version

Produced by Byron Lee. (a) This rude boy classic later appeared on *The Harder They Come* soundtrack. The persistent reggae rhythm is unbeatable, while the CROOKS/DEKKER/ROBINSON team's vocals are a nigh on perfect blend of admiration and admonishment, encapsulating Jamaica's own fascination and frustration at its young outlaws.

PUNCH 81 Fussing & Fighting/Man I Should Be

ERNIE SMITH

DUKE 119 Bend Down/Heaven Help Us All

HORSE 6 Sunday Morning/One Three

IAN SMITH & INNER MIND

BULLET 490 Devil Woman/Nenn Street Rub

SLIM SMITH

(X) COUNT OSSIE, WINSTON WILLIAMS

CAMEL 81 Spanish Harlem/Slip Away

ESCORT 851 My Love Come True/This Feeling

(b) The backing band provide a dreamy atmosphere to this cover of the CARLTON & HIS SHOES' hit, while Smith's vocals soar into gorgeous falsetto before returning to earth with soulful passion.

ESCORT 852 Life Keeps Turning/My Girl

ESCORT 859 My Girl/RICO: Plus One

JACKPOT 779 Will You Still Love Me Tomorrow/Keep on Walking

PAMA SUPREME 334 Send Me Some Loving/I'm Lost

SUPREME 219 Stay/You're My Everything

DONALD SMYTHE

PUNCH 83 Where Love Goes/THE HURRICANES: You Can Run

SONNY

ACKEE 127 Love & Peace/LARRY & ALVIN: Throw Me Corn

THE SOUL CATS

(X) KING CANNON

THE SOUL DEFENDERS

Crucial Studio One session band formed around 1970 and featuring JAH PRIVY (guitar), VAL WHITTAKER (guitar), FESTUS WALKER (bass), VIN MORGAN (drums) plus keyboard players BOBBY KALAPHAT, RICHARD ACE, AUBREY ADAMS, and JACKIE MITTOO. Vocalists included ALTON ELLIS, NANA MCLEAN, and JOSEPH HILL of CULTURE — see entry on page 83.

BANANA 354 Way Back Home/SOUL REBELS: Stand for Your Rights
Produced by Coxsone Dodd.

THE SOUL MAN

(X) MELLOTONES

THE SOUL REBELS

(X) SOUL DEFENDERS

THE SOUL SISTERS

(X) DENNIS BROWN

THE SOUL SYNDICATE

(X) ROCKIN' HORSE

THE SOULETTES

JACKPOT 766 My Desire/Bring It Up
Produced by Bunny Lee.
JACKPOT 767 All of Your Loving/LLOYD CLARKE: Love Me
Produced by Bunny Lee.

THE SOUND DIMENSION

(X) DENNIS BROWN, THE HEPTONES, JERRY JONES, MAD ROY, FREDDIE MCKAY, NANA MCLEAN, LASCELLES PERKINS, SELECTED FEW

THE SOUNDS COMBINE

ESCORT 862 African Museum/Version

SPEED

BULLET 477 There's a Train/Blue Moon

JO SPENCER

DYNAMIC 415 Bed of Roses/Forgive Me

CINDY STARR

(X) THE TEARDROPS

FITZROY STERLING

ESCORT 858 Girl Tell Me What to Do/Be Careful
PAMA 820 My Sweet Lord/Darling That's Right

LESTER STERLING

NU-BEAT 095 Iron Side (Part One)/COXSONE'S ALL-STARS (Part Two)
Produced by Coxsone Dodd. Reissued as ASHANTI 409.
SMASH 2321 Sir Collins' Special/Version

RAPHAEL STEWART

PUNCH 71 Put Your Sweet Lips/JUSTONS: Stand by Me

TINGA STEWART

b Neville Stewart (JA). Winner of the 1974 Festival Song competition and composer of the 1975 winner for his brother, Roman Stewart.
SONGBIRD 1048 Hear that Train/CRYSTALITES: Version
Produced by Derrick Harriott.

THE STICKERS

BULLET 492 One Night of Sin/Version

STONE

(X) CARL DAWKINS

STRANGER & GLADDY

CLANDISC 230 Tomorrow/DYNAMITES: Version
Produced by Clancy Eccles.
SUPREME 227 My Application/TADDY & THE DIAMONDS: Oh No My Baby

THE SWANS

(X) LEE BOGLE

TADDY & THE DIAMONDS

(X) STRANGER & GLADDY

THE TARTANS

ESCORT 843 A Day Will Come/ROBI'S ALL-STARS: Version

THE TEARDROPS

ACKEE 126 Let Me Be Free/CINDY STARR: Sentimental Girl
BIG SHOT 582 Two in One/LARRY'S ALL-STARS: Rock a Boogie

THE TECHNIQUES

BANANA 350 Since I Lost You/RILEY'S ALL-STARS: Version
Produced by Martin Riley.

THE TECHNIQUES ALL-STARS

(X) ANSELL COLLINS

TEDDY

DJ by night, a printer at Graphic Arts by day.
HIGH NOTE 053 Homebound/GAYTONES: Chapter 3
Produced by Sonia Pottinger. (a) Over the CONQUERORS' "Won't You Come Home," Teddy doesn't do much more than agree with the singers' own exhortations.
UPSETTER 353 Elusion/THE UPSETTERS: Big John Wayne
Produced by Lee Perry.

THE THIRD & FOURTH GENERATIONS

Studio band for JOE GIBBS. (X) PETER TOSH
PUNCH 91 Rudies Medley/JOE GIBBS & THE SOUL MATES: Rude Boy Version
Produced by Joe Gibbs.

NICKY THOMAS

TROJAN 7807 If I Had a Hammer/Lonely Feelin'
Produced by Joe Gibbs. (a) A bouncy version of the old religious favorite, the call and response is particularly perky, and all is fueled by the strong beat.
TROJAN 7830 Tell It Like It Is/BBC

TIGER

(X) CLANCY ECCLES, THE VERSATILES
CAMEL 70 Guilty/United We Stand
NU-BEAT 075 African Beat/Black Man Land
NU-BEAT 088 Have You Ever Been Hurt/Our Day Will Come

THE TILLERMEN
DUKE 109 Be Loving to Me/Judgement Rock

TOMORROW'S CHILDREN
(X) KEN LAZARUS

TONY & CHARMERS
Featuring LLOYD CHARMERS. (X) LLOYD CHARMERS

TOP CAT
PUNCH 63 Iron Bird/Cat Hop

PETER TOSH
BULLET 486 Maga Dog/THIRD & FOURTH GENERATIONS: Bull Dog
Produced by Joe Gibbs. (a) The distinctive stop-start rhythm swirls across this Joe Gibbs' production, but doesn't soften Tosh's nasty lyrics, a dear Jane letter would have been infinitely preferable to this kicking, no matter how sweetly the backing singers croon "sorry" in the background.

THE TRANS AM ALL-STARS
(X) JAMES BROWN

THE TROJAN ALL STARS
(X) ETHIOPIANS

THE TROPICAL ALL STARS
(X) PLAYBOYS

THE TWINKLE BROTHERS
BIG SHOT 593 You Took Me by Surprise/Version
BIG SHOT 600 It's Not Who You Know/I Need Someone
GREEN DOOR 4007 Miss Labba Labba/The Best Is Yet to Come
JACKPOT 768 Do Your Own Thing/BOY WONDER They Talk About Love
TROPICAL 002 Love Sweet Love/HERON ATTAR: Poor Man's Life

LLOYD TYRELL
ESCORT 855 One Woman/THE CHARMERS: What Should I Do

U-ROY
(X) PAT KELLY
DUKE 105 Love I Tender/JOYA LANDIS: When the Lights Are Low
Produced by Duke Reid. (a) The clopping rhythm and twangy guitar turns Presley's "Love Me Tender" inside out, as the DJ excitedly raps about love and loving.
DUKE REID 2516 Testify/TOMMY MCCOOK: Super Soul
Produced by Duke Reid.
DUKE REID 2518 True True/On the Beach
Produced by Duke Reid. (a) The DJ adds further bounce and enthusiasm to the charming KEN PARKER oldie. (b) PARAGON JOHN HOLT was happy to hand over some of his greatest songs to the DJ, and this exquisite number sent the DJ into special paroxysms of delight. "Wow! woo!" he exclaims time and again, between extorting the band "to swing" and inviting the listener to join the party.

DUKE REID 2519 Flashing My Whip/Do It Right
Produced by Duke Reid. (a) THE PARAGONS croon "Only a Smile" in the background as U-Roy inexplicably flashes his whip and bouncily brags his way across the rock steady grooves with no sympathy whatsoever for the trio's heartbreak. At one point, he even coolly suggests that lead vocalist JOHN HOLT "smile a while and give your face a rest." (b) U-Roy shows rock steady trio the THREE TOPS how to do it right, picking up the simple lyrics and running with them.
TREASURE ISLE 7064 Everybody Bawlin'/Ain't that Loving You
Produced by Duke Reid. (a) THE MELODIANS' rock steady gem of the same title provides a sonorous backdrop for U-Roy to toss in some of his most loved catchphrases, exhortations, and exclamations. (b) ALTON ELLIS' magnificent cover gives the DJ something to fall in love with. U-Roy echoes the singer's words and encourages him to ever more passionate heights.
UPSETTER 375 Earthquake/Suspicious Minds
Produced by Lee Perry. (a) A duelling cut set to the "What a Confusion" rhythm, featuring two different, double tracked U-Roy toasts.

U-ROY & HOPETON LEWIS
(X) HOPETON LEWIS
TREASURE ISLE 7059 Drive Her Home (Parts 1/2)
Produced by Duke Reid. (a) Hopeton Lewis belts out the rather suggestive lyrics to ERIC MORRIS' 1964 hit "Number One." U-Roy, of course, gleefully joins in to push this cut to its ultimate limits.

U-ROY & TOMMY MCCOOK
TREASURE ISLE 7062 Behold/Way Back Home
Produced by Duke Reid. (a) U-Roy yips and chats his way through a charming, flute heavy Tommy McCook backing track.

THE UNTOUCHABLES
BULLET 460 Can't Reach You/CARL DAWKINS: Natural Woman
Produced by Lee Perry.

THE UPSETTERS
(X) DENNIS ALCAPONE, DAVE BARKER, CARL DAWKINS, PAUL FREEMAN, DAVID ISAACS, MAX ROMEO, MAHALIA SAUNDERS, TEDDY, THE WAILERS, ROB WALKER, WINSTON WRIGHT
UPSETTER 352 Heart & Soul/Zig Zag
Produced by Lee Perry.
UPSETTER 361 Apasetic/All Africans
Produced by Lee Perry. (b) A LITTLE ROY composition and performance, also featuring EWAN GARDINER (vocals), PETER TOSH (guitar), and BUNNY LIVINGSTON (drums).

THE UPSETTING BROTHERS
SUPREME 229 Not You Baby/DREADLOCK ALL-STARS: Version

UXBROWN & SCOTTY

Duo featuring SCOTTY of THE CHOSEN FEW.

HIGH NOTE 056H Unbelievable Sounds/GAYTONES: Version
Produced by Sonia Pottinger.

THE VEGETABLES

BANANA 332 Holly Rhythm/KING STITT: Back Out Version

VERNE & SON

aka THE MAYTONE'S VERNON BUCKLEY & GLADSTONE ANDERSON.

GG 4523 Little Blue Boy/Version
Produced by Alvin Ranglin. (a) The rhythm was later re-used by SAMUEL THE FIRST for "Walking Stick" and UK toaster JUDGE DREAD for "Big Six." In its original form, however, it clops behind a self-pitying extrapolation of the original nursery rhyme, and doesn't really go anywhere.

THE VERSATILES

NU-BEAT 076 Give It to Me/TIGER: With Hot
Produced by Joe Gibbs.

THE VERSION BOYS

(X) TEDDY MAGNUS

THE VICEROYS

BULLET 470 Rebel Nyah/Feel the Spirit

THE VICTORS

ESCORT 846 Me a Tell Yuh/LLOYD'S ALL-STARS: More Echo

THE WAILERS

(X) DAVE BARKER

BULLET 464 Soul Town/Let the Sun Shine on Me
Produced by the Wailers.

BULLET 493 Lick Samba/Samba
Produced by the Wailers. (a) A calypso flavored offering offset by the pulsing reggaefied bass, with MARLEY leading the call and response vocals.

GREEN DOOR 4005 Trench Town Rock/Grooving Kingston
Produced by the Wailers. (a) The Wailers' message of hope and solidarity to Trenchtown, Kingston's infamous slum neighborhood, wrapped in an anthemic melody and a solid mid tempo reggae rhythm.

PUNCH 77 Down Presser/JUNIOR BYLES: Got the Tip
Produced by Lee Perry. (a) PETER TOSH reworked the spiritual "Sinner Man" (a Wailers Studio One hit) for this anthemic rootsy single, for which Perry found a suitably insistent rhythm and the Wailers give absolutely flawless vocal performances.

SUMMIT 8526 Stop this Train/Caution
Produced by Leslie Kong.(a) TOSH at his best, setting this single afire with his marvelous soulful vocals, the Wailers harmonize comfortingly in the background. (b) Rootsy reggae number based on the consequences of a driving offense. The guitar work is particularly notable, as is the palpitating

rhythm, with the harmonies slipping and sliding across the grooves while MARLEY's delivery is equally strong.

SUPREME 216 I Like It Like This/?
Produced by Lee Perry. (a) The 1971 rerecording of 1968's "Don't Rock My Boat," later retitled "Satisfy My Soul."

UPSETTER 354 Mr Brown/UPSETTERS: Dracula
Produced by Lee Perry. (a) An organ heavy reworking of "Duppy Conqueror," but who is Mr Brown? The Wailers never really answer that question on this dubby number.

UPSETTER 356 Kaya/UPSETTERS: Version
Produced by Lee Perry. (a) A production showcase, all simmering rhythm, pretty guitar riffs, and an overwhelmingly dreamy atmosphere, the perfect soundscape for MARLEY and the Wailers to exclaim over the wonderful effects of ganja. In 1978, the song would title an entire Marley album. Hmmm, it wasn't *that* good.

UPSETTER 357 Small Axe/All in One
Produced by Lee Perry. (a) One of Perry's more intriguing rhythms sets the scene for this classic rasta rebel single, as MARLEY swings from singing to sermonizing, with LIVINGSTON and TOSH angelically harmonizing in the background. (b) Perry found the perfect reggae rhythm for this medley of classic Wailers' singles, including "Bend Down Low," "Long Time," "One Love," "Simmer Down," and many more.

UPSETTER 369 More Axe/UPSETTERS: Axe Man
Produced by Lee Perry. Also released as UPSETTER 372. (a) An alternate vocal distinguishes this from the original "Small Axe". (b) Burru percussionists BONGO HERMAN and LES characterize this version.

UPSETTER 371 Dreamland/UPSETTERS: Version
Produced by Lee Perry. (a) LIVINGSTON was at his best on this dreamy single, which Perry promptly graced with an inappropriately upbeat rhythm. But the singer's sonorous vocals, supported by the yearning harmonies of TOSH and MARLEY, brought to life this vision of paradise.

THE WAILING SOULS

BANANA 335 Walk Walk Walk/KING SPORTY: Love Me Version
Produced by Coxsone Dodd.

GREEN DOOR 4014 Harbour Shark/Version
Produced by Wailing Souls.

ROB WALKER

(X) TOMMY MCCOOK

JACKPOT 761 Hear My Heart/Puppet on a String
Produced by Bunny Lee.

UPSETTER 366 Run Up Your Mouth/UPSETTERS: Version
Produced by Lee Perry. (a) Single released credited to the HURRICANES in Jamaica.

DENNIS WALKS

MOODISC 101 Time Will Tell/Under the Shady Tree
Produced by Harry Mudie.

NORMAN T WASHINGTON

GAS 159 It's Christmas Time Again/If I Could See You

MARLENE WEBBER

ACKEE 120 Natengula/Natengula-Kera

ACKEE 122 Cumbaya/Hail Hi Freedom

SMASH 2322 Hard Life/COLLINS ALL-STARS: Version

(a) The persistent reggae beat and the enthusiastic keyboards totally overwhelm Webber's soft, delicate vocals. The young boy with a spoken word hard-life tale-to-tell stands up proud, however.

TROJAN 7815 Stand by Your Man/CLANCY ECCLES: Credit Squeeze

Produced by Clancy Eccles. (a) Tammy Wynette's version may be better known, and HORTENSE ELLIS' is certainly more cloying. But Webber's owes little to either, with a fuller, lusher instrumentation, and barely a nod to the song's original C&W roots.

THE WEST INDIANS

DYNAMIC 413 Never Gonna Give You Up/REBELLIOUS SUBJECTS: Never Give Up

Produced by Byron Lee.

DELROY WILLIAMS

TROJAN 7813 Down in the Boondocks/Baby Make It

WINSTON WILLIAMS

JACKPOT 757 Love Version/SLIM SMITH: Ball of Confusion

WILLIE & LLOYD

CAMEL 80 Marcus Is Alive/GLADIATORS: Freedom Train

DELROY WILSON

BANANA 333 Just Because of You/I Love You Madly

Produced by Coxsone Dodd. (b) There's a hint of the Temptations about Wilson's vocal, but the backing is pure SOUL DEFENDERS.

JACKPOT 763 Better Must Come/Version

Produced by Bunny Lee. (a) The stop/start rhythms were deliberately created to cash in on the latest dance craze, the John Crow Skank. Lee's dubbish production, all reverbing synthi-drums, is sheer genius, but it was Wilson's lyrical promise of better days for the downtrodden that sold the song. Michael Manley astutely used the title as the slogan for his PNP party's victorious campaign the following year, adding further weight to the single's legacy.

JACKPOT 769 Cool Operator/I'm Yours

Produced by Bunny Lee. (a) This smash hit was built on a superbly complex rhythm, over which the ever-cool Wilson lets loose with some of his most effective pickup lines to impress the even cooler operator of the title.

JACKPOT 770 Try Again/THE AGGROVATORS: Try Again Version

Produced by Bunny Lee.

JACKPOT 780 Keep Your True Love Strong/Nice To Be Near

JACKPOT 781 Peace & Love/JEFF BARNES: Who Is Your Brother

SMASH 2317 I Am Trying/COLLINS ALL-STARS: Version

SMASH 2318 Satisfaction/Version

SMASH 2323 What It Was/LLOYD CLARKE: Chicken Thief

ERNEST WILSON & FREDDY

GAS 168 What You Gonna Do About It/DOBBY DOBSON: Halfway to Paradise

JACKPOT 765 Let Them Talk/The Truth Hurts

SHARK WILSON & THE BASEMENT HEATERS

aka ERNEST WILSON of THE CLARENDONIANS.

ASHANTI 400 Make It Reggae/Version

WINSTON & ERROL

PUNCH 74 Goodnight My Love/There Is a Land

WINSTON & PAT

BULLET 475 The Same Thing for Breakfast/Sweeter than Honey

WINSTON & RUPERT

MOODISC 106 Musically Beat/Let Me Tell You Girl

WONDER BOY

JACKPOT 764 Just for a Day/He Ain't Heavy

HAZEL WRIGHT

(X) THE ETERNALS

WINSTON WRIGHT

(X) CHARLES, PAULETTE & GEE, JOHN HOLT, THE SLICKERS

CAMEL 71 Silhouettes/That Did It

Also released as DUKE 111.

UPSETTER 378 Example/UPSETTERS: Version

Produced by Lee Perry.

YOUNG AL CAPONE

GREEN DOOR 4012 Girl Called Clover/Version

THE YOUTH PROFESSIONALS

(X) CARL DAWKINS

ALEX ZANETIS

MOODISC 102 Guilty/JOLLY BOYS: Do fe Do

ZIMM & DEE DEE

GREEN DOOR 4006 You've Got a Friend/GROOVERS: Cheep

THE ZOOMS

HORSE 8 Skinny Dippy/Sweet Bread

1972

CHARLIE ACE

(X) GABY & WILTON, GARY WILTON & CHARLIE ACE

THE AGGROVATORS

(X) CORNELL CAMPBELL, ALTON ELLIS

LAUREL AITKEN

BIG SHOT 605 Take Me in Your Arms/Two Timing Woman

Produced by Laurel Aitken.

CAMEL 90 Africa Arise/GI GINGRI: Holy Mt Zion
Produced by Laurel Aitken.

PAMA 857 Reggae Popcorn/Darling Darling
Produced by Laurel Aitken.

DENNIS ALCAPONE

(X) BYRON LEE & THE DRAGONAIRES

ACKEE 146 Power Version/BLUESBLASTERS: Martie
Produced by Coxsone Dodd. (a) Unusually, the DJ toasts over a classic ska song, merrily cock-a-doodling, splattering his raps like a machine gun, and shaking up the song.

ATTACK 8027 Fine Style/WINSTON SCOTLAND: On the Track
Produced by Tony Robinson. (a) The DJ at his most melodic, with rock steady harmonies and beat providing perfectly timed backing. A sublime blend of the toaster to a classic track.

BULLET 509 Dub Up a Daughter/TONY'S ALL-STARS: Version
Produced by Tony Robinson. Also released as GREEN DOOR 4041.

DUKE 131 Sky's the Limit/HUDSON ALL-STARS: Limit Version
Produced by Keith Hudson.

DUKE 147 Get in the Groove/Dynamite Version
Produced by Dennis Alcapone/Dennis Brown.

GRAPE 3035 Rasta Dub/UPSETTERS: Version
Produced by Lee Perry.

PRINCE BUSTER 24 Giant/PRINCE BUSTER: Science
Produced by Prince Buster.

TECHNIQUES 918 Look into Yourself/TECHNIQUES ALL-STARS: Yourself Version
Produced by Winston Riley. (a) The sparkling melody and clambering beat boosts the DJ's own natural exuberance, as Alcapone sermonizes upon the righteous before breaking into song.

TROPICAL 019 Worldwide Love/CARL MASTERS: Gable Up

UPSETTER 381 Wonderman/Place Called Africa
Produced by Lee Perry.

UPSETTER 388 Master Key/UPSETTERS: Keyhole
Produced by Lee Perry.

THE AFRICAN

SIOUX 006 Cock Mouth Kill Cock/ERROL T: I Need You Now

BOB ANDY

GREEN DOOR 4047 Life/HARRY J ALL-STARS: Version
Produced by Harry J.

SIOUX 020 Everyday People/HONG GANG: Smoking Wild

HORACE ANDY

ATTACK 8026 Feel Good/PHIL PRATT ALL-STARS: Feel Good Versio
Produced by Phil Pratt.

COUNT SHELLEY 02 Jah Jah Children/
Produced by Count Shelley.

ANSELL & ELAINE

CAMEL 98 Presenting Cheater/RON WILSON: Official Trombone

PETER ASHBOURNE

(X) FABULOUS FIVE INC

ROY BAILEY

DUKE 146 Run Away Child/Wedding March

DAVE BARKER

BIG SHOT 614 Are You Sure/I Don't Know Why

THE BELTONES

ACKEE 150 Wrapped Up In Love/SOUND DIMENSION: Pasero
Produced by Coxsone Dodd.

LORNA BENNETT

BLUE MOUNTAIN 1013 Breakfast in Bed/SCOTTY: Skank in Bed
Produced by Harry J.

VAL BENNETT

(X) CLARENDONIANS

BEVERLEY'S ALL STARS

(X) MAYTALS, MELODIANS

BIG YOUTH

See entry on page 34. (X) UPSETTERS

BLUE BEAT 424 Chi Chi Run/JOHN HOLT: OK Fred
Produced by Prince Buster. (a) Based upon an old mento song, the DJ's signature toast soaring over JOHN HOLT's cover of the DELROY WILSON hit "Rain from the Skies."

DOWNTOWN 492 Ace 90 Skank/KEITH HUDSON: True True to My Heart
Produced by Keith Hudson. (a) Hudson actually dragged a motorcycle into the studio to capture the sound of the revving engine for this tribute to the Honda, accompanied by a slow, pulsing rhythm perfect for Youth's da-da-da-da-doe-wa-doe wa-doe rap.

THE BLUESBLASTERS

(X) DENNIS ALCAPONE

BOB & MARCIA

TROJAN 7854 But I Do/I Don't Care

BONGO, LES & BUNNY (X) BONGO HERMAN

ATTACK 8041 Feel Nice Version/Quick & Slick
Produced by Prince Tony. (b) WINSTON SCOTLAND joins in.

KEN BOOTHE

CAMEL 91 Ain't No Sunshine/LLOYD & HORTENSE: You Are Everything

DYNAMIC 453 Tears from My Eyes/CONSCIOUS MINDS: Version

PAMA SUPREME 369 Look What You've Done/LLOYD CHARMERS: Version

THE BOSS ATTACK

FAB 187 Hell-El/TEARDROPS: Let Me Be Free

BROTHER DAN

(X) POOCH JACKSON

AL BROWN

FAB 186 Ain't Got No Soul/TEARDROPS: I Got a Feeling

BUSTY BROWN

PAMA SUPREME 356 Throw Away Your Gun/TWINKLE BROS: Sad Song

DENNIS BROWN

(X) U-ROY

ASHANTI 402 It's too Late/Song My Mother Used to Sing

DUKE 139 What About the Half/Version

EXPLOSION 2068 Black Magic Woman/PHIL PRATT ALL-STARS: Part 2

Produced by Phil Pratt. (a) Excellent remake of Fleetwood Mac's "Black Magic Woman," completely restructuring (and in a way, re-contextualizing) the song's original samba/blues feel.

PRESSURE BEAT 5513 Money in My Pocket/JOE GIBBS ALL-STARS: Money Love

Produced by Joe Gibbs. (a) Co-written by Brown and Gibbs, this was the ultimate showcase for the young vocalist, and arguably remains his greatest single. The singer's smooth style, convincingly delivered, slides across the grooves, buttressed by the solid beats and charming melody.

RANDY'S 528 Meet Me on the Corner/IMPACT ALL-STARS Version

Produced by Randy's.

RANDY'S 526 Cheater/TOMMY MCCOOK & IMPACT ALL-STARS: Harvest in the East

Produced by Randy's.

SONGBIRD 1074 Silhouettes/CRYSTALITES: Version

Produced by Derrick Harriott. (a) Brown takes on the much-covered Rays' golden oldie. The bells are a nice touch, the beat's unstoppable, and the singer gives it his all.

ERROL BROWN

SONGBIRD 1082 People Make the World Go Round/Version

Produced by Derrick Harriott.

FUNKY BROWN

SIOUX 018 African People (Indian Reservation)/JUMBO STERLING: Elizabethan Reggae

Produced by Roosevelt and Jack Price.

JACKIE BROWN

HIGH NOTE 060 Last Dance/GAYTONES: Version

Produced by Sonia Pottinger.

JAMES BROWN

ASHANTI 408 Mama Don't Want to See You/Version

LENNOX BROWN

BULLET 501 High School Serenade/WINSTON SCOTLAND: On the Track

Also released as GREEN DOOR 4023.

BROWN'S ALL STARS

(X) TINGA STEWART

RAD BRYAN

ATTACK 8040 Standing in the Park/BRYAN ALL-STARS: Stand Up Version

BRYAN ALL STARS

(X) RAD BRYAN

JUNIOR BYLES

BULLET 499 Beat Down Babylon/UPSETTERS: [version]

Produced by Lee Perry. (a) One of Perry's first sessions to use the NOW GENERATION as the UPSETTERS, the rhythm is determinedly laid back, MIKEY CHUNG's guitar lead is classic rock and the whipping sound is Perry. Add Byle's phenomenal vocals and you've got all the ingredients of a rebel classic.

DYNAMIC 432 Pharaoh Hiding/Hail to Power

Produced by Lee Perry. (a) The biblical story takes on new meaning in the then current climes, with lyrical allusions to the current balance of Jamaican political power. Effectively built around a nursery rhyme like melody, it's powered by a strong, and so typical Perry beat. (b) A dub version of "Pharaoh Hiding" featuring some entertaining horns, and that great rhythm. Also released as PUNCH 109.

RANDY'S 523 King of Babylon/UPSETTERS: Nebuchadnezzar

Produced by Lee Perry. (a) Byle's definitive summing up of Rasta beliefs, which also contains allusions to the utter disillusion surrounding the incumbent government. In the background, producer Perry finds an intriguing rhythm equal to the lyrical power within.

UPSETTER 387 Festival Da Da/UPSETTERS: Version

Produced by Lee Perry. (a) Junior Byles' entry to the Festival Song Competition came third, with an infectious sing-along chorus, loping along rhythm, THE JAMAICANS' excellent backing vocals, and Byles' own excellent delivery. (b) An alternate mix of the a-side is further dignified by an opening Rastafarian announcement from Scratch.

THE CABLES

JACKPOT 787 Come On/Come on Version

Produced by Bunny Lee.

CORNELL CAMPBELL

CAMEL 95 My Confession/PAT KELLY: Daddy's Home

DYNAMIC 446 My Confession/AGGROVATORS: Star Dust

Produced by Bunny Lee.

GREEN DOOR 4042 Dearest Darling/Star Dust

CAREY & LLOYD

DJ duo featuring CAREY "WILDMAN" JOHNSON AND LLOYD YOUNG (THE GROOVERS).

GRAPE 3025 Come Down/DYNAMITES Version

Produced by Clancy Eccles.

THE CARIFRA ALL STARS

(X) BILLY DYCE

CAT & NICKY CAMPBELL

DJ CAT CAMPBELL and his brother. (X) PETER TOSH

LLOYD CHARMERS

(X) KEN BOOTHE, SHIRLEY & THE CHARMERS

CAMEL 101 Jamaica Song/Out of Love

THE CHARMERS

PAMA SUPREME 346 Show Business/DEBBY & LLOYD: Guide

PAMA SUPREME 355 Desiderata/Desiderata Music

THE CHOSEN FEW

SONGBIRD 1070 Do Your Thing/Your Thing

Produced by Derrick Harriott. (a) The Chosen Few are less adventurous than on their last journey into Isaac Hayes country, opting for a true-to-the-original cover with just the syncopated beat to set it apart.

TROJAN 7864 Ebony Eyes/Version

(a) Classic Chosen Few, where the song itself really doesn't matter, it's the range of the vocals which staggers.

TROJAN 7882 Everybody Plays the Fool/You're a Big Girl Now

CHUCKLES

DUKE 144 Reggae Limbo/ZAP POW: Broken Contract

GEOFFREY CHUNG & THE ALL STARS

HARRY J 6645 U.F.O.

MIKEY CHUNG & NOW GENERATION

b Michael Chung, 1954 (Kingston, JA). Distinguished guitarist formed the MIGHTY MYSTICS in 1968 with GEOFFREY CHUNG (keyboards) and VAL DOUGLAS (bass). When the band broke up, Chung and Douglas formed the Now Generation. Line-up included AUGUSTUS PABLO, GLEN STAIR, JOE COOPER (keyboards), KEITH ROWE (guitar), TIN LEGS (drums), and others. Members were regularly used by LEE PERRY and LLOYD CHARMERS among others during the early 1970s.

GREEN DOOR 4032 Breezin'/NOW GENERATION: Version

(a) The guitarist gives this instrumental cover a gorgeous, bittersweet taste of surf, counterpointed by the lush keyboards, and gently rocked away by the tight rhythm section.

THE CIRCLES

SIOUX 017 Mammy Blue/POOCH JACKSON WITH THE HARRY J ALL-STARS: King of the Road

Produced by Harry J.

THE CLARENDONIANS

ATTACK 8039 Bound in Chains/STUD ALL-STARS: Chains Version

Produced by D. Brown & P. Austin.

CAMEL 96 Darling Forever/Version

Produced by Coxsone Dodd.

PAMA 847 This Is My Story/VAL BENNETT: Caledonia

JIMMY CLIFF

ISLAND 6132 Trapped/Struggling Man

Produced by Jimmy Cliff.

ISLAND 6139 The Harder They Come/Many Rivers to Cross

(a) Produced by Jimmy Cliff. (b) Produced by Leslie Kong. (a/b) Classic Cliff and, perhaps, the coupling which best sums up his early 1970s output. Certainly no compilation could survive without this pair (although one or two try), the one a slow-burning slab of foreboding, the other a soaring hymnal.

STRANGER COLE

JACKPOT 791 My Confession/LASCELLES & HORTENSE: The Might Organ

PAMA 848 The House Where Bombo Lives/Our High School Dance

TROPICAL 011 Mail Man/Version

ANSELL COLLINS

(X) LLOYD YOUNG

DAVE COLLINS

aka DAVE BARKER. The new pseudonym was selected by producer LAWRENCE to associate the singer with ANSELL COLLINS, following the success (as DAVE & ANSELL COLLINS) of "Double Barrel" and "Monkey Spanner."

RHINO 103 Shackatac/Smooths & Sorts

Produced by Larry Lawrence.

RHINO 105 Ride Your Pony/You for Me

Produced by Larry Lawrence.

THE CONSCIOUS MINDS

(X) KEN BOOTHE, BB SEATON

ENGLAND COOK

EXPLOSION 2063 Samba Girl/NOW GENERATION: Samba Version

PADDY COREA

EXPLOSION 2066 Soul & Inspiration/STAGS: You Must Be Trying My Faith

COUNT OSSIE & HIS MYSTIC REVELATION

(X) SOUL DEFENDERS

ASHANTI 404 Rasta Reggae/Samia

COXSONE'S ALL STARS

(X) LESTER STERLING

THE CRYSTALITES

(X) DENNIS BROWN, BONGO HERMAN, SCOTTY, ROMAN STEWART

DON D JUNIOR

aka DON DRUMMOND JUNIOR. (X) KEITH HUDSON & CHUCKLES

DANDY

TROJAN 7857 What Do You Want to Make those Eyes at Me For/Talking About Sally

DAVE & ANSELL COLLINS

RHINO 106 Keep on Trying/Give Me Some Light

TECHNIQUES 915 Karate/Doing Your Own Thing

Produced by Winston Riley.

CARL DAWKINS

DUKE 133 My Whole World/A Broken Heart

NORA DEAN

(X) WAILING SOULS

BIG SHOT 611 Night Food Reggae/PROPHETS: Jacko

DEBBY & LLOYD

Featuring LLOYD CHARMERS. (X) THE CHARMERS

DESMOND DEKKER

RHINO 107 Beware/?

TROJAN 7876 It Gotta Be So/The First Time for a Long Time

GEORGE DEKKER

Half-brother of DESMOND DEKKER, frequently appearing alongside him on sessions. From 1968 a member of THE PIONEERS.

TROJAN 7879 Time Hard/SIDNEY GEORGE & JACKIE: Fall in Love

Produced by Sidney Crooks. (a) The synthesizer intro is spectacular, setting up one of Dekker's most dynamic performances. No matter that "every day things are getting worse," Dekker's irrepressible vocals (and that synth again — catch the instrumental break!) are unbeatable.

DENZIL DENNIS

DUKE 142 I Forgot To Be Your Lover/I've Got to Settle Down

PAMA SUPREME 350 South of the Border/GRAHAM: Long Island

PAMA SUPREME 375 Mama We're All Crazy Now/ROY SHIRLEY: A
  Lady's a Man's Best Friend

THE DIAMONDS

SONGBIRD 1079 Mash Up/DYNAMITES: Version

PHYLLIS DILLON

SIOUX 009 In the Ghetto/NYAH SHUFFLE: Night of the Long Knives

DION & THE THREE TOPS

BIG 331 Three Tops Time/UNDERGROUND PEOPLE: Tops Version

ERIC DONALDSON

DYNAMIC 431 I'm Indebted/(version)

DYNAMIC 439 Miserable Woman/The Lion Sleeps Tonight

DYNAMIC 445 Blue Boot/(version)

DYNAMIC 452 Little Did You Know/(version)

KARL DOUGLAS

BLUE MOUNTAIN 1007 Somebody Stop this Madness/Ain't No Use

THE DRUMBEAT ALL STARS

(X) SIR HARRY

KEBLE DRUMMOND

(X) PHIL PRATT ALL STARS

SHENLEY DUFFUS

DYNAMIC 451 Peace/UPSETTERS: Version

Produced by Lee Perry.

GRAPE 3031 Sincerely/Version

PAMA 859 At the End/Good Night My Love

UPSETTER 380 Bet You Don't Know/UPSETTERS: Ring of Fire

Produced by Lee Perry. (a) Based on Johnny Cash's "Ring of Fire." One line is sung in Amharic (Duffus was teaching the language at the time).

ERROL DUNKLEY

(X) BONGO HERMAN

CAMEL 87 Black Cinderella/PHIL PRATT ALL-STARS: Our Anniversary

Produced by Phil Pratt.

BILLY DYCE

aka RANSFORD WHITE of THE INSPIRATIONS, THE UN-TOUCHABLES.

GG 4532 Be My Guest/U-ROY: Way Down South

Produced by Alvin Ranglin. Also released as PAMA 835.

GG 4534 Take Warning/TYPHOON ALL-STARS: Warning Version

Produced by Alvin Ranglin.

GG 4536 Undying Love/CARIFRA ALL-STARS: Version

Produced by Alvin Ranglin.

GG 4537 Time Is Still Here/GG ALL-STARS: Version

Produced by Alvin Ranglin.

THE DYNAMITES

(X) CAREY & LLOYD, DIAMONDS, CLANCY ECCLES, CHRIS LEON, HOPETON LEWIS, MELODIANS, SOUL TWINS

THE EAGLES

DUKE REID 2522 Your Enemies Can't Hurt You/Version

CLANCY ECCLES

ATTACK 8037 Ganga Free/THE DYNAMITES: Ganga Version

Produced by Clancy Eccles.

CLANDISC 239 Hallelujah Free at Last/DYNAMITES: Sha La La

Produced by Clancy Eccles.

ADINA EDWARDS

DYNAMIC 454 Talk About Love/Don't Forget to Remember

RUPIE EDWARDS

BULLET 494 I'm Gonna Live Some Life/RUPIE EDWARDS ALL-STARS:
  Rock In

Produced by Rupie Edwards.

BIG 333 Press Along/Version

Produced by Rupie Edwards.

BIG 335 Jimmy as Job Card/Riot

Produced by Rupie Edwards.

BIG 337 Christmas Parade/UNDERGROUND PEOPLE: Santa

Produced by Rupie Edwards.

RUPIE EDWARDS ALL STARS

(X) RUPIE EDWARDS, HEPTONES, MAX ROMEO, BB SEATON

MIKE ELLIOTT

ACKEE 151 Milk & Honey/Burst a Shirt

ALTON ELLIS

ACKEE 148 Let's Stay Together/Version

ACKEE 502 Too Late to Turn Back Now/IMPACT ALL-STARS: Version
Produced by Randy's.

BIG SHOT 602 I'm Trying/Luna's Mood

CAMEL 94 Wonderful World/FAB DIMENSION: Version

GRAPE 3029 Big Bad Boy/HUDSON'S ALL-STARS: Version
Produced by Keith Hudson. (a) Ellis' take on the Johnny too Bad theme, with the soulful singer admonishing "You ought to be good," but sympathetically recognizing the difficulty involved. Sonorous backing singers reinforce his sternness.

JACKPOT 796 Play It Cool/AGGROVATORS: King of the Zozas
Produced by Bunny Lee.

PAMA 840 Girl I've Got a Date/Eat Bread

PAMA SUPREME 347 Moon River/I Can't Find Out

PAMA SUPREME 361 Working on a Groovy Thing/HARLESDEN SKANKERS: Version

SPUR 3 All That We Need Is Love/KEITH HUDSON: Better Love
Produced by Keith Hudson.

HORTENSE ELLIS & STRANGER COLE

GREEN DOOR 4035 Bringing in the Sheaves/Version

JUNIOR ENGLISH

BANANA 368 Anniversary/Girls Like You

PAMA 841 Miss Playgirl/Once in My Life

PAMA SUPREME 368 Garden Party/Version

ERROL & HUGH ROY JUNIOR

PUNCH 105 Darling Ooh Wee/GOD SONS: Merry Up Version
Produced by Glen Brown.

THE ETHIOPIANS

GG 4533 Israel Want to Be Free/TYPHOON ALL-STARS: Israel Version
Produced by Alvin Ranglin.

PRINCE BUSTER 38 You Are for Me/Playboy
Produced by Prince Buster.

TECHNIQUES 919 Promises/TIVOLIS: Version
Produced by Winston Riley.

EXODUS

(X) LLOYD THE MATADOR

THE FAB DIMENSION

(X) ALTON ELLIS

THE FABULOUS FIVE INC

Vocal duo comprising GLEN RICKS and LLOYD LOVINDEER of FABULOUS FLAMES.

HARRY J 6640 Come Back & Stay/PETER ASHBOURNE AFFAIR: Version
Produced by Harry J.

FAMILY MAN

DOWNTOWN 491 Herb Tree/STUDIO SOUND: Holy Poly

FERMENA

PAMA 839 Come What May/Version

BUNNY FLIP

PRESSURE BEAT 5510 Shanky Dog/JOE GIBBS & NOW GENERATION: Boney Dog
Produced by Joe Gibbs. (a) Actually WINSTON SCOTLAND's "Skanky Dog." (b) An instrumental version of "Magadog," the horns' bite are much less ferocious than TOSH's lyrics, but twice as fun.

FLOWERS & ALVIN

Vocal duo featuring LLOYD FLOWERS and producer ALVIN RANGLIN. (X) MAYTONES, SHORTY PERRY

BULLET 512 Howdy & Tenky/SHORTY PERRY: Sprinkle Some Water
Produced by Alvin Ranglin.

EDDIE FORD

PRESSURE BEAT 5512 A You Wrong fe Trouble Joshua/KENNETH POWER: Joshua Row Us Home

SHARON FORRESTER

ASHANTI 403 Silly Wasn't I?/NOW GENERATION: Version
(a) Forrester's emotive vocals shine on this upbeat single, which features a surprisingly lush orchestration.

LEE FOSTER & ANSELL COLLINS

CAMEL 102 The Man in Your Life/Version

FRANCIS

FAB 182 Rocking Machine/SOUL CLANS: Flying Rhythm

WINSTON FRANCIS

CAMEL 99 Ten Times Sweeter than You/Fat Boy

RHINO 102 A Little Today a Little Tomorrow/Love Thy Neighbour
Produced by Bruce Anthony.

RHINO 108 Blue Moon/Now That I'm a Man
Produced by Bruce Anthony.

THE FREEDOM GROUP

RANDY'S 525 Sing a Song of Freedom/IMPACT ALL-STARS: Version
Produced by Randy's.

THE GABLE HALL SCHOOL CHOIR

TROJAN 7881 Reggae Christmas/Candy Man

GABY & CABLES

DUKE 129 Only Love Can Make You Smile/Version

GABY & WILSON

CAMEL 92 Only Love/CHARLIE ACE: 10 Commandments of Joshua
Produced by Charlie Ace.

BUNNY GALE

(X) SKIDDY & DETROIT

THE GAYTONES

(X) JACKIE BROWN, JULIEN & THE GAYTONES, MAX ROMEO

BILL GENTLES

BULLET 506 Pure in Heart/Clean Hands

WESLEY GERMS

UPSETTER 390 Whiplash/UPSETTERS: Version
Produced by Lee Perry.

THE GG ALL STARS

(X) BILLY DYCE, MAYTONES, DEL WILLIAMS

JOE GIBBS ALL STARS

(X) DENNIS BROWN, BUNNY FLIP

GI GINGRI

(X) LAUREL AITKEN

THE GLADIATORS

ACKEE 149 Sonia/SOUND DIMENSION: Solas
Produced by Coxsone Dodd.

GLEN

SONGBIRD 1081 Smokey Eyes/Version
Produced by Derrick Harriott.

THE GOD SONS

Featuring TOMMY MCCOOK and RAD BRYAN. (X) ERROL
& HUGH ROY JUNIOR, CARL MASTERS

GREEN DOOR 4024 Merry Up/Version
Produced by Glen Brown. (b) A deliciously funereal instrumental, packing a bass line which registers on the Richter scale. KING TUBBY's remix, "Tubby's at the Control," would launch his career.

GRAHAM

Vocalist GRAHAM HAWK. (X) DENZIL DENNIS, OWEN
GRAY

OWEN GRAY

PAMA SUPREME 351 Time/GRAHAM: Harlesden Street
PAMA SUPREME 358 Hail the Man/I'll Follow You

OWEN GRAY & GRAHAM HAWK

PAMA SUPREME 360 Amazing Grace/SKETTO RICH: Don't Stay Out
  Late

WINSTON GRENNAN & J JACKSON

Session drummer Grennan (d 10/27/2000) and bassist Jackie Jackson of THE AGGROVATORS etc. (X) SHORTY
PERRY.

WINSTON GROOVEY

PAMA SUPREME 349 What You Gonna Do/Why Did You Leave
PAMA SUPREME 364 Sylvia's Mother/Here Is My Heart

THE HARLESDEN MONKS

PAMA SUPREME 352 Time/Harlesden High Street

THE HARLESDEN SKANKERS

(X) ALTON ELLIS

DERRICK HARRIOTT

SONGBIRD 1068 Over the River/Version
Produced by Derrick Harriott.

SONGBIRD 1071 Since I Lost My Baby/Version
Produced by Derrick Harriott. (a) Harriott takes the Motown out of the Temptations' hit and turns it into an upbeat dancefloor-bound single, leaving the listener to assume that losing his baby was really all for the best.

SONGBIRD 1078 Being in Love/Version
Produced by Derrick Harriott.

SONGBIRD 1084 Don't Rock the Boat/Version
Produced by Derrick Harriott.

THE HEADMASTERS

(X) TREVOR LAMBERT

THE HEPTONES

ACKEE 407 I Miss You (Parts 1/2)
Produced by Geoffrey Chung.

ACKEE 414 Let Me Hold Your Hand/Version
Produced by Geoffrey Chung.

ASHANTI 411 I'm in the Mood for Love/TOMMY MCCOOK & THE
  NOW GENERATION: Eight Years After

Produced by Joe Gibbs. (b) Loosely based on the early 60s hit "I'm in the Mood for Love," this instrumental is MOR to the hilt, but the smoothness of the horns, the pretty lilting flute, and the champagne piano are all so perfect you'll wish everything sounded this good.

ATTACK 8036 Save the Last Dance for Me/Be the One
Produced by Joe Gibbs. (a) The Heptones' cover versions are rarely up to the standards of their usual work, but this take on the Coasters' golden oldie is one of their better, probably because no one fussed too much with the arrangement, and Gibbs gave the trio a solid mid-tempo beat to work around. Also released as DUKE 143, PAMA SUPREME 367.

GREEN DOOR 4020 Hypocrite/JOHNNY LOVER: Straight to the Head
Produced by Joe Gibbs.

PAMA 843 You've Lost that Lovin' Feeling/RUPIE EDWARDS ALL-
  STARS: Version

(a) Produced by Rupie Edwards. Overwrought rendition of the old Righteous Brothers hit.

PRINCE BUSTER 37 Our Day Will Come/PRINCE BUSTER: Protection
Produced by Prince Buster. (a) A cover of the old Ruby & The Romantics hit; a syncopated beat and a lush keyboard give it a bit of flair, but surprisingly the Heptones still can't quite beat the original.

BONGO HERMAN

(X) SCOTTY

BIG 332 Eternal Drums/ERROL DUNKLEY: Darling Ooh Wee

(b) A slow and steamy romantic jewel, Dunkley sings out his devotion with such overwhelming passion that the emotion virtually oozes from the grooves.

GREEN DOOR 4049 African Breakfast/BONGO HERMAN & LES & BUNNY: Chairman of the Board

SONGBIRD 1069 We Are Praying/CRYSTALITES: Version

Produced by Derrick Harriott.

WINSTON HEYWOOD

DYNAMIC 441 Stop the War/Version

DYNAMIC 457 Seek & You'll Find/Version

JOE HIGGS

SIOUX 005 The World Is Spinning Around/REACTION: Hallelujah

SIOUX 014 Wave of War/JUMBO STERLING: Shaft

SIOUX 021 Lay a Foundation/JACKIE ROWLAND: Lay a Foundation Version

NEVILLE HINDS

UPSETTER 384 Blackman's Time/UPSETTERS: Version

Produced by Lee Perry. (a) The horns bleat out "Pop Goes the Weasel," the keyboardist plays another tune entirely, the rhythm section lays down a slow reggae beat, and Hinds sings out a shopping list of demands — "food to eat, freedom of speech," et al, on this particularly odd, but brightly impassioned single.

THE HOFFNER BROTHERS

BULLET 513 The King Man Is Back/SHALIMAR ALL-STARS: Version

Also released as GREEN DOOR 4039.

JOHN HOLT

(X) BIG YOUTH

FAB 188 A Little Happiness/DELROY WILSON: Diamond Rings

GG 4529 Keep It Up/A Love Like Yours

Produced by Alvin Ranglin.

JACKPOT 790 Don't You Know/Riding for a Fall

Produced by Bunny Lee.

PAMA 845 I'll Always Love You/SLIM SMITH: 3x7 Rock & Roll

PAMA 852 Pledging My Love/I Will Know What To Do

PRINCE BUSTER 40 Close to Me/Version

Produced by Prince Buster.

PRINCE BUSTER 41 Get Ready/Version

Produced by Prince Buster.

PRINCE BUSTER 42 Rain from the Skies/Version

Produced by Prince Buster.

PRINCE BUSTER 43 The First Time/Version

Produced by Prince Buster.

HONEYBOY

BANANA 375 Homeward Bound/Peace in the Land

THE HONG GANG

(X) BOB ANDY, MONTEGO MELON, ROOSEVELT SINGERS

KEITH HUDSON

(X) ALTON ELLIS, BIG YOUTH, U-ROY, DELROY WILSON

SPUR 1 Darkest Night on a Wet Looking Road/Version

KEITH HUDSON & CHUCKLES

DUKE 145 Satan Side/DON D JUNIOR: Evil Spirit

Produced by Keith Hudson.

THE HUDSON ALL STARS

(X) DENNIS ALCAPONE, ALTON ELLIS

DELLA HUMPHREY

FAB 183 Dreamland/Version

I-ROY

GREEN DOOR 4030 Hot Bomb/THE JUMPERS: The Bomb

Produced by Lloyd Campbell. (a) I-Roy toasts on the theme of love across the stripped down version of the flip. (b) Rock steady set to a reggae beat, as The Jumpers harmonize their way across a tale of puppy love grows up; the falsetto was probably less shrill when they were kids.

GREEN DOOR 4044 Make Love/STAGE: Tic Toc Bill

Produced by Bunny Lee.

THE IMPACT ALL STARS

(X) DENNIS BROWN, ALTON ELLIS, FREEDOM GROUP, JOHNNY LONDON

THE IN CROWD

(X) SCORPIONS

THE IN FLAMES

PAMA 842 Rocket Man/I'm All Broke Up

HARRY J ALL-STARS

(X) BOB ANDY, JAY BOYS

HARRY J 6641 Down Side Up/Version

Produced by Harry J. (a) A CAREY JOHNSON toast built over the JOE HIGGS hit "The World Is Spinning Around," while the All-Stars provide the mellow groove and mood.

POOCH JACKSON

(X) CIRCLES

SIOUX 013 You Just Gotta Get Ready/BROTHER DAN: Django's Valley

Produced by Dandy Livingstone.

SIOUX 016 Once Bitten/KING REGGAE: Slave Driver

JAGO

DUKE 134 Rebel Train/Babylon Version

JAH FISH

GRAPE 3034 Vampire Rock/MOD STARS: El-Sisco Rock

THE JAMAICANS

DYNAMIC 430 I Believe in Music/Version

DYNAMIC 442 Are You Sure/Version

DYNAMIC 456 Sunshine Love/Version

JIMMY JAMES & THE VAGABONDS
STATESIDE 2209 A Man Like Me/Survival

THE JAY BOYS
(X) T. MAN & T. BONES, TREVOR SHIELD

HARRY J 6644 African People/HARRY J & THE ALL-STARS: Version
Produced by Harry J. (a) The Jay Boys misappropriate "Indian Reservation," a hit for both Don Fardon and Paul Revere & The Raiders . . . well, in which case, why not? They give it a rootsy air, while the barely-altered lyric still works in the new island context.

JD (THE ROC)
SIOUX 008 Superbad/MONTEGO MELON: Lucky Dip
Produced by Duke Reid.

JJ ALL STARS
(X) LLOYD YOUNG

AL T JOE
DUKE 148 Vision/Young & Unlearned
DYNAMIC 429 Oh What a Price/The Prisoner's Song

JOE'S ALL STARS
(X) RAY MARTELL

BLOSSOM JOHNSON
(X) JOHN SHAFT

CAREY JOHNSON
Popular DJ, also recorded as duo LLOYD & CAREY.

BANANA 369 Correction Train/SOUL DEFENDERS: Version
Produced by Coxsone Dodd. (a) Over the SELECTED FEW's "Selection Train," Johnson proves one of the less forceful DJs, but an entertaining one regardless. His freakish recital of sundry nursey rhymes certainly rubbed off on JUDGE DREAD.

DOMINO JOHNSON
GREEN DOOR 4045 Summertime/THE SWANS: Grazing

BARBARA JONES
BULLET 507 Sad Movies/SIR HARRY: Deejay Version

SAMMY JONES
(X) TWINKLE BROTHERS

SIOUX 002 Mendocino/THE RUM RUNNERS: Sugar Brown
SIOUX 011 You Are My Girl/HONEY BOY MARTIN: Unchained Melody

JUDGE DREAD
b Alex Hughes 1945/d 3/13/98. English DJ who came to fame with a string of extraordinarily, childishly, suggestive reggae singles.

BIG SHOT BI 608 Big Six/Version
Produced by Alex Hughes. (a) VERNE & SON's "Little Boy Blue" rhythm, over which the title character's sexual and other escapades are documented with schoolboyish atten-tion to detail: "Rasta-far-I, Rasta-far-me, Little Boy Blue in a ganja tree, a-smoking the weed." Absurd, but utterly delightful.

BIG SHOT BI 613 Big Seven/Version
Produced by Alex Hughes. (a) More priceless puerility: "Jack be nimble, Jack be quick, Jack jumped over the candlestick, silly little boy should've jumped higher, goodness gracious, great balls of fire."

JULIEN & THE GAYTONES
JULIEN was JUDY MOWATT (aka JEAN), later of the I-THREES.

HIGH NOTE 059 She Kept on Talking/GAYTONES: Talking Version
Produced by Sonia Pottinger.

THE JUMPERS
(X) I-ROY

THE JUNCUNO SINGERS
BANANA 366 I'd Like to Teach the World to Sing/Rope of Sand

KATINA
CACTUS 3 Don't Stroke My Pussy/Version
CACTUS 4 Don't Stick Stickers on My Paper Knickers/Version

PAT KELLY
(X) CORNELL CAMPBELL

PAMA SUPREME 353 I'm Gonna Give Her All the Love I've Got/
   MAYTONES: As Long as You Love Me

KING REGGAE
(X) POOCH JACKSON

TREVOR LAMBERT
DUKE 132 Bald Head Teacher/HEADMASTERS: Version

LARRY'S ALL STARS
(X) DELROY WILSON & U-ROY

LASCELLES & HORTENSE
Vocal duo featuring LASCELLES PERKINS and HORTENSE ELLIS. (X) STRANGER COLE

KEN LAZARUS & CREW
EXPLOSION 2064 Hail the Man/Where Do I Go?
Also released as LONDON HLH10379.

LEE & THE CLARENDONIANS
GREEN DOOR 4038 Night Owl/Version

BYRON LEE & THE DRAGONAIRES
DYNAMIC 435 Make It Reggae/DENNIS ALCAPONE: Go Johnny Go
Produced by Byron Lee.

JOHN LEE
EXPLOSION 2060 Stagger Lee/Musical Version

CHRIS LEON
DYNAMIC 450 I Didn't Get to Sleep at All/DYNAMITES: Version

CARL LEWIN

PUNCH 98 Nobody Told Me/WING: Don't Play that Song (Instrumental)

HOPETON LEWIS

ATTACK 8035 Starting All Over Again/DYNAMITES: Version
Produced by Tommy Cowan.

DYNAMIC 436 Come Together/Going Back to My Hometown

DYNAMIC 447 Good Together/Version

REGGIE LEWIS

Guitarist Lewis aka ALVA LEWIS.

UPSETTER 391 Natty Natty/UPSETTERS: Version
Produced by Lee Perry.

THE LION'S DEN

(X) THE UNIQUES

LITTLE BOY BLUE

(X) DELROY WILSON

LLOYD & CAREY

Featuring DJ CAREY JOHNSON. (X) PAT SATCHMO

ATTACK 8029 Scorpion/THE MAYTONES: Hands & Feet
Produced by Alvin Ranglin. (a) A solid reggae beat and snatches of keyboards provides the DJ with ample space to roust and rap, in this entertaining toasted warning to country girls out for the first time in the big bad city.

ATTACK 8032 Do It Again/GARY RANGLIN: Watch It
Produced by Alvin Ranglin.

LLOYD & HORTENSE

(X) KEN BOOTHE

LLOYD & KEN

PUNCH 110 Have I Sinned/Version

LLOYD THE MATADOR & THE ETHIOPIANS

SIOUX 010 The Train/EXODUS: Julia Sees Me
Produced by Lloyd Daley.

LLOYD & THE NOW GENERATION

(X) LLOYD ROBINSON

RUE LLOYD

GREEN DOOR 4033 Loving You/Version

GREEN DOOR 4036 Cheer Up/Version

JIMMY LONDON

RANDY'S 521 It's Now or Never/IMPACT ALL-STARS: Version
Produced by Randy's.

RANDY'S 527 Jamaica Festival 72/IMPACT ALL-STARS: Version
Produced by Randy's.

JOHNNY LOVER

(X) THE HEPTONES

JOHNNY LYNCH

ATTACK 8038 Don't Believe Him, Donna/Beyond the Reef

G MAHTANI ALL-STARS

(X) LLOYD YOUNG

JOE MANSANO

SIOUX 022 Trial of Pama Dice/JACKIE ROWLAND: Lonely Man
Produced by Joe Mansano.

KEN MARSHALL

PAMA 844 Shake It Loose/TOMMY MCCOOK: Version

RAY MARTELL

SIOUX 012 She Caught the Train/JOE'S ALL-STARS: Tony B's Theme
Produced by Joe Mansano.

HONEYBOY MARTIN

(X) SAMMY JONES

HARRY J 6643 Have You Ever Seen the Rain/Spanish Harlem
Produced by Harry J.

THE MARVELS

PAMA 832 Do You Know You Have to Cry/Love Power

PAMA SUPREME 348 What a Hurricane/If You Love Her

CARL MASTERS

(X) DENNIS ALCAPONE, MAX ROMEO

BIG SHOT 604 Va Va Voom/GOD SONS: Rebel

THE MAYTALS

ATTACK 8042 It Was Written Down/Sweet & Dandy
Produced by Leslie Kong.

BLUE MOUNTAIN 1020 Christmas Song/I Can't Believe

DYNAMIC 438 Redemption Song/Version
Produced by Warwick Lyn. (a) Nobody preaches with more conviction than the Maytals, and this optimistic sermon brings sweet, harmonious salvation to all listeners.

SUMMIT 8536 Thy Kingdom Come/BEVERLEY'S ALL-STARS: Version
Produced by Leslie Kong.

SUMMIT 8537 It Must Be True Love/BEVERLEY'S ALL-STARS: Version
Produced by Leslie Kong.

TROJAN 7865 Louie Louie/Pressure Drop 72
Produced by Warwick Lyn. (a) Later featured on the *Funky Kingston* album, this is the Maytals' definitive cover, a defiant performance which swaggers with a rude boy intent that establishes this among the greatest ever renditions of the oft-covered chestnut.

THE MAYTONES

(X) PAT KELLY, LLOYD & CAREY, MAX ROMEO

GG 4530 Donkey Face/GG ALL-STARS: Version
Produced by Alvin Ranglin.

GG 4531 As Long as You Love Me (Parts 1/2)
Produced by Alvin Ranglin. (a) The vocal group take a pleasant ballad and harmonize it to new heights, the reggae beat keeps the song simmering, while the keyboards adds some intriguing little flourishes.

GRAPE 3028 If Loving You Was Wrong/FLOWERS & ALVIN: In a de Pum Pum

Produced by Alvin Ranglin. (b) The lilting intro and accommodating bass leads you to believe you're in for a tender little love song — and maybe you are. But if this is the duo's idea of sweet seduction, it's no surprise the girl expects them to "do their work themselves."

PAMA 846 I'm Feeling Lonely/GG ALL-STARS: Version

Produced by Alvin Ranglin.

TOMMY MCCOOK

(X) HEPTONES, KEN MARSHALL, WAILERS

TOMMY MCCOOK & RAD WILSON

BIG SHOT 606 Tubby's Control/More Music

RICHARD MCDONALD & GLEN BROWN

DUKE 141 Boat to Progress/Version

TESSA MCDONALD

DYNAMIC 455 Life Is the Highest/Recarnate

FREDDIE MCKAY

BANANA 370 Drunken Sailor/SOUND DIMENSION: Version

Produced by Coxsone Dodd.

GEORGE MEGGIE

BULLET 504 Hard to Believe/MAX ROMEO: Softie

PUNCH 112 People Like People/MAX ROMEO: Softie

MELLO & THE MELLOTONES

SUMMIT 8538 Haile Selassie/Old Man River

THE MELODIANS

ATTACK 8025 This Beautiful Land/MELODIOUS RHYTHMS: Version

ATTACK 8031 Without You/DYNAMITES: Instrumental

Produced by Clancy Eccles.

BULLET 496 Tropical Land/U-ROY & SLIM SMITH: Love I Bring

DUKE 130 The Mighty Melodians (Parts 1/2)

PUNCH 111 Round & Round/THE UPSETTERS: Version

Produced by Lee Perry.

SUMMIT 8534 The Time Has Come/BEVERLEY'S ALL-STARS: McIntosh

Produced by Leslie Kong.

THE MELODIOUS RHYTHMS

(X) MELODIANS

MONTEGO MELON

(X) JD (THE ROC)

SIOUX 004 Swan Lake/THE HONG GANG: Reggae Mento

JACKIE MITTOO & THE REGGAE BEAT

LONDON HLU10357 Wishbone/Soul Bird

THE MOD STARS

(X) JAH FISH

JOHNNY MOORE

(X) POMPHEY

DERRICK MORGAN

GRAPE 3032 Send a Little Rain/MORGAN ALL-STARS: Version

JACKPOT 793 Let Them Talk/Bringing in the Guns

JACKPOT 794 Won't Be this Way/Ain't No Love

JACKPOT 797 Me Naw Run/All Night Long

JACKPOT 802 Festival 10/Version

PRINCE BUSTER 60 Tears on My Pillow/KEITH REID: Worried Over You

Produced by Prince Buster.

PUNCH 107 Forward March/Plenty of One

THE MORGAN ALL STARS

Studio band behind DERRICK MORGAN. (X) DERRICK MORGAN

MURT, TURT & PURT

aka MAX ROMEO, NINEY HOLNESS and LEE PERRY. (X) MAX ROMEO

NINEY & THE OBSERVERS

BIG SHOT 607 Hiding by the Riverside/Red Sea

Produced by Niney. (a) The spiritual is revised into an attack on Prime Minister Hugh Shearer and his government, to the accompaniment of gospel female backing singers, and a rhythm sliced and diced from "Beg in the Gutter."

BIG SHOT 609 Beg in the Gutter/Version

Produced by Niney. (a) Machine gun rhythms and a distinctive jolting bass line drive this sparse number, a fitting platform for Niney's damning view of current societal conditions. "What happened to better?" he demands to know. "Everything is worser."

BIG SHOT 610 Everyday Music/Observing

Produced by Niney. (a) Sly Stone's "Everyday People" is radicalized by Niney's deft hands, the piano carries the signature snatch of melody while the beat stutters insistently along, and Niney does his best DAVE BARKER impression, "one time . . . two time" all the way across the song.

BULLET 503 Aily & Ailaloo/Version

Produced by Niney. (a) MAX ROMEO and LLOYD CHARMERS duet on this marijuana manifesto whose musical arrangement is kept deliberately simple to focus attention directly on the lyrics.

DOWNTOWN 494 Get Out My Life/Version

Produced by Niney.

DOWNTOWN 495 Hi Diddle/Version

Produced by Niney.

NORA & BUNNY

Duo featuring NORA DEAN and BUNNY LEE.

TROPICAL 015 Butterfly/TROPICAL ALL-STARS: Fly Version

THE NOW GENERATION

MIKEY CHUNG's backing band. (X) MIKEY CHUNG, ENGLAND COOK, BUNNY FLIP, SHARON FORRESTER, HEP-

TONES, LLOYD & THE NOW GENERATION, TOMMY MCCOOK, LLOYD ROBINSON, BB SEATON

NYAH SHUFFLE

(X) PHYLLIS DILLON

THE OBSERVERS

SONGBIRD 1083 International Pum/Reggaematic
Produced by Niney Holness. (a) The "Rasta Bandwagon" rhythm is transformed into the slacker anthem of—it doesn't matter what color or nationality we are, "Chinee or Coolie . . . every pum is the same pum pum." (b) MAX ROMEO sings, Niney yips, and a John Crow Skank rhythm is deconstructed into such a disjointed pattern that it's fit only for marionettes. But the anthemic chorus overcomes all.

JOHNNY OSBOURNE

TECHNIQUES 916 See & Blind/TECHNIQUES ALL-STARS: Rema Skank
Produced by Winston Riley.

KEN PARKER

DUKE REID 2521 Jimmy Brown/Version
Produced by Duke Reid. (a) A cover of the Browns' 1959 smash hit "The Three Bells" set to a simple but steady reggae beat, over which Parker and a backing vocalist gently sing.

LLOYD PARKS

RANDY'S 524 Stars/Version

BOBBY PATTERSON

ACTION 4604 I'm in Love with You/Married Lady

EUGENE PAUL

PAMA 838 Beautiful Sunday/Take Care Son
PAMA SUPREME 357 I'll Take You There/Beautiful Baby

LEE PERRY

UPSETTER 385 French Connection/UPSETTERS: Version
Produced by Lee Perry.

LEE PERRY & DENNIS ALCAPONE:

UPSETTER 389 Back Biter/UPSETTERS: Version
Produced by Lee Perry.

SHORTY PERRY

b Perry Williams. (X) FLOWERS & ALVIN
ATTACK 8043 Musical Goat/WINSTON GRENNAN & J JACKSON: Stinging Dub
(a) Based on PAULETTE & GEE's "Feel It," Shorty coolly sing-songs his way across an old rock steady fave, occasionally stopping to stir up the crowd.
EXPLOSION 2067 Sprinkle Some Water/FLOWERS & ALVIN: Howdy & Tenky
Produced by Alvin Ranglin.

THE PIONEERS

SUMMIT 8535 Story Book Children/SIDNEY GEORGE & JACKIE: Gorgeous Marvellous
Produced by Sidney Crooks.

THE PITTSBURG ALL STARS

(X) U-ROY

THE PLATONICS

ATTACK 8033 Blue Moon/After Midnight
Produced by Sidney Crooks.

POMPHEY

GREEN DOOR 4029 Jamaica Skank/JOHNNY MOORE: Bing Comes to Town

KENNETH POWER

(X) EDDIE FORD

PHIL PRATT ALL STARS

(X) HORACE ANDY, DENNIS BROWN, ERROL DUNKLEY
PAMA 851 Feel Good All Over/KEBLE DRUMMOND: Dangerous
Produced by Phil Pratt.

PRINCE BUSTER & THE ALL-STARS

(X) DENNIS ALCAPONE, HEPTONES
PRINCE BUSTER 14 Big Sister Stuff/Satta Amasa Gana
Produced by Prince Buster.
PRINCE BUSTER 15 Protection/Cool Operator
Produced by Prince Buster.
PRINCE BUSTER 16 I Stand Accused/My Heart Is Gone
Produced by Prince Buster.
PRINCE BUSTER 19 Four in One Medley/Drums Drums
Produced by Prince Buster.
PRINCE BUSTER 32 Still/Sister Big Stuff
Produced by Prince Buster.
PRINCE BUSTER 47 Baldhead Pum Pum/Giver Her
Produced by Prince Buster.

THE PROPHETS

(X) NORA DEAN

GARY RANGLIN

(X) LLOYD & CAREY

THE REACTION

(X) JOE HIGGS

THE RECORDING BAND

(X) JOE WHITE

WINSTON REED

PAMA SUPREME 365 Breakfast in Bed/RANNY WILLIAMS: Guitar Shuffle

ALTYMAN REID

(X) ROY SHIRLEY

ALTYMAN REID & ROY SHIRLEY

GREEN DOOR 4026 A Sugar (Parts 1/2)

KEITH REID

(X) DERRICK MORGAN

THE RHYTHM FORCE

TROPICAL 013 Satta Call/Version

SKETTO RICH

(X) OWEN GRAY & GRAHAM HAWK

CYNTHIA RICHARDS

PAMA SUPREME 366 Mr Postman/SKIN FLESH & BONES: Version

RICO & HIS BAND

(X) SLIM SMITH

LLOYD ROBINSON

GREEN DOOR 4028 I Can't Forget/LLOYD & THE NOW GENERATION: Version

ROCKIN' HORSE

RANDY'S 522 Hard Time/Change Your Ways

AUDLEY ROLLINS

EXPLOSION 2062 Repatriation/HUGH ROY JUNIOR: Version
Produced by Lloyd Charmers. (a) Rollins gives a passionate performance on the returning to Africa theme, bolstered by a reggaefied beat and an anthemic melody. (b) "Get on the freedom train," the DJ toasts, then goes on to add even more fire to this version of the a-side.

MAX ROMEO

(X) GEORGE MEGGIE

BIG 334 Are You Sure/RUPIE EDWARDS ALL-STARS: Version
Produced by Rupie Edwards.
CAMEL 85 Rasta Bandwagon/MURT TURT & PURT: When Jah Speaks
Produced by Niney Holness. (a) LEE PERRY does the spoken word bits, while Romeo sweetly sings on this slow skanker that drives a truck through the pretensions of a new generation. (b) HOLNESS, PERRY and Romeo revive Niney's best "fire" and "lightning" imprecations, with Perry spitting out the warnings, while his fellow conspirators echo his words and make odd noises in the background.
CAMEL 86 Public Enemy #1/How Long Must We Wait
Produced by Niney Holness. (a) Powered by one of Niney's greatest (and still employed to this day) rhythms, "#1" is a Rasta classic, which turns the Public Enemy concept upside down by making the wanted man neither rude boy nor gangster, but Satan himself. Romeo passionately delivers the sermon, filled with Biblical stories and allusions.
DYNAMIC 444 We Love America/SOUL RHYTHMS: We Love Jamaica Version
GG 4535 Is It Really Over/MAYTONES: Born to Be Loved
Produced by Alvin Ranglin.
HIGH NOTE 058 Pray for Me/GAYTONES: Pray for Me Version
Produced by Sonia Pottinger. (a) Reggae rockers go to church accompanied by a New Orleans-esque horn section, on an upbeat spiritual that will have you clapping along, if not actually shouting out loud. Also released as PAMA SUPREME 345.

PAMA SUPREME 359 Are You Sure/CARL MASTERS: Va Va Voom
Produced by Rupie Edwards.

GENE RONDO

COUNT SHELLY 05 Happy Birthday Sweet 16/Meditation
Produced by Count Shelly.
DOWNTOWN 490 Wanna Be Like Daddy/STUDIO SOUND: A Little More
Produced by Dandy Livingstone.

THE ROOSEVELT ALL STARS

(X) HUGH ROY JUNIOR

THE ROOSEVELT SINGERS

SIOUX 025 Heavy Reggae/HONG GANG: Smoking Wild

JACKIE ROWLAND

(X) JOE HIGGS, JOE MANSANO

SIOUX 015 Indian Reservation/JUNIOR SMITH: I'm in a Dancing Mood

HUGH ROY JUNIOR

(X) AUDLEY ROLLINS, DELROY WILSON

ASHANTI 405 King of the Road/ROOSEVELT ALL-STARS: Version
ATTACK 8030 This Is a Pepper/JOHN HOLT: Justice
JACKPOT 806 Two Ton Gullet/Version
SIOUX 024 The Wedding/LLOYD'S ALL-STARS: Buttercup

BRUCE RUFFIN

RHINO 101 Mad About You/Save the People
RHINO 109 Coming on Strong/Crazy People Strong
TROJAN 9000 Songs of Peace/You Are the Best/We Can Make It

THE RUM RUNNERS

(X) SAMMY JONES

DOROTHY RUSSELL

DUKE REID 2524 You're the One I Love/Version

LEROY SAMUELS

PUNCH 113 Trying to Wreck My Life/Version

PAT SATCHMO

ATTACK 8024 What's Going On/LLOYD & CAREY: Tubby's in Full Swing
Produced by Tony Robinson.

THE SCORPIONS

GREEN DOOR 4019 Breaking Your Heart/THE IN CROWD: Version

WINSTON SCOTLAND

DJ who recorded a number of excellent cuts with PRINCE TONY ROBINSON. (X) DENNIS ALCAPONE, BONGO HERMAN, LENNOX BROWN

GREEN DOOR 4027 My Little Filly/BUNNY BROWN: My Girl
PUNCH 100 Butter Cup/RONALD WILSON: I Care

SCOTTY

(X) LORNA BENNETT, JOE WHITE

HARRY J 6642 Skank in Bed/BONGO HERMAN: African Breakfast
Produced by Harry J.

SONGBIRD 1080 Clean Race/CRYSTALITES: Version Train
Produced by Derrick Harriott. (a) On this hilarious single, we find Scotty cleverly rapping and rhyming across a flashy beat and a funky guitar, until Harriott interrupts halfway through to throw his weight around. "I make the hits, not the public . . ." he boasts, stealing the song right out from under the hapless DJ.

BB SEATON

BIG 336 I Want Justice/RUPIE EDWARDS' ALL-STARS: Justice
Produced by Rupie Edwards. Also released as PAMA 864.

BULLET 514 I Miss My Schooldays/CONSCIOUS MINDS: Version

CAMEL 100 Lean on Me/NOW GENERATION: Samba Pa Ti
Cool renovation of the Santana instrumental.

PAMA SUPREME 374 Sweet Caroline/Eleanor Rigby
(a) The Neil Diamond chestnut turns out remarkably well transplanted onto a reggae rhythm; which is more than can be said for (b) the old Beatles number, taking its place in a reggae hall of shame, which is already overflowing with Lennon-McCartney numbers.

JOHN SHAFT

DOWNTOWN 488 Forever Music/BLOSSOM JOHNSON: The Boy I Love
Produced by Dandy Livingstone.

THE SHALIMAR ALL STARS

(X) HOFFNER BROTHERS, LLOYD YOUNG

WINSTON SHAN

CAMEL 88 Audrey/So Nice

TREVOR SHIELD

ASHANTI 407 Rough Road/THE JAY BOYS: Rough the Road

ROY SHIRLEY

(X) DENZIL DENNIS, ALTYMAN REID

PUNCH 103 Don't Be a Loser/Jamaican Girl

PUNCH 108 A Sugar/ALTYMAN REID: Version

SHIRLEY & THE CHARMERS

BULLET 502 Rum Rhythm/LLOYD CHARMERS: Version

SIR HARRY

(X) BARBARA JONES

BULLET 519 Mr Parker's Daughter/U-ROY: On Top of the Peak
Produced by Alvin Ranglin.

DOWNTOWN 493 Meet the Boss/Musical Light
Produced by Dandy Livingstone.

DUKE 136 Apples to Apples/DRUM BEAT ALL-STARS: Good Life

SKIDDY & DETROIT

GRAPE 3030 The Exile Song/BUNNY GALE: In the Burning Sun Joh-Ho

SKIN FLESH & BONES

Group led by ALFRED "AL" BROWN, and featuring CYNTHIA RICHARDS, LLOYD PARKS. (X) CYNTHIA RICHARDS

RICKY SLICK

DYNAMIC 449 Family Man/Version

THE SLICKERS

EXPLOSION 2061 Bounce Me Johnny/Version

K SMILEY

PRESSURE BEAT 5514 Tippertone/Do It to Me

JUNIOR SMITH

(X) JACKIE ROWLAND

SIOUX 023 I Don't Know/JUMBO STERLING: My Sugar Ain't Sweet

SLIM SMITH

(X) JOHN HOLT

CAMEL 89 Take Me Back/Where Do I Turn
Also released as JACKPOT 788.

DYNAMIC 428 Just a Dream/Send Me Some Loving
(a) The warmth emanating from both voice and instrumentation is palpable on one of Smith's finest solo performances. (b) It's records like this which make one wonder about the fuss made over the great Motown stars of the 1960s; Smith could sing them all under the table. This yearning little ballad allows him to pull all his best tricks out of his voice box, the backing is as understated as the heartache is broad, while the backing vocals come in late enough that, when they do turn up, even Smith sounds glad of the company.

EXPLOSION 2074 The Time Has Come/Blessed Is the Man

JACKPOT 786 I Need Your Loving/You've Got What It Takes

JACKPOT 789 Rain from the Sky/You're No Good
Produced by Bunny Lee. (a) Smith covers the DELROY WILSON hit, and although he brings his usual conviction, the melody just doesn't play to his strengths.

JACKPOT 798 Closer Together/Blinded by Love
Produced by Bunny Lee.

JACKPOT 799 Turning Point/Money Love
Produced by Bunny Lee. (a) Smith gives another heartfelt performance, but is done in this time by a band and arrangement which really don't seem to be taking the song too seriously.

PAMA 850 The Time Has Come/RICO & HIS BAND: Version

PAMA SUPREME 373 A Place in the Sun/Stranger on the Shore

THE SOUL CLANS

(X) FRANCIS

THE SOUL DEFENDERS

(X) CAREY JOHNSON

ACKEE 147 Sound Almighty/COUNT OSSIE: Meditation
Produced by Coxsone Dodd.

THE SOUL REBELS

BANANA 374 Listen & Observe/What's Love
COUNT SHELLY 03 I'm the One Who Loves You/I-ROY: War Zone
Produced by Count Shelly.

THE SOUL RHYTHMS

(X) MAX ROMEO

THE SOUL SYNDICATE

GREEN DOOR 4021 Riot/Smoke without Fire
(a) Dynamic Keith Hudson produced cover of a Hugh Masakela instrumental, dominated by JOHNNY MOORE's trumpet.

THE SOUL TWINS

CLANDISC 238 Don't Call Me Nigga/DYNAMITES: Joe Louis
Produced by Clancy Eccles.

THE SOUND DIMENSION

(X) BELTONES, GLADIATORS, FREDDIE MCKAY

THE SPARKS

PAMA 833L You Don't Care/TONY'S ALL-STARS: Version
Produced by Tony Robinson.

LLOYD SPARKS

BIG SHOT 601 You Don't Care/TONY'S STARS: Version

STAGE

(X) I-ROY

THE STAGS

(X) PADDY COREA

JUMBO STERLING

(X) FUNKY BROWN, JOE HIGGS, JUNIOR SMITH

LESTER STERLING

ASHANTI 410 War Is Not the Answer/
COXSONE'S ALL-STARS: Version
Produced by Coxsone Dodd.

JUMBO STERLING'S ALL STARS

SIOUX 019 Hot Dog/JUNIOR SMITH: Saturday Child
Produced by Jack Price.

ROMAN STEWART

SONGBIRD 1075 Changing Times/CRYSTALITES: Version
Produced by Derrick Harriott.

TINGA STEWART

TROPICAL 018 A Brand New Me/BROWN'S ALL-STARS: Nice Version

THE STINGERS

UPSETTER 395 Preacher Man/Version
Produced by Lee Perry.

THE STUD ALL STARS

(X) CLARENDONIANS

THE STUDIO SOUND

(X) FAMILY MAN, GENE RONDO

THE SWANS

(X) DOMINO JOHNSON

SYD & JOE

BULLET 498 Three Combine/I'm the Nearest to Your Heart

SIDNEY, GEORGE & JACKIE

aka THE PIONEERS — SIDNEY CROOKS, GEORGE DEKKER, JACKIE ROBINSON. (X) GEORGE DEKKER, PIONEERS

ERROL T

aka ERROL THOMPSON. See entry in DIRECTORY OF PRODUCERS. (X) THE AFRICAN
ASHANTI 406 Jamaica Born & Bred/Version

T. MAN & T. BONES

SIOUX 007 True Born African/JAY BOYS: Tropical Chief
Produced by M. Johnson.

THE TEARDROPS

(X) BOSS ATTACK, AL BROWN

THE TECHNIQUES ALL-STARS

(X) DENNIS ALCAPONE, JOHNNY OSBOURNE

THE THIRD & FOURTH GENERATIONS

(X) PETER TOSH

OWEN THOMPSON

CAMEL 103 Must I Be Blue/Version

THE TIVOLIS

(X) ETHIOPIANS

TOMMY

DYNAMIC 433 Geraldine/Reverend Leroy

TONY & HOWIE

BANANA 371 Fun It Up/Version

TONY'S ALL STARS

Studio band for "PRINCE" TONY ROBINSON. (X) DENNIS ALCAPONE, SPARKS, LLOYD SPARKS

PETER TOSH

PRESSURE BEAT 5509 Dem a fe Get a Beating/THIRD & FOURTH GENERATIONS: Version
Produced by Joe Gibbs. (a) Thematically a precursor to the WAILERS' "Get Up Stand Up," Tosh takes on the wicked in this rebellious ditty with a surprisingly soothing musical arrangement. The PNP naturally heard the song's righteous call, and used it during their 1972 election campaign. At long last, the "Pirate" beat boards a proper song.

PRESSURE BEAT 5511 Medicine Man/CAT & NICKY CAMPBELL: Hammering
Produced by Joe Gibbs. (b) The Campbells' distinctive DJ styles — one a high pitched shriek/yodel, the other a take on DENNIS ALCAPONE — vie over NICKY THOMAS' version of "If I Had a Hammer."

TROPICAL ALL STARS

(X) NORA & BUNNY

THE TROPICAL SHADOWS

BIG SHOT 603 Our Anniversary/Version

THE TWINKLE BROTHERS

(X) BUSTY BROWN

SIOUX 003 The Happy Song/SAMMY JONES: Little Caesar

THE TYPHOON ALL STARS

(X) BILLY DYCE, ETHIOPIANS, U-ROY

U-ROY

(X) BILLY DYCE

DUKE 137 Live It Up/DENNIS BROWN: Baby Don't Do It

DUKE REID 2520 Rock to the Beat/Love Is Not a Gamble

Produced by Duke Reid.

DYNAMIC 448 Festival Wise (Parts 1/2)

(a) The DJ's rich vocal toast brilliantly counterpoints ERIC DONALDSON's falsetto on this gala single, with an organ standing in for steep drums, but still giving the proceedings an island flair.

GRAPE 3026 On Top the Peak/TYPHOON ALL-STARS: Race Attack

Produced by Alvin Ranglin. The DJ's on top of the world, or at least at his peak, on this version of ERIC DONALDSON's "Lonely Nights." The rhythm saunters gaily along while U-Roy surfs along its crest, a non-stop barrage of banter that perfectly hits the beat with every phrase; one of his best.

GREEN DOOR 4034 Hudson Affair/KEITH HUDSON: Hot Stick Version

Produced by Keith Hudson. (b) DJ PHILLIP SAMUELS sings along to the old hit. Sadly his vocal abilities don't equal the singer's, but he makes up for it with enthusiasm.

PUNCH 104 Nanny Skank/PITTSBURG ALL-STARS: Skank Version

U-ROY & SLIM SMITH

(X) MELODIANS

THE UNDERGROUND PEOPLE

(X) DION, RUPIE EDWARDS

THE UNDERGROUNDS

HIGH NOTE 061 Skavito/Savito

Produced by Sonia Pottinger.

THE UNIQUES

TROJAN 7852 Mother & Child Reunion/Corner Hop

(a) Pointless revamp of the Paul Simon original, which itself actually sounds more authentically reggae than this.

TROJAN 7866 Lonely for Your Love/LION'S DEN: Chick a Bow

THE UPSETTERS

(X) DENNIS ALCAPONE, JUNIOR BYLES, SHENLEY DUFFUS, WESLEY GERMS, NEVILLE HINDS, REGGIE LEWIS, MELODIANS, LEE PERRY

UPSETTER 393 Crummy People/BIG YOUTH: Moving Version

Produced by Lee Perry. (b) Big Youth gets the crowd skanking along to this version of the WAILERS' hit "Keep on Moving."

UPSETTER 394 Water Pump (Parts 1/2)

Produced by Lee Perry.

THE VULCANS

BIG SHOT 612 Dr Spock/Joe Kidd

THE WAILERS

CBS 8114 Reggae on Broadway/We've Got a Date/Stop that Train

Produced by Johnny Nash/Danny Sims. (a) Higher hopes rode on this 45 than are evident from either song or peformance. Recorded in London, the band hoped it would lead to a long term major label deal — and ultimately it did. Just not with CBS.

GREEN DOOR 4022 Lively Up Yourself/TOMMY MCCOOK: Lively

Produced by the Wailers. (a) Picking up the party where "Soul Shakedown" ended, this steaming mid-tempo number was both written and produced by MARLEY, and features a sublime rhythm, sultry brass and a sparkling melody. Also released as PUNCH 102.

GREEN DOOR 4025 Guava Jelly/Redder than Red

Produced by the Wailers. (a) Marley at his most wistful, the Wailers at their sweetest, but all are almost brought down by the overly busy arrangement.

PUNCH 101 Screwface/Faceman

Produced by the Wailers. (a) Not one of their best, with lots of good, but conflicting, musical ideas which really never come together.

UPSETTER 392 Keep on Moving/African Herbsman

Produced by Lee Perry. (a) A sublime blend of Motown and spiritual, "Moving"'s theme of a man unjustly accused of murder is delivered by the Wailers with deep conviction. Perry kept the arrangement simple and the rhythm steady. (b) A soft, sweet number, written by Richie Havens.

THE WAILING SOULS

PUNCH 106 Dungeon/NORA DEAN: Kiss Me Honey

PUNCH 114 You Should've Known Better/Version

Produced by Wailing Souls.

JOE WHITE

DYNAMIC 440 Kenyatta/RECORDING BAND: Version

SONGBIRD 1072 Trinity/SCOTTY: Monkey Drop

Produced by Derrick Harriott.

KC WHITE

DYNAMIC 434 Man No Dead/Version

DEL WILLIAMS

GRAPE 3027 Searching for Your Love/GG ALL-STARS: Version

Produced by Alvin Ranglin.

RANNY WILLIAMS

(X) WINSTON REED

NEVILLE WILLOUGHBY

DUKE 140 Wheel & Turn Me/Hey Mama

DELROY WILSON

(X) JOHN HOLT

BULLET 520 Here Come the Heartaches/You'll Be Sorry

COUNT SHELLEY 14 What Is Man/LITTLE BOY BLUE: Never Let You
   Down

Produced by Douglas Williams. (a) The singer has a grand time with this self-composed litany of adages for proper living, with Williams keeping it simple, just a sharp rhythm and a light keyboard accompaniment.

JACKPOT 792 Who Cares/HUGH ROY JUNIOR: Version

JACKPOT 795 Same Old Song/Stay by Me

Produced by Bunny Lee.

JACKPOT 804 Cheer Up/Loving You

SPUR 2 Addis Ababa/KEITH HUDSON: Rudie Hot Stuff

Produced by Keith Hudson. (a) This sublime version of the R&B classic "House of the Rising Sun" was treated to a hefty funk and roots work-out, and gifted with new repatriation lyrics emotively delivered up by Wilson.

DELROY WILSON & U-ROY

BANANA 367 Keep On Running/LARRY'S ALL-STARS: Version

GARY WILSON & CHARLIE ACE

BULLET 511 Babylon Falling/CHARLIE ACE: Make It Love

RON/RONALD WILSON

(X) ANSELL & ELAINE, WINSTON SCOTLAND

WING

(X) CARL LEWIN

LLOYD YOUNG

Ex-THE GROOVERS, also recorded with CAREY JOHNSON.

BULLET 500 Bread & Butter/SHALIMAR ALL-STARS: Version

DUKE 135 Soup/JJ ALL-STARS: Version

Produced by JJ Johnson.

GREEN DOOR 4037 Shalimar Special/G MAHTANI ALL-STARS:
   Version

TECHNIQUES 917 High Explosion/ANSELL COLLINS: Version

Produced by Winston Riley. (a) Young intertwines himself with THE TECHNIQUES' "You're My Everything," as he toasts about love and enthusiastically riles up everyone in sight.

ZAP POW

Session band featuring DWIGHT PICKNEY (guitar — ex-SHARKS), MIKE WILLIAMS (bass), JOE MCCORMACK (trombone), DAVID MADDEN (trumpet), MAX EDWARDS (drums), and vocalist BERES HAMMOND. (X) CHUCKLES

HARRY J 6650 Lottery Spin/Version

Produced by Harry J. (a) Exactly what it says, a musical edition of the lottery drawing (winning numbers: 0-3-7-8), and very funky it is as well.

10-STAR ALBUMS

JAMAICA

ABYSSINIANS: **FORWARD ONTO ZION** page 19

HORACE ANDY: **INTO THE LIGHT** page 24

BIG YOUTH: **REGGAE PHENOMENON** page 36

BLACK UHURU: **SHOWCASE** page 41

DENNIS BROWN: **WESTBOUND TRAIN** page 46

BURNING SPEAR: **MARCUS GARVEY** page 53

JUNIOR BYLES: **BEAT DOWN BABYLON (LP with bonus tracks)** page 56

JOHNNY CLARKE: **ROCKERS TIME NOW** page 75

JIMMY CLIFF ET AL: **THE HARDER THEY COME** page 79

CULTURE: **TWO SEVENS CLASH** page 84

CHAKA DEMUS & PLIERS: **ALL SHE WROTE** page 95

DILLINGER: **CB200** page 98

RUPIE EDWARDS: **IRE FEELINGS: CHAPTER AND VERSION (compilation)** page 105

I ROY: **TEN COMMANDMENTS** page 126

KING TUBBY: **DUBBING WITH THE OBSERVER** page 140

LUCIANO: **THE MESSENGER** page 158

BOB MARLEY & THE WAILERS: **EXODUS (expanded edition)** page 172

ZIGGY MARLEY & THE MELODY MAKERS: **CONSCIOUS PARTY** page 177

MAYTALS: **FUNKY KINGSTON** page 180

SUGAR MINOTT: **HERBMAN HUSTLING** page 191

MUTABARUKA: **THE MYSTERY UNFOLDS** page 193

NINEY THE OBSERVER: **BLOOD AND FIRE 1971–72 (compilation)** page 196

LEE PERRY: **RETURN OF THE SUPER APE** page 213

PRINCE BUSTER: **FABULOUS GREATEST HITS (compilation)** page 222

PRINCE FAR I: **UNDER HEAVY MANNERS** page 224

MAX ROMEO: **WAR IN A BABYLON** page 250

GARNETT SILK: **IT'S GROWING** page 257

PETER TOSH: **LIVE AT THE ONE LOVE PEACE CONCERT** page 292

WAILING SOULS: **ALL OVER THE WORLD** page 299

TAPPA ZUKIE: **MPLA** page 303

TRINIDAD, ETC.

ARROW: **HOT HOT HOT** page 27

BANKIE BANKS: **MIGHTY WIND** page 30

BLACK STALIN: **I TIME** page 38

BROTHER RESISTANCE: **DE POWER OF RESISTANCE (compilation)** page 43

CRAZY: **JUMP LEH WE JUMP** page 83

TERRY GAJRAJ: **FUNKY CHATNI** page 110

EDDY GRANT: **LIVE AT NOTTING HILL** page 113

JOHN KING: **CROP OVER FESTIVAL CLASSICS: TUNES OF THE CROP WINNERS, 1979–1995** page 137

KROSFYAH: **THE BEST OF (compilation)** page 142

LORD KITCHENER: **KLASSIC KITCHENER (compilation)** page 153

LORD MELODY: **I MAN** page 154

MIGHTY SPARROW: **HOT AND SWEET** page 188

MUNGAL PATASAR: **NIRVANA** page 208

SUNDAR POPO: **COME AND SING AND DANCE WITH THE CHAMP (compilation)** page 219

RAS (LORD) SHORTY: **ENDLESS VIBRATION** page 226

ROARING LION: **SACRED 78S (compilation)** page 244

DAVID RUDDER: **NO RESTRICTION: THE CONCERT** page 255

SUPERBLUE: **FLAG PARTY** page 277

XTATIC: **CHARGE aka MACHEL ARTS** page 301

BIBLIOGRAPHY

CALYPSO & RELATED

Bacchanal! The Carnival Culture of Trinidad: Peter Mason (Temple University, 1998)

Calypso Calaloo: Early Calypso Music in Trinidad: Donald R Hill (University Press Of Florida, 1993)

Calypso from France to Trinidad: Raphael De Leon (Port of Spain, 1988)

Calypsonians from Then to Now pt 1/2: Rudolph Ottley (Arima, 1994/98)

Caribbean Currents: From Rumba to Reggae: Peter Manuel with Kenneth Bilbey and Michael Jargey (Temple University Press, 1995)

Carnival Canboulay & Calypso: Traditions in the Making: John Cowley (Cambridge University Press, 1998)

East Indian Music in the West Indies: Peter Manuel (Temple University Press, 2000)

Forty Years in the Steelbands (1939–1979): George Goddard (Karla Press, 1991)

Kaiso! The Trinidad Calypso: Keith Q Warner (Three Continents Press, 1982)

The Political Calypso — True Opposition in Trinidad & Tobago 1962–1987: Louis Regis (The Press University of the West Indies, 1999)

REGGAE & RELATED

A Scorcher from Studio One Parts 1 & 2 (TSI Publications, 1998)

Bass Culture: When Reggae was King: Lloyd Bradley (Viking, 2000)

Catch a Fire: Timothy White (Omnibus Books, 1991)

Bob Marley: Stephen Davis (Schenkman Books, 1990)

People Funny Boy: The Genius of Lee "Scratch" Perry: David Katz (Payback Press, 2000)

Record Selector: Ska to Reggae Vols 1–18: Roger Dalke (TSI Publications, 1979–95)

Reggae: The Rough Guide: Steve Barrow and Peter Dalton (Rough Guides Ltd, 1997)

The Rastafarians: Leonard E Barrett Sr (Beacon, 1997)

Reggae Bloodlines: In Search of the Music & Culture of Jamaica: Stephen Davis and Peter Simon (Da Capo, 1992)

Reggae Island: Jamaican Music in the Digital Age: Brian Jahn & Tom Weber (Da Capo, 1998)

Roots Rock Reggae: Chuck Foster (Billboard Books, 1997)

Stir It Up: Reggae Album Cover Art: Chris Morrow (Chronicle Books, 1999)

Virgin Encyclopedia Of Reggae: Colin Larkin (Virgin, 1998)

Wake the Town and Tell the People: Dancehall Culture in Jamaica: Norman C Stolzoff (Duke University Press, 2000)

In addition to the above, many modern CD compilations offer extensive and, frequently, invaluable, liner notes.

Photo Credits

Barker, Dave, 210, 215, 372, 389, 413, 415, 438–439, 443, 455, 468, 490
Barnes, Esther, 138
Barnes, Jeff, 439, 468
Barnes, Lloyd "Bullwackie," 23, 24, 342
Barnet, Eric, 392, 413, 439
Baron, 72, 258, 274
The Barons, 439
Barovier, Carl, 278
Barrett, Aston "Family Man," 162, 163, 165, 167, 171, 176, 210, 248, 257, 289, 291, 296, 297, 413, 439, 446
Barrett, Bunny, 439
Barrett, Carlton, 162, 163, 165, 167, 171, 176, 210, 248, 289, 296
Barrett, Howard, 117, 118, 119
Barrett, UB, 439
Barriteau, Carl, 62
Barrow, Errol, 136
Barry, Al, 439
Basdeo, Panday, 73
Basdeo, Sheila, 110
Bashir, Na'im, 78
Bass, Billy, 413
The Bassies, 372, 392
Bastide, Andrew De La, 204
Battle Axe, 16
The Beas, 392
Becket, 72
Beckford, Dean, 101
Beckford, Ewart, 292
Beckford, Keeling, 414, 439, 468
Beckford, Lyn, 392, 414
Beckford, Theo, 90, 259, 260, 263, 324, 327, 330, 335, 342, 352, 414
Beckles, Winston, 275
Beenie Don, 95
Beenie Man, 31, 32–34, 46, 98, 124, 148, 195, 270, 279, 294, 301
The Bees, 372
Bees, Andrew, 41
Beginner, 242
Belafonte, Harry, 59–60, 143, 152, 154, 243
Belasco, Lionel, 60, 61, 63, 64
Bell, Frederick, 392
Bell's Group, 330
The Beltones, 392, 414, 468, 490
Benjamin, Nisha, 71–72
Bennett, Bruce, 414, 468
Bennett, "Deadly" Headley, 114, 262, 414
Bennett, Fay, 459
Bennett, Jo Jo, 372–373, 439, 468
Bennett, Lorna, 490
Bennett, Louise "Miss Lou," 192, 238, 239, 241
Bennett, Mikey, 46
Bennett, Roy, 392

Bennett, Val, 219, 392, 414, 439, 468, 490
Benson, George, 209–210
Bent, Rupert Gypsy, III, 279
Bentley, Kris, 123, 124
"Benyeh," 96
Berbice and the Original Pioneers, 109
Berridge, Ron, 111
Berry, Chuck, 143
Bert Innis and his Combo, 5
Bertram Ennis Combo, 364
Betancourt, Sterling, 204
Beverly's All Stars, 342, 392, 414, 439, 468, 490
Big Charlie, 342
Bigger D, 468
Biggie, 439
Biggs, Barry, 439
Big Joe, 201, 282
The Big L, 414
Big Youth, 34–37, 56, 68, 97, 101, 107, 115, 140, 193, 194, 195, 221, 236, 238, 247, 251, 252, 281, 282, 292, 295, 391, 490, 506
Billy & Bobby, 335
Billy Boyo, 293
Bim, Bam & Clover, 439
Bim & Bam, 260, 439
Bimbo, 256
The Binders, 117
Binns, Sonny SS, 414, 439
Bins, Tony, 468
Binz, 352
Bishop, Maurice, 11
Bits'n'Pieces, 268
Black, Pablove, 221
Blacka Dread, 157
The Black Beatles, 439
Black Disciples, 51
Black Faith, 390
Black George, 439
Black & George, 414
Black Harmony, 156
Black Hat, 12
Blackman, Abbi, 225
Blackman, Garfield, 225
Black Power, 2
Black Power movement, 239, 252, 319
Black Scorpio, 86
Blackskin Prophet, 224
Black Sounds Uhuru, 39
Black Stalin, 37–38, 72, 82, 112, 113, 152, 187, 218, 225, 272, 274, 506
Black Uhuru, 38–42, 45, 51, 102, 103, 147, 195, 236, 253, 268, 270, 271, 298, 506
Black Wizard, 11
Blake, Cyril, 62, 151
Blake, Keith, 392

Blake, Paul, 88
Blake, Ralph, 392
Blake, Winston, 414, 439, 469
Blakie, 37, 152
Blazing Fire, 12
The Bleechers, 210, 414, 439, 469
Blender, Everton, 256
The Blenders, 414
Blind Blake, 9
Blondie, 117–118
The Blood Fire Posse, 88
Blue, Bobby, 440
The Blue Beats, 264, 325, 330, 342
Blue Boy, 82, 83, 272, 276–277
See also Superblue
Blue & Ferris, 392
Bluegrass Experience, 121
Blue Rivers & The Maroons, 392
The Blues Blasters, 490
The Blues Blenders, 342
The Blues Brothers, 144
The Blues Busters, 144, 264, 325, 327, 330, 352, 362, 373, 469
The Blues Masters, 335
Blue Ventures, 273
Bob & Andy, 414
Bob & Marcia, 117, 390, 469, 490
Bobby & Tommy, 222
Bodie, Kirkland, 9, 275
Bodu, Ignatio "Papa," 4
Bogle, Lee, 469
Bolo, Yami, 89, 93, 192, 195, 196, 270, 302
Bomber, 152, 225, 273
Bonaparte, Belgrave, 204
Bond, Bridgitte, 342
Bond, Joyce, 373, 388, 392, 415, 440, 469
Bongo, 80
Bongo, Les & Bunny, 490
Bongo, Omar, 170
Boodhram, Sharlene, 73
Booker, Cedella, 171
Boothe, Ken, 129, 144, 155, 156–157, 195, 196, 245, 264, 294, 303, 341, 368, 373, 391, 392–393, 415, 440, 469, 490
Boothe, Milton, 393, 415
Bop, Ranny, 440
Bop, Tony, 479
Bop & The Beltones, 393
Boss All Stars, 440
The Boss Attack, 490
The Boss Sounds, 440
Bostic, Onika, 50
Boswell, George, 194
Botheration, 440
Bounty Killer, 32, 34, 46, 88, 148, 197
The Bovver Boys, 440

Bowen, Arnold, 186
Bowers, Ben, 320
Bowie, Lester, 265
Boy Friday, 469
The Boys, 393, 415, 440
Boysie, 440
Boy Wonder, 469
The (BP) Renegades Steel Orchestra, 236–237
Bradford, Andrew, 49
Bradshaw, Anthony, 52–53
Bradshaw, Devon, 53
Bradshaw, Sonny, 335, 469
Brady, Carl, 143
Braham, Ernel, 362
"Brains," 96
Braithwaite, Junior, 158, 159, 160, 288, 295
Branson, Richard, 107
Breedlove, Nathan, 265
Breeze, Jean Binta, 238, 239, 241
The Brentford All Stars, 440
The Brentford Road All Stars, 114
Brevett, Lloyd, 162, 262, 263, 265, 266, 342, 352
Brevett, Ruth, 265
Brevett, Tony, 265, 469
Brevett All Stars, 469
Brigadier Jerry, 46, 89, 303
Briggs, Barrington, 440
Brigo, 82, 225
British 2-Tone, 90, 91, 100, 102
Brooks, Baba, 263, 323, 335, 342, 353, 362–363, 373, 415
Brooks, Cedric "IM," 198, 266
Brooks, D, 440
Brother Book, 240
Brother Dan, 490
Brother Dan All-Stars, 393, 415
Brother Ebony, 273
Brother Joe & The Rightful Brothers, 139
Brotherly Brothers, 120
Brother Marvin, 273
Brother Ray, 273
Brother Resistance, 42–43, 136, 240, 241, 506
Brown, Al, 393, 469, 491
Brown, Barry, 190
Brown, Bertram, 102
Brown, Biddy, 74
Brown, Busty, 210, 393, 415, 440, 469, 491
Brown, David, 393
Brown, Dennis, 20, 34, 35, 37, 43–49, 128, 129, 134, 155, 156, 169, 193, 194, 195, 221, 236, 268, 271, 294, 302, 305, 440, 469, 491, 506
Brown, Errol, 210, 491

Brown, Funky, 121, 491
Brown, Glen, 34, 35, 293, 365, 380, 393, 415, 440, 499
Brown, Hux, 74, 103, 179
Brown, Irving, 441
Brown, Jackie, 116, 125, 469, 491
Brown, James, 159, 178, 470, 491
Brown, Jim and Badoo, 141
Brown, Junior, 223
Brown, Kent, 327, 332, 337
Brown, Lennox, 415, 441, 491
Brown, Mark, 393
Brown, Marlene, 291
Brown, Noel, 393
Brown, Pamela, 441
Brown, Teddy, 441, 470
Brown, Trevor, 470
Brown, Vincent, 441
Brown, William, 470
Brown Bo, 273
Browne, Cleveland "Clevie," 88
Browne, Glen, 79
Brown's All Stars, 491
Brown Sugar, 156
Bryan, Carl "Cannonball," 342, 393, 415, 441, 470
Bryan, Des, 470
Bryan, Dougie, 179
Bryan, FitzVaughn and Orchestra, 320, 325
Bryan, Rad, 138, 268, 470, 491
Bryan, Radcliff, 40, 78
Bryan All Stars, 491
Bryant, Marie, 335
Brynner, 5
Bubbles, 335
Buccaneer, 49–50, 88
Buchanan, Manley Augustus, 34
Buckley, Vern, 436
Bulgin, Lascelle "Wiss," 133, 134
Bullocks, Lester, 97
Bundrick, Rabbit, 164
Bunny, Jah, 189
Bunny Flip, 494
Bunny & Keimanairies, 470
Bunny Lee All Stars, 425
Bunny & Ruddy, 393
Bunny & Skitter, 197, 330
Burke, Sonny, 342, 348, 352, 363, 374
Burning Band, 53
Burning Flames, 7, 27, 50–51, 274, 301
Burning Junior, 52
Burning Spear, 51–54, 103, 167, 197, 253, 279, 441, 470, 506
Bushe, Albert, 208
Bustamente, Alexander, 12
Buster Poindexter, 27
Busty & Cool, 330
Butler, Leslie, 373, 393

Butler, Ron, 28
The Buttercups, 393, 415
BWIA Invaders, 113
BWIA National Indian Orchestra, 207, 218
Byles, Junior, 54–56, 195, 210, 211, 213, 271, 470, 491, 506
Byles, Kerrie, 54
Byron, Cheryl, 239, 240, 241
Byron Lee's Ska Kings, 356

C

The Cables, 114, 393–394, 415, 441, 470, 491
Cadogan, Alison Anne, 56
Cadogan, Lola, 56
Cadogan, Susan, 55, 102, 155, 211, 294, 391
Caine, Tubal & The Cimarrons, 441
The Caledonians, 415
Calliste, Leroy, 37
Calvert, Jeff, 9
Calypso Joe, 273, 415
Calypso Prince, 113
Calypso Rose, 5, 66–67, 112, 113, 273
Calypso Serenaders, 62, 151
Calypso/Soca, 57–66
  belair songs, 58
  bongo songs, 58
  Calypso goes international, 59–62
  carnival tent, 58–59
  early years, 57–59
  essential compilations, 63–64
  impact of World War II, 62, 63
  kalinda songs, 58
  lavway songs, 58
  leading Calypsonians, 64–66
  picong duel, 63
  picong duels, 59
  road march, 58
  the Young Brigade take over, 62–63
The Cambodians, 470
Cameron, Ray, 373
Campbell, Aston & The Conquerors, 373
Campbell, Bill, 470
Campbell, Cat, 287, 492
Campbell, Cecil Bustamente, 219, 260
Campbell, Clive, 114
Campbell, Cornell, 76, 138, 139, 268, 335, 343, 491
Campbell, Dennis, 220
Campbell, Fitzroy, 373
Campbell, Michael, 99
Campbell, Naomi, 352–353, 456–457
Campbell, Nicky, 492
Campbell, Nola, 415
Campbell, Pete, 470
Candy, 441

Inventor, 58
The Invitations, 477
I-Oses, 302
Irie, Clement, 30
Irie, Michael, 32, 294
Irie, Nolan, 294
Irons, Devon, 211
Irons, Neville, 399
I-Roy, 20, 49, 101, 103, 107, 124–127, 140, 141, 195, 201, 202, 211, 213, 281, 282, 292, 295, 391, 477, 496, 506
Isaacs, 236
Isaacs, David, 210, 213, 365, 399–400, 423, 477
Isaacs, Gregory, 34, 38, 43, 45, 46, 48, 103–104, 127–133, 139, 155, 156, 193, 195, 216, 223, 253, 271, 272, 294, 302, 450–451, 477
Isaacs, Kevin, 132
Ismay, Sammy, 365
The Israelites, 423, 451
Israel Vibration, 87, 133–135, 253, 294
Issels, Rita, 359
The Itals, 104, 379, 423, 477
I-Threes, 36, 167, 171, 176
Iwer George, 152

J

Jabba, 264
Jack, Billy, 451, 478
Jackie & Millie, 356, 365
Jackie's Boys, 478
Jack Radics, 89, 95
Jackson, Carlton, 211
Jackson, J, 495
Jackson, Jackie, 74, 77, 103, 179
Jackson, LaToya, 78, 199
Jackson, Lloyd, 478
Jackson, Pooch, 496
Jackson, Siggy, 323, 351
Jackson, Vivian "Yabby You," 35, 97, 102, 253
Jack & The Beanstalks, 423
Jacobs, Carol, 255
Jaffe, Lee, 163
Jagger, Mick, 112, 268, 270, 290
Jago, 496
Jah Bop, 195
Jah Fish, 496
Jah Jerry, 219
Jah Lloyd, 282
Jah Screw, 293
Jah Stitch, 23, 190, 223, 282
Jah Thomas, 147
Jah Woosh, 104
Jai, 226
Jamaica Fats, 365
Jamaican Actions, 400

Jamaican Federation of Musicians (JMF), 281
Jamaican Foundations, 400
Jamaican Labour Party (JLP), 12, 13
The Jamaicans, 379, 400, 423, 451, 478, 496
The Jamaican Shadows, 379
Jamaica's Greatest, 356
Jamaica's Own Vagabonds, 345
Jamari, 22
James, Bobby, 451, 478
James, Busty, 451
James, Devon, 265, 266
James, Jimmy, 332, 337, 345, 365, 478, 497
James, Philip & The Blues Busters, 356
James, Tony, 400
James, Winfield, 12
James, Winston, 451
Jamoo, 226, 273
Jarrett, Irvin "Carrot," 121, 278
Jarrett, Micky, 46
Jarrett, Winston, 210, 423
Jawan, Nau, 70
The Jay Boys, 423, 451, 478, 497
Jay & Joya, 400
The Jay Lads, 478
Jazz, Maxi, 93
JD (The Roc), 497
Jean, Wyclef, 33, 34
Jerry, Jah, 260
Jerry & The Freedom Singers, 451
The Jesters, 478
Jethro Tull, 77
The Jetliners, 365
The Jet Scene, 478
Jewels, 92
Jigsy King, 270
Jimbilin, 478
Jim Brown and Badoo, 141
The Jivers, 400
The Jiving Juniors, 260, 325–326, 328, 332
JJ All-Stars, 400, 423, 451, 478, 497
Joe, 451
Joe & Ann, 345
Joe Gibbs All Stars, 495
Joe's All-Stars, 423–424, 451, 497
Joe the Boss, 451
Johansson, David, 27
John John Band, 203
Johnny Arthey Orchestra, 468
Johnny Ma Boy, 136
Johnny & The Attractions, 379
Johnny & The Blue Beats, 345
Johns, Lydon, 424
Johnson, Anthony, 98
Johnson, Blossom, 497
Johnson, Carey "Wildman," 491, 497, 498

Johnson, Cluett "Clue J," 260, 263
Johnson, Domino, 451, 497
Johnson, JJ, 209
Johnson, Ken, 61–62
Johnson, Linton Kwesi, 102, 103, 239, 240, 241
Johnson, Mark, 28
Johnson, Pete, 451
Johnson, Roydel, 139
Johnson, Wycliffe "Steely," 86, 88
The Jolly Boys, 183, 451
Jonas, Melanie, 455
Jones, Barbara, 478, 497
Jones, George, 275
Jones, Grace, 40, 41, 268, 272
Jones, Jennifer, 444, 451
Jones, Jerry, 452
Jones, Ken, 452
Jones, Lloyd, 452
Jones, Puma, 198
Jones, Sammy, 424, 452, 478, 497
Jones, Sandra "Puma," 39
Jones, Solomon, 452
Josephs, Chuck, 343
Josey Wales, 86, 158, 293
Josh, 424
Josh & Herbie, 332
Joshua, 199
The Jubilee Stompers, 452
Judge Dread, 221, 246, 391, 497
Juice, Sly, 40
Julien & The Chosen Few, 478
Julien & The Gaytones, 497
The Jumpers, 497
The Juncuno Singers, 478, 497
Jungle Brothers, 93
Junior, B, 365
Junior, Hugh Roy, 103
Junior Delgado, 45
Junior Dread, 211
Junior Hibbert, 92
Junior Tucker, 169
Junkanoo, 28

K

Kaiser, Henry, 275
Kaiso Kid, 12
Kaiso-Quero, 273
"Kaisoul," 112
Kalaphat, Carol, 223
Kalinda, 80
Kalphat, Bobby, 400
Kamosa, Ini, 193
Kamoze, Ini, 268
Kancha, 72
Katina, 497
Kay, Janet, 49, 156
Kayamb, 237
Kaye, Shirley, 379

Keith, 478

Keith & Enid, 322, 326, 328, 332, 337, 345

Keith & Tex, 379, 400, 424

Kelley, Charlie, 400

Kellman, Bertrand "Butch," 237

Kelly, Pat, 76, 245, 400, 424, 452, 478, 497

Kelly, Steve, 28

Kelso, Beverly, 158, 159, 160, 295

Kenyatta, Jomo, 51

Kewla, Jay, 109

The Khandars, 356

Khiomal, 137

Kidare, Roy, 345

Kid Gungo, 424

Kid Loops, 93

Killer, 72

Killimanjaro, 86

The Kilowatts, 400

Kindred, 43, 136, 241, 273

King, Benny, 359

King, Bertie, 320

King, John, 136–137, 276, 506

King, Peter, 400

King, Sherwin, 141

King, Teddy & Buster's All-Stars, 379

King, Tony, 424, 452, 478

King Burnett, 213

King Cannon, 424, 478

King Cannonball, 400

King Chubby, 452

King Crimson, 77

King Cry Cry, 222, 478–479

King Dennis, 452

King Dick, 320

Kingdom, Bobby & The Blue Beats, 328, 332

King Fighter, 64, 379

King Horror, 424, 452

King Jammy, 298

King Joe Francis, 356, 365

Kingniah I, 7

King of Surinam, 70

King Onyan, 7, 50

King Perry, 365–366. *See* Perry, Lee

Kingpin, Lloyd, 454

Kingpin, Lord, 452

King Radio, 59, 63, 64, 242

King Reggae, 497

King Rock & Willows, 379

King Rocky, 356, 400, 401

King Short Shirt, 7, 137–138

The Kings of the Caribbean Steel Band, 320

King Solomon, 64

King Sparrow, 321, 366

King Sporty, 295, 452, 472, 479

King Stitt, 19, 222, 281, 287, 293, 391, 424, 452, 479

The Kingstonians, 379–380, 400, 424, 452, 479

Kingston Joe, 345

Kingston Pete & Buster's All-Stars, 379

King Sutch, 452

King Swallow, 137

King Tony, 295

King Tubby, 23, 32, 75, 88, 101, 102, 138–141, 195, 201, 211, 212, 265, 292, 293, 506

King Victor All Stars, 452

Kinsey, Don, 167

Kitchener, 273, 274

Knibbs, Lloyd, 262, 263, 265, 266

Knight, Kenneth, 248

The Knights of the Round Table, 400

Kongos, Ashanti Roy, 224

Kool & The Gang, 78, 79

Kravitz, Lenny, 29

Krosfyah, 141–142, 273, 506

"Kumina" drumming, 197

Kurass, 452

Kuti, Fela, 240, 255

L

Lace, Joe, 452

Ladonne, Pattie, 424

Lady B, 258

Lady Explainer, 12

Lady Gypsy, 273

Lady Saw, 28, 33, 87, 149

Lady Shabba, 87

Lady Spice, 16

Lady Trinidad, 151

La Fud Dil All Stars, 479

Laing, Denzil, 424, 468, 479, 481

Lake, Cecil "Cepeke," 15

Lambert, Barry, 210

Lambert, Trevor, 497

Lamont, Eric "Bingy Bunny," 48, 86, 476

Landis, Joya, 245, 400, 424–425, 479

Landor, Diana, 400

Laro, 182, 326

Laro, Winston, 452

Larry & Alvin, 400, 479

Larry's All Stars, 479, 497

The Lashing Dogs, 17

Last, Johnny, 452

LaTouche, Patrick, 109

Lavette, Betty, 401

Lavway or road march, 5–6, 58, 109

Lavway songs, 58

Lawrence, Azie, 320, 321, 328, 345

Lawrence, Diane, 380, 401

Lawrence, Gene, 380

Lawrence, Larry, 452

Laxton & Oliver, 425

Layne, Lancelot "Kebu," 42, 238–239, 240

Lazarus, Ken, 356, 452, 479, 497

Lazo, 10

Leacock, Carolyn, 137

The Leaders, 401

Lebo M, 79

Lee, Bobby, 380

Lee, Bunny, 74, 194, 210, 267, 288, 293, 356, 388, 452–453, 479, 499

Lee, Byron, 14, 50, 76, 142–147, 225, 272

Lee, Byron & The Dragonaires, 14, 50, 186, 188, 236, 263, 264, 326, 328, 337, 345, 356, 366, 401, 425, 453, 479, 497

Lee, Donald, 479

Lee, Don Tony, 380, 401, 425

Lee, George, 425, 453

Lee, John, 497

Lee, Lai Fung, 151

Lee, Warren, 425

Lee & The Clarendonians, 497

Legend, 38

Leggo Beast, 46, 47

Leggs, B, 479

Lennon, John & The Bleechers, 453

Len & The Honeysuckers, 356

Leon, Chris, 497

Leon, Owen, 347

Leonie & The Joe Nolan Band, 425

Leon & Owen with Drumbago All-Stars, 332

Leroy & Rocky, 401

Les Dawson Blues Unit, 220

Leslie, Alvin, 400, 425

Les & Silkie, 453

Letang, Norman, 121

Letts, Don, 252

Lever Brothers Camboulay Steel Orchestra, 237

Levy, Barrington, 86, 88, 136, 147–149, 190, 192, 236, 269

Levy, Ben, 366

Levy, Carl, 453

Lewin, Carl, 479, 498

Lewis, Alva, 210, 248, 380, 401, 425

Lewis, Hopeton, 144, 244–245, 380, 401, 453, 479, 487, 498

Lewis, Ian, 121

Lewis, Jerry, 56

Lewis, Joey, 111

Lewis, Marvin, 113, 137

Lewis, McCartha, 66

Lewis, Nigel, 113, 137

Lewis, Peter C, 301

Lewis, Rasta Roy "Brother Resistance," 240, 241

Lewis, Reggie, 498

Lewis, Roger, 121

Lewis, Roy, 42

Melody, 64
Melody, Bob, 223, 426
Melody, Courtney, 139, 303
Melody, Frank, 22
Melody, Johnny, 381
The Melody Enchanters, 338
The Melody Makers, 109, 236
   See also Marley, Ziggy and The
    Melody Makers
Melon, Montego, 499
Mento, 181–183, 260
Menudo, 27
Menz, Junior, 103, 117
Merchant, 152
Merrick's Orchestra, 64
The Merrits, 456
The Merrymen, 367, 481
The Message, 456, 481
The Metronomes, 96
Mexicano, 112
Mighty Arawak, 81
The Mighty Atwell, 62
The Mighty Avengers, 367
Mighty Bomber, 5
Mighty Bonnet, 16
Mighty Chalkdust, 240
Mighty Cypher, 64, 183
Mighty Destroyer, 12, 64
The Mighty Diamonds, 103, 107, 169,
   194, 236, 253, 271
Mighty Douglas, 381
Mighty Duke, 183–184
Mighty Intruder, 12
Mighty Jaunty, 16
Mighty Killer, 63, 151
Mighty Pat, 15
Mighty Power, 5, 273, 381
Mighty Raja, 12
Mighty Rebel, 12
Mighty Roots, 12
Mighty Session, 16
Mighty Sparrow, 5, 11, 37, 59, 72, 82,
   111, 144, 152, 154, 183, 184–189,
   255, 258, 320, 326, 328, 333, 381,
   402, 426, 456, 481, 506
Mighty Splinter, 7
Mighty Spoiler, 183
Mighty Springer, 7
Mighty Squeeze and Tallpree, 11
Mighty Terror, 113, 320, 321
Mighty Trini, 72
The Mighty Vikings, 381–382
Mikey General, 158
Miller, Angus, 150
Miller, Glen, 367, 382, 402
Miller, Herbie, 37
Miller, Jacob, 121, 147, 195, 201, 253
   See also Inner Circle
Miller, James, 481

Miller, Nelson, 53
Millie, 357, 367, 402, 427, 456
Mills, Rudy, 382, 427
Milton & Denzil, 456
The Milwaukee Coasters, 402
Minott, Echo, 293–294
Minott, Lincoln Barrington, 189
Minott, Sugar, 40, 86, 88, 98, 100, 139,
   156, 189–192, 193, 194, 195, 201,
   268, 269, 506
The Minstrels, 382, 403
Miranda, Marcia, 73
Miss Jane, 403
Mister Most, 427
Mitchell, Cyril, 186
Mittoo, Donat Roy "Jackie," 18, 209,
   262, 263, 265, 367, 382, 403, 427,
   456, 481
Mittoo, Jackie & The Reggae Beat, 499
Mittoo, Jackie & The Sound
   Dimension, 427
The Modifies, 456
The Mods, 323, 389
The Mod Stars, 499
The Moffat All Stars, 456
Mohammed, Feroz, 109
Mohammed, Kamalludin, 70, 71
Mohammed, Moean, 300
Mohammed, Sham, 300
Mohammed Ali, 159
The Mohawks, 390, 403, 427, 456
Monsoon, 482
Montano, Machel, 113, 241, 301
Montego Melon, 499
Monty & Roy, 329
Monty & The Cyclones, 329, 333
Moodie, Ameil, 403, 427
The Mood Reaction, 456
The Moon Boys, 427
Moonilal, Bisram, 225
The Moonlighters, 338
Moonsplash Music Festival, 30
Moore, Egbert, 151
Moore, John, 202, 262, 263, 265
Moore, Johnny, 197, 288, 294, 382,
   403, 427, 499
Moose, 456
Mootoo Brothers, 72
The Mopeds, 403
Morgan, Derrick, 90, 138, 219, 220,
   246, 247, 249, 260, 261, 322, 323,
   324, 326, 329, 331, 333, 336, 338–
   339, 344, 347, 350, 353, 357, 363,
   367, 382, 390, 396, 403, 418, 427,
   444, 456, 482, 499
Morgan, Earl, 114, 115, 116
Morgan, Sammy, 456
The Morgan All Stars, 499
Morgan Heritage, 236

Morgan's All Stars, 456, 482
Morris, Eric, 220, 260, 263, 322, 334,
   339, 347, 357, 367
Morris, Hemsley, 378, 403
Morris, Leonard, 203
Morris, Milton, 427
Morris, Monty, 144, 264, 329, 382, 403,
   427, 456
Morris, Naggo, 115, 224
The Morwells, 55
Moses, Pablo, 105
Moss, Bill, 427, 456
The Mothers Sons, 456
Motta, Stanley, 182, 263, 305
Mott The Hoople, 77
Mough Band, 184
The Movers, 357
Mowatt, Judy, 36, 116, 167, 194, 478
Mr Calypso, 482
Mr Foundation, 382, 403, 427
Mr Midnight, the Supreme Ruler of
   Sound, 117
Mr Miller, 404, 427
Mr Vegas, 124
Mr Versatile, 427
Mudada, 273
Mudie's All Stars, 456, 482
Muir, Bobby, 322
Multi National Force band, 27, 50
Mundell, Hugh, 201, 202
Murphy, Carl, 482
Murphy's All Stars, 482
Murray, Sandra, 347
Murt, Turt & Purt, 499
Murvin, Junior, 168, 211, 252, 253, 386
Muscovada, 15
The Music Blenders, 482
The Music Doctors, 427, 453, 456
Music Through Six, 404
The Muskyteers, 427
Mutabaruka, 36, 47, 131, 158, 191,
   192–194, 198, 239, 240, 241, 246,
   270, 506
Muttoo Brothers Band, 243
MYOB, 456
Myrie, Mark, 30
Mystic Revelers, 236
Myton, Cedric, 216, 418

N

Naked Funk, 93
Nangle, Ed, 404
Nap Hepburn, 5
Nash, Johnny, 144, 155, 161, 163, 166,
   289
Nash, Tony, 457
Natasha, 274
National Alliance For Reconstruction
   (NAR), 2, 73

THE REGGAE BOX
The Reggae Box: The Routes of Jamaican Music charts the course of this vital music from Independence in 1962 to the summer of 2001. From the early jazz- and R&B- influenced Ska outfits to the tradewind soul of Rock Steady, from the global breakthrough of Reggae to the tough rub-a-dub rhythms of Dancehall, it's all here, from the international hitmakers to the local performers who defined and advanced the music.
4 CD Box Set
87 Songs!
CRUCIAL 48-PAGE BOOKLET FEATURING:
3 HISTORICAL ESSAYS
DETAILED TRACK ANNOTATIONS
RARE PHOTOS & EPHEMERA
REGGAE GLOSSARY
The Heavyweight Sounds Are On
A UNIVERSAL MUSIC COMPANY
TAKE A HIT
www.hip-o.com
© 2002 Universal Music Enterprises, a Division of UMG Recordings, Inc.